CANINE LEXICON

Andrew De Prisco
and
James B. Johnson

CANINE LEXICON

Andrew De Prisco
and
James B. Johnson

Featured photographer, Isabelle Français

Publisher's note: As concrete particles from the fallen Berlin Wall have become treasured relics, our present-day world community struggles with constant change. The authors and publishers of this *Lexicon* implore our readership's pardon for suddenly dated geographic and political references throughout the book, over which we simply have no control.

Distributed in the UNITED STATES by T.F.H. Publications, Inc., One T.F.H. Plaza, Neptune City, NJ 07753; in CANADA to the Pet Trade by H & L Pet Supplies Inc., 27 Kingston Crescent, Kitchener, Ontario N2B 2T6; Rolf C. Hagen Ltd., 3225 Sartelon Street, Montreal 382 Quebec; in CANADA to the Book Trade by Macmillan of Canada (A Division of Canada Publishing Corporation), 164 Commander Boulevard, Agincourt, Ontario M1S 3C7; in ENGLAND by T.F.H. Publications, PO Box 15, Waterlooville PO7 6BQ; in AUSTRALIA AND THE SOUTH PACIFIC by T.F.H. (Australia) Pty. Ltd., Box 149, Brookvale 2100 N.S.W., Australia; in NEW ZEALAND by Ross Haines & Son, Ltd., 82 D Elizabeth Knox Place, Panmure, Auckland, New Zealand; in the PHILIPPINES by Bio-Research, 5 Lippay Street, San Lorenzo Village, Makati, Rizal; in SOUTH AFRICA by Multipet Pty. Ltd., P.O. Box 35347, Northway, 4065, South Africa. Published by T.F.H. Publications, Inc. Manufactured in the United States of America by T.F.H. Publications, Inc.

Dedication

To homeless and unhappy dogs
and to the dogs with whom we share our homes:
"Old Man" Sam, a loyal friend of ten years,
Tengu, the monster Shiba, and the fabulous Kabuki,
Chelsea, our *Ya-yah*,
plus
Celia, Cookie's heeler,
and Shandy.

Preface

Lexicon we define as the common language of a specific field of study: this lexicon attempts to record the terminology and topics relevant to the dog fancy. The international world dog community, particularly the English-speaking world, has not seen a comprehensive opus on dogs since *Hutchinson*, and the canine universe has stretched expansively over the past half century, making it ever more difficult to stay abreast of continued developments.

Marked by its fascination with the new, the peculiar, and the beautiful, the dog fancy does expand in new directions, embracing/resisting change. New breed creation and discoveries, new sporting events and titles, updated standards, new colors, improved terminology, changing trends and fads all characterize the dog fancy, a veritable living, breathing, panting thing … hence, undertaking a contemporary lexicon to chart the canine cosmos might be akin to counting cells, stars, or unregistered curs—other tasks impossible to ever truly accomplish. Just as scientists, astrologists, and breed statisticians encounter limits, so too have we, the author-compilers of this lexicon, faced limits, principally time, resources, and the impossibility of collaring all that is current.

The mere accumulation of the many thousands of pertinent entries certainly approaches the impossible, let alone the task of providing current and accurate information for each topic included. This printed volume thus stands only as a statement in time, a fleeting moment in dog history—a reflection of dogs today—it, of course, can be neither comprehensive nor complete, in the truest sense.

Nonetheless, the authors invite you to thumb through the dog fancy's "impossible dream"—an endless and colorful passageway through today's dogs. Compiled on these pages are nearly four thousand entries covering the world's recognized breeds of dog, as well as legions of canine ghosts (extinct and lost breeds), a nursery of canine infants (brand new breeds and recent discoveries from around the world), plus every species of wild canid (wolves, foxes, jackals, and others). In addition to the breeds and species of canines, this book touches upon the history of the domestic dog, its ancestors, its variations and types as well as groups of dogs (terriers, mastiffs, sighthounds, etc.). A catalog of show terminology focusing on the language of breed standards, an overview of dog shows, obedience, field, agility, and similar trials and events are combined with working-dog lingo, current trends and tests, and other related terminology. The book also serves as a primer for ownership, addressing selection, health care, accommodations, breeding, and common veterinary parlance.

The authors are young(ish) and thus fool(ish) enough to have attempted this gargantuan feat [granted we're wet behind the ears, but our ears are the sharpest and biggest in the fancy—and always erect (*See also* Erect ears)]. We have painstakingly spied on every breed fancy, read everyone's book, visited and interviewed and eventually bothered breeders, vets, handlers and judges around the English-speaking world, and beyond. The result of our research and espionage is not a dry Websterian canon from A to Z, but a readable, resourceful and—God knows—colorful kaleidoscope of dogs, dogs, dogs.

In order to render the world of dogs in its truest, most vivid and eccentric colors, the authors must confess to having been guiltlessly catholic in selecting topics for inclusion. Since we have accepted the impossibility of a "complete" lexicon, this volume attempts to capture the dog fancy here and now, recording the slightest stirrings and even those spurious developments spurned by more conservative fanciers, assembled here to portray the completer contemporary picture.

For the sake of "user-peruser-friendliness," the book is arranged alphabetically and is thoroughly cross-referenced so that information can be accessed as swiftly as possible. Three kinds of cross-references are employed: "*See*" directs the reader to the article title that discusses this term; "*See also*" functions merely to indicate supplementary related reading; and "which *see*" refers the reader to the previously mentioned article for further information.

For color, we have the incomparable work of the globe-romping photographer Isabelle Français—a multilingual dervish of talent and energy who has fearlessly embarked upon the continents, barged in on the most respected dog people and barked at their dogs. The result of her traveling and barking and snapping and developing can be seen throughout this volume: priceless moments captured on film of stunning, unusual dogs, many of which the world would not otherwise see. This volume showcases nearly a decade of Ms. Français's work, including photographs of some of the most unique animals probably anyone has seen. We are honored to work with this dedicated, delightful professional!

The authors must here acknowledge the hundreds of breeders, exhibitors, and owners who have cooperated with Ms. Français. In deference to the publication at hand, we have determined that identifying dogs by name, owner, handler, breeder, pedigree, etc., would be inappropriate and inevitably a hindrance to the user of this volume. Other considerations also prevented the inclusion of complete identifications in many cases. We sincerely regret our inability to provide every owner with his due credit. With the thousands of possible photographs at the authors' disposal (thanks to the enormous color library at T.F.H.), it is hoped that the selection of an owner's dog brings with it a sense of pride and inward satisfaction that no purple-ribbon award could otherwise bestow. Any identifications included were deemed necessary by the authors for the appropriateness of the illustration to the article at hand.

Lastly, the authors hope that this volume brings readers a welcome resource of information and that our efforts result in owners' knowing and loving their dogs ten-thousandfold more.

Acknowledgments

Riotous applause to everyone who has contributed to making this *Lexicon* a reality!

To Isabelle Français, for her limitless talents, photographic prowess, sense of humor, lack of predictability, and unreserved energy. Without Isabelle, this book could not have been possible.

To the countless, nameless, selfless owners of the dogs that grace and illustrate this book—our most sincere "thank you!"

To Robert and Bernice Martin, for being there and for allowing us to "be there" so that this book could be written. Thanks again.

To Kellie and Michael, for love and support.

To our tireless editorial consultants, for appreciated guidance.

To editors and typographers at T.F.H., Deirdre Connolly, Marcy Myerovich, Mary Alice Griffin, Julie Lloyd, and Kathy Gleason.

To Dr. Herbert R. Axelrod, for perceiving the need for such a volume in the dog world, and for being **bold** enough to produce it and persuasive enough to shackle us into assembling it!

To Walter Hutchinson, Doggie Hubbard, Caius, Linnaeus, God, Walkowicz and Wilcox (you're in good company!), for having tread the boards before us.

To Neal Pronek, for his insight into the dog community and for his fondness for fine canine literature.

To Rick Tomita, for guidance and countless favors.

To our photo contributors, who willingly offered illustrations of new and less familiar breeds.

To dog writers everywhere, for their generous contributions to cynology and dog lit.

"I am secretly afraid of animals, of all animals except dogs, and even of some dogs. I think it is because of the *us-ness* in their eyes, with the underlying *not-us-ness* which belies it, and is so tragic a reminder of the lost age when we human beings branched off and left them, left them to eternal inarticulateness and slavery. 'Why?' their eyes seem to ask us."

—*Edith Wharton*

(1862-1937)

A.A.D.
Advanced Agility Dog. *See* Agility trials

Abdomen
Structured of firm muscular tissue, the body cavity between the hindquarters and the chest. Consisting of muscular walls and the belly (the floor), the abdomen is supported above the spinal column's lumbar portion.

Abdomen, paunchy. Excessive, untucked, flabby abdominal walls creating a pendulous underline. "Pot belly" in extreme cases.

Abdomen, tucked-up. Tight, upcurving abdominal walls creating an obvious concave underline.

Aberdeen Terrier
See Scottish Terrier

Abortifacients
Drugs used to induce abortion. Only limited success has been found with such chemicals. Drug-induced abortions commonly result in complications due to side effects, surviving puppies, and misuse. Abortifacients are not recommended by many specialists.

Abortion
The premature expulsion of embryos from the uterus by surgical, chemical, or natural means. If a fetus or part of a fetus is left in the uterus, which is likely in dogs due to the varied, multiple offspring of typical litters, serious infection may occur, possibly resulting in death. The first indication of infection will be high fever, dry nose and lethargy. The immediate services of a veterinarian are necessary. Most experienced professionals strongly recommend against abortion in dogs, for the risks are just too great. Even among bitches who become pregnant during their first season, the danger of abortion often outweighs the danger of carrying and delivering the pups. Abortion is not a method of birth control. It is a last resort only when the risks to the bitch's caring and delivering of the pups outweighs the high risks of abortion.

Abscesses
A swollen or inflamed area of body tissue, with pus usually present, which may result from numerous causes, including bone splinters, animal bites or other injuries which break the skin or other protective membrane. The swelling is usually the result of the body's combating a bacterial invasion. A process of lancing, draining, and flushing and the administering of antibiotics are two common treatments for most abscesses. Hot compresses may also be used in some cases. Professional care is recommended. Old, malnourished, diseased, and other relatively weak dogs are more subject to abscess than are other dogs.

Abscesses, anal glands. These largely obsolete glands situated on either side of the rectum of the dog secrete a yellowish fluid. Because so many dogs live a domestic, often sedentary, life, these glands do not excrete this fluid but rather retain it, causing abscess and swelling. If such should result, veterinary care is required. Only a professional can correctly open the sacs and remove the foul matter.

Abscesses, mouth. One of the most common causes of dental problems in canines is the build-up of plaque and tartar on the teeth. Excessive build-up may result in swollen and diseased gums, with abscesses often occurring. In acute cases of tartar build-up, a professional scraping may be necessary; however, allowing your dog free access to safe chew products, like the effective

Abdomen, tucked-up. The Whippet, like most other sighthounds, exhibits a markedly tucked-up abdomen. Photo by R. Reagan.

Nylabone® chew products, should reduce the accumulation of plaque and tartar on your dog's teeth and thereby prevent abscess. Other causes include receding gums, broken or cracked teeth, and blows to the mouth area. An abscess in the mouth may occasionally show itself as an additional abscess under the eye, known as dental fistula, which *see*.

Abscesses, muscle. As a result of injury, often a puncture wound, muscle tissue may be invaded by bacteria. An abscess will usually result, and the condition then becomes quite serious, possibly culminating in lost tissue and/or chronic lameness. Warning signs include: favoring a muscle, swelling, soreness, and lethargy. Professional care is required.

was thought to be due to the lack of "certain bodies in their blood," malnutrition, and/or extreme climatic conditions. In Africa, the dogs were used for hunting purposes and as companion animals. In appearance the dog strongly resembled the Standard Xoloitzcuintli. Its color was sandy or mottled and it sported rose ears.

Acalasia

Most commonly inherited but also caused by environmental factors, acalasia refers to a defect found somewhere along the line from the esophagus anterior to the diaphragm. The defect is a pocket in which foods and liquids will collect, never completing their journey to the stomach. This collected matter is later

Abyssinian Sand Dog. Of all extant breeds, the Standard Xoloitzcuintli bears the most likeness to the extinct Abyssinian Sand Dog. Photo by I. Français.

Abyssinian Sand Dog

This dog, also referred to as the African Hairless Dog, is one of the first documented hairless dogs. It is believed that all hairless breeds derive from African specimens (*Canis africanis*) which were transported to various countries. When first introduced to England, the dogs were considered freaks; while the exact cause of hairlessness is not known today for certain, originally the hairless quality

vomited. Surgery is difficult, but other treatments, such as feeding from an almost vertical position, have sometimes proven successful. Signs include: vomiting, malnutrition, and choking. *See also* Vomiting

Acarus

One of the parasitic mites that can cause mange. *See* Mange

Acceptance, female's
See Breeding

Accommodations, indoor

Caring for the dog indoors requires the provision of a place to sleep, a place to piddle, and dishes and bowls from which to eat and drink. It is recommended that the owner provide each dog with its own quiet corner. Supply this area with a dog bed to which the dog can retire at any time and add a toy or two and a chew device in addition.

Dogs enjoy the crowd, but they require quiet times too. As regarding the place to piddle, the reader is referred to coverage under the heading House-breaking, in which the various methods of this training are discussed as well as the tools and territory allotment required. Feeding dishes and water bowls are available at your local pet shop. These containers should be of sturdy construction and an easyclean composition. *See also* Bedding

Accommodations, outdoor

Most dogs, especially the large and sporting breeds, require time spent outdoors. For some dogs, this time involves daily walks with their owners. However, many owners do not have time available on a daily basis to fulfill the dog's outdoor needs in this fashion. Some dogs have considerable outdoor requirements. Such breeds as the Anatolian Shepherd, the Great Pyrenees, and the Mastiff are best suited to a home with a large yard in which the dog can roam, stretch, and feel useful. Generally speaking, most of the mastiffs, flock guards, terriers, sporting and working dogs need considerable time spent outdoors where they can exercise and expend their energy. Accommodating your dog in his outdoor existence involves consideration of the breed, the environment, and the needs of dogs in general.

Naturally, some breeds are better suited to outdoor life than are others, and most dogs have a climate in which they do best. Determining qualities and characteristics of your breed is the best start in the consideration of your dog's outdoor accommodations. Kennels, dog houses, dog pens, outdoor runs, fenced-in yards, and spikes and chains are considerations that the dog owner must face. If the dog(s) will spend a considerable number of hours outdoors, a dog house or kennel is probably a necessity.

Both kennels and dog houses must be dry, draft free, and comfortable for the dog. For a single dog, a dog house is

Accommodations, indoor. Dog crates provide the pet with its own haven and also assist in training and housebreaking. Affenpinscher photographed by I. Français.

Accommodations, outdoor. Owners unable to provide a completely fenced-in property smartly opt for outdoor pens. Great Pyrenees photographed by R. Reagan.

excellent. Many fine commercial dog houses are available at your local pet shop or, if not, at a local pet supply dealer. Most commercial dog houses are properly designed to keep your pet warm and dry; these houses are constructed of sturdy material which is long-lasting and prevents parasite infestation. It is possible to build your dog his house, but doing so is time-consuming and often more costly than simply purchasing a ready-made home. Additionally, most owners would construct their dog's house of bare or painted wood. Wood can allow many parasite infestations and prove difficult to keep clean and sanitary. For owners with several dogs, there are two options: either a kennel or a dog house for each of the dogs. Many owners opt for the kennel. A kennel is a shelter of several individual compartments, each of which is independent and well suited

Accommodations, outdoor. The spike and chain, though not recommended as a sole outdoor provision, can provide temporary outdoor restraint. Photo by I. Français.

to a dog's inhabitancy. The building of kennels takes time, money and great planning. Both houses and kennels must be kept clean, which means free of parasites, excess dirt, and of course feces. Bedding should be supplied which allows the dog to keep warm at all times and provides a comfortable place in which to rest and sleep.

Exercise pens are typically wire enclosures that allow the dog adequate space to exercise and breathe the fresh air.

These pens are essentially of two types: permanent and portable. The permanent type is free-standing and can be quite large, providing ample space for most breeds. A cement or other hard-surface floor that allows for good drainage, easy cleaning, and parasite-free space is recommended for permanent pens. Portable pens are very popular with people who travel with their dogs, whether to show or to resort. Of course, if you have the space, nothing beats the fenced-in yard for safe exercise for your dog. Remember, exercise pens should not replace regular daily walks.

The dog spike and chain is an age-old way of restraining the dog outdoors. The spike and chain keeps the dog in one small area. The use of dog spikes has been questioned in recent years, and some researchers suggest that permanently chaining the dog out of doors can be detrimental to his development as a pet. The same applies to runs, contraptions made of line and lead that allow the dog to run the length of the line while on the lead. Dogs need human attention; they need to feel part of the pack. Chaining the dog outdoors is fine as a temporary method of providing fresh air but is not a way to house a dog as it is unsafe. The same applies to dog houses and kennels. The dog can fare well outdoors when well provided for, but human supervision is essential.

Acetabulum

The cuplike socket of the hip bone. Located at the junction of the ilium, ischium and pubis, the acetabular socket holds the thigh bone or femur. The formation of the acetabulum is key to the disorder known as hip dysplasia, a serious disease affecting many breeds.

Achilles tendon

The most prominent tendon in the dog, the Achilles tendon is of the greatest length and strength. The Achilles anchors and creates an extension for the calf muscles onto the fibular tarsal bone at the hock. In the short-coated sighthounds especially, this tendon is most apparent.

Achondroplasia

A type of dwarfism that affects the limbs (or the long bones) of younger dogs. Such irregular development does not detract from the bones' strength nor the regular growth of the head and body. In the dachsbrackes and bassets, achondroplasia typically equips these dogs to go to ground and is of genetic origin. *See also* Dwarfism

Acne

Inflammation of the skin glands caused by dirt entering the pores. Bacteria results, erupting in pus. Pimples may pop up more on breeds with oily muzzles than other dogs. A number of acne lotions have proven effective on this minor canine condition. The emotional/psychological effects of acne on a dog are not similar to the human teenager who refuses to return to high school. No pimple-faced Poodle, to our knowing, has ever foregone its obedience class for fear of scarring embarrassment.

Açores

See Cão de Fila de S. Miguel

Acromegaly

A disease resulting from a pituitary gland tumor causing overproduction of the growth hormone. Such gigantism affects growth patterns in height, weight and skin as well as the bones of the extremities—the head, hands and feet. The Mastiff, the Dogue de Bordeaux, and the Neapolitan Mastiff serve as perfect examples of acromegalic breeds. These breeds (some of which weigh in excess of 165 pounds) have been selectively bred for the acromegalic trait, and as such acromegaly is not a disease in the primary definition of the word. The giant breeds, such as the Giant Schnauzer and the Great Pyrenees, should not be associated here since their extremities are perfectly in proportion to their bodies.

Action

Gait, movement. The way a canine moves: trots, walks, runs. The pelvic muscles in combination with the thigh muscles create action. Different breeds move differently. Gait is an important part of conformation competition, and surely the most interesting to an audience member. Breed standards describe action or gait variously, attempting to describe the desired movement. A kaleidoscope of terminology pervades in the show ring: east and west movers, free gait, hard-driving action, mincing gait, reachy action, rolling gait, rotary motion, shuffling action, springy action, tottering action, and waddling gait, which *see*.

Acupuncture

An ancient medical practice of China in which sharp needles are used to relieve pain. These needles are inserted and rotated at specific points of the body, according to the specific pain or condition that is to be alleviated.

A.D.

Agility Dog. *See* Agility trials

Acromegaly affects the extremities of many mastiff breeds. Neapolitan Mastiff photographed by I. Français.

Addison's disease

The disease presents itself as a hormonal deficiency, specifically the adrenocortical hormones, and is most commonly seen in young to middle-aged dogs. The cause is usually not known. Known also as hypoadrenocorticism, the signs are commonly non-specific and progress in varied degrees of intensity (one step back and two steps forward). Loss of weight, appetite, vitality, and tolerance may all be signs, as may vomiting, diarrhea, dehydration, among others. A professional diagnosis is necessary. It is a serious disease, with acute cases treated as medical emergencies.

Administering medication. Liquid medication must be poured at the side of the dog's mouth, as administering it directly on the tongue or throat can result in choking. Photo by S.A. Thompson.

Adenocarcinoma

A deadly malignant tumor that originates in glandular epithelium (the cells which form a gland). Adenocarcinoma can quickly destroy the gland, as well as spread throughout the body. Uncommon in dogs, this cancer has still claimed its share of canine lives and is one form of lethal breast cancer. The most common sign is a visible lump at the affected area. Immediate medical attention is necessary. Unfortunately, once detected, it is usually too late. *See also* Cancer

Adenoma

A non-inflammatory growth or benign tumor most commonly found in the bitch's mammary gland.

Administering medication

Medication comes in three common forms: liquid, pill, and gas. Liquid medication is either injected into the blood stream or administered via the mouth. Injections should only be given by a trained professional and are therefore not of practical concern for the pet owner. Giving liquid via the mouth, however, demands a few precautions; if performed incorrectly, the dog could suffer inhalation pneumonia, choking, or other serious complications. To administer a liquid, pull the lower lip away from the gum so as to form a lip pocket; then let the liquid trickle at a moderate rate into the pocket and past the tongue, not allowing the liquid to land directly on the tongue, as inhalation is the likely result. To administer a pill, gently force the dog's mouth open by holding his head back and applying pressure to the jaw with your hand that is over the top of the dog's muzzle; then place the pill as far back on the dog's tongue as possible; close the dog's mouth and gently massage his throat. In this way he will swallow the pill. Gas is rarely given by other than a professional, and should you, as a pet owner, have to administer the dog a gaseous substance (such as oxygen), make certain that you are provided with detailed and understandable directions pertaining to dosage and administering, as well as possible complications of which to be aware; all should be provided by the prescribing physician of your choice.

"Adonis"

The first registered dog in the American Kennel Club stud book. This English Setter was entered in 1878.

Adrenal glands

Through their production of adrenalin (also called epinephrine), which acts upon the heart and blood vessels, these glands regulate the blood pressure. Additionally, they help determine the level of salt in the urine and the breakdown of fats and sugars. These glands are located near the kidneys. Adrenalin is sometimes used in conjunction with a local anesthetic to reduce bleeding during surgery.

Advanced Agility Dog

Second title for agility competitions, A.A.D. *See* Agility trials

Affenpinscher

Comically serious, the Affenpinscher is remarkable in its smug contentment and self-importance. Its name to English-speaking fanciers is unfortunately meaningless. In German, the word *affen* means "to mock"; *pinscher*, terrier. The description *affenartig* means monkeylike, of course appropriate in describing the Affenpinscher's expression. The Affen was the first of the monkey-faced canines. Today he shares this somewhat dubious distinction with the Brussels and Belgian Griffons. And even though the Affen predates these breeds, he is less popular and ironically posed as a key ingredient in their creation. Even more popular is the Miniature Schnauzer which also employed Affen blood.

Doubtless the Affenpinscher is an old breed dating back to the seventeenth century. Artistic renditions of these little terriers verify the accuracy of the breed's 300-year existence. It is believed that the breed once occurred in two sizes and that the smaller of the two has survived as today's toy terrier. The larger size, possi-

within the last 100 years, as he was still to be found at the turn of the century. Through the years, the Affenpinscher has retained his true terrier spunk, though his muzzle has shortened. Years ago, the Affenpinscher and the (smooth) Miniature Pinscher were considered two varieties of the same breed, differing only in coat type.

Affenpinscher, red.

Affenpinscher, black. Photographs by I. Français.

bly the extinct Deutscher Rauhhaariger Pinscher (Wirehaired Pinscher), was as much as eight inches taller than the present-day Affen and referred to as the Rattler. Black was the Rattler's most common color. His disappearance occurred

The British have taken very little liking to the Affenpinscher; in America his popularity is moderate but growing. Perhaps the peak of the Affenpinscher's popularity occurred a couple of centuries ago on the European continent.

ESSENTIALS OF THE AFFENPINSCHER: This definitely terrier-type toy, with bushy eyebrows and shaggy facial hair, is the original monkey dog. His head is round, achieved in part by the well-domed forehead. The large round eyes are black and brilliant. The ears are small and set high. The muzzle is short and tipped with a black nose. Though the upper jaw is a "pinsch" shorter than the lower jaw, the teeth should never show. Height should never exceed 10.25 inches (26–27 cm). Weight: 7–8 pounds (3–4 kg). The entire coat is harsh, wiry and medium long. The preferred color is black, but black and tan, red, and dark gray are also seen.

Afghan Hound, fawn. Photo by Bergman.

Afghan Hound

The great windhound of Afghanistan, the Afghan Hound also runs in large numbers along the Borderland and in Northern India, where it is known as the Barakzai, Kurram Valley Hound. It is not clear how these greyhound types made their way from the Middle East into northern Afghanistan, the country which provide its present name. Also referred to as Tazi and Baluchi Hound, the Afghan Hound, as we know him today, is one of the most ancient of dogs and, many believe, is the dog that Noah granted visa on his Ark. Although the whole truth may never be told, the Afghan's pedigree is without a doubt

pre-Christian in age. Portraits of the Afghan's ancestors appear engraved upon cuneiform pillars and tablets. Native Indian and Asian hunters prize their individual strains and guard them with jealous care. In Afghanistan, the breed is used to guard sheep and cattle and to hunt deer, wolves, gazelles and foxes. The leopard and the panther are the Afghan Hound's most impressive game—it has been known to hunt and kill big cat single-handedly. Its approach to hunting is not the typical courser's—the breed is more inclined to slay its prey, although it can be trained not to.

One account many years back described with awe the intelligence and demeanor which those Afghan Hounds guarding an Indian fortress displayed. Appearing to have no leadership, human or other, the dogs assume their patrol stations, usually in pairs. Their duties are executed with Royal Guard precision and are totally self-imposed (so it appears). The writer called these dogs "the hounds of Chaman."

"Zardin," imported by Captain Banff, was the first Afghan to be exhibited at a British Kennel Club show. This championship show in 1907 deemed Zardin the perfect Afghan Hound. Queen Alexandra personally admired Zardin, her especially requested palace visitor. In England, the breed excelled because of its beauty, intelligence and varied abilities as a guard and companion. The breed received Kennel Club status in 1926; in the U.S., the breed progressed slowly but was accepted within ten years of its arrival in 1926.

The Afghan Hound is unique among the sighthounds. Its luxuriant coat and tufted extremities give this dog an exotic, smart appeal. The breed's intelligence and sense of nobility are keen. Unlike many dogs, this dog's self-esteem is elevated, on a par with that of any cougar, peacock or swan.

ESSENTIALS OF THE AFGHAN HOUND: Aristocratic, dignified, and aloof, the Afghan, with its head held proudly and its eyes to the distance casts a striking appearance, exotic, Eastern. The expression, the long silky topknot, the peculiar coat pattern, prominent hipbones, and large feet stand as distinctive Afghan features. The head is of good length, showing much refinement, the skull evenly balanced with the foreface. The jaws to be long and punishing, with the teeth set in a level or scissors bite. The ears are long, reaching nearly to the end of the nose. The eyes almond shaped (almost triangular). The nose of good size and black in color. The neck of good length, strong and arched. The backline appearing practically level from shoulders to loin, which is strong, powerful and slightly arched. The height at the shoulders to be equal to the distance from the chest to the buttocks; the brisket well let down and of medium length. Height: 24–28 inches (61–71 cm). Weight: 50–60 pounds (23–28 kg). The forelegs are straight and strong, with great length between the elbow and the pastern. The coat hair is thick and silky, fine in texture; the ears and all four feet to be well feathered. The hair is short and close from in front of the shoulders and also backwards from the shoulders along the saddle from the flanks and the ribs upwards. The breed is shown in its natural state. Colored in solids, bicolors, and tricolors; white markings, especially on the head, are undesirable.

African Hairless Dog
   See Abyssinian Sand Dog

African hunting dog
   An unusual dog, the African hunting dog, *Lycaon pictus*, is a diurnal hunter with little fear of man. The Cape hunting dog, the African wild dog, and the hyena dog—this animal's alternative names are beginning to outnumber its square miles of roaming ground. The African hunting dog, though a highly structured and most efficient hunter, is limited to sub-Saharan Africa and finds itself more and more restricted to national parks. Diurnal in habits and fearless of man, this dog, hunting in packs of up to 40, can be a serious threat to the farmer's livestock, and farming and development are largely what has pushed this animal into the parks. Unique, the African hunting dog is the only wild dog that is spotted in color: a bright pied of black, white, and yellow. Also unusual are its non-existent dewclaws and large odd-shaped ears. Pups are raised communally, and behav-

ior is easy to observe in the wild. Often compared to the German Shepherd Dog in size, this African dog stands from 24 to 30 inches (61–76 cm), weighs 60 to 80 pounds, and has a head-to-croup length of around 44 inches (112 cm). A dog of vocal inflections, it has an alarm, a communal, and a play "bark." Dreaded in its native land, the African hunting dog is said never to miss its prey.

Afghan Hound, brindle. Photo by Putnam.

African hunting dog. *Lycaon pictus*, adult and pup.

African Lion Hound
   See Rhodesian Ridgeback

African sand fox

A wild dog and member of the genus *Vulpes. See* Foxes

Afterbirth

Term used to refer to the placenta and fetal membranes which are typically discharged from the womb after the birth of the pup. It is imperative that this spongy organ be expelled by the bitch shortly after the birth of each pup. Breeders are encouraged to watch for this expellation after each delivery. A veterinarian can administer substances which help in the removal of any retained afterbirths, after the birth of all pups. *See also* Breeding

Agalactia

A contagious viral disease resulting in lowered or non-production of milk by a nursing bitch. It usually appears in warm weather, and is accompanied by fever and loss of appetite. Abscesses may also form. In chronic cases, the mammary gland itself may atrophy.

Age. The life expectancy of dogs varies from breed to breed, and dog to dog. Photo by R. Pearcy.

Age

A dog's year, comprised largely of dog days, has been equated with seven of man's years, primarily by housewives and other dubiously informed scholars. While the assertion works in some situations, it cannot be applied in all. Generally, puppies reach an age comparable to adolescence within their first year. A popular alternative rule of thumb asserts that the first year is roughly equivalent to the first 16 years of human life; the second

year, approximately seven years; the third, six years; and all subsequent equalling five years each. This theory has substantial merit but is also not perfect, nor can it be applied to all dogs or breeds of dog. Some breeds mature faster than others. The Bernese Mountain Dog, for instance, grows at a tremendous rate. The Bullmastiff, on the other hand, develops at a much slower pace, often not reaching full maturity until its second or third year. Various factors are involved in a breed's aging process: metabolism, diets, hardiness and environment.

Small dogs, such as the toy dogs and smaller "non-sporting" or "utility" dogs, tend to live longer than the larger breeds, such as the tall mastiffs and sighthounds. The Methuselah of the dog world is the 27-year old Labrador Retriever named "Adjutant" (1936-1963). Of course, this long-lived Lab is quite an exception . . . similar tales of longevity are turned by yogurt-eating Georgians, still jigging well into their hundreds. Chihuahuas and Pomeranians, for example, often live into their late teens, while Great Danes and Irish Wolfhounds often do not reach their ten-year mark. Modern-day living and medical and healthkeeping advances insure man and dog longer, more healthy lives.

Agility Dog

First title for agility competitions, A.D. *See* Agility trials

Agility trials

A modern competitive sport involving man and dog which celebrates and capitalizes on the obedience and intelligence of the canine species, agility began sweeping the United States during the late 1980s. The sport began in the United Kingdom in 1977. In agility trials, the handler directs his dog over a timed obstacle course; the scoring revolves around faults, as in equestrian jumping events. The fast pace and flashy appeal of these trials makes agility one of the most exciting of canine spectator sports. Among the obstacles used in agility are the A-frame, weave poles, table, pause box, seasaw, dog walk, crossover, pipe tunnel, collapsed tunnel, and various jumps such as the broad jump, brush jump, tire jump, bar jump and others. Other obstacles are used in events but have not been approved by the United States Dog Agility Association (U.S.D.A.A.). It is this sponsoring organization that is responsible for the sport's growth in the United States. The association was organized in 1986 and remains in close correspondence with Britain and other European countries in which agility has become popular. Agility competitions are offered for both purebred and mixed-breed dogs, as are obedience trials. Flyball and scent-hurdle racing, two agility events, have been incorporated into the obedience competitions in some of the major kennel clubs. Presently there are three available titles for dogs competing in the sport: Agility Dog, Advanced Agility Dog, and Master Agility Dog (A.D., A.A.D., and M.A.D, respectively). The classes offered include: Tournaments, Starters, Novice, Open, Gamblers, Pairs Relay, Team, Snook and Jumping Class. Undoubtedly, agility offers new and fun opportunities to all dog lovers; more information is available from the U.S.D.A.A., P.O. Box 850955, Richardson, TX 75085.

Aggressive tendencies
See Behavior modification

Ahk-Taz-eet
See South Russian Steppe Hound

Aichi
An ancient Japanese dog used in combination with the Smooth Chow Chow to create the Sanshu, which *see*.

Aidi
See Chien de l'Atlas

Ainu Dog
The Ainu Dog is the native dog of the Ainu tribe of Japan. Today the Ainu is often called the Hokkaido-Ken since the tribe has resided on the Hokkaido island since the influx of Japanese onto the mainland. The Ainu tribe, whose history is very closely tied with the Ainu Dog, first settled in Japan some three thousand years ago—apparently with their dogs. The Hokkaido, which has changed very little over the years, is one of the oldest of

Japanese breeds and has played an important role in the history of other Japanese breeds. The Ainu's ferocity, cour-

age, and loyalty are very appealing characteristics and were probably bred for through the years. The Shar-Pei, Chow Chow and polar bear are usually the only mammals that are accredited with black-blue tongues; however, it is not uncommon for this dog to flash a blue tongue. This of course suggests some connection to one (or both) of those Chinese breeds.

The Ainu has proven a fearless and determined hunter, guard, and defender, and at the same time a loyal and well-

Agility trials are competitive events offered to both purebred and mixed breed dogs.

Ainu Dog, red. Photographs by I. Français.

behaved dog. The dog's ever alert and suspicious nature lent itself to the required role of village guardian.

ESSENTIALS OF THE AINU DOG: A medium-sized, very sturdily built dog with a squared head, pricked ears, three-cornered eyes, and a clear-set nose. Musculature tough and clean cut with noteworthy endurance. The skull and forehead broad and slightly flat. The cheeks well developed, and stop shallow but defined. The eyes are relatively small, set well apart and dark brown in color. The neck is powerful and muscular, free from dewlap. The withers are high, back straight and tough. The loins moderately broad and muscular. The forechest is well developed. The chest deep and moderately broad. The tail is set on high, thick and carried over the back, vigorously curled or sickle curved. The shoulders moderately sloping. The hindlegs powerful. Height: 18–22 inches (46–53 cm). Weight: 45–65 pounds (20–30 kg). Coat: medium short, erect and double. Color: gray, brown, red, white, salt and pepper, or brindle. Secondary sex characteristics are strongly marked.

Ainu-Ken
   See Ainu Dog

Air travel
   See Traveling with your dog

Airedale Terrier
   Largely a descendant of the now ex-

tinct Black and Tan Terrier, the Airedale Terrier is named for the river of Aire in the district of Yorkshire. Its development, beginning in the mid-nineteenth century, is accredited to local otter hunters of Airedale and Wharfdale who desired a terrier not only to work otter and other sundry vermin but also to be large enough to double as a home protector. Various large, working strains of ratting terriers (dogs all larger than a modern-day Fox Terrier) were crossed with the Otter Hound to obtain a dog substantial enough to tackle an adult badger or otter. The Otter Hound contributed not only weight and substance but uncanny swimming ability. The oversized ears sometimes seen on Airedales today are attributed to this cross to the Otter Hound. Later, the introduction of Irish Terrier (and possibly even the Welsh Terrier) blood led towards the setting of size and type.

   Of course, the result of these careful crosses is a kingly, undeniably versatile terrier that can fight and beat large-size vermin in confined corners. Due to the Airedale's size, however, the dog cannot actually "go to ground" in the usual sense, and this detail has caused many to question whether the Airedale is truly a terrier (which of course is derived from the Latin *terra*, meaning earth or ground). Among the names which this super terrier acquired are Working Terrier, Waterside Terrier, and Bingley Terrier. Airedale Terrier has persisted for the past century, however.

   The Airedale is perhaps the most adaptable, versatile dog of all. In addition to his terrier abilities, which include quarry larger than most terriers themselves, the Airedale is trainable as a gundog. Hunters who have developed their Airedale in this area reveal that he is superb in setting, retrieving and flushing—abilities he finds surprisingly natural. Many have found (and will find) the Airedale preferable to Springers and Cockers when it comes to working big duck, since a duck of any size

Airedale Terrier, tan with black saddle. Photo by I. Français.

cannot deter the Airedale. In the water, the Airedale exhibits swift, agile and powerful swimming ability.

Germany was perhaps the first country where the British Airedale's many abilities were discovered. Germany employed these large dogs as cart pullers, guard dogs, frontier dogs, police dogs, and war dogs. Ironically, the Airedale's last function, that of a combating war dog, flourished in World War I against the British, its very creators. European and Asiatic nations alike have employed the Airedale as a military assistant, relying on its easy trainability, great determination of character and devotion to duty. Trained Airedales that worked in the Russo-Japanese War illustrated the breed's superhuman intelligence. " . . . they became a source of embarrassment to the Japanese victors . . . by always finding and directing to the Russians first and the Japanese soldiers last, for the Airedale's scent is remarkable," writes Hutchinson.

As a companion and show dog, the Airedale is an obedient and splendid dog that has taken home countless exhibition awards. In appearance, the well-groomed Airedale "is as handsome as possible." Pet Airedales still exhibit a natural watchdog instinct and are dutiful guard dogs. Hutchinson purports in his enviably British tone: "Tramps dislike the Airedale excessively. They know perfectly well the menace of his voice; so much so that they give a wide berth to the house where they know an Airedale is kept."

The Airedale of course has delighted owners off the European continent as

Airedale Terriers
photographed by
I. Français.

well; in the United States, the breed has a strong following and it is a frequent sight in the home and ring. Owners must place considerable effort in the upkeep of the Airedale's coat. While stripping a terrier usually is no tremendous chore, stripping a terrier coat as large as the Airedale's cannot help but be a project. Of course, clipping the Airedale's coat should be a capital offense! In obedience trials, the Airedale is a consistent champion. Other nations such as India, Japan, Australia, Canada, South Africa and others have welcomed the Airedale Terrier as well.

ESSENTIALS OF THE AIREDALE TERRIER: The Airedale is a well-muscled, fairly cobby dog with a durable wire coat. Skull long and flat, not too broad with stop most imperceptible. Jaws, deep, powerful and strong, showing strength of foreface. Body short, strong and level. Ribs well sprung; chest deep, not broad. Hindquarters are long and muscular. Coat is dense and hard, wiry. Color is tan, except for dark markings on sides of head; legs tan, body dark grizzle or black. Saddle is black. Height: 22–24 inches (56–61 cm). Weight: 44 pounds (20 kg). Ears, smallish, folding and V-shaped. The slackless body is supported by column-like, straight forelegs, complemented by well-bent hindlegs, giving the dog free, propulsive movement.

Aitches

The pelvic tubers, rather exclusively referring to the Sussex Spaniel's body.

used very successfully in many flock-guarding programs.

ESSENTIALS OF THE AKBASH DOG: A solid white coat. Keen hearing and superior strength. The coat, which can be either smooth or long, is always double. Height: 28–34 inches (71–86 cm). Weight: 85–140 pounds (39–64 kg).

Akbash Dog, white. Photo by I. Français.

A.K.C.

Abbreviation for the American Kennel Club, which *see.*

Akbash Dog

A native flock-guarding breed of Turkey, the Akbash Dog is a durable and tremendously resourceful component of the agricultural life of that country. Thousands of years ago, the dog's prototypes were embraced by local shepherds and adapted to their specific needs. These dogs are said to have accompanied wandering Eastern travelers to Turkey and to be a cross-pollination of Eastern mastiffs and sighthounds. The breed's ranginess and acute eyesight (assumedly the contribution of the long-legged fleet hounds) along with the Akbash's white coat, which enables the shepherd to distinguish between dog and predator, make the Akbash a vital part of the shepherds' well-being in Turkey. In the United States, the Akbash Dog has been

Akita

The Akita represents an ancient Japanese breed type. The name Akita or Akita Inu comes from the province Akita where the dogs were originally, principally found. The common belief is that these dogs were originally bred for the hunt. In fact, Akitas have been commonly and successfully used for hunting such prey as wild boar, deer and black bear. Others, however, feel that Akitas were developed for fighting. Supporting their claim, they refer to the Japanese zest for the dog pits and cite examples of same-sex hunting pairs being too hostile and aggressive to work together effectively. When the Japanese (and European) dog-fighting sport declined, the dogs were employed for hunting purposes. Whatever the original impetus, the Akita was fixed from large Japanese (nordic) type dogs which could be found about three hundred years ago.

Japanese dogs are chiefly divided into

three categories or sub-groups depending on size. The largest of the native Nipponese dogs is the Akita and is basically alone in this size division. The Shika-Inus, the medium-size dogs, and the Shiba-Inus, the small-size dogs, comprise six or more other Japanese breeds. The Japanese Shiba Inu breed is the smallest of these. The Sanshu Dog, Kai, Kishu, Shikoku, and Ainu Dog populate the Shika-Inu division.

With the influx of non-Japanese dogs into Japan (especially the German Shepherd Dog and Pointers) in the early twentieth century, native breeds in Japan suffered in popularity and purity. The Society for Preservation of Japanese Dogs was established for the said purpose of preserving the native breeds of Japan. After World War I, the Akita was protected because it was becoming so scarce. The Akita Inu Hozankai Society of Japan was organized later in 1927 to preserve the Akita specifically. The Akita was so rare in the 1930s that only the very wealthy could afford or the very lucky could acquire a specimen.

Of the Japanese breeds, the Akita has gained the highest level of public attention—irrefutably. In the United States, the breed has only been known since the early 1970s. It was granted full AKC recognition in 1973.

These dogs are very proud in their way and somewhat independent. While they prove even-tempered companions for many and effective guardians for others, Akitas can be sometimes somewhat detached in nature; this quiet aloofness is often misinterpreted as a lack of loyalty or affection. Nonetheless, these are beloved family dogs that have delighted households around the world for many years. Loyalty is proverbial.

ESSENTIALS OF THE AKITA: A large dog with a bearlike expression created by the massive skull, broad muzzle and black nose, stand-offish coat, and small, triangular, slightly rounded ears. The head is massive, but in balance with the body. Skull is flat between the ears, which are erect. Neck is thick, comparatively short and very muscular. The body is longer than it is high. Chest is wide and depth of

chest is half the dog's height. Height: 24–28 inches (61–71 cm). Weight: 75–110 pounds (34–50 kg). Coat: medium short, harsh and double, with no feathering. Any color is acceptable, including pied and brindle. The tail is large and full, set high and carried in a single or double curl. Back is level with firmly muscled loin and moderate tuck-up.

Akita, red sable. Photo by J. Langden.

Akita Inu
See Akita

Alangu
A hunter and watchdog of the Tanjore and Tiruchinapalli districts of India, this

Akita, cream. Photo by Alverson.

Akita, variant, brindle. Photo by Français.

Alapaha Blue Blood Bulldog, spotted.

dog is known for its short coat and noble carriage. While good-natured and un-wavering, this dog is ferocious when on duty. Red, fawn, and black, each with a black mask, are the most common colors. He stands 27 inches (68–69 cm) tall and pricks high-set ears.

Alano

This scenthound/mastiff creation is a formidable canine with sublime hunting abilities. The Alano derives from the Celtic Hound and various mastiff types. The Dogue de Bordeaux and English Mastiff are believed to be its close rela-tions. The breed retains the large head and powerful body of its mastiff forefa-thers. The back is convex without being excessively long. The color is red with a black mask. The ears are tipped, of mod-erate length. The muzzle is mastiff-like: short and broad. The chest is broad and the thighs powerful. It is used as a pack hunter of wild boar, maintaining the scenthound's love of the chase and tire-less endurance. Alano is also an alternate name for the Great Dane, which *see*.

Alapaha Blue Blood Bulldog

This local American bulldog type has been in the Lane family of Rebecca, Geor-gia for generations. PaPa Buck Lane pioneered this nearly lost "plantation dog." The first dog to be developed into the ideal mold was named "Otto," a name which substitutes for the breed in its locale. These dogs are most trainable and among the most competent of bull-dog-type guard dogs. Lana Lou Lane, the founder's granddaughter, continues the breeding program tradition and has set a registry for the breed. To date there are about fifty dogs in the U.S.

ESSENTIALS OF THE ALAPAHA BLUE BLOOD BULLDOG: A well-developed, unexagger-ated bulldog with a broad head, natural drop ears, and a prominent muzzle. The Alapaha weighs approximately 100 pounds (47 kg) and is 24 inches (61 cm) at the shoulders. Females are usually sub-stantially smaller and weigh an average of 78 pounds (34 kg). In color the Alapaha can be black, white, blue marbled, buff, brown and spotted. The ears and tail are never trimmed or docked. The body is sturdy and unquestionably muscled.

Alariasis

An infection caused by flukes (*Alaria arisaemoides*) which are ingested by the dog. They pass on to the bronchial tract and into the small intestine, where they mature and feed on intestinal contents.

Alarm dogs

There are two kinds of alarm dogs: dogs that bark and sound an alarm and dogs that bark, sound an alarm and do something. The former category embraces the smaller dogs which may unflatteringly be called yappy: Shih Tzus, small Poodles, Maltese, and other toy-sized dogs. The Pekingese is one of the most famous dogs for alarm purposes; in its home country, the Peke would yap whenever someone behaved out of line and yap for the Emperor's royal entrance—though today he's not yappy. The latter category includes those guard dogs that are not quite man-stoppers: the Shetland Sheepdog, and Welsh Terrier, to name just a few. These dogs will attempt to protect their masters but generally do not possess the ability to tackle a man.

Alaskan Malamute

A native of Alaska and the Arctic region, the Malamute as a breed can be traced back to the Mahlemut tribe that inhabited Alaska as far back as can be determined—they are rarely mentioned without their dogs. These dogs were used chiefly for hunting and fishing tasks. The settling of Alaska surely affected the Alaskan Malamute's historical role. Dogs in large numbers were used for hauling and transportation purposes. It didn't take white men very long to realize that the Arctic husky types were the horsepower of the snow-covered tundra and that no animal could compare to them in endurance and stamina.

The Alaskan Malamute is but one of the sledge dogs of the Arctic region. The exact derivation of these Eskimo dogs is not known and is often debated. The dogs' close resemblance to the wolf is one source of controversy. Head type and facial expression strongly suggest the possibility of crosses to the wolves of the Arctic. The Arctic wolf, which is principally white in color, can be twice the size of today's Malamute. While experimental crosses between wolves and "huskies" in captivity are executed today routinely, crossing in the wild between these two canids may be entirely different. Worth remembering is that the Arctic wolf is the only animal on the tundra of which the Eskimo dogs are fearful. These sledge dogs are surely the product of an icy Darwinian survival struggle, a struggle that endured for at least 2,000 years. Employed by white men, Eskimo dogs are responsible for the successful strides made in Arctic and Antarctic exploration. One of the most common beliefs is that these dogs crossed the Bering Strait into Alaska following the migrating tribes.

Malamutes were highly prized as

Alaskan Malamute, black/white. Photo by I. Français.

workers and beloved companions. It is no wonder that today's breed is such an affectionate companion that has retained a good share of its working abilities. While the wolf seems a wild, unruly animal, it is quite gregarious with its own, as are the Malamutes, also attributable to their long-time pack existences.

Alaskan Malamutes.

The Alaskan Malamute must combine the grueling endurance and untiring dedication to work (especially as a sledge dog) and the docile nature required of a companion/family/team dog. It is a dual-natured dog composed of two highly esteemed characteristics: love of work and love of man.

ESSENTIALS OF THE ALASKAN MALAMUTE: The Alaskan Malamute creates a strong, dense, power-packed impression. The skull is broad and slightly rounded between medium-sized ears, rounded at the tips. The muzzle is massive, narrowing only slightly at the nose. Body is strongly and compactly built. The back should be straight and gently sloping to the hips. Loins well muscled, not short to interfere with movement. The shoulders are moderately sloping; forelegs heavily boned and muscled, straight to pasterns. The coat is double with an outer coat of thick, coarse guard hairs; the undercoat is dense, measuring one to two inches in length. The tail has a thick brush and should not be tightly curled. Height: 23–25 inches (59–64 cm). Weight: 75–85 pounds (34–39 kg). Coat varies in length;

medium short most common. Color: gray through black, with white markings.

Albanian Greyhound

A large sighthound of Greece used primarily in the coursing of hare and small deer. In its homeland, it is referred to as Ellenikos Ichnilatis. Resembling the Saluki, this Greek courser is clearly related to the Eastern greyhound types. One of the tallest of the world's sighthounds, the Greek Greyhound stands as high as 31 inches (79 cm). In color it is typically black and tan with a white blaze on the chest. The sizable, pendant ears and tail are fringed and carried gracefully. It is capable of working and giving tongue over both mountain and plain.

Albanian Wolfdog

This flock guard of Albania is similar to the German Shepherd Dog but does not function in the Alsatian's herding capacity. The shepherds were highly protective of their Wolfdogs, quite needlessly so in consideration of the dog's reputed ferocity. Once, these dogs were exhibited at the London Zoo and were most noted for their fierce carryings-on.

Albinism

Congenitally, the lack of pigmentation in the eyes (irises), skin and hair.

Alentejo Herder

See Rafeiro do Alentejo

Alert

1) Any dog at attention.
2) A racing dog that is quickly out from the starting box.

Allergy

Like people, dogs can be allergic to outdoor and/or indoor surroundings, such as carpet fuzz, pillow stuffings, food, pollen, etc. Recent experiments in hyposensitization have proven effective in many cases when injections are given with follow-up "boosters." Sneezing, coughing, nasal discharges, runny, watery, eyes, etc., are all symptomatic.

Almond eyes

Noticeably pointed at either corner, eyes oval in shape (e.g., Basenji).

Alopecia

An inherited skin problem which may affect all breeds. Alopecia refers to an unusual loss of hair under seemingly normal conditions, e.g., no infection or imbalance, no itching or chewing. There is no certain treatment or cure.

Alopex lagopus

A wild dog commonly known as the Arctic fox, which *see*.

Alpenlandischer Dachsbracke

See Alpine Dachsbracke

Alpine Dachsbracke

Alpine Dachsbracke, known as the Alpenlandischer Dachsbracke, is present-day Austria's foremost coldtrailing deer hunter and has been for generations. Austria developed the Alpine to fulfill its need for a robust, larger dachsbracke with the requisite drive to withstand the high-altitude Alps. The Alpine is a professional on deer, but also excels on rabbit and fox. This many faceted, multi-utility dog is pure Austrian, developed strictly from indigenous dachsbrackes. Never popular as a pet, the Alpine boasts an impressive following of hunters and gamesmen in the areas where he is popular. Knowing well the task he was bred to do, this hound is an easykeeper for his master.

ESSENTIALS OF THE ALPINE DACHSBRACKE: A hardy, solidly built hound with short but not contorted legs. The head is broad and of moderate size. The breed is most commonly seen in stag red, although black/tan and red with black ticking are also typical. The coat is described in the standard as dense and coarse but not wire. White on the body is undesirable; chocolate, black or gray-blue disqualifies. Height: 13–17 inches (33–43 cm). Weight: 33–40 pounds (15–18 kg).

Alsatian

See German Shepherd Dog

Alunk

This little known Indian breed is practically naked and is that country's only hairless miniature. It is also referred to as Sonangi. Untypical of the hairless breeds, this mottled-skin menace is a furiously

Alpine Dachsbracke, black/tan. Photo by I. Français.

effective watchdog with the ferocity which hardly befits a miniature. Occurring from Tanjore to Kanyakumari, the

Alpine Dachsbracke, black-ticked red. Photo by I. Français.

dogs are said to resemble the Mexican Hairless. The Kuchi, which *see*, is also from the Tanjore district.

Amaurosis

Amaurosis, also known as familial amaurotic idiocy, is a condition that affects the German Shorthaired Pointer breed and is marked by nervousness and decreased trainability. It is possibly a hereditary condition transmitted through the simple autosomal recessive. Progressive ataxia and impaired sight may follow. Vets can prescribe certain drugs for improvement. For hunters especially, there is nothing more frustrating than a well-conditioned dog that cannot learn even the simplest of work commands.

Amble

A gait in which front and hindlegs on the same side, as a pair, move in unison with one another. This gait is slower than the pace where both legs of the said pair are raised simultaneously; in the amble, the hindleg leaves and returns to the ground slightly earlier. This action is correct for the Old English Sheepdog walking or trotting.

American Black and Tan Coonhound
See Black and Tan Coonhound

American Blue Gascon Hound

The American Blue Gascon Hound is the red, white and blue rendition of the French Gascony hound so admired by sportsmen for its cold-nose and big voice. Those hunters, favoring the blue-ticked hounds of the Old Line strain, broke away to promote the Big n' Blue. Wilson "Bluetick Bill" Harshman receives credit for giving the breed its nickname, the title of his book containing stories about the Old Line strain. Aficionados of the American Blue Gascon formed an association to promote the breed since many huntsmen were focusing attention on the Redbone Coonhound, the Treeing Walker, and the Tennessee Treeing Brindle. These smaller scenthounds excelled in the latest trend of the night hunt because the emphasis was on speed and the number of coons treed. The organization has done well to preserve interest in the breed, and today the Big n' Blue is one of the few hunting dogs capable of pursuing bear, big cat, and wild boar, in addition to small quarry. This is a very able hound that possesses a special-

ized skill. Incidentally, in the hunter's home, this is a fearless guard dog and a worthy companion.

ESSENTIALS OF THE AMERICAN BLUE GASCON HOUND: An extremely large, big-voiced hound, the Big n' Blue stands up to 32 inches (81 cm) in height and weighs up to 110 pounds (50 kg). The breed is heavily ticked; the roaning and ticking over its usually well-speckled white coat give the impression of a grizzled appearance. Any color or combination of colors is acceptable.

bulldogs. Whether it is guard work, farm work, or field competition, this breed rises to the challenge. However, he has never been accepted into the show circles. Despite his versatility and proven worth in a vast number of areas and his ability to pass type with reliability, he remains unrecognized by the major registries of the world. The American Bulldog is registered by the Game American Bulldog Club and the breed continues to gain recognition in the United States and in Europe.

American Bulldog

During the 1800s, a time of massive European emigration, strong-bodied bulldogs with hearts of steel and games of granite were brought to the U.S. Once settled, these bulldogs were put to many uses and developed into many different types of dog. Some variations disappeared, others, by proving their value, flourished. The American Bulldog of today represents one of the true utility-type variations of the nineteenth-century

ESSENTIALS OF THE AMERICAN BULLDOG: Head large, with a broad skull and powerful jaws; the small high-set ears, when uncropped, are flap or rolled; the muzzle is short. Complementing the broad skull are well-muscled broad shoulders. The tail is usually docked, but, if not, is carried low. Height: 19–25 inches (45–64 cm). Weight: 65–105 pounds (30–48 kg). The smooth coat is colored (in order of preference): red brindle, other brindles, solid white, red, fawn, and piebald.

American Bulldog, white. Photo by I. Français.

American Cocker Spaniel

The American Cocker Spaniel is of direct relation to the English Cocker Spaniel, which in turn traces its lineage back to the spaniel types of Spain. Spaniels in America probably go back farther than the United States, and spaniels in England go back at least 400 years more. However, authorities state that both American and English cockers trace their distinct spaniel type to an English dog named "Obo," who was whelped in 1879 and owned by James Farrow.

The American Cocker Spaniel, or sim-

min (rabbits, rabbits, rabbits) which they called "Span, Span, Span"; the land they called *Hispania* or Rabbitland; the dogs to catch the "Span" Spaniels. And, although the French rendition of the word's etymology may be more precise, Ms. Woolf's account is surely more fearless and enjoyable.

The original separation of American versus English dogs was based on weight; those weighing between 28–35 pounds (13–16 kg) were dubbed English, while those weighing under 13 kilograms (28 lbs) were called American.

American Cocker Spaniel, buff.

ply Cocker Spaniel, as Americans refer to him, is the most popular of the spaniel breeds in the States. The writer Virginia Woolf (despite her name not an author renowned for canine studies) does however offer a colorful theory on the evolution of the word "spaniel" in our beloved English language and its affiliation with Spain. Circa 238 B.C., when the Carthaginians landed in Spain, they were encircled by well-sprung, long-eared ver-

Subsequently, American Cockers were bred for desired traits (size, head, body, build, etc.), and through the years they changed from both the original cockers and the modern English Cockers: their skull became higher and more domed, and the muzzle became shorter. It was in the 1940s that the two breeds were recognized as separate. The American Cocker is today the smallest member of the sporting family, and although still called an effective hunter's helper, the Cocker certainly makes more vocation of companionship and showmanship than field work.

The first Cocker to arrive in America is said to have sailed on the Mayflower, accompanying the Pilgrims in 1620. This poor lonesome dog, however, cannot be attributed to springing forth too many Cockers since he had none of his kind with which to cavort. After about a century, spaniel importation increased as settlers were enthralled with the vast and abundant wilderness of the unexplored colonies.

Mr. M.P. McCoon's liver and white Cocker was the first entered into the American Kennel Club stud book, within a couple of years of the issuance of the first edition in St. Louis, Missouri. The breed formally took hold in 1881 when the American Spaniel Club formed; a total of 117 dogs were registered that first year. This number of course includes both Cockers and Field Spaniels, the difference being only size (Fields weighed over 28 pounds, 16 kg).

The appearance of a well-groomed Cocker Spaniel is one of undeniable beauty; the dog's charming personality, thoroughly winning, merry and free, is no subtle hint as to this dog's ceaseless popularity in the U.S. especially. Today the Cocker is America's most loved national dog and he continually jockeys the Poodle and Labrador Retriever for the highest number of annual registrations.

ESSENTIALS OF THE AMERICAN COCKER SPANIEL: The Cocker Spaniel is a small gundog of sturdy and compact build. His cleanly chiseled and refined head is a most appealing physical feature. He stands well up at the shoulder on forelegs that are straight and hindquarters that are muscular. The topline slopes slightly to the rear of the dog. The muscular quarters allow for considerable speed and endurance. The skull is rounded. The cheeks have no protuberance. The

eyes are round but their rims give them a slightly almond-shaped appearance. The ears are lobular, long, and well feathered. The coat is long, silky, and abundant. Color may be solid black, including black with tan points; any solid color other than black, all with tan points allowed; or particolors (roans are classified as partis). Height: 14–15 inches (35–38 cm). Weight: 24–28 pounds (11–12.5 kg). The A.K.C. standard states, "Above all he must be free and merry, sound, well balanced throughout, and in action show a keen inclination to work…"

American Cocker Spaniel, solid black. Photo by J. Langden.

American Cocker Spaniel, tricolor. Photo by J. Ashbey.

American Eskimo

The American Eskimo is a member of the spitz family, a family that traces its lineage back six millennia to the Peat Dog of the New Stone Age lake dwellers.

American Eskimo, Toy.

American Eskimo, Miniature.

Remains of these prototypes have been uncovered in various European countries. The American Eskimo resulted from Americans breeding white German Spitz and promoting the variety. Initially these dogs were quite larger than the Standard American Eskimo that stands only 19 inches (48 cm) high. This fostering began about 100 years ago. Although the American Eskimo, once referred to simply as "Spitz," is a keen part of America's native-dog heritage, to this day it is only registered by the United Kennel Club. This American registry recognizes two size variants: Standards and Miniatures. Popularity in their American homeland is continually growing. While the breed's popularity has often been focused on the West Coast, today Eskies are blooming on the East and elsewhere as well. A Toy variety has also been developed, but is not registered by the UKC. The Toy American Eskimo seems to be a perfectly acceptable and expectable offshoot of the Eskimo breeds, especially since the Toy German Spitz has been favored for many years, be it the Victorian Pom or the Pomeranian. It is

unfortunate that more show rings aren't graced by these snow beauties' presence. Europeans have favored the tiny pure-white Pomeranians or Toy German Spitzes, but these really do not compare to the undeniably sweet expressions of the American spitzen.

The Eskie's agreeable temperament makes him ideal for most any living situation. These are principally companion dogs and are rarely used for any work purpose. "Beauty without vanity" aptly describes the Eskies that have made flawless companions to Americans for generations. They are intelligent and hardy dogs that are trainable and obedient. In the snow, they are most content and incorrigible.

ESSENTIALS OF THE AMERICAN ESKIMO: Proportionate and balanced, the American Eskimo, in any size, is the typical model of the northern working-type dog. Triangular ears, slightly rounded at the tips, ring with the celebrated nordic character. A thick coat and a richly plumed tail carried over the back complete this picture of elegance, alertness and beauty. The head should denote power in its wedge shape and perfect proportion to the body. The body is strong and compactly built. The face is foxy and the

muzzle is pointed. The back is straight, level and broad. The coat is preferably pure white; cream or biscuit is permissible. The coat covers the body with soft straight hair, with a noticeably thicker mane forming a ruff on the neck. The Standard American Eskimo is 18–35 pounds (9–16 kg) and stands 15–19 inches (38–48 cm). The Miniature is 10–20 pounds (4.5–9 kg) and stands 11–14 inches (28–36 cm). The Toy is 11–12 inches (28–31 cm) and weighs 6–10 pounds (2.5–4.5 kg).

hounds were imported by the Gloucester Foxhunting Club; these along with foxhounds from France and Kerry Beagle-type hounds from Ireland form the basis of the American Foxhound.

The nature of fox hunting has changed over the years and is still different from country to country; and in America, from state to state. Initially, fox hunting would have been more accurately labeled fox exterminating. Foxes preyed on farmers' livestock and destroyed property. The hounds were used to track down and

American Eskimos, Standard.

American Foxhound

The American Foxhound developed from English, French and Irish packhounds imported to America in 1650 by Robert Brooke. These Crown colony working hounds remained in the Brooke family for three centuries. English scent-

destroy the foxes. As the fox population diminished and hunters became enamored by the fox's natural ability to deceive and escape, the exterminating became more of a sport. The hounds were now employed only to scent and find the fox, not to kill it. In many northern states, fox hunters still kill the prey, while in most southern states, fox sportsmen hunt for the chase. Southern hunters know the individual running patterns of each fox in their area and enjoy seeing their hounds corner the fox that evaded them the weekend before.

American Foxhound, tricolor. Photo by I. Français.

Initially, however, the American Foxhound fulfilled the colonists' need for a methodical, enduring scenthound to cover the wide wooded area to pursue fox and other quarry, more out of necessity than for sport. As most of the colonists were British, it is most likely that a good percentage of the American Foxhound's original stock were Foxhounds from England. The breeds' similar appearances today would validate this assumption.

In type the American Foxhound has varied over the years as well as contributed to the development of other American scenthound breeds. Many American Foxhound strains have persisted over the years and it is not difficult to confuse an American with an English Foxhound. Independent and strong-willed, Foxhounds excel in pack hunting. Although the American Kennel Club registers very few of the breed each year, this breed makes up a good percentage of all American working dogs.

ESSENTIALS OF THE AMERICAN FOXHOUND: This long-eared hound is sufficiently tall and lightly boned for a hound. The head is fairly long; the skull slightly domed at the occiput; the muzzle long and square; the ears are of no moderate length, set at eye level and nearly reach the tip of the nose; the eyes large and set well apart. The shoulders are sloping and are not loaded; they are clean and muscular. Unlike the English Foxhound, there is a slight tuck up of loin that reflects the topline. Legs and feet sound. The medium-length coat is close and hard and comes in any color. The tricolor combination is believed to be the most popular and is frequently seen in the show ring. Height: 21–25 inches (53–64 cm). Tail has a slight curve, not carried in a squirrel fashion.

American Hairless Terrier

The American Hairless Terrier is the only indigenous hairless breed of the United States. Its genesis dates as far back as 1972. In a litter of mid-sized Rat Terriers, a completely hairless female was born. It became the prized pet of Willie and Edwin Scott of Louisiana, who bred it and produced another pair, male and female, that was used to stabilize the new breed. The Scotts, working under the guidance of their geneticists and veterinarians, have devoted their efforts to producing the breed they've aptly named the American Hairless Terrier.

These dogs are unique among the hairless breeds of the world; they differ substantially from the hairless types of Asia and Africa in that no coated variety is needed to obtain hairless pups, as the hairlessness gene is not semi-lethal dominant but autosomal recessive. Furthermore, these dogs do not have absent premolars or any of the breeding complications usually associated with the hairless breeds. For these traits, the Scotts' nude puppy and its progeny are truly remarkable, promising and noteworthy in the canine world!

The temperament of these dogs is pure terrier, although their lack of hair prevents them from performing the tasks on which their Rat Terrier parents thrive. Hairless dogs have become the choice of many owners who are looking for a unique twist or who are allergic to the hair of other dogs. Extra care is required to protect the dog from irritants that might otherwise prove unaffecting.

ESSENTIALS OF THE AMERICAN HAIRLESS TERRIER: In build, the American Hairless Terrier is identical to the medium-sized

Rat Terrier. The American Hairless is a well-muscled dog with a deep chest, strong shoulders, solid neck, and powerful legs. The ears are carried erect when the dog is alert; the tail is customarily docked. Height: 9–14 inches (23–36 cm). Weight: 7–14 pounds (3–6.5 kg). No coat. The skin color can be pink with gray, black, golden, or red spots.

American Kennel Club

The American Kennel Club is the official registry for purebred dogs in the United States. The organization publishes and maintains the Stud Book and handles all litter and individual registrations, transfers of ownership, and so on. It keeps all United States dog show, field trial and obedience records; issues championships and other titles in these areas as they are earned; approves and licenses all dog show, obedience trial, and field trial judges; licenses or issues approval to all championship shows, obedience trials and recognized match shows; creates and enforces the rules, regulations, and policies by which the breeding, raising, exhibiting, handling,

and judging of purebred dogs in the United States are governed. Clubs, not individuals, are members of the American Kennel Club, each of which is represented by a delegate selected from the club's own membership for the purpose of attending the quarterly A.K.C. meetings as the representative of the member club, to vote on matters discussed at each meeting and to bring back a report to the individual club of any decisions or developments which have occurred.

The A.K.C. is a non-profit organization which has been established since September 17, 1884. Over 400 autonomous dog clubs comprise the body. The club is the largest registry in the States; second is the United Kennel Club, which *see*. The American Kennel Club has represented over 35,000,000 dogs since its inception over a hundred years ago.

The Westminster Kennel Club show held in Madison Square Garden, New York City, New York (also the hometown of the A.K.C.) is the most prestigious of American dog shows and is licensed by this registry. *See also* United Kennel Club, Group systems

American Hairless Terrier. This is founder Willie Scott's first male, Trout Creeks Snoopy.

American Kennel Club. Best of Breed competition underway for Norwich Terriers at the Westminster Kennel Club Show.

American Mastiff
See Bandog

American Pit Bull
See American Pit Bull Terrier

American Pit
Bull Terrier, solid
fawn, uncropped.

American Pit Bull Terrier

Undeniably used in the dog pits of yesterday and today, the American Pit Bull is equally an undeniably outstanding canine, possessing intelligence, strength, courage, and an undying willingness to please. Dog fighting was once a legalized sport around the world, including such civilized countries as the U.S. and Great Britain. Just as thoroughbred horses are bred and raised to be the best at their sport, so were the pit fighting dogs. Traits bred for included: gameness, ideal fighting size (30–40

pounds; 13.5–18.5 kg), musculation, fearlessness, dedication.

Developed from the bull-and-terrier types of yesterday, the American Pit Bull Terrier displays tenacity and accompanying strength that are unparalleled in the canine world. As rich and captivating as the breed's history is, the Pit Bull's future is more worthy of commentary. No dog in the history of mankind has stirred up more attention than the Pit Bull Terrier, with the possible exceptions of Pavlov's dogs and Snoopy®. Recent ordinances and laws have placed bans on "pit bulls" in certain locales. The pit-bull paranoia is not entirely a new phenomenon; similar witch hunts were initiated in the early 1900s in the U.S., calling the dogs "monstrous" and dangerous. Pit-bull bans do not isolate the American Pit Bull Terrier (as recognized by the U.K.C.) as *the* pit bull. Pit bulls in this context can affect any dog with any bull-and-terrier in its blood. Such breeds then include the American Staffordshire Terrier, Staffordshire Bull Terrier, Bull Terrier, Miniature Bull Terrier, and the American Pit Bull Terrier. Additionally, any crosses therein are also affected: Bandogs, Pit Bullmastiffs, etc. Even the mild French Bulldog and Boston Terrier have fallen suspect under various anti-pit-bull laws. The situation is considerably difficult and dogs often need to be proven "vicious" to be dangerous.

American Pit Bull Terrier, light fawn with white.

The A.P.B.T., as registered by the U.K.C., *is* an individual breed of dog and does not refer to just any ill-bred, mindless warrior-type mongrel. Registered Pit Bull Terriers have long pedigrees to prove their blue blood. In the America of times unfortunately gone by, the Pit Bull was a much loved, much trusted, worthy companion. The loveless unworthies who have capitalized on the breed's abilities for illegal dog-fighting activities or other comparable lowlife behavior are chiefly responsible for the banning and witchhunting that have been sweeping the U.S. The media, however, should not go unscathed, for it is also responsible for escalating isolated incidents in its usual unrelenting and attention-getting way.

The Pit Bull's future has been perhaps irreparably undone and everyone is to blame except the dog itself. The "little rascal" is too set on pleasing his owner, and ironically this is the root of his own undoing. Accompanying this need to please are remarkable abilities of all kinds. Pit Bulls excel in practically every canine task: herding, guarding, hunting, policing, and ratting.

ESSENTIALS OF THE AMERICAN PIT BULL TERRIER: The bricklike head, which is especially broad between the cheeks (to house the powerful jaws), is carried upon a thickly muscled, well-defined neck. The neck runs into a deep, thick, well-sprung chest. In size, the dog's length

exceeds slightly the height of between 18–22 inches (46–56 cm). Weight is varied, even among dogs of the same height; weight can be between 30–80 pounds (14–36 kg), with 35–55 pounds (16–25 kg) being common. The coat is short, glossy, and stiff to the touch. All colors are acceptable, with or without markings. The ears set high on the skull, can be cropped or uncropped; tails should not be docked.

American Pit Bull Terriers, black with white, red with white, cropped. Photo by I. Français.

American Staffordshire Terrier, brindle with white.

American Staffordshire Terrier, brindle with white. Photographs by I. Français.

American Staffordshire Terrier

The AmStaff is first cousin to the Staffordshire Bull Terrier of England, which is a cross between the Old Bulldogge of England (who was for many years the premier bullbaiter) and, most likely, the Fox Terrier. The Old Bulldogge is not to be confused with the Old English Bulldog; if there is a resemblance, it is more between the Staffordshire Terriers, especially the larger AmStaff, and the Old Bulldogge. American fanciers desired traits that differed from those of the English fanciers, i.e., greater height and weight and more substantial body features, especially the head and chest. While both the American and British Staffs have well-developed cheek muscles, the AmStaff's conformation is more impressive due to the emphasis once placed on its pit-fighting prowess. Thus, the two Staffs grew apart in type. In 1936, the AmStaff was recognized as a separate breed by the A.K.C.

Despite their pit-fighting history and the harsh criticism that they are vicious,

day of pit fighting, these dogs were known by those who knew them well as gentle with humans. AmStaffs are known as "pleasers" and not as maulers. Their willingness and ability to achieve the desired goals of their master are renowned and prized.

ESSENTIALS OF THE AMERICAN STAFFORDSHIRE TERRIER: Well-put together, muscular and stocky, the American Staffordshire Terrier should project the impression of tremendous power for his size. Height: 17–19 inches (43–48 cm). Weight: 40–50 pounds (18–23 kg). The skull is broad, and the cheek (or jaw) muscles are clearly noticeable. Uncropped ears are commonly preferred. The tail is short in proportion to body size; it is not docked or curled. Coat: short and glossy, close lying and harsh to the touch. The AmStaff is

these dogs are loyal, trustworthy, and, above all, affectionate. Even in the hey-

seen in all colors, including solid, particolor, and patched.

American Staffordshire Terrier, black and white.

American Toy Terrier
See Toy Fox Terrier

American Water Spaniel, chocolate. Photo by I. Français.

American Water Spaniel

The American Water Spaniel traces its lineage to various water spaniels, including the Irish and old English Water Spaniels, and the Curly-Coated Retriever. This lineage is assumed, however, for it remains undocumented. It is very likely that other breeds were used in the course of the breed's development. This is not to detract from the breed's "purity" or functionability, however, for the breed is a true worker and continues to breed true to type today.

The American Water Spaniel is friendly and outgoing, possessing the character typical of other spaniels. As a field companion, the American Water Spaniel is quick, intelligent, obliging, and enduring. More of a working dog, the American Water Spaniel rarely participates in the sport of conformation.

ESSENTIALS OF THE AMERICAN WATER SPANIEL: The physical characteristics of emphasis are size, head properties, coat texture and color. Height: 15–18 inches (36–46 cm). Weight: 25–45 pounds (11–20 kg). The body, sturdy and muscular, is not too compact. The skull, of moderate length, is rather broad and full. The forehead is covered with short smooth hair. The muzzle is square; the jaws are strong and of good length. The remarkable coat is closely curled and of sufficient density to resist heat, cold, and moisture—it is not coarse, however. The powerful legs

have a medium-short curly feather. Color: solid liver or dark chocolate, small amount of white on the toes or chest permissible. The general appearance is of a medium-sized, sturdy dog of typical spaniel character.

AmerToy

See Toy Fox Terrier

Amniotic sac

The enclosing membrane of the embryo.

Amoebic dysentery

A protozoan disease that dogs can carry and exhibit which can be transmitted to man by his consumption of water or food contaminated with the saliva of an infected dog. The disease is characterized by symptoms similar to other dysenteries; they are: abdominal cramps and pains in varied degrees and diarrhea that can be bloody.

Amputation

The surgical removal of a body part, usually a limb. Amputation is performed when no alternatives are presented to save the life of the affected animal.

A.N.K.C.

Abbreviation for the Australian National Kennel Council, which *see*.

Anal sac obstruction

The sacs on either side of the rectum, just inside the anus, at times can become clogged. If the condition persists, it is necessary for the sacs to be opened, so that they do not become infected and/or abscess. Pressure is applied by the veterinarian and the glands release a thick, horrible-smelling excretion. Difficulty in elimination and/or the dog's "walking" on its rump are common signs of clogged anal glands.

Anal sacs

Located inside the rim of the anal sphincter on each side of the rectum, the anal sacs, or glands, function as storage chambers for the coating secretion that affects the odor of the stool. Seemingly a dubious function, the distinctive and distinctively noisome aroma enables pack animals to locate one another. Blockage of the anal glands is often caused in domesticated canines due to incorrect diets: lanky, inadequately plump stools cause sac expression during defecation. Owners should check the anal glands regularly. Veterinary attention is often required to forestall abscess.

Analgesia

Absense of sensitivity to pain or the lack of power to move a part of the body. The condition may be induced by drugs which act on the brain or central nervous system.

Anasarca

Dropsy of the connective tissues of the skin. It is occasionally encountered in fetuses and makes whelping difficult.

Anatolian Karabash Dog

See Anatolian Shepherd Dog

Anatolian Shepherd Dog

The Anatolian Shepherd Dog, or Karabash Dog, emerged in Turkey as the dominant guard dog. Its original work was hunting lions, although today the breed is used principally for defense of flocks. Its canine lineage is most assuredly mastiff, as it derives from crossing the most formidable of Turkish guard dogs, most of whom were of mastiff descent. Visitors to Turkey report seeing these assertive and wary gladiators on the hillsides, wearing spiked collars. This is the traditional indicator that a dog has successfully tracked and downed a wolf—only deserving canines receive this collar; it is a sign to heed and respect. The Anatolian is accepted by the Kennel Club and makes a bonding companion animal. Its wariness and outgoing confidence have waned slightly but they are positively still intact.

Anatolian Shepherd Dog, black-masked fawn. Photo by I. Français.

ESSENTIALS OF THE ANATOLIAN SHEPHERD DOG: This well-built shepherd and guard possesses fine proportions and impressive musculature. The head should don a black mask, evident in its Turkish name (Karabash); a powerful jaw and moderate stop. Height: 27–31 inches (68.5–79 cm). Weight: 85–150 pounds (39–68.5 kg). The breed occurs in brindles, tricolors, and solids, cream to fawn; white dogs also occur.

Anatolian Shepherd Dogs photographed with shepherd master in Turkey.

Anatomy, topographical

Dealing with the exterior appearance and identification of the various anatomical components of the dog.

Ancestors of the dog

Observing the Canadian Eskimo Dog or the Siberian Husky, it is no wonder that domestic dog was begot from wolves. Of course, observing an Ibizan Hound, Neopolitan Mastiff, Brussels Griffon or Chow Chow, one might surmise the giraffe, hippopotamus, monkey or brown bear (respectively). The wolf, like the domestic dog, belongs to the genus *Canis*; the group also includes coyotes, jackals and dingoes.

The evolutionary process is illustrated in the following genealogy: *Miacis—Cynodicitis—Tomarctus—*wolves—domestic dogs. *Miacis*, a forest-dweller of 40 million years ago, was a ferret-sized tree climber with a long sinuous body, heavy tail and short, flexible legs. Its paws had five retractable toes. It was carnivorous and markedly more intelligent than the animals on which it preyed. *Cynodicitis*, 10 million years after *Miacis*, was larger than its tiny forebear but still no bigger than a mink. These were fast-running ground animals whose claws were less retractile with more developed forelimbs, an animal more adapted for running than climbing. From *Cynodicitis*, all true running hounds as well as the African hunting dogs (*Lycaon*) evolved. From various descendants of *Cynodicitis* also emerged bears and raccoons. *Tomarctus* dwelled on the plains about 20 million years ago. This is the most doglike of the three and the believed ancestor of wolves, jackals, foxes and wild dogs as well as present-day domestic dogs.

The dog (*Canis familiaris*) evolved some 12,500 years ago and was the first animal domesticated by man. This domestication is believed to have occurred during the Paleolithic Period or the Old Stone Age, prior to the end of the Pleistocene Ice Age. Cave etchings, Danish kitchen middens (garbage heaps) and lake dwellings indicate that Europeans of the New Stone Age domesticated a wolflike dog. A similar canid has been documented in the succeeding

Ancestors of the dog. Nordic dogs bear a close and telling resemblance to the Arctic wolf.

Ancestors of the dog. This working Siberian Husky is convincingly lupine, appearing quite undomesticated.

Ancestors of the dog. Since wild dogs and domestic dogs interbreed without difficulty, experiments with wolves, dingoes, jackals, and dogs have been successful. Hybrid wolf photo by I. Français.

Bronze and Iron Age as well. Bone remains uncovered of the primitive dogs of the tropical zones of Africa and Asia were deposited near Mullerup on the west coast of Zeeland, Denmark.

The wolf is the main progenitor of domestic dog: it is known that the American Indians kept pariah-type dogs that closely resembled the coyotes; Eskimos' sledge pullers appear to be closer related to the Arctic wolf. It is not suggested that domestic dog could have had more than one progenitor, i.e., German Shepherds evolved from gray wolves and Basenjis from jackals. This notion falters, and it is clear that man's imposed specialization of breeds and the wide expanse of environment affected the development of the domestic dog.

Evidence of the kinship of our dogs and wolves is uncovered in their identical dentition and the fact that they can be interbred and produce fertile progeny. The Eskimos have been known to cross their huskies with wolves to increase their dogs' size. Many of the social habits of the wolf family have been transmitted to the domestic dog. Dog's loyalty and affection for man are surely manifestations of the wolf's social behavior. Dogs, like wolves, also hunt in packs and share in the excitement of their fellow pack-

mates. Whereas wolves and dogs interbred without difficulty, this is not true of dogs and jackals. Jackals have four less chromosomes (*Canis familiaris* has 78), but studies indicate that a careful breeding program could produce a fertile jackal-dog. Foxes, while members of the wild canid family, do not participate in the origin of dog and never cross with the dog.

One study, described by author Lois E. Bueler, has shown that wolf cubs will respond very socially to German Shepherd pups and adults, basically accepting them as wolves. The same wolf cubs, however, were most protestant towards

the white Samoyeds introduced in the same manner. The white coat, curled tail and different scent indicated to the wolves that this was not one of their own.

Ancestors of the dog. Wolves and domestic dog utilize like hunting methods.

Recent studies incorporate the pariah or dingo-type dogs as the missing link between the wolf and domestic dog. The dingo of Australia is slighter in build than the wolf and not nearly as muscular. The aborigines have domesticated these wild dogs with regularity for millennia and dingoes (like wolves) are able to interbreed with domestic dogs. The dingo's story is neither clear nor conclusive. Some believe that it is the last remnant of the wild ancestral dog. Without taking issue, the dingo is a canine and possesses many characteristics similar to those of domestic dog. *See also* Breed development, Dingo

Anchor hound
A Beagle that holds back at the spot at which the rabbit makes a check.

Anchored
The condition of not moving on a trail.

Anemia
A decrease of red blood cells, which are the cells that carry oxygen to the body tissues. Causes are usually severe infestation of parasites, poor diet, and blood disease. The disease is sometimes fatal.

Anesthetics
Those drugs used to allay pain, usually to make surgery or other medical procedures possible. These drugs may be administered orally, by injection, or by vapor (gas), with two or more of these types sometimes used in conjunction, especially injection and vapor.

Anestrous
When a female does not come into heat. *See also* Bitch.

Aneurysm
A rupture or dilation of a major blood vessel, causing a bulge or swelling. It may be caused by strain, injury, or when arteries are weakened by debilitating disease or old age. Surgery is needed to remove the clot.

***Angiostrongylus vasorum* infection**
See Heartworm

Anglo-Français
The designation Anglo-Français is presently employed for three French packhounds: the Grand Anglo-Français, the Anglo-Français de Moyenne Venerie, and the Anglo-Français de Petite Venerie. These hounds, divided by size, represent the working packs of France, dogs which have resulted from crosses of English and French hounds, as the name translated would indicate. The Foxhounds of Great Britain (loosely the English Foxhound) are the principal dogs involved in crossbreeding with the French packhounds to produce the largest of the three, the Grand. The Harrier, a breed also of British heritage, crossed with medium-sized French hounds (Porcelaine and Poitevin possibly) to produce the Moyenne. The Beagle and smaller French hounds produced the Petite. It should be noted that these crosses, with the likely exception of the Petite, were not "planned breeding" as such, and the resulting "breeds" came

about more naturally than other contrived breed geneses.

These are not show dogs, although some occasionally attend an exhibition, but strictly utilitarian dogs. The Grands are very elegant hounds that hunt in packs and are capable of working most any game, big or small. Most hunters attest that these dogs have an inbred knowledge of the game they hunt and possess spectacular noses. The Moyennes surely thrive on pack work and are potentially unstoppable on a myriad of hopping, crawling, and flying game. Developed for work on smaller game, the Petites are superb on rabbit, quail, and pheasant. This dog is considered the "least pure" of the French-English Hounds and is probably the youngest as well as the smallest. Type is essentially set, but many an overly cautious Frenchman still labels him a hound-in-progress. As is the case with all three sizes of the Anglos-Françaises, a wirehaired version once existed. These dogs have effectively disappeared as interest in them waned.

This dog is gentle and kind but is primarily utilitarian. The noble and appealing appearance of the dog may attract non-hunters to the breed, but it should be emphasized that this is a pack hunter who must be worked to be happy. Of the three sizes of Anglos-Françaises, the Petite adapts the most readily to life in-

doors. He has made this transition to house companion more gracefully than either of his big brothers.

Anglo-Français de Moyen Venerie, tricolor.

ESSENTIALS OF THE ANGLO-FRANÇAIS: The Anglo-Français de Petit Venerie, the smallest of the three, is most compact and

Anglo-Français de Petit Venerie, tricolor. Photographs by I. Français.

Anglo-Français, Grand.

Anglo-Français, Grand, black and white. Photographs by I. Français.

stands only 16–18 inches (40–46 cm), weighing 35–44 pounds (16–20 kg). The Anglo-Français de Moyenne Venerie is the middle-size French-English Hound, a tidy size, standing 20 inches (51 cm) and weighing 49–55 pounds (22.5–25 kg).The largest of the Anglo-Français breeds of hound, the Grand Anglo-Français is a big-boned dog with a solid body trunk. The Grand stands 24–27 inches (61–69 cm), and weighs 66–71 pounds (30–32 kg). Excluding size, these three breeds are all quite alike in appearance. The head is moderate in comparison to the

Anglo-Français Tricolore
See Anglo-Français

Anglo-Spanish Greyhound
A crossbred Spanish sighthound type that was once popular in Spain. The breed was devised by crossing the Greyhound proper with the Galgo Español, or Spanish Greyhound. *See also* Galgo Español, Greyhound

Angulation
Angles created by bones meeting at their given joints. The angulation of the

Anglo-Français de Petit Venerie, orange and white. Photo by I. Français.

body; the ears are pendulous and appear to spring from the head. The eyes are superscribed by delicate tan shadings. These tan markings complement the black and white coat. Rather generous ear leather adorns an aristocratic head. The breed comes in three color varieties: black and white, tricolor, and orange and white. Its coat is typically hound: short and sleek; an occasional wire coat may still occur. The Petite is the most graceful in appearance of the Anglos-Françaises. The body of all three of these hounds is muscular and efficiently constructed.

shoulder, stifle and hock are those most commonly referred to in the dog world. The degree of angulation, that is, desired amount of angulation, varies from breed to breed and is broadly interpreted.

Animal baiting
Animal baiting prevailed in seventeenth-century Europe. This now illegal activity is markedly one of the most demented and illustriously cruel undertakings of modern mankind. Bull, bear, and boar baiting were the first of these "sports" to be enjoyed. Baiting was popu-

Animal baiting. The English Bulldog today is far removed from its more surly, athletic bullbaiting predecessors.

Animal baiting. The Neapolitan Mastiff, in Roman times, was a formidable bearbaiter.

lar with all classes of society. The dogs were intended to lay the baited animal by the ears; eventually grappling the animal by the snout or nose became increasingly popular, thus the smaller dogs were favored and received the most tumultuous approval of the spectators. A bulldog was considered to be any dog that could function in the "sport" of bullbaiting; those bulldogs bred in England during the early 1800s were more specifically of mastiff origins, selected for particular traits. The Bulldog of Britain, one of the world's most distinctive and admired canines, while no longer possessing the ability to function in a sporting capacity, does maintain the short legs and undershot jaw for which many of the bulldog types were bred. Bullbaiting was the most widespread of the animal baiting "sports." The authors admittedly compromise the use of the term "sport," since there is nothing redeemingly sportsmanlike in any baiting activity. Like

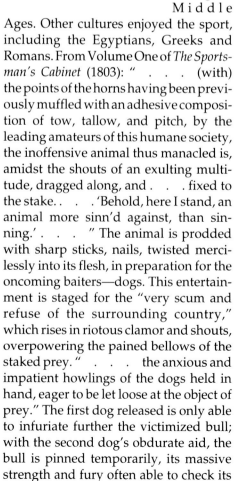

these other sports, bullbaiting was a terrible, frighteningly brainless diversion: "the most cruel and infernal practice that ever entered the mind of man, under the prostituted appellation of sport to the multitude." Bullbaiting was patronized by all classes of people and was very popular in England during the Middle Ages. Other cultures enjoyed the sport, including the Egyptians, Greeks and Romans. From Volume One of *The Sportsman's Cabinet* (1803): " . . . (with) the points of the horns having been previously muffled with an adhesive composition of tow, tallow, and pitch, by the leading amateurs of this humane society, the inoffensive animal thus manacled is, amidst the shouts of an exulting multitude, dragged along, and . . . fixed to the stake.. . . 'Behold, here I stand, an animal more sinn'd against, than sinning.' . . . " The animal is prodded with sharp sticks, nails, twisted mercilessly into its flesh, in preparation for the oncoming baiters—dogs. This entertainment is staged for the "very scum and refuse of the surrounding country," which rises in riotous clamor and shouts, overpowering the pained bellows of the staked prey. " . . . the anxious and impatient howlings of the dogs held in hand, eager to be let loose at the object of prey." The first dog released is only able to infuriate further the victimized bull; with the second dog's obdurate aid, the bull is pinned temporarily, its massive strength and fury often able to check its

suppressors. "In the midst of his sufferings, if the minds of his hellish tormentors have not been sufficiently satiated with repetitions of what has past, collateral aids are called in to rouse his powers" (the object being to "prevent the unfortunate subject of mangled misery from dying too easy a death"). "Instances are common where fires have been made under the very body of the bull, when too much worn down and exhausted, by the jerks of the chain and the worrying of the dogs longer to exert himself; patiently he stands, with the blood streaming from his mangled nostrils, totally insensible to the inhuman twistings of his tail almost to the point of dislocation . . . "

English laws in 1835 banned the brutal sport of bullbaiting and the large bulldogs, which reveled in the gore and cheers of a manic crowd, soon found occupation in the pit. Dog fighting—one dog against another dog—is the brainchild of those dedicated sportsmen evicted from their bullbaiting arena. Mastiff-sized bulldogs were crossed with small, game terriers to yield a smaller, more agile dog with no small amount of brute strength. Hence, we see the birth of the bull-and-terrier dogs. *See also* Fighting dogs.

Bullbaiting preceded most of the other animal-baiting sports, since enthusiasts rationalized the activity with the erroneous expectation that baiting would tenderize the meat of the bull. The palmy era of bear baiting ensued in about 1550 when it was England's most popular form of entertainment. Incidentally, the height of bear baiting overlapped the pinnacle of Shakespeare's writing career, so the Bard had unruly competition to fill his theatre. The poet alludes to "Sackerson" in *The Merry Wives of Windsor*, a popular bear of the day. The sport was held in the metropolis as well as in smaller communities. Bear baiting was the most expensive

form of baiting for the spectators, so the lower classes weren't often privileged with the luxury. The Romans, during

their occupation of England beginning in 55 B.C., probably practiced bear baiting as well.

Among the other animals used for baiting were the badger, lion, ass, monkey and rat. Often a cockfight would warm the crowd up for a lively badger-baiting exhibition. Bull-and-terrier dogs were frequently used on badgers. Badgers were either tied by the tail to a ring in the center of the arena or placed in a box.

Animal baiting. Bull-and-terrier dogs such as the American Pit Bull Terrier were developed after the demise of baiting sports.

Exactly what the entertainment was is difficult to surmise, and this sick diversion is closest perhaps to ratting. Rat baiting involved putting a dog in a pit with a population of rats and timing the dog's performance: x rats in a given time period. One dog named "Billy" is said to have killed 4,000 rats in the course of his 17-hour career. One match lasted about five minutes and incurred the death of at least one hundred rodents.

Animal baiting. The Dogue de Bordeaux of France is credited with appalling mauling bouts with asses and apes.

Monkeys were also matched against bulldogs. This trend lasted less than a quarter of a century in England. The monkey was given a wood stick about a foot long and its job was to cudgel the dog to death before the dog could kill it. Monkeys surprisingly held their own against the dogs. Accounts of bouts indicate that monkeys could maneuver themselves on the bulldog's back and hold tight, free of the dog's jaw, and beat the dog 'til its skull was fractured. One fierce monkey named "Jacco Macacco" was notorious for killing dogs in the pit by biting the jugular vein of its opponent. Jacco was never defeated in the pit.

Lions weren't frequently used for the baiting sport. A few accounts reveal that three bulldogs were released on a lion in the caged arena. Of the stories known from these absurd bouts, the lions usually remained unscathed and the dogs

usually died. Jackasses or donkeys were also infrequently used for baiting. The jackasses didn't lend themselves to the competition of the sport. There are records of bouts with asses and even apes which took place in Paris during the seventeenth century. *See also* Humane societies, Rats

Animal bites
See Bites, animal

Animals, classes of
Most animals can be grouped into one of three classes: omnivores (plant and animal-matter eaters), herbivores (plant-matter eaters), and carnivores (animal-matter eaters). Dogs, though they require a good supply of animal matter (meat), are classified as omnivores, for they do require both plant and animal matter to survive in a healthful condition. For more details on the dog's dietary requirements, *see* Feeding, Dietary requirements, Nutrition.

Ankle joint
Synonymous with hock joint, borrowed from human anatomical terminology, not frequently used.

Ankylosis
The joining of bones or fibrous parts into a single part, thus resulting in a stiff joint where a movable joint is normal. Such fusion of bones is a serious fault in a canine.

Anthrax
An acute, often fatal disease that can affect most all warm-blooded animals. It is caused by the spore-forming bacteria *Bacillus anthracis*. In dogs the disease is rare but occurs worldwide; it is usually contracted by the dog's eating the remains of dead-from-the-infection animals. Antibiotics have proven helpful if the disease is caught in its early stages. It can be contracted by man.

Antibiotics
Drugs lethal or inhibiting to all, some, or one bacterium but essentially harmless to the host if administered in prescribed amounts. There are many antibiotics—penicillin, streptomycin, and tet-

racycline are a few of the well-known ones. Some are broad spectrum: they attack unselectively all bacteria. Others are used to combat a specific strain or form of bacteria. Because there are possible side effects and complications, antibiotics must be used only on a prescribed basis, under the supervision of your vet.

Antibodies

When the healthy body is invaded by an antigen, a reaction occurs which triggers the production of proteins having the specific capacity to attack, destroy, or otherwise neutralize the antigen. These proteins are called antibodies.

Anticonvulsants

Drugs prescribed to lessen, control, or eliminate convulsions.

Anthelmintics

Drugs administered to destroy flat worms and/or round worms are very commonly known as platyhelminths and nemahelminths respectively.

Antihistamines

Both prescribed and over-the-counter drugs used to alleviate the effects of histamine, a chemical produced during allergic reactions to such things as bee stings, grass, foodstuffs, etc.

Antiperistalsis

A term given to the reverse action of the normal procedures of the stomach or intestine, which brings the contents closer to the mouth. *See* Vomiting

Antipyretics

Drugs or methods used to reduce temperature during fevers. These may take the form of cold baths, purgatives, ice packs, etc.

Antisialics

Term applied to substances used to reduce excessive salivation.

Antitoxins

Substances administered to counteract the effects of a poison that has entered the body.

Annual specials

Prizes which are offered by specialty clubs to their members for competition at all (or certain) American Kennel Club shows during the fiscal year of the specialty club.

Anus

The opening at the end of the dog's alimentary canal. *See also* Constipation, Diarrhea, Digestive system

Apartment

Apartment and city life requires adjustment on the part of most dogs. Persons living in apartments or luxury condominiums must compromise in their choice of the ideal dog to suit their needs. The ideal dog indeed is the dog that requires less ex-

Apartment. Residents of apartments and condominiums must abide by legal and safety restrictions. Unattended Cavalier King Charles Spaniel and Bearded Collie in a London apartment.

ercise, unless an owner is capable of providing a dog with multiple daily, regular—not occasional—walks. No matter how perfectly decorated or spacious-appearing your condo is, and no matter how exquisitely the colors and the background would complement his well-groomed coat, a Borzoi is not the dog for you! Some breeds adjust amazingly well to apartment life: terriers and toys are perhaps the rule of thumb. Many dogs, including the smaller ones, such as Beagles and Miniature Poodles, need a considerable amount of exercise to offset their hardy appetites. Many an obese Beagle or Poodle has displayed the unsightly "eyes" of a "couch potato."

Apish. Affenpinschers, the little monkey dogs, mug for photographer I. Français.

The authors do not wish to convey that no large breed of dog has ever survived well in an apartment setting. Many such owners satisfactorily keep Scottish Deerhounds or Mastiffs, to exemplify some larger canines. However, these dogs are not able to thrive, that is, be at their physical and psychological bests. Were the same dogs kept by the same owners where they were accommodated with ample running room (i.e., a large backyard or fenced-in pen), they would be incomparably more robust, healthy and happy. Many experts have determined that owners who are inclined towards nervous habits or subject to slight psychological abnormalities have a greater

negative effect on their pets when they reside in the close confines of an apartment dwelling.

Apartment residents need also to be aware of the legal matters that may concern keeping a dog in an apartment. Many landlords allow dogs in their buildings; a percentage of these charge a monthly fee to their residents who opt to own a dog. Some landlords refuse to allow any canine to reside in their buildings. Such regulations should be responsibly adhered to—sneaking around your landlord is never a pleasant (or easy) endeavor, particularly at the end of the month. Housing contracts often include clauses about dog ownership. These clauses should be read carefully for the safety and equity of you and your dog.

Because most dogs bark, apartment dwellers have the added responsibility of training their dog and teaching it appropriate manners. Your lovely Basset Hound or Beagle may be perfectly mannered during the day but become instinctually musical at night. While true dog lovers most often enjoy the exuberant Basset baritone, your next-door neighbors are bound to be less enthusiastic. Proper training surely pays off in this respect. *See also* Housebreaking, Behavior modification, Training

Apex
    See Occiput

Apish
    Monkeylike, referring to expression. *See* Affenpinscher, Brussels Griffon

Apomorphine
    A crystalline alkaloid substance produced from morphine, used as an emetic and an expectorant.

Appearance, hard-bitten
    Rugged and tough, used in A.N.K.C. standard to describe the Australian Cattle Dog and Australian Terrier.

Appearance, purebred
    Maintenance of an aristocratic and quality appearance. Most purebred dogs appear thoroughbred, though certainly many a manmade breed lacks this quality.

Appearance, symmetrical

Well-blending, harmonious flow to a dog's appearance that is desirable in many breeds. Ultimate symmetry and balance are paramount in most dogs, excepting a number of dogs whose fanciers aim to accentuate (unscrupulously, grossly, or rightly so?) a particular feature, disrupting an existent symmetry. In many cases, symmetry mustn't be a strictly subjective determination: dog fanciers must agree that a giant-pawed mastiff breed with a pea-sized toy head is simply not symmetrical, and likewise not desirable.

Appearance, varminty

Not an undesirable trait: detailing the cheeky, rascally, and self-assured expression of the West Highland White Terrier, Cairn Terrier, and perhaps a number of other lovable, varminty, varmint-undoing terriers.

Appenzell Mountain Dog

See Appenzeller

Appenzeller

A native Swiss dog known for its great strength and courage as a guard. The Appenzeller is a premier working dog, mastering the tasks of cart pulling, cattle droving, and flock guarding. The breed is of ancient stock: it is believed to represent crossings of the ancient molossus with various herding dogs of Switzerland. The thesis rests on the belief that sometime during the first century B.C., as Roman legions passed through the land of Switzerland, dogs of war were left

behind or straggled and taken in by natives. Impressed with the size and strength of these dogs, owners crossed the molossus with their herders to increase strength and size. The crossings proved successful, and the believed result, with much perfecting through the years, is today's Appenzeller.

ESSENTIALS OF THE APPENZELLER: A strong, well-built, and hardy animal, the Appenzeller is a versatile working dog capable of herding, guarding, cart pulling, and other physical employments. Slightly longer than his height of 19–23 inches (48–59 cm), the Appenzeller weighs between 50 and 55 pounds (23–25 kg). The coat is short, smooth, and worn tightly to the body. Musculature well developed; skeletal structure strong, with a deep and powerful chest.

Appearance, symmetrical. The solid stance of a remarkable purebred, the Wire Fox Terrier. Photo by Ludwig.

Appenzeller, tricolor. Photo by I. Français.

Color: tricolor (black and tan with white on the chest, blaze, tail, and toes). The tan coloration is always between the black and the white.

Appenzeller Sennenhund
See Appenzeller

Appetite
Dogs have the inherent ability not to overeat; however, as the result of boredom, anxiety, or other factors a dog will overfeed. Although a dog may consume a normal amount of food, lack of exercise may contribute to obesity. Appetite is also affected by climate and temperature, exercise, pregnancy, illness and worms, and preference for given foodstuffs. If fed quality food in appropriate amounts under normal healthy conditions, a dog should eat just enough to maintain his health and strength, without tending toward malnutrition or obesity, *which see*. *See also* Diarrhea, Feeding, Nutrition, Pregnancy, Vomiting, Worms

Apple head
Skull is rounded in every direction to various degrees. The general head shape is an inverted hemisphere. The Chihuahua remains the most apple-headed of all dogs. *See* Domed skull

Apple head unbobbingly portrayed by a champion Chihuahua.

Apple skull
See Domed skull

Apricot
A fruity-orange-colored coat.

Apron
The wealth of longish hair that extends from the mane into the sides and under the neck and the frontal chest. The Rough Collie and the Shetland Sheepdog exemplify this coat accoutrement. Known also as bib or ruff.

Aptitude, inherited
A dog's ability to function well at given tasks is governed in part by his inherited traits. *See also* Training, Canine behavior, Breed development

Aquiline nose
See Ram's nose

Arabian Greyhound
See Sloughi

Arched loins
See Loins

Arched neck
See Crested neck

Arched skull
A skull that curves convexly (or arches) either from side to side or from stop to occiput, not in all directions as with a domed skull, which *see*.

Arctic fox
The Arctic fox, *Alopex lagopus*, inhabits only the polar regions and, together with the polar bear, roams farther north than any other land mammal. The range of the Arctic fox is termed circumpolar, which means that it ranges the region surrounding the North Pole, bordering the Soviet Union, Alaska, Canada, and Greenland. Known also as the blue or white fox, this canid, alone among the wild dogs, goes through a seasonal color change. The Arctic fox's natural habitat is the frozen tundra, but it has adapted to other hunting grounds as well. Reflective of its domain, the Arctic fox is plushly coated, has a long and bushy tail, small ears, and short legs and face. Overall, the Arctic fox is low-set and rounded in appearance. Feeding on rodents and sea birds and scavenging whenever available, the Arc-

tic fox typically hunts alone. The coat of the Arctic fox is of great value, and the species is hunted throughout its region of inhabitancy. Gray wolves, wolverines, and other foxes also prey on the Arctic fox, making his continued survival testimony of his cunning and enduring adaptability.

Arctic Husky
    See Siberian Husky

Ardennes Cattle Dog
    See Bouvier des Ardennes

Argentinean Mastiff
    See Dogo Argentino

Ariége Pointer
    See Braque d'Ariége

Ariégeois
    The Ariégeois, a pack harehound from France, emerged in 1912 from three French medium–small-sized hounds. Those used were the Bleu de Gascogne, the Gascon-Saintongeois, and the Chien d'Artois. In southern France, he is sometimes referred to as the Bastard Hound, but he is slowly becoming more accepted as a fixed-type hound. Nonetheless, his acumen in pack hunting over most any terrain cannot be denied. Pack trials are still held by the Gaston Phoebus Club at the Ceron Villa in southern France. Although originally developed for hunting small game, the Ariégeois has adapted well to suburban living.

Arctic fox in winter coat and snow.

ESSENTIALS OF THE ARIÉGEOIS: Perhaps the pinnacle of elegance in the French hound family, the Ariégeois is a finely built and mostly slender dog. He is rather small, standing 22–24 inches (56–61 cm) tall and weighing about 66 pounds (30 kg). His short coat is tricolored: black patches with a few scattered tan markings (mostly on the head) mottling a

Ariégeois, tricolor. Photo by I. Français.

white background. The Ariégeois's head is surely the key to the breed's elegance: it sports a soft, intelligent expression. The ears are long, easily extending past the muzzle when outstretched.

Arm

Consisting of the upper arm, forearm and elbow, the anatomical area between the elbow joints and shoulders. Included are the humerus and muscles.

Armant

A herding dog developed in a village in Upper Egypt from crosses of Briard-type dogs of Napoleon Bonaparte's French army and native working dogs. Cattle and other livestock were necessar-

These able working dogs were quickly seized by the hard-toiling soil workers and herdsmen of the region. Lastly concerned with type or fashion, these pragmatists freely bred any dogs that worked well. Hence, the Armant, one result of the crossbreeding of native Upper Egyptian herding dogs of the early 1800s and the "deserters" of Napoleon's French army, was born.

Unknown are the breed's numbers today. It is believed that few if any specimens today are true to Armant type, although many dogs work the herds of Egypt and other countries with at least a drop of this excellent herding dog's blood. Various Armant types are known to work today as guard dogs, shepherd

Armant, black with tan. Photo by I. Français.

ily marched behind troops traversing beyond their native land. The reason: provision. Rugged, hard-bitten dogs able to work blister-footed herds for grueling hours over unfamiliar grounds were vital to large-scale military movement. The multi-thousand-mile marches of the broad-conquering Roman, French, and other armies deposited innumerable canine stragglers, which have evolved into many different breeds. The Armant is one such dog, descended from the strays and others, likely wandering for food or during the course of retreat.

dogs, and occasionally as sporting dogs. Although no longer registered by the FCI they are fine workers, but their tumultuous homeland is not conducive to the propagation of the breed. Characteristics of specimens vary, such as the ears, which are either prick or drop, and the tail, which is either long with a "shepherd's staff curl" or docked.

ESSENTIALS OF THE ARMANT: The Armant is a medium- to large-size dog, square in body and powerfully built. The ideal specimen stands 22 inches (56 cm) tall and weighs between 50–60 pounds

(22.5–27.5 kg). The sturdy, straight back and well-tucked belly give the body an accurate appearance of strength and virility. The coat, long and woolly to shaggy and rough, provides substantial protection from the elements, thus adding to the dog's overall ability and performance. Color is typically a shade of solid gray, although black, black with tan, and occasional white markings may also be seen.

Arteriosclerosis

Hardening of the arteries, a condition more common in older dogs, comes to all dogs, as it does to most all mammals, if they live to an old enough age. The condition is often noticeable by a change in the color of the eyes and in the relative size of the pupils of the eyes—the pupils, once deep black, attain a grayish, milky tint, not to be confused with cataracts. The tiny blood vessels of the eyes develop thick walls. When the thickness becomes too great, the pupil will dilate to allow more light to enter. Loss of hearing, as well as memory and other losses, may also be attributed to arteriosclerosis. As the condition increases, blood vessels continue to harden, and much of their elasticity is lost, thus placing a greater stress upon the heart. Exercise must therefore be adjusted accordingly, and lethargy may be witnessed. Although more common in older dogs, the condition is not limited to them.

Artesian Norman Basset
See Basset Artésian Normand

Arthritis

Arthritis, inflammation of the bone at the joint, is more often experienced by older dogs than younger ones. In actuality, however, any dog at any age can suffer from arthritis. Like an affected human, a dog tends to experience more acute discomfort in damp weather. Often, visible swelling around the joints is a reliable indicator of the presence of arthritis. During the course of the dog's regular activity and exercise, an owner may detect the dog's pain. It is vital to the dog's health that a veterinarian uncover the exact location and extent of the condition. A radiographer is able to evaluate

the specific condition and then trace the improvement of the patient.

Articulation

Two bones meeting to clarify a joint, i.e., the humerus and radius articulate the elbow joint.

Artificial insemination

A practice that is becoming more common in recent years. Owners of dogs who live too far from quality stock and owners of dogs difficult to mate are opting for artificial insemination, under the guidance of a professional.

Artificial respiration

The manual forcing of air into the lungs when breathing is stopped but the heart still beats, usually as the result of shock or injury. Should the heart stop, CPR, if possible, should be performed.

Aryan Molossus

Afghanistan's mastiff is a highly endangered fighting dog that reportedly can weigh up to 200 pounds. Its size and body structure would indicate that the Turkish flock guards (Anatolian Shepherd, Kangal Dog) and the Tibetan Mas-

Arthritis. Large breeds, such as the Mastiff, and older dogs too, more often suffer from arthritis. Exercise can always help. Photo by R. Reagan.

tiff are blood relations to this Afghan. Tribesmen bred these dogs for protection purposes and herding/flock guard work to which its ancestors attribute the dog's natural protective inclinations.

The Aryan Molossus adds a new twist to the world of fighting dogs. In Afghanistan, dog fighting is not simply a "sport"—dogs were used to settle disputes between tribes. Each tribe involved in the altercation chose one dog to combat in the pit—the tribe that belongs to the winning dog (that is, the surviving dog) therefore wins the dispute. In order to tell one dog apart from the other (most dogs are dark brindle), the tails were each painted a different color.

Today the number of these Molossi has diminished as a result of the Soviet occupation of the country. It is reported that the dogs have been moved to various mountains to keep them from the grip of the Russian military.

A.S.C.O.B.

Abbreviation for "Any Solid Color Other Than Black," one of the varieties of the American Cocker Spaniel.

Ascites

A collection of serous fluid in the abdominal cavity, causing swelling and shallow breathing. It may be a result of heavy parasitic infestation or a symptom of liver, kidney, lung or heart diseases. Also known as dropsy, the disease requires immediate veterinary attention.

Aseptic necrosis

A condition in which the head of the femur bone, held in the hip socket, degenerates due to infection.

Ashen

A lightish gray; term used to describe the color of some Afghans.

Aspergillosis

A fungal disease contracted from poultry and often mistaken for tuberculosis since the symptoms are quite similar. It attacks the nervous system and sometimes has disastrous effects on the respiratory system. The fungus growth in the body tissue spreads quickly and is accompanied by convulsions. There is often a bloody discharge from the nose.

A.S.C.O.B. American Cocker Spaniel in solid buff. Photo by I. Français.

A.S.P.C.A.

Abbreviation for the American Society for the Prevention of Cruelty to Animals. *See* Humane societies

Aspirin

Used as a pain reliever, aspirin also thins the blood, thus easing it through clogged veins, swollen body areas, etc.

Aspirin, like all other drugs, should be given only if recommended by a professional veterinarian.

Assistance dogs

Assistance dogs include all those dogs which are used to assist disabled individuals. Guide dogs for the blind, signal dogs for the hearing impaired, service dogs, therapy dogs and specialty dogs are all subjected to intense training programs to equip them with the necessary know-how to handle any potential situation. *See also* Therapy dogs, Seeing Eye® dogs, Service dogs, Signal dogs, Specialty dogs, etc.

Asthma

Acute distress in breathing attacks may occur suddenly at irregular intervals and last as long as half an hour. The condition may be hereditary or due to allergy or heart condition. Antihistamines are effective in minor attacks.

Ataxia

Muscular incoordination or lack of movement causing an inhibited gait, although the necessary organs and muscle power are coherent. The dog may have a tendency to stagger.

Atelocynus microtis

See Small-eared dog

Atlas

A volume of illustrations, charts; a book of maps; any person who carries a tremendous burden on his shoulders, such as the mythological god Atlas carry-ing the world upon him, or any author that endeavors to produce an opus of definition one, or a similar lexicon.

Atlas Sheepdog

See Chien de l'Atlas

Atopy

Manifestations of atopy in the dog are visible in persistent scratching of the eyes and nose. Onsets are usually seasonal—

Assistance dogs. The dog's natural intelligence and willingness to serve have availed it to man in countless ways. These guide dogs in training and 4-H Club girls were photographed by Robert Pearcy.

the dog allergic to, say, ragweed will develop the condition when ragweed is in season, or say, house dust all year 'round (or during spring house cleaning). Most dogs afflicted with atopy are multi-sensitive and are affected by something several months out of the year. Treatment is by antihistamines or systemic corticosteroids, or both.

Atresia

(Imperforate anus) A congenital condition resulting from halted embryonic development. Signs include tenesmus, abdominal pain and swelling, retained feces, and the lack of an anal opening.

Attack dog

Any dog who is trained to assault an intruder. Dogs can be trained to attack on command and/or on an intruder's encroachment upon the parameters (often territorial) set by the trainer of the dog. Attack dogs are most often employed as guard dogs, which *see*, for either home or professional use. The owner of an attack dog must consider the laws pertaining to such ownership. Most often, the owner of a dog is legally responsible for the injury inflicted by a dog, especially if the dog is trained to do so. Also, under many jurisdictions, an attack dog is considered a weapon, and laws governing its possession as well as employment are strictly enforced.

Most owners of attack dogs seek the protection afforded by such an animal; such protection can be of person or property, private or commercial. As with guard dogs, and indeed more so, attack dogs should be trained under the guidance and supervision of a professional. Most important in the selection of an attack dog is the breed's temperament. Not all dogs can be trained to inflict serious injury on another animal, especially not a human being. Besides fearlessness, the dog must possess willingness to display aggression,

Attack dog. The Fila Brasileiro, the native mastiff of Brazil, is a professional and unstoppable guardian.

intelligence to differentiate between friend and foe, and obedience to cease attack upon command. A dog who lacks any one of these qualities and who is forced into attack training is a prime candidate for the vicious dog appellation and impoundment. A dog lacking the necessary temperament is likely to turn on his owner out of confusion and/or frustration.

Some breeds that have excelled in attack dog training include: the American Pit Bull Terrier, Bullmastiff, Doberman Pinscher, Dogue de Bordeaux, Fila Brasileiro, German Shepherd Dog, Giant Schnauzer, Neapolitan Mastiff, which *see*. *See also* Guard dog, Schutzhund, Training

Attitude run

A short sled-dog race for fun.

Australian Cattle Dog

The continent's pride and joy is the product of six decades of crossing and crisscrossing various breeds in an attempt to produce a herder stolid enough to work the rugged Australian environment. The Australian Cattle Dog, commonly called the Blue Heeler and also known as the Australian Queensland Heeler, carries the infusion of Bull Terrier, Dalmatian, Australian Kelpie, Red Deer dingo and two blue-merle, smooth-coated Collies.

Exceedingly distressed with their dog's inability to work the wild native cattle of Australia, herdsmen began serious breeding programs to produce an able dog. During the 1830s, ambitious cattlemen crossed the Smithfield Collie with the wild dingo. The litter was known as Timmon's Biters: they were more reserved and barked less than the overactive Smithfields but bit too hard for the job. Ten years later, Mr. Thomas Hall crossed two blue-merle, smooth-coated Collies with working dingoes. The half-breeds proved a

notable success. Further crosses to Timmon's Biters and other experimental crossbreeds, as well as the Dalmatian, Bull Terrier and etc., yielded this silent, hard-nipping but not distressing cattle herder. The breed has bred true since the year 1893.

Australian Cattle Dog, blue and tan. Photo by T. Dorizas.

The Blue Heeler is so versatile that, in addition to cattle, he can work horses, goats, and even ducks with skill and

Australian Cattle Dog heeling cattle. Photo by R. Wood.

panache. As a rule, the breed maintains a touch of the unruly and unrefined—all to his greater ability. He is 100% working dog, fearless and determined.

Australian Cattle Dog, blue and tan.

Australian Cattle Dog, red speckled.

ESSENTIALS OF THE AUSTRALIAN CATTLE DOG: A strong, compact, and balanced dog of symmetry, strength, and substance. The essential characteristics of the breed are the ability to control and move cattle in all environments and to protect and guard stockmen, herd heads, and property. The Australian Cattle Dog is naturally suspicious of strangers but amenable and easily trainable. The head is balanced with the body and general conformation; skull broad and slightly curved between the ears; cheeks muscular but not coarse. The quarters are broad, blending and well developed. The chest is deep and muscular. The outer coat is medium-short and medium textured; the undercoat is short and dense. The coat forms breeches behind the quarters and "broom" of the tail. Color should be red, blue or blue-mottled, with acceptable markings being black, blue, and tan, preferably evenly distributed. Height: 17–20 inches (43–51 cm). Weight: 35–45 pounds (16–20.5 kg).

Australian Greyhound
See Kangaroo Hound

Australian Kelpie
This native Australian breed developed from English North Country Collies of the Rutherford strain, which were well-built, thick-skulled, smooth-haired, semi-prick-eared dogs of stamina and courage. It is unlikely that many early herdsmen of Australia would have concerned themselves with the preservation of type. It is believed that they crossed the many Rutherford Collies with other proven herding dogs in the endless attempt to better the working dog, ending in the production of the Kelpie, known also as the Barb. Although many still assert that the Kelpie is a dingo cross, their position lacks supporting data. At most, dingo blood reached the Kelpie indirectly through crosses with native working dogs, which, although they are believed to have occurred, are suspected of happening only infrequently.

Today nearly 100,000 Kelpies are employed on the continent of Australia. Besides being outstanding herders of cattle, goats, poultry and rein-

deer, Kelpies also find work as search and rescue and detection dogs, which is surprising in consideration of their relatively small size. Though no common sight in the show ring, the Kelpie is registered by the major bodies of the United States, Britain, and of course Australia.

ESSENTIALS OF THE AUSTRALIAN KELPIE: Lithe and active, depicting hard musculation with great suppleness of limb. The dog must be fit to endure with ease a full day's labor; must be free from any suggestion of weediness. Head slightly rounded at the topskull between the ears. Muzzle to be slightly shorter than length of skull. Eyes almond shaped and medium in size. Ears pricked, of fine leather, strong at the base. Neck of moderate length, strong and slightly arched. Shoulders clean and muscular, well sloping, with the shoulder blades close at the withers. Forelegs are of strong but refined bone. The ribs are well sprung; the chest deep rather than wide. Length of body slightly exceeds height as 10 to 9. Height: 17–20 inches (43–51 cm) Weight: 25–45 pounds (11.5–20.5 kg). Coat, double: short, dense under and hard, straight, weather-repellent outer. Colors include black and red, each with or without tan; fawn, chocolate and blue.

Australian National Kennel Council

Established in 1958, the Australian National Kennel Council or A.N.K.C. is the principal registry of Australia. It influences the national kennel clubs of New Zealand, Indonesia and other Australasian nations. The A.N.K.C. recognizes the same breeds as the Kennel Club of Great Britain, and adopts the same standards except for the Australian national breeds: the Australian Cattle

Dog, the nation's pride and joy; Australian Kelpie; Australian Terrier; and Australian Silky Terrier. The most prestigious of dog shows in Australia is the

Australian Kelpie, chocolate.

Melbourne Royal Show which is held each September and ranks among the world's largest conformation shows. The show has taken place annually since the late 1800s. Under the A.N.K.C., males and females are judged separately. The

Australian Kelpie, black and tan, working sheep.

Challenge Certificate system and the group system of Britain are employed by this registering body as well. *See also* Kennel Club of Great Britain, Group systems, Kennel clubs

Australian Native Dog
   See Dingo

Australian Queensland Heeler
   See Australian Cattle Dog

Australian Shepherd
   This well-known frequenter of American ranches was not developed on the hills or plains of Australia or New Zealand but born and bred in the U.S.A. These dogs have existed in America for at least a century and very likely longer, based on references that include descriptions of the dogs by native American Indians.

tralian Cattle Dog) and the Border Collie. It is likely that other collie types have also been bred with to generate the Aussie. The Australian Shepherd has become requisite on countless American farms and ranches. He is able to steer the multitudes of sheep and direct the trampling herds of cattle by nipping at their heels, while practically crawling on his belly.

If the breed's "workaholism" ethic doesn't grab one's attention, its blue eyes and handsome looks most assuredly will. However, casual fanciers are religiously discouraged from taking on an Aussie. His strong herding instincts must be utilized or his true talents are wasted. In the western U.S., the dogs are used extensively on stock as varied as ducks to water buffalo.

ESSENTIALS OF THE AUSTRALIAN SHEPHERD: Sound and symmetrical in appearance, the Australian Shepherd maintains a strong, active working condition. The head is strong and long, broad between the ears and tapering. The ears are small and carried drop. Eyes can be brown, amber, blue, flecked or odd-eyed. Neck is strong, and chest is deep rather than broad, both covered with profuse coat. The back is long and straight. Hindquarters well muscled and angulated.

Australian Shepherd, blue merle.

Although provocative accounts of these herders connecting them to the lost Atlantis still surface, the authors offer the following (less romantic and less warped) theory. Imported Pyrenean Shepherds (Bergers des Pyrenees) are a known base stock of today's breed. Other known contributors include the Smithfield Collie (also used to create the Aus-

The tail is bobbed, whether naturally or artificially. Color varieties include: blue merle, red merle, black, liver, red, with or without tan markings. Height: 18–23 inches (46–58.5 cm). Weight: 35–70 pounds (16–32 kg). The body is well balanced and well muscled. The combination of the whole is a sharp, beautifully put-together canine.

Australian Shepherds, red and white, blue merle.

Australian Shepherd hurrying the flock.

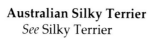

Australian Silky Terrier
See Silky Terrier

Australian Terrier

The Australian Terrier, perhaps the only well-known terrier breed (excluding the Silky Terrier) not created in Great Britain, was actually created by the British in Australia. As far back as the early nineteenth century, ten-pound blue and tan broken-coated terriers were popular in Australia as were sandy-colored dogs.

Australian Terrier, blue/tan. Photo courtesy of Cathy Lester.

The Australian Terrier was created from a blend of imported terriers from northern England and Scotland. Although the actual crossings are not recorded, Scottish Terrier, Cairn Terrier, Skye Terrier, Dandie Dinmont Terrier, Manchester Terrier and Irish Terrier are the usual suspects, each contributing individual traits to the creation of this Broken-Coated Toy Terrier, as the Aussie was originally named. This little terrier was handy on rabbit and prized for his ability to handle snake. His feisty, jumping-bean approach allowed him the dexterity to spring into the air and maneuver himself behind the snake's neck in order to kill it. Of course, the Australian Terrier's confident attitude made him a terrific watchdog.

The British at home naturally were not too enthusiastic about this new jaunty terrier that wasn't produced within Mother England's womb. While type was set in 1872, not until 1936 did the Kennel Club of Great Britain go to ground and grant "official" recognition. In sooth, the Aussie wasn't too keen upon leaving its native Australia. The American Kennel Club did not accept the Aussie until 1958. Overall, this terrier has not gained the acclaim of most of the British terrier breeds. The Silky Terrier, of course, has achieved considerably more press.

ESSENTIALS OF THE AUSTRALIAN TERRIER: A low-set, sturdy dog, long in proportion to his height, and hard bitten in appearance. The head is long, the skull flat and of moderate width. The muzzle is strong and powerful. Ears are small and set high, prick or dropping forward. Bite level. Neck on the longish side. Hindquarters are strong with slightly bent hocks. The soft silky topknot protects the eyes when working or when going to ground. The body is of solid construction; the ribs are well sprung; the chest is moderately deep and wide. Height: 10 inches (25.5 cm). A.K.C. Weight: 12–14 pounds (5.5–6.5 kg). K.C.G.B. Weight: 10 or 11 pounds (4.5 or 5 kg). Coat: harsh, straight, and dense. Color: blue/tan or clear sandy.

Austrian Brandlbracke

The Austrian Brandlbracke is seemingly a close relative of the hounds of Celtic origin and is thus related to the walking hounds of Switzerland. His racy appearance and size would indicate a laufhund or two contributing to his composition. The Brandlbracke's black and tan color, however, suggests that this hound is a spin-off of the hounds of that coloration popular in France and many other European nations in past centuries.

Whatever his roots, the Brandlbracke, sometimes called simply the Austrian Hound, less often the Carinthian Brandlbracke, and at home as either the Österreichischer Glatthaariger Bracke and

Österreichischer Bracke-Brandlbracke, brings to twentieth-century hunters an acute sense of smell and the ability to

track a large variety of game. In trailing, the breed is silent and marvelously effective. The breed is not known outside of Austria, but there it is a popular hunting dog and companion.

ESSENTIALS OF THE AUSTRIAN BRANDLBRACKE: With flat pendant ears, a deep chest, and a thick coat, the Austrian Hound stands from 18–23 inches (46–59 cm) and weighs in at up to 50 pounds (23 kg). This hound possesses surprising strength, despite its loosely limbed body. In color the breed is unexceptionally black and tan with white markings tolerated on neck, chest and feet.

Austrian Hound
See Austrian Brandlbracke

Austrian Shorthaired Pinscher
In appearance the Austrian Shorthaired Pinscher is a heavy Pinscher (Standard Pinscher). Likely the breeds are similarly rooted, considering the similarity in geography and general type. In Austria, where he is known as the Österreichischer Kurzhaariger Pinscher, he has a long history but is no longer a usual sight. Outside Austria, the breed is not known. At home, it is used princi-

pally as a working dog and watchdog known for his zealous bark.

ESSENTIALS OF THE AUSTRIAN SHORTHAIRED PINSCHER: Body appears broader than high; the head is broad; ears wide. Height: 20 inches (51 cm) and usually smaller. Wide, developed chest responsible for the necessary appearance of width exceeding height. The breed can be red, black, brown, fawn, brindle or black/tan, with limited white markings common. The tail is docked or left to curl over the dog's back.

Austrian Smoothhaired Hound
See Austrian Brandlbracke

Autoimmune conditions
A dog is said to be suffering from an autoimmune condition when its immunity system rejects part of the body which can be red blood cells, bone marrow, or other components of the body.

Autoimmune hemolytic anemia
Condition in which the immune system rejects and destroys red blood cells. Can often be treated and corrected.

Austrian Brandlbracke, black and tan.

Austrian Shorthaired Pinscher, red with white. Photographs by I. Français.

Automobiles. Rural dogs have fewer automobile mishaps. Photo by S.A. Thompson.

Automobiles. Tailgating Bearded Collies rest up in parked car.

Automobiles

Many dog owners who live in the country or less populated suburbs fail to realize that the number one killer of dogs in the United States is automobiles. Owners could prevent these fatalities by not allowing their dogs to run off their leashes when near the street. Even the most well-behaved dog may foolishly run into the street after an arousing aroma or similarly enticing bitch. City dog owners rarely allow their dogs to run free. Leash laws, for the most part, prevent owners from experimenting in this way. In the suburbs, however, owners are frequently more inclined to allow their dogs to wander around the neighborhood. Merely knowing that your dog "knows his way home" is never a reason to allow your dog to roam at will. Dogs are not rational creatures, and therefore, no matter how smart you think your dog is, are not ca-

pable of looking after their own safety. Country owners have less to concern themselves with; yet, dogs living in the country are less inclined to be aware of the dangers of automobiles, and so many country roads tend to be more unpredictable and curvy.

Many dogs are fascinated by automobiles, others are simply annoyed. Car chasing is a common proclivity of both kinds of dogs. Needless to say, this is a dangerous and risky situation for all parties involved. The dog, again boisterously displaying his irrationality, and the driver of the car, other passing cars, and children in the street are all potentially at risk. Owners are encouraged to discourage car chasing.

Dogs seem to have various "rationales" for chasing automobiles: racing to see if it can outrun the passing car; stopping the car because it is bothersome or annoying; warning the car that it shouldn't be on the dog's territory; reacting to the "growl" of the car's engine; seizing the car's tires. This latter proclivity, usually a pit bull's or mastiff/terrier's inclination, is extremely dangerous. The incredible grip of a pit bull's jaw may indeed prove its demise, as the dog's skull is flattened on the pavement by the spinning tire.

Some dogs simply bark at passing cars, every passing car. While this habit is less dangerous, it is equally undesirable. Essentially, the common-sense remedies will work best. Clapping a newspaper may intimidate a yapping dog. Puppies are of course easier to train than an adult dog who practices his pastime on barking at cars, bikes, and pedestrians.

Autopsy
See Necropsy

Auvergne Pointer
See Braque d'Auvergne

A.V.M.A.
Abbreviation for the American Veterinary Medical Association.

Azara's fox
See Forest fox

Azawakh
The Tuareg tribes of Mali, in the southern Sahara, cultivated their Sloughi to work as a hunter and guardsman. The dogs are "fleet footed enough to catch gazelles, hares and the European mouflon, courageous enough to ward off big predators, untiring like a camel and beautiful like an Arab horse." The Azawakh's hunting method is pure sighthound: he does not kill the prey but rather hamstrings the quarry until the master arrives. Seated in the master's saddle at the onset of the hunt, the full-grown Azawakh is released when the gazelle is sighted. Reaching speeds of over 40 mph, the Azawakh can course continuously for over five hours.

Almost without exception it was impossible for a Westerner to obtain an Azawakh. The Tuareg nomads led an existence which was stark and uncompromisingly difficult. The Azawakh was the vital component in their hunting. Only the strongest male whelp was not culled at birth, since their sparse lives couldn't accommodate more than the absolutely necessary number of dogs. Naturally, an occasional female was chosen for reproduction purposes. These dogs were as highly prized as a camel.

Fortunately for the European fancy, Dr. Pecar, a Yugoslavian hunter of excep-tional prowess, received an Azawakh male as a gift during one of his visits to Mali. He had admired the Azawakh among all the greyhound breeds that he knew. Later he acquired a female for slaying a bull elephant which was antagonizing a Tuareg tribe. Pecar's male and female became the foundation sire and dam for the European Azawakh. Today Switzerland, Germany and Yugoslavia have strong Azawakh fancies.

ESSENTIALS OF THE AZAWAKH: In general appearance the breed is swift, graceful, lean and well muscled. The head is slender and pear-shaped and embellished by no fewer than five warts. Black eyerims and nails, the five obligatory warts, and white markings are paramount to the Tuareg nomads. The skull long, chiseled, tapering from the set-on of the ears to the eyes and again to the nose. The neck of good length, substantial and strong. On long and muscular legs, the Azawakh stands high, with good length from elbows to pasterns. Height: 23–29 inches (58–74 cm). Weight: 37–55 pounds (17–25 kg). The back long; the chest deep; good tuck up; the tail thin and curled. The coat is soft and short in various shades of sable with white markings.

Azawakh Hound
See Azawakh

Azores Cattle Dog
See Cão de Fila de S. Miguel

Azawakhs in color by I. Français.

B.A.C.
Beagle Advisory Committee.

Babble
The superfluous barking of a hound that is making a lot of noise over little or nothing.

Babesiosis
One of perhaps four tick-carried protozoan diseases which can be carried by the brown dog tick. The disease affects the red blood cells. The symptoms include: fever, rapid pulse and breathing, loss of appetite and discolored urine.

Babiche
Strips of rawhide used to join the parts of a dog sled.

Baby teeth
The sharp baby or milk teeth are the puppy's first set of teeth. These temporary teeth number 32 in all and begin to fall out at about the twelfth week. *See also* Dentition, Dental care.

Back. Rhodesian Ridgeback displays its unique and strong back. Photo by R. Pearcy.

Back
Portion of the topline that begins just behind the withers and ends at the loins/croup intersection. Technically, this is the lumbar and thoracic regions of the spine. In general, the dog's back is considerably muscular and broad—the sinews and expanse necessary for its functional requirements are level and are in proportion to the body (usual ratio 10:9). Many breeds do not fall into these general parameters and the individual standards describe the specific back and back type for each breed.

Back tracking
The line which moves back after reaching a check rather than locating and running the new line. *See also* Backtrack

Back types
As dogs are different in so many respects, their back types vary greatly. Terminology has evolved to describe and differentiate between the many types, the desirable and undesirable. The following represents the existent canine terminology.
Arched over loins. A straight back that arches over the loins. This is caused by muscle development, indicating the desired body strength, and varies widely from breed to breed. Examples of such type are the Dachshund and the Rhodesian Ridgeback.
Camel. A dip, varying in degrees from breed to breed (and dog to dog), behind the shoulders, arching in front and over the loins, and then dropping at the rump. A form of roach back and synonymous with hump or humped back.
Carp. Dipping like a camel back, this type of roach back is less extreme in the initial dip and the arch is less high.
Dip or dippy. Same as hollow back.
Dropping through withers. Due to a looseness of shoulder, this type back is undesirable and affects the section directly behind the withers.
Flat. A back which is both straight and horizontal. Thus it is the same distance from the ground at the shoulders and over the loins. There should be no dip in the back whatsoever. Synonymous to table top back.
Hollow. Concave or sagging along the whole longitude. Same as dipped, saddle, slack, soft, swampy and sway.

Horizontal. Same as flat, which *see.*

Hump. Same as camel, which *see.*

Level. Not straight or flat by definition but rather a back that is of equal height at the withers and over the loins.

Long. The distance from the withers to the rump considerably exceeds the height at the withers. When used as a fault, a long back would be one that is longer than the breed standard requires.

Overbuilt. Padded, overly muscular development over the rump area. Often the back line rises, but not always.

Roach. A back that is arched or convex to some extent. Depending on the degree of arch, a roach back can be referred to as any of a number of types: camel, carp, wheel (all of which *see*). A roach back is often listed as a fault or disqualification although in some breeds it is desirable (e.g., Bedlington). The Manchester Terrier standard mentions a slight roach back.

Saddle. Concave same as hollow back.

Short. Less than height at withers or simply short in relation to the standard requirement. The Dachshund exemplifies short in back.

Slack. Due to lack of structural fortitude, this less severe type of hollow or sway back is also deemed a fault. Slackness of back can be detected directly behind the withers or as an excessive amount of space between the posterior ribs and hip bones.

Sloping. Height calculated at the withers exceeds height at the loins. Such a back slopes downwards toward the rear. The Doberman Pinscher is an example of a sloping back, but this trait is not desirable in all breeds and in some is expressly listed as a fault.

Soft. A back with a minimal tendency to sag, a mild hollow back.

Straight. Not referring to level of back but rather one that runs in a straight line without an arch. A slope forward or backward is possible.

Swampy. Same as hollow, which *see.*

Sway. Same as hollow, which *see.*

Table top. Same as flat, which *see.*

Wheel back. A roach back with a markedly exaggerated curve that runs from withers to tail in a continuous line. The Bulldog is a fine example.

Backbone
Spinal column.

Backcast
A swing in the opposite direction from the progress of the hunt which results in the dog's coming up from behind.

Backing
The action of a hunting dog coming to a stop upon seeing another dog on point or upon the command of the handler who sees the other dog's situation. This is called sight backing or backing on command.

Backline
Anatomically speaking, the entire topline from the rear end of the withers to the tip of the tail. Secondly, in dog sled racing, the line from the harness to the towline, sometimes called the tugline.

Backskull
See Skull

Backtrack
To move in a direction different from that in which the game is moving; moving towards where the game came from, not where it is going.

Back types:
Wheel back displayed by the English Bulldog.

Bacteria

Bacteria exist everywhere. They may be present in the air, in food, water, or waste. Quite often harmful bacteria are living inside the host, waiting for weakness to occur so that they may strike. Bacterial diseases and infections are often treated with plenty of rest, lots of fluids, and antibiotics. A bite, a burn, a common cold, all can lead to bacterial infection. *See also* Abscesses, Antibiotics

Bad breath

Bad breath can be an indication of a number of conditions. Tartar is the most common cause of bad breath; pyorrhea, ulcerative stomatitis, loose and rotting teeth, gingivitis, bleeding gums, gangrenous pneumonia, constipation, chronic nasal catarrh and indigestion comprise the various foul-smelling possibilities. Since bad breath is a signal that there is something else worth checking into, a visit to your vet is the best bet.

Bad habits

See Canine behavior, Problem dogs

Badger

Combination of black, gray, white, and brown hairs in various proportions of intensity. Badger is synonymous with beaver, hare, jasper, and blaireau and is most usually the coloration of the patches on a background of white. The Great Pyrenees and the Petit Basset are two examples of this coloration.

Badger pied

Badger in combination with white.

Baganda Hunting Dog

An ancient pack hound of Africa used to hunt big game, from gazelles to elephants. In appearance, it is shorthaired, prick-eared and ring tailed; in color the Baganda can be fawn, brown, or black and white.

Bagirmi Dog

A medium-sized, sharp muzzled pied African hunting dog with prick ears.

Bakhund

See Old Danish Bird Dog

Balaeric Hound

See Ibizan Hound

Balance

The mellifluous and proportionate symmetry exhibited in canine conformation. A well-balanced dog is one whose anatomical parts are correctly proportioned to one another.

Badger. French wirehaired cousins, the Petit and Grand Bassets Griffons Vendeens, alternate shades of badger. Photo by I. Français.

Balanced head

Skull and foreface in nearly even proportions (or lengths).

Balanitis

The medical term for constant discharge of pus from the penis. This condition often causes spotting of clothing or quarters and causes the dog to clean himself constantly. If the condition, which is bacterial in nature, becomes serious, the area may have to be cauterized.

Balkan Hound

The Balkan Hound is but one of the Yugoslavian scenthounds that is recognized by the F.C.I. and the national registry of Yugoslavia. These hounds are all rather similar in type, vary slightly in size, and are of comparable abilities. The F.C.I. recognizes nine individual breeds. In Yugoslavia, the Balkan is known as the Balkanski Gonič. Almost without variation, these hounds were descended from Eastern-type hounds brought over by the Phoenicians. It is generally accepted that the Phoenicians traded sighthounds in the eastern Mediterranean region; these dogs slowly made their way across the European continent. Selective breeding by these hunters, who hunted equally for sport and necessity, perfected and perpetuated the Balkan type. Today the Balkan is a favorite packhound choice of many regional Yugoslavian hunters, who perceive hunting as more than a weekend pastime.

ESSENTIALS OF THE BALKAN HOUND: A sturdy, neither too long- nor too short-bodied hound with short, dense and somewhat hard coat. The ground color is foxy red, the upper part of the body being black. The head should be long. Plenty of bone. The skull is somewhat domed, slight stop. Head from above is broad and long in appearance. The muzzle long and broad. Ears, medium length, lying close to the head. Topline slightly sloping from the withers to the croup. Straight and well placed fore and hindquarters. Shoulders sloping, well knit, and muscled. The Balkan Hound is black and tan saddled, foxy red or wheaten with the same black saddle, with black marks over his eyes. Height: 17–21 inches (43–53 cm). Weight: 44 pounds (20 kg).

Balkanski Gonič

See Balkan Hound

Baluchi Hound

See Afghan Hound

Bandog

" . . . vaste, stubborne, ougly . . . of a burthenous body . . . terrible and frightful to behold" (Caius, 1576). Bandog, in the dog world, originally referred to those mastiffs which could be found in Europe as early as the fifteenth and sixteenth centuries. The term *bandog* or band-dog meant dog that had to be tied up. These ancient alaunt types are believed to be the progenitors of the present-day Mastiff and Bulldog. A kennel of Bandogs kept in the Parish Gardens were described in 1600 by Camden: these dogs "are so strong and bite so hard that three of them are enough to seize a bear, and four a lion." The Bandogs were used for protection as well as fighting in the arenas against bears, bulls, lions, etc.—

The existing Bandog is a crossbred mastiff, rather the lurcher of the dog-

Bandog, in its original sense, "dog that had to be tied."

fighting world. These dogs are sometimes called Swinford Bandogs or American Mastiffs. The former alternative name credits John Swinford, D.V.M., the developer of this dog. Swinford first began his breeding efforts in the early 1970s. The most common breeds crossed to acquire a Bandog are a male American Staffordshire Terrier and a large female English Mastiff. Other options include the Pit Bull Terrier and Neo or Pit Bull and Bullmastiff. The term Pit Bullmastiff describes this latter cross. Today the Bandog is used relatively commonly by dog-fighting enthusiasts, we are told.

In size, these dogs weigh approximately 125 pounds (58 kg) and are enormously game. The dogs have no following in the dog-show world and since it is difficult to locate reputable Bandog breeders, cannot be recommended as pets.

Bandog crossbred from Neapolitan Mastiff bitch and American Pit Bull Terrier male.

Bandy

Fore or hindlegs outwardly bowed. *See* Legs, bandy

Bangara Mastiff

Bangar, a specific part of Tehri Garhwal, India, developed a version of the Tibetan Mastiff to herd and guard sheep and yak. This Indian dog stands 23–25 inches (58–64 cm). The color variations span black and tan through apri-

cot. The coat is coarse; the muzzle, mastifflike; tail, set high; body, compact.

Banjara Greyhound

The Banjara is one greyhound indigenous to India. It finds its origin in either the Sloughi and/or the Afghan Hound. The general body type does not differentiate this sighthound from others of the group. As dog exhibition and the fancy in general have not evolved in India as they have in the West, and as a dog's function affords its following, the working coursing hounds of India may not breed true, for the sake of breeding true. A traveler to India conveys that pure Banjaras are difficult to locate since most dogs indiscreetly breed with the common pariah dogs.

The Banjara's relationship to his master is proverbial: this mutual respect and admiration breeds pure. The dogs are used for various hunting and general work jobs. No Banjaras are known outside of India.

ESSENTIALS OF THE BANJARA GREYHOUND: This sighthound is a fine upstanding hound with a sturdy, defined conformation. The head, long and narrow, is high-held and houndy; the neck is lengthy and supple. The back is medium broad and muscular. He is described as being stouter than the Saluki with a squarer muzzle. The coat is rough but silky and generally black, mottled with gray or blue. The ears, legs, and tail are feathered generously. Height: 27–29 inches (68–74 cm). Weight: 50–65 pounds (23–30 kg).

Bantu Dog

A South African hunting and watchdog valued by the Zulu people. Its body type is slender and smallish. The muzzle is pointed and the ears project outward. The tail is slightly curled and covered with sparse hair.

Bar

Australian term for arm or humerus.

Barak

Yugoslavian term for hound. *See* Bosnian Roughhaired Hound

Barb

See Australian Kelpie

Barbet

The Barbet is most likely the forerunner of the modern Poodle and at one time was probably *the* water dog of Europe, for the frequency of references and illustrations suggests great popularity. The Barbet is often cited as being one of the oldest of all French breeds, but the true date of his origin may never surface. Sources point to the breed's remarkable resemblance to the old English Water Dog, both having the characteristic tight, curly coat. Though commonly field workers who remain unclipped, some show specimens are clipped today in the manner of the Poodle, frequently in the lion clip. The Barbet is also said to be the ancestor of the bichons and many Continental sheepdogs. He is excellent at waterfowl work and is undeterred and unimpeded by icy conditions. His determination turns retrieving abilities and hunting instincts into pliable tools for land hunting as well. The Barbet

is a companionable dog, though if kept in the home requires considerable care to keep clean and odor free.

ESSENTIALS OF THE BARBET: The general appearance is essentially that of a generic water dog. The coat is long, woolly and given to waviness or curling; some specimens may even possess a slightly corded coat. The coat is considered waterproof and is to be dense enough to provide good all-weather protection. In size the Barbet is medium, standing about 22 inches (56 cm). Weight is also medium, 35–55 pounds (16–25 kg). The feet are large and round, constructed for efficient mobility in the water. Color possibili-

Barbet, chestnut.

Barbet, black with white.
Photographs by I. Français.

ties include black, chestnut, fawn, gray, and white with or without markings; mixed colors are common.

Barbet, black. Photo by I. Français.

Barbone
See Poodle

Barenbeiser
German term meaning bear biter. *See also* Animal baiting

Bare pasterns
Pasterns that are not longhaired. In the Afghan Hound, such pasterns are referred to as cuffs.

Barking
Dogs communicate in a variety of ways: facial expression and body movement, eye contact, howling, growling, and of course, barking. Owners are reminded that barking is a dog's most vital means of communication. A dog may bark to warn, to ask, or even to please. It is often the case that problem barking is actually a learned response, the dog's having been conditioned through some action-reward sequence. A key to understanding your dog is understanding his bark, listening carefully to the tone, the pitch, and the actions that coincide with the bark. A key to solving many barking problems is determining the original action-reward sequence and reversing the learned response. This may take some consideration, time and patience, but it often works. Other things to consider with a problem barker is the dog's environment. A dog who is cold, frightened, or otherwise affected may bark constantly until the condition and its effects are relieved. *See also* Canine behavior.

Barrel
See Ribs

Barking is one of the dog's most fundamental means of communication, as this Bloodhound resonantly demonstrates. Photo by C. Meade.

Barrel chest
See Ribs

Barrel hocks
See Cow hocks

Barreled vent
See Vent, barreled

Barukhzy Hound
An ancient native Indian sighthound which figures in the development of the Baluchi Hound or Afghan Hound, which *see.*

Bas Rouge
See Beauceron

Basenji
The Basenji may be one of the purest of all domesticated canines. The Basenji, a member of the pariah family, is believed to have emerged from a diversity of early canid types, in a definite form which has developed into a distinctive pure breed.

In Central Africa (Zaire), the Basenji has been employed by natives for a variety of hunting chores. These little pariah types are used to hunt and destroy the Long-toothed Reed Rat, which threatened the natives' kraal, or village livestock. Natives, particularly those north of the Zambesi, used the dogs as excellent terriers. They are effective in hunting; with little training, the Basenji points, retrieves and drives game to the net; he is also able to track wounded quarry.

Previously, the dogs were favored by the pharaohs of ancient Egypt. However, like the other favored canines of the Egyptians, with the fall of the culture, the dogs were adopted by tribes throughout the Congo.

European explorers in the Congo during the late 1800s commented on the Basenji's inability to bark. Basenjis emit soft and low growllike noises, a hoarse yelp, peculiar to this breed alone.

Before 1895, the Basenji was not known to the Western World. The first two dogs to leave the Congo for England were exported by a British explorer whose name never makes even cynologists' footnotes. The dogs were entered in Crufts as "Lagos Bush Dogs"; both dogs died of distemper and the breed interest stagnated for twenty years. Distemper also killed the six Basenjis imported by Lady Hellen Nutting in 1923. Walter

Basenjis, photographed in Zaire.

Hutchinson refers to the breed in the mid-30s as the "Congo Terrier" and indicates that genuine specimens were acclimated in European zoos. He describes the dogs as having the straight legs of a Scottish Terrier, a tail that is inclined to curl, "with a suggestion of bushiness"; he also reports a noticeable feature of a ridge of longer hair running down the dog's spine.

1936 marked the first successful importation and breeding of Basenjis in England. The famed Bongo of Blean and Bokoto of Blean produced the first English litter to survive.

Basenji, red and white. Photo by I. Français.

Basenjis experience a single yearly cycle that is light triggered—this is common to all pariah dogs. Photo by V. Serbin.

The first two Basenjis to be brought to the States in 1937 were imported by Mrs. Byron Rogers. Distemper was not known to the dogs of Africa, and the dogs were thus extremely vulnerable to the disease. Both Mrs. Rogers's dogs were victims of distemper too. In 1942, Massachusetts was blessed with two surviving African-bred puppies. The American club was formed in 1942; A.K.C. recognition followed the next year.

One of the most notable pioneers of the Basenji breed in the western hemisphere is Miss Veronica Tudor Williams, who worked diligently in building her strain from Congo dogs. Present-day breeders continue to look to Zaire for stock to improve American and British lines. In the U.S. and England, the breed is known in red/white, black/white and tricolored, while in Zaire the breed is seen frequently in various brindles. Some of these handsome and eye-catching specimens are making their way into the United States.

One of the most common misconceptions about the barkless Basenji is that it

derives from a nordic strain of spitzen. No previous or future evidence supporting this theory can substantiate its truth, since it is indeed a fallacy. David Cavill, in his book *All about the Spitz Breeds*, is puzzled by the Basenji's "curious" inability to bark but relies on the breed's curled tail and dense coat as its close "anatomical resemblance" to the spitzen family. Although no wild canid possesses a curled tail, there were primitive African dogs that had curled tails and these are surely the Basenji's prototypes. This is not the Basenji's only connection to the pariah family. The true proof of the Basenji's inclusion in the pariah group can be found in its breeding pattern. All other domesticated dogs have two fertile periods per year. Wolves, pariahs, dingoes and Basenjis have only one. Further, as Lois Bueler, student and author of *Wild Dogs of the World*, points out, "in domestic dogs the hormones of the ovaries and pituitary which control the sexual cycle act independently of external stimulation, but in wolves, dingoes and Basenjis the pituitary must be stimulated by light changes to trigger a new cycle." Studies in breeding have shown this dependence on light changes to be a function of the recessive gene. While the spitz family may amply and correctly claim a link to wolves (as do all dogs), no member of that nordic family has a single annual cycle nor the dependence of the pituitary on light changes for stimulation. This evidence surely unhitches the Basenji permanently from its alleged spitzen relations.

In the U.S. and England, the Basenji is shown in the Hound Group; this categorization is probably one the kennel clubs' silliest, although the Basenji's absolute uniqueness does make grouping most difficult. In addition to the breed's soft yodellike vocalization, the coat is one of its most remarkable and beautiful features. As a home companion choice, the Basenji is a sublime candidate. His short coat requires little to no grooming; additionally he is cat-like in his daily primping. Basenjis tend to scrap with other dogs but are entirely affectionate with their human charges.

ESSENTIALS OF THE BASENJI: The Basenji is a finely built, light dog with gazellelike grace. The ears are pointed, erect and slightly hooded, sitting well forward on the top of the head. Facial wrinkles, fine and profuse, appear on the forehead when the ears are pricked. The head is flat, well chiseled and medium width, tapering toward the nose; stop slight. The jaws are strong, with perfect, regular scissor bite. The neck is of good length, without thickness, well crested and slightly full at the base of the throat. The body is balanced with a short, level back. The shoulders are well laid back, muscular, not loaded. Hocks are strong and muscular, well let down, turned neither in nor out. The feet are small, narrow and compact. The tail is set high, curls tightly over the spine and lies close to the thigh in a single or double curl. The coat is sleek and close; the skin pliant. Height: 16–17

Basenji, black/tan. Photo by R. Reagan.

inches (40.5–43 cm). Weight: 21–24 pounds (9.5–11 kg). Accepted colors include red, black/tan and black, all with white markings. In their native Zaire, however, Basenjis occur in merles and brindles as well.

Basenji, brindle, imported to the United States from Zaire. Photo by I. Français.

Basque Shepherd, blue merle.

Basket

The section of the dog sled which carries either the passenger or cargo.

Basque Shepherd

A most recent extension of the Australian Shepherd, this "little dog blue" is but an Aussie with a tail. Since most stories about the Australian Shepherd's beginnings point to the Basque territories of Spain, the new name seems appropriate.

Basque Shepherd, tricolor. Photographs by I. Francais.

While many similar dissensions from breed standards have arisen, this one may prove meritorious. Not docking the dog's tail makes for a more balanced animal, with greater agility as a herder. Additionally, promoters look forward to less spinal-column complications by not contending with the breeding of bob-tailed dogs. These same breeders also discourage merle-to-merle matings so as to avoid genetic defects associated with that potentially lethal cross. *See also* Australian Shepherd, Merle

Basset

French term for a short-legged scenthound; equivalent to the German term *dachshund*. The French have a number of basset types which developed in the Vendee, Bretagne, Normand and Gascogne regions.

Basset Artésian Normand

More efficiently constructed than his crooked-legged British counterpart, the Basset Artésian Normand is a short, straight-legged utility French hunter. In the 1600s, short-legged dogs from Artois were used to hunt badger. It does seem that these type hounds have always been available in France. In order to work in unruly terrain, brush and briar, the Artésian Basset needed straight legs that would neither hinder his speed nor drain his energy. Not as entrancing or handsome as the Basset Hound of England, these strong-bodied dogs, though considered handsome by their owners, were developed strictly for utility. Once referred to as the Basset d'Artois, the Basset Artésian Normand was developing in two distinct and unrelated types.

Leon Verrier is credited with directing the efforts of early nineteenth-century breeders who were torn between propagating the straight-legged, flat-headed Norman type of the Count Le Coulteus de Canteleu. The more refined "classic" appearance was the aim of one Louis

Lane, who had no concern for his crooked-legged, droopy-eared dwarf's hunting ability. The latter type, although exaggerated for greater appeal, lacked the requisite stamina to hunt. The standard developed by Leon Verrier around 1900 assisted in determining the desired blend. The two great Wars were not kind to the breed and today's existing specimens are greatly indebted to Leparoux de Combree, who worked hard at preserving the breed after World War II.

ESSENTIALS OF THE BASSET ARTÉSIAN NORMAND: A short, straight-legged hound. Cone-shaped ears, in generous proportion, give the head a noble and esthetic appearance. Its short coat is either tricolor or bicolor (orange and white). Height: 10–14 inches (25–36 cm). Weight: 33 pounds (15 kg). The muzzle is long, refined, and arched. Smooth muscles and a moderate amount of wrinkles and dewlap are appropriate.

Basset Fauve de Bretagne

The Basset Fauve de Bretagne is the smaller of the two hounds that derive from the Brittany area. The larger, the Griffon Fauve de Bretagne, was used to hunt wolves that threatened the prosperity of livestock and the agricultural well-being of the area. The Basset version of the Brittany hound was achieved by crossing the larger version with low-legged hounds from the Vendee area and surrounding neighborhoods. The earlier specimens of the Basset type probably looked more like terriers than the distinctive look of the Basset Fauve that we know today.

The breed's stubby, somewhat crooked legs have warranted extensive usage as a hunter in briars and heaths. In addition to its French homeland, the

Basset Artésian Normand, tricolor. Photo by I. Français.

Basset Fauve de Bretagne photographed by I. Français.

breed is becoming popular in Great Britain, where it is also recognized by the

Basset Fauve de Bretagne. Photo by I. Français.

Basset Hound, tricolor.

K.C.G.B. Variations on the "basset" theme are growing continually more popular as companion dogs more so than as hunters. Despite this Basset's efficiency in the field, he is a beguiling and affectionate homebody as well. *See also* Griffon Fauve de Bretagne

ESSENTIALS OF THE BASSET FAUVE DE BRETAGNE: Sporting a coarse, hard coat of varying shades from fawn to golden wheat, this hound stands about 14 inches (35.5 cm) high and can weigh from 36–40 pounds (16–18 kg). Its elongated head is outlined by medium-length ears and rests on a short muscular neck. The chest is wide and deep; the sternum prominent; the ribs are slightly barreled. The forelegs straight or slightly crooked. Strongly boned with slightly sloping pasterns. Shoulders slightly sloping. The tail, set on high, is thick at the base and tapers to a point. Color variations include red-wheaten and fawn. The coat is never long or woolly.

Basset Hound

The modern Basset Hound of England is a distinctive and refined breed of scenthound. Like the hounds of the Marquis de Tournon described in 1867, Basset Hounds are long, low hounds, shaped much like a Dachshund with forelegs crooked at the knees, with much more bone and larger head than the Beagle. They were not the dark tan color of Dachshunds but rather the color of Foxhounds with a certain amount of white about them. They had deep heavy bones, more like the Foxhounds than the Beagle. Today, the Basset's bone construction and head are more often likened to the Bloodhound's. This description predates by 31 years the first written standard for the Basset (1898).

However, much before the drawing of any standard, the Basset Hound was being bred by medieval monks. These industrious friars conjured up this low-to-the-ground hound to work in heavy cover. Still, it was on the British Isles that

Basset Hound.

the Basset fully bloomed. It was the hounds of the Marquis de Tournon, described above, named "Basset" and "Belle," that were imported into England. The English breed is thus directly related to the French bassets. British nobility, like French royalty, favored the short-legged hounds. After a great deal of selective breeding and the cessation of French basset importation, the British Basset Hound branched off from the Normand and Artesian bassets.

If given the choice, the Basset will trail deer, but he can be used on a variety of game, including rabbit, pheasant, and even raccoon. Basset Hounds are hunted in packs; they are slow but irrefutably effective. The Basset's voice on the trail

the Basset has achieved substantial popularity as a home companion in both England and America. Whether a result of the breed's pack existence or the good example set in their former monastic dwelling, the Basset Hound is most often brotherly and warm-hearted. Despite their charm and classic appearance, Bassets can be stubborn and lazy, so proper discipline and regular exercise are imperative to survival.

ESSENTIALS OF THE BASSET HOUND: Distinct wrinkles adorn a large, well-proportioned head; the breed's expression is aristocratic and intelligent. Relative to size, this is the most heavily boned dog in dogdom, standing 14 inches (35–36 cm) or less and weighing 40–60 pounds

Basset Hound, tricolor.

epitomizes the hounds' music. The opportunity to experience the Basset's well-tuned vocalization is still prime in Great Britain and America, where these dogs are used for hunting and field trialing. Despite the Basset Hound's ponderous appearance, he is agile and consistent on the trail.

Unlike most of the other scenthounds,

(18–27 kg). The skull is domed with stop and occipital bone prominent. The head is of medium width at brow and tapering slightly to muzzle. The ears are set on low, long, reaching well beyond the muzzle. The neck is muscular and well arched. Shoulder blades well laid back, shoulders not heavy. Forelegs short, powerful, of great bone. Upper forearm inclined slightly inward. The body is long and deep throughout length; breast bone prominent, but chest neither narrow nor unduly deep; ribs well rounded and sprung, carried well back. Back broad, level. Hindquarters standing well out, stifles well bent, feet massive and well knuckled up. The coat is short and smooth, lying close without being too fine. In color the Basset Hound is typically black, white and tan (tricolor) or lemon and white (bicolor), but any hound color is accepted. Its undocked tail must be carried gaily.

Bat ear

Erect ears, relatively broad at the base and rounded at the top, opening directly to the front (e.g., French Bulldog). *See also* Tulip ears

Bat-eared fox

The African bat-eared fox, *Otocyon megalotis*, is a peculiar wild dog of the family Canidae. Though foxlike in appearance and indeed also known as the long-eared fox, the big-eared fox, the black-eared fox, and Delalande's fox, this native African wild dog is anatomically unique enough to be the sole member of its subfamily, *Otocyoninae*. Its many ear-oriented common names are the result of its proportionately giant-sized ears which are oval in shape and about 4.5 inches (11.5 cm) long; however, its true peculiarity is its skeletal structure. An insect-eating dog, the bat-eared fox has molars that are seemingly fused, which is highly uncharacteristic of a canid. Long and lean,

the bat-eared fox stands 12 to 14 inches (30.5–35.5 cm) tall, is 24 to 25 inches (61–63.5 cm) long, and weighs from 6 to 11 pounds (3–5 kg). The animal ranges in color from dark gray to brownish gray on its back, blending to buff or whitish buff on the belly, flanks, and throat. When alarmed, this fox gets low to the ground and flattens its ears to either side of its head, in an effective attempt to escape detection. An expert at evasion, and necessarily so, this foxy fox instinctively doubles back in its tracks, confusing the

SUPERSTITION
KENNEL CLUB

SKC **BEST IN SHOW**

Basset Hound, tricolor.

Bat ear. French Bulldogs display their hallmark earage. Photo by I. Français.

Bathing. In warm weather an outdoor bath on the lawn is practical and enjoyable. Participating in this practical family fun are a well-rinsed Golden Retriever and a well-soaped Old English Sheepdog. Photographs by Robert Pearcy.

sniffer of the hottest or even coldest nose of the scenthounds on the plains and open bushlands of its native territory. The bat-eared fox seeks protection, restful time, and a place to rear its young in the burrows which it constructs in the sandy soil. Social animals, several foxes will build their burrows in close proximity, travel in groups of six or more, and raise their young communally. Though most active during the transition hours of dawn and dusk, these foxes will also hunt at night and are commonly active during the day. Unselective in their feeding habits, bat-eared foxes add rodents, birds and their eggs, lizards, fruits and tubers to their insect consumption. Besides the devastation that hunters and farmers have wantonly afflicted upon this canid, the bat-eared fox suffers considerably from disease and an ever-decreasing range to roam.

Batak Spitz

A medium-sized, extremely vocal hunting and watchdog of Africa. In appearance the dog is thick coated, long limbed, with either a short or a ring tail. Color ranges from black through white, either whole or particolored.

Bathing

Bathing in dogs is an important aspect of grooming. The general rule of thumb, however, is that bathing should occur as infrequently as possible. Dogs should be bathed when really necessary or a few days before a show. Dogs that are kept primarily indoors and are neither exhibition nor working dogs can be bathed as infrequently as two times a year. Dogs younger than six months of age should

never be bathed. Keep the coat clean by brushing or other dry makeshift means (i.e., a damp washcloth or a mild sponge bath). Likewise, senior citizen canines should not be bathed with any frequency. The dog's skin and hair are different than human's. Oil glands in our skin afford us the ability to endure frequent or daily baths and shampoos. Therefore, common sense dictates that products made for human use are not appropriate for use on a dog. There are many manufacturers and developers who produce exclusive canine products. These soaps and shampoos do not strip the oil from a dog's coat, rather they add to the coat. The use of a quality dog soap and/or shampoo eliminates the necessity for additional applications, since most topnotch products are developed to execute a variety of tasks: defleaing, conditioning, cleansing, etc.

There is no single, definitive method to bathe a dog. Experienced groomers can only offer advice that may prove effective. Effectiveness is a function of how clean the dog gets, how quickly, and how dry the owner stays during the accomplishment of the former goal.

Before bathing, be sure to brush the dog's coat. This removes hair and debris, separates the hairs and stimulates circulation. Dematting before giving a bath is also recommended.

Properly securing your dog in the tub will add to his safety and to your continued dryness. A nylon leash and collar helps to keep the dog still during the bath. Once your dog is old enough to be bathed—and the actual need arises—it is a good idea to acclimate him to the bathing procedure. Trying to bathe a six-year-old Doberman for the first time will be an experience that will soak your memory for years to come and one you may not attempt again single-handedly or without a wetsuit. The leash can be attached to a single hook on the wall, if the dog is well trained and duly tolerant. Smaller dogs can be bathed in a basin, while some of the larger breeds will extend past the confines of the family bathtub. These larger dogs will need to be bathed outdoors in more mild weather.

Dog groomers use tubs that are about waist-high and often rely on previously induced training. A rubber non-slip mat is also necessary. A well-sudsed German Shepherd slipping, panic-stricken, and paddling for dear life is surely starting out on the wrong paw. Once the dog is secured in the tub, wet the coat thoroughly with warm water, using a hose with a spray attachment. The head should be done last. Water should be run freely down the tub drain so that the dog does not have to stand in neck-high water. This also makes management on your part easier. Work the shampoo through the hair with your hands—no pet store device works more efficiently than your ten fingers—and add water as necessary to acquire a healthy lather. Be certain to wash the *entire* dog—under the stomach, under the tail, between the foot pads, under the ear leather, and "between the legs" too. Be careful when washing the dog's head—avoid getting shampoo in the dog's eyes and ears. Even though a great many pet shop shampoos are tear-free, it is still desirable to avoid getting any soap in the dog's eyes to avoid any potential irritation. Cotton gently inserted into the dog's ear opening can prevent soap and water from entering the ear canal.

When the dog's coat is well lathered, rinse with warm water, using a spray with a considerable water stream. Rinse the head back from the eyes so as not to allow soap to enter the eyes. Rinse around the ears carefully. If the dog was egregiously soiled, repeat the lathering and rinsing process. It is vital to remove all soap from the coat.

Squeeze the water out of the coat with your hands or use a blow dryer set on *low*, once the dog is removed from the tub. Towel dry the dog on the mat or allow the dog to cage dry. If the weather is amenable, letting the dog dry in the sun is also a viable conclusion. Do not let the dog roam for inevitably he will find mud—or make mud or more mud.

Long-coated and larger dogs naturally present more of a bathing challenge than do smooth-coated, smaller dogs. Obviously a 150-pound well-coated Tibetan Mastiff is going to present more of a chore than a five-pound smooth Chihuahua. Owners must alway be aware of drafts since a wet dog is especially vulnerable to colds. *See also* Grooming

Bathing. Former First Lady Nancy Reagan rinsing an antsy terrier. Photograph by M.A. Fackelman-Mener, The White House.

Bavarian Mountain Hound, black-masked red, and German hunter. Photo by I. Français.

Battak
See Sumatra Battak

Bavarian Mountain Hound

The Bavarian Mountain Hound, known on its home German slopes as the Bayrischer Gebirgsschweisshund, is the foremost blood-trailing deer hunter in Bavaria (and possibly Germany too). Various crosses of Bavarian hounds brought forth the Bavarian Mountain Hound. Popular conjecture contends that the Hanoverian Hound and Tyrolean Hounds are the most probable

forebears. Tracking in the mountainous regions of Bavaria requires the most agile and coldtrailing ability. This

schweisshund (or simply, bloodhound) fulfills this need with a vengeance. The Bavarian is a specialist on the cold trail and must be worked consistently for maximum utilization of talents. Not for the part-time or weekend sportsman, the Bavarian is chiefly employed by foresters and game wardens.

ESSENTIALS OF THE BAVARIAN MOUNTAIN HOUND: This bloodhound is shorter and lighter than others. He stands only 20 inches (51 cm) high, and reveals much endurance and persistence as a hunter. And although he is comparatively light for a bloodhound, he is in possession of an impressive musculature. Weight: 55–77 pounds (25–35 kg). Black-masked fawn to red and brindle are color possibilities for his glossy, short, thick coat.

Bavarian Schweisshund
See Bavarian Mountain Hound

Bawler
A hound that has a drawn out crying or bawling type of voice.

Bayrischer Gebirgsschweisshund
See Bavarian Mountain Hound

Beady eyes
A fault in many breed standards. Eyes that are round, smallish and queerly sparkling project an inappropriate expression for the given breed.

Beagle
The smallest of hunting hounds, the Beagle has been a recognizable dog for time immemorial. The Beagle may have been begotten from Celtic hounds crossed with smaller French and British hounds. For centuries in England, Beagles or Beagle prototypes are reported to have been hunted in packs by royalty. Beagles go on record as hare-hounds, since hunting the hare and rabbit is responsible for much of the breed's fame. Although the Beagle's origin is attributed to Britain, it was in America (and Canada) that the Beagle prospered. Beagles arrived in the States during colonial times and assisted the colonist greatly in hunting small game. Hunting the North American cottontail rabbit has boosted the Beagle's demand and subse-

quent popularity. No one, of course, denies that the Beagle's charm and good looks add to his consistent appeal.

While only myth remains about the Beagle's actual beginnings, it is clear that the Beagle types were bred to Harrier types for the sake of improvement, as a matter of course. The Cotswold Beagles (*circa* 1700), the North County Beagle, more slender than the Cotswold, and the Fox-Beagle were all crossed with Harriers. This surely improved type as well as increased size. Today's Beagle must be regarded as composite blends of all the various Beagle types that preceded our modern dog. In the early twentieth century, Hutchinson's staff purported that any modern Beagle can be categorized in one of the following five groups:

"(*a*) An almost obsolete group of which the individual members have the appearances and characteristics of miniature editions of the old and now extinct Southern Hound;

(*b*) The rough-haired Welsh Beagle forms a group which is in a class by itself;

(*c*) The largest group includes the majority of present-day Beagles, and these must be regarded as blends of original Beagle blood with Harrier or Foxhound strains, or both;

(*d*) A modern group consists of hounds having the appearances and characteristics of miniature present-day Foxhounds;

(*e*) The Pocket or Rabbit-Beagle forms a small group by itself, has more prominent eyes and other distinctive features, and stands only about ten inches at the shoulder."

In the late eighteenth century, the size of many Beagles was far diminutive to its present-day standard. While the American standard prohibits Beagles from standing over 15 inches (38 cm) tall, the British standard allows for one more inch of height. Both heights are substantially larger than the "pocket" sized Beagles of centuries past. These little handfuls were often carried on the master's horse in a pack in a sack. When the larger hounds were hot on the trail, the leather sack was opened and the smaller dogs would join on the trail. These tiny dogs still occur in an occasional litter today. Some breeders, daring and experienced, still promote

these smaller working and apartment dogs as "Pocket Beagles." Although not recognized by the major registries, these

Beagle, tricolor, on the field.

dogs are popular in certain circles.

The Beagle's hunting acumen is versatile and impressive. In England, Beagles were originally used exclusively on common brown hare, blue or mountain hare, or other aberrant hopping quarry. In addition to hare and rabbit, the Beagle is used on quail and pheasant, as well as small land animals. Larger sized Beagles (and Harriers) have been employed in the leopard hunt too.

As breed names go, the Beagle's name is unique and its origin quite unknown. Some believe it meant "smallest of hounds," but there is no record of the word's usage in the writings on Venerie before Henry VII, though there is no doubt that Beagle prototypes were already extensively used on hare hunting for centuries in Britain.

Beagles, lemon and white, in the ring.

Beagles are happy companion dogs that have ranked in the top ten breeds in America for many years. These are people-oriented, affectionate hounds that can thrive on a solely suburban lifestyle. There of course is no doubt that the Beagle knows his first love (hunting) well and should be worked. In temperament the Beagle is gay and content. Of course, disposition can explain only a part of the breed's tremendous popularity. Longevity, good looks, and intelligence are also notable pluses. Over-vocalization and a trace of

Beagle, lemon and white. Photo by Graham.

stubbornness are cited by some owners as potential concerns. Crate training is advised by many breeders.

The Beagle is also one of the world's most hardy canines and this plus has amplified the call for laboratory work. The Beagle's small size and consistency of weight make it ideal for medical experimentation and research. Colonies of Beagles are bred for this purpose. *See* Research dogs

ESSENTIALS OF THE BEAGLE: The Beagle is essentially a small foxhound, solid and "big for his inches." His inches can be under 13 (33 cm) or 13–15 (33–38 cm)—two varieties. The Beagle is sturdy and compactly built. The head is of fair length, powerful not coarse. Stop well defined. Nose broad. Ears are long with rounded tips, reaching nearly the end of nose. Neck is sufficiently long, slightly arched, showing little dewlap. Forequarters are straight and upright; the hind, muscular. Shoulders well laid back, not loaded. Chest let down to elbow. Topline straight and level. Stifles well bent. Feet tight and firm. Tail sturdy and moderately long. Any true hound color is allowed; the coat is close, hard and of medium length. Weight: 18–30 pounds (8–13.5 kg).

Beagle field trials
See Field trials

Beagle, tricolor.

Beagle Harrier

The Beagle Harrier is a creation of French sportsman Baron Gerard to hunt deer. The Beagle Harrier is surely more of a crossbreed than a pure breed. As the name implies, two British hounds were crossed to produce the Beagle Harrier. This dog is a foxhound of average height (between the two component breeds). Of course, Gerard's creation is of dubious genius. Since the Beagle and the Harrier's histories are so intertwined and since these two breeds were once considered a single one, Gerard's foxhound brings the development full circle. In effect, however, the Beagle Harrier undoes years of selective breeding to distinguish the Beagle from the Harrier.

Today the breed makes a rare but delightful appearance at rare breed dog shows, and is more frequently seen in small packs in France. His abilities are surely topnotch on deer and hare; his temperament is lively and pleasant.

ESSENTIALS OF THE BEAGLE HARRIER: Heavily boned, sturdy, and stocky is this breed. In size the Beagle Harrier stands between 15–19 inches (38–48 cm), conveniently filling the gap between its two closest foxhound relatives. Weight: 44 pounds (20 kg). The typical hound coat, short, smooth, and thick, can be any hound color. Although no importance is placed on color, a tan-dominated tri is common. Its V-shaped ears are set high and goodly sized, though not large.

Beagling

Beagling, referring to the sport of hunting with Beagles, is a term coined by Beagle fanciers who use their breed for hunting. *See* Beagle

Bear coat

Faulty long coat in the Shar-Pei, over an inch in length.

Bear ears

An undesirable ear that is rounded at the tip (e.g., a fault for the Samoyed).

Beagle Harrier, tricolor. Photo by I. Français.

Beard

Facial furnishings comprising thick and stand-offish hair that adorn the chin, cheeks, and lower jaw area. Most commonly seen on the wirehaired breeds, the beard is a key characteristic for many such breeds. The Wire Fox Terrier, Bouvier des Flandres, Black Russian Terrier, and Afghan Hound are varied examples of bearded breeds. In the wire-hairs, the beard is usually complemented by bushy eyebrows and whiskers as well.

from the Polski Owczarek Nizinny (Polish Lowland Sheepdog) when members of the breed were left on the shores of Scotland and bred to native working dogs. The Bearded Collie, bearing enlightening similarities to the Old English Sheepdog and the Polish Lowland Sheepdog, may indeed be descended from like stock. These tousled gray dogs are documented as existing in Scotland as early as the sixteenth century, and pictures of the Beardie go back at least to the Gainsborough portrait of the Duke of Buccleigh in which the dog is also depicted.

The Bearded Collie has always been a hard-working herding dog of exceptional ability; he has also enjoyed popularity as a companion and showman over the years. The breed suffered periodically during the first half of the twentieth century, reaching near extinction during World War II. The breed was preserved and maintains a steady show and work following today. Some feel that he is the up-and-coming sheepdog showman and companion: the Beardie is blithe-some and lighthearted and sometimes rambunctious. The breed's North American stronghold was begot first in Canada; it was fully accepted into the A.K.C. as recently as 1976.

ESSENTIALS OF THE BEARDED COLLIE: A powerful dog of great activity and agility, the Bearded Collie should never appear heavy and lethargic or thin and weak. Height: 20–22 inches (51–56 cm). Weight: 40–60 pounds (18–27.5 kg). Built for unending motion, the dog possesses a deep chest that allows plentiful heart and lung room; ribs well sprung. Shoulders slope well back. Back level. All limbs are strong. An alert, inquisitive countenance is characteristic of the breed. The coat is double, with soft, furry and close undercoat and flat, harsh, strong and shaggy outer coat, free from woolliness and curl, though slight wave permissible. Color can be: slate gray, reddish fawn, black, blue, all shades of gray, brown and sandy, all with or without white markings.

Beard on a gray and white Bearded Collie. Photo by I. Français.

Bearded Collie

An undoubtedly old herding breed of indefinitely obscured beginnings. It is commonly accepted that the breed developed on the British Isles, but the theories of such evolution differ considerably. Some authorities assert that the Bearded Collie is one of the oldest breeds of Britain, descending from the Magyar Komondor and arriving in Britain centuries ago. Another states that he evolved

Bearded Collie, gray and white. Photo courtesy of Chris Walkowicz.

Bearded Collies blowing in floral field.

Bearlike coat

Harsh, thick outer jacket, usually referring to the coat of the Eskimo Dog. The coat is 3–6 inches (7.5–15 cm) in length. The undercoat, woolly and dense, is about one-third of this length.

Beauceron, black/tan.

Beauceron

A strong, agile, very adaptable working dog of France; the breed, known also as the Berger de Beauce, was originally developed as a hunter of wild boar; but as the game vanished he found new employment as a herder and guarder of livestock, and eventually as a military and police dog. These dogs also serve today as guide dogs for the blind and guard dogs of home and business. Contrary to what his name implies, this French shepherd does not trace his origin to Beauce; instead, he shares Brie with his cousin, the Briard, as his place of birth. The name Beauceron, or Berger de Beauce, was chosen to differentiate the two breeds, which do both, by the way, exist in Beauce. The Beauceron is also called the Bas Rouge in his homeland. The name comes from the breed's distinctive red coloration, also called red stockings, on the lower portion of its legs.

Although in appearance the two breeds are distinct from one another—the Briard is longhaired, among other differing qualities—they likely derive from the same general stock. Indeed many French shepherd dogs trace their ancestry to common stock, and the Beauceron and the Briard, emerging in the same region, probably shared blood. A mastiffy workman of great strength, courage, and intelligence, the Beauceron has yet to achieve the same degree of popularity as the Briard. Strong-willed yet amenable to training, the Beauceron makes a fine companion and protector. His frequency in the European show ring is increasing and members of the breed are finding their way across the Atlantic to the U.S. and Canada where their reception has thus far been warm.

ESSENTIALS OF THE BEAUCERON: Strong, able, and highly adaptable dog of excellent herding skills and easily trainable intellect and disposition. The Beauceron is well constructed and muscular while remaining quick and agile. Movement to be smooth, powerful and effortless. The head is long and flat-topped or slightly rounded. Its coat must be short and close. On the head, the coat is smooth and flat-lying, while the legs, tail, and flanks are slightly fringed. The neck is thick and muscular. The chest is deep. The back is strong, straight, with croup slightly rounded. In color the exhibition-sanctioned Beauceron is necessarily black/tan, black, or harlequin. The breed also occurs in tawny, gray, or gray/black—these colors have since been banned from the show ring. Height: 25–28 inches (63.5–71 cm). Weight: 66–85 pounds (30–38.5 kg).

Beauty spot

A mark of colored hair gracefully conspicuous in the center of the white blaze on the top of the head. In the two British

Beauceron, blue merle. Photographs by I. Français.

toy spaniels, the King Charles Spaniel and the Cavalier King Charles Spaniel, these patches are referred to respectively as "spots" and "lozenge marks."

Beaver

Badger coloration.

Bed sores

Bed sores, external skin damage caused by the animal's weight on a particular area for a prolonged length of time, are common among the large, largely sedentary breeds and also among whelping mothers and sick or aging dogs that are bedridden. Owners can provide the softest bedding materials possible to ease the dog's discomfort. Vets commonly treat bed sores.

Bedding

Dog beds are particularly popular with owners of small dogs, and ideal for pups of most all breeds. Coming in various sizes, these beds can be purchased to suit most breeds. Dog beds provide a place for the dog to sleep and nap, thus keeping him off the furniture. These beds can be taken with you when you move or travel with your dog; the sight and smell of the familiar bed will ease anxiety.

Since many dogs greatly cherish their bedding area, it is an owner's responsibility to provide the cleanest and most hygienic sleeping accommodations possible. Wood wool (or fine wood shavings) are perhaps the most comfortable and lasting of bedding materials. Foam rubber is a popular option. A number of wood shavings (other than wool) become hard and uncomfortable too quickly. Pet shops are well stocked with dog beds and the proprietor will be pleased to give an up-date on the latest models. *See also* Accommodations, indoor

Bedlington Terrier

The Bedlington Terrier, known in its pre-pedigree years as the Rothbury or Northumberland Fox Terrier, acquired its present name in 1825 when Mr. Joseph Ainsley referred to "Piper" (undecidedly "Young" or "Old") as a Bedlington Terrier. The first dog documented as the predecessor of the Bedlington breed was owned by Squire Trevelyan and was whelped in 1782. One Northumbrian piper named James Allan was the original owner of Rothbury Terriers. This musically inadequate otter hunter belonged to the line of Yetholme gypsies, tinkers by trade. Allan's Rothburys were mercilessly game on otters, rats, and badger. "Peachem" and "Pincher" were Allan's two favorite terriers. As terrier crosses were common in the early nineteenth century, it is difficult to ascertain which of the British terriers were amalgamated to yield the Bedlington. If the Dandie Dinmont in fact predates the fixed Bedlington, it was likely a key ingredient; scholars disagree which breed

Bedlington Terrier, blue. Photo by I. Français.

came first. The Whippet and Otter Hound are the other two dogs generally thrown into the gene pool. Regardless, the result is a distinctive terrier with an assortedly sordid history. The Bedlington has not always been a well-groomed, soft show terrier, glowing with unsubtle ovinity, but was once a very hard game dog used by gypsies in northern England as a poacher and pit fighter. The dogs were fancied by many walks of life, including miners and pitmen, as hunters and ratters. The fast-paced industrialization that swept Europe forced this overly snarly contender to mellow and concede to today's more fanciful fancier's type, which does not know the likes nor loathe

the rat nor fancy dust-ups with his kind.

ESSENTIALS OF THE BEDLINGTON TERRIER: A light-made, lathy and graceful dog, not weedy or shelly, he is strong, hard and muscular—conformation is of utmost importance. Fairly long in the body with natural arched loin and a long rat tail. Head and skull narrow, head is pear-shaped. Jaw long and tapering. Ears filbert-shaped, low set and hanging flat to the cheek. Body is muscular yet flexible, flat, ribbed deep through brisket. Back roach and loin arched. Muscular, galloping quarters, fine and graceful, allowing a distinctive light action in slower paces. The natural coat, preferably linty and weather-resistant, is a blend of hard and soft hair with a tendency to curl (often appearing as wool). Height: 15–17 inches (38–43 cm). Weight: 17–23 pounds (7.5–10.5 kg). Coat color possibilities include blue, liver, sandy, or each with tan.

Bedouin Shepherd Dog

A rugged, stalwart canine with a solid frame and unyielding durability, the Bedouin Shepherd Dog is a medium-sized pariah-type dog. The coat is equally durable and stands up well to the desert sun and sandstorms. In color the Bedouin dog can be any variety of solids or merles.

The desert dwellers of the vast Sahara desert and the Arabian peninsula are known as Bedouins. These nomads roam with their camels, asses, and herds of goats and sheep in search of water and pasture. Excluding the much revered

Saluki, the Bedouins essentially despise dogs and their herding dogs are rather neglected. Nevertheless, the Bedouin Shepherd Dogs are a noteworthy component to the survival of these peripatetic peoples who must move across unirrigated land with their irritated, discontented flocks. These dogs, semi-domesticated from wandering pariahs, must survive on the shepherd's meager diets of millet, mutton, and dates, supplemented by an occasional locust or lizard.

The famed dog writer and gustatory accountant, Ernest H. Hart, tells of these dogs in his travelogue. They were maintained as herders of camels and goats, not pleasant or amenable beasts to persuade.

Beds
See Bedding

Bee sting tail
Used specifically to refer to the tail of the pointer, a short, straight tail that narrows to the tip.

Bee stings
Although a common occurrence, bee stings on dogs must be inspected for signs of infection, retained stingers, and allergic reactions. If no reaction is present, a cleansing as for a minor wound should suffice for treatment, first removing the stinger if present.

Beefy
Doggie slang referring to an overly muscular or conditioned animal. Usually not complimentary and referring to excessive musculation or over weight.

Behavior
See Canine behavior

Behavior modification
The key to behavior modification is defining the behavioral goal and channelling your efforts towards conditioning the desirable response. The term "successive approximation," while meaningless to the non-therapist, technically describes this process. Benjamin L. Hart, D.V.M., Ph.D., was the first to attribute this term to the canon of canine literature. Owners may wish to modify their dog's behaviors and reactions for

various reasons. The most common of these undesirable inclinations or habits are destructive tendencies, fear reactions, excessive barking, and aggressiveness. The source of each of these problems can be learned or genetic. Shyness and fear-biting, for instance, are genetic problems which cannot be "cured" by successive approximation or another modification process.

Destructive tendencies such as gnawing on furniture, uprooting gardens, urinating indoors, or destroying other property should not be tolerated by owners. While each of these aversions can be learned, destructive tendencies can be inherited to a degree. Puppies in a gang or strays running in packs can act more destructively than any single individual would alone. This pack instinct can be derived from wolves who hunt and fight in packs. Nevertheless, a dog in your home may become destructive for a number of reasons: a plea for attention, disapproval of his condition, unadulterate spite, pathological fear of being left alone, release of frustration or plain boredom. Destructiveness usually occurs when an owner is not home; this is usually a key to understanding the source of the dog's tendency. Successive approximation entails modifying the dog's reaction to your departure, making him proud of his good behavior while you are away. Such a process takes time and consistency to execute.

Fear reactions or phobias, such as to lightning and thunder, can also be modified. Dogs with this phobia "freak out" during storms, taking cover under furni-

ture, whimpering, and piddling on the carpet. One method of modification is to obtain a recording of a thunder storm and slowly accustom the dog to the sounds, beginning at the lowest possible volume and increasing it at each sitting. Fear of the dark, fear of other people, and fear of the outdoors can also be approached in a like manner.

Barking in dogs of course is a means of communication and expression with their world, their owners, and passersby. This is not to say that modifying an overly vocal dog is defying the First Amendment—violating his freedom of speech. Barking is a natural response in most dogs; many inherit the predisposition as a warning or alarm. Dogs bark out of boredom, excitement, discomfort, hunger, fear, etc. Excessive barking can be inherited or learned. There are many methods of preventing a dog from barking. If barking is linked to receiving a

Behavior modification. Exuberant barking can be a problem. Breeds like the Siberian Husky may be more barkingly boisterous than other breeds.

reward upon the command "Speak," do not reward the dog for obliging your command. Extinction and punishment

Behavior modification. The overly aggressive and territorial instincts of the guardian breeds need to be channeled by the owner. This Tibetan Mastiff is too surly and recalcitrant to serve properly as a home protector.

Behavior modification. Be consistent in defining the rules of the house. Basset Hound with upper hand and/or permission.

are frequently attempted methods of extinguishing a dog's barking. Some owners have attempted drenching their dogs from an upstairs window whenever he barks outside. The dog is intended to associate the punishment with the act and therefore stop. Others have found that wet dogs bark louder than dry ones. The use of electric shock collars, activated by the dog's barking or by the owner's remote control, have proven both dangerous and rather ineffectual. Common sense applied to an individual situation is probably the overall best answer. Debarking, or removing the dog's vocal apparatus, as well as euthanasia have been considered by owners. It is vital to remember that barking is the dog's most important means of communication and depriving a dog of sound will scar him psychologically his entire life. If

an owner thinks euthanasia is his only answer to the barking problem, he is not fit to own a dog and should bring the dog to a shelter.

Aggressiveness and dominant behavior are common problems with dogs. There are various types of aggressive behavior: competitive, between two dogs; intermale, between two males; fear-induced, either sex responding out of fear; pain-induced; territorial; predatory, dogs attacking other animals or livestock; maternal and learned, as displayed by trained guard dogs. Each type needs a different degree of modification. Conditioning competitive dogs and proper consistent training should alleviate outward aggressiveness. Of course, certain dogs, the bull-and-terrier and mastiff breeds, generally exhibit dominant behavior over other dogs. Intermale aggression (the same as competitive aggression if involving two males) can be approached in a like manner. Obedience training and discipline from an early age can assist in eliminating shows of dominance or viciousness. Any dog can show aggressiveness if provoked. Dogs such as Toy Poodles and Yorkshire Terriers tend to be one-man or one-woman dogs and exhibit aggressiveness (relatively speaking) towards any person who attempts to approach them or their master.

Learned aggression can be curbed by praise and rewards. Rewarding a dog can work reciprocally as well. Refraining from praising a dog or giving it attention is often the answer to curtailing a dog's noted animosity towards a particular family member. *See also* Canine behavior, Training, Temperament Test

Belgian Cattle Dog
 See Bouvier des Flandres

Belgian Griffon
 The Belgian Griffon, one of the small wirehaired urchins of Belgium, is recognized by the F.C.I. as an individual breed. In the A.K.C., the breed is categorized as a Brussels Griffon, which *see*. The original Griffon resembled a small terrier, half-Barbet and half-Griffon (Affenpinscher). There was a silky tuft on the head, and the muzzle was long and tapered. In the 1800s, the English Toy Spaniel was used to decrease the size and shorten the snout; it also eliminated much of his working ability. As the breed gained in popularity, Barbets, Dutch Smoushonds, Yorkshire Terriers, and Pekingese were likely used to perfect the desired type. The Pug, very popular in nineteenth-century Belgium, is known to have been introduced into the bloodlines, and this infusion brought about the short coat and, hence, the Petit Brabançon, a close relative.

Belgian noblewoman Queen Henrietta Maria delighted in the Belgian Griffons (all three types), and during her time, no one in the Belgian ruling class dared to be seen without a monkey-faced

toy griffon at his side. At the breed's post-WWI height, there were estimatedly 5,000 brood bitches in the city of Brussels alone! At this time, breeders were able to command dear prices for their progeny. While a number of countries may have partaken in the communion which produced these griffon breeds, there is no doubt that Belgium is the one nation in which the breeds prospered most.

Belgian Griffon, black, cropped.

Belgian Griffon, red, uncropped. Photographs by I. Français.

ESSENTIALS OF THE BELGIAN GRIFFON: Square and well balanced with a long hard coat. The head is large and round, with a domed forehead. The ears are small and set high. Eyes well apart, very large and prominent, black. Brisket is broad and deep, ribs well sprung, back level and short. Neck of medium length, arched. Forelegs of medium length, straight in bone, well muscled. Hind legs also muscular. Height: 7–8 inches (18–20 cm). In size the Belgian Griffon comes in two varieties: one weighing up to 6.5 pounds (3 kg), and the other up to 11 pounds (5 kg). Color for either variety can be black, black/tan, or red/black grizzle. Griffons customarily receive tail docking to a short length. In the U.S., the Belgian (called Brussels) is shown cropped or uncropped. In England the uncropped ears are semi-erect.

Belgian Malinois

See Belgian Sheepdog, Malinois

Belgian Mastiff

Also known as the Chien de Trait, this once respected canine suffered the fate of many big dogs and many native European breeds. Through the course of history, with its depressions, wars, and changing styles, dogs used for protection and dogs that required substantial amounts of food and space passed from the face of the earth. The breed was known in Belgium for its drafting abilities; it was principally employed as a cart puller. The Belgian Mastiff was also once an effective guard dog also employed for tracking and search work as well as other canine duties. Today there are no known dogs in existence, and the breed has been placed on the F.C.I. suspended list. The Belgian Mastiff resembled many of the large French hounds, and he is therefore believed to have originated in France, changing type specifics during his residence in Belgium. Like other cartpullers, the Belgian Mastiff had its tail docked to avoid unwieldy mishaps with the wheels on winding roads. As other breeds used for guard and tracking work became popular, this mastiff's numbers dwindled further. The Société Royal Saint Hubert claims the Chien de Trait to be extinct today.

ESSENTIALS OF THE THE BELGIAN MASTIFF: A strong, well-muscled, strongly boned animal, of good range of movement and keen intelligence. The skull to be large and solid, revealing its mastiff heritage; muzzle strong, rather blunt, and well set on. Neck thick-set and muscular. The shorthaired, loose-fitting coat is of brindle or fawn, with dark mask and/or infrequent white markings possible. Height: 27–32 inches (69–78 cm). Weight: 100–110 pounds (45–50 kg).

Belgian Sheepdog

In the U.S., the name Belgian Sheepdog applies to the solid black Belgian Sheepdog, Groenendael which *see*. *See also* Belgian Sheepdog, Laekenois; Belgian Sheepdog, Malinois; Belgian Sheepdog, Tervuren

Belgian Sheepdog, Groenendael

With prick ears and a keen expression, the Groenendael has existed in his native Belgium since at least the late 1800s, confirmed by a study of Belgian herding breeds conducted by Professor Adolphe Reul in 1891. The longhaired black "variety" sheepdog was found breeding true in its rather confined area of distribution around the village of Groenendael; the specimens observed proved consistent in

Belgian Sheepdogs, Groenendael, black, as always. Photo by I. Français.

physical type. It is safely assumed that the breed traces to similar stock as the various other shepherd breeds of Germany, France, and especially Belgium; the four Chiens de Berger Belge, or Belgian Sheepdogs, (the Groenendael, Laekenois, Malinois, and Tervuren) all exhibit similar body conformation, differing only in color and coat type.

Regarded as the foster father of the breed, Nicholas Rose lived in the village of Groenendael. He purchased what are considered by many the foundation bitch and stud of the present breed; their names were Picard d'Uccle and Petite. With the two, Mr. Rose established his kennel. Among the first litters were the great Pitt, Baronne, and Duc de Groenendael, dogs found in many first class pedigrees today. The kennel, as well as the first Belgian Sheepdog club, traces to 1893. The club was the *Club du Chien de Berger Belge*, and it was the first to adopt a written standard for the breed(s). The name Groenendael was officially chosen for the breed in 1910. The American Kennel Club continues to employ Belgian Sheepdog as a breed name for the Groenendael. Not just a sheepdog, the breed's versatility and inherent protective qualities make it an ideal watchdog and family guardian. The breed's refined yet rugged good looks make it an effective showman as well. Not apprehensive with strangers, the Belgian Sheepdog never shows timidity or fear. With his family, he is zealous for their attention and very possessive.

ESSENTIALS OF THE BELGIAN SHEEPDOG, GROENENDAEL: Strong, square, balanced and defined. The overall impression is one of canine nobility and intelligence. The skull and muzzle of equal length. The ears are distinctly triangular, stiff and erect, set high, of moderate length, and well rounded at the base. Neck is well muscled, without dewlap, and broadens to the shoulders. The overall body is powerful but elegant. Chest is deep and well let down; ribs moderately well sprung. Belly moderately developed, neither drooping nor excessively tucked. Hindquarters well muscled and powerful without overangulation; hocks well let down. Height: 22–26 inches (56–66 cm). Weight: about 62 pounds (28 kg). The coat is long, straight and abundant, with a medium-harsh texture. The color is black or black with limited, specified white markings—small to moderate patch or strip on chest, between pads of feet and on tips of hind toes; frosting (white or gray) on muzzle.

Belgian Sheepdog, Groenendael. Photo by I. Français.

Belgian Sheepdog, Laekenois

He, of the four Belgian Sheepdog breeds (the Groenendael, Laekenois, Malinois, and Tervuren), is the rarest today; all four exhibit similar physical characteristics, yet each differs from the other in coat type and color; all reportedly descend from the same component stock and share ancestry with various sheepdogs of France, Germany, and other European countries. This variety of Belgian Sheepdog originated in Antwerp

Belgian Sheepdog, Laekenois, fawn. Photo by I. Français.

and its surrounding region. Both a herder and a guard, the Laekenois developed into a watchman, guarding the fine linen-lined fields, where valuable cloths were bleached in the sun and rain. The breed's name Laekenois traces to the Chateau de Laeken, one of Queen Henrietta Maria's royal residences. In fact, during the Queen's reign, the breed was a favorite both of shepherds and the Queen. The Laekenois's rough, shaggy coat allowed him all-weather performance, which, coupled with the rugged, athletic body, made for an unbeatable dog. Today, however, the breed is the least numerous of the Belgian shepherd dogs, owing to factors which are largely unexplainable: the breed remains an undeterred protector and a natural herder. Conceivably, the Laeken's unconventional—even bizarre—appearance has spooked a potential American following. The Laekenois is an adaptable companion with a strong will and great intelligence. Owners are advised to initiate discipline and training

at an early age. The breed's dominant personality and inborn guarding instincts combine to make a competent working canine.

ESSENTIALS OF THE BELGIAN SHEEPDOG, LAEKENOIS: A medium-sized, balanced, intelligent dog who is attentive, hardy, and ever alert. The Laekenois must be of fine proportion, of proud carriage, and of graceful strength. The skull and muzzle of equal length. The ears are distinctly triangular, stiff and erect, set high, of moderate length, and well rounded at the base. Neck is well muscled, without dewlap, and broadens to the shoulders. Chest is deep and well let down; ribs moderately well sprung. Hindquarters well muscled and powerful without overangulation; hocks well let down. The Laekenois's wire coat is harsh, dry and not curly. There should be no hint of locks of fluffy fine hair in rough coats. Coat length to be about 2.5 inches (6 cm) on all parts of body. Height: 22–26 inches (56–66 cm). Weight: 62 pounds (28 kg). Coloration ranges from fawn to mahogany, with black overlay.

Belgian Sheepdog, Malinois

The first of the Belgian Sheepdogs to establish type, he is the short-coated fawn variety and, like the other *Chiens de Berger Belge*, is named for his believed region of origin—the Malinois was most populous in the area of Malines when the oft-cited study of Professor Reul was conducted. Professor Adolphe Reul of the Belgian School of Veterinary Science collected data through field study and observation of the various sheepdogs of Belgium in and around the year 1891, and he is largely responsible for the categorization and cognomization of the various sheepdogs today. Once as many as eight, the Belgian Sheepdogs are now four recognized breeds. The first to perfect in type, breed true, and the first to rise to notable popularity, the Malinois became the gauge of his mostly similar brothers, who were labeled collectively as the *Berger Belge á poil court autre que Malinois* (that is, Belgian short-coated sheepdog other than Malinois). Presently, the Malinois's popularity borders on moderate. Recognized by the A.K.C. in 1965, the breed has gained popularity but slowly.

strength. The breed must have fine proportions and proud head carriage. The impression is of graceful strength. The skull and muzzle of equal length. The ears are distinctly triangular, stiff and erect; they are set high, of moderate length, and well rounded at the base. Neck is well muscled, without dewlap, and broadens to the shoulders. The overall body is powerful but elegant. Chest is deep and well let down; ribs moderately well sprung. Hindquarters well muscled and powerful without overangulation; hocks well let down. Color can be all shades of red, fawn, gray with black overlay; typically double pigmented, wherein each light-colored hair is blackened. Black mask, not to extend above the eyes, and black ears are typey. Tail should have a darker or black tip.

As with that of his cousin, the Laekenois, the marginal popularity of the Malinois is regrettable: the Belgian Sheepdogs are hardy working dogs of gifted intelligence, courage, and ability, compatible in the modern home and field. The breed is diligently watchful and never shy; members are increasingly employed as police and protection dogs. In temperament, the Malinois should demonstrate a steady, proud evenness; nervousness and pugnacity are to be discouraged. The breed makes an easy care, delightful companion and family dog.

ESSENTIALS OF THE BELGIAN SHEEPDOG, MALINOIS: A medium-sized, well-proportioned dog of high intelligence and good

Height: 24–26 inches (61–66 cm). Weight: 62 pounds (28 kg).

Belgian Sheepdog, Malinois, fawn with black.

Belgian Sheepdog, Malinois. Photographs by I. Français.

Belgian Sheepdog, Tervuren

A longhaired, fawn- to mahogany-colored herding dog of Belgium, one of the four recognized Belgian Sheepdogs. He bears closer resemblance to the Groenendael than to his other two cousins and is believed to have a history that runs parallel to that fraternal breed. It is accepted that all of the four *Chiens de Berger Belge* descend from common stock, and that their physical conformation has remained essentially identical to each other for over a century, with of course the exception of coat type and color.

Belgian Sheepdog, Tervuren, photographed in Tervuren, Belgium.

M. Donhieux is noted as the founder of the Tervuren variety. Brewer M. Corbeel crossed two black-tipped fawn longhaireds. One of the litter, a bitch named "Miss," was purchased by Mr. Donhieux and crossed to the renowned Picard d'Uccle. (Picard d'Uccle is also one of the foundation stock which created the Groenendael.) The result of this cross became the prototype for the Tervuren.

During the 1940s the breed neared extinction until the 1950s when an attractive Willy de la Garde Noir brought revival to the breed. The Terv today maintains a steady following on the Continent and in Great Britain and North America.

Hinderously close in resemblance to both the German Shepherd Dog and the Groenendael, the Tervuren has not attained the popularity and rating that it commands. The Tervuren is agile and multi-talented and is used as a police, military and guide dog. He is among the most delightful of the shepherding breeds. He should be led with a strong hand—owners find him affectionate and responsible once trained.

ESSENTIALS OF THE BELGIAN SHEEPDOG, TERVUREN: A dignified dog, with fine proportions and proud carriage of head—conveying an overall impression of graceful strength. Muzzle of medium length, tapering gradually towards the nose, which is black with well-flared nostrils. The ears are distinctly triangular, stiff and erect; they are set high, of moderate length, and well rounded at the base. Neck is well muscled, without dewlap, and broadens to the shoulders. The overall body is powerful but elegant. Chest is deep and well let down; ribs moderately well sprung. Hindquarters well muscled and powerful without overangulation; hocks well let down. Height: 22–26 inches (56–66 cm). Weight: 62 pounds (28 kg). The coat, which ranges in color from red to fawn to gray, with the characteristic black overlay, is double pigmented, wherein the tip of each light-colored hair is blackened. The tail is medium length.

Belgian Shorthaired Pointer

The likely result of crosses of the Grand Bleu de Gascon and the Old Danish Pointer, this good-sized and strong pointer is closely related to and resembles the French braques. He was selectively bred to hunt over the rough terrain common in Belgium. Hence he was constructed for power rather than quickness. With the diminution of quarry and the influx of German and French pointers to this hunter's world, the Braque Belge fell from favor in his native land. He is probably extinct today, and has been placed on the F.C.I. suspended list.

Thoughtful, easily trained and a natural hunter, what the Belgian Shorthaired Pointer lacked in speed he made up for in both strength and intelligence.

ESSENTIALS OF THE BELGIAN SHORTHAIRED POINTER: A good-sized, well-built hunting dog in type and conformation similar to the typical Continental pointer. The distinguishing characteristic is the coat color: a heavily ticked white (appearing slate gray) with varied brown patches. The Belgian Shorthaired is also more thickly built than the typically lighter Continental pointers. Height: 24–26 inches (61–66 cm). Weight: 55 pounds (25 kg). The head is moderately broad; the ears are small; and the tail is usually docked. With good sufficiency of leg, the breed is built more for power than speed.

Belgian Tervuren
See Belgian Sheepdog, Tervuren

Belladonna
This "herbaceous panacea" is a harmful pest, to the point of being deadly to canines. Signs of ingestion can include: loss of depth perception, dry mouth, weak rapid pulse, and fever.

Belly
The muscular floor of the abdomen.

Belton
The word used to describe the ticking or roaning color found in the English Setter. The term was originally employed by the founder of that breed, Edward Laverack. Beltons can be either light or dark, and today we recognize five different variations: blue belton (blue and white), orange belton (orange and white), lemon belton (lemon and white), liver belton (liver and white) and tricolor (blue belton with tan patches under the eyes). *See also* English Setter

Bench
An elevated platform, divided into stalls, on which dogs are kept on exhibit when not being judged.

Bench show
A dog show at which the dogs competing for prizes are "benched" or leashed on benches.

Bench show committee
The committee of a show-giving club which is given general responsibility for all arrangements in connection with the show; the committee to which the American Kennel Club looks for enforcement of all its rules at the show.

Bengal fox
A wild dog and a member of the genus *Vulpes*. *See* Foxes

Bergamaschi
See Bergamasco

Bergamasco
Considered an intermediate type flock-working dog: a large herder of strong, broad features and flock-guarding instincts. Judging from ability, he is a herding dog of excellence, whose guarding instincts and abilities simply add to his overall performance. An impressive blend of characteristics, the Bergamasco, or Cane da Pastore Bergamasco, is a long-time herding dog of northern Italy. Shar-

Bergamasco, gray. Photo by I. Français.

ing traits with the Briard, the Polish Lowland Sheepdog, the Bouvier des Flandres, and various Eastern herders, he is a likely contributor to any number of European herding dogs, yet his exact composition remains successfully obscured in the far-away past. Many cynologists point to those ancient world-over traders, the Phoenicians, as having brought ancestors of the breed to Italy in their ever-bartering existence. Whatever its Italian start, the breed has undoubtedly existed and served well in its present working form for centuries. From avail-

able sources we assume the breed sprang from the Bergamo region near Milan; hence the name Bergamasco.

Few extant breeds of dog possess the heavy corded coat. On the Bergamasco, it provides warmth and insulation while establishing an impenetrable buffer zone against kicking herds and slashing predators. He is a remarkably intelligent animal with the uncanny ability to sense members of the herd solely from the scent of their mother. With courage and accuracy, the Bergamasco retrieves straying ovines and their lost or wounded little ones in life-endangering storms; yet the breed has but narrowly escaped extinction. He is an adaptable and witty companion and worker and deserves consideration which he has yet to receive from the twentieth-century dog fancy.

ESSENTIALS OF THE BERGAMASCO: The Bergamasco is an affectionate and closely bonding stock guard possessing a thick corded coat. The back portion of the coat is of woolly consistency, while the front portion is composed of rough, wiry hair, referred to as goat hair. Vital to the quality of a specimen is its retainment of the inherent instincts and abilities to herd and to protect. The skull is strong and broad between the ears. The stop is well defined; the eyes are dark; and the muzzle is broad and strong. The body is intensely muscled but flexible and lithe. The chest is deep but not too broad, with good spring of rib allowing for plenty of heart and lung capacity. The back is straight and strong. There is good length of leg. The tail extends to the hocks and curls up at its end. Height: 22–24 inches (56–61 cm). Weight: 57–84 pounds (26–38 kg). Color can be all shades of gray, including salt and pepper (flecked with various colors).

Bergamese Shepherd
See Bergamasco

Berger Polonais de Valée
See Polish Lowland Sheepdog

Berger
French term used interchangeably with shepherd or sheepdog.

Berger da Castro Laboreiro
See Cão de Castro Laboreiro

Berger da Serra de Estrela
See Estrela Mountain Dog

Berger de Beauce
See Beauceron

Berger de Brie
See Briard

Berger de Savoy
See Savoy Sheepdog

Berger des Pyrenees a Face Rase
See Bergers des Pyrenees

Berger des Pyrenees, Smooth Muzzled
See Bergers des Pyrenees

Berger du Languedoc
The shepherding personnel of the Languedoc area in France are grouped under the name *Le Chien de Berger du Languedoc* and in reality consist of five types of Languedoc herders. These include the Camargue, the Larzac, the Grau, the Farou, and the Carrigues. The proficient Cevennes Shepherd (Berger du Languedoc) is the bigger, stronger, more vigorous *chien* of the French herding family. Principally employed in Lower Languedoc and Lower Provence, France, these dogs necessarily developed into formidable mountain guards as well as skillful flock manipulators. However,

through the course of time, with its changing demands, the breed's numbers

Bergamasco, gray. Photo by I. Français.

neared zero: the breed is now suspected of being extinct. The F.C.I. has dropped the breed from its official registry.

Throughout his hard-worked history, the Berger du Languedoc served French shepherds as a multi-functional canine who worked alone with the shepherd and his allotted 450 sheep. The dogs were highly regarded in their time and reportedly would slay wolves with themselves suffering only minor injury. The fall of the breed is attributed to the commercialization of herding and the flagitious World Wars of the twentieth century.

ESSENTIALS OF THE BERGER DU LANGUEDOC: In height these dogs range from 16–22 inches (40.5–56 cm). For the sake of resilience, they are double coated. The outer coat offers a varied fawn, often dark, spotted on the head and forehead; the undercoat usually includes white hairs. These are working shepherds, and a specimen's degree of conformation is directly related to its effectiveness as a working dog.

Berger Picard
An old, possibly the oldest, sheepherding dog of France, the Berger Picard, or Picardy Shepherd, is reportedly Celtic and related closely to both the Beauceron and Briard.

The setting was ninth-century France; the conception, the Berger de Picard: though problematic it remains the accepted beginning of the breed. Today the Picardy is still found working the flocks in the Pas-de-Calais region near the Somme in northern France, where he has proven his stupendous herding skills for centuries. Never of tremendous numbers, the breed suffered acutely at the hands of war in the 1900s. To extinction this ancient French Celt was nearly driven. Not willing to let slip this jovial yet rambunctious canine, lovers of the breed teamed efforts, and presently the Berger Picard strides toward recovery. Yet he remains of limited numbers even in France and very few specimens are found elsewhere in the world.

The Picardy Shepherd can be a fine home and family guardian. He is unfaltering in his assertiveness and is equally untiring in his affections. Easycare and lovable, the breed and its fanciers hope for a bright future.

is slightly elongated. The chest is deep; the back is long. The legs are of good length, sturdy and strong. The tail is crook. Height: 21–26 inches (53–66 cm). Weight: 50–70 pounds (23–31 kg). The rough, tousled coat is his distinctive characteristic. The coat is colored in various shades of fawn or gray. White is a discouraged coat color, but white specimens have been known to occur.

Berge Polonais de Vallée
See Polish Lowland Sheepdog

Bergers des Pyrenees
As Paris is to painting and as Lyons is to cooking, the Pyrenean Mountains are to shepherd dogs. Emerging from these flock-filled mountains is a wondrous herd-working team: the Great Pyrenees as guardian and the Berger des Pyrenees as guide. Known also as the Labrit and the Petit Berger, the Berger des Pyrenees is bred for speed, reaction, agility, and endurance. The vital, characteristic shaggy coat, whether long or medium in length, gives the protection to resist the worst of weather conditions. Also endearing the breed to shepherds of all persuasions is the Labrit's infrequent fueling requirement when working the long haul. In short, the breed is created to persist, defeating the odds and scaling the obstacles.

There exist three varieties of this remarkable herder: the Pyrenean Shepherd Dog (goathaired and longhaired) and the Smooth-Muzzled Pyrenean Shepherd Dog. All are equally effective, the sole difference being their respective coats. The Pyrenean Shepherd totes a long or goathaired, shaggy coat that will cord if unkept, while the Smooth-Muzzled carries a medium-length shaggy coat that turns to short smooth hair on the muzzle;

Berger Picard, gray. Photo by I. Français.

Essentials of the Berger Picard: One of the tallest of all herding dogs. In general, the Berger Picard is a versatile working dog, protected by a rough, durable, all-weather coat and instinctively protective of his flock and human family. The head is strong, with moderate breadth between the ears; the ears are narrow at their base and rather small, resulting in their standing naturally erect; the muzzle

Bergers des Pyrenees, (*top*) longhaired, gray fawn; (*center*) Smooth-Muzzled, fawn; (*bottom*) pair of Bergers on active duty in France. Photographs by I. Français.

Bergers des Pyrenees, (*top*) Smooth-Muzzled, fawn; (*lower left*) goathaired, black; (*lower right*) longhaired, blue. Photographs by I. Français.

hair should never cover the eyes of the Smooth-Muzzled dog, also known as the Berger des Pyrenees a Face Rase. The three varieties are the results of the relative isolation created by the terrain and the shepherding conditions in the rugged Pyrenean Mountains. Evolving according to necessity, the Bergers des Pyrenees seem to have forever inhabited their altitudinal native land. Their exact beginnings remain unknown.

ESSENTIALS OF THE BERGERS DES PYRENEES: A quick and agile herding dog with profuse coating that provides sufficient protection from the elements incurred during the performance of his bred-for task. The skull is strong but not very broad; muzzle tapers distinctly from eyes to nose; ears high set, cropped short and blunt; eyes dark, with intelligent and alert expression. Neck strong and of moderate length. Chest deep. Back straight and strong. Height: 15–22 inches (38–56 cm). Weight: 18–32 pounds (8–14.5 kg). The Pyrenean Shepherd can be found in a number of varieties, each differing slightly in coat length and color. The three most commonly seen types include the longhaired, which is shaggy and will cord if not attended to; the goathaired, which is medium in length and considered the typical breed coat, equipped with cuffs and breeches; and the Smooth-Muzzled variety, which has a medium shaggy coat, with minimal hair on the face and front legs.

Each variety can occur in fawn, brindle, black, gray, or blue, with white points; additionally, the Smooth-Muzzled variety can be harlequin.

Berghund
German for mountain dog or flock guardian.

Berner Laufhund
The scenthounds of Switzerland have served hunters for a millennia or more. Considering the nation's limited geography, it is amazing that the various types have not interbred to produce a Swiss scenthound amalgamation. Instead, the Swiss Hound Club and the notion of distinct types have fostered a number of individual breeds. The Fédération Cynologique Internationale recognizes nine breeds. The Berner Laufhund and the Berner Neiderlaufhund are two such Swiss

Berger des Pyrenees, longhaired, fawn. Photo by I. Français.

Berger des Pyrenees, Smooth-Muzzled, harlequin.

Berner
Neiderlaufhund,
tricolor.

scenthounds. These two breeds differ only in size; the Neiderlaufhund is the smaller.

Named for the Alps in which they are apt to hunt, the Berner breeds excel on roe deer, stag and a variety of other game. These dogs, as well as the other laufhunds, are believed to have descended from the ancient Celtic and Phoenician hounds and to have types determined by the Middle Ages.

ESSENTIALS OF THE BERNER LAUFHUND: The Berner Laufhund and the Berner Neiderlaufhund comprise the two types of Bernese Hounds; the latter is also called the Small Bernese Hound. Both breeds possess a soft undercoat covered by a dense, hard outer coat in black and white (with prescribed tan markings), often considered a tricolor. Ticking or roaning is minimal. The taller smaller stands 13–17 inches (33–43 cm) and weighs 30–40 pounds (13.5–18 kg). Both breeds possess elongated body trunks, a lean head and a strong muzzle. The Neider is more compact and short-legged compared to the well-boned yet lighter body of the Laufhund. The Neider

Berner
Laufhund, tricolor
with ticking.
Photographs by I.
Français.

stands from 18–23 inches (46–59 cm) and weighs 34–44 pounds (15.5–20 kg); the is the only Swiss hound that can be seen in a wire coat.

Berner Laufhund, tricolor. Photo by I. Français.

Berner Neiderlaufhund, wire, tricolor. Only extant scenthound of Switzerland that still occurs in the wire coat. Photo courtesy J. Sutter.

Berner Neiderlaufhund
See Berner Laufhund

Berner Sennenhund
See Bernese Mountain Dog

Bernese Hound
See Berner Laufhund

Bernese Scenthound
See Berner Laufhund

Bernese Mountain Dog

The native Swiss dog to gain the most world-wide popularity and recognition. He remains, however, undeservingly

Bernese Mountain Dogs, Swissy tricolor. Photo by I. Français.

sparse in number. An undoubtedly hardy dog of great strength and endurance, the Bernese can also be trained at a variety of canine tasks. So why the lack of popularity? One possibility is the breed's high metabolism, which necessitates a diet different than the typically high-protein one fed to most dogs. These dogs also require plentiful hours of exercise on a regular basis. However, the Berner

breed seems ideal for active owners who enjoy quality time with their dogs—especially those owners willing to take the time to train their dogs at a few household chores.

The Bernese Mountain Dog is also known as the Berner Sennenhund. He is, as are all other sennenhunden, the believed descendant of the ancient molossus dogs introduced to Switzerland by the Roman legions sometime during the first century before Christ. Crossbreeding with native or available working stock, working dogs were created to aid inhabitants with the daily chores of life. Bernese Mountain Dogs achieved great acclaim as sturdy and dependable cart pullers of enthusiastic and pleasing temperament. They are easily trained at a variety of tasks and make excellent companions and family dogs.

ESSENTIALS OF THE BERNESE MOUNTAIN DOG: Compact yet well proportioned. Well endowed with muscle and bone. Chest broad. Head is marked by strong jaw, dark, almond-shaped eyes, V-shaped drop ears and a definite stop. Coloring is pure Swiss: black with tan markings and white preferably on chest, feet and tail tip, and as blaze on forehead. The dense coat of medium length, slightly

Bernese Mountain Dog in the ring. Photo by Kernan, courtesy of Lilian Ostermiller.

wavy hair grows long on the carried-low tail. Height: 23–27.5 inches (59–70 cm). Weight: 87–90 pounds (40–44 kg).

Bertillon

A racing dog's record of identification. Age, breeding, owner, color, sex and all distinguishing marks such as scars, color of toenails, etc., are recorded on the bertillon card.

Best in Group

Award given to dog adjudged best of all Best of Breed winners in its group.

Best in Show

A dog-show award to the dog (or bitch) adjudged best of all breeds.

Best in Specialty Show

Award given to best dog in a specialty show.

Best of Breed

Award given to dog adjudged finest of any competing in its breed.

Best of Opposite Sex

Award given to dog or bitch selected after BOB as the finest of the opposite sex.

Best of Winners

The dog (or bitch) which is selected by the judge as the best of all entries in the regular official classes of a breed.

Bhotia

See Himalayan Sheepdog

B.I.S.

Best in Show.

B.I.S.S.

Best in Specialty Show.

Bi-lateral cryptorchid

See Cryptorchid

Bichon

A type of curly coated small water dog which developed on various islands. Some of the bichon types existing today are the Havanese from Cuba, Bolognese of Italy, Maltese of Malta, Coton de Tulear of Madagascar, and the Bichon Frise of France and Belgium.

Bichon a Poil Frise

See Bichon Frise

Bichon Bolognese

See Bolognese

Bichon Frise

Centuries ago, the Bichon Frise was popular in France and Spain. More than any other breed, perhaps, the Bichon has been depicted in the portraits of the royal families of both countries. The island of Tenerife, one of the Canary Islands off the coast of Spain, produced the Bichon Tenerife or the Bichon Frise, as he is known today. Bichon types developed on different islands in the Mediterranean

and are miniaturized water retriever types. It is believed that the same stock that produced the Portuguese Water Dog and the Barbet also spurred the various bichon types. The bichon of Malta (the Maltese, today) is assuredly a close relative of the Bichon Frise. Whether the bichons were in Tenerife, Malta, Havana, or Bologna (etc.), these dogs were curly coated and principally white.

An alternative position maintains that Phoenician sailors first brought the Bichon to Tenerife, and from this island the breed made its way to the Continent. In either event, the Bichon waned slightly for some time until it was "rediscovered" by Italian sailors in the 1300s. By the 1500s, these dogs were enjoying the royal patronage of the court by such nobles as Francis I and Henry III. In Spain, the Bichon was favored by the Infantas and Goya, and other painters of the Spanish school found the handsome Bichon bois-

Bichon dogs, curly and white, photographed by R. Pearcy.

terously fitting to preserve on canvas.

At a certain point in the Bichon Frise's history, around the nineteenth century, royal families grew tired of their curly tykes and turned to other dogs. The Bichon took to the streets and became associated with the commonfolk, who rather willingly adopted him and his well-meaning demeanor. For a time the breed

Bichon Frise. Photo by I. Français.

was employed as an entertainer, accompanying circus acts and jigging to the organ grinder's grunts and arpeggios. Post-World War I brought a much needed revival that reinstated the breed to its former noble status.

The breed's name was derived by the president of the 1934 International Canine Federation, Madame Nizet de Leemans. Its proper plural is Bichons Frises. Because of the post-WWI combined efforts of the Toy Club of France and the Friends of the Belgian Breeds, the Brichon Frise was acknowledged as a French-Belgian breed by the International Canine Federation (F.C.I.).

Etoile de Steren Vor, owned by newly American Mr. and Mrs. Francois Picault, whelped the first-born American Bichons. Seventeen years later, in 1973, the breed received full recognition status by the American Kennel Club. In Great Britain where a silky coat is desirable, the Bichon is grouped among the Toys; in the U.S. where a coarser but curly coat is required, the breed is classed in Non-Sporting. The Bichon is forever the happy little dog, with a lively, carefree approach to life. His bouncy stride and pleasant voice contribute to his irresistible appeal.

ESSENTIALS OF THE BICHON FRISE: The Bichon is a well-balanced dog of smart appearance. The coat is naturally white and curling loosely. Head must be in balance with the body; skull slightly rounded, not coarse. The ears hang close to the head and are well feathered. The neck is well arched and rather long. Shoulders oblique; legs straight, perpendicular; pasterns short and straight. Thighs broad and well rounded; stifles well bent. Tail is normally docked. The coat is fine with corkscrew curls. A coarse not silky coat in the U.S. is desirable, while in Great Britain, a silky coat is required. Not flat or corded. The undercoat is soft and dense. Height: 9–12 inches (23–31 cm). Some kennel clubs allow cream or apricot markings on the white coat for dogs younger than 19 months of age. Dark pigment is preferred under the white coats of adults, and black, blue, or beige markings are often found on the skin.

Bichon Havanais
  See Havanese

Bichon Maltiase
  See Maltese

Bichon Tenerife
  See Bichon Frise

Bicolor

Two-colored. In hounds, white and a second color. In other breeds, it can mean black and tan (i.e., the Manchester Terrier) or black and sable (i.e., the German Shepherd Dog) or any other two colors in a given canine.

Big n' Blue

See American Blue Gascon Hound

Bile

A secretion of the liver which aids in digestion. *See* Digestive system

Billet

The droppings of a fox.

Billy

The Billy is the beautifully conceived nineteenth-century creation of M.G. Hublot du Rivault and named after the city in Poitou. Rivault combined three now extinct French hunters: the Céris, Montaimboeuf, and Larrye. Respectively, these pack-hounds contributed small size and orange spots, fortitude and speed, and a superlative nose. M.G. Hublot du Rivault's described recipe brought forth the Billy. At one time, the Billy was believed to be a more ancient strain derived from hounds from Louis XII of Southern Hound and St. Hubert Hound forebears. The three-dog recipe, however, is the more reliable theory. The Billy is a pack hunter, like his forebears, and is superior on deer.

ESSENTIALS OF THE BILLY: This elegant, handsome Frenchman is distinguished by his lemon/orange spotted white sports jacket; the coat is short and smooth. His expression denotes intelligence and alacrity. Height: 23–26 inches (58–66 cm). Weight: 55–66 pounds (25–30 kg). The Billy has a lean head and slightly curled flat ears. A light, well-placed trumpet quality marks his vocal timbre, which is capable of great variation in volume and intensity.

Biopsy

Any of several procedures by which a tumor is determined cancerous and/or by which the specific type of cancer is determined. The veterinarian or veterinary surgeon will remove all or part of a growth that is suspected of being cancerous and send it to a specialist laboratory that will perform the biopsy. Results can usually be expected in less than a week. All removed growths should be subjected to a biopsy.

Bird dog field trials

See Field trials

Bird dogs

The breeds of hunting dog that are considered bird dogs essentially comprise the entire family of pointers, setters, spaniels, and water dogs. The group overlaps the gundog group with the exception of a couple of breeds such as the Weimaraner that work for tracking large game. Spain commonly takes claim for the progenitors of today's bird dogs.

Billy, white with lemon. Photo by I. Français.

Bird-work

The act of a gundog finding and handling game birds.

Birdy

When a bird dog works his ground closely, carefully, and intensely, he is called "birdy."

Birth

The act by which the puppy enters into the world in a living state. *See* Breeding

Birth defects

Cleft palates, hare lips, and other disorders ranging from the easily treated to the quickly fatal are called birth defects when found in newborn pups. They can be the result of hereditary conditions, dietary deficiencies, or contact with dangerous substances (such as DDT), or can be the product of any number of other equations—though the three stated are the most common.

Bitch. Rough Chow Chow bitch spending quality time with puppy.

Bisben

The mastifflike Bisben of the Himalayas is a sheepdog with outstanding hunting abilities. Generally resembling a European shepherd dog, the Bisben has a long, thick coat and a long thick tail. Not as large as a mastiff, these dogs possess ferocity and resilience; their physical similarities to the Turkish shepherd dogs and character suggest bloodlines similar to the ancient flock guards of Anatolia.

Biscuit

A heavily shaded cream or off-white color, e.g., Samoyed, Pekingese.

Biscuits

Essentially treats, biscuits come in a wide variety of sizes, shapes and flavors. They are typically of little nutritional value but are greatly enjoyed by most dogs; they often lack the hardness and abrasive power to effectively serve as a dental device.

Bitch

The female of the canine species. The female differs from the male in her possession of female sex and reproductive organs and her level of female hormones. Bitches of a breed in general tend to be smaller than males of the same breed but should closely resemble the male in all other physical characteristics. Bitches are said to be of different temperament than males, though there are numerous exceptions to this rule. Certainly the bitch has motherly instincts that no male could equal, but in general males and females are similarly suited for the various tasks that we demand of dogs.

The brood bitch is a female who is used for breeding purposes. Like the stud dog, she should be of as great a quality as possible; she should possess no notable faults, be of desirable temperament, and come from a line of quality dogs. Regardless of the good quality of the stud, the bitch's faults and weaknesses can appear in subsequent litters. An outstanding bitch from a mediocre line is a chance breeder at best, for she may carry many undesirable qualities in a recessive state that can appear in subsequent breedings. It has been stated and is generally held as true that the brood bitch is the true foundation of any breeding program. If your desire is to start a kennel or breed dogs for any reason, choose the finest bitch that you can acquire, for there is no supplementing for a poor brood bitch in any sound breeding program. For a discussion of the brood bitch during her pregnancy, *see* Pregnancy.

Bite

Relative position of the upper and lower teeth when the mouth is closed.

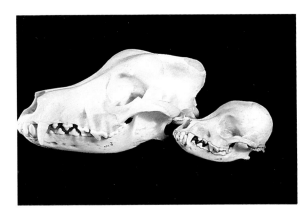

Bite types

Breed standards describe variously the desired and undesired types of canine bites.

Irregular. Condition in which one or more incisors have erupted abnormally. Irregular bites of lesser degrees are sometimes pardoned in the show ring, but severe irregularities cannot be tolerated. Often incisor alignment is deemed of secondary importance to the strength and development of the jaw.

Level. The equal length of the upper and lower jaws. Not to be confused with pincer bite.

Overshot. A receding, inferiorly constructed lower jaw in which the lower incisors make no actual contact with the upper jaw mates due to the distance. Pig-jawed, swine mouth, shark mouth and parrot-jawed are other nomenclatures identifying this condition.

Pincer. A bite in which the upper and lower incisors meet directly together when the mouth is closed. Viselike bite, another name for this bite, well describes this bite which is desirable in the Airedale Terrier and other breeds as well.

Scissors. Upper teeth closely overlapping the lower teeth and set squarely to the jaws. The perfect scissors bite should erupt at about 90° and is therefore level with the jaws. Teeth desirably are uncrowded and evenly situated, with their cutting edges in horizontal alignment.

Scissors reverse. Lower teeth slightly overlapping the upper teeth. This means that the lower incisors contact directly the outer surfaces of the upper incisors. The Mastiff is an example of such a breed; this slight unevenness, however, is not detectable when the mouth is closed.

Undershot. The lower jaw is noticeably longer than the upper, causing the lower

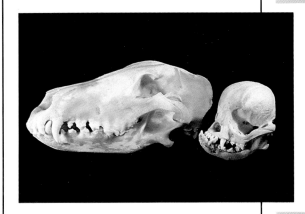

to protrude and often turn up. No physical contact between the two jaws occurs with this type bite. The British Bulldog is the example most frequently cited. In the Bulldog's case, this bite was deemed desirable for its intended holding function.

Bites, animal

If an animal, especially a wild animal, bites your dog, that animal should be caught and quarantined, to protect the dog in case it

Bite types. Overshot bites on different skull types.

Bite types. Scissors bite (*left*) and undershot bite (*right*).

Bite types. Undershot bite on brachycephalic skull.

should contract rabies or another dangerous disease. All bites, regardless of how small, need tending. While a trip to the veterinarian is recommended, the least measure must be watching the dog closely for any signs of complication or disease contraction. Professional testing will be required for an accurate diagnosis. Bites from large animals, including large dogs, may result in broken bones and internal bleeding. Such bites require special attention. Bites from cats have a history of causing complications in dogs.

Snake bites are likely in locations with snake populations, as many dogs have no inherent fear of these cold bloods. Dogs may taunt or attempt to kill a snake which they come across. If snakes inhabit your locale, read up on the species, their population and their bite marks. Venomous snakes have a typical bite pattern. A bite from such a snake will require special attention and immediate veterinary care. Snake-bite kits should be included in your canine first-aid kit.

original strains. Simon Kenton and the Poe brothers, Simion Shirk, Holmes Lingo, and Don Stringer are among the usual litany of strain founders. Of course, the most famous of strains is the Old Glory line which lasted for over 130 years. The roster of the Black and Tan's forebears is surely impressive: the eleventh-century Talbot Hound, the Kerry Beagle of Ireland, the English Foxhound, the Bloodhound, and the American Virginia Foxhound. Breeders were selective in attaining the desired coat color. While not the fastest hound on the trail, the Black and Tan is an effective hunter. Much like the Bloodhound in his tracking method, the Black and Tan is cold-nosed and methodical in the hunt. Americans crafted the breed for the task of treeing coon and opossum. The Black and Tan's stamina and strength have also beckoned his use on big cat and wild boar.

The American Kennel Club recognized the breed in 1945; this acceptance marked the first of the American coon-

Black and Tan Coonhound. Photo by Petrulis.

Black and Tan Coonhound

The American Black and Tan Coonhound is the product of selective breeding which employed a number of famous hounds to be recognized. Others may follow, but most hunters aren't particularly concerned with "official" recognition for their dogs. For fanciers who desire to show their dogs, recognition is vital; for hunters, recognition may not rival hog's spit. The United Kennel Club, however, does register various coonhound breeds and also sponsors hunting and competition events (including the favorite night hunts). In the show ring, however, Black and Tans have made good progress. Breeders are encouraged to promote the dog's working abilities. The A.K.C. standard opens with "The Black and Tan Coonhound is first and fundamentally a working dog, capable of withstanding the rigors of winter, the heat of summer, and the difficult terrain over which he is called to work." Logically, a racy, thin or inadequately muscled dog cannot meet the working dog requirements and such traits should be frowned upon in any circle.

ESSENTIALS OF THE BLACK AND TAN COONHOUND: Solid carriage: a muscular and well-proportioned body structure. The graceful droop of loosely fitting skin and extensive ear leather gives the Black and Tan a distinctive quality. Head is cleanly chiseled with medium stop. Skull should tend toward oval outline. Ears low set and well back. The neck is muscular, sloping, of medium length, extending into powerfully constructed shoulders and deep chest. Ribs, round, well sprung. Back, level and strong, with slope from withers to tail. Forelegs, strong; hindlegs, muscular and well boned. Height: 23–27 inches (58–69 cm). Weight: 55–75 pounds (25–34 kg). Desired color: coal black with rich tan markings. The coat is dense and short.

Black and Tan Terrier
    See Manchester Terrier

Black-backed jackal
    Canis mesomelas. See Jackals

Black Fell Terrier
    See Patterdale Terrier

Black Forest Hound

The oldest and only indigenous scenthound of Czechoslovakia, the Black Forest Hound is still used today on wild

boar. He is a tracker par excellence. His similarities to the Polish Hound and the closeness of geography make his relationship with that breed seem probable. Other sources speculate that the Balkan Hound and the Transylvanian Hound crossed with the Czesky Fousek or similar gundogs yielded this hound. Outside Czechoslovakia, the Black Forest Hound, known as the Slovensky Kopov, is little known. In the show ring, the breed has made notable progress, but today its primary function is hunting boar and other large game in the mountainous regions of its homeland. As a guard dog and police assistant, the Black Forest has also done remarkably well.

ESSENTIALS OF THE BLACK FOREST HOUND: A sleek-looking though wirehaired hound in a black/tan coat pattern. The coat of the Black Forest Hound can be 2 inches (5 cm) in length but remains close to the body. Structurally the body is somewhat elongated and lightly boned but sufficiently strong. Height: 18–20 inches (46–51 cm). Weight: 44–49 pounds (20–22 kg).

Black Forest Hound. Photo by I. Français.

Black Mouth Cur

A sturdy and relentless hunter, the Black Mouth Cur represents one popular type of working cur used in the southern United States. Also known as the Southern or Yellow Black Mouth Cur, this cur is formidable on bear and boar. Of course, like many of the curs and coon dogs of the American South, the Black Mouth is prime on raccoon and squirrel. Today, as has been the case for many generations, the southern states are well populated with cur-type dogs that are used by local hunters and sportsmen. With medium-sized game, the Black Mouth catches and kills it. This dog, once on the trail, does not give up. It is also proficient at treeing and baying.

lengthy. This dog's chest is deep and very solid.

Black Norwegian Elkhound

See Norwegian Elkhound

Black Russian Terrier

The Black Russian Terrier, called Chornyi in the Soviet Union, is a large terrier breed that appears a great deal like an uncropped Giant Schnauzer. The Giant Schnauzer, known by the Soviets as the Russian Bear Schnauzer, is a popular breed in Russia, prized for his guard-dog abilities. The German giant ratter, however, was more Western than the Soviets might have liked, and they therefore set out to produce a Russian version

Black Mouth Curs are used by sportsmen on big game like wild boar.

As unrelenting and overpowering as this cur appears at work, he is kind and protective with his family, preferring the ladies for company and being especially protective of children. Loyalty and fearlessness are the norm.

ESSENTIALS OF THE BLACK MOUTH CUR: Sturdy, muscular, and well structured. Height: 16–25 inches (40–64 cm). Weight: 45–95 pounds (20–43 kg). The short coat comes in a variety of shades of yellow and fawn. The irrefutably powerful muzzle is black, giving this cur his name. The tail is left natural and can be quite

of the German dog they liked so much. Crosses of the Giant Schnauzer with the Rottweiler and the Airedale Terrier produced the Chornyi. This rugged, aggressive man-stopper is used primarily as guard and protector. The breed's thick coat is ample protection from the severity of Soviet winters. While popular in the Soviet Union, very few dogs have been exported; some dogs, however, appear in European exhibition.

ESSENTIALS OF THE BLACK RUSSIAN TERRIER: Strong and robust. The body is square and powerful. The coat is coarse and thick and measures as long as four inches (10 cm). As the name indicates the most common color, the breed also occurs in salt and pepper. Height: 25–28 inches (63.5–71 cm). The head is accentuated by heavy facial furnishings and flop V-shaped ears. Structurally, he is heavy boned and thick overall.

Black/silver

A true black and silver has the solid black body with grayish silver markings above the eyes, on the cheeks, under the ears, on the forechest, on the feet and inside of the legs, and under the tail (e.g., Miniature Schnauzer).

Black Spaniel

A former gundog type known in Britain, the Black Spaniel is the likely ancestor of many Continental spaniels, frequently referred to in various breed texts.

Black/tan

Just like the black/silver except the grayish silver points are tan in color (e.g., Rottweiler or Doberman).

Black/tan saddled

The tan marks, as in the black/tan, are much larger, including the back of the head, upper legs, neck, and belly, and leaving the black only as a "saddle" on the back, as well as on the top of the neck and tail (e.g., German Shepherd Dog).

Black tongue

1) The desired bluish tongue on the Shar-Pei and Chow Chow.

2) A condition named for the discoloration of the victim's tongue soon after death—a deep purple, suggestive of black. The condition is believed to be related to an acute B-vitamin (niacin) deficiency and is very rare in dogs today. It is most often treatable with large doses of the vitamin.

Blaireau

See Badger

Blank

A foxhunting term used to refer to a cover or section of the country in which no fox is found.

Blanket

1) A large colored area covering the back and sides (or even the neck). The Beagle, Gascon Saintongeois and the

Levesque are fine examples of hounds that exhibit blanket coloration.

2) The light satin blanket that is worn by a racing dog; it is colored and numbered to correspond to post position in a race.

Blanket finish

A dog-racing term that refers to a loosely bunched field at finish which,

Black Russian Terrier, black. Photo by I. Français.

Black/tan coloration exhibited by the Rottweiler.

supposedly, can be covered by a normal-sized blanket.

Blastomycosis

A rare infectious disease involving the kidneys and liver. The animal loses its appetite and vomits frequently. Laboratory examination is necessary to determine presence.

Blaze

A white streak marking the front of the skull, or a white broad area bedecking the chest, found in many breeds. Smaller or narrower types are known as "stars" and "stripes." The Papillon exhibits a blaze on its head, while the Airedale Terrier exhibits one on its chest.

Bleeding

Bleeding is best stopped in small wounds by applying pressure to the wound. It is preferred that the wound first be covered with a sterile, non-stick material, so that the wound is not reopened when the material is removed. For deep wounds, pressure should be applied to the wound and medical assistance should be attained as soon as possible. Transport should be by stretcher. If the dog is in danger of death from bleeding, a tourniquet can be applied. A simple tourniquet can be made of any cloth torn to strips, wrapped around the limb above the wound, and tightened with the twisting of a stick or other rod that can be inserted between the strips of cloth. When properly applied, a tourniquet will reduce the flow of blood to the limb, possibly causing cell necrosis. It should therefore be only applied in an emergency. *See also* Blood clots

Blenheim

The red/white color pattern of English toy spaniels.

Bleu d'Auvergne

See Braque d'Auvergne

Bleu de Gascogne

The province of Gascony, in southwestern France, boasts a number of purebred scenthounds. These dogs are more pure than most of the world's hounds in that they are believed to be the direct descendants of Gallic scenting dogs and the hounds traded by the Phoenicians. Presently four breeds include the phrase Bleu de Gascogne in their names. The Grand Bleu de Gascogne, the largest of these hounds, is descended directly from the extinct Grand Chien Courant, and is one of the few existing breeds able to make that claim to fame. The Grand is used on deer and boar primarily. Centuries ago, this tremendously tall scenthound was used on wolf. Today only the Grande Bleu de Gascogne has achieved recognition outside of France; the Kennel Club of Great Britain has granted championship status to this breed.

The Petit Bleu de Gascogne, slightly smaller than the Grand, was bred down directly from the Grand for use on smaller game. The only wirehair of the Gascogne breeds, the Petit Griffon Bleu de Gascogne, is the rarest of the four. Many of today's smoothhaired hounds were once popular in a wire coat, but as this went out of vogue, fanciers abandoned the variety. The fourth breed is the basset (or short-legged) version of the Grand. It is known as the Basset Bleu de Gascogne. When the hounds were needed to hunt smaller quarry in higher altitudes or thickly briared terrain, a basset version became necessary. Hence, this Basset derived. Both the Petit and the Basset are expert on rabbit and other small quarry. All of the Gascognes are cold-nosed in hunting style.

ESSENTIALS OF THE BLEU DE GASCOGNE: There are four breeds which are classified as Bleus de Gascogne. The largest of the four, the Grand Bleu de Gascogne, reaches 28 inches (71 cm) in height; he is one of the world's tallest scenthounds. Efficiently built (on the leggy side) he has a strong, large head. Weight: 71–78 pounds (32–35 kg). The Petit Bleu de Gascogne stands from 19.5 to 23.5 inches (49.5–60 cm) high and

weighs 44 pounds (20 kg). The Basset Bleu de Gascogne stands 12–14 inches (30–36 cm) and weighs 35–40 pounds (16–18 kg). These first three hounds share the same short coat: thick but not too fine. The fourth Bleu is the Petit Griffon Bleu de Gascogne; this melodiously voiced basset boasts a unique coat: rough and wiry. All four Bleus are considered tricolors—mostly white, with tan on parts of head and black spots on head and body. This coat is heavily roaned, creating a blue effect.

Bleus de Gascogne, Petit and Grande.

Bleu de Gascogne, Basset. Photographs by I. Français.

Bleu de Gascogne, Petit Griffon.

Blonde. A bombshell of an Afghan Hound. Photographs by I. Français.

Blind

A device in or behind which a hunter and his dog conceal themselves from the possible flight of birds in the hope that the game will come within gun shot. *See also* Blind retrieve, Blindness

Blind retrieve

A retrieve performed without the dog's seeing the fall. In order to complete such a retrieve, a dog must be "given a line" by the handler or handled to the fall, or come upon the fall or the scent of it by chance. A blind retrieve is often referred to without the accompanying word "retrieve," as in "two marked falls and a blind," and in this sense must not be confused with a blind used for concealment, which *see*.

Blindness

Cataracts are the most common cause of blindness in dogs. Surgery may postpone the loss of sight but usually cannot prevent it. As the dog loses his vision, his other senses will intensify to compensate as best they can. The dog will rely even more heavily on his nose and ears to take him through his regular routine. It is not advisable to change residences if you have a blind dog, since he will feel more lost than ever. Progressive Retinal Atrophy (which *see*), a hereditary eye disorder, can also lead to blindness. Any of a number of irritations or seemingly innocent swellings of the eyes may cause blindness or partially impaired vision if unattended. *See also* Eyes, problems of

Blinking

A backing from, circumventing, or otherwise leaving game after becoming aware of it. Blinking is a serious fault, usually resulting from a dog's fear of punishment should the bird be flushed. A very sensitive dog may even be afraid of the explosive flush of a bird or shy from the gunshot that usually follows a flush.

Bloat

Gastric dilation-volvulus or gastric torsion, bloat is more likely to affect the larger breeds, this condition's fatal culmination is a distended stomach full of bacterial toxin pressing against vital organs. The signs are an expanded abdominal region, resounding hollowly when tapped. Immediate veterinary care is imperative. Death may occur. If the dog survives, the stomach may not return to its normal size.

Blocky

Squarish, actually wider than tall, i.e., the blocky head of the Boston Terrier. Otherwise blocky indicates that the head is coarser and broader than desirable.

Blonde

An intense, clear yellow coloration, e.g., Afghan Hound.

Blood clots

Blood clots are both necessary and dangerous. When a blood vessel is broken, either by puncture, laceration, or other injury or procedure, a clot must form to stay the loss of blood. If no clot forms, as is the case in some hemophiliacs, death may result from even the smallest of vessel openings. Blood clots are dangerous when they become too large, blocking the passage of blood in a given vein. It sometimes happens, especially after surgery, that a blood clot will dislodge, travel through the blood stream, and clog another vessel; with no blood supply, cell necrosis in the given body area will result. Where the clot dislodged, there may be hemorrhaging. Dangerous blood clots evidence such signs as swelling, degeneration and gangrene, soreness, and discoloration. After injury or surgery, it is especially important to watch for dangerous blood clotting. *See also* Blood vessels, Hemorrhage, Circulatory system

Blood vessels

Dogs, like humans, have both veins and arteries, major vessels and small capillaries. As part of the circulatory system, veins carry freshly oxygenated blood from the heart to the organs and muscles of the body, while arteries bring the oxygen-depleted blood back to the heart to be replenished. Capillaries are tiny blood vessels found in all body parts; it is through the capillaries that blood is received by the body and in turn received by the arteries. Blood vessels are composed of an elastic material, propelling the blood through contractions and dilations coupled with the pressure created by the pumping heart. *See also* Arteriosclerosis, Bleeding, Blood clots, Circulatory system, Heart, Hemophilia, Hemorrhage, Stroke

Blooded

When hounds kill their quarry, the quarry is said to have been blooded. The young or inexperienced hunter is "blooded" by anointing him with fox blood at his first kill.

Bloodhound

The Bloodhound represents Man's quest for perfection and Nature's gracious acquiescence. It is not too clear, however, that the Catholic Church unprotestingly sanctified the Bloodhound's

Bloodhound, black/tan. Photo by C. Meade.

unblemished quintessence, or so one legend says. Saint Hubert, a prince of the faith, is the acknowledged "father" of the Bloodhound breed. Hubert thought it not unbecoming to his sacred oaths and office to indulge in the blood-chilling pleasures of the blood-sniffing chase. According to a particular legend, the unprostrating St. Hubert, one Good Friday (shortly after 3 p.m.) encountered a stag in the woods bearing a crucifix between its antlers. (This stag's head-held crucifix was not red and blue and, therefore, shouldn't be confused with that more colorful stag of St. John de Martha and Trinitarian fame.) St. Hubert interpreted the stag's message and knew that unless he mended his woodsman ways, he would suffer eternal perdition (or at least a millennia in Purgatory—the stag wasn't clear on this most important detail).

The glorious hounds of our patron saint of hunting were not solely black and tan (or red) but rather solids in black and white, plus black and tans. The fame of St. Hubert's hounds, later known as Black and Tan St. Huberts, spread to the Ardennes district where they were used for hunting purposes. After Hubert's death, abbots preserved the strain with zeal and exactness, following the founder's flawless example. The King of France, for many years after Hubert's death, received three couples of Black and Tan St. Huberts annually.

Although some purport that Bloodhounds were in England prior to the Norman Conquest, it is commonly believed that descendants of St. Hubert's hounds at the time of the Norman Conquest became known as Bloodhounds. To be more precise, the blacks and black and tans took on the name Bloodhound, while the whites were called Talbot Hounds. While the Talbot is extinct today, some believe that its blood, if diluted, was contributed to the Staghounds of western England.

The writings of Gratius, feather and inking before the Christian era, tell of Sleuth-hounds entering Britain from Gaul. These hounds of Gaul are believed to be the same stock from which Hubert chose his miracle sniffers.

Bloodhound, renowned tracker and sniffer.

their deer-tracking expeditions. Later, when a swifter hound became desirable, the Bloodhounds (or Talbots) were crossed to Greyhounds (or a like, leggy running hound) to produce the Foxhound. Just as in the study of history, cynology experiences the continuous repetition of events. Americans, in the twentieth century, sought a swifter hound than the slow but deliberate Majestic Tree Hound, and the coonhound breeds rose to the need.

Individual fanciers and families have always conducted private breeding operations and progenerated a particular type or "breed." Since canines are the most diversified of all mammals on earth, it is not possible for men to think that we can categorize all "purebred" dogs in the world. Today it is believed that over 800 pure breeds of dog may exist. The F.C.I., incidentally, recognizes but half of that number. The Bloodhound or St. Hubert Hound was bred in many families in England and France without interference of other blood. Some of these strains persisted for over 300 years. William Rufus, Thomas Nevill, and Edwin Brough are historical examples of breeders of separate St. Hubert strains in the early nineteenth century. Likely all of these "purebreds," similar though different, contributed to the make-up of today's Bloodhound.

Through the centuries, the Bloodhound has thrived as a hunter of unquestionable acumen. In the nineteenth century, this slow and deliberate huntsman was used on deer in addition to its usual game of wolf and big cats. In America, blessed (at one time) with vast open wilderness, the Bloodhound's exquisite nose could be used to its full glory. Scenting is the Bloodhound's forte—tracking for the sake of tracking, in the Bloodhound's mind, is worthwhile. Unlike the coonhounds and other trailing scenthounds, the Bloodhound doesn't revel in the find but rather in the tracking. No ill-meaning bone in this dog's body well explains the breed's tendency to greet a tracked criminal with a muddy paw and a slobbery kiss.

More than any other breed of dog, the Bloodhound has been commissioned to track the undesirable—from sheep steal-

In early days, the slow-moving, extraordinarily nosed Bloodhounds well accommodated the sport-loving Plantagenets and other Normans and suited

ers to crack venders and every fetid felon in between. Many a Bloodhound's nose has convinced the Bench of a criminal's guilt. Additionally, like the Fila Brasileiro in Brazil, the Bloodhound has been employed to track down runaway slaves through swamps and similarly unruly terrain. Sometimes, too, the Bloodhound is given a break from the pursuit of uncouths and offenders, and is used to track lost children (or adults). In the seventeenth century, dogs used for these tracking purposes were referred to as Sleuth or Slough Hound, and were given preference and special exemptions (perhaps comparable to the types of privileges rightly given to Guide Dogs and other service dogs today).

The Bloodhound's appearance is as unique and outstanding as the abilities described. Exaggerated earage and flews aptly drape this miraculous, excessive dog. Its voice is often compared to the pedal notes of the king of instruments: "Full, sonorous, and musical, it is not extravagant to compare these deep-mouthed notes with the peal of an organ in a cathedral," as the late Major Whyte Melville poetically put.

The first Bloodhound to grace a British show ring appeared in 1871. The breed has proven in the United Kingdom, America, and many other nations to be a captivating show dog and a delightful companion. In temperament, the Bloodhound is amiable. In intelligence, this dog is wise and knowing. When a Bloodhound responds to a command in a leisurely, deliberate way, it is not that he doesn't comprehend but rather that he is likely re-evaluating the virtue of your request. The breed's size somewhat limits its popularity. These dogs need room to exercise and are most content when

patrolling the estate grounds of a large home. A strong and highly capable dog, the Bloodhound assumes the role of watchdog with ease, and its warning bark is anything but subtle.

Bloodhound, sentinel and companion. Photo by C. Meade.

ESSENTIALS OF THE BLOODHOUND: The largest and most powerful of the hounds, the Bloodhound can weigh up to 110 pounds (50 kg) and stand as high as 27 inches (69 cm). The head is among the breed's most impressive features, perhaps the most beautiful in all dogdom. Wrinkles, dewlap and excessive skin adorn a noble head that epitomizes character, indelibly. The ears are thin and soft to the touch, extremely long, set very low, falling in graceful folds with an inward

Bloodhound, black/tan champion. Photo by Graham.

Blue Lacy, blue (gunmetal gray).

curl. The skull is long and narrow, occipital peak very pronounced. The neck is long, the shoulders muscular and well sloped backwards; the ribs are well sprung; and the chest well let down from between the forelegs, forming a deep keel. Forelegs, straight, large in bone. Hind, muscular. Back and loins strong. The coat, thick, hard and short, can be black/tan, tawny, or red/tan. The Bloodhound's eyes are neither sunken nor prominent.

Bloom

The sheen of a coat in fine condition. A show dog's coat, lustrous and full, like a perfect flower, is in bloom.

Blue

There are four distinct colors that are called "blue"; all are inherited differently: 1)*Blue (dilute)*: Dogs born solid steel or gunmetal gray, *always* with a gray nose and paw pads (e.g., blue Great Dane or Chow). 2)*Blue (silvering, graying)*: There is another "blue" that starts black and fades to a blue-gray in adulthood, *always* with a black nose (e.g., Kerry Blue Terrier). 3)*Blue (ticking)*: Another "blue" is created by black roaning on white, *always* with a black nose (e.g., Grand Bleu de Gascogne). 4)*Blue merle*: This is a marbled gray on black, *always* with a black nose, sometimes with blue eyes. Can also be called harlequin or mottled (e.g., merle Collie).

Blue, in terms of eye color, is usually connected with eye pigmentation dilution. It is acceptable (even desirable) in some breeds, such as the Dalmatian.

Blue and Tan Manchester Terrier

Once known in England, an extinct variety of the Manchester Terrier. The breed figures in the ancestry of many European terriers.

Blue belton
See Belton

Blue eye
Refers to the bluish cast to the eyes of some dogs, usually young ones, when affected by parvoviral gastroenteritis and canine hepatitis, which *see*.

Blue Gascony Basset
Basset Bleu de Gascogne. *See* Bleu de Gascogne

Blue Heeler
See Australian Cattle Dog

Blue Lacy
A quintessential herder of the American West. Entering the state of Kentucky in 1858, the Blue Lacy is named for both his inherited blue-color gene and his founding fathers, the Lacy brothers. The Blue Lacy, bred consistently through the years for herding and droving ability, reportedly stems from Greyhound/scenthound/coyote crosses, though others believe that he is likely a blend of hard-bitten feral dogs which frequented the southeastern U.S. In either case, authorities think it likely that droving dogs also added blood to the breed stock. The Blue Lacy is related to the Catahoula dogs of the American South, and both are fearless and effective herd-working dogs of great strength.
A common sight for decades on southwestern American ranches, the Lacy faced grave challenge with the coming of motorized herding. Though they have survived, they have yet to regain their numbers or popularity. Owing to their undaunted ability and untiring desire to work, they remain, conquering all the requisite tasks, even the most demanding rancher admits. They possess gentle sureness and an earnest willingness to obey. Easy to train and easy to handle, Lacys are spectacular workmen.
ESSENTIALS OF THE BLUE LACY: This ranch dog should be sturdy and lean and, above all, effective at its trade. Of common and typically cur appearance, he is the ranch dog of the American South. Weight: 40–50 pounds (18–23 kg). Though called the Blue Lacy, colors include: tan, black/tan, yellow, cream, and the fundamental gunmetal gray. Although the breed is known for its solid-colored coat, bicolors and tricolors occur; regardless, the coat is tight, sleek, and exceptionally clean in appearance. *See also* Catahoula Leopard Dog

Blue merle
See Merle, Blue

Blue Paul
These solid blue or solid red Scottish gladiators resembled the fighting Staffordshires of England in body type but could weigh twice as much. The blue

Blue merle: the Collie.

Blue (silvering, graying): the Kerry Blue Terrier. Photo by I. Français.

dogs were known in Scotland as Blue Pauls, and the reds as Red Smuts. The name Blue Paul derives from a Scottish yarn about the pirate Paul Jones who reportedly brought the dogs from abroad to the district of Kirkintilloch.

The dogs were popular with the gypsies of that district who maintained that the dogs originally came from the Galloway coast, lending more color than blue to the Paul Jones tale. Like the bull-and-terrier breeds from which they derived, the Blue Pauls were game to the death in the ring. These dogs remained mute even in the height of battle, very much like the Tosa of Japan.

In appearance, the Blue Paul was similar to the Bullmastiff of the late 1800s. The dog was a smooth coated, cobby dog weighing about 45 pounds (20.5 kg), standing 20 inches (51 cm) at the shoulder. The head was large, the muzzle short and square. The jaws and lips were even, without overhanging flews. The stop was slight; eyes, dark hazel. The ears, set on high, were invariably cropped. The face was wrinkleless but the eyebrows were contracted or knit. Mr. James B. Morrison of Greenock, England, reports that the last Blue Paul exhibited was shown in the late 1880s.

Blue Picardy Spaniel
See Épagneul Bleu de Picardie

Blue tick
A white hound with small splashes of black mixed with the white giving the coat the effect of blue.

Bluetick Coonhound
The Bluetick Coonhound is one of the American coonhounds recognized by the United Kennel Club. Capital scenthounds from the famed cities of France were continually imported into America. These Gascony-type hounds were crossed with working dogs in the Louisiana area (foxhounds and curs alike) and afforded us the Bluetick Coonhound. The original French imports were then labelled French Staghounds or Blue Gascons. The Bluetick is a versatile hunter who can be used to tree raccoon or track fox or even cougar. Now hailed as a native American, the Bluetick Coonhound displays what appears to be a streak of Indian war paint between his eyes, a sure indicator of this dog's fearless and warriorlike approach to the hunt. The Bluetick is "a free tonguer on the trail, with a medium bawl or bugle voice when striking or trailing; many change to a steady chop when running, with a steady, coarse chop at the tree."

The coonhound breeds of America are hunters through and through and functional abilities are always considered first. Appearance, if considered, is secon-

Bluetick Coonhound, tricolor. Photo by I. Français.

dary. If a dog is able to fulfill its given task, its conformation is thereby fitting. Originally, the Blueticks were registered by the U.K.C. as English Coonhounds. Today the English Coonhound is red-ticked. Like the Black and Tan (and countless dogs of all types), today's Bluetick is the result of dedicated, consistent breeders' developing long-standing strains. The most notable of Bluetick strains are the Ozark Mountain and Sugar Creek lines.

A competitive and arduous sportsman, the Bluetick is the choice of many American hunters. It does remarkably well indoors and promises to be a fine companion and guardian to the family it loves. The breed's devotion to its family is only rivaled by its fervor on the field.

ESSENTIALS OF THE BLUETICK COONHOUND: Speckled in blue, this tricolor coonhound boasts a wonderfully unique, shiny, medium-length coat. Its heavy ticking is actually composed of black-colored hairs on a white background, creating a bluing effect. This is a middle-sized, rather racy hound with longish, lightly boned legs. Height: 20–27 inches (51–69 cm). Weight: 45–80 pounds (20–36 kg).

Blue tongue

1) Desired blue-black tongue of Shar-Pei and Chow Chow.

2) A condition suggesting congestive heart disease, which may be recognized by the dog's loss of breath, vigor, strength, etc., and a bluish color to tongue and gums, and a weak, rapid pulse.

Blunt muzzle

A truncated square muzzle typical of many breeds (e.g., Pointer, Mastiff).

Blunt-tipped ears

Ears that are rounded or blunt. The Cardigan Welsh Corgi possesses perfect blunt-tipped ears.

B.O.B.

Best of Breed.

B.O.S.

Best of Opposite Sex.

B.O.W.

Best of Winners.

Boarding kennels

Boarding kennels are service facilities designed for housing and caring for dogs—ideally, boarding kennels offer a controlled and safe environment for your pet. Modern-day owners, taking advantage of modern-day travel conveniences, have a more frequent need for such services. Owners are fortunate to have a great many boarding kennels from which to choose. The decision as to which facility to patronize is an important one that should not be made in haste. Practically every city has at least one boarding kennel. The more efficient and large-scale kennels can have over 100 runs; many smaller facilities, often no less efficient and more personalized, offer comparable services. Owners should address themselves to the types of services a kennel offers: indoor or outdoor facilities; proper ventilation— heating and air conditioning; cages or runs; available canine recreation or playtime; supervision; pickup/drop-off option; etc.

Find out about the facility's reputation, status, experience, or membership in a national association. In the United States, the A.B.K.A. (American Boarding Kennel Association) is the principal organization. If an owner puts the appropriate amount of time into choosing a facility, his dog's stay in the kennel— whether for a weekend or a month—will be a pleasant experience.

Bobtail

Old English Sheepdog's alternative name. A bobtail may also refer to a docked or non-existent tail. *See* Old English Sheepdog

Boarding kennels must be clean and well run for any responsible owner to consider patronizing.

Body

That section of the dog's anatomy that starts at the chest and ends at the abdomen. The thoracic and lumbar sections of

Bolognese, white. Photo by I. Français.

the spine comprise the upper portion of the body; the belly (or abdominal floor) and sternum enclose it on the bottom portion. The abdomen is separated from the chest by the diaphragm.

Body length

Usually determined by examining the distance from the shoulder point to the rearmost projection of the thigh, the point of the buttocks. In particular breeds, the body length may be determined differently as is thus indicated in the standard.

Body scent

The scent which comes directly from the body of a bird.

Body spots

Colored patches on a dog's skin, usually detectable through the coat—not the same as patches on the coat. Jack Russell Terriers, white Bull Terriers, pointers and many primarily white or light-colored hounds exhibit body spots.

Body temperature

See Temperature

Body, loosely slung

The pelvis and/or shoulder at-

tachment to the body is looser than ideally desired, resulting in a wobbly or disjointed gait.

Bohemian Terrier

See Czesky Terrier

Bolognese

The bichon of Bologna, Italy, the Bolognese, is believed to have descended from the bichons of southern Italy and Malta. Of course the city of Bologna in northern Italy provides his name. Like the Bichon Tenerife (Frise), the Bolognese enjoyed popularity with the nobility during the 1500s. He was graced by the company of such greats as La Pompadour, Philip II of Spain, and Catherine of Russia. One early representation of the breed appears in Kirchner's model of the Meissen factory (1730s). Some purport that this bichon was developed from the long-extinct Shock Dog, a type of European water dog that was petite enough to nap on one's lap. The Bolognese made its way to Britain initially two hundred years ago, by way of the Canary Islands, where it is believed to have existed since the 1400s. Through the years, the Bolognese was bred for companionship; it is without a doubt one of the closest bonding of dog breeds.

Bolognese puppies in a basket, an Italian delight.

ESSENTIALS OF THE BOLOGNESE: Weight: 5.5–9 pounds (3.5–4 kg). The coat is long and soft to the touch. The hair is tufty, with no undercoat. Almost all Bolognese are white, though an occasional specimen with blonde markings is seen; the blonde markings, while not encouraged by the F.C.I., are considered acceptable. He is of square build and is solid for his size of only 10–12 inches (25–31 cm).

Bolting

In hunting terminology, bolting refers to taking off, ceasing to hunt to the gun. A dog may do this to demonstrate his scorn for the handler or to escape the discipline he is undergoing.

In Beagling, applied to the rabbit, bolting indicates that the rabbit has suddenly moved away from the spot at which it was sitting; applied to hounds, a bolter is a dog that runs in a straight line away from its handler, sometimes far enough away to be out of hearing.

Lastly, the word is frequently connected with eating habits: the intake of food without chewing; swallowing whole, or nearly so. Many dogs bolt their food with little or no obvious effect on their digestion or physical condition. This is because the average dog has very powerful digestive juices in his stomach and intestines, and these suffice well without considerable salivary fluids and tooth mastication.

Bone

In canine terminology, bone is interchangeable with the quality, strength and substance of bone. Expressions such as fine bone, nice round bone, heavily boned, and good bone structure reveal but a glimpse of the bone lexicon. Each express clean, properly structured and ample bone. Other terms such as delicate, spindly, coarse and heavy gesture towards other bone types; such adjectives are relatively self-explanatory.

Bone shape

The shape of a bone in a cross section, i.e., cylindrical, flat, round and oval.

Bones for eating

Natural bones—non-manufactured, that is—are not necessary for a dog's nutrition but do contribute in other ways. Bones are fun! Besides recreation, bones can clean a dog's teeth and remove tartar accumulation. For a dog to get the most benefit from a natural bone, its owner must provide the right kind of bones. Chicken and other small and/or splintery bones are not suitable for any dog. The best bones are hard and supple: a heavy knuckle or shank beef bone are ideal in both respects. Of course, smaller dogs will need smaller bones than larger dogs. Bones can be boiled for a couple of minutes. While bones seemingly complete a dog's day and chase away the Monday blues, they should not be provided on a daily basis. Bones can wear away a dog's tooth enamel. Some owners, conscious of the potential of a dog's choking or the bone's splintering, opt to avoid bones altogether. Such owners are encouraged to provide a synthetic bone for assistance in tartar resistance and as a means of wearing away doggie tensions. Both the Nylabone® and the Gumabone® have proven the most effective of synthetic bones: these are produced from annealed nylon and polyurethane, respectively, with an applied hambone scent. *See also* Nylon bones

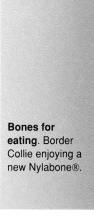

Bones for eating. Border Collie enjoying a new Nylabone®.

Bordeaux Bulldog

See Dogue de Bordeaux

Border Collie

A strong-eyed herder of the old-type collie, the working collie, as he is commonly called, possesses the ability to manipulate a herd or a number of its members with his "hypnotic" eyes. The Bor-

der Collie is deemed the closest purebred representative of the old collies of Scot-

Border Collie, black and white, maneuvering the stock.

land, believed to be the "first" collies. The strong-eye characteristic is perhaps more developed in the Border Collie than in any other breed; his fine-focused ability allows him to move, stop, steer, or otherwise guide a herd without the need to nip the heels or bark. Besides consuming less physical energy, the strong eye is an advantage to the herder because nipping risks the receiving of a kick and the frightening of the herd.

The fertile grazing Border area between Scotland and England has been patrolled and managed by the working collie for hundreds of years, and he has bred true to working type for many of them. Beauty and strict conformation to a predetermined standard have never been the strivings of Border breeders. On the contrary, the ability to perform defines the typey dog. It is the demands of herding that have shaped the breed to its present form so effectively, one might add, that the abilities of the Border has cost many "inferior" breeds their employment in the pastures.

The term "collie" finds renewed and rightful meaning in the Border Collie. The Border Collie is a rugged working dog full of love, life, and independence. He would sacrifice all for his ability to work the ranging lands where flocks and herds roam. His instincts are razor sharp, and his intelligence is superb. And yet, he is an affectionate and bonding companion dog.

Border Collie, rough, chocolate and white. Photo by I. Français.

ESSENTIALS OF THE BOR-
DER COLLIE: A well-pro-
portioned dog of smooth
outline, graceful carriage,
and perfect balance. In
definition: a tenacious,
hardworking sheepdog.
The skull is fairly broad;
muzzle tapering to nose;
stop very distinct. Eyes
oval shaped and set wide
apart. Ears set well apart,
of medium size and tex-
ture. Neck is of good
length, strong and mus-
cular. Front legs parallel.
Shoulders well laid back.
Overall, body to be ath-

letic in appearance, with well sprung
ribs, a deep chest and deep, muscular
loins. The tail, set low, should reach at
least to the hock. Height: ideally 21 inches
(53 cm), with bitches slightly less. The
Border Collie weighs 30–45 pounds
(14–20 kg). The coat may be either of two
varieties: medium long or smooth
coated. Both must possess a weather-resistant double coat. Color varies considerably; white, however, should not predominate. Dark colors most common.

Border Collie,
smooth, chocolate
and white, ears
upright. Photo by
I. Français.

Border Collie,
rough, blue merle.
Photo courtesy
Pepperland
Kennels.

Border Terrier

The Border Terrier is the common working terrier used by hunters and farmers in the Border area between Scotland and England. In this region, the Border was used to destroy the burrowing and deceptive foxes which preyed upon livestock. Appearance was never a concern of these workmen, strictly function; likewise, the Border Terrier's conformation is key to its functional abilities. The first written record of the breed dates back to 1880—an article describing the terriers of Northumberland and Westmoreland. The Border Terrier described here, if not exactly the equivalent of today's standard, was of the general type desired today. Through the course of development, the breed has been called the Reedwater Terrier and the Coquetdale Terrier. Sufficiently legged to keep pace with the horses on the hunt yet squat and plucky enough to go to ground, the Border is truly an ideal worker. This dog's instincts are strong and cannot be ignored.

Border Terrier, red. Photo by I. Français.

ESSENTIALS OF THE BORDER TERRIER: Efficiently put together, the Border Terrier is medium boned, strong and active. Head is like that of an otter, moderately broad in skull, with short, strong muzzle. Ears small V-shaped, dropping forward close to cheek. Forelegs are straight and not too heavy in bone. Body is deep and narrow, fairly long. Ribs not overly sprung; feet, small; tail moderately short, thick at base then tapering, set high and carried gaily. The jacket, ranging from red to wheaten in color, is slightly broken, tightly fitting and excessively wiry. This is a working dog, and the conformation is dependent on its functional abilities. Weight: 11.5–15.5 pounds (5–7 kg). Height: 11 inches (28 cm).

Bore out

The interference of a racing dog that carried another contestant wide.

Boredom

The lot of many working dogs is a continuous rigorous daily routine: herding dogs running hundreds of sheep, throwing themselves at the wandering woolly mass to subtly suggest the shepherd's request or endlessly staring with requisite intolerance and persistence to persuade the sheep to move on; cattledogs droving unruly herds, nipping heels and dodging misguided kicks; flock-guarding dogs surveilling the mountainside day and night. House and family dogs, however, without such noble and time-consuming tasks, run around, look around, bark a bit, sit and sleep. As is the case with humans, dogs get bored too. Many new owners address themselves diligently to the chore of amusing their new family member. Pet shops have a considerable number of doggie recreational devices (toys, balls, bones, etc.). It needs to be said that dogs do not need to be entertained— exactly. Dogs may sit closer to the television when it is on. This is more likely for warmth or the appeal of the different noise than a particular affinity for Lucille Ball or Fred Flintstone. Some owners, however, insist that their dog will only watch TV if a certain show is on or that their dog only likes commercials—these persons have dogs that either are attracted to certain sounds (commercials are usually louder than the programs they interrupt) or are simply peculiar.

Spending time with a dog is a worthwhile endeavor for both the dog and the owner. Exercising and running with the dog are healthy physically and psychologically. Frisbees® or other flying disks are usually enjoyed by dogs. All of this helps to relieve your dog's boredom.

Borzoi

1) Generic Russian term for sighthound or greyhound. The Borzoi is but one of the Russian borzois; the Tasy, Taigan, and South Russian Steppe Hound (which *see*) are others.

2) The importance of esthetics and

ain. The Russian Wolfhound, as the Borzoi was called, was bred for prowess in this glorious sport. Two Borzois, of compatible speed and stamina, were needed to course one wolf, both simultaneously gripping the wolf behind its ears, throwing it over, and pinning it to the ground. The hunter then took over the gagging and tying.

Although in the Soviet Union today there is much pride for their winning windhound, the period following the 1917 Bolshevik revolt associated the Borzoi with the ruling class. Many kennels of beautiful Borzois were destroyed. Many

symmetry in the Borzoi has not always been a quintessential concern. Speed, strength, fearlessness and coursing intelligence were the most valued Borzoi traits, as coursing wolves was a dangerous and difficult sport. The Russian royal family favored the Borzoi, much the way the British royal family embraced the Greyhound. Wolf-coursing became the national sport of Russia, ceremonial and extravagant—beyond the red coats and shod thoroughbreds chasing fox in Brit-

Borzois that work in the Soviet Union today—mostly in southwestern Russia—are imported from European stock. Of course, the Borzois of Europe were imported originally from Russia or received as gifts by European nobility and dignitaries. The dogs were known outside Russia since their first appearance in the late 1800s. During her reign, Queen Alexandra of Britain received many champion-quality Borzois from the czar.

The Borzoi, upon arrival in England,

Borzoi, white with gray and tan. Photo by I. Français.

Borzoi, white with black. Photo by I. Français.

Borzois, red and brindle. Photo by R. Reagan.

found no wolves to course and, because of its natural beauty, became an ornament in elegant homes and a favorite in the show ring. In the U.S., his lot was painfully similar. Coursing events are organized by parent clubs and provide the non-hunter Borzoi with a fine outlet for his energies and talents. The Borzoi is a strikingly exquisite dog but not ideal for every lifestyle. Apartment and condo dwellers must look elsewhere. For owners with an adequate amount of space, here is a dog of unparalleled style and grace. He is even-

tempered and always a perfect gentleman or lady.

ESSENTIALS OF THE BORZOI: Graceful, well balanced, aristocratic, dignified, and elegant, the Borzoi is a dog of beauty and gives every suggestion of speed, courage and power. The head is slightly domed, long, narrow, and in proportion with the body; eyes dark and keen, with intelligent expression; ears small, pointed, and delicate—set high but not too far back. Jaws strong, with teeth set in complete scissors bite. Neck slightly arched and well muscled. Shoulders clean and sloping well back. Chest narrow, ovally cut, with great depth of brisket. Front feet oval; hindfeet, harelike. Tail long and rather low set. The Borzoi should stride with the appearance of effortless power. The coat is long and silky (never woolly), flat and wavy. Height: 28–31 inches (71–79 cm). Weight: 75–105 pounds (34–48 kg). Although white usually predominates in the coat pattern, any color or combination is acceptable.

Bosanski Barak
See Bosnian Roughhaired Hound

Bosnian Hound
See Bosnian Roughhaired Hound

Bosnian Roughhaired Hound
Not purely a scenthound, this Yugoslavian dog, the Bosnian Roughhaired Hound is likely derived from crosses of sighthound and/or pariah. Hunters of nineteenth-century Bosnia strove for a dog with keen hunting abilities and a wire coat to withstand foul weather and difficult terrain. This dog's ingenuity and adaptability in the hunt can be attributed to his diverse background. Boar, fox and hare are among his quarry.

ESSENTIALS OF THE BOSNIAN ROUGHHAIRED HOUND : This wire-haired hound sports a long (4 inch/10 cm) coat of a stubbly texture, covering a thick undercoat. This is the classic wire coat, complete with beard and mustache. Height: 18–22 inches (46–56 cm). Weight: 35–53 pounds (16–24 kg). Shades of gray, yellow, tricolors and bicolors are acceptable colors.

Bossy shoulders
See Shoulder types

Boston Terrier
Although Bostonian through and through, the Boston Terrier originally derived from a cross of the English Bulldog and the English White Terrier. American breeders in Boston began this cross sometime in the 1800s. Considerable crossbreedings were soon conducted, and by 1893 emerged a dog bred down from the English colored Bull Terrier, the Boxer, the Pit Bull Terrier, and other pithy terriers. These early Bostons were once shown in the category of "Round-headed Bull and Terriers, any Color." The original creation, called the Boston Bull, weighed in excess of 60 pounds (27 kg). It took generations to relieve the Boston of the undesirable heavy traits which it inherited from both the English Bulldog and the Bull Terrier. During its evolution, before its presently accepted nomenclature, the breed was called the American Bull Terrier and the Bullet Head.

While today's breed is much of a toy

dog, the Boston still possesses a degree of the Bull Terrier's zest for activity. Terrier in name only, this elegant pet is well-mannered and docile. In the U.S. the Boston Terrier is one of the very few native

Boston Terrier, brindle with white.

Boston Terrier, brindle with white.

breeds that has remained popular. It is said that in the 1930s the Boston, while not overly populous, was overly dear; a fine specimen would cost about $500.00 (£2,000). The breed's numbers continued to increase, and through the 1950s the Boston ranked first in A.K.C. registration statistics. Since 1920, the Boston has remained fending well in the top 20 breeds. The breed made its way to England around 1932, through the efforts of the thankfully insistent Mrs. G. McCormick-Goodhart. Among the first British nobles to own a Boston is the Countess of Essex. New Zealand, Canada and Australia also enjoy healthy Boston fancies.

Because of the Boston's small size and large head structure, Caesarean section operations are often the norm for delivery of puppies.

ESSENTIALS OF THE BOSTON TERRIER: The Boston is a smooth-coated, short-headed, compactly built, well-balanced, short-tailed dog of medium station. The preferred color is brindle with evenly distributed white. The breed comes in three weight varieties: under 15 pounds (6.5 kg), 15–20 pounds (6.5–9 kg), and 20–25 pounds (9–11.5 kg). The coat is short and smooth, usually colored in brindle with white markings. Black with white markings is also seen. The skull is square, and the cheeks are flat. The muzzle is short, square, wide, and deep; it must be in proportion to skull. The eyes are wide apart, large and round, dark in color. The neck is of fair length, setting neatly into shoulders. The chest is deep and goodly wide; shoulders, sloping; ribs, deep and well sprung. Hindlegs set true, bent at stifles, short from hocks to feet. Feet, round, small and compact.

Boston Terrier, brindle with white. Photo courtesy of R. L. Breum.

Bottle feeding
See Puppies, Feeding

Botulism
A condition caused by the ingestion of the toxin of *Clostridium botulinum*, which is found in decomposing animal tissue and sometimes

plant matter. Botulism results in motor paralysis and can be quickly fatal. Intoxication is evidenced by such signs as motor paralysis, troubled eyesight, difficulty in chewing and swallowing, and

order to keep the game in sight while trailing the quarry.

Bourbonnais Pointer
See Braque du Bourbonnais

general progressive weakness. Treatment with a prescribed antitoxin may prove successful, with early detection contributing to the likelihood of recovery. Prevention involves proper feeding and not allowing your dog to consume decaying matter, as is commonly found in trash cans.

Bouledogue Français
See French Bulldog

Bounce
Gait characterized by over-jubilation, more buoyancy and springiness than necessary.

Bouncer
In Beagling, a bouncer can refer to the hunter when he performs the function of a brush beater by starting the game for the hounds to follow. A hound is called a bouncer when it proceeds to leap up in

Bouvier
French for bovine herder or cattle herder. Today there are many less bouviers in Belgium than in times past. Only the Bouvier des Flandres has managed to become an internationally known purebred. The Bouvier des Ardennes can still be found in limited numbers in Belgium. The others from Roulers, Paret and Moerman have been lost.

Bouvier Bernois
See Bernese Mountain Dog

Bouvier des Ardennes
A long-established cattle-working dog native to the Ardennes region of Belgium, the Bouvier des Ardennes is one of the world's rarest dogs. Today farmers still keep these hard-working dogs to work as herders and agricultural watchdogs. Likely only a few teams of these dogs still exist, and among these

Bouvier des Ardennes, red. Photo by I. Français.

very few can trace lines to the original breed members of the last century. The breed was apparently developed from crosses with the Flandres dog to the Belgian Sheepdog, Malinois, and perchance the Briard of France, with the intention of creating the premier cattle-working dog of this cattle-populous region. The breedings were largely successful, and the Ardennes Cattle Dog was once a promising cattle dog of respected ability; it was believed in the 1940s that the dog would achieve international popularity and widespread ownership. Although some 13 specimens reached as far west as the U.S., the breed never did take root out-

Bouvier des Flandres, gray. Photo by I. Français.

side its native region of Belgium. Today the Bouvier des Ardennes is an obscure dog that is threatened with extinction.

ESSENTIALS OF THE BOUVIER DES ARDENNES: Occurring in a variety of colors, the Bouvier des Ardennes represents a mid-sized Belgian cow herder. The head is moderately broad and long; the eyes are dark; and the ears are traditionally erect though today often found drop. The body is nearly square and is efficiently built: chest, deep; back, medium length, straight and strong; loins, muscular. The legs are medium in length and heavy in bone. The tail is usually docked. Coat, of moderate length, coarse and profuse,

shorter on the head and legs. Height: 22-24 inches (56-61 cm). Weight: about 55 pounds (26 kg).

Bouvier des Flandres

Stepping to the fore in the twentieth century, this Belgian cattle dog has existed in its native region of Flandres for centuries—instrumental to the subsistence of many a cattle breeder. With strength, courage, and skill, and an inherent guarding ability, the Bouvier des Flandres droves cattle with force and command while protecting herd and master from malplotting intruders, whether man or animal.

The exact beginnings and component stock of this Flandres dog remain unknown, or unremembered as some scholars utter, and for decades France and Belgium have disputed the "possession" of this rugged working breed. His history is one of trial, triumph, and near decimation. For centuries the breed worked humbly through the daily chores of droving and cart-pulling, rarely leaving his native region. Bred for ability, the breed absorbed blood from other herding breeds available to the Belgian cowman. Other bouvier types were born, and the Flandres dog was threatened as a breed by both the experimental blood and the burgeoning of other cowherding dogs. Ever efficient and undeterred, the Bouvier survived. At the turn of the nineteenth century, the breed's abilities as a guard again spurred interest. Its guardian devotion, however, proved nearly to be its undermining. A guard dog and soldier during the War years, the breed's ranks fell to near-extinction levels. Revived by diligent breedings that included outcrossing, the Bouvier of today enjoys an unprecedented devoted fancy. As a family pet and protector, he is reliable and affectionate, never taking his job lightly.

ESSENTIALS OF THE BOUVIER DES FLANDRES: He is of concentrated construction and rugged appearance. Of considerable importance is the tousled double coat, so that when separated by hand the skin is barely visible. The outer hairs are coarse to the touch, dry and mat, and the undercoat is soft and dense; together they form an all-weather protector. Color is anywhere from fawn through black, including salt and pepper, gray, and brindle. Head and skull are in proportion to build and stature. The general impression is of massiveness, accentuated by a beard and moustache. The head is clean-cut; the skull well developed, flat and somewhat longer than wide. Muzzle is broad, powerful and well boned, with upperline straight. Ears are set on high; they are triangular, very flexible, and in proportion to head. Neck is well muscled and strong. Chest deep, level with elbows, well sprung but not cylindrical. Tail is customarily docked to two to three vertebrae. Movement is powerful, driving, free and easy. Weight around 88 pounds (40 kg). Height: 23–27 inches (59–68 cm).

Bouvier des Flandres, fawn. Photo by I. Français.

Bow hocks
See Cow hocks

Bowed front
Front in which the forearms curve outwardly from the elbows and then inwardly near the wrists. The Pekingese and Tibetan Spaniel are among the breeds with this front; however, it is more commonly referred to as faulty construction and may be related to a genetic imperfection or a general health disorder.

Box
A boxlike barrier from which the racing dog starts in a race.

Box buster
A racing dog that comes very fast out of the starting box, sometimes pushing through the doors before they are fully open. Earlier starting boxes were equipped with a hinged front or lid that covered all eight starting stalls. Dogs often hit this lid before it could be raised. *See also* Dog racing

Box-broken
Dog trained to race from starting box.

Boxer

Beer, rubber and the Boxer fend high on the list of man's greatest "synthetic" achievements. The Boxer, the most stout, elastic, and unbreakable of these, springs forward for its loyalty and reliability as a companion to man. Curiously this dog, not known today for its bite, was derived

deters opponents and wakens fear in unfamiliars by his menacing appearance and impressive physique. Truthfully, however, the Boxer is the "lickiest," most loving among breeds, sweet and even-tempered, playful with family and their friends, unusually good with kids and embarassingly accepting of other pets.

So how does such a patient, non-aggressive dog derive from such blood-thirsty forefathers? Developed in the latter half of the nineteenth century, the Boxer owes its creation to the fraternity of the toughest bulldogs of the era. The Great Dane and Old English Bulldog are usually counted among his ancestors, as are a terrier or two.

One popular theory, and a very provable one, names "Tom," an all-white bull-dog, as the sire of the first Boxers, and "Meta," a check Boxer as their mother. The white markings that splash and flash on the Boxer's coat as well as the common occurrence of an all-white puppy in a litter today prove Tom's input and slake the doubts of other Thomases. The first Boxers, campaigned in 1894 by German sportsmen, differed from the original dogs, and as the breed rose to world prominence, it became notably more refined and stylish, as type was bred for and achieved. The breed's elevation to a companion–exhibition animal was spurred by its ejection from baiting bouts with bulls, as these gruesome matches were outlawed. The English Bulldog follows a similar evolution.

Boxer, brindle with white.

from canines bred to do just that—*bullenbeisser*, bull biter in German. From these hard-biting animal-baiting ancestors, the Boxer has retained fearlessness and raw strength, attributes he successfully applies in his contemporary role as defender–companion.

Today's breed is a lithe, stylish, and refined animal, a mover in show and obedience rings, a smart and biddable and non-drooling family pet. Only owners of fine Boxers grasp the breed's true character: this forboding powerhouse

The Boxer is accredited for being one of the first breeds trained for police work by the selective German people. The breed's intelligence, determination and terrific athletic skill endow the Boxer with performance ability in many arenas. As a watchdog, his ears are keen, his voice big and strident; as a guard dog, he can bring down a man with ease without biting. This is a spirited, confident animal, not undeserving of his scrappy title "Boxer." The often told story behind the breed's name is traced to the dog's inherent way of beginning a match, whether a fun tournament with a friend or a dispute with an instigating kennel mate: his dukes up, front paws extend like a professional pugilist.

Much to love in this dog of dogs, the Boxer is an affectionate and clean pet, quiet unless disturbed. This proud, somewhat cocky canine rightly gains ring-side fans and followers to cheer him on—he is a true knock-out of a dog!

ESSENTIALS OF THE BOXER: The Boxer is a medium-sized, sturdy dog, of square build, with short back and strong limbs. Under the tight-fitting coat lies well-developed musculature, together presenting a clean, refined appearance. Great attention is paid to the head and the harmonious proportion of the muzzle to the skull. The skull is lean, without exaggeration, and shows no wrinkle; the muzzle is broad, deep and powerful, never pointed—the upper jaw has a slight taper; the dark mask is confined to the muzzle and is in distinct contrast to the color of the head. The jaw is normally undershot. The topskull is slightly arched, and the occiput is not too prominent. The cheeks should be flat and not bulge. The neck is round, strong, muscular, and clean throughout, not short. Of square build, the chest is deep, reaching to the elbows; the ribs are well sprung. The topline to be straight and slightly sloping; the tail set high. Both fore and hindquarters well muscled, angulated and strong throughout. Height: 22.5–25 inches (57–64 cm). Weight: 53–71 pounds (24–28 kg). Colors are fawn or brindle, with or without white markings.

Boxer, fawn with white. Photo by I. Français.

Boykin Spaniel, solid liver. Photo by I. Français.

Boykin Spaniel

Larger than a Cocker, he is, without coincidence, similar in size to both the American Water Spaniel and the Springer Spaniel (two important contributor breeds). During the early twentieth century, dog fanciers from South Carolina witnessed the creation of a new breed of dog. Two ambitious hunters of the Boykin community in search of the pre-

mier turkey dog began with a stray; this dog proved so responsive to the experienced training of these men that it was bred to spaniel bitches of various breeds (of special importance were the obliging Springers and American Water Spaniels). Other contributors were Pointers and Chesapeake Bay Retrievers. Turkey dogs needed patience to remain quiet and alert until the fowl was called and shot; not until then could the dog move or generate any noise.

The Boykin is a fantastic swimmer. His fine nose and enthusiasm in the field make him a versatile hunter. He fits wonderfully into the small crafts used by southern hunters of water fowl. So successful is he that South Caro-

lina has made the Boykin Spaniel its official state dog.

ESSENTIALS OF THE BOYKIN SPANIEL: Height: 15–18 inches (36–46 cm). Weight: 30–38 pounds (14–17 kg). His coat is not too dense and, though it varies between wavy and curly, it is typically straight for a water spaniel's. The coat can also vary in its degree of tightness to the body; it is, of course, to be waterproof. The large ears are set high and covered with long wavy hair. The muzzle is broad and elongated. The tail is docked and feathered. Color is solid liver.

Bracco

Italian for pointer.

Bracco Italiano

Believed to be one of the oldest Italian gundogs, the Bracco Italiano is certainly the oldest extant and most successful of all the Italian Pointers. It has been asserted that the evolution of the Bracco Italiano concurs at some point with that of the Segugio Italiano, both sharing a similar ancestor. However, this claim lacks valid supporting evidence. More plausibly, native Italian hounds were bred to old Continental gundogs, and offspring were selectively chosen for retrieving, scenting, swimming and other abilities, thus leading to the emergence of the Bracco. The breed originated some time in the early 1700s but has changed little over the years, holding on to a given (yet desirable) stubbornness that is characteristic of the breed. He is energetic yet level-headed in the field. Along with the

Bracco Italiano, brown with white. Photo by I. Français.

Segugio, the Bracco remains one of the prized hunting dogs of Italy.

ESSENTIALS OF THE BRACCO ITALIANO: Squarely built and very agile, with preferred "dry" limbs and a goodly amount of muscle. The skull is round; the ears are folded; and the muzzle is convex. The expression, a truly distinguishing feature, is unchangingly nervous. The coat is short, dense, and fine; finer on the head, the neck, and the lower parts of the body. Tail is customarily short. Color: white, orange and white, chestnut and white, orange roan, and chestnut roan. Color faults are: all black or chestnut, black and white, tricolor, and black and tan. Height: 22–26 inches (56–66 cm). Weight: 55–88 pounds (25–40 kg).

Bracco Navarrone
    See Perdiguero Navarro

Brace
    Paired dogs of a kind. Braces are used in field trials, sled-dog races, obedience trials as well as conformation competition.

Brace-mate
    Each paired dog in bird-dog field trials is called a "brace-mate" of the other.

Bracelets
    A Poodle's unshaven hair on the hindlegs, when groomed in the Continental clip. *See also* Clipping the Poodle

Brachycephalic skull
    See Skull types

Bracke
    German term for the scenthound that was promoted in various areas, marked for their superb noses and excellence on hare, fox and boar.

Braco Carlos VIII
    An ancient pointing dog of Spain, the Braco Carlos VIII (or Braco Navarro) is a likely contributor to the gene pool of many Continental gundogs, particularly those of central France. The dog enjoyed a moderate status in the early 1800s and was named for the monarch who kept a large kennel of these hunters. The breed was moderately sized with a short coat,

usually white with brown markings. The coat is often ticked or occurs with tan markings. It resembled the Perdiguero Navarro, which differs slightly and is a more modern creation.

Braco Navarro
    See Braco Carlos VIII

Brake
    The metal fork stepped on by the driver to bring the sled to a halt; a fork on the underside of the sled which hits the ground and stops the sled.

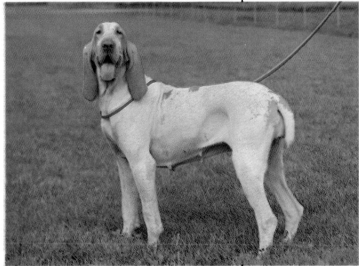

Braque
    A French term denoting the French type of pointer which is marked by its racy elegance and its enduring propensities on the field.

Braque Belge
    See Belgian Shorthaired Pointer

Braque Dupuy
    An old breed of braque that shows definite qualities of his ancestors in his houndy appearance. The breed is typically tall, uncommonly fast, and always elegant—qualities that lead some to believe that a Greyhound (or Sloughi) cross occurred. The French Revolution nearly decimated the Dupuy population, and only a few specimens were preserved in the Abbey of Argensols.
    Though workmanlike and no-nonsense, he is somewhat hasty in his charac-

Bracco Italiano, orange roan. Photo by I. Français.

ter. He owns a good nose and is always active on the hunt. The Dupuy can blaze enviable speed over open ground, and though he can work the water, owners claim that he may prefer not. The Braque Dupuy should demonstrate versatile gundog skills in addition to his fine pointing ability.

ESSENTIALS OF THE BRAQUE DUPUY: Large and somewhat high on the leg, the Braque Dupuy is the tallest of the French braques. Height: 25–27 inches (63–68 cm). In general appearance he is to be sleek and elegant, with skin tight to the body, a narrow head, little stop to the forehead, and a muzzle tending towards convex. The chest is deep and narrow, and there is a noticeable tuck to the belly. The tail is set low. Weight: 49–62 pounds (22–28 kg).

Braque d'Ariége

Once a slow and steady hunter, this Braque, through the turn of the twentieth century, was considered the closest representative of the old French braques. Considered somewhat of historical interest, the Braque de Toulouse, as this braque is also known, was held in high regard by the proud hunters of the area. With the depletion of game of all sizes and the changing face of the landscape, it was realized that a swifter dog would be needed for effectiveness. Breeders knew that it would be better to preserve the survival of the breed, by making it again functionally useful, than to maintain the breed's physique at the risk of extinction. Crossings to swifter, lighter boned dogs, mostly the Braque Saint-Germain but also the Braque Français, produced an Ariége more fleet footed and graceful. He remains, however, one of the largest and most powerful of the French pointers.

Unlike most of the other French pointers which were named for the locale in which they originated, the Braque d'Ariége is not descended from native hounds of his region. This is certain because the local hound of Ariége is strictly a twentieth-century development. The most acceptable theory known regarding the Ariége's creation is that it represents an old cross between the Spanish Pointer and the Bracco Italiano.

ESSENTIALS OF THE BRAQUE D'ARIÉGE: Powerful, elegant, and graceful, the Ariége is a tireless worker of slow pace designed for work on rough terrain. The low set tail is docked, as is common with most Continental pointers. Other features include: a possible dewlap, scroll ears, hare feet, and a square muzzle which tends to be convex. Height: 23–27 inches (58–68 cm). Weight: 55–65 pounds (25–30 kg). The short coat is fine and rather tight fitting. Color is white with orange or chestnut spots; ticking on body is common.

Braque d'Auvergne, black on white. Photo by I. Français.

Braque d'Auvergne

A hard-mouthed but fine retriever of high intelligence, outward affection, and unending enthusiasm on the field. It has been stated that the Braque d'Auvergne is directly descended from the Braque Français but by skillful selection developed into a breed uniquely its own. Another equally interesting suggestion is that the breed traces to Malta—an idea based on the belief that members of the

Maltese Order, which once contained French knights, brought these dogs back to France with them when that Order was dissolved in 1798. Unfortunately, both suggestions are devoid of any evidence from which to conclude.

ESSENTIALS OF THE BRAQUE D'AUVERGNE: A well-built yet lean, medium-sized dog presenting grace, speed, and power. The chest is deep and large, the loins are short. There is a good length of leg. Forelegs are straight. Hindlegs possess little angulation. He is hare-footed. The coat is spotted black on white, forming a blue shading with large black patches; he is without any tan markings. Although the black markings are not prescribed, they must appear on the head, covering the ears and eyes. A body color of speckled black on white is also seen. Height: 22–24 inches (56–61 cm). Weight: 50–62 pounds (23–28 kg).

Braque de Toulouse
See Braque d'Ariége

Braque du Bourbonnais

An able and efficient sporting dog which evolved from hounds indigenous to central France. He is a believed descendant and fair representative of the old French braques. As suggested by his name, the Bourbonnais Pointer originated in the province of Bourbon. An old breed, it is believed to be represented in a sixteenth-century woodcut. This depiction closely resembles the Bourbonnais in its present form. The breed's history was disrupted by the French Revolution. However, throughout the 1800s, breed purity was carefully preserved. Unfortunately, commercialized breedings were conducted in the early 1900s to meet the demands of a suddenly insatiable public. Soundness and ability were suddenly at great risk. WWI and WWII then further decimated the breed. Committed show and hunt fanciers did preserve enough stock to keep the breed alive. After the Second World War, dedicated fanciers worked to revive the breed to a level equitable with the best of Continental pointers. The Bourbonnais of today is an all-around hunter and can be used on all types of game.

ESSENTIALS OF THE BRAQUE DU

BOURBONNAIS: The Bourbonnais is a fairly large, muscular dog who combines hardiness, strength and elegance. Neck is supple but muscular and not long. Chest is very deep, possibly extending below the elbows. Back, well muscled and slightly curving in the male; straighter in the bitch. The head is rather pear-shaped and smooth in outline; the topskull is rounded. The ears are medium length and triangular. The muzzle is strong, broad, and conical. The jaw is preferred slightly overshot. Sometimes referred to as the tailless pointer, the Braque is born with either a rudimentary or an absent tail. Height: 22 inches (56 cm). Weight: 40–57 pounds (18–26 kg). Color is white with liver, brown or orange; roan ing throughout.

Braque du Bourbonnais, white with liver. Photo by I. Français.

Braque Français de Grande Taille

A breed native to the Pyrenees region of France, it nearly suffered extinction at the turn of the twentieth century. Dr. Castets and Monsieur Senac-Langrange, two canine authorities, are credited with saving the breed. Today the breed base is solid and slowly growing, and the future looks bright for the breed.

He is a sizable gundog who once enjoyed great popularity with hunters of his native region. He is closely related to the Spanish Pointer and is described as looking like the extinct and much talked about Southern Hound. His appearance certainly verifies any supposition of hound in his blood. The breed's characteristic way of scenting is high nose, but it can ground nose as well. With his nose lifted high into the air, this dog is keen on a scent. The dog's temperament is well balanced, and he proves both an able hunter and a pleasant companion.

Braque Français de Grande Taille, white with chestnut.

ESSENTIALS OF THE BRAQUE FRANÇAIS DE GRANDE TAILLE: Body is well muscled and strong but lean, elegant and enduring. Head is broad, and muzzle is slightly convex. The coat is short, thick and dense. In color, the Large Braque is white with chestnut patches, with or without ticking. Height: 22–27 inches (56–68 cm). Weight: 45–71 pounds (20–32 kg).

Braque Français de Petite Taille

The Braque Français de Petite Taille, like the Grande Taille, developed from the Spanish Pointer (and likely the Italian Pointer as well). This dog is a more refined version of the Pyrenees-type Braque Français and was fostered in the Gascony region. Like the Grande's, his hunting style is also high-nosed; he is particularly good in harsh marsh and thick cover. This dog's small size makes him an agile and easily maneuvering hunter. Owners relate what a joy he is to have indoors, although he loves to be outside too.

ESSENTIALS OF THE BRAQUE FRANÇAIS DE PETITE TAILLE: In body type and conformation the Petite Taille is mostly similar to the Braque Français de Grande Taille, which *see*. The Français's muzzle is shorter than the larger French Pointer's, and his ears, set higher and shorter, hang flatter to the head. Both breeds share the same white and chestnut coloration, although the Petite's chestnut markings are often more extensive. The head is slightly more tapered and refined. Height: 19–23 inches (48–58 cm). Weight: 37–55 pounds (17–25 kg).

Braque Saint-Germain

French pointers, as well their English counterparts, believably, owe their heritage to the Spanish Pointer. As a braque type with orange and white coloration,

Braque Français de Petite Taille, white with chestnut. Photographs by I. Français.

the Braque Saint-Germain can be traced to the dim time of Louis XV or before. Paintings hanging in the Louvre today indicate the dog's antiquity. However, it seems probable that the various braques of the eighteenth century were all considered as one breed with only color variations separating them. If one strives to determine a more definite lineage of the Braque Saint-Germain, it must be stated that the true type of the breed emerged not until the reign of Charles X, hence the breed is sometimes referred to as the Braque Charles X. One account cites that the actual breed as we know it today is the result of an English Pointer-French Braque cross.

ESSENTIALS OF THE BRAQUE SAINT-GERMAIN: Elegant and well proportioned; of supple build; fleet yet strong. The chest is deep, providing good lung capacity. The neck is strong and of moderate length. The stop is less pronounced than the English Pointer's; the snout is less elevated, and the muzzle is less square. The nose is wide-nostriled, broad and dark pink. The ears are medium sized and attached level with the eyes, standing well out from the head. The coat is short, not too fine, and never hard. In color the Saint-Germain invariably is a dull white base with bright orange splashes. Height: 20–24 inches (51–61 cm). Weight: 40–57 pounds (18–26 kg). The tail is long and tapering.

Brasilian Molosser
  See Fila Brasileiro

Brazilian Greyhound
  This Brazilian sighthound, also known as the Veadeiro Catarinense, represents calculated crossbreeding between various foxhound and sighthound types. This hound is able to hunt by sight or scent. In appearance it is a moderately sized dog with a well-domed skull with a well-defined stop, suggestive of its scenthound blood. A long thin tail and a fine mouse gray coat verify the breed's sighthound ancestry.

Brazilian Mastiff
  See Fila Brasileiro

Braque Saint-Germain, white with orange. Photo by I. Français.

Brazilian Terrier
  If a nation has vermin, a nation has terriers. Not every terrier from every rodent-infested locale in the world has been brought to the fore by its native farmers or villagers. The Brazilian Terrier, known also as the Terrier Brasileiro, is one of Brazil's two native breeds which have received international attention. Brazil's pride, its Fila Brasileiro, is inarguably one of the world's most impressive canines. The Terrier Brasileiro is an excellent ratter and has been extant for at least a century; they are popular as house companions at home. Outside Brazil,

Brazilian Terrier, tricolor.

these dogs are still relatively unknown. It is believed that they derive from crosses of British Jack Russell Terriers to the Chihuahua and Pinscher.

ESSENTIALS OF THE BRAZILIAN TERRIER: The breed weighs about 15–20 pounds (6.5–9 kg) and is always a tricolor, predominated by white, with head and saddle markings in black and tan. The ears are drop; the neck is rather long; the muzzle tapers moderately and is not broad; the stop is noticeable. The legs are light boned, and the chest sound. The coat is short and smooth.

Brazilian Tracker
See Rastreador Brasileiro

Break
1) Change in coat color from puppyhood to adolescence, i.e., a black/white Bearded Collie breaks into its slate gray coloration at four months.
2) The development of the Cocker Spaniel's skull, when the topskull and foreface plane begin to separate.
3) The the crease line in the ear lobe, separation of the upright and dropped portion of the ear (i.e., the Rough Collie).

Breaking
1) Chasing a flushed bird or moving on or retrieving before the command to move on or to retrieve has been given.
2) Training generally or specifically to be steady to wing and shot.

Breastbone
Sternum.

Breasts
Female dogs, bitches, like female humans, have organs which contain the mammary glands and allow for newborns to nourish themselves with the milk produced by the glands via the teats. About four weeks into pregnancy the bitch's breasts may begin to swell, gradually becoming firmer until they reach their determined size. Lactation, the process of producing milk by the mammary glands, occurs during the actual nursing of the pups, although small amounts of milk may be excreted prior to the birth of the pups. The breasts will remain enlarged through the weaning process, after which lactation will cease and they will gradually return to normal. *See also* Breasts, problems of, Pregnancy, Weaning, Bitch

Breasts, problems of
Tumors, injuries, and infections are the three most common causes of problems in the breasts.
Infection. Infection, caused by a bacterial invasion, may occur in the breast area for numerous reasons, including: cuts, surgery, bruises, poor diet, and allergic reactions. Bacteria may even enter through a teat and infect the breasts.

Breasts. Mastiff bitch nursing puppies. A bitch's breasts remain enlarged until after the weaning process is over. Photo by R. Reagan.

Mastitis is one such breast infection, whether it occurs before or after weaning, and it is one of the major causes of puppy death. Whether a bitch is nursing or not, or sterile or not, all infections of the breast area demand prompt action. With the availability of antibiotics and quality care, it is senseless to let any breast infection go unguarded.

Injury. The underbelly is known for its vulnerability, and that is where the breasts of bitches are located. This area is very subject to cuts and scrapes, especially if the bitch frequents wooded or brushy areas, as would a hunting dog. Another common injury to the breast area is bruising, often the result of a missed jump, kick, an automobile accident, etc. In such cases, if the knock is severe, internal injury, including injury to the mammary glands, may result. Because of the multiple, often serious, complications possible, veterinary diagnosis and treatment are recommended.

Tumors. There are two basic types of tumors: cancerous (malignant) and benign. Of the two most common tumors found in canines' breasts, adenocarcinoma is a deadly one, while the common mixed tumor is mostly harmless. Tumors are often noticeable as lumps in the breast area. Any abnormal lumps or other formations (growths) on or around the breast deserve prompt veterinary investigation.

Caked breasts, which are swollen breasts, which can often occur after weaning, are usually no more than the body's attempt to shut down the milk factory. If there is no accompanying infection, caked breasts, though they may be swollen and tender, are little cause for concern. The condition, given time, should clear; if prolonged, persisting for

more than a few days, a veterinarian should be consulted.

Pseudopregnancy. Though hardly a disorder, this is a concern of many dog owners. The fact is pseudopregnancy, which is largely the swelling of the breasts of an unmated bitch who has passed through a heat, is a normal response to ovulation. It is only when the breasts fail to swell after a heat that con-

cern should be acted upon. Of course, should the swelling be excessive or prolonged, consult a veterinarian.

Breathing difficulty
See Respiratory ailments

Breech
Adjective describes the area created by the inner thigh muscles around the buttocks of the dog.

Breech birth
The abnormal but not unusual presentation of the pup in a feet-down position in the birth canal. Many pups can be born in this position, but many others require special assistance on the part of the owner and/or a trained professional.

Breasts, problems of. Polish Hound photographed on farmer's field in Poland. Large litters may give a dam problems if she is left unattended, resulting in the fatality of one or more whelps.

Breeches

In long-coated dogs, the breeches are fringing of longer hair on the upper thighs (sometimes lower as well). The Keeshond serves as an example. Breeches can be, and are, used interchangeably with culottes, pants and trousers. On short-coated dogs, the breeches are formed at the junction of the inner and outer thighs by longish hair in ridgelike pattern.

Breed

Purebred dogs more or less uniform in size and structure, as produced or modified and maintained by man.

Breed development. Illustrating the variation in type of *Canis familiaris*, the domestic dog: English Setter, Afghan Hound, Boxer, and Bulldog. Photo by R. Pearcy.

Breed development

The family of dogs includes both domestic dogs, such as the Poodle, Basset Hound, and Greyhound, and wild dogs, such as the gray wolf, red fox and raccoon dog. Each of these members of the family Canidae vary, to various extents, in size and type. Some of the earliest recorded domestic dogs of Europe increased in size as a result of their improved diets and close association with humans. These dogs grew larger than their wild dog counterparts who needed to fend for themselves for food and shelter.

The evolution of dog breeds is bound more inseparably to the history of man than it is to Nature herself. Dog did not evolve completely on its own. Where man went, dog followed, or was pulled or did pull. A certain amount of selection was employed by the peoples who kept dog. Northern peoples, for instance, favored the larger, more robust dogs which were best able to accommodate their draft and transport needs. This type of "selection" is assuredly unconscious.

The dramatic increase and decrease in dog sizes are due to the sophisticated tinkerings of man. The European trend followed the Near East affinity for canine diversification. Man began selecting for particular types, consciously interfering with the animal's evolution. The development of the sighthound type in Mesopotamia and Egypt is a marked example of selecting for a slender, long-legged, narrow-skulled hound. The sighthound type, decidedly different than other types, is designed for a particular function. These people, tampering as it were, sought a dog that was slender (requiring little food); long-legged (increasing running capability and speed); narrow-skulled (to "slice" the wind while in flight). Similarly, Europeans developed dachshunds and dachsbrackes, short-legged dogs small enough to enter a badger's hole and extract the occupant. Easterners (and Westerners too) developed tiny dogs (to fit into a lap or a pocket) with luxuriant coats in beautiful colors or sleek, silky coats (aesthetics, esthetics!) to function as ritzy companions for the nobility. The short deformed snout of the bulldog gave it the ability to maintain a nosehold on a bull or other imposing creature.

Many of the natural inclinations or instincts of the dog have been recircuited by man. Very few hunting dogs still maintain the instinct to pursue and instantly kill the prey. Foxhounds are among the most enthusiastic of hunters but do not mangle the precious red fox upon running it down. The retrievers remain suitably interested in hunting to seek out the felled bird but are not inclined to disfigure or devour the find—even though his master is a good 100 yards away. Many terriers go to ground with verve and spirit but are trained not to dismember the squirming cornered quarry. Dogs, like their ancestral wolves, do hunt and work singly or cooperatively in packs. They remain primarily gregarious animals. Dog's immense fondness for man, deserving or not, stems from the close-knit family unit still exhibited by wolves. Ironically, twentieth-century man might improve the present state of his living condition were he to emulate the cooperative lifestyle of the wolf. Wolves work together—male and female sharing the work load, bonding for life, and participating in the rearing (and education!) of the young. Wolf cubs enter "what's out there in the world" as well-versed, well-loved, well-nurtured, well-prepared members of the woods society. The wolf's hunting method employs hearing, sight, and smell. Most domestic dogs, however, have one or two of these abilities sharpened: the greyhound types rely on sight; the scenthounds rely on smell; terriers often rely on sound. There are certain breeds today that are able to employ all three of these senses quite adeptly. The Podengo Portugues   and the Ibizan

Hound, as well as the scenthound types of Yugoslavia, exhibit strong abilities in all three areas.

It would be more accurate to look at the dogs engineered by man as specific

Breed development. Draft dogs today continue to work in their bred-for capacity.

Breed development. The Sloughi represents the sighthound type of Morocco. Photo courtesy Club for Native Moroccan Breeds.

Breed development. *Les chiens courant*, the packhounds of France, are divided into different breeds according to locales, colors, and sizes. All are most gregarious with each other. Photo by I. Français.

types more so than specific breeds. Regardless of the dog, these types were identified and differentiated by size and function. Specific colors, character traits, expressions—ideals we deem important in "breeds" today—were not yet of the essence. There were guard dogs or fighting dogs (mastiff types), hunters, herders, vermin catchers (terrier types), draft dogs (nordic types), dogs for pleasure (toy dogs), dogs that hunted by scent (scenthounds), etc.

Developing beyond these general types merely involved the engineering and further interference of man. People in different parts of the world developed dogs for their needs, and people in neighboring countries busied themselves developing practically the same dog. For instance, both Finland and Sweden developed a spitz-type herding dog. Today two breeds exist, the Swedish Lapphund and the Finnish Lapphund, although only a native Finn or Swede can likely differentiate. Britain has created breeds of its own without batting an eye. The British affinity for the German Spitzen, namely the Wolfspitz and the Toy German Spitz, materialized two well-known "breeds": the Keeshond and the Pomeranian, respectively.

Pointer types were developed in most European countries. The earliest of the pointer types, the English Pointer, was likely used in the development of other pointers: the Perdigueiro Portugueso, the pointer of Portugal; the Perdiguero de Burgos, the pointer of Spain; the

Braque Francais, the pointer of France; and the Bracco Italiano, the pointer of Italy. In times prior to man's need to organize and categorize (even pre-Benjamin Franklin), these five dogs would be considered among pointer types; today, however, not only are they each individual breeds, but some of them have specific variants within themselves.

The great flock guardian dogs of Europe present a similar phenomenon. For the purposes of the shepherd, a flock guard necessarily was big, powerful, well coated, and white. His strength and size were required in his combat with threatening wolves; his coat protected him from the harsh mountain elements; his color helped the shepherd differentiate from the wolf and allowed a certain camaraderie with the sheep. France created its mountainous white guard: Le

Chien de Montagne des Pyrenees, the Great Pyrenees or Pyrenean Mountain Dog; Italy ripened La Cane da Pastore Maremmano-Abruzzese, the Maremma Sheepdog; Poland brought forth the Owczarek Podhalanski, the Tatra Mountain Sheepdog; Greece produced the Greek Sheepdog; and Rumania, the Rumanian Sheepdog.

Importing and exporting dogs also contribute to the creation of breeds. Scenthounds and herding dogs brought to America with immigrant Europeans inevitably contributed to a number of America's cur and coonhound breeds; just as British immigrants to Australia effected the establishment of spin-off breeds: the Australian Terrier and the Silky Terrier, Australia's pride and joy toy terriers.

Essentially man has been pleased with his breed-diversification efforts. Over 800 breeds are estimated to exist in the world today. Only about 400 of those breeds are recognized by the Fédération Cynologique Internationale (F.C.I.), the world's central registry. In the U.S. and Britain, only about 150 breeds are recognized. While many breeders and dog fanciers strive to maintain existing breeds, others continually venture forth into the unknown. Not all of man's ex-

periments have proven successful. Bantamizing the one-pound Chihuahua or three-pound Toy Poodle cannot lead to a desirable end. The general good of the dog must remain foremost in all breeders' minds.

Breed development. The woolly Kuvasz of Hungary stands out as but one of the white flock-guard breeds of Europe. Photo by I. Français.

Breed development. Terriers have been developed and trained not to mangle the quarry they catch. Jack Russell Terriers upon their captured fox.

rived from its larger brothers (looking much like a white Toy German Spitz); the Kyi-Leo, derived from the Shih Tzu and the Lhasa Apso; and the Old English Bull-dogge, derived from various mastiff/bulldog types to recreate the lost functional bulldog. Since we can be sure that man's curiosity and longing for improvement will endure, so too will the development and concocting of new canines. Fortunately for Man, Dog is abundantly tolerant of our endeavors and loves us just the same. *See also* Domestication of dog, New breed creation

In the Soviet Union, a number of breeds have been formulated to equate many Western dog breeds. The Moscow Watchdog impersonates well the Saint Bernard; the Moscow Longhaired Toy Terrier masquerades in the Papillon–Longhaired Chihuahua venue. Other recent breed creations worthy of note are the Toy American Eskimo, de-

Breed standard

A written description of what the ideal specimen of a given breed should look like. Purebred dogs are evaluated on their adherence with the standard. Of course, even the finest champion of champions still falls shy of *the* perfect

dog. Each dog-registering organization adopts a standard of perfection for each breed of dog that it recognizes. Standards are usually drawn up by each breed's parent club or fostering organization, and upon recognition to championship status, a standard is adopted by the given registry. Standards vary from country to country and from registry to registry. In America, the two major registries, the American Kennel Club (A.K.C.) and the United Kennel Club (U.K.C.) recognize many of the same purebreds, but their standards vary in wording, emphasis, and content. The American registries' standards also vary from those of the Kennel Club of Great Britain (K.C.G.B.), etc., even though they recognize many identical dogs. Presently the Australian National Kennel Council (A.N.K.C.) recognizes all of the breeds of the K.C.G.B. and adheres to the British standards, except for breeds that are native Australian, such as the Kelpie, Cattle Dog and Australian Terrier. The Fédération Cynologique Internationale (F.C.I.), the international dog registry, recognizes more breeds than any other single registry and has adopted standards for each of the hundreds of breeds it registers. Lastly, individual smaller registries sprout up all over the place and register dogs that are not recognized by a major registry (as well as others). These private registries usually function similarly, though on smaller scales. *See also* American Kennel Club, Judging dogs

Breeding

Breeding is the practice of mating two animals with the intention of creating offspring. The foremost goal of all breeding should be the production of sound, healthy animals of quality equal or superior to their parents. Dogs having any given weakness should not be crossed to any other dog having the same weakness but should be crossed to such a dog that will serve to eliminate the weakness. Any animal having serious physical or genetic faults should not be bred, as doing so only weakens the breed as a whole and creates nothing but problem-ridden, heart-breaking pups.

Breeding. A healthy litter of Rottweilers posed around their whelping box.

There are many reasons to breed dogs, but some reasons are undoubtedly more valid than others: the two outstanding reasons to breed dogs are the propagation and the betterment of a breed. Reasons such as financial gain and educational experience are not adequate reasons in themselves, though they can contribute to the experience of breeding dogs. Above all else must be the well-being of the mated pair and their offspring. In breeding, this begins with the diet and soundness of the brood bitch and stud dog and ends with all the pups being placed in suitable homes. Breeding demands responsibility and knowledge. Breeding is not for everyone—indeed it is for relatively few. The following discussion outlines the major facets of breeding dogs, including the selection of a compatible pair, the actual crossing of the dogs, the

bitch's carrying the pups, the delivery and location of the pups in suitable homes.

Pairing dogs involves the selection of a male (stud) and female (brood bitch) who best complement each other's traits and characteristics by accentuating the strengths and eliminating the weaknesses. A study of genetics and how it applies to the canine will make clearer how traits are passed from parent to offspring by chromosomes and DNA. Each parent contributes a sex cell, the ova of the female and the sperm of the male, and each of these cells possesses the genetic material that will compose the offspring. Traits called for by the DNA will be exhibited depending on other factors, including their dominance or recessiveness. A dominant trait will show over a recessive one, but the animal can still carry the recessive gene. Therefore, it is important for the breeder to have both a good knowledge of genetics and a good idea of the breeding that went into the lines from which both the stud and bitch spring. Dogs with inheritable defects, such as hip dysplasia, eclampsia, and others, must never be bred. In the United States, it is generally held that no dog should be bred that is not certified by the Orthopedic Foundation for Animals, meaning that the dog has been radiographically proven not to possess hip dysplasia. *See also* O.F.A.

For the health and safety of the bitch, both she and the male should receive a veterinary examination prior to the actual breeding. The bitch must be physically mature, of sound body and temperament, have no parasites, infections, or other inhibitory conditions, be up to date with all inoculations and other shots, and be of sound nutritional health. The age at which a bitch can safely carry and deliver a litter varies from breed to breed. Typically the smaller breeds can, and in some cases should, be bred earlier than many of the larger breeds which mature at a slower pace. Your veterinarian can assist you in your determination of the bitch's readiness for mating. Pregnancy is a time of great strain and stress on the female, making it imperative that she be of overall soundness. The male should be examined for disease, parasites, and other undesirable conditions, as well as temperament and physical soundness. Once the ideal mates are selected and each successfully completes the veterinary examination, the actual mating can be planned.

Preliminary considerations involve a contract, a location, and the bitch's heat. A contract should be written and signed by both parties involved, specifying all fees and procedures, as well as what actions will be taken if specific conditions arise, i.e., miscarriage, failed fertilization, the birth and/or survival of a single dog. A contract can also be written and signed by future owners of the pups prior to the actual breeding; these contracts ensure homes for the pups, saving much strife and stress for the breeder after the whelp. Contracts should be specific and consider the possibility of a failed breeding.

Location is also a consideration. Stud owners prefer to have the bitch visit the stud, which may be better in many cases due to the territorial tendencies of the male. For inexperienced breeders, mating conducted at a veterinarian's practice or professional breeder's kennel may be an option to consider. For some breeds, special equipment is necessary, such as a breeding rack, a muzzle, or other device. Professionals can list for you the items which they have found useful. It is im-

an increase in appetite. This swelling continues until a few drops of blood drip from the vulva. Bleeding continues from four to fifteen days; the consistency of the bleeding can vary from breed to breed and individual to individual. Before the bleeding stops, the discharge changes to a pale reddish color. The second sign is the bitch's willingness to mate. This can be seen in her teasing or even assuming the mating stance. The bitch will mate repeatedly during this acceptance stage. But, as eggs are fertilized, chemical and physical changes occur, and the bitch

Breeding. Pairing the right stud dog to the right brood bitch is a delicate, even formal, matter. Chow Chows. Photo by C. Barnard.

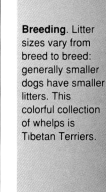

Breeding. Litter sizes vary from breed to breed: generally smaller dogs have smaller litters. This colorful collection of whelps is Tibetan Terriers.

portant to be prepared and to expect anything.

The first signs that the bitch is in season are a slight swelling of the vulva and

soon forbids males from mating with her. Because the female typically has many eggs and not all of these are fertilized in one mating session, it is possible for the litter to be sired by more than one father. Such is not desirable, and many kennel clubs refuse to register dogs of two-father litters.

The gestation period for dogs varies between 58 and 65 days from the date of copulation. The prepared owner should count these days from the first mating and be ready for either an early or late delivery. As pregnancy progresses, the bitch's abdomen will swell with the expanding uterus and her mammary glands will fill with milk. Throughout her pregnancy, she requires a substantial diet rich in vitamins, minerals, and easily digestible proteins. Regular inspections by the veterinarian can be scheduled, especially if she is a first-time mother.

Breeding. A pregnant Vizsla bitch. Photo by I. Français

As with good food, exercise is essential to the healthy pregnancy. The bitch should be walked regularly at a moderate pace until the latter stages of her condition, at which time exercise should taper to a close at the bitch's bidding.

All supplies should be on hand at least by the middle of the pregnancy; a whelping box should be constructed or acquired and the bitch should be given the chance to become familiar with it. Additional contracts for the sale of the pups can be signed at this time, or if no prospective buyers are yet reached (an undesirable state), advertising and screening buyers should begin in earnest.

Whelping is the process during which the pups are expelled from the womb. As whelping nears, the bitch's behavior will change; she may become fidgety and attempt to wander; she will often construct a nest of sheets, bed covers, throw rugs, etc.; and in the end she will refuse food; such behavior can last two or three days without demanding the owner's concern. The bitch should be led to the whelping box and allowed to rearrange it according to her liking. The whelping box should be large enough for the bitch to move and turn around in comfortably. All whelping supplies must now be at hand, and the veterinarian should be notified. The owner should be patient. In long-coated dogs, it is wise to remove the abdominal hair a few days in advance of the date of expectation.

The most reliable sign that the bitch is soon to whelp is a two to three degree Fahrenheit drop in her temperature (normal is about 101.5°F, 38.6°C), after which she should deliver within 48 hours. True labor begins as the pups begin to pass into the birth canal; it is evidenced by an earnest effort on the part of the bitch to expel the pups. Once true labor begins, no more than two hours should pass without the appearance of a pup. After the first is born, the others should follow at somewhat regular intervals. If the bitch shows any signs of trouble throughout the whelping process or should any pup not emerge in due time, a vet should be contacted immediately. The new breeder must remember that whelping is an exceedingly strenuous process. Total whelping time varies with the breed and the individual dog. As rough parameters, small dogs generally require under five hours, while larger dogs require six to twelve hours.

As each pup is born, the bitch should instinctively remove the sac in which the pup is contained, remove any mucus, and stimulate its breathing. Many dogs will sever the umbilical cord by biting, but some owners will have to cut the cord themselves. Should the bitch ignore the newborn, the owner must intervene by removing the sac, clearing the mucus, and starting the pup's breathing—lost seconds can result in lost dogs. Each pup

Breeding. The whelping box must be placed in a warm, quiet location where the dam feels comfortable and familiar. Petit Basset Griffon Vendeen bitch and litter.

must be followed by an afterbirth. After the pup is cleaned and cared for and receives its first feeding, it should be placed in a separate box that is well heated and bedded; doing so prevents its interfering with or being rolled on by the mother. When all the pups are delivered, cleaned and fed, the bitch is often injected with a substance that causes the release of any retained afterbirths or pups, either of which will cause severe infection and complication. The bitch may wish to get up and stretch her legs or she may simply wish to rest a bit; either is fine, but she should be coaxed outside to relieve her bladder. She should be offered nourishment in the form of broth, milk or other nourishing liquid. Many authorities advise against feeding the bitch any solid food for the first few days. Little inclined to leave her newborns, the mother will likely need encouragement to take a break, stretch and relieve herself for the first few days.

The bitch and her pups should be given a couple weeks' peace, after which contracted buyers can view them. Visitors should be kept to a minimum. Pups typically receive their shots sometime around their sixth week of age and are usu-

ally ready for their new homes by the seventh to ninth week of life. *See also* Bitch, Outcrossing, Inbreeding, Linebreeding, Pregnancy, Reproductive system, Stud dog, Weaning

Breeding. The birthing of a Collie. Courtesy of Doris Blakely.

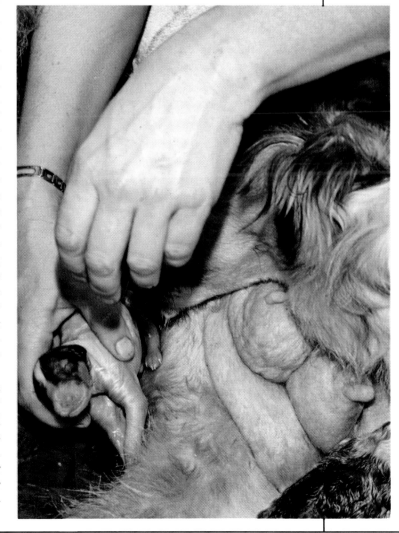

Briard

The Berger de Brie is a large French herder of distinctive appearance and very fine herding abilities. The Briard's physical and working characteristics suggest descent from the Chien d' Aubry, or Aubry's dog, a centuries-old dog depicted and described in French legend and art—a dog believed to have origi-

Briards, fawn and black. Photo by I. Français.

nated in the Middle Ages by crosses with Oriental sheepdogs and French guard dogs. However, the Briard's exact origin remains riddled with uncertainty and is basically impossible to determine. Large herding dogs with guardian abilities were created and propagated to protect shepherds and their sheep from wolves, poachers, and other threats, and they have existed in Europe believably as long as the shepherding trade itself. The Briard is a close relative of another French herder, the Beauceron; these two large shepherds were once considered two varieties of a single breed, the Briard but a goat-haired Beauceron. The Briard, known by many a Francophile as the Berger de Brie, is still managing the unruly woolly masses in French provinces today. Likewise, he is a familiar sight in show rings and competitions in both Europe and America. The breed retains its fearless guardian instincts and acute herding skills to this day, yet it has matured into an affectionate, well-mannered dog.

ESSENTIALS OF THE BRIARD: Without ever appearing coarse, the Briard combines strength of muscle and sturdiness of bone with free movement and agility; the general appearance is rugged, supple, muscular and well proportioned. Intelligent in expression, the eyes are bright and wide open, and must always appear dark. The skull is slightly round and slightly longer than wide. Muzzle is square and strong, never tending towards snipiness. Neck is of good length, strong, arched and muscular. Shoulders, well angulated and laid back. Chest, broad and well let down, with medium spring of rib. The back is firm and level. The coat is coarse, dry, and hard, providing complete protection from the elements. The Briard comes in black, various grays, and tawny, with deeper shades preferred and white seriously discouraged. In height he stands from 22–27 inches (56–68.5 cm) at the withers. Ideal weight is 75 pounds (34 kg). The tail is long, well covered with hair, with upward hook at its tip.

Brick

Nose coloration on a light-colored Shar-Pei.

Brick-shaped head

A lengthy, rectangular head; equal skull and muzzle widths (e.g., American Pit Bull Terrier).

Bridle

The collection of ropes gathered with a ring to which the towline is attached.

Brindle

A color pattern existing in varying extremes, dark to light, which is effected by darker hairs forming bands and producing a striping on a background of lighter colored hairs, usually yellow, tan, or brown. The Boston Terrier, Tennessee Treeing Brindle, and Greyhound are but a few breeds in which brindles occur. Brindles are also described by color, i.e., blue brindle and red brindle. In their native land, Basenjis also come in brindle.

Briquet

See Chien d'Artois

Briquet Griffon Vendeen
See Griffon Vendeen

Brisket
Most often used to refer to the breastbone or sternum, but sometimes referring to the chest area in general.

Bristle coat
Short, piglike coat, referring to the Shar-Pei. Bristly coats sometimes simply denote wire or broken coats. *See also* Wire coat

British Bulldog
See Bulldog

Brittany
A truly unique gundog possessing both setterlike and spaniellike characteristics. Until 1982 the breed was referred to as Brittany Spaniel by the A.K.C. In its manner of working, however, the breed functions more like a setter. Though in size it is smaller than the typical setter, it is also leggier than the average spaniel. From what basic stock then does the Brittany stem?

Hunting accounts and illustrations dating back to the 1700s depict the Breton (or Brittany) Spaniel. This Brittany, however, is not the Brittany of today. The modern Brittany begins his history at the start of the 1900s, when one Arthur

Enaud devised a breeding program to rejuvenate the old Breton, which at that time was waning into obscurity. The old dog was physically and temperamentally suited to his native habitat—rough and thicketed country.

In 1896, the first Brittany Spaniel graced a show ring in France, under the working-name "Short-tailed Brittany." The Club de l'Epagneul Bretagne formed in 1907 and drafted the first standard. In 1931, the breed found its way to the States; it was granted A.K.C. recognition three years later; the American national parent club, the American Brittany Club, was formed in 1942.

Today's Brittany is greatly suited for the show ring yet still remains a versatile hunter of good pointing and retrieving ability. The all-around abilities of the Brittany make it a gundog in the most European sense. While the breed was once deemed a spaniel (the U.K.C. still refers to it as the Brittany Spaniel), it is a dog of superior pointing abilities, more a pointer than a flusher. The decision to "flush" the "Spaniel" from the breed name was surely justified, since "Brittany" says it all and does it all!

Brittany, orange and white. Photo by I. Français.

ESSENTIALS OF THE BRITTANY: The deep chest, short but strong loin, broad hindquarters, and sloping forequarters are all essential qualities for this active and energetic canine. The tail, if existent, is customarily docked to 4 inches (10 cm) and carried level; there should be a small twist of hair on the tip. The coat, which is fairly fine but dense, lies flat or slightly wavy; excessive feathering to be penalized. Color: orange and white, liver and white, black and white, roan, or any of these colors in a tricolor pattern; ticking is allowed. The nose is dark and its pigmentation corresponds to the coat color (is in harmony with it). Height: 17.5–20.5 inches (47–50 cm). Weight: 28–33 pounds (13–15 kg).

Brittany Spaniel
See Brittany

Broad in skull
Reference to the length of skull between the set-on of the ears. A dog who is broad in skull is said to possess a goodly mass for the breed, a desired trait in some standards, a fault in others.

Broad jump
In obedience trials, four separate hurdles painted white, built to telescope for convenience, largest measuring five feet (150 cm) wide and seven inches (17.5 cm) high. Spaced so as to cover a distance equal to not less than two-and-a-half times the height of the dog at the withers, except that the maximum shall be no more than six feet (180 cm). This applies to all breeds save those excepted in the high jumps, which are limited to twice the height of the withers. In removing hurdles, the highest is removed first.

Broke down
When a contestant in a dog race pulls up suddenly, indicating internal or external injury, it is said that he "broke down."

Broken coat
A crinkly wire coat, most often applied to terriers. A broken coat is comprised of a harsh outer coat and a dense, soft undercoat. The Stichelhaar or German Brokencoated Pointer has a coat which is 1.5 inches (3–3.5 cm) in length, hard and bristly and lying close to the body. At full length, such a coat can resemble coconut matting. In the Jack Russell Terrier, the broken-coated variety is slightly different than the wire.

Broken color
A solid-colored coat which is interrupted by patches of a different color. Ofttimes, white coats with darker colored spots.

Broken-down pasterns
See Down in pastern

Broken ears
Malformed or badly shaped ears cited as a fault in many breed standards. Broken or broken-down ears are commonly incurred by injury or as a result of abnormal construction of the ear cartilage.

Broken-up face

Face type describing brachycephalic breeds in which the face is "interrupted" by the exaggeration of the features: the pronounced stop, folds in the skin, pug nose, and undershot jaw (e.g., Bulldog).

Bronchitis

Inflammation of the mucus lining in the respiratory tract, the windpipe or trachea, and lungs. Dampness and cold are usually responsible, and the symptoms usually follow a chill or may be present with cases of pneumonia or distemper. Symptoms are a nagging dry cough, fever, quickened pulse rate, runny nose, perhaps vomiting, and congested nasal passages which must be kept open. Old dogs are particularly affected. It is a highly transmissible disease, and isolation from other animals is important. Antibiotics are often prescribed.

Brood bitch

See Bitch, Pregnancy

Brown nose

A nose that is colored brown, acceptable in a number of breeds (e.g., German Shorthaired Pointer, Sussex Spaniel), sometimes depending on the coat color of the specific dog. A brown nose on a chocolate Labrador Retriever is acceptable, whereas the same nose on a black Labrador would be an egregious fault.

Brows

Formed by the frontal bone contours above the eyes, these ridges or superciliary arches are considered part of the forehead and vary in prominence from breed to breed. To exemplify extremes in prominence, the Dogue de Bordeaux's brows are most prominent while the Collie's are very slightly prominent. The brows are also key to the expression of a number of breeds. A flewy mastiff's brows impart a pendulous air while the Sussex Spaniel's loose brows make his expression frown.

Brucella canis

See Canine brucellosis

Bruises

This common injury to man occurs less so in dogs. A bruise is bleeding be-

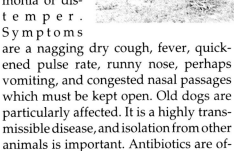

Broad jump being executed by a Chesapeake Bay Retriever. Photo by R. Reagan.

Broken coat exhibited by a Jack Russell Terrier.

neath the skin, the result of broken blood vessels. A bruise close to the surface is usually visible as a typically reddish to brownish discoloration, fading to yellowish as the injury heals. However, a dog's coat may make such observation difficult. With deeper bruises, such as those of internal organs, visible signs other than unusual behavior, etc., may not be present. Minor bruises are not serious concerns—they heal. Serious bruises, which include some surface bruises, can be dangerous to the point of resulting in death. A bruised muscle, especially the heart muscle, requires special care. If your dog takes a bad knock, whether it is by a car, a club, or a fist, it is best to seek veterinary counsel. Ice can be used to ease the swelling and control the spread of the bruise, but aspirin should not be given, as it thins the blood, thus counteracting coagulation (which seals the rupture to stop the flow of blood).

Bruno Jura Laufhund, black/tan. Photo by I. Français.

Bruno de Jura
See Bruno Jura Laufhund

Bruno Jura Laufhund
The Bruno Jura Laufhund represents the type of Swiss laufhund that developed in the Jura area of Switzerland. These dogs are very similar to the French hounds, from whom they likely descend. The broad head with heavier wrinkles differentiates the Jura from the other laufhund breeds. Their coats, many occurring originally in smooths and wires, are free of white markings. The Bruno Jura Laufhund's oversized ears and skull size, hallmarks of this native Swissy, point to the St. Hubert-type hounds common in Belgium. It has a reputation as a finder of game and hunter of unstinting energy; hare, fox and small deer are among its quarry. *See also* Saint Hubert Jura Laufhund

ESSENTIALS OF THE BRUNO JURA LAUFHUND: Ambling close to the ground, the Jura Hound is an elongated, robust mountain dweller. He stands from 17–23 inches (43–59 cm) high and weighs from 33–44 pounds (15–20 kg). His short coat is most commonly seen in a classic black/tan or saddled pattern, but it can also occur in solid bronze, yellow or red. He is not as heavily boned or exaggerated as the St. Hubert variety.

Brush
1) Any bristle-type grooming tool.

2) A bushy, average length tail or the relatively short fur covering some tails. The Tahltan Bear Dog flails a unique tail; its flaglike tail, ever so prominent, is perhaps the epitome of the brush.

3) In gait, brush can refer to the fore and hindlegs touching one another at the inside; this is unnatural and undesirable movement.

Brush coat
The coarse coat of the Shar-Pei longer than the horse coat—approximately three-quarters inch in length.

Brussels Griffon
The Brussels Griffon, while today a proper and beloved toy dog, was once renowned for his expert destruction of rats and other roaming rodentia. Griffon d'Ecurie or Stable Griffon was his name. This griffon "brusselled" in Belgium as a patrol dog for urban cabbies—a cap the monkeylike passenger donned with style. These original griffons looked more like terriers than they presently do. This is not surprising, considering that various terriers were used in their creation. The Affenpinscher was likely the instrumental stock to the early griffon's composition. In the 1800s, the English Toy Spaniel was used to diminish the size and shorten the snout. As the breed

gained in popularity, Barbets, Smoushonds, Yorkshire Terriers, and Pekingese were likely used to fine-tune desired type.

All three griffons of Belgium, including the Belgian Griffon and smooth-coated Petit Brabançon, were at one time considered one and the same breed. Of course, today the A.K.C. and the K.C.G.B. register all three breeds as Brussels Griffon or Griffon Bruxellois, respectively.

Like the Affenpinscher, whose popularity has never reached the level of the Brussels, the breed has never been on the top of the A.K.C. hit parade. The Brussels sports a tough mug and is a "toy" in size alone. The breed's rough-and-tumble personality wins it lifetime admirers, if its less-than-pretty-boy face does not. In the U.S., the Brussels's ears are cropped and the tail is docked to about one-third. These mini-terriers are not inclined to their traditional chores, though they are most amenable to more gentlemanly activities: swimming, backpacking, and hiking for starters.

ESSENTIALS OF THE BRUSSELS GRIFFON: This red-coated griffon of Belgium has a long wiry coat of harsh rough hairs. His color is called "clear red." Brussels Griffons are squarely and solidly built dogs who weigh between 6–12 pounds (2.5–5.5 kg) and stand 7–8 inches (18–20 cm) high. They move with a free gait and push off with a good drive. The well-balanced body is short backed, with well-sprung ribs and a strong loin. The chest rather wide and deep, legs straight and medium in length. The head is large, compared to body, rounded and not domed, wide between ears. The ears are semi-erect, high set; smallness is desired. *See also* Petit Brabaçon, Belgian Griffon.

Buck
An object used for training or practice as a substitute for a bird; it is also called a retrieving buck.

Buhund
Norwegian for homestead dog. *See* Norwegian Buhund

Bulging eyes
A severe degree of protruding eyes. Bulging eyes can be caused by simple overly large eyeballs or excessively small sockets or may even be related to a hyperthyroid condition or glaucoma.

Bull Terrier, white.

Bull Terrier, colored.

success at the show and slaughter in the pits. These two goals the Bull Terrier achieved. They are among the most refined of showmen and the most relentless of gladiators in the rat pits. In fact, the Bull Terrier has had a double history. It holds records for the most rats killed in minutes, hours, and other time parameters, and yet it quickly became the stylish breed of the English gentleman. Known also as the "White Cavalier," these dogs were bred by gentlemen for gentlemen, to protect and serve unto the death yet never to instigate a quarrel.

In the 1860s, fanciers concluded that all white would be the color of this "new" and most fashionable breed. James Hinks then quickly created an all white specimen that became the prototype of the breed for several years. Culling the piebald pups and breeding white dogs to white bitches led Hinks to creating his pure white coat. Some writers have suggested that Hinks also incorporated the Dalmatian in his quest for a reliable solid white dog. The complications in physical type that would have resulted from these crosses, however, make such possibilities most unlikely. Today, the breed is recognized in two color varieties: all white, and colored (any color other than white or any color with white markings).

Contrary to the original concept of breeding the bull-and-terrier dogs,

Bull-and-terrier

Dogs created in the nineteenth century from agile mastiff-types and game terriers for the purpose of the rat and fight pits. Extant forms today include the American Pit Bull Terrier, Bulldog, Bull Terrier, and the Staffordshire terriers.

Bull Terrier

In the 1850s, after years of experimentation, James Hinks of Birmingham, England, thrust upon the world a new bull-and-terrier dog, one who further removed some of the undesirable traits of the then existing Bulldog (the roach back, the over-angulated legs, and the undershot jaw). The Bull Terrier was originally created in large part from crosses of bullbaiting bulldogs and the now extinct English White Terrier, possibly with later crossings to the Spanish Pointer to add size. These dogs were designed with a dual nature in mind:

Hinks concentrated on appearance and not fighting ability; a handsome gladiator who cannot hold his sword and shield ably is soon a dead gladiator. When Hinks was challenged that his dogs were incompetent pit contenders, he matched his 40-pound bitch Puss of Brum against the never wary Mr. Tupper's 60-pound bull-and-terrier cross. Not only did Puss emerge victorious from the bloody bout but she hurried to the Holborn dog show later that day where she won a red ribbon for the jubilant Hinks. Although this story is contested by serious cynologists and others with little faith in chivalry and romance, the authors have seen judges make equally dubious choices in the conformation ring. The real question is: Just which judge did Mr. Hinks know on that victorious day?

Easily trained, fearless, and clean, the Bull Terrier makes an excellent companion and guard for the small home or apartment.

ESSENTIALS OF THE BULL TERRIER: Fearless and energetic yet kind and well mannered, the Bull Terrier is symmetrical, strongly built and muscular. The head is long, strong, deep, not coarse; with well-sunken small dark eyes, clean lips, and a level or scissors bite. The ears are small, thin, and close together. The neck is long, muscular, arched, and clean. The body is well rounded, with a noticeable spring to the rib. The legs should be big boned but in balance with the body. The forelegs should be perfectly straight. The tail should be short, set on low, fine, and ideally carried at the horizontal. Height: 21–22 inches (53–56 cm). Weight: 52–62 pounds (24–28 kg). The coat to be short, flat, harsh to the touch, and with a fine gloss; the skin to fit tightly. The Bull Terrier can be white or colored. On the white dogs, markings on the head are the only

ones permissible; any other markings are severely faulted in the show ring. The colored Bull Terrier can be any color other than white or any color with white markings. Blue eyes are a disqualification in both color varieties.

Bullbaiting
See Animal baiting

Bulldog
Centuries ago, the probable crossing of the Old English Mastiff and feisty terrier types produced a dog with the courage, strength and tenacity to successfully combat a furious bull. These dogs, fast, fearless, and powerful, were the foundation stock of today's Bulldog breed. The sport of bullbaiting originated in Britain during the thirteenth century, though animal baiting was practiced at least from the Roman era. The sport rose quickly to feverish heights, and the dogs of the sport, born on the British Isles, became the pride of the English people. Fanciers of the sport and of the dogs took no account of the beauty, type, or grace of the dogs. These dogs were bred to be able savages nearly insensitive to pain. In 1835, bullbaiting was made illegal, and the existence of the able-bodied bulldogs

Bulldog, lemon and white.

was threatened. Lovers of the breed then stepped in and attempted to preserve the breed. Today, though he retains the name, the Bulldog is a much changed bulldog. *See* Animal baiting

Of all the dogs sharing the old bull-baiter ancestry which have survived, the Bulldog is likely the breed that has changed the most in outward appearance and type. First distinguishable as a breed in the early 1700s, the forefather Bulldogs entered the show ring in the 1860s. From that time onward, the Bulldog was bred for a new type, always more eccentric, at least temporarily culminating in the breed as we know it today. It was just shortly after the sport of bullbaiting had waned under legal pres-

ham, and London no doubt, was well populated with early Bulldogs. Nottingham Frank, a blue pied dog weighing 18 pounds (8 kg) was renowned in the area in the mid-1850s; he was bred by the ever-smirking Mr. Smedly in 1853.

While the Bulldog of today is not particularly noted for his speed and agility, he is celebrated for his rolling gait. The breed has been selectively bred for this action, which its fanciers do not find abnormal, though admittedly peculiar. The standard asks for a gait that is unrestrained, free and vigorous; it is loose-jointed shuffling and sidewise moving. Coincidentally, the Bulldog has not been deemed particularly quick in its mental agility either. Stonehenge as early as 1887

Bulldog, fawn.

sures that the Pug was incorporated into the bloodlines to alter the pit dog's appearance. The dogs which strutted their smug Pug faces in the show rings of the 1850s and 60s did indeed reveal this Pug ancestry. Dogs were said to have weighed as little as 20 pounds (9 kg).

Nottingham, like Sheffield, Birming-

described the breed's intellectual prowess thusly:

"F. Cuvier has asserted that this dog has a brain smaller in proportion than any other of his congeners, and in this way accounts for his assumed want of sagacity. But though his authority is deservedly high, I must beg leave to doubt the fact as well as the inference; for if the brain is weighed with the body of the dog from which it is taken, it will be found to be relatively above the average, the mistake arising from the evident disproportion between the brain and the skull. . . . I was able to obtain the fresh brain of a pure bulldog for the purpose of comparison in 1879, and from an examination have no doubt of the fact being as above stated. The mental qualities of the bulldog may be highly cultivated, and in brute courage and unyielding tenacity of purpose he stands unrivalled among quadrupeds, and, with the single exception of the game-cock, he has perhaps no parallel in these respects in the brute creation."

Nonetheless, and with all due respect to Mr. Walsh, the Bulldog is indeed one of humanity's most unique and exquisite of canine types. Despite the dogs' laid-back approach to life, these are determined and undeniably charming dogs, the gold rim around the proudest Briton's highly-held teacup, the tightest pucker of his stiffest upper lip.

ESSENTIALS OF THE BULLDOG: A thick-set, heavy, low-slung body of medium size, with a smooth coat, wide shoulders and sturdy limbs. The general appearance of the Bulldog should suggest great stability, vigor, and strength. The breed moves with a distinctive style and carriage, giving a characteristic "roll." Of considerable importance are proportion and symmetry, both to be harmonious. The skin should be soft and loose, especially at the head, neck and shoulders; the head and face to be covered with heavy wrinkles, with two loose pendulous folds that form a dewlap from the jaw to the chest. The skull to be very large, and its circumference should measure at least that of the height of the dog; the head should appear high and be short from the point

of the nose to the occiput. The cheeks well rounded; eyes to be set low down in the skull and as far from the ears as possible; ears are set high and are termed "rose-eared" in shape; the ears should never be cropped. Nose to be large, broad and black; flews should be thick, broad, pendant, and very deep, completely over-

hanging the lower jaw at each side. Neck short and thick. Shoulders heavy, wide

Bulldog, chestnut and white. Photo by I. Français.

Bulldog, brindle and white. Photo by J. Ashbey.

spread, slanting outward, and strongly muscular. Chest deep, with ribs well rounded. Back short and strong, very broad at the shoulders and comparatively narrow at the loins. Forelegs short, stout, and muscular. Hindlegs strong, muscular, and slightly longer than forelegs. The tail may be straight or screw but never curled or curly. Height: 12–14 inches (31–36 cm). Weight: 40–50 pounds (19–25 kg). Coat color may be: various brindles (commonly red) and white and pied (white with any of the various brindles); dudley, black and black with tan are highly undesirable.

Bullenbeisser

German term for bull biter. *See also* Animal baiting

Bullet wounds

All bullet wounds, even grazes, should be treated by a veterinarian. The lead content of many bullets, as well as the possibility of internal bruises from even slight grazes, makes all such injuries serious matters for concern.

Bullmastiff, fawn. Photo courtesy of Adele Pfenninger.

Bullmastiff

Of truly utilitarian birth, the Bullmastiff was created to hunt down, overtake, and immobilize a man upon command. Not bred to maul or kill, the breed possessed the strength, courage and wisdom to combat an armed intruder, if necessary, and to hold a man at all costs until the master arrived. During the 1800s, estates suffered extensive pillaging of their livestock and game. The raiders were known as poachers, and it was a direct result of their theft that the ferocious bulldogs were bred to the Herculean mastiffs to produce the Bullmastiff, a breed then commonly known as the "Gamekeeper's Night Dog." The original crosses led to a 60-percent mastiff to 40-percent bulldog breed type. Poaching was punishable by death, and one can imagine the desperate struggles that must have resulted from the fear of being caught in the act. The Bullmastiff, with his strength, speed, and determination, was awesome at estate policing. These original dogs were less refined than today's dogs who possess definite type.

In modern times, the Bullmastiff is principally employed as a watchdog and companion for the families that adopt him. These are large watchdogs with a distinctive appearance and a giving and high-spirited temperament. Like many other dogs developed for a specific purpose in a limited region, the Bullmastiff has done well to extend its numbers throughout the world. The breed is accepted by the A.K.C. and K.C.G.B., representing the two most influential national registries, and has substantial, active fancies in Sri Lanka, India, Cambodia, France, Germany, Italy, Denmark, Canada, Mexico and several of the South American countries.

The Bullmastiff, though a big dog with a dark history, is a loving dog that you can trust with your person and your property. Ever watchful and always enduring, his spirited ways delight the owner. Fanciers are strongly advised to seek a dedicated breeder with proven stock. These are ideal dogs with children and seldom bark without cause; their excitability is minimal, making for a pleasant, easy-to-live-with and reliable watchdog. Docility is often associated with the breed, but its

broad and muscular, denoting power. Height: 24–27 inches (61–69 cm). Weight: 110–130 pounds (50–59 kg). The coat is short and dense and provides good weather protection. Color possibilities include: fawn, brindle, or red, with a black mask common.

Bull neck

A neck characterized by any or all of the following: power, shortness, coarseness, thickness, musculation, and masculinity. A crest often accentuates.

high spirited personality can be never less than friendly and never more than wary.

ESSENTIALS OF THE BULLMASTIFF: A symmetrical dog, powerfully built but active. The foundation stock of the breed was 60% Mastiff and 40% Bulldog. Great strength, endurance, and alertness are apparent in the breed's overall appearance. The head is large and square, with a fair amount of wrinkle; the forehead flat; the muzzle short (in ratio to the skull as one is to three), broad, and nearly without taper; a dark muzzle is preferred, as is a level bite, though slightly undershot allowed. Neck slightly arched and nearly equal to the head in circumference. Body compact, with a wide, deep chest, not loaded and slightly sloping shoulders, and a short back that gives the appearance of a well-balanced dog. Hindquarters

Bumping

Flushing a bird which should have been located and pointed. Bumping also refers to the swing a dog takes in quartering his territory.

Burmese wild dog

Similar to the Indian wild dog, this canid is more strongly built than the Malay wild dog. This wild dog may still be found in Burma.

Burns

Burns are frightening experiences for both you and your dog. A dog can easily go into shock and suffer convulsions from a burn. For all but the most minor burns, veterinary care is recommended. For minor thermal burns, cooling the affected area with a substance such as ice can ease the pain as well as the severity of the injury. Caustic and acid burns require special attention. Besides seeking medical attention, the affecting chemical must be removed from the dog as soon as possible. For most substances, other than oil-based ones, a thorough flushing with water is in order; for oil-based substances, vegetable oil can be used to flush the area. Get help as soon as possible.

Burr

An unnatural cartilagenous growth on the interior of the external ear canal.

Burrow

The underground home of small animals, such as rabbits.

Bursitis

Similar to rheumatism and arthritis, bursitis is the inflammation of the capsule, called the bursa, in which a joint moves. *See* Rheumatoid arthritis, Arthritis

Burst

Any fast part of a run, generally the first part of a foxhunting expedition. When a fox is killed in a "burst," the hounds have burst him.

Bus travel

See Traveling with your dog

Bush dog

A wild dog of South America. In appearance more like an otter or badger, the bush dog, *Speothos venaticus*, is found from eastern Panama to southwestern Brazil, from the east coast of Brazil to the Andean Cordillera, preferring a tropical environment and meals ranging from small animals to large river-dwelling rodents and deer. Indefatigable, bush dogs hunt in packs of up to a dozen members, are avid swimmers and divers with notable underwater mobility, and reportedly demonstrate potential tameability. Lengthy and low set, the bush dog stands about 12 inches (30 cm) at the shoulder but is 25 to 27 inches (62.5–67.5 cm) long, excluding the about 12-inch tail. The coat is coarse and not dense, making it of little value to furriers. The bush dog is rare, largely because its preferred domain, savannah and forest with close proximity to water, is quickly being destroyed by the forever march of man. A den dweller that communicates by chirping, whistling, and clicking noises, the bush dog's wild behavior remains unknown and largely unstudied.

Butterfly nose

A nose that appears spotted, that is, speckled by unpigmented areas. Butterfly noses are common on a number of harlequin or merle-colored dogs (e.g., Cardigan Welsh Corgi, Great Dane), but are consid-

Butterfly nose acceptable on the blue merle Cardigan Welsh Corgi. Photo by I. Français.

ered faults in some breed standards. Adolescent dogs (and puppies) tend to have partially pigmented noses that will usually fill out in time. Judges are more lenient on such dogs in light of their immaturity.

Buttocks

The musculature that surrounds the pelvis's ischiatic tubers; the rear portion of the upper thigh.

Button ears

Semi-erect ears distinguished by the upper portion folding forward toward the eye and the lower part remaining upright. Resultingly the orifice of the external ear canal cannot be fully seen. *See also* Semi-drop ears ·

Buying the board

Refers to the action of a bettor purchasing all combinations, in quiniela or daily double wagering.

Bye

In a stake of a field trial that contains an uneven number of dogs, the dog whose name is drawn last is called the "bye" and runs alone, unless the judges choose a brace-mate for him.

Byelorussian Ovtcharka

See East European Shepherd

Buttocks. The impressive, tight musculature of a Staffordshire Bull Terrier.

Buttocks. A hind view of a callipygous young Cocker. Photo by S. Miller.

Ca

Spanish dialect for dog. The Perro de Pastor Mallorquin is known as the Ca de Bestiar; the Perro de Presa Mallorquin, the Ca de Bou; and the Ibizan Hound, the Ca Eivissencs in their native Spain.

Ca de Bestiar
See Perro de Pastor Mallorquin

Ca de Bou
See Perro de Presa Mallorquin

Ca Eivissencs
See Ibizan Hound

Cairn Terrier, sandy. Photo by I. Français.

Cabriole front
See Fiddle front

Caesarean section
An operation performed to deliver puppies, which are unable to pass through the cervix and be delivered normally. Caesarean sections are performed most often when a pup is too large, presented in breech position, or for some other reason cannot be passed; when a bitch is long overdue for delivery and she is in danger; or when the bitch dies for any reason and the pups can be rescued. The procedure is major surgery, and the bitch and pups are both at risk.

Caffeine
A stimulant that affects the heart muscle directly. It has several beneficial uses to dogs with specific conditions. It should only be given, in any form, under the advice and supervision of a professional. See also Heart

Cage dryer
A drying device which attaches to the cage so that a dog may be dried in the cage. See also Grooming

Cairn Terrier
Said to resemble the original Highland Terrier, today's Cairn Terrier is the general stock from which arose the Scottish Terrier, Skye Terrier, Clydesdale Terrier (a no-longer seen silky version of the Skye) and West Highland White Terrier. The Highland Terrier lived to exterminate vermin: badgers, otters, foxes, setting the example for all his descendants. The Cairn Terrier is called such because of his smaller size and the ability it gave him to sniggle into cairns, the small openings in stone grave markers. Bishop of Ross, John Lesley, writes of the Cairn Terrier's ancestors in his Historie of Scotland from 1436 to 1561, published in 1830, "a dog of low height which, creeping in subterranean burrows, routs out foxes, badgers, martens and wild cats from their lurking-places and dens."

Recognized by the Kennel Club of Great Britain in 1910, the Cairn has become one of Britain's most popular terriers and ranks in the top ten British breeds. Its rise to fame was not an effortless one. Until the Cairn made its way into the show ring, it was virtually unheard of outside its home circles. Efforts were made to categorize the dogs as "Short Haired Skye Terriers," since Skyes were already firmly established by this time. Nonetheless, the breed's gay personality and competitive size make it a choice terrier and pet.

ESSENTIALS OF THE CAIRN TERRIER: The skull is broad with a noticeable indentation between the eyes. Jaws and muzzle strong. Ears are small and pointed, erect, not too closely set. Forelegs should not be out at elbow. Legs are covered with hard hair. Body is compact, with a straight, medium-length back, and well-sprung deep ribs. Strong hindquarters. Coat is double with profuse hard outer coat. The undercoat is short, soft and close. Head well furnished. Foxlike facial expression. Tail, undocked, short, well furnished not feathery, gay carriage. Height: 9–12 inches (23–30.5 cm). Weight: 13–16 pounds (6–7.5 kg). Colors include red, sandy, gray, brindle or nearly black. Muzzle and ears typically dark pointed. A.K.C. allows for any color except white.

Calamine lotion

Mostly zinc (98%), this is a heavy metal substance to which dogs are sensitive and which must be used only under professional recommendation.

Calcaneus

Point of hock. The uppermost point of the large fibular tarsal bone in the hock or ankle joint.

Calcium

A metallic element necessary for good bone structure as well as other healthful conditions. It must be received in appropriate amounts (approximately .6% of the dietary intake coupled with .4% phosphorus and adequate amounts of vitamin A and D which are necessary for absorption and assimilation). Excessive calcium intake does not lead to big bones but only to complications. A depletion of calcium can result from either a lack of intake or an inability to absorb calcium.

Calculator

One who calculates winning wagers in mutuel betting.

Calculi, urinary

See Urine

Calculus

An abnormal stony mass in the body. Tartar accumulations, the most common problem with dogs' teeth. *See also* Dental care, Periodontitis, Nylon bones, Tartar

Calorie

A small calorie is the amount of heat needed to raise one gram of water one degree centigrade. A large calorie is the amount of heat needed to raise one kilogram of water one degree centigrade; often used in measuring the energy of food.

Cairn Terrier, brindle.

Camel back

See Back types

Cameroons Dog

A lanky, prick-eared, shortcoated hunting dog of Africa. Of medium size, the Cameroons Dog can be any color, either pied or variegated.

Canaan Dog

Legend has it that a Canaan Dog was tied to the dais of Queen Jezebel by a golden chain. The Canaan Dog is the national dog of Israel and has been known in the Middle East for centuries. He is of pariah origin, although many communities of non-wild (semi-) Canaans have existed in the Negev Desert and have been employed by the Bedouins and other nomadic tribes as herders and sentry dogs. The breed is believed to

Canaan Dog, red brown and white. Photographs by I. Français.

Canaan Dog,
sandy.

have descended from two different Israeli strains of pariahs. Before the efforts of dog people, the dogs were roaming the Canaan area in a feral state, much like the dingoes of Australia or the Singing Dogs of New Guinea. Various types of pariahs range from Iran and India to South Asia, into Japan and, of course, Australia.

Dr. Rudolphina Menzel of Israel, the dog person chiefly responsible for the salvation and stabilization of the breed, studied the strains in the 1930s. Menzel's observations and efforts led to the establishment of a standard. She noted that the dogs in their feral state ranged in appearance from a larger, double-coated flock-

guard type dog to a smaller rather sighthoundy looking dog (similar to the Small Podengos). Antonius, a fellow cynologist, participated in much exhaustive research as well and was chiefly responsible for locating the sheepdoglike pariah in Asia Minor and Egypt.

The American Kennel Club accepted the Canaan Dog into its Miscellaneous Class in 1989. The breed is versatile and intelligent, having proven itself in police, assistance, and Red Cross work. A non-aggressive but resourceful watchdog, the Canaan Dog is a protective and companionable dog.

ESSENTIALS OF THE CANAAN DOG: A medium-sized, notably delicate dog, well proportioned and of a general spitz type. The head is blunt and wedged, the skull slightly rounded. The body is strong with a straight topline and is tautly muscled throughout. The coat is medium short, harsh and straight; the tail is bushy and curled over the back. Colors include sandy to red brown, white and black. Dark and white masks are acceptable. Gray and black/tan are frowned upon. Height: 19–24 inches (48–61). Weight: 35–55 pounds (16–25 kg). A sharp, fast trot is characteristic of the breed.

Canadian Eskimo Dog
See Eskimo Dog

Canadian Kennel Club
The Canadian Kennel Club (C.K.C.) is the national registry of Canada. Prior to the American Kennel Club's 1884 inception, twenty years of dog shows were locally run in Canada. The C.K.C. was formed in 1888, just four years later. The Canadian registry recognizes American judges, just as Canadian judges are able to function in the U.S. Also shared are most of the American regulations, a similar judging system and most breed standards. The organization sponsors over 1,200 dog events annually, including

Canaan Dog,
white and black.
Photographs by I.
Français.

championship exhibition shows, field trials and tracking events. The Canadian Kennel Club is responsible to the national government for the registering of pedigreed animals. Laws prohibit the selling of purebred puppies without properly registering the litter with the C.K.C. Dogs are identified by tattoo or nose print. The Club divides its purebreds into the six groups: Sporting, Hound, Terrier, Working, Non-Sporting, and Toy; in addition to a Miscellaneous Class. Not all dogs are categorized exactly as the A.K.C. delineates and no Herding Group exists in Canada. The breeds which the A.K.C. groups as Herding are shown in the Working Group.

Canary Dog
See Perro de Presa Canario

Cancer
Cancer by definition is the state of uncontrolled cell reproduction, forming a malignant tumor that destroys beneficial tissue locally or by metastasis. Unlike the cells of the dog that compose his organs and other body parts, cancer cells are not checked in their growth. They will continue to grow at a rapid rate, eventually destroying the organism that allows for their life. Normal cells are stopped in their growth; when the liver reaches full size, its cells stop reproducing except to replace lost cells.

Non-cancerous tumors are called benign; they are typically slow growing in comparison to the malignant tumors; they rarely metastasize; and they rarely recur after their removal. Benign tumors often do not present a threat to life; malignant tumors are most always life-threatening and deserve immediate medical attention.

There is no one cause for the disease as a whole, and dogs are at high risk of contracting many forms of cancer. Common in dogs are skin, bone, testicular, ovarian, mammary, and lymphatic cancers, and the causative factors are often as varied as the forms of cancer themselves. Hormones, worms, environment, virus and many other factors have been shown to cause or at least contribute to cancer in the dog.

Ovarian cancer is one of the greatest killers of non-spayed bitches, with mammary cancer adding considerably to the numbers, while testicular cancer slays many male dogs; studies suggest that hormonal production is the prevailing factor in these types of cancer. Studies also have shown that other forms of cancer are more common in "whole" dogs of both sexes than in neutered dogs of the

same breeds, especially males of the species. Such studies suggest that hormones and hormonal production are contributing factors to a variety of cancers.

Stress resulting from weight has been blamed for the incidence of bone cancer among the giant breeds, and sunlight has been shown to cause various forms of skin cancer in man and dog. Lymphosarcoma is the most common lymphatic tumor in the dog, and its cause remains inconclusive. Air pollution, insecticides, preservatives, mental stress and numerous other factors have all been shown to increase a dog's likelihood of contracting cancer of one form or another.

Fortunately for dogs, there are treatments available, including chemotherapy, to which dogs tend to respond better

Canadian Kennel Club. A remarkable and intelligent Canadian hunter, the Nova Scotia Duck Tolling Retriever is recognized in its native Canada as well as internationally. Photo by I. Français.

than do humans. Of course, the best treatment is prevention: proper feeding, healthful accommodations, neutering if feasible, and regular check-ups all help reduce the dog's likelihood of contracting cancer.

Cancer. Many medical studies have suggested that the Boxer is one of the most prone to cancer. Other breeds particularly susceptible include the Great Dane, Irish Wolfhound, and Doberman Pinscher.

One of the keys to treatment is early diagnosis. All dogs should be inspected at least once monthly, older dogs twice, by their owners. The seven signs which the owner should be aware of are the same as those of humans as established by the American Cancer Society: 1) Change in bowel or bladder habits 2) A sore that does not heal 3) Unusual bleeding or discharge 4) Thickening or lump in breast or elsewhere 5) Indigestion or difficulty in swallowing 6) Obvious change in wart or mole 7) Nagging cough or hoarseness. Lameness, joint inflammation and pain, as well as other physical abnormalities, are all worthy of investigation as possible signs of cancer. Oral tumors are common in older dogs, and all owners must be certain to check the animal's mouth when conducting their routine cancer check. Proper diagnosis involves laboratory testing of the removed tumor or a portion of it, known as biopsy, which *see*.

Candle flame ears
British term for erect and prominent flame-shaped ears sported solely by the Toy Manchester Terrier.

Cane
Italian for dog. The Maremma Sheepdog is known as the Cane da Pastore Maremmano-Abruzzese, the Bergamasco as the Cane da Pastore Bergamasco, and the Volpino Italiano as the Cane de Quirinale in their native Italy.

Cane Corso
See Sicilian Branchiero

Cane da Pastore Bergamasco
See Bergamasco

Cane da Pastore dell' Italia Centrale
See Maremma Sheepdog

Cane da Pastore Maremmano-Abruzzese
See Maremma Sheepdog

Cane di Macellaio
See Sicilian Branchiero

Caniche
See Poodle

Canidae
The family of animals which includes domestic and wild dogs, wolves, dingoes, jackals, and foxes.

Canine
A sharp-pointed tooth located next to the incisor teeth; the dog has four canine teeth, two upper and two lower; also known as fangs.

Canine adenovirus 1
(CAV1) The virus responsible for infectious canine hepatitis. The virus is capable of surviving outside the host for weeks or months, where it can be contracted by dogs and other animals. *See* Hepatitis, canine.

Canine adenovirus 2
(CAV2) Related to canine adenovirus 1, this virus is the cause of infectious canine tracheobronchitis, or kennel cough, which *see*.

Canine behavior

Wagging tails, lapping tongues, pointing paws, ground-scratching hindfeet, growls, grunts, and grimaces: Why does my dog do that? Canine behavior and instincts are equally complicated and fascinating. Determining the intelligence of our canine comrades is dependent on sensory abilities, physique and the nature and extent of an individual dog's experience. The amount of stimulation that a dog receives also contributes to the degree of its intelligence. Poodles are usually considered the most intelligent of all dogs; whether Poodles are smarter due to the size of their skulls and "brain room," as some studies purport, or because Poodles tend to be people-dogs, and therefore over-stimulated, is not to be exacted. Many canine behaviorists habitually compare the dog's intelligence to the cat's and man's. It is virtually impossible to prove that a dog is more intelligent than a cat: cat fanciers assert that their cats are too smart to succumb to the foolish requests and "commands" of their owners. Dogs do fulfill most any request or command directed to them. Intelligence and trainability, however, should not be confused. The Aristotelian notion that only man can *reason* differentiates man from dog; while dog can learn and remember, it cannot rationalize to make a decision. ("If I run around the yard in the morning, I may escape the afternoon rain.") Dogs have proven to be among the most trainable of all domesticated animals. Gorillas, horses and chimpanzees join the ranks as most trainable. Cats are certainly less trainable, or at least less conducive to training. Compared to hermit crabs, gerbils and tropical fish, cats rate exceedingly well.

Canine capabilities, greatly dependent on instincts or hereditary aptitude, vary from breed to breed, and even dog to dog. The ability of the pointing breeds

to point, retrievers to retrieve, and herders to gather cooperative or uncooperative objects together illustrate the various capabilities of canines. Most breeds possess a hereditary aptitude for their inbred task. Herders more instinctively take to maneuvering sheep than could a Bedlington Terrier. Certain breeds can be taught to do practically anything. Bed-

lingtons could be taught to herd sheep though they would do it with less natural skill and grace than would a Border Collie. The Bedlington, incidentally, might get very mixed up in the woolly crowd

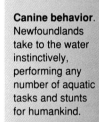

Canine behavior. Newfoundlands take to the water instinctively, performing any number of aquatic tasks and stunts for humankind.

Canine behavior. Man has done well to channel the talents and physical abilities of dog. A mass of woolly cords, the Komondor bonds and blends with its sheeply charges. Photographs by R. Pearcy.

too. American Pit Bull Terriers, Australian Shepherds and German Shepherds have reputations of outstanding trainability, practically capable of competing with the specialists in any given field.

Canine capability is closely associated with the species's greatly developed senses. While dogs' eyes are not as keen as man's (excluding a few hawkeyed sighthounds), they are exceedingly better at night. The shape of the dog's skull affects its vision as well: the long-nosed sighthounds possess a binocular vision of about 70 degrees, the brachycephalic, short-nosed breeds (bulldogs, pugs) have about 80 percent binocular vision. Hearing in a dog is probably twice as good as in man. Again, the placement of the ears on the head affects their abilities. Man's ears, on the side of his skull, are able to determine only vague sound directions. The dog's ears are set high on its head, and its mobile ear pinnas are ideally constructed for the precise location of sound. They may be pointed in the same or separate directions. The ultra-

sonic dog whistle (which to man is silent) demonstrates a dog's ability to perceive frequencies inaudible to man. A dog's olfactory senses exceed that of humans' by

40 times. The number of olfactory cells in the dog's nose is about 200 million, in man there are only five million. Of course, the scenthounds have the keenest of all canine noses: the Bloodhound and Otterhound lift their nose to all other dogs. *See* Nose. The canine gustatory and tactile senses are secondary to the former three. Dogs, we believe, can taste food, not that much tasting is involved when an energetic dog bolts his food. The sense of touch, likewise, is restricted. Dogs experience tactile sensations on their hard pads and through their coats. These are generally less relevant to their instincts and abilities. *See also* Senses. Let it be said, however, that most dogs love to be petted.

Communication is another important aspect of canine behavior. Body postures, facial expressions, vocalization, exchanges of odors and body gestures comprise the various ways which dogs communicate. Man's primary mode of communication is speech; in dogs, however, it is difficult to surmise how effective auditory communication actually is. Canine vocalization can be divided into four categories: whimpers, growls, barks and howls. Just as a human baby cries to communicate, so too a dog vocalizes—often the owner (or parent) must rationalize the "speaker's" intention.

Puppies particularly mew and whine to indicate stress: general discomfort, hunger, coldness, or pain. Older dogs express their distress through whines, whimpers and yelps.

Growls indicate a dog's antagonistic intentions. A growl is a dog's way of posing a threat, submitting a warning, and giving its protagonist a chance to back off or withdraw his provocation.

Barking, of course, is the most frequent form of vocal communication among dogs. The pariah-derivative dogs, such as the Basenji, do not bark as such but instead vocalize in a yodel or howl. Dogs bark for many reasons: alerting their owner, expressing excitement, announcing an alarm, and convincing their listener are just some of these reasons. Just as men have different tones of voice, dogs' barks range from ferocious and blood-chilling to inquisitive and charming. Of all dogs, perhaps, the Finnish Spitz has the most widely acclaimed bark. In Finland the breed is called the Barking Bird Dog, and his barking talents are regularly demonstrated in the show ring. This tradition has been cautiously transferred to American show rings. Other breed fanciers (who apparently do not equally revel in their dog's voices) are fearful of what the outcome of 20 Finskies vocalizing would inspire from the hundreds of other dogs in the ring. (What a beautiful display of dogdom—how often dog show people forget that their prized champions are but *dogs*.)

Howling, the last manifestation of vocal expression, is less common in domestic dogs than in their wolf ancestors. There are notable, resonant exceptions: the nordic dogs tend to howl more frequently, as do a number of the scenthounds. Coonhounds and Beagles are inspiringly vocal on the moving trail.

Howling is surely a communal affair, rather like a good ol' American sing-a-long (without Mitch).

The olfactory is also a very important means of communication in dogs. Urination, vaginal secretions, feces, anal gland secretions, saliva and other bodily secretions are potential sources of communicative scents. Of these, urine is seemingly the most important. Dogs urinate for various reasons besides the obvious necessary elimination: demarcation of territory, attraction of a mate, creating signature-bearing landmarks, etc. Males, more so than females, urinate with a will. The male's well-guided stream, clearing his

Canine behavior. Finnish Spitzen stand quietly in the ring.

Canine behavior. Members of the mastiff and bulldog breeds have been bred for fearlessness and strength. A convincing and virile American Bulldog.

lifted leg, onto a vertical tree, hydrant or post is indicative of its prominent place in canine society. While many dogs are ambipedal (will lift either leg), others prefer a particular leg.

Canine behavior. Doberman Pinschers, bred for guard work, require more time to train for sled work than do traditional draft dogs—plus they don't have snowshoes.

Social behavior in the dog encompasses interaction with other canines, sociability with non-canines (humans, cats, canaries, etc.), reproductive strategies, hunting methods, and participation in the rearing of young. While many dogs are naturally aggressive towards other dogs, some dogs are very docile and submissive. Canine aggressiveness can

be to varying ends: possession, confidence, reinforcement of an initiative, or simply bluffing. Terriers, for instance, are instinctively straightforward in their encounters with other dogs. These assertive excavators are traditionally sparred in the show ring for their "gameness." The American Pit Bull Terrier, of course, has the market well "cornered" in the area of gameness. Other dogs, with strong guard instincts, demonstrate profound intolerance of another canine's trespassing on their territory. The mastiff breeds and similarly aggressive flock guardian breeds have the strongest such instincts. Defending their masters is another typical instinct of such boisterous personalities (hence, these breeds usually make great watchdogs). Territorial bouts may break out in kennels, but usually these are not vindictive struggles to the other's end. The hound breeds, accustomed to pack life, tend to be more docile and gregarious towards their fellow canines. These dogs also acknowledge the superiority of a given dog as pack leader.

Over the years, dogs have excelled as workers and hunting companions over various terrains and weather conditions. In the United States and England today, however, the vast majority of dogs are kept as family pets. The most popular of domestic dogs kept as pets have adapted well to life with humans. A family environment has proven to be conducive to well-rounded dogs and people. Educa-

Canine behavior. Female Shiba clearly disinterested in the advances of her suitor. Threat displays often are means of bluffing and flirting. Photo by I. Français.

Canine behavior. Cattle dogs instinctively take to livestock. Golden Retrievers, however, exposed to the family cow, may soon learn to herd and heel high and even low (i.e., *moo*).

tional studies show that children who have been raised with a dog learn many valuable lessons in responsibility, care and social awareness. Dogs have learned to function as companions, watchdogs, guardians, babysitters, and playmates. Additionally, properly acclimated and trained dogs tend to do well with other family animals. Certain dogs, often regardless of breed, do not like cats. Terriers and bull-and-terrier breeds perhaps demonstrate the most poignant distaste for the feline.

The hunting strategies of dogs are communal like that of their wild dog ancestors. Such strategies are greatly respective of existing food conditions. Reproductive strategies function similarly. Wolves hunt in packs and pair off into a dominant/subordinate relationship. Both parents participate in the rearing of the young. Domestic dog does not adhere consistently to the patterns set by wolves. Since behavior is greatly influenced by both instinct and environment, domestic dog lives in more varied environments than any other domestic animal. For this reason, such patterns are irregular from breed to breed, dog to dog,

country to country, village to village, etc.

Dogs that live in a pack environment will tend to be rather cloned, while dogs that live in a one- or two-dog home tend to develop personalities "doggedly"

Canine behavior. An obedient and versatile Rottweiler retrieving in the water.

their own. Purebred dogs can be described generally by breed. Breed standards indicate the "desired temperament"—such as gay, fearless, sporting, affectionate, chary with strangers, reserved or extroverted. Such adjectives, generally true as are horoscopes for humans perhaps, cannot purport to pinpoint the exact qualities of every member of a given breed. Just as an aloof Saluki is considered usual, many Saluki owners attest that their dogs are happy-go-lucky and affectionate. *See also* Training, Behavior modification, Senses, Puppies

Canine brucellosis

One of the very few venereal diseases contracted by dogs, this bacterial infection is spread by contact with genital discharges and saliva. It is one cause of abortion in females and sterility in males. Aborted puppies typically are dead or weak, with few surviving. It isn't curable.

Canine distemper

See Distemper

Canine ehrlichosis

A truly troubling disease, canine ehrlichosis is endemic in many sections of the U.S.A. and occurs throughout the world. The common transmitter of the disease is the seemingly ever-abundant brown dog tick. Blood transfusions are a second way of transmission. Anorexia, depression, and loss of vitality are possible signs. Clinical diagnosis is necessary, with lesions occurring non-specifically, discolored lungs common, and widespread

hemorrhaging occurring in acute cases. The disease can be fatal.

Canine heartworm infections
See Heartworm

Canine hepatitis
See Hepatitis, canine

Canine hospitals
As medicine and the quality of care advance , so too does the number of canine-specific medical establishments. Hospitals and clinics dedicated to the treatment of animals can be found throughout the United States, where there are over 5,000, as well as in Britain, Canada and Australia. These facilities are equipped with boarding kennels and staffed by veterinary professionals. Some hospitals offer an ambulance service as well. *See also* Clinics

Canine infectious tracheobronchitis
Inflammation of the trachea and bronchial tubes, also known as kennel cough, which *see*.

Canine malignant lymphoma
A progressive, typically fatal disease of dogs, characterized by abnormal proliferation of cells of the lymphoid organs (lymphosarcoma) or bone marrow (lymphocytic leukemia), usually resulting in their becoming solid, and thereby malfunctional. The signs of the disease are variable, depending largely on the organs affected. There remains no known cause or cure, but it is not believed to be transmittable, and judiciously applied chemotherapy has proven helpful in treating the disease. *See also* Cancer

Canine parainfluenza
(CPI) A virus which can cause what is commonly known as kennel cough, which *see*.

Canine parvovirus
See Parvovirus

Canine pemphigus
Known also as pemphigus vulgaris, this autoimmune disease, although uncommon, can be fatal if not treated. Pemphigus is characterized by lesions on various parts of the body, commonly the mouth, anus, penis, vulva, nail beds, and around the nose. Because of the dog's relatively thin epidermal layer, these lesions can spread rapidly, especially because of the susceptibility of secondary infection. The disease is treatable in many cases.

Canine reovirus
A virus capable of causing respiratory disease in dogs.

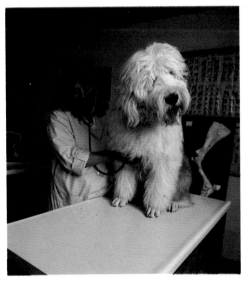

Canine rheumatoid arthritis
See Rheumatoid arthritis

Canine typhus
See Leptospirosis

Canis adustus
The side-striped jackal. *See* Jackals

Canis aureus
The golden jackal. *See* Jackals

Canis familiaris
Canis familiaris is the scientific name for domestic dog. Domestic dog, that is all purebred an l mixed-breed dogs not wild or feral, represents the most varied animal species in existence. Cynologists speculate that there are nearly 800 specific dog breeds in existence. These dogs range from three inches to 40 inches high at the shoulder; from one to 200+ pounds in weight.

Canis hallstromi
See New Guinea Singing Dog

Canine hospitals are well staffed with competent veterinarians and animal specialists. Photo by R. Pearcy.

Canis latrans
A wild dog native to North America which is commonly called the coyote, which *see*.

Canis lupis
The gray wolf. *See* Wolves

Canis mesomelas
The black-backed jackal. *See* Jackals

Canis rufus
The red wolf. *See* Wolves

Canker
A bacterial infection of the ear in which the ear may drain, have a dreadful odor, and ooze a dark brown substance all the way out to the ear flap. Causes of canker can be mites, dirt, excessive hair growth in the ear canal, wax, etc. A daily cleaning and administering of antifungal ointment or powder are in order until the condition is cured. Symptoms are the dog's shaking his head, scratching his ear and holding the head to the side. See your veterinarian for specific instructions prior to treatment.

Canned dog food
See Feeding

Cannibalism
Cannibalism in dogs is most rare. The tragic occurrence that a bitch should kill and devour her litter is generally what is referred to as cannibalism among dogs. There are no documented cases of adult

dogs fighting to the death, and the winner dining over the fallen dog. Cannibalism in a number of wild species is more common: females killing their litters or even males doing so.

Rodents driven by stress or other circumstance may slay and devour their young. In dog, a domesticated animal, however, cannibalism cannot be aptly explained by stress. It is conceivable that certain wild canines may exhibit a degree of cannibalism, but even this is largely unsubstantiated. Dangerfield and Howell set forth the following curious, unexplained example of domesticated canine cannibalism: "A Gordon Setter, which was known to have devoured two previous litters, whelped a third time. She was watched closely until the puppies were four weeks old and the weaning process had begun. Yet the bitch devoured the entire litter during one night." Some breeders attest that such behavior is due to a hereditary imbalance or more succinctly to insanity. Others believe that the imbalance is related to the bitch's diet. The psychology of dogs is difficult to draw conclusions on—regardless, the Gordon Setter bitch, whether bereft of reason or bran, did not whelp a fourth time.

Cannon bone
Pastern or metacarpus. More commonly used in equine terminology.

Cannonballing
Generally applied to dogs' staging a desperate surge near the end of a race, where they drive through a field of contestants in a somewhat reckless manner.

Canter
Less regular in step than the walk, the canter is essentially a slow gallop.

Cão
Portuguese for dog.

Cão da Serra da Estrela
See Estrela Mountain Dog

Cão da Serra de Aires
A mid-sized, shaggy herder indigenous to the southern plains of Portugal. The breed reportedly has worked the

flocks of his native land for generations. An all-purpose dog of herding and droving abilities, the breed doubles as a guardian as it works its clutches, whether

it be equine, ovine, bovine, porcine or other. The breed is particularly adept at the retrieval of flock stragglers. Portuguese owners relate that these "monkey dogs"—as they are called in their native land—have been a part of the farming operation and family life for as long as they can remember. Although he appears similar to the Berger des Pyrenees of France and the Catalan Sheepdog of Spain, no reliable evidence is forwarded to suggest a reliable descent. These dogs are reliable and clever and make outstanding working dogs. Though they do well at an exclusively outdoors life, they do enjoy a cozy couch, blanket, or rug and always reciprocate a kind hand with a loving look.

ESSENTIALS OF THE CÃO DA SERRA DE AIRES: A surly but efficiently built herder known for its quickness and cleverness. The dog is of moderate size and may range in weight from 26–40 pounds (12–18 kg). The skull is broad between the ears and strong; muzzle of fair length, square with only slight taper. Eyes are dark. Ears are set high and hang straight to the skull. Back of good length; croup rounded. Set high on strong legs. Feet are particularly adaptable to rough terrain. In color this dog comes in shades of fawn, gray, wolf, black, brown, and yellow.

Particolor and white are frowned upon. The coat is long and given to waviness. The hair is longer on the head, giving the dog bangs and a wiry muzzle. Height:

16–22 inches (40.5–56 cm). Ears are sometimes cropped. Tail is left full length, reaching to hocks.

Cão de Agua
See Portuguese Water Dog

Cão de Castro Laboreiro
The Cão de Castro Laboreiro, also known as the Portuguese Cattle Dog, is an all-weather guardian of flocks and herds in Portugal. The Cão necessarily had to be tough enough to combat wolves and other fearless predators, and as such,

Cão da Serra de Aires, gray.

Cão de Castro Laboreiro, brindle. Photographs by I. Français.

Cão de Fila de S. Miguel, brindle. Original illustration by AnnMarie Freda.

had to be equally (and more) dauntless. Although he is not well known in the English-speaking world, he is popular in Portugal where he has recently begun a career in conformation. His voice is unique in producing musicality of a different sort: an octave-climbing, chromatic vocalization makes him an effective and even entertaining watchdog. Nevertheless, these dogs are work dogs who thrive on hard daily routines. Their dedication to their work and their master is proverbial.

ESSENTIALS OF THE CÃO DE CASTRO LABOREIRO: Muscles are densely packed, giving him a well-built overall appearance. In height he is greater than his length. Despite his concentrated and slightly elongated appearance, he is exceedingly quick and mobile. Height: 21–25 inches (53–63.5 cm). Weight: 50–75 pounds (23–34 kg). Coat: short, harsh, and waterproof. Color: various shades, most commonly gray to black-gray.

Cão de Fila
See Fila Brasileiro

Cão de Fila de S. Miguel
The recent creation of Portuguese cattle farmers, this breed, also known as the Açores or Azores Cattle Dog, has links to an ancient breed of Portuguese cow herder. Presently recognized by the national registry of Portugal, the Cão de Fila de S. Miguel works on the S. Miguel

Island of the Azores and is reportedly used extensively for cattle herding. Its color is always brindle; size is medium with a massive head and ears cropped to rounded tips. Height: 19–24 inches (48–60 cm). Its temperament is described as strong, and it is a reliable watchdog. Only a few specimens have yet been exported from the S. Miguel Island.

Cap
The color pattern which extends down towards the eyes and around the skull. The cap, darkly colored, meets a lighter colored face and thereby forms a widow's peak. The Siberian Husky and Alaskan Malamute possess caps.

Cape
An extension of the neck ruff, this profuse hair growth shawls the dog's shoulder region. The Schipperke sports such a cape.

Cape fox
A wild dog and a member of the genus *Vulpes*. *See* Foxes

Car travel
See Traveling with your dog

Carbohydrates
Combining six parts of carbon dioxide with five parts of water to make starch, all carbohydrates come from plants. Dogs cannot digest starch well without its first being cooked—or partially digested by another animal, usually a prey. Dogs require balanced amounts of carbohydrates, including starch and its converted substances, to maintain good health. Quality dog foods will provide this, and they usually supply nutritional information that includes the carbohydrate amount either on the can or bag or through written information. *See also* Feeding, Nutrition.

Carcinoma
Any of several kinds of cancer composed of epithelial cells (cells that consist of one or more layers and have very little intercellular space). *See* Cancer.

Cardiac diseases
See Heart problems

Cardiac failure

The heart may stop pumping for any number of reasons, commonly because of surgery, shock, or old age; in all cases, it is known simply as cardiac failure or cardiac arrest. If a veterinarian or other professional is close at hand, the heart may be stimulated through chemicals and/or artificial respiration; otherwise a knowledgeable layman may be able to perform artifical respiration *which see. See also* Heart, Heart problems

Cardigan Welsh Corgi

A smallish, low-set heeling herder of ancient origin that has puzzled cynologists and opened the history of this distinctive Welsh breed to conjecture. There are two known Corgi breeds: the Cardigan and the Pembroke. For years the two were held as distinct varieties; today they are fervently defended as separate breeds by their fanciers. Theories continuously emerge regarding the age of one or the other breed, many attempting to prove the greater antiquity of one dog over the other: it is often stated that the Cardi is the older Corgi, arriving in Wales with the Celts circa 1200 B.C., and the Pembroke landed not until the tenth century A.D. (The earliest known reference to these herders dates 920 A.D.) While these dates may be accurate, it is thought that the two dogs trace to similar ancestral stock and developed parallel in time, distanced geographically, accounting for their similar yet unique breed characteristics.

The Corgi's natural calling is the driving of livestock, a task accomplished by nipping at the animals' heels, spurring their movement and direction. This nipping quality gives him the label of heeling dog. The breed has changed little over its long history, with the exception of some refinement for the show ring and temper-

ing for the pet home; he retains his fine working ability and is still found working cattle, horses and other livestock, especially in his native Wales. They are

active and loving companions: truly the big dog in the small package. He is gentle and amicable with family and friends.

ESSENTIALS OF THE CARDIGAN WELSH CORGI: A low-set frame that is long in proportion to height. In general appearance he is sturdy and tough, capable of excellent mobility and endurance. The

head is foxy in shape and appearance, skull wide and flat between the ears,

Cardigan Welsh Corgi, brindle and white.

Cardigan Welsh Corgis, blue merle and white, tricolor. Photographs by I. Français.

tapering toward the eyes, above which it is slightly domed. Moderate stop. Length

Cardigan Welsh Corgi, red and white.

Carolina Dogs, gold. Photo by S. Etherington.

of foreface in proportion to head as three is to five. Eyes rather widely set with corners clearly defined. Ears erect, large but proportionate to size of dog; tips slightly rounded; base moderately wide. Shoulders well laid and sloping. Legs short but body well clear of ground. Feet turned slightly outwards. He is an all-weather dog, thanks much to his dense double coat: harsh outer, soft and thick inner. The overall coat appearance is smooth. The legs must be short and slightly bowed for best utility in his herding field. Height: 10.5–12.5 inches (27–32

cm). Weight: 25–38 pounds (11.5–17.5 kg). In addition to possessing the foxlike brush tail, which his cousin the Pembroke does not, the Cardigan is considerably heavier and longer. Lack of balance and oversize or undersize are severely discouraged.

Caries

A pathological change causing destruction of the enamel on teeth and subsequent invasion of the dentine; in other words, a cavity in a tooth. This may result in bad breath, toothache, digestive disorder, etc., depending upon the severity. Cavities in dogs are rare, though we hear more and more of false teeth being made for dogs and occasionally even root canal work for show dogs. *See also* Dental care, Periodontitis, Cavities

Carinthian Brandlbracke
See Austrian Brandlbracke

Carlin
See Pug

Carlin à Poil Longue
Bred from the Pug, this longhaired variety of that breed was once known in France. *See* Pug

Carnassial teeth
Consist of the four premolars of the lower jaw and the first molars of the upper jaw.

Carnivorous animals
Animals which are strictly meat eaters are known as carnivores. Dogs, once thought of as being carnivorous, are actually omnivorous, which *see*; they eat and require both animal (meat) and vegetable (plant) substances. *See also* Animals, classes of; Feeding; Nutrition

Carolina Dog
The Carolina Dog comes out of the American Deep South and is of an ancient pariah type which greatly resembles the larger sized Dingo. A number of such pariah types existed in the United States. Many of these dogs were favored by Indians and used for various tasks, herding for one. The Kentucky Shell Heap Dog and the Basketmaker

Dog are examples of ancient pariahs on the North American continent. Aptly nicknamed "Old Yaller," the Carolina Dog has proven adaptable to domestic life despite its strong flight instinct and general uneasiness with humankind. Free-roaming dogs can still be found in parts of South Carolina, where they are studied and captured by ecologists, including noted authority Dr. I. Lehr Brisbin, Jr. These scientists strive to learn more about these unique canines, their relation with the dingo and other pariahs

as well as their role in the development of modern American breeds.

ESSENTIALS OF THE CAROLINA DOG: A lightly constructed pariah-type dog with pointed ears; long, arched neck; wedge-shaped muzzle and a smallish head. The chest is well developed, and the coat, short and dense, is yellowish gold. Height: 22 inches (56 cm). Weight: 30–40 pounds (13.5–18 kg).

Carpal joint
Wrist, carpus. On the front leg, the joint connecting the forearm and the pastern.

Carpathian Sheepdog
See Rumanian Sheepdog

Carre's disease
See Distemper

Carrot-shaped tail
A short tail that is wide at the base and tapers to a point. This tail is typically carried erect.

Cars
See Automobiles

Cart training
When there is no snow, training sled dogs with a three- or four-wheel cart is known as cart training. Carts also are used in racing in warm climates that do not have snow. *See also* Draft dogs, Sled dogs

Cast
The search a bird dog makes in any one general direction without an abrupt turn.

Cast off
The releasing of a dog at the start of a hunt or beginning of the contest between the two dogs of a brace at a trial.

Castor oil
A typically fast-acting and effective cathartic, or laxative, castor oil is sometimes given to constipated dogs. It is best to contact your veterinarian first.

Castration
A decision facing a great number of dog owners every day is whether or not they should have their male castrated, or neutered. Common castration involves minor surgery in which the testicles are removed, often with the sac in which they are contained. There are many arguments for and against castration, and the more popular of these are presented here.
Fanciers in favor of castration cite that castrated males will be less inclined to wander, that the male's common practice of marking his territory with urine will be curbed, that dogs otherwise given to

Cart training is a popular method of training sled dogs off-season. Siberian Huskies preparing for the race.

viciousness will be mellowed, and that, with so many euthanized unwanted or lost dogs, castration is the responsible action for anyone not wishing to breed dogs. It is also claimed that a dog will not "miss" his sex drive, especially if the operation is performed prior to the dog's completion of his first year of life, though conclusively supporting this claim is nearly impossible.

Cat bites. Though smaller than most dogs, cats are well endowed with sharp teeth and claws to taunt, teach and tatter the family mutt.

Those in opposition to castration cite as their major arguments that it is unhealthy, unnatural, and detrimental to a dog's performance. The "unnatural" argument is easy to understand. There are many people—some dog fanciers included—who believe that nature should take her course. They are not without justification, as nature is an effective and efficient process. The claims that it is unhealthy, as well as detrimental, to performance rest on the similar basis of the dog's chemistry altered as a result of his missing testicles. Indeed, the chemistry is changed, if for no other reason than the necessary drop in the testosterone

level, a chemical produced primarily by the testes. Supporters of castration claim no change in either a dog's health or performance, but those in opposition have a rational concern.

Whatever your stand on castration, it is a consideration that should be confronted by every dog owner. The decision should rest largely on the individual circumstances and not on individual preference. Both positions have their support; it is recommended that the dog owner discuss the castration procedure and effects with a veterinarian prior to making this important decision. There are many concerned groups that offer assistance and advice, and there are some that can refer the owner to sources or provide free or inexpensive operations.

Castro Laboreiro Sheepdog
See Cão de Castro Laboreiro

Cat bites
"They fight like cats and dogs": The eternally believed antagonism between cat and dog perhaps tips our tongue among all animal relationship citations. Today the relationship is most commonly a jealous one, the dog resentful of any affection bestowed upon his feline housemate. Other antagonisms stem from both the dog's chase and play instincts—instincts that present themselves quite differently in cats. For whatever cause, the effect of a cat bite is often with serious consequences. Cat bites tend to cause infection in dogs, and it is necessary to keep the wound both open and clean until no further signs of infection are present. Cat-bite infections that form under sealed skin can abscess, causing considerable pain, as well as large affected tissue areas. Prompt veterinary consultation is strongly advised.

Cat feet
Round, close-cupped, compact, and circular describe the dog's feet known as cat feet. They appear, as does a feline's, close together with the center toes extending a hair longer than the outer two. The Boxer and Sussex Spaniel are but two of the many dogs that have cat feet.

Catahoula Cur
See Catahoula Leopard Dog

Catahoula Hog Dog
See Catahoula Leopard Dog

Catahoula Leopard Dog
A definitive livestock worker who originated in the American South and specializes in the rounding up of wild, unruly pigs and cattle. The breed is known for its fearlessness and aggression; it is believed by some to represent old crosses of Spanish dogs of war brought by the explorers with native Indian dogs, with the likelihood of hound infusion evidenced in the dog's drop ears and willingness to tree and trail. The State of Louisiana is cited as the point of origin, particularly the area of Catahoula, the parish of which the breed is the namesake. For the right owner, this is a protective yet dominating canine. He is a hard-working, dedicated dog of remarkable dexterity and courage.

ESSENTIALS OF THE CATAHOULA LEOPARD DOG: A hardy stock dog, exceptionally tough and fearless. An aggressive and hard heeler, unquestionably suited for working rough stock. Head large but in proportion to body; skull broad between the ears and flat; cheeks strong but not prominent; muzzle very strong, never snipy. Chest, reaching to the elbows, is deep, allowing for good heart and lung capacity. Back is level, long and strong. Legs of strong solid bone and taut muscle. Tail is set high, level to the back, and is carried down, reaching to the hocks. Coat is short and dense and colored in a merle or black/tan pattern. Height: 20–26 inches (51–66 cm).

Weight: 40–50 pounds (18–23 kg). Color is an especially notable feature: eye color and coat color working in a very complementary and expressive way.

Catalan Sheepdog
Historically, the Gos d'Atura Catalan is a versatile dog who satisfies numerous chores in his native Catalonia, a region on the Mediterranean in the northeastern corner of Spain. The Catalan Sheepdog performs well as a herder of sheep and cattle, a police dog, and a messenger dog in times of war. The breed is native to Spain, but his region of origin was settled by French who crossed the border from the Pyrenees region. There are two varieties of the Catalan Sheepdog; both are well

Catahoula Leopard Dog.

Catalan Sheepdog, fawn. Photographs by I. Français.

suited to work either sheep or cattle, and they are renowned for their horse-working ability. The longhaired type is known as the Gos d'Atura Catalan, and the short-coated variety is known as the Gos d'Atura Cerda; in Castilian the two varieties are called Perro de Pastor Catalan de pelo largo and Perro de Pastor Catalan de pelo corto, respectively. Their natural guardian instincts combined with their ability to herd make these dogs capable of handling a flock by themselves.

Catalan Sheepdog performs exceptionally as a cattle dog. Photo by I. Français.

His disposition and handy size suit him ideally as a house dog and companion. He is fierce, unafraid and effective as a herder—owners are not recommended to pamper and spoil this dog, for his natural instincts must remain part of his personality. As a working companion he is a more well-rounded and even-tempered dog.

ESSENTIALS OF THE CATALAN SHEEPDOG: The head is large but in definite proportion to body; skull should be well formed and strong; distinct stop; strong muzzle with level topline. The ears are set high and sometimes cropped to stand erect. The breed is memorable for its whimsical flowing beard and mustache. Height: 18–20 inches (46–51 cm). Weight: 40 pounds (18 kg). The coat is usually lengthy and wavy, although a rare short-coated variety exists. In color the Catalan can be fawn with black tips, black, black/tan, grizzle or brindle.

Catalog

A book which all show-giving clubs are required to publish and which shows the particulars on every dog entered at the show, prizes offered, the scale of championship points awarded at that show, and other data pertinent to the event at hand.

Cataracts

Common in old dogs, as they are in old humans, cataracts are an eye disorder in which the lens of the eye, an otherwise crystalline component, is affected with a whitish opaque quality. Cataracts can cause partial or total blindness. Surgical removal is possible in some cases.

Catch dog

A dog used to catch and hold a hunted animal in order for the hunter to capture it alive.

Cattle dogs

Farmers developed dogs for their purposes. Cattle and hog farmers could not rely on the small, less aggressive sheep and turkey dogs to maneuver their unruly herds. Therefore, a cattle dog needed to be aggressive, sizable and intelligent. Farmers and butchers as well had use for these dogs. Butchers needed dogs to help manipulate their herds through the streets on their way to market. The dog's speed and agility were as important as its intelligence. In order to move a particularly stubborn cow, a dog would have to determine the right foot to "heel" or bite. If the dog were to bite the foot on which the animal's weight did not rest, it could be instantaneously kicked and probably killed. These dogs necessarily had to be quick—of mind and body. Farmers docked the tails of their cattle dogs probably for the safety of the dog, to prevent the hogs or cows from grabbing on to the dog. Among the world's breeds that perform this type of work are the Old English Sheepdog, Australian Cattle Dog, Australian Kelpie, the English Shepherd of the U.S., the Stumpy-Tail Cattle Dog of Australia, Lancashire Heeler of Great Britain, and the Bouvier des Flandres of Belgium. Although used less frequently as cattle dogs today, the Welsh Corgis are competent working

heelers and drivers. Some of the more versatile sheep herders are also capable of cattle droving: the Border Collie and the Australian Shepherd (of the U.S.) are exceptional examples of this kind of herding prowess.

Cattle dogs. Rottweilers are rarely used today for cattle droving, the task for which they were originally bred.

Cattle dogs. A quick-thinking and swift heeler, the Australian Shepherd.

Caucasian Ovtcharka

The Caucasian Ovtcharka is but one of the ovtcharkas that are found throughout the Soviet Union, Turkey, and Iran. Primarily these are working dogs that vary

Caucasian Ovtcharka, dark fawn.

greatly in type. Unlike dogs that are bred for "purity" or to adhere to a given written standard, the Caucasian Ovtcharka is bred for function first and appearance second (if at all). The most uniform specimens exist in the Georgian Republic of the U.S.S.R. Dogs which have escaped exportation bans are working in East and West Germany as guard dogs. The Germans, who have always been enamored of the pure as well as the powerful, perhaps compromise in their employment of the Russian ovtcharkas. These are strong-willed, strong-bodied dogs that can be trained for guard duties but are often frightfully unmanageable. No home has yet reported happily housing the ovtcharkas as strictly pets yet.

ESSENTIALS OF THE CAUCASIAN OVTCHARKA: This very Russian canine is quite a large dog, usually standing between 25–28 inches (63.5–71 cm) tall. Weight: 105–145 pounds (46–65.5 kg). Contributing to its massive appearance is the profuse medium-long coat. There is heavy feathering and a bushy tail on these dogs as well. The weather-resistant coat is especially effective at keeping out the cold. In its native country, the Ovtcharka's ears are cropped short, which gives the dog a soberingly wolfike appearance. Never bred specifically for color, the breed varies in gray, fawn, tan, pied, brindle, and white. The F.C.I. prohibits brown dogs.

Caucasian Sheepdog

See Caucasian Ovtcharka

Caudal vertebrae

Tail vertebrae. Coccygeal vertebrae.

Caucasian Ovtcharka, brindle. Photographs by I. Français.

Cavalier King Charles Spaniel

The Cavalier King Charles Spaniel is the result of man's trying to recapture a piece of history, immortalized on canvas. The long-nosed type of King Charles Spaniels to be spied in the paintings of Van Dyck and Hogarth and other seventeenth- and eighteenth-century painters clearly illustrate these old Blenheim Spaniels. In the 1920s, an inquisitive American named Roswell Eldridge queried into the existence of the "Blenheim Spaniels of the Old Type." So acute was his curiosity and so earnest his desire to "preserve" the type that he offered £25 for spaniels representing the "Old Type" at Crufts, England's most prestigious dog show.

Working toward the breed's current level of popularity (in England, the breed is among the top ten!), Mrs. Hewett Pitt is recognized as the first lady of the Cavalier. A dog by the name of "Ann's Son" owned by Miss Mostyn-Walker is the first "long-nosed" specimen of note.

The breed gained Kennel Club status in 1944 and has enjoyed continually growing recognition. The 1960s saw the breed in the arms of British royalty; Princess Margaret's affection for the breed boosted the Cav's popularity in Great Britain. Despite the breed's tremendous popularity in the United Kingdom, American fanciers haven't achieved more than Miscellaneous Class recogni-

Cavalier King Charles Spaniel, Prince Charles (tricolor).

Cavalier King Charles Spaniel, ruby.

tion for the Cav in the U.S. However, the English Toy Spaniel (King Charles Spaniel), a close relative of like size and origin has been recognized in the U.S. since the year 1959.

Cavalier King Charles Spaniel, black/tan.

ESSENTIALS OF THE CAVALIER KING CHARLES SPANIEL: The highly important head is almost flat between the ears; the stop is shallow; the muzzle is well tapered. The eyes are noticeably large, dark, and round, but should never be too promi-

nent. The body is short-coupled, with good spring of rib and a level back. Legs of moderate bone, well-turned stifle. The feet compact and cushioned, well feathered. Height: 12–13 inches (30–33 cm). Weight: 10–18 pounds (4.5–8.5 kg). The coat is long, silky and free from curl. He should be free of trimming and have plenteous feathering. Colors: black/tan, ruby (solid red), Blenheim (red/white), and Prince Charles (tricolor).

Cavities

Rarely occurring in dogs, cavities affecting teeth require veterinary care and the affected teeth will likely need to be removed. Prevention involves a sound diet and free access to quality chew products at all times.

C.C.

Abbreviation for Challenge Certificates, which *see*.

C.D.

Companion Dog; this suffix signifies that the dog has completed three tests in the Novice A or B classes of obedience trials under at least two judges, and with at least six dogs in competition: has made scores of 170 or better out of the possible 200, and in each instance has received at least 50 percent of the allowable score for each individual exercise.

Cavalier King Charles Spaniels, Blenheim (red/white).

C.D.X.

Companion Dog Excellent; this suffix signifies that the dog, after first acquiring the C.D. degree, has completed three tests in the Open A or Open B classes of obedience trials, under at least two judges, and with six dogs in competition, has made scores of 170 or better out of the possible 200, and in each case has received at least 50 percent of the value of each individual exercise.

Cellulitis

Inflammation of the loose subcutaneous tissue of the body. A general condition which can be symptomatic of several other conditions or diseases.

Cemeteries for dogs

The role of dogs in human society is unlike that of any other domesticated animal, with the possible exception of cats. Funerals for dogs, of course, are no new concept. It is believed that the pharaohs of Egypt included their favorite sighthound in their burial plans and that some Oriental toy dogs were chosen to accompany the Emperor into the great beyond. The largest funeral for a dog ever held was hosted by a pseudo-monarch, and over 10,000 mourners attended this mongrel's "royal" send-off.

Today there are professional canine funeral chapels that provide a number of unique services to dog owners, including a variety of caskets, head stones, embalming or restoration, and burial. While this may be an excessive gesture on the part of the bereaved household, such a formal good-bye may help with the mourning process.

Cerdocyon thous

See Forest fox

Cereals

Made of such products as corn, oats, rice, wheat, soybeans, and barley, cereals are sometimes given to canines that re-quire supplementing in a given area of their diet, especially carbohydrates, in which many cereals are high. Various cereals can be purchased or made, following the directions on component packages or recipes of various sources.

Cerebellar hypoplasia

A leading cause of seizures in canines, this brain disorder is a developmental defect in that the cerebellum forms incorrectly, causing such symptoms as uncoordination, irregular behavior, and involuntary actions. Brain tumors are likely present, and it is usually best to have the affected animal euthanized.

Cerebellum

Composed of three lobes and located behind and below the cerebrum, this part of the brain is known as the muscle control center, for it is believed to coordinate muscular movement.

Cerebrum

The upper and primary part of the brain of vertebrate animals. It is composed of two approximately equal-sized parts, left and right, believed to control the opposite side of the body to which they are located as well as the voluntary and conscious behavior and process.

C.E.R.F.

The Canine Eye Registration Foundation is an organization specializing in registered dogs whose eyes have been thoroughly tested for problems.

Certificate

A mutuel ticket, or receipt. In the early days of dog racing, betting was illegal and tickets sold were claimed to represent stock certificates in the track's earnings, interests in earnings of the dogs rights to enter claims for dogs, seat reservations, and many other variations of mutuel wagering.

C.D.X. degree was earned by this multi-titled Weimaraner: this is Ch. Eb's Glory Be of Skytop, C.D.X., U.D., T.D. Owner, Helen Remaley.

Cervix

Although it can be any necklike part, possibly of the urinary bladder, it is usually used in reference to the "stem" of the female's uterus, through which offspring must pass in normal delivery. The cervix is at the bottom of the uterus and extends to the vagina. *See also* Breeding, Vagina

Česky Fousek

See Czesky Fousek

Česky Terrier

See Czesky Terrier

Cestodes

Parasitic worms, flat worms and flukes can affect dogs. The eggs of cestodes are passed through feces, and can there be detected by professional inquiry. *See also* Flatworms, Flukes

Cevennes Shepherd

See Berger du Languedoc

Ch.

A prefix used with the name of a dog or bitch that has been recorded as a Champion by its registry as a result of defeating a specified number of dogs in specified competition at a series of licensed or member dog shows. In the U.S., under the A.K.C., championship is awarded upon completion of 15 points, including two majors—the total number under not less than three judges, two of whom must have awarded the majors at A.K.C. point shows. In Great Britain, the title is awarded upon the earning of three Challenge Certificates. In England, Champions are entered in the open class; there is no special class for Champions only. *See also* Champion

Chaining dogs

Lengths of chain are used to stake a dog outdoors; usually they are about six feet in length and are attached with snaps to the dog's collar and to the stake. Many authorities strongly recommend against chaining the dog outside for the majority of the day and certainly as a means of permanent accommodation. See Accommodations, outdoor

Challenge

In fox hunting, the first hound to open on finding scent "challenges."

Challenge Certificate

Challenge Certificates are awarded by the Kennel Club of Great Britain and the majority of British Commonwealth countries. These certify that a dog has won a legitimate competition against other purebreds at a sponsored event and that the dog is worthy of receiving the title of Champion. Three Challenge Certificates are required for the attainment of the Champion title.

Chambray

An ancient French hound which resembles the Billy; it is larger and more muscular than the Billy, standing 28 inches (71 cm) at the shoulder. It is deep chested and strong bodied. The coat is fine and short and colored in white and fawn. This particolor pattern fades with age and older dogs are always seen in pure white. Dogs with fawn heads have a darker spot on the top of the skull.

Champagne

A term adopted by fanciers to describe a darkish shade of tannish red, or even lighter. The authors intend to pop a bottle when such inane terminology is erased from the canine lexicon.

Chaining dogs. An outdoor spike and chain serve effectively as a means of temporary restraint. Temporarily restrained here is an American Bulldog. Photo courtesy John Blackwell.

No dog becomes a Champion until it is so officially recorded by the American Kennel Club. *See also* Ch.

Change

The hounds' act of leaving the line of one quarry for that of another.

Character

Temperament or disposition of a dog. Each breed is noted for possessing a character that is unique, more or less, to itself. Character is inherited, and breeds that are true to character are thereby ideally suited for their particular function. That is to say that the protectve and gentle character of the Great Pyrenees well befits its role as flock or estate guard, while the self-esteem and combativeness of the Pekingese complements its long-time role as toy and alarm dog.

Charnique

A large coursing dog breed which developed in Spain.

Chart Polski

Besides Poland's Owczarek Nizinny and Podhalanski, the nation can boast a third purebred dog, the Chart Polski, the newest member of the sighthound group. The Polish Sighthound is a tall, angular, strongly muscled, shorthaired coursing greyhound. This ancient breed's revival takes place in Poland where it is used for hunting purposes.

The Arabian Greyhound is believed to be the breed's predecessor and the modern-day Borzoi is said to have sprung from Chart Polski lines. Centuries ago in East-

Chart Polski, white with black.

ern Europe, these dogs were used on a variety of game, including rabbit, fox, wolf, and deer.

In Poland, the breed has been recognized since 1981; the Polish Kennel Club thereby acknowledged that this revived breed is indeed the same animal depicted in paintings from centuries ago. Owners

Chart Polskis. Photographs by I. Français.

describe the breed as "exceptionally intelligent and elegant, a wonderful dog to live with—very affectionate and clean and obedient." In the late 1980s, approximately 100 Chart Polskis lived and worked in Poland; the number steadily increases, and some dogs are known to have entered the U.S. The first American-bred litter was born in Maryland in 1991.

ESSENTIALS OF THE CHART POLSKI: A large muscular dog, clearly stronger and less slight of figure than other shorthaired sighthounds. It is neither heavy nor lymphatic. Height: 27–32 inches (68–80 cm). The head is strong and lean; skull should be flat on top with stop barely marked. Topline of muzzle and skull should be slightly divergent. A small nose hump is desirable. The expression of the eyes must be piercing; they are dark in color, but can range from amber to dark beer. The back is straight in the chest area and moderately arched in loin area. Stomach tuck-up is noticeable. Hindlegs are long and well muscled, fairly well angulated and somewhat laid back. Skin is elastic and tight; hair is springy to the touch, fairly hard, not wiry nor silky. Pants and brush tail are desirable. All colors and combinations are permissible.

Cheeky. The Staffordshire Bull Terrier exhibits very pronounced cheek muscles.

Chasing
Running after the flushed bird. Hound's following a visible fox.

Chastek paralysis
Actually a vitamin deficiency resulting from excessive consumption of raw fish, leading to paralysis; this condition is more common in wild canids than it is in domestic dogs that are not commonly fed raw fish.

Check
A temporary or permanent loss of the correct line by hounds, either because of scenting difficulties such as presented by the terrain or other factors, or possibly because the quarry has deliberately established a break in the line.

Checking
Confirming the position and progress of the handler, usually as one cast is being completed or one piece of cover negotiated before proceeding to the next.

Cheek bumps
Faulty over-development of cheek muscles or incorrect bone formation cause the cheeks to bulge beyond conformation to the breed's standard.

Cheeks
Below the eyes, the skin regions beginning at the lips and reaching back to the masseter muscles area. Cheeks are often described in breed standards, and specific phraseology has developed. Developed musculation in the cheeks is termed fleshy in cheeks; structurally lean in the cheeks is known as clean in cheeks; coarse or prominent cheeks are referred to as cheeky.

Cheeky
Bulging in the cheeks, sometimes the result of over-developed cheek muscles. This characteristic is desirable in some breeds, though undesired in others.

Cheilitis
Inflammation of the lips.

Cheiloschisis
See Harelip

Cherry eye
When the third eyelid becomes enlarged, the Harder's gland becomes visible as a small piece of red flesh. At this time it is common for the eyes to discharge profusely. Determination of the cause and prescription of the cure involve veterinary counsel. *See also* Eye anatomy, Entropion

Cherry nose
See Dudley nose

Chesapeake Bay Retriever

As his name bears witness to his origin, the Chesapeake Bay Retriever was born on the famous ducking shores of the Chesapeake Bay bordering Virginia and Maryland. The first dogs emerged in the early years of the nineteenth century, but it took a good century for type to reach perfection. These dogs are ideally constructed for the task of waterfowl retrieval, and though they have received more than their share of criticism for broad heads and other less than "refined" physical characteristics, the breed is truly ideal for its purpose. These dogs are also of fine health, good intelligence, and even temperament.

Concerning the birth of the breed, there exists a tale to which many fanciers of the breed adhere: it is the well-knit, well-loved tale of the stranded Newfoundland vessel. The captain of this tossed ship gave two Newfoundland-type dogs to a Mr. George Law, who had aided the sailors of the vessel in their time of need. The tale continues with these Newfie-type dogs'

and tan hounds have contributed to the spinning of the Chessie, since both the

coat and eye color of the breed suggest such a bloodline.

The Chessie is a relentless worker, with great courage and power and a will of tempered steel. The breed is revered as the unsurpassed water retriever. First-hand data speak of individuals of the breed retrieving 1000-plus fowl in a given hunting season.

ESSENTIALS OF THE CHESAPEAKE BAY RETRIEVER: Skull broad and round with a medium stop. Nose medium with a short muzzle. Ears small, set well up on the head, hanging loosely. Eyes medium large, yellowish or amber in color. Neck medium length and very strong. Shoulders sloping, free, and powerful. Chest strong, deep, and powerful—barrel round and deep. Body of

being bred to the then-common yellow and tan coonhounds, thus happily yielding the Chesapeake. Feasibly, the yellow

Chest capacity. The Staffordshire Bull Terrier's well-developed chest is preferably deep in brisket. Photo by Missy Yuhl.

medium length, neither cobby nor roached. Legs straight, with good bone and muscle. Dewclaws on hind legs must be removed. Tail to extend to hocks. Coat is short and thick, never over 1.5 inches (3.8 cm) in length, with a dense, fine woolly undercoat. Hair on face and legs must be straight, with tendency to wave on shoulders, neck, back and loins only. Coat texture is of definite importance:

must be weather resistant, especially to water and cold. Color: any color varying from dark brown to faded tan or dead grass, which varies from tan to dull straw color. Height: 23–26 inches (58–66 cm). Weight: 64–75 pounds (29–34 kg). Eyes are yellow.

Chest

Thorax, brisket. The anatomical region between the neck and abdomen. Composed of thirteen thoracic vertebrae above and thirteen ribs on either side, with the sternum below. Eight sternaebra or individual bones, attached by blocks of cartilage, comprise the sternum. This is the formation of the dog's chest or floor of the thorax.

Chest capacity

Depth, length and width determine the dimensions of the chest. The chest, as the protectorate of the heart, lungs, and other vital organs, must be of optimum development for the overall, sustained health of the dog. Chest types also affect the capacity of an individual breed's chest. The differences in chest shapes are related directly to rib contours. Many breed standards require a dog to be deep in chest, which means that the depth of the chest extends minimally to the point of the elbow. Chest depth is measured from the withers to the end of the sternum. Shallow in chest would indicate that a dog is insufficiently deep in chest.

Chest measurements

See Chest capacity

Chest types

Barrel. A chest formed by rounded or well-arched ribs. Not always desirable.

Egg shaped. The most common canine chest, generally oval or pear in shape.

Shallow. Insufficiently deep in chest.

Well developed. The desired chest dimensions of a given breed for its optimum functioning.

Well ribbed up. Adequate chest development with good length of ribs.

Well sprung. Ribs springing out, denoting correct shape.

Chewing

In adult dogs the desire to chew stems from their instincts for tooth cleaning, gum massage, and jaw exercise—as well as the need to vent periodic doggie tensions. Young dogs have similar instincts; chewing cuts the puppy teeth, induces the growth of permanent teeth (under the milk teeth), assists in normal jaw development, and settles the permanent teeth into the jaw. A dog's need to chew, however, must be directed by its owner. If provided with the proper chew device, the chewing instinct will provide the dog with clean, healthy teeth and gums. *See* Dental care, Periodontitis

Cheyletiella dermatitis

A condition in dogs caused by mite (*Cheyletiella yasguri*) infestation. It is highly contagious and can affect humans. These mites can survive free from the host. The typical condition shows scaling (false dandruff), with excessive scratching, alopecia and inflammation almost always accompanying.

Chief steward

1) Official acting as supervisor and coordinator of stewards at a large dog show.

2) The chief steward takes the other officials along the dog sled trail and determines their individual posts. He remains at the start/finish line.

Chien

French word for dog.

Chien Canne

French name for the Poodle, which *see*.

Chien Courant de Bosnie a Poil Dur

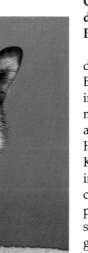

This medium sized Bosnian hunting hound, formerly known as the Illyrian Hound and the Keltski Gonič in Bosnia, is a competent pursuer of both small and large game, ranging from hare to wild boar. Its powerful build and pendant ears have led historians to believe that the Celtic Hound is its likely ancestor. This proposition has been doubted by modern-day cynologists. Standing 22 inches (55 cm) at the shoulder and sporting a long head and a harsh coat, the Illyrian Hound is a robust and consistent tracker.

Chewing is essential for the proper development of the teeth and good dental hygiene. This famed Shiba Inu busily chomps on a new Gumaknot®.

Chien de l'Atlas, white. Photographs by I. Français.

Chien d'Artois

The Chien d'Artois, also known as the Briquet, is one of the oldest French scenthounds; its history parallels the Normand, Vendeen and Poitou, all of which are scarcely found. Nineteenth-century French hunters boasted *"les chiens de petit équipage"* (packs of small dogs) made up of the Briquets. The original Artois's over-popularity during the 1800s and the indiscriminate crosses to British gundogs nearly decimated the purity of the Artois type. Fortunately, the packs of Prince de Conde and those worked at Chantilly

Chien d'Artois, tricolor. Photo by I. Français.

still retained the original type. Two concerned dog men, Ernest Levair and M. Therouanne, worked for 20 years to re-establish the almost lost type. By the turn of the twentieth century, their efforts were rewarded by true-breeding dogs of the old type. Despite the insufferable losses of World War II, today the descendants of the remaining pure Artois are growing in number. They are used on hare and other small quarry in small packs. The Briquet is recommended for work in thick briar and difficult terrain. No ordinary scenthound, the Chien d'Artois is also capable of pointing, one of the few advantages of its ancestors' having been crossed with the gundog breeds.

ESSENTIALS OF THE CHIEN D'ARTOIS: An efficiently bodied and fine-proportioned little hound with a broad skull, dark eyes, and a merry tail. The Briquet has a smooth dense coat comprised of fine

hairs. The tricolor pattern is broken and brilliantly colored in white, dark fawn, and charcoal. Height: 20–23 inches (51–59 cm). Weight: 40–53 pounds (18–24 kg). The flat, large ears and slightly creased facial skin give this hound an unmistakably likeable expression.

Chien de Berger Belge

See Belgian Sheepdog, Groenendael; Laekenois; Malinois; Tervuren

Chien de Berger Egyptian

See Armant

Chien de l'Atlas

The Chien de l'Atlas or Aidi works in Morocco as a flock guard, protecting large herds of sheep and goats. The breed's original employment was the defense of North African nomads and their belongings. In Morocco today, the Aidi is also a reliable hunting companion and, paired with the swift-moving Sloughi, the Aidi exhibits strong scenting ability. The Aidi is a high-energy dog which only recently has found his way into the pet world. His traditional role as worker—guardian of people and animals and hunter—has imbued him with tremendously broad protective instincts. Once acclimated, the breed has done well in the home as a companion and watchdog. The breed has also been referred to as the Douar Dog.

ESSENTIALS OF THE CHIEN DE L'ATLAS: The Aidi's height at the shoulder is between 21–25 inches (53–63.5 cm). His lean yet thickly muscled body is protected by a coarse weather-resistant coat. The protection of the coat and the power of the muscles are essential and characteristic. The preferred color is white; however, black, black and white, tawny, and a dilute red may also occur. The typical Atlas Sheepdog weighs about 55 pounds (25 kg) and always remains symmetrical.

Chien de Montagnes des Pyrenees

See Great Pyrenees

Chien de Pays

See Griffon Nivernais

Chien de St. Hubert

See Bloodhound

Chien de Trait
  See Belgian Mastiff

Chien des Garrigues
  An extinct French shepherd that resembled the Berger du Languedoc, differing only in its smooth coat and white or gray coloration, frequently mottled by dark patches.

Chien d'ours de Tahltan
  See Tahltan Bear Dog

Chien Français
  The determination of the Chien Français grouping resulted from the 1957 pack surveys conducted in France. These purely Celtic canine descendants developed variously from the Gascon-Saintongeois and the Levesque and were once countless. These French Hounds have been divided into three distinct breeds, each employing the nomenclature Chien Français. The Chien Français Tricolore, Chien Français Blanc et Noir, and the Chien Français Blanc et Orange—the distinction in color only. These are pack hunters: there is little concern for an "ideal" conformation; functional, working concerns are foremost. Today they specialize on deer but are efficient on most quarry. Only the three listed breeds exist today. At one time, however, many other variations on the Chien Français existed. Mostly attributed to the diminished role that the French court plays in the contemporary social life of the country, the number of packs has dramatically declined throughout France.
  Coming to modern man exclusively as hunters, these dogs are elegant in appearance and affectionate with enviable adaptability to game and terrain.
  ESSENTIALS OF THE CHIEN FRANÇAIS: Well balanced and sturdy. Three breeds are recognized under the distinction Chien

Français. These determinations are made on the basis of color: three colors exist today. Le Chien Français Blanc et Noir is

black and white, Le Chien Français Blanc et Orange is orange and white, and Le Chien Français Tricolore is tricolor (black, white and tan). The Blanc et Noir has tan markings on his face but should not be confused with the Tricolore. The coat is always short and smooth. Bicolor dogs weigh up to 66 pounds (30 kg) and stand 29 inches (74 cm) high; the Tricolore is about ten percent smaller.

Chien Français
Blanc et Noir.

Chien Français
Tricolore. Photographs by I. Français.

Chien Français Blanc et Noir
  See Chien Français

Chien Français Blanc et Orange
  See Chien Français

Chien Français Tricolore
  See Chien Français

Chien Loup
  See Keeshond

Chien Français Blanc et Orange. Photo by I. Français.

Chihuahua, longhair.

Chihuahua

The Chihuahua, named after the state in Mexico, is the smallest canine in recorded history, weighing as little as one pound! Some sources trace the breed to South America; it is believed variously that the dog, or dogs similar to it in size and type, was revered by the Aztecs as a sacred dog, fostered by the ninth-century Toltecs when it was called Techichi, or developed and kept by the Incas. The origins of any canine on the South American continent invite problems to which countless natural historians have addressed themselves. If dogs indeed existed in the Americas, particularly in Incan civilization, they were saved by the Spaniards that arrived there. Other reports, however, indicate that the conquistadors only found tree-climbing, mute, mutant rodents or rodentlike curiosities in South America. It is even doubtful that the earliest figurines that resemble the Chihuahua are even of the canine species. Likewise, the belief that the deceased Atzec leaders were entombed with their Chihuahuas is also untrue, although bitterly romantic, we admit. No authentic Aztec grave has ever produced the remains of any dog, mummified or otherwise.

The Chinese, some believe, had their hands in the breed as well, with their incessant fetish for bantamization. The Chinese were dwarfing dogs as they were trees and fish. The Chinese contribution to the breed more likely occurred in a latter-day cross to the Chinese Crested. The smallest of the Portuguese Podengos, a dwarfed pariah type, bears an exceptional, eye-raising similarity to the Chihuahua. The Chihuahua breed as we know it today descends from selectively bred American stock. It is also not clear whether or not the Longcoated Chihuahua antedates the Smooth. Some believe the Long was developed on American soil using Smooths and Papillons. Another source indicates that Longs were to be found in Colombia and Brazil before the said American development.

The Chihuahua's origins will never be fully understood, but for Chihuahua enthusiasts the forming of hypothesis and spinning of myths ease the disappointment of cynologists frankly asserting: "We just don't know." We cannot pretend to know more.

This Chihuahua's conquest of the dog world begins in Mexico City in 1895, and the little dog inched his way up to El Paso, Texas in minimal time. The aptly named "Midget" was the first Chihuahua to be registered by the A.K.C.—the year was 1904. Today the Chihuahua in the States ranks at the very top of the registration list and is one of the continent's most beloved companion dogs. Although the Chihuahua is "a tad" too tiny for sporting, dogs during the early half of this century were said to be game retrievers and hunters of vermin.

ESSENTIALS OF THE CHIHUAHUA: The Chihuahua is small and dainty, compact with brisk forceful action and a saucy expression. The apple domed skull blends into his lean cheeks and jaws. The head is topped with large ears that are held erect when alert, but have their position for repose (a 45° angle flares at the sides). The body is level on the back and slightly longer than high. There are two coat types: Smooth, a close glossy coat of a soft texture; and Long, a flat or slightly curly, soft-textured coat with an undercoat preferred. Either coat type can be any color—solid, marked, or splashed. Weight: 1–6 pounds (.5–3 kg). The neck is slightly arched; the shoulders, well laid, lean and sloping; ribs, well sprung; brisket, deep. The hindquarters are muscular; hocks, well let down. Feet small and dainty.

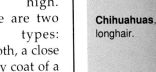

Chihuahuas, longhair.

Chihuahua, smooth.

Chihuahuas, longhair, solid, splashed and marked.

Children and dogs. Junior Showmanship proves a great experience for the youth involved. This proud young lady poses with her winning Chihuahua.

Children and dogs

Many of the world's most popular breeds get along famously with children. Gundogs and hounds in particular take well to children and don't seem to mind a little yanking on their ears or the fondling of their noses. Basset Hounds, Beagles, Golden Retrievers, English Springer Spaniels, to name a few, are among those breeds with great reputations with children. Even some of the larger breeds prove ideal: the Great Pyrenees, Saint Bernard and Old English Sheepdog have inbred patience and kindly hearts which enable them to endure even the most undisciplined of urchins.

Parents should exercise discretion when choosing the breed of dog for a child. When it comes to child companions, some breeds of dog, it must be said, are more risky to own than others. Well-informed parents exercising sound judgment can provide their child with a sensible canine companion. *See also* Choosing a dog

Children must be taught the appropriate way to handle a dog, especially a puppy. A puppy, delicate like an infant, has a soft spot on the top his head and must be held with the utmost gentleness. "Baby puppies" should not be handled by children. A puppy's bones, tendons, and muscles are generally delicate and can be injured quite easily. Before allowing a child to hold a puppy, teach the child how to stroke and pet the puppy gently. Adults must reinforce the idea that a puppy is a living thing and different than the child's teddy bear. Once the pup is old enough to be handled, adults should demonstrate for the child the proper way to lift a puppy. A dog should always be supported with both hands, *never* lifted by the scruff of the neck. One hand placed

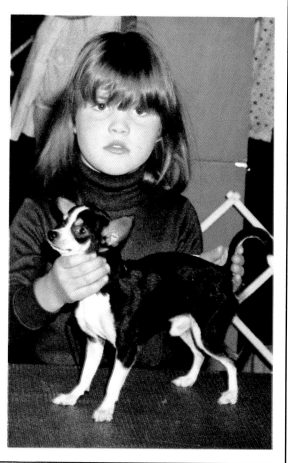

under the chest, between the front legs, and the other hand supporting the dog's bottom end will be comfortable and effectively restrain the animal while it is being held.

Owning a dog offers a child many benefits: adults who grew up in the company of a dog will attest to the fact that the dog played a vital part in their childhood and that the benefits are innumerable and somehow ineffable.

The authors attempt to materialize and enumerate some such benefits. It is the unconditional love and commitment that a puppy offers a child that activates the young owner's sociological and psychological development. A puppy teaches the child kindness; the puppy is alive and only responds to the child's equable and considerate treatment. A dog provides its owner with a constuctive pastime, occupying the child's time and often keeping him out of trouble. The dog induces responsibility: many times a puppy is the child's first real responsibility. As adults would agree, caring for a dog (feeding, grooming, cleaning, exercising, etc.) requires time and commitment. While a young child cannot handle the entire lot of responsibility, sharing in some responsibility, however, can give the child satisfaction and likewise due reward. Puppies build character: ownership of a dog gives the child confidence and self-esteem ("This is *my* dog!"), as well as pride. Children often come out of their shell to tell others about their much loved pet, thus aiding in socialization too. Learning that love can be returned as reciprocally as it is showered is also another important life lesson that dog ownership can impart to a child. Certain breeds, of course, require a little more effort before they will return such affection: these dogs perhaps teach a lesson that most find out well into adulthood. Lastly, puppies can teach a child about death, understanding its meaning by talking to their parents.

Children and dogs. Canine companions, such as this elementary (though not simple) Bobtail, frequently boost a child's confidence and aid in socialization.

Children and dogs share many quiet moments together. American Pit Bull Terriers, when properly reared, are excessively fond of children.

Children and dogs. Glimmering with pride, this youngster is surely the first on his block to own a Kyi-Leo.

Children and dogs meet children and dogs quite spontaneously. Helming this encounter are a longhaired Dachshund and a black retriever. Photo by S. Miller.

Children and dogs. Puppies draw forth a child's personality, often giving the child confidence and self-assurance. This evocative tyke is a Sloughi puppy. Photo by E. Moreau-Sipiére. Photo courtesy of Mosica Arabians.

Children and dogs. Parents are reminded that bringing a new puppy in the home may be perceived by the child as bringing in a new baby. Sensitivity and common sense must be employed. Cradle full of rough Chow Chow puppies.

Chilla
See South American foxes

Chiloé
See South American foxes

Chin
The lower muzzle at the junction of the lower jaw bone halves.

China eye
See Walleye

Chinese Cresteds, Powderpuff. Photo by I. Français.

Chinese Crested
The Chinese Crested is one of the world's few modern hairless dogs. Hairless mutations have occurred throughout the history of the dog. Mostly these dogs were culled, either by their own inability to adapt to their environment, the difficulty of persuading a willing suitor, or actual extermination by owners shocked by their Quasimodo-mishap. The hairless breeds, while admittedly a mutation, are not freaks, in the truer sense of the word. Their nakedness has been regarded unkindly, but in more recent centuries, dog fanciers in Africa, China, Spain, and Mexico have been intrigued by the uniqueness of these breeds.

Geographical and conformation similarities have linked the hairless breeds to the pariah types of Africa. Today's hairless breeds, excluding the new American Hairless Terrier, all probably derive from like stock. Such dogs as the African or Abyssinian Sand Dog, the African Elephant Dog, and the Turkish Hairless or Naked Dog have yielded today's Chinese Crested, Peruvian Hairless and Inca Orchid, Mexican Hairless, and Xoloitzcuintli. Much evidence also points to the hairless dog's development in Turkey.

Although rare in its name-giving China, the Chinese Crested is enjoying ever increasing popularity with the Western World. The first Chinese Crested to be exhibited in the U.S. appeared in 1885. The breed remained in vogue for a few decades, but then fell from its crest of popularity. In 1986, within 100 years of its original exhibition, the Chinese Crested was reinstated in the A.K.C. Miscellaneous Class; in 1991, the breed was accepted into the Toy Group.

Hairless dogs do not breed with the same genetic soundness as other breeds. Inherent in all the hairless breeds, again excepting the American Hairless, are the absence of premolars (or front teeth), a condition sex-linked to the hairlessness; occasionally missing toenails; and breeding difficulties. Necessary for the counterbalance of the hairless gene, a semi-lethal gene, is the powderpuff or veil-coated variety. Coated dogs occur in litters of hairless dogs; they are double-coated, silky specimens with complete dentition and manicures. These dogs do not display hairlessness but do carry the gene. Their progeny consist of hairless and coated puppies. The veil-coat is known as a Powderpuff.

The Chinese Crested is perhaps the most handsome of the hairless breeds. The crest or tuft of hair on its head gives it an appeal that the other dogs do not possess. They do require special care to keep them suitably protected; their hairlessness makes them especially susceptible to ultraviolet rays, cold and dampness, and other environmental conditions.

ESSENTIALS OF THE CHINESE CRESTED: A medium- to fine-boned dog, with a smooth hairless body, with hair on feet, head and tail only or covered with a soft veil of hair. The hairless dog's body is seen in two types: deer type, which is racy and fine boned; and cobby type, which is heavier in bone and body. The skin is an important feature: it is fine-grained and smooth. In the variety known as the

Chinese Crested, lavender.

Chinese Crested. Photographs by I. Français.

Powderpuff, the coat consists of an undercoat with a soft veil of long hair. The skull is slightly rounded and elongated. Cheeks are cleanly chiseled, lean and flat, tapering to the muzzle. The nose is a prominent feature, narrow, as is the muzzle. Head presents a graceful appearance. The ears are set low; the neck is lean, free from throatiness. The body is supple, medium-long. Chest, broad and deep. Height: 9–13 inches (23–33 cm). Weight: 5–10 pounds (2–5 kg). The tail, as with the crested head, is coated, creating a plumelike impression. In the Powderpuff variety, all colors occur. On the hairless members, the skin is from pink to black, including mahogany, blue, lavender, and copper; it can be solid or spotted.

Chinese Crested Dog
See Chinese Crested

Chinese Fighting Dog
See Shar-Pei

Chinese Greyhound
A variation of the English Greyhound which occurred in China. This breed of sighthound is much smaller than the Greyhound proper, bearing a resemblance to a Whippet/Italian Greyhound cross, but is probably the product of expert dwarfing on the English type dog. The ears are large and carried erect or pointing forward. The tail is slightly fringed; the coat is short and smooth. In color the Tschika, as it is also known, ranges in various shades of fawn or brown, with a white blaze desirable.

Chinese Hound
Known as Ma-chu-gou in China, the Chinese Hound is still believed (by some) to be the Phu-Quo Dog in the form in which it was brought to France but did not survive. Its heavy greyhound body type, short coat and ridged back have linked it to extinct longhaired packhounds once found in Kashmir, Nepal and Eastern Tibet. These dogs are no longer believed to occur in China and join the ranks of their contributing ancestors.

Chinese Shar-Pei
See Shar-Pei

Chinese Temple Ch'in
The ancient temple dwellers of the Orient form the basis of a number of well-known companion dogs; the Japanese Chin, Pekingese and Shih Tzu are among the popular breeds. A modern-day resurgence of the ancient Chinese Temple Ch'in has begun sweeping the dust off the sacred icons which once adorned the entrances of Oriental temples. Physically this revived breed appears most like the Japanese Chin, and indeed maintains a blood relation. The new Temple Dog was resuscitated through a breeding program which matched a believed Temple Dog male with a large Chin female. Japanese Chin fanciers and breeders have long regarded the larger Chins as possible links to the Temple Dogs of the past. The nose of the Temple Dog is longer than the Chin's, and this, in addition to the larger size, differentiates the two breeds. Presently the breed is not recognized, although a standard has been drawn and appearances at American rare breed shows have commenced. The dwarfish pug-faced Orientals promise to take the canine world by storm as they are ferociously charming, with a prized ferocious look too.

ESSENTIALS OF THE CHINESE TEMPLE CH'IN: A small dog, short-legged, heavy boned; with a deep broad chest, narrow hips, and a long body. The head is massive, domed and carried on a thick neck. The coat is long and profuse, usually parting down the middle of the back. There is a heavy mane which is at its longest and thickest on the chest and neck. The tail is carried over the back, curled to the right or left and is a luxuriant plume. The face has large, expressive eyes, a short muzzle, and a flat up-turned nose below the eyes. The ears, front legs and rear legs are heavily feathered. The gait is ponderously rolling, lionlike. The color is white with black markings; black mask, black ears, black saddle, and black at the base of the tail most generally seen, but any markings are acceptable. Very rare are solid colors and red or yellow markings. Height and weight vary tremendously: 2–20 pounds (.9–9 kg); 3–14 inches (8–36 cm). There are four size possibilities, divided into classes: giant, classic, miniature, and sleeve. *See also* Japanese Chin.

Chinook

An early twentieth-century American creation, the Chinook was the brainpup of Arthur Walden. Walden desired a dog that was as fast as the arctic husky dogs and as strong as the larger sledge pullers. Walden considered the dog a "half-bred Eskimo," part mongrel and part St. Bernard. The breed's year of incipience is 1915. The Chinook possesses a pulling power comparable to any snow-shoed arctic horse. The name was given to the breed to commemorate "Chinook," the founder's favorite and most untiring sled dog. Admiral Byrd's Antarctic expedition was powered by Chinook dogs, each of which towed an average load of over 150 pounds (69 kg).

In addition to sledge pulling, the breed also excels at protection work. A tad strong willed, these dogs need to be taught early who is head dog. These are large dogs with surprising longevity, an average healthy dog living 10 to 15 years. Besides being good-looking and healthy, the breed is among the most pleasant of the nordic dogs—a group of dogs with highly favorable temperaments. Chinook fanciers presently work hard to increase the breed's numbers and popularity.

ESSENTIALS OF THE CHINOOK: The body is muscular, compact and well balanced; the chest is deep; moderate bone and flexible musculature are prominent. The coat is medium and close lying. The muzzle is powerful, and the teeth are enduring. In color the Chinook is tawny (a golden fawn). The breed's ear carriage, rather wind-blown and bending, gives the dogs a curious and entreating glint. Weight: 65–90 pounds (29–40 kg). Height: 21–26 inches (53–66 cm).

Chippendale front

See Fiddle front

Chippiparai

The hare-hunting Chippiparai, also called Thambai, is an excellent hunter of India with the ability to flush game. Its intelligence and trainability have also made this dog useful at police work in India. This southern greyhound stands on long legs, with a racy well-built body.

Chiselled

Usually referring to the head or foreface (especially below the eyes) describing the clean-cut lines desired. The allusion is to the craft of sculpture, and the finely or well-chisel ed skull is one that reflects refinement, especially if covered by close-lying skin. The Whippet, for example, has a chiselled muzzle.

Chinook, tawny. Photo by I. Français.

Choke collar

A collar that tightens around the throat of the animal when pulled. *See* Collars, Training.

Cholecystitis

A condition affecting the gall bladder. The onset is usually during the time an animal is suffering from infectious canine hepatitis. Removal of the gall bladder, which thickens and becomes highly vascular, can effect a complete cure. *See also* Hepatitis, canine

Choosing a dog

The first aspect of responsible dog ownership actually surfaces before purchasing your dog. Selecting the right dog or breed requires sensible forethought, a little research, and full consideration of the necessary factors. An owner's income and lifestyle, the size of his home, and the climate in which he lives are all worthy of initial consideration.

Choosing a dog. Resisting a Chinese Shar-Pei puppy presents problems to even the most rational and unimpulsive person. Photo by R. Pearcy.

Since dog ownership is essentially an emotional undertaking (among other things), it is nearly impossible to convince a determined potential owner that the dog he wants isn't the *right* dog for him. So many whimsical, impressionable dog lovers are so seduced by a puppy in a store window that they purchase the dog without even partial consideration of what ownership entails. Certain breeds are indescribably attractive as puppies: Shar-Peis, Basset Hounds,

Chow Chows, Clumber Spaniels, etc. If more people approached dog ownership responsibly, so many fewer dogs would end up in the pound, homeless, or worse.

Potential owners are faced with three primary determinations: puppy vs. adult dog; male vs. female; purebred vs. mongrel. The presence of children in a houshold affects the first consideration. If the child is very young and still requires constant care, bringing in a second "baby" may be too much for the new parents (and owners) to handle. Puppies, however, will attach themselves more definitively to the family more so than a full-grown dog, which may have reservations. Many people trust puppies more than adult dogs. Adult dogs, however, previously housetrained and well mannered, may present fewer complications than a puppy.

The question of male or female is truly a matter of preference. Generally speaking, the bitch is easier to handle and train; female dogs tend to be more affectionate and obedient. Females have less tendency to roam and are usually more even tempered (a plus in a household with children). Males tend to be more independent and dominant, perhaps less whimsical and doting. Castration must be considered for a male that is not intended to be bred. This may reduce his need to roam around and relieve his sexual tensions. It is not at all uncommon for castrated males to continue to roam, however.

The last determination addresses the owner's intentions for his dog. If the owner wishes a dog solely as a pet and companion, a mongrel or mixed breed will suit his needs famously. Additionally, mongrels are cost-efficient and usually can be acquired for a minimal fee. However, if the owner is looking for a show dog or obedience trial contender, he must purchase a pedigreed dog. Furthermore, most breeds of dog have convincing reputations. For instance, if an owner is looking for a hunting companion, he is wise to choose from the sporting, gundog or hound groups; if an owner desires a guard dog or man-stopper, there are breeds that regularly perform such tasks; if an owner is looking for an even-tempered dog or simply a "looker," various breeds have these particulars to offer.

No matter what dog you decide to adopt—puppy or adult, male or female, purebred or mongrel—there are certain physical vital signs for which the new owner should be looking. Dogs should be well filled-out; a pot belly likely indicates bad nutrition or internal parasites. The dog's eyes should be clear, free of redness and discharge. Dull eyes can indicate that the dog is not healthy. A moist nose without discharge: nasal discharge may indicate an upper respiratory infection. The dog's teeth, after five months of age, should number 32 and be free of discoloration. Missing teeth are usually apparent (breeders don't particularly appreciate prospective owners counting the teeth of every dog in their litter). General

listlessness is to be avoided; such dullness should not be confused with shyness or caution. The ears should be pink

and not inflamed. Calling the dog to check for deafness is also a good idea. A small swelling protruding from the naval is an indication of a hernia. The coat should be checked for visible external parasites, such as fleas, ticks, etc.

Having the seller take the dog's temperature is not a usual request by a new owner, but the seller should be willing to comply. A certificate of inoculation should also be acquired upon purchase. A purebred dog should be accompanied by a pedigree as well as a registration certificate from the national kennel club. Persons purchasing a purebred for show purposes should also acquaint themselves with the breed standard (the essentials of a given breed as well as its disqualifications).

The question of where to buy a dog, of course, depends on the kind of dog you desire. While your

Choosing a dog. Pet shops offer potential dog owners the opportunity to see a variety of dogs, as well as an array of products necessary to the proper care of a dog.

Choosing a dog. Well-known Boxer and Shiba Inu breeder Rick Tomita of Jacquet Kennels (Oakland, New Jersey) embraces a handsome litter of Boxers. Knowing your breeder is tantamount to getting the right start with the right dogs. Photographs by I. Français.

Choosing a dog like the Tibetan Spaniel will likely entail finding a reputable breeder, since these adorable little dogs are too rare to be acquired from commercial sources.

Choosing a dog. Observing a litter of puppies, like these feisty and charming Affenpinschers, gives the potential dog owner an idea of the overall quality of the dog or dogs being considered. It is also advisable to see the dam of the litter as well. Photographs by I. Français.

pet shop can provide a selection of pet-quality dogs of the more popular breeds, it is not likely that it can provide show-quality Lundehunds or even Sealyham Terriers, for instance. No pet shop in the

world could stock every possible breed. Quality pet shops sell dogs from reputable breeding stock—make sure your pet shop proprietor has the answers to *all* your questions and can provide you with specifics and the paper work to back up

his statements. If your desire is a show-quality animal, a breeder is your only real option. Just as there are quack pet shops, there are quack breeders. These poorly informed, untrained breeders capitalize on the popularity of a particular breed, purchase a "show-quality" couple and crank out litters bi-annually (or *worse!*). These operations are known as puppy mills and are to be avoided. Incidentally, poorly operated pet shops often rely on puppy mills for their canine stock. Reputable breeders usually have a number of dogs in their program and are dedicated to the betterment of the breed—making money is never a prime concern. A good breeder may let a dog go for less than its worth if he is assured an ideal, loving home. Such breeders will not usually allow their show-quality dogs to enter homes where they will be solely pet dogs. The reputation of a breeder depends on his dogs excelling in the conformation ring. Likewise, a good breeder will not sell you a pet-quality animal and encourage you to enter the show ring, since this will tarnish his reputation as a breeder.

The process of choosing a dog should not be rushed. It must be approached intelligently and rationally. Friends and family can volunteer unbiased advice to help make the decision easier. *See also* Breeding, Children and dogs, Pet shops, Mongrels

Choosing a dog. If owning a dog that is a purebred is not a priority, a mixed-breed dog may fit the bill just fine. Mongrels make loving and faithful companion animals. Photo by R. Pearcy.

Chopper

A hound with a short staccato voice on line, giving tongue in abbreviated chopped notes.

Chops

Very deep flews, referring specifically to the Bulldog.

Chorea

Brain damage as a result of severe distemper. It is characterized by convulsive movements of the legs. It is progressive and if it affects the facial muscles, salivating or difficulty in eating or moving the jaws may be evident. Sedatives may bring relief, but the disease itself is incurable.

Chornyi

See Black Russian Terrier

Choroiditis

Inflammation of the choroid coat of the eye which is to be regarded as serious. Immediate veterinary inspection is required possibly by a specialist.

Chortaj

The Chortaj of Russia is one of the nation's many indigenous running hounds. These hunters have withstood the sands of time and still can be found hunting on the wide open steppes. The tradition of hunting on horseback, accompanied by a pair of gazehounds and a falcon, comes from the Cossacks and Tartars and is upheld by Soviet huntsmen today. The Chortaj, along with the South Russian Steppe Hound, is still used to hunt the abundant game found in these open plains. The 1952 Cynological Congress chose the Chortaj as one of the indigenous Russian breeds worthy of preservation. Although a number of Russian breeds have been exported to the United States, the Chortaj still remains exclusively in the Soviet Union, where it is kept largely as a hunter.

ESSENTIALS OF THE CHORTAJ: A large hard-coated dog with a long neck, rose ears, and arched body. The build is stouter and coarser than the Greyhound with which the Western World is acquainted. The coat is thick and smooth to the touch. In color the Chortaj is usually solid, but this is of little consideration. The overall appearance is well balanced and sinewy. The head is long, without stop, and narrow. The chest is broad and deep; the tuck-up is severe. Height: 25–26 inches (63–66 cm).

Chortaj
photographed in the Soviet Union by Vladimir Pcholkin.

Chow Chow

The Chow Chow, the principal indigenous dog of China, is a long-time breed of dog that has served man in countless ways: hunters, caravan guards, night-watchmen for the sampans and junks, sled pullers, flock dogs, companions, on the polar bear. In China, the native land, the Chow Chow was never perceived as the friend of man. Unlike the Malamutes and Samoyeds, the Chow was never a beloved companion of the men for whom it worked. Likewise, breeding practices were strictly utilitar-

watchdogs, and show dogs. Additionally, the omnivorous Chinese, living in a nation that does not boast a great meat output, also used the Chow for sustenance. It is no new news that the Chinese ate their dogs. Chows as well as Shar-Peis were used for food: "A chow in every pot." On a high feast day or most any day, the Chow could be found offered at the butcher's or the deli. When the smooth variety of Chow was first exhibited in England in 1870, it was promoted as a curiosity, "the Edible dog," and exhibited as such.

A union of northern breeds of the Arctic and heavy Eastern mastiffs probably produced the Chow. The breed, of course, derived from the same ancestor as Western dogs, a creature believed to be akin to the bear. Today the Chow is commonly compared to a bear—a teddy bear, most usually, though. Incidentally, the Chow's blue-black tongue, while also possessed by the Shar-Pei, is also found

ian. It would have been unlikely for the Westerner to enter China to locate "purebred" Chows, as one might go to Ireland to find a "purebred" Glen of Imaal. Cynologists and other historians alike root the Chow in 11th-century B.C. China, making it one of the oldest breeds known to man. The Chow Chow is frequently depicted in art and literature, although most of the earliest depictions have been lost.

Presently, in both the U.S. and Great Britain, the Chow Chow is growing increasingly popular, quickly working its way up the breed registration list. While the longhaired Chow is more popular the world over, the smooth-coated Chow continually grows in popularity. The smooth is easier to care for than the long coated. Along with the Chow's stirring following in the U.S., the Shar-Pei also grows popular—both native Chinamen. The smooth Chow Chow may owe some of its newest found popularity to the

Chow Chows, smooth, red.

Shar-Pei, since it more closely resembles what a wrinkly Shar-Pei puppy should look like grown up than does an adult Shar-Pei itself! Both varieties, in physical abilities and intelligence, are sure-footed and impressive to behold.

ESSENTIALS OF THE CHOW CHOW: The Chow is a perfectly balanced dog. Short coupled, active and compact, the massive muscular body is squarely built (body squares at the shoulder). The head is large and proportionate. The skull is flat and broad with little stop. Eyes, almond-shaped, dark and small. The characteristic expression is essentially of independence. A distinguishing characteristic is the blue-black tongue. The ears are small and carried stiffly. The teeth are strong and level; neck, strong and slightly arched; forelegs, straight and well boned; shoulders, muscular; chest, broad and deep; back, short and straight; loins and hind legs, muscular. Two coat types exist: a long coat which is dense, abundant, standoffish, and, of course, long; and a smooth coat which is shorter and more plush. The color may be any clear color, including black, tan, cream, blue, and red. Height: 19–20 inches (48–51 cm). Weight: 45–70 pounds (21–32 kg).

Chow Chows, rough and smooth, red.

Chow Chows, smooth and rough, tan, black and red. Photos by D. Valadez.

Chrysanthemum Dog
See Shih Tzu

Chrysocyon brachyurus
South American wolf commonly known as the maned wolf, which *see*.

Chute
The first several feet behind the starting line are referred to as the chute.

Circuit
A series of dog shows, the dates for which are arranged through the cooperation of a group of clubs so as to permit exhibitors to travel from show to show in direct route. There usually is a short interval between shows, and a circuit may include a dozen or more cities. *See also* Shows and showing, Classes at shows, etc.

Circular eyes
Describes the Smooth Fox Terrier's desired eye type.

Circular feet
Round, well-padded feet (e.g., Sussex Spaniel). *See also* Cat feet

Circulatory system
The heart and a vast network of blood vessels, both large and small, compose the cell-feeding system. The heart receives blood via two large vessels, the anterior and posterior vena cava. This blood is sent first to the lungs where the by-product carbon dioxide is exchanged for the much needed element, oxygen, which is carried by the red blood cells. The rejuvenated blood is then brought back to the heart where it is pumped to all parts of the body, nourishing every cell. The arteries return the depleted blood to the heart where the process resumes. The main filtering organ of the blood is the spleen, the most important function of which is to clean the blood, culling quantities of bacteria and other pests, as well as retiring aged red blood cells through liquefication.

Chow Chow, rough, red.

Cirneco dell'Etna

Like the Ibizan Hound and Pharaoh Hound, the Cirneco dell'Etna likely had an older ancestor of the coursing type which originated in the Mediterranean region. In Sicily, the Cirneco has bred true to type for many years, free from planned, accidental, unsupervised or otherwise, crossbreeding; he is the only dog that hunts on the hills of Mount Etna. Compared to the Pharaoh and Ibizan, the Cirneco is smaller. Its hunting acumen rests in coursing hare and rabbit. Its light-footed and delicate approach also makes it effective on ground birds.

The interest in the Cirneco dell'Etna has been steadily waning in its native Italy. Breeds of dog like the Pharaoh and Ibizan have become more commonplace, although both breeds are relatively uncommon. The Cirneco may be the perfect choice for the potential owner who cannot decide on which sighthound he wishes to adopt. It is hoped that new dog enthusiasts will actively pursue this ideally sized easycare dog and not let the breed enter into volcanic oblivion.

Cirneco dell'Etna. Photo by I. Français.

broad and the tuck-up is more moderate than many of his fellow sighthounds. The coat is short and smooth. In color the Cirneco is fawn-red, with white markings permissible. Height: 17–19 inches (43–48 cm). Weight: 18–26 pounds (8–12 kg).

Cirrhosis

The degeneration of liver cells which are replaced by fibrous tissue. The condition is typically caused in dogs by chronic or repetitive attacks on the liver by disease, toxins, and/or parasites. It can also be caused by a low protein diet and malnutrition. This progressive disease can be fatal and deserves prompt treatment.

C.K.C.

Abbreviation for the Canadian Kennel Club, which *see*.

Classes at shows

Dog shows are regularly divided into classes. A class categorizes dogs' age, experience, and breeding. The five classes used at American and Canadian shows are Puppy, for dogs six to twelve months of age; Novice, for dogs that have not won three ribbons (or other first places); Bred-by-Exhibitor, for dogs shown by their breeder-owners; American-Bred (or Canadian-bred) for non-champion dogs whelped in the U.S. (or Canada) from matings in their respective countries; and Open, for dogs over six months of age. Dogs winning any class compete for class winners: Winners Dog or Winners Bitch. The two dogs winning this distinction compete for Best of Breed with the champions.

In Great Britain, breeds initially competed separately, each in a class designated for their breed. This system has since necessarily folded. Today the British show class system is divided into Members' shows and Open shows (including Champion shows). Among the classes offered within these two categories are puppy, junior, maiden, novice, tyro, debutante, under-

ESSENTIALS OF THE CIRNECO DELL' ETNA: A finely built sighthound with upright ears placed prominently on his head, the Cirneco dell'Etna is exceedingly sleek and clean-cut. The head is well chiseled, the nose self-colored. The chest is fairly

graduate, graduate, post graduate, minor limit, mid limit, limit, open, veteran, and field trial. For a popular breed as many as 18 classes can be offered per sex.

Classifications

The list of breeds for which the show offers competition and the classes (regular and special) which are offered.

Claw

The correct terminology for the dog's toenail, as it is commonly referred.

Clean cut

Flowing and trim features, used most commonly to describe the head.

Clean head

Head free of wrinkles, over-musculation or other lumps.

Clean neck

Dry neck. Neck that is tightly skinned and free of loose skin, dewlap, or wrinkles, e.g., Sloughi.

Cleanliness

Keeping a dog healthy and parasite-free is largely dependent on the cleanliness of his living area. A dog's bedding, water and food bowls, crate, and run all require regular cleaning and disinfecting. Sanitation control should be a preventive measure. Fleas, ticks and other parasites can be avoided by spraying the surrounding areas of your home and dog's outside area with a non-toxic insecticide. The continued health of your dog—as well as your own—will prove all of these preventive measures worth the effort. *See also* Accommodations, indoor; Accommodations, outdoor

Cleft lip

See Harelip

Cleft palate

A congenital defect in which the two hard palate bones, which when formed correctly will seal the palate, grow incompletely or improperly, leaving a space between them. The condition is believed to be both hereditary and dietary, and is especially common in short-muzzled dogs. It also has occurred in studies controlling various vitamin-A deficiencies. In minor cases, the condition is often treatable. The condition is easily visible upon inspection of the palate. Acute conditions often require the culling of the affected animal.

Clinics

Typically established and run by humane societies or canine interest groups, clinics are a type of canine hospital where a dog can receive treatment at low cost to the owner. In recent years there has been a marked increase in clinics specializing in spaying and castration. Clinics are often run on a non-profit basis, and a local clinic, if available, can very often be contacted through the local phone directory. *See also* Canine hospitals, Veterinarian.

Clipped keel

See Keel

Clipped tail

Same as docked tail, which *see*.

Clipping the Poodle

The origin of clipping the Poodle is linked largely to the dog's employment as a water dog, and later as a circus performer. Huntsmen used the Poodle as a gundog, a role the dog performed with enviable acumen. Its forte as a retriever, however, was in the water, and the abundance of its coat hindered its speed and

Classes at shows. Crizwood's Flag Is Up, a Wire Fox Terrier, takes Winners Dog. Photo by J. Ashbey. Courtesy of C. and W. Wornall.

agility in the water. Hunters shaved the dog's hindquarters to permit greater freedom in the water. Later the dog's superior canine intelligence brought the breed popularity as a circus performer: the imaginations of theatre people to mold and clip the Poodle's coat into amusing, eye-catching shapes—pompons on the legs and tails, saddles, caps, bracelets, anklets, ribbons, bows, artificial coat dyes, etc.

leg above the puff are visible. The rest of the body is left in full coat but may be shaped in order to insure overall balance.

In the third acceptable clip, the "Continental," the face, throat, feet and base of tail are shaved. The hindquarters are shaved with optional pompons on the hips. The legs are shaved, leaving bracelets on the hind legs and puffs on the forelegs. There is a pompon on the end of the tail. The entire shaven foot and a

Clipping the Poodle. Miniature Poodle in English Saddle clip.

The American Kennel Club allows the dogs to be shown in four specific clips, in addition to the corded coat. The A.K.C. Poodle standard describes the four permitted clips. The "Puppy" clip, with the coat long, is acceptable for dogs under one year of age. The face, throat, feet and base of the tail are shaved. The entire shaven foot is visible. There is a pompon on the end of the tail. In order to give a neat appearance and a smooth unbroken line, shaping of the coat is permissible.

The "English Saddle" clip involves shaving the face, throat, feet, forelegs and base of the tail, leaving puffs on the forelegs and a pompon on the end of the tail. The hindquarters are covered with a short blanket of hair except for a curved shaved area on each flank and two shaved bands on each hindleg. The entire shaven foot and a portion of the shaven

portion of the shaven foreleg above the puff are visible. The rest of the body is left in full coat but may be shaped for overall balance and appeal.

In the "Sporting" clip, a Poodle shall be shown with face, feet, throat, and base of tail shaved, leaving a scissored cap on the top of the head and a pompon on the end of the tail. The rest of the body and legs are clipped or scissored to follow the outline of the dog, leaving a short blanket of coat no longer than one inch in length. The hair on the legs may be slightly longer than that on the body.

Topknots, hair on the skull from stop to occiput, of all four A.K.C. clips can be held in place by elastic bands or left free.

Some owners, however, are not interested in the show ring and wish to clip their Poodle in a lesser known style which accentuates the particular dog's personality. Undoubtedly, the Poodle coat is the most tremendous and impressive of all coats in dogdom, and the conscious owner can capitalize on his dog's uniqueness and the quality, abundance and versatility of this magnificent coat.

Of course, any one of these styles has many variations which only your personal choice should govern. The creative Poodle pet-owner should "never" feel restricted. If an owner intends to clip the dog himself, it is most practical for the novice clipper to start with the simpler cuts until he has acquired confidence and dexterity. Getting the advice of professional groomers is priceless and relatively without cost.

Among the possible non-regulation super trendy clips are the Summer, Shawl, Baby Doll, Clown, Town and Country, Royal Dutch, Dutch band, Kerry Blue style, Bedlington Terrier style, Water Spaniel style, Monkey, Cowboy, Sailor Boy Bell-bottom, and Hillbilly clips.

The Summer clip is a convenient one to use to keep the dog cool. It involves a clean face, and shaving the body, leaving pompons on the feet and tail. The Shawl clip is very similar to the English Saddle clip, except that the saddle-shaped indentations are not used. The heavy hair of the mane extends down the front leg to the dewclaw, and the back

(which is trimmed for a heavy, hedgelike appearance) extends down the back leg to the dewclaw. The hair on the front legs

is trimmed straight down for a very clean appearance. This is a good preliminary clip if you intend to exhibit your dog in the future.

The Baby Doll clip (sometimes called the Bolero) is also a take-off on the English Saddle. The muzzle (whiskers are optional) and the throat to the pith of the neck are shaved. The sides and back of the neck are clipped so that the mane drapes around the throat like a necklace. The top-knot on the head is scissored a little

Clipping the Poodle. Standard Poodle puppy in Puppy clip.

Clipping the Poodle. Standard Poodle in Sporting clip. Photo by Booth.

closer than in the previous clips and rounded. Desirably, the Poodle gains large leg-of-mutton-looking shoulder pads and a large bouffant on the rump.

Clipping the Poodle. Toy Poodle in Continental clip. Photo by Gilbert.

The front leg below the elbow is shaved to the first knuckle, leaving a full pompon below. The paws are shaved clean. The hindlegs are shaved farther than in the English Saddle clip, since the Baby Doll is meant to be an exaggeration. The pompons are scissored round. The ears are shaved leaving very large round-bottomed tassels on the ends of them. The belly is shaved leaving a narrow band around the center of the body to separate the legs of mutton and the bouffants.

The Clown clip is easy to care for and ideal in the hot summer months or in perennially warm climates where the Poodle's heavy coat might cause him discomfort. The muzzle is shaved or whiskers are left, as you prefer. A large pompon is left on the head, terminating in a decided point on the back of the neck between the ears. Blend the pompon into the hair on the back of the neck after the body is shaved. The ears are usually left full but evened off at the bottom. If you wish, they can be shaved down with or without tassels. The entire body is shaved, except that large pompons are left on the feet and on the tail as in the Continental clip.

The Town and Country clip is sometimes called the Master; this is similar to the Sporting clip, but more exaggerated. Most dogs in this clip have the whiskers left on and a full topknot on the head which terminates in a point at the back of the neck. This clip should look very crisp. The body is shaved to the elbows on the front legs and a little lower on the rump in the back than in the Sporting clip. The paws are clipped a little higher than the dewclaws. The puffs on the legs should be full, not blended at the edges into the body hair, but with a very definite line of demarcation. A pompon on the tail, and the ears full.

The Royal Dutch clip, or Dutch Boy, is a popular Poodle clip in America. The muzzle is shaved, and full whiskers are left. These should begin at the back corners of the mouth. Square them off by combing them forward then scissoring straight along the bottom edges and straight up and down at the front of the mouth. The ears usually have ball-like tassels. Full ears are also very attractive with this clip. Leave full pompons on the head and tail. The neck and throat are shaved. A strip is shaved all the way along the ridge of the back to the base of the tail. Between the last rib and the point where the loin joins the hindleg, a medium-width band is shaved around the stomach. The shoulders and rear legs need to look very full, and the Poodle look short at the same time. The paws are shaved to the dewclaws. Fully comb out the hair on the legs and then scissor this hair evenly for a hedgelike look.

The Dutch Band clip is very similar to the Dutch Boy but has a squarer look. The face hair beneath the eyes should be fuller than in the Dutch Boy. The whiskers should be full, but the muzzle shaven. Tassels on the ears are squared off instead of ball shaped as in the Dutch Boy. The neck and throat are shaved to the pith, leaving a very definite rounded edge on the ruff, like a necklace. The ruff is left full to the last rib. Both front and rear legs are left full, and the paws are not shaved but scissored square. The band around the stomach is shaved. This clip should be very crisp, so make sure that all the lines are sharp and definite. The pompons on the tail and head should look square. This is achieved by combing the pompons up and scissoring them flat on top. Then scissor them straight up and down on the sides.

The Kerry Blue Terrier style clip is primarily for those who like the appearance of the terrier breeds. The appearance of the Bedlington Terrier can also be adopted by the Poodle. These two are novelty clips and no serious Poodle fanciers should subscribe to the folly of masquerading their Poodle as a different breed. The Water Spaniel style clip is a utility type clip, and is especially useful in the event that you should err on the head topknot.

The Monkey, Cowboy, Sailor Boy Bell-bottom and Hillbilly clips are absurd styles, which rather exaggeratedly (even vulgarly) shape the coat. The authors withhold the information to discourage owners from getting too carried away with any inane clipping styles. While creativity is an unchallenged essence to life, so too is dignity. *See also* Poodle, Corded coat, Grooming shows

Clitoris
A small glandular organ lying close to the opening of the vagina; its function is a matter of debate. The clitoris swells at times, believably enhancing intercourse.

Cloddy
Heavy, unrefined, stubby in general appearance.

Close-coupled
Short coupled. *See* Coupling

Close-cupped feet
See Cat feet

Clostridia
Rod-shaped bacteria responsible for some food poisoning and gangrene, among other infections.

Clipping the Poodle. Miniature Poodle in corded coat. Photo by I. Français.

Clown face
A bicolored head which is divided (by color) longitudinally through the center. The Smooth Fox Terrier is one breed that is made-up thus.

Clumber Spaniel

A spaniel with a definite sense of identity, the Clumber is bulky and low set, with deliberate yet dignified motion and a steady, determined pace. The actual origin of the Clumber is likely lost forever. Based on physical qualities, authorities point to the Clumber's origin: its long and low body might indicate the use of the Basset Hound; the heavy head and visible haw suggest the infusion of the early Alpine Spaniels (thus a relation to the St. Bernard). Not much can be ascertained as fact, but the need for heavier that supine hunters desired a more sluggish gundog in order for them to keep up with him, flattering their snail's-pace style and thereby avoiding any overexertion during their weekend exhibitions.

The Clumber Spaniel responds well to training and, although slow, makes a fine tracker and retriever. As a companion, the Clumber Spaniel is excellent; his noted qualities are loyalty, affection, and discrimination.

ESSENTIALS OF THE CLUMBER SPANIEL: The low-to-the-ground Clumber is a unique spaniel, rather long and heavy, weighing between 55 and 85 pounds (25–38 kg). Height is 19 to 20 inches (48–51 cm). Head is massive, and body is heavy-boned. The head has a marked stop, a flat top skull, and a large protuberance at the occiput. Muzzle, medium in length; nose, large and square; ears, broad and set low, triangular in shape and slightly feathered. The dense, weather-resistant coat is straight and flat but not harsh. There is noticeable feathering of the underbelly and legs; a neck frill is also present. The coat color is predominantly white, with either lemon or orange markings. The muzzle and ears are frequently freckled with such markings.

Clydesdale Terrier

See Paisley Terrier

C.O.C.A.

(The Confederation Canina Americana) C.O.C.A. consists of the national kennel clubs of South and Central America. The countries involved in this amalgamation include Brazil, Mexico, Argentina, Venezuela, Colombia, Peru, Chile, Uruguay, and Paraguay. The organization has successfully managed to unite the efforts of Latin American kennel clubs and minimize existing disharmonies among them.

Clumber Spaniels, white with orange markings. Photo by I. Français.

spaniels to work denser terrain is one acceptable impetus for the Clumber's inception. A second, more entertaining if not more reliable, reclines on the notion

Coarse

Used to describe the bulky, plain, unrefined qualities in the physical properties of a dog. Coarse, in terms of coat types, would indicate a rough or wire texture. *See also* Wire coat

Coarse head

An overly broad head marked by lumpy bone and extraneous musculation. Always considered undesirable.

Coarse shoulders

See Shoulder types

Coarse skull

See Thick in skull

The coat is the dogs' protection against heat and cold. The practice of clipping a dog's coat to keep it cool during the hot months may not be wise, for in some breeds the soft undercoat acts as insulation against heat. If a dog is clipped, the time it takes for the coat to grow in must be considered—it may take nine months or even longer in some breeds.

The coat can be a sign of a dog's good or ill health. An overly dry coat can be a sign of vitamin deficiency or other illness. A sparse or patchy coat can suggest parasitic infestation, especially if accom-

Coat

The hair covering the dog's skin. Most breeds of dog have coats, and the majority of these are double-coated, that is, possess two coats—an outer coat and an undercoat. The outer coat, the coat that is readily visible, is usually comprised of long, coarse, and/or stand-offish hair; the undercoat is usually soft, short and smooth, providing the necessary insulation. Many smooth-coated breeds are single coated but not all single-coated breeds are smooths. The Maltese, for instance, is a long but single-coated breed of dog.

panied by raw or flaky skin. An oily coat can be a sign of poor diet or lacking care. The change in day length and especially the change in temperature will affect coat growth. A dog's coat that does not respond to the changing seasons with either shedding or coat growth may be signaling disorder or complication, depending, of course, upon the breed.

Most coat types require some degree of grooming, which *see*. It is usually the combination of good grooming habits and a sound diet that promotes a healthy coat on any dog, whether it is long or short coated.

Coat. The longhaired Lhasa Apso requires extensive grooming in order to actualize such an elaborate show coat.

Coffin head profiled by the Borzoi. Photo by R. Reagan.

Cobby

Well packaged: compact, thick-set, shortish. Refers to both height and length (e.g., Pug, King Charles Spaniel).

Coccidia

Protozoa, when found in large enough numbers in the intestines, will damage the intestinal wall, often leading to bloody diarrhea. *See also* Diarrhea

Cocked ears

Semi-prick or semi-drop ears that are characterized by forward-bending tips. Sometimes referred to as tipped ears (e.g., Shetland Sheepdog).

Cocked-up tail

A tail carried erect in a breed in which the correct or preferred tail carriage is level with or below the level of the topline.

Cocker Spaniel

See American Cocker Spaniel, English Cocker Spaniel

Cocking spaniels

Small spaniels which could negotiate the willows and alders in the bottom lands, beneath the level at which they intertwine, to flush the quick-rising woodcock from its boring operations. There are two noteworthy cocking spaniels today, the American Cocker Spaniel and the English Cocker Spaniel. In both breed's native countries they are known simply as Cocker Spaniel. In America, the Cocker is one the nation's most popular breeds. At one time, the Welsh Springer was referred to as the Welsh Cocker. *See* Gundogs, American Cocker Spaniel, English Cocker Spaniel

Coffin head

Long, narrowish head that appears coffinlike in shape (e.g., Borzoi).

Coin tail

A tightly double-curled tail desirable in the Basenji and Shar-Pei.

Cold line

The faint scent of fox, which may be minutes or hours old, depending on scenting conditions.

Cold nose

Refers to the excellent scenting ability of a hound able to work an old or cold trail. A "cold-nosed" hound has superior scenting ability.

Colds

It is extremely unlikely that your dog will get a cold in the same way that a person gets a cold. When a dog shows signs similar to those of the common cold, they are probably the result of other causes.

Collar

Coat coloration outlining the neck area, most often white (e.g., Basenji, Collie). A royal collar is the symmetrical and well-balanced white coat markings that surround the neck (e.g., Old English Sheepdog).

Collarette

Moderate ruff formation around the neck (e.g., Belgian Sheepdog, Malinois).

Collars

Collars and harnesses are of great use everyday; they should be worn by the dog at all times. Attached to the collar or harness should be an identification tag and a dog license, as well as any necessary medical information that could save your dog should he get lost—such as allergies, disorders, etc. The pup should be introduced to the collar at about six weeks of age. It should be suitably sized and not one he will grow in to. Comfortable with his collar, the dog should be easier to train on the lead. Choke collars are not recommended for pups, though they can be useful in training so long as they are used with care; opinion varies on the use of choke collars, especially the spiked version known as the training collar, which is not recommended.

Elizabethan collars. Named for its faint suggestion of the fashionable collars of Elizabethan England, the Elizabethan collar is a protective device that is worn around the dog's neck and prevents his scratching his head or chewing his body. These collars can be purchased at a local pet shop or veterinarian's office. Elizabethan collars are most commonly used to preclude the dog's irritation of an infection or applied bandage or preparation. It must be remembered that scratching and chewing are signs of a condition. Preventing the dog from scratching is not extinguishing the condition but thwarting the signs. Chronic scratching and/or chewing should be inspected by your veterinarian.

Flea collars. The common parasite of dogs, the flea, can cause a host of complications to the dog. Flea collars can help prevent or limit flea infestation by repelling and/or killing fleas on or near the animal. These collars have a limited life and should be replaced as directed. Flea collars alone do not prevent flea infestation but good husbandry and other measures must be employed. The owner should be cautioned: some dogs may have an allergic reaction to the chemicals contained in the flea collar. Watch carefully. If symptoms appear, discontinue use and visit your regular veterinarian.

Collars. A choke collar is an excellent training device.

Collars. Puppy collars acquaint the young canine with collar wearing and leash training, and provide a means for identification.

Collie

1) Working type sheepdog, a generic term. Besides the Collie (Scotch Collie), there are the Border Collie, Shetland Sheepdog, Welsh Collie, and New Zealand Shepherd.

Collie, Rough, sable and white. Photo by I. Français.

2) The Collie is a member of the truly ancient herding "race" which claims as its land of origin the country of Scotland. There are two varieties of the breed: the Rough and Smooth Collie, and both are sometimes referred to as Scotch Collies,

suggestive of their native land. The title Collie is a derivative of the name Colley Dog which was given to the breed many years ago by Scots farmers who employed the dogs at herding the native mountain-dwelling sheep called colleys, an ancient ovine which is the forebear of the renowned black-masked and black-footed Highland sheep of Scotland today. Originally primarily black in color, the breed, even in its nineteenth-century heyday, scarcely presented the classic "Lassie" coloration (sable/white).

The necessity to Scottish inhabitants of grazing livestock deemed the breeding of hard-working, rugged Collies tantamount to their survival: the Scots were very demanding with their dogs and highly selective in their work-oriented breeding practices. It is believed that the Smooth Collie developed in the region of Northumberland County, England, where cattle droving became its forte, and that the Rough Collie developed as a sheep herder in the Highlands of Scotland, where the climate is more extreme in its coldness. There is, however, little doubt that both varieties of Collie spring from the same well—both breeds coming from identical ancestry.

The Collie of the present retains many of its once-bred-for qualities and can still be seen working herds in Scotland, New Zealand, Australia, and other at least partially pastoral countries. The breed is known for its efficiency in working relatively large herds and seems to delight in the challenge.

Believed to have entered the British Isles as far back as 55 B.C., the Collie became the twinkle in the dog fancier's eye in the second half of the nineteenth century. Queen Victoria of England is often cited as responsible for the "discovery" of the breed, for it was she who first brought the Collie to the attention of the general public—or at least brought an attention that penetrated lastingly. The [Collie] Queen came upon the dogs during her royal visit to Balmoral in Scotland in the early 1860s. From that time onward there has been a fancy of the breed that has focused on physical type. Known at that time as the Scotch Sheepdog, the Collie first entered the show ring at the Birmingham Dog Society show in England in the early 1860s. Following the royal lead, America first admitted Collies to the ring in 1878 at the Westminster show of that year. Today most of the breed please their owners in the home and in the show ring, and not on the pasture. Known for their intelligence and willingness to please, Collies fare well in obedience trials. Regardless of their variety, members of the breed are never timid or sullen: the ideal Collie is blessed with an expression and disposition that are absolutely distinctive to its breed.

ESSENTIALS OF THE COLLIE: Collies present a dignified impression marked by certitude, alertness, and intelligence. The standard for the Rough Collie states that, in general appearance, "Appears as dog of great beauty, standing with impassive dignity, with no part out of proportion to whole." The Smooth Collie standard is essentially similar, with the added clause, "giving the appearance of working capability." The Collie's lithe working body is marked by a clean, firm, sinewy neck that carries one of the most expressive heads in dogdom. Of special importance are: the eyes (obliquely set and almond shaped), the skull in proportion with the body, and the tipped ears in proportion with the skull; viewed from front or side, the head re-

sembles a well-blunted clean wedge; viewed in profile, top of skull and top of

muzzle lie in two parallel straight lines of equal length divided by a slight, but perceptible stop. Ears are small and set not too close together on the top of the skull; when alert they are carried semi-erect. Body is slightly long in comparison to height; back is firm with a slight rise over the loins; chest is deep and fairly broad behind the shoulders, and ribs are well sprung. The coat may be either rough or smooth, with the former being long and

Collie, Rough, tricolor.

Collie, Smooth, sable and white.

dense and the latter being short, smooth, and double. Color can be sable and white, tricolor or blue merle. Height is between 22–26 inches (56–66 cm), and weight varies between 50–75 pounds (23–34 kg), always with good proportion, never oversized or undersized.

Color

The hairs of dogs, as those of other mammals, possess three kinds of pigments: black, brown, and red or tan. Dilu-

describe non-solid coats. Each term has specific nuances and conditions of which an owner must be aware. A bicolored Cocker Spaniel and a tricolored Afghan Hound are surely undefined variables in the show rings.

The politics of colors is colorful to say the least. With some breeds, colors are immaterial and of no importance. For example, the Wire Fox Terrier does not favor one color or another, *except* that white should predominate; brindle, red

Collies in color. Rough Collies in all three recognized colors: sable and white, tricolor, and blue merle.

tion factors may render these pigments lighter, or they may be removed entirely by genes producing white spotting or albinism. Hair length and texture (and sometimes skin pigmentation) affect the appearance of hair color.

Dogs have occurred in practically every dilution of every color dreamable. More so, the dog fancy has done its best to complicate the matter by applying specific terms to each color occurring in each breed. For instance, the cream- or tan-colored Cocker Spaniel is called buff; a similar color in the Doberman Pinscher is called Isabella. Additionally, sometimes the same term means different things in each breed—sable is a different color pattern in Collies than it is in German Shepherds. The differentiation between the particolors (more than one color) has been difficult too. Particolor, bicolor, tricolor, pied, roan, brindle, and merle all

liver or slaty blue are objectionable—*otherwise*, color is of little or no importance. A brindle Fox Terrier owner might sneer at the apparent *non sequitur* that has been in print for years. There are breeds where color really plays no role: the Greyhound, Chihuahua, and the Foxhound. Color, in general, is a superficial consideration in dogs, barring albinism (which *see*); the color of working dogs in particular is immaterial. It is believed, however, that shepherds were color conscious: white flock guards bonded better with the sheep; dark herders with splashes of white related to and influenced the flock with greater success. Since the color of the Greyhound or Bulldog didn't affect its performance on the field, in the pit, or on the track, colors were never deemed of any importance.

Colors have been so important to some breeds, on the other hand, that the breed name reflects it: The Soft Coated *Wheaten* Terrier, Irish *Red* and *White* Setter, American *Black* and *Tan* Coonhound, Kerry *Blue* Terrier, German *Wolf*spitz, West Highland *White* Terrier and the Russian *Harlequin* Hound.

Certain breeds necessarily forbid particular colors. Most terrier breeds are prejudiced to whites—solid white or just markings. Colors also have defined breeds (at least initially). The Cairn Terrier in white of course would be a Westie; the Newfoundland in parti, a Landseer; the white German Toy Spitzen soon gained favor in the U.S. as "American Eskimos"; the neglected black German Longhaired Pointer found friends elsewhere and became the Grosser Münsterländer. Certain breeds are divided by color: there are three different Cocker Spaniels, each shown individually—Black, Any Solid Color Other Than Black, and Particolor; there are two Bull Terriers—Colored and White; and four Cavalier King Charles Spaniels—Blenheim (red/white), Black/tan, Ruby (solid red), and Prince Charles (tricolor).

Color fads undulate like other superficial emphases in the show ring. At one time, there was a tremendous demand for cream-colored Pomeranians, today the color is less common. Today's Boston Terriers are favored in the brindle and

white pattern, today's Bulldog standard lists the order of preference for the five color possibilities, red Miniature Pin-

schers dominate the show ring, while most solely pet MinPins tend to be black and tan.

Show ring terminology for colors can be rather intriguing. Some colors such as grizzle, liver, slate, and drab yellow do not ring as mellifluously as harlequin, blue speckled, apricot and Isabella. Perhaps the most pleasing of all color terms is sand, used to describe the desert-dwelling Sloughi. Additionally, the authors have found that most dog owners are not aware that the Dalmatian can be liver and white, that Poodles can come in bright red and that certain "underground" Poodles, in particolors, and that the skin of some Chinese Cresteds is actually lavender! Isn't it a wonderful, colorful world of dogs! *See also* Merle, Blue

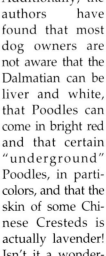

Color. Rough Chow Chow exhibiting cream coloration.

Color. Samoyed exhibiting the biscuit coloration. Notice how similar in hue the biscuit color is to the cream of the Chow Chow.

Color. Unusual and/or often discouraged varieties: (*top*) Brittany in black and white; (*middle*) Staffordshire Terrier in black/tan; (*lower right*) Basenji in brindle; (*lower left*) Doberman Pinscher in solid white.

Color. (*top*) White in the German Shepherd Dog is not desirable to breed purists. Today white shepherds are considered as a separate breed at rare-breed shows. (*middle right*) Miniature Smooth Dachshunds looking dapper in dapple.

Color. (*middle left*) German Wirehaired Pointer in black and white known as the German Drahthaar. (*bottom*) West Highland White Terrier, once a simple white and cull-worthy Scotch terrier!

Color blindness

Dogs see the world in shades of gray and thus in human terms would be considered color blind. A dog distinguishes objects by scent more so than sight; therefore, switching your dog's dark blue dish to a dark green dish would go unnoticed if the plastic didn't smell stronger on the new green one.

Combs

Combs come in many shapes and styles. The most commonly used comb is the fine-medium combination. It is important that the comb is comfortable in your hand and that the teeth are properly spaced for the particular coat on which you are working.

Combs. A well-combed Afghan Hound vending a wide selection of combs and brushes. Photo courtesy of Hindes (England).

Colostrum

The puppy's first milk received from the bitch; this milk contains important antibodies which help the pup to combat possible disease.

Coma

The state of deep and prolonged unconsciousness, usually the result of an injury or disease affecting the brain. Dogs that suffer coma are most times best put to death in a humane manner.

Combination

Mutuel ticket that combines straight, place, and show.

Commisures

Lip corners, where the upper and lower edges of the lips meet at the sides of the muzzle.

Communal pad

Also known as metacarpal pad. *See also* Feet anatomy

Compact

The definitive union of body parts, not to be confused with cobby, which *see*.

Compact coat

A close-lying, short-medium length coat with a dense undercoat.

Compact feet
See Cat feet

Companion Dog
A dog that has won certain minimum scores in Novice Classes at a specified number of A.K.C.-licensed or member obedience trials. C.D. is the usual suffix employed. *See also* Obedience trials

Companion Dog Excellent
A dog that has won certain minimum scores in Open Classes at a specified number of A.K.C.-licensed or member obedience trials. C.D.X. is the usual suffix employed. *See also* Obedience trials

Comparative anatomy
Although man is an erect-standing, bipedal mammal, he is quite similar skeletally to the dog. With the obvious exception of man's walking on two feet and dog's walking on all fours, the dog is missing a clavicle or collar bone. The essential skeletal components, skull (of course different in itself), scapula, humerus, pelvis, femur and metatarsals are existent in both human and canine. Another difference is the dog's humerus or upper arm, which is attached to the chest wall along its entire length, whereas in man the humerus is entirely free. Dog, unlike man, walks specifically on its "toes," whereas man walks on his entire foot (including the metatarsals). It is interesting to note that no other animal exhibits as much variation in skeletal formation as the domestic dog. This is of course an obvious statement if one considers the differences apparent in the giant breeds from the toy breeds. In general, it is fair to say that man's body is more flexible than the dog's: man with his triple-digited fingers, thumbs, and ball-and-socket arms bows only to the flexibility of one particular canine—the Norwegian Lundehund, with all its double-jointed majesty.

Compiègne Pointer
See Braque Saint-Germain

Compression
A serious condition affecting the brain, it is often the result of a serious blow or fall. Loss of balance and coordination, bloody nose and ears, and vomiting are common signs. Additionally, the pupils may be of unequal size. The dog should be set to rest and kept warm while veterinary care is immediately sought.

Conception
Occurs when the sperm penetrates and fertilizes the egg. It marks the beginning of the life process. The fertilized egg becomes an embryo, which in turn becomes a fetus, and when mature is born into the world. *See* Breeding.

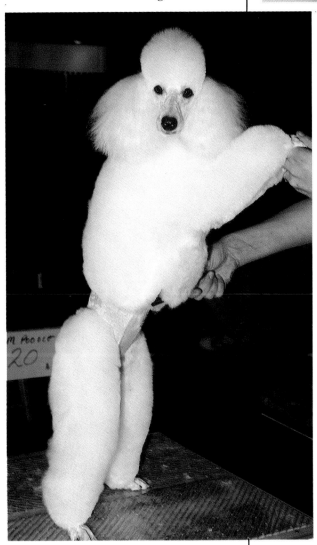

Comparative anatomy. Poodle on two feet impersonates upright man (though this talented canine still lacks a clavicle!). Photo by I. Français.

Concussion
A condition of impaired function, typically of the brain, it is often a result of a serious blow or injury. Common signs include shallow breathing, weak pulse, pupil dilation, pale lips, and a general coolness to the body. The dog should be subjected to rest until veterinary treatment is available.

Condition

An animal's general fitness and health as determined by the animal's external and behavioral signs. A finely conditioned working dog, of course, has a more rigid standard to live up to than would a homebound Havanese, although both dogs must be in optimal physical and psychological states in order to be considered in good condition.

Cone-shaped head

The triangularly or conically shaped skull that is commonly seen on dogs (e.g., the Dachshund).

Conformation

The outward appearance and physical formation of a canine, including the symmetry and balance of the composite of its parts. In canine terminology, conformation is applied to show ring competition and denotes the overall quality of a dog's structure, form, and arrangement of the parts.

Conjunctiva around the eyelids are visible on this Basset Hound.

Congenital hip dysplasia

Refers to the condition of hip dysplasia that is inherited. *See* Hip dysplasia

Congo Dog

See Basenji

Congo Pygmies' Bush Dog

Standing about 17.5 inches (44.5 cm) tall, this little-known African is used by natives for hunting. Shorthaired and long-headed, this prick-eared dog is remotely similar in appearance to the Basenji, who also derives from the Congo area. In color the Congo Pygmies' Bush Dog is yellowish fawn. These dogs are hunted by the Pygmies in great numbers on such large game as lion and elephant. They are known for their fearless and furious hunting approach which effectively and devilishly fells the game.

Conjunctiva

The mucous membrane lining of the eyelids, both upper and lower. On most breeds, these pinkish lines are not visible. In a select group of mastiffs and mastiffy hounds, such as the St. Bernard and Bloodhound, the conjunctivae are visible to a certain degree. *See also* Haw-eyedness, Ectropion.

Constipation

A direct result of too little water or blockage in the intestines, constipation can signal poor diet, digestive disorder, or an enlarged prostate gland, which blocks all but small or loose stools. Bones are perhaps the most common cause of constipation; when insufficiently digested, they pack in the intestine, causing blockage. Such foods as rice, bonemeal, and others are "binding" foods, in large doses drying the intestines, causing constipation. Other causes of constipation include: old age, pregnancy, and intestinal impaction.

Contact dermatitis

Skin irritation caused by sensitivity to a substance with which a dog comes into contact. Determining the substance and removing it, if possible, from the dog's living area is recommended. If impossible, shots to control or neutralize the reaction may be prescribed.

Continental clip
See Clipping the Poodle

Continental Toy Spaniel, Papillon
See Papillon

Continental Toy Spaniel, Phalene
The Épagneul Nain of Belgium, a favorite of royalty, is the ancestor of both the Phalene and the Papillon. In the United States and Great Britain, the Phalene is but a variety of the Papillon. The F.C.I. registers the two dogs individually. All F.C.I.-registered Papillons must have erect ears; Phalenes, completely drop. As *papillon* in French means butterfly, when the ears fail to emulate a butterfly, they are called *phalene,* or moth.

The Phalene has always been loved by a select few, but he never achieved prolonged popularity, as did the Papillon in France during the early 1700s. No sound evidence connects the Continental Toy Spaniels to the Chihuahua, despite an obvious similarity to the long-coated variety of that breed. In France today, the Phalene is called le Chien Ecureuil, or Squirrel Dog, in honor of its tail, not its quarry. Incidentally, dogs of the breed have been effectively used as rabbitters and ratters. *See also* Papillon.

ESSENTIALS OF THE CONTINENTAL TOY SPANIEL, PHALENE: The skull should be rounded between the ears, the muzzle one-third the total length of the head, pointier and thinner than the skull, with stop accentuated. Ears should be large, with rounded tips, heavily fringed, set well back and completely dropped. The neck is of medium length. Shoulders are well developed and sloping back. The chest deep; forelegs straight and fine boned. The topline is even; the ribs well sprung; belly slightly arched. Height: 8–11 inches (20–28 cm) The coat is long, usually profuse, with the abundant flowing undercoat. Movement is light and free, suggestive of ethereal power and grace. The long tail is set high and well fringed. Color is particolor: primarily white, with patches of any color except liver; color should surround the eyes and cover the ears, leaving a white blaze on the foreface.

Contractible ears
Ears in which mobility is such that the external ear leather can be folded and turned up in a most peculiar way—backwards or at right angles upwards so that the ear opening is shut. These ears are the exclusive property of the Norwegian Lundehund. This ability enables this industrious ex-puffin hunter to close its ears to avoid water or rain getting inside.

Contusion
A closed wound of ruptured small blood vessels and soft tissue damage. Synonymous with "bruise," contusions are not common in dogs and, unless serious or extensive, require little care. The application of cold to the affected area immediately following the injury can minimalize swelling.

Convalescent dogs
See Older dog

Convulsions
Some causes of convulsions are brain injury, cerebellar hypoplasia, diabetes, eclampsia, encephalitis, epilepsy, fever, foreign bodies, heatstroke, hypoglycemia, poisons, salmon poisoning, and vitamin deficiencies.

Continental Toy Spaniel, Phalene, particolor. Photo by I. Français.

Coolout shelter

Covered runway in which racing dogs may be walked after a race while they are cooling down.

Coonhounds

Coonhounds are scenthounds that are used to tree raccoon. The treeing instinct is deeply bred in these dogs. While the foxhound is one of the variety's ancestors, the hunting style is somewhat different. America is the home of the five known coonhound breeds: the American Black and Tan, Redbone, Bluetick, English, and Treeing Walker. Other varieties exist but are not recognized on a large scale basis. The United Kennel Club recognizes all five breeds; the American Kennel Club presently recognizes only the Black and Tan. Most raccoon hunting takes place in the southern U.S. The dogs have also been used on opossum, rabbit and deer.

Coonhounds. American Black and Tan Coonhound poses with coon skins.

Copper

Necessary in small amounts for good health, proper levels can prevent hookworms, when adequate iron and protein are also fed.

Coprophagy

Coprophagy, also known as stool eating, can be caused by dietary insuffi-ciency, hunger, pleasing smell, and desire to retrieve. It can lead to disease and illness. If vitamins and minerals are lacking or food is insufficient, proper feeding can be the cure. Feeding parboiled green vegetables may mask the odor, and changing the bacterial content of the intestines, through cultured foods, can give an odor to the stool that is unpleasant to the dog. Common in pups and all dogs is the desire to chew; nylon (or safe) chew products are the best way to satiate chewing, if this desire is the cause. Worms are another cause of coprophagy, and deworming is the answer to such. Coprophagy should not be allowed, and it is not "normal" behavior. Determine the root and extract it. Occasionally coprophagy becomes a habit, and although the root is expunged, the habit continues.

Copulation

The uniting of the dog's penis with the bitch's vagina. In canine matings, because of the unique design of the dog's penis, mating involves special considerations. *See* Breeding

Corded coat

Nature's interweaving of the outer and undercoat to produce individual cords for the protection and warmth of the dog. Only a handful of dogs possess this peculiar coat: the Puli, Komondor, and Bergamasco. Each of these breeds functions as protectors of flocks, and their corded coats provide them with an impenetrable buffer against the flock's predators. The presently unfenceable German Sheeppoodle is known to have had a corded coat. A Poodle's coat will also cord if correctly encouraged, as will that of the Berger des Pyrenees. The cords are separate from one another and are not one unkempt matted mass. Corded coats require a great deal of attention in order to keep clean and untangled.

Corkscrew tail

A tail that is spirally twisted or curled; similar to a double-curled tail or curled tail except that the second curl descends lower instead of enravelling itself inside the first curl.

Corky

In terms of temperament, spunky or vital. Infrequently applied to terriers.

Cornea

The large, round, transparent area of the eye.

Cornish Greyhound

The original show-type Greyhound that developed in Cornwall, England. This name was applied to distinguish these show-stock dogs from the coarser coursing types. *See also* Greyhound, Coursing

Corns

Hard callouses affecting the soles of a dog's feet. These are thick painful growths that typically occur on the feet. They are reportedly caused by friction and are not especially common in dogs. Should the dog walk with a limp, the foot should be checked for such growths, especially between the pads. A veterinarian should be consulted regarding treatment.

Coronaviral gastroenteritis

Reported around the world, CG is highly contagious. The signs are milder than those of parvoviral infection, but include anorexia, depression, vomiting, and diarrhea. The most common cause is ingestion of fecal matter of infected canids, including dogs, foxes, and coyotes. Although no effective treatment has been found, therapy includes large doses of fluids and selective antibiotics. A vaccine is also available.

Correction

The independent re-evaluation of the conditions of a flash or short point, and

moving on. Usually a bird has been in the brush and has left.

Corsac fox

A wild dog and a member of the genus *Vulpes*. *See* Foxes

Corded coat illustrated by the Komondor. Photo by R. Reagan.

Cortisone

A corticosteroid, one used for anti-inflammatory purposes, this drug is often prescribed for allergic reactions, arthritis, and other inflammatory conditions and problems.

Coton de Tulear

The Coton de Tulear is a bichon type that developed in southern Madagascar and the surrounding areas. When troops of the Indian Company settled on the island of Bourbon in 1665, the ancestor of the Tulear bichon accompanied them. The Chien Coton "La Reunion" is believed to be the breed's direct ascendent. The original bichon type extends back possibly one thousand years or more. Bichon type was diversified as new areas

Coton de Tulear. Photo by I. Français.

were settled by the Europeans and the breeding stock of the bichon in the given area was necessarily limited. It is even possible in some cases that native dogs of other types were crossbred. The Maltese, the bichon of Malta and one of the world's most recognized bichons, was used to stabilize the Tulear when its numbers were dangerously low. The Coton has enjoyed the favor of the Madagascar upper class for some years; today, however, he is woven thinly in Madagascar. The breed gained F.C.I. recognition in 1970 and looks forward to continued progress and popularity. On the Continent, the breed is becoming exhibited more and more frequently, although there are comparably few in the world today.

ESSENTIALS OF THE COTON DE TULEAR: The ideal coat is cottony or fluffy rather than silky. *Coton*, of course, translates to "cotton." The outer coat is long and white; no undercoat is present. Other than the pre-

ferred all-white dogs, specimens with champagne heads or body markings, as well as those with black and white, have helped to distinguish the breed from other members of the bichon family. Height: 10–12 inches (25–31 cm). Weight: 12–15 pounds (5.5–7 kg). Under the fluffy coat, the Coton de Tulear is a dog of balance and symmetry.

Coughs

The three common canine coughs are dry, kennel, and reverse. *See* Distemper, Kennel cough, Snorting, respectively. Coughing can also be the sign of a weak heart. *See* Heart, problems. Persistent or severe coughing is definite reason to seek veterinary care for your dog.

Couples

A brace or pair of hounds or sheepdogs. A link with a swivel-snap at each end allows scenthounds to be coupled together. The number of hounds in a pack is traditionally enumerated in couples. A thirteen hound pack is six and a half couples. The expression originates from the practice of keeping hounds coupled cast away on the hunt.

Coupling

The part of the body joining the dog's chest to the hindquarters; the coupling is the entire muscular region joining these two body parts, including the loins. The short and powerful coupling associated with the short distance between the last rib and the hindquarters area is termed short-coupled or close-coupled. Loosely coupled or long coupled, on the other hand, refers to a lengthy distance and resulting structural inferiority.

Coupling, open Insufficiently muscled loins or flanks. A fault listed in the Flat-Coated Retriever breed standard.

Course

To chase game by sight and not by scent. *See* Coursing, Sighthounds

Courser

A track racer that runs wide or from side to side of the track like a coursing dog attempting to head off the hare.

Coursing

The coursing of wild game is one of man's oldest sports—stretching the expanse of four milennia. Gazelles, wolves, deer, antelope and hare are among the coursing hunter's quarry. Coursing, unlike hunting, concerned the matching of one dog's speed against another; hunting, of course, chiefly involved the catch and the kill. The Celts are believed to have introduced the sport of hare coursing to the Romans and Greeks in 150 A.D.

In the East, the Saluki or Gazelle Hound, as it was known, was used to course gazelles. In Mali, the highly prized Azawakh, seated high on its nomad master's camel, was released in the coursing of gazelles as well. Other Eastern greyhounds, such as the Rampur Dog, the Poligar Dog, Banjara Greyhound and the Mahratta Greyhound of India, were used in the hunt. Since many of these dogs were providing food for their masters, coursing was as much a sport as it was a necessity.

In Russia, wolf coursing captured the fancy of the nobility. The great dukes and royal families kept large kennels of dogs for the sole purpose of coursing the wolf.

fanfare and Russian national pride, prewar Russians hailed the coursing event with much of the fervor which the British attached to the fox hunt. Wolf coursing required two dogs of compatible speeds to pursue a single wolf; the dogs seized the wolf by its ears, both dogs gripping at the same moment in order to throw it over. The dogs were then required to pin the wolf until the hunter arrived.

Great Britain boasts the Greyhound, the fastest dog to ever glide across the earth, the race horse of the canine world. Coursing hares, foxes and stag demanded the attention of the general public. Eventually hares became the principal animal coursed. From the romantic glory days of wolf and gazelle coursing, the sport had degenerated to the point where five or six dogs would race after bunnies in a fenced-in area. And while coursing meetings and organizations emerged, the sport became nothing short of killing already-captured bunnies. Greyhound owners would host coursing events to watch their dogs chase hares in the enclosure. Since the owners didn't actually see the first dog overcome the hare, it was usually an unsolved mystery to determine whose dog won the race. Other equally common and disappointing hare coursing moments occurred when the hare would only hop a few yards before five Greyhounds, in full

Coursing. The swift-moving Sloughi has been trained to course a variety of game including rabbit, gazelle and coyote. Photo courtesy Mosica Arabians.

The Borzoi, known as the Russian Wolfhound for good reason, excelled in the sport. Decorating the sport with glorioso

stride, toppled over it and crushed it.

A relief from this folly-ridden sport (for the hares, at least) was the advent of

Coursing. The confines of a manmade track and pursuing already captured bunnies have deflated the romanticism of the hunt. Lurcher photographed by I. Français.

the sport of lure coursing. Chasing a mechanical bunny around a track alleviated the mindless killing of rabbits on public fields. In the glare of artificial lighting, a dummy hare would be chased by six "thoroughbred" Greyhounds. The dogs soon attained the status of quality racehorses. The focus was now more concentrated on the performance and competiton of the dogs, as the original coursers from centuries past intended. *See also* Dog racing, Greyhound

Covering ground

The ratio of distance between the ground and brisket and the distance between forelegs and hindlegs. In terms of gait, the phrase would indicate an easy, economical motion with good reach of stride. This term is most frequently applied to working hounds.

Covert cover

A wood, thicket, or other place where a fox is sheltered.

Coyote, *Canis latrans*.

Cow hocks

Hocks turning inward and feet outward, in the manner of cattle. Such a condition restricts action and represents a physical abnormality. The brushing up of the pasterns against one another when walking is the explanation of the restricted action. In the opposite condition, bow hocks or barrel hocks, the hocks turn outward and the feet inward. Bow-hocked dogs usually have a waddle to their walk and seem to stand wide behind.

Cow-hocked gait

Hindlegs that incline inwardly and tend to rub the interior of the rear pastern in passing. This type of gait is faulty and restricts the animal's ability to move freely.

Cowley Terrier

An extinct small terrier type of England.

Cowlick

A small tuft or swirl of hair protruding in an alternate direction from the rest of the coat— the logic or semi-logic being as if it were groomed by the tongue of a passing bovine.

Coydog

A predatory animal, probably a cross between a wolf and a western coyote, that now ranges widely throughout the U.S.

Coyote

The coyote, *Canis latrans*, is a wild dog native to North America and an animal that intrigues man with its poignant ability to survive. Coyotes once roamed in strong numbers throughout western North America, as far north as Alaska and as far south as Mexico. With the coming of the white man and the transformation of the terrain, the coyote's numbers decreased, due to widespread poisoning efforts by man, hunting, trapping, and other methods of extermination. The cunning coyote survived and survives and has even extended its range northeast into Quebec, New York State, and Maine. In appearance the coyote is best likened to a small wolf, standing no more than 26 inches (66 cm) at the shoulder and weighing from 20 to 50 pounds (9–23 kg). The distinctive feature between either the similarly sized gray or red wolf and the coyote is the head: the latter typically has a larger brain case, a more slender muzzle, and longer tooth row. Also distinguishing from the wolf, the coyote does not form large packs but hunts alone or in pairs.

Coursing. Sequence of photographs depicting Sloughis coursing coyote in the open plains of the American Midwest. Photos by P. Szura.

The scientific name, *Canis latrans*, literally means "barking dog," and barking, accompanied by howling and other similar sounds, is this wild dog's characteristic way of communicating.

Crab-eating dog

The crab-eating dog was once the common name of the forest fox (*Cercydon thous*), a South American fox known for its crayfish- and crab-eating proclivities. The natives of southeastern Uruguay claim that crosses between their domestic dogs and the crab-eating dog were once especially valuable. There may be some truth to the romantic tales of these natives since there are reports of successful fox/dog crosses (none, though, that have been substantially supported). *See* Forest fox.

Croatian Sheepdog, black. Photo by I. Français.

Crabbing

The British terminology for sidewinding: the spinal column deviates in such a way that a rear leg passes on the inside of the forefoot, while the other does so on the outside of its partner, as opposed to traveling in line.

Crank tail

A tail that extends level with the topline at the base but which then drops at a 90° angle and curls at the final quarter of its length.

Crash

When the pack gives tongue together on finding a fox.

Crate training

A method of housebreaking. *See* Housebreaking, Training

Creaseless

Wrinkleless, free from creases in the skin, e.g., Greyhound.

Crest

The uppermost portion of the neck, from nape to beginning of withers. In the hairless breeds, crest would refer to the stray twist of hair that tops the head (e.g., Chinese Crested).

Crested neck

Well-arched neck, appearing so due to firmly developed neck muscles.

Crinkly coat

The slight wave in a wire coat (e.g., Wire Fox Terrier).

Croatian Sheepdog

A flock-working canine native to the province of Croatia in present-day Yugoslavia. Probably related to the latter-day Hungarian Water Dog and the increasingly popular Puli, the Croatian Sheepdog has been a recognizable entity for about one thousand years. The Hrvas̆ki O̅vcar, as the breed is known at home, is smaller and more agile than his two likely guardians, the Karst Sheepdog and the Sarplaninac, and takes full advantage of their brawn should the flock be threatened by any intruder. The Croatian is the definitive herder of his native land and is a common sight among its ovine multitudes. As a herder, he is a fast and active performer with strong instincts and reflexes. His stand-offish approach to the flock may be less conventional than some other herders but surely no less effective.

The Croatian is a virtually weatherproof canine with a comparably adaptable disposition. He is wary of strangers and often plays the pugilist; he is, however, most amenable to training.

ESSENTIALS OF THE CROATIAN SHEEPDOG: The head is wedge shaped; skull, moderately broad and slightly domed; ears, set high; muzzle, long, tapering, but not pointed. The chest is wide but not excessively deep. The hindlegs are lean and muscled and have marked angulation, which allows for unilaterally free direction. The back is straight. The dog is well muscled overall—never thin or rangy. This athletic body, built square and set high on the leg, is somewhat veiled by the long, dark-colored coat, which is given to feathering and density; coat is smooth on the face and front of the legs. The tail can be docked, curled, or long and bushy. Color is often black or black-gray, with white markings on the legs, feet and chest. Height: 16–21 inches (40.5–53 cm). Weight: 30–45 pounds (13.5–20.5 kg).

Crook

The arrangement of the forequarters with inward twisted pasterns on bassets and other low-legged hounds.

Crook tail

A crook tail can be used as a synomym for crank tail, which *see*, but a crook tail is more likely to be the term selected when such a tail type is a fault.

Crooked front

Forearms incline inwards and often appear curved from elbows to wrist. Such construction is typical of the short-legged or basset breeds.

Crooked mouth

Any mouth that deviates from a normal bite; often used to equate wry mouth, which *see*.

Cropped ears

Ears that would otherwise be drop ears but are diminished in size by the surgical removal of a portion of the auricular cartilage. *See* Ear cropping

Cropper

A foxhunting term for a bad fall.

Crossbreds

A crossbred dog, or cross-breed, is one which is the result of a two-breed mating, i.e., the cross of a Pit Bull Terrier male to a Neapolitan Mastiff bitch. A crossbred can also be the result of two dogs having the same two breeds in each of them, i.e., the cross between two 50/50 Olde Bulldogge and English White Terrier dogs. Unfortunately for the dog world, many crossbred dogs are simply the result of unplanned matings, while others represent a wanton cross of two different purebred dogs for the mere sake of producing a litter. Other crossbreds, however, are quite different, and many form the basis for a new breed, such as the Leonberger, Moscow Watchdog, Beagle Harrier, Kyi-Leo, or Bullmastiff for example. These breeds, among many, began as a simple cross by a knowledgeable breeder with a specific intention in mind. *See also* New breed creation

Crossing over

Feet cross over one another as well as a center line beneath the body. An insufficiently deep chest is the usual cause of this abnormal type of gait.

Crossbreds. The Catahoula Bull Terrier, a recent crossbred resulting from the Catahoula Leopard Dog and the Bull Terrier.

Crossbreds. Rottweiler–American Pit Bull Terrier cross resulted in this dog, which will prove to have no real effect on the dog world.

Crown at the top of the Rhodesian Ridgeback's ridge. Photo by I. Français.

Crouch

Unnatural or exaggerated hind-limb angulation causes a crunching or gathering-up of the hindquarters. Crouch can also be due to stress or unsure disposition. As a result, the rump/croup area appears markedly lower than the forequarters, with an arched, bending backline. Never a desirable trait.

Croup

The part of the back from the front of the pelvis to the root of the tail.

Croup, sunken

An all-breed fault, a croup with insubstantial musculation and having concave appearance.

Crown

In the canine world, crown has acquired three definitions: a) the dome or topskull. b) the visible part of the tooth above the gum line. c) the caterpillarlike swirl that begins the ridge on the Rhodesian Ridgeback's back.

Cruelty to animals

Whether intentional or unknowing, cruelty to animals is a problem plaguing the civilized world today as a decaying remnant of dark ages. For a discussion of cruelty and the humane societies estab-

lished in the hope of combating the disorder, *see* Humane societies.

Crufts Dog Show

See Kennel Club of Great Britain

Crupper

The croup section closest to the tail.

Cry

The sound that a hound makes when trailing or running quarry. It is different from the bark of common dogs and varies noticeably at different phases of the chase. Also called voice and tongue.

Cryosurgery

Procedure in which malignant tumors are exposed to cold to destroy the cancer cells.

Cryptorchidism

A dog's having a retained testicle, that is, a testicle not fully descended into the scrotum. This retained testicle can turn cancerous in the dog's later life, and removal may be recommended by your vet. Surgery is also possible to relocate the retained testicle in its proper scrotal sac; this surgery is held as unethical by most dog fanciers. Cryptorchids are forbidden in the show ring. They should not be bred, due to the possibility of passing this undesirable, often dangerous, trait.

Cub

The young of the fox.

Cuban Mastiff

A bulldog/mastiff cross that was located in Cuba in the 1830s. This dog was presented to the Zoological Society of London in 1832. This very strong, well-muscled dog was used in bull fights in its native land and is believed to have greatly resembled the sixteenth-century English Mastiff.

Cuffs

The pastern regions on an Afghan Hound, when covered by short hair, are sometimes called cuffs.

Culling

The process of selection in which the fate of individuals of the litter is determined. Culling must occur at all levels of breeding. Sickly, diseased pups, pups born with serious malformations, etc., should in all humanity be put down. Any dog other than those of utmost soundness should not be bred. Breeding only outstanding dogs limits the need for culling. No matter how crucial the need for culling, it is always a heart-rending task. *See also* Breeding, Infanticide

Culotte

The Schipperke's trousers—longish hair breeching at the rear upper thighs.

Culpeo

See South American foxes

Cumberland Sheepdog

The Cumberland Sheepdog is the working dog of the shepherds of the Peak district, the East Cheviotdale, Westmoreland and, of course, Cumberland. These shepherds have made little effort to popularize or preserve the breed outside of their British locales. The German Shepherd Dog was employed in the early 1900s to resuscitate the dwindling stock. The breed was an intelligent and industrious performer that excelled in the sheepdog trials during the early twentieth century. Today the Cumberland is numerically weak or non-existent.

In appearance, the body is rather long and lithe; the head is broad between the ears, tapering to the muzzle. The coat is heavy, dense and water resistant. The color is black with white self markings. Average height about 20 inches (51 cm).

Cuon alpinus

See Dhole

Cur

Curs, a group of dogs expressly American, derive from various American and European stock, including schweisshunds, scenting hounds and native Indian cur or pariah dogs. The term "cur" should not be confused with mutt or mongrel. While mongrels are

dogs of no known (or pinpointable) purebred ancestors, the curs are specific strains of dog that were accomplished for hunting pursuits. Curs mostly hunt larger game. The Black Mouth Cur and the Mountain Cur are formidable pursuers of wild boar and bear. They are usu-

ally silent on the trail and are able to hunt as well as tree. In size the curs vary greatly; the tiny Stephens Stock can weigh as little as 35 pounds (16 kg) while the Black Mouth Cur can weigh as much as 95 pounds (43 kg). Appearances vary equally. The dog known in American fiction as "Old Yaller" was of cur origin, and probably looked most like the Mountain Cur, one of the cur breeds. None of these breeds are recognized by either major American registry. Among these hardy hound curs are the Treeing Tennessee Brindle, Plott Hound, Stephens Stock, Black Mouth Cur, American Blue Gascon Hound, and the Leopard Cur.

Cur. Mountain Cur, a lesser known American cur, performing at a daytime trial. Photo by I. Français.

Curled tail

A common tail type, especially among the northern breeds, curled tails are broken into two basic groups (single and double curl), although there exist many varieties therein. Curled tails are just that, tails that curl. These tails can curl tightly over the back or loosely over the back, with numerous degrees of tightness or looseness, in single curls or double; these tails can also fall over the loin, curl over the back and fall down the side, curl over the hip, and lay, lie, or fall in numerous other fashions.

Curly coat

Tight, full curls providing a dog protection from the elements and water. The Irish Water Spaniel and the Barbet possess curly coats, as do the bichons and other water dogs.

Curly coat on a liver Curly-Coated Retriever. Photo by I. Français.

the old English Water Spaniel is possibly the water spaniel contributor. The Curly-Coated Retriever is likely the first dog used for serious and extensive retrieving work in England. Although the breed's ability has made it known around the world, it has at best maintained moderate numbers in relation to popular purebred dogs. Its following, however, is truly a dedicated group of fanciers. Owners assert that the dogs are easycare and exceedingly pleasant as companions. The curly coat requires little grooming.

ESSENTIALS OF THE CURLY-COATED RETRIEVER: The general appearance of the breed is of a strong, intelligent, active dog. The head is long but well proportioned, and the muzzle is long but never snipy. Eyes are large but not prominent and either black or dark brown in color. Height: 25–27 inches (63–69 cm). Weight:

Curly-Coated Retriever

An enthusiastic and hard-working gundog, which based on written accounts of the dogs traces back to at least 1803. It is suggested that small Newfoundlands were used in the early construction of the breed, likely for their excellent water performance—a characteristic ideally desired in a retrieving dog. Another often-cited component breed is the Irish Water Spaniel, though

70–80 pounds (32–36 kg). He is a squarely constructed dog. The body essentials include well-sprung ribs, deep chest and well-muscled hindquarters. The coat is composed of crisp, small curls and is a most distinctive and important feature; even the tail, which is left at its natural length, is covered with curls, though the muzzle and foreface have shorter, smoother hair. Coat color is either black or liver.

tisonelike substances are given over a long period of time, several years usually. Though signs can vary from case to case, possible signs include: wasting, trembling, sagging abdomen, and weakness. Most dogs exhibit change in their skin and coat, both becoming very thin and dry, with the skin wrinkled and the coat rough. Treatment is possible with the correct diagnosis.

Curly-Coated Retriever, black. Photo by I. Français.

Curtain

Some racing lures are drawn into escapes at the end of a race; where there is no such hiding place, a curtain is drawn across the track to conceal the lure after a race and prevent dogs from continuing around the track. Sometimes an additional curtain behind the dogs traps them in a small space and makes it easy for handlers to collect them.

Curved shears

Used to achieve curved lines on a dog's coat, especially in the shoulder, flank, and chest areas.

Curved slicker brush

Slicker brush with heavier pins which works extremely well on heavily long-coated dogs, such as the Old English Sheepdog.

Cushing's syndrome

Hyperadrenocorticism, or cortisol excess, is the result of overproduction of cortisol, a cortisonelike substance, by the adrenal glands. It may also occur if high doses of cortisone or cor-

Cushion

The outstanding thickness of the upper flews. In a number of breeds (the Boxer, Pekingese), this is a highly desirable trait. On the feet, cushion refers to well-developed padding, i.e., well cushioned.

Cut

In shepherding, this term refers to a number of sheep. When a shepherd selects a number from his herd to take to market, this is called a "cut."

Cut. Australian Shepherd moves a "cut" of sheep from the rear.

Cynology experts rely on ancient remains to help reconstruct the genesis of present-day breeds. Aztec pottery effigies found in burial sites in Colima, Mexico, have linked the Chihuahua with the ancient Techichi, the round hairless pariah rendered in clay in this photograph by S.A. Thompson.

Cut-up
See Tuck-up

Cute
A coursing term that refers to the dog's cleverness in coursing hare; the dog heads off the hare, compels its running mate to do most of the work, and collects points without great effort.

Cutting-back
A term used at field trials that refers to the dog's going back towards the handler after a forward cast has been made.

Cynaosis
A definite blueness seen in and around the mucous membranes of the face; i.e., tongue, lips and eyes. It is usually the result of a circulatory obstruction or heart condition.

Cynodictis
See Ancestors of the dog

Cynology
The term cynology refers to the study of dogs. Cynologists concern themselves primarily with the history and evolution of domestic dog, behavioral patterns and the development and diversification of breeds. Cynology in terms of breed histories and development is limited by a number of factors. Since the concept of purebred dogs and the large scale recording of pedigrees is a product of the late nineteenth century, there is little reliable evidence prior to 1873, when the Kennel Club of Great Britain was formed. Cynologists often rely on art work, especially paintings, to get a clear picture of what a particular kind of dog looked like. Of course, using paintings as the sole source of a breed or type's anatomical conformation is dangerous without fully appreciating the style of painting the artist embodied. Even the great portrait painters of the seventeenth and eighteenth centuries romanticized their sub-

jects for their greater glory, greater approval, and greater stipend. The writings of early commentators such as Samuel Pepys and Johannes Caius contribute a rare wealth to the study of dogs, but it is impossible to visualize definitively the appearance of a given dog without seeing its picture (i.e., what does "a broad skull" mean in modern terms). Breed histories, therefore, are based more often on conjecture, hypotheses, and legends than on archeological, scientific or documented evidences. Nonetheless, breed histories are well worth reading since they can teach us about the dogs we love, make us think about their behavior, and maybe reinforce our knowledge of a specific historical period.

Cystitis

A condition of the urinary tract that is characterized by inflammation and/or infection of the bladder.

Cynology. Medieval French manuscript, characteristically illuminated, commemorates the blessing of the hunt. Cynologists uncloak little-known customs about dogs and keepers' traditions from such documents. Photo by I. Français.

Cynology. Victorian postcard based on Pug painting which was printed in England. Inferences from old dog paraphernalia like this give breed historians convincing information about physical types and pet traditions.

Cysts

Non-cancerous or benign growths caused by the secretions of the sebaceous glands. Though unsightly, they are usually harmless and easily removed by minor veterinary surgery.

Ovarian cysts are a common problem of the ovaries, leading to sterility and discomfort, and usually dictating the removal of the ovaries. Ovarian cysts are not reported to affect good health.

Czech Coarsehaired Pointer

See Czesky Fousek

Czesky Fousek

A native Czechoslovakian gundog especially adept at pointing. It is a dog that

ESSENTIALS OF THE CZESKY FOUSEK: In general appearance, a large and tallish dog standing on good length of leg. The head is broad between the ears, with a medium stop; the ears are folded; the dark eyes are alert in expression; the muzzle on the sides and undersides is bearded. Chest is deep; neck, thick. Hindquarters are well-muscled, with hindlegs well angulated. The tail is customarily docked to two-fifths length. Height: 24–26 inches (61–66 cm). Weight: 60–75 pounds (27–34 kg). Coat: rough outer, soft and thick inner; bristly in feel and appearance, giving an overall shaggy appearance of the dog. Color: brown or brown and white; ticking or markings may be present.

Czesky Fousek, brown. Photo by I. Français.

does best in the care of experienced hunters, for it loves to work the field. The breed has a strong following in its native land and enjoys present popularity. In keeping with the history of Czechoslovakia, the breed has suffered a rough twentieth century. Flourishing through the late nineteenth and early twentieth centuries, the breed was nearly decimated by the two World Wars. With its numbers near zero, concerned fanciers turned to the infusion of German Wirehaired and German Shorthaired Pointer blood to save the breed. As a result, the breed today bears fair resemblance to both these German Pointers.

Czesky Terrier

Czechoslovakia's terrier, the Czesky Terrier, is a twentieth-century creation. The genetic research and successful breeding program of Dr. Frantisek Horak are responsible for yielding an elegant, functional terrier. The two foundation breeds for this new breed are generally accepted as the Scottish Terrier and Sealyham Terrier, although the Dandie Dinmont is the likely tag. One of the breed's hallmarks, its fading coat color (either blue-gray or light coffee), was likely donated by the Dandie's color gene. Horak's work was most appreciated by the Czech sportsmen who were disheartened by the Deutscher Jagdterrier's abilities, a small-sized terrier small enough to go to ground but not always capable enough to hold its own against fox or badger. The Czesky unearther was suitably sized and substantially strong enough to take care of larger quarry as well. Horak was as pleased with the dog's working attributes as he was with his attractive looks.

A breed full of character and good nature, the Czesky is quickly gaining ground in the United States as a home companion. His obedience and ability, not to mention his lovely coat, have made him the choice of many new fanciers.

ESSENTIALS OF THE CZESKY TERRIER: A fine, silky coat that comes in blue-gray or light coffee. Drop ears and well-furnished eyebrows and beard, a long head with a moderately full muzzle. Robust and hardy, the Czesky weighs in at 20 pounds (9 kg), the average being closer to 16 pounds (7.5 kg). Height: 10–14 inches (25.5–35.5 cm).

Czesky Terrier, light coffee.

Czesky Terrier, blue-gray.

Czesky Terriers, puppies. Photographs by I. Français.

Dachsbracke

German type scenthound used for slow, close ground work. *See* West-phalian Dachsbracke, Deutsche Bracke

Dachshund

1) German term for a short-legged scenthound used for badger; equivalent to the French *basset* and the Swiss *neiderlaufhund.* Of course the Dachshund is the best example of this type of working dog.

many of his functions defy usual hound abilities. Because of the Dachshund's inherent ability to go to ground, it is frequently mislabelled as a terrier. The breed's solid construction and natural determination enable it to tunnel, with a digging ability that rivals the craftiest of terriers. The Miniature Dachshund, the smaller of today's two accepted sizes, is known as the Kaninchenteckel or Rabbit Dachshund, for its ability to enter a rabbit's hole and chase it upwards. In

Dachshunds, Standards, long, wire, smooth.

2) The Dachshund, known in Germany as the Teckel, has a long and much debated history. The word "Tekal" from which the German *Teckel* derives can be found inscribed on the base of an ancient Egyptian sculpture—an Egyptian king seated with three rather curious, if not familiar, doglike animals. Apparently a race of long-backed, short-legged dogs existed in Egypt at a very early date. These dogs were clumsy, egregiously eared 30-pounders and the said forebears of our current-day multi-talented Dachshund. In German, *Dachshund* translates as badger dog, reflecting the breed's original function.

In type, this is a true hound, although

addition to tracking and scenting, the usual functions of hounds, Miniature Dachsies go to ground like the most tenacious of terriers. Longhaired Dachsies have been known to retrieve in water, giving many a setter a swim for the mallard. The Standard Dachshund's abilities extend past the badger, its original quarry, to include rabbits, fox, deer, ferret and stoat.

The Dachshund, with its many varieties, is able to please most anyone. Both sizes, Standard and Miniature, come in three coat varieties: long, smooth, and wire. Dachshund fanciers are among the most avid, committed of dog lovers—their determined preference and loving bias towards their breed is perhaps metaphorical of the Dachshund's natural tenacity. While a member of the hound family, the Dachshund is pure terrier in disposition: feisty, stubborn, and industrious—and always loyal.

In England, as early as 1866, the Dachshund made its way into the show ring. However, the first Dachshund to capture British attention was "Dashy," owned by Queen Victoria, nearly 30 years prior. For the British (and Americans as well, for that matter), the Dachshund was more of a companion and show dog than a hunter. The Germans, less interested in "ideal" conformation points and more in function, used their dogs extensively. The larger sized dogs,

people, the breed was truly intended to be a working dog. A Dachshund seizing its prey shows no mercy—there is unsullied hatred towards its designated prey.

Dachshund, long, black with tan.

Dachshund, wire, yellow.

Dachshund, smooth, red.

the Standards, were used for tracking badger, stag and boar, while the smaller, the Miniatures, were used for rabbit hunting. It should be said, in all fairness, that the British frequently employed the Dachshund as a rabbitter and ratter. The German standard was not drawn up until 1888, nine years after the British had drawn up their standard. The most telling point of dissension in these two important standards is the way in which the Germans chose to measure size. Unlike the British and American standards that measure by height, the Germans divide classes by chest circumference, which determines how large a hole the dog can enter. While the Dachshund's temperament is amiable with most

The smooth is the purest and original Dachshund, perhaps. The wirehaired variety is believed to have evolved through crosses to wire terriers or wire

bassets. Early writers reported that the wirehairs were bred from crossing

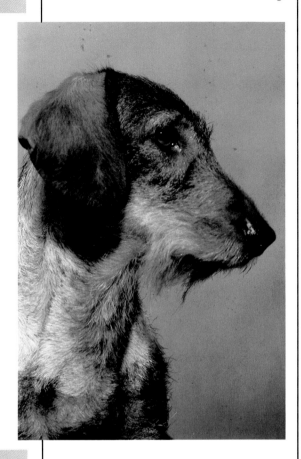

Dachshund, wire, red/yellow, with shadings.

Dachshund, smooth, dappled.

smooths with roughhaired pinschers. The result was a Dachshund with a small-ish, short head. The Dandie Dinmont

Terrier was then used to acquire the appropriate head. Even today, in long-

haired Dachsie litters, pups possess a touch of the Dandie's soft tuft on the head. The longhaired variety may be as old as the smooth but many believe it derived from crosses to the Field Spaniel. One school of thought purports that the longhaired Dachshund was used to perform groundwork for the Salukis in Abyssinia, while others trace the breed to Egypt, like the smooths. The similarity to the bassets of France has always been an option when excavating the Dachshund's long-lost roots. Some believe that the longhairs derived from the bassets of La Vendée in France. The longhair's ability to retrieve and work in water makes a cross with a low-legged spaniel, such as the Field or Sussex, a likely possibility.

The Miniature Dachshund was bred in Germany around 1900. The desire was to get a Dachshund with the smallest chest dimensions possible; of course, by virtue of its being a Dachshund, the dwarf rabbit dog would still have tremendous strength and stamina. Dwarf Pinscher and Black and Tan Terriers of the old type were used to bantamize the standard-size Dachshund. The Miniature that most influenced the breed in its early days was owned by Staffelstein Kennel and named Zwerg von Barrach. The new tiny dogs were used instead of ferrets and worked to extract rabbits from thick undergrowth and holes.

Through tough times in both Britain and America, the Dachshund today maintains a great number of fanciers and is surely one of the most recognizable of all the world's canines. The Dachshund is as intelligent and clever as he is clean and industrious. One of the most hardy of dogs, the breed ideally is energetic and active. Owners are encouraged to be disciplinarian and discretionary.

The long back invites physical problems, thus dogs should not be allowed to jump off furniture. Proper training and eating habits will help to keep your Dachshund in fine physical condition.

ESSENTIALS OF THE DACHSHUND: A lengthy, low-to-the-ground hound with a deep chest and a compact muscular body. Six varieties exist: two sizes and three coats. The Standard Dachshund weighs in from 15–25 pounds (6.5–11.5 kg); the Miniature Dachshund at less than 9 pounds (4 kg). The smooth coat is short, thick and shiny. The wire coat is uniformly tight, rough and coarse, complete with a beard and fine undercoat. The long coat is soft, sleek and glistening. The breed's color possibilities can be one-colored (reds and yellows), two-colored (black, chocolate, gray with tan; white with yellow), or dappled (merle, harlequin and brindle). Regardless of size and coat type, the Dachshund conformation is the same. The head, appearing clean cut, should taper uniformly to the tip of the nose. Ears, long but not dramatically, are set near the top of the head. They are not pointed or narrow but rather beautifully

folded. The neck is fairly muscular; the front is compact, deep, long, broad and

muscular to endure the exertion of the underground. Legs are short and muscled. The trunk is long and fully muscled; the back, with sloping shoulders and short rigid pelvis, should lie in the straightest possible line. The breast bone should be strong and noticeably prominent, depressing a dimple. Paws compactly closed with arched toes. Tail set in continuation of the spine.

Dachshund, long, dappled.

Dachshund, Standard, smooth, black with tan.

Dalmatian

There is no doubt that the Dalmatian is an ancient breed. The Dalmatian has been known as a breed in England since the 1700s, but models of a spotted dog date back to ancient Greek friezes. E.C. Ash, the noted author of *Dogs and Their History*, refers to spotted dogs that appear on a tablet dated circa 2000 B.C. Authorities claim Dalmatia, a western region of Yugoslavia, to be the birthplace of the breed.

Dalmatians have been employed at numerous tasks over the ages, including: dogs of war, border patrols, cart pullers, sheep herders, vermin exterminators, dogs of the hunt (retrieving, scenting, birding, and pack hunting), circus performers, and of course coaching dogs. He remains the only recognized carriage dog in the world and has been used with great success since at least the Middle Ages. Some believe that these dogs actually

Dalmatians, white with black.

enough, under the pole between the leaders and the wheelers. The dogs were adopted by the fire departments of the 1800s because of their outstanding way with horses.

Above all, some say, the Dalmatian is a congenial and pliable pet. However, the dog's strength and stamina can be too much of a challenge for some owners, as the dogs are extremely enduring and determined. Dalmatians are dedicated and loyal and always eager to please.

ESSENTIALS OF THE DALMATIAN: A strong, muscular, and active dog, free from coarseness and lumber. In temperament, outgoing and friendly, free from nervousness and aggression. The head, of fair length, is flat and broad between the ears. Neck is fairly long, arched, light and tapering, free from any throatiness. Chest not wide but deep, with good spring of rib. Hindquarters rounded, with good turn of stifle and well-defined

worked with chariots of ancient Greece, Rome and Egypt. Dalmatians are known for their ability to work horses under the rear or front axles and, amazingly

hocks. With great freedom of movement, the Dalmatian is built for moderated speeds over good distances. Coat coloration of virgin white base with defined

round black or liver spots. Not intermingling and clearly defined, spots should range from the size of a dime (one pence) to the size of a half-dollar (fifty pence piece). The coat hairs are short, hard, and close set. Weight: 50–55 pounds (23–25 kg). Height: 19–23 inches (48–58 cm).

Dam

See Bitch, Pregnancy

Dandie Dinmont Terrier

This short-legged terrier was developed as an otter and badger specialist in seventeenth-century Great Britain—more specifically, in the Cheviot Hills and Coquetdale. The Allans, also of Bedlington fame, are said to have kept this type of rough-coated Border terrier. Farms in Lyndlea and in the Teviotdale Hills also had very similar terriers, and it was these terriers that so impressed Sir Walter Scott to influence their inclusion in his novel *Guy Mannering*, published in 1814. His character Dandie Dinmont gave its name to this breed of terrier. Whether selective breeding or pure blissful serendipity, the Dandie was derived from various running dogs and hounds. Often the Otter Hound is purported, but

the physical characteristics would prove this largely erroneous. The Dachshund and the Bedlington Terrier (if the prototype antecedes the Dandie's creation) would have provided a number of the Dandie traits that are unique: short, crooked legs, domed head, round eyes, scimitar-like tail, arch of loin, and the soft silky hair atop its head.

Although the Dandie Dinmont of today doesn't possess the gameness to bolt after badger, he is a kindly and dependable soul that makes a particularly obedient and lovable house dog. His appearance sets him apart from the other British terriers and Dandie people are proud of their dandy terrier.

ESSENTIALS OF THE DANDIE DINMONT TERRIER: Longer than he is tall, the Dandie Dinmont ambles on short, crooked legs, head strong and large, broad between the ears with a well-domed forehead. Ears set low, hanging close to cheek, lightly feathered. Long flexible body with good spring of ribs. Low at shoulders, the back is arched over loin and dropping again to root of tail. Top of head covered by a soft, bouffy hairpiece; wiry tail. Height: 8–11 inches (20–28 cm). Weight: 18–24 pounds (8–11 kg). The coat is crisp and is comprised of both hard and soft hairs. Penciled or

Dalmatian, white with liver.

Dandie Dinmont Terrier, pepper. Photo by I. Français.

piley, the coat is pepper (bluish black to silvery gray) or mustard (reddish brown to pale fawn).

Danish Broholmer, brownish yellow. Photo by I. Français.

Dandruff

As common in canines as it is in man, dandruff is the natural flaking of skin caused by the constant replacement of cells of the epidermal layer. Too frequent bathing can deplete the skin of its natural oils and lead to excessive flaking. Regular brushing accompanied by infrequent baths will likely control dandruff. Some dogs' coats allow dandruff flakes to pass unnoticed, while others retain the flakes, making the case seem more acute. Excessive dandruff can signal many other potential conditions or complications. Lack of fat intake, mange, and allergies are three likely dandruff causes. In acute cases, proper veterinary treatment can aid the condition.

Danish Broholmer

Established in the nineteenth century, this Danish mastiff enjoyed moderate popularity in his native country throughout the early 1900s. The breed was employed for guard and utility work, especially in rural areas and more especially with the well-to-do classes. With the coming of the two World Wars and the economic crisis that afflicted all of Europe, the Broholmer's numbers dwindled. Also affecting the popularity of the breed were other dogs that came to the fore as guard and utility workers during the twentieth century, among them the German Shepherd Dog, the Rottweiler, and the Boxer. It was not until the 1970s that activity was focused on preserving the breed. The current breed base is small, yet type is well established.

The Danish Broholmer resulted from the crossing of English Mastiffs with "local dogs," which were received from Germany years earlier. The Danes accepted the gifts of English Mastiffs from the English royalty, just as they had accepted gifts of German Mastiffs from the German royalty. The Danish Broholmer is a watchful, faithful, and fearless dog who remains good-natured and easily trained. His size and power, however, require that an owner be sure of himself as a master, willing to give the dog the necessary training, discipline, and exercise.

ESSENTIALS OF THE DANISH BROHOLMER: A big, powerful, and rectangular mastiff type, standing 27.5–29.5 inches (70–75 cm) tall and weighing 115–140 pounds (52–63 kg). The head is comparatively broad and big. The muzzle is short, with pendulous lips. The chest is powerful, broad, and deep. The back is long, with the croup slightly sloping. The coat is short and coarse. Color: light yellow with black nose and mask; brownish yellow with black nose and dark points; lighter colored eyes allowed; black with white markings on feet, tip of tail, and chest allowed. Tails are long and high-standing.

Danish Dachsbracke

See Strellufstöver

Danish Farm Dog

A resurgence of the Danish Farm Dog has swept the European fancy. This native Danish dog is a revived remnant of draft dogs from nineteenth century Europe, although slighter in build than those cart-pulling dogs of yesteryear. This medium-sized short-coated dog can

be any combination of colors against a white background. Farmers today are making use of this all-purpose canine, and appearances in the show ring are becoming surprisingly commonplace. It is not registered presently with the F.C.I.

Dapple

Mottling or spotting on the coat, rather unpatterned and irregular darker patches, splotches and marks on a lighter colored background. Some examples of dappled dogs include some Dachshunds and the Catahoula Leopard Dog. *See also* Merle

DDT

Once used with frequency as a pest control, widely sprayed to exterminate mosquitoes, DDT has been found to be highly carcinogenic and the cause of many birth defects. Keep your dog away from the chemical, and do not visit areas that you suspect of being treated with the toxin.

Dead ears

Ears without mobility or life, irresponsive and sluggish. Likely not appearing on hounds, dead ears are houndlike in appearance.

Deadgrass

The desired coloration of the Chesapeake Bay Retriever. Deadgrass is the color of dead grass, more or less—darker tans through lighter yellows. The origination of the term is traced to a famous, late Chessie breeder in Maryland whose kennel of dogs partook in an orgy of urination on his lawn; he later commented "my grass is dead, like my dogs"—it is believed that he was referring to their color.

Deafness

Deafness in dogs, while not uncommon, usually occurs in older dogs. Dogs that have grown deaf need to be cared for with special consideration for their condition. Older dogs do not understand that their hearing has dimin-

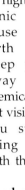

Danish Farm Dog, tricolor.

Danish Farm Dog, bicolor and tricolor. Photographs by I. Français.

ished; instead, they perceive their world to have grown quieter. Dogs most often lose only partial hearing; complete deafness is not a usual occurrence, with the exception of dogs of certain breeds born solid white. It is not known precisely why these dogs are born deaf, nor is it clear why older dogs tend to lose their hearing.

Deafness can be avoided by the owner's proper care of his dog's ears. The floppy-eared breeds tend to be more subject to ear ailments since dirt is more often retained in the ears, as is water, hence infection or irritation. Dogs with upright or cropped ears are less susceptible to early deafness. A dog that shakes its head, cocks his head oddly, or paws at his ears abnormally, should be taken to the veterinarian to have his ears checked for possible infection. Regular cleaning of the ears, removing wax and dirt build-up, will help prevent avoidable infection. Excessive wax production is the most common cause of deafness in dogs.

A very loud noise or explosion can cause deafness. It is not uncommon for a paralysis of the auditory nerve to accompany (or follow) distemper. Growths or warts sometimes block the auditory canal—deafness shortly follows. Inflammation of the ear (external otitis) and fluid leaking from ear (otorrhoea) can be caused by irritating the ears in cleaning or from the dog's excessive scratching of its ears. Temporary deafness has resulted from the use of certain prescribed drugs. *See also* Ear disorders

Deafness can be acquired or congenital. The Dalmatian breed is commonly affected, though no breed can be labelled definitively as such. This howling Dalmatian seemingly is in good ear.

Death, care of remains

How your dog is cared for after his death falls largely under the jurisdiction of local and state ordinances. It is suggested that the owner learn the specific laws pertinent to canine ownership and make the necessary arrangements as soon as possible. Burial, including funeral ceremonies, has become popular in many communities, with professional services available. Cremation is another very real possibility in an increasing number of communities, and these too may include services. Perhaps the most common way that dogs are cared for after their death is through the veterinarian. It is a rare practice where a vet does not have the facilities or abilities to care for a dead dog. *See also* Cemeteries for dogs

Death, common causes

In these days of increased owner awareness, easily available and nutritionally sound foods, and fine medical care and facilities, the most common cause of death is old age (if we exclude the too common euthanization of the lost and/or unwanted). Cancer, heart disease, and kidney disease, in that respective order, are the most common final and fatal stressors. The second most common cause of death is car accidents.

Death, coping with loss

The passing of a canine friend can be a traumatic experience for many dog owners. Through the years, the bond between person and dog grows to emotional depths, forming a rich and meaningful relationship. All life must one day end, and knowing simply that you gave your dog the best possible life you could should ease the always untimely separation. As many psychologists point out, remember the good times and the happy moments, remember your dog in his playful days of puppyhood, his awkward days of adolescence, funny habits, his healthful maturity, and his reclining elder years. Speak to friends, fellow dog people, and organizations set up for animal welfare; they all should lend a shoulder of empathy.

Death, postmortems

You may be asked or you may request

that a study into the cause of your dog's death be conducted. If you allow your dog's remains to be studied, you are likely contributing to science and to better care for canines in the future. The consideration is, of course, for the owner to make, and it is one that can require considerable mind searching. Remember, the choice is yours; exercise your right, and do what you think is best.

Debarking
The removal, usually surgical, of the dog's vocal apparatus. This practice is considered cruel by many fanciers. It should be considered only as a last resort when elimination is a necessity.

Deep-set eyes
Eyes well sunken into their sockets (e.g., Chow Chow).

Deerhound
See Scottish Deerhound

Defecation
The expellation of the contents of the bowels. *See* Digestive system

Dehydration
A state in which the water level of the dog is far below normal. Dehydration can be a dangerous state and often is the result of some common signs of illness, such as diarrhea, vomiting, fever, and lost appetite. Persistent diarrhea, especially with accompanied vomiting, is a leading cause of dehydration, a condition that may require hospitalization. A dog requires water daily, especially when worked hard and during the hot months.

Delaney System
See Systems

Delayed shot
In field trials, the handler is charged with a delayed shot when he flushes the bird and waits an appreciable time before firing the shot in order to gain more control over his dog.

Delirium
A temporary state of extreme mental excitement, marked by restlessness and hallucinations. Delirium can accompany fever or other abnormal conditions, such as some poisonings, injuries, and shock.

Dematting
Dematting—removing, undoing, untangling hair clumps and knots in the dog's coat—should be the first step in any grooming procedure. Just as the degree of matting will vary from breed to breed (and from dog to dog!), so too will the dog's tolerance. Some dogs do not seem to mind the tugging and pulling involved, as if any display of attention will do; other dogs are upset by the slightest tugging at their coats. Dematting should not cause the dog severe stress. If the dog is totally intolerant of the necessary dematting, it may be necessary to shave the coat and attempt to groom the new coat more regularly.

Pet stores sell dematting formulas, special chemicals that can simplify the procedure. A slicker brush and a matting comb are also useful tools available at supply shops.

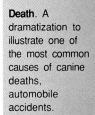

Death. A dramatization to illustrate one of the most common causes of canine deaths, automobile accidents.

Demodectic mange
See Mange

Den
The home of the fox.

Den bark
The peculiar cry of the hound when the fox is run to earth during the hunt.

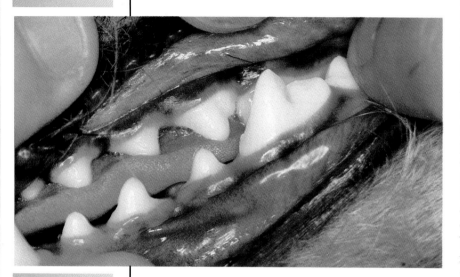

Dental care. Clean teeth are not a coincidence or the product of luck. Owners must provide the appropriate outlets to keep their dogs' teeth healthy.

Dental care. Scaling the teeth removes tartar and plaque build-up and is usually performed by a veterinarian. Photo by V. Serbin.

Dental care
Canine dental care should always be preventive in nature. While cavities commonly plague the mouth of humankind, other problems lurk in the canine oral cavity. Pits, discoloration, breakage, worn enamel, the accumulation of tartar or calculus (plaque), and gum abscesses are potential dental/oral problems of dogs. The most common of these are tartar and plaque which can be readily detected on the teeth of the dog. Dental problems are often cued by bad breath. Regular veterinarian check-ups ensure good teeth development.

Owners, however, need to take an active role in their dog's dental health. Getting to the root of the canine dental dilemma, owners need to recognize that no less than 75% of all canine dental problems serious enough to require a vet's assistance, and nearly 98% of all canine teeth lost, are attributable to periodontal disease. Owners must claim responsibility for their dog's health, and tooth care is no minor aspect of the care required. Daily brushing with a salt/baking soda solution is the best answer, but many owners find this task tedious or find their dogs not amenable to the treatment. Granted, with some breeds this would be quite a feat. The simpler (and possibly more effective) way to avoid, reduce and fight periodontal disease and calculus build-up is through the use of a thermoplastic polymer or nylon chew device. There are a number of such items on the market. The original in this case is also the best. Nylabone® is the highest quality nylon chew device available; its softer counterpart, the Gumabone®, is equally effective in fighting tartar accumulation. Both these products are scented and come in a range of sizes. The Gumabone® products have been clinically studied, and now scientific proof states that, used regularly, the device reduces calculus build-up by 70%. The independent research of Andrew Duke, D.V.M., uncovered this find in 1989. Such devices are also therapeutic, allowing the animal to work off its "doggie tensions." *See also* Nylon bones

It is necessary to realize that all dogs chew—this is not *intended* to be a destructive pastime. Therefore, providing the dog a productive outlet for his need to chew is advised by all veterinarians. Rawhide chews and natural bones are the most common choices of pet owners, not necessarily the best. Because these are

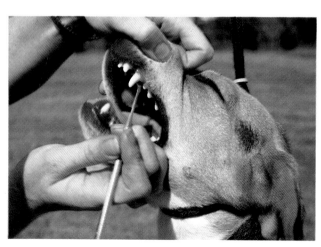

flavorful to dogs, they treat it as food. Rawhide can be harmful to the dog if ingested. Consult your veterinarian before providing your dog with rawhide chews. Natural bones are probably better than rawhide, but not much. Chewing on natural bones may wear his teeth away prematurely; owners should not provide their dogs with such bones on a regular basis. Hard bones are better than soft bones which may break apart; particles lodged in the dog's throat can cause choking.

Most dentists today attest that brushing is not enough, hence regular dental "cleaning" appointments are vital, as is flossing. Fortunately for those aforementioned who cannot brush their dog's teeth, it is not necessary to apply human dental floss to our dogs. Nylafloss® is a revolutionary product that is constructed of nylon rope-like strands that are chewed by the dog. Gently tugging on the ropelike device directs the strands between the dog's teeth, much the same way that dental floss works for humans.

Dentition

The canine dentition, which is the order and arrangement of the dog's teeth,

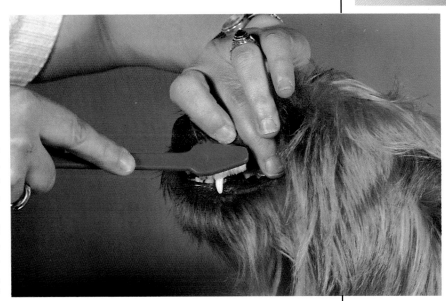

consists of highly specialized structures designed for biting, tearing, cutting and grinding—basically the tool of a meat-eater. The outside of the dog's tooth is constructed of pearly white enamel; this outer exposed portion is known as the crown. Beneath the enamel is dentine, which comprises the bulk of the structure. The neck refers to the tooth at the

Dental care. Brushing the dog's teeth is a first step in good dental hygiene. Australian Terrier.

Dental care. A lucky and well-instructed Akita puppy getting good use from his Gumabone Wishbone®. Photographs by I. Français.

permanent counterparts. The canines, sometimes called eye teeth or fangs, number four and sit on each side, upper and lower, of the incisors. The canines are the largest and strongest teeth in the canine mouth. They are slightly curved in shape with blunt tips. Both upper and lower jaws have eight premolars situated at the sides. The rearmost teeth are the molars: there are six in the lower jaw and four in the upper. Unlike the other teeth, there are no molars in the temporary dentition.

Show dogs are required to have all 42 teeth, 20 in the upper and 22 in the lower. Most of the recognized hairless breeds exhibit an absence of premolars.

gumline; the root is the portion of the tooth that is embedded into the jaw bone. Cementum covers the root; it is a thin bonelike substance. Composing the sensory nerves is soft tissue called pulp.

Dogs, like humans, are equipped with a temporary and permanent dentition. The dog's permanent teeth are 42 in number, the milk teeth (or "puppy" teeth) number 32. While the temporary teeth most assuredly fall out as designed, the permanent are only permanent with proper care—in dogs as well as humans. *See* Dental care

Dogs have four types of teeth: incisors, canines, premolars and molars. The incisors, the smallest of the 42, sit three on each side of the middle of the upper jaw and three on each side of the lower jaw. These 12 teeth are present in the deciduous set and are replaced by their

Depth perception

The ability to determine the distance or depth of a fall even when the terrain is flat or monotonous with no distinguishing landmarks.

Dermatitis

Dermatitis is defined simply as an inflammation of the skin. In dogs, there are four more or less common types of dermatitis. They are: atopic, cheyletiella, contact, and nasal solar.

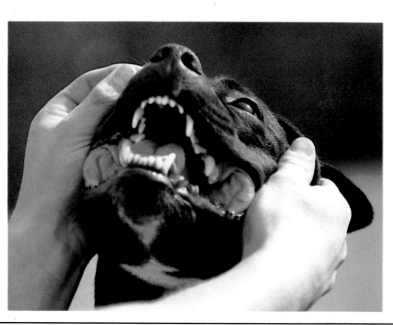

Dermis

Also called "the true skin," the dermis is the underlayer of the skin, lying directly below the epidermis, the upper layer. It contains many capillaries, glands, and other living cell structures. It is highly sensitive.

Destructiveness

The term destructiveness in dogs implies that the offending canine intends to destroy, in a malicious or a harmful way. In puppies especially, destructiveness is the incarnation of their curiosity—closets, pantries, garages, and basements have a multitude of unexplored and tantalizing objects. Owners need to acknowledge this intense puppy curiosity and realize that, while a puppy can pulverize valuable property, he can also hurt himself in the process. Nevertheless, while a puppy's vandalism is inherently innocent, his destructiveness needs attending. Owners must adopt a policy and adhere to it: one which promotes the respect of possessions and appropriate behavior.

An older dog may tend towards destructiveness as a plea for more attention from its owner, much in the way a child might. Such a dilemma is alleviated by establishing a regular time of intense interaction between the owner and the lonely dog. Obedience tricks and rewards will make the dog feel loved and important. If the destructiveness persists, isolating the dog from the rest of the family for a half hour (immediately after his ransacking) will reinforce that his behavior will not yield the results he intended. Dogs, like puppies and like people, hate to be ignored.

Deutsche Bracke

The Deutsche Bracke or German Hound is the only official bracke recognized in Germany today. This bracke comes from those hunting dogs promoted in Sauerland and Westphalia. At one time, western Germany was well inhabited by packs of these hounds which were lower stationed than most other European hounds and more stur-

dily constructed. The ram's nose and stiff-cartilage ears were also typical. Said to have evolved from generic Celtic hot-nosed hounds, the Deutsche Bracke worked in the German forests, hunting fox, hare, and boar. Of all brackes that once assisted German hunters, only the Deutsche Bracke still exists to remind us of the type of hounds that once flourished. Extinct relations include the Sauerlander Holzbracke and the Westphalian Bracke. The breed is used today on both hot and cold trails, silently and giving tongue. A multi-talented, rather average-looking huntsman's dog that hasn't

received much attention as a show dog, this dog is a versatile scenter that can even be trained to retrieve.

ESSENTIALS OF THE DEUTSCHE BRACKE: A tricolor, smoothhaired bracke, the German Hound is low stationed and well boned. For his inches, this hound is a powerful and robust dog of superior ability. Height: 16–21 inches (40–53 cm). Like many of the other German hounds, the Deutsche Bracke possesses stiff ears that lie close to his head and the standard ram's nose profile. In size he is closest to the British Harrier, while in appearance he resembles the Scandinavian Stövare.

Deutsche Dogge

See Great Dane

Deutsche Sauerlandbracke

See Deutsche Bracke

Deutsche Bracke, tricolor. Photo by I. Français.

Deutsche Schaferhund
See German Shepherd Dog

Deutscher Drahthaariger Vorstehhund
See German Wirehaired Pointer

Deutscher Grossspitz
German name for the Giant German Spitz. *See* German Spitzen

Deutscher Jagdterrier
See German Hunting Terrier

Deutscher Kleinspitz
See German Spitzen

Deutscher Kurzhaariger Vorstehhund
See German Shorthaired Pointer

Deutscher Langhaariger Vorstehhund
See German Longhaired Pointer

Deutscher Mittelspitz
See German Spitzen

Deutscher Wachtelhund, brown roan. Photo by I. Français.

Deutscher Spitz
See German Spitzen

Deutscher Stichelhaariger Vorstehhund
See Stichelhaar

Deutscher Wachtelhund
A small German gundog of many typically spaniel features, including a wavy coat. The breed today closely resembles a centuries-old spaniel that once existed in England and on the Continent but has since died out. The Wachtelhund also suffered near extinction, but in 1897 a band of spaniel breeders focused their efforts and revived the breed. Today the Deutscher Wachtelhund, or German Spaniel, enjoys solid popularity with the German people as a hard working and efficient huntsman.

Watchel in German means "quail," and these dogs certainly possess a masterful ability on quail. In no way an exclusivist, the Wachtelhund is an all-around bird dog. His scenting ability makes him especially popular with hunters who hunt heavily thicketed woodland. He can also be trained to retrieve and is a good water dog. Based on use and ability, it seems probable that Continental water dogs are his prime component stock, although it is likely that various sporting spaniels, including the Cocker, are also in his blood.

ESSENTIALS OF THE DEUTSCHER WACHTELHUND: A solid dog with a no-nonsense character. The overall appearance is of a compact, robust animal set fairly low to the ground. Muzzle and skull of equal length, with slight arch to the topskull. No stop noticeable. Muzzle elongated but not pointed. Ears set high and wide, hanging flat behind the eyes, touching the eyes when pulled to them. Well-muscled, with powerful quarters and good spring of rib. Length to slightly exceed height. Coat to be wavy, thick and long. Coat on muzzle and foreface shorter and smooth. Tail docked. Height: 16–20 inches (40–51 cm). Weight: 44–66 pounds (20–30 kg). Color is dark brown, often with white markings on the chest and toes; other colors are white with brown patches and white mottled with brown. Brown roans and brown harlequins are preferred to the caille-colored dogs.

Devocalization
See Debarking

Dewclaws
Fifth digit on the inside of the legs. Most canines are born devoid of dewclaws or have them removed shortly after birth. There are, however, a handful of breeds that require retained dewclaws: Great Pyrenees, Beauceron, and Briard. The Norwegian Lundehund possesses two dewclaws on all four feet, just one aspect of its most unique anatomy. Only on the Lundehund are the dewclaws actually functional.

When asked when to remove the dewclaws, the appropriate response could be, "as soon as possible." At several days of age, the dewclaws are easily and relatively painlessly removed. They must be removed under the guidance of an experienced breeder or vet, as pain and excessive bleeding may otherwise result.

Dewlap
Loose pendulous skin under the throat. The Bloodhound and the Fila Brasileiro are two stupendous examples of heavy dewlap.

Deworming
Most often by chemical means are worms removed from the canine host. Depending on the individual dog and condition, the species of worm, and the extent of the infestation, a specific course of action will be determined by the vet. There are medications that attack worms at various stages of their development, i.e., larval, mature, etc.

DHL
A vaccine that is usually given to a pup at about six weeks of age, serving as an inoculation against distemper, hepatitis, and leptospirosis.

Dhangari Dog
The Dhangari Dog of Maharashtra is a herding dog that moves with the caravan and doubles as a nightwatchman and hunter as well. These Indian working

dogs stand 20 inches (51 cm) high, bitches are considerably smaller; weight is 20–25 pounds (9–11.5 kg). The Dhangari is probably extinct due to countless crosses to pariah types and mongrels.

Dhokhi Apso
See Tibetan Terrier

Dhole
Known also as the red wolf, the red dog, and the Indian or Asian wild or hunting dog, the dhole is a wild dog that ranges from India through mainland China, southeast Asia, and north to southern Siberia. Commonly referred to in texts on the wildlife, especially the wild dogs, of Asia, the dhole, *Cuon alpinus*, stands between 17 and 20 inches (43–51 cm) and weighs 22 to 40 pounds (10–18 kg). It fairly resembles a small wolf in size though this varies considerably according to geographic location. A brightly colored topcoat of red and a profuse fox brush tail, the dhole is easy to distinguish from other wild dogs. Differing from domestic dog and other members of the genus *Canis*, the dhole has up to eight pair of teats and only 40 teeth. Preferring to roam in heavily wooded regions of its native lands, the dhole hunts and is most active during the early morning and early evening hours. It has been witnessed in the mountainous re-

Dewclaws should be removed from a puppy as early as possible, if removal is desirable.

gion of Tibet at elevations exceeding 13,000 feet (3,900 m); at such heights and on the steppes where the vegetation is sparse, the dhole is most active at night. With great endurance and tremendous agility, this wild dog preys on larger animals with ease. Its pack and family instincts are similar to members of the genus *Canis*, yet its communicative barks, yelps, whines, and chatters are distinctive to it alone. The dhole displays no willingness or intention to join the howls or antics of other wild dogs when kept captive in close proximity, and it is believed that this exclusion is consistent in the wild.

Diabetes insipidus

(DI) Occurring in dogs, this disorder of the antidiuretic hormone secreting control results in good quantities of normal but dilute urine. It is classified by veterinarians as a pituitary disorder. Excessive urination and dehydration are typical signs. The condition requires professional diagnoses and can often be treated with prescribed doses of the missing antidiuretic hormone.

disease. Signs include: unquenchable thirst, frequent urination, and weight loss with increased appetite and accompanying weakness.

Diamond

The black-colored thumb mark on the forehead of the fawn-colored Pug.

Diaphragm

The partition of muscles and tendons between the abdominal cavity and chest cavity. *See also* Chest

Diaphragmatic hernias

See Hernias

Diarrhea

Regardless of how dry a given food is when it enters the stomach, it leaves that digestive organ and passes into the intestines as a semi-solid well-surrounded with fluids. As the matter travels the intestines fluid is removed until, completing the run of the large intestine and entering the colon, it is well formed and adequately consistent. Anything that offsets the liquidation and subsequent

Diarrhea. The diet of a puppy, especially, must remain consistent in order to maintain proper digestive-system functioning. Photo by R. Reagan

Diabetes mellitus

Likely the most common endocrine disorder in dogs, usually affecting middle-aged dogs (over five years old). According to *The Merck Veterinary Manual* (1986), the risk to females is approximately five times greater than it is to males, with Samoyeds and Dachshunds known to be the most susceptible. Routine testing can spot the disease at an early stage; otherwise, noticeable signs are not present until the later stages of the

dehydration process of digestion can cause the disorder known as diarrhea.

The most common cause of diarrhea in healthy dogs is a change in diet. Dogs are creatures of habit, and this adage applies to their digestive systems as well. A change in the type, quality, consistency, or even quantity of food can cause a case of diarrhea. In such instances, the case is short lived, meaning that the dog's system adjusts to the new diet and the digestive balance is regained. An exception is when the animal is allergic to the new food. In such cases, diarrhea will be prolonged, with other allergic reactions possible. A change of diet is recommended. It is therefore necessary that the dog owner use caution in changing a dog's diet. All such changes should be gradual, allowing the dog time to adjust. New owners must learn what the new dog's diet has been and stick to it at first, changing it gradually if desired.

Parasites, particularly whipworms, are another cause of diarrhea. When parasites are present in the digestive tract, they are often noticeable within the stool itself or by the occurrence of bloody excrement. Periodic stool checking by your veterinarian is deserved by your dog. When unchecked, parasites in the digestive system can kill an animal.

Just as humans suffer from the "intestinal bug" so are dogs affected by infectious intestinal bacteria. Such infections are visibly determined by reddish discoloration suggestive of irritation around the anal opening. Bacterial disorders can be self-correcting but should be inspected by a veterinarian, who may prescribe antibiotics and/or a change in diet. Oftimes the same signs are due to the presence of a virus.

Another cause of diarrhea that should be considered, especially in dogs receiving medications, is the possibility of toxemia. Poisoning, whether it is in the form of accidental ingestion or reaction to a prescribed medication, can cause diarrhea. Diarrhea can be the first sign of trouble in poisoning, and the possibility should be investigated. Early determination can save the dog's life.

The absence or presence of vomiting in conjunction with diarrhea is important in determining the specifics of the case. Vomiting suggests that the disorder includes either the small intestine, the stomach, or both. The absence of vomit-

ing suggests that the disorder is localized within the large intestine.

The dangers of diarrhea include dehydration, malnutrition and anorexia, weakness that brings susceptibility to other disorders, and in some cases blood loss and intestinal damage.

Persistent diarrhea must not be ignored and should be investigated immediately. All dogs will have their day, and an occasional loose stool or two is not to be alarming.

Diet
See Feeding, Nutrition

Digestive system
This highly efficient system of organs converts foods into substances that are usable by the body, either as fuel or as stored, potential food. In short, the nutrients needed by the body to perform its many tasks, including digestion, are prepared for use by the body by the digestive system. The primary components of this system are: the teeth and mouth (for mastication); the tongue (the dog's primary tool for getting food into its mouth); the throat, including the esophagus, pharynx, larynx, and epiglottis (the pharynx and larynx start the food down the esophagus, which leads the food to the stomach,) and the epiglottis, (a flap-

Digestive system. Mother's milk provides easy digestibility and nutrition for very young puppies.

like cartilage mechanism closes over the windpipe to prevent food from entering it); the stomach (its elastic walls house and mix the food while digestive juices break down the food); the large and small intestines, which further break down the food; the pancreas organ producing digestive enzymes and regulating the power of the body to handle blood sugar); and the excretory organs (by which remains of the digested food are removed).

Digestive system. Growing puppies will gradually adapt to a diet of solid foods.

Though all the aforementioned components are vital to digestion, the primary organs are the stomach and the intestines. While in the stomach, food is subjected to considerable doses of acidic substances which primarily break down proteins and fats, leaving starch digestion, begun by the salivary glands, to the intestines. The stomach prepares all its food contents for further and complete digestion in the intestines and, through contractions, moves food into the small intestine. The exit of the stomach is called the pylorus; it connects the stomach to the duodenum, a thick area of the small intestine that receives bile from the liver and starch-digesting substances from the pancreas. Bile breaks up fat into tiny components, and enzymes turn starch to dextrin, which is later turned into glucose by another substance, secreted into

the small intestine. In the small intestine, proteins and fats are also reduced to their component parts, amino and fatty acids. Once so broken, all can be absorbed through the intestinal walls and pass into the lymph and blood. Microscopic, hairlike projections, called villi, line the walls of the intestine, increasing immensely both its surface area and its efficiency of absorption. The large intestine is largely responsible for removing excess water through absorption from the remains of the food. With digestion complete, including absorption, the remains pass to the colon, from which they are soon excreted.

A system of many parts, including many organs, the digestive system is affected by numerous and varied problems, ranging from diarrhea to abscessed gums to ingested foreign objects. The major and most common disorders are covered under separate entries, which include: Diarrhea, Feeding, Puppies, Housebreaking, Vomiting, Worms.

Digit
Toe.

Digitalis
A stimulant which, though commonly used, may prove toxic. Careful observation is recommended while the patient is receiving doses of digitalis. Mild diarrhea is a common first sign, while depression, vomiting and cardiac difficulty signal trouble.

Digitoxin
A medication given to a dog with congestive heart failure. Dosage is of course adjusted to the severity of the condition and size of the individual animal affected.

Dingo

The Australian dingo, or warrigal, is a wild dog of great antiquity but not a native of Australia. It is believed that the dingo was brought by primitive man to the continent of Australia as a semi-domesticated feral dog. Fossil remains of the dingo in Australia date to the late Pleistocene period. As a carnivore in a land of grass-eating animals, the dingo found life in its new land tastefully simple—with a plentiful supply of easy catches, the dingo flourished and became an undetachable part of the Australian wildlife. Its effects on prehistoric Australian ecology are assumed to be considerable. With the coming of European man and his sheep and rabbits, the dingo population burgeoned and the ecological

years, the dingo controlled the rabbit population, allowing grazelands for man's sheep but eventually outnumbering its own food supply. Later, when poisoning was employed to further extinguish the rabbit population, dingoes began to prey on sheep, and man in anger hunted the dingo. With fewer dingoes, rabbits ran rampant, decimating the grazelands. Thus began and continues the vicious ecological cycle of Australia.

Despite its origins and certain similarity to the basic domestic dog, the dingo is unquestionably a wild dog and likely to remain unbroken for years to come. A few Australian breeders of herding dogs have crossed their domestic stock with "tame" dingoes to improve the breed's or strain's endurance and tolerance to the

Dingo of Australia may represent the dog in its most natural state.

balance of Australia was further upset. Rabbits, like the dingo, found life in the grassland quite easy, with few predators and abundant food; the dingo, graciously accepting, found the rabbit a welcome addition to its diet of marsupials. For

rugged Australian environment. Such crosses have given varied degrees of success. Most notable is the Australian Cattle Dog, which *see*.

In the wild, dingoes may hunt alone or in family units, but rarely in packs. Dingoes shy from man and have reverted to the ancient canine way of life. They communicate in yelps and howls and can be heard howling together before the hunt. The dingo's head is characterized by rather small rounded ears, carried erect. The tail is well furred, appearing bushy. The coat's length, density, and texture vary according to climate. In color the dingo is commonly tawny; however, it can be any color from white through black, including an occasional brindle; albinos are also reported. Height: 19–23 inches (48–58.5 cm). Weight: 50–70

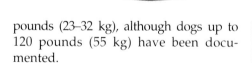

pounds (23–32 kg), although dogs up to 120 pounds (55 kg) have been documented.

Dirofilariasis
  See Heartworm

Disc (intervertebral) abnormalities
  Between each bone in the spine is a connecting structure called an intervertebral disc. When the disc between two vertebrae becomes irritated and protrudes into the spinal canal it forms lesions and is painful. This is a disease which particularly affects the Dachs-

hund because of its long back in comparison to the length of its legs. Paralysis of the legs, reluctance to move, and loss of control of body functions may be symptoms. X-ray and physical examination will determine the extent of the condition. Massage helps circulation and pain relievers may be prescribed. Veterinary surgery is sometimes successful and portable two-wheel carts which support the hindquarters may increase the affected dog's mobility.

Disc, spinal
  See Spinal column

Discs, intervertebral
  See Intervertebral discs

Dish face
  Foreface converges with the nose tip above the usual stop. A dish face is required of the Pointer as well as a number of other European pointers but is a listed fault for the German Shorthair.

Dishing
  Similar to crossing over and weaving and referred to in the Wire Fox Terrier standard as a fault.

Dislocation
  Synonymous with separation, dislocation is the term used to refer to the coming apart of two bones at the joint at which they are normally "fused" by ligaments, muscles, and tendons. Dislocations are more likely to occur in the knee, shoulder and hip regions than in other regions of the dog. A dislocation is a painful injury and can be detected by the dog's severe favoritism of or inability to apply pressure to the affected part. Veterinary care is recommended. Rest and relocation are likely courses of action.

Disqualifications
  Disqualifications are built into every breed standard; most of these egregious faults are specific to that breed. For example, broken down or cropped ears disqualify a Chihuahua from competi-

Dish face illustrated by the Braque St.-Germain of France. Photo by I. Français.

tion; brindle markings disqualify the Italian Greyhound. There are a number of commonly listed disqualifications such as a dudley or butterfly nose, incorrect jaw, over weight limit, and cow hocks.

The following disqualifications are applied to all dogs intending to compete in a conformation exhibition. A dog that is blind, deaf, castrated, spayed or that has b e e n changed in appearance by artificial means (with the exceptions of breed standard's permitting cropping or docking in a given registry) and a male dog that does not have both testicles normally located in the scrotum will not be permitted to compete in the open class. A dog that is lame shall not be permitted to compete; judge will determine if a given dog is lame. In regis-

tries that permit ear cropping, any dog whose ears have been cropped incorrectly is ineligible to compete.

Dogs that show signs of a communicable disease or are known to have been in contact with such a disease shall not be permitted on show grounds.

Disqualifications. A distinctly long coat on the Weimaraner breed is severely penalized and disqualifies the dog from American competition. This variant has allured new followers to develop these handsome dogs despite traditional fanciers' disproval.

Disqualifications. A white ground color in the Boxer disqualifies it from competition. Tracing the breed back to its English White Bulldog beginnings explains this common occurrence in the Boxer. Many such Boxers are affected by deafness. Photographs by I. Français.

Distemper

This once epidemic disease ravaged litters around the world, spreading panic and sorrow with its airborne viral contagion. Today the disease is under good control. There are distemper shots, which every young pup should receive at an early age, and there is a greater understanding of the infection, its causes and

Doberman Pinschers, black/tan and Isabella; cropped ears.

its complications. The disease is characterized by persistent high temperatures, gastrointestinal and respiratory complications, and often pneumonic and neurological complications. The disease is viral in origin and affects members of the Canidae family, including foxes and wolves, as well as members of the Procyonidae family, including raccoons, and other related families. Therefore, it is possible for a dog to acquire the disease from animals other than other dogs. It is not, however, contagious to man. The disease is spread through the air, and infection occurs after inhalation.

Distemper teeth

Refers to puppies' permanent teeth which, upon eruption, are affected with pits and eroded enamel that are the result of sustained fever during early puppyhood. Neither of the effects are self-correcting. The term originates from the time when distemper was rampant in the canine world and many puppies suffered from "distemper teeth" as a result. The use of the word "distemper," therefore, does not infer that distemper is the single disease which will produce pitted teeth. Such ruined and discolored teeth can be the result of any disease, even a rather mild one, incorrect dietary intake, or parasitism. *See also* Dental care

Distended pastern joint

Enlarged wrist or metacarpal joint giving the pasterns an undesirable, untidy appearance.

Diuretics

Drugs used to increase the quantity of urine released from the body.

Divided find

In field trials, when two dogs are found pointing and the judges are unable to determine which found a bird first, each is credited with a divided find.

Divided placements

When the performances of two dogs in a field trial are considered equal, the judges sometimes divide the purses. This is mostly done in third-place wins.

Divided point

The situation occurring when two or more dogs encounter game and point, each independent of the other and unaware of the other's point.

DMSO

Chemical capable of penetrating the skin. It can be used to carry some drugs to the ligaments, tendons, and other components. Vets often prescribe this to treat acute pulmonary edema.

D.N.F.

In dog racing, D.N.F. indicates "Did not finish," i.e., the race.

Doberman Pinscher

With the idea of creating a mountain of a terrier that retained all the agility, game, and action of the best ratter, Louis Dobermann began a breeding program between 1865–1870 in Apolda, Thueringen, Germany. Herr Dobermann, a tax collector, had the need for a dog that would protect him from both the irate, negligent tax payers and their snarling guard dogs. The Wagner of the canine universe, Dobermann worked with terrier, herder, and mastiff motifs and themes to complete his super-terrier masterpiece. His access to all dogs that he brought in through his employment as dog catcher plus his own fine kennel stock afforded Dobermann the opportunity to develop the canine par excellence. At this task Herr Dobermann admirably succeeded. In a remarkably short period of time, about 15 years, the Doberman's type was perfected.

From the beginning of the 1900s, the Doberman Pinscher spread quickly to other European countries, and by the 1930s the breed reached the U.S. and Canada. In the U.S., Doberman Intelectus was the first dog whelped on American soil and registered by the American Kennel Club. Intelectus's dam, Doberman Hertha from the Hohenstein Kennels, was the first of the breed to achieve A.K.C. championship; the year was 1912. It is believed that a descendant of Dobermann himself brought this first-rate member of the master canine race to the United States.

In Great Britain, the Doberman Pinscher (where he is called simply Dobermann) was first exhibited in 1933; the daring Elizabeth Craig (Mrs. A.E. Mann to her friends), writer and dog enthusiast, presented the only dog of German origin at the Crystal Palace Kennel Club Show in London. Despite the stir this caused, the breed did not build in number until after the Second World War. The first club in England was founded in 1948.

The great surge in popularity that the Doberman has witnessed during the twentieth century has predictably brought the overbreeding problems that must be confronted and overcome. However, the breed today remains a dog of outstanding quality and ability, used for guard, police, military, and obedience work—despite the crude and wanton breeding practices of some money-minded individuals.

Doberman Pinscher, black/tan.

Many Dobermans participate in protection training. These dogs are commonly employed for such guard-dog functions. The North American Working Dog Association (W.D.A), recommends that dogs be trained in Schutzhund work, which *see*. Schutzhund work involves Tracking, Obedience and Protection; these areas of concentration are designed to mold the dog into the most capable and obedient guardian that it is capable of being. While the Doberman does well in Schutzhund, it does not compete with the German Shepherd Dog, who excels in these tests and training like no other breed.

Nevertheless, Dobermans are highly trainable and duly intelligent. The German standard for the breed stresses the

ideal dog's working abilities; likewise the American and British standards have

Doberman Pinscher, red/tan; uncropped ears.

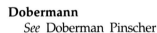

Doberman Pinscher, red/tan; cropped ears.

compact and powerful, showing no exaggeration of muscle or bone. Topline sloping from withers to croup; chest reaching to the elbows. The head is long and dry, with a gradual taper from between the ears to the point of the muzzle. The jaws must be solid and powerful, never hinting at snipiness. The bite to be scissors. Coat: smooth, short, hard, thick, and close lying. Color: solid ground color of either black, red, fawn, or blue, all with tan markings. The ears are usually cropped and held erect in the U.S.A. and uncropped and held naturally in Great Britain and Germany.

followed the German lead. The German Kennel Club standard begins: "The Dobermann Pinscher should be built muscular and powerful, but not clumsy and massy; neither should he be greyhound-like. His appearance must indicate s w i f t n e s s, power, and endurance. Temperament should be lively and ardent."

ESSENTIALS OF THE DOBERMAN PINSCHER: The body is medium size, square, and suggestive of power, courage, stamina, and nobility. The breed stands 23–28 inches (59–71 cm) tall and weighs 66–88 pounds (30–40 kg). The build is

Dobermann
See Doberman Pinscher

Dock

Amputation of a section of the tail vertebrae of a four or five-day-old puppy. A great many breeds are docked, and breeders have a standard number of vertebrae to dock, which varies from breed to breed. Docking today is upheld mostly for traditional if not valid reasons. Historically, however, a great number of dogs' tails were docked to protect them from injury, i.e., some gundogs' tails were docked so that they would not be snagged or torn in the brush.

Docked tail

A tail that has been artificially shortened or removed, usually to a length prescribed or desired by a breed standard.

Dog bite statutes

While biting is the dog's primary means of protection, courts tend to lean towards the bitten party. Dog bite cases are the most common suit for which damages are brought. Many legal systems impose absolute liability on the dog's owner for any injury or damage done by the dog, regardless of fault. Dog Bite Statutes, as these no-fault clauses are known, concern dog bites as well as any such accrued damage. Depending on the jurisdiction, one party or the other will have to prove that he was not at fault. The elements covered by a statute include the nature of the injury, the location of the event, who can sue and be sued, defenses and actions of the victim.

Dog box

The compartment mounted on a truck in which dogs are transported to and from the racing site.

Dog food

Commercially prepared foods for dogs. *See* Feeding

Dog fox

The male fox.

Dog house

An outdoor enclosure designed to safely harbor a dog comfortably for a temporary or for a prolonged period. Dog houses should be watertight and free from drafts. Dog houses can be purchased commercially or self-constructed *See* Accommodations, outdoor

Dog racing

The first dog race on record took place at Welsh Harp at Hendor, near London, in 1876. A 400-yard rail was assembled in the grass and the competing Greyhounds chased a mounted artificial hare, pulled by a sledge. Even though the afternoon diversion was successful, no enthusiasts emerged to organize any lasting sport. It wasn't until the late 1890s that a dog racing event made its way to America. This first dog race, which took place in Miami, Florida, also did not stir up sufficient enthusiasm for the dog racing sport to take a strong hold.

The sport in America leaped into popularity when the Tucson, Arizona

Dog racing. Organized racing and coursing events among fanciers today are becoming increasingly popular. Whippets at a dog-club event.

track opened in 1909. This was the first modern track. Other tracks followed: Houston, Texas; Tulsa, Oklahoma; and Miami, Florida. The Belle Vue Stadium in Manchester was started by Canadian

rules and regulations of competition.

Presently the dog racing sport flourishes in three countries: England, America, and Australia. In all three nations, the Greyhound is the principal dog. Other sighthound breeds, however, do participate in races: Whippet, Afghan Hound, Ibizan Hound, Irish Wolfhound, Saluki, Sloughi, and Pharaoh Hound. In the U.S. and England, the Whippet is the second most popular racing dog. In Spain, the Galgo Español (or the Spanish Greyhound) is the principal racing dog; in Hungary, the Magyar Ağar (or Hungarian Greyhound). In India, while a number of native greyhounds exist, organized dog sports do not flourish as they do in the West, and these dogs are used more often for hunting and coursing as opposed to racing.

Dog racing. Inflamed, named, and numbered, Greyhounds darting through the starting gates.

Dog racing. The graceful and lean Pharaoh Hound in full stride. Photo by P. Mayberry.

Brigadier General Critchley, American Charlie Munn, and Sir William Gentle (and their backers). In England, their Manchester track was the first to open (1926); tracks in London and Liverpool trailed closely behind. About the same time, the Greyhound Racing Association was formed to service the fast-growing dog sport: training kennels for the race dogs were established. The National Greyhound Racing Club, formed in 1928,

The fastest Greyhound on record is Pigalle Wonder, who set the world record of 28:44 seconds for a 525-yard dash (the standard oval track) in the Derby heats. (Only great Greyhounds in their prime break 29:00 seconds, a feat which

focused more on the interests of the public, the licensing of courses, and the

Pigalle did 24 times.) Other greats of the past tracks include: Endless Gossip,

Trev's Perfection, Mile Bush Pride, Bally-nennan Moon, and Mick the Miller. This latter, a two-time Derby winner, is accredited with tremendously enhancing the sport's popularity in England.

Racing Greyhounds are retired around four to five years of age, after which they are typically euthanized—tens of thousands are put to death annually. Today there is a growing concern over these fine animals, and several organizations work diligently to place retired Greyhounds in caring, capable homes. The standards set for ownership are typically high, but if you're up to the challenge, it can be a rewarding one. These dogs have proven adaptable, affectionate, and more people-oriented than might be expected. Don't be misled, however, as the ex-racing Greyhound is a big, robust canine with considerable exercise requirements. Life expectancy, however, is usually about eight years due to the rigorous track workouts and steroids involved with training. Additonally, close supervision and a well-fenced yard are requisites. Interested persons are encouraged to contact their local humane society and/or a nearby track for information about Greyhound placement organizations.

Dogo
Spanish for dog.

Dogo Aleman
See Great Dane

Dogo Argentino
Dr. Antonio Nores Martinez, in the 1920s, distinguished himself and Argentina by producing that nation's first native purebred dog, the Dogo Argentino.

The Dogo was bred to hunt, in packs, the vicious big game of wild boar, mountain lion, and jaguar. The terrain of his native land demands fit animals. The Dogo can traverse great distances at considerable speeds and yet retain enough strength to conquer his quarry. The Dogo combines a number of breeds, including: a base of the Old Fighting Dog of Cordoba (the breed itself a blend of Spanish Mastiff, Bull Terrier, old Bulldogge, and early Boxer); harlequin Great Dane; Great Pyrenees; English Pointer; and to a lesser degree, Irish Wolfhound and Dogue de

Bordeaux. Thus the breed combines strength, stamina, agility, hunting ability, fearlessness and a cool yet all-weather white coat color. The Dogo Argentino is intrepid and untiring. The essential requirements are exercise and obedience training. An impassable guard, the Dogo is gaining international respect and popularity.

ESSENTIALS OF THE DOGO ARGENTINO: The Dogo is smooth-muscled, symmetrical in appearance, and very powerful. The skull is massive; the jaws strong; and the neck thick and powerful. Height: 23.5–25.5 inches (60–65 cm). Weight: 82–95 pounds (37–43 kg). The coat is short, smooth, thick, and glossy. Color is always white.

Dogo Argentino, white. Photo by I. Français.

Dogs as delicacy. The Shar-Pei remains one of few authentic Cantonese dishes not offered in white cartons by American Chinese restaurants.

Dogs as delicacy

The omnivorous East, comprised mostly of nations that do not produce much meat, relied on unconventional means for food—unconventional compared to Western standards. The concept of eating our dogs, to our Western mindsets, is a foreign and frightening thought, distasteful at best. As we open our minds to the cultures of Eastern lands, many "unconventional," surely non-Western, ideas arise. The concept of walking into our neighborhood grocery store or corner delicatessen and seeing "Diced pug," "Loin of chow,"

"Poodle tongue," or "Peke liver" next to our sirloin or pot roast is beyond our most outstretched notions.

In the Cantonese language, the word "chow" means food, just as the slang word means in English. In China, the Chow Chow, one of the West's most beloved and popular dogs today, was originally raised as a watchdog and as a broiler specialty. Although the extent to which the Chinese ate dog flesh is not entirely known, it is positive that they did partake of dog meat on a regular or semi-regular basis. Dog flesh was a favorite delicacy and, just as in the U.S. Americans think turkey and ham on our holidays, the Chinese think dog on their New Year's day. Perhaps in the more remote areas of China today, dog flesh is still eaten with some regularity. There is not a super-abundance of dogs in China today, and with regard to the expense of purchasing a dog, eating it is not foremost on the Chinese mind. Smooth Chow Chows,

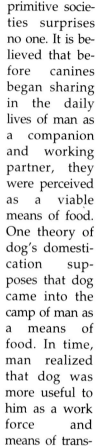

when first imported into England, were uncuriously billed a curiosity: "the Edible Dog."

The fact that dog served as food in primitive societies surprises no one. It is believed that before canines began sharing in the daily lives of man as a companion and working partner, they were perceived as a viable means of food. One theory of dog's domestication supposes that dog came into the camp of man as a means of food. In time, man realized that dog was more useful to him as a work force and means of transport and discontinued the regular eating of its flesh. This theory, however, is perhaps the most dubious of dog's domestication process.

During World War II, and other periods of inescapable starvation, Europeans were forced to consume their stable dogs and house pets. When dog historians and cynologists refer to the Great Wars as being unkind to dogs, they refer not simply to men not breeding and showing dogs, but resorting to such unthinkable occurrences. Likewise, it is commonly believed that many starving Eskimos on uncharted tundra resorted to eating the weakest of their fan-hitched huskies. Of course, in consuming their only means of transportation, they reassured their doom. A Russian laika student of yesteryear, Prince Andrew Shirimsky-Schichmatow, indicates that the Chinese greatly savored the flesh of any laika that wandered too far south. His studies indicate that nearly a million laikas were consumed by the Chinese, although it is likely that Chow Chows were included in this figure.

The Telchichi dog, a believed forerunner of today's Chihuahua, is said to have been "castrated and ate" by the tribes that raised them. Peruvian Indians raised their beloved Inca Orchid dogs as pets but did not refrain from featuring one of their hairless brothers as an occasional main course. Likewise, the Aztecs used their hairless dogs, the Xoloitzcuintli or Tepeizeuintli, as sacrificial offerings and belly warmers. Since the hairless varieties were more valued than the coated varieties, the coated dogs were likely spitted and charcoaled first.

The Poi Dog of Hawaii, the pineapple bouncing delicacy of the Polynesian Islands, is one of two canines in the history of "civilized" humankind to have no other function but to provide food for the natives. The dogs were fed poi (a paste made from ground, baked, and fermented taro root) to fatten them for eating. The dog's lack of chewing contributed to their flat, broad skulls; their mandibles flattened from continued disuse. The Poi Dog's extinction, largely attributed to the slothfulness and malformity of the functionless dog, indicates to the dog world today that dogs cannot be raised in the manner of hogs or pigs and still survive.

The second dog used solely as a food source is the Philippine Edible Dog, raised on the Philippine Islands. The practice of eating this dog has been the custom of the tribes of northern Luzon for years. If the practice has been discontinued, it is due to pressure placed on the tribes by American authorities on the island. The dogs were well fattened, stuffed with rice and local seasonings and roasted over wood embers. To the feasting natives, dog flesh is more of a delicacy than pork or ham.

The authors have had the rare opportunity to talk to persons who have consumed the flesh of dog in foreign countries. It was served with great pride to them and would have been perceived an insult to not partake in their offering. We are told the flesh is very tender, with a taste unlike any meat known to Western palates. When asked, our interviewee assured us that it did *not* taste like chicken. *See also* Sumatra Battak

Dogs as delicacy. When first exported to England, the Smooth Chow Chow was delectably labelled "the Edible Dog."

Dogue
French for mastiff.

Dogue de Bordeaux

The Dogue de Bordeaux, known variously as the French Mastiff and Bordeaux Bulldog, is a truly ancient breed of France said to have descended directly from the Molossus of Rome. The breed's large brachycephalic skull, deep protective instincts, and overall massive build speak of this direct relationship. A frequent

Dogue de Bordeaux, golden. Photo by I. Français.

sight on French estates for centuries, the Bordeaux dog is a fearless guardian. Employed as a hunter of pigs, bears, boars and wolves, these formidable titans were never over-esteemed by their twelfth-century French masters. During the Middle Ages, the dogs were used for cattle droving. For many generations, the dogs were employed as both war dogs and flock guardians. Their fearlessness and power are formidable and can be aptly compared to most any dog that has ever intimidated the likes of men, wolves, and bears. Frequently used in baiting sports as well as dog fights, the Bordeaux has proven himself versatile through the ages. With the outlawing of animal baiting, Dogues were pitted against Dogues and provided hours of blood-stirring and -spilling entertainment for the onlooking French peasants and noblemen. Never a dull moment, a full-grown jaguar would be introduced to liven up a less than exciting match.

In times of the breed's popularity, two sizes of Bordeaux existed: the Dogue and the Doguin. The former, the larger, weighed in excess of 100 pounds and was used in bear baiting; the latter, used to bait bull and ass, weighed in at about 80 pounds. Today only the larger size, the Dogue, is still found.

Though the breed struggled through much of the the twentieth century, it is gaining moderate international popularity as a fine guard and companion. In many respects, the breed is similar to the Bullmastiff of Great Britain, although it is a far more ancient pure breed. In size these dogs are comparable, as are their general appearances.

The red-masked Bordeaux took to the big screen in 1989 with American film comedian Tom Hanks, who was much enamored with this French giant and particularly impressed with its intelligence, cooperative nature and slobbering abilities.

ESSENTIALS OF THE DOGUE DE BORDEAUX: The breed's acromegalic features include its massive head, superabundant wrinkles, and exaggerated paws. The body is well balanced and muscular. Furrowed with wrinkles, the broad round head is tremendous and the largest in the canine world. The eyes are oval, set far apart, large, not bulging; the supraorbital ridges are pronounced. The ears are small and hanging. Neck very strong and muscular. The chest is powerful, broad, deep, let down below the elbows. Back broad and muscular; loins short. The shoulders well sloped, protruding slightly from the withers. Hindquarters elongated, with thighs well let down and muscular. Feet strong with closed toes. Height: 22–27 inches (59–69 cm). Weight: females over 88 pounds (41.5 kg); males over 100 pounds (46 kg). The coat is fine, short and soft to the touch. In color the Dogue is fawn, mahogany, golden, or black speckled—warm tones desirable. Black or red mask a must.

Dolichocephalic skull
See Skull types

Domed skull

Synonymous with apple skull, the term used in the Chihuahua standard; a domed skull is sloping on all sides, somewhat like one-quarter of a globe. Such a skull has a rounded and smooth appearance.

Domestication of dog

Dog, it is assured, was the first animal to be domesticated, excluding man himself possibly. Actually, domestication usually refers to taming a wild animal to the "home life" of man and breeding that animal for his purposes. Many animals have been tamed by man and put under his domain—arguably, all animals have been put under man's domain. The lion, for instance, has been tamed by man but never to the extent that it is worthy of man's trust. Even the most domesticated of lions might snack on his master's pet Siamese when his master is away. Other slithering and crawling animals have been domesticated to man's curious avail: rats, gerbils, chipmunks, snakes and skunks. The rat, especially, which in

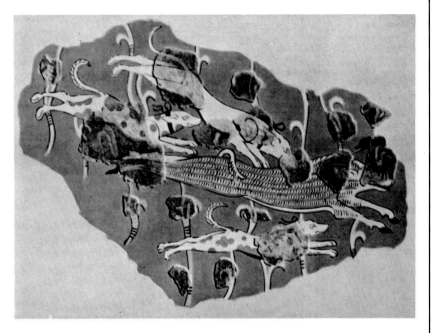

accord with Günter Grass's portrait, is one of the most intelligent and industrious of all animals and even makes an affectionate companion for any human able to swallow his distaste for rodents. Even so, the rat, like the lion, does not enjoy the rank of the dog (or the cat) as a domesticated companion.

The domestication of dog occurred about 13,000 to 15,000 years ago. Denmark provides us with the most authentic ancient relics of early dogs. It is not clear, however, whether these fossils date 10,000 B.C. or 6,000 B.C. Dog has been found in domesticated form

Domestication of dog. Frescos of Far East origins document early canine involvement in hunting and coursing expeditions.

Domestication of dog. Theoretically, the husky dogs of the North developed from the Nordic wolves; these early wolf-dogs were used as draft dogs. Pack of Greenland Dogs.

throughout tribal Africa before colonial days. In Europe, the Mediterranean, the Near East, and Asia, domestic dog has been known for as many years as man has cared to record his history. The canine species adapted with more versatility than perhaps any animal; its universal adaptability, hardiness and ease of transport qualify dog's compliance with man's migrations and global moves.

Domestication of dog. Pariahs of New Guinea and other dingo types support the "garbage dump" theory which purports that wild dogs approached man's camps or settlements for a free meal.

Historical documents and artistic renderings from Europe and the Near East, although more recent than the Danish finds, do substantiate the fact that domestic dog played a dear role in evolving society. Whether simply serving as house companions (i.e., the Egyptian House Dog) or for purposes of hunting, guarding, coursing, etc., dog was actively involved in these ancient cultures.

At least four individual theories have arisen to explain how wild canines transformed into the domestic canines. Per-

haps the least popular of these theories is that man encaptured wild dog for food. While it is no mystery that man has eaten dog, as he has eaten most every other animal on the earth (surely including himself) whether or not raising dogs for food would yield the kind of domestication the dog exhibits today is at least questionable.

The pariahs of New Guinea, New Ireland, Australia and Polynesia shed credible light on a second theory. Some well-known dog experts purport that, just as the pariahs were lured by the garbage heaps of civilized man, wild dog may have been drawn to the camps of man because of the easy availability of food. The dogs slowly tolerated the approach of man and eventually served as refuse collectors, cleaning up the heaps which attracted vermin as they did the dogs.

One popular theory contends that wolf cubs were brought home by men after slaying the wolf mother. The cubs, initially functioning as pets for the hunter's children, soon joined man in his hunt for food. The scent of men on the grown-up wolf cub differentiated it from the other wolves and hence the domesticated variety persisted. This theory recently has been invalidated by evidence that disconnects domestic dog from the gray wolf, directly. Assuredly, the gray wolf and the dog share a number of characteristics: skeletal compatibility, behavioral similarities, like dentistry. Modern researchers point out the larger size of the northern gray wolf with its much heavier dentition—an animal too large to be the immediate forebear of the domestic dog. More likely, then, dog was derived from one of the subspecies that occurred in the southern border of the wolf's range. The Indian wolf, one such subspecies, is medium sized with smaller carnassials. The dingo and other pariah types may also have partaken of this evolutionary process. The dingo may be the missing link between the gray wolf subspecies and the domestic dog.

Domestic dogs' lifestyles, different than those of wolves or wild dogs, explains a number of the differences between the two animals. The smaller dentition in domestic dog logically derives from the kinds of foods fed it by its keeper, man. Not having to tear into the side of a fallen gazelle would tend to diminish the necessity for a large, powerful jaw. Variations in size, excluding the extremes in domestic dog, do not truly comprise a major difference since, in fact, the wolf and its subspecies vary quite substantially themselves.

Naturally, *Canis familiaris* or domestic dog has adapted, evolved and changed more dramatically than any other animal. Dog was required to adjust to the living conditions of the men who kept him and whom he served. *See also* Ancestors of the dog, Breed development

Domino
Reverse facial mask pattern on the face of some breeds (e.g., Saluki, Tazi, Afghan Hound).

Dorsal
On or near the back. Opposite of ventral, which *see*.

Douar Dog
See Chien de l'Atlas

Double
When the pursued fox turns back on its course. Also refers to a double fall: two birds shot down at the same time.

Double coat
The dog's usual coat, consisting of an outer coat and an undercoat: two-ply. *See* Coat

Double curled tail
See Coin tail

Double handling
Show-ring jargon for planting a distracting or encouraging second party outside the ring to better a show dog's chances. This juvenile practice is frowned upon in the professional world.

Double suspension gallop
See Gallop

Double-jointedness
In most breeds of dog, double-jointedness is a physiological abnormality where the joints (often the hock joints) are capable of odd contortions not typical of the canine species. Slipped hocks, for instance, is a mild form of such a condition. The exception to the rule is the Lundehund, which possesses a double-jointed neck, practically allowing the head to rest on its back, two double-jointed toes (five triple-jointed ones), and double-jointed forelegs. So much for purebred "abnormalities."

Down
All dogs in the obedience trial, but not more than 15 at a time, must lay down for three minutes in the Novice class with their handlers across the ring; five minutes in the Open classes with handlers out of sight. *See also* Training

Down-faced
The plane of the foreface and the plane of the skull incline downwards; the tip of the nose is therefore below the level of the dog's stop.

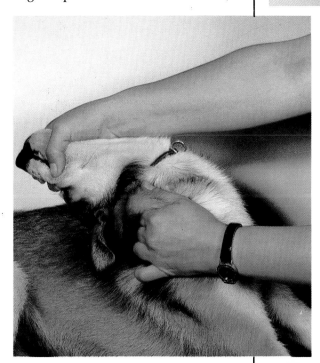

Down in pastern
Down on pastern; weak or faulty metacarpus set at a pronounced angle from the vertical. Same as broken-down pasterns and falling pasterns.

Draft
To remove hounds from a pack during a selection process in preparation for a hunt or competition.

Double-jointedness. The Norwegian Lundehund's double-jointed neck is but one of its adapted abnormalities. Photo by I. Français.

Draft dogs

Draft dogs, dogs that are used to pull loads, can be divided into two general categories: cart pullers and sled pullers. The cart pullers of Switzerland, Belgium and the Netherlands are principally of mastiff origins. Switzerland boasts the most glorious and colorful variations on the draft dog: there are four breeds which have arisen for this purpose: the Bernese Mountain Dog, Entelbucher, Greater Swiss Mountain Dog and Appenzeller.

In Belgium, the Belgian Mastiff functioned as a draft dog. In the days of draft

would pull an average load of about 300 pounds. A Belgian ordinance forbade the use of dogs which were smaller than 24 inches at the shoulder. The dogs were also competent gundogs and coursers, of sublime intelligence and fortitude. Belgian owners fed their dogs almost exclusively on horse meat and, incidentally, regularly attested that the dogs were more resourceful than a donkey or mule, not to mention cheaper to maintain and more amenable to work.

Denmark, too, enjoyed the service of draft dogs. The extant Danish Farm Dog is likely an offspring of such dogs. Milk-sellers and bakers are just a few of the merchants who greatly profited from the use of these dogs.

Other than the three aforementioned nations, no other European country professed great interest in draft dogs of their own. With the arrival of modern transportation modes, draft dogs have lost

Draft dogs. The Greater Swiss Mountain Dog, the largest and most powerful of the draft dogs of Switzerland, is a descendent of the ancient Roman mastiffs.

dogs in Belgium, for instance, these harnessed singular pullers rendered optimum service for the industrialist and agriculturist alike. A Belgian organization dedicated to the improvement of draft dog services (early twentieth century) was headed by a Professor Reul, who then defied any public authority to suppress the use of draft dogs in Belgium. "A disastrous economic revolution would be the consequence. Penury and poverty would enter thousands of homes where a relative affluence is apparent now." The club strove for a "better harnessed" system of draft dogs pulling "better-moving" vehicles. One draft dog

their place in twentieth-century society. By 1967, the use of these dogs had been abolished on the Continent.

Sled pullers, the second type of draft dog, were the horses of the nordic landscape. Today six known breeds fall into the category of nordic draft dog: the Siberian Husky, Alaskan Malamute, Greenland Dog, Eskimo Dog of Canada, Chinook of the U.S. and Northeasterly Hauling Laika of the old U.S.S.R. All six of these breeds are still employed for draft purposes. Of course the Siberian Husky and Alaskan Malamute have international reputations as companion animals as well. *See also* Nordic dogs

Drag

The trail left by an animal in transit; scent left as it drags its body and tail through grass, brush, sand or whatever the terrain. Drag also refers to a bag or sack of material strong with the scent of the game in question, which is used to lay down a trail for trials, or, in this day of scarcer game and more frequently encountered high-speed highways, for a foxhound hunt, wherein the trail is laid with a drag in the most interesting manner possible for a safe but sporting ride by the field.

Drag hunt

A hunt (foxhounds, pack master of hounds, whippers-in, field master, field) which depends upon a drag rather than live fox for the line. The term draghound has been loosely applied to refer to a number of hounds that participate in the sport of drag hunting.

Dragging

When a sledge dog is dragged along by his neckline, either after he falters or if he is merely lagging behind.

Draghound

Any number of British scenthounds which were used for the sport of drag hunting. *See* Drag hunt

Drahthaar

See German Wirehaired Pointer

Draw

In gundog field trials, 1) to move upon game cautiously; 2) the manner of determining the sequence in which dogs will compete in field trials is called the "draw" or "drawing." The names of the dogs are written on individual slips of paper and folded and placed in a receptacle. They are then "drawn" out, one at a time. The first dog drawn competes with the second, etc. Should there be an uneven number, the last dog "drawn" is called the bye.

Drentse Patrijshond

A strong, all-purpose hunting dog revered in his native Holland as a dog of great strength and willingness on the field. Originated in the Dutch province of Drentse, from which he takes his name, the Drentse Partrijshond resembles the

half-spaniel, half-setter dogs that are the believed ancestors of most gundogs. Known in his native land since at least the 1500s, the Dutch Partridge Dog is portrayed in a head study by Henrick

Draghound is a type of scenthound with a physical conformation similar to a small greyhound, ideal for swiftness on the trail.

Drentse Patrijshond, red and white. Photographs by I. Français.

Goltzius (1558–1617) in which the dog appears much like today's breed. However, with few dogs extant today, the breed is facing a serious challenge, while interest in its survival wanes.

Both a pointer and good retriever, he takes well to water and quite naturally to the gun. Gentle, meek and obedient, he does not respond well to aggressive training. He makes a fine companion and is ideal for the sporting but sensitive owner-hunter.

ESSENTIALS OF THE DRENTSE PATRIJSHOND: A medium-sized but very strong dog. The refined head, not large, is broad between the ears and slightly prominent at the cheeks. The neck is thick and strong, of good length. The dog's body is well

the 1900s and hunts fox, hare and deer. Born for the hunt, the Drever or Swedish Dachsbracke is a vociferous and industrious worker with capabilities far beyond one's expectations. Some have tried this able-bodied dachsbracke against larger game, such as wild boar. The Drever is quick enough and smart enough to dodge the game and bark like hell to warn the hunter. He is rarely shown but has turned up at an occasional exhibition. He has become somewhat popular in Canada, where he has been recognized since 1956.

ESSENTIALS OF THE DREVER: A solidly built dog close to the ground, the Drever flaunts characteristic white markings on his face, feet, neck, chest and tail tip. He

Drever, tricolor. Photo by I. Français.

built and of good bone. Back straight; chest solid. The tail is left long, resembling a setter. Height between 23–26 inches (58–66 cm). Weight: 45–50 pounds (21–23 kg). The coat is coarse and straight. The extensive feathering on the legs, feet, tail, and ears gives the coat a longer overall appearance.

Drever

A popular hunter and companion in Sweden, the Drever derives from the Westphalian Dachsbracke and the Strellufstöver. The Drever developed early in

stands from 11.5–16 inches (29–41 cm) high and weighs about 33 pounds (15 kg). A well-proportioned head is placed atop a long, strong neck. The legs are straight and not crooked like the Dachshund's. This dog is standardly described as somewhat less than medium size. In appearance he is rectangular, compact and of good stature. The coat is complete with hair straight and close.

Drive

Powerful hindquarter propulsion denoting sound locomotion.

Drooling

Drooling and slobbering are the complaints of many owners of big, happy, sloppy, wet-mouthed dogs. Of course, certain breeds drool more habitually than others: among the salivating offenders are the Saint Bernard, Mastiff, Dogue de Bordeaux, Neapolitan Mastiff, Bloodhound, and any number of flamboyantly flewsy dogs. When dogs salivate excessively it is important to find out the source of irritation; a splinter or an infected tooth is common. An irritated stomach may also cause excessive salivating. Other concerns for the owner to be aware of are the possibility of convulsions, encephalitis, insect stings, lip ailments, poisoning, tongue injuries and warts. To the owners of those habitual offenders mentioned above, the authors cannot offer any spongy reconciliation in the form of a new solution to the dripping dilemma—towels have worked fine in the past, however.

Droop

Excessive slope of the croup.

Drop ears

Naturally folding, hanging, pendulous ears. Many of the gundog breeds (Cocker Spaniels, Irish Setters, etc.) possess full drop ears, which hang straight down from their position on the head. Drop ears can also refer to any ear that is not fully erect, such as an ear that tilts over at the tip.

Drop on recall

This is done at obedience trials in the Open classes only; the dog sits at one end of the ring and the handler goes to the other end and calls his dog, dropping him on signal from the judge. He then calls him in as in the regular recall.

Dropped muscle

Rupture of inner loins or shoulder muscles of the dog in a coursing event.

Dropping on point

Some bird dogs drop to the ground when scenting birds. Standing upright on point is preferred. Dropping on point is caused by over-cautiousness or fear of flushing the birds, although some handlers train their dogs to drop on point, as a precaution against breaking to shot.

Dropsy

Abnormal accumulation of fluid in the tissues of body cavities. Also referred to as edema when accumulations manifest themselves below the skin. In the stomach region it is called ascites. Lack of exercise or poor circulation, particularly in older dogs, may be the cause. While the swellings are painless, excess accumulations in the stomach can cause digestive distress or heart disturbances, and may be associated with diabetes. Occasional diarrhea, lack of appetite, loss of weight, exhaustion, emaciation and death may occur if the condition is not treated. *See also* Ascites, Edema

Drooling. While larger mastiff breeds drool for the sake of drooling, excessive salivation can indicate a medical problem worth checking. Mastiff photographed by I. Français.

Drótszörü Magyar Vizsla

The roughhaired variety of the Vizsla, which *see.*

Drover dog

See Cattle dogs

Drowning

Most dogs can swim but some cannot; and, in truth, it seems that those who can swim are in greater danger of suffering death by drowning. This possibility results from the desire and curiosity of those dogs who can swim, for they are the likely candidates to enter a swimming pool or garden pond or other body of water that is not easily exited by a dog. The stamina and endurance of most dogs are great, and these qualities extend to their ability to stay afloat. However, too many dogs drown each year in swimming pools and other artificial bodies of water. It is imperative that the owner prevent the dog's entering by the construction of a fence or other adequate barrier.

Drowning. Dogs in swimming pools must be closely supervised; by law, all swimming facilities must be enclosed by a fence for safety reasons.

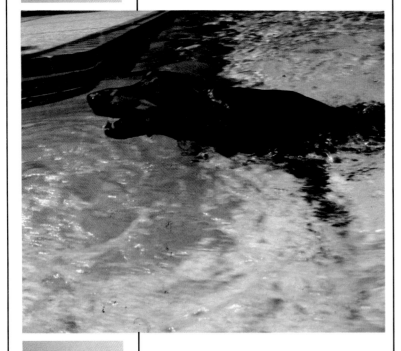

Dry

Basically wrinkleless, taut skin on head, neck or body; the Whippet, for example, exhibits a dry neck. In the German Shepherd Dog breed standard, dry refers to hard, lean condition.

Dry bath

Designed to clean the dog without getting him wet, dry baths are usually sprayed or sprinkled on and brushed off after the given time has elapsed. They are generally fast and easy and can be medicated, flea control, or other specialty type. *See* Bathing, Grooming

Dry dog food

Also called kibble, dry dog food is a commercial preparation of various foodstuffs amalgamated to provide a balanced diet. Dry food, as implied, lacks moisture and typically is crunchy. High quality dry food is often employed as a base diet for adult dogs and supplemented with canned food and an occasional treat. *See* Feeding, Nutrition

Dry neck

See Clean neck

Dual champion

A dog that has won both a bench show and a field trial championship.

Ducat

Mutuel ticket.

Dudley

Unpigmented nose color, or generally shaded to body color. Always deemed a fault. Flesh-colored or unpigmented.

Dudley nose

A flesh colored or badly pigmented nose. A commonly listed fault in breed standards that is sometimes referred to as cherry nose, putty nose and flesh nose. *See also* Butterfly nose

Dumb rabies

See Rabies

Dumbbell

A wooden object shaped like the gymnasium work dumbbell; size and weight vary with the size of the dog performing at the given time in the obedience trial.

Dummy

An object used for training or practice as a substitute for a bird, also called a retrieving buck.

Dunker

The Dunker or Norwegian Hound was created towards the middle of the nineteenth century by Herr Wilhelm Dunker. Dunker crossed his most competent scenthounds with the Anglo-Russian Hound (now referred to as the Russian Harlequin Hound) to create a swift hound that would hunt rabbit by scent instead of sight. Herr Dunker was pleased with his creation's abilities and distinctive appearance. The merle gene's transfer from the Harlequin Hound explains the unique saddle that the breed wears. His deep chest and strong lungs give him endurance in the hunt. At one time, the Dunker was crossed with the Hygenhund, another outstanding Norwegian scenthound, for the sake of attaining a dog with the best qualities of both breeds. This cross wasn't as immediately successful as desired since some of each breed's better characteristics were lost or infelicitously diluted. Thankfully, both breeds have remained pure ever since. Although not known outside his native Norway, the Dunker delights hunters and owners with his trustworthy and reliable conduct. As a watchdog, he is valuable, comfortably served by his confidence and quick wit.

ESSENTIALS OF THE DUNKER: A dog of striking elegance and extraordinary balance, the Dunker illustrates the illustrious, cleanly lined, sleek scenthound conformation. The head should be clean cut and of fair length, having no loose skin. The ears should not be set on too high; the leather must not be too short. The neck should be rather long, having no loose skin hanging. The back should be straight, strong and not too long; the loins to be broad and muscular. The chest is spacious and well rounded. The forelegs should have strong bone; the shoulders should be long, sloping and muscular. The hindlegs well angulated. Height: 18–22 inches (46–56 cm). Weight 35–49 pounds (16–22 kg). The breed's short coat is uniquely colored: tan with a black (splotchy) or blue-marbled saddle. Despite the Dunker's moderate size, he is sufficiently powerful.

Dunker, tan with black saddle. Photo by I. Français.

Duplex dresser
Stripping knife with a removable razor blade.

Dupuy Pointer
See Braque Dupuy

Dürrbächler
See Bernese Mountain Dog

Dusicyon culpaeolus
See South American foxes

Dusicyon culpaeus
See South American foxes

Dusicyon fulvipes
See South American foxes

Dusicyon griseus
See South American foxes

Dusicyon gymnocercus
See South American foxes

Dusicyon inca
See South American foxes

Dusicyon sechurae
See South American foxes

Dutch Partridge Dog
See Drentse Patrijshond

Dutch Sheepdog
See Schapendoes

Dutch Shepherd

Any one of three varieties of herding dog native to the Netherlands. The Longhaired, the Roughhaired and the Shorthaired are the three types of Dutch Shepherd; all are similar in physical conformation, except in coat type, and all are judged by the same breed standard. In this respect, the breeds are like the Belgian Sheepdogs, of which there are four coat/color varieties.

These Dutch breeds of shepherd dogs have been known in their present forms at least since the early 1700s; it is known that specimens of the breeds were taken with Dutch emigrants, immigrants to Australia. The breeds likely trace back to the 1500s, and it is very probable that the Belgian and Dutch Shepherds are descended from very close stock, with the Dutch Shepherds receiving a later infusion of German Shepherd blood. The various Dutch Shepherds have remained true to type over the years, although their sharp decline in popularity during the late nineteenth and early twentieth century resulted in slackened breeding practices and subsequent registrations. The Dutch Shepherds are among the most competent of all shepherd dogs at such tasks as guard work, herding, field trials, and companionship. They are noble and very intelligent dogs.

ESSENTIALS OF THE DUTCH SHEPHERD: The three varieties of Dutch Shepherd (Longhaired, Roughhaired, and Shorthaired) are judged by the same breed standard. They are, with the exception of coat type, essentially the same in physical conformation. Overall, strong, enduring, and agile workers, with mass well proportioned and in relation to bone structure. Head is of good length and width but not long or broad, well chiseled and refined, but should never appear less than strong; ears set high and carried erect; muzzle tapering slightly to the nose but never snipy. The neck is of moderate length, arched and strong. Shoulders well laid. Chest deep. Back strong. Hindquarters well muscled and with good angulation. Height: 23–25 inches (58.5–63.5 cm). Weight: 66 pounds (30 kg). The Dutch Shepherds come in three very different coat varieties, each of which is recognized by the F.C.I. The Longhaired's coat is long, straight, flat and harsh; the Roughhaired's jacket is medium long and wiry; the Shorthaired's hair is fine and dense. Although the coat types vary, the color possibilities remain the same for each: various shades of brindle, including gray, yellow, silver, red or gold brindle, and blue.

Dutch Smoushond

The Dutch or Hollandse Smoushond today is slightly different than the breed of the late nineteenth century. The original breed was created by a Dutch merchant who began gathering and selling yellow German Coarsehaired Pinschers (a dog said to be a predecessor of today's Schnauzer breeds). Abraas, by name, was one of the few in the breeding profession who was making a profit. At the time, the yellow whelps were looked down upon, much like a particolored Poodle perhaps. Abraas was able to take these German rejects and sell them in Holland, thus beginning the Dutch Smoushond breed. These straw-colored pups became quite popular and remained so until World War II, the war which ultimately decimated the breed. Well after the War, a fan of the Smoushond in Holland began a campaign to recreate the yellow breed. By the mid 1970s, the Smoushond was re-established. These dogs are being nurtured by a parent club in the Netherlands and presently there is no interest in promoting them abroad.

ESSENTIALS OF THE SMOUSHOND: A coarse wire jacket of medium length must come in yellow, preferably dark straw, and is complete with facial accoutrements—beard, mustache and eyebrows. Height: 14–17 inches (35.5–43 cm). Weight: 20–22 pounds (9–10 kg). The body is well balanced and moderate in size and stature.

Dutch Spaniel

See Wetterhoun

Dutch Steenbrak

A *Hollandse* twist on the Deutsche Bracke of Germany, the Dutch Steenbrak is a smaller rendition of that hot-trailing hound. These dogs were derived from Celtic hounds and provincial farm dogs.

Dwarfing

The art of dwarfing has been associated with the Chinese for centuries: not just dogs—trees, plants, fish, women and other animals. The result of the Chinese toy-factory efforts is a number of the world's most renowned toy breeds. The "sleeve" dogs of China and Japan include the Pekingese, Shih Tzu, Japanese Chin, Tibetan Spaniel and Pug. The sleeve dogs were called such because they could easily fit into the emperor's sleeve. These dogs were allegedly much smaller than today's toy breeds. Each of these toy dogs enjoyed unique favoritism from the reigning nobility. Many such Oriental dolls were fashioned to replicate the much homaged lion: the Pekingese and Shih Tzu particularly. The term "lap dog" has a similar origin. These dogs

ideally fit into the emperor's (or some other worthy noble's) lap.

Britain and France, like other countries all over the world, have produced their fair share of dwarfs. Britain especially favored the toy spaniels: the English Toy Spaniel or King Charles Spaniel, the Cavalier King Charles Spaniel, and the Papillon (a decidedly French credit).

It seems that no group of dog has escaped the dwarfing frenzy of imposing humanity—dwarfing dogs is a notion often looked down upon as small-minded by other dog people, even be-

Dutch Smoushond, straw. Photo by I. Français.

littled. Even the mighty, massive mastiffs have their assembly of little people: the Pug, Boston Terrier, French Bulldog, Miniature Bulldog and Miniature Bull Terrier are of incontestable mastiff beginnings. One of the primary reasons that the British so scathingly pooh-poohed the arrival of France's French Bulldog was that its Frenchmen creators had successfully dwarfed the Briton's beloved Bulldog, a hurdle they themselves had not adequately overcome.

Among the miniature gundogs, the toy spaniels of Britain and France, the water dog/bichon types such as the Bichon Frise, Maltese, Bolognese, Papillon and Coton de Tulear, and of course the Toy Poodle. There have been comparably fewer scenthounds miniaturized, perhaps the Pocket Beagle and arguably the Miniature Dachshund (and the family of related dachsbrackes) are the most common.

The nordic breeds have also been dwarfed with enviable results: the Pomeranian and/or the Toy German Spitz, the Toy American Eskimo, the Japanese Spitz, and the Volpino Italiano. Among the sighthounds, however, the notion isn't quite as popular. The Italian Greyhound has been in existence so long that modern-day dog historians cannot pinpoint its reason for coming into existence, although most likely the dog derives from the larger greyhound types.

The terriers, inevitably—since they are mostly small already—contribute a number of dwarfs to the toy dog category: the Affenpinscher, Brussels and Belgian Griffons, Petit Brabançon, Toy Manchester Terrier, Toy Fox Terrier, and Yorkshire Terrier, to name just a few.

Toy dog breeders warn against breeders seizing extremes and becoming obsessed by their diminutive whelps. The smaller the bitch gets, the more often the births need to be by Caesarean section. This is often the case with Teacup or Tiny Toy Poodles. Boston Terriers and English Toy Spaniels are other examples of dogs that often require C-section. It is these breeding and general health problems that should alert dog fanciers to when their efforts have reached beyond fruition. The dogs' continued health and ability to thrive must remain foremost in all dwarfing men's minds. *See also* Toy dogs, Toy Group

Dwarfism

Not to be confused with miniaturization or bantamization, dwarfism is believed to be the result of a pituitary defect and has been reported in a variety of breeds. The results are uncharacteristically small size for the breed and almost inevitably an early death. *See also* Achondroplasia

Dwelling

The unnecessary lingering of hounds on scent.

Dying

Losing the trail.

Dwarfing. Contented and coddled, the proverbial lap dog enjoyed the attention of the nobility in many Asian and European nations.

Dysentery

A contagious condition in which the animal is infected with amoebic organ-

affected muscles having a variety of degenerative and atrophic changes. Lameness and other suggestions of dys-

Namise

isms. Dysentery affects the intestinal tract and is characterized in severe cases by acute abdominal pain and bloody, mucous-containing diarrhea.

Dysgerminoma

A malignant ovarian tumor. Symptoms are fever, vaginal discharge, vomiting and diarrhea. Tumors vary in size, though more commonly are of the large size and, from reports to date, the right ovary is more commonly affected. Radiotherapy may be successful; if not, surgery is required.

Dysplasia

A condition, often congenital, characterized by a disorderly or faulty growth of certain bodily tissues. The two most common dysplasias in dogs are elbow and hip dysplasia, which *see*.

Dystrophy

Faulty development or degeneration. There are many reported examples of disorders and conditions in dogs that suggest a similarity to various types of muscular dystrophy in humans, with

trophy should be investigated by a trained professional.

Dwarfing. The Oriental penchant for dwarfing pet dogs has produced such tiny leonines as the Pekingese, posing here with an ornamental Foo Dog. Photo by Namise.

Dwarfing. Viably dwarfing the Bulldog of England was perfected by the French—this badger-wearing miniature is the French Bulldog.

Ear anatomy

When first considering the ears of a dog, one is inclined to look at the external ear or auricle—the ear lobe or leather. However, the canine ear is comprised of three parts: the external ear, the middle ear and the inner ear. The ear lobe or pinna is comprised of auricular cartilage and on either side is covered by skin. The outer side of the lobe is typically covered

Ear anatomy. With drop-earred breeds like the Weimaraner, the internal ear anatomy is protected by the natural fold of the ear leather; however, such ear types are prone to ear infections.

by longer fur than the inner side. Functionally, the lobes perform to capture air vibrations or sound and funnel them through the ear drum, middle ear and finally the inner ear. Characteristically, a breed's ear is vital to its individual expression. The carriage, size and shape of a particular dog are expressly considered in that dog's appearance.

Ear, break of

Where a semi-drop ear bends or folds (e.g., Airedale Terrier).

Ear carriage

The physical arrangement of an ear as it is placed on the skull, taking into account its appearance and function. The carriage of the ear affects the breed's

expression. For instance, a drop-eared Doberman Pinscher has a distinctly different expression than an erect-eared Dobie. Lazy, erect, drop, dead, upright, alert and folded are descriptions commonly applied to ear carriage. The Collie's folded tipped ears surely give that breed an expression that no other breed competes with (except perhaps the Shetland Sheepdog).

Ear cropping

The routine surgical procedure to remove part of the ear cartilage. The desired erection of normally drop or pendant ears is the principal reason for this surgery, which is carried out in pups between 10–16 weeks of age. Today, cropping on show dogs and pets is strictly cosmetic, whereas, historically, cropping was necessary in order to avoid or lessen injury incurred in the deterring of natural adversaries that preyed upon livestock and flocks. The mastiff breeds, too, were cropped in order to avoid their ears being ripped in the fighting ring. In England, ear cropping has been expressly prohibited since about 1900. Hutchinson's definition of cropping surely relays the British position: "Cropping. A useless practice of amputating portions of a dog's ear in order to make them supposedly more shapely, pointed and erect." Australia and a number of European countries (in addition to England) have outlawed cropping, although it is still common practice in most American states. Incidentally, more and more of the usually cropped breeds (Doberman Pinschers, Boxers, and Great Danes, for instance) are being exhibited with natural ears in the U.S.

Ear disorders

The most common signs of trouble in the ear are chronic scratching, unusual head carriage, and persistent shaking of the head. The dog may scratch its inner ear with its claws and then proceed to lick the claw. The ears of all dogs require regular care in the form of both cleaning and inspection.

Hematomas, or blood blisters, of the ear are often the result of chronic shaking and/or scratching; they are also commonly caused by repetitive nipping of the ear by another dog, often a pup's instigative nipping of an older dog. The signs are swelling and soreness relative to the severity of the condition. Minor conditions can cure themselves but serious ones can require corrective surgery.

Otitis externa, or inflammation of the external ear, is most common in breeds having pendant ears and/or excessive hair around the ears. The condition is usually the result of uncleanliness and can be prevented with regular cleaning of the ears and removal of excessive wax. *Acute otitis externa* is a serious condition in which more than the external ear is

infected. Signs include chronic head shaking and scratching. The ear appears sore and is painful when the area around it is touched. The cause is often a foreign body or external parasites. Immediate attention should be sought and no medication should be given unless prescribed by the inspecting veterinarian. *Chronic otitis externa* is often the result of uncleanliness of the ear for a prolonged time. The signs are similar to the aforementioned but the condition is often more difficult to cure. Veterinary assistance is recommended.

Otorrhea refers to a condition that is characterized by a bad-smelling discharge in the ear and also known as a canker, which *see*.

Otitis media, infection of the middle ear, often follows an untreated case of *otitis externa*. The signs are more acute than those of the external infections, and the dog is obviously under much stress. The ear is carried low and shows clear signs of pain and infection. Veterinary care is imperative at this point. No treatment should be attempted without veterinary counsel.

Ear disorders. Owners must regularly inspect their dog's ears: keeping the ears clean and waxless prevents possible infections.

Ear cropping. A young Boxer puppy with ears taped after ear cropping surgery. Photo by V. Serbin.

Ear feather
See Fringe

Ear leather
The flap of the ear. *See* Ear anatomy

Ear lobe
Leather, pinna. *See* Ear anatomy

Ear mites
Tiny insects that live parasitically in the outer ear canals of dogs and cats. Cats are the primary carriers. Unlike dogs, cats seem little affected by the presence of ear mites and can live many happy years shaking and depositing mites around the house and yard. The dog, in his explorations, contracts the mites with his roomy auditory canals. Dogs are seriously troubled by mites, and they will scratch their ears to pieces in an attempt to be rid of the pests—all for naught unfortunately. Increasing the complication is the likelihood of secondary bacterial infection of the ear, noticeable by a distinctive, unpleasant odor. The presence of ear mites is heralded by a reddish brown wax deposition in the ear. By smearing a wax sample on white paper, minute reddish mites are visible—helpful is the assistance of a microscope. Pet-shop remedies can work, but if a secondary infection is found, veterinary care is recommended.

Ear types
Classification of canine ears is a difficult and convoluted topic. It can be stated that ear types can be generally classified into three groups: erect or pricked ears; drop or pendant ears; and semi-erect or semi-drop ears (depending on whether the glass is half-full or half-empty). Part of the difficulty is elucidated upon realizing that the same ears on a different breed will look absolutely different, depending on their placement on the skull, carriage, and relation to the facial features. This volume separately treats each of the following ear types: Bat ears, Bear ears, Blunt-tipped ears, Broken ears, Button ears, Candle flame ears, Cocked ears, Contractible ears, Crop ears, Dead ears, Drop ears, Erect ears, Filbert-shaped ears, Fleshy ears, Flop ears, Fly ears, Folded ears; Full drop ears; Hanging ears; Heart-shaped ears; High set ears; Hooded ears; Hound ears; Inward constricted ears; Lobular ears; Low set ears; Pendant ears; Prick ears; Propeller ears; Rolled ears; Rose ears; Round-tipped ears; Semi-drop or semi-prick ears; Sharp-tipped ears; Triangular ears; Trowel-shaped ears; Tulip ears; Upright ears; U-shaped ears; V-shaped ears; Vine-leaf ears, which *see*.

Earrings
Terminology refers to the ear fringes of the Kooikerhondje.

Ears, set-on
The junction from base of outer ear to skull. Determinations (set on low, set on wide, set on high) depend principally upon the level of the eyes and the width of the skull. Set on low would indicate ears that are attached below the eye level; set on wide, ears that are wide apart; set on high, ear attached above or at the level of the eye.

Earth
The hole of some burrowing animal which has been appropriated by a fox, or which the fox goes into for safety.

East African Dog

A powerful medium-sized hunting dog of Africa with a broad skull and a long tail.

East and west movers

The front feet thrown out to either side (sideways) away from the center line. Undesirable gait, unusual terminology.

East European Shepherd

The East European Shepherd is a direct descendant of the German Shepherd Dog. The breed originated in the region of the Soviet Union known as Byelorussia from selective breeding of German Shepherd Dogs that arrived in that region during the 1920s. It took a relatively short period of time for the breed to acquire traits which made it more suitable to the Russian climate and the desires of the Russian people: the breed is now more square, slightly brawnier, and in possession of a denser coat than the German Shepherd Dog. The East European, also known as the Byelorussian Ovtcharka, emerged with perfected type just prior to the Second World War. The destruction brought to the Soviet Union during the period was not escaped by the breed. Employed as dogs of war and guardians of property, many a loyal dog was lost during those flagitious years. The breed survived and has become one of the most popular breeds of the western Soviet Union. A courageous companion and worker, the East Euro is pleasant, personable, intelligent and determined.

ESSENTIALS OF THE EAST EUROPEAN SHEPHERD: A solidly built working dog, set nearly square, with a long, strong back, deep chest, substantial hips, and a far-reaching, enduring gait. Head is proportionate to size of body, never coarse, fine, or long; skull is broad between the ears and overall thicker than the German Shepherd Dog's; forehead is slightly domed; muzzle strong, clean and closes tightly. Eyes of medium size, almond shaped; dark brown is the preferred color. Neck is strong with well-developed musculature. The body is covered with a dense double coat capable of excellent insulation and all-around weather protection. Colors can be black and black/tan (with saddle); whites and brindle are allowed but rarely seen. Height: 24–29 inches (61–74 cm). Weight: 78–105 pounds (35–48 kg).

East Java Dog

A pariah type dog found in the mountains of Java, one of the islands of Indonesia. Its conformation was like the other pariah types, including a thick coat, narrow tapering skull and a reddish-blackish coloration.

East European Shepherd photographed by V. Pcholkin.

East Siberian Laika

The working laikas of the Soviet Union may indeed represent the link be-

East Siberian Laika, piebald. Photo by I. Français.

Eclampsia can affect a nursing bitch if she is not provided with an ample supply of calcium and phosphorus. Photo by V. Serbin.

tween the wolflike spitzen and the world's doglike dogs. The East Siberian Laika today is more of a conglomeration of these working "barkers" than an individual breed. (*Laika* in Russian means barker.) Soviet breeders are working sedulously to establish type. Historically the laikas were used for pulling and hunting. Among their quarry are the bear, elk, reindeer and marten. Only the strongest of the pack is used on the larger game whose powerful brawn is capable of breaking the back or snapping the neck of prey held within the dog's unrelenting jaws. Today many of the East Siberians can be seen as city companions. They are highly trainable and, with appropriate discipline, very obedient.

ESSENTIALS OF THE EAST SIBERIAN LAIKA: Coat, short-medium and stand-offish, of either solid or piebald white, gray, tan, red, or black. The coat is plush; the tail is thickly furred and curls over the dog's back. The neck is thickly muscled and strong. The head is covered with shorter fur; the ears are carried erect. Height: 22–25 inches (56–64 cm). Weight: 40–50 pounds (18–23 kg).

East-west feet

Forefeet turning out from the center line. Such feet often accompany narrow fronts and/or shallow chests.

East-west front

Pasterns improperly positioned cause the feet to turn outward, from the center line.

Eastern expression

See Expression

Eastern Greyhound

See Chortaj

Eclampsia

The true cause of eclampsia is not fully known. Studies indicate that small, highly excitable breeds are more likely victims than other canines. The disease is typically contracted by the bitch after the whelp and during the nursing process. Common signs include: restlessness, rapid breathing, and over-excitement.

The disorder can quickly develop into ataxia and convulsions. The course from onset to spasms may take only between 8 and 12 hours. Prevention is achieved by feeding a balanced diet which includes good quantities of calcium as well as other required nutrients to the expectant and nursing bitch. *See also* Bitch; Nutrition; Breasts, problems of

Ectropion

Condition marked by haw-eyes or everted eyelids, the opposite from entropion (where the eyelids turn in). Ectropion is most frequently seen in the bull type, short-nosed breeds and necessitates veterinary attention before the inflammation becomes too severe.

Eczema

Eczema is another form of skin irritation which may confine itself to redness and itching, or go all the way to scaly skin surface or open, wet sores. These are sometimes referred to as "hot spots." A hormone imbalance or diet deficiency may be the cause. Find the cause and remove it. Medicinal baths and ointments usually provide a cure, but cure is a lengthy process and the condition frequently recurs.

Edema

The abnormal accumulation of fluid in the cells and/or body cavities, resulting in swelling, discomfort, and eventual toxemia. Edema is often a sign and the result of failing kidneys or other problem of the urinary tract, which includes the ureters, bladder, and the urethra.

Egg-shaped head

Head construction required of the Bull Terrier. Head is shaped like an egg, that is, oval and broad.

Egyptian Sheepdog

See Armant

Ehrlichosis

See Canine ehrlichosis

Elbow

The joint in the forelimb created by the junction of the arm and forearm. In dogs, the elbows are close to the adjoining chest wall. "Out at elbows" and "out in elbows" are both phrases which indicate that the elbows have drifted from their desired positions. This construction or malconstruction usually precludes unsound and uneconomical movement. Tied in elbows is the contrary construction, which is also incorrect and hinders proper gait.

Elbow dysplasia

A condition characterized by an abnormal development of the elbow joint. It is often difficult or impossible to determine prior to two years of age, at which time X-rays are still necessary for conclusion. Progressive lameness with favoring of the affected joint is the most common sign. Corrective surgery is often the only corrective measure. Because the condition is believed to be congenital, no dog having the condition should be bred.

Elbow joint, problems of

Whether present at birth or acquired by injury, a condition known as ununited anconeal process is the common elbow joint ailment. It can be diagnosed by X-ray and can often be corrected.

Elghund

Norwegian term for moosedog, but it is usually translated as elkhound. Dogs of this type are from the Scandinavian countries; they are robust spitz types used to hunt large game. *See also* Jämthund, Norwegian Elkhound, Nordic dogs, Spitz

Eligibility

In order for a dog to be eligible to compete in a dog show, it must be a registered purebred of known ancestry. No dog blind, deaf, castrated, spayed,

Ectropion and entropion are conditions affecting the eye lids of particular breeds. Entropion, which *see*, can be surgically corrected if attended to promptly, as is the case with this Shar-Pei puppy.

lame or whose appearance has been physically altered may compete. Neither shall a dog carrying or exposed to a disease be granted eligibility. In registries where ear cropping is permissible, improperly cropped ears disqualifies as would cropped ears in an area where the practice is prohibited.

All the tests of obedience are progressive and may be entered by any purebred dog of either sex, registered with the national breed club that is sponsoring the event, or eligible for such registration subject to the rule that dogs may not enter any form of competition regulated by the governing body. Bitches in season may not be entered in Obedience test classes or tracking tests in most countries, and a dog that exhibits viciousness must be disqualified from obedience trials or tracking tests.

Elizabethan collar
See Collars

Elkhound
See Norwegian Elkhound

Ellenikos Ichnilatis
See Albanian Greyhound

Elterwater Terrier
A strain of terrier once known in Great Britain, but which is now extinct.

Emaciation
The state of chronically low body weight characterized by protruding bones, little muscle mass, and greatly reduced fat cells. Emaciation can be the result of starvation, parasites, or disease.

An emaciated dog demands immediate medical attention.

Embolisms
See Blood clots

Emetic
A substance used to induce vomiting.

Emphysema
An incurable disorder of the lungs that is the result of excessive and prolonged stress, usually in the form of previous disease, to the lungs. This stress causes lung breakdown, disabling portions of the lung tissue and forcing the dog to breathe harder to achieve adequate oxygen levels in the body.

Empyema
Accumulation of pus or purulent fluid in a body cavity, resembling an abscess. Another term for pleurisy.

Encephalitis
Brain fever associated with meningitis. An inflammation of the brain caused by a virus, rabies, or perhaps tuberculosis. It may also be caused by poisonous plants, bad food or lead poisoning. Dogs go "wild," running in circles, falling over, etc. Paralysis and death frequently result. Cure depends on extent of the infection and the speed with which it is diagnosed and treated.

Endocarditis
Inflammation and bacterial infection of the smooth membrane that lines the inside of the heart.

Endometritis
Inflammation of the lining of the uterus. *See* Uterine infections

Endurance
Stamina and perseverance, endurance is a highly desirable quality in most breeds of dog. Dogs that work are especially in need of endurance. The sledge-pulling dogs and hunting dogs (scenthounds, gundogs, and sighthounds) are all celebrated for their terrific stamina. Wilcox and Walkowicz relate one of the most amazing stories of canine endurance in their *The Atlas of Dog Breeds*

Endurance can no better by illustrated than by the Nordic sledge dogs. Siberian Huskies in shape can pull tremendous weights for extended periods of time.

of the World. Of the great American sled dog breed, the Chinook, they depict a seven-dog team pulling an 800-pound sledge load over 502 miles of ice and snow-covered roads in a mere 90 hours. Not a single dog limped upon reaching the destination and some reportedly had actually gained weight.

Enema

An injection via the anus, enemas are most often employed to relieve constipation and fever. Cold enemas are sometimes appropriate for treating a dog for heat-stroke, which *see.*

English Beagle

See Beagle

English Bulldog

See Bulldog

English   Cocker Spaniel

The English Cocker is no doubt one of the oldest types of land spaniel existing today. He, like all other "true" spaniels, traces his ancestors back to the spaniels of Spain. This spaniel family has existed in Spain, and many of the countries to which the spaniels spread, for centuries. Prior to the 1600s, all spaniels were considered as but a single group of dog, with the variously sized dogs occurring in the same litter. The larger spaniels were used for flushing or springing game, while the smaller spaniels were primarily used for hunting woodcock. In due course, the names springer and cocker, or woodcock, spaniels were respectively employed.

In 1892 the The Kennel Club of Great Britain recognized two spaniels (Springers and Cockers) as separate breeds,

with the English Cocker called simply the Cocker Spaniel. Deserving of mention is

English Cocker Spaniels, orange roan and blue roan. Photo by I. Français.

the fact that, even after official recognition of the separate spaniel breeds, both types (or breeds) still appeared in the same litter, with size alone the distinguishing factor. Indeed, the two "breeds" shared the same color pattern, many of the same abilities, and many of the same ancestors. It was only after years of selective breeding that truly distinctive gundog breeds emerged.

The nineteenth century marked a time of further spaniel diversification, with at least two other lines of spaniel development. One involved dogs that eventually sprung the Sussex, Field, and American Cocker Spaniels, and the other eventually bringing the English Toy Spaniels.

The English Cocker Spaniel Club of America was formed in 1935, with the two-fold determination to promote the breed in America and discourage cross-

English Cocker Spaniel, particolor.

English Cocker Spaniel, particolor. Photographs by I. Français.

breeding with the ever-popular American Cockers. The club's first specialty was held in May, 1936, and employed the British standard of the time. Whereas the Canadian Kennel Club recognized the

the strong American Cocker fancy. A second factor is that, whereas the English Cocker existed in a relatively pure state in its native land at this time, breed purity was questionably infiltrated with American Cocker blood. Hence, under the direction of Mrs. Geraldine R. Dodge, the breed club of America began an extensive search into the history and pedigree of the English Cocker back to 1892. This study was completed in 1941. This research proved instrumental in achieving the breed's A.K.C. recognition. Today the breed enjoys popularity and fixed type on both sides of the Atlantic and retains the fine hunting abilities that make it both a treasured companion and a prized hunting dog.

ESSENTIALS OF THE ENGLISH COCKER SPANIEL: The general appearance of a merry, sturdy, sporting dog, well balanced and compact, of square build. Skull cleanly chiseled yet well developed; muzzle square; stop distinct; eyes full but not prominent; ears lobular, set low on level with eyes.

English Cocker in 1940, the breed did not receive American Kennel Club recognition until January, 1947. Part of the hesitancy of the A.K.C. to grant recognition to the English Cocker can be attributed to

Neck moderate in length and muscular. Body to be strong and compact, with sloping fine shoulders, deep chest, and wide muscular hindquarters. Tail should be set on slightly lower than topline.

Movement should be a true through action with great drive that covers ground well. Weight: 26–34 pounds (12–16 kg). Height: 15–16 inches (38–41 cm). The coat is flat and has a silky texture; it is not profuse and never curly. The legs and body are well feathered above the hocks; the ears are also covered with a fine feathering. Colors are various, including self, parti, and roan.

English Coonhound

The English Coonhound, an American coonhound breed, comes from the original hunting hounds of Virginia. The English Coonhound does not descend directly from Great Britain although many British foxhounds likely partook in the creation of most, if not all, coonhound varieties. The breed was originally called the English Fox and Coonhound—in an attempt to describe its capabilities. The breed has also been effective on opossum, bear and cougar. This coonhound was fashioned to work the rugged American terrain. Upon the granting of individual breed status to the Black and Tan and Redbone, all other treeing coonhounds were labelled English Coonhound. While the breed today is mostly redtick in color, all varieties of colors can occur, including tricolors and blueticks. In working style the English is fast and

hot nosed. The loose grouping of all coonhounds under this nomenclature

has mixed the breed's ability a bit—many can be slower moving and cold nosed in hunting approach. These dogs are mild-mannered gentlemen with good looks and manly drive. With children they are affectionate and gentle.

ESSENTIALS OF THE ENGLISH COONHOUND: A thinly boned, slender hound with an elongated head and longish tail. As his alternative name suggests, the breed usually occurs in redtick (a white background marked by copperish red patches

English Coonhound, bluetick.

English Coonhound, redtick. Photographs by I. Français.

and specks); however, it can also be blue-tick, tricolor, white-red, white-black, white-lemon or brindle. Height: 20–27 inches (51–69 cm). Weight: 40–65 pounds (18–29 kg). His slender conformation is no good measurement of his strength and endurance.

English Coonhound, tricolor.

English Foxhound, tricolor. Photographs by I. Français.

English Foxhound

The English Foxhound, known at home in Great Britain simply as the Fox-hound, is a dog that traces its roots well back to the 1200s. Fox hunting, not a sport, but a necessity, originally followed stag hunting. Extracting and exterminating the destructive foxes from the British landscape required a great company of horses and dogs to scour the country to extirpate the said vermin As the number of foxes dwindled and/or the British became enamored with the chase of the fox, fox hunting became more of a sport than a killing expedition. Many wealthy land owners kept large packs of hounds for use in the sport. The general

pack existence of today's English Foxhound's ancestors may be one reason that the breed is rarely kept as solely a home companion. Seventeenth-century British noblemen such as Brocklesby, the Earl of Yarborough; Milton, the Earl of Fitzwilliam; Berkeley, Lord Fitzharding; Badminton, the Duke of Beaufort; and Belvoir, the Duke of Rutland were famous pack owners. It is believed that Brocklesby's hounds contributed to the make-up of all Foxhound strains in England. All of these packs laid the foundation for the present breed.

Fox hunting required dogs that were lighter in bone and faster on leg than the St. Hubert Hound, which had been a most popular hunting companion. Leicestershire, the center of fox hunting in Britain, was populated by breeders committed to improving the dog's abilities. Originally, the St. Hubert or Talbot Hounds were crossed with lighter-boned running hounds, probably small greyhound types. During the sport's golden age, well over 200 packs of foxhound reportedly existed. Type varied substantially as emphasis always remained on ability to perform.

The English Foxhound descends from these pack dogs and is still able to func-

tion in that hot-nosed, solid-voiced capacity. Although never popular as solely companion dogs, these are simple, gregarious dogs with affectionate and obedient temperaments.

ESSENTIALS OF THE ENGLISH FOXHOUND: A medium-sized foxhound, the English Foxhound has a level back and rather angulated hindquarters. His short coat is either tricolor or bicolor. The head should be of full size, but by no means heavy. Neck long and clean, without throatiness. The shoulders, long and well clothed with muscle without being heavy, especially at the points. Back is very muscular, as is loin. The body is well muscled and tight. The limbs must be as straight as a post, without knuckling over. Good depth of rib, most symmetrical in body, and brainy in expression describe the ideal dog. Height: 23–27 inches (58–69 cm). Weight: 55–75 pounds (25–34 kg). Grace and strength must prevail. The English Foxhound is a few inches larger than its cousin, the American Foxhound.

English Greyhound
See Greyhound

English Mastiff
See Mastiff

English Pointer
See Pointer

English Saddle clip
See Clipping the Poodle

English Setter

Authorities place the origin of today's English Setter back in the 1500s, when even then the breed was known as an effective bird dog in England. There exist at least three varied opinions regarding the early development of these dogs. Some old writings suggest that the breed is an offshoot of various land spaniels which originated in Spain. A slightly different theory contends, based on evidence gathered largely from documents of early sportsmen, that the old English Setter was created by crosses between the old Water Spaniel, the old Spanish Pointer, and early Springer Spaniel types. However, these claims are questioned in *Partridge Shooting and Partridge Hawking* by Hans Bols, 1582. In this text evidence (both pictorial and verbal) is presented to the fact that spaniels and

setters were distinctly different at the time that these suggested crosses would have occurred. The earliest known text which believably speaks of the setter

breeds, *Of Englishe Dogges*, by Dr. Johannes Caius, was translated from the Latin by Abraham Flemming and published in 1576. In this work, setters are described in great detail as dogs which made no noise either with foot or with tongue but which would approach their quarry with great stealth and then would lie on their bellies and creep forward like worms. But whether Dr. Caius was referring to the ancestors of the modern setters is not clear. Hence, there remains a question regarding the early beginnings of the breed. What is clear is that the English Setter has proven himself for the past two centuries to be an outstanding field dog, show dog and friend.

Edward Laverack is often credited as the "founder" of the modern-day English Setter. Around the mid-1920s, Mr. Laverack acquired from the Rev. A. Harrison two dogs, whose names were "Ponto"

English Setter, orange belton.

English Setter, blue belton. Photo by S.A. Thompson.

English Setter, orange belton.

and "Old Moll." To grant credit where credit is due, it must be added that Rev. Harrison reportedly kept his setter lines pure for some 35 years. From his first two dogs, Mr. Laverack succeeded in producing fine progeny which today is considered the key foundation of the breed.

The first breed show to include the English Setter took place on January 28, 1859, at Newcastle-on-Tyne, England. From that point onward, the breed grew in popularity at the show and breeders seriously focused on producing quality specimens.

Charles Raymond of Morris Plains, New Jersey, in the mid-1870s, after which the breed grew consistently in popularity, both at the show and in the field. The English Setter has retained a healthy level of popularity in the U.S., his homeland, and other European countries, where the breed is loved for its beauty and respected for its utility.

ESSENTIALS OF THE ENGLISH SETTER: A dog of exquisite style and graceful movement: quick, easy, and true. The English Setter is a mid-sized, active dog. He denotes balance and symmetry and has no exaggerated points. Height: 24–25 inches (61–64 cm). Weight: 40–70 pounds (18–32 kg). The coat is flat and of good length; feathering is seen on the body, legs, and tail. Color possibilities: blue, liver, orange belton, lemon belton, black, lemon, liver, and orange and white; also all white. Heavy dark patches and solid coloring are avoided by most fanciers. The head, carried high, gives the characteristic expression of the breed. The head is long and reasonably lean; stop well defined; skull oval from ear to ear. The eyes are bright, mild and expressive, with color ranging between hazel and dark brown (darker considered better).

Among the first of the breed to enter the U.S. were the pair purchased by Mr.

English Shepherd

The English Shepherd of today is a well-conceived conglomeration of the old-type collies: the Scotch Collie, the Border Collie, and other proven herder types. These crosses occurred in the United States, which, despite the breed's rather misleading name, is the country of origin. The base stock of this most agile farm dog was the old-type British shepherd dog that existed on the British Isles before the time of Christ. Though these old-type shepherd dogs have contributed to numerous herding breeds, the English Shepherd is said to be the extant breed that is their closest representative. The English Shepherd is a blessing to many American stock farmers. The breed has a strong hold, and breeding programs emphasize working quality. The result of this striving is the agile, hardy, pliable worker that herds loose-eyed with the degree of physical action adjusted accordingly to the individual stock members.

Owing to his acute sensory perception, the English Shepherd is an alert, responsive dog. He is level-headed and never given to aggression or lethargy. He makes a good companion but must receive adequate exercise to maintain his instinct and appealing disposition.

ESSENTIALS OF THE ENGLISH SHEPHERD: English Shepherds have a slightly thickset, very solid appearance. The muzzle is medium short and tapered to the dark pigmented nose. The ears are rather high set and button. The eyes are clear and dark. The facial expression should be caring and attentive. The forelegs are straight, and the hindlegs are slightly bent, denoting the power and quickness necessary for an effective herder. The coat is short on front of face and legs but medium long on body and tail; feather-

English Shepherd, tricolor. Photo by I. Français.

ing is noticeable. Color possibilities for the breed include black and tan, tricolor, sable and white, and black and white. Height is medium, 18–23 inches (46–58.5 cm), and weight is moderate, 40–60 pounds (18–27 kg).

English Springer Spaniel

All true spaniels trace their origins back to the spaniels (also called épagneuls) of Spain. Prior to the 1600s, all spaniels were considered as but a single group of dogs, with the variously sized dogs occurring in the same litter. The smaller spaniels became the forefathers of today's English Cocker Spaniel, while from the larger spaniels sprang the springers. The larger of the spaniels was especially adept at flushing, or springing, game in the field, hence their acquired name. In 1892 The Kennel Club of Great Britain recognized the two spaniel types as separate breeds. For many years prior to breed status, and for some years after, springers and cockers not only appeared in the same litters but were actually bred

English Shepherd, black and white, in obedience training. Photo courtesy D. Karr, E.S. Club.

English Springer Spaniel, liver and white. Photo by I. Français.

to one another. This practice was soon outlawed by the two breed clubs, and great strides were made towards standard conformation. The Kennel Club of Great Britain granted breed recognition in 1902. The American Kennel Club granted recognition in 1927.

The proper English Springer must be a dog of ability. He is a fine hunter, excelling at springing game. He is hardy yet well-behaved and quick to learn and respond. He is a fine showman and an unbeatable companion. In short, he is an all-around dog—even making his way to the White House under President George Bush.

ESSENTIALS OF THE ENGLISH SPRINGER SPANIEL: Symmetrical, compact, strong, and merry. Of all the British land spaniels, the English Springer is highest on the leg and raciest in build. Body neither too long nor short; chest deep; loins well-muscled; and skull of medium length and fairly broad. Height: 19–20 inches

English Springer Spaniel, tricolor.

(48–51 cm). Weight: 50–55 pounds (23–25 kg). The coat is straight, close lying, and never coarse; extensive feathering can be seen under the body and on the legs and ears. Colors are liver and white, black and white, and either color with tan or liver markings (tricolor).

English Toy Spaniel

The English Toy Spaniel is the King Charles Spaniel. The Cavalier King Charles Spaniel is neither, although it was once categorized lumpishly with the King Charles as English Toy Spaniel. Today the English Toy Spaniel is one breed with four different coat color options.

Prior to the twentieth century, spaniels of various sizes and types occurred in the same litter; a single litter could theoretically contain a cocker, a springer, and a "toy." Breeds, as we conceive of them today, did not exist. These "toys" were not the toy spaniels we see today; they were merely small variations (runts) of the larger gundogs. Man, always in search of companionship, would occasionally keep one of these dwarfs. As the desire for small dogs increased, breeders realized the value of these one-time culls and began breeding smalls to smalls. Eventually type was fixed. The King Charles's well-domed skull is a distinctive feature of the breed and likens it more to the Pekingese than to any gundog.

The breed acquired its present name under the Court of Charles I. The Toy Spaniels that we dub "English" today may in fact be related to similar lap-sized spaniel types of Holland. One authority, the late Baroness Wentworth,

traces the breed to a century prior to Charles I. "It was probable that they were also imported by Anne of Cleves and by William, Prince of Orange, who was a native of Holland. The Duke of Marlborough may also have secured some during the wars with Flanders, for though the liver-and-white Spaniel has now died out (1930), their type of head was occa-

sionally recognizable in the Marlborough Spaniels." The English Toy Spaniel

English Springer Spaniel puppy, black and white.

English Toy Spaniel, Blenheim. Photos by I. Français.

English Toy Spaniel, Prince Charles.

English Toy Spaniel, King Charles. Photo by Phoebe.

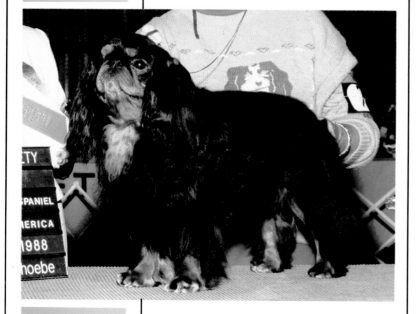

likely developed from the small cocking Blenheim spaniels of yesterday and these Dutch toy spaniels. Crosses to the Japanese Chin and/or the Pekingese and/or other Oriental toy dogs later affected the breed's physical attributes. The domed head is attributed to these crosses with Oriental sleeve nappers.

The study of dog origins is as intriguing as its sources are eclectic. One writer substantiates the authentic antiquity of the Prince Charles variety of English Toy by citing a "Lost and Found" ad in a 1667 edition of the *London Gazette*. The authors present the ad here with dumbfounded respect for the canine researcher so inspired to thumb through three centuries' worth of *London Gazette* classifieds to uncover it: "Lost in the Dean's Yard, Westminster, on the 25th of October, a young white Spaniel about 6 months old, with a black head, red eyebrows, and a black spot on his back, belonging to His Highness Prince Rupert. If anyone can bring him to Prince Rupert's Lodgings in the Stone Gallerie of Whitehall, he shall be well rewarded for his pains." The

color description is clear and authentic; the size of the dog, however, is not indicated. Nonetheless, the breed has been admired by British royalty for centuries and is traditionally permitted into courthouses, due to the edict of the dissolute, diluted Charles II whose fondness for the breed (to the point of "silliness") evolved the judgment. Some authorities discount this tale.

This breed is known for its quiet contentedness. It is an ideal house dog, quickly learning the house rules and quickly befriending the house ruler. Years of listening through the doors of Parliament have made this dog a diplomatic and sensible tyke, with a good ear for conversation.

ESSENTIALS OF THE ENGLISH TOY SPANIEL: Refined, compact and cobby. Weight: 9–12 pounds (4–5.5 kg). Height: 10–10.5 inches (25–27 cm) tall. The skull is rather large in comparison to body size, most well domed. Good specimens exhibit a head absolutely semi-globular (sometimes extending beyond the half circle). The eyes are very large and set wide apart, and the ears are very long and set quite low. The preferred bite is slightly undershot, with never a protruding tongue. The forelegs are short and straight; the shoulders well laid back; elbows close to the rib cage. Chest is wide and deep; back short and level. Hindquarters are sufficiently muscled; stifles well bent; hocks well let down. Coat: long, straight, and silky, with ample feathering on the ears, legs, and tail. Color: black/tan (King Charles); tricolor (Prince Charles); red and white (Blenheim); solid chestnut red (Ruby).

English Toy Terrier
See Toy Manchester Terrier

English Water Spaniel
This British collielike dog is believed to have been bred from water dogs (including the Poodle) and various native spaniels. Selective breeding developed this cross into a hardy working spaniel-type with a curly coat. The breed emerged in the early nineteenth century and despite certain attempts to reestablish it, it has been absorbed into the muddy pools of obscurity.

Entelbuch Mountain Dog
See Entelbucher

Entelbucher

Brought to Helvetia circa 2000 years ago by the Romans, mighty mastiff-type dogs were crossed with varied Swiss dogs to create the Swiss mountain dogs which are among the most ancient of all Switzerland's breeds. The Entelbucher calls Entelbuch in the Canton of Lucerne his birth place. He is the smallest of the four Swiss mountain dogs. The Greater Swiss Mountain Dog and the Bernese Mountain Dog each have larger international followings; the Appenzeller and the Entelbucher remain popular primarily in Switzerland. The Entelbucher was embraced by Lucernese shepherds as a guard dog and was used as a farm dog and cattle drover. The Entelbucher's size makes him a superior all-purpose dog.

ESSENTIALS OF THE ENTELBUCHER: A square, sturdy dog with typical working dog features. The head is well proportioned to the body, strong with a flat skull. The body is robust and compact and most efficiently conceived. Height: under 20 inches (51 cm). Weight: 55–66 pounds (25–30 kg). The tricolor coat is black and tan with white on toes, tail tip, chest and blaze; the tan always lies between the black and white.

Entelbucher Sennenhund
See Entelbucher

Enter

When young hounds are first put in a pack they are said to be entered.

Enteritis

Intestinal inflammation of serious import. It can be massive (generalized) or confine itself to one spot (localized). Symptoms are diarrhea, bloody at times, vomiting and general discomfort. Antibiotics are prescribed and fluids, if the diarrhea and vomiting have been excessive. Causes are varied; may follow distemper or other infections or bacterial infection through intestinal worms. In severe cases, hospitalization and intravenous feeding may be prescribed.

Enterotoxemia

Toxins and gases in the intestine, as a result of bacterial infection. As bacteria increase in the intestine, intermittent diarrhea and/or constipation results from maldigestion. If the infection reaches the kidneys through the circulatory system, nephritis results. The digestive system must be cleaned out by use of castor oil or colonic irrigation and possibly by antibiotics. Only a veterinarian should diagnose the condition and prescribe the remedy.

Entelbucher, tricolor. Photo by I. Français.

Entropion

Entropion, inverted eyelids, is an abnormality which is likely congenital and due to muscle spasms and contractions. The eyelid's inverted position is a source of constant irritation. This condition is more common in small-eyed or pig-eyed dogs (e.g., Shar-Pei) and, if detected early enough, can be surgically corrected before any egregious damage is done. The opposite condition is known as ectropion, which *see*.

Entry

The signed application of an exhibitor for the admission of his dog to competition at a show; the entry form is the contract between the exhibitor and show-giving club. Also, a term used for a dog nominated by its owner or trainer for a race; any starter, or any dog listed for starting in a race.

Eosinophilic cyositis

Inflammation of the muscles that dogs use for chewing. Persistent attacks usually last one or more weeks. They come and go over long periods of time, coming closer and closer together. Difficulty in swallowing, swelling of the face, or even the dog's holding his mouth open will indicate the onset of an attack. Anti-inflammatory drugs are the only known and prescribed treatment.

Épagneul

French term for spaniel.

the Épagneul Français, he may be of northern descent. The most likely component stock is the Chien d'Oyssel. Not a true spaniel, the Bleu is closer to a setter in physical characteristics. The Épagneul Bleu de Picardie, like his close relative the Épagneul Picard, is lighter in bone, better in nose, and more prolonged in stamina than the old French Spaniel type. Specially suited for hunting in the woods and marsh, he is responsive, obedient, and bonding with his master. His work ethics are astounding. His specialty is snipe in the marsh.

Épagneul Bleu de Picardie, black and white.

Épagneul Bleu de Picardie

A native of France and a good-natured gundog and companion, the Bleu de Picardie was created by crossing the blue belton English Setter with the Épagneul Picard (also a French breed). Considering that the English Setter was also created by crosses with Picards, crossing the two breeds seems both probable and desirable and not the ill-conceived crossbreeding that is too commonly seen today. Historically speaking, the original Picard's development traces to Spain, likely during the fourteenth century, although it has been suggested that, like

ESSENTIALS OF THE ÉPAGNEUL BLEU DE PICARDIE: Courageous yet good natured. A fairly tall dog, up to 25 inches (64 cm), of solid, square build. Head is medium and lacks exaggeration. Tail is long and low set. The coat is fairly long, dense, and hard; on the ears and tail it is finer and longer. Color: black (often called blue) and white, with heavy ticking but without red markings; red on head and feet is more acceptable. Weight: 44 pounds (20 kg). He has a gentle nature which is denoted in his deep brown eyes and candid facial expressions.

Épagneul Breton
See Brittany

Épagneul Ecossais
A small setter of France which unfortunately can no longer be located.

Épagneul Français
Two rather interesting theories exist concerning the origin of this breed. One purports that the breed was formed on the Barbary Coast, whence it spread to Spain and then to France, where it was bred with type in mind. A second asserts that the breed is of Scandinavian descent, probably Danish, and is supported by the institution of the Order of the Elephant, by King Christian I in 1478, in memory of the spaniel named "Wildbrat." Based on the latter assertion, it is assumed that Wildbrat is the forefather of the Épagneul Français. Authorities today assert that the breed is closely related to both the Small Münsterländer and the Drentse Patrijshond. Although popular in France, these dogs are little known and even less seen elsewhere. With hunting becoming more and more a sport and less a necessity in France—as it is most of the world over—these dogs are more popular companions than ever before. They are docile and friendly, though they may be wary of strangers. They are quiet, only barking for reason. They remain, however, proven gundogs.

ESSENTIALS OF THE ÉPAGNEUL FRANÇAIS: In general appearance, the French Spaniel is a sturdy dog of calm expression. The head is squared; the skull is slightly domed; it is joined to a short, strong, thick neck. Chest is deep and fairly broad.

Height: 21–24 inches (53–61 cm). Weight: 44–55 pounds (20–25 kg). Coat: short, tight, flat, and straight, with feathering on the legs, ears, underbelly and tail. Color: white with liver markings.

Épagneul Français, liver and white.

Épagneul Nain Continental Papillon
See Papillon

Épagneul Nain Continental Phalene
See Continental Toy Spaniel, Phalene

Épagneul Français, liver and white. Photographs by I. Français.

Épagneul Picard, tricolor.

Épagneul Pont-Audemer, liver and white. Photographs by I. Français.

Épagneul Picard

The Épagneul Picard probably stretches its origin to Spain, although, like the Épagneul Français, it may be of northern descent. The likely lineage trails back to the Chien d'Oyssel. The Épagneul came into being in the fourteenth century. Really not a spaniel, the Épagneul is closer to a setter in physical characteristics. The Épagneul Picard is lighter in bone, better in nose, and more prolonged in stamina than other standard French spaniel types.

Specializing in hunting snipe in the marsh, the Picardy also does very well when hunting other water fowl and even some land game. He is an especially affectionate mate, bonding closely to his master and family. The Picard requires moderate exercise for an active dog, and is gentle and undemanding.

ESSENTIALS OF THE ÉPAGNEUL PICARD: Standing up to 25 inches (64 cm) tall and weighing around 44 pounds (20 kg), the Picardy is an enduring dog built for strength and stamina. The long coat is fairly dense and hard; the ears and tail are covered with finer and longer hair. Tail is long and low set. Coloration is a liver, tan, and white tricolor with heavy ticking. The eyes are a rich brown and set fairly on a moderately long head. The nose is well designed for sufficient scenting ability.

Épagneul Pont-Audemer

A native gundog of France who specializes in water work. He is a dual-purpose dog who is both a fine pointer and retriever. The breed today is in danger of extinction. Authorities point out the European hunter's current craze for all-purpose dogs and their general apathy towards the preservation of breed type as being partially responsible for the breed's demise. The Pont-Audemer's aptitude for water work and general appearance and type suggest that the old English Water Spaniel or the Irish Water Spaniel played an important part in the development of this French spaniel breed. It is also likely that the Poodle and/or Barbet were contributors to the early Pont-Audemer stock. Because the breed's numbers have always been limited, inbreeding has been a recurrent problem. The Irish Water Spaniel has been used at least once to help regenerate the breed, and recent crossbreeding has been reported. The breed is a water dog par excellence and is beautifully suited to handle the marshes. His land abilities are also notable. A catch phrase used to refer to the Pont-Audemer is: "He goes where the hunter can't go."

The Pont-Audemer, scarce as he may be, is a sublime hunting companion. He enjoys the hunt as a sport and approaches a weekend with his master with an eager and light heart. He loves the water and captivates many a land hunter with his natural ability to point. Specimens today are mostly found in the hands of serious hunters of wetlands and marshes. For them, no other dog will do.

ESSENTIALS OF THE ÉPAGNEUL PONT-AUDEMER: The Pont-Audemer is a marvelously handsome spaniel. The head is a distinguishing feature; longer than the typical spaniel; furnished with a topknot. The face is smooth. The coat is long, curly and woolly, providing excellent protection against water. In color the Pont-Audemer is solid liver or liver and white (with or without ticking). The body is medium sized and thick set. Height: 20–23 inches (51–59 cm). Weight: 40–53 pounds (18–24 kg).

Épagneul Pont-Audemer, solid liver adult and liver and white ticked puppy. Photo by I. Français.

Epilepsy

Similar to the disorder in man, epilepsy is characterized by irregular seizures lasting one to two minutes with no other physical malformities present. Urination and defecation during the seizure are common, with the animal soon regaining control after a moment of disorientation and wonderment.

Epiphora

A constant tearing which stains the face and fur of dogs. It is a bothersome condition which is not easily remedied either with outside medication or by surgical tear duct removal. There has been some success in certain cases reported from a liquid medication given with the food and prescribed by veterinarians. This condition may be caused by any one or more of a number of corneal irritations, such as nasal malfunction or the presence of foreign matter in the superficial gland of the third eyelid. Surgery may be recommended by the inspecting vet.

Erdelyi Kopo
See Transylvanian Hound

Erect ears

Upright or prick ears which are either blunt or pointed and tipped (e.g., German Shepherd Dog, Cirneco dell'Etna, Keeshond).

Ermenti
See Armant

Erz Mountain Dachsbracke
See Alpine Dachsbracke

Eskimo Dog

Considered by many to be the most genuinely industrious sledge dog of all the arctic breeds, the Eskimo Dog finds its fountainhead in Greenland. To the northern Canadians and the Inuit people, the breed is known as Kingmik. When first discovered, the Eskimo Dog pro-

Eskimo Dog, copper and white.

vided the long-searched-for answer to the transport problem that Eskimos faced. As a sledge dog, each Eskimo Dog on hitch is capable of pulling about 100 pounds at speeds of 7 miles per hour. The Eskimo Dog is the legitimate Husky, the name loosely used to refer to the Siberian Husky who has effectively usurped much of the fame that the Eskimo rightly deserves. Surely the term "husky" has degenerated to refer to any sledge dog type. Originally the name was applied to the Eskimo Dog by explorers. The Siberian Husky, the more popular "husky," is quite a small fry compared to the Husky of Canada. Nonetheless, the Eskimo Dog is quite akin ancestorwise to both the Siberian Husky and the Samoyed. At one time, most likely, all three breeds were one and the same. The various and indubitably distinctive husky types emerged quite naturally, and miraculously. Probably no other type of dog has cov-

ered (without the help of aircraft, ocean liner, etc.) the geographical expanse of the huskies: from East Cape, Siberia, across Alaska, Arctic Canada, Baffin Land, Labrador to Greenland—approximately 3,400 miles! Of course, such a broad domain explains the Eskimo Dog's type variance. Over the years, crossing with "civilized" canines has hindered the pure Eskimo. The Eskimo Dog's pads are believed to be the toughest in the canine world: "a dog is only as good as his feet" is a popular adage employed by sledge masters. Additionally, the Eskimo Dog's weight differs greatly; the Canadian Kennel Club indicates the weight to range from 60–105 pounds (27–48 kg); working dogs' variation is more expansive: from 40–135 pounds (18–61 kg). Dogs weighing over 100 pounds (45 kg) are said to lack the requisite stamina for long trips. The ideal weight is 70–80 pounds (32–37 kg). Just as weight differs, so does coloration. Most often the Eskimo Dog's coloration adheres to the wolf's coat colors. The most striking combination is probably the black and white. Dogs which descended from those of the famed Lieutenant-Commander MacMillan from Baffin Island, trained by E. P. Clark, were white-bodied dogs with coal black heads and are still hailed as the most glorious strain the breed has known. This strain was wiped out by a distemper epidemic some years ago. Of course, today in England and especially Canada, many undeniably beautiful Eskimo Dogs grace the dog fancy.

Among the breed's game, the polar bear is its most impressive object of pursuit. The breed's power and tremendous size avail it to a great number of people. As a working sledge dog, he is peerless; as a companion, he is a loyal friend and a favorite among the children. Unlike the Alaskan Malamute and American Eskimo (among others), the Eskimo Dog does not necessarily thrive in warmer, more temperate climes.

ESSENTIALS OF THE ESKIMO DOG: Heavy coated and powerful, the Eskimo Dog is hardy with hard muscles. Its tremendous freight capacity is evident in its broad big-boned shoulders, heavily muscled legs, deep chest and overall balance. The head is broad and wedge shaped. This is a compact and efficiently built canine. Height: 20–27 inches (51–69 cm). Weight: 60–105 pounds (27–48 kg). The outer coat is long, 3–6 inches (7–15 cm) in length, and coarse; the undercoat is impenetrable and abundant. Dogs come in any color or combination.

Esquimaux
See Eskimo Dog

of the Soviet Union. No specimens are available outside the Soviet Union.

ESSENTIALS OF THE ESTONIAN HOUND: Not excessively tall or heavy, the Estonian is an ideal-sized hound with a brilliant black/tan jacket that is short and dense. The muzzle is somewhat long and the teeth are of maximum strength. His ears are long and tend to fold as they hang. Standing only 18–21 inches (46–53 cm) high, he is longer than he is tall.

Estonian Hound, black/tan. Photo by V. Pcholkin.

Estonian Hound

The Estonian Hound, known as Gontchaja Estonskaja in the Soviet Union, is a small, low-stationed scenthound. Russian breeders set out to develop a more compact, more controlled hound to work hare and fox. The larger hounds already available were destroying the countryside's wild goat population.

These breeders and hunters located in the Estonian Republic (north of Moscow, on the Baltic Sea) began developing the Estonian Hound. Crossing Beagles to local hounds effectively reduced the dog's size; mixing in the Swiss Neiderlaufhund contributed early maturation and voice; and a splash of the English Foxhound for endurance culminated in the present-day breed. This hound is good-natured and personable with his own, but tends to be wary of strangers. This quality and his convenient size have made him an increasingly popular watchdog in various republics and areas

Estrela Mountain Dog

Large flock-guarding dogs accompanied those peoples that migrated from Asia into parts of the Iberian peninsula. The Estrela Mountain dog or the Cão da Serra da Estrela, as he is known in Portugal and Spain, represents the kinds of dog that guarded the flocks of the Transumancias of Portugal. Like many other flock guards, the Estrela sheepdog has a mastiffy appearance, and it is quite likely that Spanish Mastin blood can be attributed to its lineage. In Portugal, he is known and respected for his fearlessness and consistency. The best guarded flocks in Portugal almost invariably are overseen by the Estrela. The breed has a growing fancy in Great Britain and some of its natural abilities are being put to use by British pet owners.

As a guard, companion, and show dog, the Estrela has been successful. Owners report that breeding is difficult, as is handling. A firm hand is essential to keep this dominant canine in tow. Bitches sometimes tend not to become impregnated at a given time; patience and persistence are the keys to breeding the Estrela Mountain Dog.

Estrela Mountain Dog, wolf gray.

ESSENTIALS OF THE ESTRELA MOUNTAIN DOG: An average height of 27 inches (68.5 cm), with some specimens standing as tall as 29 or 30 inches (74 or 76 cm). For his height, his weight is moderate, usually between 66 and 110 pounds (30–50 kg). The colors recognized by the K.C.G.B. are fawn, brindle, and wolf gray; although other colors may occur, they are deemed unacceptable. The skull is large and no-

ticeably rounded. The overall appearance of the dog is that of mountain-moving power. The coat can be either of a long type or a short type; both are thick and medium-harsh.

Estrus cycle
See Bitch, Breeding, Heat period

Eurasian
The re-creation of the ancient type German Wolfspitz was the chosen whim of one Julius Wipfel of Bergstrass in Weinheim, Germany. Crossing the Chow Chow and the present-day German Wolfspitz, Wipfel whipped up his first batch of "Wolf-Chows," as he called them. The selected pups were crossed with a Samoyed-type sledge dog, and this cross begot the Eurasian. By the 1960s, the breed was established and popular in its native country. The breed is often called Eurasier as well.

Very people- and affection-oriented, the Eurasian is a natural watchdog, exceptionally wary of strangers. He is an easily trained animal that is docile and peace-loving. The Eurasian is mostly seen as a companion in Europe, although some specimens can be found in the United States.

ESSENTIALS OF THE EURASIAN: This handsome, well-coated, medium-sized spitz is beautifully balanced in both physical

Eurasian, fawn.
Photographs by I.
Français.

conformation and temperament. The Eurasian possesses an abundant stand-off coat, long enough to withstand the cold yet short enough to reveal the muscular contours of the body. The head strongly resembles the wolf: it is wedge shaped and well in proportion to the body. The muzzle and skull lengths are proportionately the same. The top of the skull is flat. The ears are set high and not too far apart; they are triangular in shape, erect and of medium size, directed forward. The neck is of medium length, good depth and very muscular. The body is strong and not short. The back is firm, straight; the chest is shorter than the loin area. The tail is set high, round and firm, of medium thickness and tapering towards the tip. Forelegs straight; hind slightly angulated. Skin is tight, of good thickness. Height: 19–24 inches (48–61 cm). Weight: 40–70 pounds (19–32 kg). Dogs can be red, fawn, mahogany, wolf-gray, or black in color; white and pintos also occur. Only solids are registered by the F.C.I.

Eurasian, red.

practice of killing an animal in the most humane way when it is suffering from an incurable disease or irreparable injury. "Euthanasia" is also applied to the prac-

Eurasian, brown. Photographs by I. Français.

Eurasier
See Eurasian

Euthanasia
From the Greek, the term translates to "kind death." Ideally, euthanasia is the tice of exterminating animals that are unwanted, unclaimed, or "unfit" for society. Though the way of extermination *may* be painless, it is in no way kind, and thus the term is misleadingly applied.

Ever-gentle slicker

Fine-wire pin brush, lighter in weight, to be used on Poodles and matting toy dogs such as Yorkshire Terriers.

Ewe neck

Upside down neck or concave neck also describe the ewe neck which is marked by a concave rather than a convex topline. An appreciable, unappreciated anatomical flaw.

Exercise is vital to your dog's health. Multiple daily walks, especially for large dogs, should be routine for all owners. This tot is being walked by an eager Great Pyrenees.

Exercise

Diet and exercise are the two most important components in your dog's health. While some breeds need substantially more exercise than others, it is fair to assume that all dogs need exercise daily. Dogs that live in an apartment environment will need to be taken out for at least a ten-minute romp several times a day by the owner or another complying family member. Dogs that are fortunate enough to be expended a fenced-in yard or sizeable run will get a good amount of exercise on their own. Nonetheless, these dogs should also be walked on a leash for a ten- or fifteen-minute period.

Fulfilling a dog's exercise requirement is one primary responsibility that hinders people's getting a dog. It is a consideration well worthy of thought. Dogs need to be walked on a regular basis—that is, at least daily, or after each meal, if the dog is confined to an indoor existence. Even the smaller dogs—most toys included—need to be taken for a regular walk. The fresh air (or the urban facsimile thereof) and sunshine will do your dog and you much good. An appropriate amount of exercise will benefit the dog physically and psychologically; of course, all dogs do not have identical exercise requirements. The taller sighthound types and large herding dogs, for example, will need more exercise than the smaller hound types and toy dogs. Older dogs and pregnant dogs also will need exercise adjusted accordingly. *See also*, Bitch, Older dogs

While a sedentary, inactive lifestyle is not to be favored for even the most slothful of Bassets or contented of perched Pekingese, too much exercise can be also undesirable. Common sense functions as your best barometer: do not over run your puppy in hot or humid weather; likewise do not exhaust a dog that rarely runs a great deal. Such exertion can cause irreparable physical problems with any dog, regardless of age.

Exportation of dogs

The exporting and importing of dogs has long been a popular form of exchange from country to country. It is generally accepted that much of the development of our diversified domestic dog is due to broad exportation. The Phoenicians, for example, are perhaps the most famous of dog exporters. These world-traveling traders recognized the appeal of various "different" Eastern and African dogs to the European continent as well as the hardiness of the dogs as cargo and made big business from their expeditions.

Britain, a nation that has created more breeds of dog than any other, enjoyed perhaps the greatest influx of foreign pedigrees. Today the importation and exportation of dogs are not as simple as in the past centuries. Quarantine laws and bans regulate the entrance of many dogs into certain lands. Dogs in Australia, for instance, can be quarantined for as long as nine months. The famed British Crufts Show, for example, once featured the exhibition of many "rare," never-before-seen imported dogs. Quarantine laws have limited the number of such dogs from appearing at this and other European shows. Surely Mr. Cruft, the Barnum of the dog world, would have frowned on limiting the appeal and exoticism of his canine spectacle.

Most of the British Commonwealth

countries in the West Indies as well as Australia bar the importation of North American dogs into their countries.

After World War II, Japan took a tremendous interest in Western purebred dogs. Their fascination with the Alsatian (German Shepherd), Pointer and the Bulldog led to a great number of imports.

Today the United States imports a number of dogs from all over the world. America, as well as many other nations, has been stung by the pedigree bug. In America, the "new" and "foreign" capture the public's eye, increasing the need to import a myriad of products, including dogs. Petit Bassets from France and England as well as Shiba Inus from Japan and England, for instance, are being imported with increasing regularity.

Another aspect of exchange can be observed in the importation of semen. The frozen dog-semen program that was initiated at the University of Oregon Medical School in 1968, the first research endeavor in this field, indicated that canine semen stored in liquid nitrogen exhibited dashing motility upon thawing. While the authors are not encouraging every reader to investigate the prospect thoroughly, a number of American breeders in particular are taking advantage of certain technological advances to improve their breeding stock. For instance, certain Borzoi owners in the States have cooperated with Soviet kennel owners and accomplished the necessary arrangements. Other Rottweiler enthusiasts have made contacts in Germany for the betterment of their breeding programs. With the medical advances in the field of frozen sperm and the increasing trustworthiness of international over-night postal services, more and more breeders may begin clanging testtubes with fellow foreign dog enthusiasts. *See also* Gift dogs

Exportation of dogs. Many nations have forbidden the exportation of native dogs. Today it is most difficult to acquire an Azawakh from its homeland Mali. Historically these dogs were never sold, but offered as gifts on certain rare occasions.

Exportation of dogs. This armful has taken the States by storm, and American importations of the little French basset, the Petit Basset Griffon Vendeen, are steadily increasing. Photo by I. Français.

features and is often described in the standard. In the Pug standard, for instance, the eyes are key to the breed expression: "soft and solicitous in expression." The Schip-

Expression: (*top*) monkeylike (Belgian Griffons); (*middle*) ineffably sweet (Collie); (*bottom*) the "Samoyed smile."

Expression

Dogs, perhaps more so than most non-human animals, possess individual facial expressions that are typical of their breed or often unique to themselves. Owners are usually in tune to their dog's thoughts and moods. For most, interpreting their dog's every twitch and sigh is practically instinctive, just as one's dog understands its owner's moods and emotional states. Breed expression is keenly linked to facial

perke standard defines expression as "questioning, sharp and lively, not mean or wild." A wealth of adjectives has been attached to "expression" to facilitate capturing the nuance that only the dedicated fancier can detect or identify. Oriental (e.g., Afghan Hound), frowning (Chow Chow), gruff (Black Russian Terrier), monkeylike (Belgian Griffon), apelike (Affenpinscher), saucy (Chihuahua) and somber (Boxer fault) are but a few of these modifiers.

Expression: (*top*) dignified and gentle with deep, faithful, far-seeing eyes (Saluki); (*bottom*) courageous, bold, self-esteemed and combative (Pekingese).

Extension

The opening of a flexed joint, opposite of flexion, which *see*.

parent cornea (front) reveals the iris, usually colored. The pupil is the dark hole in the iris.

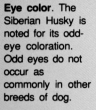

Eye color. The Siberian Husky is noted for its odd-eye coloration. Odd eyes do not occur as commonly in other breeds of dog.

Eye anatomy

Not unlike the human eye, the canine eye functions as light rays penetrate the cornea in front; the lens focuses on the rays; and the retina receives the projection. The image, thus created, is transported through the optic nerves for visual impact and mental recognition. The upper and lower eyelids enclose the eyeball. The conjunctiva, a pink mucous membrane, lines the eyelids's inner surface. Inside these two eyelids, the corner or inner canthus of the third eyelid (*Membrana nictitans*) is formed. This lid, more obvious in some breeds, is not consciously controlled as are the inner and outer lids. Although the white part of the dog's eye is not usually seen, it surely exists and is called the sclera. The conjunctiva blends into the sclera. The trans-

Eye brows

Covering the superciliary ridges or skull's supraorbital processes are the brows, skin and hair that are above the eyes. *See* Brows

Eye color

Pigmentation in the iris produces eye color. The pigment known as melanin varies in distribution and thus affects the darkness of the eye. Dark eyes are most common in dogs; dark brown to brown eyes indicate a good amount of melanin which is evenly distributed. Lighter colored eyes indicating a lessening of melanin concentration are less common in dogs and, depending on breed, can be deemed a fault. Bird of prey eyes are amber to yellow in color and are sometimes referred to as hawk eyes because of their glazed, harsh quality. Such eyes are a fault in the German Shorthaired Pointer for instance. In the Curly-Coated Retriever standard, hazel-colored eyes, referred to as gooseberry, are listed as a fault. Odd eyes refer to two differently colored eyes (usually one light brown and one blue) occurring in the same dog. Siberian Huskies are noted for their oft-occurring odd eyes. Odd eyes are not common in most all other breeds. *Also see* Walleye, Eye types.

Eye disorders

The most common eye disorders are entropion, ectropion, conjunctivitis, keratitis, cataracts, and progressive retinal atrophy, which *see*. *See also* Blindness

Eye rims

In canines, the eye rims, those margins above and below the eyelids. Must be congruently and tightly in place in order to forego any possible eyelid problems. While this is the most vital consideration, breed standards more often refer to a breed's desired eye rim color. Black or dark is most common.

Eye types

The shape of the aperture enclosed by the eye rims. Eye types vary greatly in dogs, and understanding the differences between the many terms which apply to them can be almost farcical. Dog show illuminati appear rather in command of the couple of dozen terms that apply to eye types. The following can be found in this volume for the sake of enlightenment: Almond eyes; Beady eyes; Bulging eyes; Circular eyes; Deep-set eyes; Eyes set square to skull; Full eyes; Glassy eyes; Globular eyes; Goggled eyes; Haw eyes; Obliquely placed eyes; Oblong eyes; Oval eyes; Overhung eyes; Pig eyes; Prominent eyes; Protruding eyes; Receding eyes; Ringed eyes; Round eyes; Triangular eyes; and Well-sunken eyes, all of which *see*.

Eyelids

See Eye anatomy

Eye color. Bird of prey or hawk eyes are a fault in the German Shorthaired Pointer. Photo by R. Moat.

Face
Foreface, that is, the eyes, nose, mouth, cheeks and lips.

Fading puppies
Once used to refer to all neonatal deaths, the term fading puppies is now applied to pups that succumb to cold and die in the first few days of life. Pups are unable to shiver for the first few days of their life and cannot of their own accord provide enough heat to prevent chilling if kept in temperatures below 70°F. Usually the bitch gives her pups warmth, but should she not, it is up to the breeder to supply the necessary temperature. Heat-

ing pads and overhead lamps can be used, optimally in conjunction with a room temperature that is maintained at or above 70°F.

Faking
Disguising by unethical means a known fault in a show dog. Examples of faking, for the sake of information rather than the encouragement of ungodly creativity, include dyeing the coat, chalking to accentuate white markings, inserting a marble into the scrotum to fake a missing testicle, improper grooming to mask a defect, and plastic surgery to correct ear carriage or tail fault. Oftimes owners fake

faults in photographs as well and the publisher of this book has rejected numerous photos for faking: some contributors paint in the dog's absent eye twinkle, blacken an undesirable white marking or even paint in hair on their own head!

Falconry
The sport of falconry has its beginnings with sportsmen of the Far East as far back as 4,000 years; while the partnership of man and dog has been commonplace for time immemorial, the partnership of man and hawk peals with ancient and exotic clangor. Dogs, too, have been used in falconry for many years. Etchings of Magyar huntsmen working with hawks and their hunting dogs, Vizslas, of course, date back 1,000 years. Among the quarry of this industrious hunting triangle: rooks, magpies, grouse, partridges and rabbits. In the desert, the Azawakh of Mali has a history of working with falcons; in Continental Europe, falconers have made use of the German Longhaired Pointer and other Continental pointers. Birds of prey quickly adapt to these partnerships with dogs, and falconers deem this the height of the form. Young aristocrats in Britain today partake in falconry with great gusto. In the U.S., 46 states permit licensed hunting, and despite modern firearms and hawk-eyed binoculars, the hawking sport has a steady fancy. *See also* Ferreting, Sighthounds

Fall
The shot bird, killed or crippled.

Fall of Hair
See Veil

False pointing

Pointing when the game is not there. It may be that the game was there, and left a scent or that the dog is simply delirious from six hours in the marsh. Some dogs learn that they can stop and rest or get special attention from the handler if they assume the pointing stance. Such learning calls for quick un-learning.

False pregnancy

Pseudopregnancy. *See* Breasts, problems of; Breeding

Fancier

Any person who is interested and active in the sport of purebred dogs; the owner of this book.

Fang

Canine teeth. *See* Dentition

Far turn

The turn at the end of the backstretch of a dog race; it is farthest from the finish line and the grandstand.

Farou

See Berger du Languedoc

Fasting

The self-denial of food for oneself. Sickness, obesity, and depression are but three of many possible causes.

Fatty tumor

See Lipoma

Fawn

There are two different colors which can be referred to as "fawn."

1)Fawn (brown): A tan color ranging from light chamois to red wheaten, often with shadings of the red or even black tips on the hairs. *Always* with a black nose. Genetically, this color is the same as sable (e.g., Boxer). 2)Fawn (gray): There is another color sometimes called "fawn" which is a pale grayish brown dilution of brown and blue. These dogs *always* have a pale gray to flesh-colored nose (e.g., Weimaraner).

F.C.I.

Abbreviation for the international dog registry known as the Fédération Cynologique Internationale, which *see*.

Feather

Plumage or fringing on a dog refers to the longer hair on the ears, tail, belly and back of legs. Flag and fringe are used synonymously although fringe often applies expressly to the ears of a specific breed (e.g., Skye Terrier).

Feathering

When the scenthound moves its stern from side to side with liveliness, indicative of its having found an interesting scent, but not in sufficient quantity to speak to it, he is said to be feathering.

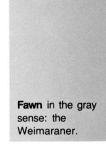

Fawn in the gray sense: the Weimaraner.

Fédération Cynologique Internationale

The canine authority representing numerous countries, principally European, all of which consent to and agree on certain practices and breed identifications. Recognizing each breed of the countries it includes, the F.C.I. registers over 400 breeds—each of the breeds that are federated are thus eligible for International Championship.

The purpose of the F.C.I. is to bring international uniformity to the breeding, exhibiting, and judging of purebred

dogs. Initially the organization represented only European countries: its founding 1911 membership included France, Belgium, Austria and Holland. Belgium has always been the location of the F.C.I.'s headquarters. For address, *see* Kennel clubs.

The organization has extended considerably since its original five European nations. Today the organization includes 19 European countries, 12 Latin American, 2 Asian, 1 African and 11 others (including Great Britain and South Africa). The United States has never sought inclusion.

The organization sponsors both national and international shows. The hosting country determines the judging systems. Breed standards are adopted in accord with each dog's accepted country of origin. Therefore the French standard for the Petit Basset Griffon Vendeen will function as the F.C.I. standard as well.

Despite the F.C.I.'s prominence and near 400-dog registry, the organization is scarcely heard of in the United States (you now are among the few informed elite). Quarantine laws limit the number of persons who would otherwise attain the F.C.I.'s most prestigious International Champion title. In England, an imported dog can be quarantined for up to six months; in Australia, up to nine months. The organization's other two titles are the International Trial Champion and the International Beauty Champion, which *see*.

Feeding

Feeding may seem like a simple concept: open a can, transfer the processed protein into a weighted bowl, and serve it once daily—the dog will be happy, healthy, and long lived. Unfortunately, it isn't that simple. The dog is a specialized animal with specific feeding requirements. It can be said that poor nutrition, the result of improper feeding practices, is the number one cause of disease and other unhealthy conditions of dogs today. While a dog may survive for years on a can-a-day feeding regimen, chances are he will not thrive, will not be his best, regardless of the love, training, and accommodations that he is provided. Proper feeding is truly a major base of the dog's health and longevity—provided, of course, he is of sound breeding.

Canned, kibble, semi-dry or moist, biscuits, treats, and bones: kinds of foods are many, and many commercial foods are fine, provided that they supply a well-balanced meal of easily digestible protein and carbohydrates, as well as

adequate amounts of fats, vitamins and minerals. However, it must be remembered that such "foods" as biscuits and treats generally have little nutritional value and can spoil your dog's appetite for the foods he needs. Treats and biscuits should be reserved for dogs who eat their meals well and show signs of nutritional health. The smart owner reserves treats for rewards, using them to shape the dog's behavior to desired ends. Bones are best left out of the diet, especially of puppies and older dogs.

From puppyhood through maturity, continuing through old age, the dog's digestive system changes with the changing demands of the dog's body. The following paragraphs outline the changing dietary needs of the growing dog as they apply to feeding. Of course, you should feed your dog according to his physical size, rate of metabolism, and amount of exercise.

Pre-weaned puppies receive their nutrients via their mother's milk, with few exceptions. Occasionally, there will be weak or otherwise needy pups that require bottle feeding, and these little souls should be provided with a recommended simulated bitch's milk. For the majority, however, the quality of their diet largely depends on their mother's dietary soundness. The nursing mother should be fed several meals a day of high-quality commercial food, with supplements in the form of milk, fresh meat, boiled vegetables, and vitamins, if recommended by your veterinarian. Such supplemental feeding will provide the bitch with the

necessary calcium, iron, phosphorus, and other vitamins and minerals that she needs to keep her strength and feed the pups well. In large litters, it is likely that supplemental feeding of the pups will be required to ease the burden placed on the dam and add bulk and strength to the numerous pups. In small to average sized litters, the pups usually feed exclusively from the dam until the onset of the weaning process.

Weaning is the puppy's transition from mother's milk to solid food. The weaning process can begin anywhere

Feeding. These two-week-old Doberman pups require feedings every few hours. The hard-working provider should be offered small highly nutritious meals at regular intervals.

Feeding small litters places considerably less stress on the nursing dam. For healthy dogs, such as these Borzois, supplemental feeding is rarely required in litters of less than five. Photo by I. Français.

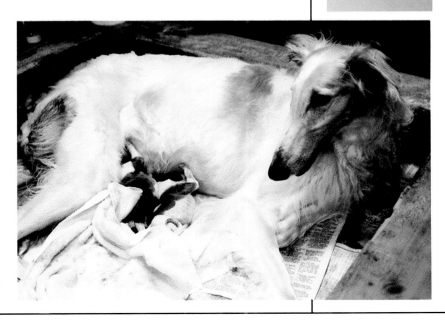

Feeding. With the weaning process well underway, this three-week-old Fox Terrier litter is just learning how to eat.

Feeding. Breeders recommend the use of a commercial weaning cereal to meet the nutritional needs of growing puppies. This Petit Basset dam demonstrates lapping for her litter.

between the third and fifth weeks of life, with most pups becoming completely weaned by their fifth to sixth week of age. When the pups are weaned is often decided by the dam. She will become less and less inclined to nurse and begin frightening the pups away as they feed. Weaning can also be initiated by the breeder. As the pups are weaned, they will begin taking their meals away from the mother. These first meals should be high in protein, vitamins, and minerals and served warm in a thin to medium pastelike state—importantly, they must be easily digestible. It is recommended that one use a puppy weaning cereal, one specially made with the nutritional needs of the growing puppy in mind. As wean-

ing continues, the pups will take more and more of their meals away from the mother until they feed exclusively on the foods their owner supplies them. When the pups are completely weaned, most owners begin to incorporate moistened kibble and small amounts of canned foods to increase the pups' caloric intake, especially in the protein area. Certain breeds, however, have very high metabolisms and mature faster than others; these dogs do not require high-protein diets. The Bernese Mountain Dog is an example of such a dog.

From six to twelve weeks the pups should be fed four times a day. The pups' diet should remain high in protein, vitamins and minerals, and should remain easily digestible. Canned foods and moistened kibble can continue to be added to the diet, but the progression must be gradual. This is a time when many pups head to new homes. New owners must be instructed by the breeder or pet shop exactly what the pup has been eating. The new owner should continue to feed the same foods in the same manner—necessary changes or supplementing of the diet must come gradually, for the pup's system cannot adapt to drastic change. Diarrhea, vomiting, possibly leading to anemia or other complications, can be avoided if the pup is kept on the same diet that changes slowly.

At about twelve weeks, the pup can be put on a schedule of three meals a day. His diet should now consist largely of quality puppy food, semi-moist or moistened, supplemented with a few spoons of canned food and vitamin and mineral supplements as recommended by your veterinarian.

Five to ten months of age is a period of rapid growth in most breeds. At this time it is most important that the pup receive adequate amounts of calcium, protein, and other nutrients. Veterinary counsel is recommended. Feeding should be in the form of moist kibble and canned foods, a few table scraps if desired, and supplementing as recommended by your vet. Feeding twice daily has proven effective for this time. Each breed is unique and every dog is an individual. Regardless of the countless feeding charts found, there really is no general specific rule regarding the amount of food required. The owner must gauge the amount of food by the dog's appearance and activity. If the dog appears thin and is always hungry, by all means feed the poor thing. On the other hand, if the dog is solidly built for his breed but is seemingly ever-hungry, it is may simply be the dog's need to chew; in which case try a safe and effective chew product. If the dog is heavy and lethargic, an unusual state for a pup, his exercise should be increased and his intake decreased; he should also see a vet.

By their first year of age, most breeds are reaching their physical maturity, a point at which their bodies are almost completely developed. All dogs, especially the large and giant breeds, continue to fill out after they reach their full height. Feeding should continue twice daily, including one moderate meal and one smaller meal, the order of which should be determined by the owner. For dogs who are more active during the day, it may be wise to feed their smaller meal in the

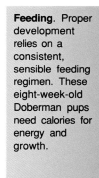

morning and reserve their larger meal for the evening hours. This is common practice among owners of working dogs, who have found that feeding a large meal to their dogs in the morning hours got the dogs off to a slow start. If you and your dog are active in the evening hours, running, playing, or other, a larger meal in the morning and a small meal at night might be the best answer. So long as feeding is regular and provides the dog with

a complete, well-balanced diet, the dog should adapt to any normal feeding routine without exception, barring fussiness.

Feeding. Proper development relies on a consistent, sensible feeding regimen. These eight-week-old Doberman pups need calories for energy and growth.

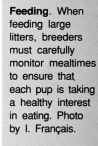

Feeding. When feeding large litters, breeders must carefully monitor mealtimes to ensure that each pup is taking a healthy interest in eating. Photo by I. Français.

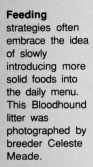

Feeding strategies often embrace the idea of slowly introducing more solid foods into the daily menu. This Bloodhound litter was photographed by breeder Celeste Meade.

Feeding. The individual needs of each puppy can vary, despite the apparent likeness of littermates. Feeding a litter of eleven healthy Golden Retrievers for eight to ten weeks can surely become a costly venture for the breeder.

When the dog reaches his physical maturity, at about one year of age for most breeds, he must be weaned to adult

food. As with puppy weaning, this process must be gradual. Begin by introducing a few spoons of adult food and proportionately decreasing the puppy food, either can or kibble, adding a spoon or two every other day until the dog is feeding solely on adult kibble and can, with scraps and/or treats issued accordingly and judiciously. If the young dog shows any adverse reaction, most commonly diarrhea, fall back to his last ration until the signs clear—if they last more than 72 hours, less if severe, contact a veterinarian. If all goes well, your dog will be eating his adult food in a week or so. If in doubt, a slower change is probably better and less likely to have adverse effects. Vitamin and mineral supplements can most likely be halted at this time, provided your dog is healthy and fit. It is of utmost importance to check the label to learn the contents of the dog food. It

should list the products and the nutritional information or give an address to which you can write. A dog does not necessarily need variety in his diet. The dog's taste buds are much less developed than human's; what this means is that so long as the dog is provided with a nutritionally sound, well-balanced diet, he should enjoy it for many years to come. Too many changes in the dog's diet can lead to a finicky eater and a dog with digestive upsets. Your dog derives pleasure from a full stomach and not from broad palatal experiences; therefore, choose the best possible food for your dog, with the help of your veterinarian, local breeder and pet shop proprietor, and stick to it. Any dog should have water available to him at all times.

The older dog can require a special diet. As the digestive system ages, it often has difficulty breaking down some food substances and absorbing others. Dogs with a faltering system may require a special diet, at the recommendation of

your veterinarian. It is safe to assume that most older dogs do better on easily digestible diets that ease the wear and tear on their aging systems. Vitamins and minerals may have to be reintroduced to the dog's diet, depending upon his condition.

One of the major problems facing older dogs, and many adult dogs for that matter, is obesity. Many dogs are simply overfed. It is not merely their metabolism as many an owner has excused himself. The responsible owner considers his dog's age, activity level, and metabolic rate (not just one of these) and feeds accordingly. If the owner notices a few pounds being added to his dog's structure, one of three things should be done: either the dog's activity level should rise or his ration decreased or both. *See also* Nutrition, Obesity, Vitamins

Feeding. Older dogs may become more finicky eaters as their metabolisms change. Photo by I. Français.

Feet anatomy

Four individual digits comprise the average dog's foot; on each toe or digit are three phalanges; the toenails grow from the lowest phalanx of the toe. The toes are webbed, that is, connected to one another by skin and tissue. Certain breeds, of course, have more webbing than other breeds; the water dogs, for example, have feet that are unmistakably

Feeding habits are unique from dog to dog. Demonstrating this feet-first is a thirsty English Bulldog.

webbed. The Labrador Retriever and the Otterhound are examples of such breeds. Toe and foot shapes are often described in a given breed standard: well split up, tightly knit, close cupped and arched are examples of the terminology employed to describe the feet.

On the lower part of the foot (underneath), the toes are cushioned. These digital pads are composed of fatty tissue and elastic fibers; they are structurally thick, rugged and often darkly colored. The canine forefeet are most commonly larger and wider than the hind feet. *See also* Feet types

feet; Semi-hare feet; Snowshoe feet; Splay feet; Spoon-shaped feet; Spreading feet; and Webbed feet, which *see.*

Feist
See Rat Terrier

Femur
The thigh bone or femur is the longest single bone in the body; it extends from the hip to the stifle and supports the upper thigh area.

Fence-jumper
A racing dog that bolts the course, running across the infield in an effort to head off the lure.

Fennec
The species *Fennecus zerda* is a well-adapted desert-dwelling fox that has several specialized features justifying its classification in a genus separate from the *Vulpes* foxes. The fennec is very small, standing around 8 inches (20 cm) at the shoulder and weighing all of about 3 pounds (1.5 kg). The head of the fennec is smaller than Rüppell's sand fox, the foremost desert dweller of the vulpine foxes. The muzzle is fine and the teeth are poorly developed. Fennecs are of a light color, with soft, fine fur that thickly covers the animal. Able to withstand North Africa's extremely high daytime temperatures which quickly change to cold nights, this desert fox is well suited to hunt and survive in his arid land. The animal is omnivorous and is able to survive on a variety of diets. Quick and nimble, fennecs are effective predators of small desert animals. Specimens have been kept in domestic captivity, but they have proven annoyingly boisterous and active through the dark hours. Of course, these animals are not available at local pet

Fennec,
Fennecus zerda,
the desert fox.

Feet types
Most canine feet are round or slightly oval in shape but there are a variety of other possibilities: Cat feet; Circular feet; Close-cupped feet; Compact feet; Corny feet; East-west feet; Ferrety feet; Flat feet; Hare feet; Oval feet; Paper feet; Round

shops, and it is strongly recommended that you not seek their companionship in your home.

Fennecus zerda

A small desert-dwelling fox commonly known as the fennec, which *see*.

Feral

By definition, feral refers to an untamed state of existence, or a returning to a wild state after a period of domestication. Feral dogs, sometimes termed pariahs, are those dogs which exist without the assistance or interference of man. The Dingo of Australia must be counted among feral dogs, some say; that is, it is believed that the Dingo was once domesticated but has reverted to a wild state. Theoretically all feral dogs will eventually resemble the dingo-type. Other canines, such as the New Guinea Singing Dog, are also perceived as feral canines; in some taxonomical records, the Dingo and New Guinea Singing Dog are considered separate species from Canis familiaris. *See also* Dingo, New Guinea Singing Dog

Ferreting

Ferrets have been used in conjunction with hunting dogs for generations. Working with ferrets involves entering the ferret into a hole in the ground and catching whatever comes out after it. Ferreting can make use of nets, guns, hawks and dogs, of course. It is the hunter's responsibility to coordinate the efforts of the ferrets and the dogs so that both animals' abilities are being utilized to the full. Most U.S. states, however, have banned any form of hunting involving ferrets and hawks. Ferrets' principal quarry is rabbits, rats, and sometimes

foxes. Agile and quick sighthounds are the most handy dogs to hunt in conjunction with ferrets—Whippets and Greyhounds in particular. Gundogs are far too slow to catch a rabbit in the open; terriers can do a respectable job on an exodus of bolting bunnies, catching a couple at least. Of course, the sighthounds have little trouble and usually enjoy the course. Even the tiny Italian Greyhound has been used as a courser in this type of hunting. Dogs tend to get bored if the hunter opts to use a net and doesn't allow the dogs to snag the rabbits themselves. *See also* Falconry

Ferrety feet

Poorly knuckled, inadequately padded feet that are narrow, long and flat.

Fetlock

An excessively sloping p a s t e r n ("overbent fetlocks" cited as a fault in Irish Wolfhound standard).

Feral. These specimens, photographed in Spain, represent a type of Galgo Español that differs from the domestic breed and may exist in a feral state. Photo by I. Français.

Ferreting requires that a hunter acclimate the dog to the ferret for the maximum utilization of the animals' skills. This collie-lurcher appears quite timid with his musteline workmate.

Fiddle front fearlessly bowed by a Petit Basset Griffon Vendeen.

Fever

The normal body temperature for the average dog is 101°F. A temperature of 103° or above is considered a fever in most breeds. Fever is a common sign that something is wrong with the dog. Depending on the accompanying signs, fever may suggest any of many diseases and disorders, commonly bacterial or viral infections. High fevers can cause delirium, fits, hallucinations, and various other such abnormalities. Chronic or high fever needs veterinary diagnosis and care. *See also* Temperature

Fiber

Foodstuffs used as roughage.

Fibula

The smaller of the tibia/fibula combination that supports the lower thigh.

Fiddle front

Cabriole front or Chippendale front, indicating a fore assembly that is fiddle-shaped. In such a construction, the elbows are set wide apart, the forearms slope centerwise, and the feet and pasterns turn outwards.

Field

Those, other than master and hunt staff, who follow the hounds on a foxhunting venture. *See also* Scenthounds, Packhounds

Field Ch.

Prefix indicating Field Champion, which *see.*

Field Champion

A dog that has defeated a specified number of dogs in specified competition at a series of A.K.C.-licensed or member field trials. Field Ch. is the usual prefix employed. *See also* Field trials

Field Spaniel

It is unquestionable that all modern-day spaniels are descended from the same basic stock which traces its origins back to the spaniels of Spain. Of course, the Field Spaniel is no exception. More specifically, the Field Spaniel is descended directly from the stock that has become the English Cocker Spaniel of today. The breed was developed in the early 1800s by hunters who desired a dog heavier than the Cocker but which retained the same merry disposition and affectionate personality. The Field Spaniel was designed with stamina, docility, and gentleness in mind. These dogs were to be soft in mouth, loyal to the master, eager on the hunt, and affectionate in the home. To these ends, breeders gloriously succeeded. However, by the mid-1800s, interest in these dogs in the show ring brought modifications in type, eventually creating a ludicrously proportioned, functionally inept dog with an exaggerated, long, weak body; sagging underbelly; cumbersome head; and crooked legs. Sensible breeders returned the Field Spaniel to reasonable working condition by the turn of the twentieth century, but it would take great effort to salvage the *breed* from its nearly ruinous state and repair the image thus created. It is assumed that both English Cockers and English Springer Spaniels were used in this regenerative process. For some time all respect seemed lost, and breeds' numbers slipped dangerously. By the 1950s, there were too few specimens for the Kennel Club of Great Britain to continue granting championship status. Dedicated fanciers persisted, and by 1969 the awarding of Challenge Certificates was reinstated in Great Britain. The breed's numbers today remain limited on both sides of the Atlantic, with but a handful of litters registered each year. Those who love the breed love it dearly, and the Field Spaniel, though small in number, looks forward to a promising future and remains recognized around the world.

ESSENTIALS OF THE FIELD SPANIEL: Without exaggeration or coarseness, the Field Spaniel should be a dog of soundness and great perseverance. The head is at once to convey the conviction of high breeding, character, and nobility; skull well developed; muzzle not too wide across, to be

Field Spaniel, liver. Photo by I. Français.

long and lean, never snipy or square. Eyes dark hazel to nearly black, in accordance with coat color. Ears long and wide, set low, with nice setterlike feathering. Neck long and strong. Body moderate in length, well ribbed up, straight or slightly arched. Shoulders sloping and well laid back; chest deep and well developed. Legs of fairly good length with flat straight bone. The coat is flat or slightly waved—not too short. Feathering is abundant but not overdone. In color the Field Spaniel is black, liver. golden liver or mahogany red, or roan; or any of these with tan. The breed also comes in bicolors (with white). Height: 18 inches (46 cm). Weight: 35–50 pounds (16–22 kg).

Field trials

Field trials are similar to obedience trials in that they involve dog's working relationship with man. There are many different kinds of field trials: Basset Hound, Beagle, Bird dog or Pointing breed, Dachshund, Foxhound, Retriever, Spaniel, and Coonhound. Each breed or group competes individually in trials specifically designed to test the dog's ability to perform its bred-for function.

The scenthounds are tested on hunting and trailing, speed and driving, as well as endurance. Foxhounds are disqualified for babbling, loafing, skirting or

cutting and, of course, quitting. The first Foxhound trial was held in Albany Hills, Maine in 1889.

Beagles, as recognized specialists on the prolific cottontail rabbit, are tested on their ability to pursue Molly hare, cottontail rabbit. The first Beagle trial was held by the National Beagle Club in 1890 in Hyannis, Massachusetts. At a cottontail trial, Beagles are run in braces (pairs); at a hare trial, all entries run together. In all working and/or competing Beagles, ability and desire to hunt are primary concerns. Upon finding the game, the dog must drive it energetically and enthusiastically. Quality performance is of the essence. Not all quality working Beagles excel in field trial competition;

Field trials. Canadian Dual Champion Glenmajor's Dunk's Top Boss is a major field dog in Canada and the first dual Champion GSP.

Field trials. Champion Jam Spirit Hurrah, owned by John and Sami Simons, a pro Weimaraner at a gundog trial.

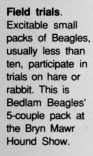

Field trials. Excitable small packs of Beagles, usually less than ten, participate in trials on hare or rabbit. This is Bedlam Beagles' 5-couple pack at the Bryn Mawr Hound Show.

many fine performers are too excitable among their fellow Beagles and become nervous or timid. In addition to a fine nose, properly used voice, and hunting enthusiasm, a Beagle must be determined and independent, not depending on his bracemate's cry.

Gundog trials, including pointing, bird dog, and retrieving competitions test the quality of the hunting dog's performance on the field. Retriever trials attempt to promote and develop the quality of the retriever breeds as well as to demonstrate the intelligence of such trained dogs. Retriever trials, although artificial or set-up, do not test the dog in any task unrelated to actual hunting. Additionally, sportsmen participating learn proper training and the expansive abilities of their dogs. Both training and natural ability are considered in judging any gundog trial. Scent-

ing ability to a retriever is the most important quality. A highly successful retriever will quickly and thoroughly work out the area of the fall as well as mark it properly, responding to the hunter's command without a moment's hesitation. Return of the game must be prompt and tender.

Bird dog trials are demonstrations of the bird hunters in competition with fellow dogs. The first such trial was held in Memphis, Tennessee, in 1874. Judging a bird dog field trial involves interpreting individual dog's work, evaluating and selecting the most efficient and professional performance.

The first spaniel field trial was held in 1899 and included events for both cockers and springers. Today trials for these spaniel types are held individually. All of these trials provide means to evaluate nose, speed, facing cover, marking, overall style and thoroughness, pace and control. Spaniel trials differ from bird dog trials in that water work is often involved and the dogs must work directly from the gun.

Growing in popularity and now sanctioned by the American Kennel Club, coonhound trials include night championship chases, where dogs are released on the scent of a raccoon into an unfamil-

 iar dark woods to tree the animal, and daytime water races, where dogs swim across a lake or bay after a raccoon encaged on a raft. A water race also ends with the dogs' treeing the animal once they have crossed the bay. Titles awarded for coon trials such as Grand Nite Champion, Nite Champion, and Senior Nite Champion illustrate how these events have become more legitimized through licensing by major organizations—previously these spurious and spontaneous events were marked by heavy wagering and big prize money. *See also* Obedience trials, Agility trials, Sheepdog trials

Fighter

A racing dog that impedes or interferes with another contestant during a race. Not necessarily a vicious animal, one that tries to head off and impede a contestant. The English equivalent is "savager."

Fighting dogs

Although dog fighting was outlawed in England in 1835, the mystique of the "sport" (pardon the degenerate appellation) echoed throughout the succeeding century. The majority of dogs that fit into the category of fighting dogs are of bull-

and-terrier backgrounds. Mastiff blood gave the dogs the requisite power; terrier blood provided the speed and agility necessary for maneuvering around the pit. The fighting dogs of Europe encompass many such breeds: the Staffordshire Bull Terrier, the Bulldog, the Boxer and the Bull Terrier, in addition to the more mastiffy Dogue de Bordeaux and the Neapolitan Mastiff. The fighting dogs of the East include such dogs as the Shar-Pei, once known as the Chinese Fighting Dog, and the Tosa Inu of Japan. The Akita is often considered to be a fighting dog, though this is a much contested point. The American Pit Bull Terrier and American Bulldog are also of bull-and-terrier origins. Afghanistan too offers a unique pit fighter in the Aryan Molossus. While dog fighting in Afghanistan is sometimes engaged in as sport, various tribes fought dogs to settle disputes. The owner of the surviving (winning) dog would thus win the dispute; disputes may have involved land settlements, herd ownership, etc. Some-

how this concept of dog fighting seems more humane, at least in that the dogs' lives substituted for human lives. In the

Field trials. Coonhound trials involve a wide variety of exciting events. This English Coonhound participates in a water race at a United Kennel Club field trial. Photo by I. Français.

Fighting dogs. Although treadmills require very specialized knowhow, many fraternity members of the "Bulldog" (the American Pit Bull Terrier) utilize this device to generate stamina.

sport of dog fighting, however, dogs' lives are sacrificed for entertainment purposes, a pastime that no rational being can rightly justify.

The nadir of dog fighting in modern times occurred during the latter part of

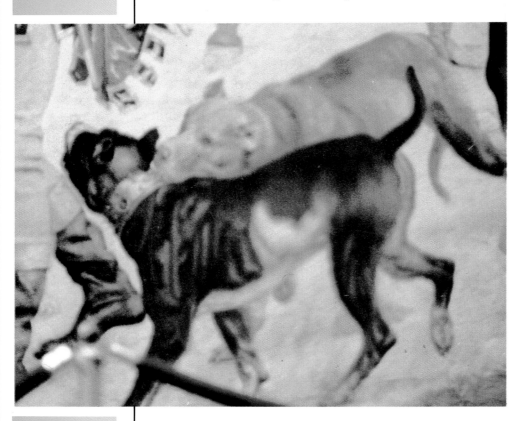

Fighting dogs. Artistic renderings and paintings can be used to document the history of dog fighting and its prominence in public entertainment.

the eighteenth century, when the sport was among the most popular of all sports in England. Two dogs would enter the pit with their seconds (usually their owners). The pit was divided by a scratch mark in the center, and the challenger would cross the line onto its opponent's half, thus commencing the match. The match procedure of sending the challenger over the scratch line was repeated until one of the dogs refused to cross the scratch, was physically incapable of doing so, or was killed.

Although dog fighting has been outlawed for well over a century and a half, these fights still occur in the U.S., Japan, Russia, and many other equally civilized (and less civilized) nations. The magazine *Bloodlines*, published by the U.K.C., for a time ran ads announcing "conventions"—a euphemism necessarily adopted to mislead non-bulldog

people. Surely pitbull men were convening to gossip about last week's Purple Ribbon winners or the tacky housedress of a particular judge.

Many persons involved in dog fights believe that the dogs *enjoy* fighting and prefer to rough and tumble with a worthy opponent than to strut in the show ring or lounge around the home. While it is often suggested that not many dogs die in these matches, more realistic figures reveal that dogs typically only fight a few times before they are but a meaningless statistic. Bulldog men or pit enthusiasts see things much differently than do non-bulldog people. Dr. Carl Semencic writes: "Another misconception that non-dogfighters often have about dogfighters is that they are a vulgar lot of low-class individuals and that the poor animals involved in the match are at the mercy of a pack of bloodthirsty near-idiots. . . .The common denominator among these people is not their stupidity but rather their interest in the match. Furthermore, the owners of the dogs involved in the match do not want to see their dogs damaged; certainly they don't want to lose their dogs, and they often have a fair amount of money riding on their dogs to win the match at hand and future matches—not to mention stud fees."

If indeed the dogs "*enjoy*" the match, this cannot justify the conducting of dog fights. The bulldog (that is any dog used in pit fighting) did not develop naturally like the Saluki or the Basenji, but rather these dogs were manufactured by persons who wanted to have game warriors to fight against one another. Were we to selectively breed for a different inhumane proclivity, could we justify it to by

saying, "but the dogs *enjoy* it." While dog racing has arguably inhumane aspects, it is lengths ahead of the dog fighting sport: has a pit bull ever survived as many matches as a Greyhound has raced? Also interesting in Dr. Semencic's statement is how pitmen don't want to see their dogs damaged because they are investments, as if money is more important than humane treatment. *See also* Animal baiting

Fila

Portuguese for line; applied to a number of Brazilian breeds.

Fila Brasileiro

Mastiff types indigenous to the Iberian peninsula, including the Spanish bulldog, were brought to Central America by Portuguese and Spanish conquerors in the sixteenth century, along with European-bred Mastiffs and Bloodhounds. These powerful and professional dogs were crossed with native dogs to create the Fila Brasileiro. The Fila's extraordinary scenting ability and houndy appearance support this incorporation of Bloodhound lines.

Despite their size and definite mastiff

Fila Brasileiro, black/tan. Photo by I. Français.

lines, these dogs are agile and enduring. They are used to drove untamed cattle and are commonly employed on ranches and as tracking dogs. Reports tell of swift and determined Filas employed during the times of the Brazilian struggles for independence. In the early decades of the nineteenth century, the Fila Brasileiro proved competent as a tracker of runaway slaves from São Paulo and Minas Gerais farms. Outside his native country, the Fila is valued primarily as a guard dog. In Portugal, in the sixteenth century, the "dogs of Acores," as the Fila's forebears were labelled, were used as protectors of home and property.

As a rule, the Fila is suspicious of strangers and committed to his human family. Brazilian breeders in the late 1970s enthusiastically responded to the demand for Filas in the United States and Germany by exporting stock, which has helped to form a base for Fila breeding in these countries. In recent years, the quality of Fila stock and the availability of dogs have dramatically improved. Frequenting rare-breed shows in the United States, the Fila has captured the attention of many big-breed fanciers, especially owners of Bullmastiffs.

ESSENTIALS OF THE FILA BRASILEIRO: Of typical mastiff type, the breed is well boned and rectangularly structured, compact in build yet symmetrical in outline. The head is massive, with a thick skull and broad, strong muzzle; the lips are thick and pendulous. The neck is extraordinarily strong and muscled; dewlap at the throat. Topline: croup set higher than the withers. Body: strong, broad, and deep. Hindlegs parallel; forelegs straight to pasterns and parallel. The Fila can be any color, solid or brindle, except white or mouse gray. The skin is thick and loose all over the body. At the neck it forms a generous and prominent dewlap. Height: 24–30 inches (61–76 cm). Weight: 95 pounds (43 kg) and over.

Fila da Terceiro

A Portuguese guard dog which descended from the Rafeiro do Alentejo, the nation's formidable flock guardian. This rather large and square dog is employed principally in the Axorean Archipelago of Portugal. The dog can weigh as much

Fila Brasileiro, brindle.

Fila Brasileiro, red.

as 100 pounds (45 kg) and stand 24 inches (61 cm). The body is lowset, strong and heavy; the head is broad and heavy, with a short, blunt muzzle. In color, the dog is fawn in various shades or white with yellow or brown markings. The coat is short and smooth. *See also* Rafeiro do Alentejo, Rastreador Brasileiro

Filbert-shaped ears of the Bedlington Terrier.

Finnish Hound, tricolor. Photos by I. Français.

Fila de S. Miguel
See Cão de Fila de S. Miguel

Filbert-shaped ears
The uniquely shaped ear lobes of the Bedlington Terrier which impart to the breed a foppish look all its own. These dangling nut-like accessories ofttimes resemble pompons.

Filled-up face
Cleanly muscled facial contours, smooth. In brachycephalic breeds, the term has been used to equate well-cushioned.

Find
When hounds first smell scent of the quarry and open on it, they are said to have made a find. Also, in field trials, when a dog makes an individual point on game, he is said to have made a "find."

Finishing a dog
Refers to completing a dog's championship, field trial or obedience trial title.

Finlandskaja
See Karelo-Finnish Laika

Finnish Hound
Taller than its Scandinavian brothers and resembling the American Foxhound in size, the Finnish Hound was originally shown in Finland in 1870. Since that time, type has been improved through various selective crossings. Today's Finnish Hound has only been known to man for little over one hundred years. He has a mixed ancestry like most of the scenthounds; crossings of the English Foxhound as well as French, German and Swedish hounds brought forth this handsome, finely finished Finn. He is very much the hunter and approaches the sport with enthusiasm and skill.

ESSENTIALS OF THE FINNISH HOUND: A large, robust hound with moderately loose skin and generously proportioned ears. In color pattern, he is always tricolor, with white markings on the front and underbody (including feet and tail tip). Height: 22–25 inches (56–64 cm). Weight: 55 pounds (25 kg).

Finnish Lapphund
The development of the breed known today as the Finnish Lapphund traces back to the dogs kept by the Lapp people. These European natives lived in the area known as Lapland, which includes Sweden, Finland and parts of northern Russia and Norway. The Lapland Dog, as it was

once known, was brought to England by the Normans. The Finnish Lapphund is a natural herder and was employed originally on reindeer. Over the years, as reindeer herding subsided, the dogs were used rather effectively on sheep and cattle. The dogs that were adopted by Finnish dog lovers became known as Finnish Lapphunds, while the dogs that endeared themselves to the Swedes became known as Swedish Lapphunds. To avoid creating unnecessary animosity, the F.C.I. recognizes each as a separate breed, whether or not they are actually different dogs. Today the handsome Lapphund of Finland is used as both a companion and draft dog.

ESSENTIALS OF THE FINNISH LAPPHUND: A medium-sized spitz, strongly built (considering size), with a gloriously plush coat. The head is square and the muzzle is slightly elongated. The neck is long, without dewlap. The chest is deep, and the shoulders are well angulated and long. The ears are pointed, medium size, quite far apart, rather broad at the base. The forelegs have strong bones which are straight. The body is firm; the back is strong, straight and considerably broad and strong at shoulders. Brisket deep and longish. Hindlegs are well boned; dewclaws permit-

ted. Tail is medium long or slightly shorter. In color the Finnish dog is most any color, provided that it dominates over any white symmetrical markings present. Height: 18–21 inches (46–53 cm). Weight: 44–47 pounds (20–21 kg). The coat is plentiful, long and thick, with heavy underwool. Fringing is generous on the legs and tail; shorter on head and leg fronts.

Finnish Spitz

The Finnish Spitz has long been the most popular dog in its native land. In the U.S., the breed is just breaking ground and gaining fanciers. The American Kennel Club granted full breed recogni-

Finnish Lapphund, black/tan.

Finnish Lapphunds, black/tan, red/tan. Photographs by I. Français.

tion in 1987. Britain has recognized the breed since 1935, however. The Finsk Spets or Suomenpystykorva (the names by which it is known in Finland) is a descendant of the dog which, centuries ago, accompanied the ancestors of the Finns, who lived in small clans in their primeval forests and subsisted by hunting and fishing. Following the arrival of newcomers to the area, the Finsk Spets followed their owners north, and hence the only purebred specimens were to be found in northern Finland, Lapland, and

Finnish Spitz, red. Photo by J. Callea.

Russian Karelia. The individual efforts of two foresters, sharing the name Hugo and a cabin, are hailed as the breed's modern-day fathers: Hugo R. Sandberg and Hugo Roos. This Finn, sometimes called the Finnish Cock-eared Hunting Dog and the Barking Bird Dog, is used for hunting bird as well as squirrel and hare. In Finland he is highly loved for his wonderful voice, and at exhibitions at home the distinction of "King of the Barkers" is awarded to the dog with the most melodious yodel.

On the field, the Finnish Spitz is a talented birder. His award-winning bark alerts the hunter, while his frozen point indicates a bird's hidden position. In the 1800s, repeated crossings with various Scandinavian hunters unhappily degenerated the natural field abilities of the breed. Breeders worked towards re-establishing the breed's original capabilities by focusing on unaffected (un-

crossed) Finnish Spitzen. Today field trials continue to stimulate the breed's natural abilities. The breed still enjoys the hunt and works most efficiently on bird. The Finsky is an intelligent and mindful hunter—he is believed to show disappointment when the hunter aims poorly and misses the bird he spotted, and to show indignation when an uncouth hunter doesn't reward him with the bagged bird's feet for his part in the hunt.

Courageous though cautious, the Finnish Spitz is a decisive, independent soul. As a pup, he is not prone to fondling. Rather catlike in his distribution of affection, the breed is strong-minded and sensitive.

ESSENTIALS OF THE FINNISH SPITZ: A lively dog of medium size and striking brilliant red coloration. The Finnish Spitz has small, cocked, sharply pointed ears; medium-sized eyes, set slightly askew; and a generously plumed tail, curving vigorously from the root into an arch. All of these features add to its alert bearing. The body is almost square in outline; the back is straight and strong; the chest deep. Hindquarters strong; hocks comparatively straight. The tail curves forward, downward and backward, then presses down against the thigh. The coat varies in thickness; overall, it is dense, moderately short and stand-off. The undercoat is soft, short and dense. On shoulders, particularly in the males, hair is considerably longer and coarser. Height: 15–20 inches (38–53 cm). Weight: 25–35 pounds (12–16 kg).

Fins

Hair on the feet of the longhaired Dachshund.

Finsk Spets

See Finnish Spitz

Finnish Spitz.
Photo by R.
Holmes.

Finsk Stövare
See Finnish Hound

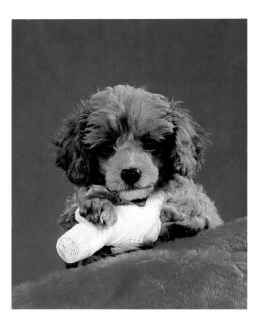

First aid

Because accidents are not predictable, owners often have to care for an injured dog first before a veterinarian can be reached. Often emergency help by the owner saves a dog's life and lessens the chance of permanent damage. Injured animals often resist help because of the intensity of their pain. Nipping in fear and pain is common, so approach an animal with utmost caution. A muzzle can be slipped over the dog's mouth. A bandage or piece of cloth will suffice as a makeshift muzzle—as will a silk tie or kerchief, in times of desperation.

A first-aid kit on hand is a time saver—and in an emergency, time is of the essence. Typically, a first aid kit should contain a thermometer; surgical scissors; rolls of three- and six-inch bandages; surgical cotton; petroleum jelly; enema equipment; bulb and hypodermic syringes; flea powder; tweezers; opthalmic ointment; anti-diarrheal; hydrogen peroxide; merthiolate; antiseptic powder; alcohol; aspirin; mineral oil; dressing salve; styptic stick; hot water bottle; sedatives and the vet's or veterinary hospital's telephone number.

Automobile accidents; bee stings; animals bites; burns; broken bones; choking; cuts and abrasions; dislocations; drowning; electrical shock; heat and sun stroke; porcupine fights; shock; food poisoning; and snake bites are just some of the potential mishaps for which an owner should be prepared.

Fish eye
See Walleye

Fistula

An abnormal opening, or tract, through which fluids drain. They can occur in any part of the body and are usually caused by injury in the form of foreign-body penetration, i.e., splinter, glass fragment, needle, etc.

Flag
See Feather

Flagging

Moving the tail while on point, which is an indication of lack of intensity or that the game has moved out from under the point. *See also* Softening

Flagpole tail

A long tail typically carried at a right angle to the body.

Flank

The fleshy region near the abdominal floor and hindquarter junction.

Flanks, drawn up

Flanks that are well tucked up.

Flared nostrils

Nostrils that are opened widely (e.g., Bouvier des Flandres).

Flash point

The momentary point expected of young pointer dogs before they develop the intensity and training to hold indefinitely. *See also* Pointing dogs

Flashings

The white markings on the Cardigan Welsh Corgi which color its chest, face, feet, tail tip and neck. These flashings are part of the Corgi's striking appeal and are cited as the reason that the solidly colored Swedish Vallhund (Vasgotaspets) can never rival the Corgi in popularity or appeal (except in Sweden, of course).

Flat feet

Feet that appear flat due to inadequately arched toes.

Flat ribbed

Chest cross-section that reveals that the ribs appear flat rather than round; this chest shape is usually deemed undesirable but not exclusively so.

Flat skull

A skull that is not arched from side to side nor from stop to occiput but is flat in all directions.

Flat tail

A term that refers to the tail that is flattish in appearance.

Flat withers

Low at shoulders or withers. Structure where the topline runs nearly horizontal. Dogs so affected show poorly demarcated withers.

Flat-Coated Retriever

Originating in Great Britain as a specialist land retriever, the Flat-Coated was commonly employed on estates throughout his native country during the nineteenth century. For his aptitude, the title "game-keeper's dog" was coined to refer to him. The breed has evolved to become a fine water and land retriever with the added skills of flushing and upland game hunting. He works close to the hunter and is a highly trainable, calm and patient professional. The breed is known for its affection and intelligence.

It was the Lesser Newfoundland, or St. John's Newfoundland, that contributed to the creation of the Flat-Coated Retriever. The Lesser Newfoundland should not be confused with the modern-day Labrador Retriever, which differs in coat, size, and

composition. The breed attained classification for the second British dog show,

held in 1860. J. Hull, whose breeding efforts began in 1864, is credited with establishing the breed and providing a quality base from which the Flat-Coated could spring. Following Hull's establishing of stock, the breed gained great popularity in Britain. The breed's famous patron, H.R. Cooke, bred quality Flat-Coated Retrievers for over 70 years. Throughout the twentieth century, however, the breed has given way to the Labrador and Golden Retrievers, and other popular retrievers and gundogs. Immediately following World War II, breed numbers were so low that it was nearly lost to extinction. Stock was strengthened, and by the mid-1960s, the

Flat-Coated Retriever, liver.

Flat-Coated Retrievers, black and liver. Photographs by I. Français.

breed was securely re-stabilized. Ending on a positive note, fanciers of the breed feel that the decline in popularity has kept these dogs out of the hands of commercial breeders and in the hands of those truly dedicated to the preservation of soundness, type and working ability. This is a gundog of strength and substance with unmistakable refinement and elegance.

Flesh-colored nose on the Pharaoh Hound. Photo by I. Français.

ESSENTIALS OF THE FLAT-COATED RETRIEVER: The ideal appearance of the Flat-Coated is "power without lumber and raciness without weediness." The head is long and clean; the body, symmetrical, with wiry muscling and a deep chest, proud carriage, and a waving tail to project its undaunted style—all of these in silhouette comprise the breed's uniqueness. Height: 22–23 inches (56–59 cm). Weight: 60–70 pounds (27–32 kg). The Flat-Coated can be solid black or liver. The proper coat is of moderate length, dense and full, with a high luster—as inferred, the ideal is flat-lying and straight.

Fld. Ch.
Prefix for Field Champion, which *see.*

Flecking
Created by specks or spots of color, flecking is synonymous with speckling and ticking (when referring to coat coloration). In reference to eye coloration, flecks indicate walleye—sparse coloration in specks on the iris.

Flemish Draught Dog
See Belgian Mastiff

Flesh-colored nose
A "dudley" that is desired: an evenly pigmented nose that would be called a dudley on a breed that shouldn't have a flesh-colored nose. The Pharaoh Hound and Cirneco dell' Etna are two examples of breeds with flesh-colored noses.

Flesh marks
Small areas of the nose that are not colored properly. When such flesh marks touch, a butterfly nose takes wing.

Fleshy ears
Ears made of overly thick cartilage or that are coarsely skinned; a fault in the German Shorthaired Pointer.

Flews
Sometimes used to refer to the dog's lips, flews are the skin that hangs from the muzzle, around the mouth. Flews are fleshy and, in some breeds, pendulous. The Bloodhound epitomizes pendulous flews. *See also* Dewlap

Flexion
The closing of a joint, antonymic with extension, which *see.*

Flighty
Uncertain, changeable; applicable to both scent and hounds.

Flock guardians

Domesticated dogs were needed to protect domesticated sheep from the large predators that found them accessible and effortless prey. These domesticated dogs were necessarily massive and powerful with punishing jaws, unfaltering courage, vigilance, and patience. Additionally, the dogs also needed to be trustworthy enough not to stray or to lunch on a newborn lamb or goat.

Many European nations, whose prosperity depended partly on livestock, thus required such a dog to protect their woolly capital. Sheep and goats were raised on the mountainsides of France, Spain, Portugal, Italy, Romania; on the high plains of Turkey and the Caucasian range of Russia. Just as sheep all think alike, so too did their tenders. French, Spanish, Italian, Romanian, Greek, Portuguese, Turkish and Russian shepherds

purposes—to help the shepherd differentiate his dog from the wolf and to allow the sheep to bond closer with the dog (since it too was white). Even though these flock-guard types were not known to stray or travel very far, the dogs of these various countries all look remarkably similar. Size varies considerably as each breed developed according to the climatic requirements and altitude of their posts. There are slight differences when one gets close up: one might notice that the Maremma Sheepdog you sighted from across the slope is actually a Greek Sheepdog with its right ear cropped.

Most of the breeds that were developed as flock guards have remained working dogs. The Great Pyrenees (or Pyrenean Mountain Dog), Kuvasz, and Komondor are among the most popular flock guards kept solely as pets today. It is important that the fancier understand

Flock guardians. The mountainous expansive terrain of Spain is patrolled and protected by the massive Spanish Mastiff.

coincidentally all conceived the same ideal type of dog to guard their flocks: big, white and furry. Flock guards are almost invariably white: this color has two

the difference between a flock guard and a sheepdog or herder. Flock guards are strictly sentinels—they do not work the sheep or maneuver according to the shepherd's signals. Such is the role of herding dogs, canines that are generally

tamized mastiff, and the Papillon is a bantamized gundog, no such miniaturi-

Flock guardians. While the flock guardian must be fearless enough to combat wolves and other predators, it must also be sufficiently gentle and even-tempered to relate to its charges. Akbash Dog becoming acquainted with kid goats.

considerably smaller, who depend on their large fellow canines to protect them. Some of the most notable tag-team sheepdog teams are the French guard and herder, the Great Pyrenees and the Berger des Pyrenees; the Portuguese, the Estrela Mountain Dog and the Cão da Serra de Aires; the Italian, the Maremma Sheepdog and the Bergamasco; and the Polish, the Owczarek Podhalanski and the Polish Lowland Sheepdog (Polski Owczarek Nizinny).

Aside: The Flock Guardian breeds are the only group of dogs that have not been miniaturized; whereas the Pug is a ban-

zation has ever been accomplished with the great flock guards. *See also* Herding dogs, Instinct tests

Floor stand dryer

Works well for blow drying on the table, as well as cage drying. A good-quality dryer should swivel and have a post that can be raised and lowered.

Flop ears

Ears that fail to remain erect. Flop ears are not to be confused with drop ears which are naturally pendant. Flop ears are not necessarily deemed a fault.

Flock guardians. Blending well with wool, the corded Komondor enjoys a close rapport with his ovine charges. Photo by R. Pearcy.

Flossing

No dedicated dog owner can deny the importance of dental care. Dentists encourage all patients to floss, and now flossing is possible for dogs too. Of course, human dental floss is not the answer, though canine devices are available. Nylafloss® is a revolutionary product that is designed to save dogs teeth and keep them healthy. Experts have purported that this product is the most effective way of fighting plaque build-up in dogs. The product is made of 100-percent nylon products and works on accumulations beneath the gum line. Dogs without exception love to tug on Nylafloss®, and never perceive what good it does their teeth. Large dogs must be supervised with the device. *See also* Dental care

Flossing can be accomplished through the Nylafloss®, as this young German Wirehaired Pointer demonstrates. Photo by I. Français.

Flower

Shar-Pei term for a non-solid-colored dog, i.e., particolored. Also applied to a badly pigmented tongue.

Fluffies

Slang for long-coated Pembroke Welsh Corgis. Undesirable fluffiness of coat in any breed.

Flukes

Small parasites common in both freshwater and marine fishes. Dogs can acquire these parasites by eating raw fish, a fluke itself perhaps. Only one of the fluke-related diseases, salmon poisoning, is treatable. The possibility of contracting any fluke-related disease, including salmon poisoning, can be virtually eliminated if the dog is not allowed to consume raw fish.

Flush

The rise of a game bird. To cause a game bird or birds to fly.

Flushing spaniels

Spaniels flush. Flushing is defined as springing birds from cover. Flushing spaniels are dogs that quarter their ground within range of the gun—from 20–75 feet (6-22.5m), usually about 35 feet (10.5m), locate their game, flush it for the shot, then remain steady to mark the fall and retrieve the bird on command. In the mid-1800s, litters of spaniels varied greatly in size and dogs were classified in accordance with utility. The flushing spaniels were developed from setters and are in reality setters with pointing abilities. Flushers are useful on pheasant and other large game birds. Many retrievers can also be trained to flush. Great Britain receives credit for the creation of six individual flushing spaniel breeds: the Sussex, English Cocker, English Springer, Welsh Springer, Clumber, and Field. America has two flushers: the Cocker and the Boykin Spaniel. As American as the coonhounds, this latter was used to hunt wild turkey! *See also* Gundogs, Retrievers, Cocking spaniels, specific breeds, etc.

Flute
See Median line

Flush
demonstrated by the all-around German Shorthaired Pointer. Photo by R. Pearcy.

Fly ears
The unpreferred and partial erection of prick-ears. This incorrect carriage can be permanent, due to an incorrect placement of the ear or cartilage weight, or temporary, as a result of an illness or condition. Secondly, fly ears can be ears that tend to stray from the sides of the face. In sighthounds, fly ears indicates the correct position to be assumed when ears are alert.

Flying off
Refers to when a sheepdog yields to the sheep instead of holding his ground.

Foiled
When the ground has been much traversed by cattle, sheep, horses, hounds, etc., it said to be foiled.

Folded ears
Drop ears that hang in folds (longwise) rather than remaining flat to the head of the dog.

Folic acid
A substance obtained from green leaves and other plant and animal substances that exhibit vitamin B activity. It is used for medicinal, including preventive medical, purposes, e.g., the treatment of anemia.

Follicular hormone
A hormone secreted by the ovaries during the female's heat, affecting the bitch's behavior.

Food
Any substance taken into and assimilated by the dog to keep it alive and enable it to grow and repair tissue. *See* Feeding, Nutrition

Foot pads
See Feet anatomy

Foot
In coursing, fleetness or speed is referred to as foot. *See also* Feet anatomy, Feet types, Sighthounds

Forearm
Same as lower arm, this is the region between the elbow and wrist. In addition to the muscles and tendons, the forearm is made up of the radius and ulna.

Foreface
The front of the face situated in front of the brain case, sometimes called the muzzle.

Foreleg
See Forequarters

Forepaw
That part of the foot below the wrist; the paw.

Forequarters

The dog's front assembly: forelegs or thoracic limbs, including the shoulder blades and forefeet. Just below the first and second thoracic vertebral spines is the base of the shoulder blades which are rather large, flat, triangular bones and the forequarters' uppermost component. Muscle and ligaments connect the shoulder blades to the first rib and the adjacent thoracic vertebrae. The humerus head fits perfectly into the glenoid cavity, the depression found at the lower end of the shoulder blade; the shoulder joint is thus formed. The arm or humerus, a long and relatively straight bone, is found below the scapula; the angle this forms determines forequarters angulation, a most essential factor in movement. The forearm region is assembled through the carpus or wrist and the ulna and radius. These two latter bones are fused lengthwise and run down to the carpal joint. The metacarpus or pastern is the region between the carpus and the foot; it is comprised of five thin metacarpal bones. The foot or paw is the last component of the dog's forequarters assembly.

Forequarters angulation

The slope of the shoulder blades toward the rear at a given angle. Depending on the longitudinal axis of the humerus, 90° or more is considered ideal angulation. There is much variation on this ideal in many breeds.

Forest fox

One of several South American wild dogs, the forest fox, *Cerdocyon thous*, is a long, unfoxy-looking animal. Known also as Azara's fox, the crab-eating dog, and the savannah fox, the forest fox has numerous subspecies well distributed throughout the Guiano-Brazilian subregion, an area of South America that is thickly carpeted with tropical and semitropical forests. Not foxlike in type, the forest fox has distinctively short ears, nails, and coat. Its forehead has a distinctive bulge, and its lower jaw is notably concave. The forest fox weighs about 15 pounds and extends about 27 to 28 inches (68.5–71 cm) in length before adding the 11 or 12 inches (28–30.5 cm) for the tail.

The forest fox roams and hunts singly, in pairs, in family groups, but not in packs. Relatively little is known about the wild behavior of this South American canid, though we know it feeds on a

Forequarters construction affords balance and symmetry to the animal. The French Bulldog has forelegs that are short, straight and set wide apart. Photo by I. Français.

variety of small animals, including the cottontail rabbit. Interesting is this fox's apparent proclivity to be tamed, based on its observed behavior in captivity. If raised from an early age, the forest fox can be trained to hunt with man in the dense, dark forests of South America.

Form

Variously applied to the racing performance of a dog: good form meaning consistency; bad form, inconsistency. The printed past performance record or the seat or kennel of the rabbit or hare are also termed forms.

Foster mothers. The maternal instincts of an experienced dam can be readily evoked in cases of emergency. This Shar-Pei bitch acted as foster mother to this healthy litter of Rottweilers.

Foster mothers

Should the dam suffer death during delivery or prior to the weaning of the pups, it may be possible to employ another bitch as the "mother" of the pups, to provide nourishment and the early stages of training and love. One should work in conjunction with an experienced breeder or veterinarian, for foster mothers do not always prove successful. Bottle feeding will likely have to supplement the feeding of the pups, especially until the foster mother's milk production reaches its peak. Gray wolves are renowned for their use of foster mothers. It is not unheard of for a wolf cub to survive the death of both its parents prior to its being weaned. Domestic dogs, like their wild counterparts, have a natural parenting instinct that is not hard to evoke.

Fox Collie

A medium-sized working sheepdog of Scotland which has been lost to the proficiency of other Scottish herders.

Fox Paulistinha

See Brazilian Terrier

Fox Terriers

See Smooth Fox Terrier, Wire Fox Terrier, Toy Fox Terrier

Fox-brush tail

See Brush tail

Foxes

Wild dogs of the genus *Vulpes* include: the red fox (*V. vulpes*), kit fox (*V. velox*), corsac fox (*V. corsac*), Bengal fox (*V. bengalensis*), hoary fox (*V. cana*), Tibetan sand fox (*V. ferrilata*), Rüppell's sand fox (*V. rüppelli*), African sand fox (*V. pallida*), and cape fox (*V. chama*). Together, vulpine foxes comprise the largest and most widespread group of wild dogs. For the most part, foxes are more solitary creatures than other wild dogs. Foxes commonly hunt alone, and some foxes, such as the red fox, live solitary lives, except during their mating season. Two species are found in North America: they are the red and the kit fox. The red fox, once thought to be indigenous to North America, has since been proven to be the same as the Eurasian red fox. The kit fox, once common throughout the Great Plains region of the U.S. and Canada, was largely exterminated in the 1800s by the widespread poisoning, trapping and shooting that prevailed through the century. The Eurasian red fox has increased its numbers in many regions of Europe and Asia as a result of the mass agriculturization, which it finds more conducive to survival than the dense, dark forests. The corsac fox, found throughout central Asia, is one of the more social of the foxes and is extensively hunted for its pelt in the Soviet Union. The hoary fox is also found in central Asia, where adapting to arid environments has made its survival possible. The Tibetan sand fox, also well adapted to arid survival, is found in the mountainous region of Tibet and is able to inhabit elevations of over 13,000 feet (3,900 m). Also indigenous to Asia is the

Foxes. The red fox, *Vulpes vulpes*.

Bengal fox, which is found throughout India and resembles a small red fox in size. The most highly adapted of the vulpine desert-dwellers is Rüppell's fox, which has the large ears characteristic of the desert dogs but is distinguished by its white-tipped tail. Hardy and very adaptable to the ways of modern society, foxes serve the important ecological function of killing many rodents and other pests. Unfortunately for the fox, man has found its pelt more valuable than its service to the environment and its good sport on the chase more pleasing than Sunday mornings spent in a pew. *See also* Arctic fox, Gray fox, Forest fox, Semyen fox, South American foxes

in appearance. In a more general sense, the word has been used to describe overall appearance (e.g., the Cairn Terrier).

Foxes. The red fox, *Vulpes vulpes*, cub.

Foxhound

See English Foxhound, American Foxhound, Scenthounds

Foxlike head

Head of essentially triangular shape, long with the base being noticeably narrower and the foreface clean (e.g., Finnish Spitz).

Foxy

Adjective used most commonly to describe head types and meaning like a fox. The Finnish Spitz and Norwich Terrier have heads foxy

Fracture

The actual breaking of a bone. The general fractures are: hair-line or greenstick, simple, and compound. A hair-line fracture is one in which the bone is

French Bulldogs, bicolor and brindle.

French Bulldogs, fawn and white. Photographs by I. Français.

cracked but not separated. These fractures are more common in pups and young dogs than in older dogs because of the more flexible constitution of the younger dogs' bones, thus the term "greenstick" is sometimes applied. Such fractures typically do not require resetting but often require wrapping and splinting. A simple fracture is one in which the bone is broken into at least two separate pieces. The pieces can easily shift out of alignment and therefore require resetting. Simple fractures require splinting. A compound fracture is so-called because the injury of a completely broken bone is compounded by the puncturing of body tissue (including the skin) by the bone. In such breaks, the bone must be reset and often pinned in its proper place.

Free gait

The natural, effortless, consistent movement desired of many breeds, especially the working and sporting dogs, since such gait is applicable to their intended work.

Freezing

The reluctance of a gundog to deliver a retrieve to hand, sometimes to the point of absolute refusal.

French Bulldog

Allegedly the baiter of enraged asses, the French Bulldog has encountered quite a stable of disrespectful, stubborn types. The imaginative and inspired proposition of Mr. George R. Krehl states that the French Bulldog was developed in Spain. A figurine flittering the Frenchie's trademark bat ears dating 1625 is labelled "Dogue de Burgos, España." This Burgos bullbaiter, actually used to bait donkey not bull, was the hypothesized ancestor of the French Bulldog. The French allegedly took this donkey baiter back to Paris where it was fashionably bantamized into the present-day breed. While it is true that nineteenth-century Europe heralded the bull-

dog and the sport of bullbaiting, the French Bulldog's development is principally based in France from British Bulldog stock, not Spanish. The British had long tried to miniaturize their beloved national dog but experienced only minimal success. These Toy Bulldogs were taken to France where the French developed the breed. British fanciers were not amused. The name "French Bulldog" was bemoaningly received by the British and the dogs' very existence was ignored. The first dogs to be brought to England (1893) were called "nondescript"—the concept of calling a spin-off of the Union-Jack flapping Bulldog "French" was indescribably inappropriate and tasteless. In 1905, with about 100 fine examples in the country, the Kennel Club began registering the breed under the name Bouledogue Français. America, not France or England, however, boasts the first Frenchie club, whose historic Waldorf-Astoria specialty set an uptown norm for posh purebred fanciers in the United States.

ESSENTIALS OF THE FRENCH BULLDOG: The heavy bone, big ears, and well-muscled body all contribute to the exceeding handsomeness of the French Bulldog. The breed's hallmark assuredly is its bat ears, which are medium sized, wide at base, rounded at the top, set high, carried necessarily upright and parallel. The short smooth coat contributes greatly to the clean appearance and enhances the solid build. His head is large and square. The muzzle is short and broad. The body is short and well rounded; the chest, deep, broad and well ribbed. The back should be broad, with a slight fall close behind the shoulders. Forelegs short and stout, straight and muscular, set wide apart. The hind legs strong and muscular, longer than the fore. The feet are moderate in size, compact and firmly set. The tail is straight or screw. In weight, there are two varieties: under 22 pounds (10 kg) and 22–28 pounds (10–13 kg)—which is rather large for a toy. Colors include brindle, fawn (with or without white markings), pied, and white.

French front
Front in which the feet angle outward. The name is derived, presumably, from the position assumed by a ballet dancer.

French Hound
See Chien Français

French heartworm
See Heartworm

French Mastiff
See Dogue de Bordeaux

French Bulldog, fawn.

French Pointer–Gascony type
See Braque Français de Petite Taille

French Pointer–Pyrenees type
See Braque Français de Grande Taille

French Shorthaired Shepherd
See Beauceron

French Spaniel
See Épagneul Français

Fresh
The opposite of cold, when applied to the line—scenthound terminology.

Frictionless gait
Gait in which the movement is free and tireless and in which there is no contact between extremities.

Frigidity
Typically applied to females, it is the inability or refusal to become sexually aroused, even upon skillful manipulation and maneuvering. Frigidity is not common in dogs, though there is a higher reported incidence in toy dogs. Frigidity can be the result of physical and/or psychological conditions. Often the bitch is unfamiliar with her surroundings, including the male, and her sexual drive is overridden by fear. Other suggestions include hormonal imbalance and physical malformation.

Frill

Formed between the apron and the mane, a ridge composed of hair (long or short, depending on breed) that stretches down the sides of the neck from the ear base towards the prosternum.

Fringe

Feathering. Long hair that drapes over the ears, covers the tail, or supplements the chest and belly fur on a number of breeds. The Skye Terrier and Briard epitomize ear fringing, the Shetland Sheepdog is fringed on the chest, and the Afghan Hound is elegantly fringed on its tail. *See also* Feather

Fringe cascading down the ears of the Épagneul Pont-Audemer of France.

Frog face

In brachycephalic breeds, a nose that extends farther forward than usual. The French Bulldog's expression caused by its uptilted nose became a source for the term: English Bulldogs that exhibited a similar nose type were derogatorily dubbed "Froggies" to commemorate their unfortunate likeness to that "unsightly Frenchman."

Front types

The dog's front, when speaking of types, generally refers to the assemblage of elbows to feet. Breed standards have employed specific terminology to describe the various front types; many of these terms are rather self-explanatory; others need explanation to be correctly understood: Bowed front; Cabriole front; Chippendale front; Crooked front; East-west front; Fiddle front; French front; Gun barrel front; Horseshoe front; Narrow front; Pigeon-toed front; Pinched front; Steep front; Straight front; True front; and Wide front, which *see*.

Frontal bones

The bones involved in the formation and shape of the forehead. Frontal bones assume different pronunciation and levels of angulation—this varies, of course, from breed to breed.

Frostbite

A dog suffers frostbite when it is subjected to low temperatures for a prolonged period of time. Different breeds certainly have different tolerances to cold. One must fully consider the coat type, body fat, acclimatization, etc., of their dog in reference to its tolerance of cold. *See also* Accommodations, outdoor

Frosting

The replacement of colored hairs (particularly on the face and muzzle) with white hairs. Similar to graying in humans, frosting usually affects older dogs but can occur prematurely and does so as a matter of course in a handful of breeds. *See also* Older dogs

Frothing

Many dogs froth at the mouth. Frothing is characterized by a foamy, often white, discharge of the mouth that tends to linger on the lips and in the lipfold, and drips down droollike from the muzzle. In itself, frothing is not abnormal and is no sign for alarm. When subjected to long travel or other forms of stress, the dog may froth without its signifying disorder. Frothing can, however, signal disease. If your dog froths regularly or ever froths in conjunction with fits or behavior abnormalities, he should receive veterinary care.

Froufrou

A tuft of hair left intentionally on the tail during grooming.

Frown

Wrinkled skin across the head and

eyes leaves a preoccupied or worried expression on the face of the dog, as if he were frowning. *See also* Expression

Frozen semen
See Exportation of dogs

Full cry
The chorus of music from a pack of hounds. American hounds generally give their best cry at full speed.

Full drop ears
See Drop ears

Full eyes
See Protruding eyes

Fungal infections
Infections caused by a class of infecting organisms that produce highly resilient spores which mature and reproduce when conditions are right. Most fungal infections that affect the dog are on the skin; the most notable perhaps is ringworm, which *see*. Also affecting dogs is aflatoxicosis, which is mostly acquired by the ingestion of moldy cereals. Dogs rarely contract other fungal infections, such as ergot, largely because of commercial dog food and the relatively little plant matter that dogs consume.

stance) include beards, moustaches, and bushy eyebrows.

Furious rabies
See Rabies

Furnishings
A wealth of hair on the extremities of some dogs. Furnishings are frequently found on the legs, tail, head, muzzle, ears, etc. Facial furnishings (in the German Wirehaired Pointer, Bouvier des Flandres, and Giant Schnauzer, for in-

Furrow
See Median line

Fusospirochetosis
See Trenchmouth

Futurity Stake
A class at dog shows or field trials for young dogs which have been nominated at or before birth.

Furnishings on the face of the Bouvier des Flandres. Photo by I. Français.

Gaily carried tail
See Gay tail

Gait is a sure indicator of sound construction. The Siberian Husky's gait is characteristically smooth and seemingly effortless. In the show ring, the breed is gaited on a loose lead at a moderately fast trot.

Galgo Español, smooth, brindle. Photo by I. Français.

Gait

The way a dog moves—movement, action, gait—is a reliable indicator of how soundly structured the animal is. In the show ring, gait is an important part of conformation competition. Different breeds are required to move in particular ways; the need for the sporting and working breeds especially to move in a certain fashion is linked to their ability to perform the work they are intended to do. The following terms describe the dog's gait, both desirable and undesirable: amble, canter, cow-hocked gait, crabbing, crossing over, dishing, frictionless gait, gallop, goose-stepping gait, hackney gait, moving close, over-reaching gait, pace, paddling, plaiting, side-winding, single tracking, stilted gait, toeing-in, trot, walk, and weaving, which *see*.

Galgo Español

Named for the Gallic peoples that once inhabited the Iberian peninsula, the Galgo Español is an ancient breed of running hound. It is plausible that the Galgo shares like roots with the Ibizan Hound. For many centuries, the Galgo bred true and was employed on farms in Castile and Andalusia as a guard and hunter of small game. On the race track, the Galgo is a professional and a race dog par excellence. At one time, an attempt prospered to create an Anglo-Spanish Greyhound, by crossing the Galgo and the English Greyhound. This dog was hardy and less resistant than the Galgo. It lacked the size of the Greyhound but nonetheless achieved considerable popularity in Spain for a time. Imperio II owned by Marqués de Corpa was a champion Anglo-Spanish Greyhound from the 1930s. What the world's necessity for another sighthound is escapes these authors. Fortunately many breeders have turned toward the extant sighthounds and promoted them. Due to their size and the requirements thereof, large sighthounds are not overly popular in any Western country. This is a capable and adaptable hound that is most apropos for the sport of racing. Spanish fanciers promote the Galgo as a companion dog and courser. This breed, the Galgo Español, is recognized by the F.C.I. and

should not be confused with the aforementioned, unrecognized Anglo-Spanish Greyhound.

ESSENTIALS OF THE GALGO ESPAÑOL: Symmetrical formation: the body is lithe and balanced; the head is long and narrow. The ears are small and rose-shaped; they hang straight down. The legs are long, and the tuck-up is defined. Height: 26–28 inches (66–71 cm). Weight: 60–66 pounds (27–30 kg). Color variations include: cinnamon, chestnut, red, black, and brindle; solid or in combination with white. The conformation is practically identical to the English Greyhound but on a proportionately smaller scale.

Gall bladder

A membranous sac attached to the liver, in which excess fall, or bile, is stored and concentrated.

Gallop

A four beat gait in which the dog, moving at the fastest possible speed, is ultimately suspended during motion. The Greyhound has a gallop that is all its own; consisting of tremendous leaps, the Greyhound gallop (also known as double suspension gallop) leaves the dog airborne for extended periods of time. The gallop pattern is comprised of the feet moving in this order: right fore, left fore, right hind, left hind; upon beat two (left fore), the dog's suspension begins.

Gallstones

Rare in dogs, gallstones are known as bilary calculus and are formed of either cholesterol or calcium salts. Gallstones can block the flow of bile, causing severe pain, jaundice, and other symptoms. Responsible feeding of salts and fats should prevent these deposits.

Gammel Dansk Honsehund

See Old Danish Bird Dog

Gangline

Center line fastened to the sled to which the dogs are hitched. Same as towline, which *see*.

Gangrene

The decay of tissue, or the death of tissue, resulting from lack of adequate blood supply to the tissue. Also known as tissue necrosis. Gangrene can result from injury, amputation, and other causes,

such as frostbite. Gangrenous tissue must be removed, sometimes at the cost of an entire limb or body part. The application of a tourniquet, which *see*, can result in gangrene to the area of the body on the side of the device from the heart.

Garlic

Allium sativum (or garlic) is a strong-smelling bulbous plant of the lily family, the bulbs of which are commonly used to season food. Garlic collars and garlic tablets are sometimes employed to combat flea problems. The odor of garlic is believed to act as a repellent against fleas. The practice is not always effective, and some dogs are equally repulsed (and repulsive) by the garlic odor. It is, however, a generally safe way to attempt to curb flea inhabitancy on the dog.

Galgo Español, wire, fawn. Photo by I. Français.

Gallop. Afghan Hound in full suspension. Photo by C.A. Grove.

Gas

Large amounts of proteins as well as strong vegetables, such as onions and cabbage, can cause the accumulation and expellation of gas. Anxiety and nervousness are also contributing factors in the dog's flatulence. Occasional gas is normal and to be expected. Chronic gas is usually telling the owner that something is wrong, either with the dog's digestive system or the diet which the dog is being fed. Older dogs are especially prone to gas, and their diet may have to be adjusted to the easily digestible foodstuffs. Sharp changes in the diet are always to be avoided; they can cause gas as well as diarrhea. *See also* Feeding

Gascon-Saintongeois

In the 1840s, the Baron de Virelade created the Grand Gascon-Saintongeois by crossing the few remaining specimens of two nearly extinct French hunters, the Grand Gascony and the Saintongeois. The Saintongeois was a renowned wolf slayer that had fallen into disuse upon the decline of the French nobles. The Gasconies were also quite rare, and Virelade's efforts saved these breeds from total obsolescence. The Grand Gascon-Saintongeois adapted well to its forebears' quarry of roe deer and other large game. Furthermore, the breed sustained its forebears' good looks and impressive size, legginess and rather loose skin. The smaller version of the breed, called the Petit Gascon-Saintongeois, was developed to work specifically on hare and smaller game. The Grand is often referred to as the Virelade, after its founder. While not known outside France, the Gascon-Saintongeois is still a popular pack hunter in France.

ESSENTIALS OF THE GASCON-SAINTONGEOIS: The Grand is a robust, big and leggy hound with long, exaggerated ears and a handsome head, the occipital peak of which is very pronounced. The Petit, like its larger brother, possesses these qualities but on a smaller scale. In height, the Grand is 25–28 inches (63.5–71 cm) and weighs 66–71 pounds (30–32 kg). The Petit in height is approximately 22.5–25 inches (57–63.5 cm) high. Both varieties possess a tricolor coat pattern which is specifically detailed with tan spots on the head only and black spots on the upper body. Ofttimes the white background has black ticking throughout. The coat is short, dense and smooth.

Gaskin

The lower thigh (e.g., of the Bloodhound).

Gastric torsion

See Bloat

Gastritis

Inflammation of the stomach caused by any of many factors—spoiled food which tends to turn to gas, overeating, eating foreign bodies, chemicals or even worms. Vomiting is usually the first symptom though the animal will usually drink great quantities of water that more often than not it vomits. A determination of the cause is the first step towards a cure.

Gastroduodenitis

Inflammation of the stomach and duodenum.

Gastroenteritis

See Coronaviral gastroenteritis, Parvovirus

Gate

Attendance at a race; the number of spectators passing through the entrance gates.

Gaunt head

Terminology employed in the Vizsla and Belgian Groenendael breed standards meaning clean or lean. The drawers and/or translators of these standards were indiscreet or simply inept in their word choice, if one considers the primarily unflattering definition of the adjective employed.

Gay tail

The tail carried up, very high, or over the dog's back. When the tail is carried higher than the carriage described by the standard, the term gay tail is often applied.

Gazehound

Alternative term for sighthound, which *see*.

Gee

Term indicating a right turn to a sled dog; not to be confused with "O gee," when the said sled dog has mistakenly turned left.

Genetics

Begetting the desired get requires that the breeder possess three essentials: knowledge of genetics, careful selection, and time. While a breeder's short-term goals may be accomplished by breeding "best-in-show" stud to "best-in-show" bitch, such a crude program, weeding out weedy, poor specimens, can only inevitably yield limited results. Mendelian genetics enables us to evaluate dogs

not for their phenotype (what they appear to be) but for their genotypes (what they will *produce*). Close examination of the pedigree of both the sire and dam allows a breeder to select from the genotype of dogs, instead of the phenotype. A dog with a single fault may be unwisely discarded without ever considering if that dog will reproduce that fault. Addi-

tionally, breeders must not approach all dog breeds in a like manner, since dominant and recessive characteristics are different from breed to breed. In Cocker Spaniels, per se, the black color is dominant and the buff recessive; in German Shepherds, sable is dominant and black recessive. A dominant trait means that the dog will pass on that trait to a majority of the progeny and not skip a generation; a recessive trait can remain buried, tending to skip one or more generations and is expressed in the offspring only when both animals carry that recessive trait.

While humans have 46 pairs of chromosomes in each reproductive germ cell, dogs possess 39 pairs. A chromosome is an assembly of genes in a line, much like

Genetics. Breeders dealing with the hairless breeds must be aware of lethal gene combinations. In the Chinese Crested, the Powderpuff (or coated variety) must be employed in mating, as hairless-to-hairless pairings will be unsuccessful. Powderpuff mother and hairless pup photographed by I. Français.

beads on a string. Genes are the basic units of inheritance that are transmitted from generation to generation. Every species has a definite number of chromosomes—all dogs regardless of breed have 78—which are arranged in pairs and carry the traits that the animal inherits. The chromosomes of each contributing

therefore any two domestic dogs theoretically could produce fertile progeny. Wolves and coyotes should be included in the domestic dog's litany of fertile crosses, since both these species also have the requisite number of chromosomes. Incidentally, many coyote hunters have been distressed to find their rioting hounds violating a female coyote in heat. For this reason, many hunters find it useful to keep a robust, sensible though unscrupulous female hound in the pack to keep the impressionable males in line. It is not clear whether Matthey's work on the jackal, numbering its chromosomes at 74, is correct. Some experimental wild dog breeders (Herre, 1964) indicate that fertile crosses between jackals and domestic dogs have been accomplished. More recent studies indicate that jackals also have 78 chromosomes and that fertile progeny have been produced (Wurster and Benirschke, 1968).

Genetics. Although both the Saint Bernard and Pomeranian possess the correct chromosomatic material to reproduce, matings such as this one—particularly with a Pomeranian bitch—would prove an abomination. Photo by I. Français.

parent separate, and one-half of the genes from the chromosomes (one of each pair) of the sire unite with one-half of the genes from the chromosomes of the dam. Thus, one-half of the genes from each combine to comprise the new individual.

All breeds of dog have the same number of paired chromosomes, and

Since domestic dog is the most diversified of all animal species (this book describes over 600 breed variations of *Canis familiaris*), a number of interbreed differences should be taken into account. To exemplify with the most extreme example, mating a one-pound Chihuahua to a 200-pound Tibetan Mastiff would surely invite unimaginable complications. One common breeding misconception is that breeding a big dog to a small dog will yield a medium-sized dog. More likely, the mating will produce big dogs and small dogs. Woe to the female Chihuahua alluded to above—since such a dam could probably fit into the skull of its prospective Tibetan Mastiff puppy progeny. "More" wisely, the Tibetan would be the dam and the Chihuahua the sire. (Artificial insemination might also be advised, since the male Chihuahua might not quite conceptualize the task set before him.)

Many interbreed differences revolve around superficial traits (such as hair texture, color, ear carriage, length of tail, etc.), while general physical conformation is surprisingly similar. There are other considerations such as the achondroplastic legs of the basset and dachshund type dogs, the brachycephalic skull types of the bulldogs types, thyroid metabolism, and uric acid secretion which can affect interbreeding factors. Basenjis' single estrus cycle, similar to that of dingoes and wolves, also presents a consideration for crossing that breed. Behaviorally, breeds vary a great deal: aggressiveness, emotional reactivity, trainability, protectiveness, gameness, hunting instincts, etc.

Genetic analysis of hereditary instincts links the study of genetics to canine social behavior, since such interactions occur in regular and predictable patterns. The three types of interactions which affect genetic analysis include mother–offspring, littermate, and dog–human. A study has proven that heredity can affect the mother's maternal behavior, including nursing and retrieval of a stray whelp. Various litter studies have proven that different breeds interact as littermates differently. In certain breeds, the dominance–subordination scenario is played out quite early, and antagonistic behavior between males is common; females may tend not to fight but express their dominance vocally; absolute dependence on littermates may also occur.

Breed standards commonly describe the temperament typical of a breed. This is a reflection of the breed's personality and its interaction with humans (and other dogs as well). Some breeds are amenable to excessive handling, while others remain aloof until they are completely acclimated to a person's scent, etc.

Genetics. Pursuing a natural mutation in a breed, such as long hair on a smoothhaired breed, can lead to developments like this Longhaired Whippet. It cannot be clearly ascertained whether or not a different longhaired breed was introduced to create this new line of silken windhounds. Photo courtesy of W. Wheeler.

Genetics. Since the domestic dog and gray wolf both possess 39 pairs of chromosomes, crosses will theoretically produce fertile progeny. Hybrid wolf photographed by I. Français.

Genes affect canines at every level of organization; their primary effect is through enzymes which modify the

speed of biochemical reactions; secondary effects of genes are manifested on the cellular and physiological levels. How genes exactly affect the physiology and behavior of the dog (or any animal) is not quite understood, although the secondary effects can also be exhibited indirectly through behavior. Of course, the genetic composition of a particular breed or population can be altered by social, behavioral, and physiological factors, as affected through the processes of selection and evolution. *See also* Canine behavior, Breeding, Hairless dogs

Gentian root powder
Used to curb the eating of stools. *See* Coprophagy

Gentian violet
Has been used at 1:1,000 parts strength as an antiseptic for external use.

Geophagy
The eating of dirt, which is believed to be caused by factors similar in origin to those of the eating of stool. *See* Coprophagy

Geriatrics
Care of the elderly. Caring for the older dog requires patience and understanding of the aging process and the changes that occur in the older dog. *See* Older dogs

German Boarhound
See Great Dane

German Broken-Coated Pointer
See Stichelhaar

German Hound
See Deutsche Bracke

German Hunting Terrier
The German Hunting Terrier, known as the Deutscher Jagdterrier in Germany, was created by Bavarian sportsmen through crossing the Welsh Terrier and the old-fashioned Broken-Coated Terrier, a black and tan British dog. Its progeny was crossed with both varieties of Fox Terriers: this latter cross explains the breed's two coat types. Four Bavarians were involved in the project: C.E. Gruenwald, Chief Forester R. Fiess, Dr. Herbert Lackner, and Walter Zangenbert. The result is a terrier that has been called a hunting machine, merciless to its quarry. This working terrier, although appearing a

friendly tyke, is not a house dog and responds kindly only to his master, unless otherwise instructed. Additionally,

the German Hunting Terrier is capable of working on most game, with a wondrous nose, doubling as a land or water retriever.

ESSENTIALS OF THE GERMAN HUNTING TERRIER: The Jagdterrier is small and game, standing no taller than 16 inches (40.5 cm). Well-muscled and vigorous, this breed can come in one of two coats: the shorter is smooth and coarse; the rough is very wiry and broken. In color, it can be black/tan, red, or chocolate/tan. Clearly visible cheeks and a sturdy muzzle give its angulated head a determined look. Its ears are V-shaped and sit much like a Fox Terrier's. Weight: 20–22 pounds (9–10 kg).

German Longhaired Pointer

Developed from longhaired gundogs that populated Europe during the 1800s, the German Longhair, or Langhaar, made his first show appearance in Hanover in 1879. He has been known nearly as long as other German Pointers and shares some common ancestry with them. Despite the Longhair's rather gentle, soft appearance, the breed is expected to perform the same rigorous hunting tasks demanded of all German gundogs, and the breed proudly lives up to these expectations. The Longhair, in order to be true, should

avoid both red and black coloration—such colors would indicate the bloodline's being violated by the Irish Setter, Newfoundland, or Gordon Setter. Each of these three admittedly handsome dogs were often carelessly crossed with the Longhair, with the result being coarse, improperly colored dogs.

His hunting affinity centers on feathered game and he is a pro in the water. At one time, he was a notorious falconer and hawker. The breed is recognized by both the F.C.I. and the Canadian Kennel Club. The breed's popularity is best described as moderate but stable.

This enthusiastic all-around hunter must be provided an outlet for his energy. He is a fun-loving, easygoing dog

that enjoys being with his master. Although hunting is a passion, other outdoor diversions can be undertaken and enjoyed. The coat is not so long as to require extended grooming sessions, the tail is left long and beautifully adorned, and the feathering is never removed.

German Hunting Terrier, smooth, black/tan.

German Longhaired Pointer, solid liver. Photographs by I. Français.

German Longhaired Pointers, solid liver and bicolor. Photo by I. Français.

German Shepherd Dog, black and tan.

ESSENTIALS OF THE GERMAN LONGHAIRED POINTER: The Langhaar is a sturdy dog with a solid liver coloration. In size he is comparable to the other German pointers, with the long coat his distinguishing feature. Height: 24–27 inches (61–69 cm). Weight: 55–77 pounds (25–35 kg). The coat, of medium length and harsh texture, is shiny and wavy, never appearing coarse or silky. White spots or a white chest often occur, although a solid-colored dog is preferred.

German Pinscher
See Pinscher

German Roughhaired Pointer
See Stichelhaar

German Sheeppoodle
A rare, if not extinct, sheepdog of Germany with a distinctive cording coat. The breed's ancestors are the Water Dog and the Barbet. It evolved in Germany as the Pudel, bearing similarities to the popular Poodle whose coat also cords. In Germany it was often referred to as the Schafpudel and bears "a heavy and uncouth appearance." It is a large dog, standing 24 inches (61 cm) at the shoulder. The color is typically white with pied or shadings common. German shepherds have long regarded the breed's guardian abilities.

German Sheeppudel
See German Sheeppoodle

German Shepherd Dog
One of the oldest and one of the most versatile of all shepherd breeds, the German Shepherd, according to the noted authority, Captain Max von Stephanitz, traces back some 6000 years. Another authority writing on the antiquity of the breed cites a formerly overlooked line in Tacitus, the famed Roman historian who spoke of "the wolf-like dog of the country around the Rhine." Though the true age of the German Shepherd may never be known, experts agree that the breed has existed in the region today called Germany for centuries. The concurrence is understandable when we realize that the German Shepherd embodies the old shepherd dog prototype and is ideally suited for the task of herding and flock herding. The resemblance of other Continental herding dogs, such as the Dutch Shepherds and Belgian Sheepdogs, to the German Shepherd Dog is remarkable though not uncanny.

It would be inaccurate to limit the German Shepherd Dog's talents to the

pasture in attendance to a flock (a role it is still able to fulfill). The breed's finesse and sagacity at a myriad of tasks speaks well of its unshakable popularity. A guard dog, guide dog, Red Cross worker, police assistant, military and messenger dog, as well as flock herder, paint a more complete portrait of the breed's abilities.

The long-held British name for the

breed, Alsatian, was derived from the region called Alsace, from which the first British imports were brought. After the First World War the breed was termed the Alsatian Wolfdog.

Dogs of any breed, especially those that attain great popularity, easily become the victims of both poor breeding practices and press sensationalism. The German Shepherd Dog worked as a diligently responsible, ever-alerted herd and guard for centuries in its native land. The close of the First World War sent the soldiers home, and the arms of many of them held a member of an outstanding German dog breed. We could only guess at the number of German Shepherd Dogs that entered Great Britain and the United States from Germany after the War. So versatile and affectionate were the dogs that they quickly rose to the fore of breed popularity, which opened, and indeed subjected, the breed to overbreeding of poor specimens with money as the sole underline. Nervous and unevenly tempered dogs resulted. An occasional incidence of biting would hit the press hard, and generalizations would be drawn, conclusively. In a decade, registrations in Great Britain dropped from 6,357 in 1928 to 1,778, and the breed faced a grave danger on the Isles. Rumors spread regarding the breed as a wolf hybrid, untrustworthy, unsuitable as a dog: utter nonsense. Many a dog would not have recovered nor survived such an onslaught. The German Shep-

herd Dog reburgeoned, proving its superior quality and intelligence. Today the best German Shepherd Dogs are among the best dogs in the world. The inferior specimens, however, are indeed poor.

ESSENTIALS OF THE GERMAN SHEPHERD DOG: Active and enlivened, the German Shepherd Dog immediately impresses with strength, agility, and form in a medium-sized, deep bodied, smooth and

German Shepherd Dog.

German Shepherd Dog, black.

substantial animal. The ideal dog denotes at once noble bearing and quality performance. The cleanly chiseled head

carries moderately pointed well-proportioned ears, held erect when alert; medium-sized almond-shaped eyes, as dark as possible; and a powerful jaw, set in a scissors bite. The neck too is clean-cut, strong and muscular. The body is deep

German Shepherd Dogs, black and tan.

and solid, never bulky or lanky. Shoulder blades are long and obliquely angled; they are laid on flat and not placed forward. Chest is deep and capacious; ribs are well sprung and long. Moderate tuck up. The withers are higher than and slope into the level back. The back is straight, very strongly developed and relatively short. (The desired overall length is derived not from a long back but from the relation of length to height: the sum of the forequarters, back, and hindquarters to the length from ground to wither.) Weight: 75–95 pounds (34–43 kg). Height: 22–26 inches (56–66 cm). The tail is bushy and hangs in a slight saber curl. The dog has a medium-length double coat. The outer coat is harsh, straight, and dense; it lies close to the body. The head, legs, and paws are covered with short hair, the neck with longer, thicker hair. Color varies in black and tan, with most variations being acceptable. Strong rich colors are in preference.

German Shorthaired Pointer

A versatile and all-purpose gundog capable of effective hunting in both field and water. The breed is descended from very old working-stock schweisshunds (slow working scent hunters) which have inhabited Germany for centuries. Prior to the nineteenth century, this stock represented an amorphous group with no distinct type emergent. As the century progressed, German breeders began fixing type, in search of the ideal gundog. The base stock for the German Shorthair is believed to be the old German Bird Dog, which was added to already existent Spanish Pointer blood. Prior to the 1870 Kurzhaar Stud Book, however, no actual records were kept of the breed, and therefore component stock can only be assumed—the early Shorthair likely received blood from a variety of native scenthounds. The dog that resulted from these crosses was much heavier, longer eared and slower than today's breed. For their ends, this dog was not sufficient. Breeders then crossed to the English Pointer to create a lighter and faster German pointer. Continued crosses to outstanding English Pointers improved stance, refined type, and above all to the hunters, further developed the Shorthair's nose. Also of great importance to German hunters is the dog's obedience. This quality has been consistently bred for through the ages, and the breed today is unquestionably loyal and heeds unhesitatingly its master's command. No one can deny this gundog's superior abilities or intelligence.

The German Shorthaired Pointer was first registered by the A.K.C. in March, 1930. These dogs have proved outstanding at Field Trials. The first A.K.C.-licensed Field Trial for the breed was held by the parent club on May 21, 1944.

ESSENTIALS OF THE GERMAN SHORTHAIRED POINTER: An aristocratic, well-balanced, symmetrical animal indicative of power, endurance and agility. First impression should be keenness, denoting total enthusiasm for work without any indication of nervousness or flighty character. In absolute symmetry: clean-cut head of reasonably broad skull, broad and fairly high set ears, deep chest, powerful back, good quarters, strong muscle, good bone, well-carried tail, and hard coat. The dog's outline is graceful

and well balanced. The size of the Shorthair is of prime importance: he must be neither too large nor too small. Height: 23–25 inches (58–64 cm). Weight: 55–70 pounds (25–32 kg). Solid liver or liver and white (with or without ticking) are the desired colors. A true water dog, this breed has webbed feet.

German Shepherd Dog. Solid white GSDs are disqualified from competition. A small contingency, however, still promotes this agile and attractive breed variant. Photo by I. Français.

German Shorthaired Pointer, liver and white ticked.

German Shorthaired Pointer, liver with ticking.

German Shorthaired Pointers, solid liver and liver with ticking.

German Spaniel

See Deutscher Wachtelhund

German Spitzen

Developed in Germanic countries as companion and utility dogs, the spitz breeds were popular in Germany, Austria, Holland and Great Britain. The spitz-type dogs are considered to be among the most ancient of canines known to man. They have contributed to the make-up of a great many of today's breeds, including many shepherds. Fossils of prehistoric dogs found in Scandinavian countries, Russia and Switzerland bear likeness to these spitz types. The family of German spitz is divided principally by size and color, as opposed to conformation. Viking travelers' bringing of dogs into Germany and Holland briefly explains these dogs' root-taking. Around Germany, the different colored spitzen were each associated with specific areas: the grays were found along the Rhine in the districts of Mannheim and Stuttgart; the blacks in Wurtenberg; and the whites in Elberfeld.

The largest of the German Spitzen is the wolf gray German Wolfspitz, which is considered one and the same with the Keeshond by the F.C.I. Large German Spitzen, taken into England, were soon called Keeshond, who has also received fame as the Dutch Barge Dog. These dogs today have subtle differences, and the Keeshond is recognized as an individual breed throughout North America and Britain, where it is quite popular. Nordic herding dogs with profuse harsh coats were probably transported to the Germanic countries during the Middle Ages. These dogs spread throughout the European continent and progenerated the shepherd breeds as well as the spitz varieties, of which this breed is the oldest. The Wolfspitz once frequented a number of German and French neighborhoods, particularly Elberfeld, Düsseldorf, Aix-la-Chapelle, and Credfeld. The French referred to him as Chien Loup, which translates roughly to the current-day name. These dogs were agile workers and proficient herd-

ers. Their given tasks acquired them names of "dogs of the vine grower" and "dogs of the carrier."

The Giant German Spitz or Great Spitz is known in German as the Deutscher Grossspitz. The Standard and the Small German Spitzen are the most common of these breeds. These two sizes are combined into one breed by the Kennel Club of Britain and divided by size: the Standard or Mittel, the Small or Klein. The Small variety has been called variously Miniature German Spitz as well as Victorian Pom, reflecting its being favored by

German Spitzen, Mittel German Spitz, solid white. Photo by I. Français.

Queen Victoria at one time. The smallest variety is the Zwergspitz or Toy German Spitz, which is a popular lap dog in Germany and other European countries. In the U.K. and U.S., the Toy German Spitz makes no progress since its "spin-off" and clone, the Pomeranian has taken its place. The Pomeranian was so named in England and is actually but a Zwergspitz, although it has since developed its own standard and likewise, its claim to fame. Thus, the German Spitzen's popularity in America (and for the most part, Great Britain) is limited by the favoritism shown to the Pomeranian, Keeshond,

and American Eskimo—all of whom stem from German Spitz stock. Even in Germany today, these breeds are waning in numbers and popularity as they are not the chic dogs they once were. The German Spitzen are of equable disposition, exhibiting a healthy amount of confidence; they are happy and up-beat companions.

ESSENTIALS OF THE GERMAN SPITZEN: A well-knit, nearly square outline befits all varieties of the German Spitzen. Its profuse fur coat does not cover the dog's substance; the body is compact, well ribbed up and rounded. Overall body proportion is of utmost importance. Head is medium large, broad in skull, narrowing in a wedge-shaped nose. Moderate stop is noticeable, muzzle is not long. Ears are small, triangular, set rather high—perfectly erect. The forelegs are straight with length in proportion to a well-balanced frame. Loins moderately short, chest fairly deep; level topline; moderate tuck up at loins; hindquarters moderately angulated with hocks moderately well let down. Feet small and catlike. The coat is double, consisting of a soft dense undercoat and a long, rough-to-the-touch outer coat, most profuse on forelegs and trousers. In color the German Spitzen are most typically solid—black, orange, brown, wolf gray or white. Particolors exist. The Wolfspitz is wolf gray only. Size: Zwerg—under 8.5 inches (21.5 cm). Klein—9–11 inches (23–28 cm); Mittel—11.5–14 inches (29–35.5 cm). Giant—16 inches (41 cm) minimum. Wolfspitz—18 inches (46 cm) minimum.

German Spitzen. (*top*) Zwerg German Spitz, solid red; (*middle*) Klein German Spitzen, particolor; (*bottom*) Mittel German Spitz, solid red. Photographs by I. Français.

German Spitzen. (*top left*) Mittel German Spitz, solid black; (*top right*) Klein and Mittel German Spitzen, solid red; (*middle*) German Wolfspitz, wolfgray; (*bottom*) Mittel German Spitz, bicolor. Photographs by I. Français.

German Wirehaired Pointer

The German Wirehair, known as the Deutscher Drahthaar in his native country, is an all-purpose gundog and repre-

German Wirehaired Pointer, liver with ticking.

sents a counter-reaction to the increasingly specialized gundogs of the 1800s. German hunters, known for their demanding requisites of a working canine, could not tolerate dogs that worked only one kind of game or performed only one hunting function. Therefore, by the mid-1800s, they began their selective breeding for the ultimate "all-rounder," a dog that could point, retrieve, and flush, and work under any environmental conditions on a given terrain.

Recognized in his native Germany in 1870, the Wirehair is a fairly new breed of dog. The development of the German pointers, including the Wirehair, was an essentially simultaneous concurrence; each breed developed from similar stock but became individualized with the efforts of regional breeders. The early German Wirehair was mostly a conglomeration of Griffon, Stichelhaar, Pudelpointer, and German Shorthair—breeds which themselves represented amalgamations of each other as well as the Foxhound and the Poodle. Through continued selective breeding, which included further crossings to emphasize desired points and especially to perfect the desired coat type, the German Wirehair was created.

The German Wirehair's introduction to the U.S. has been one mixed with controversy. The practices of the German

German Wirehaired Pointer, liver and white.

breeders differ from those accepted by the A.K.C. In Germany, crossbreeding is generally accepted, provided that breeding is done with the sole intention of perfecting the abilities and attributes of the dog. Stud lists are adopted and crossbreeding is granted when the need is justified. The A.K.C., however, disagrees with such practice and feels that specimens of a given breed should be crossed only to others of the breed. When A.K.C. breed status was granted, the mixed pedigrees of many Wirehairs prevented their admittance. One trait not allowed by the A.K.C. but welcomed by many European fanciers is the black coloration. There exist today many fine Wirehairs in America that are not registered with the A.K.C. They find their home in various performance-oriented registries and continue to excel as fine hunters and companions. The breed's protective coat enables it to work well in thicketed brush or chilling waters. As with the terrain,

weather seems practically inconsequential to the dogs. They are built for endurance and are unsurpassed in courage and determination.

ESSENTIALS OF THE GERMAN WIREHAIRED POINTER: Essentially pointer in type, the breed is sturdily built, lively and intelligent. The head is moderately long, with a broad skull, medium stop, fairly long muzzle, and rounded but not too broad

Gestation

The period beginning with conception and ending in the delivery of the litter. Gestation in domestic dogs ranges from 58 to 65 days, with 63 an average. *See* Breeding, Brood bitch

German Wirehaired Pointer, black and white. This color variation is not accepted in American show circles and is referred to by its fanciers as the German Drahthaar. These dogs are excellent all-around hunting dogs, epitomizing the *vorstehhunden*. Photo by I. Français.

ears. Eyes brown and overhung with bushy eyebrows. Neck of medium length and slightly arched. Body slightly longer than high, of deep chest with well-sprung ribs, short, straight, strong back, and apparent tuck-up. The coat is weather resisting and, to some degree, water repellent. Distinctive outer coat is straight, harsh, wiry, and rather flat-lying (from 1.5 to 2 inches in length). Undercoat dense in cold but nearly invisible in hot seasons. Height: 24–26 inches (61–66 cm). Weight: 60–70 pounds (27–32 kg). In color the Wirehair is solid liver or any combination of liver and white. Although not accepted in the A.K.C. registry, the breed can also be black and white. Other color possibilities that are frowned on by all registries include solid black and tricolor.

German Wolfspitz
See German Spitzen

Get
Puppies. *See* Breeding, Puppies

Ghost running
A Beagle following a non-existent scent or trail.

Giant breeds
A number of dogs fit into the category of giant breeds. While the group is predominated by the mastiffs, such skyscrapers as the Giant Schnauzer, a giant among the terriers; the Scottish Deerhound, Irish Wolfhound and Greyhound, among the sighthounds; the Great Pyrenees, Maremma Sheepdog, and other large flock guards; and the Bloodhound also rightly deserve their placement in the group. Among the towering mastiffs are the English Mastiff, Great Dane, Bullmastiff, Tosa Inu, Dogue de Bordeaux and Tibetan Mastiff. There are many others worthy of mention and

the authors apologize to any omitted and offended collosians. In general, the giant breeds need owners with big yards, big salaries, big fences, and big commitments. These Brobdignabians predictably have large appetites and need plenty of room to stretch their long limbs. They also tend to be shorter lived than the medium to small size dogs. *See also* Mastiff breeds, Acromegaly

Giant breeds. Owners considering adopting a giant-breed member must have a surplus of space, money and time for proper training. This Bullmastiff belongs to Dr. Carl Semencic, who is also the photographer.

Giant Schnauzer

A large working/herding breed developed in the south of Germany for the purpose of cattle droving. The breed originated sometime in the fifteenth century and was commonly employed by German farmers into the eighteenth century. Because of its large size and considerable feeding requirements, the breed lost favor for a time with hard-pressed stockmen. With the coming of the railroad and urban development, the breed regained popularity with butchers, who needed strong, dependable dogs to move the herds of massive bovines with tight control. Also, dogs were needed to guard the cattle traders who, without credit cards or check books, were forced to carry large sums of cash on their person. To this task, Giants took like Newfoundlands to water. Giants, known as Riesenschnauzers in their native land, quickly became the mascots of beerhalls and other meeting places of the German working classes during the 1800s. It is stated that during this period of the breed's popularity crosses and selective breedings occurred that likened the breed to the Standard Schnauzer. The Müncher Dog, as the Giant was once called, remains the largest of the Schnauzers and also the most powerful. He is favored as a guardian breed by many demanding owners and proves most effective at his duty. He retains his cattle-working ability and is still employed, though rarely, as a drover dog throughout the world.

The Giant Schnauzer is one of the hardiest of all working breeds; his harsh terrierlike coat and strongly developed musculature make him a canine with which no "intelligent" animal should wish to contend: vigorous in body and mind and adaptable to all kinds of weather and living conditions, the Giant Schnauzer is surely an all-around dog. Despite his grand size, he needs relatively less exercise and obedience training than do many of the other large, long-legged breeds.

ESSENTIALS OF THE GIANT SCHNAUZER: In muscular composition and robustness, the Giant Schnauzer casts an imposing and dauntless figure of canine power. Correct body conformation is of utmost importance. Head is strong, of good length, narrowing from ears to eyes and then gradually towards the end of the nose. Jaws, strong with a perfect, regular and complete scissor bite. Ears, v-shaped, set high and dropping forward

Giant Schnauzer,
solid black.

to temple. (In the U.S. and Germany, the ears are customarily cropped.) Neck is moderately long, strong and slightly arched. Shoulders, flat, well laid back. Forequarters, straight. Muscle, smooth and lithe rather than prominent. Bone, strong. Chest, moderately broad and deep. Ribs, well sprung. Body, square. Tail is set on high and carried at an angle slightly above topline; customarily docked to two joints. The concentrated, short-coupled, and powerful frame accommodates an effortlessly free and driving gait. Height: 23.5–27.5 inches (59–70 cm). Weight: 70–77 pounds (32–35 kg). The coat is of medium length, harsh and wiry, just short enough for smartness on body and slightly shorter on neck and shoulders; undercoat is woolly. In color the Giant can be solid black or pepper and salt.

Gift dogs

Giving dogs as gifts, talismans, and tokens of goodwill has been a custom of various societies throughout the world. The Oriental countries have historically offered their tiny toy dogs as tokens of peace and benevolence. Commodore Perry was "very, very glad" to receive sleeve dogs from his Japanese hosts in the 1860s. The Tibetan Terrier and Tibetan Spaniel were also gift wrapped for visitors to Tibet as tokens of good luck for travelers. Ambassador Pecar received an Azawakh for his assistance to the Tuareg

Giant Schnauzer,
pepper and salt.
Photographs by I.
Français.

Gift dogs. This Shiba Inu was a gift to American breeder Rick Tomita. When exportation of quality dogs from native countries is so limited, gifts like this "Japanese Boy" prove extremely beneficial. Photo by I. Français.

tribe, a token of great esteem from a people who never allow their dogs to leave their land. Talbot and Southern Hounds as well as various pack hounds of France were frequently sent to European monarchs on a regular basis to ensure goodwill between nations. Dogs, not fighting dogs, but honorable, sincere domesticated canines, will continue to dissolve international tensions and borders. Correspondence between East and West, exchanging breeding stock for the improvement of breeds in different lands, and sharing national dog treasures

continue to open man's eyes to the beauty and glory of lands different than his own. Japan is a sublime example of importing and exporting dogs. Although much of the exchange has diminished, today Japan has its fair share of English Pointers and German Shepherd Dogs, and like-

wise, the West has many beloved Akitas and Shibas for which to be grateful. *See also* Exportation of dogs

Gigantism
See Acromegaly

Gingivitis
Acute or chronic inflammation of the gums. The condition is characterized by congestion and swelling; if untreated, gingivitis can lead to periodontitis, which *see*. Gingivitis is caused by a local irritation or infection, or it can be secondary to a systemic condition. A narrow red band around the neck of a tooth may be an indication. A veterinarian's aid is necessary. Scaling and brushing regularly is usually advised.

Girth
Measurement of the chest circumference taken behind the withers at the point of maximum development.

Giving tongue
A scenthound on the trail gives tongue, that is, bays and howls. The scenthounds (including the American coonhound breeds and the French packhounds) are gifted, variously, with musical and expressive voices capable of exciting the huntsmen and their fellow packmates as well.

Glass eye
See Walleye

Glassy eyes
A fault indicating eyes that are glazed and exaggeratedly unintelligent in appearance.

Glaucoma
A condition that results in excessive pressure on the eye, causing pain and possible blindness. There is possible treatment if the disorder is detected in an early stage. In some cases, surgery is necessary to save a dog's vision. If pain, protrusion, or other eye abnormalities are detected, a visit to the vet is in order.

Glaucous
A grayish blue coloration (e.g., Old English Sheepdog).

Glen of Imaal Terrier

The Glen of Imaal Terrier receives its name from the Glen of Imaal, a region in County Wicklow in Ireland, where this little terrier has been in existence for a long time. The Glen of Imaal is a splendidly game terrier, fearless in attacking its quarry. Unlike many other terriers, the Imaal is compact enough to go to ground after badger or fox and game enough to fight its chosen vermin to the death. In times gone by, the breed is said to have participated in dog baiting, one dog against another. Unlike the Pit Bull Terriers, these dogs fought in an open field and not a pit. Specimens from the baiting days are said to have weighed up to 50 pounds (22.5 kg)—today's dogs weigh about 35 pounds (16 kg). Common mostly in Ireland, the Glen of Imaal is recognized by the Kennel Club of Great Britain and has an active fancy in England. The breed's moderate size and good health make it an ideal home or apartment dog, for the right owner.

ESSENTIALS OF THE GLEN OF IMAAL TERRIER: The body is long, ensuring the image of great substance. The head should be of good width and fair length, with a foreface of power, and a pronounced stop that tapers to the nose. The ears can be rose or half pricked but not large. The neck muscular, of moderate length. Forequarters must be short but of great bone; chest wide and strong with front legs bowed. Body is deep and long, longer than high. The topline straight. Loins must be strong; the ribs well-sprung. Hindquarters strong and well muscled. Height: 14 inches (35.5 cm). Weight: 35 pounds (16 kg). A soft undercoat underlies a rough-textured, medium-length coat, which is tidied to project a clean outline. The Imaal can be wheaten (from a light wheaten to a golden reddish), blue (not giving toward black), or brindle.

Globular eyes

Reasonably prominent round eyes that do not bulge (e.g., Chihuahua).

Glomeruli and tubules

Minute collecting components of the kidney instrumental in the filtration of urine.

Glossitis

Inflammation of the tongue.

Glossy coat

A healthy coat with a sheen and a shine. *See also* Coat

Glucose

A crystalline, natural-occurring sugar found in most food substances.

Glycerin

Also known as glycerol, a thick liquid created by processing fats and oils. It is used as a solvent and as a lotion for treating some skin conditions.

Glen of Imaal Terriers, wheaten. Photo by I. Français.

Glycogen

Produced and stored in the body, this substance is easily converted into body-useable energy.

Gnarled tail

A malformed, twisted tail with joints appearing larger and more pronounced than desired, knotted or fused (e.g., Boston Terrier fault).

Go

Same as start, begin, etc. For a sled dog, response to this word is crucial.

Goathair

Medium-length, harsh coat on the Berger des Pyrenees, Briard, and other herders.

Goggled eyes

Staring, protruding eyes with a hint of bulge. A fault in the Cocker Spaniel.

Goiter

Any enlargement of the thyroid gland, usually noticed as a swelling in the lower portion of the neck region, is commonly termed "goiter."

Golden jackal

Canis aureus. See Jackals

Golden Retriever. Photo by Thacker.

Golden Retriever

A very popular gundog breed that traces its roots to England and is employed today primarily as a companion, showman, obedience and field trial dog; the breed can still perform well as a retriever on both land and water and is increasingly employed as a seeing eye and therapy dog. Sir Dudley Majoribanks (Lord Tweedmouth) is often credited as the father of the breed. It is documented that he acquired a Yellow Retriever, named Nous, in Brighton England, in 1865. To increase the intelligence, courage and ability of his new acquisition, as well as to stride towards the attainment of his desired retriever type, Lord Tweedmouth crossed the Yellow Retriever with the now extinct Tweed Water Spaniel, a hardy water worker who then frequented the British seacoast. The first cross is reported to have been sometime between 1867–68. This first crossing produced four yellow puppies. One female of the litter, named Cowslip, was later mated to a second Tweed Water Spaniel. A bitch was again retained from the litter for breeding purposes. She was later crossed to an offspring of another bitch from the first litter. Breedings continued, with crossings to an Irish Setter and yet another Tweed Water Spaniel reported. It is also believed that a Bloodhound may have been crossed into the line to improve scenting and add bone. Yellow Retrievers, now know as Golden, began their ascension to popularity in the late 1800s. The breed's first Field Trial victory occurred in 1904. Goldens made their show ring debut in 1908 and were listed as Flat Coats (Golden). The A.K.C. first registered the breed as such in 1925. Throughout the 1930s and 40s, the popularity of the Golden grew, though they were at that time used primarily as hunting retrievers. Today, Goldens are used successfully at a variety of tasks, including field work, obedience, showmanship, companionship, and help for the disabled.

There is an oft-cited story of the Golden's development that is worthy of mention in any text on the breed; it involves the acquisition of Caucasus sheepdogs by Lord Tweedmouth, who purchased the dogs upon a captivating glimpse at their performance of feats in a traveling circus. The ancient Caucasus sheepdogs were the much trusted flock guards for Russian shepherds who entrusted their charges to these slow-working, enduring dogs. These Russian dogs were determined defenders and killers with the unique proclivity to cease attack on command. Transported to Scotland, they became known as the Guisachan Retrievers. The story is not well supported but remains a colorful tale worthy of preservation.

ESSENTIALS OF THE GOLDEN RETRIEVER: Symmetry, power, and balance. The Golden Retriever is primarily a hunting dog and should be witnessed in hard working condition. Head is broad in skull and slightly arched, without prominence of frontal or occipital bones. Muzzle is straight and blends smoothly and strongly into skull. Expression of the eyes to be friendly and intelligent. Body is well balanced, short coupled and deep through the chest. Ribs long and well sprung, never barrel shaped. Back strong and level, with slight slope at the croup. Tail well set on, thick and muscular at the base. The quarters are broad and strongly muscled. The coat is dense and water repellent with good undercoat. The quality of the coat and the wealth of free-flowing feathering are essential to the Golden. In color the breed is rich, lustrous golden in various shades. Height: 21–24 inches (53–61 cm). Weight: 60–75 pounds (27–34 kg).

Golden Retriever. Photo by I. Français.

Golden Retrievers.

Gonads

The organs that produce reproductive cells: in males, the testicles; in females, the ovaries. *See* Breeding

Gone away

In foxhunting, when the fox has been found and the pack takes off at a fast rate.

Gone to ground

When the fox or badger has retreated into the earth, a drain, den or other underground shelter.

Gonič

Yugoslavian word for hound.

Gontchaja Estonskaja

See Estonian Hound

Gontchaja Russkaja

See Russian Hound

Gontchaja Russkaja Pegaja

See Russian Harlequin Hound

Goose neck

Swan neck. A tubelike, long neck that lacks both power and cresting; the neck base is no wider than the neck/head junction.

Goose-stepping gait

Gait characterized by accentuated lifts of the forelimbs. The forefeet and pasterns are fully extended before replaced onto the ground.

Gordon Setter

Originating in Scotland, the Gordon Setter has been known at least since 1620, when the "black and fallow setting dog" was praised by a writer as the "hardest to endure labor." He is a true setter with a truly old heritage and distinctive appearance, resembling the English or Irish Setters in general type. It is believed that the Gordon Setter existed for decades

prior to the written praise as a proven setter, but not until the late 1700s did they come to the fore. The fourth Duke of Gordon is credited with setting the breed before the world's dog fancy. It was to his kennels that writers came to report on the dogs and to his kennels that other kennel owners came to purchase fine quality dogs. It is reported that George Blunt and Daniel Webster imported a brace of the Duke's Gordons in 1842, so attracted were they to the dog's coupled beauty and hunting ability. For years following, Gordons were continuously imported by avid enthusiasts. Gordons were quick to win the hearts of American huntsmen

with their kiss of beauty and promise of a bag full 'o game.

With the coming of the field trial competitions, the Gordon's popularity waned slightly, for although he is unbeatable as a one-man shooting dog, the Gordon is slow in comparison to other gundogs and therefore at a disadvantage in the field trial. There is a current attempt to increase the Gordon's speed through selective breeding. Of course, the primary consideration is the preservation of the Gordon's superior bird-finding ability.

"A most petable dog," the Gordon Setter is celebrated for his beauty as well as his loyalty and obedience. A quiet and serene dignity graces this handsome set-

Gordon Setter. Photo by I. Français.

ter, who is a biddable and kind companion animal.

ESSENTIALS OF THE GORDON SETTER: Marked by good size, sturdy build, and plenty of bone and substance, active, enduring, and at the same time stylish. Head rather broad, large and finely chiseled—the heaviest in the setter group. Back strong and fairly short; ribs well sprung; shoulders fine at the points and well laid back. The tail is short and should not reach below the hocks, carried horizontally or nearly so; thick at the root and tapering to a fine point. Color is black and tan. Height: 23–27 inches (58–69 cm). Weight: 45–80 pounds (20–36 kg). The coat, with its clearly defined mahogany on sleek black, is moderately long and flat. The feathering is distinctly long and fine. Gait should be bold, strong, driving, and free-swinging.

Gos
Spanish dialect for a herding dog.

Gos d'Atura Catalan
See Catalan Sheepdog

Gos d'Atura Cerda
See Catalan Sheepdog

Grading
Method of classifying racing dogs according to their past performances.

Grand Anglo-Français
See Anglo-Français

Grand Basset Griffon Vendeen
See Griffon Vendeen

Grand Bleu de Gascogne
See Bleu de Gascogne

Grand Gascon-Saintongeois
See Gascon-Saintongeois

Grand Griffon Vendeen
See Griffon Vendeen

Grand Nite Champion
Title earned by hound who, after attaining Nite Championship, wins an additional three first places in Coonhunt competition.

Gordon Setters photographed by I. Français.

Grass

Grass is one of your dog's favorite wonders of nature, next to trees and flowering bushes perhaps. Most dogs find the grass refreshingly enticing—dusted by a passing female, pre-scented by another territorial male, or just fun-smelling. While grazing on the front lawn won't necessarily cure any particular ailment that your dog has, it may induce vomiting. As long as the grass hasn't been sprayed with an insecticide, there is no cause for alarm.

Great Dane, harlequin, cropped ears. Photo by I. Français.

Gray fox

A distant relative of the domestic dog is the gray fox, *Urocyon cinereoargenteus*. Existing from southern Canada through northern South America, the gray fox stands 14 to 15 inches (35.5–38 cm) tall, weighs from 7 to 13 pounds (3–6 kg), and has a total body and head length from 21 to 30 inches (53.5–76 cm), excluding the 14- to 15-inch (35.5–38 cm) long tail. With coarse fur and no woolly undercoat, the pelt of the gray fox is of much less value than that of his relative, the red fox, *Vulpes vulpes*. Living among the pines or on thinly shaded arid regions, the gray fox is found in uplands as well as at sea level, preferring the warm, dry climes. His home is a den. He hunts in small packs or family groups, and he is the only

wild dog to scale trees regularly. Feeding on rodents, insects, rabbits, birds, other animals, and fruit, the gray fox, like many other foxes, is most active during the dark hours. Though the mortality rate is high, and this animal is easy prey to traps, guns, and other manly inventions, the gray fox survives and remains a relatively numerous canid.

Gray Norwegian Elkhound

See Norwegian Elkhound

Gray wolf

A wolf of the genus *Canis* that is found in North America, Europe, and the Soviet Union. It is probably the best known of all wolves to English speaking peoples. *See* Wolves, Ancestors of the dog

Great Dane

A large mastiff of great strength and courage portraying a definite elegance. The ancestor of the Great Dane is believed to trace its roots back as far as dynastic Egypt; as with many of the most romantic, less-than-gripping attempts to validate the authenticity of a breed, the Great Dane's wall-climbing, pyramid-dwelling ancestors can be spied on tombs of pharaohs from the Fourth dynasty. While it was certainly in Germany where the breed was developed and refined, early attempts to improve these mastiffs were exerted by the Celts who brought the dogs into Ireland and England. This early component stock believably incorporated the Irish Wolfhound, creating Europe's most impressive canine of the period. The Alans brought their mastiffs with them upon invading Gaul, Italy and Spain in the fifth century. Ironically, there is nothing of Danish origin in the development of the breed, the title "Great Dane" being but one choice of many common names of the breed, others including German Mastiff, Deutsche Dogge, Dogo Aleman, Alano, and German Boarhound. It is believed that a

cross to the Greyhound may be responsible for the breed's agility and slender body type.

The breed enjoyed great popularity in Germany during the 1800s, and it was the chosen dog of the renowned Bismarck, who employed the dogs as his personal guardians. Once found on nearly every German estate, German Mastiffs were commonly used for boar hunting, a sport that required great strength, speed and courage. It was during these times that ear cropping became typical of the breed, the cropping performed to protect from tearing of the ears during the hunt.

In England, the breed club was formed in 1885; four years later, in 1889, the American parent club, the Great Dane Club of America, was founded. Both the American and British standards, the official description of the ideal specimen, were based upon quite literal translations of the German standard, which was adopted by the Great Dane Club of Germany in 1891. Additionally, the French, Indian and Dutch standards are all based on that first German standard.

To be or not to be a Great Dane owner is contingent upon the size of one's home, yard, and bank account. The dogs need to feel involved with the home life activities, and their feeding requirements are grand. Some believe that the Great Dane has become too gentle to be a man-stopper, although his size and strength would qualify him for this work, were he properly raised.

ESSENTIALS OF THE GREAT DANE: Smoothly muscled and well formed, the

Great Dane, brindle, cropped ears.

Great Dane, fawn, cropped ears.

Great Dane, brindle, uncropped ears.

Great Danes, black, cropped ears.

appearance is both massive and elegant. The head is long and refined yet shows great strength. The nose bridge broad with a noticeable ridge; the stop strongly pronounced. The ears should be high and of medium size. Neck is long and arched. The shoulders well muscled; the chest deep, with ribs well sprung. Sufficiency of bone and tremendous substance are paramount. The Dane should move with a long, easy, springy stride, with no tossing or rolling of the body. Height: 28–32 inches (71–80 cm). Weight: 100 pounds (45 kg) and over. Coat colors: black, blue, brindle, fawn and harlequin. The coat should be short and thick, smooth and glossy. Crossbreeding of color varieties is seriously discouraged except as specified by the Great Dane Breeder's Code of Ethics, which can be acquired by contacting the national breed club.

Great Dane, blue, cropped ears.

Great Pyrenees

Just as the greatest works of art cannot be fully understood and should not be unravelled for fear of losing some of their glow, so too is the Great Pyrenees. Exactly which breeds contributed to the make-up of this great French guard cannot be discerned. The Kuvasz of Hungary, the Maremma Sheepdog of Italy, and the Anatolian Shepherd Dog of Turkey are all candidates and bear similar, though not precise, appearances to le Chien de Montagnes des Pyrenees, as the French call their Great Pyrenees. And on the great Pyrenees mountains has the Great Pyrenees worked for thousands of years. Early in the twentieth century, however, the breed was scarce, and the efforts of Bernard Senac-Langrange and M. Dretzen are cited as rescuing the breed from near extinction. Of the flock-guarding breeds, the Great Pyrenees or the Pyrenean Mountain Dog, as the British call him, is considered the strongest. Like the polite Frenchman he is, the pet Pyr of today does not impose his strength and he is truly one of the gentlest of the gentle giants. In France, the working Pyrenees, whose white coats are often patched with badger, guard their sheep and cattle from wolves, bears, and other stock thieves. The Pyr works in conjunction with the smaller Berger des Pyrenees (which *see*), which does the actual herding of the flocks and herds. He is also employed by farmers and ranchers on a variety of livestock.

Historically the Great Pyrenees has been favored in France: respected as a dog of war of undaunted ability, the Pyrenees has captured the heart of many a royal lady who has taken handsome specimens home to Paris to guard the estate. Today the Great Pyrenees is a familiar sight in British and American show rings. Far more docile and easygoing than his ancestors or his working cousins in France per se, the pet Pyrenees makes a flawless companion who is gentle and ever so patient with children. His coat, solid protection from the harsh clime of the Pyrenees mountain tops, requires a good deal of brushing to keep in tip-top shape.

ESSENTIALS OF THE GREAT PYRENEES: Wedge-shaped head, v-shaped ears carried close to the head. Little stop with dark eyes. The chest is flat sided and rather deep. The legs heavily boned; the feet closely cupped. Front feet equipped with single dewclaws; the hind, double dewclaws. The white coat of this giant can also be patched with badger, gray, or tan, as is rather common in France and England. Standing as high as 32 inches (81 cm) and weighing from 90–130 pounds (41–59 kg). The medium-long, slightly coarse and undulating coat is equipped with a pure white undercoat. Height at the shoulders should equal height from the shoulder blades to the root of the tail.

Great Spitz
See German Spitzen

Greater Saint John's Dog
See Saint John's Dog

Greater Swedish Elkhound
See Jämthund

Great Pyrenees, white.

Greater Swiss Mountain Dog
A working dog originating in the rugged Swiss Alps, the Greater Swiss is a larger breed than the closely related, though more popular Bernese Mountain Dog. The breed traces its descent to the Alpine Mastiff and has been known to exist since the eighteenth century. The breed was created as a strong and able cart puller, a task at which it was commonly employed. The relation of the Greater Swiss Mountain Dog and the smooth-coated St. Bernard became intertwined as the latter became more popular and the former faded out of favor. Crossbreeding

Greater Swiss Mountain Dog, tricolor. Photographs by I. Français.

to Saints partly explains the large size of the Mountain Dog today. Second of the Sennenhunden only to the Bernese Mountain Dog in popularity, the Greater Swiss has found friends in the United States, where it is recognized, as well as Great Britain and Canada.

Greater Swiss Mountain Dog, pup. Photo by I. Français.

ESSENTIALS OF THE GREATER SWISS MOUNTAIN DOG: The short, shiny weather-resistant coat is of the typical Swiss tricolor: black and tan with white. Weighing as much as 130 pounds (59 kg), the Greater Swiss is the largest of the four Swiss mountain dogs. Height: 23–29 inches (59–74 cm). Rectangular and well put-together, the body is well ribbed with strong loins. The back is flat and not too long. The chest is broad.

Greek Greyhound
See Albanian Greyhound

Greek Harehound
Indigenous to Greece, the Greek Harehound is an ancient breed that shares its root with the Balkan Hound of Yugoslavia. Its extraordinary inclination to hare

has lent itself to high specialization. The dog possesses a fine nose and beautifully resonant voice. Once used specifically as a packhound, the breed is used today in duos or trios. A pleasant and good-willed personality continues to satisfy Greek sportsmen, who will do with no other. He is not known outside his native Greece.

ESSENTIALS OF THE GREEK HAREHOUND: Distinctive for his elongated head and ram-shaped nasal canal, the Greek Harehound stands from 18–22 inches (46–56 cm) high and weighs 38–44 pounds (17–20 kg). The coat is short and coarse and reddish tan in color with black saddle and white markings. The breed has moderate-sized ears and coffee-brown eyes that project an intelligent and alert expression.

Greek Herder
See Spartiate

Greek Sheepdog
The Greek Sheepdog has mastered through the centuries the art of guarding a flock and protecting it from predators of all sorts. This solid white, solid shepherd is solid shepherd, no nonsense, and not a pet. Although in appearance the Greek Sheepdog may look like the Great Pyrenees, Kuvasz, or Maremma Sheepdog, this is not a gentle giant. Greek shepherds who work with these dogs say that they are fearless and feared by any intelligent creature on two or four legs. These shepherds also have continued an ear cropping practice peculiar to the breed. According to their forefathers' tales, cropping the right ear of the dog would improve its hearing (which was already keen). Whether or not this helps the dogs' hearing, it gives an unbalanced appearance to the head, suggestive of the dog's discordant personality.

Some speculation leads cynologists to believe that the breed's similarities to the Akbash Dog of Turkey is no coincidence as migrators from Turkey likely brought their sheepdogs with them as they traversed the land. This is not to say that the Akbash Dog begot the Greek Sheepdog but that years of breeding with local and semilocal stock likely produced the Greek breed. The dog today is used strictly as a working dog and is never kept as a pet. A log is sometimes attached to the dog's collar to curb its energy and potential viciousness.

ESSENTIALS OF THE GREEK SHEEPDOG: Coat: solid white. The body is sound and muscular. The chest is deep and the legs heavily boned. Weight: 75–100 pounds (34–45 kg). Height: 25–28 inches (63.5–71 cm). The Greek Sheepdog traditionally has its right ear cropped.

enabled them to locate seals' breathing holes in the ice. The Grønlandshund, as he is also known, is strictly a work dog and not kept frequently as a pet. Its personality is not as people-oriented as many of the nordic and spitz breeds. Pack dogs, especially, never given the opportunity to establish a personal relation with the lead human, must show their loyalty and even affection in their unstinting work ethic.

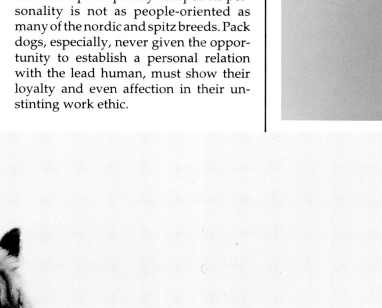

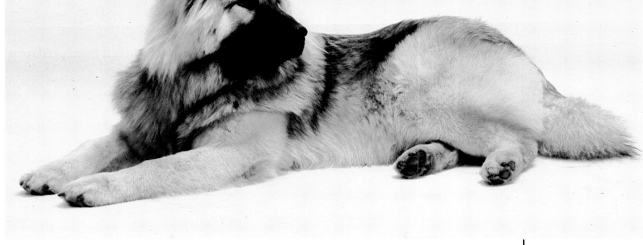

Greenland Dog

Recognized today as an individual breed, the Greenland Dog represents the standard working "husky-type" dog. It is one of the nordic hauling breeds that has survived until the current day. Modern innovations on the ice-laden landscape (snowmobiles and other mechanically propelled vehicles) have broached the disappearance of dozens of husky varieties. Even today, with the dedicated efforts of concerned individuals, the Greenland Dog is not populous in its native Greenland. The dogs' employment in Greenland included sledge work as well as hunting. The dogs' keen noses

ESSENTIALS OF THE GREENLAND DOG: The Greenland Dog is a powerful polar spitz, built for endurance at arduous and strenuous work as a sledge dog in arctic conditions. The head is broad and slightly domed; the stop pronounced though not abrupt. Muzzle wedge-shaped and strong. The ears are rather small and triangular, rounded at the tips, carried erect. A muscular body, well defined and rigorous, it is higher at the withers than it is long. Chest very capacious; back straight; loins straight and broad; croup slightly sloping. The profuse hard coat should be double. Tail fully plumed, curled over the back.

Greenland Dog, gray. Photo by I. Français.

Height: up to 25 inches (64 cm). Weight: at least 66 pounds (39.5 kg). Members of the breed can be any color: white, gray, or black, and a little tan in any proportion.

Greyhound

1) Used generically as a synonym for sighthound. *See also* Sighthounds, Borzoi, Afghan Hound, etc.

2) The "speed merchant" of the canine world, the Greyhound was designed for the specific task of running. The hunting Greyhound needed to be fast and strong enough to course the fleetest of running quarry, regardless of size, and overtake it. This sometimes required the dog to change directions at maximum speeds—a task impossible for any dog or other animal that was not expressly designed for speed.

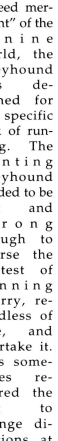

Greyhound, brindle. Photo by I. Français.

The breed's eyesight and speed are surely proverbial—eyes is to Greyhound as nose is to Bloodhound is a cynologist's easiest analogy.

By speed and sight did the Greyhound overtake its prey, without relying on doggedly tracking it down. The breed, isolated by the treeless expanse of open desert, was able to ingrain exactitude of type with no interference from other dogs. The Arabs, thus, are the originators of the dogs we know as Greyhounds.

The Greyhound was among the highest favored of all dogs: the pharaohs and other ancient Egyptian, African and Asian leaders had images of their Greyhounds engraved into their tombs and bas reliefs. Additionally, etchings, paintings and drawings were frequently commissioned by the wealthy who owned and greatly favored the Greyhound. In 1016, only the elite were permitted to own a Greyhound, as the Canute Law edicted: "No meane person may keep any greyhounds." Of course the law was redundant since no *meane* person could afford a *greyhound*, which rivalled the cost of a serf.

The Greyhound's movement from its Arab origins can be traced through North Africa to Greece, then to Gaul and finally England. In the course of this geographic movement over time, development and crosses changed the Greyhound prototype. The Saluki, Ellenikos Ichnilatis or Greek Greyhound, Persian Greyhound, and Chinese Greyhound participated in this Greyhound evolutionary process, affecting or being affected. Egypt, China, and Persia (Iran) are other countries through which the Greyhound moved. The Greyhound's role in the creation of the world's sighthounds is unparalleled by any other running canine.

The development of the Greyhound, to a large extent unhampered by man, yielded the world one of the most perfect animals to dwell among us. As a historical note and an illustration of man's incurable dissatisfaction and quest to perfect the already perfect, an eighteenth-century breeder (and rather bad playwright) named Lord Orford decided that he should develop a *faster* Greyhound. His theory, soon put into practice, included the infusion of Bulldog blood to increase the Greyhound's persistence. Orford was impressed by the pit Bulldog and its unyielding determination in the fight. Other dogs such as the Scottish Deerhound, Lurcher, and Italian Greyhound were also used.

Orford's theory proved effective, despite the absurdity it initially invoked. Dogs from Orford's programs were promoted as the fastest and sturdiest of running dogs. Races and coursing events were used to prove the superiority and prowess of Orford's dogs over pure Greyhounds. The undefeated "Czarina" was Orford's favorite cross. At age thirteen, Czarina whelped her first litter. "Snowball" we know was a male; we do not know whether he was white or black, nor if he was truly a great dog. Some believe that Snowball and his brother "Major" are the sole stud source for the lot of Great Britain's Greyhounds. The appellation Snowball became the stamp of excellent work. Other great early Greyhounds included Fiery Furnace, Father Flint, Mutton Cutlet, Smutty Face, Mingo, Beaded Brow, Latto and My Jim. Hutchinson's

Greyhound, white with brindle. Photo by Gilbert.

Greyhound in motion. Photo by R. Pearcy.

Chart of the Greyhound traces the earliest of British Greyhounds.

For centuries, the Greyhound coursed large game: antelope, wolves, and deer. Rabbit, however, was never its primary prey. The "sport" of coursing hares developed and was certainly a dubious one. Actually, its initial purpose was to entertain the dog's owners and his friends, none of whom wanted to dine on the kill. As a matter of fact, it became no more than a matter of killing rabbits, since the owners could never tell which dog reached and killed the rabbit first. The senseless slaughter of rabbits, as these coursing events had become, were often sponsored and attended by the king and his court. The British townsfolk and their clubs supported similar outings. Whether the Greyhounds chased live hares in open or closed areas, or whether the Greyhounds chased decoy rabbits around a said track, the sport's popularity waned through the years, following the trends and such.

And yet Greyhounds remain a noble breed, despite their having to engage in the mindless diversion of men. Dog races are still held in the U.S. and Britain. Some

seems a common sight—one immediately associated with racing and great speed (be they dogs or buses). It is a shame, however, that in America as well as England, the breed's pet qualities have been disregarded. Despite the Greyhound's tremendous size (which precludes many small-home dwellers from adopting a Greyhound), the breed is an affectionate and expressive dog. This is a gentle and loving companion animal. In order to maintain his health, adequate space and suitable exercise are essential.

ESSENTIALS OF THE GREYHOUND: Generously proportioned and upstanding, the Greyhound is strongly built, symmetrical and powerful. The head is long, with a flat skull and slight stop; the jaws powerful and well chiseled; teeth set in a complete scissor bite; eyes bright, oval, and obliquely set; and the ears small, rose shaped and of fine texture. The neck is long and muscular; the shoulders are clean and well laid back, muscular without being loaded; elbows free and set well under the shoulders. The chest is deep and capacious; the ribs deep, well sprung, and carried well back. The body and hindquarters feature ample propor-

Greyhound placing in the World Dog Show 1988. Photo by I. Français.

Greyhound, brindle. Photo by I. Français.

organizations established to find homes for retired running Greyhounds are working to prevent these proud performance athletes from being senselessly destroyed. In America, the Greyhound

tions and are well coupled to enable good ground to be covered in a stance. Hindquarters to show great propelling power; loin arched; stifles well bent; hocks well let down. The tail is long, set rather low, strong at root, tapering to a point, and carried low, slightly curved. There is definite suppleness of limb, which emphasizes in a marked degree the distinctive type and quality of the Greyhound. The body is capacious, with an arched loin and powerful quarters. The lengthy legs and feet are sound and supple, ever important to the dog's traditional function. The coat is short and smooth, fine and close, and can be colored in any shade, solid or brindle. Height: 27–30 inches (68–76 cm). Weight: 60–70 pounds (27–31.5 kg).

Greyhound Braque
See Braque Dupuy

Griffon
French term which refers to the wirehaired or rough-coated scenthounds. From the word *greffier*, meaning clerk, "griffon" indicated clerk's dog. *See* Petit Basset Griffon Vendeen, Griffon, Fauve de Bretagne, Griffon Nivernais, Griffon Vendeen

Griffon Belge
See Belgian Griffon

Griffon Bruxellois
See Brussels Griffon

Griffon d'Arret a Poil Laineux
See Barbet

Griffon Fauve de Bretagne
In a tawny and tousled coat, the Griffon Fauve de Bretagne is a long-time member of the French pack of scenthounds. The breed was developed by the sheepmen of Brittany to track wolves that threatened grazing flocks on the peninsula. This wirehaired, robust hound proved too smart and able for its own good: by the late 1800s the threat of sheep-chomping wolves in Brittany was minimal, and the dogs became a non-essential to the flock keepers.

The restoration of the breed occurred years after the fall of the Brittany wolf, and local wirehaired hounds with desirable traits, as well as Vendeen hounds were employed to save/recreate the breed. Today's breed closely resembles the medium-sized Vendeen hound, the Briquet Griffon Vendeen. The Griffon Fauve de Bretagne is but one of two purebred scenthounds from Brittany, the second was developed from the Griffon

and it is known today as the Basset Fauve de Bretagne. This basset version of the Griffon has a strong following and is recognized in Great Britain as well as France. *See also* Basset Fauve de Bretagne.

ESSENTIALS OF THE GRIFFON FAUVE DE BRETAGNE: In solid shades of wheaten to red, this hardy working hound weighs approximately 44 pounds (26.4 kg) and stands 20–22 inches (50–55 cm). The coat is rough and medium, never long or woolly. The forelegs are straight; the hind somewhat angulated. The head is small, and the ears big and typically hound. The feet are well furred. The chest is wide and deep; the sternum prominent; the ribs slightly barreled. The shoulders are sloping. The tail, set on high, is thick at the base and tapers to a point.

Griffon Fauve de Bretagne, fawn. Photo by I. Français.

Griffon Nivernais

Today's Griffon Nivernais of the Nivernais district of central France was

Griffon Nivernais, black and tan.

Griffon Vendeen, Grand, fawn. Photographs by I. Français.

called Chien Gris de St. Louis (St. Louis's Gray Dog) during the thirteenth century, named after the admiring Louis IX. It is not clear how the breed evolved. Rough-coated sighthounds of Phoenician origin or similar leggy Eastern herders are likely contributors. Whatever the origin, these dogs have remained popular in France through the centuries. Four centuries after Louis IX, the Sun King Louis XIV also favored the Nivernais dogs. A smaller variety known as the Griffon Nivernais de Petite Taille existed at one time but is no longer located. The breed contributed to the gene pool of the original scenthounds. Specifically bred for hunting boar, today they are used in the U.S. and Canada as well as other countries on various quarry, including bear. After the French Revolution, the breed scattered and it required a revival movement around the year 1900 to get the

breed back on its feet. Chien de Pays (Local Dog) was the name chosen for the Nivernais during the revival.

ESSENTIALS OF THE GRIFFON NIVERNAIS: A woolly, rugged coat on a sturdy well-muscled body. Coat on head is well-furnished, including beard, mustache and bushy eyebrows. Height: 21–25 inches (53–64 cm). Weight: 50–55 pounds (22–25 kg). The breed comes in a variety of colors—the preferred color is gray (in varying shades), but black/tan, tawny, fawn, and roan may occur as well.

Griffon Vendeen

The roughhaired scenthounds of the Vendee area are among France's and the world's most ancient strains of packhounds. Four individual breeds today bear the name Griffon Vendeen. The largest of the four, the Grand Griffon Vendeen was originally used to hunt wolf and boar during the fifteenth century. The Briquet Griffon Vendeen is used on hare and hunted in small packs or singly. This medium-sized dog has become more popular as a one-hunter's dog and, unlike the Grand, has a renewed handful of followers. The third breed, the Grand Basset Griffon Vendeen, is the larger of the two basset varieties. Prior to 1950,

both basset varieties occurred in the same litters and the smaller variety, the Petit Basset Griffon Vendeen, was deemed an individual breed. Both basset varieties are used on hare and feathered game. Depending on where you go in France, these breeds can be seen hunting anything from deer and wild boar to pheasant and quail. Today of the four Griffon Vendeen breeds, the Petit Basset is the most popular and is a jaunty home companion. *See* Petit Basset Griffon Vendeen

Crosses of the white Southern Hound (now extinct) and rough coated hounds of Italian origin yielded the Grand Griffon. Later crosses to the Griffon Nivernais, another French wirehaired hound, helped improve type. At one time the breed was called Chien Blanc du Roi or the King's White Hound. For centuries, French kings used the Chien Blanc du Roi in the region of Vendee.

A lesson in etymology: the word *griffon* in French today translates as wirehair but actually derives from the word *greffier* which means clerk. These were *chiens du greffiers* or clerks' dogs because it was they who cared for the king's kennel of hounds.

ESSENTIALS OF THE GRIFFON VENDEEN: Displaying patches of orange, gray, tawny, or black/tan on a bright white background, the Grand Griffon Vendeen can stand as high as 27 inches (69 cm). His coat is wire—hard and rough—never woolly or soft. Weight: 66–77 pounds (30–35 kg). Slightly smaller than the Large is the Briquet Griffon Vendeen (Medium Vendeen Griffon), which stands only about 22 inches (56 cm) tall and weighs no more than 53 pounds (24 kg). The Grand Basset Griffon Vendeen (Large Vendeen Basset) stands 15–16.5 inches and weighs 40–44 pounds. All the Griffon Vendeens possess the same hard and rough coat of like color patterns.

Grizzle

An admixture of black and white hairs creates this color, which is in the blue-

gray/silver-gray neighborhood. G also can contain a degree of red mi with black.

Griffon Vendeen, Briquet, tawny.

Griffon Vendeen, Grand Basset, tricolor. Photographs by I. Français.

Grølandshund
See Greenland Dog

Grooming

Grooming, for health, cleanliness and beauty, benefits your dog. While mud puddles, unexplored basements and fresh topsoil have their charms, dogs generally like to be clean. Dogs clean themselves by rolling in the grass and

dog to grooming is also helpful for his general obedience training.

Dogs' coats can be smooth and short, long and silky, coarse and wiry, medium, medium-short, medium-long, or absent. Each of these variations requires different grooming approaches. The long-haired breeds will need more extensive grooming and brushing than the smoothhaired breeds. The condition of a

Grooming needs vary from breed to breed. Keeping the cords of an adult Komondor clean and untangled requires much time and patience. Photo by I. Français.

licking; they are substantially less consistent and efficient than their feline counterparts. An owner's regular grooming sessions (brushing, nail clipping, wiping the eyes and ears, checking the teeth, and occasionally bathing) are necessary to the dog's general health and happiness. Dogs with well-kept coats are less likely to suffer from external parasites, such as fleas and ticks, which can lead to skin disorders and other problem-causing conditions.

As any owner who has attempted to bathe a previously unbathed six-year-old Mastiff will attest, it is best to begin grooming sessions when the dog is still a puppy. Consistent regular sessions for ten or fifteen minutes will acclimate the puppy to the grooming procedure. Most dogs, properly introduced to grooming, enjoy the attention and treatment they receive during the session. Acclimating a

dog's coat greatly influences the dog's general appearance. While a long-coated show dog may seem ineffably glamorous, a poorly groomed long-coated dog is a monster of a different kind. A badly groomed Beagle or Greyhound certainly looks comparably better than a badly groomed Lhasa Apso or Old English Sheepdog. Longhaired dogs, therefore, must be groomed as frequently as necessary to keep their luxuriant coats looking their best. Wire coats require plucking to remove the dead hair and provide a trim appearance. Smooth coats can be efficiently cared for by using a hound glove, brush or cloth.

Grooming should regularly take place in the same location so that the dog associates the room with the procedure. Setting up a grooming table (a stand made especially for dog grooming) helps to facilitate most dogs ideally. The taller or

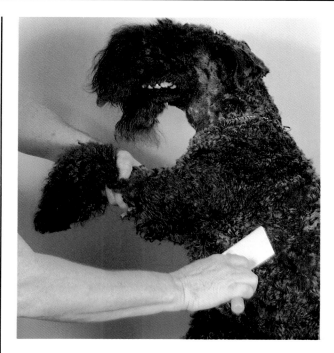

heavier dogs will need to be groomed on the floor or outdoors. Assigning a daily or bi-daily time for grooming will help regulate the dog and remind the owner of his responsibility.

A number of grooming tools are essential. Fortunately, pet shops stock a myriad of grooming accessories and most any product can be obtained there. *See also* Bathing, Nail clipping, Clipping the Poodle, Shedding, Dental care, Plucking, Grooming shows

Grooming posts

Polelike utensils that attach to grooming tables specially designed to secure the dog during grooming. They come in various styles and sizes. If you wish to groom large dogs, the post should be at least 48 inches (122 cm) high in order to give stability when raised to accommodate large dogs. Posts that go through the table (as opposed to those that fasten to the table edge) are most convenient, as you can move freely around the table without bumping into them or catching clipper cords on them. A second post can be attached to the back of the table in order to attach a "belly band" loop. This band prevents the dog from sitting down. Grooming loops should always be nylon and should have a secure lock that is easy to open, but secure enough so that the dog cannot slip out easily.

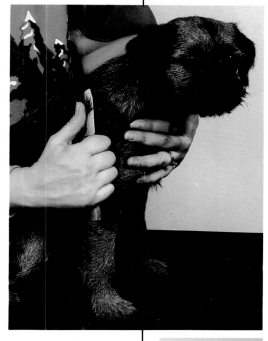

Grooming shows

Grooming shows are becoming increasingly popular. These colorful exhibitions primarily feature Poodles, Bedlington Terriers, and other breeds that lend themselves to creative grooming. The dogs that participate in these shows are assured exclusion from the show ring for some time, depending on the exaggeration of the clip chosen. Some owners choose a particular motif or theme and

Grooming. Slicker brush used on the coat of the Kerry Blue Terrier to remove dead hair and for purposes of dematting.

Grooming. Stripping knife used for upkeep on the coat of the Border Terrier.

Grooming. Pin brush used on long-coated breeds such as this English Cocker Spaniel. Photographs by I. Français.

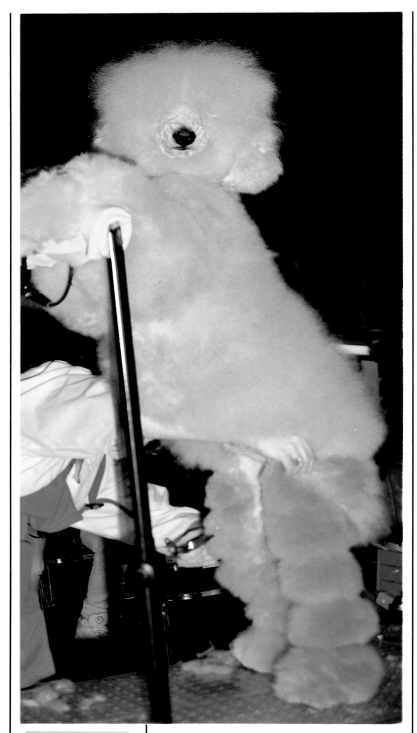

Grooming shows are a favorite of Poodle fanciers. This Standard Poodle impersonates a renowned Sesame Street® character. Photo by I. Français.

the dogs don't seem to mind the attention, many of the participants look less than dignified. *See also* Clipping the Poodle, Grooming

Grooming table

Standard grooming tables are 24 inches x 36 inches (61 cm x 91 cm); however, there are smaller tables, which measure a third less. If you are not grooming large dogs, use the smaller table. Some dogs behave better if they do not have a lot of room to dance around on. All tables should have a top made of rubber or some other non-skid material that is easy to disinfect.

Grosser Münsterländer Vorstehhund
See Large Münsterländer

Grosser Schweizer Sennenhund
See Greater Swiss Mountain Dog

Ground scent

The scent left by game on the ground or bushes, weeds and grasses as it moves about through them.

Group systems

The American Kennel Club and the Kennel Club of Great Britain each possess individual systems of grouping the dogs that they register. The British system relies principally on two major distinctions: Sporting and Non-Sporting, into which the six groups are divided. Under Sporting, the club includes the Hound Group, the Gun Dog Group, and the Terrier Group; under Non-Sporting, the Utility Group, the Working Group and the Toy Group.

The American Kennel Club uses similar group names but organizes somewhat differently. The A.K.C. divides its breeds into seven groups. The Sporting Group contains the hunting dogs: pointers, setters, spaniels (including the Brittany) and retrievers. In the British registry, these hunting breeds are called Gun Dogs. The Hound Group, like the British group, contains both the scenthounds (Beagles, Bassets, Bloodhounds) as well as the sighthounds (Borzois, Whippets, Greyhounds). The Working Group contains the police, guard and protection dogs, the draft dogs, and other

dress the dog (and themselves) to follow that idea. Some of the more memorable examples are carousel horses, unicorns, and celebrities. Various accessories and dyes may be involved in elaborate grooming procedures. Many feel that these shows are demeaning to the animals involved and only function to amuse the owners and spectators. While

medium–large-sized dogs with definite working abilities. The fourth group is the Terrier Group, fired by both short-legged and long-legged terrriers; this group also coincides with the British. The Toy Group contains all the potential lap and pillow dogs, including the Shih Tzu, who is grouped in the Utility Group of the K.C.G.B. The A.K.C. Non-Sporting Group, the sixth, coincides with the Kennel Club's Utility Group. While it is usually meaningless to define something by what it is not, the Non-Sporting Group is comprised of the dogs that do *not* fit into the other six categories; these breeds are versatile and exceptional as companion dogs. The last group and most recent installation is the Herding Group, which consists of the herding dogs, breeds which, in England, are placed in the Working Group.

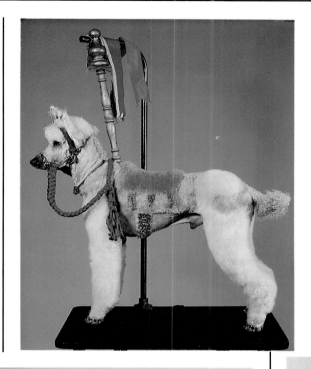

The Fédération Cynologique Internationale divides its dogs into ten groups: Shepherd Dogs; Watchdogs and Working Dogs; Terriers; Dachshunds; Hounds for Big Game; Hounds for Small Game; Pointers; British Gun Dogs; Fancy Dogs; and Greyhounds. Since the F.C.I. must categorize over three times the number of dogs as either the A.K.C. or the K.C.G.B., the above, more-specialized system meets their needs.

The Australian National Kennel Council, the Singapore Kennel Club, and the Kennel Union of South Africa share the same group system as the Kennel Club of

Grooming shows. Poodles remaining diverting and dignified, considering the costumes and props: pedigree pooches disguised for carousel ride, vacation in the tropics, and the set of a famous educational children's program. Photographs by I. Français.

Great Britain. The Canadian Kennel Club adhered to the group system of the A.K.C. until the Herding Group was established in 1983. All dogs in the Herding Group were previously shown in the Working Group, where these breeds reside in Canada today.

Growling

A dog's way of vocalizing a threat—a subtle but communicating warning. Often accompanied by intensive staring and the flashing of jowls. *See* Canine behavior

Gruff expression

See Expression

Guard dog

Any dog kept for the protection of person and property. There is a distinction between a guard dog and a watchdog: a guard dog not only watches and alerts but also threatens the intruder to the point of retreat or combat; a watchdog simply watches the home and alerts others to the intruder by barking. While the watchdog may possess the physical ability to stop an intruder, it typically is not of the temperament to do so.

Guard dogs can be categorized into two general groups: home guardians and professional guardians. Some home guardians are professionally trained, but most are simply trained by their owners, who rely heavily on the dog's instincts, which should include a dominant temperament, a wariness of strangers, territorialism, and a natural inclination to protect. Breeds that have proven suitable as home guardians include: the Bouvier des Flandres, Bull Terrier, Bullmastiff, Doberman Pinscher, German Shepherd Dog, Giant Schnauzer, and Rottweiler, which are but a few of the many breeds suited for home guard work. In short, many of the mastiff and flock guardian breeds excel at the task of home protection.

Most professional guard dogs are highly trained to perform their given role. Professional guard dogs include those employed by factories and warehouses, shopping malls and department stores, banks and security services. Dogs employed by the police and military can also be labeled as professional guardians,

Guard dog. A properly trained Rottweiler serves as an imposing and confident guardian of home and property. Photo by. DiBenedetto.

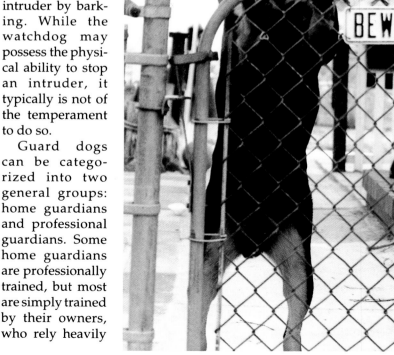

but their tasks are often more varied and/or highly specialized than most other professional guardians, i.e., bomb and drug scenting, search and rescue, etc. Professional guardians are typically obedient to one master only, who is responsible for feeding and caring for the dog in all ways. These dogs will not accept food from strangers and will tolerate another person only if the master's tone and command suggest that all is well. Professional guard dogs are usually trained to attack on command and fight until the opponent quits struggling.

For owners who want a truly effective and reliable guard dog, it is recommended that they not leave their quest to chance. By contacting breeders and owners of their desired breed, potential owners can better decide if a given dog is the breed for them. Reading up on the demands of guard duty and training and comparing these requisites to the temperament and physical abilities of their prospective breed, owners can better make an educated selection of a truly worthy home guardian. Also, training a dog to be effective at guard work should not be left to the unknowing. Improper training can lead to a useless animal at best, a vicious one at worst. Many a poorly trained guardian has turned on its owner or trainer, and many a one has attacked an innocent member of the family or a welcome guest.

Above all, a guard dog must be discriminating; he must correctly perceive danger and act accordingly. A guard dog must also be extremely obedient to members of his human family, both defending and ceasing attack upon command. Training a dog to this degree often requires the assistance and advice of a professional trainer. Perhaps the surest ways of attaining a quality guard dog are choosing a member of a breed that best suits your personality and attending training classes together. A properly trained dog is an unbeatable companion and protector, but an improperly trained one is nothing but a nuisance and a threat to all who come near him.

Guard dog. Akitas require professional training in order to function as effective guard dogs. While the dogs possess the size and power desirable in such a protector, Akitas are equally headstrong and aloof, and therefore need proper channeling of their abilities.

Guard hairs

The longer, smoother, stiffer hairs that grow through the undercoat and normally conceal it.

Gums

Gums in dogs, like gums in humans, are formed by the mucous membrane and the underlying tissues that cover the bony sockets of the teeth and the neck of erupting teeth. Gums and teeth can be at the root of many canine diseases, mostly gingivitis and pyorrhea or pyorrhea alveolaris.

Gingivitis is an acute or chronic inflammation of the gums; it is characterized by congestion and swelling. It is more often caused by local irritation, by spread of infection from other mouth areas, or a secondary result of systemic disease. Plaque and calculus are the most common local causes; others include

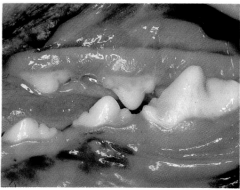

physical trauma, foreign bodies, dental caries, and irritation caused by broken teeth. Likewise, most diseases of the mouth also cause gingivitis as a result of the inflammation. Simple gingivitis can be diagnosed by a narrow bright red band around the neck of the tooth. The gums will be tender and bleed easily, if probed. Enlarged, spongy gums and the presence of pus are signs of the condition. Gingivitis must be treated by a veterinarian; if ignored, it will cause the gums to become more swollen, leading to ulcerate subgingivitis and hypertrophy.

Pyorrhea alveolaris is a condition characterized by the formation of a slowly developing exostosis at the root of an affected tooth. Such a condition greatly hinders the extraction of the tooth. *See* Periodontitis.

Care of the dog's gums, of course, cannot be divorced from the care of its teeth. Owners need to address themselves to providing the right kinds of

canine products to assist in the cleaning and maintaining of their dog's teeth and gums. Simulated chew bones, more so than natural chew bones and rawhide, provide the necessary regular stimulation for the gums to keep them clean and free from food decay, which eventually leads to the two conditions discussed. *See also* Dental care, Nylon bones

Gun barrel front

Parallel and straight, the forearms and pasterns are positioned vertically. Same as true for straight front.

Gundog field trials

See Field trials

Gun Dog Group

The Gun Dog Group of the Kennel Club of Great Britain categorizes those dogs which hunt from the gun; these are almost exclusively feather hunters. These setters, pointers, spaniels and retrievers are categorized in the Sporting Group in the U.S. Nevertheless, they are the same multi-talented, ever-popular gundogs. *See* Sporting Group, Group systems, Gundogs

Gundogs

The term gundog refers to any breed of dog that works from the hunter's gun. The gundog breeds are often divided into five subgroups: pointers, retrievers, water dogs, flushing spaniels, and setters. These subgroups, however, serve only as a guideline, since many, many of the gundogs cross over subgroup lines. The European pointers, for example, were bred not just to point but also to work in the water, to work cover, to track wounded birds by land and by water,

and to retrieve. Examples of these multi-faceted canines are France's Braque Français and Braque d'Auvergne, Italy's Bracco Italiano and Spinone Italiano, Spain's Perdiguero Navarro, and Germany's Weimaraner and Pudelpointer. The Pointer, a.k.a. the English Pointer, is not nearly as versatile as any of the above since it was developed for the specialized task of pointing only. Its name Pointer is therefore most fitting.

Retrieving gundogs are dogs such as the well-known Golden Retriever and Labrador Retriever that were developed to retrieve felled feather. Since many retrievers were required to retrieve from water, the difference between retrievers and water dogs is difficult to discern. Water dogs differ in their coat type more so than in their ability. A water dog's coat is typically curly and heavy—coats belonging to the Poodles and Portuguese Water Dog are exemplary of the water-dog coat. It is difficult to understand at first how a dog like the Labrador Retriever, with his *webbed* feet, is not among the water dogs, likewise the passionately water-bound Chesapeake *Bay* Retriever and the Nova Scotia Duck Tolling Retriever. Similarly, the Curly-Coated *Retriever* is among the water dogs. Nonetheless, the body types and coat types especially differentiate the two subgroups. The small bichon types, with their curly coats, also represent the water dog type.

The setter gundogs are distinguished by their long fringed tails and feathering. The term setter preceded the term spaniel; the early setters were characterized by their crouching hunting style. Such early setters contributed to the gene pool of both our contemporary setters and spaniels. The flushing spaniels were developed from setters and are in reality setters with pointing abilities. Flushing is defined as springing birds from cover. Great Britain deserves almost all credit for the family of flushers. With the exception of the American Cocker and a couple of crossbreeds from British breeds, the flushers are entirely British. Among them: the English Cocker, the Clumber, Sussex and Field Spaniels, and the English and Welsh Springers. The British also excelled at miniaturizing many of these spaniel types: the King Charles Spaniel and the more outgoing Cavalier King Charles Spaniel. France's Papillon and Phalene Continental Toy Spaniel were also conceived from similar elegant notions.

Gundogs. The Weimaraner is one of the most versatile of gundogs, able to retrieve, track, point, and flush. This winner Weimaraner holds a retrieved ground bird.

Gundogs. The handsome English Springer Spaniel is essentially a setter with pointing abilities. Photo by I. Français.

Gundogs. The instincts of gundogs remain strong even today. While the Golden Retriever contends as a pet and companion animal, it is still effectively used by hunters. This obedient Golden has retrieved a downed ringneck pheasant to its master.

The gundogs are without a doubt the most intelligent of all dog types; additionally they are generally acknowledged as the most handsome and genuine, explaining their enormous popularity in the United States and the world over. Sitting high at the top of A.K.C. registration stats, jousting for the tippy top spots are the Poodle, Cocker Spaniel, Labrador Retriever, and Golden Retriever.

Even so, many of the lesser known gundog breeds are inordinately deserving of the attention of more purebred fanciers. Among them: the Nova Scotia Duck Toller (of Canada), Chesapeake Bay Retriever (of America), Portuguese Water Dog, Kooikerhondje (of the Netherlands) and a favorite handsome Frenchman that is finally growing in numbers, the Braque du Bourbonnais.

Gyp
Female racing Greyhound.

Gundogs in training. These young Chesapeake Bay Retrievers are playing fetch with their owner on the shore of a lake. Photo by R. Reagan.

Gundogs are truly smart, even tricky. The Nova Scotia Duck Tolling Retriever's trademark method of luring ducks to shore is as unique as it is ingenious.

Hacking

Overhandling by giving repeated commands, usually of a type that inhibits a dog's work instead of leaving him to his own initiative.

Hackles

Hair on the neck and back raised involuntarily in anger or fear.

Hackney gait

High lifting of the forefeet in the manner of a hackney pony. Deep shoulder angulation and upright pasterns facilitate this movement that is usually considered abnormal. The Italian Greyhound, for one, requires this type of gait even though it is generally an undesirable energy-consuming motion that can ensure little endurance.

Hair

Hair makes up a dog's coat. Hairs are fine, threadlike outgrowths through the skin from follicles. The follicles have little erector muscles within them which can cause the dog's hair to stand up straight. *See also* Coat, Coat types

Hair, fall of

Longer hair on the top of the head that fringes and falls forward over the face, eyes, and/or ears (e.g., Yorkshire Terrier). *See also* Veil

Hairless dogs

Hairless dogs have long been associated with the species *Canis africanis*, a type of coatless dog that developed in the North African/Middle Eastern area. The Abyssinian Sand Dog (also known as the African Sand Dog) is one such ancient African dweller. Not long ago, the hairless dogs were considered but mutations, not constituting a veritable breed. Of the existent hairless breeds, only one breed, the American Hairless Terrier, has been selectively bred for the hairless trait. Other hairless breeds carry the hairless gene which is a dominant lethal gene. Dogs are born heterozygous, able to produce both hairless and coated progeny. Hairless dogs tend to have missing premolars and sometimes eyeteeth. The coated variety is known as powderpuff, in the Chinese Crested. The coated variety (the non-mutant progeny) therefore does not suffer from these dental abnormalities and is necessary in perpetuating the breed. Hairless dog to hairless dog matings usually result in stillborns or pups with severe abnormalities because the offspring is not ensured to receive the necessary recessive gene for coat. Theoretically the American Hairless Terrier does not possess a lethal gene and its progeny are homozygous and may produce hairless dogs; therefore, no coated variety, as such, is necessary. Of course, the Rat Terrier, from whom the American Hairless was developed, can be considered the coated variety, although the hairless breed is flourishing without intervention of their coated cousins.

Hairless dogs have occurred in the Middle East and North African areas for centuries. Some extinct hairless types include the African Sand Dog; African Elephant Dog; Small African Greyhound; Turkish Hairless Dog; Guatemalan Hairless; and Nubian Dog. Among the breeds that exist today are the Chinese Crested; Mexican Hairless; Peruvian Inca Orchid; Inca Hairless Dog; and Xoloitzcuintli, which *see*.

Halden Hound

See Haldenstövare

Haldenstövare

The Haldenstövare of Norway is named for the town of Halden in the southeastern corner of that country. The breed's roots are implanted in the scenthounds (especially foxhounds) of various European countries. It still, however, possesses a distinguishing appearance unlike any other recognized hound and has been deemed purely Norwegian. This is a hound of remarkable scenting ability, so proficient that it can work by itself on the varying game of Norway. Like most of the other Scandinavian *stövare*, the Halden Hound does not work in packs and is able to rough it over the most rigorous of terrains. Speed is another of the Halden Hound's strong points. Not popular outside Norway, the Haldenstövare is a trustworthy companion and a most competent hunting dog.

ESSENTIALS OF THE HALDENSTÖVARE: This deeply chested, able-bodied hound possesses a distinctive tricolor coat: a short, shiny jacket of predominating white blotched by black spots and brown shadings. Height: 20–25 inches (51–64 cm). Weight: 45–60 pounds (20–27 kg). The dog's feet are specialized to amble it through treacherous Norwegian terrain.

Hallmarks

Physical trait expressly identified with a breed. Examples of hallmarks in the purebred world include the spectacles on the Keeshond, the saddle on the Afghan Hound, the warts on the Azawakh, the kissing spot on the Blenheim variety of the Cavalier King Charles Spaniel and the spots of the Dalmatian.

Hallstromi Dingo

See New Guinea Singing Dog

Halo

The dark skin that surrounds the eyes of the Bichon Frise. These are usually black, circular and rather narrow and are key to capturing the breed's typical eye expression.

Hamilton Hound

See Hamiltonstövare

Hamiltonstövare

The Hamiltonstövare was developed in the late nineteenth century by Count A.P. Hamilton in an attempt to achieve the superlative working hound. Hamil-

Hamiltonstövare, tricolor. Photo by I. Français.

ton crossed his English foxhounds with three Germanic dogs of noteworthy ability, the Curlandish Hound, the Hölsteiner Hound, and the Heiderbracke. Hamilton Hounds are hunted singly and possess many universal hunting dog qualities, as they are able to trail, flush, and bay upon finding the wounded quarry. The snow-covered forests of Sweden do not deter his superb abilities. In its native Sweden, the Hamilton Hound is among the most popular and populous hunting dogs; it has also done well in the show world. When these dogs were originally imported into Britain, they were erroneously called Swedish Foxhounds. Today the Hamiltonstövare is recognized by the Kennel Club of Great Britain (by its appropriate name).

ESSENTIALS OF THE HAMILTONSTÖVARE: This sleek tricolor foxhound boasts a rather long and elegant head, with ears that lie flatly and are not too pendant. He is robust and hardy. His possessions include: deep chest, well-tucked flanks, and high-toed feet. The coat is double, becoming thicker as the Swedish winter approaches. His musculature and composition are clean in appearance. Height: 20–24 inches (51–61 cm). Weight: 50–60 pounds (22–27 kg).

Hams

Muscular groupings on the upper thigh (from the hip to the stifle). In some breed standards, the term hams is loosely applied to incorporate both the upper and lower thighs.

Handlers may specialize in a breed or a group. Seen gaiting this Best in Show Doberman Pinscher is professional handler Carlos Rojas. Champion Warwick's Zanuck of Chalmar is owned by M. Jacobson and M.J. Lewis. Photo by Mack.

Handicapper

One who classifies or grades dogs according to their racing ability; one who makes selections.

Handle bar

Topmost portion at the rear of the sled which the driver holds.

Handler

A handler is the person who is at the human end of the leash while the dog is in the show ring. The handler may or may not be the owner. Likely, if the handler is not the owner, he is a professional handler, one who is paid to handle other people's dogs. Much of the dog's performance in the show ring is dependent upon the experience and know-how of the handler. Though not in the U.S., handlers in some places can be licensed by the national kennel club and expected to meet certain minimum requirements.

Hanging ears

See Drop ears

Hannoverscher Schweisshund

See Hanoverian Hound

Hanoverian Hound

The Hanoverian Hound or the Hannoverscher Schweisshund was developed in Hanover, Upper Saxony, in the nineteenth century. The city gameskeepers crossed lighter Celtic dogs from the Harz mountain regions with heavy tracking dogs of St. Hubert type to yield the Hannoverscher Schweisshund. A schweisshund is a hound that is a blood tracker: when the game is hit, the schweisshund follows it until it falls, then leads the hunter to the animal.

Today these dogs are used mostly as tracking dogs, and they are praised for their unfaltering noses. At tracking, the Hanoverian is far superior to the best of gundogs trained for the purpose. Many times when a German Shorthair or a similarly competent hunter is unable to follow a week-old trail, the Hanoverian is commissioned to bring the quarry home.

Not recommended for non-hunters, the Hanoverian is a dedicated sportsman who requires an equally committed human enthusiast. As a solely companion animal, the Hanoverian is not a likely candidate and will probably never be.

ESSENTIALS OF THE HANOVERIAN HOUND: Low on leg and somewhat heavy, the Hanoverian is essentially a medium–large-sized dog that is thick in appearance. The head carries its large, stiff ears high. Height: 24–27 inches (51–61 cm). Weight: 84–99 pounds (38–45 kg). His chest is large and round, and his build is thicker than that of many of his hound brothers. Colors vary in shades of red, with streaks of black creating a brindling effect. Dogs occur with and without black masks.

Happa Dog

Once a short-coated variety of the Pekingese, also from China. The dogs, said to resemble tiny bulldog types, were first exhibited in England in 1907. Little is known or heard of these dogs and they have quietly passed into obscurity.

Hard-driving action

Undesirable action that is not free and easy but rather jerky and exaggeratedly forceful and determined, consuming a great deal of energy.

Hard mouth

The type of carry that is undesirable in a gundog; opposite to soft mouth, such a hold disfigures a fowl, rendering it inedible (by humans).

Harder's gland

A small gland of the eye that becomes visible as a small piece of red flesh when the third eyelid is enlarged. *See* Cherry eye

Hardpad

A condition in which the dog's foot pads become very hard. Other signs of the condition resemble those of distemper. The condition can be prevented through the appropriate distemper inoculations. Dogs that survive the condition will drop off their hardened pads. *See also* Distemper

Hare

White/gray/black/brown admixture of hairs. Color common in hounds (e.g., Basset Griffon Vendeen). *See* Badger

Hare feet

Center toes are more than a hair longer than the outer toes, giving the foot a rabbitlike appearance—longer, with unarched toes.

Hare Indian Dog

Possibly a relation to Canada's Tahltan Bear Dog, the Hare Indian Dog was a sledge dog of North America that also doubled as a hunter for the Indians who kept it.

Harehound

A hound used principally on hare.

Harelip

Congenital defect resulting in incorrectly formed lips, usually occurring at the junction of the maxilla and premaxilla. It can vary in degree and affect the upper and/or lower lip. Known also as cleft lip and, medically, as cheiloschisis, harelip often occurs in conjunction with

cleft palate, and both are believed to be passed hereditarily, although nutrition, stress, and drugs can also be contributing factors. Depending on its degree, harelip may be surgically corrected.

Hark forward

A huntsman's cheer to encourage his hounds to work forward.

Harking in

The action by one member of a brace of hounds in joining a bracemate that has started game and given voice.

Harlekinpinscher

See Harlequin Pinscher

Hanoverian Hound, brindle. Photo by I. Français.

Harlequin
coloration on the
Great Dane.

Harlequin

Pied color pattern of black or blue-gray on a white background. The color patches are usually of like sizes and appear ragged. The harlequin Great Dane is an example of a dog that is harlequin

through and through whereas the saddle of the Dunker and Russian Harlequin Hound are harlequin while the body is colored otherwise.

Harlequin Pinscher

The Harlequin Pinscher developed from selected smaller Pinschers (Standard Pinschers) specifically for their harlequin coloration. Merle-colored dogs were occurring in certain litters of Pinschers. Since the dominant gene is not existent normally in the Pinscher, a cross to another dog must have introduced it. The Berger des Pyrenees or Shetland Sheepdog are possible contributors since both carry the dominant gene. A number of other small herding dogs and small hounds also carry the gene; few if any terriers do. The Harlequins were promoted as companion animals with distinctive esthetic highlights. The breed is extant in Germany although not terribly popular. He makes a fine home companion.

ESSENTIALS OF THE HARLE-QUIN PINSCHER: Well muscled and dry, the Harlequin's

body is square without a cobby appearance detracting from its elegant lines. A sufficiently deep chest and a slightly tucked belly give the dog a brawny but sleek appearance. Height: 12–14 inches (30.5–35.5 cm). Weight 22–26 pounds (10–11.5 kg). Its short smooth coat is spotted gray, or black, or dark on a white or clear ground, with or without tan markings. Like most other pinschers, the ears are cropped to a point and the high-set tail is docked.

Harness

The canvas or nylon webbing that covers the dog and is attached to the lines.

Harrier

The original West County Harrier was begot by skillfully combining the Beagle with the St. Hubert Hound. Harriers are believed to date back to the thirteenth century at least. Many Harriers, not necessarily from West County, were brought to the U.S. during the turn of the nineteenth century. In the early twentieth

Harrier, tricolor.
Photo courtesy
B.M. Burnell.

century, however, there was one single pack of Harriers reportedly left in West County, England. In order to preserve the type, locals crossed in the Foxhound with the existing true specimens. This addition of Foxhound blood made this slower, medium-sized dog considerably faster. Hare is his natural quarry, and hare hunting antecedes even stag hunting in Britain. Some packs of Harriers were used alternately on hare and fox. Although the Harrier's popularity has been hindered by its slightly larger relative the English Foxhound, the breed enjoys its moderate status. Despite their strong natural instincts, the Harriers make fine home companions (especially for country dwellers) and are recommended for non-hunters and sportsmen alike. Like their Foxhound cousins, Harriers tend to bond more with their fellow canines than with their human acquaintances; this is attributed to their many generations of pack existence.

ESSENTIALS OF THE HARRIER: This well-balanced, active, medium-sized foxhound comes in a full range of hound colors, although tricolors are most common. He is full of strength and quality. The level back, deep chest, and marvelously proportioned head mounted on a neck of ample length give this hound a sturdy, competent appearance. The shoulders slope into the muscles of the back, clean and not loaded on the withers. Ribs deep, well sprung. Deep chest with plenty of heart room. His square stance is supported by his straight legs and round catlike feet. Height: 19–22 inches (48–56 cm). Weight: 48–60 pounds (21–27 kg).

Hatzruede

The Hatzruede, which translates as dog used for the chase, is believed by some to be a forerunner of the Great Dane. These dogs replaced the ancient Chiens de Combat and were popular German forest hunters during the Middle Ages: wild boar, bear and wolf were among its quarry. Laws dating back to the seventh century refer to the Boarhound (*Canis porcatorius*), and reliefs from the twelfth century show Hatzrueden heads. The dogs occurred in

both Germany and England. In England, the Hatzrueden are believed to have resulted from Mastiff/Irish Wolfhound crosses.

Hauling

A shepherding term that refers to the dog's bringing in the sheep.

Haunch

Muscular development surrounding the loin and leg.

Haunch bones

Hip bones or ilium.

Harrier
photographed by
I. Français.

Haut-Poitou
See Poitevin

Havana Silk Dog
See Havanese

Havanese

The Havanese is a member of the bichon family. His coat, construction, and jaunty manner all point to the little white dogs so popular with the Spanish centuries ago. These dogs probably found their way with the Spanish settlers of Cuba, where the breed attained a certain distinctiveness from the other bichons. The breed has been facing a crisis through the 1900s but is presently on the rise in popularity, having some dedicated breed enthusiasts who are actively campaigning for its preservation in the U.S.A. In 1991, the breed was accepted by the United Kennel Club.

ESSENTIALS OF THE HAVANESE: Never primped, clipped or altered in any way, the Havanese gives a rugged impression in a diminutive dog. The breed stands 8–11 inches (20–28 cm) high and is nearly square in build. Weight: 7–12 pounds (3–5.5 kg). The legs are strong and allow for free and easy movement. The profuse coat varies from wavy to curly. The Havanese comes in a wide range of possible colors, including cream, gold, silver, blue, black, and many other colors.

Haw

Term indicating a left turn to a sled dog.

Haw eyes

Eyes with a large amount of conjunctival membrane visible, a result of pouching lower eyelid due to looseness. *See* Haw-eyedness.

Haw-eyedness

Ectropion. Lolling, sagging lower eyelids caused by loose skin, exposing a substantial portion of the conjunctival lining. With a few photogenic exceptions (e.g., the Bloodhound, St. Bernard, Basset Hound), haw-eyedness is an undesirable feature, as it provides a gap to collect secretory pooling. The usual tight-skinned eyelids of canines allow for unimpeded tearing, flowing, and drainage. Haw-eyedness can eventually lead to chronic conjunctivitis, initiated by bacteria infestation of the eyes and leading to inflammation and excessive tearing. *See also* Ectropion, Conjunctiva

Hawaiian Poi Dog

While both U.S. non-continental states each have indigenous purebreds, only Alaska's Malamute breed has survived the test of time; Hawaii's Poi Dog, the islands' native dog, has been extinct for nearly two centuries. The Poi Dog's role in the culture of the Polynesian people was quite different than that of the Mahlemut's sled-pulling lifesaver. This pariah type dog was referred to on the islands as Ilio, its scientific name is *Canis pacificus*. It is believed that these dogs first came to Hawaii with the Polynesians about 1,000 years ago. Similar dogs were found on Tahiti as well as on the Sandwich Islands. The Poi Dogs were an important part of the Polynesians' way of life. The females in the tribe took care of the dogs and even nursed Poi puppies, believing that this would increase their protective instincts. They were obviously prized as companions, especially for children, and habitually enjoyed hobbling about with the penned hogs.

The Polynesians, however, did not differentiate between dogs as pets and dogs as food. These pariahs were raised almost exclusively as items of food. The dog's flesh was a celebrated delicacy. The custom of feeding the dogs breadfruit and poi (a granular paste based on the taro root) served to fatten them for the purpose of human consumption. This vegetarian diet also explains the formation of the dogs' skulls, which were large and flat from the lack of chewing. Their bodies were stubby and overweight for their height. Lack of exercise and stimulation created the world's most indolent and plumply doleful of pineapple-rolling pariahs. In color the dogs were usually tan or rust-yellow; white and other colors also occurred. The hair was smooth, the muzzle sharp, the back long, and the ears erect. Legs were typically short and crooked.

A program was conducted in the Honolulu Zoo in the early 1800s to attempt to save the scarce breed; the experiment, which persisted for 12 years, was abandoned. These zoo-kept dogs were the last known Poi Dogs. It is indeed a shame that such a fascinating canine has been lost to the dog world, although in reality, the dogs are probably more interesting to read about than they would be enjoyable as home companions. Had the Poi Dog survived to see the advent of the dog show craze, would it have added a little zest to the ring and made judges re-evaluate the emphasis on gait, as the dogs wobbled about the ring or slept on their benches? We guess not. *See also* Dogs as delicacy, Sumatra Battak

HD
    See Hip dysplasia

Head
    The foremost part of the skeleton usually including all the bony structures associated with the skull.

Head chopped off
    Term used when a racedog is beaten to the first turn; headed off at the turn.

Head planes
    Profile view of geometric dimensions or bends of the topskull and foreface. The former determined from occiput to stop and the latter from stop to nose tip. Breed standards occasionally describe head planes and always in relationship, one to the other, i.e., parallel, converging, etc.

Head trailing
    A subtle method of trailing in which a dog runs ahead of his bracemate while watching out of the corner of his eye for the bracemate's change of direction and then changes direction accordingly. A casual observer might think the wrong dog is trailing.

Havanese, black and white. Photo by I. Français.

Headed
    When the fox is made to turn back during the hunt, he is said to be headed.

Heads up
    A fox hunting term used to refer to when the hounds searching for scent raise their heads from the ground.

Heart

Though no animal is perfect, their hearts are nearly so. The canine heart, as is the human heart, is a most efficient pump of blood. It is literally the "heart" of the living being. The heart is a muscle, composed of smooth muscle tissues. It is controlled unconsciously, which means that it takes no conscious effort to make the heart pump blood. A healthy heart in a healthy animal reacts to the demands and stress placed on the animal, supplying at all times an adequate blood supply to the living cells that compose the body. Excessive stress, whether the result of overexertion, disease, heartworms, congested blood vessels, or other, can damage the heart, forcing it to work even harder to provide adequate circulation. Regular exercise at moderate to high levels conditions the heart, and a nutritious diet with proper fat and cholesterol

Heart. Veterinarians routinely monitor a dog's heartbeat. Photo by R. Pearcy.

levels maintains the health and efficiency of this vital organ. *See also* Circulatory system, Heart problems

Heart problems

When a dog owner speaks of problems of the canine heart, the first concern that comes to mind is often heartworms. Indeed, these copepods are a major cause of death in dogs. However, canines also suffer heart enlargement, heart attack, leaky valves, infection and inflammation, and congestion.

An enlarged heart is often the result of overexertion by the immature dog, whose heart is still in its developmental stages. All pups and young dogs most certainly need exercise. To work your dog hard and/or to work your dog for long hours, however, is to risk an enlarged heart. Dogs that suffer from this disorder respond poorly to activity and have a relatively short life expectancy.

Heart attacks (cardiac arrest) happen in dogs just as they do in humans, and obese, sedentary, high-fat and cholesterol-consuming canines are, like their human counterparts, prime candidates for the occurrence. The onset of an attack is not easy to detect in dogs. Panting, pain, glassy eyes, paralysis, and other abnormal behaviors can all be signs. Unfortunately, it is often the ceasing of the heartbeat that signals the owner to the problem. If detected at an early stage or if the attack is a minor one, there is veterinary treatment possible. If you suspect that your dog is suffering from a heart ailment, contact a vet immediately; keep the dog quiet and warm, and follow closely the instructions given by the vet.

Leaky valves are often detectable to the "naked" ear when the ear is pressed against the dog's chest. Leaky valves provide a hissing sound and perceptible vibrations. There is no general treatment or

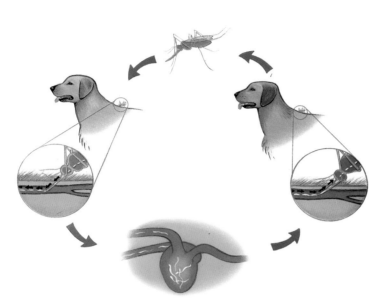

cure, though the vet will likely prescribe a diet and exercise program.

The surrounding tissue of the heart can become infected with harmful bacteria. Breathing can be labored or short, and the pulse may either rise or fall. Breathing and/or pulse irregularity should be inspected by the veterinarian as soon as is possible. Treatment is possible, and cure is likely.

A congested heart gives signs in the dog's lethargy, apathy, shortness of breath, weakness, and sometimes bluish discoloration of the tongue and gums after exertion. These signals are definite calls to action. If the cause is congestive heart disease, there is treatment. *See also* Circulatory system, Heart, Heartworms

Heart room, plenty of

Terminology employed in breed standards to indicate maximum chest capacity for the sake of optimum stamina.

Heart-shaped ears

Ears whose cartilage is generally shaped to resemble a geometric heart (e.g., Tibetan Mastiff).

Heartworm

A disease complex caused by the filarial worm *Dirofilaria immitis*, the adults of which occur primarily in the right ventricle and pulmonary artery. Signs of the dog's infection include gradual weight loss, decreased exercise ability, and coughing when subjected to physical stress. In severe cases, a dog may have a high temperature, accumulated abdominal fluid, and other signs. The duration and acuteness of the infection will dictate the symptoms, and any one dog may show all signs or only one.

The infection is reported around the world, with the highest incidents reported in tropical and subtropical regions around the world. The disease is spread by female mosquitoes of various species, which deposit the heartworm microfilariae when they bite a dog. Within the dog, the microfilariae remain active for one to three years. They develop further only when they are ingested by another mosquito. Within this second mosquito, the filariae develop to the infectious larval stage. Upon biting a dog, the larvae are deposited, travel through the dog's bloodstream, and settle in the heart, where they mature and grow, causing damage to the organ.

The infection is diagnosed through blood tests, and treatment is accordingly initiated by a veterinarian. Because it is nearly impossible to protect any dog that is out of doors from mosquito bites, prevention without the use of foreign substances is difficult. Mosquito repellent for animals can be used; keeping your

Heartworm life cycle: a carrier mosquito bites a dog and deposits microfilariae; the filariae travel through the blood stream, lodging in the heart to reproduce. The carrier dog is later bitten by an uninfected mosquito, which thereby acquires uninfectious microfilariae.

dog away from mosquito-infested areas is also recommended. There are chemicals that can prevent the disease, but these drugs can only be administered under the recommendation of a veterinarian; daily or monthly edible pills are common preventatives for heartworm.

Another type of heartworm, known as French heartworm or *Angiostrongylus vasorum* infection, involves smaller heartworms that are occasionally found in the right ventricle and pulmonary artery of dogs in the U.S., Europe, and the U.S.S.R. Cardiac hypertrophy and hepatic congestion are some signs that occur in acute cases, as well as the tendency to bruise easily, caused by the lessened ability of the blood to clot.

Heat

A single dog sled race.

Heat exhaustion is extremely dangerous to dogs. Do not overtax your dog with exercise or extended periods in direct sunlight. Of course, never leave a dog in a closed car unattended.

Heat exhaustion

Known also as heat prostration, this is a condition caused by overexertion, especially in hot weather. Overweight and older dogs are likely candidates, as are young pups. Dogs must not be overworked, overplayed, or overexcited in hot weather. The dog suffering from heat exhaustion should be cooled and allowed to rest. Water should be made available, and a close eye must be kept.

Heat period

The time when the bitch is fertile and can be impregnated; The season in which a bitch is receptive to the advances of male dogs. Domestic dogs typically have two heat periods a year. Known also as season and estrus, the bitch's heat period is a time that demands special care on the part of the owner. Her behavior may change due to hormonal changes that occur during this period. She will emit a scent that attracts males. To prevent harassment from dogs and unintended impregnation, the bitch in heat should not be allowed outside alone and must be taken away from her yard to relieve herself. *See also* Breeding, Bitch

Heatstroke

Heatstroke or sunstroke can be identified by a number of signs: excessive panting, rapid breathing, vomiting, rapid pulse, weakness in the limbs, staggering, or collapse. Leaving a dog in a closed car during the summer months is one sure way to induce sunstroke—never leave a dog in a closed car for any length of time. Overweight and older dogs are more susceptible to suffering from sunstroke and therefore should not be left in the direct sun for any length of time.

Sponge an affected dog with cold water; if using a tub, keep the water cold and shallow. A cold water enema, if practical, can also be effective. Dry off the dog and contact your vet.

Heel

1) Tarsus or hock joint. *See also* Foot anatomy. 2) In obedience trials, the dog is to walk at the left side and with its head even with or in line with the left knee of its handler. This applies in free heel and heel on leash. *See also* Training

Heeler

A heeler is a dog that herds cattle by nipping at the animals' feet. *See* Australian Kelpie, Australian Shepherd, Australian Cattle Dog, Lancashire Heeler, Cattle dogs

Heidewachtel

See Small Münsterländer

Height

In dogs, height is determined correctly as the distance from the highest point of the withers to the floor when the dog is in the proper upright stance. Accurately determining the height of certain dogs (i.e., the giant breeds and a handful of toy breeds) has been a point of dissension in the dog world for a number of years. Firstly, owners of the giants tend to "round up" a few inches while owners of the toys, down an inch or so. The tallest dog in the world is the Irish Wolfhound, indisputably. The American standard calls for the breed to average 32 to 34 inches (81.5–86.5 cm) while dogs are reported to stand as tall as 36.25 (92 cm) and more. On the other end of the scale, a number of toy dogs would joust for the distinction of shortest dog in the world. The Chihuahua, Yorkshire Terrier and Pomeranian all stand but a few inches. Of course, smaller dogs from the toy breeds as well as such bantamized tots as the Teacup Poodle and Pocket Beagle can stand even below six inches (15 cm).

Problems inherent in dogs this small, such as breeding and general care, should deter the over-popularity of dogs any smaller than the standards require and therefore advise.

Hellenic Hound

See Greek Harehound

Height in the domestic dog varies considerably. The Toy Poodle, on the lowest end of the yardstick, stands less than ten inches (25.5 cm) high.

Height. The Apollo of dogs, the Great Dane can stand over 32 inches (81.5 cm) at the shoulder.

Hellinikos Ichnilatis
See Greek Harehound

Hematomas

Deposits of blood between layers of skin, most often occurring in the flap (or leather) of the ear. The cause is bruising, often the result of excessive scratching, non-puncturing nips from another animal, or other vessel-breaking occurrences. The ears swell with blood and fluid until they appear as water-filled balloons. Minor surgery that involves draining, cleaning and a few sutures may be the recommended treatment.

Hemobartonella

Hemobartonella canis, a bacterial parasite of the red blood cells, is characterized in acute cases by anemia. The disease is often self-curing and rarely diagnosed. Antibiotics can often provide a cure.

Hemophilia

A condition having two main types; Hemophilia A is more common than Hemophilia B. The A type is reported in all breeds as well as in hybrids and mongrels. Both hemophilia A and B are inherited defects that can be passed by carriers as well as affected dogs. They are the believed result of improper breeding practices, which include excessive in-breeding and not culling deficient offspring. Hemophilia A and B are characterized by an animal's inability to stop bleeding. Though carried by both sexes, the disease seems to exist only in males.

Hemorrhage

The escape of large quantities of blood from a blood vessel. A hemorrhage sometimes occurs after surgery and birth. Accidents and injuries can also cause a hemorrhage.

Hemorrhoid

A painful swelling of a vein in the region of the anus, often with bleeding.

Hepatitis, canine

Infectious canine hepatitis (ICH) is a contagious disease of varying signs from mild fever and congestion to severe depression and inability of the blood to clot. The disease is reported around the world and affects other animals besides the domestic dog, including foxes, wolves, and other carnivores. Different from the hepatitis that affects humans, ICH cannot be contracted by man. Viral in nature, canine hepatitis is commonly transmitted via the excreta (urine, feces, or saliva) of affected animals and quickly infects the animal. Common signs include lethargy, thirst and dehydration, diarrhea, vomiting, and refusal to eat. Abdominal swelling may be present due to an inflammation of the liver. Fever too is a common sign. Canine hepatitis demands immediate medical attention. The disease can be fatal but can be treated if caught at an early stage.

Herbivorous animals

Those animals that consume only plant matter. Though dogs can survive for a period of time with exclusive plant consumption, they require animal substances to live long and flourish. *See also* Animals, classes of; Carnivorous animals; Omnivorous animals

Herding dogs

Herding dogs, like flock guards, were developed in every country that produced livestock for its well being. These dogs derive from ancient nordic and spitz type dogs and still retain a number of these features. Many of the herding dogs are double coated, with prick ears and tapering muzzles. Other herders are descendants of the Tibetan sheepdogs that migrated with peoples into eastern Europe.

Herding dogs need to be both intelligent and agile. Arguably these are the most obedient of all dogs, following precisely the signals of their shepherd masters. Such precision and intelligence explain why these dogs excel in obedience trials; of course, their natural instincts fully explain why these dogs do well in sheepdog trials. Most every European nation developed its own herding dog. Additionally, Asian and African nations also produced similar dogs. Egypt has long been assisted by the Armant (or Ermenti), a dog that today functions as a herder and competent guard dog. Tibet, the locale of the ancient sheepdog types, yields the Tibetan Terrier and the Shih Tzu. Ensuring that "sheep may safely graze," Germany yielded the Giant Schnauzer, Hovawart and German Sheeppoodle (now extinct). The German Shepherd Dog, also of course of German origins, today rarely functions as a herder since his size and trainability have qualified him for other work. Finland's sheep are herded by the Lapin-porokoira; Portugal's by the Cão da Serra de Aires; Spain's by the Perro de Agua

and Catalan Sheepdog. Belgium produced four varieties of its sheepdog, the Belgian Sheepdog: the Malinois, Groenendael, Tervuren and Laekenois. Netherlands followed suit with four of their own.

France and Britain have output quite a sum of herders; among the most popular of these breeds are the Briard, Collie, Border Collie, Bearded Collie, Old English Sheepdog and Shetland Sheepdog.

Herding dogs. One prominent French herdsman, the Berger de Beauce or Beauceron, is a strong, self-efficient worker. This Beauceron was photographed in France by I. Français.

Herding dogs. It requires a dog of terrific stamina and reflex to move a large flock from one destination to another. This Austalian Shepherd works in Colorado.

The United States has also developed a number of its own herding dogs: the

Herding dogs
lend themselves
to a variety of
livestock, from the
very large to the
small and fragile.
Strong-eyed
Australian
Shepherds
herding plains
bison bull (*above*)
and Barbado ram
(*below*); Border
Collie pushing
ducks along
(*right*).

English Shepherd, Australian Shepherd and Blue Lacy are some of the most versatile of dog breeds to have yet surfaced.

The versatility of the herding dog group is astounding. While most of the breeds were derived for herding sheep and goats, these dogs adapt most readily to ducks, turkeys and other poultry as well as hogs and cattle. The size of herds varies greatly; some agricultural establishments may have but a couple of dozen sheep for a dog to maneuver while other larger farms can assign as many as 1,000 sheep to one dog.

Herding dog enthusiasts today concern themselves with perpetuating their breed's working qualities. While national recognition (by the A.K.C., for example) helps a breed fancy

accelerate the nation's interest, it can also lead too many people astray. Some Border Collie people have a difficult time conceiving "a standard of perfection" for their breed since not every great working dog looks the same: some are black and white, others are brownish and white, some are solid, some are shorthaired, others long. Coat type and color are less important considerations compared to the dexterity and skill of the dog. Granted there are Border Collie fans who have long, well-thought-out dissertations (poorly worded though they be) concerning the sheep's psychological reaction to dogs of a particular color (less than 30% white induces the sheep's "Little Red Riding Hood" complex), but color considerations in the show ring are more frivolous than such work ethic philosophies. It is said that short-coated herders, with insulated undercoats, fend better in

cold climates since long-coated dogs tend to ice up.

Herding Group

Established in 1983, the A.K.C. Herding Group is that group of purebred dogs who were originally used for herding purposes. These breeds previously were included in the Working Group. The group is a rather international potpourri of sheep and cattle manipulators; it includes such herders as the Old English Sheepdog, the Welsh Corgis, the Australian Cattle Dog, the Bouvier des Flandres, the German Shepherd Dog, the Puli and Briard.

Herding dogs. The natural instincts of herders manifest themselves while the dogs are still puppies. Belgian Tervuren puppy approaching a mini-gaggle of geese.

Herding dogs. Australian Kelpie puppies experiment with sheep.

Herding dogs. Moving low to the ground, this Australian Shepherd effectively shoes and heels and shoos the cattle into the pen.

Heredity

The transmission of characteristics from parents to offspring by means of genes in the chromosomes; the tendency of offspring to resemble parents or ancestors through transmission of genes. In dogs arguably the transmission of desirable traits is more vital to the improvement and general betterment of the breed. While people manipulate the breeding of dogs—mating the sturdiest female to the sturdiest male—society's approach to human coupling is somewhat different. While humans marvel over a newborn's possession of his mother's nose, a bitch's whelps all possessing her ears, nose, tail and coat color is no surprise to the bitch or its owner. As a rule, purebreds breed true, meaning they pass on their specific traits to their young, necessarily. *See also* Genetics

Heredity illustrated by parent and offspring chocolate Labrador Retrievers. Photo by I. Français.

Hermaphrodite

An animal that possess an anatomy suggestive of both sexes. The degree to which the genitalia suggests one sex or the other varies; sometimes it is strongly evident, other times more subtle. Regardless, such an animal is most commonly sterile. Hermaphrodites in dogs, as in humans, are not common. *See also* Masturbation, Homosexuality

Hernias

Hernias include a wide range of protrusions, which can be of tissues or organs. These abnormal protrusions can occur through normal or abnormal open-

ings. Some hernias are common in dogs, such as umbilical hernias, and some are of hereditary susceptibility.

Umbilical hernias are rarely of great concern. Their result is merely a fatty tissue deposit in the navel region. Corrective measures include regularly applied pressure to the protrusion or, in acute cases or cases of breeding bitches, corrective surgery. Professionals do not agree that umbilical hernias are the result of the bitch's biting the umbilical cord too close to the navel.

Inguinal hernias, which occur in the groin, scrotal hernias, which occur in the scrotum, and perineal hernias, which occur in the anus (typically of males), are all hernias of greater seriousness, many of which require surgery, depending on the case. Any protrusion in these areas requires immediate veterinary care.

Diaphragmatic hernias occur as a result of excessive strain. The diaphragm is the thin membrane located between the chest and abdominal cavity; and it is essential for breathing. In a diaphragmatic hernia, the diaphragm is torn and may be forced into the chest cavity, with some abdominal organs possibly following. Corrective surgery is likely necessary. Weak breathing, pain and vomiting are all possible signs.

Herpes virus

Canine herpes viral infection is known to occur only in canines. The disease is usually contracted by puppies as they pass through the vagina of an infected mother. The disease is often fatal to infected newborns.

Hertha Pointer

A breed of pointer that traces its roots back to 1864 and the retreat of the Danish army after defeat in the Danish-German War. During the retreat, several soldiers came upon a stray bitch of general gundog type. She accompanied the soldiers for the remainder of their retreat and became known to them as "Hertha." Upon arrival in Denmark, the bitch was given to one of the soldiers' friends, a true hunter and well-known supervisor of the vast state forests of Jutland. During the same period, the Duke of Augustenborg, Frederik Christian, kept a renowned

on feet, tail, chest and neck. Comparable to the Pointer of Great Britain in size, the Hertha tends to appear slightly sleeker. Height: 23–26 inches (58–66 cm). Weight: 45–60 pounds (21–27 kg).

Hertha Pointer, orange-red.

kennel of orange and white English Pointers. The owner of Hertha acquired one of the Duke's dogs named "Sport," and later bred the dog to Hertha. Thus began the breed today know as the Hertha Pointer.

The breed has not been granted breed status by the F.C.I. or any other major registry, but there has been a group formed to preserve and further the breed. There is believed to be political undercurrents that are working against the breed. These dogs have bred true since 1864 and are continually increasing in numbers in Denmark.

These are athletic and robust hunters who are praised by their Danish owners for their keen desire to work and unstinting ability to learn. Their hunting instincts are sharp, and they use them to full advantage on the hunt. They are readily adaptable to the home environment and prefer to sleep indoors.

ESSENTIALS OF THE HERTHA POINTER: The moderately sized Hertha is a solid orange-red dog of typical pointer type. A minimum of white markings may occur

Hiccoughing
A normal reaction in dogs, hiccoughing is involuntary contractions of the diaphragm, commonly caused by the improper swallowing of foodstuffs. Puppies may commonly hiccough, especially after receiving milk. It is only when the dog's hiccoughs last for more than several consistent hours that the owner need be alarmed.

Hide
Depreciatory term used to refer to a racing dog of fair or ordinary class.

High in shoulders
See Shoulder types

High in withers
Structure in which the withers slope downwards to the rear (e.g., Pointer, Spinone Italiano).

High jump
In obedience trials, used in Open Classes only, but used in Utility Class as part of one exercise. Side posts four feet

(120 cm) high are positioned with the jump bar five feet (150 cm) wide, so constructed as to provide adjustment for each two inches (5 cm) from 12 to 36 inches (30.5–91.5 cm). Base board is eight inches (20 cm) wide, including space from ground or floor.

High jump taken by Airedale Terrier in an obedience competition. Photo by R. Reagan.

High set ears

Ears set no lower than eye level are considered high set (e.g., Bulldog).

High velocity dryer

This dryer can be used while a dog is still in the tub. It blows the water down the hair shaft and off the hair with tremendous force. As it has no heating element, it uses very little electricity.

Himalayan Sheepdog

This breed of Indian flock guard may still be found along the Himalayan borders from eastern Nepal to Ladakh in Kashmir. The Himalayan Sheepdog is commonly called Bhotia. While the dogs are typically black and tan or black with white markings, a sub-variety colored in golden brown or solid black exists in the Kumaon hills. These dogs are as versatile as any of the mountain-dwelling guards of Europe and are capable of both herding and guarding. Dogs in Chambria were reported to bear resemblance to large black Labrador Retrievers with longer hair.

Reserved by nature, these heavy-boned, medium-size shepherds are astonishingly alert and nocturnal by nature. The head is medium size; stop, slight. The eyes are deep set and close, the ears triangular, drop medium length, set on high. The quarters are powerful and well muscled. The tail is thick and bushy; the feet are cat. The coat is long and harsh with a thick undercoat. Weight: 50–70 pounds (23–31.5 kg). Weight: 19–25 inches (48–63.5 cm).

Hindquarters

The ilium, ischium and pubis comprise the pelvic limb or hindquarters. The acetabulum or hip socket is positioned lower than the two main bones into which fits the femur or thigh bone. The pelvic slope is thus determined by the angle formed between a vertical line drawn through the iliac wing and ishial tuber. The longitudinal axis of the femur likewise determines the pelvic angle. In articulation with the tibia and fibula, the femur forms the stifle joint. Firmly anchored in the trochlea, the narrow groove formed by the femur is the patella or kneecap. The patella, the lower end of the femur, and the upper portion of the tibia and fibula comprise the stifle (or knee) joint. Stifle angulation is determined by the longitudinal axis of the femur and the tibia/fibula, which form the dog's lower thigh region.

The tarsus (or heel) is comprised of seven tarsal bones. The hindfeet are most similar to the forefeet except that they are smaller, thinner, and longer.

Like the forequarters, the hindquarters are an important component of the canine anatomy, and, as such, breed standards employ terminology to describe the ideal and undesired hindquarter types. Drooping hindquarters appear so due to deeply sloping and lengthy pelvic girdle; haunch bones higher than the pelvic tuber. Light in hindquarters either indicates slim and racy construction or muscle development less than ideal. Hindquarters straight behind specify hindquarters that do not extend past the tail set-on and are therefore inadequately constructed for power and drive (e.g. Chow Chow). Hindquarters too far under indicates that the rear assemblage is crouched too closely under the body, with hocks too directly underneath and often the pasterns steeply sloping. The opposing situation, where the dog's hocks and rear pasterns are placed too far back, is termed hindquarters too far back.

Hindquarters, angulation

The slope of the thigh bones (femur and tibia/fibula). References to angulation sometimes incorporate the angles of the pelvis or the hock joint.

Hip bones

Haunch bones or ilium.

Hip dysplasia

Congential hip dysplasia, the malformation of the hip joint's ball and socket, is present in the dog at birth. Such a defect can involve the absolute dislocation of the hip or simply a bad fit into the socket. Hip dysplasia, or HD, implies the faulty conformation of the femur head or acetabulum. It is manifested in lameness, the inability to maneuver on slippery surfaces, the disinclination to jump, hopping gait, and an unusual resistance to activity. While hip dysplasia appears to be simply a hereditary disorder, the dog's environment has a significant bearing on the development of the disorder. While no breed is 100-percent hip dysplasia free, German Shepherd Dogs, Rottweilers and Saint Bernards tend toward more occurrences than other breeds. Generally, the malformation can be observed once the dog is five to six months of age. A veterinarian can verify hip dysplasia through X-ray. The effect of the defect is lameness—the dog is unable to stand up straight and unwilling to get up. Since the defect is genetically determined, dogs with the disease should not be bred so as not to perpetuate the disease in a line.

The Orthopedic Foundation for Animals, Inc., dedicates itself to the control of this disease and others. *See* O.F.A.

Hip joint

The fusion point between the iliac wing and the ischiac tuber. *See also* Hindquarters

Hip socket

Acetabulum, the socket into which the femur or thigh bone fits. *See also* Hindquarters, Hips

Hippopotamus muzzle

The desired meat or bone mouth of the Shar-Pei.

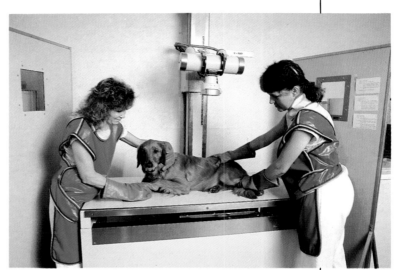

Hips

Generally speaking, the area around the upper thigh and rump junctions; technically, the femoral head and pelvic acetabulum articulation. Hip joint.

Hives

The result of an allergic reaction, hives are large inflamed areas on the dog's skin that commonly itch. Relief can be attained through the use of cold compresses and/or antihistamines. See your veterinarian.

Hoary fox

A wild dog and a member of the genus *Vulpes*. *See* Foxes

Hock

Joint between the lower thigh and rear pastern. The term hock has been employed variously and technically incorrectly as "the point of hock" or as "the whole of the rear pastern." The hock, also known as the tarsal join, is made up of seven bones, viz., astragalus, os calcis, scaphoid, two small cuneiform bones, large cuneiform, and the cuboid.

Hip dysplasia. That a dog is hip-dysplasia free requires an X-ray examination. For truly conclusive results, the dog must be anesthetized since the hip contortions necessary are painful. Photo by R. Pearcy.

Hock types

The shape, contours, angulation, and positioning of the hocks of dogs vary from breed to breed (and dog to dog). Breed standards have turned many a phrase to indicate the desired and undesired hock types: many an ad hoc committee has churned hock terms for hours to capture the desired nuance of angulation or hock contour. The terminology "well let down," when hacking through hock talk, arises frequently and many word variations on this popular construction exist. Well let down hocks describe the hock that is properly positioned from the ground for a given breed. Hock let down is closely linked to the acuteness of the hock joint angle. Hocks close to the ground, let down in hocks, and set low hocks are phrases with the same meaning. The snatch or thrust of hocks refers to powerful, purposeful flexion of the hock region.

Hock types. Well let down hocks on an Akita.

Straight hocks indicate that a greater than ideal angle between the lower thigh and rear pastern regions exists. High in hock is the phrase raised to indicate overly long rear pasterns or the inadequate slope of the metatarsi for a particular breed of dog. As such, the area from hock to ground is greater than ideal; thus the dog is not well let down. Hocks square with body indicates hock points positioned in line with the rearmost edge of the upper thigh. Weak hocks is a term used in the general sense to denote that the hocks are insufficiently angulated or let down. Well bent hocks or well angulated hocks is the opposite of straight hocks and indicates that the hock joints are properly angulated for the breed of dog in question. The undesirable conditions termed bow and barrel hocks and the opposite (and equally undesirable) cow hocks are discussed under the latter, which *see. See also* Sickle hocks

Hodgkins disease
See Canine malignant lymphoma

Hokkaido-Ken
See Ainu Dog

Hold hard
A warning to riders in the hunt to slow up and not press the hounds closely.

Holders
Canine teeth as termed in the Rhodesian Ridgeback standard.

Hollandse Herdershond
See Dutch Shepherd

Hollandse Smoushond
See Dutch Smoushond

Homosexuality
Incidents of homosexuality are known in the dog community. Commonly male puppies will mount each other with typical adolescent curiosity. Most usually this mounting diversion ends by the dog's adulthood. Nevertheless, it is not unusual for two male dogs to continue mounting one another or participating in sex play. Homosexual masturbation is as common as masturbation itself. Cases of male dogs exist where one male penetrates and ejaculates into the anus of the other. Owners usually discourage such "aberrant" proclivities although they are mostly harmless (as long as kept out of the sight of guests).

Pseudo-hermaphrodites, that is dogs having both male and female organs, have also encouraged homosexuality in the canine castle. Male dogs may attract other male dogs with such secondary sex characteristics. Such hermaphrodites possess more developed, larger nipples, a pendulous, soft scrotum with especially soft testicles, and a larger and more flabby penis. The testicles secrete a female hormone which can cause abnormal behavior in both dogs involved, as well as skin disorders.

For whatever reasons, fewer incidents of "lesbianism" have been reported. Nonetheless, it is not all that uncommon for two female dogs to mount one another, especially if one is in heat. Just as the male's erect penis is stimulated to orgasm when rubbed against his male partner, the female's clitoris is stimulated, bringing the bitch to a clitoral orgasm. This sex play usually doesn't persist too far and usually desists by adulthood. One of the most remarkable cases, however, involved two adult female French Bulldogs that were inseparable for years. *See also* Masturbation

Honest

A hound that has no faults in the field trial is said to be honest.

Honor a line

When a hound gives tongue on the line of a known quarry.

Honorable scars

Scars on a dog's body suffered as a result of work for which he was bred. Such scars should not detract from the conformation judging of a dog as long as the injury does not interfere with the dog's functional abilities.

Honoring

Remaining steady while another dog is sent to retrieve.

Hooded ears

Rather small ears with forward curving edges (e.g., Basenji).

Hook

A meat hook attached to the bridle of the sled by a line to hold the team in place. It can be driven into the ground or attached to a stationary object.

Hook tail

See Upward hook tail

Hookworm

Intestinal-tract parasite that can cause anemia and other ill conditions, especially in puppies, who can acquire these worms through infected mother's colostrum and milk. Hookworms are two-stage parasites: eggs are excreted by an infected animal and mature in several days on warm moist soil, where they can be ingested by canine passers-by. Diagnosis requires a stool sample. There are several species of hookworm that can infest our dogs. *Ancylostoma caninum* predominates in tropical and subtropical areas, while *A. braziliense* in Florida up through the Carolinas, and *Uncinaria stenocephala* in Europe, Canada, and northern U.S.A. *A. caninum* and *A. braziliense* can infest animals through the skin.

Horizontal tail

Whip tail or bee sting tail, which *see*.

Horseshoe front

Although the forearms are straight, the elbows are more inwardly inclined than the wrists (e.g., Bedlington Terrier).

Hospitals for dogs

See Canine hospitals, Clinics

Hooded ears of the Basenji. Photo by I. Français.

Hot boxer

Star dog in a dog race.

Hot nose

Hot nose refers to a scenthound that excels on a trail with a new or fresh scent. *See also* Cold nose

Hot spot

See Eczema

Hottentot Dog

A spitzlike dog native to Africa which figures largely in the development of the Rhodesian Ridgeback. The Hottentot, also called the Kaffir Dog, was first described by Hahn in 1896; the dog may have possessed a ridge on its back like its descendant, but also a bushy tail. The dogs were used for hunting purposes by the Hottentot people from which the dog derives its name.

Hound ears

Not the ears of a hound but instead referring to an undesired full drop ear. In the Airedale Terrier, for example, hound ears are a fault.

Hound glove

A grooming tool that slips over the hand more like a mitt than a glove but which nonetheless polishes and shines short coats, such as those of the Doberman Pinscher, Boxer and Basset Hound.

Hound Group

Most national kennel clubs employ the delineation Hound Group. This group includes both scenthound and sighthound breeds, making for an overall curious integration of body types, personalities and coats. Standing high above the crowd are the taller sighthound types—the Afghan Hound, Greyhound, and Irish Wolfhound; holding their ground with a distinctive air are the medium-sized Rhodesian Ridgeback and Otterhound; disinterestedly peering away is the majestic Bloodhound; equally uninvolved (but looking up) are the low-grounded Basset Hound and Dachshunds; interested, but worlds apart, is the Norwegian Elk*hound* (no hound at all!); uniquely indescribable and looking in all directions is the pariah-born Basenji. The group is nearly as diverse as those utilitarian pedigrees in the Non-Sporting Group. England inexplicably groups the Finnish Spitz and Norwegian Lunde*hund* within its Hound Group. While the A.K.C. Non-Sporting Group is typically criticized for its categorizations, it is probably the Hound Group which is the most confusing. *See also* Group systems, Scenthounds

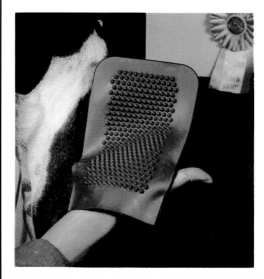

Hound Group. Best in Group competition for Hounds that hunt small game at an exhibition of the Fédération Cynologique Internationale.

Hound glove used to touch-up the coat of shorthaired dogs, such as the Boxer.

Housebreaking

Housebreaking is the foundation training upon which all subsequent training is built. Successful housebreaking also sows the seeds of future person-to-pet relationships. Housebreaking is, therefore, a vital process that must be undertaken intelligently. The owner should know the basics of canine intelligence and behavior and use this knowledge to his full advantage. Dogs are essentially clean animals, and most dogs want nothing better than to please their masters. Therefore, a pup must be introduced to and kept in a clean environment, taught how to keep it that way, and praised for *all* correct behavior.

Dogs simply do not have the muscular control necessary for complete housebreaking until they reach three or four months of age. Demanding a dog to be housebroken before this time simply leads to frustration and disappointment for both the owner and the dog. If the appropriately aged dog is allowed to relieve himself in the desired location every time he has to go and is praised for doing so, he will quickly become successfully housebroken. There are many proposed ways to housebreak a dog, the most common of which are paper training and crate training.

Crate training is now the most recommended method of housebreaking a pup. For many years owners were instructed to paper train their dogs, but paper training allows the dog to relieve himself in the home, and this is what most owners are striving to eliminate eventually. Crate training does involve a financial expenditure, for the owner must invest in a dog crate, or portable kennel. This crate is to serve as the puppy's own home. It is a place for him to call his own and a place for him to keep clean. Upon bringing the pup home, introduce him to the crate. In it should be a blanket, towel or other suitable bedding, a safe chew toy, and any other objects that you feel are necessary to make the pup feel welcome and at home—these objects should be few in number and not clutter the crate. The

crate should be large enough to allow the pup to move around comfortably but not

so large that he can sleep in one corner and relieve himself in another. During the day, the door of the crate should be left open, allowing the dog freedom to enter and leave. The crate should be located in a restricted area; a location in which the owner can keep a close eye on the dog, preventing his sneaking off to mess in a far corner of the house. During the night or any time that he cannot be supervised, the dog should be kept in the

crate. He should then be taken to his proper area of evacuation as soon as the owner returns or morning arises. Housebreaking is achieved in this manner: immediately following each feeding, the pup is taken outside until he relieves himself; as he does, he must receive warm praise that tells him he is doing the right thing; after evacuation, the pup is led back to his area, which will be clean

Housebreaking. The location of a puppy's "potty papers" should be clearly indicated to the trainee. This Boxer pup receives where-to-go directions from its young instructor.

Housebreaking. Every time the puppy piddles on paper, praise and petting are paramount. Photos by V. Serbin.

Housebreaking. Crate training reinforces the puppy's understanding of "where to go" (and where *not* to) since the dog's natural instinct is not to soil its den. Bullmastiff youth photographed by I. Français.

and pleasing to the animal. Instinctively wanting clean quarters, the pup will be little inclined to defecate or urinate in his area; if he does, the mess must be cleaned immediately not to allow the pup to get accustomed to the mess. The dog should not be scolded: relieving himself is natural. If the pup goes other than in the desired location, it is not his fault but yours, for you did not let him outside at the appropriate time. By praising the pup each time he goes in the appropriate place, and by keeping clean his home quarters, the pup will quickly learn the desired location for relieving himself. Remember that the puppy's excretory system is limited in its capacity to retain waste; the pup will have to be led to his location eight or more times a day; these should be regularly scheduled and immediately follow each meal. Crate training, therefore, demands time and dedica-

tion of the owner, but the rewards are well worth the effort.

Paper training is best suited to the dog owner who does not have the time or physical ability to take the pup out regularly, eight or more times a day, or for owners of small dogs whom they wish to remain indoor companions for the duration of their lives. The dog should be confined to a limited area. When paper training begins, the entire surface area should be covered with newspapers. When the dog relieves himself on the paper, he should be praised. Except for dogs who are to remain indoors, paper training is not a substitute for outdoor training; the pup must still be taken on regular walks, especially following each meal. Gradually, the paper area should dwindle, working towards the pup's chosen spot to relieve himself. Most pups will have a chosen spot, but if they don't it is the owner's judgment that determines what area is to remain covered. The pup should be encouraged to go on the remaining papered area, and whenever he does he should be praised. If he misses the papers he should not be scolded, and his nose should never be rubbed in the excreta. Praise alone for doing what is right is the best way to train any dog. As the papered area becomes ever smaller, it can be moved closer and closer and finally out the door, at which time the pup should be completely housebroken. If a mishap occurs, the dog was not let out at the appropriate time.

Housebreaking adult dogs involves essentially the same process. The dog should be confined to

a limited area and be allowed outside regularly, especially after meals. The adult dog's digestive system works slower than a pup's, making it advisable to take the dog out about one hour after a meal, rather than immediately following it.

Dogs that "refuse" or cannot be housebroken either have a disease or are improperly trained. Veterinary inspection can narrow the possibilities, and professional training can often break the unhousebreakable dog.

Sick dogs should not become unhousebroken. An accident that occurs should not be punished, as it is only a sign that you are not providing the sick dog with the additional outings that his system needs. A dog suffering from diarrhea will need an ever-present location in which to relieve himself, for bodily control simply is not there. *See also* Puppies, Training, Children and dogs

Hovawart

Hovawart as a breed name is derived from the German *Hofewart*, which means loosely "estate guard"; the dog is of German origin and is an effective herder and home and stock guardian. The Hofewart of old were favored by many German barons and others of the royalty: they were prized protectors of livestock and game. References to the breed occur in both written and pictorial form and date back to the fifteenth century. The breed described and depicted closely resembles the Hovawart of today. There exist two opposing theories regarding the Hovawart's origin in its present state.

One theory contends that the breed is the re-discovered direct descendant of the

Hovawarts, black/gold, blonde, and black.

Hofewart of the 1800s, a time when the breed faded into obscurity. A dedicated group of fanciers entered the Black Forest and the Harz region of Germany in the early twentieth century in search of the said canine; based on careful research they believed that the breed had receded

Hovawart, blonde. Photographs by I. Français.

to this obscure area but still existed in a relatively pure form. According to reports, the group exited successfully, and through strict breeding practices perfected the breed to its present state.

A second theory states that breeds such as the German Shepherd Dog, Newfoundland, Kuvasz, and possibly others were crossbred to produce the believed accurate type, based on the existing references and artwork. Regardless of the means, the Hovawart is safely established with the dog fancy of Germany and England. A loyal canine who is protective, watchful and willing, the Hovawart is a fine guard and watchdog. Gentle, patient, and tolerant, he is an excellent companion.

dard is quite explicit in its detail of the breed's color pattern. The coat is long in appearance but short on face and forelegs. Height: 24–28 inches (61–71 cm).

Hrvaški Ovčar
    See Croatian Sheepdog

Huckle
    Pelvic wing portions above the back line.

Huenerhunden
    German term for bird dogs.

Hugged rail
    When a dog is raced close to the inner rail, or fence, to save distance.

Humane societies
    With the stated intention of preventing cruelty towards animals, these organizations are formed. Humane societies typically adopt a code listing the rights that animals are entitled to and state the ways in which these rights can be provided and upheld. Rights may include medical treatment, housing and protection from abuse, and euthanasia. For the greater part of the history of the English-speaking world, animals maintained no rights. Their master was their god. In 1822, the English Parliament passed the Ill-treatment of Cattle Bill, which provided protection to many of the man-owned animals, but not to pets. Following this lead, the English Society for the Prevention of Cruelty Toward Animals (S.P.C.A.) was formed, and in 1840, under the Queen's direction, Royal was added to the society's title, making it now the R.S.P.C.A. By an act passed in 1849, the Royal Society granted protection to all domestic animals, including pets. Meet-

Hovawart, black/gold. Photo by I. Français.

ESSENTIALS OF THE HOVAWART: A medium-sized, strong but not heavy herder. The head is strong, the skull broad and free from wrinkles. The eyes are typically dark, toning with pigmentation, and oval in shape. The ears are triangular, hanging, and set medium to high. The body is well balanced, equipped with a strong, level topline, deep brisket and moderately deep loins. Shoulders well sloping. The tail is long and bushy. The gait is free, supple, and tireless. Soundness is very important, and there must be no stilted action. The backline and head may tend to drop at high speed. The average weight of this working dog is between 65–90 pounds (30–40.5 kg). The coat can be black/gold, black or blonde; the staning with fair success in its early years, the R.S.P.C.A. continued to grow in its responsibilities with the Act of 1876 that granted protection to laboratory animals and the Act of 1900 that granted protection to zoo-kept animals.

The American Society for the Prevention of Cruelty toward Animals was formed in 1866 by the well-intending Henry Berg. It was largely a New York-based institution, and many American cities followed suit in the next few years. The humane societies of America today remain primarily on a local level, and the laws and their enforcement can vary from place to place and time to time. Some societies are concerned with all animals, while others concentrate on those animals used for research or other arguably inhumane purpose. Humane societies today can be public or private, non-profit or commercial. They can be large or small, corrupt or sincere. Selecting a dog from an animal shelter as a pet may well save that dog's life, but the potential owner must exercise discretion. For more information about the humane societies near you, check your local or county phone book.

Humerus
Arm, *see* Forequarters

Hungarian Greyhound
See Magyar Agăr

Hungarian Hound
See Transylvanian Hound

Hungarian Pointer
See Vizsla

Hungarian Puli
See Puli

Hungarian Sheepdog
See Komondor

Hungarian Vizsla
See Vizsla

Hunger
See Appetite

Hurdle and bar jump
In obedience trials, the hurdle is as high as the high jump and graduated in the same way. Uprights are four feet (120 cm) high and set five feet (150 cm) apart, with the bar placed so as to fall if hit. The bar is two and a half inches (6 cm) in diameter and painted in alternating black and white sections of about three inches (7.5 cm). Adjustable by two inches from 12 to 36 inches. *See also* High jump

Humane societies frequently find themselves in situations where a lost or injured animal must be restrained in order to be admitted.

Hurdle and bar jump easily executed by a dashing Golden Retriever. Photographs by R. Pearcy.

Husky

Generic term for Eskimo-type dogs. In general, the laikas can be considered huskies as can any other nordic draft breed or type. *See* Alaskan Malamute, Eskimo Dog, Siberian Husky, Nordic dogs, Draft dogs

Hütespitz

An upstanding German sheepdog of medium size. The back is broad and

Husky is commonly used as an alternative name for this sled-puller, the Greenland Dog. Photo by I. Français.

strong; chest deep; shoulders sloping; coat moderately long, profuse and harsh to the touch. The color is white with occasional fawn markings. A pastoral passing relation of the German Spitz family, the Hütespitz is not recognized by a major registering body.

Hybrid

A hybrid technically is an animal which derives from two distinct races or species; in canine terms, a hybrid is synonymous with crossbreed. *See also* Mongrels, Wolf hybrids

Hydraulic tables

Coming in various sizes and shapes, these are used by professional dog groomers. They can be raised, lowered, and turned in a full circle. Although hydraulic tables are more costly than standard models, the ease of control and the comfort it gives a groomer return the initial investment. These efficient tables are useful for all dogs, particularly the large breeds.

Hydrocephalus

A condition also known as "water head" since a large amount of fluid collects in the brain cavity, usually before birth. This may result in a difficult birth and the young are usually born dead or die shortly thereafter. Euthanasia is recommended for those that do survive since intelligence is absent and violence to themselves or others is liable to occur.

Hydronephrosis

Due to acystic obstruction, the kidney collects urine which cannot be passed through the ureter into the bladder, causing the kidney to swell (sometimes to five times its normal size) and giving pain in the lumbar region. The kidney may atrophy if the condition goes untreated.

Hydrophobia

The fear of water; has been reported in varied degrees in dogs. Also an alternative term for rabies, which *see*.

Hydrothorax

Water in the chest cavity; may follow an injury, infection or other abnormal condition of the chest region.

Hygenhund

The Hygenhund came forward from the breeding program of one F. Hygen. This Norwegian fancier and hunter crossed the old Hölsteiner Hounds with a potpourri of Scandinavian hounds (and German hounds as well) to attain his Hygenhund. Hygen proudly gave his own name to his creation, which essentially looks like any other Scandinavian hound he used to create it—differing subtly in size and color. Although the Hygenhund has never been a popular or international dog, nothing can take away from this hunter's instinctive abilities and expertise.

ESSENTIALS OF THE HYGENHUND: A solid, tight build complements this short-coupled hound. The breed is long bodied with a short and strong back. The head is medium sized, a little broad, neither heavy nor long. The skull appears slightly domed. The muzzle is clean and broad and rather deep. The legs are solid and sinewy. Forelegs straight in bone but well angulated. Height: 19–23 inches (48–59 cm). Weight 44–53 pounds (20–24 kg). The coat is straight and dense, without being excessively short. The Hygenhund commonly comes in yellow with white markings, although red/brown and other colors also occur. The toes are well arched and close together.

Hygenstövare

See Hygenhund

Hygiene

See Bathing, Cleanliness, Grooming

Hymen

Located approximately one to three inches (2.5–7.5 cm), depending on the breed, within the bitch's vagina, it is a mesh of tissue that runs vertically across the vaginal canal. The hymen should be investigated by a veterinarian prior to breeding commencement.

Hyperkinesis

A condition marked by persistent hyperactivity. Affected dogs have boundless energy and can be unmanageable and incorrigible.

Hyperthermia

One treatment for cancer; involves submersing the body in water above body temperature coupled with X-ray therapy. *See also* Cancer

Hygenhund, red/white.

Hypoadrenocorticism

See Addison's disease

Hypoglycemia

Low blood sugar. Can be the effect of stress, over work, exercise on an empty stomach, or genetic causes. Convulsions, dry heaves, and blackouts are some possible signs. The condition occurs in many of the tiny breeds, e.g., Teacup Poodles, Yorkshire Terriers, etc. Often a teaspoon of honey can revive the ailing tot.

Hypoparathyroidism

Signaled by muscular twitches, depression and, in acute cases, convulsions, the condition is the result of an underactive parathyroid gland. The condition, if prolonged and untreated, can cause soft, weak bones—the effect of mineral depletion. Secondary hyperparathyroidism is a similar condition that results from excessive secretion of the parathyroid.

Hysterectomy

The surgical removal of all or part of the uterus, either because the organ is threatening to the well-being of the bitch (cancerous, etc.) or as a means of preventing pregnancy (spaying). *See* Spaying

Ibizan Hound

Resembling the large-eared type grey-hound that kicked up sand in Egypt many millennia ago, the Ibizan Hound was favored and used for hunting by the pharaohs. These ancient dogs are traced back as far as 3400 B.C. Art work and artifacts bearing strong resemblance to the Ibizan have been unearthed from the time of Hemako, whose dynasty dates 3100 to 2700 B.C. A black varnished wood replica of Anubis, "the Watchdog of Death," was found in the tomb of Tutankhamen and projects the same image as the Ibizan today.

nent collars, suggestive of their some-what deceptive strength, and riding side-saddle on Hannibal's elephant in his Ital-ian invasion. At one time, the Ibizan, conscious of his blue blood, was believed to refuse to mate with any dog not of his Mallorcan tribe.

The survival of the Ibizan has been attributed to the Phoenicians, who dis-covered the island of Mallorca in the eighth or ninth century. It is not known exactly how the Ibizan trekked its way from Egypt to Mallorca but the history of that island has been affected by a great many powers: Carthaginians, Romans,

Ibizan Hound, smooth, chestnut and white. Photo by I. Français.

Unlike the Greyhound, the Ibizan, founded on the island of Majorca, can hunt by sight, scent, and even sound (making them soundhounds). It is be-lieved that the Ibizan is one of the most ancient of dogs and that its development parallels that of the earliest Egyptian windhounds. Nonetheless, the Grey-hound and Saluki are possible ancestors. A touch of Egyptian Mastiff may account for the stouter physique of the breed, and the relative isolation of ancient Egypt facilitated the purity of the Ibizan type. The Pharaoh Hound of Malta is said to have similar origins, of course develop-ing in a different geographic location. History finds the Ibizans wearing promi-

Arabs, Egyptian, Chaldeans and Vandals all entered and conquered.

Today Spain is considered his home country; many dogs worked in the Span-ish province of Catalonia, where they are known as Ca Eivissencs. In France, due to their association with French poachers, they were banned. The Charnique, as the French would say, was valued for its silent hunting abilities. In Spain and Mallorca, however, the breed continued, in packs or singly, hunting rabbit, par-tridge, and larger game. The breed's hunting style is unique: these are not gundogs—the Ibizan is able to scent, flush and course the prey. A tireless hunter, the Ibizan is to be both agile and controlled. He retrieves to hand and has the ability to jump great heights without a take-off run. If ever a dog should lose sight or scent or sound of its prey, it will stand on its hindlegs to get a better overview of the situation. These are extrasensory, super-intelligent canines with limitless abilities.

In 1956, the first Ibizans were imported to the U.S. by Colonel and Mrs. Seoane of Rhode Island. Actual A.K.C. recognition followed in 1979. The Ibizan in the States today enjoys only a moderate following.

ESSENTIALS OF THE IBIZAN HOUND: The tall and narrow Ibizan Hound is distinguished by his outstanding upstanding ears and fine build. The head is fine and long, and the clear amber eyes possess an expression unique to the breed. The skull is flat, with a prominent occipital bone; the stop is not well defined, and the muzzle is sightly convex. The neck is lean, muscular, and slightly arched. The forequarters are rather steep, with short shoulder blades, long straight legs, and erect pasterns of good length. The back is level and slopes slightly from the hip bones to the rump. The rib cage is long and flat; the body is short coupled and well tucked up at the waist. The tail is long, thin, low set, and reaches below the hock. The coat can be shorthaired or wirehaired; in both varieties the coat is hard, close and dense. The wire coat is 1–3 inches (2.5–8 cm) in length, with a mustache and slight feathering on the back, thighs and tail. In color the Ibizan Hound is white, chestnut

(lion tawny) or, most commonly, a combination of these colors. Height: 22–29 inches (56–74 cm). Weight: 42–55 pounds (19–25 kg).

I.C.F.
Abbreviation for the International Canine Federation. *See* Fédération Cynologique Internationale.

Iceland Dog
More of a herder than a hunter, the Iceland Dog was conceivably introduced to Iceland by Norwegians, who referred to the ancient breed as the "Friaar-Dog." Studies of the breed done in 1877 by Dr. Fitzinger divided it into two categories, a

Ibizan Hound, wire, chestnut with white.

Ibizan Hounds, wire, white with chestnut. Photographs by I. Français.

division which no longer persists in Iceland. The coat and undercoat are its principal divergences from the Greenland Dog. The Icelandic breed's coat is not

Iceland Dog, wheaten.

Iceland Dog, wolf sable. Photographs by I. Français.

quite as long as its polar cousin's jacket. The Sirjanskaja Laika is believed to resemble the breed in many respects as well. Although the breed didn't quite take in the United Kingdom when introduced at the turn of the twentieth century, concerned British breeders, working with native Icelandic fanciers, reconstructed the breed after a severe outburst of distemper in the early 1900s.

The breed's need for working is less intense than many of the other nordic herders. In his heyday, he was a confirmed enemy of the snow fox and crow; today, however, his hunting instincts are quite dormant, making him a fine easy-going companion.

ESSENTIALS OF THE ICELAND DOG: The compact Iceland Dog is a typical nordic spitz, having pricked ears and curled tail. From the side, the dog is rectangular, longer than high, the ratio depending on individual harmony. There are two types of coats, but at all times thick and efficiently water-repellent. The head is wide between the ears, the skull somewhat domed. Cheeks are flat, muzzle short, tapering evenly toward the nose. The ears are firm and erect, wide at base

and very mobile. The neck of medium length and strong. The body is strong though not coarse; the chest deep; ribs well sprung. The croup is short and rounded. The forelegs straight; the hindlegs strong and well angulated. The tail is set high, well curled and thickly furred. The coat can be either medium length or longer haired. Both types are double. Wheaten, wolf-sable, off-white, and black are the color possibilities. White markings and black mask often accompany. Height: 12–16 inches (31–41 cm). Weight: 20–30 pounds (9–14 kg).

Iceland Spitz
See Iceland Dog

Icelandic Sheepdog
See Iceland Dog

Ichthyosis
A skin condition under elbows and hocks. Scaliness and cracked skin cover the area which particularly comes in contact with hard surfaces. Rubbing lubricating oils into the skin and keeping the animal on soft surfaces are two possible solutions.

Ilio
See Hawaiian Poi Dog

Ilium
The bone surrounding the acetabulum. See Hindquarters

Illyrian Hound
A Yugoslavian running hound breed. See Chien Courant de Bosnie a Poil Dur

Illyrian Sheepdog
See Sarplaninac

Immunity
When bacteria invade the bloodstream, a reaction occurs. The body, largely through the action of the lymphatic system, can develop chemicals that act to destroy the specific bacterium that invaded. These chemicals, termed antibodies and antitoxins, are produced efficiently only when no antibiotics are administered. Immunity developed in this way is known as "acquired immunity." Inherent immunity is passed hereditarily, from parent to offspring. Some acquired immunities are believed to be capable of transmission, thereby becoming inherent in the offspring. Passive immunity is typically short lived. It is the immunity sometimes acquired when antibiotics or other drugs are administered to help combat invading bacteria.

Immunotherapy
Cancer therapy involving injections to stimulate the immune system in the hope that the body will then reject and destroy cancer cells. Research is ongoing.

Impetigo
Skin disease seen in puppies plagued by worms, distemper or teething problems. Little soft pimples cover the surface of the skin. Sulfur ointments and ridding the puppy of the worms will help.

Impotence
The male's inability to maintain an erection and therefore impregnate a bitch. See also Frigidity, Infertility

Impoundment
Dogs roaming at large, unlicensed and uncollared, are the most likely candidates for impoundment. Although the laws vary from place to place, animal control authorities are equipped with the right to impound, sell, and/or destroy dogs. A dog, as its owner's legal property, is afforded certain legal rights. A dog cannot be confiscated without proper notice or even a court hearing. The dog that has been knighted a nuisance or has proven reckless, damaging property or generally violating the sound pollution boundaries or a neighbor's continued peace of mind, can be confiscated and impounded. The owner is most usually notified before the impoundment as well as before the destruction of

the animal. Often the owner is allowed to defend the dog's "right to life" in court.
Pounds are required to keep the dog for a prescribed period of time before they can take any permanent action. The usual period is from one to fourteen days. Owners who find their problematic pooch at the pound must have the dog vaccinated and licensed (if not previously done), pay a fine and a fee for the facility's "service." Dogs that are not claimed are either offered for adoption or destroyed in a humane manner. Most pounds reserve the right to require a new owner to spay or neuter the dog.

Inbreeding
The practice of breeding two closely related dogs, possibly father–daughter or mother–son. Inbreeding is sometimes

Impoundment.
Unattended dogs roaming the streets are prime candidates for impoundment. Tranquilizer guns may be employed in certain situations. Photo by R. Pearcy.

used by experienced breeders to focus on desired traits present in the immediate family. Much debate centers heatedly around the practice of inbreeding. While it is believed to intensify some desired traits, it has also been found to intensify undesirable traits, generate unsound specimens with such hereditary conditions as hip dysplasia, cleft palates, hemophilia, etc., and result in overall unsound litters, many specimens of which require culling. Despite these and other complications, inbreeding remains a useful practice for experienced and knowledgeable breeders who do not abuse it. Inbreeding is not recommended for other than responsible professionals.

Inca Hairless Dog, blue-gray. Photo by I. Français.

man breed club that acquired the Inca Hairless Dog's F.C.I. recognition in 1985. Peru has two distinct hairless breeds: the Peruvian Inca Orchid is larger than the Inca Hairless and more deerlike in structure. The larger sized Inca Orchid grows to twice the weight of the Inca Hairless. The coated Inca Hairless Dog is rather inconspicuous in its appearance, looking rather like "any other dog," or any other sighthound, perhaps.

Like all other hairless breeds, the Inca Hairless Dog needs daily care for his skin, since it is very vulnerable to the sun's rays and to nicks and cuts. For the dog lover who is allergic to dog (or cat) hair, a hairless dog may be the perfect option. A handful of these can be found in the U.S. today.

ESSENTIALS OF THE INCA HAIRLESS DOG: The Inca Hairless Dog comes in three size variations: the small, 9–18 pounds (4–8 kg); the medium, 18–26 pounds (8–12 kg); and the large, 26–55 pounds (12–25 kg). Height varies accordingly. The skin is scaly and soft to the touch. In color the skin should be dark. Coated dogs can vary in color, with lighter colors and fawns often occurring. On the top of the Hairless Dog's head is a fuzzy tuft of hair. Smaller tufts occur on the edge of the ears, feet and tail.

Incontinence

Urinary incontinence is the partial or total loss of control of urinary excretion. It can result from the female's loss of estrogen due to spaying. The condition is not common and can be treated. Other causes of urinary incontinence include disease, tumors, growths, and internal injuries.

Infanticide

The act of killing a puppy, often for the sake of other pups and/or the mother herself. Puppies are culled for various reasons, often because their inherent defects would provide misery throughout their lives. In large litters, too large for the bitch to safely feed, the weaker members of the litter are sometimes culled for the sake of the others. If the pups are sound and promising, there

Inca Hairless Dog

Hairless dogs as such have existed in Peru for centuries. The dogs were highly prized companions of the Incan civilization. While few breeders living in Peru still actively breed the Inca Hairless Dogs, there are a number of breeders in Germany. It was the efforts of the Ger-

is little call for infanticide. Bottle feeding, whether exclusively or as a supplement, should be attempted before any healthy pup is put down. It is rare that a bitch will cull a pup, unless the pup has a defect that the bitch is aware of and instinctively kills it. *See also* Cannibalism, Culling.

Infectious canine hepatitis
See Hepatitis, canine

Infectious canine tracheobronchitis
See Kennel cough

Infectious jaundice
See Leptospirosis

Infertility
There are degrees of infertility, in dogs as well as in other animals. A male occasionally may prove impotent, unable to maintain the erection necessary for impregnation. Apparently potent males, capable of erection and ejaculation of semen, can be analyzed for fertility. The quality and quantity of the dog's semen affect the animal's fertility. With bitches, however, infertility can only be determined after an actual mating. Sterility can be the cause of infertility, as graphically explicit as it may sound. A sterile

bitch is referred to as "barren."

Owners can encourage their dogs' fertility by keeping the dog in shape and well nourished. Obesity is a common factor in infertility. Vitamin and mineral supplements are most often beneficial. Since the Victorian notion of plump, busty females has been long deflated, the most fertile bitch is hard and conditioned.

Breeders convey that timing is essential in capitalizing on a bitch's fertility. Coupling should occur in the eleventh day of estrus and then two days later. Immature males and aging males may not be fully fertile. Heredity, hormonal disturbances, and environmental factors all also contribute to the fertility (or infertility) of a dog. *See also* Breeding, Bitch, Stud dog, Exportation of dogs

Infield
That part of the racing course enclosed by the racing strip or track.

Inguinal hernia
See Hernias

Inhalation pneumonia
See Pneumonia

Inner thigh
See Thigh

Inoculation
The injection of a disease agent into an animal, usually to cause a mild form of the disease in an attempt to build up an immunity.

Insecticides

Any substance used to kill insects, including parasites. Insecticides can also be toxic to dogs and must be used only with discretion.

Inside rabbit

Lure that travels on the inside of the racing strip.

Instinct testing

Purebred fanciers became interested in instinct tests during the 1980s; the American Kennel Club encouraged breed clubs to dedicate themselves to traditional functions of their individual breeds. The dog, in its many diversified domestic forms, possesses strong instincts to perform in a given capacity. Purebred dogs that have never seen a farm, woods, desert or lake are surprising their owners with their innate instinctive abilities. Trials are being promoted by the major kennel clubs to develop each breed's natural instincts. Among the established tests are hunting tests, herding tests, lure coursing, terrier trials, weight pulling and sledding. Certain breeds are receiving special attention: coaching tests for Dalmatians, water rescue for Newfoundlands and Landseers, sledding for the Nordic breeds, etc. The results of these tests and response from the purebred community have been overwhelming—a positive new direction for the dog fancy to lean, taking the sole emphasis off conformation.

Insurance for dogs

Accident and life insurance for dogs are not usual. Home owners' or renters' policies more usually cover liability for dog bites or damage done by a dog to a neighbor's property. Most insurance companies, however, abide by a "one-bite rule." The second (and succeeding) times that your dog bites someone, liability will be assumed by the owner. Owners of vicious dogs (dogs deemed "vicious" by a judge or termed a "pit bull") may fail to obtain a policy that covers canine liability as a result of owning a high-risk pooch. Separate canine liability insurance can be obtained through certain companies but this almost invariably is very expensive. Most home owners' policies cover only dogs that are pets; kennel dogs kept for breeding purposes are often excluded from such a policy. It is common for dogs to be insured when being shipped by air, rail or sea.

Int. Ch.

Prefix for International Champion.

Instinct testing encourages dogs to develop their born-for abilities, performing tasks far-removed from today's daily routine. Belgian Tervuren performing in a herding test.

Instinct testing. Bearded Collie attempts duck-herding!

Interbreeding

Mating two dogs of different breeds, usually with the intention of creating a new breed. *See also* New breed creation

Interdigital pyoderma

Abscesses that occur with regularity between the toes of some dogs. An occasional abscess of the toe region does not constitute the condition. It can be treated with antibiotics.

Interim

Term used to designate a standard for a breed which is recognized but which has yet to be granted championship status by the Kennel Club of Great Britain. *See also* Kennel Club of Great Britain, Breed standard.

International Beauty Champion

One of two titles awarded by the F.C.I., this title is based on accumulating either one or two types of aptitude certificates and prizes in several countries under a number of different judges. The obedience trial title is known as an International Trial Champion.

International Canine Federation

See Fédération Cynologique Internationale

International Trial Champion

One of two titles awarded by the Fédération Cynologique Internationale, this title, recognizing the dog's excellence in obedience work, is based on accumulating either one or two types of aptitude certificates and prizes in several countries under a number of different judges. The conformation title is known as the International Beauty Champion.

Intervertebral discs

Circular structures composed of soft cartilage found between each spinal vertebrae which allow frictionless and smooth spinal movement. *See also* Disc (invertebral) abnormalities, Spinal column.

Intestines

Intestines comprise the lower part of the alimentary canal and are instrumental in the digestive system. There are essentially two parts, the small and the large. The intestines begin at the exit of the stomach and extend to the anus. *See* Digestive system.

Intimidation

Using the flushing whip, riding crop, leash or other object in a threatening manner when a gundog is on point or the birds are being flushed.

Intussusception

While its causes are not well understood, intussusception is the folding of layers of the intestine atop one another in a collapsing telescopelike fashion. Bleeding from the rectum is often the first noticeable sign, and upon closer inspection, it will be noticed that there is a swollen region of the abdomen affected by the collapse. Surgery is often the only possible treatment. The condition is not common in dogs.

Inu

Japanese word for dog. *See also* Akita, Tosa Inu, Shiba Inu, Shika Inus, Ainu Dog, Sanshu Dog, etc.

Instinct testing. Border Terrier making the scent-filled acquaintance of his rodent opponents at a terrier test. Photo by I. Français.

Inward constricted ears

Common in puppies whose ears are becoming erect, inward constricted ears angle towards the center line of the skull. In due time such lobes will stand naturally erect.

Iris

Dark (or usually dark) colored membrane that encircles the pupil. *See* Eye anatomy, Eye color

Irish Blue Terrier

See Kerry Blue Terrier

Irish Red and White Setter. Photo by I. Français.

Irish Red and White Setter

An Irish breed of setter that is actually older, although less popular, than the more abundant solid red Irish Setter. Prior to the nineteenth century, the Red and White Setters were the preferred setting dogs of hunters and setter fanciers. There are abundant records that establish the dogs' fine quality and genteel following. By the turn of the nineteenth century, however, the solid red dogs became the vogue and the Red and Whites suffered, eventually retreating to remote corners of hunters' dens. The last "original" Red and White was reported at the Strabane show of 1908, in Ireland. However, because the red-and-white gene is recessive, Red and Whites did and still do crop up in solid red litters. In the 1920s, the breed could be seen with one Rev. Noble Huston of County Down as working field dogs, not exhibition dogs. Another Catholic priest, Rev. Doherty, represented a group that wanted to revive the breed some decades later, and in the 1940s a breed club was formed. Shortly thereafter, a family by the name of Cuddy took interest in the breed and their contribution has been remarkable. Most specimens today trace their roots back to Cuddy dogs. In the 1970s, the Irish Kennel Club designated the monitoring and preservation of the breed to the Irish Red Setter Club. Through their efforts and determination, the breed today is solidly established, no longer reliant upon solid red litters for breeding stock. The Irish Red and White Setter enjoys recognition by the Kennel Club of Great Britain and looks forward to promising future growth.

If not as graceful as the Irish Setter, the Red and White is equally as proficient in field work and as untiring and jubilant in enthusiasm. The Red and Whites are slightly shorter, wider, and more thickly set on the body; their ears are set higher; and they have less long, heavy feathering than the Irish Red. The Red and White remains a friendly and devoted companion and hardy toiler.

ESSENTIALS OF THE IRISH RED AND WHITE SETTER: The athletic and powerful Red and White is a well-proportioned dog, without lumber. The head is broad with a noticeable stop. As the name indicates, the coat color is a clear particolor—a pure white base with solid patches in red; roaning is not permitted but mottling and flecking are common and pardonable. The coat, slightly coarse, is finely textured with thin feathering. Height: 23–27 inches (58–69 cm). Height: 40–70 pounds (18–32 kg).

Irish Red Setter

See Irish Setter

Irish Red Terrier

See Irish Terrier

Irish Setter

The "Modder Rhu," as he was called in Gaelic, or "Red Dog," traces his history back to the fifteenth century. The true component stock of the breed remains conjecture, but the commonly accepted theory states that the breed was the eventual result of English Setter, Spaniel, and Pointer crosses, with the positive likelihood of a Gordon Setter cross also occurring. The Irish Red Setter was the name originally chosen for the breed in America, in part to distinguish it from its older and once more populous counterpart, the Irish Red and White Setter. Whereas these setters are definite particolors, with white often predominating, the Irish Setter is accepted in self-color only, with no more than small, inconspicuous amounts of white allowed. The Irish Red Setter did not appear in England until the early 1800s, when several prestigious breeders of Irish Setters began to select exclusively for self-colored dogs. Several years later, when the breed was more solidly established, Stonehenge (Walsh) wrote: "The blood red, or rich chestnut or mahogany color is the color of an Irish Setter of high mark." These words mark the beginning of the great ascent of the breed, for from that point on the popularity of the breed grew steadily. The breed today is recognized and well loved around the globe, with acceptance and good numbers in all major registries.

A trainable hard worker, the Irish Setter is a thorough gentleman and a beguiling canine friend. Tractable and handsome, this is the ideal dog for the weekend hunter or owner seeking a loving, faithful companion with elegant good looks.

ESSENTIALS OF THE IRISH SETTER: An active, aristocratic bird dog, rich red in color, substantial yet elegant in build. The head is long and lean; the muzzle is moderately deep. Throat is moderately long, strong but not thick. The body is suffi-ciently long to allow a straight and free stride; shoulder blades long, wide and sloping well back; the chest deep; the ribs

Irish Setters, red.

well sprung; the legs sturdy, strong, and nearly straight, with plenty of bone. The coat, short and fine on top with long, silky feathering on ears, legs and chest, is rich chestnut or mahogany, with no sign of black. White on chest, forehead, etc., shall not disqualify. Height: 25–27 inches (63–69 cm). Weight: 60–70 pounds (27–32 kg). Feathering as straight and flat as possible. The gait must be lively, graceful

Irish Setter, red. Photographs by I Français.

and efficient. Balance is an important feature of the Irish Setter's overall appearance; a specimen must be at least balanced and at best beautiful.

Irish Terrier

The Irish Terrier is an old breed of Irish terrier. It is difficult to say how old. As a breed, these terriers became organized in 1879; before that time, most any terrier in Ireland was called "Irish Terrier." The

Irish Terriers, red, adult and puppy. Photo by I. Français.

spun and respun story of the 1872 Irish Terrier Dublin "Specialty" exemplifies the ruckus which the Irish Terrier breed underwent. This specialty show was every judge's nightmare. Fifty dogs were entered for competition, but there was no standard. Entered were Irish Terriers (i.e., terriers who lived in Ireland) of all walks of life: some were actually Cairn Terriers; others aspired to be. The Irish Red Terriers, as the breed became called, were classed variously, including an "Under 9 pounds" category (a bitch today weighs 25 pounds!). In the "Open Class," a class asking for trouble, the winner was a 30-pound bitch—solid white! The famous pedigreed specimens of Mickey Dooley named "Daisy" and

"Fry" were also entered. These two dogs ironically boasted the oldest pedigrees in existence. Most of the dogs entered had dubious pedigrees; many were notes from their owner saying, "bred by owner or Mrs. Mulligan, ask her." The breed club's establishment in 1879 put an end to this wonderfully Irish chaos. Nonetheless, the Irish Terriers were expert on grounding rats, unburrowing rabbit, badgering badger and outfoxing fox. Additionally, the breed can be used as a gundog and is able to retrieve, flush, and point. These are trainable, eager and confident dogs with stout hearts and much character.

ESSENTIALS OF THE IRISH TERRIER: Harmonious and symmetrical, its moderately long body is slackless and strong and should not appear cloddy. The head is also long, narrow between the ears, free from wrinkles with hardly perceptible stop. Drop V-shaped ears are characteristic of the breed, as is a well-trimmed beard, neither profuse nor absent. Neck of fair length, gradually widening, well carried and not throaty. Loin should be muscular and very slightly arched, ribs fairly sprung, rather deep than round. Hindquarters strong and muscular. Feet strong, tolerably round and moderately small. Height: 18 inches (45 cm). Weight: 25–27 pounds (11.5–12.5 kg). The coat is dense and wiry in texture, of rich quality with a broken appearance. The dog should be whole-colored in shades of red through wheaten.

Irish Water Spaniel

Persian manuscripts dating 4000 B.C. indicate the presence of "Water Dogs" in Ireland. Legal documents from the Christian era specifically mention "Irish Spaniels"—many believe that these writings (circa 17 A.D.) are the first references to spaniels in black-and-white history. Pinpointing the ancestry of the Irish Water Spaniel is quite problematic. The Poodle was probably a descendant of the Water Spaniel and therefore isn't the progenitor as once believed. The most reliable theory purports that the breed is the result of dogs brought into Ireland through Spain from beyond the Caucasus by the earliest inhabitants of Ireland.

Never shy, the Water Spaniel is bold and eager. He is courageous and effective in the field, especially when retrieving waterfowl. Grooming is a necessity but never a tortuous chore.

ESSENTIALS OF THE IRISH WATER SPANIEL: A strongly built, upstanding dog that should not appear leggy or tucked. The body is of medium length, pear-shaped at the brisket, and muscular. The head, rather sizable and high in dome with a prominent occiput, peaks in a topknot that consists of long, loose curls that do not bewig it. Height: 21–24 inches (53–61 cm). Weight: 45–65 pounds (21–30 kg). The proper coat is vital: it should be tight with crisp ringlets on the body, the neck, and slightly down the rattail; it is longer with loose curls on the legs and smooth on face and elsewhere. Color is a rich dark liver with plummish tint peculiar to the breed (sometimes called puce-liver).

Irish Wolfhound

"He would lay down his life rather than fail you." The Irish Wolfhound, one of the most written about and wondrous of the world's mighty canines, has attended the needs of mankind: protecting our young, removing nuisances, evoking smiles, provoking tears with its loyalty. The breed standards traditionally have compared the Irish Wolfhound to the lighter Scottish Deerhound and the heavier Great Dane. The comparison is not a random one: it is likely that one of the Great Dane's smooth-coated ancestors and dogs of Deerhound type contributed to the creation of the Irish Wolfhound. The most respected cynologists are sure that the Wolfhound's history parallels that of the Deerhound. Of course, the Celtic peoples of Ireland have long favored the large sighthound types. Upon the invasion of Delphi in 275 B.C., the Celts took home

Irish Water Spaniel, puce-liver. Photo by I. Français.

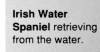

Irish Water Spaniel retrieving from the water.

sighthound types.

Having fascinated fourth-century Rome with its size and very presence, the breed has always been venerated for its massiveness and brute force. Of course, the dogs which Symmachus, the proud owner of the seven Wolfhounds, traipsed down the streets of Rome were about 150 pounds (67.5 kg) each and stood over three feet (91.5 cm) at the shoulders—even larger than many of the molossians that tumbled with black bears in the Roman arenas. In the fifteenth and sixteenth centuries, its hunting of wolves was foremost. One Wolfhound named "Aibe," while lacking the ladylike succor and curves of Helen, inspired a battle

the Wolfhound and its hunting prowess and undying loyalty to its master and family. The Irish, of course, can boast the most moving, alluring and genuine of any people's folklore.

H.D. Richardson in the 1840s, when much of the Irish Wolfhound population was dissolved, attempted to revive the great dogs by publishing an article in a penny newspaper. Captain G.A. Graham, however, is the man who deserves the fancy's gratitude for his work in recovering the lost breed, using the few existing strains of Wolfhound and necessary crosses to Danes and Borzois. The breed was first exhibited in the 1870s and has since remained.

The Irish Wolfhound is friendly and kind, although he can make a fierce and proverbially competent watchdog. The tallest dog in the world, which he is, needs plenty of room to stretch his record-making limbs and is therefore not the choice for apartment dwellers or condo inhabitants. Coursing and running events are offered for active enthusiasts in the U.S. and Britain.

Irish Wolfhound.
Photo by Tatham.

GROUP
FIRST
OVIDENCE COUNTY
ENNEL CLUB
FEB
1988
TATHAM PHOTO

when its owner refused King Cormac's offer of six thousand cows . . . or was it the king of Ulster offering four thousand? . . . regardless, it was most assuredly a lot of milk and manure for any man to resist!

Along with the last wolf killed in Ireland (approximately and allegedly 1780), went the population of the beast's slayer about fifty years later. More so than with any other breed, legends persist about

ESSENTIALS OF THE IRISH WOLFHOUND: Of great size, strength, and symmetry, the Irish Wolfhound, the tallest breed of dog, ideally stands up to 34 inches (86 cm) tall. The commanding and tousled appearance is nothing short of impressive, being very muscular yet very graceful in build. The head is long and carried high, with the frontal bones of the forehead very slightly raised and very little indentation between the eyes; the muzzle is long and somewhat pointed; the ears are small, rose shaped, and of a fine velvet texture—preferably dark in color, hanging not close to the face. The neck, very strong and muscular, is rather long and well arched, without dewlap or loose skin about the throat. The chest is very deep; the breast wide. The back is long, and the loins are arched. Hindquarters are muscular, with good bend of the stifle and the hocks well let down. The tail is long and slightly curved. The coat is rough and harsh, especially wiry on the head. Gray brindle, red, black, pure white, fawn, wheaten, steel gray, and other dark self-colors. Weight: 90–120 pounds (40.5–55 kg).

Irregular bite
See Bite types

Isabella
Term employed in certain breed standards to distinguish a specific fawn coloration (e.g., Doberman Pinscher, Bergamasco). Isabella is the dilute of brown and has been called palomino, camel's hair, and mouse-gray.

Ischium
Along with the ilium and pubis, the ischium comprises half of the pelvic girdle. *See* Hindquarters.

Istrian Hound
The Istrian Hound can be found in Yugoslavia in both smooth and wire coats. Rightly, these dogs are considered two individual breeds. The Smoothhaired Istrian Hound (Kratkodlaki Itrski Gonic) and the Wirehaired (Resasti Itrski Goñic) are each recognized individually. Crosses of Phoenician sighthounds and European scenthounds produced these Istrian hunters. These are

the oldest of the Yugoslavian scenthounds and can be differentiated from other similar breeds by their snazzy orange and white coloration. They are prized for their bloodtrailing abilities and admired for their basso voices on the trail. These dogs are expert on fox and hare but wild boar is their favorite quarry. Their handsome appearances have earned them fanciers in show circles; however, these dogs still function primarily as hunting mates.

ESSENTIALS OF THE ISTRIAN HOUND: The Istrian Hound's two coat types are separated into two individual breeds, with no interbreeding allowed. The Smooth weighs in from 35–50 pounds (16–23 kg)

and stands 18–21 inches (46–53 cm) high. The Wire can exceed those measure-

Istrian Hound, smooth, white with orange.

Istrian Hound, wire, white with orange. Photographs by I. Français.

ments by about 3 pounds (1.5 kg) and a couple of inches (5 cm). White with orange/yellow markings on the ears aptly describes both coat colors. The main difference, of course, is in coat type: the Smooth's coat is short and fine; the Wire's coat is 2–3 inches (5–8 cm) in length and comes with a woolly undercoat. Both breeds are racy and catfooted.

Istrian Sheepdog
See Karst Shepherd

Italian Coarsehaired Pointer
See Spinone Italiano

Denmark, Frederick the Great, and Queen Victoria also invited the Italian Greyhound to cross his legs on their thrones and poofs.

Ancestrally speaking, the Italian Greyhound belongs to the sighthound family; it is actually the flawless model of the classic English Greyhound in miniature. Throughout European history, the breed has been known in its exquisite and delicate form, having enjoyed immense popularity in the sixteenth and seventeenth centuries.

While the breed has never regained the status and popular attention that it once enjoyed, the Italian Greyhound has

Italian Greyhounds, mouse, white, and fawn. Photo by I. Français.

Italian Greyhound

Italian Greyhounds are likely the first dogs ever bred strictly for companionship. Ornamental and sincere, these tiny dogs were pets of the Greek, Egyptian and Roman nobilities. The breed, authentic in its antiquity, has been preserved on canvas, in stone, and through spices. Artists Blake, Carpacio, Van Dyck and Watteau are among the many who have painted the Italian Greyhound; sculptors and craftsmen have rendered this tiniest of sighthounds in stones and metals. Mummified dogs have been found in tombs of pharaohs which greatly resemble the perfectly miniaturized Greyhound we know today. Besides the great pharaohs of Egypt, such royalty as Mary Queen of Scots, Charles I, Queen Anne of

a moderate following today. In the United States, the breed is fortunate with a strong, active parent club continuing to promote it as an outgoing, sturdy companion dog. In the show rings of Great Britain and the U.S., the breed is increasingly on the rise.

The petite Italian Greyhound, though not shy, takes time to bond; he is a discerning dog, choosing his bed, his meals, and his friends with the utmost care. He is both loving and lovable—the perfect companion for those looking for an intelligent, elegant dog with a definitive sense of history.

ESSENTIALS OF THE ITALIAN GREYHOUND: A greyhound in miniature. Slender, lithe and light, the Italian Greyhound is elegant and graceful. The A.K.C. standard specifies height as 13–15 inches (33–38 cm) while the K.C.G.B. requires a weight of 6–10 pounds (3–10 kg). The head is long, flat, and narrow. The ears are rose shaped, not pricked, soft and fine and placed well back on the head. The eyes are rather large, bright and attentive. Highly refined in appearance, the Italian Greyhound has an arched neck and a high-stepping gait, making it resemble quite resolutely the larger sighthounds. The chest is deep and narrow, ribs and brisket of good length, back slightly arched. Forelegs straight; hindlegs parallel when viewed from behind. Stifle well bent, the hocks well let down.

Italian Hound
   See Segugio Italiano

Italian Pointer
   See Bracco Italiano

Italian Segugio
   See Segugio Italiano

Italian Spinone
   See Spinone Italiano

Itching
   A salivating flea scurrying up a dog's rib, grass fungi creeping up a dog's cringing spine, an irritating perennial twitch—all levy an itch. Pruritis (perhaps the elitist's catchword for itching) has caused vets and dermatologists to scratch their perplexed brows for years. Dogs itch rather seasonally, generally late summer through early fall—thus the condition "summer eczema." Itchiness is often accompanied by the loss of hair. Some vets attribute the condition (at least partially) to flea bite dermatitis, the dog's allergic reaction to the flea's saliva. Some irritant in summer moisture or simply parasites moving from one place to another may cause itching. Pet shops carry flea shampoos and yellow oil lotions which can be of some temporary relief. Steroids have been used to curb itching, but only in desperate cases.

Itrski Gonič
   See Istrian Hound

Ivicene
   See Ibizan Hound

Italian Greyhound, white with mouse. Photo by I. Français.

Jabot

Longish hair on the neck and chest of the Schipperke. A furnishing placed similarly on different breeds is called an apron.

Jack Russell Terrier, smooth, white with brown.

Jack Russell Terriers, puppies

Jack Russell Terrier

The Jack Russell Terrier of today is essentially a Fox Terrier crossbred with a number of other terriers, but not necessarily the descendants of the terriers that worked with Parson Russell of Devon, England. Reverend Russell was a fox hunter who employed and developed a strain of terrier capable of performing the task of fox hunting. The "purebred" Jack Russell of today is only recognized by the United Kennel Club. To be true to the strain which the Parson favored, the dogs must not look like a Bull Terrier,

with broad chest or egg-shaped heads, nor be too short on the leg. For Russell's purposes, a terrier that was part Bull Terrier possesses the tendency to kill the quarry; and, as the fox was a dear quarry, destroying it upon catching it was undesirable. Russell actually favored the wirehaired terriers since in smoothhaired dogs he suspected Bull Terrier blood. Further, dogs too short on the leg were not able to keep up with the Parson's pack of galloping hounds, a necessary attribute. There have been tendencies toward both these undesirable traits which have festered in the Jack Russell breed up to modern day. A number of persons still perpetuate the squat, egg-headed JRs. Although some fanciers are working toward acceptance in the U.S., recognition was never important for Jack Russell, one of the founding members of the K.C.G.B..

Jack Russells are frequent sights on horse farms. Terriers on horse farms are logical necessities—horse food (corn, oats, etc.) attracts rats, hence the need for a ratter. The Jack Russell is a competent ratter, able to keep pace with the best of them. Additionally, much of the breed's popularity can be attributed to its easygoing, people-loving personality and adaptability to house or apartment life.

ESSENTIALS OF THE JACK RUSSELL TERRIER: An elegant and sprightly little terrier that is well balanced and well structured. Three coat types—broken, rough and smooth—all come predominantly white with tricolor, brown, or black markings. Height: 9–15 inches (23–38 cm). Weight: 12–18 pounds (5.5–8.5 kg). The chest is not so broad as to interfere with the dog's entering a fox hole. The body is longer than it is tall. The tail is docked, leaving approximately four inches (10 cm) on the adult specimen. The ears are dropped Vs. The muzzle is long and rather pointed.

Jackals

There are three jackals of the genus *Canis*; they are: *Canis aureus*, *C. mesomelas*, and *C. adustus*, commonly known respectively as the golden jackal, black-backed jackal, and side-striped jackal. The golden jackal is the most common of these three Old World animals and boasts a number of common names, including: Asian, common, gray, Indian, silver-backed, and yellow jackal. In appearance the golden jackal resembles a small, light-weight wolf, but the species varies considerably in physical specifics from location to location. Maximum height is around 16 inches (41 cm), and weight is usually no more than 25 pounds (13 kg). Distribution is mostly south of the wolf's, ranging from North Africa to south of the Sahara. It is also found in southeastern Europe, the southwest Soviet Union, and across the Near East.

The golden jackal does not construct elaborate dens but prefers to inhabit simple burrows, often taking over those of other animals. The voice of the jackal is described as a series of three or four ascending wails followed by three quick yelps. Jackals are unselective dogs that feed primarily on rodents and small birds. The animals usually hunt singly or in pairs but will occasionally be seen carousing in a small pack.

The black-backed jackal is a re-

stricted native of Africa, where it is a well-known and commonly seen scavenger. In some parts of Africa, its natural prey is now extinct, and the black-backed jackal has adapted to prey on livestock and the remains of felled game and other dead animals. Distinctive is this jackal's coloration: dark saddle marking from the neck to the set-on of the tail, with the sides of the head and the outer legs a reddish

Jack Russell Terrier, wire, white with brown. Photo by I. Français.

Jackals. The black-backed jackal, *Canis mesomelas*.

hue, and the throat, chest, and belly ranging from to sand to white. This jackal has several calls, which it employs on the hunt. The height is about 19 inches (48 cm), while weight hovers around 20 pounds (9 kg).

Also native and restricted to Africa is the side-striped jackal, which is infrequently seen by man. Known also as the Rhodesian jackal, this animal ranges the open woodlands and savannahs of central Africa. Both larger and more wolflike in appearance than the other (and more common) jackals, this jackal usually stands no lower than 20 inches (51 cm) at the shoulder and weighs around 30 pounds (13.5 kg).

Jacket
Synonym for coat, most often employed when discussing the coats of terriers. *See* Coat.

Jagdgriffon
A large herding dog once found in its native Austria. The breed was similar in basic construction to the Briard of France, and, to a lesser extent, the Ovtcharkas of the U.S.S.R. The Jagdgriffon may have contributed blood to the Leonberger.

Jämthund, gray.
Photo by I.
Français.

Jämthund
The Jämthund is the largest of the extant Swedish elkhound types. The dog's name comes from the Jämtland district of Sweden. The breed may find its

origin as a hunter of bear in Norway, but history finds him more commonly hunting moose in Sweden. Since the sport of bear hunting is no longer common practice, the elkhounds stake their fame on such quarry as lynx, wolf, and moose. In Scandinavian countries, the Jämthund has been commonly employed to hunt elk, a sport and necessity. The Elkhound breeds are as ancient as any breed of dog known to man. Popular in its homeland of Sweden as a hunter and companion, these are lively, hardy dogs that hunt efficiently and methodically.

ESSENTIALS OF THE JÄMTHUND: The Jämthund is the taller and heavier brother of his close-resembling and more popular relative, the Norwegian Elkhound. The Jämthund weighs around 66 pounds (30 kg) and stands between 23 and 25 inches (59–64 cm) tall. His long legs are thick boned; his hindlegs are especially well muscled with slight angulation. The deep chest, moderate tuck, and brawny shoulders give an athletic look, which is substantiated by his vigorousness on the hunt. He has, as do the other Elkhounds, a narrowing taper to the skull, beginning at the erectly carried ears, and a curling tail carried over the body. The coat color may be any shade of gray, with white or lighter gray markings common.

Japanese Akita
See Akita

Japanese Chin
The Japanese Chin, or Japanese Spaniel, shares its history with the embroidered likes of the Chinese Pekes. Tapestries, vases, ornaments and silks are among the renderings of these Oriental toys which reinforce its antiquity. These lion dogs of Peking were presented to the emperor of Japan by the emperor of China; likewise, Chinese teachers, spreading Buddhism to Japan, are believed to have taken their sleeve dogs with them. The lion, of course, represented the deity Buddha and the Pe-

kingese, known as the Lion Dog, symbolized the omnipotence of the divine one. These dogs were perceived as royal and sacred. The Chinese bred these dogs selectively and ceremonially, under keen supervision. In the sleeves of his respectful master, the Chin gained profound admiration of the human species and subtle, loving understanding. The Japanese selective breeding for specific traits yields the dissension between the Chin and the Pekingese today.

A second theory persists which involves a Korean emissary giving the breed as gifts to the Japanese emperor in 732 A.D. Neither theory has been proven or disproven and both are equally probable (or improbable). Regardless, the receiving Japanese are most responsible for the perfection of the Chin as we know it today.

American commander Commodore Perry, in 1853, brought a pair of Chins to the reigning Victoria after the forced harmony of his "Pacific overture" in Japan. In 1880, the Chin made its British show-world debut; the Rothchilds, Lady Samuelson and Queen Alexandra are among the earliest of British fanciers; within four or five years, the breed club was on its feet.

The specimens originally brought into Europe were smaller than the dogs we know today. It is believed that English Toy Spaniel blood was infused to "adjust" the Chin's mite-size. Importation into the United States occurred during the later decades of the nineteenth century. August Belmont of New York received two of the very first American imports. Although Belmont's dogs didn't populate the States with tiny Spaniels, they did spur a greater wave of newcomers. Ten dogs appeared in the 1882 New York

show. Japanese Chins were called Japanese Spaniels prior to the A.K.C. acceptance in 1977. The dogs have also taken strongholds in France, Switzerland, Austria, and Germany.

Japanese Chin, red and white.

ESSENTIALS OF THE JAPANESE CHIN: Aristocratic and elegant, compact and smart, the Chin comes in two varieties according to weight: over 7 pounds (3 kg) and under 7 pounds—the rule is: the smaller the better. The Chin has a large head and

Japanese Chin, black and white. Photographs by I. Français.

large, dark, prominent eyes set wide apart. The Chin is an ornate dog, with a profuse coat of long straight and silky hair. The thick feathering tends toward stand-offish, thus creating a visible mane; the feathering on the upper legs creates the effect of breeches. The legs are straight, of fine bone. The body is square and compactly built, wide in the chest, cobby. Length of body equal to height at withers. Hindquarters are straight with profuse feathering. Colors include black and white or red and white in a broken pattern.

Japanese Middle Size Dog
See Sanshu Dog

Japanese Shiba Inu
See Shiba Inu

Japanese Small Size Dog
See Shiba Inu

Japanese Spaniel
See Japanese Chin

Japanese Spitz, white. Photo by I. Français.

Japanese Spitz
The Japanese Spitz is a small spitz type that became popular in Japan. The breed is believed to have descended from the Samoyed, although he bears a strong resemblance to the American Eskimo, a spitz that is a derivative of the German Spitzen. Japanese bred smallish Samoyeds to continually reduce the dog's size—the end result being the Japanese Spitz. Creation of the breed commenced in the late 1800s; the breed is of worldwide distribution today, but is still fighting to attain a firmer foothold.

The term Japanese Spitz once referred to the group of small nordic-type dogs that reside in Japan, the family of Inu. Today the Shiba Inu has grown to be the most popular of the group. The American Eskimo, also solid white only, is widely beloved in its native U.S., and this breed will likely preclude the growth of the Japanese Spitz breed's popularity.

ESSENTIALS OF THE JAPANESE SPITZ: The Japanese Spitz is pure white with a profuse, stand-off coat; the tail is carried curled over the back in nordic fashion. The coat is short on the bottom half of the legs, with breeches on the hindlegs and feathering on the forelegs. The head is medium sized, without coarseness; moderately broad and slightly rounded. The ears are carried prick; the muzzle tapers slightly; the eyes are dark, and the nose and lips are black, together contrasting with the pure white coat. The neck is strong and arched, of moderate length. The quarters are well proportioned and balanced. Height: 15 inches (38 cm). Weight near 13 pounds (6 kg).

Japanese Terrier
The Japanese Terrier was created during the early eighteenth century in Japan. Smooth Fox Terriers, imported from Holland, and a blend of other European terriers and indigenous Japanese dogs yielded this Nipponese terrier. These are variously referred to as Mikado Terriers, Oyuki Terriers (for the snow white coat), and Nippon Terriers. These little dogs, although small enough to warrant their being solely toy companions, can function effectively as gundogs as well as terriers. The Japanese Terrier is a respected retriever and a skilled water

worker, able to retrieve a bagged duck or downed goose. Certain specimens were fostered exclusively as toys. Not popular in Japan, the breed has a slight but growing fancy on the Continent.

ESSENTIALS OF THE JAPANESE TERRIER: A smooth-haired, smooth-muzzled terrier that is predominantly white with sparsely distributed specks of black and tan. The refined, elegant type of this terrier evokes the affecting winds of the smaller sighthounds. A small docked tail and a proportionately small head placed on its well-muscled body give the breed a distinctive appearance. Height: 12–15 inches (30–38 cm). Weight: 10–13 pounds (4.5–6 kg).

Japanese Tosa
See Tosa Inu

Jasper
A clearish, ofttimes red, brown or yellow variation of quartz used to describe the badger colored patches on the Great Pyrenees. Although in the United States the Great Pyrenees is most commonly solid white, in Great Britain and other European countries (France), the Pyrenean Mountain Dog (as he is known in England) is frequently patched with badger or jasper.

Jaundice
Not a disease but a condition, jaundice is a warning sign that a disorder or disease is affecting the liver. Jaundice appears as a yellowish discoloration of the eyes, skin, gums, and mucus membranes. Possible causes include: toxemia, tumors, and an occluded bile duct. Any condition that prevents bile from enter-

ing the intestine can cause this bile to become absorbed into the blood and consequently cause a yellowing of bodily tissues. Urine too may become discolored, and stools tend to turn grayish and sticky. Any such condition is known as obstructive jaundice. A common cause of obstructuve jaundice in dogs is the presence of roundworms, which enter the bile duct and grow to obstruct it. Two other common causes include duct inflammation and gallstones. Canine hepatitis, which prevents the liver from properly functioning, and anemia may also cause jaundice. Both jaundice and obstructive jaundice require the investigation of a veterinarian.

Javanese Dingo
Originating on the Java island, the Javanese Dingo is a pariah type which has been found in Indonesia for centuries. Like the Dingo or Warrigal, it is not recognized by its native registries and likewise enjoys all the privileges of its Australian cousin.

Jaws
The two bony parts that hold the teeth and frame the mouth; the lower jaw, known as the mandible, is hinged and movable, while the upper jaw, or maxilla, is not. Both jaws consist of right and left halves, which are firmly connected at the mandibular symphysis (center front), and house 22 teeth. The canine jaw usually meets in a scissors bite, that is, equally; undershot and overshot jaws are considered serious faults, unless otherwise indicated in a specific breed standard (i.e., the Bulldog requires an undershot jaw). Jaws are used principally for

Japanese Terriers, tricolor. Photo by I. Français.

eating purposes but there are exceptions: the Greyhound uses its jaws for hunting; the terriers almost unanimously use their jaws to execute their task; the bullbaiting dogs use their jaws to clamp onto their opponent's nose and hold. The term "punishing jaws" has been applied to well-developed overall jaws, capable of downing and killing their prey—the Afghan Hound, for instance, is endowed with such jaws. A tight-lipped jaw is one that appears thin lipped, closely tracing the jaw outline. *See also* Bite types

Jeweled eye
See Walleye

Jindo, fawn, owned by Ted and Judy Rabinowitz. Photo by I. Français.

Jindo

The Korean government has been most protective of its native and highly treasured Jindo. While the history of the breed remains uncertain, legends say that the dogs found their way to the island of Chindo, southwest of the Korean mainland, on a Mongolian "turtle" ship. The Jindo on the island has remained pure and still bears many eastern dog traits (small ears, curled tail, sharp expression). Dogs have been smuggled out of Korea and in the U.S. abide mainly with Korean Americans. Jindoes on mainland Korea have become more mongrelized due to interbreeding with other dogs. Since 1938 both Japan and

Korea have considered the breed a national natural treasure. It is useful as a ratter and hunter of weasils and groundhogs. The dogs are loyal but aloof, protective of family and good with children.

ESSENTIALS OF THE JINDO: A well-balanced, double-coated spitz-type dog, the Jindo has a spirited bold expression, deep-set almond eyes, erect, small ears, and a dense coat. The skull is eight-sided and the muzzle is moderately pointed. The tail is short and curled up. Height: 16–23 inches (40–59 cm). Weight: 30–40 pounds (66–88 kg). Colors include many shades of yellow (from reddish fawns to browns).

Joints

Joints mark the junction of two bones. The articular ends of these bones are exceedingly smooth; some are convex, while others are concave. The convexities fit accurately into the concavities, and the two surfaces glide freely, one over the other, lubricated as they are by joint oil. The joint proper is completely surrounded, enclosed and strengthened by a fibrous capsular ligament, and upon the inner surface of this is found the synovial membrane which secretes synovia (joint oil). At various points, strong bands of tough fiber, known as ligaments, cross the joint from above to below and retain the bones in position. Their location must of course depend upon how the joint moves. Many joints are further strengthened, and maintained intact, by masses of muscular tissue which surround them—an example, the hip joint. The shoulder and the hip joint are known as ball and socket joints, and such joints allow for great range of movement. Some joints have pads or discs of cartilage interposed between the two bones; another type of joint also has cartilage present but allows for little movement. The stifle joint, which *see*, of the dog's hindleg corresponds to the human knee and is perhaps the joint most likely to present any complications to the dog. Some common joint disorders and conditions include: arthritis, lupus erthematosus, and osteoarthritis, which *see*. For problems related to specific joints *see*: Elbow joint, problems of; Knee, problems of; Hip joint, problems of; Spinal joints, problems of.

Jowls

In canine terms, pendulous or heavy lips (e.g., Bulldog).

Judge

The person who is chosen by the show-giving club to determine the relative merits of all dogs entered in a conformation show. Judges are licensed by the appropriate registering body, but each show must select its own judging panel. To be licensed, a judge-candidate must satisfactorily fulfill the requirements of length of time participating in the dog sport, litters bred, champions owned and bred, passing written and oral examinations, and attending symposiums, workshops, etc. Some judges serve without compensation, while others expect a full allowance for their expenses; some serve professionally and receive a flat fee for their services and expenses.

Judging dogs

Nothing perhaps is more overwhelming for the first-time attendant at the Westminster Kennel Club Show than to

show judge, in absolute intimacy with the breed standard, weighs and balances the sum of each entrant's parts to determine which dog is the finest. As imperceptible and seemingly subjective as it is

to observe a judge pulling one Dalmatian out of a line-up of 25—when the novice's eyes see nothing but spots—it is more amazing to observe the same judge choose Best in Show from six or seven totally different, all absolutely remarkable dogs. Such is the phenomena of judging! The cynic's response, inspired by cloudy prejudices and howling politics, asserts that the judge was paid off or is faking it. *Au contraire*, ye of little faith and poor sportsmanship—ask a judge to point out for you the good points and bad

Judging dogs. Carefully studying the conformation of two Dogo Argentinos in a Rare Breed show is Dr. Carl Semencic.

Judging dogs. For an American judge, this is the show of shows. Akita Best of Breed at the Westminster Kennel Club Show (1981).

watch the prowess of the judge pulling out the "right" dogs from a line-up of dogs that look as like as like can be. A

points of any dog he/she judges, and you will discover that the judge is in total command of the essentials of each breed—and the nuances and subtleties that lurk below.

Each breed must be more or less a certain size: weight and height; more or less look a certain way; basically wear a smooth, woolly, wiry or non-existent coat, and more or less walk a certain walk. It is, of course, fortunate that essentially purebreds are the sole contestants in such conformation exhibition. Without a standard on which to rely, no judge would have any basis for his determination, other than pure subjectivity.

No longer emphasized today as strongly as in years passed, a Scale of Points for each breed could be relied upon by judges. This scale, often included at the end of the breed standard, assigned a point value (out of 100) to each of the dog's body parts, gait, expression, etc. Today not every A.K.C. standard employs a Scale of Points, and none of the K.C.G.B. standards include one. Many judges, breeders and exhibitors believe that the scale was the most effec-

tive way of conveying what is and is not important in the breed. From the scale, the desired traits could be clearly emphasized. For instance, the French Bulldog standard assigns 40 points to the head and two points to the coat; in the Chihuahua, the head and coat each receive 20 points. Certain standards replace the Scale of Points with a listing of features in order of importance (e.g., Scottish Deerhound and Irish Wolfhound). Breed standards that use neither must clearly emphasize in the text which features are most important. The standards for the Collie and German Shepherd, for example, are excruciatingly explicit in emphasizing points of utmost importance in the text.

Responsible judges, like sensible breeders, consider the overall soundness of a dog, without overly emphasizing one specific show point, a fashionable exaggeration or near-grotesque feature. Determining, therefore, the pernicious, injurious fault from the easily rectified, inconsequential fault is paramount. For example, the staggered gait of a Bullmastiff should be more consequential than the oversilkiness of a Bichon Frise.

While there are dissenting idiosyncra-

sies in judging procedures from country to country, and from registry to registry, essentially the ring procedures are the same—the dogs are evaluated for their merits individually and in comparison to the competition. Generally a judge con-

siders the major points first: head type, balance, the arch of neck and length; placement of shoulders, depth of chest, spring of ribs; turn of feet; musculation and angulation of the hindquarters; the set of the tail. Gaiting is observed after the judge has evaluated the major conformation points.

Jugoslavenski Planinski Gonič
    See Yugoslavian Mountain Hound

Jugoslavenski Trobojni Gonič
    See Yugoslavian Tricolor Hound

Jugoslovenski Ovčarski Pas Sarplaninas
    See Sarplaninac

Jump demand
    In obedience trials, applicable to retrieving the dumbbell over an obstacle in the Open Classes and for the first half of

the hurdle and bar jump exercise in the Utility Class. The jump is never less than 1.5 times the height of the dog at the withers, but never more than three feet (91.5 cm), except in cases of such breeds as Bullmastiffs, Great Danes, Great Pyrenees, Mastiffs, Newfoundlands, and St. Bernards, which must jump the height of the withers.

Jumped
    When a pack of hounds has been working a line slowly and suddenly makes the fox go away at full speed, the fox is said to have been jumped.

Jumper
    Hurdler. A dog that races on a track of hurdles.

Junior Showmanship
    This class for boys and girls ten to sixteen years of age focuses on the junior's ability to handle his/her dog. The dog's conformation is not a factor in Junior Showmanship competition. Junior Showmanship, popular in the U.S., Mexico and Canada, developed originally as an informal outing; its popularity influenced the A.K.C. to formalize the events with its usual boilerplate regulations. National championships are held annually as part of the Westminster Dog Show in New York. *See also* Shows and showing

Jura Hound
    See Bruno Jura Laufhund, Saint Hubert Jura Laufhund, Laufhund

K-9 Corps

Military-employed dogs that work as police dogs in times of peace and war. In the Vietnam War, the K-9 Corps saved virtually thousands of lives. In peace time, the dogs are used as museum guards, drug detectors, mine detectors and government patrol dogs. *See also* Police dogs, War dogs

Kabyle Dog

See Chien de l'Atlas

Kaffir Dog

See Hottentot Dog

Kai Dog, medium brindle. Photo by I. Français.

Kai Dog

The Japanese Kai Dog or the Tora Dog can be loosely categorized as a Shika-Inu, or a medium-sized dog. A discussion about dogs in twentieth-century Japan must begin with the large importation of Western breeds into Japan after the First Great War. The Japanese were so greatly impressed by the abilities of the Pointer and Alsatian that native breeders took to these newcomer canines and abandoned their Japanese dogs. Canine researcher and breeder Haruo Isogai in the 1930s was the first to divide Japan's native dogs by size; Isogai's study attempted to regroup and revive the native breeds of the land. The Kai Dog was often referred to as a "deerhound" and is a fine hunter, though rarely seen outside his native country. In 1990 the first Japanese Kai were imported to the U.S.: three females and one male.

The name Tora Dog (*tora* means tiger) is derived likely from the brindle coat, although some believe the dog's wild, untamable disposition influenced the choice. Incidentally, the Kai does *not* hunt tiger, as he would be hard pressed to find tigers roaming the Japanese countryside. He is considered a one-man dog that also gets on well with other dogs. The physical characteristics of the Kai Ken are dependent on the individual dog's bloodline: descendants of "Dairo," the deerhunter, are thin, long-bodied, fox-faced and light-footed; descendants of "Kaikuro," the boar hunter, are thick, stocky, bear-faced, and sure-footed.

ESSENTIALS OF THE KAI DOG: The Kai is a medium-sized dog, standing 18–23 inches (46–59 cm) tall, and is of the classic Japanese canine type. He is distinguishable from his other mid-sized Japanese relatives by his narrower skull, slightly more tapered head, and less than domesticated nature. Dogs found in the mountainous regions are extensively worked and may weigh between 35–45 pounds (16–21 kg); dogs inhabiting the homes and kennels of non-hunting fanciers may weigh as much as 60 pounds (27 kg). Coat is short, straight, and somewhat coarse. The most common colors are: black brindle (Kuro-Tora), red brindle (Aka-Tora) and medium brindle (Chu-Tora).

Kaikadi

This unique Indian breed is specific to the nomads of Maharashtra. It is known for its exceptionally fast and quick snapping abilities, possessing skills similar to any farm terrier. In the jungle the Kaikadi is game at chasing both monkeys and rotund (though aerobic) jungle rats. In size these dogs stand 15–18 inches (38–46 cm) with long thin legs, well muscled. The head is thin and long; the eyes are very prominent; the ears erect. Colors are variegated—white, tan and black are dominant.

Kangal Dog

To protect the robust livestock prided by the Kangal shepherds of Turkey, a powerful dog was developed. From peoples capable of producing animals as exquisite as the Arabian horse and their robust Turkish livestock, the Kangal Dog or Karabash comes, offering elegant movement, soundness, and structure. In performance, the Kangal Dog is a wondrous sight; in dedication and endurance, this dog is prized like no other in the Kangal region. The component stock which shepherds utilized to create the breed has been effectively concealed, but the short coat and curled tail suggest more than a hint of the Nordic breeds. These shepherds are refreshingly obedient and always loyal, even though they are never kept as strictly pets, since this would be to deny them of their natural guarding duties. This approach to the flock is subtle but highly effective. Not the massive force of some of the more aggressive flock guards, the Kangal Dog is a wary and able protector.

ESSENTIALS OF THE KANGAL DOG: Color: graying dun or chamois, with a black mask. The limbs and body yield a sturdy balanced construction. His shoulders and thighs are especially muscled. The thick straight forelegs and powerful neck contribute to this overall impression. Height: 28–35 inches (71–89 cm). Weight: 75–150 pounds (34–69 kg). The coat is dense while remaining essentially short and smooth.

Kangaroo Dog

See Kangaroo Hound

Kangaroo Hound

The Kangaroo Hound was derived from selective crosses of Greyhounds and Deerhounds in order to hunt kangaroo. Although this springy marsupial is protected by Australian conservation laws today, at one time it was a verifiable pest and crop destroyer. Dogs were needed to help course and diminish the high kangaroo population. The kangaroo can travel at unbelievable velocities; and, when it is overtaken by one of these powerful running hounds, it has the good sense to hop into the water and thus force its assailant to attack swimming. Or, backed against a tree, the kangaroo is formidable, equipped with invincible legs and a sweeping monster tail. A kangaroo willingly and viciously fights to the death. The dog bred to hunt the kangaroo had to be equally quick-footed and quick-witted—and plenty strong.

If any Kangaroo Hounds exist today, they are found on remote stations in Australia, where they may be employed to catch small game for the ranchers. Australian Greyhounds, generally smaller than the Kangaroo Hounds that diminished the kangaroo population, are more likely to still exist.

ESSENTIALS OF THE KANGAROO HOUND: The robust and powerful Kangaroo Hound is a dog comparable to an oversized English Greyhound and can weigh as much as 80 pounds (36 kg). The head is narrow and lengthy, the ears tiny and rose shaped. The body is well ribbed with a deep chest. The legs are long and powerful. Height: 27–30 inches (68–76 cm). Can be any color, often with white predominating, although solid black dogs were known. The coat of these hounds is medium in texture: a rough coat that appears smooth but is coarse in actuality.

Kangal Dog, dun. Photo by I. Français.

Karelian Bear Dog, black with white. Photo by I. Français.

Karabash
See Anatolian Shepherd Dog, Kangal Dog, Akbash Dog

Karelian Bear Dog
The Karelian Bear Dog has functioned as both a guard dog and hunter in the area once known as Karelia, found in northern Europe (now the Karelo-Finn-

ish republic of the U.S.S.R.). This region has always been populated by tough big-

game hunting canines. Among this avid hunter's game are the buck, hare, and moose. He is also fearless enough to fight the wolf and therefore functioned as a protector by hunting these large wild canids. In Finland, his established homeland, the dog is used mostly on elk and is the favored dog of native big-game hunters. The breed's popularity has crossed the borders of a number of Scandinavian countries as well. He is known variously as the Karelsk Björnhund, the Karjalankarhukoira, and the Karelischer Barenhund.

Not the usual choice for the casual pet owner, the Karelian Bear Dog is a hunter of unyielding bravery and determination. The true outdoors enthusiast and dedicated hunter can look to this hard-working breed, as have some dog men in Canada.

ESSENTIALS OF THE KARE-LIAN BEAR DOG: Robustly built, well boned and of moderate size, the Karelian Bear Dog is slightly longer than he is high. The outer coat is straight and stiff; the undercoat is soft and dense. In color he is black with a slight brownish or dull cast preferred. White markings are distinct and occur on the head, neck, chest, abdomen, legs and tail. The head is shaped as a blunt wedge. The ears are cocked and point outward slightly. The body is sturdy and the back is well developed. Height: 19–23 inches (48–59 cm). Weight: 44–50 pounds (20–23 kg).

Karelian Bear Laika
See Russo-European Laika

Karelischer Barenhund
See Karelian Bear Dog

He is a lightly built dog with a bushy tail. Weight: 25–30 pounds (11.5– 14 kg). The coat is dense and stand-offish. Most common colors are red with a white chest, intermingled with gray or black hair, and fawn of various shades.

Karelian Bear Dog, black with white. Photo by I. Français.

Karelo-Finnish Laika

Finnish doglore refers to the Finlandskaja or the Karelo-Finnish Laika as a cross between a fox and a nordic-type dog; indeed, the muzzle has a very fox-like suggestion. The breed originated long before the national boundaries of the present-day Scandinavian countries or Soviet Union. The Karelo-Finnish Laika and the Finnish Spitz were once probably the same breed. Later, however, with the drawing of hard-line national parameters, and the claiming of all inhabitants existing within them as the given country's, two distinguishable breeds emerged. The Karelo-Finnish Laika hunts small game, including various birds and hare, at which it proves exceptional.

ESSENTIALS OF THE KARELO-FINNISH LAIKA: The Karelo-Finnish Laika has a skull that is not broad between the ears; this feature coupled with the circular eyes, appearing mistrustful rather than sly, gives the breed a more jackal-like, rather than foxlike, expression. The neck appears disproportionately thick, due to the long profuse ruff which extends to the cheeks. The back is moderately long, slightly exceeding the dog's height of 15–19 inches (38–48 cm).

Karelsk Björnhund
See Karelian Bear Dog

Karelskaja
See Karelo-Finnish Laika

Karjalankarhukoira
See Karelian Bear Dog

Karst Shepherd
The Karst Shepherd or Krasky Ovcar is a sturdy flock guard from Yugoslavia. This sheepdog is one of the nation's oldest canines and, although he appears similar to the flock guard breeds of neighboring European countries, he probably

Karelo-Finnish Laika, red-fawn. Photo by V. Pcholkin.

Karst Shepherd, iron-gray. Photo by I. Français.

antecedes most of them. In the Karst region, this dog has been protecting herds and flocks for centuries. The breed is scarcely seen outside Yugoslavia but can be found in conformation competition in some European countries from time to time. Less aggressive than many of the larger flock guards, the Karst Shepherd or Istrian Shepherd, as he is occasionally called, is energetic and efficient. He is dedicated to his task, but very often this loyalty must be earned; he is necessarily wary of unfamiliars.

ESSENTIALS OF THE KARST SHEPHERD: This iron-gray shepherd weighs from 58–88 pounds (26–40 kg) and stands 20–24 inches (51–61 cm) high. Hardy and mus-

cular, the Karst Sheepdog can flourish in a rugged mountain climate. The breed has a relatively long water-resistant outer coat and an insulating undercoat. The Krasky possesses "spectacles," lighter rings of coat around the eyes. The ears are high set and rather small. There is noticeable feathering on the angulated hindlegs, the moderately tucked belly, the deep chest, and thick tail. The coat ideally has dark shadings throughout; the black mask is essential.

Kaukasische Schaferhund
See Caucasian Ovtcharka

Kawkasky Owtscharka
See Caucasian Ovtcharka

Keel
The term used to indicate the curved outline of the Dachshund's lower brisket from the prosternum to the end of the breastbone. An unusually short sternum, blending into the abdomen's lower line is called clipped keel.

Keeshond
A descendant of the German Wolfspitz, the Keeshond entered the British dog scene, via Holland, as the Dutch Barge Dog, named aptly for its producing homeland. In that country, the dog was used as a good-luck companion on sea-faring vessels and as a handy guard and vermin controller. The spitz dog in wolf-gray was most favored in the Netherlands (particularly in the southern provinces of Brabant and Limburg) and became the mascot of the common Dutch Patriot Party, led by Cornelius (Kees) de Gyselear. Unfortunately, when the House of Orange (and their apricot, smug Pugs) triumphed, the Keeshond was snubbed, dubbed the affiliate of a defeated party. Only country dwellers, farmers and river boatsmen remained interested in the Kees's Keeshonden. The British interest in the breed was sparred by the yachting Miss Hamilton Fletcher (later Mrs. Wingfield Digby) when she noticed the Laputan Pom gaily gaiting on the deck of a Dutch barge.

The British Keeshond (now popular the world over) is the progeny of the Wolfspitz of Germany crossed with a negotiable and negligible percentage of Dutch imports. Today, the F.C.I., the world's all-encompassing registry based in Belgium, does not differentiate the Keeshond from the Wolfspitz and only recognizes the latter. In Holland, the dog is typically smaller and darker in coat color. Its employment as a "barge dog" has been solely historical for centuries now. Hutchinson relays that the Keeshond has not been seen "trotting restlessly up and down the deck of the slow-moving barges and guarding the gangway whilst its master went ashore" since the later 1800s. These dogs were fuller in coat and ruff than the Keeshonden found in Holland in the early twentieth century. In the 1930s, Holland could not boast a great number of Keeshonden and most of their dogs were discovered on farms "running in circles round and round their wooden kennels, tied to these by heavy, cumbersome chains," or an occasional specimen would be a vendible of gypsies and tinkers.

The Keeshond and the Pomeranian have surely excelled in popularity over all of their other German Spitz cousins. The Keeshond's sporting instincts may be developed or restrained at will. With training, this incisive rabbiter and ratter will either ignore or pursue the given quarry. The Keeshond is adored today as a sensible watchdog, ideal companion and dapper show dog.

ESSENTIALS OF THE KEESHOND: The distinguishing characteristic of the breed is the "bespectacled" face. These "spectacles" are actually delicately drawn lines that angle slightly upward from the outer corner of each eye to the lower corner of the ear; completing the spectacled effect are distinct markings and shadings that form short but expressive eyebrows. This highly expressive, distinctly marked head is set upon a well-balanced, me-

Keeshond, wolf-gray.

dium-sized, short-coupled body. The head is wedge shaped; the muzzle of medium length, neither coarse nor snipy. The ears are small, triangular in shape, mounted high on head and carried erect. The neck should be moderately long, well shaped and well set on shoulders; covered with a profuse mane. The body is compact with a short straight back, sloping slightly downward towards the hindquarters; chest well-ribbed, barrel, well rounded, deep and strong; belly moderately tucked up. Forelegs straight and well feathered, hind slightly bent. The tail set high, moderately long and well feathered, tightly curled over the back. The coat is harsh, straight, and stand-off. A dense ruff on the neck and profuse trousers on the hindquarters are formed by the coat. Color is a mixture of gray and black, with no black below the wrist or hocks. Dutch specimens at one time could be seen in solid black and solid white, the latter color being more common. Height: 17–19 inches (43–48 cm). Weight: 55–66 pounds (25–30 kg).

Keeshond, wolf-gray.

Kelb-tal Fenek
See Pharaoh Hound

Kelef K'naani
See Canaan Dog

Kelpie
See Australian Kelpie

Keltski Gonic
See Chien Courant de Bosnie a Poil Dur

Ken
Japanese for dog. The Japanese Tosa Inu is sometimes called the Tosa Ken, and the Ainu Dog, the Ainu Ken.

Kennel
1) An organized establishment for breeding and/or boarding dogs. *See also* Accommodations, outdoor; Boarding kennels 2) In foxhunting, the fox's lair.

Kennel blindness
Applicable to a breeder who sees no faults in his own stock but at the same time is quick to criticize lesser faults in other breeders' production.

Kennel Club of Great Britain
The Kennel Club is the principle dog-registering organization of Great Britain. Founded in 1873, the registry has remained since its inception a prestigious and influential body in the life of the nation's dog world. The Kennel Club has always strived to bring the various British dog societies under one central authority that would set uniform dog-show and dog-trial rules. Further, its mandate specifies that the body will maintain a register for all of the breeds which it recognizes. The Kennel Club approves the standard for each recognized breed by which the breed is judged. Today over 1,700 canine organizations and clubs fall under the Kennel Club's auspices. Nearly 8,000 shows, obedience and field trials are sponsored by clubs annually.

The title Champion, awarded from the Kennel Club, is one of the most difficult of all titles to attain. Championship is dependent on the accumulation of three Challenge Certificates (C.C.s) from three different judges. Only a limited number of C.C.s are available at any given show. Less popular and new breeds are offered fewer C.C.s than the more popular breeds, since the number of dogs registered per year directly affects the number of C.C.s offered.

Recognized breeds are divided into six groups: three Sporting Groups: Terriers, Hounds, Gun Dogs; three Non-sporting: Utility, Toys and Working. Like the A.K.C., new breeds and other breeds with lesser numbers are relegated to a Miscellaneous Class and provided with an interim standard.

The Kennel Club acquired the already-famous Crufts Dog Show from Charles Cruft's estate upon his death in 1938. This spectacular all-breed exhibition was initiated in 1891, sponsored by Queen Victoria, and attracted unusual entries from all over Europe and Asia. When this grand circus of a show was placed under the more judicious auspices of the British Kennel Club, it necessarily became more restricted. The number of entries was limited and Champions were given preference; additionally certain quarantine laws precluded many foreign dogs from competing. Today Crufts is the largest and most prestigious dog show in Great Britain and attracts over 50,000 spectators annually.

Kennel clubs

Nearly every country in the world has at least one national kennel club. These clubs function to register purebred dogs and to improve the general conditions in which dogs live in their countries.

The addresses of some of the world's major kennel clubs follow; these clubs can provide more information on their organization and regulations that apply to dog showing, registration, etc. *American Kennel Club,* 51 Madison Avenue, New York, NY 10010 U.S.A.; *Australian National Kennel Club,* Royal Show Grounds, Ascot Vale, 3032, Victoria, Australia; *Canadian Kennel Club,* 2150 Bloor Street West, Toronto 12, Ontario, M6S 4V7, Canada; *Fédération Cynologique Internationale,* Rue Leopold-II, 14B-6530 Thuin, Belgium; *The Kennel Club of Great Britain,* 1 Clarges Street, Piccadilly, London W1Y 8AB, England; *United Kennel Club,* 100 East Kilgore Road, Kalamazoo, MI 49001-5598, U.S.A. *See also* American Kennel Club, Australian National Kennel Club, Canadian Kennel Club, Fédération Cynologique International, Kennel Club of Great Britain, States Kennel Club, United Kennel Club

Kennel cough

Also known as canine infectious tracheobronchitis, this respiratory disease is an inflammation of the trachea and bronchial tubes, resulting in coughing spasms that are particularly acute after rest or an alteration of the environment (i.e., going from indoors to outdoors), or at the commencement of exercise. Kennel cough is often a secondary disease to heart disease, enteritis, and parasitism. Inhalation of smoke and/or other noxious chemicals can also cause the infection. In all cases, kennel cough is a highly infectious disease that can easily pass from one animal to another, including cat-to-dog transmission; the disease

therefore can easily rampage in a kennel where many animals are kept in rather close quarters, and this fact is why the disease acquired its common name. Proper diagnosis of both the disease and its causative agents is necessary for effective treatment, which often includes rest,

warmth, proper hygiene, and prescribed drugs (especially antibiotics). Prompt treatment greatly increases the likelihood of a sound recovery.

Kennel cough certainly has deterred many a concerned owner from lodging his dog in a kennel. While their concern is justified, owners should be aware that through ever-increasing knowledge and access to chemo-medical advances, kennel cough and other equally dreaded diseases are coming well under control, and many kennels boast of their years-long record of no outbreaks. Investigation of the potential kennel, keeping an eye on maintenance and cleanliness and asking any and all appropriate questions should help the owner determine if the kennel is worthy of his dog.

Kennel sickness

Term used to refer to a type of influenza that is accompanied by diarrhea and vomiting. Once common to racing Greyhounds.

Kennel tick

Brown dog tick, *see* Ticks

Kennel clubs. Afghan Hound and Shetland Sheepdog compete in a 1985 exhibition of the Japanese Kennel Club. Photo by Matsu.

Keratitis

A condition characterized by a bluish white discoloration of the cornea of the eye. The white of the eye may turn a reddish color but not necessarily. This typically accompanies serious disease or illness. It is also known as blue eye.

Kerry Beagle

The Kerry Beagle, appearing like an inferior Bloodhound, is a direct descendant of that St. Hubertesque breed. Cynologists believe that the Kerry, although used initially on stag, was one of the first dogs used exclusively to hunt hare. Though a common sight around Tipperary and Kerry in past centuries, the Kerry Beagle galloped into the twentieth century with but a few packs. In its native Ireland, the Kerry was hunted in packs during the 1800s with the field following on foot. Surely the term beagle in the Kerry's name is a curious one of unknown origin. Beagle, by many, meant "smallest of the hounds," a description which does not describe a dog that reportedly stood to 26 inches (66 cm) high in days gone by. Some of these Irish hounds were brought with immigrants into the U.S., where they contributed to other hound strains. In 1902, a dog author named Rawdon Lee indicated that the Kerry still existed in Ireland. Today, while the breed is not plenteous, fanciers are working hard to revive the Kerry's status. Drag trials in Ireland too have spurred resurgence in this ancient breed.

ESSENTIALS OF THE KERRY BEAGLE: A close-coated hound, the Kerry Beagle appears as an unexaggerated Bloodhound: smaller, less wrinkled skin, less keen nose. Black/tan is the most common color pattern, although other varieties are known, including tricolor, mottled, and tan/white. Height: 22–26 inches (56–66 cm). Structurally, this hound is strong and firmly built.

Kerry Blue Terrier

Not until the nineteenth century can historians detect references to the Kerry Blue Terrier of Ireland. This Irish terrier, however, is said to go back much farther. Urban folk in southern Ireland attest that the dog has always been an integral part of country life. The Kerry has roamed the Kerry mountains and been utilized by natives of the region as a terrier, herder and sportsman. Irish lore tells of the

Kerry's ancestors surviving a shipwreck in Tralee Bay in the late eighteenth century. One tale tells how the dogs paddled "home" from a sinking Spanish Armada vessel. Some aver that Irish Wolfhounds owned by the squires had a paw in the Kerry's development. More concretely, we surmise that the Kerry Blue is of the same gene pool that produced the Irish Terrier and Soft Coated Wheaten Terrier. The Kerry is admired for its ability to take an otter single-handedly in deep water. Its propensity for ratting is natural. He is also useful at guarding homes, children and livestock. The Kerry became the mascot of the Irish patriots and their rally

Kerry Blue Terrier, blue. Photo by I. Français.

for independence from Mother England. The Kerry was not shown in America until 1922, when he competed at Westminster. Kerry fanciers must be praised for their devotion to the breed and for remaining faithful to the Kerry's natural abilities. The scissoring that occurs in the American ring is minimal compared to the foppish chicanery that goes on in some breeds. In Ireland, the breed is shown in its natural coat. Spunky, good-humored and typically terrier in temperament, the Kerry is a well-rounded, much-loved international blue-blooded purebred.

ESSENTIALS OF THE KERRY BLUE TERRIER: Strong and well balanced. Next to his bluish color, the Kerry's most distinctive feature is his square head, proportionately lean, with slight stop, and flat over the skull. Ears, small to medium V-shape, carried forward but not high. Neck, clean and strong. Shoulders are flat with elbows close to sides. Body short coupled with deep chest and level topline. Large well-developed hindquarters. Tail set high and carried erect. The Kerry's coat is characterized by its dense, silky growth, soft and plentiful, and unusual eye-catching color. The Kerry breed's sturdy construction provides it with freedom of movement and activity. Height: 17.5–20 inches (44–51 cm). Weight: 33–40 pounds (15–18 kg).

King Charles
The black/tan variety of the English Toy Spaniel.

King Charles Spaniel
See English Toy Spaniel

Kink tail
A bent, sharply angled or snapped tail. Such a malformed tail is usually due to foreshortened tendons on the one side which force the tail sideways. Genetic factors or an injury may also be the cause of veritable vertebral deformity.

Kirghiz Borzoi
See Taigan

Kishu
The Kishu, one among the Shika-Inu classification of Japanese dogs, has its beginnings in the mountainous areas of the Mie and Wakayama prefectures, where it is the *matagi's* dog. His closest relatives are the Kai Dog and the Shikoku; he is also related to the Ainu Dog. Neglected like the Kai after World War I, these ancient dogs depended upon Mr. Isogai's efforts to resuscitate the national Japanese dogs for their survival. The mid-sized dogs couldn't compete with the larger, jauntier German Shep-

herd Dog that had recently drawn attention. Although once used primarily on

Kerry Blue Terrier, blue.

Kishu, white. Photographs by I. Français.

deer, the Kishu is marvelously skilled at hunting boar.

ESSENTIALS OF THE KISHU: The Kishu is a mid-sized dog of classic Japanese type. It is distinguished from the Kai Dog, a fellow Japanese dog, by his broader skull, although narrower than the Shikoku; and from the Ainu Dog by his more lengthy body. The head is massive, skull flat and broad between the triangular, erect ears. The body is slightly longer than high; the chest is wide, ribs well sprung, brisket well developed. The back is firmly muscled and straight. The Kishu possesses a short, straight, coarse coat, a curled-over-the-back tail, erect ears, and tapered skull. In height the breed is 17–22 inches (43–46 cm) tall. It is fringed on the cheeks and tail. Its most common color is white but can be red, sesame or brindle.

Kiss mark on the left cheek of a Manchester Terrier. Photo by I. Français.

Kiss marks

Tan marks on the cheeks of black/tan breeds or Swiss-colored breeds (black/white with tan). The Doberman Pinscher exemplifies the former, the Appenzeller, the latter.

Kissing spot

Term lovingly awarded and aptly describing the lozenge mark on the Blenheim variety of Cavalier King Charles Spaniel. *See also* Spot

Kit fox

A wild dog and a member of the genus *Vulpes. See* Foxes

Kleiner Münsterländer Vorstehhund

See Small Münsterländer

Knee joint

Stifle joint on the rear leg, not to be confused or used synonymously with the wrist or carpal joint.

Knee problems

The knee joint, also known as the stifle joint, is a complex joint subject to many problems. A separated kneecap, known also as a luxated patella, is perhaps the most common knee injury suffered by dogs. This condition has also been known to occur from abnormal bone alignment. Surgical correction may be necessary in any case. Torn ligaments are another very real possibility facing your dog's knees. Ligaments can be torn, or ruptured, during any activity, including, playing, running, retrieving, flushing, and even walking. When a dog suffers this condition, he refuses to put weight on the affected limb. Preliminary inspection of the feet, foot pads, and bones will help eliminate such possibilities as punctures, cuts, and breaks. Because of the delicacy of the knee joint, all conditions affecting the joint should be reported to a veterinarian as soon as possible. Too often homemade splints and bandages simply do not work, and, commonly, they aggravate the initial problem. *See also* Arthritis, Lameness

Kneecap

Patella. The bone which is found in the groove at the bottom end of the femur.

Knitting

See Plaiting

Knuckling over

The forward bending of the leg at the carpal joint when the dog is standing. Faulty construction is usually at the crux of the problem, and knuckling over is common in both the long-legged hounds (e.g., American Foxhound) and the short-legged hounds (e.g., Basset Hound, whom it disqualifies).

Koban Copeği

The native name of the Anatolian Shepherd Dog, which *see*.

Kombai

Native to the Ramnad district of India, the Kombai was once hailed aristocratically in southern India. The Shenkottah is believed to be its closest relative. This powerful, exceedingly fast hunting dog had the ability to cover large expanses of land, regardless of obstacles. The Zamindars and other Indian tribes used these dogs for hunting. They were once popular as pets and watchdogs but have become extinct.

Komondor

Of the herdsmen's dogs of Hungary, the Komondor is the largest. A guardian of sheep and cattle, the Komondor has been employed in Hungary for centuries. It is believed generally that these dogs are of Eastern origin and were transported to Hungary by nomadic Magyars over one thousand years ago. A breed as distinctive as the Komondor, distinguished by its mass of white cords, is not necessarily related to the world's other corded canines, the Bergamasco of Italy or the Puli, also of Hungary. The Komondor's coat is no freak of nature, but rather a gift. Protecting the dog from inclement weather and from the treacherous jaws of its wolf predators, the corded coat provides an impenetrable buffer zone to the Komondor's skin—similar, in a way, to the Shar-Pei's prickly, thick coat, protecting it from the snarling mouths of combatants. As an accessory to its function as flock guard, the corded coat has proven highly effective.

The Komondor's unique appearance has gained him ringside fans in both the United States and Great Britain. In addition to his role of show dog and companion, he has been effectively employed as a police dog and guard. The Komondor's coat takes a good amount of grooming in order to keep clean and unmatted. The cords should be separate; breeders wrap hairs around a central hair to reduce the matting. In temperament, the Komondor

Komondor, white. Photo by I. Français.

is protective and obedient. A firm hand will acclimate an assertive Komondor puppy to the home/family lifestyle. Of course, there is never room for aggression in the training procedure.

ESSENTIALS OF THE KOMONDOR: A large muscular dog with strong well-boned limbs. The muzzle of the Komondor is shorter than the skull, but their planes are parallel. The skull is covered with hair. Nose: black, sometimes slate. The body is slightly longer than high. Hair is shortest at neck and head and becomes progressively longer, reaching maximum length at the thighs and tail. Back is straight and strong; chest deep; hindlegs well angulated; and overall structure, thick boned. Weight: 80–150 pounds (36.5–69 kg). Standards specify height at 25.5 inches (64.5 cm) for dogs, although larger working specimens are common. The coat is invariably white and corded.

Komondor, white. Photo by I. Français.

Kooichi Dog

This native dog of the Powinder tribes of Afghanistan is also commonly called the Powinder Dog. It is a medium-sized guard dog, weighing between 70–90 pounds (31.5–41 kg) and standing 22–25 inches (56–63.5 cm) at the shoulder. These dogs are most aggressive towards strange dogs; nomads typically dock the ears to avoid tearing during a fight. To the Powinder people, the dogs are excessively friendly. These dogs are very well kept by the nomads and are most independent, detesting confinement of any sort. The dogs have not been domesticated outside their native circles, despite certain attempts.

Kooiker Dog

See Kooiker-hondje

Kooikerhondje

Although believed to have been a common companion of Dutch duck hunters for many years, the Kooiker, as we know him today, is a rather new addition to the gundog gang. In 1942, the Baroness v. Hardenbroek van Ammerstool sought specimens to reestablish the Kooiker Dog that had saved Prince William of Orange and was illustrated by seventeenth-century Dutch painters. The Baroness was successful in creating the modern-day Kooiker within a few years. In hunting style, the Kooikerhondje is unique. He functions as a decoy, attracting wild ducks into traps with his fringed white tail. The hunters, admirably concerned in natural reserves, net the birds and ring young or endangered specimens. The Kooiker is an industrious and undeterred sportsman. For his intelligence, stamina, and quick reflexes, he can be compared to the best of the working gundogs. A lively, good-natured and affectionate dog, the Kooikerhondje is both a fine hunter and a good companion for old and young alike.

ESSENTIALS OF THE KOOIKERHONDJE: Light and graceful, the Kooikerhondje is a medium-sized dog, resembling a spaniel or small setter. The head is in proportion to the body, with good arch to skull and defined stop; the ears are set on high.

With a slight wave, the Kooiker's coat is moderately long with fringe adorning the legs, ears, chest, and tail. The ears, well feathered, are jeweled by black tips that are referred to as earrings. The breed color is always red and white. Height: 14–16 inches (35–41 cm). Weight: 20–24 pounds (9–11 kg).

Korthaar Hollandse Herdershond
See Dutch Shepherd

Korthals Griffon
See Wirehaired Pointing Griffon

Kostrome Hound
See Russian Hound

Krasky Ovcar
See Karst Shepherd

Kratkodlaki Itrski Gonič
See Istrian Hound

Kooikerhondje, red and white. Photo by I. Français.

Kromfohrländer

The Kromfohrländer was created by Frau Ilse Schleifenbaum rather unintentionally. This Westphalian townswoman crossed what now seems to be a Griffon Fauve de Bretagne with a tousy fawn-colored dog given to her by passing American soldiers in 1945. She so delighted in her first litter from the cross that she worked to perpetuate the type. Within ten years, the breed was established and recognized. It is a sound sportsman but more of a companion dog, as was the frau's intention.

ESSENTIALS OF THE KROM-FOHRLÄNDER: A robust and well-proportioned dog whose coat type may vary from rough and wiry to medium-long and straight. In color the breed is mostly white with varying shades of tan marking its head and saddle. The ears are pointed and fold over the top of the skull. The muzzle is not too pointed, with powerful jaws. Height: 15–17 inches (38–43 cm). Weight: 26 pounds (12 kg).

Kromfohrländers, wires and smooth, white with tan. Photographs by I. Français.

Kuchi

This longhaired Tanjore native is an Indian rat and squirrel hunter. He stands about 10 inches (25 cm) high and weighs about 15 pounds (7 kg). A thin build and a heavily feathered tail complement this companionable terrier.

Kuri Dog
See New Zealand Native Dog

Kurzhaar
See German Shorthaired Pointer

Kuvasz

The Kuvasz is believed to have inhabited Hungary since 1100 A.D., when it was transported with the Kurds. Some authorities maintain that the Kuvasz is a relation of the Komondor who was brought by the Huns from the steppes of Russia. A protector by name, the Kuvasz has derived from ancient Eastern people known as the Sumerians. The Turkish word *kawasz*, "armed guard of the nobility," probably gives the Kuvasz his name.

In the United States, the Kuvasz enjoys moderate popularity. In temperament, size, ability and appearance, the Kuvasz is an ideal, intelligent, well-mannered canine with a lot to offer Americans. That the Kuvasz is not more popular is perhaps one of the puzzlements of the canine world. Great Britain, even more so, has ignored the Kuvasz breed and has not registered it with the K.C.G.B. A dog with stamina, scenting ability, guarding ability, good looks, power, charm, etc., etc.,

Kuvasz, straight coat, white. Photo by I. Français.

In the fifteenth century, during the time of King Matthias I, the dogs were used to hunt wild boar. The Kuvasz has played various roles in the history of the European continent and was often the companion of rulers. Hunting, however, was never this Hungarian working dog's primary function. In Hungary, the Kuvasz is the foremost guardian of flocks. Its size and strength, which were advantages in its boar-battling days, were equally applicable to its role as flock guardian. Although not the largest of canines, the Kuvasz, standing 30 inches (76 cm) at the withers, is a substantially sized dog with good bone: a dog, however, of outstanding agility, able to maneuver about the flock as necessary.

will surely gain a more stable stronghold in America and Britain as the dog world opens its eyes and homes.

ESSENTIALS OF THE KUVASZ: A medium to large-sized, well proportioned dog with a moderately long coat in white or ivory; it may be straight or slightly wavy. Height: 22–26 inches (56–66 cm). Weight: 80–120 pounds (37–55 kg). Legs are strongly boned. In addition to the dog's symmetrical carriage, the highlight of its appearance is the head, with its handsomely majestic expression especially denoted in the dark glistening eyes. The broad skull begins after a mild stop. The powerful jaws are concealed behind an exquisite muzzle.

Kuvasz, curly coat, white.

Kyi-Leo, black and white particolor. Photographs by I. Français.

Kyi-Leo

The Kyi-Leo is certainly one of the newcomers to the world of dogs. The "breed" was established in 1972, after an original cross with the Lhasa Apso and the Maltese. Mrs. Harriet Linn acquired one of the first specimens in 1965 from San Jose, California. Linn's commitment and enthusiasm for the breed are greatly responsible for the Kyi-Leo's presence in the dog scene today. The breed is a sturdy and adaptable dog with many of the best qualities of both its tiny ancestors. Twenty years of linebreeding are responsible for the establishment of the desired type. The Kyi-Leo originated in California and has entered the hearts of many fanciers, and he has an active group of supporters.

Breeders focus on character and disposition. The Kyi-Leo is gentle and bonds closely with his immediate family. He re-

tains the Lhasa's wariness of strangers and thereby makes a good warning or alarm dog. He is not known to bark without reason or to be shy of people. The coat will require brushing and a little trimming, but no clipping is involved. Today the Kyi-Leo is known in the U.S. and Canada only.

ESSENTIALS OF THE KYI-LEO: In height the Kyi-Leo stands 8–12 inches (20–31 cm) tall, with 9–11 inches (23–28 cm) being preferred. He is well boned for his size, with good muscle tone. He is light on his feet and quite agile. The coat is long and thick; it hangs straight or slightly wavy; there is a natural part that tends to form along the spine, contributing to the breed's neat and attractive look. Color is

Kyi-Leo,
particolor.

usually black and white particolor, but gold and white and self-colors are also seen; the color of some specimens may fade from black to slate.

Kyi-Leo,
particolor.
Photographs
courtesy of Harriet
Linn.

KyiApso

In considering the development of the world's dog breeds, one must first acknowledge that some breeds are intentionally created (by experimentation, crossbreeding, etc.) and others simply develop as a response to a given environment. Once humans set a gene pool and begin to acquire the desired features with some consistency, a breed is considered a purebred. The new breed being promoted in the United States known as the KyiApso or the Tibetan Bearded Dog represents the latter type development, namely an ancient hardy dog that developed in the protective "cocoon" of the Tibetan plateau, an isolated geographical region considered "one of the most demanding" on Earth.

produced seven pups from two imported dogs. It is hoped that by the turn of the century, three or four genetically separate American KyiApso lines will be established so as to form a breeding basis in the West. The finalizing of a breed standard is presently contingent on increased importation of breed representatives and the progress the dogs make in the West with selective breeding and improved nutrition (a diet of commercial canned food happily replaces a peck of picked pikas).

Purebred fanciers in the West approach native Tibetan breeds with consternation and apprehension. In addition to such up-and-coming Tibetans as the Tibetan Terrier, Spaniel, Mastiff and the more established Lhasa Apso, there are

KyiApso photographed with Tibetan Mastiff in Tibet. Photo courtesy of Daniel Taylor-Ide.

While the KyiApso allegedly is an ancient dog indigenous to Tibet, its official importation to the U.S. and the establishment of a breeding program were undertaken as recently as 1990. This program is accredited to dog breeder Daniel Taylor-Ide of West Virginia, who spent a number of years working in Tibet where he met these very unique dogs. The first litter born in the U.S. in 1991

other known native types, such as the Sha-Kyi, Do-Kyi, and Yun-Kyi (these latter two dogs would likely be considered Tibetan Mastiffs). The Tibetan Mastiff, the largest of these dogs, has caused particular befuddlement in the West. Initial accounts of the breed in Tibet claimed that the dog could weigh in excess of 220 pounds (132 kg), while later reports thinned the dog down to about half that size. Reports about the KyiApso first reached Western ears and journals in 1937, when an article was printed in the *American Kennel Club Gazette* in March of that year. Since there were no conclusive details on the whereabouts of this dog, and due to the limited accessibility of Tibet, decades passed without Western dog folk getting involved with investigating the native dogs of Tibet.

Located at the foot of the holy Mount Kailash, the KyiApso is a working dog used for hunting and protection purposes by nomads, alerting its keepers to the approach of strangers: humans, wolves, and snow leopards. The dog is moderately sized, weighing no more than 85 pounds (51 kg), with a sinewy, lean construction and guaranteed lithe movement, useful to a dog that must chase down its own food (often pika and hare), run with herds of yaks, goats, and sheep, and keep up with its peripatetic keepers. The lack of food in the plateau, the harsh, incredibly cold weather, and the necessity of fighting off Tibetan wolves qualify the KyiApso's physical build: lean and leggy, heavily coated for protection against the elements, and sufficiently stoic and sturdy to be bigger than its natural opponents. Other noteworthy features of the breed are its beard (in Tibetan *apso*) and its deep, sonorous bark (which is described in the standard as sepulchral). Due to the traditional importance of this dog's bark, the Tibetan KyiApso Club states that dogs with exceptional resonant barks are preferred to small-voiced dogs (similar to the Kennel Club of Finland favoring a Finnish Spitz with a clear, enthusiastic yodel).

This breed should not be mistaken for either the Lhasa Apso, a smaller dog developed in lower elevations of Tibet, or the Kyi-Leo, a crossbred developed from the Lhasa and Maltese in the U.S. *See also* Kyi-Leo, Lhasa Apso, Tibetan Mastiff, New breed creation, Breed development

ESSENTIALS OF THE KYIAPSO: Stoic, independent, territorial and playful, the KyiApso temperamentally is unique and sound. The head appears large due to the distinctive facial furnishings—beards are mandatory. The stop is marked; ears pendant and V-shaped. The body is well-balanced; topline level; tail set high and

carried in a forward full plume; neck muscular and broad. The forequarters are broad and powerful; hindquarters are muscular, bowed slightly from crotch to hock. Movement is a unique rolling yet vertical topline gait. The coat is firm, full, and long though not as long as the Lhasa's; it is weather-resistant and double, undercoat soft and dense. Colors vary but black and tan and black with white chest spot are most common; other colors include golden, white and chocolate. Height: 22–28 inches (55–70 cm). Weight: 65–85 pounds (39–51 kg).

Kyushu
See Kishu

KyiApso, black and tan.

KyiApso, golden. Photographs courtesy of Daniel Taylor-Ide.

Labor

The state of active attempt to expel the fetus. Labor is characterized by intense muscle contractions and panting. The onset of labor is marked by a reddish vaginal discharge. Labor is completed when the last pup is born, at which time the state becomes known as postpartum. *See also* Breeding

Labrador Retrievers, yellow, chocolate and black. Photo by I. Français.

Labrador Retriever

Superb and undaunted, the Labrador propels itself through ice-caked harbor waters to search and retrieve, an inborn ability long employed. About the turn of the nineteenth century, boats that carried salted cod from Newfoundland to Poole Harbour, Great Britain, landed the reported ancestors of the Labrador. These dogs were short-limbed, sturdy swimmers with short dense coats and short, thick tails like an otter and were probably employed by the boatsmen to tow ropes ashore on the shelving beaches. So attractive were the dogs that offers hurled to Newfoundland sailors for their dogs never ceased. Oft cited is the Earl of Malmesbury's attraction to and acquisition of the early Labrador dogs, known at the time as the Saint John's breed of water

dog. These dogs are believed to be one of the two common types of dog found on Newfoundland at the time, the other dog evolving into today's Newfoundland breed. Although the exact origin and evolution of the Labrador in his native land remain uncertain, it is known that the breed was long employed and long respected for his excelling ability and fine intelligence. Even at its early introduction to the British Isles, the breed was known for its superiority as a gundog. In 1830, the noted British sportsman, Colonel Hawker, said of the breed, "by far the best for any kind of shooting."

The breed was quick to gain a strong foothold in England, and fanciers consciously bred for type. The Earl of Malmesbury stated: "We always call mine Labrador dogs, and I have kept the breed as pure as I could from the first I had from Poole, at that time carrying on a brisk trade with Newfoundland. The real breed may be known by its close coat which turns the water off like oil and, above all, a tail like an otter." During the time of the Labrador's ascendency in Great Britain, the breed was quickly losing ground in its native land, taxed out of existence. Additionally, the English quarantine laws of the time dampened imports of the dogs to the point where breeding stock was limited to those dogs already on the Isles. Fortunately they were largely of excellent quality and in the hands of serious breeders, for outcrossing to other types of retrievers was necessitated. The characteristics of the Lab proved prepotent, and type remained essentially unaffected. The practice of crossbreeding was soon discouraged, however, and the breed undoubtedly benefitted from the selective breeding that prevailed. Labradors were first recognized by the Kennel Club of Great Britain in 1903.

In addition to Lord Malmesbury's contribution to the early Labradors, the third Viscount of Knutsford also had an active hand in the preservation of the true Lab. The colorful story of his travelling to Newfoundland in search of fine specimens during the time of quarantine, which ended in his being told to go to England and visit the kennels of Holland-Hibbert (his own kennels!), is often retold over the tea of countless dedicated fanciers. Adding a touch of feminine refinement to the history of the Lab was Lady Howe, an owner of countless quality Labs, a judge of the breed, and the author of one of the early texts on the breed published in 1957. Lady Howe kept and bred many champions, including Banchory Bolo and Bramshaw Bob, and her contribution to the breed will be forever appreciated.

Research on the breed has continued, and the working over of the Duke of Buccleuch's stud book led breed historians to believe that the two stud dogs that laid the foundation of the modern Labrador were Mr. A.C. Butter's Peter of Faskally and Major Portal's Flapper, whose pedigrees date back to 1878.

The Labrador Retriever was first recognized by the American Kennel Club in 1917 and has proved truly a breed to capture the American heart. The intelligence, the warm affection for man, the field dexterity, and the undying devotion to any task make the Labrador Retriever a dog for all dog lovers.

The popularity that the breed faced during the latter half of the twentieth century, coupled with the limited breed base that it began with in the late 1800s, has given strain to the breed of the present. Though less affected than could have been expected, owing largely to its true superiority as a canine, Labradors must be selected with care and consideration. While the best Labs are among the finest dogs of the world, the worst specimens can be pretty bad. Potential owners are encouraged to exercise their discretion and research skills, avoid the puppymill breeders, and find themselves the best of canine companions, for home and/or field.

Labrador Retriever, black, with retrieved mallard duck.

ESSENTIALS OF THE LABRADOR RETRIEVER: The ideal Labrador should be a strongly built, short-coupled, very active dog;

fairly wide over the loins, and strong and well-developed in the hindquarters. The coat should be close, short, dense, double, and free from feather. The skull should be wide, with a slight stop; the head clean cut and free from fleshy cheeks. Bite level. Ears set rather far back and somewhat low. Brown or black is the preferred eye color. Neck powerful; shoulders long and sloping; the chest of both good width and depth. Forelegs straight from shoulder to ground; hocks

Labrador Retriever zealously taking to the water.

well bent; legs of medium length and in proportion to body. One of the breed's distinctive features is its otter tail: very thick towards the base and gradually tapering to the tip, with no feathering but thickly covered with dense coat. The coat is comprised of short dense hair, without wave or feathering. Height: 21.5–24.5 (54–62 cm). Weight: 55–75 pounds (25–34 kg). Labradors come in three solid colors: black, chocolate/liver, and yellow (from light cream to red fox). Though brindles occur, and were once common in the Saint John's dogs of old, brindle is not an accepted color in the breed standard.

Labrit
See Bergers des Pyrenees

Lachrymal glands
Glands that produce tears, found at the inside corners of the eyes.

Lacing
The characteristic trot of the back legs, a short trot with hinds moving closely together; not considered a fault in the Chart Polski.

Lactation
The process by which milk is produced by the mammary glands of the bitch for ingestion by the pups. Lactation is believed to be onset by a change in hormonal levels. Additionally, stimulation of the teats spurs the lactation process. Cessation of stimulation (sucking) as well as "normal" hormonal levels which recur sometime after delivery stops lactation. *See also* Breasts; Breasts, problems of

Laekense
See Belgian Sheepdog, Laekenois

Lagota
See Truffle Dog

Laika
Russian for barker (or dog). The laikas are nordic sledge-pulling dogs used extensively in Siberia and elsewhere. *See also* East Siberian Laika, West Siberian Laika, Karelo-Finnish Laika, Russo-European Laika, Nenets Herding Laika

Lair
The locality where a fox generally stays above ground in the daytime.

Lajka Ruissisch Europaisch
See Russo-European Laika

Lakeland Terrier
The Lakeland Terrier is the farmer's terrier of the Lake and Border Districts in England. Its role was not a glamorous one, but rather a vital necessity to rid the farmer's ground of foxes that would kill sheep and poultry. Fox hunting with Lakelands never progressed to the well-dressed, for-the-sport level; it had always been an extermination process. The Lakeland, unlike the Jack Russell or Fox Terriers, killed the prey upon seizing it. The very quality that Reverend Jack Russell loathed was paramount in the Lakeland Terrier. The shape of the

Lakeland's muzzle indicates its rat-crushing ability. Contrarily, in the south, terriers were not intended to tackle and mutilate the quarry, but instead to hold it, unscathed and contained for the next hunt. Therefore, the more finely chiseled muzzles were favored in the south. For time immemorial have the Lakeland Terriers worked in these districts. Groups of Lakelands worked in conjunction with packhounds. They are not diggers but rather untiring patrols, with the ability to kill. As a companion dog, the Lakeland has become rather popular. He is recognized through much of Europe (of course in Ireland and England) as well as the United States, Canada and Australia.

ESSENTIALS OF THE LAKELAND TERRIER: Smart and workmanlike in general appearance, soundly put together and square in build, the Lakeland is compact and well balanced. The head is also square: the length of the muzzle equaling that of the skull. The length of head from stop to tip of the nose should not exceed the length from occiput to stop. Ears moderately small, V-shaped and carried alertly, not too high or low set. The shoulders must be well laid back with straight, well-boned legs. Reasonably narrow chest. Back is moderately short, well coupled. Hindquarters muscular, with long powerful thighs. Feet compact, round. The outer layer of its two-ply coat is hard, wiry and waterproof. The undercoat is soft. Color: blue and tan, black and tan, red, wheaten, red grizzle, liver, blue or black. The tan on a Lakeland is light wheaten to straw. Height: 13–15 inches (33–38 cm). Weight: 17 pounds (8 kg).

Lalande's Dog
See Bat-eared fox

Lameness
Lameness in the dog can occur from the lodging of a foreign object in the dog's paw, or from other patent causes such as cuts, blows, bits or fractures. Limping is generally the indication of a dog's lameness—the dog may whimper and hop on three feet due to the disuse of the affected limb. One of the most avoidable causes of lameness is unclipped toenails. Severely neglected toenails on a dog that never runs on pavement can progress to the point of lameness. Owners must properly attend to their dogs' claws for this and other reasons. It is wise to check your dog's feet regularly. Cut pads require immediate attention. Foreign objects that lodge themselves in the dog's paw need to be removed promptly in order to avoid further infection and lameness.

Rheumatism, eczema (between the toes or on the pads) and cysts between a dog's toes are other causes of lameness. Long-backed dogs and toy dogs are sometimes more inclined towards lameness caused by other than foreign objects. Patella luxation occurs moderately often in toy dogs; lesions to spinal discs, which can be treated surgically many times, are fairly common in long-backed dogs.

Lakeland Terrier, black and tan. Photo by Dave Ashbey.

Lancashire Heeler

A British breed representative of crosses between Corgis and Manchester Terriers. The Lancashire maneuvers the herd by nipping the heels of its members, as do the Welsh Corgis. The Lancashire

Lancashire Heeler, black/tan. Photo by I. Français.

Heeler resembles the Corgis in another way: he is low to the ground and very agile, two qualities necessary in any breed that works the heels of stock, for such dogs face the constant risk of a swift and lethal kick from a frightened or otherwise irritable animal. Characteristics of the Manchester Terrier are evidenced in the breed's primarily black coloration, abounding energy, sleek build, and lighter head construction. The Lancashire's type was perfected during the 1960s and 1970s, and the breed has excelled ever since that time. Courageous, athletic, and determined, the Heeler is also a fine ratter, watchdog, and rabbit hunter. Other names of the breed include Ormskirk Terrier and Ormskirk Heeler.

ESSENTIALS OF THE LANCASHIRE HEELER: A low-set, strong and active cattle worker and terrierlike ratter and rabbitter. The head is always in proportion to the body; the skull is flat and wide between the ears, tapering towards the eyes which are set wide apart. Ears are erect; drop ears are undesirable. Shoulders well laid, with elbows firm against the ribs. Body is well sprung. Topline firm and level, never dipping at the withers or falling at the croup. The tail is set on high and left natural. The coat is seasonally long or short—wintertime reveals a plush coat with a visible mane; the summer, a sleek shiny coat. Height: 10–12 inches (25.5–30.5 cm). Weight 6–12 pounds (2.5–5.5 kg).

Landseer

In the U.S., considered simply a black-and-white variety of the Newfoundland, the Landseer has hence become known by F.C.I. and affiliated clubs as a separate breed. Landseers rode a wave of popularity during the first half of the nineteenth century, at which time the dogs identically resembled the Newfoundland in bodily composition. Bred selectively for specific type, the Landseer has become lighter boned and slightly taller than the typey Newfy.

Named for the artist whose renderings brought fame to the black and white particolor Newfoundland, this breed owes much to the romantic realism of Sir Edwin Landseer's canvasses. As were the other Newfoundland dogs, the Landseer was employed to give assistance to fishermen on the shores of the island of Newfoundland. The dog's ancestor is clearly the Greater St. John's Dog, the larger of the two types of St. John's Dogs that were the first stage of evolution of these fishing swimmers. The dogs are natural rescue dogs and are greatly inclined to the water. They are said to be the strongest swimmers among canines.

For the owner seeking a dog of singular beauty, strength and unequaled faithfulness, the Landseer is indeed an ideal choice. Breeders work hard to attain the perfect markings as prescribed in the breed standard, and the dogs have retained much of their working ability.

ESSENTIALS OF THE LANDSEER: White with black markings only. The preferable markings are black head with narrow blaze, evenly marked saddle, black rump extending to tail. Beauty in markings is considered greatly important in the show ring. The coat is dense, flat and double; it is waterproof. The head is broad and grand in size. The body is muscular and well ribbed; the chest is fairly broad. The feet are webbed and well shaped. The Landseer is slightly taller than the Newfoundland and lighter in frame. Height: 26–31.5 inches (66–80 cm). Weight: 110–150 pounds (50–68 kg). The gait is free and rolling.

Langhaar
See German Longhaired Pointer

Langhaar Hollandse Herdershond
See Dutch Shepherd

Lank
The adjective curiously employed in the alliterative breed standard of the Skye Terrier to mean lean (e.g., "long, low and lank").

Lapinkoira
See Finnish Lapphund

Lapinporokoira
The Lapinporokoira was bred from Finnish Lapphunds crossed with such herding dogs as the German Shepherd and working collies. The result was an exceedingly durable dog, able to withstand extremely cold weather, work long hours over great distances, and retain the strength to control a large herd with great command. Truly an intermediate between the nordic and herding dog, a spitzlike herder, the Lapponian Herder, as the breed is also known, is a dog of fine herding abilities, especially suited for working domesticated reindeer in northern climes. The breed served its livestock-owning employers until the coming of the snowmobile to Scandinavian herdsmen in the twentieth century. Breed numbers fell and breeding practices slackened. However, with the rise of fuel prices and the cost of motorized herding equipment, interest in the breed was renewed. In 1966 a standard for the breed was written, thanks in part to the con-

Landseer, black and white particolor.

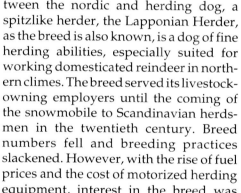

Lapinporokoira, black/tan. Photographs by I. Français.

cerned Olli Korhonen, then chairman of the Finnish Kennel Club. The cooperation that exists between the employers and the breeders of the Lapinporokoira today ensures the working quality of the dogs. Stockworkers are primarily interested in dogs, while breeders care for the bitches. Each season, owners of dogs in search of working stock take their proven animals to breeders, and matings are conducted. The dog owner gets his stud fee, usually a male pick of the litter, and the breeder sells the remaining males and retains the best females for future breeding purposes. So long as the need for outstanding herders remains present in the northern climes, the future of the breed remains bright.

Large Münsterländer, black with white. Photo by I. Français.

ESSENTIALS OF THE LAPINPOROKOIRA: The head is strong; skull moderate between the ears, with slight taper, less so than in typical spitz-type breeds. The ears are triangular and set high, standing erect. Good depth of chest and spring of rib are desirable. Body well boned and sturdily muscled. The tail, bushy, is set and carried below topline; may curl but not to the degree found typically in spitz breeds. Double coated, the Lapinporokoira varies in color from white with dark shadings to black and black/tan, the latter combinations being more popular. The outer coat is glossy, long and hard; the undercoat is soft and woolly. Height: 19–22 inches (48–56 cm). Weight: 66 pounds (30 kg) maximum.

Lapland Reindeer Dog
See Lapinporokoira

Laporotomy
A surgical procedure in which the abdominal cavity is opened in search of problems and complications that could not otherwise be diagnosed.

Lapphund
The nordic herding dogs of the Lapp people. *See* Swedish Lapphund, Finnish Lapphund

Lapplandska Spetz
See Swedish Lapphund

Lapponian Herder
See Lapinporokoira

Lapponian Vallhund
See Lapinporokoira

Large Blue Gascony Hound
See Bleu de Gascogne

Large French Pointer
See Braque Français de Grande Taille

Large French-English Hound
See Anglo-Français

Large Münsterländer
The Large or Grosser Münsterländer stems from the generic base of *huenenhunden*, German bird dogs, which until the late 1800s remained an amorphous group of dogs commonly interbred. It was not until the late 1800s that concern for type emerged. As it did, however, and as it grew, breeds emerged. One such emergent breed was the German Longhaired Pointer. When the breed club for the Longhair adopted its standard, it accepted only liver/white specimens, to the exclusion of the many black/white specimens still around and still occurring in litters of liver/whites. Some German hunters, many from the region of Münster, were concerned primarily with ability and continued to propagate the black/white dogs. In 1919 a club was formed for the breed, which is today recognized by the Kennel Club of Great Britain as the Large Münsterländer. Although not plenteous, the

breed is a recognizable and valued hunter in England, Germany and Canada. The breed's smaller counterpart, the small or Kleiner Münsterländer, is derived from similar stock, colored in liver and white and appears quite setterlike.

ESSENTIALS OF THE LARGE MÜNSTERLÄNDER: The Large Münsterländer possesses a well-balanced conformation suggestive of easy, steady movement and drive. The breed's head is sufficiently broad and slightly rounded; it is solid black with a white snip or star allowed. The coat is long and dense, not curly or coarse. Feathering on ears, front and hind legs and tail. The body is white with black patches, flecked and/or ticked. Height 23–25.5 inches (58–65 cm). Weight: 50–70 pounds (23–32 kg).

Large Portuguese Hound
See Podengo Português

Large Portuguese Rabbit Dog
See Podengo Português

Large Spanish Hound
Name alternatively used for the Sabueso Español de Monte. *See* Sabueso Español

Large Swiss Mountain Dog
See Greater Swiss Mountain Dog

Large Vendeen Griffon
See Griffon Vendeen

Larva
The early free-living immature form of any animal that changes structurally when it becomes an adult. *See also* Fleas, Worms, Ticks

Laryngitis
See Pharyngitis

Lateral
Adjective used in breed standards to indicate "of the sides."

Latvian Hound
The Latvian Hound is a relative newcomer to the world of purebred dogs. In Latvia, one of the Soviet Baltic states, boar and deer hunting required multipurpose, swift-moving hounds to follow and flush the game. It is a curious hunt in which the dogs and hunters must sport in a specific 1600 x 1600-foot area of woods; therefore, the dogs must be super-obedient. The Latvian derived later when the Forestry Department declared that dogs over 20 inches (51 cm) tall would be excluded. Immediately, hunters needed to turn to the basset types. Crosses of the Curland Hound, a long-legged dog derived from Lucernese and Polish hounds, were crossed with Dachshunds and Beagles. The result was the Latvian Hound whose type has only been stabilized since 1947.

ESSENTIALS OF THE LATVIAN HOUND: General basset type with short straight legs, a strong arched back and a tight-lipped, wedge-shaped head. The feet are cat. The coat is hard and dense and the color is black and tan. Height: 16–19 inches (40–48 cm).

Laufhund
A Swiss term that means walking dog or dog that follows on foot. It is applied to various scenthounds of Switzerland, including the Schweizer Neiderlaufhund, Bruno Jura Laufhund, Saint Hubert Jura Laufhund, Jura Neiderlaufhund, Berner Laufhund, Berner Neiderlaufhund, Luzerner Laufhund, Luzerner Neiderlaufhund.

Laxatives
Laxatives and cathartics are substances administered to relieve constipa-

Laufhunds of Switzerland: these tall specimens include the Bruno Jura Laufhund, Berner Laufhund, and Luzerner Laufhund.

tion. There are such substances to relieve specific conditions. Such substances labeled as laxatives and cathartics should therefore be given only after the condition has been properly determined.

Layback

1) The position of the nose of the brachycephalic breeds such as the Pekingese and Bulldog, rather appearing as if it were rolled up against the lower foreface.

2) In some breeds, refers to proper shoulder angulation.

Leash training should not be rushed. Puppies need to feel comfortable with the leash before attempting to lead them along their first walk. Photo by S. Miller.

Lead dog

The dog at the head of the team, usually the fastest, most experienced and best trained.

Lead poisoning

The element lead is found in many substances and is toxic when ingested. Small amounts of lead are usually harmless, but small quantities can accumulate in the body to cause severe reactions. Early signs include bluish discoloration to the gums and head pain. In acute cases, trembling, severe cramps, muscular weakness, convulsions, coma, and death are all signs of lead poisoning. The most common cause of lead poisoning is the ingestion of paint.

Leadout

Groom employed by a dog-racing track to lead contestants from paddock to starting barrier and return them after a race is completed.

Leaky roof

Derisive term used to indicate a dog-racing track of low class, belonging to the "leaky-roof" circuit.

Leash

The leash is the primary means of physical restraint and manipulation that pet owners have for their dogs; the leash is an essential tool in the training process; and, even with well-trained dogs, the leash is reasonable protection against your dog's darting in front of a car, combating another canine, defecating on your neighbor's lawn, and other such dangerous and/or embarrassing occurrences. Every dog owner should own a leash and use it whenever appropriate. In a growing number of cities and towns, leash laws are in effect, often with regulations regarding the appropriate size, length, and use of the dog leash. Owners are encouraged to learn about the laws relative to them and adhere to such laws. Dog leashes are available at pet shops everywhere, giving little excuse to the pet owner whose dog escapes him.

The puppy must soon be made comfortable with a collar and leash, and these must be used whenever the pup is outside a confined area. The collar for the pup must never be too tight or too loose.

The leash required by most obedience classes is one about six feet (180 cm) long, flat, and made of strong sturdy leather or webbing, which of course is too long for daily walks. *See also* Collars, Training

Leash laws

Leash laws require that a dog be under the control of its owner at all times. This requirement denotes that the dog may need to be physically confined, leashed or muzzled. All responsible owners realize that no dog should ever be allowed to roam free.

Leather

Lobe of the outer ear composed of cartilage. Most frequently referred to in the hounds and gundog breeds.

Leather end

Ear tip which lacks any or much hair on an otherwise fully coated ear. The Brittany is an example.

Leg

In obedience competition, a "leg" is earned when a dog scores 170 or more out of the possible 200 points and attains more than half on each exercise. Obedience titles require the earning of three legs. *See also* Obedience trials

Leggy

Tall, though not rangy, and appearing well off the ground. Usually considered a fault and caused by overly long legs or an insufficiently deep chest.

Legs, bandy

Outwardly bent forearms or hindlegs which curve out laterally from hip to hock. *See* Cow hocks

Lemon belton

See Belton

Length

See Body length

Leonberger

For purely esthetic reasons, the mayor of Leonberg, Herr Heinrich Essig, attempted to breed a canine that would resemble the heraldic lions on his city's coat of arms. The cross between a Landseer Newfoundland and a Saint Bernard, then crossed to a Great Pyrenees, in 1907, produced a strong, furry leonine canine that became the pride of Herr Essig. The breed, when first introduced to the dog world, was dismissed as a mere cross of two breeds, which it was. Soon thereafter, however, the breed's exceedingly good looks captured the heart of animal lovers, and the breed rapidly gained popularity. The dogs are said to have worked as herders, but this theory is basically unqualified or undeveloped. The breed today enjoys recognition in England and on the European continent.

A force to be reckoned with, this canine resembles the mighty lion in appearance and attitude. He is laid-back and content, though livelier than his Saint Bernard ancestors. Gentle and genial, he enjoys companionship and makes a wary and able watchdog.

ESSENTIALS OF THE LEONBERGER: The skull is wide and moderately deep. The stop is slight; no wrinkles should be noticeable on the head. The ears are set on high and lay close to the head. Strong and muscular, the body is slightly longer than high. The coat is medium-soft to hard, fairly long, lying close to the body, despite considerable undercoat. Height: 29–32 inches (72–80 cm). Weight: 80–150 pounds (37–67 kg). Color: light yellow, golden to red-brown, preferably with black mask. The tail is well furnished and flown at half mast.

Leonberger, red brown with black mask, puppy. Photo by I. Français.

Leonine

A quality desired of a number of breeds and meaning lionlike. The lion as the king of the jungle has been hailed by many a dog lover (and hunted by twice as many). Creating a canine to resemble or impersonate (as it were) the lion has been the obsession of a number of canine fanciers. The Chow Chow standard employs the term, but it is just one of the dogs which appear leonine. The Leonberger, Löwchen, Pekingese and Shih Tzu are some examples of dogs that feign a distinctly lionlike appearance. The Buddhists traditionally venerate the lion, and the Chinese have made continuous attempts to pay the great beast homage

through the cultivation and grooming of their dogs. The Löwchen, of course, goes by the pseudonym Little Lion Dog and is often clipped in a leonine fashion. The lion clip is sported by this miniature canine as well as others including the Portuguese Water Dog and the Barbet. The color fawn of the Ibizan, by the way, is referred to as lion color.

Leopard Cur

The Leopard Cur is an American native breed derived by settlers of the American South. A tough dog capable of protecting the early settlers from Indian attacks, working the unruly, semi-wild livestock, helping to provide settlers with food, and even fighting for their keepers were all requisite tasks of the cur-type dogs of America. In the 1700s, North Carolina was the state in which the Leop-

ard Cur specifically thrived. European dogs (British and French primarily) probably contributed to the development of these dogs. Early Spanish settlers, conquistadors with war dogs, French settlers with various working hounds and their sturdy herder from Beauce, the Beauceron (perhaps the harlequin variety), as well as British and Irish settlers with their hounds and herders (merle Collies likely) all fit into the development of cur dogs in America. In this instance, cur refers not to a mixed breed but rather to a kind of dog with superior hunting skills. In addition to the European dogs, native American pariah types likely have contributed to the gene pool.

Considering the difficulty of the Leopard Cur's tasks, the dog needed to work hard and skillfully. Controlling cattle and hogs, hunting large cat such as the eastern mountain lion, and chasing and treeing raccoon were among the dog's diversified chores about the farmstead. The Leopard Cur's varied gene pool procured all of these wondrous skills. Incidentally, the name Leopard Cur does not indicate that the dog hunts leopard (as "coonhound" indicates that a dog hunts coon) but rather modifies the desired coat coloration of these dogs: a leopard spot or merle.

ESSENTIALS OF THE LEOPARD CUR: A sinewy, muscular body empowers this hound of strength and character. The merle color in this breed is considered "leopard-spotted"; other colors include black/tan, blue, brindle, and yellow. The coat is dense and smooth. Weight: 45–77 pounds (20–35 kg). The muzzle is elongated; the ears are moderately sized.

Leopard Tree Dog
See Leopard Cur

Leptospirosis
A contagious disease of animals, including man and dog, which may be without symptoms or result in such conditions as fever, jaundice, hemoglobin free from red blood cells, and death. The infection is commonly acquired from skin or mucous membrane contact with urine or, less frequently, from the ingestion of urine-contaminated water or feed. The typical spirochete responsible for the disease are *canicola* and *copenhageni*, though there are others. In the U.S., brown rats are the primary carriers of *copenhageni*. All dogs may be affected by the disease, but there seems to be a greater incidence in males. The disease can be severe and can have a sudden onset, characterized by slight weakness, anorexia, vomiting, high temperature, and mild conjunctivitis possible. The condition is often treated with antibiotics and other substances. Clinical diagnosis is necessary.

Lesion
Damage to an organ or other body part. Lesions are the result of injury, condition, and disease, of which they are often a sign.

Lesser Saint John's Dog
See Saint John's Dog

Lethal genes
Genes which can have a deleterious (and usually fatal) effect. If the lethal gene is recessive, both the male and the female must possess the gene in order for the resulting progeny to be affected. Among possible lethal genes are those for cleft palate, hemophilia, whelp absorbtion, and hairlessness. Additionally, bilateral cryptorchidis is a semi-lethal gene trait. One also notes that the results of crossing two merle-colored dogs can result in double-nosed progeny that may be blind, deaf, or sterile. Two merle dogs therefore, should never be mated, according to some authorities.

Leukemia
Layman's term for canine malignant lymphoma, which *see*. *See also* Cancer

Level mouth
A mouth in which both the upper and lower jaws are of equal length and in which the upper and lower incisor teeth are lined up horizontally and touch when the mouth is closed.

Levesque
Melding three breeds, Rogatien Levesque brought forth the Levesque in 1873, attaching his name to the creation. The Levesque's ancestors include the Bleu de Gascogne, the Grand Gascon-Saintongeois, and the English Foxhound. The Levesque is one of the Batard breeds of France. These French hounds were considered to be the superior pack-hounds of any hunter's day. Swift and well built, the Levesque was intended to work in packs on a variety of game. Today the Levesque is very rare, and few true specimens can be found even in France. Cynologists believe that all remaining specimens of the Levesque were used in creating the Chien Français Blanc et Noir.

Leopard Cur, merle (leopard spotted).

ESSENTIALS OF THE LEVESQUE: A strictly tricolor scenthound of good size, the Levesque is a slender but muscular dog. Expression-wise, it is intelligent and lively. Height: 26–28 inches (66–71 cm). Weight: 55–66 pounds (25–30 kg). The coat is typically hound—short and smooth. The head is long and rather large, the ears are big and houndy, laying close to the head. The overall impression is imposing and memorable.

Lexicon

The particular language of a specific field of study or interest. A volume which defines common (and sometimes obscure) terms used in a given field, e.g., a canine lexicon.

Lhasa Apso, golden.

tive terrier-type canines for the purpose of guarding the interiors of temples. These dogs became the foundation stock of the Lhasa Apso. It was not until the seventh century that these Lhasas were bred to emulate, at least in appearance, the revered lion. The Lhasa visually imitated the holy lion—the symbol of the Buddha's dominance over the animal kingdom. The *Abso Seng Kye*, or the "Bark Lion Sentinel Dog," was secure and cozy under the surveillance of the grand Tibetan Mastiff. The Tibetan people were greatly respectful of the tiny Lhasas whom they believed were the reincarnations of pious lamas who failed to attain Nirvana. The name "Apso" has had many interpretations: it may indeed be a corruption of *Rapso* which means goatlike in Tibetan. The breed's shaggy, flowing hair looks quite like a Tibetan mountain goat. Lhasa, of course, is the capital city of Tibet.

The honorable Mrs. Baily brought the first Lhasas to England, in the year 1921, which were given to various dignitaries. The breed appeared in exhibition in 1929. Across the Atlantic as well, the Lhasa made way and was accepted by the American Kennel Club in 1935. The Lhasa remarkably retains some of his once-valued instincts for guarding the home and family; therefore, he tends to be wary of strangers. His lively though assertive nature is appreciated in the home as well as in the show ring.

Lhasa Apso

The Lhasa Apso is chiefly a companion dog with a rich history of interaction with man, as a talisman, a companion, and a symbol of divinity. Deep within the largest continent in the world, in the ancient land of Tibet, there existed small brachycephalic dogs bred from the na-

ESSENTIALS OF THE LHASA APSO: The Lhasa is an appealing dog, with a long dense coat of heavy hairs laying straight.

Lhasa Apso, honey.

Color can be golden, sandy or honey, preferably with black tips on the ears, tail, and beard; other colors include grizzle, slate, smoke, particolor, black, white, and brown. The well-feathered tail is carried over the back in a screwlike fashion. The head, well furnished with whiskers and beard, is narrow and moderately sized.

The muzzle is of medium length. The ears are pendant and well feathered. Forelegs straight; all legs well fringed. Height is between 10–11 inches (25–28 cm). The length from point of shoulders to point of buttocks longer than height at withers. Ribs well up; strong loin, well-developed quarters and thighs.

Lhasa Apso, cream.

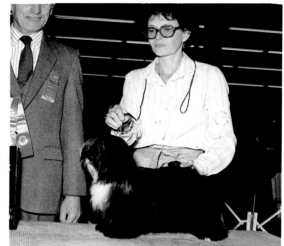

Lhasa Apso colors vary in hue and intensity. Since no one color is preferred over another, identifying colors correctly has never been an important matter. Black tips on the ears are desirable in honey, sandy and golden. Hues of red-golden, smoke, sandy, and black with white chest markings are equally attractive.

Liberian Dog

A small terrier of West Africa used on a variety of game. It was probably brought to the continent by European settlers. The Liberian Dog is neat in appearance. Its muzzle is broad; ears prick; and stop well defined. The dog is used for ratting purposes.

Lice

Small, flat wingless insects that live parasitically by burrowing into the dog's skin and feeding on the dog's blood. Lice are too small to be easily detected. The likely sign of lice infestation is weight loss. Increased scratching may cause hair to fall out, leaving bald, irritated patches of skin. Lice reproduce quickly and can infest humans. A louse in the house is cause for immediate action, which includes burning the dog's bedding, treating the dog with a prescribed insecticide, and inspecting and sanitizing yourself well as well.

Licensed show

A show given under American Kennel Club rules and awarding championship points by a club which is not a member of the American Kennel Club.

Licenses

Regardless of the country and state in which you reside, your dog likely will need a license. Essentially a license is a tax on your dog. Governments tax everything else, why not our dogs too? Dogs, incidentally, are the only domesticated pet to be taxed. Such "privilege" also equips an owner with certain rights as well as liabilities. The issued tag must be worn by the applicable canine at all times. Thankfully, licenses can be acquired through the mail. Depending on the city in which you live, a license may only be applicable in that particular city; others are more state- or district-wide. Dogs that change owners usually do not need a new license. In some regions, spayed or neutered dogs, just like the various assistance dogs, may receive discounts or exemptions.

Dog owners who breed dogs for selling (even if you sell only one!) may require a kennel or breeder's license. A "hobby kennel" license may be the other option for the one-time breeder of the family pet. Be sure of the legality of your breeding actions, since fines usually exceed fees substantially.

Lick granuloma

A thickly calloused area of the skin that results from the dog's chronic licking of the area. The affected area is typically hairless and irritated. Treatment usually involves anti-inflammatory steroids and a covering of the affected area. If the dog can be made to stop licking the area, lick granulomas may heal on their own. Interesting is the fact that snake venom was once the preferred cure for the lick granuloma, with cobra venom the most desirable. Such cures are no longer prescribed.

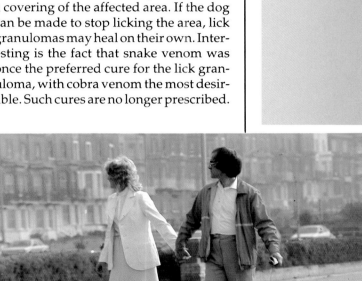

Life expectancy
See Age

Life insurance
See Insurance for dogs

Line

In scent-hunting, the track of the quarry as indicated by its scent.

Linebreeding

Mating two related dogs that have at least one generation separating them. Intended as a "safer" type of inbreeding, linebreeding employs a more diverse gene pool by not crossing dogs that are directly related, e.g., brother/sister,

Licenses. Legal restrictions on dog ownership vary from state to state or county to county. Urban dog owners must acquire the license required by their own cities. Photo by R. Pearcy.

mother/son. This more diverse pool lessens the problem of fixing faults in a line, while at the same time ensures consistent quality offspring to the degree that the parents and their ancestors are of good quality. Linebreeding provides the base for most responsible breeding programs today. *See also* Breeding, Bitch, Inbreeding, Outcrossing, Stud dog

Linty coat
Downy, soft coat of the Bedlington.

Lip-fold pyoderma
An infection that can occur in breeds in which there exist folds of skin along the lower jaw. The infection usually creates a foul odor, which causes some observers to confuse the condition with that of halitosis, a condition caused by bad teeth or gums. Antibiotics are proven effective in treating the condition. Rarely will a breed without the folds acquire the infection.

Lipoma
A fatty, benign tumor, found usually in overfed animals. Proper diagnosis is required to differentiate this relatively benign growth from malignant tumors. Unless the lipoma becomes excessively large, corrective measures are usually stalled. Removal typically involves only minor surgery.

Lippy
Pendulous or overhung lips. *See* Lips

Lithuanian Hound, black with tan. Photo by V. Pcholkin.

Lips
The fleshy areas that surround the mouth cavity, covering the teeth. In dogs, unlike in humans, the lips are more difficult to delineate, as they usually blend into the muzzle, cheeks and chin. The lower lips cover the lower teeth and blend in with the chin area from the lip margins, where they begin. The upper lips begin below the nose and continue through the lip margins; they cover the upper teeth. The lips are usually narrow and heavily pigmented. "Lips" is sometimes interpreted to mean flews and is not among the most common terms employed in the canine lexicon. Fluttering lips, pendulous lips, houndlike lips, overhung lips, and underhung lips all loosely describe loose, deep, greatly developed lips. *See also* Flews, Muzzle

Liptok
See Slovak Cuvac

Listed dog
A dog entered at a dog show but which is not registered in the American Kennel Club Stud Book. Such an unregistered dog may be shown for 30 days upon the payment of a listing fee for each show. Thereafter, it may be granted an extension if the owner can prove that he is unable to register the dog due to technical difficulties (inability to procure a signature, etc.). In such a case, the American Kennel Club may grant permanent listing privileges to the dog upon the payment of the fee whenever shown. The fee is required to cover the added cost of maintaining a record of show wins on a dog that is not included in the registration files.

Lithuanian Hound
The Lithuanian Hound is a creation of twentieth-century Russia. The Curland Hound, a long-legged, nineteenth-century Baltic hunter derived originally from scenthounds of England, Poland and the Lucernese area of Switzerland. In attempting to recreate the original-type Curland Hound, industrious Russian breeders crossed Bloodhounds, Beagles, Polish Hounds and a potpourri of native

hounds to conjure up the Lithuanian Hound. He is effective on hare and fox. The boar, the Lithuanian Hound's intended quarry, proves too wild and deadly for this hound to pursue. Many Lithuanian Hounds were slain by wild boars during the 1976–77 hunting season. Hunters and breeders reevaluated the breed standard and abilities. Even if the Lithuanian Hound falls somewhat shy of the old Curland Hound in the hunt, he has unpassable speed and great persistence. No specimens are known outside of the Lithuanian Republic.

ESSENTIALS OF THE LITHUANIAN HOUND: The body structure of the Lithuanian Hound goes against the grain of the typical scenthound. Moderately tucked flanks seem almost to contradict the sturdy, heavily boned body of this hound. He is an impressive sight: muscular, sleek and determined. Height: 21–24 inches (53–61 cm). Color is always black with limited tan markings. The dog possesses less heavy bone than many a hound his size. The Lithuanian's tail is rather long and held low.

Litter

An ideally sized litter is one of four or five whelps. This population is manageable for the brood bitch. Since bitches only have eight nipples, more than eight pups causes obvious problems—excessively large litters may require employing a foster mother or a little extra human intervention to avoid the strain and drain on the bitch. Many of the smaller breeds may whelp only one or two pups: Pomeranians and Papillons frequently have litters of one or two. The larger breeds tend to have larger litters, say seven to nine pups: Labrador Retrievers, German Shorthaired Pointers, Irish Setters. The record for the largest litter goes to an English Foxhound that whelped 23 in 1944; A Saint Bernard whelped a close second with 22 (unfortunately only half of each litter survived). The sporting breeds tend to have the largest average litters—all over six whelps per litter. One Irish Setter of note whelped 17, 16, and 15 in three successive years.

Little Lion Dog
See Löwchen

Liver

1) A brown color ranging from reddish to chocolate, *always* with a brown nose and paw pads (e.g., Irish Water Spaniel).

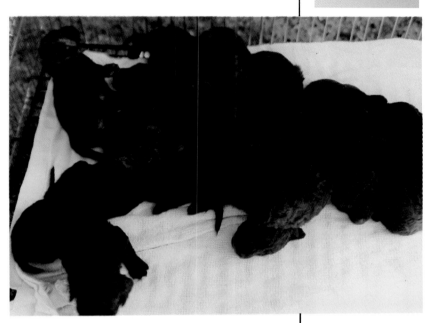

2) The liver is a large gland and serves numerous functions, including an aid in digestion, excretion, blood clotting, and the breakdown of red blood cells. The liver is vital to life. Fortunately its size and capacity allows it to withstand much wear and tear from disease, poor diet, and other stresses for many years. As the dog ages, the liver shrinks and hardens, and fats cells begin to infiltrate. Digestive disturbances, weight loss, swelling of the abdomen, muscle atrophy and weakness, vomiting and diarrhea are all signs of potential liver malfunction. Excreta can change; foamy urine and tan or black feces are also signs. Treatment for a diseased or infected liver requires skill, care and patience. Immediate veterinary care is necessary and can save the dog's life. Medication, diet, and a variety of other treatments may be prescribed depending on the specific condition that affects the dog's liver.

Liver belton
See Belton

Litter of liver puppies—a good-sized family of newly born Irish Water Spaniels.

Liver-colored nose
See Brown nose

Liver-colored dogs always have brown noses. This is a fine example of a liver-roan English Cocker Spaniel photographed by I. Français.

Livestock
Livestock is defined as any animals that are commercially valuable. This definition excludes both pets and wild animals. Most regions protect livestock from dog attacks in one way or another. The dog must be caught in the process of attacking, preparing to attack or fleeing from the area. Some jurisdictions consider a dog trespassing on farmland a direct violation and authorize the killing of any such animals. It is always wise to be aware of the laws which will affect your dog's actions.

Loaded shoulders
See Shoulder types

Lobe
The cartilage of the external ear. *See* Ear anatomy

Lobular ears
Ear shape particular to a number of the spaniel family (e.g., English Cocker, English Springer).

Local breed clubs
On a smaller scale than the national clubs, local breed clubs accept members and establish goals. Members are typically breed owners and are dedicated to the improvement and furthering of the breed. Breed clubs are excellent sources of contacts and most clubs have established networks to assist members with locating handlers, groomers, and breeders. Local breed clubs often organize, run and support events ranging from field trials to bench shows, to therapy visitations. Local clubs give you a chance to support, further, and affect your breed. Newsletters are published by local breed clubs, and if potentially interested, one should contact the local club and ask for information. A listing of local clubs in your area can be acquired by contacting the national breed club and requesting applicable information.

Lockjaw
See Tetanus

Loins
Lumbar area that begins as the rib cage ends and ends as the pelvis begins. In dogs, the loins are often requested to be of a particular type, contour, angulation, etc. Arched is perhaps the most common loin type. Such loins must be strong and agile as called for by the particular musculature of a given breed, not structure. Lean loin development, that is, without excessive muscular development, is often requested through the phrase "light in loins" (e.g., Staffordshire Bull Terrier). Sagging loins are undesirable in any animal and are caused by loins that are poorly muscled or simply too long. The backline in such a dog tends to sag or sway. *See also* Tuck-up

Longhaired Dutch Shepherd
See Dutch Shepherd

Longhaired Whippet

It is not uncommon for a sighthound breed to develop more than a smooth coat type—and the Whippet is no exception. A recent addition to the dog world (and a cause of considerable controversy), the Longhaired Whippet is an elegant, silky-coated version of the smoothhaired Whippet. It is not recognized by the American Kennel Club as an individual breed or an acceptable coat variation of the Whippet breed. *See also* Whippet, New breed creation.

Loose shoulders
See Shoulder types

Loss
When a pack of scenthounds can no longer follow the line, they are said to have come to a loss.

Lost back
Long back muscles of the racing dog torn loose from anchorage from over-exertion in a race.

Lost dogs
Because many dogs have a tendency to wander and because many owners are irresponsible about controlling their pets, dogs get lost. An abandoned dog is also a lost dog, unless the person who abandoned the dog foolishly "abandoned"

Longhaired Whippet, fawn with white. Photo by L.M. Gray.

Longhaired Whippet, white. Photo by Richard Robyn. Photographs courtesy of W. Wheeler.

him two blocks from home and the dog finds his way back. There are of course some very romantic tales of dogs' being "lost" in Tucson, Arizona, and finding their way home to New Brunswick, New Jersey. These tales are great to read about but provide little comfort for the owner of a lost dog. People who find a lost dog should report it to the necessary authorities. There are lost and found organizations in a great number of cities and towns. Newspaper ads and radio stations prove very helpful in cases of this sort. Owners should be thorough and calm about their search. Usually, spreading around photographs of the dog will help in positively identifying the animal as well.

Loulou Finnoi
See Finnish Spitz

Low at shoulders
See Shoulder types

Low in withers
See Flat withers

Low-set build
Minimal or limited distance from the ground of the brisket or underline to the floor. Dogs possessing low-set builds include the Dachshund and Czesky Terrier.

Low-set ears
Ears that originate at eye level or below, depending on the breed.

Low-set tail
Typically a tail set below the level of the topline. *See* Tail

Löwchen
Whether the Löwchen, commonly named the Little Lion Dog, developed in Germany or from French bichons and water dogs is yet unknown. Various sources reveal the breed to be of Russian, Mediterranean and French beginnings. France is the nation that is usually attributed as the breed's own. Nonetheless, it is known that the Lion Dog enjoyed popularity in Italy, Spain, France and Germany as early as the 1500s. This popularity continued through to the 1800s; Goya is but one of the great artists who chose to capture the Little Lion Dogs on canvas. The lion clip, as used on the Portuguese Water Dog, was the fashionable norm for the Löwchen's coat. With the coming of the twentieth century and the two World Wars, the popularity of the Löwchen waned. By 1960, he was granted the title "rarest breed" by the *Guinness Book of World Records*. The efforts of Madame M. Bennert of Brussels helped the struggling Lion Dog after the Second World War; she and Dr. Richert

Löwchen, fawn.

Löwchen, grizzle. Photographs by I. Français.

Löwchen, white. Photo by I. Français.

Löwchen, dark gray. Photo by I. Français.

receive credit for the Löwchen's continued existence today. While not especially popular in the U.S. (where it is still not recognized), the Löwchen is on the rise, enjoying his Kennel Club and Australian recognition.

ESSENTIALS OF THE LÖWCHEN: The Löwchen is little and clipped in the traditional lion clip, including tail topped with a plume. The dog is strongly built, well balanced and active. Height: 10–13 inches (25–33 cm) tall and weighs 8–18 pounds (3.5–8.5 kg). His long silky coat is wavy but never curly. He can be any color or any combination of colors. The head is short; the skull wide in proportion; the eyes are round, dark, large, and intelligent; the ears are long, pendant, and well fringed. The neck is of good length. The hindlegs are well muscled, straight. Forelegs are fine and straight; shoulders well laid back. Tail is of medium length.

Lower arm
Anatomical region including the radius and ulna.

Lower jaw
Mandible. *See* Jaws

Lower thigh
Area encompassing the tibia and fibula bones. *See* Thigh

Lowlands Herder
See Polish Lowland Sheepdog

Lozenge mark
Kissing spot or beauty spot. A chestnut colored spot found on the top skull of the Blenheim variety of both the King Charles Spaniel and Cavalier King Charles Spaniel. The lozenge mark is considered a hallmark of each breed.

Lucernese Hound
See Luzerner Laufhund

Lumbar
Loins region. *See* Loins

Lumber
Excessive musculation or bony development to the point of superfluity. The phrase most commonly employed to point to this characteristic as undesirable is "without lumber."

Lumpy shoulders
See Shoulder types

Lundehund
See Norwegian Lundehund

Lung
Two in all, the lungs are large organs housed in the chest and vital to respiratory processes. Entering the lungs via the bronchial tubes, which branch into numerous bronchioles and further into air sacs, oxygen is absorbed by the lungs. Surrounding the millions of air sacs are tiny capillaries. These capillaries receive this oxygen and exchange carbon dioxide, which is expelled by the lungs. The oxygen is then carried to all parts of the body via the circulatory system. Carbon dioxide is one of the waste products of the body, and oxygen is a primary fuel. *See also* Circulatory system, Lungworms, Respiratory system

Lung room, plenty of

Chest capacity optimum for maximum lung and heart development.

Lungs, problems of

See Lungworms, Hookworms, Edema, Emphysema, Pleurisy, Pneumonia, Tumors, Cancer

Lungworms

These parasites, common to many large mammals, fortunately do not commonly affect the dog. Lungworms are roundworms, which *see*. These roundworms live in the lungs of the host and produce eggs. The eggs are coughed up by the host and then swallowed. They pass through the host's digestive system and are released in the stool. New hosts then acquire the worms when coming into contact with the infected feces. Thus are lung worms propagated.

Lupus erythematosus

A common joint affliction. Proper diagnosis requires laboratory tests. Treatment is variable, but anti-inflammatories have proven effective.

Lurcher

The name *Lurcher* derives from the Romany word meaning to rob or plunder; the nomenclature was determined by the Romanies, although the tinkers of Ireland also favored the dog. Often not considered a breed as such, the Lurcher is more of a crossbreed, usually three-quarters sighthound. The most common combinations are Greyhound/Terrier and Greyhound/Collie. The Collie crosses often are not sizable enough for the Lurcher's intended work.

It is difficult to describe the Lurcher since, by definition, a standard of perfection is not appropriate. These dogs are generally tall and firm, with a rough coat. Size is dependent on the two breeds (or dogs) crossed. Gypsies traditionally scoff at any Lurcher that is not predominantly Greyhound, since the lesser Lurchers are ineffective for a day-long hare hunt. The stringent training method of the gypsies is frowned upon in some Lurcher circles, since the

pups begin working at six months. Only the top-producing pups are kept; the rest are used as barter. Ideally, the Lurcher should have the nose of a Foxhound, the feet of a Greyhound, and the eye of a hawk. His hard coat is necessary for performance over harsh thick-thicketed terrain. Important features of the Lurcher include a long strong back, good spring of rib, and a lengthy neck. Color is never of importance.

Lurcher, particolor.

Lurcher, black with white chest blaze. Photographs by I. Français.

Lurcher, red-fawn. Photo by I. Français.

Luzerner Neiderlaufhund, tricolor.

Lure

Electrically-pro-pelled stuffed or artificial rabbit that is attached to an arm that extends out over the dog-racing track.

Lure coursing

See Coursing

Luxation

Dislocation of a joint, e.g., carpal luxation. *See also* Subluxation

Luzerner Laufhund

The Luzerner Laufhund and the Luzerner Neiderlaufhund represent the two sizes of native hounds that can be found in Lucerne, Switzerland. The scenthounds of Switzerland necessarily had to be lighter and smaller than many other dogs that performed similar functions, due to the more mountainous, less cultivated geography of Switzerland. The taller of the two, the Luzerner Laufhund was likely bred from the Petit Bleu de Gascogne of France. These two hounds share many similar features, including a fine sense of smell.

These dogs can be used on a wide variety of game, including roe deer and boar. The Neiderlaufhund, the shorter, was bred down from the Luzerner Laufhund by crossing in various dachsbrackes or the Dachshund. The Neiderlaufhund can be used on smaller game and it was for this purpose that this low-stationed hound was likely contrived. With the exception of size, these two breeds look quite similar. The head resembles the St. Hubert Hound with its long, folding ears and narrow skull.

ESSENTIALS OF THE LUZERNER LAUFHUND: The Luzerner Laufhund and the Luzerner Neiderlaufhund (Small Lucernese Hound) possess tricolor, heavily ticked wire coats. The main difference between them is size: the Laufhund stands 18–23 inches (46–59 cm) tall and weighs 34–44 pounds (15.5–20 kg); the Neiderlaufhund may stand from 13–16 inches (33–41 cm) but can weigh up to 40 pounds (18.5 kg). This latter dog is a shorter legged, sturdy-to-the-ground hound, while the former is taller and appears slighter in build.

Ixodes dammini, one carrier of Lyme; in its larval stage it primarily affects rodents and birds, on which it matures to its nymphatic stage and moves to such mammals as dog and man. On these higher animals the ticks reach their mature stage, at which time they seek their chosen prey. The most commonly reported signs are arthritislike conditions accompanied by fever. These conditions commonly affect the large joints and affect them recurrently. Numerous other signs are reported, and these vary considerably from case to case, with no two

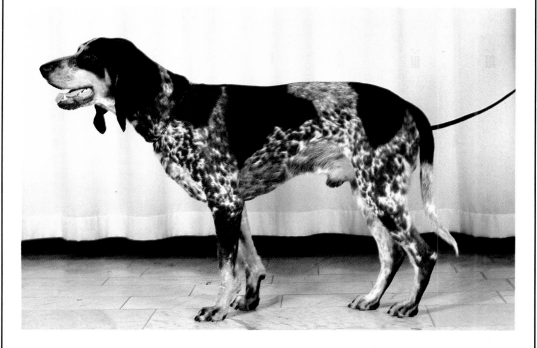

Luzerner Laufhund, tricolor. Photo by I. Français.

Lycaon pictus
See African hunting dog

Lye
A strong alkaline solution obtained by leaching the ashes of wood.

Lyme disease
A tick-carried-and-transmitted, inflammatory disease that affects many species, including dog and man. The real culprit (causative agent) is a spirochete. This spirochete, which has been tentatively named *Borrelia burgdorferi*, is transmitted by several three-stage ticks of the genus *Ixodes*. Any of the three stages, the larva, the nymph, or the adult, can carry and transmit the disease. An example is

cases necessarily giving evidence of common signs. The variability of signs makes non-clinical diagnosis difficult. Treatment with such antibiotics as ampicillin and tetracycline has proven successful. *See also* Ticks

Lymphocytic leukemia
See Canine malignant lymphoma

Lymphoma
See Canine malignant lymphoma

Lysis
The process by which clotted blood cells dissolve into fluid, whereby they can be either utilized by the body or passed as waste.

Ma-chu-gou
See Chinese Hound

Macellaio Herder
See Sicilian Branchiero

Macellaio Herding Dog
See Sicilian Branchiero

Mackenzie River Dog
Similar to the Hare Indian Dog and the Tahltan Bear Dog, the Mackenzie River Dog is a regional pariah-type dog which was used by the Indians of Canada for hunting and sledge-pulling.

Magyar Agăr,
white with brindle.
Photo by I.
Francais.

Magyar Agăr
The Magyar Agăr is also known as the Hungarian Greyhound. The present-day Hungarians are largely descended from the Magyar people who invaded and settled, in the ninth century, the area of Europe known today as Hungary. The Magyar people brought, along with their traditions and customs, their dogs. These dogs likely resembled the Sloughi and other Eastern greyhound types. In later centuries, however, the Agărs were crossbred with the Greyhound proper and hence closely resemble that breed today. It was indiscreet crossbreeding of the Hungarian courser with the English Greyhound during the nineteenth cen-

tury that is responsible for the present-day Magyar Agăr's lack of many of the hallmarks which its forebears once possessed. The Agăr's primary job was (and still is) coursing hare and fox, although with the ecological changes of the modern world, hare is more commonly coursed today. The quickness of the Magyar's feet is only rivaled by the quickness of his mind; his sight is far superior to his scenting ability. Like the English Greyhound, the Magyar is employed as a race dog, a feat his feet accommodate very well.

ESSENTIALS OF THE MAGYAR AGĂR: The Magyar is a lean and elegant dog that closely resembles the Greyhound proper. His frame is longer than square. His muscles are well developed; plenty of bone, long, sinewy legs. He stands between 25–27.5 inches (63–70 cm), slightly smaller than the Greyhound. He weighs 49–68 pounds (22–31 kg). The head is wedge-shaped when viewed from either the top or side. The skull is voluminous, the forehead fairly large. The muzzle should not be too snipy. The ears are very motile, of medium size, not so soft as those of the Greyhound. The chest is deep and capacious; back solid but springy, rather straight, only slightly arched at the loins. The coat is short and close but fairly rough, especially in winter. Color possibilities encompass various solids and brindles.

Magyar Vizsla
See Vizsla

Mahratta Greyhound
The Mahratta Greyhound, like the Rampur Dog and Banjara Greyhound, is an indigenous running sighthound of India. Today these dogs still exist but are not plenteous in number. Uncertainty prevails over the Mahratta's lineage. Whether the Mahratta is a descendant of the Saluki or a localization of other indigenous Indian sighthounds remains the essential question. The Mahratta's small size, in relation to the Rampur and other Indian dogs, makes either Saluki

descent or a pure and assuredly ancient origin the most likely hypothesis concerning development. With exceptional speed and concentrated strength, the Mahratta Dog is used successfully for coursing small and medium-sized game in the indigenous province after which he is named.

The Mahratta possesses instinctive courage and ability for the hunt. He uses these to full advantage in conjunction with his excellent eyesight, fleet feet, and able muscle. The Mahratta is used almost exclusively for the hunt; life in India makes owning a dog solely as a pet a frivolous venture. Likewise, the world of showing and breeding purebred dogs has never enraptured the Indian country as it has Japan or Western nations.

ESSENTIALS OF THE MAHRATTA GREYHOUND: The Mahratta is best described as resembling the smooth-coated Saluki, for he gives the impression of enduring speed coupled with active strength. Standing only 21 inches (53 cm) at the shoulder, the Mahratta is, however, slightly smaller than the Saluki. The Mahratta is a compact sighthound, well muscled, deep chested, and strong backed. The common color pattern consists of dark blue and tan. The coat is short and provides good protection against the various Indian elements.

Main earth

A foxhunting term used to refer to the fox's den and place of breeding.

Majestic Tree Hound

The Majestic Tree Hound was bred rather recently by American hunters to handle horse-killing big cats in the South. In creating this large and formidable hound, hunters also subscribed to the old-type cold-nosed methodical worker. American breeders chose working hounds of the St. Hubert type from French stock to create the Majestic. The working Bloodhound is his closest pinpointable forebear. Big-game hounds of the said Gascon type were crossed with other large hounds used for similar purposes in the American West. The resulting size of the Majestic seems to verify these speculations. Although the Majestic Tree Hound would not be aptly described a fast worker, he is surely sufficient in his pace.

ESSENTIALS OF THE MAJESTIC TREE HOUND: Massive and ponderous, the Majestic Tree Hound epitomizes the large working dog. One hundred pounds (45 kg) of muscle, the Majestic can be 31 inches (79 cm) tall. His coat can be any combination of colors, usually arranged on a white sky; the coat is short, thick and dense.

Magyar Agár, white with fawn.

Majestic Tree Hound, red-fawn. Photographs by I. Français.

Majestic Tree Hound, tricolor. Photo by I. Français.

Maltese, white.

Making game

Showing signs of awareness of the presence of game. This is indicated when a dog's tail action accelerates and his actions seem searching and cautious. This usually ends in a point, an accidental flush and automatic stop to flush, a flush and chase, or the search proving fruitless and the dog moving on at the previous rate and style.

Making-the-wheel-tail

An excited tail that actually curls fully over the back of the dog. The usual tail carriage is low.

Malar bone

See Zygomatic arch

Mallorquin Bulldog

See Perro de Presa Mallorquin

Malnutrition

The result of disease, condition, or inadequate feeding, malnutrition is the lack of any of the vitamins, minerals, proteins, fats, or carbohydrates necessary for good health and soundness. Malnutrition does not mean emaciation. Obese dogs can lack vitamins, minerals, or other needed components. The signs of malnutrition vary greatly from case to case. *See also* Nutrition

Maltese

It is unclear whether the Maltese originated on the island of Malta, after which the breed is named, or in the Sicilian town of Melitia. Caius writes that the breed was called Melita, of the island of Malta. The bosom-snuggled Maltese was favored by the great ladies of Rome. The Maltese society was an ancient and sophisticated people who were exuberantly proficient in the arts and highly civilized. The elegant and tiny Maltese dwelled among these people. It is believed also that in the fifth century the Greeks raised tombs to their Maltese. Appropriately, the Maltese has been celebrated in art and captured breathtakingly on the canvas of many well-known artists. Although painter Edwin Landseer prophesied the immediate extinction of the breed, the Maltese became a popular show dog in 1850 and has continued in this vein ever since. The Maltese hasn't always been solely a showpiece and home ornament: once called the Maltese Terrier, it was used on rats and had a particular distaste for felines. Were it not for the length of its exuberant coat, the breed would have been capable of handling badger as well.

After World War I, the breed was practically extinct in England. Specimens from Holland and Germany helped to revive the British Maltese. Today many Maltese trace their bloodlines to these German and Dutch imports. No frail or delicate dog, the Maltese is hardy and lively and able to withstand reasonable extremes in climes. He is described as sweet tempered, gentle mannered, sprightly in action, and vigorous. This breed delights in its small size (its size has been likened to a squirrel's and a ferret's) and its long-sitting acquaintance with humankind.

ESSENTIALS OF THE MALTESE: The pure white, profusely coated Maltese is essentially short and cobby. The body is compact and well balanced, with good spring of rib. The coat, a mantle of long and silky hair, is of good length but does not interfere with the dog's gait; the texture of the coat must be silky and never woolly. The head is of medium length and well proportioned. The eyes are oval and lively, never bulging. The drop ears are rather low set and well feathered. The neck is of sufficient length to promote the proper proud carriage of the head. Height: not exceeding 10 inches (26 cm). Weight: 4–6 pounds (2–3 kg). A solid white color is preferred, although lemon on the ears is pardonable. The tail is long haired and carried gracefully over the dog's back.

Mammary cancer

Mammary cancer is the uncontrolled growth of cells that affect the mammary gland by the destruction of mammary cells and the obstruction of mammary function. Mammary cancer is reported at a high incidence in bitches, with unspayed animals heading the list. There is a believed correlation between the lactation process and mammary cancer and between hormonal production and mammary cancer as well.

Mammary glands

See Breasts

Maltese.

Man-stopping guard dog

A term used to refer to a breed or a member of a breed that has the temperament and physical ability to inflict such serious bodily injury as to make impossible further advance or assault. Some man-stoppers include the Bull Mastiff, the Canary Dog, the American Pit Bull Terrier, and the Tosa Inu, which *see*.

Manchester Terrier

The Manchester Terrier originated in Manchester, England, supposedly from crosses of the now-extinct English Terrier or Black and Tan Terrier and the Whippet. The original crosses are accredited to a Crumpsall resident, Mr. John Hulme. Hulme's said intention was to produce a combined ratter and rabbiter. This indi-

Manchester Terrier, black and tan. Photo by I. Français.

vidualistic terrier was favored by the British working classes in the heyday of the ratting sport. One particular key dog named "Billy" went down on record for killing 100 large rats in 6 minutes 35 seconds. This exciting venture took place in a wooden box encasement. Billy's heroic abilities are believed to be typical of the early Manchesters. The British fascination with rat baiting led to the Manchester's uncommon popularity. Ear cropping also had a dramatic effect on the breed's popularity. When it was outlawed, many fanciers shied away from the breed. The Manchester's ears had become larger and heavier than anyone expected, hidden for so long by cropping at an early age. It took some doing to get the Manchester's ears to drop forward gracefully like the Fox Terrier's. Referred to in Victorian times as the "Gentleman's Terrier," the Manchester is described as ardent, lively, and good natured. His agreeable disposition, convenient size and minimal grooming needs make him an ideal companion. The

smaller version Manchester, the Toy Manchester Terrier, which *see*, was a favorite of Queen Victoria and today remains a fine companion dog.

ESSENTIALS OF THE MANCHESTER TERRIER: Sleek, finely built terrier: jet black with rich mahogany to tan markings, which do not blend into each other but form clear well-defined lines. The head is long and level with wedge shaped jaws that taper. Eyes are dark and oblong. Ears small, V-shaped. In the United States, the ears are often cropped to stand to an erect point; in Great Britain, the ears are left natural, hanging close to the head. Shoulders clean and sloped with straight forelegs. Body short, well sprung with slight roach. The feet small with arched toes. Tail tapers to a point. Height: 15–16 inches (38–41 cm). Weight is divided into two categories: 12–16 pounds (5.5–7.5 kg); 16–22 pounds (7.5–10 kg). The coat is short, firm, and glossy.

Mandible

Lower jaw, under jaw. *See* Jaws

Mane

Long and profuse hair on top and sides of the neck of some breeds (e.g., Pekingese). Shawl. Ruff.

Maned wolf

Chrysocyon brachyurus is native to South America and its range extends through Brazil, Paraguay, and northern Argentina. Distinct defines the maned wolf's appearance: very long and very thin legs, a long coat that is reddish in color and stand-offish on the back (forming a mane and giving the species one of its common names), a long neck, large pointed ears, and a sharply pointed muzzle. The animal is approximately 50 inches (127 cm) long and stands around 29 inches (74 cm) at the shoulder. The maned wolf prefers far-away lowland and thick brushland where it can practice its omnivorous and indiscriminate eating practices and stay as far away from man as possible. Its habits have been described as foxlike, but little is actually known about its social behavior and instincts. The maned wolf is not a predator of livestock and in fact is quite beneficial to man, eating various insects and weeds.

Unfortunately the animal is ruthlessly hunted, although its skin sells for little and its fur is useless as clothing. The animal's lack of cunning and lack of speed make hunting it less than sport.

Mange

Any of a number of mange-mite infestations. There are many kinds of mites, but not all cause mange. The three common kinds of mites that affect our canine pets are: red mange mites (*Demodex canis*), sarcoptic mange mites (*Sarcopters scabeii*), and ear mange mites (*Otodectes cynotis*). All these mites are so small that they cannot be identified without the use of a microscope.

Red mange, known also as demodectic mange and follicular mange, typically shows itself first as a balding patch under an eye, on a cheek or the forehead, or on the front legs. As the infestation spreads and worsens, the dog's scratching increases. If not treated, secondary complications will likely present themselves, including a bacterial infection which causes pustules and intense reddening of the skin.

Sarcoptic mange, resulting in the condition called scabies, is caused by round mites, the females of which burrow into the skin and lay eggs. Males and immatures do not burrow but live on the surface of the skin, beneath flaking and scaling pieces of skin. Scabies is one condition that is easily transmitted from dog to man, and owners must therefore be wary if they suspect that their dog is infected. Proper diagnosis requires a professional; treatment is available.

Ear mange is also caused by round mites, but these live in the ear canal, causing a substance to accumulate that resembles wax but is crumbly and dark, quite distinct from normal ear wax. This substance, if removed from the ear and observed, will reveal numerous scabs, the result of the mite's piercing the skin to feed parasitically. An ear-mite infection will cause great irritation to the dog, resulting in his shaking and scratching his head excessively. The infection will also cause a strong odor, which is more the result of a secondary bacterial infection than the actual mite infestation. There are many over-the-counter preparations available, but the owner must exercise caution; if the condition is incorrectly diagnosed or secondary conditions are present, some medications can actually do more harm than good. Seek a veterinarian's counsel.

Manila Spaniel

An ancient bichon-type lap dog that was brought to the Philippines by the Spaniards. The dog is no longer extant and in all likelihood has been absorbed into the Havanese breed. While the bichons developed in different island locales, it is wrong to consider each type distinct from the others. Today, of course, these types have each developed into separate breeds, promoted by different countries. *See* Bichon. These tiny dogs were said to possess palliative abilities capable of relieving stomach aches and the like.

Manteau

The term used for the Sloughi's mantle, comprised of black tipped hairs on the back.

Mantle

Dark-shaded portion of the coat that covers the shoulders, back and sides. The term is applied variously: in America, to the St. Bernard's coloration; in Europe, to the mantle or blanket covering the Levesque, Grand Anglo-Français, Polish Hound, and other scenthounds as well.

Mantle covering the backs of two young Polish Hounds. Photo by I. Français.

Marbled eye
See Walleye

Maremma Sheepdog

The Maremma Sheepdog is the sheepdog of central Italy that guards sheep herds. The Italian Cane da Pastore Maremmano-Abruzzese combines the names of two extinct Italian Sheepdogs: the Maremmano, a shorter coat sheepdog; and the Abruzzese, a longer bodied mountain dog. The Maremma is descended from the most ancient of the

Maremma Sheepdog, white. Photo by I. Français.

migrating Eastern sheepdogs. The Maremma's ability to work in high altitudes, its intelligence and independence make this sheepdog paramount to the Italian shepherds. The European flock guards of course are all quite similar: many are white, plushly coated, bulky or semi-bulky, and very powerful. Generally, the Eastern sheepdog prototype is accepted as the progenitor of most of these breeds. The various spin-offs developed within individual countries. The Maremma, although similar to the Kuvasz and Great Pyrenees, is less bulky; it is a very similar dog with stronger livestock instincts.

In Great Britain, the Maremma Sheepdog is recognized by the Kennel Club and competes for championship status. He is generally used as an estate guard and companion. In the United States, the Maremma is still little known although the interest is growing.

ESSENTIALS OF THE MAREMMA SHEEPDOG: This profusely coated sheepdog is thickly boned and solidly muscled. Coat must be white; any yellow or orange coloration is tolerated on ears only. Very impressive are the large shoulders and thick legs. Height: 25–29 inches (63.5–74 cm). Weight: 70–100 pounds (32–45 kg). The body is slightly longer than tall, without sway or roach. The chest is deeper than broad and the belly is moderately tucked. The stifles are moderately bent; the feet oval and toes strongly arched.

Maries disease

A condition in which excess bony deposits occur along bone surfaces. Long bones are those most often affected, causing a noticeable enlargement. Lameness and difficulty in standing result. Bony deposits can also occur in the lung tissue, resulting in coughing and difficult breathing. The cause is unknown.

Marked fall

A fall, observed by the dog, in which the dog should be able to locate and retrieve without aid from the handler, although the bird may have moved from the location of the fall. In which case the dog should be able to trail and recover it.

Markiesje

Although a new breed of gundog, the exact component stock is not fully known. It is reported that Miniature Poodle, Continental Toy Spaniel, and possibly a small Brittany or two were crossed to produce a small but effective spaniel-type hunter and retriever. Artistic renderings from Holland in the mid-1700s have been cited as verification of the Markiesje's authenticity in history. The dog is known for its light-footed step and ever-alertness. While the breed remains unrecognized and limited in number, small game hunters and show enthusiasts are taking interest in this very versatile breed. It tends to be independent and can be aloof with strangers, often quiet and reserved.

ESSENTIALS OF THE MARKIESJE: Smallish spaniel-type; intelligent, well-balanced multi-purpose dog. The head is medium sized, with a flat skull and a tapering muzzle. The body is well constructed and balanced with a capacious chest, sloping shoulders, and well-muscled quarters. The coat is long and silky; feathering is generous on the ears, legs and tail. In color the Markiesje is solid black, with or without white markings. Height: 14 inches (35 cm). Weight: 20–22 pounds (9–10 kg). The expression is undeniably clear and attentive.

Marking

Noting the location of a fall and remembering it until the bird is retrieved from that location or, should it be a runner, trailed from the fall and retrieved.

Marshall

The official in charge of a sled dog race.

Mask

1) Dark fore-facial shadings that occur on a number of breeds, e.g., Pekingese, Bullmastiff, Pug, Dogue de Bordeaux. In the breeds in which masks occur, they are often most desirable. 2) A foxhunting term that means the fox's head.

Master Agility Dog

The highest title awarded for agility competition, M.A.D., see Agility trials.

Master hair

Guard hair (e.g., Eskimo Dog).

Mastiff

There is no doubt that the Mastiff descends from ancient lines; dogs of similar type inhabited Europe and Asia deep into B.C. times. These massive canines were employed in the hunting of wild horses and lions, as well as in protecting the homes of Babylonians. The burying of terracotta Mastiff figures under the thresholds of houses was a custom of the Assyrian peoples. It was practiced to invoke the canine spirits to ward off evil spirits. Mastiff prototypes, such as the Molossus of Epirus and Babylonian Mastiff, were used as flock guards against wolves and other predators. Romans found the Mastiff in England when they first arrived—how the dogs got to England escapes our knowledge— and took them back to Rome to perform in the arenas. One early writer claims that the Roman government set up a "Procurator Cynegii" at Winchester, England, to purchase promising canines for use by the army and in the arena. These dogs are believed by many to be the ancestors of

Markiesje, black with white chest marking. Photo by I. Français.

the modern Mastiff. Yet, with all the documented evidence of "giant" dogs which resemble in general type the Mastiff of today, the origin and development of the breed continue to be speculated on by historians.

Some well-respected mastiff authorities maintain that all mastiff breeds began in the East, in the region of Tibet, and from there spread to Persia, Assyria, Babylonia, Egypt, and Greece. Others assert that the Mastiff represents one of four ancient mastiff breeds, each of which evolved independently of the other. A third mastiff-authority group maintains that the Mastiff, the English Mastiff that is, represents the "true" ancient giant from which all other mastiffs evolved. This last theory, though likely very appealing to Mastiff fanciers, is dif-

the Mastiff is believed by some to have played an integral role in the creation of the Great Dane, another old, impressive mastiff breed. This assertion is fervently denied by many fanciers, particularly Dane lovers. But whether it be the case or not, the unquestionable fact remains: the Mastiff is a breed which has impressed many, and this impression has led to its use in the creation and "improvement" of other breeds; from the first legions to enter the Isles to the newest canine fancier, people stand in awe of the emanating power, noble carriage, and devoted expression of the Mastiff.

Present-day owners are well aware of the Mastiff's need for a good deal of exercise and lots of room to move. In addition to the spacial requirements, the Mastiff demands a considerable volume of food.

In short, Mastiff ownership is not for everyone. Mastiffs aren't too fond of the show ring; although many dogs participate, they would rather meander around an estate, looking noble and being omnipotent.

ESSENTIALS OF THE MASTIFF: Massive and symmetrical in appearance, the Mastiff possesses an imposing and well-knit frame. The body is broad, deep, long and powerfully built; set on legs well apart and squarely set. Chest is wide, deep, rounded and well let down between the forelegs, extending at least to the elbow. Muscles sharply defined. There is to be no looseness in the shoulders. Legs are straight, strong, and set wide apart, heavy boned. The head, giving a square appearance when viewed from any angle, is broad with noticeable wrinkles—breadth is desired greatly. Muzzle is short and square. Mask is black and ever-

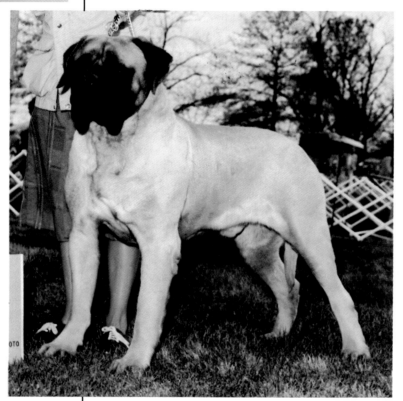

Mastiff, apricot. Tatham photo.

ficult to substantiate, for records of mastiff types found in other parts of the world outdate any records of Mastiffs in the British Isles.

Throughout the history of this most impressive breed, the Mastiff has contributed his blood to the creation of other breeds. Besides the undeniable contribution to the Bullmastiff and other breeds,

present. Ears, small, V-shaped, and rounded at the tips. Eyes, set wide apart, medium in size, never too prominent. The outer coat is moderately coarse; the undercoat is close-lying and dense. In color the Mastiff is apricot, silver fawn, or dark fawn-brindle. Height: at least 27.5–30 inches (70–76 cm). Weight: 175–190 pounds (80–86 kg).

Mastiff breeds

The breeds of dog that come down to modern man from mastiff origins are principally protectors and gladiators. The mastiff breeds were often developed partly for entertainment value, rather like the toy breeds, incidentally. The molossian arena performers of ancient Rome were vaudevillians of a nearly lost school. These dogs were discovered by the Romans in England. It is not clear how these mammoth canines developed. The Phoenicians are usually instrumental to their existence in Britain, possibly from their trade with Cornwall.

Mastiffs have always been associated with protection. The Tibetan Mastiff and the Great Dane are examples of dogs which thrived as property and estate guards. The term mastiff is believed to have derived from the Latin adjective *mansata*, meaning household—thus house dog. The comparable term *bandog* also described these dogs and signified a dog that was tied up (or leashed). The ancient Assyrians buried terracotta mastiff figures underneath the thresholds of their homes so that the spirits of the great protectorate giants would disperse the evil spirits at-tempting to enter. This custom confirms that mastiffs have long been honored as home companions and guardians.

The evolution of the great molossus of Babylonia follows the prototypes into Egypt and Mesopotamia. The Greek mastiff, the Molossus of Epirus was clearly of like origins as the great molossus. Mastiff types were also used by early European barbarians who used the dogs to guard their possessions during times of war. This evolution or migration began in the Tibetan area and gladly fol-

Mastiff, silver fawn. Photo by I. Français.

lowed two roads: one towards the Middle East and the Mediterranean; the second northwards likely by way of China and Russia.

Those mastiffs transported by Romans to fight other dogs and other baited animals were successful in their role as gladiators. The mastiffs' tremendous strength and aggressiveness made this arena sport very popular in Rome. The Alaunt, a breed of dog developed in fifteenth-century Spain, is considered the first bulldog or canine expressly used for the "sport" of bullbaiting.

Mastiffs, once beyond the days of animal baiting, were not released from the pits—the equally inhumane sport of dog fighting ensued. The breeds of fighting dogs that exist today are descended from these seventeenth- and eighteenth-century dog wrestlers. The sport of dog fighting was immensely popular in England, a nation that has historically sunk its teeth into some bloody dubious diversion. In England, the Bull Terrier, the Old English White Terrier and the old Bulldog are among the bull-and-terrier breeds (or types) used in the dog-fighting pit. These terriers gave new meaning to "game." Additionally, dog fighting took hold in other countries as well, not necessarily though possibly resulting from the scarring activity in England. Japan fought its Tosa Inu; Spain, its Perro de Presa Mallorquin; France, its Dogue de Bordeaux; Brazil, its Fila Brasileiro. Later, Argentina developed its pit fighter, the Dogo Argentino. The Canary Islands also boasted a worthy combatant, the Perro de Presa Canario, also known today as the Canary Dog.

The United States also partook in the dog-fighting sport. The American Pit Bull Terrier, standing no higher than 22 inches, has proven itself against domestic and imported canines three and four times its size. Other bulldog-type dogs have been developed but, perhaps thankfully, have gained less press and recognition. The American Bulldog, Olde English Bulldogge, and Bandog are among such breeds. These reinvented bulldogs attempt to rediscover the lost functional old English Bulldog.

Mastiff breeds. The mountainous Spanish Mastiff, weighing in as much as 170 pounds, functions as a guardian of livestock in its native *España*. This tiger-brindle world champion was photographed by C. Salas.

Despite these dogs' massive sizes, the mastiff breeds have retained an enviable level of popularity. Among the many loved mastiffs are the Rottweiler, Great Dane, Saint Bernard, Mastiff, Boxer, and Bull Terrier. The ever-popular Bulldog comes to modern fanciers as one of the most charming of companion animals, a living relic of the wondrous working breed of the past. It is quite true that the mastiff breeds have been miniaturized

with unexpected sublimity: among the miniature mastiffs are the Pug, Boston Terrier, and French Bulldog.

Mastin

Spanish term for mastiff. The Pyrenean Mastiff is known as the Mastin d'Aragon in Spain; the Spanish Mastiff, at home variously as el Mastin de Español, de Extremadura, de la Mancha or de Leon.

Mastin d'Aragon
See Pyrenean Mastiff

Mastin de Español
See Spanish Mastiff

Mastin de Extremadura
See Spanish Mastiff

Mastin de La Mancha
See Spanish Mastiff

Mastin de Leon
See Spanish Mastiff

Mastino Napoletano
See Neapolitan Mastiff

Mastiff breeds have developed in many different countries, though each share basic similarities. Whether developed for baiting bulls and bears, guarding property, or fighting one another, these dogs are powerful and massive. (*top*) American Bulldog, photo courtesy of J. Blackwell; (*middle*) Dogue de Bordeaux, courtesy of P. Curley; and (*bottom*) Neapolitan Mastiff, photographed by I. Français.

Masturbation

Sexually mature male dogs may attempt to relieve their sexual frustrations on practically anything mountable: chair legs, towels, table legs, curtains, neighbor's legs, etc. Admittedly this can be an embarrassing proclivity for the shy owner to explain or apologize. Male dogs also tend to lick themselves to erection and subsequent ejaculation.

Additionally, homosexual masturbation or sex play is common among dogs of both sexes. Males hump males; females hump females. Heterosexual foreplay in dogs often involves the female riding the male for her pleasure, thus such a "humping" instinct is normal. The rubbing of the erect penis or clitoris against the body of the other animal can lead the rider animals to orgasm. *See* Homosexuality

Maturity is reached in the various breeds at different ages. This young Komondor still enjoys romping around in his puppy coat—a mature corded coat is not seen on the Kom until it is two years of age. Photo by Ron Reagan.

It is often difficult to dismount these masturbation habits; most usually dogs beyond adolescence tend to masturbate less. Sighthound owners have been more concerned with the habit than others—but without good reason. Male dogs that habitually masturbate may be candidates for castration, which *see.*

Mat comb

Mat combs are designed to cut through mats without destroying the coat. They have a heavier tooth, are sharp on one side, and can be resharpened. Left-handed groomers can use these combs with ease as they are reversible. Some mat combs have one tooth only and have replaceable razor blades in them. Mat combs must be kept in good condition for best use.

Mătin Belge
See Belgian Mastiff

Mating
See Breeding

Mating cycle
See Breeding

Maturity

The state of physical and mental progression when all bodily systems have reached full development. Maturity marks the point when a dog is a dog and not a puppy any longer. Various breeds mature at different rates. Typically the smaller breeds mature quicker than the large breeds: whereas a Miniature Schnauzer may be physically mature at eight months and mentally mature at 12 months, a Great Dane may not be physically mature until 16 months and mentally mature until 18 months. Until the dog has reached its maturity, it must not be treated as a mature dog but as a pup, given to playfulness and irresponsibility. Hard training is best reserved for the mature dog—of course housebreaking and simple training should be long accomplished by full maturity. *See also* Puppies

Maxilla
Upper jaw. *See* Jaws

Measles

Dogs acquire measles only from man; the disease is as serious to the dog as it is to man: usually curable and passing but sometimes serious and even fatal. Once the disease is established in the dog, it can be passed to other people. Quarantine is therefore recommended in conjunction with veterinary attention.

Measurements

For conformation competition, dogs whose standards include a height or weight disqualification may be measured if the judge or an exhibitor calls for it. Measurements included in standards provide guidelines for breeders and judges. The Beagles, Dachshunds and Poodles use measurements to determine classes. British and American regulations regarding disqualifications and ineligibilities are different from one another and have tended to change from time to time.

Medelan

An extinct bear-hunting breed of Russia. The Medelan likely contributed to the creation of other hunting laikas of the Soviet Union.

Median line

The furrow that runs down the center of the dog's face which is required in some breeds. Also called a flute, the median line is a groove created by bone formation and musculature. The Vizsla and Weimaraner are two breeds that have noticeable median lines.

Medicinal baths

Liquid preparations for the treatment of and/or relief from various diseases and conditions. Medicinal baths are used successfully to treat many parasitic infestations, including tick, flea, lice, and mite. Medicinal baths are also used for treating hookworm infection and many allergic conditions. They often are prescribed by a veterinarian.

Medium Portuguese Hound
See Podengo Português

Medium Portuguese Rabbit Dog
See Podengo Português

Meet

The gathering place of those taking part in a fox hunt.

Melon pips

Tan spots above the eyes of the Basenji. *See* Pips

Member show

A show given by a club which is a member of the American Kennel Club and at which American Kennel Club championship points are awarded.

Meningitis

Inflammation of the membranes (meninges) that surround the brain and spinal cord. The inflammation is most often the result of bacterial or viral infection and is often a secondary infection resulting from an untreated middle-ear infection (itself often a secondary infection of an untreated external-ear infection). Meningitis can also be caused by bacteria that are carried by the blood stream or can concur with distemper. Symptoms include pain, depression, loss of balance and muscle coordination. Treatment is possible after proper diagnosis as to condition and cause. Meningitis is not common in domestic dogs.

Merle coloration occurs in many small herding breeds, such as the Shetland Sheepdog.

Merle

A genetic color factor usually blue-gray with black flecks. Merle most commonly occurs in long-coated breeds, with a few handsome exceptions. Examples of breeds which exhibit merle coloration include the Collie, Border Collie, Dachshund, Beauceron and Cardigan Welsh Corgi. The color should not be confused with brindle, which is also a splotchy patterned coat coloration. The merle genes are controversial in dog circles, and some concerned breeders and fanciers assert that the genetic defects associated with the color gene (blindness and deafness by age two) could be hazardous to a given line or breed and thus all merle-to-merle breedings must be avoided. This syndrome has been referred to as the "lethal white."

Mexican Hairless, coated variety, black with white.

Mexican Hairless, charcoal. Photographs by I. Français.

Merry tail

In the Cocker Spaniel, English and American, the tail is believed to be the most accurate barometer of temperament. A merry or wagging tail indicates the correct and desired temperament of the "Merry Cocker."

Mesaticephalic skull

See Skull types

Messenger dogs

Dogs used in times of war to carry messages for military units. *See* War dogs

Metacarpal pad

Communal pad; is the large pad situated at the rear of the four digital pads of the foot. *See* Feet anatomy

Metacarpus

The pasterns region. *See* Forequarters

Metatarsus

Rear pastern. *See* Hindquarters

Metritis

Infection of the whole uterus. *See* Uterine infections

Mexican Hairless

The Mexican Hairless, also known as the Toy Xoloitzcuintli and the Tepeizeuintli, came to Mexico, transported by the forebears of the Aztecs, through Asia. The hairless breeds developed most probably in Africa and, by one means or another, found their way through China to North America. The Mexican Hairless was brought to South America during the seventeenth century by traders. These dogs were once referred to as African dogs, and the irregular formation of their teeth and the absence of premolars on both jaws differentiate the Mexican Hairless from the other hairless dogs. The Aztec Indians favored these little hairless dogs and their larger brothers, the Xoloitzcuintlis, as night-time poncho warmers, general pets, and occasional sacrifices or meals. The little dogs were also revered for their "healing powers," able to relieve the elderly and sick with their palliative abilities. The breed's ancient name Xoloitzcuintli is believed to have its origins in a religious cult based in Acapulco which was devoted to these divining hairless divas.

As the breed developed in modern times, two types evolved. The more desired was the lighter, more active type as

opposed to the cloddy, untamed-appearing ones that invariably repulsed newcomers to the breed. When the breed was imported to Britain, inevitably there was confusion between it and the Chinese Crested Dog that was already known there. Today the Canadian Kennel Club recognizes the Mexican Hairless. The A.K.C. recognition of the breed was dropped in 1959 due to the lack of registrations. Hairless breeds have never appealed to the general American public. Today the Chinese Crested is the most popular of the hairless breeds.

Like all other hairless dogs, the Mexican Hairless is not a dog for everyone, requiring special attention for his skin, which is susceptible to the sun and to scrapes from objects around the house. Despite the peculiar appearance, the dog is a happy and alert canine, always willing to shed affection.

ESSENTIALS OF THE MEXICAN HAIRLESS: Smooth and soft skin where the average canine advocate expects hair of some sort—the Mexican Hairless is hairless, no body hair whatsoever. On the top of the skull should be planted a tuft of coarse hair. A little tail fuzz is not to be fustigated. A coated variety exists. The body, rather perfect in symmetry, is level-backed and broad chested. The head is slender, with a narrow skull, lean cheeks, and a pointed muzzle. The skin can be dark solid charcoal, slate, reddish gray, liver, or bronze; coffee or pink spots sometimes occur. Height: 11–12 inches (28–31 cm). *See also* Xoloitzcuintli

M.F.H.
Master of Fox Hounds.

Miacis
See Ancestors of the dog

Mid-Asian Shepherd
See Middle Asian Ovtcharka

Mid-Asiatic Borzoi
See Tasy

Middle Asian Ovtcharka
Believed to be an ancestor of the Tibetan Mastiff, the Middle Asian Ovtcharka is a unique-looking dog which is primarily found in the mid-

Middle Asian Ovtcharka, particolor. Photo by I. Français.

U.S.S.R., where it originated. Some reports say that the Middle Asian is found as far east as Mongolia and as far west as Germany. In regions of the Soviet Union, he aids and protects nomadic tribes, a chore he has performed for centuries. Sources say that the purest specimens are found today in the Republics of Kirghiz, Tadzhik, Kazakhstan, and Uzbek. The breed is of the Ovtcharka family and is a medium-sized member of the group. This Ovtcharka is a hardy and adaptable dog that has done well living in hot, sometimes waterless regions of Central Asia. To supplement their hunting abilities, natives have crossed the pure Middle Asians with Borzois. His function in middle Asia is solely that of a protector and he is never kept as a pet. Few specimens if any are known outside the Soviet Union.

ESSENTIALS OF THE MIDDLE ASIAN OVTCHARKA: The coat is short and dense, and his thick skin forms folds and wrinkles about the neck and head. His limbs denote strength but are not excessively muscled. Height: 23–28 inches (58.5–71 cm). Weight: 80–110 pounds

(37–50 kg). Color may vary, but black, white, gray, and brindle are most common; color markings are also common. *See also* Ovtcharka

Middle Asian Ovtcharka, black with white and tan markings. Photo by V. Pcholkin.

Middle-sized French-English Hound
See Anglo-Français

Mikawa Inu
This Japanese dog is reportedly a modern creation, derived from crosses of the Smooth Chow Chow and a medium-sized Akita (known as a Nippon Inu).

Milk
Milk as a supplementary food is recommended by many authorities. There are, however, precautions that the owner must exercise. Milk can have a laxative effect if the dog has not had the substance for some time, while boiled milk can be constipating and should only be given when recommended. Milk does not cause worms, as is believed by some. The false belief regarding milk and worms probably comes from the fact the pups can acquire worms via the dam's teats while nursing. Such worm acquisition, however, has nothing to do with the milk, per se. High in protein, calcium, and water, milk can be good food when given in moderation and when the dog's digestive system is acclimated to it.

The milk produced by the mammary glands of dogs differs from that produced by other animals. For example, as compared to cow's milk, dog's milk has more protein, less carbohydrates and water, and nearly four times the amount of fat. The composition of dog's milk directly reflects the nutritional needs of nursing pups.

Milk fever
See Eclampsia

Milk teeth
Baby teeth, which *see*. *See also* Teething

Mincing gait
Lacking drive and force, movement that is uneven, unpaced, and prancey.

Minerals
Chemical elements found in the body and necessary for its healthful existence. All elements are not minerals, but all minerals are elements. The primary minerals of importance to the dog are calcium, phosphorus, potassium, sulphur, choline, sodium, and magnesium; together they make up about 6% of the dog's total body composition. Other necessary minerals, found in lesser quantities and called trace elements, include iron, manganese, copper, iodine, zinc, cobalt, fluorine, and boron. A well-balanced diet should provide all these elements in the necessary amounts. It is a rare dog that needs mineral supplements. *See also* Vitamins

The two mineral deficiencies of great consequence in dogs are those of calcium and iron, which *see*. However, as all the aforementioned minerals are necessary to the dog, an absence of any one can have dire consequences. A chronically sick, weak, or otherwise affected canine should be investigated for mineral deficiency; diagnosis usually involves blood tests. *See also* Eclampsia

Miniature American Eskimo
See American Eskimo

Miniature Bull Terrier

This breed was created by selectively breeding small Bull Terriers and crossing with the Old Toy Bull Terrier, two breeds which historical evidence places in the early nineteenth century. There was considerable variance in the weight of the Mini Bulls through the first decade of the twentieth century. However, type was defined to be 12 pounds around 1914. Specimens of this size proved difficult to breed, and the breed bordered on extinction by 1918. The weight limit was then raised to 18 pounds, and the breed made considerable progress. Functionalists state that the Miniature Bull Terrier was created to assist his big brother in ratting. Others, however, claim that the smaller breed was created to counteract the growing tendency to produce ever larger Bull Terriers, with the smaller dogs "being more attractive." The present Mini Bull remains free of the problems that often haunt other miniaturized breeds. At one time, the breed was considered but a variety of the standard-sized Bull Terrier, but more recently the kennel clubs register it separately. The Mini Bull today, not bantamized to toy extremes, preserves the Bull Terrier's spirit and even disposition. These are ideal apartment dwellers due to their convenient size and alert demeanor. When reared properly in a household with children, the breed demonstrates great consideration and protectiveness over his allotted charges.

ESSENTIALS OF THE MINIATURE BULL TERRIER: Well balanced and powerfully built, the Miniature Bull Terrier stands from 10–14 inches (26–36 cm) tall, never exceeding the upper height limit and never weighing more than 20 pounds (9 kg). He is the spitting image of

his big brother, the Bull Terrier, and the same standards apply to both breeds, excluding the size parameters. (*See* Bull Terrier.) The down-faced, egg-shaped head, distinctive among the Bull Terriers, is a definite quality of the Mini Bull. The body is well rounded, with great depth from withers to brisket. The back is short and strong, as is the tail. Weight must be in proportion to the height.

Miniature Dachshund
See Dachshund

Miniature Bull Terrier, white.

Miniature German Spitz
See German Spitzen

Miniature Bull Terrier, colored. Photographs by I. Français.

Miniature Pinscher

Not a dwarf of the Doberman Pinscher as some believe, the Miniature Pinscher is an ancient breed whose origins can be traced for over 350 years. Its resemblance to the Doberman is an *ex post facto* coincidence; namely, the doing of Herr Dobermann, who greatly admired the sleek Miniature Pinscher. The MinPin was derived from large smooth-coated German Pinschers and was employed to keep down the rat population in the stables that it frequented. The breed was developed in the German Rhineland, where it was known as the Reh Pinscher, allegedly due to its similar appearance, structurally and gait-wise, to the *reh* deer, a small roe deer.

This ancient MinPin then looked very little like the refined tyke we hail today as the "King of the Toys." The present form can be attributed to selective breeding and possible crosses to the Italian Greyhound to lessen size.

The breed has been much more successful in the United States than it has been in Great Britain. The A.K.C. has recognized the breed since 1929, the same year in which the American parent club was formed. The *ritard* in the British progress was initially due to the desire to produce a MinPin with erect ears, since cropping wasn't an option as it was in the States and Germany. Today the MinPin has a marvelously international cheering section: it is the top toy dog in Holland, Italy and Denmark. While he is unanimously classified as a toy for his petite ten-pound size, in temperament he is terrifically terrier. Of course not too

BEST OF BREED OR VARIETY
WAMPANOAG KENNEL CLUB
JULY 1990
THE STANDARD IMAGE
CHUCK TATHAM

many owners use their MinPin to rat or extract other undesirables from our surrounding countrysides, but the breed still maintains much of the energy and ability that would enable him to do so. In the home, he is a great alarm dog and amenable to discipline. The show ring is dominated by stag red dogs, since this color is more plenteous. Black/tans are very popular as pets, not to suggest that they too are not admired in the breed ring. Both colors make handsome and hardy companions.

ESSENTIALS OF THE MINIATURE PINSCHER: The MinPin is well balanced, short coupled, smooth coated and sleek. The head must be in correct proportion to the body, tapering, narrow and well fitted but not too prominent foreface. Skull appears flat, tapering toward the muzzle. The ears are set high and erect. The neck is proportioned and slightly arched, muscular, free of exaggeration. The body is compact, slightly wedge shaped and muscular. Forechest is well developed; shoulders clean and sloping, moderately angulated. The legs are well muscled. He appears naturally well groomed and self-possessed. Height: 10–12.5 inches (25–32 cm). Weight: 8–10 pounds (3.5–4.5 kg). Colors available are black/tan, chocolate/tan and stag red.

Miniature Poodle
See Poodle

Miniature Schnauzer

The Miniature Schnauzer is known as the Zwergschnauzer in Germany, its country of origin. The Schnauzers are actually named for their snouts: *schnauze* means muzzle or snout. Therefore, the Miniature Schnauzer's muzzle, bearded and well furnished with soft hair, is an important and distinctive feature of the breed. Although this Miniature of the Schnauzer breeds arrived after its two larger brothers (the Giant and Standard), it is not merely a diminutive Standard Schnauzer. The Miniature Schnauzer may have been derived directly from the Standard or possibly from selectively

crossing Miniature Pinschers and Affenpinschers. The American Kennel Club suggests Poodles in their breed history— possible though not probable in any significant dosage. First exhibited as an individual breed in 1899, the Miniature Schnauzer, although today prized as one of the world's most popular and lovable companion dogs, is the only Schnauzer breed that is expressly a ratter. The Miniature Schnauzer usurps the honor of being the most popular terrier in America that is not of British descent. In the Mini's case, this is to his gain, as the temperament of this breed is not like the feisty, yappy British ratters, but rather more serene, amiable and contented.

Nonetheless, its propensity as a ratter is enviable, although most Mini owners today do not send their darling Schnauzers after upturning vermin. Such owners are not to be admonished, as this is surely the most elegant of the terriers and essentially the breed's instincts are dormant, making him one stylish and friendly terrier to be reckoned with. This is a terrific apartment dog that only needs a little exercise; he is a most dependable alarm dog.

ESSENTIALS OF THE MINIATURE SCHNAUZER: This nearly square dog is sturdy and strong—conformation in a

Miniature Schnauzer, salt and pepper. The first uncropped Miniature Schnauzer champion in the U.S.!

Miniature Schnauzer is considered more important than sheer appearance. A moderately broad chest, a strong straight back, well-muscled thighs, and a refined

head of good length comprise the dog's structure. Colors include salt/pepper, black and silver, and solid black. The coat is harsh and rough; fairly thick furnishings conspicuously adorn the head and legs. Height: 12–14 inches (30.5–35.5 cm). Weight: 13–15 pounds (6-7 kg). Ears may be cropped in America, not in England. Tails are customarily docked.

Miniature Shar-Pei

In recent years, some breeders have been striving to produce a "variety" of the Shar-Pei breed which would be smaller and retain the wrinkled appearance of the Shar-Pei puppy. Most importantly, the Miniature Shar-Pei would pass on the desired smallness and wrinkled appearance with the necessary reliability required for breed status. According to present-day Miniature fanciers, this dog is to stand no higher than 16 inches (40 cm) and weigh between 30 and 42 pounds (18–25 kg), as compared to the Standard Shar-Pei which stands from 18 to 20 inches (45–50 cm) and weighs 45 to 70 pounds (27–42 kg). The smaller specimens are referred to as Toy Chinese Shar-Pei. Fanciers claim that small Shar-Pei have been present in the breed since shortly after its arrival in the United States. American Shar-Pei fanciers and the breed club are not enthused, nor do they condone these dogs. *See also* Oriental Shar-Pei.

Miscellaneous class

Most every major kennel club has a miscellaneous class which groups breeds not yet granted full championship status. Also, breeds that show continuously low new registrations may be relegated to this class. Miscellaneous breeds may compete in obedience trials and in conformation shows limited to the Miscellaneous class. Dogs cannot earn championship points. Only when the kennel club board of directors (or a similar body) determines that a miscellaneous breed has a substantial following can it be admitted to registration in the stud book and allowed to compete in the regular show classes. Unfortunately, dog-world politics sometimes can delay championship status of a breed with a sizeable, active fancy.

Mismark

Self colors with an area of white on back between tail and withers, on sides between hindquarters or elbows, or on ears. In the Pembroke Welsh Corgi, a mismark is the lack of tan on a tricolored dog.

Mites

Any of a large number of tiny, sometimes microscopic, arachnids that are often parasitic upon other life forms. Mites that affect dogs can be classed in three general groups: mange mites, nasal mites, and sand fleas (or red bugs). Mange mites are discussed under mange, which *see*. The nasal mite (*Pneumonesis caninum*) attaches itself to the nasal wall of the dog, causing sneezing and nose bleeds. If properly diagnosed, the condition can be treated. The sand flea (*Leptus irritans*), also called a chigger, harvest mite, and red bug, attacks animals during its larval stage, when it attaches to the animal, feeds, and then drops off to molt. A sand flea infestation causes noticeable irritation to the dog, often with severe scratching, weight loss, and other signs of trouble.

Mob

To surround and kill a fox without giving it a fair chance to run.

Modelled

See Chiselled

Mole

Spots or ascended marks on the cheeks

Miniature Shar-Pei.

of some dogs, sometimes with a few stray hairs in the center. A number of the sighthounds are frequently seen with moles adorning their faces (e.g., Whippet, Saluki) as well as the Pug. *See also* Warts

Molero

In the Chihuahua, the incomplete formation or union of the frontal bones of the skull leave a space or gap which is covered by skin and hair. The defect renders such dogs vulnerable to injury.

Molossian

See Mastiff breeds

Molting comb

They come in two styles, one for shorthaired breeds and one for longhaired breeds. They do an excellent job of removing loose undercoat.

Mongolian Dog

Once a beloved pet dog of France, this imported Asian breed, toy dog in size, fell from favor and no known specimens exist today.

Mongrels

Johannes Caius, the most renowned of the world's dog writers, asserts: "Of mongrels and their mixed varieties I have little to say, for they display no signal mark of race or breed: I dismiss them as useless." With all due respect to Dr. Caius's canine prowess, it is assured that Caius never owned a mongrel or a mutt, since to know a mutt is to love a mutt.

A mongrel is a crossbred animal whose sire and dam are of indecipherable types. Mongrel and mutt are often inaccurately interchanged with crossbred; a crossbred is a dog that is descended from parents of two different recognizable breeds. Needless to say, mongrels can only beget mongrels. Needed to say, though, two crossbreds can only beget mongrels . . . for a while, that is. Many breeds, of course, are the result of selective matings of crossbred creations. *See* Crossbreds. The term "mutt" (accurately interchanged with mongrel) is believed to have derived as the truncated form of mutton-head, slang for a stupid person. Many dog experts look fondly upon passing mongrels and have a grand time attempting to decipher the dog's lineage. Of course at a certain point, all one can discern is the type of dog, i.e., mastiff, herder, hound. Some authorities believe that dogs, when left to breed randomly, will soon produce generic feral-type dogs.

As companions and house dogs, mongrels are compatible with thoroughbred dogs. In the sixteenth century, such dogs were referred to as *admonitores* due to their vigilance and resourcefulness about the house. Many persons also rely on the concept of hybrid vigor: mongrels are believed to be less susceptible to disease and frequent ailments than are purebred dogs. In a reasonable Darwinian sense, mongrels are necessarily hardy—these survivors learn to rough it and are not "reared like a hot-house vine" as are purebred dogs. It is arguable that many show ring people get so wrapped up in the exaggeration of a bodily superfluity that the soundness of the dog suffers. Additionally, only purebred dogs are subject to the "puppy mill effect"—no know-nothing doggie entrepreneur has ever set up a kennel grinding out the offspring of the neighborhood curs.

On a different note, all purebred dogs at some point were "mere" mongrels—that is to say, a purebred in the making, its undulating forebears and prototypes evolving, passing mongrels. Halfway through Herr Dobermann's Wagnerian canine experiment, all he had surely was a mutt. Thankfully that mutt resulted in the Doberman Pinscher of today. Likewise, fearless nineteenth-century Australian breeders venturing toward the Cattle Dog were making a real mess of a mongrel until their dozen-generation, half-dozen-breed formula yielded their purebred pride and joy. Such breeds, the concoctions and contortions of man, can be perceived as mongrels that breed true. This is never questioned: surely mongrels *always* breed true—mongrel yields mongrel, beautiful and simple like the dogs themselves. Additionally, mongrel fans never spend dust-filled hours staring at the hieroglyphics on Egyptian tombs trying to substantiate the antiquity of their dog's lineage. Is there a doubt in anyone's head that there were mutts meandering through the streets of ancient Greece, Rome, Egypt, Assyria, and the submerged Atlantis as well? Not too many mongrel owners rejoice in the absolute antiquity of their "un-breed." Possibly even *Tomarctus*'s first-born was but a mutt.

It seems somehow fitting that mongrels are favored in every American state. The United States, representing the melting pot of most of the world's cultures, fittingly embraces dogs of mixed backgrounds. Purebred Americans are non-existent: even the Indians started in Asia! In light of this observation, the purebred craze in America seems also fitting since various peoples continue to value and observe their forefathers' national cultures. That Italian-Americans have adopted the Spinone; to the Irish-Americans, the Kerry Blue is a marvelous American notion.

Mongrels are happy dogs, beatific and blithe, and rather demonstrative (although mongrels don't use such words). Mongrels are also democratic, rarely having to participate in a tie they didn't chose themselves. Fixed marriages are for royalty, old rich, and purebreds only!

Let it not be assumed that the authors are biased towards mongrels (or purebreds per se). Experiencing the prowess of specialized working types, whether at

an obedience trial or a sheepdog trial, a night hunt or an agility trial, purebred

dogs are amazing, intelligent and very exciting. The bottom line indeed is: a dog is a dog is a dog and all dogs are perfectly super!

Monkeylike expression
See Expression

Monsters
Abnormally large or disproportionate pups. Monsters can rupture the womb, seriously threatening the bitch. Monsters often result in miscarriage, and those that don't invariably cause birthing difficulty. *See also* Breeding

Moonflower Dog
See Peruvian Inca Orchid

Mops
See Pug

Mongrels. Never groomed for show, nor stacked, nor judged by anyone except a loving owner, mongrels simply are not standard. This ever-loving mutt, "Murph," grew up with the author and his family. Photo by James B. Johnson, Sr.

Moscovian Miniature Terrier
See Moscow Longhaired Toy Terrier

Moscow Longhaired Toy Terrier

A most recent development in the Soviet dog world, the Moscow Longhaired Toy Terrier enters the scene as a hardy and minuscule house dog that doesn't need a great deal of food or space to survive. The longhaired Chihuahua and some English Toy Terriers or Papillons are the likely candidates for the breeds used to create the Muscovian Miniature Terrier, as he is also known. The exact cross is, however, one of the better kept secrets of the U.S.S.R. Breeding efforts began in the late 1970s.

The latest craze in Russia, these Moscow Toys are the pick of senior citizens and urban dwellers. In a country where urban living quarters are rather cramped and a citizen's budget for keeping a dog is lim-

ited, a small dog with a Moscovian seal of approval is sure to be the top toy in town for some time to come. Due to the well-refined European toys used to create him, he is easily trained, easy to care for, and far more polite than the average Russian cur or street dog.

ESSENTIALS OF THE MOSCOW LONGHAIRED TOY TERRIER: As the English name suggests, the coat is longhaired, with generous feathering on the ears and legs, a ruff to the neck, and a tail that is docked. The tuck-up is substantial. The face tapers sharply and the ears are rather large. Height: 8–11 inches (20–28 cm). Weight: 4.5–6.5 pounds (2–3 kg). This handsome Muscovian mite can be solid tan; black, brown, sable, fawn, all with tan points or in solid; and merle.

Moscow Watchdog

A product of Soviet dog breeders of the 1950s, the Moscow Watchdog is much of a crossbreed. Beginning with the Caucasian Ovtcharka for its obvious watchful and assertive traits, determined breeders crossed it with the Saint Bernard to increase size—the Alpine Mastiff itself was too supine and slow in manner to gratify their needs. The end result after much selection and perfection was the Moscow Watchdog, a breed that possesses the mental and physical attributes desired by the demanding Soviet fanciers who created it.

The Moscow Watchdog is a strong and able-bodied mastiff who proves a true comrade and a watchdog—the latter feature evident in the translation of the dog's name. He is even in temperament, if properly reared, and the choice of many Russian owners in search of a fine and fearless guard. Their need for space and exercise limits their numbers. No dogs are known outside the U.S.S.R.

ESSENTIALS OF THE MOSCOW WATCHDOG: A big-boned but free-moving dog with a massive head and powerful legs. The Moscow Watchdog is well endowed with muscle and intelligence. The coat of moderate length is dense and well fringed. Coat color is always red and white. Height: 25–27 inches (64–69 cm). Weight: 100–150 pounds (45–68 kg). The tail is plumed and very long.

Moskovskaya Storodzevay Sobaka
See Moscow Watchdog

Mosquitoes
Comprising over 1,600 different species, these insects of the family Culicidae are two-winged flyers; female mosquitoes are equipped with skin-piercing mouthparts that are used to extract blood from their prey. Mosquitoes can transmit numerous diseases, including heartworm, which *see*.

Mottled
Dark, circularlike patches over a mostly light, bicolored coat pattern with a basically uniform appearance, e.g., a blue-mottled Australian Cattle Dog.

Moulting
See Shedding

Mountain Cur
The Mountain Cur, deriving from the same stock as the Leopard Cur, occurs mostly in the Ohio River Valley area. As with all the other American curs, an amalgamation of European hounds and

herders and indigenous pariah types fills this robust dog's gene pool. Specifically, it is believed that a tribe of Indian Cur may have contributed to the Mountain Cur's make-up. The breed is a superb trailer and treer.

This is not a submissive, easygoing hound. With the toughness to confront a very angry, very large cat, these silent-trailing curs have learned to be decisive and dauntless. Today Mountain Cur refers to a specific breed of dog whose essentials follow; previously, however, mountain cur referred to these dogs as well as the Treeing Tennessee Brindle and the Stephens Stock, which *see*.

ESSENTIALS OF THE MOUNTAIN CUR: A stocky, rugged working dog with a genuine, though somewhat generic, cur appearance. The coat tends to be longer than that of the other hounds but is still basically short. Colors: brindle, black/tan, blue, yellow to fawn. Weight: 35–65 pounds

(16–29 kg). The tail of this heavily structured hound is often docked. Some puppies are born without tails.

Mountain Cur, smooth, fawn/white.

Mountain Cur, rough, brindle. Photographs by I. Français.

Moustache

Facial furnishing of varying texture around the lips and sides of the face; this longish hair creates a moustache effect. Many of the wirehaired breeds (e.g., Scottish Deerhound, German Wirehaired Pointer) are endowed with moustaches.

Mousy

Small, shy racing dog, usually a young, inexperienced female.

Moustache and beard handsomely furnishing the face of the Berger Picard of France. Photo by I. Français.

Mouth

See Bite, Jaws

Mouthy

The quality of a hound that is needlessly noisy.

Movement

See Action, Gait

Moving close

The dog is moving close when the hocks turn in and the pasterns drop straight to the ground and move parallel to one another. In some cases, the dog's legs rub against one another on the inner side when passing. This gait is stressful to the ligaments and muscles and is caused by hindlimbs that are not sufficiently separated from each other during movement/gaiting.

Mudhol Hound

Dainty in appearance, though heavier than a Whippet, the greyhound of Maharashtra is known as the Mudhol Hound. This Indian sighthound is used as a hunter of jackal, deer and rabbit. The dogs weigh 20–30 pounds (9–14 kg) and are smooth coated. The head is long and thin; ears, fine in texture. The body is long and tapering. In color these dogs are typically black and tan, occasionally mixed.

Mudi

A native Hungarian breed that performs well as an all-purpose farm dog: herding livestock, ridding rodents, and helping in the hunt when commissioned. Despite its versatility and hardiness, the breed has never excelled in popularity even in its homeland; presently its numbers are dangerously low. The breed's inability to gain a stronghold on the dog owners of Hungary can in part be attributed to the ancient Magyar working breeds, the Puli and the Komondor, whose effectiveness has long been revered by the Hungarian people and the working-dog world in general. However, the few owners who do employ and favor the Mudi find him incomparable.

ESSENTIALS OF THE MUDI: An efficiently constructed dog of well-rounded ability. He is heavier and taller than the Puli. The coat is short on the head but medium long on the rest of the body, with curls the norm. In color the Mudi has limitless possibilities: black and white are common; the pied or "pepita" is a happy peculiarity of this breed. The pepita is an evenly distributed collage of colors.

Height: 14–20 inches (35.5–51 cm). Weight: 18–29 pounds (39.5–13.5 kg).

Multiple impregnation
See Breeding

Münsterländer
See Large Münsterländer, Small Münsterländer

Muscle bound
Overly developed musculature that hinders normal, easy movement; the resulting gait is lumbering and restricted.

Muscle system
A muscle is composed of functional cells known as muscle fibers. All muscles have the quality of contractibility; all are energized via nerve impulses; and all receive nourishment from blood. Together the many muscles of the living animal constitute the motive power for movement, respiration, circulation, digestion, excretion, secretion, and numerous other functions necessary for existence. The expansion and contraction of muscles generate force and movement and work are accomplished. All muscles can be classed as one of three types: skeletal, smooth, and cardiac.

Skeletal muscles are composed of long, cylindrical fibers. These muscles appear striated and are voluntarily controlled by the animal. The primary functions of the skeletal muscles are support and locomotion; they comprise approximately one-third of the animal's total body weight. Individual muscles of the skeletal-muscle group range greatly in size and shape, from the tiny muscle of the middle ear to the large muscles of the gluteal region. Most skeletal muscles are attached to bone or cartilage by means of tendons; others are joined to organs, other muscles, or the skin; a few skeletal muscles lie free beneath the skin.

Smooth muscles are composed of spindle-shaped fibers. Unlike the skeletal muscles, they are not striated. Smooth muscles are found in the walls of hollow organs, in the blood vessels, as well as in association with the glands, the spleen, the eye, and the hair follicles. Smooth muscles are known as involuntary muscles, for they are energized by impulses from the autonomic nervous system and are in many cases affected by hormonal secretions. Smooth muscles operate without the need for conscious effort or control.

Cardiac muscles form the bulk of the heart. They are distinct and distinctly arranged from the other two muscle types, yet they have characteristics in common with both of them: cardiac muscles show cross striation, as do the skeletal muscles, and they have a centrally placed nuclei, as do the smooth muscles. Cardiac muscles are also char-

Mudi, pepita. Photo by I. Français.

acterized by rhythmic contractions. The cardiac muscles are controlled by the autonomic nervous system. All muscles, to be well developed and sound, require good nutrition, regular exercise, and plenty of rest. If these three conditions are met and your dog is born of sound health, you can hopefully expect few problems with his muscles.

Musculation
The distribution, lay and development of muscle groups.

Mush
Originally a French term meaning to walk or to march, mush basically means "let's go" to a team of sled dogs. Coincidentally, it's Hollywood that capitalizes on nordic men echoing "mush" at their huskies more so than actual race people today (Hollywood makes mush of most things anyway).

Music

The sounds of hounds at bay, a specialized scenthound hunter's term.

Mute

Description of a hound which does not open, or give tongue, on the line.

Mutuel

Form of dog-racing wagering in which odds are determined by amount of money wagered, with track management claiming a percentage of all wagers.

Mutuel plant

Department or enclosure reserved for acceptance, payment, and calculation of wagers at a dog-racing track.

Muzzle

1) Consisting of the forward sections of the jaws, upper and lower, the muzzle is that portion of the skull in the front of the brain case. Depending on the skull development, muzzle types vary greatly. Comparing the short or stubby muzzle of the brachycephalic (short-faced) breeds (e.g., Pug, Bulldog) with the long wedge-shaped, tapering muzzle of the dolichocephalic (long-headed) breeds (e.g., Saluki, Greyhound), the differences in type, size and depth are rather apparent. Many terms have been employed to describe the muzzle types: Blunt muzzle; Square muzzle; Pinched muzzle; Snipy muzzle; Pointed muzzle; Short muzzle; Stubby muzzle; Tapering muzzle; Wedge-shaped muzzle; which *see*.

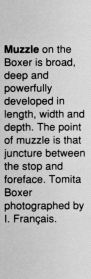

Muzzle. The tapering or long wedge muzzle of the Borzoi. This non-typy Borzoi is a real working dog in the Soviet Union. Photo by V. Pcholkin.

Muzzle on the Boxer is broad, deep and powerfully developed in length, width and depth. The point of muzzle is that juncture between the stop and foreface. Tomita Boxer photographed by I. Français.

2) Dog muzzles can be made or purchased at a pet shop. A bandage or necktie can provide a workable makeshift muzzle should the need arise. The muzzle is wrapped around the dog's mouth twice and tied above and below the chin and then around the back

of the head behind the ears. Most manufactured muzzles are made of leather or some kind of wire. Muzzles chiefly intend to prevent the dog from biting, injuring, or fighting. In case of an accident where the dog is hurt and in shock, the makeshift muzzle may help to keep the dog under control.

In some cities, owners are required to muzzle their dog when walking on pedestrian thoroughfares. This law is aimed at large dogs or potentially vicious dogs. City owners are encouraged to investigate all laws regarding dog ownership in their city.

Muzzle band

The white markings around the Boston Terrier's muzzle.

Mycoplasma

Tiny microorganisms of the genus *Mycoplasma*. They are smaller than bacteria but larger than virus and are believed to be the causative agents of some diseases, especially of the joints and lungs.

Mycotic diseases

Any of the diseases that result from mycosis, the growth of parasitic fungi, in any part of the body.

Muzzle band on the Boston Terrier.

Muzzles as restraint and safety devices on these robust mastiff-types from southwestern Europe. Photographs by I. Français.

Nail

Commonly used terminology for the dog's claw.

Nail clipper

The guillotine style nail clipper comes in a regular size for most medium-sized dogs and an extra-large size for larger breeds. The scissor-style clipper is recommended for small dogs and cats. The extra-large scissor-style clipper is excellent for dewclaws that grow excessively long. *See also* Nail clipping

Nail clipping. A viable alternative to the nail clipper is an electric file. Here pedicurist-breeder Rick Tomita files the front-paw claws of a trusting Boxer.

Nail clipping

Dogs that regularly exercise or play outdoors on abrasive surfaces will generally require less frequent nail clipping than those kept mainly in the house or on soft ground.

When clipping a dog's nails, one must be careful not to cut the "quick," a blood vessel in the nail. Cutting the quick will cause the dog pain and may result in future battles when a manicure is needed. Keeping a styptic (powder or pencil) handy in case of an emergency is well advised.

Holding the dog's paw carefully, snip off just the very tip of each nail. Ragged nail surfaces may be smoothed away by using a file. Nail clipping should not be neglected. Overgrown nails can lead to a dog's severe discomfort and even lameness in the worst cases.

Naming your dog

"The naming of [dogs] is a difficult matter, it isn't just one of your holiday games." (sort of T.S.Eliot)

Not everyone can name their Great Dane "Hamlet" or their Löwchen "Leo"—dog names should be unique and be special for each dog. Dogs with pedigrees usually need to retain a particular catch-word to identify the line, and the kennel clubs limit the number of letters that a dog's name can have. Twenty-five is usually the right neighborhood. The Mexican owner who tried to register his purebred Chihuahua as "Pedro Gonzales Chiquito Rodriques Marquez" had to settle for "Pete." Most show dogs have abbreviated names around the house, mostly for convenience's sake.

Some owners were so effective in naming their special dogs that the name became regarded as the breed name. "Barry," a premiere rescue-worker, offers his name as an alternative to Saint Bernard. Other breeds such as the Hertha Pointer (named after the creator's first bitch, "Hertha"), the Australian Kelpie, which is sometimes called the Barb (after "Barb," of course), the Chinook (named after Walden's snowshoed lead dog), and the Alapaha Bulldog which is called Otto (after PaPa's first stud "Otto").

Kennel clubs do not allow more than one dog to take the same name or else a number is attached to the name. A dog can keep its name as long as it achieves a certain number of wins in the show ring by a certain age (this varies from registry to registry). If the dog fails to meet this qualification, the name can be up for grabs again.

Nape

The region marked by the skull base and top of the neck's junction.

Narrow front

A front in which the forearms are positioned too closely—mostly considered a fault. In the running sighthounds, however, a relatively narrow front is appropriate with the dog's chest being deeper in order to compensate for the loss of capacity.

Narrow thigh

Thighs that are insufficiently muscled when observed from the dog's side.

Nasal bone

Foreface's bony section that forms the muzzle's top edge. *See* Skull anatomy

Nasal mites

Tiny parasites that infest the nasal passages of dogs. *See* Mites

Nasal septum

The bony partition that separates the right nasal cavity from the left.

National breed clubs

Organizations formed at the national level for the promotion and improvement of a breed. The national breed club is often responsible for a written standard for the breed, breeders oath, sponsorship of nationwide specialty shows, and the requisite guidance and support to local breed clubs. National breed clubs can contribute greatly to the popularity and overall quality of a breed. Active membership is imperative to the functioning of the club, and all seriously interested in the furthering and bettering of a breed are encouraged to contact the national breed club for information and needed specifics.

Navarro Pointer

See Perdiguero Navarro

Neapolitan Mastiff

The Mastino Neapolitano or Italian Mastiff is modern Italy's most well-known mollosian and collosian. The Italians have long cherished the "bandogges," or dogs that need to be tied, or "pugnaces," pugnacious protectors, as guards of their homes and property. In early times, the times of Caesar, the great mollossus was prominent in the Roman empire. Many of these dogs have been preserved on a small scale throughout the Italian countryside. The Neapolitan Mastiff is the most prominent; the Cane Corso or Sicilian Branchiero (which *see*)

are also descendants of these ancient molossian types. The breed is indeed a descendant of these ancient molossi that were transported to Rome to fight in the arenas. In their arena and pit fighting days, stoicism was key, although the type of pugnacity with which the Pit Bull Terrier approaches the match was never achieved. Piero Scanziani, a painter, after witnessing the first Neos to enter the show ring in 1946 (Naples), became an avid breeder and is honored for his efforts that brought the dogs to the public's eye. These eight resurrected molossians, exhumed by Riccardo Pacifico, with their varying yet unique appearances, startled and perplexed Italian judges. By 1949, just three years after his first encounter,

Neapolitan Mastiff, gray. Photo by I. Français.

Piero Scanziani secured the most outstanding stock of Italy and commenced a breeding program which greatly perfected the Neapolitan. Mr. Scanziani and his excellent Neos proved instrumental in the acceptance of the breed by the Italian Kennel Club (*Ente Nazionale della Cinafilia Italiana*). It was Piero Scanziani's

Neapolitan Mastiff, puppies, black and blue. Photo by I. Français.

standard for the breed that was first adopted by the kennel club; his standard remains today, though since modified.

In his native land, particularly in the southern part of the country, the Neapolitan Mastiff is an unsurpassed defender of home and property, yet he is not typically aggressive or tenacious with people. The breed continues, extending its range around the world with the formation of breed clubs in the U.S., Germany, Great Britain, and other countries. Members of the breed do tend to assume a dominant role, and owners are cautioned to be firm and consistent in their mastership. The Neo makes a good outdoor dog in mild climates when adequate shelter and plenty of room are provided. The breed is known for its messy eating habits and considerable drooling.

ESSENTIALS OF THE NEAPOLITAN MASTIFF: His appearance is massive, strong, and coarse, and yet synchronously majestic. The broad flat skull is abundant in wrinkles and folds. The nose is large with well-opened nostrils. The muzzle and lips are copious and heavy. The ears are customarily cropped short. The neck is thick set and very muscular. The chest is broad and well developed. The upper profile of the back is straight, with only the withers rising slightly above the topline. Forelegs and hindlegs are strong boned and well muscled. The tail is typically docked to two-thirds length. The coat is dense, with the texture coarse. Permissible colors are black, blue, gray, mahogany, and brindle. Height: 23–30 inches (59–76 cm). Weight: 110–154 pounds (50–70 kg).

Neck
Anatomical region between the head and shoulder area; connecting the head with the body. The cervical region of the body.

Neckline
A light line that hooks the sled dog's collar to the towline.

Necropsy
Examination of the dead, usually with the intention of identifying the cause(s) of death. There are those dog people who support the postmortems, believing that they can improve the future dogs of the world by better understanding the canine species and the diseases and conditions which affect it. Others find the practice particularly distasteful and refuse at great protest to allow past dogs to undergo the procedure. As with most everything, there are laws regarding necropsy, and the responsible owner should be aware of these regulations. If your dog succumbs to illness and you are asked to give its remains to science, the course of action is truly yours to choose.

Nederlandsche Herdershonden
See Dutch Shepherd

Negri bodies
Those substances that form in the brain of an animal that has contracted rabies. Negri bodies make possible many types of rabies diagnosis. *See* Rabies

Neider

Swiss term for short-legged, equivalent to the French term *basset* and the German *dachs*.

Nematodes

Any worms of the phylum Nematoda of worms, many of which are parasitic. Two nematodes that can prove lethal to dogs are roundworms and heartworms, which *see*.

Nenets Herding Laika

Just as the Samoyede nomads were developing and employing the Samoyed, the Nentsy tribe, an equally ancient group, fostered the Nenets Herding Laika. More accurately, each tribe developed *a dog*, with no consciousness of creating an individual breed. The concept of breed establishment and purebred dogs is not a universally accepted mindset. A working and yet warm dog, the Nenets fulfilled the tribe's guarding and herding necessities. It is also suggested that the Nenets dog actually represents the Samoyed of today in its native land, where color variation exists. The Soviet Cynological Council established national interest in this laika as their only chosen herding breed. It has since entered reindeer herding programs, and continued use is encouraged.

ESSENTIALS OF THE NENETS HERDING LAIKA: Medium in size and symmetrical in balance, the Nenets Laika is very close in type and appearance to the Samoyed. Never bred for color, the Nenets can be gray, black, white or tan as a solid or in pied pattern with white. The head is powerful and wedge shaped. The ears are triangular and erect. Substance is of great importance: while the dog should be sufficient of both bone and muscle, these should be in proportion to the overall body, never appearing clumsy. Chest deep, legs moderately long. Hindquarters very well developed; stifles well bent. The coat is inordinately profuse, often obscuring the muscular conformation and stunning outline of the dog. The coat forms a ruff and thick breeches. Ruff often more prominent on males. Height: over 16–18 inches (41–46 cm). Weight: 40–50 pounds (19–23 kg).

Neoplasm

An abnormal growth of tissue, as in a tumor. *See* Cancer, Tumor

Nephritis

An acute and/or chronic disease of the kidneys, characterized by inflammation, degeneration, fibrosis, etc. The three main causes of nephritis are bacterial infection, food toxin, and other poisons. Nephritis can also be caused by a blow to the kidney area that results in kidney damage and, consequentially, infection. Bacteria, carried through the bloodstream, can lodge in the kidney, causing damage and possibly death. The most common diagnosis of the disease is urine testing. The signs of the disease are common to many other diseases. If the dog exhibits symptoms of disease, including those already mentioned, it is wise to have a urine test performed by a professional. If caught in an early stage, the disease can be treated, often with antibiotics and, in chronic cases, a change in the dog's diet.

Nervous system

The nervous system is comprised of the brain, the spinal cord, and all the many miles of nerve fibers that transverse the body of the dog. The nervous system itself can be broken down into smaller systems: the peripheral and the central nervous systems. This division is not based necessarily on structure or function but more for the convenience of

Neider or short-legged. This little Swiss tyke is the Jura Neiderlaufhund.

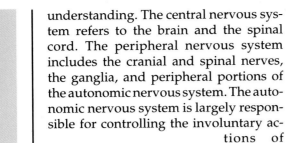

understanding. The central nervous system refers to the brain and the spinal cord. The peripheral nervous system includes the cranial and spinal nerves, the ganglia, and peripheral portions of the autonomic nervous system. The autonomic nervous system is largely responsible for controlling the involuntary actions of the body (the heart and circulatory system, the respiratory system, etc.). The nervous system in its entirety is responsible for all data transmission and processing: the brain, the central data base, receives information from the various sensory receptors, including the tactile (touch), olfactory (smell), auditory (hearing), visual (sight), and gustatory (taste), via the nerve fibers and spinal cord, and processes the information, often responding with a return message, via the same network, to the appropriate body part(s). The oft-cited though simplistic example is one's touching a hot object: a dog steps on a glowing cinder; the nerve cells of the affected paw send a message to the brain that relates the condition; the brain receives the information; and at least two things occur—the brain stores the data, forming an association between the object and the perception, in this case the pain of being burned, and also sends the commands that will tell the appropriate body parts to function (react)—thereby removing the paw from the object and alleviating the burning. This is but one way in which the brain controls behavior through its

Nervousness is an undesirable trait in any companion animal. Temperament testing programs have been developed to determine the temperamental stability of an owner's dog. Photo by R. Pearcy.

assimilation of sensory perception.

The brain, housed within the protective skull, is composed of three primary parts: the cerebrum, the cerebellum and the medulla oblongata. These are covered by three membranes: the dura mater, the arachoid, and the pia mater. *See also* Cerebrum, Cerebellum, Nervous system disorders, Spinal column

Nervous system disorders

The nervous system, composed primarily of the brain and spinal cord, is a sensitive system which, if assaulted, can easily result in serious complications, often leading to disability, involuntary action, and death. Disorders of the nervous system stem from three major sources, namely disease, injury, and malformation.

Perhaps the most serious disease that directly attacks the nervous system is rabies, which often leaves its victim dead. (*See* Rabies) Another serious disease is the often crippling distemper, which can also be fatal. (*See* Distemper) Other diseases that affect the nervous system largely do so indirectly. For example, a calcium deficiency leads to complications that impair the nervous system. Injuries to the brain and/or spinal column can also impair the functioning of the nervous system. A broken spinal cord can paralyze a dog for life. A blow to the head can result in conditions ranging from chronic head pain to convulsions, to incapacitation, to death. It is important to realize that the cells which largely compose the components of the nervous system, namely nerve cells, cannot be regenerated. Therefore, a lost nerve cell is lost forever; it cannot be replaced.

Sometimes a pup is born with a nervous-system disorder. The type and severity of the disorder can vary considerably, ranging from a handicap that can be overcome with patience on the part of the owner to the inability of the animal to function and thereby survive. Severely affected pups should be culled humanely, while less affected ones, under the discretion of the owner, should be dealt with as seems fitting. Of course, consultation with your veterinarian is most helpful. *See also* Meningitis, Neuritis, Nervous system

Nervousness

Of the dog and of the owner, nervousness is a state of chronic excitability. Nervousness can be inherited or it can be acquired. It is believed that an owner's nervousness can contribute his dog's exhibiting the same tendency, and vice versa for the nervous dog and his once calm owner. Poor breeding practices are often accused of being the cause of nervous dogs, and whether so or not, it is a good idea to have your stud or bitch temperament tested prior to embarking on any breeding program. Nervous dogs should never be bred, no more so than vicious or shy dogs should be. Sedation may be possible after consultation with a veterinarian regarding the nervous problem. In many cases, a change of environment is all that is necessary to soothe the excited dog—determine the possible causes and systematically eliminate them.

Neuritis

Inflammation of the nerves. Neuritis is a very painful condition that inhibits the dog's mobility and capacity for work. Lameness, lethargy, and obvious pain are all signs. The condition seems to worsen in damp weather.

Neurotrophic dermatitis

Inflammation of the nerve endings, causing acute tactile sensitivity and pain.

Neutering

See Castration, Spaying

New breed creation

Many purist dog fanciers today regard the creation of new breeds of dog as unnecessary and dubious, even harmful and unscrupulous. Such prejudices against new breed creation are not necessarily apt for the continued resilience of the purebred dog world. Had Herr Louis Dobermann, Captain John Edwardes, James Hinks and Sir Dudley Majoribanks yielded to such purist presumptions, we would not have the quality assistance or companionship of the Doberman Pinscher, Sealyham Terrier, Bull Terrier and Golden Retriever, respectively, of course.

By definition, breeds are sustained by man, and often breeds are conceived by man and created through conscious, careful efforts. While not every breed of dog known to man was created by man, man upholds the responsibility of sustaining each and every breed extant.

It is sometimes difficult to determine where one breed ends and a second one begins—when a breed is a breed and not a variety. Would the American Kennel Club have recognized two separate Norwich terriers had it not been for human intervention?—likely those little red terriers could have survived as a single breed, as they had for generations prior.

No fault of its own, the canine physique is probably the most adaptable on earth, and creative humans capitalize on the never-fading novelty of altering and "perfecting" it.

Variation within breeds often extends far beyond prick or drop ears, as it does with the Norwich terriers. Such dissensions in ear carriage are prompted by humans, as can be seen in the difference between British and American Boxers, Dobermans and Great Danes. Many American breeders, who have not selected for ear size or set, would experience very funky ears on their new-generation dogs should they suddenly stop cropping their puppies' ears. Variations in coat types, color and size naturally occur within breeds, and often these

New breed creation. The Doberman Pinscher was the "brainpuppy" of Herr Louis Dobermann, who set out intentionally and doggedly to create this distinctive guardian breed.

"interesting" mutations spark the attention of fanciers who then promote them. Examples of such new breed creations

from extant, well-known breeds include the Wirehaired Viszla, Longhaired Weimaraner, Longhair Whippet, and Miniature Shar-Pei. Wirehaired versions of hounds have always existed but have not always maintained the interest of the populace. Of the nine scenthound breeds of Switzerland, only one, the Jura Neiderlaufhund, can still be seen in a wire coat. The hounds of France, including the jaunty Petit Basset Griffon Vendeen, have proven more popular in their snazzy wire coats. Often color variations can spur separate breed status, as with the Landseer, Irish Red and White Setter, Grosser Münsterländer, and West Highland White Terrier; certain "unrecognized" colors occur in breeds and cause dissension or new-breed break-offs, the black German Wirehairs (Drahthaars), parti Poodles and Shar-Pei, brindle Labradors and Basenjis, and white German Shepherds are all colorful examples. Size variants also yield new breeds, intentionally or unintentionally: the Toy and Teacup Poodles, Toy Bulldog, and the basset hounds of Europe.

The gundog group, heartily stocked with tens of pointers, setters, spaniels and water dogs, provides a workable example of man's delineating breed divisions. Not so many lit-

ters ago did cockers, springers and toy spaniels occur in the same litter. All the British gundogs trace their lines to the same stock of forefathers. As a rule, perhaps, breed divisions are not formed haphazardly. Divisions among the gun dogs occurred for the sake of utility, despite certain passing contentions of the uselessness of the Field and Clumber. Less often, thankfully, breed divisions occur because of national pride or dissonance within the fancy, nationally or internationally. Two Cocker spaniels and two Staffordshire terriers may be attributable to less than utilepurposes.

The making of a new breed must resort to crossbreeding, that is mating two dogs of apparently different breeds (or a purebred to a mongrel). Crossbreeding is used for a number of reasons, and often for the sake of improving a current line. The most drastic example of crossbreeding to better a line still remains the unordinary Lord Orford's using Bulldog lines to improve the Greyhound. Of course, the Bulldog of his day was higher on the leg and far less exaggerated than the beloved ranine Bully of this century. Utilizing the blood of the Bloodhound, Basset Hound breeders were able to achieve the desirable heavier bone in the

breed. To improve the constitution, increase or diminish size, renovate the heart, or remold the head, crossbreeding has been employed and still is. Commonly, the Greyhound is employed for speed, the Poodle for intelligence, and the Pointer for ability.

Crossbreeding is the necessary tool in the creation of a new breed. The Australian Cattle Dog exemplifies the glories of a successful crossbreeding program, a veritable paradigm of canine malleability—a purebred created from the Dingo, Dalmatian, Bull Terrier, and Smithfield Collie (a working Australian sheepdog).

The envisionment of the "perfect" dog has led many great minds to strive for new breeds, as well as many demented ones. Herr Dobermann and James Hinks are surely two obsessed breed fathers. Their perfect creations were aimed at the execution of a given task. The Bullmastiff was created expressly to be a nightwatchman's dog; the Doberman to be a tax collector's guardian; the Boykin Spaniel, a turkey dog; the German Wirehair, an all-purpose gundog; the Dogo Argentino, a jaguar hunter; the Kangaroo Hound, a pouch poacher; etc. Other "perfect" dogs, however, were envisioned without any utilitarian intent whatsoever: Leonberger, Kyi-Leo and probably a hairless breed or two.

Breeds develop in specific and/or isolated areas—there are estimated to be nearly 800 individual breeds in the world today, about half of which have no official registry or recognition outside a given locale. These regional breeds slowly attract interest. Some of the most notable among these new regional breeds stirring attention include the Petit Basset of the Vendee area of France; the Chart Polski, the Polish Sighthound; the Sicilian Branchiero (Cane Corso), Italian mastiff; the Danish Farm Dog; the Markiesje, a

new spaniel of Holland; the Caõ de Fila de S. Miguel, a working mastiff of Portugal; the Alapaha Blue Blood Bulldog, American bulldog of Georgia.

Some of these regional dogs are actually recreations of extinct breeds, or at least this is the intention and contention of the creators. David Leavitt's Old English Bulldogge sets out to *be* the old Bulldog of England; and the Chinese Temple Ch'in, the ancient temple dog of China; and the Cane Corso, the long-lost Italian farm dog, the Cane di Macellaio. Pres-

New breed creation. The Pudelpointer is an alloy of poodle-types and pointers. This utilitarian concoction was stirred by Baron von Zedlitz in the latter part of the nineteenth century.

New breed creation. Completely new to Western eyes, the Çesky Horsky Pes is a modern creation of Czechoslovakian and Russian dog fanciers. These two examples were photographed in Czechoslovakia in 1990 by I. Français.

New breed creation. With walls of stone and disillusionment falling in the 1990s, new informational developments in the dog world are recently available. Two new additions to the dog world coming from the Soviet Union and Czecho-slovakia are the Prasky Krysarik (*right*), a smooth black and tan toy dog, and the larger, long-coated Chosasky Pez (*below*). Photographs by I. Français.

ently efforts to "resuscitate" the Lesser New-foundland are underway in Canada; the new breed, spurred from black La-bradors and similar black water dogs, is called St. John's Water Dog or simply Black Dog.

New breeds continue to fas-cinate and frus-trate dog fanci-ers—as long as dog and man reside in the same world, new breeds of dog will emerge. The creation of new breeds may rightly be viewed as frivolous and super-fluous, in light of the hundreds of won-derful breeds extant today, but the possi-bilities remain endless. Thus, fanciers will not be satisfied until each man has a breed of his own to bear his name for the rest of eternity—the ultimate goal of Herr Louis Doberman, Reverend Jack Russell, Perr Schiller, Hugh Stephens, and Saint Hubert (admittedly, the latter had more than a good hunting dog vying for his im-mortality).

See also Breed development, Wolf hybrids, Mongrels, Crossbreds, Patents

New breed creation. New faces in the dog world, *clockwise from right*: the Chinese Temple Ch'in; Chart Polski; Old English Bull-dogge; and the Sicilian Branchiero (Cane Corso). Photographs by I. Français.

New Guinea Singing Dog

Visitors to New Guinea would hardly be surprised that the island's indigenous dog has had a difficult time surviving. While the New Guinea Singing Dog, *Canis hallstromi*, scientifically speaking, is an adaptable, hardy dog, only the most compost-loving, heapingly industrious of centipedes and parasites can thrive in much of the relentless island environment of New Guinea. This dingo-type dog unwisely took residence on this island. The climate of the island varies greatly, as does the geography. Some dogs dwelled with natives in the ardent lowlands, while others ventured for the

New Guinea Singing Dog, owned by Philip Persky. Photo by I. Français.

nipping mountain peaks where they resorted to a feral way of life. The breed acquired its name from its howl, which is an undulating and modulating series of tones that blends in a swelling portamento. The musical quality of the sound is unlike that of any other dog— even the most beautifully voiced of the scenthounds. The breed is quite rare in New Guinea today but can be seen in zoos in the United States and Australia. In addition to a few zoo inhabitants, a new breeder in New York has been working and promoting the breed.

Essentially a wild dog, the New Guinea Singing Dog is presently tame enough to tolerate the handling of humans. He will not, however, put up with this on too regular a basis.

ESSENTIALS OF THE NEW GUINEA SINGING DOG: This medium-sized pariah is a hardy and well-balanced dog with erect ears and an average to long coat. In color he is red or shades of red, with or without symmetrical white markings. Height: 14–15 inches (35.5–38 cm). Weight: 20 pounds (9 kg). The head is fairly broad and the body duly muscular. The medium-length tail is well plumed.

New Ireland Dog

This dirty white or cream-colored dog, with black markings and white blazes, is a guard dog used in New Guinea. The head is characterized by a pointed muzzle and prick ears. The tail is less curled than that of the New Zealand Native Dog. The New Ireland Dog is one of the few dogs native to the island along with the New Guinea Singing Dog and the Papuan Dog, both of which have become rare.

New Zealand Native Dog

This native New Zealander once played an important role in the spiritual lives of the islanders as a sacrificial offering. The Maori people also valued the dog's skins for clothing and relished the dog's flesh. The dogs subsisted on leftover fish heads and remains left by the unscaling Maoris. In appearance the dog varied from a shorthaired pariah type with prick ears and a bushy, curly tail to a longhaired type resembling a small herding dog. Both types varied in color; some were spotted, others were solids in white or black. The dogs were valued as guards and companions.

New Zealand Sheepdog

While not recognized by any major dog registry, including the F.C.I., a definite type of working sheepdog has developed in New Zealand. This dog, the New Zealand Sheepdog, resembles the English Shepherd and Border Collie in appearance, though it is lower set, and its color is always solid black with mahogany markings. The dog's method of working is known as "huntaway," requiring that the dog find and maneuver a flock of sheep on a hillside, herding them uphill or downhill, as indicated by the shepherd. While no dust has yet been stirred in the American purebred fancy, New Zealand Sheepdogs have been imported into the U.S. as companion and working dogs. Temperament is gentle and steady—intelligence second to no other sheepdog.

Newfoundland

Developed from the fishermen's dogs, the Greater St. John's Dogs, the Newfoundland was prized by shore and sea dwellers on the island of Newfoundland. Possibly the companions of ancient Beothuk Indians on the island, the Newfoundland's big black water-wallowing ancestors dwelt with humans before the settling of Newfoundland by white men. The large mastiff-like Newfoundland today possesses an unquenchable affinity for the water and is a natural rescue dog.

Tales of the Newfoundland's beginnings have proven both timeless and waterproof. Captain Richard Whitbourne of Exmouth wrote in 1620 that "mastiffe-dogges" on Newfoundland did "fawn and play" in the woods of the island, often with other "wolves and beasts of the country" which came down by the shore. A century later Sir Joseph Banks of the Royal Geographic Society reported in his *Journal of a Voyage to Newfoundland*: "I had thought I should meet with a sort of dog differing from any I had seen, whose peculiar excellence was taking the water freely. I was, therefore, the more surprised when told that there was no distinct breed. Those I met with were mostly curs with a cross of the Mastiff in them. Some took the water well, others not at all. The thing they are valued for here is strength, as they are employed in winter to draw in sledges whatever is wanted in the woods. I was told indeed that at Trepassy lived a man who had a distinct breed which he called

an original Newfoundland dog but I had not the opportunity of seeing any of them."

The excerpt from Banks's journal is seeping with romanticism but does indeed highlight character traits which the Newfy of today genuinely boasts. Another sportingly energetic theory involves the amalgamation of water spaniels, bird dogs and mastiffs along with Spanish and Portuguese specimens that bedecked salt-carrying vessels.

Johann Pietrse, former president of the

Newfoundland, black.

Netherlands Club and breeder, purports "that the Newfoundland descends from French Dogs, brought to Newfoundland by the first French colonists. In that way the Newfoundland is descended from the large Pyrenean mountain dog, and a spaniel from the northern part of Spain, and similarly the Newfoundland would

Newfoundland, Landseer particolor. Photographs by I. Français.

be a close kin to our spaniel and setter." The much loved breeder and former president of the Newfoundland Club of America, Mrs. Maynard Kane "Kitty"

Newfoundland, bronze. Photo by I. Français.

Drury, notes that were it not for the Newfy's single dew claw, this latter theory would withstand the waters of interrogation; the Great Pyrenees possesses double dew claws and would have likely passed this dominant trait.

Other theories place the genesis in America, according to a study done on bones of native Indian dogs excavated in old Appalachian ruins (linking the breed to the Tibetan Mastiff or a similarly monstrous Oriental ogre); another follows through with the Tibetan Mastiff as progenitor but places the dogs among the Vikings and Leif Ericsson around 1000 A.D. (a mastiff-sized, black "Bear Dog" whom Ericsson labelled "Oolum"). This, incidentally, was Kitty's favorite theory.

No matter what his origins, the Newfoundland is a unanimously loved member of the dog world, with a character that is second to none. A dog of discriminating style and majesty, he is able to protect himself against would-be enemies yet is actually indiscriminative about his candidates for rescue—unfalteringly volunteering to save a drowning fellow canine with whom he is not friendly. Among the many qualities which the Newfy offers his owner, he is a sublime and talented backpacker; with a pack on his back, the Newfy looks forward to a weekend in the great outdoors more than he could ever a weekend on the show circuit. Newfys generally don't appreciate the show ring as much as most other breeds, despite their stunning appearances. Humility, strength and common sense do not contribute well to the Newfy's show ring mindset.

The particolor version of the Newfoundland majesty in white and black is known by the F.C.I. as the Landseer, a separate breed; in the U.S. and Britain, partis are shown simply as Newfoundlands. *See also* Landseer

ESSENTIALS OF THE NEWFOUNDLAND: A large dog with big bone and much strength. The head is broad and massive; the body is muscular, with ribs well sprung and chest broad. The neck is strong and well set on the shoulders. The topline is level from the withers to the croup. The back is strong, well muscled from the shoulders through the croup. The chest is full and deep with the brisket reaching at least down to the elbows. The forelegs are well muscled and well boned, as is the rear assembly. Feet are webbed and well shaped. The Newfy's coat is medium in length and very dense. Some feathering occurs on the forelegs and hindlegs. The undercoat is substantial and the outer coat is impressively water resistant. Height: 26–30 inches (66–76 cm). Weight: 110–150 (50–68 kg). In color the Newfoundland can be solid black, bronze, and white and black particolor (called Landseer).

Niacin
Known also as nicotinic acid, it is one of the B-complex vitamins. A deficiency of niacin can result in various complications, including black tongue, which *see*.

Nictitating membrane
See Third eyelid

Night blindness
See Progressive retinal atrophy

Nihon Terrier
See Japanese Terrier

Nippon Inu
A medium-sized version of the Akita of Japan, not recognized by any major registry. It excels as a hunter of bear, wild boar and red deer. The increasingly

popular and smaller Shiba Inu was once grouped together with its close relative, the Nippon Inu.

Nippon Terrier
See Japanese Terrier

Nite Champion
Title earned by hound who earns at least 100 points, with at least one win, in Coonhunt competition.

No
Word used to keep sled dogs on the trail should they start to veer off course, to stop them from chewing on the line, to ward off a scrap or fight, etc.

Non-regular classes
Classes other than the regular official classes of the American Kennel Club which often are provided by show sponsoring clubs. Such classes are required to be judged after the judging of Best of Winner and some winners of these non-regular classes must compete for Best of Breed. Such non-regular classes may be for dogs which have won a field trial, dogs which are locally owned, etc.

Non-Sporting Group
The Non-Sporting Group was one of the first two A.K.C. categories assigned; if a dog was not of a "sporting nature" it was relegated (seemingly appropriately) to "non-Sporting." It is not quite fair to say that all the breeds branded "Non-Sporting" are functionless, devoid of sporting or working abilities. The Dalmatian, for instance, is quite a sporting ratter, a most reliable guard dog, and quite a horse director at that. Keeshonden, Schipperkes and Poodles, no less, are among the world's most talented canines, and even most useful. These are multi-dimensional, multi-functional workers that can essentially perform any task expected of them (within reason of course). The group is quite small and once included the toy breeds as well; the creation of the Toy Group diminished the ranks considerably (although not all the toylike canines managed to squeeze their way out of the group—the French Bulldog, Boston Terrier, Lhasa Apso and Bichon Frise are still categorized as Non-

Sporters although they do function *primarily* as indoor companion dogs, despite a few inches or pounds. The British equivalent to the Non-Sporting Group is the Utility Group, probably a more useful determination. *See also* Utility Group, Group systems

Non-slip retriever
A dog bred and trained to remain with the hunter while game is flushed by other dogs or by beaters or shot from blinds as they pass. Their task is to mark the fall and make the retrieve upon command.

Non-uniting anconeal process
Elbow dysplasia, a defect which affects the elbow joint; it is commonly found in German Shepherds, Mastiffs, Bassets and Labrador Retrievers. Forequarter lameness may be an indication of the defect's presence. An X-ray can verify non-united anconeal process positively; surgery is the only option for correction.

Nootka Sound Dog
Curious nomenclature once applied to a featured spitz-type dog exhibited in the Zoological Gardens of England. The dog is said to have resembled a large Samoyed. The name might well have been contrived by a circus proprietor.

Norbottenspets
The Norbottenspets is a small spitz with an uncharacteristically short coat for a northern breed as well as a loose curled tail that hangs more toward the

Norbottenspets, white with cream. Photo by I. Français.

thigh than tightly across the back. The Norbottenspets's close resemblance to the Norwegian Lundehund suggests his descent from similar spitz types. The most contemporary research reveals a more direct bloodline connection to the ancient spitz-type dogs of the Vikings than to the other nordic spitz types. The German Spitzen's contribution is not clear. For many years, the Norbottenspets was commonly employed as a hunter of small game and as an all-around farm helper. Then, with the waning of the hunt and the farm and the introduction of foreign dogs to Sweden, the Norbottenspets became nearly extinct in the middle of the twentieth century. He is again a breed popular with native Swedes, more common as a companion than a hunter. The breed is also known as the Pohjanpystykorva.

ESSENTIALS OF THE NORBOTTENSPETS: The Norbottenspets is short, squarely built, and of strong body. The head should be powerful, dry, well built and wedge-shaped. The muzzle is moderately long, sharply tapering. The ears are high set, slightly over medium size and stiffly erect. Neck is moderately long, dry and muscular, with slight arch. The back is

short, strong and elastic. Croup moderately long and broad, slightly sloping, with well developed muscles. Chest moderately deep and long. His stand-offish double coat, although short, provides good all-weather protection. Color is white with limited spots of cream or brown (black and red are also seen). Height: 16–17 inches. (41–43 cm) Weight: 26–33 pounds (12–15 kg).

Nordic dogs

Prehistoric remains of ancient dogs, found in the Scandinavian countries, Russia and Switzerland, represent body types essentially like the German Wolfspitz, one of the spitz-type nordic dogs, as well as the Scandinavian elkhound type. The nordic dogs, some believe, are the first canines to have been domesticated by man. The nordic dogs include the spitz types, laikas, huskies, lapphunds, and elkhounds—all dogs of the Arctic snows and tundra. The prick ears and wedge-shaped heads, muscular bodies coated plushly by stand-off coats allude to their close relative the northern wolf. The spitz breeds, including the German Spitzen, Schipperke, Finnish Spitz, Samoyed, and others, are as ancient a type as the pariah types from central Asia. Much discussion degenerates about the relationship of the pariah and the spitz. The Basenji is believed by many to be descended from nordic dogs because of its prick ears and curled tail. While this assumption is incorrect, the pariah-dog Basenji does illustrate the similarity in the spitz and pariah types. *See also* Basenji.

Northern-bound Europeans and Asians selected from the early domestic-dog stock available for the thick coats, muscular frames with trim loins. These dogs became the working Eskimo's dogs, the hauling and herding laikas of the north, the working huskies.

The northern breeds can be divided effectually into four functional categories: hunting dogs, draft dogs, herding dogs and companion dogs. The bird-hunting Finnish Spitz, puffin-hunting Lundehund, bear-hunting Karelian Bear Dog and Russo-European Laika, the Japanese Shika-Inus, and the moose-hunting Norwegian Elkhound and Jämthund are the principal members of the hunting category.

The draft dogs represent both muscular and Darwinian fitness. The nordic sledge-pulling huskies, including such breeds as the Eskimo Dog, Alaskan Malamute, Siberian Husky and Greenland Dog, were absolutely indispensable to their ice-hacking nomadic owners. Weighing as much as 125 pounds, the Eskimo Dog (of Canadian fame) is the largest of these draft breeds. Rigorous experience has proven, however, that hauling huskies are ideal weighing around 80 pounds (about the weight of the Alaskan Malamute). The famed Arctic explorer Donald B. MacMillan indicates that the huskies on his North Pole trip (covering 1,000 miles of Polar ice) performed best in the 85-pound range. The first dogs to give out weighed 125 pounds; dogs over 100 pounds were essentially too heavy for such a strenuous haul.

The Antarctic expedition of Admiral Byrd employed rather unique northern pullers, American huskies known as Chinooks. The breed, created by Arthur Walden from various husky and Eskimo types, represents an ideal working draft dog. *See also* Chinook

The herding nordic dogs include the Samoyed, Norwegian Buhund (or Nordic Sheepdog), Iceland Dog, and the Swedish/Finnish Lapphunds. These dogs are some of the purest domesticated canines scarcely tampered with by man. Reindeer, cattle and sheep are among the stock which these dogs herd. The Soviet herder is known as the Nenets Herding Laika, a dog very similar to the Samoyed.

Among the nordic breeds used principally as companion animals are the lot of spitz-dog types. The German Spitzen, in

five sizes and many colors, were used for various purposes, including guard work. There are a number of nordic dogs that are today billed as toy dogs. The Pomera-

nian, Toy German Spitz, Toy American Eskimo, Japanese Spitz and Volpino Italiano epitomize companion spitzen.

The northern breeds are among the cleanest and most affectionate of dogs. The Samoyed, a fine example from the group, celebrates a long history of close association with man, attributing to its wonderfully demonstrative personality. *See also* Samoyed

Nordic Spitz
See Norbottenspets

Nordic dogs. The Siberian Husky, one of the world's most recognizable sled dogs, is still very capable of draft work.

Nordiske Sitz-hunde
See Norwegian Buhund

Norfolk Retriever
A retriever which once occurred in Norfolk, England; a dog of medium size and excellent water skills and instincts.

Norfolk Terrier, red. Photo by D. Cross.

Norfolk Terrier
The Norfolk Terrier is the breed name given to the drop-eared variety of the Norwich Terrier. In Great Britain, 1965 marked the breed split; in the United States, 1979 was the year that the A.K.C. recognized the dogs as separate breeds. The appearance and temperament have grown somewhat different over the decades since the divide. Of course the breed history is identical up to 1965. *See also* Norwich Terrier

ESSENTIALS OF THE NORFOLK TERRIER: A stocky, short-legged, drop-eared dog, compact and keen. Muzzle foxy and strong, length about one-third less than the wide and slightly rounded skull. Pronounced stop. Ears neatly dropped, carried close to cheeks, round tips. Shoulders well laid back. Neck of medium length, short and compact with well-sprung ribs. Sound hindquarters, well

muscled. Tail medium dock. The coat should be harsh and flat lying; it is longer and rougher on the neck. The body is short-backed, level and of good substance. The Norfolk colors include various shades of red, wheaten, black and tan, and grizzle. White marks are not desirable. Height: 10 inches (25–26 cm). Weight: 11–12 pounds (5–5.5 kg).

Norman Hound
A large hunting dog of ancient lineage, once known in France.

Norsk Buhund
See Norwegian Buhund

Norsk Elghund (Gra)
See Norwegian Elkhound

Norsk Elghund (Sort)
See Norwegian Elkhound

Norsk Lundehund
See Norwegian Lundehund

North Caucasian Steppe Ovtcharka
A smaller variety of the mountain-dwelling Transcaucasian Ovtcharka of the Soviet Union. It is finer in structure and higher on limb, with an overall squarer build. In color the dogs are gray, white, pied and dappled.

North Eastern Sleigh Dog
See Northeasterly Hauling Laika

North Russian Samoyed-Laika
See Nenets Herding Laika

Northeasterly Hauling Laika
The Northeasterly Hauling Laika, known in the Soviet Union as the Sewero-Wostotschnaja Jesdowaja Sobaka or the North Eastern Sleigh Dog, is likely an amalgamation of different drafting/working huskies. The breed is widely distributed in Eastern Siberia, in the region of Amur in Manchuria, in lower Kolyman and in the Anadyr River area, as well as some of the Arctic isles. The dogs are hardy and reliable sleigh dogs and used extensively for mail carriage and other professional transportation and skijoring. The dogs also provide warmth for their owners in the case of

sudden blizzards; the furry pile of hauling huskies serves as an ice-proof furnace. The dogs work four to six days per week, pulling as many as 50 miles per day, and subsisting on as little as three pounds of fish daily.

ESSENTIALS OF THE NORTHEASTERLY HAULING LAIKA: A large, robustly built sled dog with erect ears and an often curled tail. Height: 23–24 inches (58–61 cm). The head is strong, massive and broad with a flat skull and slight stop, well marked. The muzzle is short, broad and powerful. The jaws are notably strong. The ears are short and stiffly erect, with bluntly rounded tips. The body is extremely powerful; chest broad; tuck-up moderate; quarters muscular; legs lengthy and powerful. The tail types can be sickle, curled or straight, often docked. Colors: solid white or black, reddish gray, black/ tan, and pied.

Norwegian Bearhound
See Jämthund

Norwegian Buhund
Belonging to the same variety as the sheepdogs of Greenland, Siberia and Kamchatka, the Norwegian Sheepdog was once employed as a *kometik*-puller (a type of sleigh) and hunter's companion, who possessed a subtle nose. As time and necessity dictated, these dogs were adapted for work on farms as general hands and herders. Since the Middle Ages, the breed has been known to fulfill this capacity and was designated the *Buhund* (translating variously as farm dog). Slightly smaller than the Norse herder of old, today's Buhund is principally employed as a guard dog. Although not popular in the U.S., the Buhund can be found in sizable numbers in both England and Australia; in both countries, the breed is recognized by the national registering bodies.

ESSENTIALS OF THE NORWEGIAN BUHUND: The Buhund is a lightly built, middle-sized spitz with a short, compact body. The head is wedge shaped, lean, not too heavy. Skull is almost flat; the stop well defined. The ears are pointed, size and shape in harmony with head. Neck is lean and comparatively short. Forelegs are moderately angulated, with straight,

well-set elbows, and good bone. Chest is deep with well-sprung ribs. Hindquar-

ters moderately angulated. The ears are placed high and carried erect. Overall, the breed is free from exaggeration and built for arduous work. Though lean, the legs are strong. The double coat is made of a harsh, close but smooth outer coat and a soft and woolly undercoat. Height: 17–18 inches (43–46 cm). Weight: 53–58 pounds (24–26 kg). Color can be

Norwegian Buhund, wheaten.

Norwegian Buhund, red. Photographs by I. Français.

wheaten, black, red, or wolf; small symmetrical markings and black masks are allowed on the body.

Norwegian Elkhound

The Elkhound of Norway, as known in the U.S. and Great Britain, is a gray, thickly coated dog and is the oldest known breed of the Scandinavian countries. The Scandinavian elkhound breeds, three in number, are among the world's most historic breeds and have changed the least from the pristine dog type through ages of canine development. The Norwegian Elkhound actually

Norwegian Elkhound, gray. Photo by I. Français.

can be gray or black. The Gray Norwegian Elkhound is the most familiar and known as the Norsk Elghund (Gra). The black breed is a little smaller and much rarer. It is known as the Norsk Elghund (Sort) or simply the Black Norwegian Elkhound. The third breed is the Jämthund or Swedish Elkhound, which is the largest of the elkhound breeds. *See also* Jämthund

Fossils dating back to the Stone Age, discovered in Norway, bear the likenesses of today's breed; such evidence reveals the antiquity and genuine purity of the Elkhound breed. In Norwegian, *elghund,* the dog's name, really translates

to moosedog, which more accurately describes the group since there is no hound in their blood. They do, however, follow game closely, as would a scenthound, and not chase it. "Moose" is as appropriate a word choice as elk, since the dogs were used on both animals, plus lynx, bear, and wolf. In Norway, the breed has been employed principally in the pursuit of the elk, thus justifying its accepted name. (The authors acknowledge that no matter how hard one tries, "moosedog" does not ring mellifluously.) Norwegian elk hunters convey that a working dog can "wind" (scent) an elk up to three miles away. Additionally, the dogs can be used as a retriever of birds, a hunter of small game, a rabbiter, ratter, mole and stoat extractor; some Elkhounds have hunted and killed fox and otter; others have been successful at holding a stag at bay, as gun dogs, water dogs, and as herders of farmyard chickens and ducks (working with the Collie). Many current-day owners are unaware of the Norwegian Elkhound's extraordinary hunting prowess and the unique fashion in which he executes it. Barking at bay, dodging attack, and soundlessly creeping encompass his versatile approach to the hunt. Next to the Airedale Terrier, the Norwegian Elkhound is perhaps the most versatile of all breeds of dog.

Despite its antiquity, the Norwegian Elkhound, known simply as Elkhound in Britain, has not been excessively popular. Even though the breed has appeared at Crufts since the early twentieth century, its popularity as a show and companion dog is a comparatively new development. Normally friendly, they are natural protectors with great dignity and independence of character—more mannerly and unassuming than most Vikings one meets nowadays.

Essentials of the Norwegian Elkhound: A proportionately short body with a thick and rich, but not bristling, gray coat. Powerful and compact, the body is broad chested, with a straight back and well-developed loins. The ears are prick and the tail is curled over the back. The neck is of medium length, firm and muscular. The head is considered "dry," that is, without loose skin. The forelegs are firm and straight. Chest is wide and deep. The loins muscular and stomach slightly drawn up. The coat is thick, rich and hard, rather smooth-laying. The Elkhound's color is gray with black tips—a solid coat should be a medium-gray tone, neither too dark nor too light. Height: 18–20 inches (46–51 cm). Weight: 44 pounds (40 kg).

Norwegian Hound
See Dunker

Norwegian Lundehund
Originating in Vaerog, an island off the coast of Norway, this most unique canine, the Norwegian Lundehund, was developed for the specific task of hunting the puffin bird. The puffin bird could only be caught by reaching into tight crevices in the rocks, and the Lundehund has been specially equipped for this difficult task. The Lundehund is in possession of six multi-jointed toes on each foot, a double-jointed neck capable of reaching in peculiar directions and laying practically on the dog's back, and ears that close up to prevent water getting inside. These features equip the Lundehund with the particular ability to perform its very specialized task. He was also trained to search and retrieve the puffin bird's abandoned nest. An ancient theory that this dog survived the Ice Age by feeding on sea birds is unlikely, even though the dog's purity and antiquity cannot be challenged. In the late 1500s, the explorer Schonnebol wrote of these dogs on his visit to Norway.

Today the credit for the Lundehund's survival is shared by two enthusiasts and breeders: Eleanor Christie and Monrad Mostad, who worked separately though together to pull the breed through distemper epidemics in the 1930s and 40s. Today in Norway, both the colorful puffin bird and its ex-extractor (the Lundehund) are protected by government and resource associations.

The breed is recognized in Great Britain, though few have made their way to the States. As can be surmised from his greatly detailed hunting methods, he is highly intelligent, industrious and independent. Friend and photographer, Isabelle Français (whose photography this volume enjoys) relates that of the hundreds of different dog breeds that she has photographed, the Lundehund is the most difficult to portray. Whether this lack of cooperation is due to the breed's obstinacy or simply its distaste for studio photographers is not exactly known. Nonetheless, these are handsome, sharp-looking dogs that have been well acclimated to life as pets. If desired, the Lundehund's hunting abilities can be

Norwegian Lundehund, black-tipped fawn. Photo by I. Français.

rechanneled to work on other, more populous ground birds.

Essentials of the Norwegian Lundehund: A rectangular spitz dog, small, comparatively light. Strong legs with at least six toes on all four feet, of which at least five toes of the forefeet and four on the hindfeet should take part in supporting the dog. The head is clean, of medium wedge shape. The feet's six toes

Norwegian Lundehund, red.

Norwich Terrier, wheaten.

are multiple-jointed with two large functional dewclaws and eight plantar cushions on each foot. Lack of premolars on both sides in both jaws is quite common: the bite is level (often undershot). The ears, triangular and medium sized, are carried erect; they have the specific quality that the cartilage around the ear opening is able to contract, and the external ear leather is folded and turned up in a peculiar way—backwards or at right angles upwards so that the ear opening is shut. The neck is clean cut, of medium length, rather strong, and double jointed. The body is strong, with a straight back and a rather slightly descending croup. Chest is long, of medium width. The coat has a soft undercoat; the outer is rough and dense, it is short on the head and front of the legs. Height: 12–15.5 inches (31–40

cm). Weight: 13 pounds (6 kg). In color it is reddish brown to fallow, with black-tipped hairs preferred. Whites with black tips also occur.

Norwegian Puffin Dog
See Norwegian Lundehund

Norwegian Sheepdog
See Norwegian Buhund

Norwich Terrier
The little terriers known as the Norwich Terriers can be traced to the short-legged, red, red wheaten or black/tan terriers that were easily recognizable in Anglia (eastern England) at the turn of the nineteenth century. These dogs are likely crosses between the Scottish Terrier and the Cairn Terrier, but that cannot be stated for sure. Other possibilities include the Border Terrier and the more probable Irish Terrier.

One enterprising sportsman, known as "Doggy" Lawrence, began selling little "Red Terriers" to Cambridge undergrads in the 1870s. These dogs, the forebears of today's Norfolk/Norwich breeds, were likely small Irish terriers. After the decimation of World War I, Frank Jones attempted to revitalize the hard-hit stock. Staffordshire Bull Terriers and Bedlingtons, allegedly, were crossed with other small red Irish terriers to regenerate the lost Norfolk dwarf. Jones most likely used any working terrier stock he could find, and as such there is little reason to believe the Staff was involved. For a while these creations were called Jones Terriers. At other times,

when the breed was being peddled by "Doggy," it was referred to as the Cantab Terrier or the Trumpington Terrier. The K.C.G.B. recognized the Norwich Terrier in 1932. Until 1965 in Great Britain and 1979 in the U.S., Norwich referred to both the prick-eared and drop-eared varieties. Today the Norwich Terrier is the prick-eared dog, and the Norfolk is the drop-eared dog. Other distinguishing features have arisen since the dissension but for most of the two breeds' existences, they were interbred as one breed.

ESSENTIALS OF THE NORWICH TERRIER: A squat, keen dog of awesome power for his little size. Muzzle, foxy and strong, length about one-third less than the wide and slightly rounded skull. Shoulders well laid back with short powerful, straight legs. Body short and compact with well-sprung ribs. Hindquarters sound and well muscled with good powers of propulsion. Feet round with thick pads. Tail medium dock. Height: 10 inches (25–26 cm) Weight: 11–12 pounds (5–5.5 kg). Its prick ears are perfectly erect when aroused. The mouth is tight-lipped with scissor-biting teeth. The Norwich's gait should be true, low, and driving. The Norfolk colors include various shades of red, wheaten, black and tan, and grizzle. Extensive white marks are unpardonable and render disqualification.

Nose

1) The hound's scenting ability. 2) When referring to the canine anatomy, the nose consists of the cartilagenous framework and the nasal cavity. As in humans, the nose is the olfactory organ. Often dog people use the term loosely to refer to the muzzle in general or simply the external nose. *See* Nose types

Hunting enthusiasts use the term nose differently. Noses are to canines as eyes are to humans: that is, dogs use their noses routinely as they proceed through their daily endeavors, much as humans

rely on their eyes to identify objects, spot danger, or read instructions and signs. The dog's nose is his scenting instrument and is therefore of extreme importance. The scenting ability, of course, is certainly more pronounced in hounds. The Bloodhound, as the epitome of the scenthound, has a nose that defies description, or at least lends itself to absurd hyperbole. For instance, it is said that a Bloodhound's nose is at least two million times as sensitive as a human's nose. Such capability has its pluses and minuses: for instance, the honeysuckle blossoming on a spring morning would send a Bloodhound to unprecedented elation (or multitudinous nausea), while the odor of fresh garbage, its owner after a five-mile run or its own stool would be more than any human could stomach. The nose, therefore, is as key to the scenthound's ability to find its quarry as is its scent memory. Back to the miraculous Bloodhound: it is believed that a Bloodhound could still detect a drop of blood after it has been diluted by ten thousand gallons of water. In a forest, graced with its hundreds and hundreds of different scents, a tracking hound needs to remember the *one* scent, ignoring the scent of other animals, avoiding the smells left by humans (petrols and other powerfully smelling substances), and not stopping to enjoy the honeysuckle (so to speak).

Nose. All dogs have a propensity to sniff—every scent is worth exploring and enjoying. These two Dutch Smoushonds are seemingly on the track of something wonderful. Photo by I. Français.

Scent is comprised of tiny matter particles that are left by living things: it is generally believed that a hound can detect chemical changes in the quarry (such as fear, rage, and exhaustion). Dogs in general have stupendous memories for scents and recognize their owners and friends (and enemies) by their scents, at least initially. Some people have stronger scents than others (not to be confused with body odor) and dogs remember the stronger scented persons more readily.

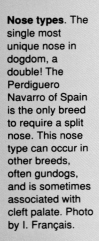

Nose types. The single most unique nose in dogdom, a double! The Perdiguero Navarro of Spain is the only breed to require a split nose. This nose type can occur in other breeds, often gundogs, and is sometimes associated with cleft palate. Photo by I. Français.

which is split down the center, is often associated with cleft palate. One breed of dog in Spain, the Perdiguero Navarro, a gundog of substantial ability but limited fame, possesses the double or split nose.

The dog fancy has developed terminology for the various nose types: some of the terms which are covered under their respective headings included in this volume are: Aquiline nose; Brown nose; Butterfly nose; Cherry nose; Dudley nose; Flesh-colored nose; Liver-colored nose; Pink nose; Putty nose; Ram's nose; Roman nose; Self-colored nose; Smudge nose; Snow nose; and Spotted nose, *which see.*

Nosebleed

Nosebleeds are usually caused by the nose being hit against a hard surface. Sneezing too hard can also initiate a nosebleed. Infection is a common cause of nosebleeds or epistaxis (as your Merck-referring vet may call it). Nasal infections should be treated by a veterinarian since ignored problems can only get more complicated, especially where the nose is concerned. Lastly, a tumor may cause a discharge of purulent materials, with or without bleeding. See your vet.

Nostrils

External orifices or openings of the nasal organ. *See* Nose, Nose types

Nostrils, flared

See Flared nostrils

Not prominent shoulders

See Shoulder types

Nose types

Dogs' noses, as well as varying in ability, vary in shade, size and placement. Regardless of breed, the nose skin is covered by relatively short short hair and the front portion, hairless. Most commonly, the canine nose consists of two nostrils which are joined at the center by the nasolabial line or philtrum. Exceptions to this rule have cropped up throughout history, and at times a number of breeds have experienced the double nose phenomenon. Such a nose,

Nova Scotia Duck Tolling Retriever

Tolling dogs, the forefathers of the Nova Scotia, have been known in the Little River district of Yarmouth County in southwestern Nova Scotia since at least the 1890s. The breed was developed there in the early twentieth century to toll (or lure) and retrieve waterfowl.

It is reportedly the result of various crosses, including the Golden, Chesapeake, Labrador, and Flat-Coated Retrievers, and possibly small amounts of Cocker Spaniel, Irish Setter, various working collies, and/or a playful spitz type or two. When at work, the dog has a speedy, rushing action, with the head carried almost level with the back and heavily feathered tail in constant motion. The Toller is known for its high degree of intelligence, easy trainability, and great endurance. He is an outstanding swimmer and a natural retriever on land and in the water. The breed's strong desire to retrieve as well as its inherent playful nature are vital to its tolling performance and have been selectively bred for throughout the course of its development. The dog prances and plays on the shore for the deceptive entertainment and subsequent attraction of offshore ducks. Once within shooting distance, the ducks are fired upon and the Toller is then sent to retrieve the kill. The breed is popular with a close knit, strongly supportive group of fanciers. Formal registration did not occur until 1945, a date which also marks the drawing of the first formal standard. The Canadian Kennel Club initiated recognition in the 1950s, and the FCI granted full international recognition in 1982. This is a breed which is fully deserving of the attention of American fanciers, particularly those bored with the Golden and Lab. The U.K.C. presently registers this Canadian breed.

ESSENTIALS OF THE NOVA SCOTIA DUCK TOLLING RETRIEVER: A medium-sized dog that is powerful, compact, balanced and well muscled, with medium to heavy bone. The head is clean cut and slightly wedge shaped. The muzzle tapers in a clean line from stop to nose. Eyes set well apart. Ears triangular, of medium size, and set high and well back on the skull. Many Tollers have a slightly sad expression when not working. While at work, however, the dog should possess the intense concentration and excitement which are characteristic of the breed. The body is deep chested with good spring of rib. The coat is double, of medium length, and water-repellent. It may have a slight wave on the back but is otherwise straight. Color: various shades of red and orange, with lighter feathering. Height: 18–20 inches (45–51 cm). Weight 37–51 pounds (17–23 kg).

Nova Scotia Duck Tolling Retriever, red. Photo by I. Français.

Novice class

In the A.K.C., the Novice class is for dogs which have not yet won three first-class ribbons, nor championship points in the Open, American-bred, or Bred-by-Exhibitor classes. In the K.C.G.B., it is reserved for dogs that have not yet won a Challenge Certificate or five first prizes. *See also* Classes at Shows In obedience trials, the Novice A class is for purebred dogs, of either sex and of any breed, that have not won the title C.D. Each dog is to have a separate handler and must be handled by the owner or a member of the immediate family. No professional handler, trainer, or kennel employee may compete. The Novice B is similar to the Novice A except either amateur or professional handlers may compete, and more than one dog may be shown by one person—but each must have a separate handler for the sit and down.

Numbers player

Race patron who bets the post position numbers of the racing dogs rather than their class or form.

Nursing

See Bitch

Nutrition

Nutrition refers to the dog's food requirements: milk is high in protein and calcium but may also be high in fat; vegetables have vitamins but lack protein. Nutritional soundness pertains to the balance of foodstuffs that sufficiently

provides the dog with all his required food components. Water, proteins, fats, carbohydrates, vitamins and minerals are what the dog demands for health and survival. Fortunately, much research has been conducted in the field of canine nutrition, and dog owners reap the benefits every time they purchase a high-quality dog food.

Approximately 70% of the canine's total body weight is composed of water. Water, two parts hydrogen and one part oxygen, is obtained in three ways by the dog: drinking, oxidizing hydrogen during the digestive process, and eating. But while the dog does have more than one way of acquiring this vital component, water always should be avail-

able to the adult dog, and he should be allowed to drink his fill at all times. It is important for the owner to realize that the water requirements of dogs are not all the same, especially when considering the larger dogs versus the smaller. Large dogs can better store water and, therefore, can perform for relatively longer hours without a drink if necessary. Most smaller dogs cannot store large amounts of water, making regular trips to the bowl a frequent necessity. Water requirements can also vary with age: most pups cannot store adequate amounts of water, and older dogs sometimes require large doses of water daily to aid their aging kidneys and digestive system. With the exception of puppies that are involved in the housebreaking process, all dogs should have water easily available at all times.

Proteins are essential to muscle growth and maintenance. All dogs have particularly high protein requirements during puppyhood and their rapid growth periods, when muscle development is at its greatest. Most quality puppy foods are high in easily digestible protein. Meat, fish, soy beans, and yeast are all good sources of protein. No one source should be provided exclusively, for the amino acid content of various protein sources differs. Amino acids are the building blocks of proteins; there are many different amino acids, each serving a specific function, and most of which are essential to

healthy existence. Dogs who are lacking in protein or various amino acids often receive supplemental diets, with milk, eggs, and various other substances

added. Milk and eggs, cottage cheese and yogurt are all valuable sources of protein and amino acids, but they must not be given in excess, for most have a high fat and cholesterol content and can also cause digestive upsets. For most adult dogs, quality commercial food, supplemented with occasional treats, provides the necessary protein and amino acids for healthful existence. Amino acid supplements should be given only with the recommendation of a veterinarian or canine nutritionist. In a starved or nutritionally

Nutrition. Commercial-brand kibble is fortified with essential protein and vitamins. Weimaraner puppy photographed by I. Français.

deficient animal, proteins are broken down effectively and converted into energy by the body.

Carbohydrates, composed of starches and sugars, are the primary energy source in human beings. Dogs, however, lack the bacteria that is essential to break down cellulose, thereby making most plant substances largely indigestible by the dog. Most plant matter, unless properly cooked, passes through the canine digestive system, serving as roughage. Roughage is important for the smooth and proper functioning of the digestive system, which means that the dog should not be on a diet that is totally digestible, unless prescribed by a veterinarian. Carbohydrates should form a primary energy source for the dog. In conjunction with roughage-type starches, easily converted carbohydrates should comprise about one-half of the dog's caloric intake. Starches are complex substances to the digestive system and must first be broken down into simple sugars to be of use to the dog. Simple sugars, fructose, glucose, and others, are excellent energy sources for the dog. If, however, they are not used they are stored by the body. An excess of energy foods can lead quickly to an overweight condition.

Fats supply concentrated energy, essentially fatty acids, and are an essential part of canine nutrition. They are a vital source of energy, provide necessary bodily insulation from both heat and cold, promote a healthy coat, and facilitate normal cell growth. Fats are found in many foods, particularly meats and dairy products. A balanced diet provides fats but never in excess. Too much fat can cause obesity and lead to digestive upsets for the day.

Vitamins and minerals are necessary for the proper breakdown, absorption, and use of foodstuffs. Of utmost nutritional importance with regard to vitamins and minerals is complementary balance, e.g., calcium cannot be correctly used by the body unless adequate amounts of phosphorus and vitamin D are also included in the diet. As with fats, carbohydrates and proteins, vitamins and minerals are supplied sufficiently to most dogs if they are fed a high-grade commercial dog food in appropriate amounts, supplemented with occasional treats if desired by the owner. Veterinary counsel is most helpful in regard to your dog's diet and his subsequent nutritional soundness. *See also* Digestive system, Feeding, Vitamins

Nyctereutes procyonoides
See Raccoon dog

Nylon bones
Nylon bones, especially those with natural meat and bone flavor added, are probably the most complete, safe, and economical answer to the chewing need. Dogs cannot break them nor bite off sizeable chunks; hence, they are completely safe. And being longer lasting than other things offered for the purpose, they are very economical.

Hard chewing raises little bristle-like projections on the surface of the nylon bones to provide effective interim tooth cleaning and vigorous gum massage, much in the same way your toothbrush does it for you. The little projections are raked off and swallowed in the form of thin shavings, but the chemistry of the nylon is such that they break down in the stomach fluids and pass through without any harmful effect.

The toughness of the nylon provides the strong chewing resistance needed for important jaw exercise and effective help for the teething functions; however, there is no tooth wear because nylon is non-abrasive. Being inert, nylon does not support the growth of microorganisms, and it can be washed in soap and water or sterilized by boiling or in an autoclave.

There are a great variety of Nylabone® products available that veterinarians recommend as safe and healthy for your dog or puppy to chew on. These Nylabone® Pooch Pacifiers® usually don't splinter, chip, or break off in large chunks; instead, they are frizzled by the dog's chewing action, and this creates a toothbrush-like surface that cleanses the teeth and massages the gums. At the same time, these hard-nylon therapeutic devices channel doggie tension and chewing frustation into constructive rather than destructive behavior. The original nylon bone (Nylabone®) is not a toy and dogs use it only when in need of pacification. Keeping a bone in each of your dog's recreation rooms is the best method of providing the requisite pacification. Unfortunately, many nylon chew products have been copied. These inferior quality copies are sold in supermarkets and other chain stores. The really good products are sold only through veterinarians, pet shops, grooming salons and places where the sales people really know something about dogs. The good products have the flavor impregnated *into* the bone. This makes the taste last longer. The smell is undetectable to humans. The artificial bones which have a strong odor are poor-quality bones with the odor sprayed on to impress the dog owner (not the dog)! These heavily scented dog toys may impart the odor to your carpets or furniture if an odor-sprayed bone lies there wet from a dog's chewing on it.

Similar to nylon bones are polyurethane chew devices. The most recommended of these dog toys is the Gumabone®. These multi-colored, variously shaped chew devices are softer than nylon bones, though still quite indestructible. Scientific studies on the quality of these chew devices have indicated that dogs that use these products have a far less chance of gum disease and tooth decay and may live longer. *See also* Dental care, Periodontitis, Gingivitis, Flossing

Nymphomania

Hormonal disturbances of the gonads, due to pituitary control, can manifest themselves in nymphomania. Excessive sexual desire is generally referred to as satyriasis; in females it is called nymphomania. A cystic condition in the female's ovaries may account for this insatiability. Surgery can correct the condition.

Nystagmus

A condition of the eyes, in which the eyes twitch from side to side. It is often a side-effect of a stroke.

Nylon bones like the Nylabone® provide both good dental upkeep as well as a tasteful pastime.

Obedience Trial Champion

An A.K.C. dog that has won the required number of points and first place wins specified to acquire the title. The requirements may change from time to time and are recorded in the American Kennel Club's obedience regulations. The employed suffix is O.T.Ch.

Obedience trials invite and involve all dogs to compete in educational and entertaining competition. All recognized breeds, as well as others, have excelled in the obedience competition. Rottweiler pictured with a dumbbell.

Obedience trials

The second most popular event in the dog sport, obedience trials were deemed a "fad" in the early days of the 1930s. Within a decade and a half, by 1948, over 200 known training classes and official clubs existed in the United States. While bench shows (or dog shows) are in effect beauty contests featuring, rather exclusively, the conformation of the dog, obedience trials consider a dog's skill, training and interaction with man. To be scored by the judges, the dog is required to complete a series of exercises or activities for which he has been trained. While conformation is of no direct importance, at least theoretically the dog's conformation—physical par—influences its ability to perform. The details of color and coat texture of course remain irrelevant, whereas the musculation, balance and assembly of the dog affect its strength, agility and endurance. Unlike bench competition, spayed and neutered as well as mother bitches are admitted into competition.

Obedience trials are divided into three levels: Novice, Open and Utility; each level excels in difficulty. Only purebred dogs that have not achieved the first title (Companion Dog or C.D.) are eligible to compete in the Novice class. The Open class awards Companion Dog Excellent (C.D.X.) and the Utility class awards Utility Dog (U.D.).

The Novice class imbues the fundamental obedience exercises which are essential to the proper behavior of any companion dog, hence the title C.D. Among the six exercises are: heel on leash, stand for examination, heel free, recall, long sit, and long down. The second level focuses on more demanding feats of obedience and agility. The seven exercises include: heel free, drop on recall, retrieve on flat, retrieve over the high jump, broad jump, long sit, and long down. The third level consists of five activities: signal exercise, scent discrimination, directed retrieve, directed jumping, and group examination. At each level a dog must score 170 points out of a possible 200—or three "legs"—and achieve at least 51 percent on each exercise. In order for a dog to acquire its Obedience Trial Championship (O.T.Ch.) it must win three first places, one at each level. Each place must be won under a different judge with the required number of dogs competing in each class.

Tracking is another aspect of the obedience trial that involves following a stranger's scent over a given terrain after the scent has aged from 30 minutes to three to five hours. The track for Tracking Dog (T.D.) title is about a quarter-mile long; for Tracking Dog Excellent (T.D.X.), the track is approximately one half-mile long.

Obedience trials. Chow Chow performing in Novice class on long sit.

Obedience trials in the Open class involve the high jump and the retrieve over the high jump. Illustrated are three breeds performing in the Open class: (*bottom left*) the Belgian Sheepdog, Tervuren, (*top right*) Rottweiler and (*bottom right*) American Eskimo.

Obedience trials. (*top right*) Border Collie over broad jump; (*middle*) Whippet performing scent discrimination in the Utility class; (*bottom right*) a C.D.X. Old English Sheepdog over the broad jump; and (*bottom left*) a C.D. Smooth Fox Terrier winning at an obedience trial at the American Fox Terrier Club Centenary Show.

Obedience trials. (*top*) Siberian Husky over the high jump; (*bottom right*) Doberman Pinscher retrieve over the high jump; (*top left*) a smiling smooth Chihuahua with his dumbbell; and (*bottom left*) a longhaired Chihuahua over the broad jump.

Odor. Pet shop and supply houses offer commercial products to help minimize doggy odors, with specially designed sprays for bitches in heat, puppy stains, etc. Photo by I. Français.

Obesity

Obesity is the over-accumulation of fat in body tissue as a result of excess energy intake. Owners too frequently indulge their infrequently exercised mature (or older) dogs. Table scraps and the lack of exercise are the plumply obvious causes. Dachshunds and Beagles are perhaps among the most indulged of pet canines. A regular exercise program, the discontinuation of all snacks, and a low-calorie dense diet comprise the necessary course of action. Owners tend to overlook the obesity of their beloved companions; this only further diminishes the dog's health, encourages his sloth and rotundity, and shortens his life.

Oblique shoulders

See Shoulder types

Obliquely placed eyes

Eyes in which the outer corners are set higher than the inner corners, i.e., Mongolian eyes. Such slanted eyes are usually deemed a fault, as most breeds of dog have eyes which are placed square to the skull. However, a handful of canines are required to have such eye type (e.g., Pomeranians, Afghan Hounds).

Oblong eyes

Eyes in which the contours are more rounded than angular and are longer than high. Essentially oval, this is the most common type of the canine eye.

Obstructive jaundice

See Jaundice

Occiput

Upper back point of the skull, a feature that varies in prominence from breed to breed. Often referred to as the peak, apex, and occipital bone. The occiput's function is to serve as a point for muscles to attach themselves.

Occipital protuberance

The prominently raised occiput typical of many of the gundog and scenthound breeds.

Odds man

Calculates approximate odds during progress of betting at a dog-racing track.

Odor

Bad breath, smelly coat, putrid ears, an unwiped backside: dogs are generally clean animals, but there are some individuals and some conditions under which some individual animals will emit one or more of the classic doggy odors.

The dog's mouth is typically a very clean place, relatively speaking of course. It has been determined that the buccal cavity of the canine is far cleaner than that of the average human. Infections, decaying teeth and gums, tartar and plaque deposits can, however, contaminate the dog's mouth and cause bad breath. A thorough cleaning is often all that is required to set the dog back on the road to sweeter breath. However, should there be infection or degeneration, corrective dental surgery may be necessary. To prevent bad breath and contribute to your dog's dental health, supply him always with a safe and effective chew product and attend to his teeth with regular trips to the veterinarian. *See also* Dental care

Coat odor is another common complaint lodged against the dog. Some dogs do naturally emit a strong doggy odor, and if your dog is to be a house dog, it pays to do some breed investigation. Generally a smelly dog is an unkempt dog. Regular grooming, which maintains the health of both the coat and the skin, largely reduces any propensity of the dog to give off odor. Bathing should be infrequent even for the odorous dog. Deodorants can prove successful in chronic cases. *See also* Grooming

Ear odor is most often a sign of ear infection, likely a secondary one brought about by mite infestation. Ear odor speaks for veterinary care. *See also* Ear mange, Ear problems

Longhaired dogs should be regularly clipped around the anus, thus preventing fecal matter from attaching to the coat and pervading the home.

Oestrus
See Heat period

O.F.A.

The O.F.A. or Orthopedic Foundation for Animals, Inc., is an organization which was founded by a number of progressive American Rottweiler breed clubs for the physical betterment of that breed. Any two-year-old or older dog of any breed is welcome to have its X-rays examined. Rottweilers are just one breed of dog that has frequent bouts with hip dysplasia, a hereditary disease that manifests itself in lameness, physical maneuvering difficulties, and implies faulty conformation of the femur and the acetabulum. *See* Hip dysplasia

The O.F.A. defines its four objectives as follows:

"1. To collate and disseminate information concerning diseases of the bones and muscles with first and major emphasis on hip dysplasia.

2. To devise and encourage the establishment of control programs to lower the incidence of musculoskeletal disease.

3. To encourage and finance research in musculoskeletal diseases.

4. To receive funds and make grants to carry out these objectives."

The controversy arises as to whether or not the O.F.A. is or should be the only authority to deem a dog "H.D. free." Many breeders still prefer to rely on their trusted veterinarian. The O.F.A. certifies dogs that are at least two years of age and

whose certified X-rays deem the animal free of hip dysplasia.

Off
Start of a race; position of dogs at the start.

Ogar Polski
See Polish Hound

Old Country Bulldog
See American Bulldog

O.F.A. The underlying goal to this foundation is to promote the breeding of physically sound animals, animals that are able to move and jump with agility and ease, as this Rottweiler demonstrates.

Old Danish Bird Dog

Known also as the Gammel Dansk Honsehund in its native land, this breed was developed in the early eighteenth century for the purpose of retrieving. Its close-working skills were soon developed and the breed today is employed at a variety of tasks, including pointing and field trialing. In the field, the dog must work fairly close to the handler and be able to take direction from him. Most desirable is the high point, but the creep and the drop are allowed. The tail should be carried lively and gaily on the hunt, with full rotation of circular motion upon scent. The breed traces to various farm hounds (likely St. Hubert type) and old pointing dogs of the Danish region. Evidence of Bloodhound blood includes the breed's heavy neck and superior nose; the Old Danish is also employed at *schweisshund* work, which is the locating of wounded deer. Morten Bak is hailed for his contribution to the dog's development, and the breed is sometimes referred to as the Bakhund, but rarely outside Denmark.

Old Danish Bird Dog, white with liver. Photo by I. Français.

The breed enjoyed quick success, but the Second World War decimated the breed to near extinction. Through the efforts of a few dedicated breeders and fanciers, the breed was preserved. The Old Danish Bird Dog (or Old Danish Pointer) is one of only two gundogs native to Denmark and boasts impressive registries each year in his native land. The Old Danish Pointer is an intelligent and trainable companion and hunter. His coat requires minimal care and he makes a fine watchdog. He is serious in his work and serious in his devotion to his master and household. He is rarely seen outside his native land.

ESSENTIALS OF THE OLD DANISH BIRD DOG: For a pointer, the Old Danish is quite small, standing only 22 inches (56 cm) in height. In general appearance, the length is to exceed the height of the dog; he is to be a strongly built and substantial gundog. Weight: 40–53 pounds (18–24 kg). The head is deep, comparatively short, with a broad skull and deep muzzle. The neck is strong and muscular, with dewlap present especially in males. The body is well developed, with a deep, broad chest and a strong level back. Hindquarters well angulated, with broad, muscular thighs. Forequarters powerful, with sloping shoulders and strong, straight legs. The coat is short and dense and colored in white with light to dark liver markings and a small amount of ticking permissible but not preferred.

Old Danish Pointer

See Old Danish Bird Dog

Old English Mastiff

See Mastiff

Old English Sheepdog

Originally developed as a cattle drover, the breed emerged in England sometime in the mid-1700s. It was quick to gain the popularity of dog fanciers and soon found itself and its distinctive rolling gait the subject of applause at exhibitions on both sides of the Atlantic. The OES is essentially a big dog, weighing 66 pounds (30 kg) or more, and this characteristic, coupled with its time-consuming coat, has kept the breed from attaining that often destructive "great" popularity. The exact composition of the OES is not determined conclusively, but judging from its characteristics and the information available, it seems likely that the dog traces to ancient herders—possibly a blend of several of them. Possible contributors include: the Bergamasco, large ovtcharkas, the Bearded Collie, the Briard, and the Armant.

An alternative name of the breed,

Old English Sheepdog, gray with white. Photo by I. Français.

Old English Sheepdog, blue with white.

Bobtail, is significant in its relation to the history of the breed. Many theories have purported the nature of the customary docking. By far the most often repeated and commonly accepted one refers to the tax exemption granted to drover dogs in England in the eighteenth century and earlier. It is stated that tails were docked to distinguish the droving dogs and thereby claim exemption. Another theory states that the breed was a chronic rabbit chaser while on duty and that shepherds docked the dog's tail to decrease its maneuverability and thereby its fun. Whatever the origin, the tradition lasts to this day: the Bobtail's entire tail is customarily docked.

Faithful and protective, the Old English Sheepdog is intelligent and trainable. His rather disdainful expression is well hidden under shaggy bangs, giving him a light-hearted yet watchful air. He is a fine, loving companion and a watchful, fearless guardian dog.

ESSENTIALS OF THE OLD ENGLISH SHEEPDOG: A strong, squarely built dog of great symmetry and overall soundness, he is to be absolutely free of legginess and profusely coated over his entire body. Colors include shades of gray, grizzle, blue or blue merle, all with or without white. The head is proportional, with a well-defined stop; the muzzle is truncated, strong and square, equal in length to that of the skull. Eyes set well apart, dark or wall. Ears small and carried flat to the side of the head. Forelegs are perfectly straight, with plenty of bone, hold-

Olde English Bulldogge, white with brindle markings.

ing the body well from the ground. Shoulders well laid back. Dog to stand lower at the withers than the loin. Body rather short and compact, with well-sprung ribs and deep chest. Stifle well turned, and hocks set low. The tail is customarily docked completely. The coat is harsh in texture and never straight, always free from curl. The hindquarters are the most heavily coated. Height: 22 inches (56 cm) or more. Weight: 66 pounds (30 kg) or more.

Old English White
See American Bulldog

Old English White Terrier
A dog which figures into the histories of many British and Continental terriers. The breed was renowned for its game instincts and toughness. Crosses between the Old English White Terrier and various bulldog types produced many of the bull and terrier breeds (Bull Terrier, Staffordshire Terriers, etc.).

Old Spanish Pointer
See Perdiguero Navarro

Olde English Bulldogge, white with fawn. Photographs by I. Français.

Olde English Bulldogge
A Bulldog that is functional and traditional at the same time, the Olde English Bulldogge is courageous and determined without being over-aggressive. Disenchanted by the English Bulldog, David Leavitt of Pennsylvania began a project to recreate the eighteenth-century Bulldog. Not so impressed by that ancient breed's baiting abilities as he was enamored of its active and able appearance, Leavitt set out to reconstruct the dog that the present-day Bulldog no longer resembles. A linebreeding scheme involving Bullmastiffs, Pit Bull Terriers, American Bulldogs and the Bulldog has reaped a modern protection dog that looks and is man-stopping, able to impede an assailant without having to bite, which is fortunate for both the intruder and the owner alike.

ESSENTIALS OF THE OLDE ENGLISH BULLDOGGE: A medium-sized dog possessing great strength and athletic refinement. The head is large in proportion to the body and is furnished with a moderate amount of wrinkles. The skull is carved between the eyes, extending up the forehead. Two-fold dewlap and semi-pendulous flews are desired. The ears are rose or button. The muzzle is short and broad. The body is cobby and muscular. The back is slightly roached and strong. The short, close coat is col-

ored with brindles of red, gray or black on white; solid white; or fawn, red or black, with or without white markings.

Older dogs

With modern-day advances in medicine and the high quality and accessibility of veterinary care, the likelihood of our dog's living longer grows. If you have purchased a healthy dog from a reputable source and taken proper care of him, you should have the pleasure of seeing the dog live to his optimum age.

Signs of old age include overweight or underweight, a slowing down of the dog's metabolism and activity, hair graying around the muzzle and face, and a dullness in the eyes. Loss of breath from regular activities indicates that the dog is slowing down. Digestive upsets, including constipation, vomiting, and diarrhea, commonly result in weight loss. The dog's hair may thin as a result of less active skin glands. Callouses will form on the elbows, and skin may thicken in places. A bitch's teats begin to sag and tumors and cysts are common in the unspayed bitch, as is mammary cancer. In both sexes, muscle tone diminishes, and the dog may become more susceptible to parasites.

Blindness and deafness may occur in the older dog. These senior citizens aren't aware that their bodies are slowing down; more likely, they think the world itself is slowing down. It is important that owners continue to pay attention to the older dog and do not neglect him because he's no longer the perfect frisbee partner or beach jogger. Older dogs tend to be more sensitive and affectionate to their owners and are most appreciative of attention in the golden years.

Generally speaking, older dogs should be exercised considerably less intensely than usual, though exercise should remain regular. The dog's caloric intake decreases along with the exercise requirement. Owners should be aware of the development of worms in the stool. Frequent grooming is also helpful to stimulate the skin. Teeth become more sensitive as the enamel wears away or teeth begin to fall out. Proper dental hygiene throughout a dog's life should keep his whites white and strong till the end of his days. *See also* Nutrition, Feeding, Grooming, Dental care, Exercise, Cancer, Blindness

Olecranon process

Point of the elbow. *See* Forequarters

Omnivorous animals

Those animals which require both animal (meat) and vegetable (plant) matter in order to live a healthy existence. The dog, like man, is an omnivorous animal. *See also* Animals, classes of

Open class

In conformation, this class is for any dog over six months of age. In obedience trials, this class is for purebred dogs, of either sex and of any breed, which have won the C.D. degree but have not been awarded the C.D.X. degree. As in the Novice class, no professional may compete, and the dog must belong to the handler or member of the immediate family.

Open coat

A type of single coat where the hairs are generously separated and are usually stand-offish, lacking undercoat.

Opiates

Substances derived from the poppy plant and which are sometimes used medicinally, often to relieve pain, as with opium and heroin, or control coughing, as with codeine.

Oral contraception

Substances, often in pill or liquid form, which are given to the bitch to prevent impregnation. Success with such substances is reported varied. Side effects and costs should be discussed with your veterinarian, who may well suggest a spaying operation.

Older dogs deserve a sensitive owner's consideration. The dog's world has slowed down considerably, grown quieter and hazier, and his muzzle has gone gray.

Otter Hound, wheaten. Photo by I. Français.

Orb
Eyeball.

Orbit
Eye socket. *See* Eye anatomy

Orange belton
See Belton

Orchitis
Inflammation of one or both of the testicles, noticeable in the dog's movement. The inflammation is painful, and a dog so affected will typically walk with his hindlegs spread slightly and held stiffly, so as not to touch the delicate organs. Treatment may involve the surgical opening and draining of the scrotum, but often prescribed antibiotics will do the job. Acute infections can cause sterility. The condition should be treated as soon as possible.

Oriental expression
See Expression

Oriental Shar-Pei
Inevitably, as a breed gains popularity, new colors and size variations often accompany its reign in the public's favor. Along with the Shar-Pei's gust of favor have arisen variations on that favorite theme. The Oriental Shar-Pei is but one of the smallish Shar-Pei variants—a purebred dog 12–15 inches in height that maintains its babyhood without the need of eye tacking or skin problems. Toys stand less than 12 inches. Developed by Michigan fancier Aaron Silver, the Oripei is a Shar-Pei hybrid achieved through crosses with the Pug. These dogs are not endorsed or registered by the American breed club. *See also* Miniature Shar-Pei

Ormskirk Heeler
See Lancashire Heeler

Ornamentation
Furnishings, which *see.*

Orphan puppies
See Foster mothers

Orthopedic Foundation for Animals, Inc.
See O.F.A.

Os penis
The bone in the dog's penis.

Osteoarthritis
Contrary to the etymology of its title, this is a degenerative and not an inflammatory joint disease. It is a painful disease and is witnessed by the dog's favoring of a specific joint or limb. Prescribed treatments exist, and the suspecting owner should seek veterinary counsel.

Osteoporosis
One result of a calcium deficiency in the dog, it is a condition that causes weak, brittle bones.

Österreichischer Kurzhaariger Pinscher
See Austrian Shorthaired Pinscher

O.T.Ch.
Prefix indicating Obedience Trial Champion, which *see.*

Otitis
Inflammation of the ear. *See* Ear problems.

Otocyon megalotis
See Bat-eared fox

Otodectic mange
Ear mange, *see* Mange.

Otter Hound

The Otter Hound, as unique as it appears, is actually a credible replica of the extinct Vendee Hound. The breed's origin probably traces back to the Southern Hound and the Bloodhound, later crossed to the Water Spaniel to create this daringly dashing hound. The domed-shaped skull, narrow head and deep flews validate the Bloodhound's contribution, while the breed's swimming ability and curly-haired pendant ears accredit the Water Spaniel's blood. The Otter Hound was developed to hunt otters, a task it no longer fulfills. The breed's nose has been compared to the Bloodhound's, one of its direct ancestors. The Otter Hound does one-up the Bloodhound as it regularly scents on land and on water. On land the scent is referred to as a "drag"; on water as a "wash."

In Great Britain, the Otter Hound has a long and romantic history. Perhaps more than any other breed, the Otter Hound has collected many kingly fanciers. The litany of the Otter Hound's royal hunt mates, at first glance, seemingly imitates Shakespeare's history plays: Edward II; Henry VI; Richard III; Henry VIII; King John; Charles II; Edward IV; Henry II and Henry VII; plus one very fine lady: Elizabeth I. Other Otter Hound trivia worth unearthing: in May 1908, the Northern Counties Otterhounds executed the longest drag then on record—23 miles from Ellishaugh Bridge to Catcleugh Reservoir and Blakehopeburn. In 1907, the longest hunt (10

hours and 45 minutes) was recorded by the Carlisle Otterhounds. And the largest otter ever bagged weighed 35 pounds, a credit to the 1909 Essex Otterhounds.

The concept of purebred Otter Hounds escapes the modern reader. In 1920, it was known that only two packs of "purebred" Otter Hounds existed in

Otter Hound, tricolor. Photo by I. Français.

England (one in Kendal and District and the second in Dumfriesshire). Otter Hounds, as a matter of course, were crossed with the finest of Foxhounds (English or Welsh) to improve the hunting ability of the dog. It was noted that purebred Otter Hounds tended to babble more than the Otter–Fox cross, which used its voice with more discretion. Furthermore, the Otter–Fox cross had superior drive and stamina: "It will stand up to the longest hunt when the pure Otterhound is shivering on the banks of the river, and experience has shown that it is of a far more sturdy physique." (Hutchinson, p. 1295) These crosses were shorter coated and therefore didn't hold the water as well, enabling the animal to dry off quicker. Today's Otterhounds thus have kept much of the Foxhound blood, whether or not present-day owners or breeders are aware.

The task of hunting otters was a rugged and arduous task that required the dog to have both strength and swimming

Otter Hound, tricolor. Photo by I. Français.

ability. Racing over rocks and gravel, darting through wooded countryside, and propelling through icy, churning tides—for hours on end—did not slow the persistent, patient Otter Hound. The breed has adapted reasonably well to trailing game other than otter, since otter hunting is hardly in vogue today. (In England, otters are a protected species.) Otter Hounds are, however, less inclined to riot after the game as would a fire-eyed coonhound. The dogs have remarkable coldtrailing ability and can be used on a variety of game.

Patience and perseverance, key to the Otter Hound's original occupation, transfer well to current-day home life. He is a fun-loving, unpredictable companion who is unfailing in his devotion to his

owner. The Otter Hound is also a terrific show dog and is recognized in England, America and Canada. Although the otters are bigger in both the U.S. and Canada, the dogs are not used for that purpose in North America. In 1991, the A.K.C. accepted the breed name as Otterhound, one word, as does the British Kennel Club.

ESSENTIALS OF THE OTTER HOUND: A rough-coated squarely symmetrical hound with its body length slightly exceeding its height. The breed's feet are large and broad and web (the toes are connected with membrane). The head is large, fairly narrow, and well covered with hair. The chest is deep; the topline is level. Shoulders are clean and well sloped. Legs heavy boned and straight. Height: 22–27 inches (56–69 cm). Weight: 65–115 pounds (29–52 kg). The body is well muscled and lean; the skin is thick; the coat is naturally stripped, and the undercoat is oily and waterproof. In length the coat can be 3–6 inches (7.5–15 cm). The Otter Hound comes in a wide variety of colors: grizzle, blue/white, wheaten, black/tan, liver/tan, tricolor, lemon/white, and reddish fawn.

Otter head

Analogy employed in the Border Terrier breed standard, likening that terrier's head to that of an otter.

Otter tail

A tail thick at the base and tapering to the tip, usually covered with short, thick fur. Such a tail is characteristic of the Labrador Retriever and as such is utilized as a rudder for the purpose of swimming.

Otterhoun

See Wetterhoun

Outcrossing

Mating two dogs of the same breed but of different lines. Breeders reserve outcrossing for introducing new qualities into their lines (e.g., larger head, more bone). However, introducing "new blood" can also introduce certain known and/or unknown variables, and most breeders avoid outcrossing for fear of losing tight control of the hard-earned quality of their puppies. If outcrossing is employed, the breeder must know and fully understand the breeding behind both of the dogs involved. *See also* Breeding, Inbreeding, Linebreeding

Out of coat

Term indicating that a long or wirehaired dog has shed its coat for one reason or another (illness, weather, etc.).

Outer coat

The harsh, longer or stand-offish exterior jacket of a double-coated dog.

Outside rabbit

Lure constructed on the outside of a racing strip.

Oval eyes

Self-defining term for eye shape, the most usually requested in dogs.

Oval feet

Similar to cat feet, but the center toes are slightly longer. Spoon-shaped, such feet are required of the German Shorthaired Pointer.

Oval skull

Mild flowing contours from the set-on of one ear to the other.

Ovaries

Small organs located behind the kidneys of bitches. The ovaries through their secretions, influence bodily development and sexual interest. The ovaries begin to influence the development of the bitch before birth and their contribution to the overall animal continues until death. In conjunction with the pituitary gland, the ovaries initiate the sex cycle. The follicular hormone secreted by the ovaries affects the behavior of the bitch in heat and also contributes to the swelling of the vulva and the bloody discharge that signals the likely receptiveness to mating. The ovaries are commonly re-

moved as part of the spaying operation, with few reported complications.

Overbirdiness

Characteristic of a bird dog that searches the same ground over and over again for the felled game.

Overfill

A term which refers to an over-development of bone or muscle above and between the eyes which contributes to an uneven, unchiseled appearance.

Overhang

A pronounced, extending forehead/brow that overhangs the nose when viewed from the side (e.g., Pekingese).

Overhung eyes

Eyes that appear tinier than they may in fact be due to the dog's overly developed eyebrows.

Oval skull illustrated by the English Setter. Photo by I. Français.

Overhung lips
See Lips

Overland
The dog's taking a wide swing around the racing track.

Ovtcharka or dog that guards the ship is a distinctive type of Russian working dog. The ovtcharka from the Caucasian Mountain area is known as the Caucasian Ovtcharka. Photo by I. Français.

Overlay
The darker shaded mantle or blanket that rests on a light background on a dog's coat. As color terminology is so convoluted in the canine world, with many words referring to the same color in different breeds or one word referring to two different colors in different breeds, so too is black overlay (e.g., Belgian Malinois) the equivalent to sable.

Over-reaching gait
When viewed from the side, a trot fault that is caused by more angulation and drive from behind than in front, so that the dog's rear feet are forced to step to one side of the forefeet to avoid interfering or clipping.

Overrun
When hounds do not check, turn back, or when they no longer scent the line, they are said to have overrun.

Oversexed dogs
See Masturbation

Overweight dogs
See Obesity

Ovtcharka
Ovtcharka (sometimes less properly spelled *Owtcharka*) means dog that guards the ship in Russian. The family is nordic in characteristics, mostly large, and all quite protective. *See also* Caucasian Ovtcharka; South Russian Ovtcharka; Mid-Asian Ovtcharka; Transcaucasian Ovtcharka; North Caucasian Steppe Ovtcharka

Ovulation
When the follicles of the bitch break open, releasing the egg to be fertilized. *See also* Breeding

Owczarek Podhalanski
The Owczarek Podhalanski, also known as the Polish Mountain Sheepdog, the Owczarek Tatrazanski, or simply, Tatra, is an indigenous mountain worker of Poland. The Tatra is probably related to the flock guardian breeds of Czechoslovakia and Hungary, although many still connect it with the Bergamasco of Italy. The Owczarek Podhalanski is still used as a flock guard that is able to hold his own against the most formidable of foes. Other times, this shepherd is used as a cart puller. In the U.S. and Canada, he has been selected for military and police work. A dog greatly dedicated to the task at hand, the Tatra is independent and quick-minded, often aloof but always on the guard.
ESSENTIALS OF THE OWCZAREK PODHALANSKI : Solid white and massive. Its coat is long and dense—both straight and wavy varieties occur, as does either pure or creamy coloration. Height: 24–34 inches (61–86.5 cm). Weight: 100–150 pounds (45–69 kg). Tatras are thick boned and muscular throughout their bodies.

Owczarek Podhalanski, white. Photo by I. Français.

Owczarek Tatrazanski
See Owczarek Podhalanski

Owner liability

There are many legal considerations involved with dog ownership. An owner is responsible—legally—for controlling his dog. Personal injury, property, and nuisance are considered typically by most authorities (national or state) to be owner-liable. The damaging of livestock, rearrangement of a neighbor's prize eggplant garden, the unsolicited fertilization of that gardener's lawn, or the biting of that gardener's scolding finger are all the responsibilities of the dog's owner. A dog is property; a dog cannot be sued, nor can it sue; a dog has no legal rights. Those fanciers who claim that the appellation "owner," attached to one who shares his home with a dog, is improper terminology will not find themselves fending well in the legal system.

Awards given by courts for damages or injuries incurred by an owner's cur vary substantially. Some courts award compensation for emotional upheaval and wear (i.e., pain and suffering). The usual rule is loss of service, economic or emotional, as the court deems appropriate and fair. The legal regula-tions concerning owner liability vary from country to country and indeed from state to state—owners should be aware of the particulars of these laws.

Owner-handler

The person handling a dog in the ring is the dog's registered owner, though not necessarily.

Oxytocin

A drug that can be used to induce labor. It is preferred over some other drugs because it affects the uterus more directly than others. Oxytocin should be administered only by a veterinarian.

Owner-handler Jeffrey Pepper with Ch. Vendric Bravo under judge Anna Katherine Nicholas. Mr. Pepper is a well-known breeder of the Golden Retriever as well as Petit Basset Griffon Vendeen.

Pace

A rolling motion to the body, a gait in which the left foreleg and left hindleg advance in unison, followed by the right foreleg and the right hindleg. Pace is associated with some breeds when they are moving slowly (e.g., Great Pyrenees, English Springer Spaniel) and with others when walking or trotting (e.g., Old English Sheepdog).

Pachon de Vitoria

See Perdiguero Navarro

Pack

1) A group of hounds that is regularly hunted together. *See also* Packhounds, Nordic dogs, Canine behavior, Wolves

2) The astrakhan-appearing and feeling portion of the lion-clipped Poodle's coat.

Packhounds, keen in nose and hollow in voice, work together as a unit. "Basset Hounds Hunting" by Vernon Stokes captures these low-legged packhounds in slow but determined pursuit.

Packhounds

Foxhounds and the older staghounds are the typical hounds which lead pack existences. Fox hunting and stag hunting required large packs of scenthounds to track the wily and fast fox and the un-staggering stag. Packhounds were kept by the nobility and upper-class families of England and France, where the sports were most prominent. French packhounds include the hounds of the Vendeen and Gascogne areas as well as the Poitevin, Billy, and Porcelaine, to name just a few. In America, the coonhound breeds are also hunted in packs, as are most of the curs.

Packs of foxhounds are usually followed by hunters on horseback, with a couple of exceptions. Other packs of foot hounds are followed by a walking field. British hounds of this sort include the Beagle, Basset Hound and Otter Hound. The Swiss have a number of scenthound breeds (which are known as laufhunds, or "walking" dogs). The Berner, Luzerner and Schweizer areas have each developed two laufhunds, one tall and one short.

Pack hunting has diminished tremendously over the years. While there are still approximately 200 foxhound packs in England, the number of staghounds and draghounds have dwindled to very few. Staghound hunting, once very popular in Ireland as well as England, involved following the dogs on horseback, much like fox hunting. Staghounds are essentially foxhounds used for stag hunting. Draghounds, standing about 20 inches (51 cm) at the shoulder, were used for drag racing. The hounds followed a trail which was placed on the ground by *dragging* a *drag* (a feces-filled sack) across the runway where the dogs were to race. For reasons unbeknownst to these authors, the excitement of watching British hounds' rioting over deer dung down an unpaved thoroughfare has waned over the years. Drag hunting today commonly involves the dragging (pulling) of an animal pelt along a determined course, often leading to a live, caged animal. Drag hunting is popular especially with American coonhunters, who employ this type of hunting as pre-season training.

Dogs that are raised in packs tend to be more dog-oriented than people-oriented. Pack existence depends on an inherent hierarchy, similar to the social organization of wolves. These are very gregarious and intuitive dogs that may not necessarily adapt themselves to life in a single-dog home where there are no fellow canines to muddle about with nor foxes to chase on Saturday mornings. Most dogs, however, are able to rechannel their pack instincts, placing their human master as "leader of the pack" and their homes as their territory. Though not hounds, many nordic dogs, namely the sled dogs, also exist in packs. Their sociability and complacent natures are comparable to other pack dogs.

Pack sense

When the hounds of a pack run in mass formation well and honor each other's cry.

Padding

Padding can refer to the desired development of the lips to foster the proper breed expression (i.e., the Boxer's lips should be well padded); secondly, padding as applying to gait, according to the American Kennel Club, is a compensating action to offset constant concussion when a straight front is subjected to over-drive from the rear—the front feet flip upward in a split-second delaying action to coordinate stride of forelegs with longer stride from behind.

Paddling

The front feet thrown out sideways in an uncontrolled fashion; this gaiting fault is named after the swing and dip of a canoeist's paddle. The swinging is caused by a pinching in at the elbow and shoulder joints. Sometimes referred to as "tied at the elbows."

Paddock judge

One who has charge of dogs before a

race, makes identification inspection, supervises weighing, grooms, etc.

Pads

See Feet anatomy

Paisley Terrier

An early type of Skye Terrier, the Paisley Terrier (or Clydesdale Terrier) wasn't as dapper as today's silky coated Skye Terrier. This is the smoothest of the Skye Terrier's forebears and the last to emerge. With the appealing size of the Yorkie and the true character of the Skye, the Paisley Terrier was immensely popular in Glasgow exhibitions in the 1860s. At this

Packhounds such as the Chiens Françaises are still quite numerous in France. These large hunting dogs thrive on the sport and work of hunting and are oriented strongly towards their fellow hounds. Photo by I. Français.

Padding of the Boxer's lips gives the breed its correct expression.

time the breed was even called the Glasgow Terrier. The popularity of the Paisley, however, flared into controversy with the advocates of the silky Skye, which of course prevailed. It was believed that a few specimens still existed in Glasgow in the 1930s. Today the true Paisleys have surely faded from the canine wardrobe.

Palate

Roof of the mouth, the fusion of the two bony-fleshy partitions which separate the respiratory and digestive passages within the head. The hard palate, in front, is composed of bone and begins behind the upper incisor teeth, forming the major part of the roof of the mouth. The soft palate is a soft, fleshy extension of the hard palate which continues backwards to end near the larynx.

An overly developed soft palate, the condition known as prolonged soft palate, occurs in some dogs, especially the shorter faced (brachycephalic) breeds. Such a condition can be most harmful to an animal.

Palate, cleft

See Cleft palate

Panting. Heavily coated dogs like these Komondorok can suffer from the heat. Shade and water are a must for all dogs kept outdoors in warm weather. Photo by R. Reagan.

Pampas fox

See South American foxes

Pancreas

The primary functions of this organ are to secrete enzymes that aid digestion and to regulate the body's use of blood sugar. *See also* Digestive system

Pancreatic degenerative atrophy

A disease also known as juvenile atrophy of the pancreas, not uncommon in young dogs. German Shepherd Dogs and Collies have a notable number of occurrences. Dogs affected by pancreatic degenerative atrophy tend to lose weight despite their unappeasable appetites. Food goes undigested and can be detected in the stools: coprophagy often accompanies the disease. The stools are soft and unformed. A veterinarian should be contacted; prescribed tablets can help management.

Pancreatitis

The two major types of pancreatitis are *acute* and *chronic*. In acute pancreatitis, the lipase and serum levels of the pancreatic enzyme are elevated, causing adverse reactions in the animal. In chronic pancreatitis, the enzyme levels decrease, causing adverse reactions in the dog. Both conditions are serious and can result in death. They are diagnosed only by a trained professional.

Panosteitis

A term sometimes used to refer to inflammation of every part of the bone.

Panting

In itself a normal action of the dog, serving mostly to cool the animal through evaporation of moisture in the mouth and throat. Dogs have relatively far fewer sweat glands than do humans. The result is that dogs rely on panting to cool themselves in excessive heat. Panting can be a sign of danger to the dog. Sharp, continuous panting is one warning sign of heat stroke, which *see*. Panting as the result of only moderate exercise can be a sign of obesity, poor health, heartworms, and many other dangerous conditions. If such is the case, a veterinary check-up is recommended.

Pants

Breeches or trousers, used in many breed standards.

Paper feet

Feet that lack sufficient padding; like ferret feet but narrowness is not necessarily present.

Papillomas
See Polyps

Papillon

The Épagneul Nain of Belgium, a favorite of royalty, is said to be the ancestor of the delicately winged, windblown Papillon. Prized for his butterflylike ears and white blaze delineating the center of his head, the Papillon is one of the foremost European toy breeds. In the 1500s, the breed was well known in Spain, although they were equally adored in France and Italy. Whether or not the bichons of Bologna, where the Papillon achieved a good deal of attention, contributed to the breed's make-up is uncertain. Many historic Papillon breeders lived in Bologna and it is no mystery that most Bolognese dog fanciers also favored the bichon types. Additionally, many Spaniards took their knapsack-napping Paps with them to South America. The breed took on well on that continent too. It is certain that the Papillon was not affected by the Chihuahua, as once purported. More likely the Pap contributed *its* long-coat genes to the creation of the Longhaired Chihuahua.

The name Papillon, meaning butterfly in French, is perhaps one of the most ex-

quisite names in dogdom. The dogs whose ears fail to stand erect are termed *phalene*, meaning moth. Not too much perception is required to surmise which type has been favored through the course of history. In France today, Papillons are called *Le Chien Ecureuil*, or Squirrel Dog, in honor of their tails, not their quarry. Incidentally, they have been effectively used as both rabbiters and ratters.

The Papillon's present-day exceptional photogenic abilities are not difficult to explain. As favorites of European royalty, the Papillon was included in many kingly and queenly portraits. Such greats as Rembrandt, Van Dyck, Watteau, Rubens, and Fragonard rendered the Papillon's whimsical and winning ways on canvas alongside such nobles as Madame de Pompadour and Marie Antoinette.

Unlike many ancient European purebreds, the Papillon didn't take a stronger foothold upon the popularity of the

Papillon, particolor.

Papillon. Photographs by I. Français.

purebred dog show at the turn of the nineteenth century. Not until the mid-1920s did the Kennel Club of Great Britain recognize the breed; in 1923, a couple of Papillons appeared in one British exhibition in the Miscellaneous Foreign Dogs Class. In America, the breed's acceptance wasn't until about a decade later. The A.K.C. recognized the Papillon in 1935.

Papillon, white with black particolor. Photo by I. Français.

These are prime house dogs and primarily indoor companions, genuinely hardy and alert; though delicate and graceful, they are untainted by colder weather. It is generally accepted that the dogs do not need "coddling" in the winter, although cuddling is perfectly accepted and expected. They are catlike in cleanliness and neat-footedness. *See also* Continental Toy Spaniel, Phalene.

ESSENTIALS OF THE PAPILLON: Finely boned and dainty, the Papillon flowers in elegance suitably French. Its distinguishing characteristic is its beautiful butterfly ears which flare out, like the widespread wings of a full-grown butterfly. It is not a cobby dog. The head is small with a well-defined stop. The skull should be rounded between the ears, the muzzle one-third the total length of the head, pointier and thinner than skull, with stop accentuated. Ears should be large with rounded tips, heavily fringed, set well back and completely erect. The neck is of medium length. Shoulders are well developed and sloping back. The chest deep; forelegs straight and fine boned. The top line is even; the ribs well sprung; belly slightly arched. The coat is abundant, silky and flowing—straight with a resilient quality. Breeches or culottes are noticeable. Height: 8–11 inches (20–28 cm). The Papillon is particolored: basically white, with patches of any color (except liver). Symmetrical facial markings are desired, including a white blaze down the face. Tail flows with plume.

Papuan Dog

First described in 1929, the Papuan is a small tribal dog that has believedly existed in its native New Guinea for centuries. It is a small, shorthaired, prick-eared pariah type which has been known to cohabitate with the natives. The Papuan is one of New Guinea's few indigenous dogs, the New Guinea Singing Dog and the New Ireland Dog among them.

Parainfluenza

See Canine parainfluenza

Paralysis

Loss of motor coordination and sensation in any part of the body is paralysis of the affected part(s). Paralysis can occur as a result of injury (a blow to the head) or disease (rabies, distemper, toxoplasmosis). Paralysis of the face muscles, often affecting only one side of the head, can be a sign of nerve inflammation, which can be treated with antibiotics, anti-inflammatories, and rest. Paralysis of the hindquarters region is often a sign of spinal cord or intervertebral disc damage, both of which are very serious conditions. Paralysis is a sign of nerve damage or disorder. Therefore, whether mild and localized or acute and widespread, all paralysis demands immediate attention from a veterinarian.

Paraphimosis

When the penis, often of an adolescent dog, protrudes through the sheath, swells, and cannot be withdrawn.

Parasite

A living organism that lives in or on a host, from which it derives sustenance but which it does not benefit. Parasitic organisms that commonly affect dogs include: fleas; lice; mites; ticks; flukes; heartworms; hookworms; roundworms; tapeworms; whipworms; babesias; coccidia; and toxoplasmas, which *see*.

Parathyroid glands

Located near the thyroid gland, the parathyroid glands secrete a hormone that is important in the regulation of calcium in the body.

Parent club

National breed club that assumes responsibility for the promotion, betterment and standing of its breed. In order for a breed to become recognized by the national kennel club, it must have a parent club, comprised of fanciers, breeders, and owners, to draw up its standard. The national registry then adopts the breed standard. *See also* Kennel clubs

southeast Asian origins that migrated to Australia, probably with aborigines; it has existed in a feral or wild state for millennia. These pariahs are kept today by aborigines, although most Dingoes in Australia live in a wild state. Evidence exists supporting the keeping of Australian Dingoes as pets by the aborigines for many centuries. Theoretically, dogs, without the tampering of humans, left to breed freely, would eventually appear very much like a Dingo.

Despite the huge land expanses that separate the various pariahs, these dogs tend to range from red to tawny, possess straight-standing prick ears and me-

Pariahs occupy a considerably important position in the development and domestication of canines. The Podengos of Portugal are believably closely related to native pariahs. Photo by I. Français.

Pariahs

The pariah group includes semi-wild and feral dogs that occur across southern Asia, Europe and eastern Africa. These "scavenger" dogs were once considered unleashed mongrels that had escaped domestication. More likely, pariahs represent a pure canid, an original strain of canine, that has never been completely domesticated. The Dingo is a pariah of

dium-length coat. Variations, of course, occur: there are long and shorthaired pariahs, black and white pariahs as well as merle or brindle pariahs. Type ranges dramatically from the heavy boned, large pariah of the Caucasus and Turkey to the sighthound type pariah of the Mediterranean area.

Pariahs have survived in a semi-domesticated state which Lois E. Beuler, author of *Wild Dogs of the World*, describes as a "more or less symbiotic relationship with man." This symbiotic relationship is closely akin to one theory of dog's domestication. Wild dogs (wolves, jackals, pariahs?) were attracted to the garbage dumps of man; man appreciated free garbage collection service. This arrangement led to man and dog's side-by-side relationship. (*See* Domestication of the dog.) The link between wolf and dog may indeed be welded by the pariah dog, in which case domesticated canines are descendants of pariahs. Modern research has not unveiled the truth or falsehood of this assertion. It is accepted that domestic dog is a descendant of the gray wolf—the evolutionary steps are not known.

Among the world's pariahs are dogs which inhabit New Guinea, Australia, Polynesia, Malaysia and New Ireland. The New Guinea Singing Dog, Australian Dingo, Hawaiian Poi Dog and Telomian are examples of these pariahs. America has a fair number of pariah types that derive from various sources; the Carolina Dog is one such dog. The most popular pets that are of pariah be-

ginnings are the Basenji, Canaan Dog, and Chihuahua. Some sources link the pariahs directly with the sighthound types; the Pharaoh Hound, Ibizan Hound, Portuguese Podengos, and Cirneco dell'Etna are among such sighthounds associated with the pariah family. Hairless dogs (which *see*) also are often associated with the pariah family.

Parotid gland
Salivary glands located to the front of each ear.

Parrot
An overshot bite.

Parson Jack Russell Terrier
See Jack Russell Terrier

Parvovirus
Canine-specific viral infection. Parvo was first recognized as a problem in the late 1970s, with two parvovirus disease forms, myocarditis and enteritis. Today only the enteritis form is seen. Parvo can be very lethal, especially to puppies, and the disease occurs worldwide. The virus is released in the feces of infected dogs, and ingestion of such fecal matter is the most common way of parvo transmission. Indicative signs include vomiting, bloody runny stools, and fever. Speedy diagnosis and treatment are a must. Today this disease is fairly well controlled, provided that owners and breeders act responsibly by keeping all shots up-to-date.

Pastern
Recognized commonly as the region of the foreleg between the wrist (carpus) and the digits. Pastern types vary greatly in strength, slope, and length. Pastern terminology includes the following: bare pasterns, distended pastern joint, down in pasterns, slanting pasterns, slope of pasterns, sunken pasterns, and upright pasterns, which *see*.

Pastore Abruzzese
See Maremma Sheepdog

Patchy tongue
An incompletely pigmented tongue, a fault occurring in breeds that have blue-

black tongues (e.g., Chow Chow, Chinese Shar-Pei).

Patents

Patenting of genetic engineering is an aspect of dogs as property which is expanding quickly. Under such a patent, new dog breeds can be patented, and the founder of the breed shall receive a royalty each time a patented animal gives birth or generates income. Founders Hugh Stephens, Johannes Plott, and David Leavitt (or their next of kin, perhaps) will take advantage of such good news. The authors are fearful, however, that 500 immediate relatives of Herr Louis Dobermann, St. Bernard and St. Hubert will suddenly emerge looking for retroactive royalties!

Patterdale Terrier

A product of the Yorkshire and Lake District of Britain, the Patterdale is a robust, sturdy working stock dog. The name Patterdale was chosen after a village in Cumbria, where the dogs are common. Breeders are solely interested in working abilities. Even today types vary somewhat. The Patterdale is mostly too vicious to hunt fox with pack hounds, unless it's fox extermination and not sport that is desired. This quality is certainly suggestive of the Bull Terrier in its blood. The Patterdale is a rather tiny dog, weighing no more than 13 pounds (6 kg), and laid-back as terriers go. This is a working dog and not solely a companion dog. It is also an astounding digger. Still common in England, there are a few select Patterdale owners in the United States. The first of these dogs were im-

ported in the year 1979.

ESSENTIALS OF THE PATTERDALE TERRIER: Cheekier and thicker than most any terrier, this well-built tiny stock dog stands only 12 inches (30.5 cm) high and weighs

12–13 pounds (5.5–6 kg). Its small size can be used as a reverse scale to measure its gameness and tenacity. The coat is weather-resistant and is short and coarse. Colors: Black, red, chocolate, black/tan.

Patti

This shepherd and guard dog was one of India's most useful dogs. While nearly extinct today, certain Tamil nomads still work this dog to protect the herds from foxes and other predators. Intelligent and hardy, these black and tan dogs are said to resemble Alsatians.

Paw

See Feet anatomy

Peak

Various meanings depending on breed: for instance in the Basset Hound, the peak refers to the rather prominent occipital crest; on the head of the Irish Water Spaniel, the peak is a coat pattern reference; in the Cardigan Welsh Corgi, it refers to head markings, i.e. widow's peak.

Pear-shaped head

The well-contoured head of the Bedlington Terrier or Austrian Pinscher.

Patterdale Terrier, black. Photo by I. Français.

Patterdale Terrier, red.

Pedigree is a formal record of a purebred dog's known ancestors. This pedigree, issued by the Japanese Kennel Club, belongs to author Andrew De Prisco's Shiba Inu Jacquet JP's Tengu. Bred by Richard Tomita, Tengu's sire is Katsuranihiki of Oikawa House ("Chibi") and dam is Kurotomi of Ome Shinjosow ("Kuro").

Pedaling

When the driver keeps one foot on the runner of the sled and pedals or pushes with the other.

Pedigree

The record of a purebred dog's ancestry is known as a pedigree. Pedigrees usually include at least three generations of a dog's descent and, almost without exception, are written. The Bedouin nomads passed down their Saluki pedigrees by word of mouth, chanted from memory, from generation to generation. Such a system today for the world's 400+ breeds would be wonderfully chaotic, to say the least. A pedigree should not be confused with a registration certificate.

tificate for absolute proof that the dog is a purebred. Remember that pedigree blanks are readily available through pet shops, and are even printed as compliments of dog food companies and certain breed periodicals.

Peintinger Bracke

See Styrian Roughhaired Mountain Hound

Peking Palasthund

See Pekingese

Pekingese

The Pekingese of Peking has preferred for centuries the company of humans rather than his fraternal Pekes. Of course the breed finds its unhumble beginnings in the Orient, but surely it has delighted more than just a billion Chinese. Ever since its introduction to England in the late 1800s, the breed has been admired and promoted by Westerners. The Peke is by definition devoted to his human charges, a task he has historically taken gravely serious. The tale of the six Pekes guarding the body of their deceased mistress during the Chinese war of 1860 is certainly representative of the breed's unwaning dedication and love for its human god, whose every step and breath is foremost in his life.

The Pekingese rolled about Chinese palaces prior to the first century. When the Chinese, under Emperor Ming-Ti, embraced the teachings of the Buddha, the dog's type began to regard the sacred lion in the Great One's teachings. The concept of "lion" was a fascinating and inspiring one to the Chinese, who never saw the lion of Africa. The tiger-lions that emerge in Chinese art verifies the people's reverence of the great "king of the jungle." For thousands of years, the Pekingese has been associated with the Chinese devotion to Buddhism. Like the Buddha lion, the lionlike Pekingese was worthy of great homage and laud. Bred by the chief eunuch, the tiny "Lion Dogs" were kept in the sacred temple. The Pekes preceded the empress

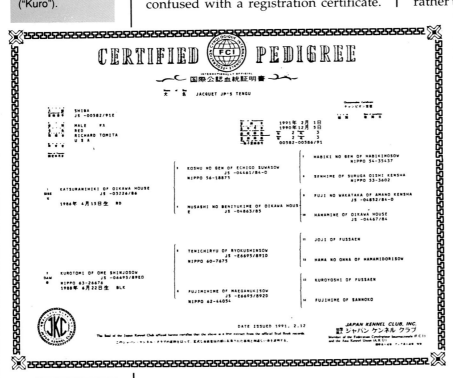

The former is merely a statement by a breeder of the dog's ancestors; it does not vouch for the pure breeding behind the particular dog or puppy. The latter, a registration certificate, is issued by the national kennel club and does indeed verify that the dog's parents were both registered purebred dogs. Do not be swayed by a pedigree paper, as handsome, official and impressive as it may appear with its litany of alliterating, tongue-twisting, title-toting purebreds; owners must insist on a registration cer-

into the Chamber of Ceremonies and announced her arrival. Four select Pekes constituted the empress's body guard. Always on guard against evil and wrongdoing, the Pekingese shared the empress's pillow, fan and egg foo yung.

Chinese vengeance is far-reaching and relentless: punishment for theft or defamation of any of the empress's dogs

Pekingese, fawn.

was slow death by torture. During the nineteenth-century "reign" of Dowager Empress T'zǔ Hsi, the overbearing and manic depressive guardian of an enthroned infant emperor, hundreds of Pekes inhabited the summer palace. For the Empress, her Pekes, particularly the sunshine-evoking golden dogs, were among the few favored. Handpainted flowers and sunfilled Pekingese adorned the silken screens and tapestries of the palace. During T'zǔ Hsi's reign (a phenomenon the feminist movement has yet to analyze), the palace ladies were strongly encouraged in the arts. The Empress herself instructed the ladies in color schemes and textures: poised and posed, the Peke sat patiently through these palette-dipping sessions. Toward the care-taking eunuchs, the new Empress was a fury, for she emphatically controlled their breeding practices. Even the age-old tradition of encouraging the

dog's short, flat faces by nailing fresh pork to a board for the dogs to lick was rigidly suppressed. Verily, the Peke couldn't candidly display his "swelling cape of dignity" in public and nibble pig dribblings in private. To illustrate the scope of the Empress's unbalanced devotion to her dogs, let us present, in her own verse, her dogs' poetic though equally unbalanced diet:

Sharks' fins and curlews' livers and the breasts of

quails, on these may it be fed, and for drink give it

the tea that is brewed from the Spring buds of the bush that groweth in the province of Han Kon, or the

milk of antelopes that pasture in the Imperial parks,

or broth made from the nests of sea swallows.

Thus shall it preserve its integrity and self-respect,

and in the day of sickness let it be

Pekingese, fawn.

Pekingese, red.

anointed with the
    clarified fat of the leg of a sacred leopard and give

In the United States, the Pekingese has been among the favored purebreds since 1909, the year of its A.K.C. acceptance.

Pekingese, black.

it to drink a throstle's egg shell—full of the juice
    of the custard apple in which has been dissolved
    three pinches of shredded rhinoceros horn—and apply to
    it piebald leeches—

England accepted the breed prior to this, in 1893. In both countries the breed has countless fans and its overall popularity cannot be "stifled." The Peke, despite his petiteness, is courageous and bold. His independence and confidence should imply combativeness rather than delicacy. The dog is accustomed to being unchallenged and foremost in his master's eyes. His coat requires extensive grooming on a regular basis.

The authors acknowledge the amusing translation of Mrs. Coath Dixey, and they advise the reader not to try this diet or remedy at home.

ESSENTIALS OF THE PEKINGESE: He is ever alert and dignified. The body is short with a broad chest. The head is wider than deep, and the skull is flat and deep between the ears. The profile is flat with the nose well set between the eyes. The shape of the body is heavy in front, with well-sprung ribs, and a broad chest. The

The Peke can be recognized in the bronze works of Korea, dating back to 2000 B.C. The breed's connection to Tibetan-type lion dogs is defined by the Dalai Lama of Tibet's yearly tribute to the court of Peking with his very fancied toy dog. As a favored animal of the Buddhist, the Pekingese was regularly portrayed in the art of that faith: tapestries, paintings, silks, and the elegant like.

Pekingese, white.

back is level and not too long for the body. Legs short. Feet flat, toes turned out, not round. The coat is long and straight, with the profuse mane extending beyond the shoulders and forming a cape around the neck. The outer coat is coarse, the undercoat thick. Weight in three categories: under 6 pounds (2.5 kg), 6–8 pounds (2.5–3.5 kg), 8–14 pounds (3.5–6.5 kg). Colors: red, fawn, black, black/tan, sable, brindle, white, and particolor. All dogs should be masked with spectacles around the eyes.

Pelvic angle
See Hindquarters

Pelvic girdle
Pelvis. *See* Hindquarters

Pelvis
Hip bone. *See* Hindquarters

Pembroke Welsh Corgi
It is known that the Pembroke is a very old breed, with written references dating back to 920–1107 A.D. The breed's early use was as a cattle drover, and it was especially popular from the fourteenth through the eighteenth centuries, when professional drovers would transport farmers' cattle long distances to the nearest market. The most commonly mentioned theory maintains that the Pembroke first entered Britain with Flemish weavers who were brought to the British Isles by Henry I of England and established in Wales. It is stated that these weavers found their Corgis indispensable and therefore brought them along, often at the cost of other posses-

sions which could not all be transported. Nineteenth-century breeders rou-

tinely crossed the Pembroke Corgi with the Cardigan—this explains readily why the breeds appear so similar today. Such crosses diminished the differences that may have once been noteworthy. Today, breeders are determined to keep the two highly enchanting, low-set herders distinct. Pembies are often born tailless, Cardigans never. Admittedly, differences exist, but these are surely more obvious to Corgi lovers than to the average fancier and casual Corgi enthusiast.

ESSENTIALS OF THE PEMBROKE WELSH CORGI: Set low, of good strength, and built solidly, the Pembroke Corgi evokes the impression of substance and stamina, efficiently packed into a small space. The head is foxy in shape and appearance, but never sly in expression; skull fairly wide and flat between

Pembroke Welsh Corgi, red with white.

Pembroke Welsh Corgi, black and tan with white. Photographs by I. Français.

the ears. The foreface is nicely chiseled to give a tapered muzzle. The ears are erect and firm, medium in size, coming to a slightly rounded point. The eyes, medium sized and oval, are set somewhat obliquely; eyes dark but not black, nor yellow or bluish. The coat is medium in length, short, and thick; it is double—the outer is longer and coarser. On the body the length varies. Height: 10–12 inches (25.5–30.5 cm). Weight: 30 pounds (13.5 kg) or less. Colors include red, sable, fawn, and black and tan, often with white. The tail is docked as short as possible—this feature in addition to the foxy expression distinguishes him from the Cardigan.

Perdiguero de Burgos, liver and white with ticking. Photo by I. Français.

Pemphigus vulgaris
See Canine pemphigus

Penciled
See Pily coat

Penciling
Black lines which run down the topside of the toes of some breeds (e.g., Gordon Setter, Doberman).

Pendant ears
See Drop ears

Penis
The male sex organ and one part of the male's reproductive system.

Pepita
Pied coloration in the Mudi.

Peppering
Black and white hairs admixed (e.g., pepper and salt Schnauzers).

Perception
The act of feeling, comprehending, recognizing, or otherwise observing or becoming aware of something. The primary ways in which the dog perceives are through sight, hearing, touch, taste, and smell. Therefore, the primary organs involved in perception are: the eyes, ears, skin, tongue, nose, which *see*. *See also* Nervous system, Nose, Canine behavior

Perdigueiro Português
See Portuguese Pointer

Perdiguero
Spanish for pointer; the Portuguese word is *Perdigueiro*.

Perdiguero Burgales
See Perdiguero de Burgos

Perdiguero de Burgos
A pointing dog, native to Spain that, although traced to old lines, is a relatively new breed in its present form. Records show that Don Alonso Martinez, during the time of King Phillip VI (1700s), penned a description of dogs having similar characteristics as the Perdiguero de Burgos, or Spanish Pointer. It has been speculated that the breed originated from crosses of various old Spanish breeds, including the Pachon Iberico and the Sabueso Hound. The original specimens were much larger than today's breed. They were more heavily built and often attained 30 inches (76 cm) in height at the withers. Most likely the infusion of Pointer blood lightened the bone and added grace to the once deliberate dogs. Whereas the breed was used almost exclusively on larger game, such as deer, it is employed today on hare, partridge and other small, quick game.

As a companion, the Perdiguero is an adaptable, likable dog that is obedient and consistent. As a hunter, the Perdiguero is sublime, able to retrieve from water and work rough, mountainous terrain.

ESSENTIALS OF THE PERDIGUERO DE BURGOS: A big dog yet without heavy bone. The head is strong, with square muzzle, sizable ears, prominent lips and noticeable dewlap. The body is well muscled yet slender. The coat is liver and white, with or without patches or ticking; in length and texture, it is short and fine. Height: 20–24 inches (51–61 cm). Weight: 55–66 pounds (25–30 kg). The temperament is quiet, trustworthy, and affectionate.

Perdiguero Navarro

A very old breed of hunting dog that has inhabited the European continent and contributed to its hunting-dog gene pool for centuries. The distinctive feature of the breed is its split or double nose. The Navarro, also known as the Old Spanish Pointer, has been instrumental in the creation and perfection of countless Continental and British gundogs through the ages. Yet the breed was not recognized by the Spanish Kennel Club until 1911, due to the dwindling numbers of Navarros. In fact, the breed was believed extinct at various moments of the twentieth century. Fortunately, a group is trying to preserve and revive the breed in Spain today, yet the task before them is challenging. The present type is virtually identical to the prototypical dog that helped produce the European setters, vorstehunds and braques of Germany and France.

ESSENTIALS OF THE PERDIGUERO NAVARRO: With a bony, sinewy conformation, the Perdiguero Navarro exemplifies the ancient pointer body type. The general appearance is coarse yet functional. The skull is strong; the muzzle square. Prominent lips and dewlap are present; the body's skin is taut. The split or double nose is a distinctive feature of the breed. Height: 20–24 inches (51–61 cm). Weight: 55–66 pounds (25–30 kg). Coat is of two varieties: smooth and longhaired. Color: white base with orange markings or liver/white with ticking.

Perineal hernias
See Hernias

Periodontitis

Periodontal disease is the leading cause of canine tooth loss; 98% of all tooth loss is attributable to periodontitis; 75% of all veterinarian-treated tooth problems are due to the disease. Periodontitis is an acute or chronic inflammation of the tissue surrounding the tooth, the result of untreated gingivitis. The disease can be local, affecting one tooth, but is more usually generalized.

Lack of masticatory exercise (chewing!) results in functional insufficiency of the jawbones and may add to periodontal disturbance and eventual disease. The

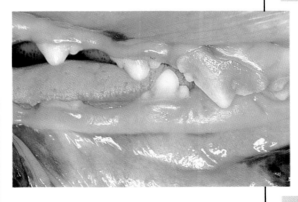

disease begins as gingivitis, which is caused by plaque and bacteria on the tooth. Certain breeds of dog are more susceptible to the disease than others because of the positioning of their teeth; food deposits more frequently in irregularly formed jaws (such as in Bulldogs and other brachycephalic dogs).

Periodontitis causes the resultant bac-

Perdiguero Navarro, liver/white with ticking. Photo by I. Français.

Periodontitis is a disease of the gums, the result of untreated gingivitis, which leads to tooth loss and possible heart and kidney disease.

terial toxins to be absorbed into the blood stream and potentially to the heart and kidneys. In the infected mouth, teeth are loosened; tartar, unsightly and bad smelling, accumulates heavily; and the dog experiences a severe loss of appetite. Long-standing periodontal disease manifests itself in simple symptoms such as diarrhea and vomiting.

Calculus must be removed by a veterinarian; a general anesthesia is recommended. Scaling, polishing and necessary extractions, and flushing the gums with a saline solution are among the vet's tasks. The disease is rarely cured but can be prevented by owners. Clean teeth are linked to chewing—owners must provide their dogs with a hard chew device to remove plaque build-up which in turn can cause the disease. Rawhide is fun but not an acceptable device for preventive dental care. *See also* Dental care, Nylon bones, Gingivitis

Perro de Pastor Mallorquin, black. Photo by I. Français.

Peristalsis

The act by which food is moved through the digestive system, which *see*.

Perro

Spanish for dog. The Perro de Presa Canario, Perro de Pastor Mallorquin, Perro Flora (Peruvian Inca Orchid) and Perro Mastin del Pireneo (Pyrenean Mastiff) are examples of Spanish *perros*.

Perro de Pastor Catalan

See Catalan Sheepdog

Perro de Agua de Español

See Water Dog of Spain

Perro de Pastor Mallorquin

The Ca de Bestiar or Perros de Pastor Mallorquin were brought to the steamy Balearic Islands, where they mutated as their need dictated, or their breedings were shepherded by rural peoples. The isolation of this off-the-coast-of-Spain island of course played a role in the development of this Spanish flock guardian. In present-day Spain the Ca can be found on farms and other rural areas, although he is not known outside of Spain. The dog has extreme abilities to withstand heat and is most territorial. Efficiently built with an easycare coat, the Perro de Pastor Mallorquin might be a fine candidate for flock guarding programs in the United States, particularly in the hotter regions. A fair number of specimens are being used in Brazil for guarding purposes.

Spanish owners focus mainly on utility and are less concerned with breed purity; of course, for purebred dog enthusiasts, this means a thoroughbred Perro de Pastor Mallorquin may indeed be a difficult find.

ESSENTIALS OF THE PERRO DE PASTOR MALLORQUIN: The head, especially on the shorthaired variety, is sharply defined; the muzzle tapers slightly, contributing to the chiseled impression, and ends in a dark, solid-colored nose. Height: 19–22 inches (48–56 cm). Weight: 45–60 pounds (20.5–27 kg). The ears should be left natural and the tail undocked. The legs should be of good length, insuring a steady, enduring stride. Coat can be either *pelo corto* (short) or *pelo largo* (long, actually medium) in length. Colors: black or dark brindle.

Perro de Presa Canario

Developed on the Canary Islands, the modern Canary Dog is a cross between the native and indigenous Bardino Majero (now extinct) and the Mastiff of England, brought over in the 1800s. These crossbred dogs were selectively bred for fighting ability. With the outlawing of dog fighting on the island and the introduction of foreign dogs such as the German Shepherd Dog, the Canary Dog faced extinction by the 1960s. Thanks to dedicated breeders, the Canary Dog was saved and today enjoys renewed popularity. Dr. Carl Semencic is responsible for the breed's growing American fancy and the name "Canary Dog." The Canary Dog requires a dominant master and an attentive human family; no member can be uncomfortable around dogs. Canaries make outstanding guards; their appearance is a deterrent and their ability a detriment to any intruder.

ESSENTIALS OF THE PERRO DE PRESA CANARIO: Powerful square head, nearly as wide as it is long; muzzle is broad; jaw is strong. The ears are usually cropped. The rump is slightly raised (set higher than the withers), giving a curved impression to the strong back. Great power emanates from the broad, deep chest and the strong-boned, well-muscled hindquarters. Height: 21.5–25.5 inches (54–65 cm). Weight: 84–106 pounds (38–48 kg). The coat is short and rough. Color: fawn or various brindles, often with white.

Perro de Presa Mallorquin

A native breed of Spain created for competition in the dog-fighting and animal-baiting rings. *España* reveled in dog fights and was engrossed in bullbaiting as a spectator sport. Even today, while bullbaiting has been outlawed, dogfights are still supported by certain, thankfully small, circles. Mallorca, one of the Balearic islands off the coast of Spain, is where this unrelenting canine calls home. Organized dogfights on Mallorca have waned and with them, the population of Mallorquin Bulldogs.

Today the breed is more commonly referred to as Ca de Bou and is exhibited in Spanish dog shows. The Ca de Bou is a tough-minded dog of medium size that is bulldoggy in appearance. Compared to

the warrior of days gone by, today's Ca is docile and biddable, though still most brave and powerful.

ESSENTIALS OF THE PERRO DE PRESA MALLORQUIN: A baiting dog standing 22

inches (56 cm) at the withers and weighing in at 80 pounds (36 kg). The head is large when compared to the body, with a wide skull. The ears are short, thin and curved. The eyes are large and oval, not showing conjunctiva. The neck is thick and strong. Back is relatively short; deep and large, short loins with deep arch to hip. Tail is strong at root and reaches hock. Forelegs shorter than hind; fore are straight and developed. Coat is short and

Perro de Presa Canario, brindle.

Perro de Presa Mallorquin, black-masked fawn. Photographs by I. Français.

hard and can be brindle, fawn or red in color, without white hairs.

Peruvian Inca Orchid, hairless.

Peruvian Inca Orchids, coated (*below top*) and hairless (*below bottom*).

Perro Flora
See Peruvian Inca Orchid

Perro Mastin del Pireneo
See Pyrenean Mastiff

Persian Greyhound
See Saluki

Perspiration
Dogs don't sweat like humans do; they perspire freely from the muzzle and the pads of the feet. They perspire from the skin only when suffering from a skin disorder; and they do indeed have sweat glands (just fewer than humans). When hot, dogs pant, breathing rapidly with their tongue lolling as a means of cooling themselves.

Peruvian fox
See South American foxes

Peruvian Inca Orchid
This vestless Peruvian dog was discovered by Spanish explorers visiting Peru. These Moonflowers were nighttime dogs that didn't like the light of the day or the rays of the sun. Inca noblemen kept the dogs in darkened rooms, surrounded by orchids during the day. In Peruvian, the breed is referred to as *Oeuchua*, meaning "dog without vestments." Incan nobility prized the lighter hued dogs and selectively bred for lightness of pigment. The breed has tooth and skin problems, and the coated variety is essential to keeping these disorders to a minimum. These disorders are not peculiar to the Peruvian Inca Orchid breed but are true for most other hairless dogs created with the dominant, semi-lethal gene for hairlessness. (*See* Hairless Dogs) Today the breed can be found in the Americas and in Europe. The Peruvian is not fond of light and the smallness of the eyes is attributed to squinting in the sunlight, or so it is said.

ESSENTIALS OF THE PERUVIAN INCA: The Peruvian Inca Orchid is a thin and lightly boned dog that resembles a tiny short-legged baby deer (without hair, of course). The head is mesocephalic: the F.C.I. standard indicates the total length is 3.85/10 of the height of the withers. Likewise, the bizygomatic width must be 5/10 of the total length of the head. The ears are erect at attention; in repose they lie toward the back. The neck is long, muscular, carried high, in an elegant and graceful way. The forelegs are well joined to the trunk. The scapulo-humeral angle will be between 100 and 110°. The hindleg muscles are rounded and elastic. The coxo-femoral angle shall be 120° and the femoro-tibial angle will be 130°. Due to the angulations already mentioned, these dogs move with a shorter gait but with a quick step which at the same time is softened and flexible. Height: 15.5–20 inches (39.5–51 cm). Weight: 20–28 pounds (9–13 kg). The skin is smooth all over and heavily mottled in any color, in combination with a pink background, or it can be solid colored. The skin is soft and pliable. As with most other hairless breeds, a coated variety exists and is full-coated in any color.

Pet shops

The well-stocked, efficiently run pet supply shop is an essential component of every owner's weekly itinerary. The responsibility of pet ownership is multifaceted and one that requires a great many supplies: leashes, beds, flea collars, collars, food, chew bones, toys, and even a good how-to or breed introduction handbook. Pet shop keepers are increasingly better informed, and experienced merchants can be very helpful in guiding the new owner towards the most efficient and safest products. Pet shops are a genuine source of advice about grooming, nail trimming, bathing, and general coat care. Of course, most pet shop keepers cannot provide you with the necessary medical advice concerning the diagnosis and treatment of an ailment.

Many pet shops are quite diversified in their offerings; catering to the dog fancy is but one aspect of a pet shop. Fish, snakes, birds, cats, hamsters, ferrets, and any number of domesticated animals are also available, of course, in addition to dogs! For most owners, purchasing a dog is a toss-up between the pet shop and the professional breeder. Pet shops most commonly offer "pet-quality" animals, that is, animals that are suited for a life as a home companion, not a career in the show ring. In most cases, the dogs offered behind the glass are purebred dogs, pet shops do not intentionally sell mutts. If

an owner intends to purchase a purebred dog, whether for show or sole pet use, he must acquire the pedigree as well as the registration certificate. Only this latter assures the owner that the dog's dam and sire (parents) were registered purebred dogs. Don't be impressed by a dog's "papers" unless they are approved by the A.K.C. or K.C.G.B. or the equivalent national registry.

If a potential owner is seeking a show-ring quality dog, a professional breeder is generally the first choice. Keep in mind

Pet shops offer top-quality products and helpful advice for owners. Considering the selection and values offered, dog owners can scarcely afford not to visit their pet shops on a weekly basis. Dachsie caught browsing by I. Français.

too that not all breeders are competent and honest and most breeders do not speak too openly critically of their own stock. Yet, more likely than not, no breeder will sell you a poorly bred dog for show purposes, since his name is also associated with the dog and his reputation rests on the quality of the animal.

Pet shops should be a place where the pet owner feels comfortable, accommodated and welcome. Today such shops eliminate the consumer's need to shop for their pet supplies in a grocery store or discount department store. Owners are best served by members of the pet trade whose sole responsibility and reliance is on the pet owner. It is no mystery that the grocery store clerk cannot recommend the appropriate canned dog food for your Bernese Mountain Dog puppy nor that the department store attendant cannot help you choose the appropriate flea collar for your Maltese. Pet shops depend on the patronage of pet lovers and make it their business to serve them in the utmost capacity.

Petit Anglo-Français
See Anglo-Français

Petit Basset Griffon Vendeen, tawny. Photo by I. Français.

ness to the ground make him ideal for hunting in rugged terrain. Hunting is instinctive, as it is with his Griffon relations. Although no newcomer to France, the Petit Basset is creating quite a stir in the U.S. and Great Britain, where active fanciers are promoting him. American television actress Mary Tyler Moore is one proud owner. The American Kennel Club entered the Petit into its Hound Group in 1991. The breed was previously recognized in Canada. In England, they are known as "Roughies." The appearance and personality of these little bassets rightly explains their sudden rise to popularity.

ESSENTIALS OF THE PETIT BASSET: A roughly coated basset that is short-legged and efficiently constructed. The coat must be hard and rough to the touch; it reaches up to 2.5 inches (6 cm) in length. A pure white background provides the woolly canvas for a palette of colors: orange, gray, tawny, and black/tan. Weight: 25–35 pounds (11–16 kg). Height: 13–15 inches (33–38 cm). The ears are graciously feathered. The body is muscular, longer than tall. The chest deep. The tail medium length, strong at base. Shoulders well laid back.

Petit Basset Griffon Vendeen
The smallest variety of the French Griffons of the Vendee area, the Petit Basset Griffon Vendeen was bred down from his larger *freres*. There are four known varieties of Griffon Vendeens, the roughhaired hounds of the Vendee area in France.

His terrifically tough coat and close-

Forelegs appear straight from front; slight crook acceptable. *See also* Griffon Vendeen

Petit Berger
See Bergers des Pyrenees

Petit Bleu de Gascogne
See Bleu de Gascogne

Petit Brabançon

The original Griffons of Belgium looked more terrier than they presently look. The Petit Brabançon is the smooth-haired variety of the Brussels Griffon. In the United States and Great Britain, the breed is considered just a variety of that breed. The F.C.I. considers the Petit Brabançon a breed unto itself. The breed has enjoyed a healthy fancy in Italy. Unlike the Brussels or Belgian Griffon, the Petit's coat is not wire. The griffons (meaning wirehairs) were created through crosses of various wire-haired terriers and toy dogs. The Affenpinscher (*pinscher* translates to terrier) was likely the prime contributor of component stock to the early Griffons. In the 1800s, the English Toy Spaniel was used to decrease the size and shorten the snout; it also eliminated much of these dogs' ability. As the breed gained in popularity, Barbets, Smoushonds, Yorkshire Terriers, and Pekingese were likely used to perfect desired type. The Pug is chiefly responsible for the smoothing of the griffons' coats, hence the Brabançon.

ESSENTIALS OF THE PETIT BRABANÇON: The Petit Brabançon is the smooth coated version of the Brussels Griffon. The coat, short and dense, can be red, red/black, red/black grizzle, black or black/tan. These are squarely and solidly built dogs that weigh between 6–12 pounds (2.5–5.5 kg) and stand 7–8 inches (18–20 cm) high. The body is composed of a short back, well-sprung ribs, and a strong loin. The head is large in comparison to the body, rounded, in no way domed. The chest is rather wide and deep; legs straight, of medium length and bone.

Petit Chien Lion

See Löwchen

Petit Gascon-Saintongeois

See Gascon-Saintongeois

Petit Griffon Bleu de Gascogne

See Bleu de Gascogne

Phalene

The drop-eared variety of a breed, most commonly referring to the drop-eared Papillon. *See* Continental Toy Spaniel, Phalene

Petit Brabançon, grizzle, uncropped.

Petit Brabançon, grizzle, cropped. Photographs by I. Français.

Phantom pregnancy

Pseudopregnancy. *See* False pregnancy

Pharaoh Hound, chestnut. Photo by I. Français.

Pharaoh Hound

Perhaps the oldest and certainly the most honorably recorded dog in history, the Pharaoh Hound graces the tombs of ancient Egyptian pharaohs with his much retained beauty and elegance. In Malta, his native land, his name Kelb Tal Fenek literally means "Dog of the Rabbit." His lineage can be traced to circa 3000 B.C. The Phoenician Hound is likely his progenitor; dogs were a usual barter of the Phoenicians, and these seafaring merchandisers arrived in Malta in pre-Christian times. For an uninterrupted 2,000 years, these dogs developed rather

purely on their isolated island and have always been popular with the Maltese countryfolk. Much about the type and abilities of these ancient dogs is revealed through observing early paintings and working out the kinks in surviving hieroglyphics. While the Pharaoh Hound retains much of his enthusiasm for the hunt, on Malta today the dog is primarily a companion since the rabbit population of Malta has been scarce for generations. Hare and rabbit, of course, are not the Pharaoh's only quarry. The dogs in Malta are said to pick up the scent of a wild deer and "course it to a standstill." Unlike the Greyhound that hunts entirely by sight, the Pharaoh is able to hunt by both sight and scent. The Maltese have also made use of the dogs' intelligence and industry by employing them as house guards. Some dogs would keep their vigil atop a flat-topped roof while the family was out or asleep.

Pharaoh Hound enthusiasts today boast of their dog's distinctive ability to blush. These dogs have been favored as companions for many years and are among the most sensitive and expressive of all domesticated canines.

Due to its proximity, Italy enjoyed some of the first Pharaoh Hound imports. Italy's own sighthound, the Cirneco dell' Etna, may have been affected by the importation of these compatible sighthounds. Although the breed was introduced to Britain in the 1930s, it had little effect. Both the U.S. and Britain began their current Pharaoh fancy in the late 60s. These sleek, genuinely good-looking dogs are continually gaining new admirers. While the Pharaoh may never be overly popular or even recognizable to the general public, those who do know him wouldn't trade him, no matter what sum a passing Phoenician might offer!

ESSENTIALS OF THE PHARAOH HOUND: The general appearance is one of grace, power and speed. The skull is long, lean and chiseled. Foreface slightly longer than the skull. The nose is flesh-colored. The mouth is powerful, the bite scissors. Ears are medium-high set, carried erect when alert, very mobile. The neck is long, lean and muscular, with a slight arch to carry the head on high. The body is lithe with an almost straight topline. Deep brisket almost down to point of elbow. Ribs well sprung. Tail is medium set, fairly thick at the base and tapering whiplike. The shoulders are long and sloping and well laid back. Strong without being loaded. The hindquarters are strong and muscular, with moderate sweep of stifle. The feet are strong, well knuckled up and firm; paws well padded. Height: 21–25 inches (53–64 cm). The coat is short and glossy, ranging in texture from fine to slightly harsh. Color possibilities pass from tan through rich tan to chestnut, with some white.

Pharyngitis

Pharyngitis and laryngitis are terms used to refer to the inflammation of the pharynx and larynx respectively. Such inflammation can be the result of a vast number of causes, and proper diagnosis is necessary before successful treatment can be prescribed. *See also* Laryngitis

Phenobarbital

A sedative and antispasmotic.

Philippine Edible Dog

See Philippine Islands Dog

Philippine Islands Dog

This South-Sea-faring pig and fowl herder of the Philippine Islands, also known as the Philippine Edible Dog, is a gallant, fearlessly spitting canine, despite its spear-spitted destiny. Like its Pacific neighbor, the Hawaiian Poi Dog, the Philippine Dog was common on the table

of pig-breeding tribesmen. These northern Luzon inhabitants of the Igorot tribe carefully bred their dogs, breeding primarily for their herding abilities. The dogs generally worked the pigs until, in their wallowing old age, they hobbled

Pharaoh Hound in coursing attire.

with their porcine charges only to share in their corpulent companions' same roasted destiny.

Outnumbering the imported Oriental sleeve dogs on the islands, the Philippine Native Dog was the most popular companion of the Philippine people. The dogs resemble a cross between the Bull Terrier and Smooth Fox Terrier. Unlike the Poi Dogs of the Hawaiian Islands, these dogs are muscular, deep chested and in full capacity of their functioning jaws. In their herding tasks, these dogs, despite their small size, are able to thwart any oncoming, pig-threatening buffalo.

Philippine Native Dog

See Philippine Islands Dog

Phillips System

See Systems

Philtrum

The line of junction between the left and right upper lip and nose halves.

Phimosis

A condition in which the opening of the sheath is too small for the penis to protrude, thereby making copulation impossible.

Pick of the litter.
This stunning litter of Japanese Shiba puppies was bred at Jacquet's Shibas by Rick Tomita. The pick of the litter, the smaller male, became author Andrew De Prisco's first Shiba. Photo by I. Français.

Phlebitis
Inflammation of a vein.

Photo finish
A close finish in a dog race that requires the use of a photo finish camera to determine the winner.

Photophobia
Though literally "fear of light," photophobia refers to acute sensitivity to light, usually accompanying such conditions as distemper, conjunctivitis, and some upper-respiratory infections.

Pica
Technical term for a depraved appetite, often caused by physical complications. *See* Appetite

Picardy Shepherd
See Berger Picard

Picardy Spaniel
See Épagneul Picard

Piccoli Levrieri Italiani
See Italian Greyhound

Piccolo Brabantino
See Petit Brabançon

Phu-Quoc Dog
The alleged ridgebacked ancestor of today's Rhodesian Ridgeback, the Phu-Quoc was brought to Africa from its native Thailand where it crossed with native African dogs. The Phu-Quoc was one of the dogs known to bear the ridge on its back. Besides the Rhodesian, the Mha Kon Klab, a lesser known (now extinct) canine of Africa also possessed the ridge. The first Basenjis described by British writers also were believed to possess this unusual fur crest.

On its native island off the coast of Thailand, the Phu-Quoc was used for hunting and guard work. The dog was medium sized with a short coat.

Pick of the litter
The pick of the litter usually refers to the first pup who is picked from the litter or to the right of the buyer or breeder to make the first selection. Often as part of a stud fee, a breeder will have pick of the litter, be it first, second, third, etc. Following then, pick of the litter can be any selection of a pup from the litter, be it first or last. Typically, when a breeder has a litter or is planning for a litter, he will sell picks of the litter to buyers. Picks may range in cost and/or may be determined solely on a first-come/first-serve basis. *See also* Breeding, Choosing a dog

Pickup

The actual picking up of the retrieve, whether it be a dummy, buck, or bird. The promptness with which a dog makes a pickup is an important part of his performance. *See also* Gundogs

Piddling

Puppies piddle when they are excited; puddles of piddle (for Poodles in particular) can be maneuvered around by controlling the source of the pup's excitement. Since urine probably does not give your home the aura or aroma that you desire, it is a good idea to attend to this housebreaking matter straightaway. If your pup piddles when you arrive home, tone down your homecoming—don't shower the dog with a wave of affection or you'll be showered twice in return. Retrievers in training also tend to piddle in their excitement for the find. Hunting dogs should not be permitted to allow a delightful bush to interrupt the retrieve. Hunters should let their dogs take care of these essentials before the sporting begins. Thus, forbidding the dog to "water" saplings in passing is for the dog's and the hunter's benefit.

Pi-dog

A mongrel type, particularly of Eastern derivation.

Piebald

A white background is superimposed with irregular, but symmetrically placed, black patches. In the Akita, the color is referred to as pinto. For preference, the color patches are well defined and cover about a third of the body.

Pied

Color type in the hounds marked by uneven patches. Generally there are three types of pied: badger pied, lemon pied, and hare pied. Badger pied consists of spots of black, gray and cream hairs superimposed on a white background. In lemon pied, the patches consist of lemon, cream or black; in hare pied, khaki, orange, gray and black.

Pied. Badger pied on a European-bred Pyrenean Mountain Dog. In the U.S., the so-called Great Pyrenees is less commonly seen with these pied markings. Photo by I. Français.

Pig eyes

Eyes that allude to porcine inelegance: too small and too close together.

Pig jaws

See Undershot

Pigeon chest

A shorter breastbone and nearly absent prosternum create this defective chest which usually constitutes a lack of endurance due to insufficient heart and lung room.

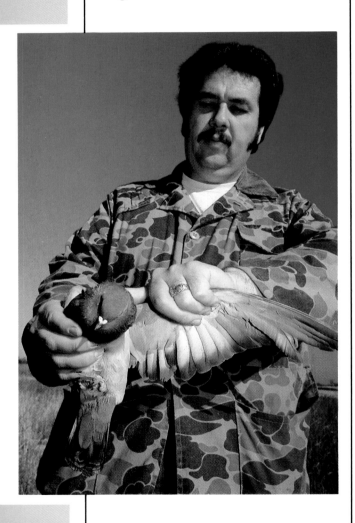

Pigeon dizzying

Pigeon dizzying—that is dizzying a pigeon—is one method of training a gundog to be steady on live game. With the bird in hand, one can dizzy a live pigeon by tucking the bird's head under its wing and moving one's arms in circular motions for about a minute. One cannot, of course, dizzy a dead pigeon, so be sure the pigeon is live and don't overdue the dizzying so that the bird remains "live." Actually, dizzying a pigeon for over a minute essentially has no greater (desired) effect on the bird, so one minute will suffice. The seemingly violated bird will then sit in the grass where it is placed for up to ten minutes, while it regains its equilibrium. Wind your student flusher toward the disoriented fowl and blow the whistle when the dog is just on flushing the bird. Ideally the pigeon will fly away, wise enough to avoid men in camouflage clothing and funny hats for the rest of its days.

Pigeon-toed front

Opposite of east-west, this front is marked by pasterns and feet turning inwards towards the centerline.

Pigeon toes

Front feet that turn inwards toward the center line.

Pigment

Coloration or markings on the coat or eyes. A well-pigmented dog, then, is one with dark eyes, dark coat markings and dark claws.

Pigmentary keratitis

A condition in which the cornea of the eye becomes inflamed and there occurs a deposition of pigment. The condition starts in the white of the eye and has been described as a black shade being slowly drawn across the eye. If caught at an early stage, the condition can be treated.

Pile

An undercoat that is good and dense.

Pily coat

A crisp jacket of harsh, thick outer hair, with a soft, close-lying undercoat.

Pimples

See Acne

Pin brush

Pin brushes come in many sizes and shapes. They are excellent for breaking up the coat and removing loose hair. Pins must be of good quality and retain their shape. *See also* Grooming

Pinched front

Same as narrow front, which *see.*

Pinched muzzle

Snipy muzzle. Terminology usually employed to indicate an undesirable, overly refined muzzle. Such a muzzle is usually weakly structured and can appear over-chiseled and pointy. In some breeds, however, a pinched or snipy muzzle is to the liking (e.g., Lundehund).

Pink nose

A very light colored nose, often refers to a fault although, as most always, there are exceptions: the Braque St. Germain has a pink nose.

Pinscher

1) German for terrier. *See also* Miniature Pinscher, Affenpinscher, Harlequin Pinscher, Austrian Shorthaired Pinscher, Doberman Pinscher

2) Pinscher is the Kennel Club of Great Britain's chosen name for the Standard Pinscher of Germany. Admittedly, German Pinscher or Standard Pinscher, in light of the number of popular pinschers, would be more descriptive nomenclature. This Pinscher, like all the other *biters* of Germany, was a farmer's terrier, capable of vermin control and guard duty. Tall for a terrier, the Pinscher could not go to ground, but ofttimes his swiftness more than compensated for this restriction. In 1879 the breed received official recognition from the German Kennel Club. Of the German pinscher breeds, the Standard is the least popular; the ever-popular Doberman Pinscher and Miniature Pinscher have effectively usurped any possibility for the Standard to gain popularity. This is unfortunate, as the Standard fills the gap between these two extreme sized pinschers with grace and efficiency. Not too large to pine in smaller quarters, the Pinscher is an adaptable, versatile dog with man-stopper abilities. The Pinscher is self-possessed and high spirited. Even in Germany, the breed is little known. The British Kennel Club also recognizes the breed and notably categorizes it in the Working Group instead of the Terrier Group. This determination, if nothing else, is a tribute to the Pinscher's versatility. Some dogs have been brought to the U.S., although their progress has received little press.

ESSENTIALS OF THE PINSCHER: A smooth-coated, middle-sized dog with well-cut eyes of good size and high-set cropped ears. The most common color is shiny black with clear tan markings. Other colors include red, dark brown with yellow, fawn, red fawn, but not biscuit fawn. Higher on the leg than most terriers, the Standard Pinscher stands 16–19 inches (40.5–48 cm) and weighs 25–35 pounds (11.5-16 kg). Although well balanced with elegant lines, the breed is not as

Pinscher, red, cropped.

sleek and taut as the Doberman. The dog's back is straight and the tail is customarily docked.

Pinscher, black with tan, uncropped.

Pit bull has been defined as any dog of bull and terrier origin. The American Pit Bull Terrier, of the U.K.C., is most commonly referred to by the term, though its fanciers prefer the term "Bulldog."

Pinto

Piebald coloration in the Akita. *See* Piebald, Pied

Pipe-stopper tail

Upright, short tail undesirable in the Fox Terrier.

Pip-head

An apple-shaped or rounded skull that is accompanied by a snipy foreface and bulging eyes.

Pips

Small colored patches above the eyes of some breeds. The Doberman Pinscher and Basenji are just two examples of breeds that have pips.

Piroplasmosis, canine

A condition which is the result of the tick-spreading protozoan, babesiasis, which *see*.

Pit bull

Since there is no breed known as "the Pit Bull," the definition of what dog comprises a pit bull is cause for much controversy. The term derives from the Pit Bulldog of the nineteenth century, those dogs of bull-and-terrier blood which were used in the sport of bullbait-

ing. A number of A.K.C. breeds derive from this stock including the American Staffordshire Terrier, Staffordshire Bull Terrier, Bull Terrier and Bulldog, as well as some tiny bullies—the French Bulldog and Boston Terrier. Of course the U.K.C.-registered American Pit Bull Terrier, which *see*, is also from bull-and-terrier stock. It is this breed that has been referred to simply as "Pit Bull" on occasion.

Laws against members of the bull-and-terrier family have disfigured the face of many jurisdictions. Insistent lawmakers, with little regard to what a "breed-specific" law means, have labelled "pit bulls" vicious, and likewise branded related breeds "monstrous" in the process. The blame for the need for such laws must be pinned to the owners of pit bulls who have capitalized on their dogs' fighting-dog instincts. These self-seeking individuals are promoting "people-mean" dogs, a quality in Pit Bulls that has never been favored. Such laws will result in outlawing both the 75-pound American Pit Bull Terrier along with the 7.5-pound Boston Terrier. With a little luck, legislators will see that the true culprits in the pit-bull phenomena are the bad owners and not the dogs, and act accordingly.

Pit Bullmastiff

A crossbred Bandog: Pit Bull Terrier and Bullmastiff. *See* Bandog

Pittenweem Terrier

Small terrier of Scotland, no longer extant, which played a role in the development of various Scottish terrier breeds.

Pituitary gland

A small double-lobed gland located near and attached to the base of the brain. The pituitary is perhaps the most instrumental regulator of the body, having direct and indirect chemical influences on many other glands and organs. The pituitary can affect: estrus, maternity, shedding, labor, gigantism, dwarfism, sexual development, metabolism regulation, obesity, and blood pressure.

Place

Second place in a race; the contestant that finished second.

Placenta

The afterbirth that accompanies the delivered pup and has been used to nourish the fetus. The placenta is composed of three parts: the chorion, the amnion, and the allantois.

Plaiting

Manner of walking or trotting in which the legs cross. Also referred to as knitting. Usually not desirable.

Plaque

A thin transparent film that is found on the surface of a tooth and contains mucin, bacteria, and other substances. Minerals precipitate on the plaque, if not removed, resulting in tartar.

Plasmacytic-lymphocytic synovitis

A common disorder of dogs in which joint disease is the only manifestation. It most commonly affects the stifle joint and evidences itself in lameness and poor motion of the hind legs. Treatment is variable and often unsuccessful. *See also* Rheumatoid arthritis.

Plate

Used in Komondor terminology to describe the matting of a neglected coat.

Pleurisy

A condition, often resulting after a case of pneumonia, in which the chest cavity accumulates fluid, noticeable in the unclear sound of the heart and lungs when heard through the chest. In "dry" pleurisy, breathing is accompanied by a rasping or grating sound.

Plott Hound

The Plott Hound's designated name honors its American founders and progenitors. Residing on "top of ol' Smokey" in North Carolina, seven generations of Jonathan Plott's family, beginning in the 1750s, bred their dogs exclusively within the family. A mix of bloodhounds and curs reportedly comprised the original stock. Dogs were bred by various family members; the strain bred by the Cables of Swain County were termed Cable Hounds, while those bred by Blain Blevin were known as Blevin Hounds, etc. The dog's working claim to fame is its coldtrailing of bear. The Plott Hound is American through and through. Southern owners report that they are quick of mind and foot.

ESSENTIALS OF THE PLOTT HOUND: A medium-sized, soundly put-together hound that is usually brindle. The coat, which is short, thick, and dense, may also occur in slate blue and buckskin; many with black saddles. Height: 20–24 inches (51–61 cm). Weight: 45–55 pounds (20–25 kg). A long, high-held tail and long ears characterize the breed. The conformation of the Plott Hound is lean muscled, rather thin boned and lithe. The tail is long and carried erect when alert. The ears are pendant and on the large side.

Plucking

The required way to care for the coat of some show-ring terriers. Plucking removes the dead hair from the dog's coat. A plucking tool (or one's hand) is used; when a stripping knife is used, it is called stripping (which *see*). Plucking can be done with the hands (index finger and thumb), but no plucking should be attempted without professional guidance.

Plume tail

Plume-shaped tail composed of long hairs creating a featherlike effect. The hair covers the entire tail or only part and spreads over the back: in the Pekingese, the hair covers the entire tail; in the Chinese Crested, the hair covers only the tail tip.

Plott Hound, slate blue. Photo by I. Français.

Pneumonia

A conditon of many types: broncho-pneumonia, lobar pneumonia, inhalation pneumonia, verminous pneumonia, and traumatic pneumonia. Fever, shallow breathing, loss of appetite, a grating/rasping sound to the breath, and possible mucus discharge are the signs common to all these types of pneumonia. All forms involve serious irritation of the lungs, and all deserve immediate veterinary treatment.

Verminous pneumonia mostly affects young pups and is the result of larval (hookworm and roundworm) invasions of the lung tissue. Inhalation pneumonia is the result of lung irritation by such as smoke, liquid, or other substances that damage lung tissue and cause labored, painful breathing.

Podenco Andaluz, long, cinnamon.

Poaching

Trespassing on private property when hunting. The classic image of poaching, of course, involves lightfooted, lightfingered Lurchers coursing hare and rabbit, followed by the shifty field.

Pocadan

See Kerry Beagle

Pocket Beagle

The Pocket Beagle is essentially a very small Beagle, perhaps standing eight inches (20 cm) high. The Pocket Beagle presents a number of breeding and health problems. Hypoglycemia is a common condition with tiny toys.

Podenco Andaluz

This ancient Spanish sighthound was first established on the peninsula at Cádiz and bears strong resemblance to the Egyptian hounds from which it likely descends. The breed has a growing fancy in Spain and is being promoted anew.

ESSENTIALS OF THE PODENCO ANDALUZ: A rough, independent animal of strong hunting instinct. Three size varieties from 43–68 cms. Three coat types: short, long and hard. Colors are cinnamon, red and white. Straight back, deep chest not touching elbow, much leg.

Podenco Canario

This sighthound developed on the Canary Islands and has many similar qualities to the Ibizan Hound. Like the Podenco Andaluz, the Canario likely developed parallel to the Podengos of Portugal. It is a highly adaptable rabbit hunter able to work in volcanic regions. Often stubborn and nervous, this Podenco is protective and intelligent, though not terribly noble in appearance.

ESSENTIALS OF THE PODENCO CANARIO: Well-muscled sighthound, preferably red and white. Height: 53–64 cm. Body long, head conic—type and overall symmetry to be emphasized. Coat is short and flat.

Podenco Ibicenco

See Ibizan Hound

Podengo Português

Employed by the Portuguese as rabbit hunters—setting and tracking—the Portuguese Hounds or Rabbit Dogs, Podengos Portuguêses in Portuguese, find their running-hound ancestors in northern Africa. Hunting in packs or singly, the Portuguese Hounds became specialists on rabbits. Various crosses—pariah, sighthound and otherwise—constitute the Podengo of today; each cross was intended to improve or redirect the dog's hunting abilities. The Portuguese Podengos come in three size varieties: the Grande is the largest and therefore is able to cover the most ground, possesses the greatest strength and can hunt large

Podenco Canario, red. Photographs by I. Français.

ting, guard work and companionship.

ESSENTIALS OF THE PODENGOS PORTUGUÊS: The Grande Podengo Português is a large sighthound type with a well-proportioned head, flat skull and pronounced stop. The muzzle is straight, the eyes small and oblique, ranging in color from light honey to dark chestnut. The ears are pricked, triangular, and sizable. The back is level; the legs are straight, with cat feet. Height: 22–28 inches (56–71 cm). Weight: 66 pounds (30 kg). The breed occurs in two coat types: short coat, which is hard and

Podengo Português
Pequeno, smooth, white.

game. The Medio is probably the fastest of the three *hermanos* and has exquisite maneuverability on rough ground. The Pequeno, for all its petiteness, is still an eager hunter, small enough to enter a rabbit warren, and also an able ratter. The running Podengos hunt in the manner of the Greyhound—singly or in pairs.

Like the Poodle, the Podengo's three size variations conveniently offer dog lovers a scale of options. Like the Dachshund, there are six possible variations (three sizes x two coat types) on the breed's theme. Like the Airedale Terrier, the breed is hardy and has sporting abilities which are many and diversified. Unlike the Poodle, Dachshund and Airedale Terrier, the Podengo has received little attention from the dog world as a companion or show dog. Portugal, of course, uses these dogs for hunting, rat-

longer than most sighthounds; wire coat, which is medium long, shaggy and coarse. Yellow, fawn, and black with white markings are the color options for both types.

The Medio Podengo Português is a moderately sized sighthound type with a well-proportioned head, flat skull and pronounced stop. The muzzle is straight; the eyes small and oblique; eye color varies from light honey to dark chestnut. The ears are pricked, triangular, and sizable. The back is level; the legs are straight, with cat feet.

Podengo Português
Pequeno, smooth, red.

Podengo Português
Medio, smooth, red and white. Photographs by I. Français.

Height: 15–22 inches (38–56 cm). Weight: 35–44 pounds (16–20 kg). The breed occurs in two coat types: short coat, which is hard and longer than that of most sighthounds; and wire coat, which is medium long, shaggy and coarse. Color may be: yellow, fawn, or black with white markings.

Point of the elbow
See Forequarters

Point of the hock
See Hindquarters

Point of the shoulder
See Forequarters

Point stealing
Moving in, usually closer than a dog that has already established a point, while obviously being aware of that dog's situation.

Point-to-point
A straight run in scenthunting.

Pointed muzzle
See Tapering muzzle

Podengo Português
Grande, smooth, red. Photo by I. Français.

The Small Podengo Português, actually a miniature sighthound type, appears like a large, very sturdy Chihuahua. It has a well-proportioned head, flat skull, pronounced stop, and straight muzzle. The eyes are small and oblique; they range in color from light honey to dark chestnut. The ears are pricked, triangular, and sizable. The back is level and the legs are straight with cat feet. Height: 8–12 inches (20–31 cm). Weight: 10–12.5 pounds (4.5–6 kg). The breed occurs in two coat types: short coat, which is hard and longer than most sighthounds; and wire coat, which is medium long, shaggy and coarse. Yellow, fawn, and black with white markings are the color options.

Pohjanpystykorva
See Norbottenspets

Point
In scent hunting, the distance, as measured in a straight line, between two localities farthest apart in any particular hunt. *See also* Pointing

Pointer
A breed native to the British Isles, the Pointer is reportedly the first dog used to "stand game," in the sense that we use the term today. The exact origin of the Pointer remains a topic of discussion. It was once held as common belief that the Pointer traced back to the pointers of Spain. This belief is still adamantly adhered to by many. An alternative theory states that the Pointer of Great Britain is a breed distinct from Continental pointers, asserting that the various pointer breeds developed separately but parallel to each other, regardless of whether or not the base stock was similar. What is certain is that the Pointer did develop in Great Britain and that it did emerge as the premier workman of its kind. It is unquestionable that Spanish Pointer was infused into the Pointer's lines, but it remains undocumented whether or not the blood was received exclusively after the Pointer's type was fixed.

The earliest references to Pointers in England date to the mid-1600s. These early dogs reportedly worked with Greyhounds on hare coursing; the Pointers were actually used to point out hares for the Greyhounds to seize. The advent of wing-shooting in the early 1700s, however, greatly changed the atmosphere of dogs and the hunt; hunting turned more to sport, with skill and performance utmost concerns. From its beginnings, the Pointer has been revered as a fine hunting dog. Eighteenth- and nineteenth-century hunters experienced the Pointer in his hunting prime. The Pointer of today remains a true-to-the-bone hunting dog with an irrepressible desire to hunt, exceptional nose, good speed, and a clean-limbed, lithe and muscular body. Pointers are celebrated for their even and kind dispositions. The breed's bearing is decidedly aristocratic, intelligent and trainable. Most Pointers today are used as field dogs, and their numbers exceed A.K.C. registrations tremendously in actuality.

ESSENTIALS OF THE POINTER: The ideal Pointer gives the immediate impression of compacted power and agile grace. The head is noble, carried proudly and presents the expression of intelligence and alertness. The body is well muscled, illustrating both stamina and speed. The skull is of medium width, approximately as wide as the length of the muzzle. The muzzle concave, ending at the nostrils to produce a slightly "dish-faced" appearance. There is a slight furrow between the eyes and a prominent stop. The muzzle should be deep without

pendulous flews. Bite level. Ears set at eye level. Eyes of ample size, rounded and intense, the darker the better. The neck is long, dry and muscular; the shoulders long, thin, and sloping. Tail to be

heavy at the root and tapering to the tip, never extending below the hock. Height: 23–28 inches (58.5–71 cm). Weight: 42–67 pounds (19–30 kg). Balance and overall symmetry are more important than size alone. Colors are commonly lemon and white, orange and white, liver and white, and black and white. Self and tricolors also occur and are accepted. Gait to be smooth and frictionless with a powerful hindquarters' drive.

Pointer, liver and white. Photo by R. Pearcy.

Pointers, in the breed ring photographed by I. Français.

Pointing

The cessation of motion and becoming muscularly intense, regardless of position, upon encountering the scent or sight of game.

Pointing dogs

The pointing breeds are those hunting dogs that have been bred and trained to seek game from various terrains. Pointing involves physically freezing to an instinctive immobility when the dog scents the presence of a bird. The Continental pointers, those pointing hunting dogs of Europe, are superior hunters, bred not just to point, but also to retrieve, trail, and flush. *See* Gundogs

Pointing dogs have been developed in many different European countries to work on ground birds. This Continental pointer is the Perdiguero Navarro of Spain. Photo by I. Français.

Points

Areas of color on the face, eyebrows, ears, legs, or feet, i.e., the Manchester Terrier is a black dog with tan points. Points, in conformation terminology, refer to a specific aspect of the dog's anatomy being referred to at a given time.

Poison

A substance that is harmful to the well being of an animal, plant, or other living thing. In chemistry, a poison can be defined as a substance that inhibits or destroys the activity of a catalyst, enzyme, etc., or that interferes with or checks a reaction, but such usage is not common canine terminology except when discussing the internal chemical function of dogs and diseases affecting them.

The most common way in which a dog is poisoned is through the ingestion of toxic substance, whether it be contaminated food, toxic plant, or insecticide or other poison.

Depending upon the substance, treatment for poisoning can vary, as poisonous substances affect the internal systems of a dog differently. For example, if your pet ingests acid, alkali, gasoline, or kerosene, do not induce vomiting: give milk to dilute the toxin and coat the internals and seek veterinary attention immediately. If you know from which container your dog acquired the poison, read the label to see if an antidote is prescribed—if not, continue to the vet. Do not waste time searching for the possible container, which may not list an antidote or which may not be found; when poisoning is concerned, time is precious.

Common poisons include: acids (hydrochloric, nitric, acetic); alkalis (many cleansers and cleaning agents); arsenic (lead arsenate, arsenic); food poisoning (bacteria-infested food); hydrocyanic acid (wild cherry, laurel, and other plants); insecticides; lead (paints, lead arsenic); phosphorus and/or strychnine (many rodent and other animal poisons); thallium (bug poisons). If you carry any of these or other toxic substances in your home, make a list of them and the recommended treatment listed on the container. When in doubt, contact the Poison Control Center nearest you.

Poison ivy

Any of several plants of the cashew family, genus *Toxicondendron*, having three-leaflet leaves, greenish flowers, and ivory-colored berries. Contact with such plants can cause a severe rash that requires veterinary treatment. Allergic reactions to the toxin can further complicate the effect and demand more serious concern from the owner.

racy, fairly big hound with less earage than many other hounds. The Poitevin is greatly distinguished for his fine symmetry, appearing more perfectly balanced than most other scenthounds. Height: 24–28 inches (61–71 cm). Weight: 66

Poitevin, tricolor. Photo by I. Français.

Poitevin

One of the longest established varieties of the French scenthounds, the Poitevin dates back to the early 1700s—probably farther. The Marquis François de Larrye is revered as the founder of the breed. The Haut-Poitou region was well populated by working packs of these handsome hounds. In order to reinstate the breed after a devastating rabies epidemic in 1842, English Foxhounds were bred with the few remaining specimens. The post-epidemic Poitevin naturally resembles the English breed more so than did its predecessors. The breed was originally employed in France as an all-day pursuer of wolf.

Today the Poitevin is fancied by a small group of houndmen in France. He is genuinely friendly and attentive. His lively and intelligent nature endears him to those that work him.

ESSENTIALS OF THE POITEVIN: In color the Poitevin is reminiscent of many English packhounds. The breed is usually hound-marked, that is tricolored with a saddle, or orange and white. This is a

pounds (30 kg). The body is tautly muscled, and the skin is considerably tight for a hound. The head is handsomely sculpted, narrow with a well-pronounced occiput.

Poitevin-Normand

A French crossbreed that resulted from pairing the Poitevin and the large hounds of Normandy. With its smooth, abundant coat and finely chiseled skull, the Poitevin-Normand bears a strong physical resemblance to the Billy. The coat is tricolor or bright red marked with white; black mantles are common.

Police dogs

The use of dogs by police did not begin until about 1910 when European forces began training dogs for various policing functions. The effectiveness and much-talked-about success of war dogs in World War II led to greater utilization of dogs' talents for guard work, scenting, and patrol tasks. The German Shepherd Dog is the breed that is most commonly associated with police work (the breed is

are used for patrolling buildings, parks, hospitals, and other public institutions. Of course, many private businesses and institutions rely on dogs for surveillance and guard duty. Dogs with keen scenting abilities (Bloodhounds, German Shepherds) are used to track escaped criminals or locate illegal drugs. City police dogs are used for riot or crowd control, street patrol, and building searches. In New York City, a Golden Retriever is employed to track stolen cars. Special police dog schools have been training dogs for these and other remarkable purposes for many years. These canines are responsible for thousands of arrests and assistance as well as for patrolling parks, schools and hospitals a few-hundred-thousand times per year. *See also* War dogs

Poligar

The Poligar is named for the chieftains of the southern Karnatak (India), evidently this gazehound's original breeders. The breed excels in pig-hunting ability. Natives bearing spears followed the Poligar hounds on foot. The breed was found in Rajapalayam, Krishnan, Mylapore, and Madras. In addition to pig, the dog has also been hunted on fox, jackal, and deer. The coat is distinct: the head is covered with sleek soft fur, while the body is protected by bristles similar to those of the wild boar. The tail is short, rarely reaching an inch below the hock; it is thickly set-on. Due to the paucity of these dogs, inbreeding and crossbreeding have likely occurred.

Police dogs. This Rottweiler is "Bear" and his Deputy Sheriff partner Roger Jernigan, who work together in Sarasota County, Florida.

Police dogs are professionally trained in attack training and schutzhund work. The German Shepherd Dog ranks among the most trainable of all police dogs.

sometimes informally referred to as the Police Dog). Among other breeds that perform police work are the Doberman Pinscher, Akita, Airedale Terrier, Belgian Sheepdogs, Boxer, Dutch Shepherds and Collie. Each of these breeds possesses above-average canine intelligence. Labrador Retrievers and Bloodhounds are also commissioned for more specialized tasks such as rescue work or searching for a lost child.

Police dogs

Polish Hound

The Polish Hound is indigenous to Poland and is employed as a hunter and watchdog. This hound has been known and bred exclusively in Poland for centuries and may be related to the tracking dogs of Austria and Germany. Its actual ancestral composition is not known, and since all dogs come from other dogs, it is safe to say that the Polish Hound has other European cousins, possibly loose-skinned, loose St. Hubert Hounds. The Pol-

ish Hound's movement at work is slow and consonant; he is a persistent and enduring tracker of various game over the most treacherous terrain. His inborn ability to locate game and his sense of direction are remarkable. Only after World War II did a resurgence to regenerate the Polish Hound's numbers occur. Today the breed is still found but is reported to be quite rare.

ESSENTIALS OF THE POLISH HOUND: Massive and ponderous, the Polish Hound is efficiently built, though lighter than the flewsy, large-headed St. Hubert. The general appearance of this hound is imposing. Height: 22–26 inches (56–66 cm). Weight: 55–71 pounds (25–32 kg). The coat is usually black/tan or black and tan saddled, in texture, short and hard.

Polish Lowland Sheepdog

The Polski Owczarek Nizinny is a herding dog native to Poland bred from the ancient Puli and long-coated herding dogs of the Huns. Authorities refer to the breed as possibly "the missing link" between many of the shaggy herders of today and the corded herding dogs of the

Polish Hound, black and tan saddled. Photo by I. Français.

Polish Hound and owner photographed in Poland.

ancient East. Undoubtedly the Polish Sheepdog has contributed to numerous herding dogs through the centuries, including the Bearded Collie and the Schapendoes, for the dogs were commonly traded by Polish sailors in seaports around the world. The necessity of producing a working dog functional on the Polish landscape and unaffected by the harsh climate spurred the probable crossing of the Puli with other mountain herders to produce a smaller dog that retained the weather-resistant coat. Although nearly sinking into extinction during the Second World War, the breed now enjoys well-deserved recognition.

rectangular rather than square. Brisket deep, with moderate spring of rib. Withers distinctly marked; back level and muscular, with broad loin. Hindquarters well angulated, with broad and well-muscled thighs. Hocks strong and distinctly angled. Tail is medium set, thick at the base and tapering; length not below hocks. Coat: whole body covered with long, dense, shaggy thick coat of harsh textured hair. The coat can occur in any color, including pied. Height: 16–20 inches (40–52 cm). Weight: 30–35 pounds (13.5–16 kg).

Polish Mountain Dog
See Owczarek Podhalanski

Polish Mountain Herder
See Owczarek Podhalanski

Polish Sighthound
See Chart Polski

Polish Water Dog
Once a common water retriever of Poland, the breed is probably extinct. The authors ignore reports that the last remaining specimens drowned in the early part of this century.

Poll
Top of the head (e.g., Wire Fox Terrier standard).

Polski Owczarek Nizinny
See Polish Lowland Sheepdog

Polycythemia vera
A disease of the blood that causes an elevation of the hemoglobin concentration. Blood-letting has been effective. The convulsions that typify its presence can be likened to epileptic fits and last for several minutes; the limbs become stiff and the body feels hot. Mucous membranes become congested. The dog may shiver, and the skin takes on a ruddy discoloration. Blood samples must be taken and analyzed periodically. If medication is given to reduce the production of red blood cells, recovery is usually likely.

Polish Lowland Sheepdog, fawn. Photo by I. Français.

ESSENTIALS OF THE POLISH LOWLAND SHEEPDOG: A medium-size, strong, cobby, muscular dog with a shaggy thick coat. The head is medium in size and in proportion to the body; skull moderately broad and slightly domed; ears medium size, heart shaped, large at base and set moderately high, drooping with fore edge close to cheeks. Profuse hair on the forehead, cheeks and chin makes the head appear larger than it really is. Nose blunt, with wide-open nostrils. Body

Polyps

Polyps and papillomas are small virus-caused growths. Polyps are typically found on the body and are easily removed. Papillomas typically occur in the mouth and may require minor surgery to be removed.

Pompon

Circular tufts of hair at the end of the tail of some breeds (e.g., Poodle, Löwchen) when clipped in a particular fashion. *See* Clipping the Poodle

Pomeranian

The Pomeranian is the perfect facsimile of its larger spitzen cousins. Dogs similar to the Pomeranian, although considerably larger than today's 3–7 pound dog, were used as sheepdogs throughout the world, not just in northern Germany. These ancestors weighed as much as 30 pounds, much larger than our much-loved Lilliputian. Distinguishing these larger dogs from the Keeshond of today would have been a near-impossible chore. When the Pom (the Northern German Sheepdog) first arrived in Britain, it was not well received, perceived as a "foreigner" with an unattractive, unkempt coat. Early breeders worked hard to master the Pom's coat. Admittedly, there are few things in the dog world more unsightly than a molting spitz in bad coat. The Pomeranian's coat today is among the most impressive in the dog world—its plushness and fullness are attributed to its Arctic Circle ancestors. The English dog fancy was slow to catch on since the nation already had its herd of sheepdogs and no need for cart pullers.

The breed is a descendant of the Ger-

man Spitzen and is the smallest from this sled-pulling family. The German Spitz family also yields the Toy German Spitz, a dog quite similar to the Pomeranian. The dog received its name from the northern German town of Pomerania, where dogs of this particular type were abundant. The British (eventually) favored the Pomeranian; Queen Victoria was much enamored of the breed and pushed for its exhibition in England. The

Keeshond is also of German Spitz origin and is the other breed that the Brits have embraced as their own. The F.C.I. does not recognize either breed because of

Pomeranian, cream. Photo by I. Français.

Pomeranian, orange sable.

their still-extant indigenous German Spitz equivalents.

Pomeranian.
Photo by Gilbert.

Pomeranian,
particolor.
Photograph by I.
Français.

The Pom's many coat colors—twelve in number—also helped promote its popularity in the United Kingdom and America. At one time, white was *the* color for Poms, but these dogs were often a tad larger, and the smaller oranges became the favored color in Germany. British fanciers were less impressed with the "drab" orange coat and began crossing the known colors to acquire the subtle shades and pastel hues which color the breed today.

The Pom is a wonderful companion dog and has been a show-ring contender in the U.S. since 1900. England recognized the dog 30 years before America. The breed's docile temperament and affectionate nature endear it to many; its vivacity and spirit make it well liked the world over.

ESSENTIALS OF THE POMERANIAN: Compact and short coupled, the Pomeranian possesses a well-knit tiny frame. The head and nose are foxy in outline; the skull is slightly flat. The ears are small and not too widely apart. The muzzle is not snipy or lippy. The neck is rather short. Not straight in shoulder. The body is short-backed and well ribbed, with a

fairly deep chest. The coat is very abundant: the outer coat is long and perfectly straight, harsh in texture; the undercoat is soft and fluffy. In color the Pom is any of 12 colors: black, brown, chocolate, beaver, red, orange, cream, orange sable, wolf sable, blue, white or particolor. Height: 11 inches (28 cm) maximum. Weight: 3–7 pounds (1.5–3.5 kg).

Pomeranian Sheepdog

A white, medium sized shepherd of Germany which stands 20–24 inches (51–61 cm) at the shoulder. The skull is narrow with a slight stop. The muzzle, tapering to the nose, is powerful. The ears are small. This dog was once commonly found in the region after which it derives its name. Today it is not registered by any major body. The Hungarian Kuvasz is the dog's probable ancestor. The Pomeranian Sheepdog is believed to be distantly related to other Continental sheep herders as well. The breed was introduced to England by Mr. A.D. Ingrams, a sheep farmer from Devonshire, where it was found to work well on both flat and hilly terrain. The dog was first shown at a Kennel Club show in 1937 and made its way to Crufts in '38. It has since fallen into obscurity. *See also* German Spitzen

Pommerscher Hütehund
See Pomeranian Sheepdog

Pont-Audemer Spaniel
See Épagneul Pont-Audemer

Poodle

"The constancy of the Poodle is un-doubted," yet there exist three distinct breeds: the Standard, the Miniature, and the Toy. The three Poodles are certainly of close relation, with the Standard the oldest and the Miniature and the Toy likely later bantamizations of the first. Exactly when the Poodle emerged is unknown, as remains its country of origin. Undoubtedly old, the breed's development borders on two countries: is the

pearance, and intelligence, the dogs were quick to take root wherever their seeds fell. Some historians believe that Germany, Russia, and France all played vital roles in the evolution of the Poodle and that each perfected its chosen color for the dog: Germany, brown; Russia, black; and France, white. Accounting for the particolored Poodles of the time remains a dispute. Lending fuel to the fire is the painting by Franz Snyder of 1595 that clearly depicts a Poodle of base white

Poodle, Standard, white.

Poodle of French descent or did the breed arise in Germany? Commonly called the French Poodle, the breed was once believed to be unquestionably French, in manner, appearance, and origin. Today, the more accepted thesis defies the French of Poodle and declares the breed brought to perfection in Germany, where it was employed as a water retriever and known as *Canis familiaris aquatius* or the "pudel," from which we have the English name for the breed. If the Poodle did not stake its beginnings in France, it is assumed that Poodles were taken to France and other countries in the ranks of armies during the 1400s. With their ability, ap-

splashed with color, giving a pied or particolored appearance.

Art and the Poodle are on familiar terms. The Poodle was the subject of many a leading animal artist of the fifteenth and sixteenth centuries. In 1490, Bernadine Pinturiccio painted his series known as the "Patient Grizeld" in which a well-trimmed "toy" Poodle is in evidence, interesting when considering that the Standard is accepted as the oldest of the three Poodle breeds. The sixteenth-century painting by Martin de Vaux, entitled "Tobit and his Dog," illustrates a clipped Poodle of undeniable type. Also, in *Book of Beasts*, 1665, is found yet an-

Poodle, Miniature, silver.

Poodle, Standard, black. Photo by Alverson.

other unmistakable Poodle dog.

Stonehenge, in his *Dogs of the British Isles*, shows a drawing of a Poodle by Albert Durer, 1471–1528, and gives this account of the breed by Mr. L. Clement:

"Clement divides it into two grand classes, one including the dog used for sporting, the other including performing, companion, and toy poodles. Scientists have told us that the Poodle's cerebral cavity is more capacious than in other dogs, and that the frontal sinuses are fully developed, also that the general foundation of the head and skull exhibit every indication of extraordinary intelligence."

As suggested, the Poodle and his early ancestors did find employment beyond the marshlands. Belgian owners used Poodles to smuggle

lace by having it tightly wound round the dogs' bodies. The lace was hidden by some covering, and the dogs were trained to give any person in uniform a wide berth. The Truffle Dog, which *see*, a breed primarily of Poodle blood, was employed long in Britain to "hunt" the edible truffle fungus, revered as a delicacy in Europe.

The more "conventional" use of the Poodle is understood from the translation of its generic French title, Caniche, which, like its other common French name, Chien Canne, translates to "duck dog." Indeed, the Poodle's primary function of yesterday was the retrieval of fallen waterfowl, a task which it completed with unerring accuracy even in the twilight hours.

The customary practice of clipping the Poodle traces back to its hard water-working days of yore. The Poodle's absolute skill and remarkable intelligence were hampered in the water by its profuse coat, which when soaked became cumbersomely heavy. Clipping has been developed over the history of the breed (to the point of absurdity some may say), but nonetheless, Poodle clipping is taken seriously by serious fanciers, and no dog in England or America struts in the show ring unclipped, not even puppies. *See also* Clipping the Poodle

A dog of diversity, the Poodle was the premier French circus dog. Travelling with his trainer, the Poodle was paraded from city to city across Europe, gaining admirers with every tent's rising. Speaking of the time was Alexander Woollcott, when he wrote of his Poodle companions: "They clearly regarded themselves as having a special relationship to the human species. A bond traceable I suppose to the fact that for a thousand years their forebears travelled with the French circuses and in all that time had no fixed point in their lives except a person; no home at all save the foot of the boss's bed wherever it might be." However interesting, it must be remembered that Poodles throughout their history were employed as water-specialized gundogs. Countless Poodles worked the fields with their gun-cocked owners in search of goose, duck, and grouse.

The development of the Miniature Poodle seems quite obvious. The breed was scaled down from the Standard for fanciers desiring similar intelligence and abilities in a smaller package. The Miniature became well loved in circuses as trick and stunt dogs and popular in homes. Many years ago, a blending of Maltese blood with the Poodle was used to re-perfect the Mini whites—but this cross was unsatisfactory and has been thoroughly bred out. The Miniature is not to be confused with the even smaller Toy Poodle, which is exclusively a companion and show dog.

Efforts in the past century to miniaturize the Miniature Poodle ofttimes resulted in a feeble-bodied smaller dog, which had a rather grotesque appearance and waned in comparison to its hand-

some forebears. Twentieth century attempts were less scornfully accepted,

and today's Toy Poodle is sturdily constructed. He was never intended for work and likewise lacks the necessary size to make him believable as a working dog. The clipping of his coat is purely traditional and doesn't feign to be more than ornamental. The Toy Poodle is quite gregarious, loves companionship, and flourishes in homes of any size. He proves truly the delightful canine, if not spoiled. The Toy tends to favor one family member, usually the lady of the house,

Poodle,
Miniature, apricot.

and will defend her honor at all costs.

ESSENTIALS OF THE POODLE: The Standard, Miniature, and Toy Poodles are

Poodle, Toy, gray.

Poodle, Standard, apricot.

customarily judged by the same standard, with size as the only variant. The Poodle is an active, intelligent, and elegant dog, squarely built and well proportioned. Carriage must be proud; construction and movement sound. The skull is moderately rounded, with a slight but definite stop; the muzzle is long, straight, and fine, with a slight chiseling under the eyes; eyes very dark, oval, and intelligent; the ears to hang close to the head (the fringe not to be excessive). Neck well proportioned. Shoulders smoothly muscled; blades well laid back and of about same length as upper foreleg. Body square; chest deep and moderately wide, with ribs well

sprung; back level; loin short, broad, and muscular. The tail is set on high and carried up, customarily docked of sufficient length to ensure a balanced outline. The coat is of considerable importance in the show ring. The curly coat to be of a naturally harsh texture and dense throughout. The corded coat is to hang in tight even cords of varying length, longer on the mane, head, and ears, and shorter on the puffs, bracelets, and pompons. The accepted clips typically include: Puppy, English Saddle, Continental, and Sporting. In Britain, a Lion clip is recommended for showing. The color of the coat can be any solid color, with clear colors definitely preferred. Color possibilities include: white, black, blue (a dark gray), gray (when light called silver), brown (dark walnut or reddish chestnut), café-au-lait (beige), cream and apricot. Though particolors do occur, they are not accepted by most registering bodies. Size: Standard, height over 15 inches (38 cm), weight 45–70 pounds (21–34 kg); Miniature, height 10–15 inches (25.5–38 cm), weight proportional; Toy, height less than 10 or 11 inches (25.5–28 cm), weight proportional.

Poodle, Miniature, café-au-lait.

Poodle, Miniature, white.

Poodle, Miniature, black, in corded coat.

Poodle, Standard, particolor. Most major registries require that Poodles be solid colored only and discourage all particolors. Photographs by I. Français.

Poodle Pointer
See Pudelpointer

Poodle Sheeppoodle
See German Sheeppoodle

Pool
Total sum of wagers bet on a race; total bets on each of various forms—straight, place, show, daily double, or quiniela.

Pooper-scooper laws
Many cities have ordinances requiring that owners curb their dogs when they are walking them in public places. These laws vary from place to place. It is always a good idea to know all laws that affect your dog and you. A pooper-scooper, of course, is a shovellike device which makes street clean-up efficient and practically imperceptible to passers-by. Many owners are embarrassed when their healthy Great Dane fills the fool-proof Zip-lock in their purse; the scoop ensures against such sticky situations.

Popping the box
The dog's coming away from the starting barrier very quickly.

Porcelaine
Believed to be the oldest French scenthound, the Porcelaine has roots in the now-extinct Montaimboeuf as well as some smaller laufhunds of Switzerland. In appearance, the Porcelaine is debatably the most elegant of the French hunters. Its name is derived from its porcelainlike appearance—sleek to the point of shiny, and delicate. The breed was necessarily reconstructed after the French Revolution but now stands on solid ground. Roe deer and hare are its specialties in the hunt. Many specimens travelled with their French owners to America and settled in the mid-East, just prior to the American Civil War. These imported Porcelaines were used in the de-velopment of a number of American scenthound breeds and types.

ESSENTIALS OF THE PORCELAINE: The solid white coat is composed of very fine hairs of miraculously short length. The color can be interrupted by orange spots on the body and especially on its notably sizable ears. Weight: 55–62 pounds (25–28 kg). Height: 22–23 inches (56–59 cm). The finely sculpted head and moderate but delicate build reinforce the appropriateness of its name.

Portuguese Cattle Dog
See Cão de Castro Laboreiro

Portuguese Hound
See Podengo Português

Portuguese Pointer
Known also as Perdigueiro Português, the breed is an ancient Portuguese dog, with paintings and written records of the breed dating at least to the fourteenth century. The Perdigueiro is derived from Spanish dogs. These dogs were used centuries ago as hawking dogs. Some look on the extinct Podengo de Mastra, a pointing hound, as this pointer's prototype. An artist by the name of Afonso III painted dogs of type similar to the Perdigueiro as early as the thirteenth century. Because breed type has been fixed

Porcelaine photographed by I. Français.

for centuries, it is probable that the breed extended beyond its native lands, whether by trade, travel, or accident. With such as the scenario it seems only

short and slightly convex (similar to the English Pointer); there exists a furrow to the brow and a defined stop. The ears are set high and hanging. The chest is deep, extending to the elbows, yet is not broad. Height: 20–22 inches (51–56 cm). Weight: 35–60 pounds (16–26 kg). This Pointer is usually seen sporting a short and smooth coat; an older type coat also occurs that is longer haired with feathering on ears, underside and tail. In color the breed is yellow or chestnut, varying in intensities—solid colors as well as Irish patterned whites. In temperament these dogs should be outwardly affectionate, loyal to the master, and energetic on the field.

Portuguese Rabbit Dog
    See Podengo Português

Portuguese Pointer, smooth, chestnut with white. Courtesy of Canil de Torres.

likely that the breed contributed to other early gundogs. The Portuguese Pointer docked in England in the early 1700s and is believed responsible for the dish face of the modern English Pointer. The breed today enjoys a wealth of popularity with its Portuguese fanciers. Dedicated breeders and serious hunters have made certain that the breed's hunting abilities have been retained; its versatility extends to pointing and retrieving skills. He is able to withstand the most severe climates and terrains and is intensely committed to the hunt.

Portuguese Sheepdog
    An alternative name for two different breeds, Cão da Serra de Aires and the Estrela Mountain Dog, which *see*.

Portuguese Watchdog
    See Rafeiro do Alentejo

Portuguese Pointer, long, red with white. Photo by I. Français.

ESSENTIALS OF THE PORTUGUESE POINTER: The body is well balanced with good sufficiency of bone, presenting an overall quick and powerful appearance. The skull is broad between the ears; the muzzle is

Portuguese Water Dog

Robust and well-endowed with muscle and strength, the Portuguese Water Dog sports the conformation of a fine Olympic swimmer. In his native land of Portugal, the Portuguese Water Dog is known as the Cão de Agua, with the long-haired and curly varieties known respectively as the Cão de Agua de Pelo Ondulado and the Cão de Agua de Pelo Encaradolado. In English-speaking countries, the breed is sometimes called the Portuguese Fishing Dog, referring to its long-time function. Some authorities suggest that the breed may trace as far back as 700 B.C., when its forefathers were employed as herding dogs on the steppes of central Asia near the Russo-Chinese border. Over the years, adapting to the terrain and task and bred selectively for working ability, the dogs developed into a definite type, very similar to a heavy-set, long-coated Portuguese Water Dog. How the dogs were brought to Portugal remains disputed, but one theory purports that Goths, a confederation of German tribes, brought some of these dogs with them on their return from the dog's native region. The theory continues to state that some tribes went to the German region and their dogs became the Poodle, while others travelled south to Iberia and their dogs became the Lion Dog, or Portuguese Water Dog. For an unknown length of time, the Lion Dog has been employed by Portuguese fishermen to herd fish into nets, retrieve overboard tackle (or escaped cod), and guard gear on shore. By the early twentieth century, the rustic Portuguese fisherman was vanishing from his shores, and his dogs were following suit. In the 1930s, Dr. Vasco Bensuade, a Portuguese shipping magnate and dog lover, made waves to save the breed. Breaking shore, a club was founded and a standard adopted. By 1954, Porties entered England. Though

accepted by the KCGB, the breed receded from the country by 1957. It entered the U.S. in 1958 and its popularity consistently grew. Today the breed is recognized and found in many countries, including the U.S., Canada, and Britain.

The breed's jaunty expression and captivating looks have brought many newcomers to investigate the Portuguese Water Dogs. These neophytes invariably find a highly intelligent, courageous and untiring companion and sportsman.

ESSENTIALS OF THE PORTUGUESE WATER DOG: He is of medium build, stands from 16–22 inches (40–56 cm) tall, and weighs anywhere between 35–55 pounds (16–25 kg). The coat is profuse, covering the entire body except on the forelegs and thighs. Two types are distinct: long,

Portuguese Water Dogs, brown and black. Photo by I. Français.

Portuguese Water Dog, white.

loosely waved, with sheen; or short, harsh and dense. Two clips are also common: the lion clip and the working-re-

triever clip. In color the Portie is white, black or brown, with or without white markings. The head is well proportioned, strong, and wide; there is a slight taper to the muzzle. Ear leather is heart shaped, thin in texture, and set well above the line of the eyes. Neck is straight, short, and nicely rounded. Brisket deep; ribs long and well sprung; back short; good tuck

up. The tail is not docked, thick at its base and tapering to its tip. The forelegs are strong and straight; the shoulders well

inclined and strongly muscled; the hindquarters are strongly muscled. The Portuguese Water Dog is of exceptional intelligence and great endurance.

Posavac Hound

The Posavac Hound is one of the native scenthounds of Yugoslavia. Generally speaking, each of these hounds developed from early Phoenician sighthound prototypes and various wandering European scenthounds. Their sleek and oftimes long body types indicate sighthound blood. Slavic hunters have appreciated and employed the alacrity and ability of the Posavac for many years. These dogs and their Greek hound relations are the only scenthounds of southeastern Europe and the Balkan area. Hare and deer are the Posavac's usual quarry.

ESSENTIALS OF THE POSAVAC HOUND: Tautly muscular, possessing seamless lines, the Posavac sports a rich red jacket, the texture of which is thick and wiry. Red is the preferred and most often seen color, although breed members can also

Portuguese Water Dog, black. Photographs by I. Français.

come in yellows and fawns, with or without white markings. Weight: 35–45 pounds (16–20 kg). Height: 17–23 inches (43–59 cm).

Posavaski Gonič
See Posavac Hound

Post
Starting position of a contestant; each position is numbered, from 1 to 8, with number 1 being stationed closest to inside of track.

Posterior
Adjective meaning of the back, opposite of anterior.

Postmortems
See Death, postmortems

Postparturition
A term used to refer to the state immediately following the bitch's delivery of pups. *See* Breeding

Pot-hook tail
The pot-hook tail is carried up and over the back, in a high-raised arc, not touching the back, a fault in the British standard for the Lhasa Apso.

Potassium
One of the minerals required by the dog. Potassium deficiency can cause paralysis and other serious conditions.

Potbelly
Swelling of the abdominal region, an undesirable characteristic in any dog. A potbelly can indicate malnutrition or internal parasites. *See also* Bloat

Potlicker
Slang term for a racing Greyhound of poor quality.

Potsdam Greyhound
A small greyhound type of Italy, similar to the Italian Greyhound. The breed, or a similar tiny sighthound type, may still be bred by local Italian breeders, and a number of American fanciers are investigating their present-day whereabouts.

Posavac Hound, fawn with white. Photo by I. Français.

Potterer
A hound that dwells too long on scent.

Pouch
Fold of loose skin that overhangs the point of hocks (e.g., Basset Hound).

Powderpuff
The coated variety of the Chinese Crested. In other breeds of hairless dogs, the equivalent powderpuffs are simply referred to as coated. Breeding of many hairless dogs is dependent upon these coated dogs since they do not carry the dominant lethal gene for hairlessness. The coat gene is the double recessive. Since a hairless-to-hairless mating produces puppies with extreme abnormalities, the coated hairless dog is essential to the propagation of the breed. Two hairless dogs can produce a coated dog—about one in three pups is born coated;

two coated dogs, of course, can only produce coated dogs, but this pairing is rarely necessary. The Chinese Crested Powderpuff and the coated of the other hairless breeds are shown in their own classes at shows, not competing against their naked siblings until Winners class and Best of Breed. *See also* Hairless dogs, Chinese Crested, American Hairless Terrier, etc.

Powderpuff puppies in the Chinese Crested result from most matings. These coated dogs are essential to the propagation of the breed and must be used in all breedings. Photo by I. Français.

Powinder Dog
See Kooichi Dog

P.R.
Suffix indicating the U.K.C. title of Purple Ribbon, which *see.*

P.R.A.
Progressive retinal atrophy, which *see.*

Prance
Springy and bouncy movement originating with the hindquarters.

Pregnancy
A state of the female that begins with the fertilization of an egg(s) within her (conception) and ends with the expellation of the conceived offspring (birth or abortion, natural or otherwise). The duration of pregnancy, known as gestation, is typically 63 days, during which time the bitch goes through many changes, physical, chemical, and psychological. During the first four or five weeks of pregnancy, there is usually little noticeable change in the bitch's body or behavior. She may be a little less inclined to feed, but this should soon pass by the fourth week. If it does not, a veterinarian should be consulted. By the fifth or sixth week, she will begin to show added girth on and around the flanks and a slight prominence to her teats and should demonstrate a marked increase in her interest in food. Exercise should be moderate and performed regularly at this time; the owner should not allow her to engage in any strenuous jumping or quick movements. By the sixth week, a trained professional can detect fetuses in the uterus through an internal examination. The owner should not attempt such a procedure, for there is great risk to the pups when an unskilled hand probes the mother's innards. At this time, feeding is of utmost importance. The bitch should be fed several times daily, and vitamin and mineral supplements should be added to the diet. Cod liver oil, egg yolk, bone meal, fresh meat, and milk have been recommended to many owners as supplements—though do not overfeed. Upon a visit to the veterinarian about this time, he can best counsel you on your bitch's dietary needs. Calcium is of particular importance to the expecting bitch; a calcium deficiency can quickly result in a disease known as eclampsia, which *see.* If she is carrying heavy, usually indicative of a large litter, the bitch will require more frequent but smaller meals served regularly. Each meal should be well balanced and easily digestible. The added pressure that a large litter exerts on the digestive system makes it difficult for the bitch to consume and pass large meals. If she suffers constipation, mineral oil or another mild natural laxative can be given, but strong preparations must certainly not be used. Throughout her pregnancy, fresh water should be available. The bitch should be allowed to drink her

fill. Water helps the bitch remove toxins that can accumulate in the blood during pregnancy and thereby prevents toxemia. During the latter weeks of pregnancy, exercise should be maintained but at low intensity; two daily walks should suffice. As delivery nears, a change in behavior that includes restlessness, nest building, and abstinence from food is to be expected. Delivery is eminent when active contractions begin. Delivery marks the end of pregnancy, at which time nursing begins. *See also* Bitch, Breeding, Nursing dam, Puppies, Reproductive system

Premature birth
Puppies born before their 58th day of development are considered premature. Such puppies are not ready to face the world, because of their prematurity. Premature birth is rare to occasional in dogs, and the common causes are injury and accident and not an inherent weakness on the part of the bitch. Premature puppies require special care. They usually need bottle nursing, for they are too small and weak to nurse from their mother; they must also be kept warm at all times. Most premature pups stand little chance of survival, though it is not unheard that entire early litters have survived, but this is most always due to the litter itself and not the owner. If your bitch delivers early, contact your vet immediately, keep the pups warm, and nurse them with simulated bitch's milk.

Premium list
The printed offering of prizes by a show-giving club which is submitted to the prospective exhibitor when requested in order to enter a dog by the owner from show secretary or superintendent.

Premolars
See Dentition

Prepotency
In breeding, a dog's ability to transmit a particular quality or feature to its offspring consistently. Concerned with genetic dominance (homozygocity), prepotency is usually a term that refers to male dogs rather than female. *See also* Breeding, Genetics

Prick ears
See Erect ears

Primary teeth
Milk teeth or deciduous teeth are the puppy's first teeth. *See* Milk teeth, Dentition

Primidone
One of many anticonvulsant drugs.

Prince Charles
The term for the tricolor pattern in English toy spaniels.

Problem dogs
A dog's problem (the possession of an undesirable trait) is defined by its owner in most cases. Problem dogs are those that bark incessantly, cannot be housebroken, jump on people or objects, run away, bite, destroy furniture or other possessions, fight with other animals, dig holes, and perform innumerable other undesirable actions. A dog that has a problem in the eyes of its owner is a nuisance, and though he may love his

Pregnancy, whelping and nursing prove stressful to the bitch. Newfoundland mother and pups photographed by R. Reagan.

dog, the relationship between owner and dog is at high risk. Many dogs that suffer the fate of abandonment, lack of care, or other forms of neglect are those that can be classed as problem dogs. Yet, many dogs that exhibit problems would not continue to do so if their owner knew just a little dog psychology. The dog is a unique animal in that it alone wishes to serve man, to please man, to heed man, and will do so willingly if reared properly. Ironically, many of the problems that dogs exhibit (i.e., barking, biting, shyness, begging) are actually taught them by their owners. A discussion of learned responses and ways to modify them is found under Behavior modification, which *see*. Additionally, many specific problems, numerous as they are, are discussed individually under their appropriate headings, e.g., Barking, Viciousness.

Problem dogs. Disciplining puppies and discouraging inappropriate behavior are the first step in avoiding the chances of a problem adult dog. Photo by R. Pearcy.

Proctitis
Inflammation of the rectum.

Progression
Form of wagering in which the bettor doubles or adds to the sum wagered each time he selects a loser on the theory that when a winner is selected a profit will be shown on series of bets.

Progressive retinal atrophy
P.R.A. is a form of blindness that frequently affects dogs; in the dog, it is a recessive trait, that is, an inherited kind of blindness. Onset occurs at different ages in different breeds. In the Collie and Irish Setter, progressive retinal atrophy can begin at four to six months of age; in the Miniature Poodle, P.R.A. can onset at age of three to five years. Poor sight or night blindness are sometimes early symptoms of P.R.A. Some other breeds that may be stricken with the disorder more commonly are Cocker Spaniels, Cardi-

gan Welsh Corgis, Cairn Terriers, Norwegian Elkhounds and a few others. Although there is no effective therapy available, selective breeding can help ensure P.R.A.'s not occurring in future litters.

Prolactin
A substance found in female dogs which is in part responsible for their motherly instinct.

Prolonged soft palate
See Palate

Prominent eyes
Eyes that protrude slightly, more so than full eyes, less so than bulging eyes.

Propeller ears
Like fly ears, these are incorrectly carried, sticking out from the head in a propellerlike fashion.

Propped
Speed is retarded, during a race, by extending forelegs and putting on the brakes; it may be a momentary hesitation or complete stop.

Propped stance
A stance adopted usually from stubbornness in which the dog outstretches his forelegs further than desired, making the forearms not perpendicular to the ground. The hindlegs, to compensate defiantly for balance, are often altered as well.

Prostate gland
A partly muscular gland that surrounds the urethra and lies at the base of the bladder. The prostate gland secretes an alkaline substance that is ejaculated with the sperm. If the prostate gland becomes infected, the secretion will contain numerous pus cells that negatively affect the sperm, often resulting in treatable infertility. Older dogs sometimes suffer from prostatic enlargement, which may be the result of infection, hormonal actions, or tumorous growths. The enlarged gland can be felt as a swelling in the pelvic region of the dog. Signs of the disorder include straining to defecate, constipation, and soft stools.

Prostatitis

Inflammation of the prostate gland. Usually caused by a bacterial infection, it is treated with antibiotics.

Prosternum

The breast bone portion that projects beyond the shoulder point when the dog is seen from the side.

Protest

A written charge which may be filed at a show by an exhibitor while within the ring or from outside the ring, by a member of a member club, the latter in writing with the superintendent or bench show committee alleging that a certain dog is being show in violation of a registry's rules. A cash deposit is required. Some protests must be adjudicated immediately by the bench show committee. Others may be determined after the closing of the show. Certain protests may also be filed with the registry after a show's closing.

Protozoan

Microscopic animals, many of which live parasitically and make dogs' days miserable.

Protruding eyes

Eyes that bulge to varying degrees. Full eyes, prominent eyes, goggled eyes, and bulging eyes all describe this condition or type of eyes.

Pruritis

See Itching

Pseudomonas

One bacterial infection that is known for its difficulty to eradicate. Specific and concentrated antibiotics prescribed by a veterinarian may be necessary to rid the infection.

Pseudopregnancy

A condition that occurs after the ovulation of a non-mated bitch. Although not pregnant, she exhibits the signs of pregnancy, including swelling of the breasts, increase in appetite, change in behavior, etc., and may even build a nest. The condition is absolutely normal and will subside with time.

Psittacosis

This disease that affects birds and people has been diagnosed in rare instances in dogs. A soft, persistent cough indicates that the dog has been exposed, and a radiograph will show a cloudy portion on the affected areas of the lung. This is a highly contagious disease to the point where it can be contracted during a post mortem.

Psowaya Barsaya

See Borzoi

Puce

Solid liver coloration on the Irish Water Spaniel.

Pudelpointer, liver. Photo by I. Français.

Pudelpointer

A manufactured breed of the late nineteenth century, created by the German Baron von Zedlitz. The Baron, as well as many of native huntsmen, desired the ultimate hunting dog, the perfect "all-arounder." He began with some 90 pointers and 7 Poodles. The pointers were a variety of both English and Continental working dogs and the Poodles disputedly either of modern-type or their older forebears—Barbets. The breed took time to perfect, but in the end it acquired many of the truly desirable qualities of the variety of dogs that contributed, including intelligence, stamina, good nose, staunch pointing, water-working ability, and a weather- and work-resistant coat.

The breed is revered by many hunters in its native *Deutschland*, and a few specimens are found working the game of Canada and the U.S. Of utmost importance is the dog's field ability. Before a specimen can be entered into the stud book of Germany, it must pass well a rigorous field trial test. This test, or series of tests, includes water, field, and woods work, as well as retrieving such game as hare and fox under a variety of demanding circumstances. Judgment is based on nose, searching, pointing, retrieving, and obedience. The breed is renowned for its field trial abilities. It is usually found in the hands of serious hunters only.

ESSENTIALS OF THE PUDELPOINTER: Standing plenty of ground, powerful and taut, the Pudelpointer is a sufficiently tall hunter. The dog stands to 26 inches (66 cm) at the withers. The coat is short, rough, and waterproof, rather tightly fitting to the body, with a fine, woolly undercoat. Chestnut to deadleaf, dark liver to autumn leaf, are the desired colors, but black occurs in dogs with concentrated Pointer blood. The chest is deep and wide, and the loins are strong. The shoulders and upper arms sufficiently angulated for good movement. The tail is docked in the manner of the German Shorthaired Pointer's.

Puerperal tetany
See Eclampsia

Puffs
Odd terminology for round bands of hair on the forelegs of Poodles prepared in either the English Saddle or Continental clip.

Pug, silver fawn. Photo by I. Français.

Pug
The Pug, a miniature mastiff, has been domesticated since 400 B.C. and finds its roots in the Orient. Like many other toy dogs, the Pug was favored by Buddhist priests and kept as a companion in the monasteries. Japan also enjoyed the companionship of the Pug for many years prior to its introduction to the European continent. In the sixteenth century, the Pug found tremendous favor in Holland. The Dutch Pug, as it was called there, was regarded with esteem after it saved the life of William, Prince of Orange, by barking and warning of the Spanish's approach at Hermingny. Incidentally, the Dutch East India Company is believed to be this brachycephalic dwarf's ticket into Holland.

As with many of the small breeds, the Pug was larger at one time, as one usually

expects a mastiff to exceed 18 pounds. The breed has had an effect on a number of beloved British dogs, including the Bulldog and the Affenpinscher. During the reign of William III, the Pug found his way to Britain and into the favor of this monarch. The first black Pugs to arrive in England came by way of Lady Brassey in 1877. Prior to this time, the West had not seen but golden (fawn) Pugs.

The name Pug initially belonged to the pet marmoset monkey, a popular home companion in the eighteenth century. "Pug Dog" was the breed's original name to distinguish it thus from this personable primate. A second possible derivation of the appellation Pug comes from the Latin. *Pug* in Latin means "fist," alluding to the dog's head in profile. This latter explanation is the less likely. Of course, the word pug in the English language has become synonymous for the breed's short, thick, turned-up (pug) nose. In Holland, the breed was known as "Mopshond," the Dutch infinitive "to grumble." This translation reveals the breed's unique impression, though if the Pug grumbles (some say he snores!), he does so as quaintly as caninely possible. In France he is known as the Carlin. *Multum in parvo*, the Pug certainly is a lot in a little package! He is massiver and more solid than most of his fellow toys and makes a hardy companion dog. Rumors of yore complained that Pugs snored and were greedy, making rotund

and resonant pets. This most assuredly is not true—while Pugs do snore in reality, they are not necessarily greedy.

ESSENTIALS OF THE PUG: In appearance the Pug is decidedly square and cobby, with a compact form, well-knit proportions and hard muscles. The head is large and round with no indentation. The nose is snubbed. The muzzle is short, blunt and square, not upfaced. Wrinkles are clearly defined on the face. The coat is fine, smooth and soft, neither short nor woolly. The chest is wide and well ribbed up. The legs are very strong, straight and moderate in length, well under. Colors include apricot, black and silver-fawn. The mask should be black; darker and more intense are desirable. Height: 10–11 inches (25–28 cm). Weight: 14–18 pounds (6–8.5 kg). The ears can either be rose or button.

Puli

A short-coupled, thickly coated, herding dog native to Hungary and a believed descendant of ancient dogs of the East. The Puli's tail, which distinctly curls over its back, contributes to and supports this general assumption. The breed came to its native land with the Magyars, one of the many tribes of nomadic Huns that migrated to eastern Europe. The Magyars settled in the region now known as Hungary around the ninth century A.D.,

Pug, black.

Puli, white, puppy. Photograph by I. Français.

and they brought with them their sheep and horses and their dogs that were used to herd and protect these flocks. The

Puli, black. Photo by I. Français.

Pulik, gray. Photo by V. Serbin.

Puli's breed name is derived from *Puli Hou*, which translated means the "destroyer Huns." Of general etymological interest, the plural of Puli in Hungary is *Pulix*, while in the U.S. the plural is *Pulik*.

That the Puli is a smaller version of the ancient Tibetan Dog is an assertion that stands up most to conjecture. Resembling the Tibetan Terrier in color and conformation, the Puli may indeed be a less sizable Komondor. As the Chinese candidly assert, Tibetans have produced both "the most beautiful women and the worst-tempered dogs." The Puli that migrated with the Magyars to Hungary retained much of this Tibetan choler. His fervor and assertiveness transfer well to his flock detail. His size and energy make him an eager herder, and his innate belligerence (since mellowed) makes him a fearless and confident guard. Additionally, the Puli's incessantly matted coat affords protec-

tion from both the elements and the dangers of herding duty. Today's Puli is lighthearted, agile and decidedly sound.

His coat requires a dedicated owner to keep it well groomed. More commonly, he is kept unclipped and uncombed—of course, keeping him unkempt keeps his keeper busy keeping the long cords clean and unmatted. *See also* Corded coat

ESSENTIALS OF THE PULI: In general characteristics, he is a sturdy and effective herding dog of extreme intelligence and medium size. The woolly, naturally forming cords that cover the tightly knit body of the Puli are the breed's trademark. The head is medium-sized; skull is slightly domed. The muzzle one-third the length of the head, ending in a bluntly rounded nose. Withers slightly higher than level of back, which is of medium length. Ribs deep and well sprung. Hindquarters strong and well muscled. Well bent stifle. Hocks set fairly low. The tail is medium in length and carried curled tightly over the rump-loin area. The coat is dense and profuse on all parts of the body. Wavy or curly, the outer coat is never silky; the undercoat is soft. The coat clumps naturally and forms cords on the adult dog. Height: 14–19 inches

(35.5–48 cm). Weight: 20–40 pounds (9–18 kg). In color the Puli is usually dark—black, rusty black, and gray—but can be apricot or white as well.

Pulmonary osteoarthropathy

A condition involving bony deposits on bone surfaces. *See* Maries disease

Pulse

What is called the pulse is actually the expansion and contraction of the blood vessels as the blood moves through them. The pulse of a dog varies according to its age, weight, size, and breed. Typically, small dogs have a pulse of 100 beats per minute or more, while large dogs tend to have a pulse of 75 beats per minute or less. Your veterinarian can help you determine if your dog's pulse is normal.

Pumi

The Pumi, like the Puli, is a hard-working herder, native to Hungary, very strong, sound and independent. The Puli was created from crosses of the Magyar's Puli with Pomeranian or Hutespitz dogs that were brought to Hungary during the seventeenth and eighteenth centuries. This was a time of considerable trading between the Hungarian, German, and French peoples, and dogs were often exchanged in conjunction with sheep and other valuable livestock.

Whereas the Puli was the premier Hungarian sheep and horse herder, the Pumi was created for the defined purpose of droving cattle. The breed has existed in its perfected type for at least several centuries and remains a favorite cattle dog of the Hungarian people.

The long coat (without the cords) is inherited from the Puli; the ear carriage and volatile temperament are derived from his drover-type relations. The Pumi's ears are arguably the most unique in all of dogdom. Like the Mudi, the Pumi is a multi-functional dog. He is primarily a cow herder but can also double as an

exterminator and triple as a watchdog.

ESSENTIALS OF THE PUMI: An active and courageous cattle drover of spirited character; the working Pumi is said never to be quiet. The head is strong; skull moderate and slightly domed; well covered with plush coat. The ears are semi-erect and set high on the skull. The neck, of good length, is strong and well muscled. Back is straight and strong. Chest is deep. Legs of good length: forelegs straight; hind legs of moderate angulation. The coat is moderately long, composed of plush curls that never cord. Any solid color except white is acceptable: shades of silver, dove gray and slate are most common. Height: 13–19 inches (33–48 cm). Weight: 18–29 pounds (8–13 kg). The tail is a fair indicator of the breed's temperament, always merry and carried high.

Pumi, white. Photo by I. Français.

Pumik, (*top*) silver; (*bottom left*) dove gray; (*bottom right*) white and gray. Photographs by I. Français.

Puncture wounds

Often deep but rarely long or wide, puncture wounds require pressure applied to stop the bleeding and a disinfectant cleaning. The owner must keep close watch for internal bleeding and bacterial infection, including tetanus. If the animal is in serious pain or shows signs of infection or internal damage, seek veterinary counsel immediately.

Punishment

Physical or verbal, smacking, scolding, or neglect punishment is not necessary in any dog-training and finds no place in any healthy person-to-pet relationship. *See also* Behavior modification, Training, Housebreaking

this show definition also serves to qualify those dogs eligible for competition in such a class.

For breeders, trainers, and pet owners, a puppy may be defined as any dog who is not physically matured. Different breeds reach physical maturity at different ages, though most breeds mature between the 12th and 18th months, with a few breeds, such as the Bullmastiff, not reaching full maturity until sometime around the 24th month. Especially among owners of the large breeds, a common mistake is to treat a fully grown dog as a mature dog and not as a puppy. A puppy is a puppy until it is mature in both mind and body. Treating a pup as a dog and correcting it for behavior it has

Puppies

The term puppy can be defined in various ways, according to the intention of the definition. For the American Kennel Club and other kennel clubs throughout the world, a puppy is any dog registered by the kennel club who is over the age of six months but under the age of twelve months. This definition serves the purpose of defining those dogs that are eligible for competition in the Puppy Class. In Australia there is also a Baby Puppy Class, and a "baby puppy" is defined as any registered dog under the age of six months but over the age of three months;

yet to learn and is unable to master can only lead to unhappiness and frustration.

From birth to twenty days is a time of great physical growth for the pup. In fact, so rapid is the rate of development that scientists have broken this short period into two parts to allow them to better understand and discuss this time of transformation. The two periods are known as the "neonatal period" (birth to 12 days) and the "transition period" (13 to 20 days). Total dependence pervades the pups' first twelve days of life: they are blind, weak, and do not have adequate energy stored to live too many hours

Puppies. A basket (or pile) of basking Shar-Pei puppies.

without a feeding. They are totally reliant upon the dam (and/or the owner) to provide their food, warmth, and stimula-

Puppies. At twenty-one days of age, these Great Pyrenees pups still experience a heavy reliance on the dam and characteristically sleep in rows, not piles. Photo by Rhonda Dalton.

Puppies. Treeing Walker Coonhound dam nursing her litter. The strongest relationship between dam and whelps occurs during the first two weeks of life. Photo courtesy of Danny May.

tion. This is a very critical time for the pups, and many succumb to disease and other conditions during this period. The pup at birth is only partially developed: its hearing, sight, metabolism, and temperature regulation are all yet to be completed. The newborn has no teeth, cannot walk, and can empty its bowels only with stimulation from the mother or caretaker. Its brain and motor coordination are also poorly developed, making the pup's response to stimuli slow and ineffective and leaving its safety in the hands of the mother. In short, the neonatal pup is a feeble, totally dependent animal that needs nutrition, warmth, and protection. Ideally these come from its mother, with helpful intervention on the part of the knowledgeable owner. It is remarkable to witness the growth of pups during this stage: they change greatly every day.

The transition period is thus called because this is a time when the dependent pups grow to the beginnings of recognition of their environment and functioning of their own accord. This period begins with the opening of the pup's eyes and ends with the coming of the startle response, which marks development of the brain and motor coordination. It is, like the neonatal, a time of remarkable development and change: physical and mental as well as emotional abilities begin to emerge.

Of importance during the neonatal and transition periods are housing, cleanliness, socialization and feeding. The original whelping box or a box of similar size should suffice for the pups' first week of life, but by the tenth or twelfth day it may be wise to move them to another box, keeping them warm and allowing the bitch easy access at all times. Cleanliness should be exercised at all times. Bedding should be changed frequently, and the owner must make sure that the bitch stimulates and cleans the pups after each feeding; if she fails, the owner must intercede. Socialization begins at birth, when the pups first meet the

bitch at the nipple and each other in the whelping box; the first jockey for nipple control and all subsequent struggles are an important part of puppy socialization, and soon each pup's personality will be hinted in the pup's vying for the nipple. The owner must ensure that all pups receive the proper amount of milk; it is not unusual, especially in larger litters, for one or more of the pups to be pushed aside at feeding time. These pups are usually the smaller and more timid ones and may require bottle feeding from the owner. Weak pups need special attention. Giving them a nipple of their own before the rest of the litter is fed is viable, as is supplemental bottle feeding. Pups who are unusually weak or seemingly sickly should perhaps be culled at the recommendation of a veterinarian or other professional. This period is the first and possibly the most trying testing ground. Pups that survive well to the end of the transition period have a good chance of making it to a healthy adulthood.

The end of the transition period marks the beginning of the "litter socialization period" (21 to 35 days). This period is so called because it marks the puppy's awareness of others in his environment besides itself and its mother. It is during the litter socialization period that the pups' personalities emerge. Each pup's senses, brain, and motor function approach near-total development, allowing the pup to perceive and respond to its environment and those that are a part of it; the pup now becomes a conscious being while gaining muscle strength and coordination. Additionally, the pup can now react emotionally to the stimuli of its environment: it will startle, whimper, or sleep contentedly. At this stage the

puppy will possess vocal cords that enable it to bark, an important tool for human and litter socialization. Because the pup is aware of its environment, cleanliness as well as acclimatization to noise and other environmental conditions are of utmost importance at this time. A pup that is forced to live with its feces will ultimately grow into a "dirty" dog that is hard to housebreak and possibly hard to train. A pup that lives in a kennel with little human contact can grow to fear, disregard, or dislike human beings—likely never to be a good pet.

A puppy's socialization with its siblings and human counterparts brings the emergence of the pack instinct: leaders and followers will emerge, and each dog will learn its contribution to the group. What makes a pack leader or dominant pup can be its size, strength, energy, or vocal ability, depending on the breed, the litter size, and the individual litter and dog. Although the pup's individuality is emerging at this stage, the pup is not yet ready for life as an independent animal; it still needs its littermates, its mother, and its breeder. The pup's environment should be relatively unchanging, contact with outsiders should be limited, and time away from the nest should be kept to short intervals. Attempting to train any dog at this time is likely futile. Let the pups be pups. They have much yet to

Puppies at a young age learn the rules of canine society through interaction with litter mates. Akitas emerging from whelping box.

learn, and there will be plenty of time for behavior modification later.

The puppy's fifth through twelfth weeks are known as its "human socialization period." This is a time when the interactions with humans are crucial in determining to a large extent how well the pup will blend into its human pack—all contacts with people imprint upon the developing dog. People should be gentle and kind with the pups at this stage. It is especially important to educate and monitor children at this time, for reckless and abusive children can instill a lifelong fear of children in the dog. The pup must come to associate pleasantness with people, and correction must be kept to a minimum. Although by four weeks of age, the beginning of the human socialization period, the pup is able to learn simple tasks, it has yet to master control of its muscles. By five weeks, the pup's curiosity is evident: it will begin to explore and learn about its environment; its brain and sensory perception become more acute and its emotional reactions are easily observed. The pup goes through what is called a "fear

period" at this stage, during which a fear of strangers, unknown sounds, and changes in the environment occur. The stage is transitory, leaving the dog a more secure and independent animal. Two more fear periods will occur; one around the eight-week mark and another during the "juvenile period." The need and desire to investigate grows stronger every day, and the pups quickly learn that there is a strange but terribly interesting world outside the litter and its box. The pup will show interest and hesitation in the people it meets. As long as the interaction is gentle and rewarding, the pup should grow into an obedient, well-acclimated dog who is a joy to the owner and a credit to its breed and breeder.

It is during this period that most pups receive their first shots, and their interaction with the vet is important. A bad first experience at the vet's can lead to lasting fear of the vet and even extend to car travel (the mode by which the pup arrived at the vet's office). Also occurring during the human socialization period is the process known as weaning.

Weaning often concurs with the second fear stage and is a moment of great importance to the pup, marking the beginning of its existence as a "mature"

animal no longer totally reliant upon its mother.

The age of seven through twelve weeks is a second transition stage. It is during this period that most pups leave their mother and kin and travel to a new home. If the pup has been properly reared to this point, it is ready to take this great step. Of course, the pup has been

Puppies. Eight-week-old Old English Sheepdog pups require daily one-on-one attention to be properly socialized. Under usual circumstances, puppies are released to homes around the eighth week so that socialization can be assumed by the new owners.

Puppies. Samoyed pups beginning to develop their own unique personalities and expressions.

weaned for at least a week prior to its exit and should demonstrate good muscle and mental ability and a fair degree of control. It should not fear humans and should be relatively secure in itself as an individual. However, it must be remembered that around eight weeks the pup goes through a second fear period in which it is important to limit changes in its environment; if, however, weaning has already been accomplished by the eighth week, the eighth week fear period may have already passed. The period is usually initiated by the dam, as she begins to threaten the pups while they nurse, and this threat behavior carries over to the pups' play and formation of the group instinct. It is during this second fear period that the pups learn the nature of dominance and submission and how to use fear in their later relationships—by eight weeks, the pup's memory is fully developed and most of what it learns at this time will affect its future interactions with humans and other animals. Therefore, while seven to twelve weeks is a good time to transfer the pup to its new home, the six to twelve days of this second fear period are a very bad time to transfer the pups; the added stress could affect the developing dog for the remainder of its life.

By the end of the second transition period, members of the litter should be eating solid to semi-solid food. All foods at this point should be softened with milk, water or another suitable liquid. The pups should at this time be introduced gradually to the outdoors, collars and leashes, and/or other concepts, objects or conditions that will have to be confronted in later life.

The "juvenile period" of a dog typically lasts from twelve weeks to six

months. All senses reach full development, usually by the twelfth week or shortly thereafter; emotional maturity is usually achieved sometime between the 13th and 16th week; and sexual development begins sometime around the 16th week and continues through to adult-

hood, with males beginning to mark their territory with urine by their eighth month. The teething process is com-

Puppies of two little-known hound breeds, the Majestic Tree Hound (*above*) and the Berner Laufhund (*below*). While most puppies in the juvenile period become more independent, many hound breeds continue to rely heavily on fellow dogs and human acquaintances. Berner pups by I. Français.

Puppies. (*top*) Even pups intended for protection work must be gently treated and reared lovingly. Dogue de Bordeaux pup photographed by I. Français.

Puppies (*bottom left*) certainly enjoy pampering, however, carriage rides must not replace the dog's lead training.

Puppies. (*bottom right*) A child growing with a dog in his life reaps certain benefits by experiencing unconditional affection. Dalmatian photo by Cheryl Fales Steinmetz.

Puppies. The highly favored Japanese son of author Andrew De Prisco, Jacquet's Tengu at five weeks, Shiba Inu bred by Rick Tomita.

Puppies. Terrier breeds, such as the Cairn (*left*) and Wire Fox (*right*), prove to be scrappy, feisty adolescents. Photographs by I. Français.

pleted and the permanent teeth are in around the 16th week. Overall, the juvenile period is a time of great enjoyment for the owner with his pup; training, including housetraining, can begin in earnest; the pup's intelligence and absorption are impressive; and his playfulness is marked and exciting. *See also* Socialization, Behavior modification, Training, Housebreaking, Children and dogs

Puppies should be acquired from a reputable source. While it may be possible to purchase healthy puppies from a backyard breeder, investigating the seller's credibility is tantamount to acquiring a healthy dog. Toy Fox Terrier puppies photographed by Tom Caravaglia.

Puppy clip
See Clipping the Poodle; *See also* Poodle, Grooming

Puppy class
Puppy classes at dog shows are designed for exhibiting canine starlets. Puppy classes begin at six months of age (on the day of the show) and are typically divided into six-to-nine-month and nine-to-twelve-month old dogs.

Puppy mills
"Puppy mills" is a colloquialism for irreputable breeding factories that produce puppies with little concern for the betterment of the breed and the quality of the animals that they are producing. Puppy mills are infamous for supplying pet shops—these farms raise thousands of dogs, most of which are physically ill, all of which are mistreated and unsocialized. These breeders are to be avoided like the plague, which their puppies may indeed be carrying. Breeding requires knowledge, dedication, and healthy working stock. Purchasing a show-quality bitch and breeding her every season cannot promise positive results in the long run. Puppy mills are largely responsible for the deterioration of many popular breeds today. These money-motivated practices do not produce unpopular breeds: a Harrier puppy mill is an oxymoron of sorts. Those breeds sitting pretty on the stats list are the ones to be most conscious of. *See also* Choosing a dog, Breeding, Genetics

Purchasing
See Choosing a dog

Pure boar bristle brush
Excellent for regular brushing. Removes loose hair and distributes a dog's natural oil from the skin down the hair shaft. Promotes a healthy, shiny coat. *See also* Grooming

Purebred -vs- mongrel
See Choosing a dog

Purple Ribbon pedigree
A Purple Ribbon or "P.R." is the prefix attached to a United Kennel Club-registered purebred dog that has six generations of known ancestors. This determination, registered and trademarked by the U.K.C. in the 1930s, also requires that all of the dog's 14 ancestors in the last three generations be U.K.C.-registered. It is the highest pedigree awarded by this American registry.

Put down
When an animal is humanely put to death. *See also* Culling, Breeding

Putty nose
See Dudley nose

Pyoderma
Pyoderma simply means pus under the skin. The two common pyodermic conditions are lip-fold and interdigital pyoderma, which *see*.

Pyometra

Term referring to pus in the uterus. *See* Uterine infections

Pyothorax

Pus in the chest cavity; may follow an injury, infection or other abnormal condition of the chest region.

Pyrenean Mastiff

Many of the flock guarding breeds that serve the region of the Iberian peninsula are believed to have descended from dogs left by the Phoenicians in the Mediterranean trading expeditions. Phoenicians, the often-cited trading folk, stocked much of their canine cargo in Sumeria and Assyria, and many of these dogs were left in Spain, where they eventually were purchased for or coerced into guard work for the great peninsular flocks. It is quite probable that shepherds throughout France, Spain, and various adjacent regions traded and re-traded various of their flock guards. Finally, however, in the mid-nineteenth century, action was taken to delineate the Pyrenean Mastiff as a distinct breed. The Pyrenean Mastiff was instrumental in maneuvering these large masses of often uncooperative ovines to and from grassy pasture. One dog per 200 sheep was the average responsibility—often five or six dogs worked a 1000-head herd.

Both the Spanish Mastiff and the Great Pyrenees contribute to the complete picture of the Pyrenean Mastiff's development. In physical appearance, the Pyrenean Mastiff is halfway between these two canines: the Great Pyrenees is more profusely coated, possesses a more graceful head and is rangier; the Spanish Mastiff is smooth coated, possesses different ears and a more definite stop. In Spain and a number of Scandinavian countries, the breed is gaining admirers and employers.

ESSENTIALS OF THE PYRENEAN MASTIFF: A sturdy, powerful build. Gray, brindle, black, or orange markings occurring on a white background describe his color. The coat is moderately long, longer on tail, neck and chest, and contributes to the massive appearance of this powerhouse. Height: 28–32 inches (71–79.5 cm). Weight: 120–155 (55–70 kg). The head is

very deep and excessive dewlap is not uncommon. The broad skull and a wealth of dewlap are suggestive of the Saint Bernard. The thick powerful legs are no less than impressive.

Pyrenean Mountain Dog

Name accepted by the Kennel Club of Great Britain for the great French guard and companion Le Chien de Montagnes des Pyrenees. *See* Great Pyrenees

Pyrenean Shepherd

See Bergers des Pyrenees

Pyrenean Mastiff, white with black.

Pyrenean Mastiff, white with brindle. Photographs by I. Français.

Pyridoxin

A chemical which, if deficient, can cause anemia.

Q-fever

A rickettsial infection common to dog and other animals, including man. It has been described as influenzalike in its symptoms in man and as rarely noticeable in other animals, though it is believed to be responsible for some abortions in sheep and goats. The infection is not often diagnosed, largely because of its lack of signs and symptoms in dogs, but animals are believed to be major transmitters of the disease to man.

Quarantine

A quarantine period for incoming canines is mandatory in most countries—it is the period during which the exported dog is isolated before being allowed to enter the visiting country. Some countries only quarantine dogs that they suspect of carrying a contagious disease; other countries quarantine all entering animals. The period varies from country to country: roughly guestimating from one to nine months. Most nations have established rabies-free licensed kennels in which the dogs are kept. It is vital that dogs under quarantine not come in contact with other dogs.

Quarry

The hunted animal.

Quarters

Refer to the four parts which comprise the bodies of quadru-

peds. Adding the prefixes "fore" or "hind" couples the two respective parts, thereby making the reference to the entire "half" of the carcass. The statement "hindquarters well muscled" would tell the reader that the rear half of the dog, including the hindlegs, hips, and buttocks, possesses good size and quality of muscle. Synonymous with the term "hindquarters" is "quarters, back." The antithetical prefix, in this case "fore," used in such a statement as "forequarters strongly developed," would direct the reader to the front portion of the body, including the front legs, shoulders, etc.

Quarters, muscular

Refers to a dog with good quantity and quality of muscle mass on the quarters, usually the hindquarters, unless otherwise stated. Such quarters give a powerful, often visibly defined, appearance.

Quick

A blood vessel in the dog's nail. Clipping the dog's nail too deeply (or closely) will result in the bleeding of the quick. "A clipped quick makes a dog cower quick." Be quick about having a styptic powder available for such emergencies. If nail clipping (which *see*) is a bad experience for your dog, he will fuss greatly each time you need to cut his nails.

Quiniela

Form of wagering that originated in Mexico. The bettor selects two entries in a race; if both finish either first or second he wins.

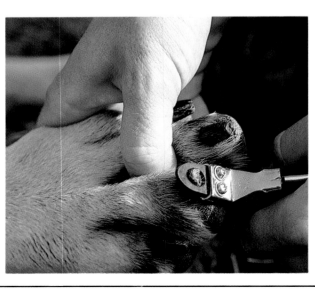

R.S.P.C.A.
See Humane societies

Rabbit-earth
A foxhunting term that refers to the burrow in which the fox frequently goes for shelter.

Rabbiter
A rabbiter is any dog that can hunt the rabbit among its quarry. While bunnies sustain a more benevolent reputation than other pests, they can indeed damage crops and farmland. Fortunately not taxonomically branded "rodentia," rabbits are not usually pursued by terriers but rather by more long-legged extractors. The hounds are the classic warren dogs—both sighthounds and scenthounds. The Portuguese Podengos are sometimes referred to as Rabbit Dogs. Among the spaniels are many competent rabbit and hare dogs. Because of the rabbit's alacrity and celerity, the sighthounds are common pursuants—especially Borzois and Greyhounds, although the latter has been fooled more often than not by cottontailed mechanical lures.

Rabies
An acute, viral, natural disease affecting dogs, and one to which all warm-blooded animals are susceptible. Although at one time all rabies viruses were thought to be the same, several distinct strains of the disease are known today. Discovering these exact strains was important in the development of vaccines. Rabies is of worldwide distribution transmitted from animal to animal by means of a bite. Virus-containing saliva is thereby introduced to the animal's muscle and/or mucous membranes, where there occurs a period of replication (reproduction). After this period, the virus travels to the brain via the peripheral nerves and spinal cord. The disease then also infiltrates the salivary glands, at which time the affected animal can transmit the disease to others. If the disease is treated before it travels to the brain and typical signs are exhibited, the chance of recovery is good. If, however, signs are evidenced, the disease is most often fatal, although cases of recovery are recorded.

The first sign of rabies is a change in behavior. This change may not be different from those resulting from indigestion, injury, poisoning or the early stage of another infectious disease. Most animals will cease consuming food and water, and many will strive to be alone. The course and accompanying signs of

the rabies infection can be divided into three phases: "prodromal, excitative, and paralytic." Depending on the length of the excitative phase, the case can be labeled as either furious or dumb (paralytic) rabies. In furious rabies, the excitative phase is the predominant phase, and the dog seems to turn mad, which is to say he becomes aggressive, vicious, and wild, often biting and clawing other animals and objects around him. The dog appears highly alert and stressed; a

Rabies is frequently transmitted to dogs from raccoons in North American territories.

simple, common noise can cause attack. There is little sign of paralysis during this stage of the disease, but it will set in as the disease progresses and is the cause of death. Dogs rarely live more than ten days after the initial signs are shown. Infected puppies reportedly seek human companionship during the excitative stage but respond to stroking by biting without warning. The paralytic form is characterized by the early onset of paralysis, typically beginning with the throat and accompanied by profuse salivation and an inability to swallow. Typically the dog's lower jaw will hang limply. Affected with the paralytic form, dogs are less inclined to bite or attack and usually die a day or so after the initial onset of paralysis, which is the cause of death.

Rabies is contagious to man and owners must exercise great caution if they suspect that their dog has contracted rabies. It is imperative to get medical attention as quickly as possible. There are inoculations against the disease, and many communities require all licensed dogs to receive such treatment.

Raccoon dog

Native to Japan and bearing a most curious resemblance to a large raccoon is the raccoon dog, *Nyctereutes procyonoides*. This wild dog stands about 15 inches (38 cm) at the withers and weighs 8 to 13 pounds (3.5–6 kg) during the summer, but as much as 20 pounds (9 kg) prior to hibernation. Originally found from eastern Siberia through Manchuria, Korea, mainland China, and into northern Vietnam, the raccoon dog has a coat of such value that the U.S.S.R released several thousand of these animals in scattered regions of the motherland, hoping that the animal would establish itself. It did, and today these valued creatures inhabit not only the western U.S.S.R. but also Poland, Finland and parts of Sweden. It is likely that it will continue to spread westward into Germany and beyond. Ironically, while the raccoon dog spreads further west, it is vanishing in the East, particularly in its native Japan, which though rich in folk-

lore regarding the dog, found it more pleasing to be rich in their fur-lined pockets and therefore hunted the canid extensively. Today the raccoon dog is limited to small portions of the Nipponese islands. Preferring the profusely vegetated river banks, the raccoon dog is rarely observed in the wild.

Raccoon dog, *Nyctereutes procyonoides*, photographed in captivity by R. Pearcy.

Racy

A racy dog is clean cut and aerodynamic, with what many feel to be a certain elegance. The Sloughi is an example of a racy dog.

Radial nerve paralysis

The radial nerve controls the movement of the front of the foreleg. When this nerve is damaged by injury, often the result of a blow against it, the signs are similar to those of a dislocation. The nerve damage is irreparable, and the dog will likely lose control of the affected limb for life.

Radius

In what is called the forearm of the dog (the length of the dog's front legs below the elbow joint) there exists a bony component which is called the radius.

Rafeiro do Alentejo

This instinctive native Portuguese flock guard developed from various Spanish mastins in the south of Portugal. The breed, at 30 inches (76 cm) at the shoulder, is one of the tallest dogs in the flock guardian group. Likely contributors to the Rafeiro, sometimes known as the Portuguese Watchdog, are the Estrela Mountain Dog and the Spanish Mastiff. Aggressive and rowdy by nature, these dogs are dauntless guards for the flocks they watch and are frequently employed as estate guards. In the U.S.A., they are currently used in flock-guarding programs, though few have been imported.

ESSENTIALS OF THE RAFEIRO DO ALENTEJO: The Rafeiro is a stocky dog, having a short neck, thick chest, well-developed limbs, and a very strong, solid back. Height: 30 inches (76 cm). Weight: 95–110 pounds (43–50 kg). The coat is medium-short and spotted; it can be composed of gray, brindle, black, red, or yellow hairs in varying amounts. Besides its build, other notable features include heavily boned forepaws, oval feet, and a generous dewlap.

Rail runner

Stays close to inner rail of track, thus saving distance.

Railbird

One who follows racing intensely; those who stand against rail or fence, opposite finish line; one who comes to the track early, before racing starts.

Rajapalayam

This strikingly beautiful ivory-colored dog is a multi-dimensional canine once popular in India. Bearing a faint resemblance to the Great Dane, this 120-pound (54 kg) dog could be found in black, silver/gray, and harlequin. Used extensively for hunting, guard work, and companionship, these noble dogs found indoor life monotonous. It is believed that a number of these dogs still exist in parts of India.

Rafeiro do Alentejo, brindle. Photo by I. Français.

Ramp

A great aid for getting big dogs in the tub or on the table. Collapsible models fold up and can be stored when not in use.

Rampur Dog

The Rampur Dog runs among the indigenous sighthounds of India. The question as to whether the breed is a descendant of the Afghan Hound or the Sloughi often arises. Based on the Rampur's entirely smooth coat, the evidence seems to point to the latter breed, yet the Rampur is both bigger and more powerful than the Sloughi. Crosses with English Greyhounds could easily account for the added bulk, but the evidence is too insubstantial to state with certainty anything pertaining to component stock. The Rampur Dog, believably enough, originated in the Indian province of Rampur. He is rarely seen outside of his native land; he is, however, an able hunter worthy of the respect of coursing fanciers around the globe.

The Rampur has the coursing instinct ingrained within him. He uses it to full advantage with his excellent eyesight, good speed, and powerful body. The Rampur is bred for the hunt; it is a rare owner who owns one solely as a pet, though they would make fine companions if properly acclimated.

ESSENTIALS OF THE RAMPUR DOG: Immediately striking is the Rampur's head, with its very pronounced stop and light-colored eyes, which contrast with the mouse-gray coat to wield a disarming impression. He is deep chested and strong backed. His limbs are muscular, allowing for speed over otherwise exhausting distances. He is strong boned, built for the punishment served in the hunt. Height: 25.5–28.5 inches (65–71 cm). Weight: 50–66 pounds (22.5–30 kg).

Range
The distance at which a gundog hunts from his handler.

Rangy
Rarely a compliment, this adjective suggests that a dog is too lengthy and of excessive height for its breed, likely possessing bones too thin.

"Rare" breeds
The concept of "rare" breeds, while not a new one, is surely a modern fad. At a show for exclusively "rare" breeds, no

"Rare" breeds are those which have not received full recognition from a national kennel club because of the small number of specimens in the country. The Japanese Shiba Inu has fast become a much-talked-about rare breed. This is the famed Jacquet's "Chibi", with handler Don Robinder, winning "Rare Breed Dog of the Year" for owner Rick Tomita. Photo by Booth.

Rampur Greyhound
See Rampur Dog

Ram's head
Convexly appearing skull and foreface, with the skull and muzzle toplines diverging and the brow as the highest point.

Ram's nose
A basically straight foreface that dips downwards with the nasal cartilage: opposite of a Roman nose that curves convexly in an uninterrupted line. The term aquiline nose is synonymous and employed in the Scottish Deerhound breed standard.

breed fully recognized by the national registering body is eligible for competiton. Breeds that are included in the Miscellaneous Class therefore do qualify to compete. Examples of frequent rare breed show contestants include the Shiba Inu, Shar-Pei, Spinone Italiano, Lundehund and Löwchen.

Rare thus becomes synonymous or interchangeable with "not fully recognized." This definition of course has its limitations. While the Jack Russell Terrier in the United States is not recognized by either national registry, its numbers are not so few as to commission the status of "rare." Rare, according to the dictionary, should mean scarce, uncommon or not frequently encountered. Breeds that qualify as scarce, by virtue of their numbers, are endangered. Examples of such rare dogs include the Braque du Bourbonnais, Braque Dupuy, Tahltan Bear Dog, Greek Sheepdog, and the Aryan Molossus, to name just a few of the many canines in the world today that are truly infrequently encountered. As time passes, the status of each of these breeds will likely change: while the Tahltan may be extinct in reality, the Bourbonnais grows in numbers steadily.

There are certain breeds registered by the national kennel club which are rather uncommonly seen. The Harrier, Sussex Spaniel, American Water Spaniel and Wirehaired Pointing Griffon are just a few examples of breeds that the average (non-show-ring) person has never seen (or heard of!). In 1988, to be specific, less than five Harrier litters were registered in the entire United States. While each of these breeds have their share of dedicated dog people, they are still numerically scarce in comparison to the dogs in good registration status standing.

Rastreador Brasileiro

The Rastreador Brasileiro (or Brazilian Tracker) was created by Brazilian hunter Oswalde Aranha Filho as a tracker of the South American jaguar. To pursue this mighty feline, a dog had to be sufficiently powerful, absolutely fearless and endowed with the stamina to track for an average of six to seven hours over practically insurmountable terrain—without losing the scent. Various varieties of American Foxhounds served as key ingredients; touches of American coonhounds were

then added (Treeing Walker and Bluetick Coons are usually cited). Another source reports that German Shepherds were being used and crossed with the Foxhounds. Regardless of the exactitude of the components, the breed is a formidable all-weather canine of superior abilities. Its whereabouts today are dubious, and most specimens may be absorbed into obscurity.

ESSENTIALS OF THE RASTREADOR BRASILEIRO: The essential features of this feisty Brazilian include a flat head, which is round with little apparent stop; metallic yellow eyes; a powerful deep chest; and a saberlike tail. This is a dog whose firm conformation is fashioned for endurance and power. The coat is short and rough to the touch. The ears are long and pendulous. Height: 25–27 inches (63–69 cm). Weight: 50–60 pounds (22–27 kg). In color the Rastreador is basically white (and sometimes brown) with blue, chestnut or black markings.

"Rare" breed shows are becoming increasingly popular. This Best in Show Tosa Inu has won the International Molosser Supermatch under judge Rick Tomita for handler Carl Semencic. Photo by I. Français.

Rat Terrier

The Rat Terrier, sometimes called Feist for good reason, is a feisty, hardy little terrier—truly an American at heart. American President Theodore Roosevelt was the breed's most famous fan and he

Rat Terrier, tricolor.

Rat Terrier type known as Feist used to hunt squirrel. Photographs by I. Français.

graciously shared his revelation with the world by naming it Rat Terrier. The early development of the Rat Terrier began in England with crosses between Smooth Fox Terriers and Manchester Terriers. At the height of the ratting craze, these dogs were prize-winning ratters. Wilcox and Walkowicz, in their delightful and soon-to-be-classic volume, *The Atlas of Dog*

Breeds of the World, describe their propensity: "Contests fired bets on how

many rats the dog could kill in a certain period of time. The record is held by a Rat Terrier that killed 2,501 rats found in an infested barn over a seven-hour span." A feat as amazing as it is nauseating. After 70 years and a mountain-high pile of rat carcasses, the Rat Terriers (not yet named) were brought to the United States in 1890. Crosses in the U.S. were orchestrated: Whippet and Beagle were included. The larger sized terriers were used to hunt as well as rat. Squirrel, coon, wild boar and deer are among the breed's quarry. Breeders are not concerned with type and type still varies, mostly in size. Toy Rat Terriers (acquired after a dose of Chihuahua) are commonly seen on farms as companion dogs. Hunters call many Rat Terrier-type dogs Feist since they are never concerned with conformation. A rule of thumb: any Rat Terrier is a Feist, not any Feist is a Rat Terrier.

ESSENTIALS OF THE RAT TERRIER: These smooth-coated "Feisty" terriers come in three different sizes: the Standard is 14–23 inches (35.5–58.5 cm) in height and 12–35 pounds (16 kg) in weight; the Midsized is 8–14 inches (20–35.5 cm) and 6–8 pounds(3–4 kg); and the Toy is 8 inches (20 cm) and 4–6 pounds (2–3 kg). In color the Rat Terriers are tri-spotted, red/white, solid red, black/tan, blue/white, and red brindle. Their bodies are compact but meaty; the heads are tiny and the muzzles pointed.

Rat tail

A thickly rooted tail covered in sparsely distributed hair or with curls (e.g., Irish Water Spaniel).

Rats

The determined vermin that has plagued mankind for time immemorial: the rat, the only uninvited animal onto Noah's great Ark, the emptier of many farmers' silos, the ill-fated quarry of the working terrier group. Terriers for centuries have extracted the squirming, long-tailed, terribly industrious rat from the countryside. Although rats have been domesticated by man and used in laboratory experiments and as pets, their principle lot in this world has not been one of harmony with man.

In nineteenth-century England, rats

were the most popular of prime-time pit victims. Dogs were pitted against rats. Rat contests—competitions in which the

dog that could speedily kill the most rats in the shortest expanse of time was the winner—were the most fashionable form of entertainment among the lower class peoples. The Staffordshire Bull Terrier, the Fox Terrier and the Rat Terrier are among early terriers used for this popular and peculiar proclivity. Although our twentieth-century sensibilities are revolted by the thought of rat carcasses heaved randomly at an enthusiastic onion-eating assembly, our violence-packed, oftimes nauseating television entertainment differs only in its two-dimensionality and its lacking the arousing olfactory and tactile sensations on which the rat pits thrived. *See also* Terriers

Rawhide

The most popular material from which dog chews are made is the hide from cows, horses, and other animals. Most of these chews are made in foreign countries where the quality of the hide is not good enough for making leather. These foreign hides may contain lead, antibiotics, arsenic, or insecticides which might be detrimental to the health of your dog... or even your children. It is not impossible that a small child will start chewing on a piece of rawhide meant for the dog! Rawhide chews do not serve the primary chewing functions very well. They are also a bit messy when wet from mouthing, and most dogs chew them up rather rapidly. They have generally been considered safe for dogs until recently.

Rawhide is flavorful to dogs. They like it. Currently, some veterinarians have been attributing cases of acute constipation to large pieces of incompletely digested rawhide in the intestine. Basically it is good for them to chew on, but dogs think rawhide is food. They do not play with it nor do they use it as a pacifier to relieve doggie tension. They eat it as they would any other food. This is dangerous, for the hide is very difficult for dogs to digest and swallow, and many dogs choke on large particles of rawhide that become stuck in their throats. Before you offer

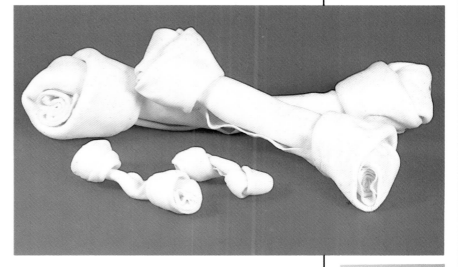

your dog rawhide chews, consult your veterinarian. Vets have a lot of experience with canine chewing devices; ask them what they recommend. *See also* Nylon bones, Dental care

Rat Terrier working dogs rank among the most industrious of the small terriers.

Rawhide chews come in many shapes and sizes and are flavorful to dogs. Photographs by I. Français.

Rear view of climbing Rottweiler puppies.

Redbone Coonhound. Photo courtesy of Dick Stratton.

Reach
Efficient and economical movement that is consistent and long-striding. Contrary to stilted action.

Reach and drive
Good reach of forequarters and drive from behind—ideal in most every breed.

Reach of neck
An appropriately long and muscled neck that is both refined and elegant.

Rear pasterns
Metatarsus; anatomical region between the hock joint and foot.

Rear views
The various ways that the hindquarters can appear when seen from either a profile or direct-view vantage point. The most common rear views are: nicely angulated, well-let-down, cow hocks, over or lacking angulation, and bandy legs.

Recall
In obedience trials, the dog sits at one end of the ring and the handler goes to the other and calls the dog in at the judge's command. The dog sits directly in front of the handler and, on the judge's command, goes to heel, sitting.

Receding chin
Usually referring to an undershot jaw, *see* Undershot.

Receding eyes
Eyes that are too deeply set into the skull resulting from excessively large sockets, insubstantial muscle tissue or small eyeballs.

Receding skull
A faulty skull that should otherwise have converging planes, forming a blunt wedge, instead has planes that diverge.

Reckless

Rough, heedless, or mild form of interference; used in Greyhound racing.

Recording fee

A fee that is collected by the show-giving club and which is remitted to the national kennel club to help defray the expense of maintaining the record of each dog.

Rectal prolapse

Diarrhea, straining from constipation or heavy infestation of parasites are the most common cause of prolapse. Rectal prolapse is the expulsion of a part of the rectum through the anal opening. It is cylindrical in shape, and must be replaced within the body as soon as possible to prevent damage. A vet should be called. Change in diet, medication to eliminate the cause, etc., will effect a cure.

Rectangular head

Head that appears rectangular in shape and is usually longish (e.g., Giant Schnauzer).

Red bugs

Sand fleas. *See* Mites

Red fox

A wild dog and a member of the genus *Vulpes. See* Foxes

Red mange

See Mange

Red wolf

A close relative of the gray wolf, the red wolf is a member of the genus *Canis* and is found exclusively in a small portion of the southeastern United States. *See also* Wolves

Redbone Coonhound

The Redbone Coonhound, one of the first recognized U.K.C. breeds of American coonhound, is also one of the most recognizable. The A.K.C. Black and Tan, perhaps, has become the most popular of the coonhound breeds, although hunters vary on this point. Red hounds are believed to have come over to America with Scottish immigrants during the 1700s. Breeders in Tennessee and Georgia desired a hound with more speed and a hotter sniffer than the existing coonhounds. In molding the Redbone, these breeders blended American Foxhound and various local curs. The result was a dog of moderate size, foxhoundish appearance and fortitude. He is used principally for

Redbone Coonhound photographed by I. Français.

Redbone Coonhound puppies are exposed to the prey at an early age in order to elicit hunting instincts. Photo courtesy of Dick Stratton.

Redbone Coonhound barking up a tree, indicating that the raccoon has been treed. Photo courtesy of Dick Stratton.

treeing raccoon but can be adapted to other game, including big cat.

ESSENTIALS OF THE REDBONE COONHOUND: A handsome, strong and robust coonhound, the Redbone stands 26 inches (66 cm) high. Weight can range from 50–70 pounds (22–31.5 kg). This is a perfectly proportioned hound with superb nose and sonorous voice. The coat is dense and short, rather hard to the touch. The Redbone is invariably solid red (with white marks not to be fussed over).

Refused
Would not leave starting box, or would not run after emerging from box.

Registration
Registration rules and procedures vary from country to country. While the purposes of registration are compatible in the United States, Britain, Australia and Canada, there are notable differences.

In the United States, an American-born puppy must derive from a registered litter in order to be registered by the American Kennel Club. The A.K.C. provides official registration papers to breeders for all litters. Upon acceptance of the breeder's litter registration application, individual registrations for each puppy are sent. Buyers should receive a bill of sale, signed by the seller. The following information is crucial for the completion of a puppy's registration application: breed, sex and color of the dog; date of dog's birth; registered names of the dog's sire and dam; name of the breeder.

In Great Britain, only purebred dogs can be registered by the Kennel Club. Upon registration, a name is given to the dog. If the dog has not won a major prize by the age of ten, the dog's name can be used by a different dog.

Registration with the A.K.C. involves both litter registration as well as individual dog registration. Bichon Frise photographed by R. Pearcy.

Redtick Coonhound
Informal alternative name for the English Coonhound, which *see*.

Since there are so many dogs registered by the Kennel Club, it has become perplexing for breeders to choose new prefixes for their kennels.

Specific regulations of each registry can be acquired from the particular kennel club.

Reh Pinscher
See Miniature Pinscher

Reindeer Herding Laika
See Nenets Herding Laika

Relief dog
Courses are limited to three or four minutes. When contestants continue beyond that time without making a kill, a fresh dog (or dogs) is sent in to make the kill and end the course.

and cervix serve identical purposes, and with the exception of the bitch's uterus, which is Y-shaped and made for multiple fetuses, the reproductive system of the female dog matches that of the female human. Estrus is quite different, however, as, in domestic dogs, estrus typically occurs twice yearly (with the exception of some breeds of pariah origin such as the Basenji) while in humans it is once monthly. The typical bitch ovulates for three to five days and must be mated during this time if she is to become impregnated. The bitch is capable of birthing a multiple-sired litter, that is she can be impregnated by more than one dog during any given heat or estrus cycle.

The purpose of the reproductive system is of course to reproduce, and to this end each of its various parts is ideally

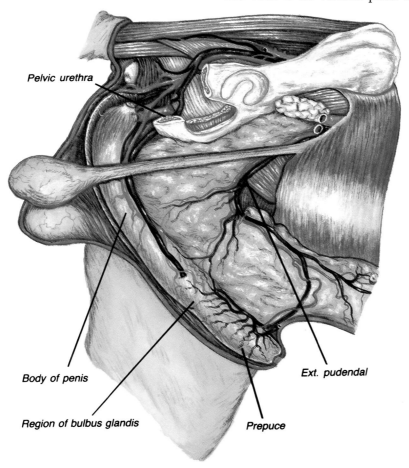

Pelvic urethra

Body of penis

Region of bulbus glandis

Ext. pudendal

Prepuce

Reproductive system: male. Illustration by Alexandra Suchenko.

Reproductive system
Male: penis, scrotum, testicles, prostate gland. The female: ovaries, uterus, vagina, and mammary glands. Essentially, not much different from the human. In both species, the fallopian tubes

suited. The goal of the male's system is the production of potent sperm to fertilize the bitch-produced egg and, indeed, to ejaculate that sperm. Sperm are produced in the testicles; these glands are housed in the scrotum, where their temperature is closely controlled to a few degrees below the body temperature. The testicles are served by several other glands and organs which together make possible the production of sperm. After its production, sperm move to the epididymis, a coiled tube consisting of three parts and having four basic functions: to provide a path for the sperm; to house the sperm; to secrete fluid onto the sperm area; and to allow the sperm to mature. The vas deferens, or ductus deferens, moves the mature sperm to the urethra, or sperm shaft, of the penis, whereby they are ejaculated. The penis of the dog is distinct in two key characteristics:

the vagina until some time passes after ejaculation. This is an inherited trait of the ancient dogs and serves to ensure the impregnation of the female.

The organs of the female that work for reproduction have four goals set before them: the production of eggs; the development of the embryo; the expellation of the developed young; and the provision of nourishment for the young. Egg production occurs in the ovaries, small organs found usually near the kidneys in female dogs. The eggs, or sex cells, are known as ova. The ova are transported by the oviducts, or fallopian tubes, to the uterus. Impregnation can occur during

Reproductive system: female. Illustration by Alexandra Suchenko.

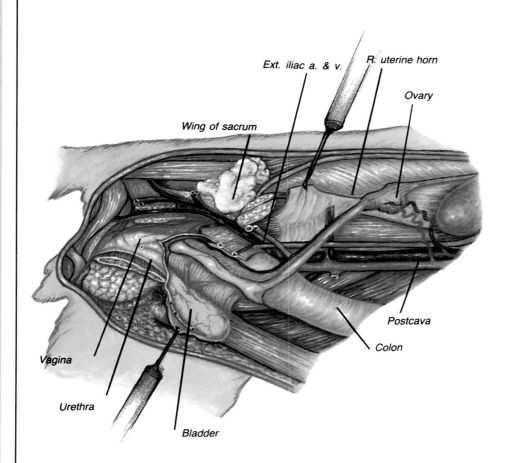

Ext. iliac a. & v.

R. uterine horn

Ovary

Wing of sacrum

Postcava

Colon

Vagina

Urethra

Bladder

within the shaft of the penis is the os penis, a bone which increases the adamancy of the erection and has a deep central groove through which the urethra passes; and at the base of the penis lays a bulb that swells with excitement and prohibits the exit of the penis from

this transfer. If fertilized, the egg becomes implanted in the uterus, a hollow, muscular, elastic organ that serves as the habitation for the development of the young. The uterus consists of a neck, called the cervix, a body, and two horns. The uterus of the dog is Y-shaped and specially adapted for the habitation of multiple developing young. The cervix, part of the uterus, also comprises the very upper part of the vagina, or birth canal. The opening of the vagina is known as the vulva. The vulva closes over the vagina to serve as protection. At the cervix is the clitoris, the function of which is not fully understood but which is believed to contribute to the stimulation of the male during intercourse. After they reach full intra-uteral development, the pups leave the uterus and travel through the vagina by the muscular contractions of the female. Once delivered and their umbilical cords severed, the pups receive sustenance from the bitch via the teats of her mammary glands. The mammary glands, through a process called lactation, produce milk regularly until weaning is completed, at which time the pups no longer feed from her and the remainder of her milk is resorbed by her body. *See also* Breeding, Os penis, Vagina, etc.

Resasti Itrski Gonič
See Istrian Hound

Rescue programs
Rescue programs are those efforts sponsored by local breed clubs to attempt to seek out and relocate lost, stray, or abandoned dogs into new homes, or to useful places in society. Many of these dogs are extracted from shelters or animal control authorities. Other dogs in need of "rescue" are those racing dogs that approach retirement or a kennel of dogs whose owner is no longer able to care for them or dies. In the U.S., over 250 breed clubs sponsor such programs, placing thousands of dogs annually. The amount of money which each club spends annually on this project cannot be determined since many of the expenses are absorbed by individual members.

Research dogs
Dogs which are used in laboratory research serve mankind in a tremendous way. The field of curative or preventive medicine has profited greatly from the contribution of laboratory dogs. Man and dog also benefit from the advances which are made through medical experimentation. The Beagle is perhaps the most common dog used as a research dog. Its tidy size, durability, early maturity, simplicity and temperament make the Beagle ideal for the purpose.

Reserve Winner
The dog (or bitch) chosen by the judge to be second to the Winners Dog or Winners Bitch. In case the win of the latter is cancelled, the Reserve Winner is advanced to the position of the dog whose win was cancelled.

Reserve Winner taken by Champion Kimchatka Sun Seeker, Samoyed handled by H. Yamashita for owner Amy Sakata. Photo courtesy of Betty Moody.

Respiratory ailments
Although respiratory diseases are not common in dogs, certain breeds are more susceptible to breathing problems than others. The Great Dane and Greyhound, for instance, may suffer respiratory ailments because of the deep narrow thoraxes, and the Bulldog and Pug may tend toward nasal inflammations because of their brachycephalic facial anatomy. The hound breeds, however, tend to have a greater resistance to cold and wet because of their outdoorsman activities.

The following respiratory ailments are covered separately in this text: Laryngitis; Tracheobronchitis; Sinusitis; Bronchitis; Bronchiectasis; Rhinitis; Pneumonia; Lung worm; Pleurisy; Neoplasms; Kennel cough.

Restraint
Excessive cautioning or handling while the gundog is hunting or on point.

Retrievers. Labrador Retriever returning shot mallard to hunter. Photo by V. Serbin.

Retained placenta
See Afterbirth, Breeding

Retinal dysplasia
A generalized improperly developed retina that can be the result of causes ranging from trauma to inheritance to injury. In acute cases, the condition may manifest itself in complete detachment of the retina. It is highly hereditary and may be revealed under ophthalmoscopic examination. Eventual blindness inevitably results. Dogs with retinal atrophy should not be used for breeding. Particularly prominent in certain breeds where current breeding trends have tended to change the shape of the head. Cataracts may accompany the syndrome and, in the Labrador Retriever, may be associated with a shortening of the forelegs. *See also* Progressive retinal atrophy

Retriever field trials
See Field trials

Retrievers
Retrievers are the largest of the gundogs, heavier bodies and often with broader skulls. As their name implies, retrievers are dogs that retrieve felled game. These are specialist hunters of water fowl, even though they work equally well on land and water. To facilitate their retrieving ability, these breeds must also be expert swimmers. The Labrador Retriever, perhaps the best, is even equipped with webbed feet! Besides the Lab, Britain has also developed the Flat-Coated and the Golden. The Chesapeake Bay and the Nova Scotia Duck Tolling are North America's two native retrievers. The Netherlands too has created its own retriever, the Kooikerhondje. *See also* Gundogs, Spaniels, Water dogs

Retrieving buck
An object used for training or practice as a substitute for a bird, also called a buck or a dummy.

Rheumatoid arthritis

The first signs of the disease are a shifting lameness and soft-tissue swelling around various joints, with the latter detectable mostly by a trained professional. As the disease progresses, it tends to localize in specific joints, evidenced by swelling and pain in them. Clinical observation often reveals cystlike areas in the subchondral bone. Cartilage erodes, resulting in a collapse of the joint space, after which angular deformities can occur as well as joint luxation. The disease can spread, affecting a large percentage of the skeletal structure. The disease is most common in older dogs. Veterinary treatment is variable and often unsuccessful. *See also* Arthritis, Plasmacytic-lymphocytic synovitis

Rhinitis

Acute or chronic inflammation of the mucous membranes of the nasal passages. It is quite common in both dogs and cats. It is seldom fatal, but requires endless "nursing" on the part of the owner for survival, since the nasal passages must be kept open so the animal will breathe. Dry leather on the nose, though there is excessive discharge, high fever, sneezing, etc., are symptoms. Nasal discharge may be bloody and the animal will refuse to eat, making it listless. The attacks may be recurrent and medication must be administered.

Rhodesian Ridgeback

Originating in South Africa from immigrating German and Dutch mastiffs, scenthounds and native Hottentot dogs, the Rhodesian Ridgeback is a powerful, intrepid hunter of the African lion. The Hottentot dog possessed the unique ridge on its back, a long and narrow coat pattern formed by hairs growing in the opposite direction to the surrounding area. Prior to these European settlers' arrival in the 1650s, there is evidence to believe that the Hottentot dog roamed the countryside in large numbers in an undomesticated state. Easy food and curiosity probably led the dogs toward the European settlers. Soon the dogs became involved in the routine of the newcomers and were utilized for guarding and hunting purposes.

Others believe that the Hottentot dogs were used as hunters by the Hottentots prior to any European intervention. This theory is enforced by the rock carved on the Valhalla farm which depicts a Hottentot chief's burial; the dog, along with oxen and humpbacked Zebu cows, are included. Historians surmise that the

Rhodesian Ridgeback, wheaten. Photo by I. Français.

dogs, like the livestock, were valued possessions of the Hottentot people.

The name "Lion Dog" comes from the Rhodesian's ability to harass a lion through constant strategic attacks which lure the preoccupied "king" towards the hunter's cocked rifle. Requisite skills for this line of canine work include: courage, agility, stamina, and strong instincts. In protecting the camps from other wild animals and unruly native tribesmen, these dogs excelled.

While the dogs had essentially developed in South Africa, many were transported to Rhodesia, where big-game hunting was common. There is specific documentation indicating that the dogs were transported to Matabeleland in 1875 to the famed hunter Cornelis van Rooyen. Van Rooyen is said to have crossed his hounds with the imported Hottentot dogs. The Rhodesian's nose and trailing ability, surely indicative of its hound blood, combined with its brute force to tackle a full-grown lion, won the admiration of these expert hunters. The name Rhodesian Ridgeback derived from the fame which these dogs won in Rhodesia on big cat, whence all of the "tall tales" emanated, plus an alliteration to boot. It was not until the 1920s that type began to standardize; for centuries prior, there existed many varieties of the Ridgeback dogs.

The Ridgeback is intensely loyal and affectionate. Though he is receptive to strangers, he remains suspicious and ready to defend. A natural performer, he will delight his owner by conquering all tasks set before him. *See also* Hottentot dog, Thai Ridgeback Dog

Rhodesian Ridgeback, red. Photo by I. Français.

ESSENTIALS OF THE RHODESIAN RIDGEBACK: The ridge of hair on the back is short and dense, in the form of a dagger. The hilt of the ridge starts at the shoulders and has two crowns or whorls where the handle finishes. It tapers to a point at the hips. The smooth tight muscles of the Ridgeback's body and the strong-boned symmetrical carriage combine to give

him free and efficient movement over great distances at good speeds. With a flat skull, the head should be fairly long and rather broad. The brow is typically wrinkled. The ears are of medium size. The muzzle should be deep, long and powerful. The neck should be fairly strong, free from throatiness. The shoulders should be sloping, clean and muscular, denoting speed. The chest should not be too wide, but very deep and capacious; ribs moderately well sprung, never rounded like barrel hoops, the back powerful, the loins strong, muscular and slightly arched. The forelegs perfectly straight; the elbows close to the body. Tail strong at insertion, tapering towards the end, free from coarseness. Height: 24–27 inches (61–69 cm). Weight: 65–75 pounds (29–34 kg). Coat: short, dense, sleek and glossy. Color: wheaten, from light through red.

Rib cage

Bony enclosing wall of the chest, which *see*.

Ribbed-up

Refers to a dog whose ribs are carried well back. *See* Ribs

Ribs

Those usually rounded, flexible bones forming the solid defense of the vital organs housed in the chest area.

There are various terms employed to refer to specific rib types or locations in breeds. Back ribs denotes latter section of the rib cage. Barrel chest is used to refer to the quality of the rib's arching, typically centimeters after the vertebral column. The opposite of barrel-shaped ribs are flat ribs (also called slab-sided and narrow ribs), ribs without the soon-occurring arch. To say a dog is deep in the ribs is to say that the chest is designed for good cardiovascular capacity; it is synonymous with "deep in chest," which *see*. Ribs carried well back refers to a rib cage that is lengthy in distance from shoulders to abdomen. Ribs that are well rounded are the equivalent of well-sprung ribs.

The term "spring of ribs" deserves special mention. It refers to the arch or lack of arch to the ribs as they extend from the back. It would seem natural that the greater the arch, the greater the chest capacity, and such is the case, within reason, in dogs. Thus, a dog that is said to have good spring of ribs is implied to have good cardiovascular ability, or substantial chest capacity.

Rickets
A disease uncommon today, it is the result of vitamin D, calcium, and phosphorus deficiencies.

Ridge
Usually referring to an atypical coat-growth pattern, this hair, growing lengthwise, along the back, against the grain of the coat, is desired of the Rhodesian Ridgeback. Deemed a freak of genetics by some, this ridge rarely occurs in other extant breeds.

Riesenschanauzer
See Giant Schnauzer

Rigging
The system of hooking sled dogs to their lines.

Rigor mortis
The stiffening of the body that occurs after death as a result of the coagulation of the muscle protein.

Ring
The roped-off enclosure (square or rectangular) in which show dogs are judged. For indoor obedience tests, an exhibition ring must be a minimum of 30 by 50 feet; and for outdoor tests, a minimum of 50 by 80 feet is required. The ground is required to be level and grass cut short.

Ring tail
A relatively lengthy tail whose tip curls in a ring or circular fashion (e.g., Afghan Hound).

Ringed eyes
Eyes in which an abnormal amount of sclera is detectable.

Ringer
Where fraudulent substitution is made in a coursing event.

Ringworm
A fungal infection caused in dogs mostly by *Microsporum canis* but also by *M. gypseum* and *Trichophytom mentagrophytes*. The infection is visible on the dog's skin as scaly circles, in which are found broken, damaged hair and lesions. The dog will tend to scratch the area,

causing increased irritation and likelihood of secondary infection. The disease is contractible by man, and it happens that an owner and his dog share both misery and company. It is most often easily treated but demands immediate attention because of its infectious nature.

Riot
When over-excited hounds run other than the intended quarry.

Roading
Often called roadwork, exercising a dog for conditioning, usually on a road and by car or horseback. Not to be confused with roading up or in, which is moving up cautiously to establish a positive point after being stopped temporarily by a faint or indefinite scent of game.

Roan
Individual colored hairs in the white markings. Red hairs create a "red roan" and black hairs give a steel gray appearance called "blue" or "blue roan" (e.g., Australian Cattle Dog).

Ring tail held proudly by the Afghan Hound.

Rocky Mountain spotted fever

A disease of both dog and man caused by *Rickettsia rickettsii* and transmitted by the ticks *Dermacentor andersoni* and *D. variabilis*. The disease is commonly called tick fever in dogs. Signs include: high fever, depression, sluggishness, and weight loss, among others. The disease often relapses during its early stage but emerges again, more acutely, a week or so later. Diagnosis requires a veterinarian, and antibiotic treatment.

Rolled ears

Inward-curling ears that are long and pendant, often possessed by hounds (e.g., Bloodhound).

Rolling gait

Ambling action; swaying movement from side to side that is typical of the low-legged, barrel-chested breeds. The Bulldog, Pekingese, and Newfoundland are fine examples of rolling gait.

Roman nose

A nose that curves convexly in an uninterrupted line: opposite of a ram's nose which dips downward with an otherwise straight foreface.

Roof of mouth

Simply another way of saying palate, which *see*.

Root

Usually immediately precedes the prepositional phrase, of the tail; it is synonymous with and refers to the base of the tail, which *see*.

Rolling gait demonstrated by the Newfoundland. Photo by R. Reagan.

Rodenticides

Chemicals or other agents used to kill rodents. Discretion must be employed to ensure that the agent is not harmful to dogs or other domestic animals.

Roll

In dog talk, used to refer to one of three things: the gait caused mostly by a chest too round (except in the Pekingese, in which such a gait is typical); or the fold of skin across the top of the nose, found particularly in some bracycephalic dogs; in fighting circles, a roll is a practice to determine gameness.

Root canal therapy

Injury to a tooth may be treated by prompt dental root canal therapy, which involves removal of damaged or necrotic pulp and placing of opaque filling material in the root canal and pulp chamber.

Ropy tail

A gnarled appearing tail that is weathered and mostly hairless.

Rose ears

Mostly small ears that fold, exposing the cartilaginous bumplike formation known as the burr (e.g., Italian Greyhound).

Rosettes

Common on many dog breeds with a typical black base coloration are small tan patches of coat on both shoulder fronts. They are particularly common on some German breeds, including the Doberman Pinscher and Rottweiler. Rosette is also used to refer to the patches of hair over the loins in the Continental clip of the Poodle.

Rotary motion

The determined and powerful gait, marked by strong thrust causing the hocks and stifles to pump in an apparently circular or rotary fashion, when viewed in profile.

Rotenone

A resinous substance derived from the roots of tropical plants and sometimes used as an insecticide, especially to kill fleas and lice.

Rottweiler

The true history of the Rottweiler remains misty to this day. With few facts supporting them, fanciers and historians sketch the development of the breed. One oft-cited history of the breed claims that the ancestors of the breed were the dogs used by the Roman legions to drove and guard livestock as they traversed the Alps. If this is true, then the Rottweiler may share heritage with the Swiss sen-

Rosettes on both sides of the chest above the front legs on these handsome Rotties.

Rottweiler, black and tan.

Rottweiler photographed by John L. Ashbey.

nenhunden (Greater Swiss Mountain Dog, Entelbucher, and others) which are also the believed descendants of the ancient Roman dogs. The history continues with the dogs following Roman troops into Germany and remaining there after the conflict. Rottweil, the city which gives the breed its name, is located on the Neckar River in the southern part of the country and by virtue of its location flourished as a city of commerce and agriculture activity. Bred for strength, courage, and droving skills, Rottweilers were employed to drove cattle from town to town, while at the same time protecting against thieves and other predators. So trusted were the dogs that it was common practice to attach to a dog the moneybag required for trade, for nowhere, including the bank, were the assets better protected.

After this period of great use, the breed suffered decline until 1914 brought the call to war. The strength and intelligence of the breed made the dogs first-round draftees. The War proved the physical and mental abilities of the Rottweiler. Since that time the popularity of the breed has been no less than steady and is often on the climb. The breed entered the U.S. in the early 1930s and was accepted into the A.K.C. ranks in 1935. The breed entered Great Britain in 1936, but it was not until 1966 that the breed's popularity warranted K.C.G.B recognition.

The dominant popularity of the Rottweiler's spin-off, the Doberman Pinscher, postponed the breed's increased popularity in the United States; in recent years, however, the breed has been climbing the registration stats like never before. Today the United States and Germany boast master races of superiorly bred Rottweilers. These dogs are highly trainable and equally intelligent. The German requirements to train the dogs in Schutzhund work (that is, attack and protection training) has sparked interest in the U.S. Many fanciers, though, are not enamored by the prospect of "stoking the fires of his aggression," as Dick Stratton puts it. The Rottweiler is a naturally protective animal with a hell of a lot of animal power. The "untrained" dog is thus suitable for the average owner's protection needs. Overstimulating these instincts has already proven harmful to the breed, as its reputation in Great Britain has been marred, much like the Pit Bull Terrier's has in the U.S. These dogs are fine animals, indeed, and their high trainability and strength can make them dangerous in the hands of delinquent, irrational owners. It must be stated that Schutzhund has much to offer the Rottweiler and its owner, but it must be undertaken sensibly and professionally. A badly trained dog is a "bad dog." Additionally, potential owners are encouraged to seek a proven, reliable breeder to avoid getting a potentially maniacal specimen, ill bred and unworthy of an owner's trust. Many dogs have also contracted parvovirus and hip dysplasia, two dread conditions. As with any breed that captures the public's fancy, puppy mills abound—do not compromise in the purchase of your dog because you are over anxious. Lastly, Rottweiler owners must always keep a close eye on their dogs since they can tend to be most accident-prone.

ESSENTIALS OF THE ROTTWEILER: A stalwart dog of fine proportion and compact, powerful form. The appearance displays boldness and courage, and the expression should indicate good humor. The head is medium in length and broad between the ears. The muzzle is fairly deep with topline level. Neck strong, round, and muscular. Shoulders well laid back. The chest is broad and deep with ribs well sprung. Hocks well angulated. Feet round and compact with toes well arched. Tail customarily docked, carried slightly above the horizontal. Gait conveys strength, stamina, and purpose. Coat is double: top coat of medium length; undercoat not visible through top coat. Color is quintessential: a glistening black with markedly defined rich tan markings. Height: 22–27 inches (56–69 cm). Weight: 90–110 pounds (41–50 kg).

Rough-coated Bohemian Pointer
See Czesky Fousek

Roughhaired Dutch Shepherd
See Dutch Shepherd

Round eyes
Circular eyes (e.g., Cocker Spaniel).

Round feet
See Cat feet

Round head
See Short head

Rottweiler, black and tan.

Round neck
A neck that is round as opposed to the more common elliptical shape (e.g., American Water Spaniel).

Round-tipped ears
See Blunt-tipped ears

Rounded skull
A skull type typified by arching from ear to ear and from stop to occiput. The arch, however, is gentle and not as rounded as in a domed skull, which *see*.

Roundworms
Two species of roundworms, *Toxocaris canis* and *Toxascaris leonina*, may infect

the dog's small intestine. An adult worm is white in color, slender, and ranges in size from one and a half to seven inches (4–18 cm) in length. Roundworms give off a toxin that is harmful to the dog, and larvae migrations to the lungs frequently cause death.

Intestinal roundworms (*Toxocara canis*) are ingested by the dog, usually through food contaminated by the ground or by nursing puppies from the dam's teats. Prenatal infestation also may occur by larval invasion through the placenta. Each worm egg contains a tiny coiled embryo which is released by the bursting of the shell in the intestine and then becomes a larva. These larvae pierce the intestinal wall, entering the bloodstream; they are carried by way of the liver to the lungs. From the lungs, they crawl or are coughed up into the esophagus, to be swallowed and again reach the intestines. In the intestines, the worms lay eggs which are voided in the stool. These microscopic eggs generally embryonate within two to three weeks and they may remain viable for years.

The life cycle of *Toxacaris leonina* is much simpler: this worm enters as larvae through the bowel wall to complete development and reenters the dog's intestines ten days later.

Puppies usually build an acquired immunity to roundworms by about six months of age. Veterinarians have medications that can destroy roundworms and other similar internal parasites at the same time. *See also* Hookworms, Nematodes, Lungworms, Whipworms, Worms

Router
Racing dog able to maintain a fast pace for a distance of 5–16 miles (8–25.5 km) or even more.

Royal collar
See Collar

Rubarth's disease
See Hepatitis

Rubber brush
One of the finest brushes for removing dust and loose hair on shorthaired breeds. Also works well on cats.

Rubber curry brush
Takes out dust and dirt on shorthaired breeds. *See also* Grooming

Ruby coloration on the Cavalier King Charles Spaniel.

Ruby
The term for solid red coloration in the English toy spaniels.

Rudder
Tail of the Otterhounds, Wetterhouns, Labrador Retrievers, or other dogs known for their swimming affinity. The noun means "tail," specifically a tail commonly used for steering while afloat.

Ruff

When long, abundant, stand-offish hair adorns the *entire* neck of a dog, that dog is said to have a ruff. The ruff, or neck ruff, is typical of many northern breeds, including the Giant German Spitz, Keeshond, Samoyed, and Chow Chow.

Rumanian Herder

See Rumanian Sheepdog

Rumanian Sheepdog

The Carpathian Mountains of eastern Rumania is the home range of the Rumanian Sheepdog (also called the Carpathian Sheepdog). This breed of rough-and-tumble sheepdog is quite similar to the Greek Sheepdog, Owczarek Podhalanski and the Slovak Cuvac, all of whom were derived from like stock. In usual practice, the medium-coated Rumanian Sheepdog was used as a protector of the flocks against wolves and other predators. Certain Rumanians that could be found farther south possess shorter coats and were used for draft and carting purposes. Shepherds in many of these Eastern European nations partake in interesting practices with their sheepdogs. Just as the Greek Shepherds crop one of their sheepdog's ears to improve its hearing, so do Rumanian shepherds dock the last third of their furry white dog's furry white tail, which the dog could then wave above its height as a signal of sorts while working in the fields. The actual purpose of this practice has escaped most cynologists and tradition simply at least is the reason. The practice of attaching a log to the dog's collar to curb his surliness and potential ferocity, a practice also used by the Greek shepherds, is also adhered to in Rumania.

The Rumanian Kennel Club recognizes two breeds of Rumanian Sheepdogs, according to coat type. Numbers and interest in this shepherd are waning; crossbreeding necessarily occurs in the attempt to salvage certain lines, and with some purity lost.

ESSENTIALS OF THE RUMANIAN SHEEPDOG: A heavily boned, thickly muscled dog with a short stout neck, topped by a head composed of a large skull, deep-set eyes, strong jaw, and thick muzzle. Height: 23–26 inches (58.5–66 cm). Weight: 70–98 pounds (32–45 kg). The dense coat is medium-long in length. Color is usually white with a pied brown, sometimes all white; reports also suggest the occurrence of brown dogs.

Rump

A small area located on the rear dorsal area of the dog, the rump fills the gap between the loin and the buttocks. Rump and croup are often used as though they referred to the same body location. They do not. Rump can be preceded by innumerable adjectives, a majority of which will refer to either the slope or the muscle make-up of the rump. A goose rump is a particular rump type that is characterized by an excessive pelvic slope.

Ruff surrounding the neck of the Keeshond.

Run

In foxhunting, the chase of the fox from find to kill.

Run out

In shepherding, the act of the dog's going after sheep.

Runner

One who acts as an assistant at the judging ring and aids the stewards in getting competing dogs into the ring when their classes are called.

Runners

Two bottom strips of wood on which the sled runs and are covered with steel or plastic strips called runner shoes.

Russian Harlequin Hound, piebald. Photo by V. Pcholkin.

Runt

Usually reserved for the smallest, weakest member of a litter, often the last born. There are many dog tales spun and wagged about runts of the litter: runts are the most affectionate; they are the most intelligent; they are long lived; etc. Such statements should not be taken as fact but as generalizations. Some runts may be anything a dog can be, but of course not all can be everything.

Runup

In coursing, the dash from slips to the hare.

Rüppell's sand fox

A wild dog and a member of the genus *Vulpes. See* Foxes

Russet gold

A particular reddish brown hue seen on Vizslas by their fanciers. It appears in the K.C.G.B. standard for the breed.

Russian Harlequin Hound

The Russian Harlequin Hound, originally known as the Anglo-Russian Hound, is a cross between Foxhounds of English importation and the Russian Hound (which *see*). English Foxhounds have been known in Russia since the time of Empress Anne (circa 1735). The present name was adopted in 1951. In size, the Harlequin Hound is smaller than its Foxhound forebears and heavier than its comrade the Russian Hound. In Russia, the Harlequin is called the Gontchaja Russkaja Pegaja.

The multi-colored coat distinguishes the dog from its quarry to eschew mishaps. The Harlequin contributed to the formation of the Dunker, a Norwegian hound created by Herr Wilhelm Dunker. The Dunker shares the Harlequin Hound's merle-colored saddle.

ESSENTIALS OF THE RUSSIAN HARLEQUIN HOUND: This squarely built tricolor hound is sturdy and competent. The well-defined stop and noticeable flews distinguish him from other Soviet hounds, as does his piebald color. In height the Harlequin stands from 22–26 inches (56–66 cm). A strong head and well-developed teeth give this working hound repute and respect.

Russian Hound

The modern-day Russian Hound, sometimes referred to as the Russian Drab Yellow Hound, is a scenthound breed indigenous to Soviet soil and possibly descending directly from the laikas. The breed's undercoat and wedge-shaped head are thereby explained. The dogs' wide-ranging voices are distinctive and expressive.

The designation "Russian Hound" once referred to three types of Russian hounds: the present breed, the Estonian Hound and the Lithuanian Hound (which *see*). The latter two now have siz-

able enough numbers to have individual breed status. Additionally, in the early 1900s, the Russian Hound's type varied considerably from region to region. The notion of "purebred" is not precisely a Russian one and dogs were bred for functional purposes.

Russian Hounds have long been favored by the Russian nobility; the Grand Duke and Czar, in their days of power, always kept packs of Russian Hounds to accommodate their partaking in the Russian national pastime: hunting. Hare is this Russian's usual game, although he is handy on an occasional fox or two as well. At home, this breed is referred to as the Kostroma Hound or Gontchaja Russkaja.

ESSENTIALS OF THE RUSSIAN HOUND: Appearing slightly longer than tall, the Russian Hound is a weighty-looking dog with a solid torso and back. The coat is moderately short and unusually dense, possessing a thick undercoat. Usually drab yellow in color, the Russian Hound can vary from yellows into reds and possess a black saddle and small markings in white.

Russian Piebald Hound
See Russian Harlequin Hound

Russian Retriever

A large gundog which is said to resemble the Golden Retriever of Great Britain. The breed may have indeed descended from certain sheepdog types and is probably extinct in its original form.

Russian Samoyed Laika
See Nenets Herding Laika

Russian Spaniel
Gundogs in Russia have existed for countless generations. Many Russian dogs of old were said to have resembled European breeds: for instance, the Russian Retriever could have nearly passed for the Golden Retrievers of its day; the

Russian Hound, drab yellow.

Russian Spaniel, white with black. Photographs by V. Pcholkin.

Russian Setter for the English Setter. The Russian Spaniel is not nearly so old as these but surely results from similar Continental gundog offspring and the ever-popular English Pointer, the usual ingredient for speed. He is multi-faceted in his hunting abilities—able to search out, flush, and retrieve. The duck, quail, corncrake, and sandpiper are among his feathered quarry; the wild goat and hare, his land quarry. The breed, however, is known to tire easily under rough working conditions.

To their Russian owners, these Spaniels are unparalleled in devotion and ability. In addition to providing impressive work on the field, they make good-natured house pets and are very reliable watchdogs.

ESSENTIALS OF THE RUSSIAN SPANIEL: The small working spaniel of Russia stands 15–17 inches (38–43 cm) high. In general appearance, he is robust and handsome, resembling a leggy English Springer Spaniel. He is well muscled overall with good sufficiency of bone. The tail is customarily docked. The desired coat is silky with good feathering on the ears and loose fringe on the belly and legs. In color the Russian Spaniel is usually white with dark marks (black, brown, liver) occurring on the body and most usually on the head and ears.

Russian Wolfhound
See Borzoi

Russkaja Spaniel
See Russian Spaniel

Russo-European Laika
The awesome Russo-European Laika is closely related to the Finnish dog, the Karelian Bear Laika. The Soviets, upon claiming the Karelia area, "embraced" the indigenous big-game hunter as their own. In an attempt to increase the Karelian Bear Laika's power and aggressive nature, Russian breeders crossed the breed with the Utchak Sheepdog, an absolutely fearless and formidable animal. The result, the Russo-European Laika, is an intrepid bear hunter, also used on boar, moose, and wolf. Although this is a handsome dog that would serve without qualm as a watchdog, it is not yet

Russo-European Laika, black and white. Photo by I. Français.

Russo-European Laika, black and white. Photo by I. Français

acclimated to urban life or habitual human contact. They are outstanding candidates for forest rangers and marshalls. *See also* Karelian Bear Dog

Essentials of the Russo-European Laika: A good-sized, strong working dog, the Russo-European Laika is short-coated and usually black and white in color. Height: 21–24 inches (53–61 cm). Weight: 45–50 pounds (20–23 kg). The muzzle is rather elongated and the jaws are punishing and strong. The tail tends to curl up although many are born tailless, a condition breeders do not favor but to which they concede. The ears are prominently placed on the top of the head and are large.

Ruwhaar Hollandse Herdershond
    See Dutch Shepherd

Saarlooswolfhond

Part German Shepherd Dog and part wolf, the breed is the result of diligent crosses performed by the founder of the breed, Leendert Saarloos, over the course of some thirty years. In the 1930s, with the

Saarlooswolf-hond, wolf gray.

cooperation of a Dutch zoo, Leendert Saarloos acquired a zoo-kept wolf bitch, which he intended to cross with a German Shepherd Dog. The impetus of his intention was his belief, based on his studies of genetics, that the domestic dog had greatly degenerated into an animal ridden with weakness. He believed that

Saarlooswolf-honden, a trio of like-looking, lupine specimens. Photographs by I. Français.

the wolf, even zoo-kept specimens, was immune to many of the diseases that affected domestic dogs. To his disbelief,

his first wolf succumbed to a debilitating virus before he could breed her. Soon thereafter, the zoo provided Saarloos with a second wolf, and the breeding program began.

The Saarloos dogs proved to be less than the breeder had initially imagined: they retained too considerably the instincts of the wolf, which made them unsuitable for traditional dog owners and certainly for any herding duty that the German Shepherd performed with alacrity. Undeterred, Saarloos continued his program, striving to perfect his dogs through careful selection of desired traits and breedings to bring the dog closer to the German Shepherd characteristics. He was unable, however, to deplete his new breed of the typical wolf characteristics, including a strong pack instinct, shyness, the tendency to roam, and the demand for territory. Through continued attempts and sedulous selection, near-success was achieved—the breed was not recognized by the Dutch Kennel Club until 1975, six years after Leendert Saarloos's death. The breed is now registered by the F.C.I.

ESSENTIALS OF THE SAARLOOSWOLFHOND: A medium-large dog with a solid carriage, showing excellent strength and mobility. The skull is moderately broad, sloping from ears to eyes. The muzzle has a definite taper to the solid dark nose. The ears are large (like the German Shepherd Dog's) and carried erect. Height: 27.5–29.5 inches (70–75 cm). Weight: 79–90 pounds (36–41 kg). The coat is medium-short and very dense; the neck is covered with a ruff. Color should indicate the wolf ancestry, being either agouti, wolf gray, or wolf brown, with limited white markings possible.

Saber tail

A curved tail carried up or down (e.g., German Shepherd Dog).

Sable

The canine coat of either brown, buff, fawn, tan, gold, gray or silver base hairs tipped with black, creating a definite overall coat pattern. The sable coloration of the Belgian Shepherd Dog, Tervuren, is expressed as: "All shades of red, fawn, gray with black overlay."

Sabueso
Spanish for hound.

Sabueso Español de Monte
See Sabueso Español

Sabueso Español Lebrero
See Sabueso Español

Sabueso Español
Two Spanish countrymen are labeled Sabueso Español: the Sabueso Español de Monte and the Sabueso Español Lebrero. The former breed can still be found in Spain and other European nations, but the Lebrero is rarely seen today. The Sabuesos' similarity to the St. Hubert Hound and his classic mastiff appearance can assure us of the antiquity of the strain. The breeds are usually traced back to the old Celtic Hound. Although the breeds are traditionally Spanish in origin, the name derives from early French inhabitants. These dogs have existed on the Iberian peninsula for many years, where the breed has remained pure. Two varieties are still known. They are powerful hunters and have been employed by Spanish authorities for tracking purposes. While hunted in packs years ago, these hounds are used singly due to their temperamental and willful dispositions.

ESSENTIALS OF THE SABUESOS ESPAÑOLES: The Sabueso Español de Monte, the larger breed, sports a white coat patched with red, which is hard and short. The breed weighs approximately 55 pounds (25 kg) and stands as high as 22 inches (56 cm). The Sabueso Español Lebrero, the smaller, is nearly solid red with patches of white on blaze, neck, chest, etc. He stands under 20 inches (51 cm) and weighs less than 50 pounds (23 kg). On both breeds, the skin, covered by glossy fine hair, is flexible and loose. The oversized ears hang freely and amusingly, and the flews and dewlap are in no scarcity. The patches on the coat vary in color (red or black), number and proximity.

Sacrum
An element of the spinal column, which *see*.

Saddle
Perhaps the most common usage refers to the usually black coat marking that runs the length of the back, often from the rear of the shoulders to either the croup or the rump, and extends down both rib cages, suggestive of the appearance of a saddled horse. Found on many hounds, such as the Bloodhound. Secondly—mantle—the term can refer to the area supported by the thoracic vertebrae (between the neck and abdomen). A third usage points to the short hair found on the back of fully mature Afghan Hounds.

Sagittal crest
It is the bony ridge that runs the length of the skull, ending in the formation of the occiput.

Sagittal suture
The fusion of the bones that form the median line, or furrow, of a dog's skull.

Sabueso Español de Monte, white with red.

Sabuesos Españoles de Monte (*right*) and Lebrero (*left*). Photographs by I. Français.

Saint Bernard

The Saint Bernard is one of few breeds whose true function is rescue work. Although it is not likely that the St. Bernard ever met Saint Bernard (the monk who lived during the twelfth century), these Barry Hounds began assisting the brothers at the Hospice in the third quarter of the eighteenth century.

steady popularity with the American public, though its numbers in England and the Continent remain limited.

The true origin of the breed as well as his conclusive history remains metaphorically buried under miles of snow. Many colorful and pardonably romantic theories persist on the origin of the wonder and snow-bound St. Bernard.

Saint Bernard, smooth, red with white. Photo by I. Français.

Today the Hospice preserves tradition and the dogs are kept busy by charming the enchanted visitors who, much to the dogs' relief, rarely need rescuing. There is belief that the original breed died out some centuries ago and that the monks had to recourse to using Newfoundland and Great Pyrenees stock to revitalize the breed. And it is believed that Great Dane blood also entered the veins of these hardy working dogs at one time or another. The breed today enjoys a large,

The somber and never ill-natured expression of the St. Bernard modifies one of the most benevolent of all canines. His disposition is steady and kindly, making a fine companion for children and adults alike.

ESSENTIALS OF THE SAINT BERNARD: A mighty and proportionately massive dog, the Saint is muscular and impressive on his every part. Shoulders are broad and sloping. Back is broad and straight. Chest is broad and deep. The head is

Saint Bernards, (*top left*) adult and puppy, (*top right*) smooth, (*bottom*) smooth and long. Photographs by I. Français.

large and massive, and the expression is unmistakably dignified. The eyes small, deep set, and dark. The coat is very dense: smooth coats lie close; long coats are medium in length and slightly wavy. In color the St. Bernard is white with red or red with white; red and brown-yellow are equally desired. Height: 25.5–27.5 inches (65–70 cm). Weight: 110–over 200 pounds (50–90 kg).

Laufhund exhibits the influence of the flewsy hounds of Belgium, namely those of the St. Hubert variety. The original St. Hubert Hound, of course, is not the Swissy hunter, but rather the Bloodhound, or officially Le Chien de St. Hubert, as he is known in Belgium. In appearance, the St. Hubert Jura Laufhund terrifically resembles the Bloodhound, with lots of earage, flews and dewlap.

Saint Hubert Jura Laufhund, tan with black saddle. Photo by I. Français.

Saint Bernhardshund
 See Saint Bernard

Saint Germain Pointer
 See Braque Saint-Germain

Saint Hubert Hound
 See Bloodhound

Saint Hubert Jura Laufhund
 A cloak, as dark as that of any Belgian monk, osbscures the genesis of this "walking dog" of Switzerland. The St. Hubert Jura Laufhund is one of two distinct breeds developed in the Jura Mountains between Switzerland and France. The Bruno Jura Laufhund, the other, bears a closer resemblance to the hounds of France, while the St. Hubert Jura

However, this hound is not even half the size of the weighty Bloodhound. The St. Hubert possesses the proverbial sniffer of the Bloodhound, and proves to be more agile on hellish terrain, with the wherewithal of a saint, or at least a blessed.

ESSENTIALS OF THE SAINT HUBERT JURA LAUFHUND: A smaller Bloodhound sums up the appearance of the St. Hubert Jura Laufhund. The body is solid and the chest deep. The head, long for the body, is characterized by loose skin and tremendous ears. Height: 18–23 inches (46–59 cm). Weight: 34–44 pounds (15.5–20 kg). Colors include tan with black saddle and black with tan points. The coat is short and hard.

Saint John's Dog

St. John's, the capital city of the island Newfoundland, is the namesake of a lost fisherman's dog. By and around the seventeenth century, two distinct types of St. John's Dogs emerged: the Lesser St. John's Dog, which contributed to the present-day Labrador Retriever, and the Greater St. John's Dog, which forms the base of today's Newfoundland. These noble working dogs had curly coats and strong, high-standing tails; the dogs occurred in solid-colored coats as well as spotted and brindles. Today both derivative breeds, the Lab and Newf, exhibit these non-solid coats: Labrador breeders still experience a stray brindle puppy in a litter and likewise certain Newfoundland breeders have specialized in the particolored dog, sometimes known as the Landseer. While today's Newfoundland is often counted among the mastiff breeds, the original St. John's Dogs were certainly closer in type to water dogs or gundogs, and early Newf specimens were much lighter in bone and smaller in size than today's bear-like sweet-tempered bully.

Reports of a revival of the St. John's Dogs (likely the Lesser) have been surfacing recently. Committed Canadian fanciers are developing a strain of Black Dogs in hope of duplicating this lost breed.

Salicylic acid

A remedy sometimes used to remove warts or slow the growth of bacteria.

Salivary cyst

Surgery is necessary when the salivary gland becomes clogged or nonfunctional, causing constant salivation. A swelling becomes evident under the ear or tongue. Surgery will release the accumulation of saliva in the duct of the salivary gland, though it is at times necessary to remove the salivary gland in its entirety. Zygomatic salivary cysts are usually a result of obstructions in the four main pairs of salivary glands in the mouth. Infection is more prevalent in the parotid of the zygomatic glands located at the rear of the mouth, lateral to the last upper molars. Visual symptoms may be protruding eyeballs, pain when moving the jaw, or a swelling in the roof of the mouth. If surgery is necessary, it is done under general anesthesia and the obstruction is removed by dissection. Occa-

Saint Hubert Jura Laufhund, black with tan points. Photo by I. Français.

sionally, the zygomatic salivary gland is removed as well. Stitches or drainage tubes may be necessary or dilation of the affected salivary gland. Oral or internal antibiotics may be administered.

Saluki, fawn. Photo by J. Ashbey.

Salivary gland

Glands located around the mouth cavity and which secrete the digestive enzyme known as saliva. Injuries, cysts, and infections can all affect the glands, often leading to serious complications. Salivary gland infection is evidenced by swelling of the neck area and under the tongue. Treatment of salivary conditions often involves surgery.

Salmon poisoning

A fluke disease, mostly reported in the Pacific Northwest and southwestern Canada. The flukes are acquired by the ingestion of raw or insufficiently cooked fish, in which cysts of flukes are present. Signs include a high fever (106–107°F), unquenchable thirst, refusal to eat, and eye discharge. Seek help immediately. Soon after the initial stage, the temperature drops and the stools become liquidlike and bloody. As the temperature continues to drop, the dog suffers emaciation and dehydration, and dies.

Saluki

Swift-moving across the desert sands, the Saluki, like the Bedouin nomads that hunted them, is an ancient, noble breed of the Arab deserts. Perhaps predating all man's other working running gazehounds, the Saluki was bred with pride and consistency. The breed is wondrous in that over the centuries it has changed substantially little since it has been utilized continually for the purposes for which it was bred. The work and the sport required a light, fleet-footed, fast dog with stamina and power; the Saluki persists to qualify with grace and precision. Pedigrees, committed not to parchment but to memory, were kept meticulously. A high standard of performance efficiency was paramount to the hunting Bedouins and Arabs. The Saluki, like the Arabian horse,

Saluki, cream. Photo by R. Reagan.

attests to the Arabs' uncanny mastery of the *art* of breeding. Dogs were inherited from generation to generation, attaching a further sense of pride and meaning to the breeding of the dogs. Tribes guarded fervently the dogs bequeathed them and, with equal fervor, chanted the pedigree tongued through oral transmission. Of course, not all dogs were respected by the Muhammadans; "ordinary" dogs (called *Kelbs*) were despised and deemed unclean. The Bedouin Shepherd Dog, a pariah type, used in Jordan, was never revered as was *El Hor*, the noble Saluki. In the Sahara, the Saluki is fashioned *Barake* or especially blessed. Unlike the sheepdogs and watchdogs, the Saluki is permitted into the sheik's tent. Salukis were never sold but presented as gifts of esteem. Much to the relief of pet shops and current-day breeders, this tradition hasn't followed the breed to the West.

On the desert, the dogs' education begins at six months, instructed by the children, on rats and jerboa. Eventually the pups are promoted to hare and gazelle—hence the breed's common name Gazelle Hound. Females were often considered more docile and adaptable. Hunting gazelle depends on the dog's strong instincts and efficient training—segregating a gazelle from its herd and running it down, often in a circular fashion, until the exhausted animal is caught and killed. The terrain on which the Salukis ran was rough and rocky. Their claws would penetrate the terrain, sinking into the sand, their vision blurred by wind-lifted sands. In Palestine, desert partridge are caught in flight by working Salukis. Falconry, using a hawk in conjunction with a leashed (and then unleashed) Saluki, is also a famous motif of this ancient desert runner. The hawk or falcon lead the dog to the prey. The dog, with eyes fixed on the hovering seeing-eye bird, leaping over deep fissures and burdensome boulders, moved at blurring speeds.

From the pre-dynastic periods, about 6000–5000 B.C., before the pharaohs, there exists a carved ivory head of a Saluki, with the long neck graced by the traditional collar. There also exists an engraving on slate of three Salukis at-

Saluki, grizzle/tan. Photo by I. Français.

tacking a gazelle. Indeed, Salukis are historically renowned for their hunting ability. In writings of the Greek expeditions of Xenophon in Arabia: "These swift hounds were known to the Greeks, and their methods of a 'straight forward chase' without employing 'net or wily inventions' are extolled." Salukis are also seen in ancient Egyptian records dating between 2000 and 3000 B.C.

The breed comes in two coat varieties: the feathered or long-coated are termed by the Arabs *Shamir*; the smooths, *Nejdi*. The long-coated were later called Persian Greyhounds because of the variety's popularity in Persia (now Iran).

Although introduced to Britain in the late 1800s, the breed was not noticed until its recognition in 1923. The A.K.C. granted status to the breed in 1927.

Today the Saluki is still a prized companion. The coursing skills and hunting instincts of this dog are truly impressive. Like the Borzoi of the Soviet Union, the Saluki has enjoyed a resurgence of popularity. These handsome dogs are once again revered for the chic, noble hounds they are. Despite their size, these dogs make fine indoor companions, catlike in their cleanliness and aloof outlook on life. Proper exercise and running space are, of course, essential.

ESSENTIALS OF THE SALUKI: "The fine-trained lop-eared hounds, with slender sides, who lightly outrun the sharp-horned white antelope." The whole appearance of the Saluki suggests grace, speed, endurance, and symmetry. The head is long and narrow; the nose is black or liver in color. The chest is deep and moderately narrow. The shoulders sloping and set well back, well muscled without being coarse. The forelegs are straight and long from the elbow to the knee. Hindquarters are strong, hip bones set well apart and stifle moderately bent.

The back is fairly broad, muscles slightly arched over loin. The feet of moderate length. The tail long, set on low, carried naturally in a curve. Height: 23–28 inches (58–71 cm). Coat: smooth and silky, with light feathering on the legs, back of thighs, and sometimes shoulders; the ears are covered with long silky hair; the smooth variety has no feathering. Colors: cream, white, golden, fawn, red, black/tan, grizzle/tan, and tricolor.

Samoyed

The Samoyed, named after the great nomadic tribe with whom it dwelled, celebrates a heritage of close intercourse with Nature and remains today untampered with or unnecessarily "improved" by man. This is the pure and ancient lineage which the Samoyed enjoys in the dog world. The Samoyede, a fishing and hunting people, inhabit the eastern shores of the White Sea in Russia, the vast tundra which extends to the river stretches of the Ob and Yenisei. The veritable inaccessibility of the tundra on which the primitive Samoyede tribe

dwelled explains the unquestionable purity of their dog. The Samoyed is the epitome of the domesticated canine. The

Daniels Studio

Samoyed dog's continual association with man has shaped the sweet and personable character it exhibits today.

The dogs were described in 1779 by the explorer Tooke who indicated that

Samoyed family photographed outdoors. An extremely affectionate and noble breed of dog.

the dogs were used for hauling and that the peoples who moved with them wore garments of the dogs' white or black furs. These dogs did not hunt but instead were used as reindeer herders, guards, and intimate pets—sledge work is not believed to have been as common a chore for these dogs as it was for the Arctic huskies. The breed's pure coloration was greatly loved by the Samoyede people: "a coat of dazzling white with silver-tipped ends which gleam like glacier points, or with a pure white coat delicately tinted with biscuit, as though reflecting the rays of the sun." Historically, however, the breed could also be found in black and white and rich sable. The Nenets Herding Laika (or Reindeer Samoyed), which *see*, is a closely related breed of the Soviet Union that resembles the Samoyed except for color possibilities. The Nenets can also be gray, black or tan. The Samoyed's solid white or biscuit coat is one of its most striking attributes today. Necessarily, the Samoyed's coat needed to be thick and durable.

Early British fanciers favored the white and biscuit dogs. The first Samoyed to come to England arrived in about 1900 via sable fur traders returning from Siberia. The Samoyed breed of today is believed to trace its descent to about a dozen Samoyeds—those imported to England. Queen Alexandra was a devoted Sammy lover and many of her kennel dogs contributed to both British and American Samoyeds. The Samoyed is also greatly renowned in Australia where the breed thrives. In the U.S., it is populous and popular.

ESSENTIALS OF THE SAMOYED: Substantiating the strikingly luxuriant appearance is a strong, active, graceful dog, capable of awesome endurance. Pure white, white with biscuit, cream or all biscuit are allowable colors. The well-balanced, medium-sized body is blanketed by a thick, soft undercoat which is penetrated only by the harsh, stand-offish hairs composing the weather resistant outer coat. The skull is wedge shaped and broad, slightly crowned, not round or apple headed. The muzzle of medium length and medium width should taper toward the nose. Stop is not too abrupt. The ears are strong and thick and erect, triangular and rounded at the tips. The neck is strong, well muscled and carried proudly erect. The chest should be deep with ribs well sprung out. The back is straight to the loin, medium in length, very muscular and neither long nor short coupled. The tail should be moderately long, profusely coated with hair and carried forward over the back. Height: 18–22 inch (46–56 cm). Weight: 50–65 pounds (23–30 kg).

Samoyedskaja
See Samoyed

Sanctioned match

A less formal show than a licensed or member show. No championship points are awarded at sanctioned matches and champions may not compete. Various classes may be provided except that nothing resembling the Winners Class will be offered.

Sand fleas

See Mites

Sanshu Dog

The Sanshu Dog is the cross-pollination of various Shika-Inus, middle-size Japanese dogs, with the smooth-coated Chow. Breeders on the Japanese mainland, in 1912, decided that a medium-sized guard dog would be ideally suited for their needs. In appearance, the Sanshu Dog looks like a diminutive Akita or a tall Smooth Chow. Some believe that the Sanshu has existed in Japan for many years and is the same dog as the extinct Indo-Chinese Phu-Quoc Dog, a guard dog imported to Europe at the turn of the century. Serendipitously perhaps, the Sanshu does bear an enviable resemblance to that lost canine. Today the breed functions as both a guard and companion; it is a greatly esteemed member of the Shika-Inu group. He is becoming a sought-after companion dog around the world and the popularity of the Shiba Inu seems to be instrumental in the West's interest in "new" Japanese breeds. *See also* Shika Inu, Shiba Inu

ESSENTIALS OF THE SANSHU DOG: A beautifully constructed dog with a sturdy, rather square body and straight stout limbs. A rather large head for his proportionately smaller body—full with the robust expression of the Akita (which is considerably larger). In color the Sanshu varies in shades of red, tan, white, gray, fawn, and pied, as well as black/tan and salt/pepper. Height: 16–18 inches (41–46 cm). Weight: 44–55 pounds (20–25 kg). The tail, rather feathered, curls loosely over the back. A smaller version of the Sanshu exists, which maintains these same physical traits, but is about 4 inches (10 cm) smaller.

Santa Elena fox

See South American foxes

Sapling

An untried race-dog pup of racing age, 10 to 18 months.

Sar Planina

See Sarplaninac

Sanshu Dog, black/tan. Photo by Rick Tomita.

Sar Tip

A breed of Yugoslavian sheepdog quite similar to the Sarplaninac. The Sar Tip is a larger and more powerful dog that is grave and undemonstrative in demeanor. *See* Sarplaninac

Saraila

A little-known Indian terrier breed existing in Assam, it is a useful house dog of a kind nature.

Sarcoma

Any of various malignant tumors that are made of and spread by connective tissue or tissue that is developed from the mesoblast, the middle layer of cells of the tumor. *See* Cancer

Sarcoptic mange

See Mange

Sarplaninac, gray. Photo by I. Français.

Sarplaninac

The Sarplaninac, although not as old a breed as either the Greek Sheepdog or the Akbash Dog, from whom this breed derives, is one of the oldest dogs native to the area now part of Yugoslavia. Performing traditional flock guarding roles, the Sarplaninac works principally in the mountain range that bears its name. The region of Macedonia, once known as Illyria, gave the breed its former name. A small but notable number of Sars have come to the United States for employment. These dogs' hard-work ethic and natural abilities speak well for the breed's potential in more and more flock guarding programs. The Sar has not yet adopted the typical American attitude toward life, that is, weekends are for play. Although the breed will show the lighter side of its personality on occasion, it is a strictly work dog that thrives when it is performing its natural task. Dogs also have been exported to Canada and are doing well.

ESSENTIALS OF THE SARPLANINAC: The body is medium in size and bone; the feathering on the underbelly and legs

and the bushy scimitar tail, however, give the appearance of a much stouter dog. Height: 22–24 inches (56–61 cm). Weight: 55–80 pounds (25–37 kg). Coat: medium in length, quite dense, either rough or smooth. Color: tan, gray, white, or black; can be pure or blend.

Saucy expression

See Expression

Sauerlander Dachsbracke

See Westphalian Dachsbracke

Savoy Sheepdog

A French herding dog developed by farmers in the Savoy area for sheep and cattle work. It is medium sized and substantial with a long body and drop ears. The coat is thick and light or dark gray (often with blue or brown patches). It stands 18–22 inches (46–56 cm) and weighs 45–55 pounds (20.5–25 kg). The head is strong and rather coarse. These are excellent and robust servants to their French shepherd masters.

Saw-horse stance

Appears as though the dog is standing on ice, with the feet slipping out and the legs spreading under him, forming obtuse rather than the desired right angles with the body.

Scabies

See Mange

Scale clerk

Weighs dogs as they reach the track from the kennel and just before leaving the paddock for a race.

Scale of Points

See Judging dogs

Scalp

Synonymous with "skin" of the skull or "flesh" of the head.

Scapula

The bone called the shoulder blade and found in the dog's forequarters, which *see*.

Scent

See Nose

Scenthounds

Celtic Alaunt-type mastiffs are believed to have yielded the dogs that we refer today as scenthounds. A scenthound, quite simply, is a dog that hunts principally by scent. The Bloodhound is perhaps the epitome of the scenthound and fittingly it is derived from the St. Hubert Hound of sixth-century Belgium. The Talbot Hound and the Southern Hound are among the earliest known scenthound types. These dogs were heavier than the lot of scenthounds that comprise the group today, still retaining much of their mastiff ancestor's bulk and size. Early breeders selected for the quality of the nose and transformed the mastiff bulk and power into speed, drive and stamina.

The scenthound group can be divided into packhounds or foxhounds, coonhounds, curs, dachshunds or basset hounds and "walking" hounds. France receives credit for producing 30–40 distinctive scenthound breeds. The Middle Ages in the feudal states that now comprise France experienced much enthusiasm for the hunt. The nobility went to great measures to raise and train large packs of hunting scenthounds. During the 1600s, hundreds of parks and forests in France were usurped for the king's dogs—a hunting pack could contain as many as 1,000 dogs! Many French scenthound breeds come in both a smoothhaired variety and a wirehaired. The wirehaired is referred to as *griffon*. *Basset* or short-legged versions of each of these taller "walking" dogs were also created. The scenthounds of Switzerland, known as laufhunds or "walking" dogs (the hunter walked behind the pack during the chase, i.e., a horse wasn't necessary), come in both sizes; the smaller size is prefixed by the word *neider*.

Great Britain boasts a smaller number of dogs,

even though the British breeds have more universal followings than any other nation's scenthounds. The Basset Hound, Foxhound, Beagle and Otter Hound are among the British contribu-

Scenthounds indigenous to the United States are largely classified as coonhounds. North America is the central location of the raccoon population, hence the development of these working treeing breeds. Bluetick Coonhound barks up a tree.

Scenthounds in France are branded *les chiens courant* or the running hounds: there are no fewer than a dozen individual breeds indigenous to France. Photographs by I. Français.

tions to the group. Fox hunting in England was approached by the nobility with unprecedented red-coated ceremony. While the extracting of the perni-

Scenthounds in England are aptly dubbed foxhounds. These hard-running sharp-scenting hounds sometimes work in conjunction with a field on horseback and a pocket terrier to do the dirty work.

Scenthounds. Bred for the desired shorter legs, the Basset Hound is considerably slower than the running foxhounds, though it is no less determined and consistent.

cious red fox from the countryside was initially but a chore that required the assistance of dogs—hounds to scent them out and terriers to exterminate them—the chase of the fox became such an obsession that the hunter soon began chasing the fox (now less populous) for the sport of it.

Germany's contributions to the scenthound pool are the dachshunds, low to the ground hounds: two Dachshunds in three coats. Other German scenthounds include the Hanoverian Hound, the Deutsche Bracke and the Westphalian Dachsbracke. These dogs each have wondrous coldtrailing noses.

The American scenthounds fall into two categories: coonhounds and curs. The coonhounds derive essentially from British foxhounds, supplemented by various Irish, German and French dogs to achieve certain ends. The raccoon, of course, is the coonhound's quarry, the masked, tree-climbing mammal that gave the coonhound its reason to come into being. The curs derive from various American and European stock, including schweisshunds, scenting hounds and native Indian cur or pariah dogs. None of the cur breeds are recognized by either major American registry. Among these hardy hound curs are the Treeing Tennessee Brindle, Plott Hound, Stephens Stock, Black Mouth Cur, American Blue Gascon Hound, and the Leopard Cur.

Schafpudel
See German Sheeppoodle

Schapendoes

A densely coated sheep herder, native to Holland and of physical resemblance to such other European herding dogs as the Bearded Collie, the Puli, and the Polish Lowland Sheepdog, the Schapendoes, or Dutch Sheepdog, is undoubtedly a very old breed. It is related to the Briard, the Bergamasco, and its British counterpart, the Bearded Collie. However, the breed never attained favor of the aristocracy and lived exclusively as a working dog, and there remains no conclusive evidence of its ancestry.

The breed has served the farmer of Holland for centuries, but its future remains questionable. In the first half of the twentieth century, many Dutch farmers lost or sold their lands and the population of Dutch Sheepdogs fell. Also during this time was a large-scale importation of Border Collies and other renowned herders. The result was a further decrease, which through the war years worsened to the threat of extinction.

Fanciers have since worked to save the breed in its native land, and specimens have appeared at European dog shows since the late 1940s. Through selective breeding, and of course supply and demand, the breed has become more of a pet than a working dog but still retains many of its herder instincts. Lively and affectionate, diligent and loyal, hardy and all-weather, the Schapendoes is a promising dog of high pet caliber.

ESSENTIALS OF THE SCHAPENDOES: A hard-working dog of distinctive shaggy appearance. The head is strongly constructed; skull is arched and broad between the ears; the part of the hair on the topskull suggests a defined furrow, which in reality is only moderate. The muzzle is broad and strong and well furnished with beard and mustache. The back is long, strong and straight. Tail set high, very thick, reaching not below the hocks. Chest deep but not broad. Hindquarters well angulated. Height: 17–20

Schapendoes, black with white. Photo by I. Français.

inches (43–51 cm). Weight: 33 pounds (15 kg). Many specimens have a wave to their coat. Coat colors are ideally between blue-gray and black; all colors, however, are acceptable.

Schillerstövare, black and tan.

Schipperke, fawn, unaccepted A.K.C. color; pet dog with undocked tail.

Schillerstövare

The ancient Schillerstövare was allegedly perfected by Per Schillers, the founder of the breed. This Swiss breeder desired a hound of lighter type, able to cover more ground with greater speed. The gene pool likely contains the German, Austrian and early Swiss hounds. Reportedly the Schiller Hound has been hunted in the Swedish forests since the fifteenth century. This is a hunter and tracker of especial use on snow hare and fox. The Schiller Hound, however, has been employed effectively on quite a variety of land game. While the Schiller dog is a popular huntsman, it does not rival the more popular Hamiltonstövare as a show dog. His hard coat enables him to withstand the cold and prolonged journeys in the snow, again adding to his hunting attributes.

ESSENTIALS OF THE SCHILLERSTÖVARE: This quick-moving hound appears more like a running sighthound than a full-bodied scenthound. The coat, which is self-colored in black and tan (with a saddle), is short, dense and smooth. The undercoat is thick. Height: 19–24 inches (48–61 cm). Weight: 40–54 pounds (18–25 kg). The body is square and gives this robust-looking hound a noble and compelling appearance.

Schipperke

The "Little Skipper," with his prick ears and nordic body shape, is most probably a descendant of spitz types and not a miniaturization of the black Belgian Leauvenaar, a provincial herder, as was once asserted. Used on barge ships in Belgium, the Schipperke likely has always been little. As a breed, it has been around for centuries and continues to breed pure. He is believed to have participated in the world's first specialty show which took place in Brussels in 1690.

The first Schipperke to be imported into England was "Flo" in 1887, owned by a Mr. Berrier. Other specimens soon followed and the Schipperke Club of England was established within three years. The first to arrive in America was about the same time; Mr. Walter J. Com-

stock of Providence imported one in 1888. The first American parent club was founded in 1905. Surely the British categorization of the Schipperke is more apt than the American: The Kennel Club of Great Britain considers the Schipperke among its Utility breeds, while the American Kennel Club labels it "Non-Sporting." The truth is that while the Little Skipper is sized between a toy and a terrier, his sporting abilities are keen. Traditionally a shipmate, the Schip has been popular ashore as well, showing an impressive propensity as a ratter, if properly trained. He can also hunt effectively on rabbit and mole. Defining a dog by what it is *not* generally proves inept, but calling the multi-talented Schip non-sporting is as incorrect as it is inept.

The British standard for the breed does not emphasize these touches as much as the American does. Generally speaking, Schipperkes today are not as robustly frilled as they were at the turn of the century. The classic culottes and jabot should never go out of style and set the breed apart from all others in the canine tribe.

ESSENTIALS OF THE SCHIPPERKE: The medium-sized Schipperke possesses a short, thick-set body that is broad behind the shoulders. The head is foxlike and fairly wide; the muzzle is tapering, not too elongated or blunt. The neck is strong and full, slightly arched, rather short. The shoulders are muscular and sloping. The body is short, thick set and cobby. Loins muscular and well drawn up from the brisket. Forelegs straight under body, with bone in proportion, but not coarse. Hindquarters somewhat lighter than foreparts, but muscular with well-rounded rump. Tail docked to no more than an inch. The outer coat is abundant and somewhat harsh to the touch—the longer hair around the neck forms a ruff and a cape, while the longer hair on the rear forms culottes and a jabot. In color the Schipperke is solid black, which is the only color accepted by the A.K.C; however, the breed also comes in a handsome range of tans and fawns, which are acceptable abroad. He is typically tailless. Weight: up to 18 pounds (10 kg).

Schipperke, black. Photo by I. Français.

Schnauzer

In German *schnauze* means muzzle. *Schnauzer* today describes three rough-coated terriers of Germany: the Miniature, Standard and Giant, which *see*.

Schutzhund

In German, *Schutzhund* means protection dog, and the concept of Schutzhund training evolved in Europe in the 1890s. This type of training involves three important aspects: tracking, obedience and protection work. Schutzhund strives to develop the full potential of the dogs it employs, making them the most competent protection dogs they are capable of being Schutzhund primarily involves the dogs of the Working Group; other breeds have also taken part, such as the Airedale Terrier. Schutzhund dogs are not attack dogs, but rather dogs that are friendly, well behaved, control-lable companions. Dogs are trained to bark before they bite and taught to seize the suspect without causing him irrepa-rable harm. Presently there is much con-cern in big-dog circles about the necessity of Schutzhund training. Opponents pur-port that protection breeds like Rottweilers and Dobermans already possess strong man-stopping instincts, and that these can be dangerous if sharp-ened too acutely.

N.A.S.A., that is the North American Schutzhund Association, got under way in the mid 1970s; early attempts to organ-ize in the States failed. The Working Dogs of America, Inc. (W.D.A.), is another Schutzhund organization, which was es-tablished at the same time.

While Schutzhund training remains favored in Germany and certain other European countries, the A.K.C. does not sanction Schutzhund work. This official stand was issued in 1990.

Schweisshund

German term for bloodhound, a scent-hound used for tracking wounded ani-mals. The Bavarian Mountain and the Hanoverian Hound are good examples of schweisshunden. These dogs are cold-nosed, to a large degree.

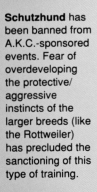

Schutzhund training has long been a part of a guard dog's education, particularly in Germany. This Alsatian works with its trainer.

Schutzhund has been banned from A.K.C.-sponsored events. Fear of overdeveloping the protective/ aggressive instincts of the larger breeds (like the Rottweiler) has precluded the sanctioning of this type of training.

Schweizer Laufhund

The Schweizer Laufhund represents one of the three basic Swiss hound types. Switzerland is graced with a hardy supply of scenthounds; the Schweizer, along with the Berner and Luzerner breeds, comes in two sizes—essentially a tall (laufhund) and a short (neiderlaufhund). The term *laufhund* in Swiss means "walking dog," or dog to follow on foot. Both the Schweizer Laufhund and its smaller brother, the Schweizer Neiderlaufhund, are likely descended from the old French hounds. The Swiss terrain dictated that these French spin-offs possess lighter, leaner conformations to accommodate their work—speculating more specifically, the Porcelaine and smaller specimens of the Chien Français Orange et Blanc.

Both Schweizer breeds are dogs with strong drive and excellent hunting instincts. Although the wirehaired versions of these breeds once existed, they no longer are seen today.

ESSENTIALS OF THE SCHWEIZER LAUFHUND: This is a rather lightweight dog that stands on rather lengthy, well-boned legs. The coat can come in either of two types: (1) a tight-fitting, dense, and short smooth variety; and (2) a standoffish outer, soft inner, double-coated roughhaired variety. Color for both varieties is white with either yellow, red or orange markings. Although red is reportedly less common, dogs with deep red markings are found. Height is 18–24 inches (46–61 cm). Weight: 34–44 pounds (15.5–20 kg). This is an attractive dog for one who prefers a more streamlined, endurance-built hound. The smaller version, the Schweizer Neider-

laufhund, is the spitting image of his brother but stands 13–16 inches (33–41 cm) high and weighs 30–40 pounds (13.5–18 kg).

Schweizer Neiderlaufhund
See Schweizer Laufhund

Scimitar tail
An exaggerated saber tail, which *see*.

Sclera
The white matter that surrounds the cornea of the eye. Visible in many breeds, as it is in humans, it is undesirable and even penalized in some breeds.

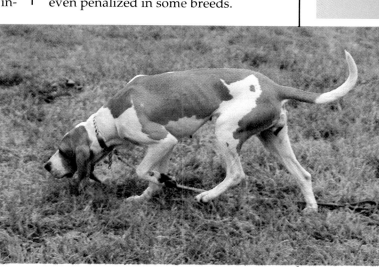

Sclerosis
See Arteriosclerosis

Scotch Collie
See Collie

Schweizer Neiderlaufhund, white with orange.

Schweizer Laufhund on the scent. Photographs by I. Français.

Scottish Deerhound

"Shagg haired" or "curled" Greyhounds have been known in Scotland

Scottish Deerhound, blue-gray. Photo by I. Français.

prior to the sixteenth century. Both Dr. Caius and Holinshed describe the dogs in their respective writings. The Scottish Deerhound has been described variously: the Rough Highland Greyhound, Scotch Greyhound, Highland Greyhound, Wolfdog, and Staghound. Today the British refer to the breed simply as Deerhound. Americans preserve the "Scottish" prefix. The breed was remarkably popular during the sixteenth and seventeenth centuries, due to the definitive Scotch diversion of deer-driving; the eighteenth century, however, backfired on the fast-driving Deerhound, as gunpowder unplugged the breed's popularity. Many powerful, though fanatical, chieftains kept the breed; they were primarily stag hunters who regarded their magnanimous hounds with pride, preserving their romantic intrigue with their coarse-coated coursers. The breed lingered in relative obscurity until a resurgence in the early 1830s.

The Deerhound's chore different than that of the Greyhound, its apparent rela-tion, reveals its slightly differing appearance. Bred to hunt the native deer of Scotland, the dog gained size and strength. To flourish in the harsh climate, it also sprouted a rough protective coat.

The Deerhound's heyday is surely but a historical footnote, and a fleet one at that. While the breed remains today in able and loving hands, those hands are limited. The breed is recognized in the both the U.S. and Britain, although neither country can boast an impressive number of annual registrations. This is a gentle and gentlemanly dog, with elegant ways and polite affection. The breed's size and need for an exercise area, however, has precluded its wide acceptance as a companion animal.

ESSENTIALS OF THE SCOTTISH DEERHOUND: The Scottish Deerhound appears as a rough-coated Greyhound; he is, however, larger in size and bigger in bone. Height 28–32 inches (71–81 cm). Weight: 75–110 pounds (34–50 kg). The head, which is carried high, is long, level, and in balance with the whole dog. The neck should be long, befitting the Greyhound character. The requisite mane may detract from the apparent length of the neck. The shoulders should be well sloped. The body, too, is long; there is great depth to the chest, which provides maximum endurance. The coat is rough and hard, with a beard and brow of softer hair. The ears are small and carried as a Greyhound's. Colors include a variety of dark self-colors, with dark blue-gray being preferred.

Scottish Terrier

Known as the Aberdeen Terrier before 1890, the Scottish Terrier typifies the rough, harsh British terrier, that is, different from the smooth black and tan terrier. More accurately, however, the Scottish Terrier typifies the Scottish terriers. In days of old, before type was set, the Scottish Terrier could be seen in most any region of Scotland and type varied from region to region. Dogs merely resembled their parents, more or less, so dogs in a particular region often looked rather the same. Dogs were adapted to work on a particular countryside. Some of these Scotties were used to extract vermin from rocks, rats from under earth, or other pests from barns, etc. These terriers were truly working terriers which all looked similar, at best. The breed we know today as the Scottish Terrier came into being thanks to Captain Gordon Murray and S.E. Shirley, who worked towards setting the type. Culling "mongrels with hair ten and a half inches long" from the show rings, Murray described the "Scottish Terrier" type in 1879, eliminating the "half-breed curs and their half-wit owners" from exhibition circles. Establishing type has certainly stabilized the Scottish Terrier's soundness and gratefully didn't detract from his natural gameness. In 1882, three years later, when the Scottish Terrier Club was established and the dogs began entering dog shows as a separate breed, type and soundness were stabilized. Although a popular companion dog, the Scottie has never been called a toy dog. His hardy, rugged terrier character defies the image of pillow-sitting tyke. The breed, popular in Europe and America, is still a competent rodent patrolman as well as a handy watchdog.

ESSENTIALS OF THE SCOTTISH TERRIER: Possessing the strength and solidity of a big dog in the compass of a small one, the Scottish Terrier is well muscled and sturdy. The Scottie's head is long, but not exaggerated in relation to the body, which is also elongated. Stop distinct. The face wears a keen, lively expression. Neck of moderate length, muscular, set on sloping shoulders. The chest is broad and hung between the forelegs. The back is proportionately short and muscular. Straight topline. Powerful hindquarters, buttocks wide. Feet well padded. Colors: black, steel, iron gray, brindle or grizzle, sandy and wheaten. White is usually tolerated on the chest only. Height: 10–11 inches (25.5–28 cm). Weight 19–23 pounds (8.5–10.5 kg). The outer coat is close lying and harshly wired; the undercoat is soft and short.

Scottish Terrier, brindle. Photo by I. Français.

Scottish Terrier.
Photograph by J. Ashbey.

Scout

The gundog handler's assistant at a field trial. When a person other than the handler is hunting for the competing dog, he is said to be scouting.

Scrambled mouth

This term refers to the situation arising in the oral cavity when the incisors are misplaced.

Screw tail

A naturally short tail twisted in a generally spiral fashion.

Scroll ears

Drop hound ears that tend to roll up, e.g., Braque Dupuy.

Scrotal hernia

See Hernias

Scrotum

Location of fully descended testicles, this sac can let loose or tighten up to regulate the temperature of the testes, keeping them always at optimal production temperature, which is slightly lower than normal body temperature. *See also* Reproductive System

Scurf

See Dandruff

S.D.

Suffix for Sled Dog degree.

S.D.X.

Sled Dog Excellent suffix.

Sealyham Terrier

The Sealyham was conceived and established in less than two and a half decades. This handsome, proficient terrier is the brainchild of the eccentric and aged Captain John Owen Tucker Edwardes, an Otter Hound enthusiast and hunting sportsman who sought the perfect terrier companion for his surly pack. Edwardes, a resident of Sealyham, Haverfordwest, Wales, planned his ideal, "proper" terrier to be light-boned enough to keep up with the hounds, agile enough to maneuver over the rocky precipitous terrain, and utterly small enough to uncover and undo the otters hiding between the

rocks—*plus*, fit the public's concept of "a popular dog."

While breed type was set around the mid 1800s, the breed didn't capture the popular attention until around 1910; one year later the Kennel Club of Great Britain and the American Kennel Club recognized the breed. Unlike many of the other British terriers, no one tried to classify the Sealyham as a variety of the Cairn or Skye Terriers: the Sealy looked so different that fanciers embraced it with no time to spare. As companions Sealys are strong-willed and assertive, and, therefore, the dog needs a firm hand to handle properly. He retains much of his ancestor's gameness, but his good looks and trainability certainly make him an incomparable show dog.

ESSENTIALS OF THE SEALYHAM TERRIER: Superbly balanced, the body is of medium length and level with a broad deep chest, well let down between the forelegs. Its head is long and broad without coarseness. The neck is fairly long and muscular. Forelegs short, strong and straight. Hindquarters powerful, thighs well bent at stifle. Feet are round and catlike. Tail carried erect. Coloration is paramount to the Sealyham look—tan or badger patches marking the pure white head and ears (without exaggeration). Otherwise, the body is solid white. Height: 10–11 inches (25.5–28 cm). Weight: 22–25 pounds (10–11.5 kg). The outer coat is hard and wiry; the undercoat is weather-proof.

Sealyham Terrier, white with badger. Photo by I. Français.

Search and rescue

Romping through the snow in red and white (or white and red), warm brandy dangling, the Saint Bernard has long been prided as the rescue breed. This dog was used at the Hospice of St. Bernard for

Second series

In field trials, after the dogs have been run as regularly drawn, the judges may select some of the contestants to compete again. This is called a second series.

Second thigh

Lower thigh. *See* Thigh

Seçoviano

See Galgo Español

Sectorial teeth

See Dentition

Sedge

Term used alternatively for deadgrass, the desired color of the Chesapeake Bay Retriever.

Seeing Eye™ dogs

A tribute to canine intelligence and trustworthiness, dogs provide sight and guidance for human members of society who are blind. In 1926, John Sinykin opened the first school for guide dogs. Sinykin was a German Shepherd breeder who initiated The Master Eye Institute (or His Master's Eyes). The first actual Seeing Eye™ dog (a trademark) was founded in 1928 by Josef Weber. The organization's purposes are threefold: to train dogs to guide blind persons; to train and teach instructors in the science and technique of educating dogs to act as guides; and to teach blind persons to use and handle the dogs properly. Leader Dogs for the Blind, another school, opened in 1939. In England, Guide Dogs for the Blind Association began in 1931. In Great Britain alone, there are approximately 1,800 guide dogs. This association, like the aforementioned American schools, trains dogs for this purpose.

Among the breeds which are most commonly used as guides are the German Shepherd, Labrador Retriever, Boxer and Golden Retriever. The temperament, obedience, intelligence and

Search and rescue expertly performed by two longhaired Saint Bernards. Photo by V. Serbin.

many years but today other breeds do the rescue work while the St. Bernard sits around looking historical. Search and rescue work requires that the dog have a good nose, an inherent sense of urgency, and certain physical abilities. German Shepherds, Newfoundlands, Landseers, and Labrador Retrievers are just some breeds employed. Excellent swimming and tracking abilities and protection from the elements are essential to the precision performance of search and rescue workers.

Seborrhea

A skin condition also referred to as "stud tail." The sebaceous or oil-forming glands are responsible. Accumulation of dry skin, or scurf, is formed by excessive oily deposits while the hair becomes dry or falls out altogether.

Sechura fox

See South American foxes

consistency of the breed are paramount in the dog's ability to assume the responsibility for its master. Dogs are matched individually according to compatibility with their prospective blind owner. *See also* Assistance dogs

Segugio

Italian for hound.

Segugio Italiano

The Segugio Italiano represents the unique hound of Italy. Of very ancient origin, these dogs are believed to be descended from crosses of the ancient Celtic scenthounds and Phoenician sighthound types. The dog's long muzzle, lack of stop, and sheer height suggest the sighthound influence. Many believe the present type a fair representation of the early ancestors. The Italian Renaissance, with its revitalization of ancient beauty and value, brought the Italian Hounds to enviable popularity. Much ceremony was attached to the hunt: horses, vibrant colors, and brass *a la Verdi* (had Verdi yet lived!). Once the hunt fell in popularity, so too did the Segugios. Today however, they are the most popular dogs in Italy and are still used on hare, rabbit and boar over most any terrain.

There are two varieties of Segugios: the shorthaired known as the Segugio Italiano a Pelo Rase and the wirehaired known as the Segugio Italiano a Pelo Forte. Both breeds are equally common in Italy.

ESSENTIALS OF THE SEGUGIO ITALIANO: The Segugio Italiano a Pelo Forte (or Roughhaired) and the Segugio Italiano a Pelo Rase (or Shorthaired) are two individual breeds of Italian Hound that vary in coat type and resultingly look unique from one another. Segugios have a tendency towards a self-color of flat black, long ears, a small skull, and a notably elongated body. The Pelo Forte is roughcoated with bushy eyebrows. The Pelo Rase's smooth coat accentuates his muscular body that covers much ground. The Segugio is a rather large dog but has the refinement that one expects with so ancient and nobility-favored a breed. Height: 20–22 inches (51–56 cm). Weight 40–60 pounds (18–27 kg). Both coats occur in black/tan and fawn.

Self-color

Although lighter or darker shadings of the same color may be allowed, de-

Segugio Italiano, smooth, black/tan.

pending on the breed, a self-colored dog must be a solid-colored dog but can be any canine color.

Self-colored nose

A nose complementary to a dog's coat color: for example, a brown nose on a chocolate Labrador Retriever.

Segugio Italiano, wire, black/tan. Photographs by I. Français.

Self-marked

A solid-colored canine with white (or "bleach") markings on the tip of the tail, the tops of the feet, and the front of the chest. *See also* Self-color

Semen

The thick, whitish fluid secreted by the male reproductive organs upon ejaculation. The semen contains the spermatozoa and other fluids.

Semi-drop ears

Cocked or tipped ears that are essentially prick ears with drooping tips (e.g., those of the Collie).

Semi-drop ears, the tipped ears on the Rough Collie. Photo by I. Français.

Semi-hare feet

Feet that appear between oval and hare feet.

Semi-open trailing

Refers to a dog that will bark some of the time on trail (e.g. chop mouth), but really begins howling when he has the quarry treed.

Semi-prick ears

Ears that are not full prick, same as semi-drop ears, which *see*.

Semyen fox

Classified as *Simenia simensis*, the Semyen fox is a little known wild dog that is native to the highlands of Ethiopia and a member of the family Canidae. Known also as the Abyssinian fox, the Ethiopian fox, the red jackal, the red dog, the red wolf, and a host of other names, the Semyen fox is foxlike in vocal expression and den behavior and has the pointed muzzle and large triangular ears of the typical fox; however, its overall appearance is clearly more like the coyote or jackal than any vulpine relative.

Because so little is known conclusively about this wild dog, it is difficult to cast any definitive judgments on its nature. It is believed to be a dweller of rocky dens and has been reported inhabiting altitudes that exceed 10,000 feet above sea level, covered with moorland. The moors most frequented by this fox are heavily populated with rodents, which form the staple of the Semyen fox's diet. Farmers of the Ethiopian highlands accuse the fox of killing their livestock and their children, acts which are unlikely in light of what is known about this rodent-eater. Numerous pups fall prey to the large birds of its moorland habitat, including various eagles. Recent motions on the part of the Ethiopian government to preserve its moorlands in the form of national parks suggest hope for this ancient highland dweller—which like so many other animals existed long before the encroachment of man.

Senility

Senility or senile decay may occur at as early as six years of age. Such development of course depends on the breed to a large extent, and the individual dog to a lesser extent. A graying muzzle and hazy eyes are signs of old age; the dog's senior citizen years are marked by less activity, overweight (or underweight) and a lethargy which affects the quickness of the mind. *See* Older dogs

Senior Grand Nite Champion

Title earned by hound who, after attaining Grand Nite Championship, wins an additional three first places in Coonhunt competition.

Sennenhund

Dog of the Alpine herdsman. Breeds to which the term sennenhund are affixed include the Appenzeller, the Bernese Mountain Dog, the Entelbucher, and the Greater Swiss Mountain Dog, which *see*. These four dogs share many similarities, including coloration, general body type, mastiff ancestry, and utility. They vary in size but all make fine herder and drover dogs and excellent watch and guard dogs. The sennenhunds found extensive employment as cart-pulling dogs for many years in the Swiss Alps and maintain a strong work ethic and willingness to please. *See also* Draft dogs

Senses

We commonly conceptualize the senses as being five in number, although there are a number of secondary senses as well. Dogs have the same "big five": visual (eyes); auditory (ears); tactile (feel); gustatory (taste buds); and olfactory (nose). Among the secondary senses, the kinesthetic or sense of movement; muscular or reflex senses; the sense of balance; the sexual sense or instinct; the sense of hunger or thirst. Beyond the first five, however, the conceptualization of what comprises a sense is somehow obscured and becomes intertwined with our notions of instincts. Additionally, dogs also have what we usually call common sense, in that they learn from their mistakes, remember them, and usually don't repeat them. Humans sometimes exhibit common sense and allegedly have exclusive rights to the powers of reasons. (The authors take this moment to assure the readers that it does not require rational beings to agree to write a lexicon!)

S.E.P.P.

Abbreviation for Siberian Evaluation Performance Project, which *see*.

Septicemia

Once known as blood poisoning, this condition is actually caused by foreign bacteria filling the vascular system. It is usually cured with prescribed antibiotics.

Service dogs

Service dogs, also known as mobility dogs, are trained to assist a physically disabled person. The dogs help the individual accomplish many everyday activities; they are also trained in a number of safety procedures, should the need arise. *See also* Assistance dogs

Set and crawl

The action of the sheepdog in crouching and crawling towards the sheep and thereby causing them to move slowly in the desired direction.

Set-on

The joining of the base of the tail and the body or the joining of the base of the ear and the skull.

Setters

Setters or "couchers" preceded our modern spaniels. These dogs couch, or creep slow and low to the ground, in scenting their winged quarry. Today's

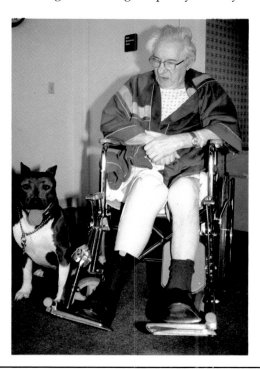

setters are among the most beautiful of the gundogs. England's Gordon Setter and English Setter, Ireland's Irish Setter, and France's Èpagneul Français, among them. The earliest setters, such as the Llewellyn, Laverack, and the Èpagneul Ecossais, contribute to the gene pool of both our contemporary setters and spaniels. *See also* Gundogs

Settle

When a find is made by one or more hounds and others, coming from different directions, join in on the line, the pack is said to settle.

Sewero-Wostotschnaja Jesdowaja Sobaka

See Northeasterly Hauling Laika

Shaggy

The appearance of dogs with profuse, usually medium to long hairs, which because of their texture, length or growth give an almost unkempt appearance.

Shanks

Thigh regions, usually upper and lower. Upper shank is the equivalent of upper thigh. *See also* Thigh

Shar-Pei

The Shar-Pei, or Chinese Fighting Dog as it was once called, is a cross of mastiff and nordic breeds. The blue tongue is a feature that it shares with the Chow Chow, an obvious contributor to the Shar-Pei's make-up. For the residents of the Chinese southern provinces (Dah Let and Kwantung), the dogs were not just gladiators vaudevilling in the pits for entertainment purposes. That was their night job—during the day, they hunted, herded and protected the Chinese peasants, who were their captivated audience later that night. The dog's piglike pliable skin gave it an advantage over its opponents, who found it most distasteful and uncomfortable when grabbed.

The Shar-Pei is a centuries-old canine whose present-day popularity is but a recent phenomenon. When Shar-Peis first made their appearances on American shores in the early 1970s, they were billed as the rarest canine in the world. Early attempts to capture the history and essence of the Shar-Pei prove inept compared to present-day norms. Dangerfield and Howell in 1971 describe the Shar-Pei: "Like primitive animals their interest is in violence; they need no urging to attack.

Shar-Pei, fawn. Photo courtesy of R. L. and Vicky Teshera.

Wherever they are and whatever they appear to be doing, they are in fact biding their time and silently waiting for the opportunity of attacking and vanquishing every other dog in sight, regardless of size." Quite contrary to these previous writings, the Shar-Pei was less successful in the pits due to its discerning and basically disinterested demeanor. Being intelligent canines, lordly and sober, the Shar-Pei bequeathed the pits to more suitable bull-like mentalities. Today the Shar-Pei's mastiff blood may instill the occasional desire to spar with fellow kennel mates.

Like the Chow Chow, the Shar-Pei has also survived in mainland China where the breed was regarded as a delicacy. In cultures different than the Western ones we live in, culinary and etiquette traditions differ greatly. Dogs have long been used as food in Eastern, Polynesian, and Indian civilizations. *See also* Dogs as delicacy, Sumatra Battak, Hawaiian Poi Dog, Philippine Islands Dog

The outlawing of pets on mainland China forced the breed into near extinction. Matgo Law, a concerned breeder, was able to stir up Western interest in the breed and effectively rescue it from mortality. Today the Shar-Pei is continually growing in popularity. The breed is among the most exceptional in the canine world. The Chinese standard for the Shar-Pei, in

its own way, poetically captures some of the allure of the breed through its evocative language. The standard requires a Wu-Lo head (a pearlike melon), clamshell ears, butterfly nose (like a Guangzhou cookie), Pae Pah legs (ham-shaped instrument), shrimp back, iron-wire tail, grandma face, iron pelle tongue, water buffalo neck, wun fish body, facing sky anus, horse's rear end, dragon leg, garlic feet, mother frog or roof tile mouth, and iron toenails.

Owners should be alerted to the potential skin problems and eye conditions that the dogs are sometimes prone to. Like the colorful Chinese standard, these dogs are irresistible and uncannily interesting, especially as puppies. Their hippopotamus heads, blue flowering

Shar-Pei, brown. Photo courtesy of Dawn Walling.

Shar-Pei, red. Photo courtesy of Elly Paulus.

Shar-Pei, chocolate, adult and puppy. Photo courtesy of P. and M. Tingen.

tongues and un-ironable wrinkles make them exceptionally unique in the canine world. Persons seduced helplessly by the Shar-Pei puppy and its wrinkles are reminded that these dogs grow up into adult dogs that may barely resemble your wallet-sized puppy snapshots.

stand-offish, is but one of the breed's peculiarities: a bluish (preferably black) tongue and mouth; a wide, blunt muzzle, well padded to cause a bulge at the base of the nose; petite, rounded equilateral triangular ears that drop close to the head; canine teeth curved like scimitars.

Shar-Pei (*opposite*), fawn. Photo courtesy of Peter Belmont, Jr.

Alert and dignified, the Shar-Pei is affectionate with his own but is usually aloof and independent. His frowning expression is no fair indicator of his disposition: he is mostly delighted to be in the presence of the people to whom he is extremely devoted. Shar-Peis tend to be one-person dogs and can sometimes be less than hospitable. The A.K.C. admitted the breed into full-championship status in October 1991.

ESSENTIALS OF THE SHAR-PEI: The extremely oversized coat, prickly and

The head is large for the size of the body, which is medium sized and powerful. Shoulders muscular, sloping. Forelegs of moderate length and good bone, straight. Chest deep, broad. Hind legs muscular, strong. Feet compact, firmly set, moderately sized. Height: 18–20 inches (46–51 cm). Weight: 35–45 pounds (16–21 kg). The color is solid in fawn, chocolate, cream, red or black. Particolored and saddle patterns also occur but are disqualified from shows.

Shar-Pei, (*above*) silver. Courtesy of Dr. D.M. Cline.

Shar-Pei, (*right*) particolor.

Shar-Pei, (*below*) black.

Shark mouth

Colorful term that refers to an overshot bite or receding lower jaw.

Sharp-tipped ears

See Blunt-tipped ears

Shaved rail

Raced too close to the inner rail.

Shawl

Around the neck of the Tibetan Spaniel is a distinctive growth of hairs; not a mane yet not a ruff, it is called a shawl.

Shedding

Shedding or *molting* of a dog's hair occurs twice a year: autumn and late spring. Although it is usually assumed that the dog sheds his coat as the seasons turn, more likely the length of daylight is connected to the shedding process. With the longer days of spring, the dog commences shedding his heavier coat to make way for his lighter coat; with the shortening days of winter, he sheds his lighter coat for his heavier one.

While some owners claim that their dogs never shed, others complain that their longhaired dogs shed non-stop from spring through winter. Regular vigorous grooming and brushing can help remove the dead hair; plucking can relieve any dead hair tufts. Dogs kept inside tend to shed for longer periods of time than dogs that live primarily outdoors. The heat of electric lights and excessive steam heat, worsened by a lack of exercise, can be the causes of these long molting periods. Sunlight, the intended overhead lamp, is more suitable to promote a shorter, more natural shedding period. Most owners agree that keeping a molting dog outdoors benefits the dog as well as the carpet and furniture.

Shedding, in shepherding

In shepherding and sheepdog trials, the dividing of a lot of sheep, such as separating the lambs from their mothers, is known as shedding.

Shed'n blade

Removes loose hair only. Pulls out loose topcoat and undercoat. The small shed'n blade takes out loose topcoat and undercoat. Good for small dogs, like Chihuahuas.

Sheepdog

Essentially there are two types of sheepdogs: herding dogs and flock guards. These differ largely in function and body types. The herding dogs are generally smaller dogs, agile enough to maneuver the flock. The flock guardians, mostly massive, are sentinels and protect their charges from attackers. *See also* Herding dogs, Flock guardians

Shedding. Longhaired breeds, such as the Bearded Collie, require daily grooming attention especially during the molting season. Brushing helps to remove dead hair and leave room for new growth. Photo by V. Serbin.

Sheepdog trials

Arguably the most exciting event in all the dog world are sheepdog trials. To improve the overall performance of working collies, organized trials for

Sheepdog trials. Border Collie following handler's signals as it pens its allotted sheep.

Sheepdog trials. Belgian Tervuren driving sheep at trial.

sheepdogs began in Bala, North Wales in 1873 and soon caught on throughout the British Empire. This first Welsh trial was organized by Lloyd Price of Rhiwlas, Wales, and was won by a Scottish collie named "Tweed," owned by James Thompson. Since the early part of the twentieth century, international sheepdog competitions have been sponsored in England, Scotland and Wales.

While the national enthusiasm of the

British for this sport has never been surpassed, other nations have reveled in the trialing of sheepdogs, including New

Zealand, Ireland, Australia, Canada, and the United States. The first competition in the U.S. was held in Philadelphia, Pennsylvania, in 1880. Other trials soon followed in New England and California. The North American Sheep Dog Society was the first to sponsor annual sheepdog events.

Sheepdog trials, regardless of the country of origin, are always competitive, exciting for the participants, and riveting for an audience. Classes are often divided into singles and doubles, where a handler works one or two dogs. Doubles are frequently referred to as braces. Among the possible events at a trial, the four traditional common events are gathering, penning, driving and shedding (separating a marked sheep from the others). Essentially sheepdog trials are a stylized kind of farm work, as each event should be a derivative or variation on a daily herding task. In most cases, events are a mere simplification of an actual working situation, since penning a half dozen sheep scarcely compares with driving 150 sheep uphill. It is estimated that a working Border Collie can work up to 1,000 sheep on its own. Just as a working sheepdog closely heeds the instructions of the shepherd or farmer, the dog in trial carefully follows the instructions of the handler. Hand signals, staffs, and whistles comprise the modes of a handler's communication with his dog. The dog's style, silence when working, accuracy and swiftness in responding to instructions are all considered in evaluating contestants. Unlike field trials, sheepdog trials require the dog to work within a time limit. Additionally, the dog's working in public, on unfamiliar terrain, under the judge's omnipresent scrutiny add to the excitement of these trials.

Among the breeds that perform with consistent success in sheepdog trials are the Border Collie, Australian Kelpie, Australian Shepherd, Bearded Collie, Belgian Tervuren, and Australian Cattle Dog, among others. As the current trend in the dog fancy underscores action and instinct-development, major dog registries are beginning to sponsor and license sheepdog trials, along with instinct tests and field trials. With a little luck, such traditional herding dogs as the German Shepherd, Belgian Shepherd and Collie, whose instincts and natural bred-for abilities have diminished or been otherwise channeled (frequently toward protection work), may regain some lost talents. Enthusiasm throughout the world for sheepdog trials continues to grow and soon other countries may follow the bright example of the British Empire where national sheepdog competitions today are spectacular, televised affairs! *See also* Field trials, Instinct testing, Obedience trials, Agility trials

Shelly

Suggests a chest that, because of its atypical dimensions, cannot provide the cardiovascular endurance necessary for the expected performance abilities of the breed of which the dog is a member.

enkottahs were able to down an adult tiger. Today, these formidable hunters are surely extinct, as may be their closest relative, the Kombai, which *see*.

Sheepdog trials. The ideal conformation of a working dog is in harmony with its task. This trial ace Snowmere Tweed is an English show champion Border Collie. Courtesy of D. Collier.

Sheepdog trials reach beyond the strictly working breeds to include such popular pet breeds as the Bearded Collie.

Shenkottah

Existing in the Trivandrum district, the Shenkottah is a powerful Indian dog used to hunt tiger. A pair of sinewy Sh-

Shepherd Spitz

German sheepdog type related to German Spitz family, believed to be extinct today. *See* Hütespitz

Shetland Sheepdog

A small collie-type dog, native to the Shetland Islands, popular today as a pet and show dog. The Shetland Sheepdog is related to the various collies of Great Britain, but whether this relation is through direct descent or only shared foundation stock is not certain. It is known that sailing vessels commonly argued by some.

The terrain of the Shetland Islands is exceedingly rough on all forms of life: the soil is rocky and there is little fauna to support man and his domesticated livestock. To adapt and survive, natives of the islands developed small, hardy cattle, sheep and Shetland ponies, and accordingly they employed small yet rugged herding dogs. These dogs are the ancestors of today's breed.

A move some decades ago by British breeders wreaked potential havoc on this ancient herder. A miniature Collie was developed (many of which resembled an inflated Papillon more than a Sheltie) and was shown with the Shetland breed. From these "contrived" miniatures was created a second type and much dissension as well. Further complicating the matter and further harming the Sheltie, a third miniaturized Collie type was created, this time a toy-sized variety. None of these dogs had the working abilities of the Shetland, and the breed overcame all potential harm.

Shetland Sheepdog, sable with white. Photo by Marx.

landed on the Shetland Islands during the 1700s, and that on board were such canines as the King Charles Spaniel, Greenland dogs, and various spitz-type herding dogs of the Scandinavian countries. It is believed that these dogs crossed with local herding dogs, and that through the course of time and the continued selection for fine working dogs, the Shetland Sheepdog emerged as a breed. The Shetland Sheepdog, though closely resembling the (Scotch) Collie, is a separate breed and not at all a bantamized version of *the* Collie, as has been

Today's Sheltie may have a bit more of the characteristics of those mini-Collies in him than did his ancestors, but his herding abilities are still basically intact and his popularity remains strong. The breed is recognized around the world by all major organizations. The Sheltie is a well-loved companion and showman across the globe; the breed's expression, sweet and unaffected, reveals his gentle and unceasingly loyal personality. These are merry, well-mannered, and plain

eye. Jaws level and clean, with teeth set in a perfect, regular and complete scissors bite. Eyes medium size, obliquely set, and almond shaped; color dark brown except in merles, where one or both may be blue or blue flecked. Ears small, moderately wide at base, placed fairly close together on top of the skull. The body is slightly longer from the point of the shoulder to the bottom of the croup than the height at the withers. The chest is deep, reaching to the elbow. Ribs well sprung. Back strong and level. The tail, set low and of tapering bone, reaches at least to the hock. Coat is double: outer coat of long and harsh hair, abundant, complete with mane and frill; undercoat soft, short and close. Height: 13–16 inches (33–40.5 cm). The Sheltie can be sable, tricolor, blue merle, and black and

Shetland Sheepdog, black and tan with white.

Shetland Sheepdog, blue merle with white. Photo by Rockwell.

bloody adorable dogs, fully deserving of their great popularity.

ESSENTIALS OF THE SHETLAND SHEEPDOG: The Sheltie is a small, long-haired working dog, free from cloddiness and coarseness. Of great importance is the symmetrical outline in which no part appears out of proportion to the whole. The head is refined, and when viewed from the top or side appears as a long, blunt wedge, tapering from ear to nose. Skull flat, moderately wide between the ears, with no prominence of the occipital bone. Skull and muzzle of equal length, dividing point the corner of the

white or black and tan. Smooth-coated specimens are most undesirable.

Shiba Inu

Developed some 3,000 years ago in Japan, the Shiba Inu is able to trace its roots to primitive times. Such ancient

Shiba Inu, red sesame. The famed import Ch. Katsuranihiki of Oikawa House ("Chibi"), owned by Richard Tomita. Photo by I. Français.

types as the Shinshu, Mino and Sanin are the proposed canines that took part in the Shiba's genesis. The Shiba Inu is the smallest of the Japanese dogs and is said to have originated from dogs brought over from the South Seas. Hunters used the little dogs on a variety of small ground birds and other small game. The breed's intelligence and quick motion sometimes availed it towards hunting assistantship on the bear or deer.

World War II nearly decimated the original Shiba population in Japan. Later, in 1959, a second blow to the population—this time a distemper outbreak—

shook the breed further. Efforts to restore the Shiba involved gathering remaining pure dogs and preserving desired qualities. From region to region, the little Japanese spitz dogs varied; in montane areas, the dogs were heavier boned, in the less rural areas, slimmer and more graceful in appearance.

The first American import of import occurred in 1977; since then, significant importation has ensued. Presently, however, due to the reluctance of Japanese breeders to cooperate with interested American dog folk (for fear of Americans deviating from the original Japanese standard, as many have with the Akita Inu), importation has slowed considerably. Fortunately, certain breeders in the States have experienced success in importing and reproducing Japanese quality. East-coast breeder Rick Tomita of Jacquet's Boxers and Shibas has produced extraordinary, exquisite examples of traditional type and temperament and consequently enjoys the respect of top Japanese breeders and judges.

In England and Australia, the breed has already received national kennel club recognition. In the U.S., the breed is entered the Miscellaneous Class of the A.K.C. in October 1991.

The Shiba personality is alarmingly his own. His tendencies repeatedly have led fanciers to compare him to the cat: he is clean, independent and industrious; he is nearly too smart to train and can be brazenly bratlike. Even so, the Shiba spirit reminds us that he is not a cat at all but a true Dog of a dog: his instincts are strong and primitive—sometimes a millenia from domestication!—and his foxlike (even wolflike) appearance unwittingly conjures images of being more in tune with the "call of the wild" than one bargains for. As pets, Shibas are full of surprises and noises that startle even life-long dog people; not frequent barkers, these inus squeak and scream to express their disapproval or another original idea, much in the style of the Basenji or an Eastern opera diva. Owners with time to invest cannot ask for a bigger dog in a pint-sized package: as Rick Tomita has put it: ". . . inside every Shiba is a dog the size of an Akita" and more. Of course, those searching for an ornamental low-key apartment dog—pretty though he be—are barking up the wrong *bonsai* with the Shiba!

ESSENTIALS OF THE SHIBA INU: The small Shiba Inu, appearing much like a dwarf-size Japanese Akita, is well balanced and sturdy. The head, appearing like a blunt triangle, is broad with well-developed cheeks. The muzzle is straight and of good depth. Forehead is broad and flat, cheeks well developed, stop moderate with slight furrow. The withers are high,

Shiba Inu, red sesame, puppy. Jacquet's Tengu, owned by author Andrew De Prisco.

Shiba Inu, red.

back straight and short. The loins broad and muscular. The chest deep, ribs moderately sprung, and belly well drawn up. The coat is plush, hard and straight, with a warm soft undercoat; coat is slightly longer on the sickle-curved, curled tail. Completing the spitz portrait, the Shiba has erect triangular ears, inclining slightly forward. The most preferred of the Japanese colors are crimson red through pale red, red sesame and black and tan. Height: 13.5–16.5 inches (34–42 cm). Weight: 20–30 pounds (9–14 kg).

Shiba Inu, black and tan. Photographs by Isabelle Français.

Shih Tzu

The Shih Tzu, like the Pekingese, belongs to the Orient and is hailed as a lion dog, the translation of *shih tzu* from Chinese. The Shih Tzu was perfected in China and is likely a dwarfed Tibetan Terrier, that is, exaggerated beyond the Lhasa. The short face was much admired in China, and the Shih Tzu was derived by crosses between these bantamized Tibetan breeds and native Chinese miniatures. Since the sixteenth century, a pair of Shih Tzus was presented to distinguished visitors as a token of good will and good luck. This tradition was initiated during the Manchu dynasty. It is customary for the Chinese to compare the dog's anatomy with tangible objects or animals; in so doing, much of the dog's personality and utility are simultaneously revealed along with the anatomical features. The Chinese standard of the breed requires a "lion head, bear torso,

In its native land of China, the Shih Tzu enjoyed the unyielding admiration and love of the nation's emperor for centuries. The West, however, did not make the Shih Tzu's acquaintance until the twentieth century. General Douglas Brownrigg brought a duo into England in 1930. The Kennel Club granted recognition in the late 1940s when a sufficient number resided in the country. America recognized the breed in 1969 and it has continued to climb the popularity scale since then. As a companion dog and show dog, the Shih Tzu has proven ideal in Canada as well. Its resilient and dignified approach to everyday life gives this breed a particularly personable appeal.

ESSENTIALS OF THE SHIH TZU: The coat is luxurious, long and dense, with good undercoat. The breed is known for its chrysanthemumlike face. The head is broad and round, wide between the eyes. The muzzle is square and short, but not

Shih Tzu, black and white particolor. Photo by Missy Yuhl.

camel hoof, feather duster tail, palm-leaf ears, rice teeth, pearly petal tongue and movement like a goldfish."

wrinkled. The ears are large with long leathers, and carried drooping. Forelegs are short, straight and well boned. The body between the withers and the root of the tail is somewhat longer than the height at the withers. Well coupled and sturdy. Tail is heavily plumed and carried gaily, set on high. The Shih Tzu enjoys an abundance of colors, and its white blazed tail is particularly prized. Height: 8–11 inches (20–28 cm). Weight: 9–16 pounds (4–7.5 kg).

Shika Inus

The Shika Inus represent the middle-size division of native Japanese purebred dogs. When European breeds were first imported to Japan after World War I, the native Japanese breeds were greatly neglected. Mr. Haruo Isogai headed a committee to help resuscitate the native breeds. Dogs were divided into three categories: Akita-Inu or Cho-ken, the largest of Japanese breeds; Shika Inu, the middle-sized breeds; and the Shiba-Inu or small-sized breeds. Among the breeds categorized as Shika Inus are the Ainu Dog, Kishu, Kai Dog, Shikoku, and San-shu Dog (which *see*). These dogs work variously as herders, watchdogs, guards and deer hunters. Among the Japanese breeds with which the world is acquainted, the Shika Inus are the least known. The larger but compact Akita, the massive surly Tosa Inu, the jaunty and lovable Shiba Inu and Japanese Spitz, to name just a few, each have noteworthy followings in the West. Today the Shikas are still found working and playing in

Japan although very few specimens are known elsewhere.

Shih Tzu, orange and white particolor. Photo by I. Français.

Shamisen

A Japanese musical instrument, similar to the lute, which originated in the 1600s and which is covered with the skin of a dog or cat.

Shikari Dog

The Shikari Dog of Kumaon, India, is a wild dog of Dhole descent. Strong and standing over 36 inches (91.5 cm) tall, it has been domesticated by the Kumaon natives and used for guard work and hunting large game. These are *very* big dogs. *See also* Dhole

Shikoku

The Shikoku originates on the Japanese Islands near Osaka. The Japanese, so taken by the abilities of the Pointer and German Shepherd Dog, promoted these newly discovered dogs and all but ignored the native breeds. The study done by Mr. Haruo Isogai in the 1930s divided the nation's dogs by size and attempted to revive the indigenous Japanese breeds. The Shikoku was one of the most ignored dogs, being larger than the less neglected Chins and Shibas and less substantial than the large Akita, which remained favored and sacred. The Shikoku is a specialist on deer and has been referred to as a "deerhound."

Shikoku, brindle. Photo courtesy of Richard Tomita.

ESSENTIALS OF THE SHIKOKU: The Shikoku is distinguishable from its fellow Shika-Inus by its smaller size and coat color. The Shikoku stands 17–21 inches (43–53 cm) high and comes in brindle (white, red, black) or red coloration. Like the other middle-sized Japanese breeds, the Shikoku has a coat which is short, harsh and straight with a soft dense undercoat. The body conformation is typically nordic: the feathered curled tail; the prick triangular ears; the good-sized head and medium-length muzzle. The dog's muscles are clean cut. It is strong, well boned and compact. The forehead is broad, cheeks well developed, the stop shallow but defined. The withers are high and well developed with a back straight and strong. The tail is set on high and carried over the back.

Shiloh Shepherd Dog

Like the White German Shepherd, the Shiloh is a variant of the GSD. American fanciers are heralding this sturdy and intelligent "new" purebred as a dog closer to the original "Alsatian Wolfdog." The breed is intelligent, protective and remarkably suited as a family companion.

Shock

The symptoms and severity of shock vary with the cause and with the nervous system of the individual dog. Severe accident, loss of blood, and heart failure are the most common causes. Keep the dog warm and quiet; get him to a veterinarian right away. Symptoms are vomiting, rapid pulse, thirst, diarrhea, cold and clamminess, and eventual physical collapse. The veterinarian might prescribe plasma transfusion, fluid, perhaps oxy-gen, if pulse continues to be too rapid. Tranquilizers and sedatives are sometimes used as well as antibiotics and steroids. Relapse is not uncommon, so the animal must be observed carefully for several days after initial shock.

Shock-headed

A dog on whose head appears a seemingly disarranged stack of hair. Employed in the British Shih-Tzu breed standard.

Shiloh Shepherd Dog. Photo by I. Français.

Short head

Round head. A shortened muzzle and broad skull contribute to this head type's round appearance.

Short muzzle

A muzzle that is stubby and shorter than half the length of the skull, typical of the brachycephalic breed (e.g., Pug, Bulldog, Shih Tzu).

Short Transylvanian Hound

See Transylvanian Hound

Shorthaired Dutch Shepherd

See Dutch Shepherd

Shot-breaking

A fault in field trials—when the gundog stands steady to the flush of a bird and breaks or chases when the shot is fired, he is charged with shot-breaking.

Shotgunning

Where a racer swerves rather wide nearing a turn, then cuts sharply across a bend to save ground.

Shoulder

The general fore-area of the dog, incorporating the upper foreleg girth and the mass immediately surrounding it, attaching it to the chest, extending to the withers, on each side. The true shoulder is the two shoulder blades and the mass of muscle, ligament, and tendon immediately surrounding them.

Shoulder blade

The bony matter of the shoulder, a predominant component of the dog's forequarters, which *see*.

Shoulder joint

Point at the front of the forequarters region formed by the lower shoulder blade and the upper arm bone. It is an important point from which to judge the front quarters of a dog.

Shoulder types

The shoulders are an important component to every breed's forequarters. The shoulder girth is one of the primary muscle groups of the body, adding to a dog's speed, strength, and agility. There are many distinctive shoulder sets. However, there are approximately seven primary shoulder types.

1) Loaded shoulders, bossy shoulders, coarse shoulders, and lumpy shoulders all refer to shoulders that are muscled to the point of excess. Such development gives the dog a brawny, often bumpy appearance that tends to seem awkward, disrupting the normally smooth flow from the neck, through the shoulders, onto the upper forelegs. Because excessive shoulder girth is inhibiting to proper and efficient forequarter movement, loaded shoulders is an undesirable characteristic, at least until the body-building craze reaches the dog fancy. A few Pit Bull fans surely have proven the authors dead wrong.

2) Loose shoulders are essentially weak shoulders. The shoulder blades are poorly attached to the chest and back area, and there seems to be a general lack of solidity to the shoulder region. There is a direct correlation between loose shoulders and weaving gait. Loose shoulders also have a negative effect on a dog's stance. Needless to say, loose shoulders are an undesirable characteristic.

3) If a dog is low at the shoulders, low at the withers, or has flat withers, the dog's withers lie below the area of the topline directly above them. Though a

fault in many breeds, low at the shoulders is desirable in a few breeds, the Dandie Dinmont perhaps best known among them.

4) Not prominent shoulders are described as shoulders in which the scapula is adequately muscled to give a smooth appearance, neither bumpy nor bony. Can be a desirable characteristic.

5) Oblique, slanting, sloping, well-angulated, and well-laid back shoulders all refer to the most frequently desirable set of the shoulders. In oblique shoulders, the longitudinal and horizontal axis form

Shoulder types: shoulder blade well laid back in the Siberian Husky; straight or loose shoulders highly undesirable.

a 45° angle, thus forming a 90° degree angle with correctly set upper arms. *See also* Angulation, forequarters

6) Steep in shoulders, straight in shoulders, and upright in shoulders refer to shoulder blades that are set so as to form an angle greater than the preferred

Shows and showing. This top-knotch Peke is being examined in the show ring. Photo by I. Français.

90° angle with the humerus (upper arm bone). Such shoulders extend their girth into the base of the neck, thus giving the neck a shortened appearance. Like most other generally undesirable shoulder types, steep shoulders negatively affect the gait of a dog.

7) Tied-in shoulders refers to shoulders in which the shoulder blades are too

hemmed in, or too firm or tight. The blades, normally moving with the action of the dog, lose their mobility, giving the dog a tense, tight, restricted motion and appearance. Tied-in shoulders are almost exclusively undesirable.

Shoulder, lay of
The slope or angle at which the shoulder is set. *See* Angulation, forequarters

Shoulder, set of
See Shoulder types

Shoulder, slope of
The angle or lay at which the shoulder is set. *See* Angulation, forequarters

Shouldering
Where a racing dog pushes or obstructs another with its body.

Show
Third position at finish of a dog race.

Show secretary
One who acts in the capacity of superintendent for a show-giving club.

Showing teeth
Nearly synonymous with showing tongue, showing teeth is an often seen characteristic of many brachycephalic dogs, i.e., the Pug, the Bulldog, and the English Toy Spaniel. Though tolerable in some breeds, it is undesirable to the point of fault or even disqualification in many others. Showing teeth literally mean that the set of the jaw permits the bottom row of front teeth to be visible often; in such cases, the tongue too is visible, hence showing tongue.

Showing tongue
Common in some of the brachycephalic breeds, it is the characteristic of common visibility of the tongue. *See also* Showing teeth

Shows and showing

The first dog show, in Newcastle-upon-Tyne, England, in June of 1859, was whelped when the sports of bullbaiting and dog fighting were banned. The laws which made these two pastimes illegal were passed in 1835. The first show divided the dogs into two classes: Pointers and Setters. As dog exhibition became increasingly popular, more and more dog shows occurred throughout England. In 1873 the organizers of the National Dog Club created the Kennel Club.

The first American show was held in 1876 by a gundog club. It is speculated that the first U.S. shows derived from hunters squabbling over whose dog was actually more handsome. In considering many hunters' distaste for the show ring, this fact is remarkably ironic. The dog sport, namely dog shows, was the initiative for the formation of the American Kennel Club in 1884. The A.K.C. is the foremost registry in the United States, followed by the United Kennel Club, another all-breed registry that was founded primarily for the registry of hunting dogs.

The A.K.C. dog sport is divided into three competitive events: conformation dog shows, field trials, and obedience trials. Conformation shows are sub-divided: all-breed and specialty. A specialty is a show for one breed only or one group only. One can enter his Lakeland Terrier, for instance, in a Lakeland Terrier Specialty or in a Terrier Specialty. Usually the less popular breeds participate in group or multi-breed specialties.

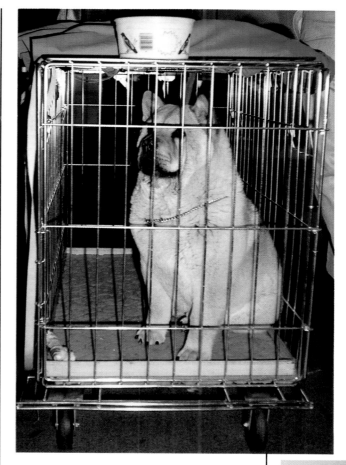

the sponsoring registry. The principle concern is that the dog comes close to the ideal conformation as described in the breed standard of perfection. The judge decides which dogs come closest to "perfection." Of course no dog could ever be absolutely perfect, in every judge's opinion.

Shows and showing. Bench shows, shows where the dogs are benched or crated when not in the ring, have become increasingly less common. Smooth Chow Chow.

Shows and showing. Specialty shows, shows where one breed or one group is exclusively featured, are sponsored by local and regional clubs on a regular basis. These Shar-Pei are competing in the Chinese Shar-Pei Club of America's tenth national specialty.

All conformation shows are run in accord with the rules and regulations of

In Great Britain, the dogs are divided into two broad categories: Sporting and

which are on the decline are placed.

Depending upon the time of year and the location of the show, the event may take place either in an indoor arena or stadium or on an outdoor field. Outdoor shows are usually held beneath a tent or canopy, since rainfall does not usually hinder competition—it does, of course, make it rather uncomfortable and intensifies (or dilutes) competitiveness between dogs, handlers, and owners.

In the United States, there are two dog shows that are both big, all-breed, and very prestigious. The New York show, held in Madison Square Garden, is the Westminster Kennel Club Show and the

Shows and showing. In America, this is the Show of shows: Westminster Kennel Club all-breed dog show held annually in Madison Square Garden, New York. Photo by I. Français.

Non-Sporting. The former category includes Working, Gun Dogs, Hounds and Terriers; the latter into Utility and Toy Dogs. The American Kennel Club divides dog similarly into seven groups: Sporting Dogs, Hounds, Working Dogs, Terriers, Toys, Non-Sporting Dogs, and Herding Dogs. Both kennel clubs have a Miscellaneous Class, into which new breeds, less popular breeds, and breeds

California show in Santa Barbara. The International Kennel Club Show held annually in Chicago, Illinois, is one of the nation's largest indoor show. In Great Britain, Crufts is the most prestigious show. It has been staged annually since 1891 and continues to be an international spectacle.

For persons not involved in the dog show world, attending a dog show is a worthwhile venture. Most people aren't aware that there are nearly 150 breeds recognized by the national registry—many of these breeds are surely not commonplace, and many of their names may not even be familiar to the average dog owner. Any person owning a pedigreed dog, with papers, is eligible to enter his dog in a dog show. The necessary details can be acquired from the national registering bodies. It is important that your dog be well groomed and looking his best—this is for your dog's own benefit and out of respect for the presiding show judge.

Shows and showing. The World Dog Show is the annual international competition for all recognized F.C.I. breeds. The 1990 show was held in Denmark. Two big winners were these multi-titled champion Dalmatian and Old English Sheepdog.

Shows and showing. F.C.I. dog show held in Barcelona, Spain: Gun Dogs competing for Best in Group. Photographs by I. Français.

Shropshire Terrier

One of the oldest recorded types of terriers, the Shropshire Terrier is an ancestral breed of working terrier whose contribution to modern-day terrier breeds has faded from even the footnotes of breed history books.

Shuffle back

Race contestant forced to withdraw from a bunched field due to crowding.

Shuffling action

Rather slothful and sloppy gait characterized by apparent feet dragging. With the exception of the slow-trotting Otter Hound, this gait is not desirable.

Shuman System

See Systems

Siberian Evaluation Performance Project

Started in July 1982, S.E.P.P. is dedicated to preserving the working qualities of the Siberian Husky. The purpose of the organization is to locate and identify world-class Siberians and incorporate them into sound breeding programs.

Siberian Husky

The Chukchis of the Kolyma River in Siberia employed what is today the Siberian Husky and fostered it as a pure "breed" throughout the nineteenth century. Among nordic dogs, the Siberian Husky is one of the most recognizable and people-oriented. Much of the breed's temperament is due to the Chukchis's fine treatment of their dogs. The Siberian Husky, the Alaskan Malamute, and the Eskimo Dog are but a few of the world's Arctic husky-type dogs. There is considerable reason to believe that these "huskies," a coined term, all stem from the same dogs but were each fostered by a different region and group of hunters. As dog sledges were the principal means of transport in Alaska, the huskies were most vital. The Siberian Husky, being 30 pounds (14 kg) smaller than the dominant Alaskan Malamute, became favored by Russian explorers as sled dogs of speed, agility and endurance, the same qualities valued by the Chukchi tribe.

The first Siberian Huskies arrived in Alaska in the early twentieth century—they were then still called Chukchis. Alaskan dog-sled racing became popular

Siberian Husky, black and white. Photo by I. Français.

at about the same time. The Siberian's speed amazed and inspired dog racers in the States. The first team of Siberians to make its appearance in the Alaska Sweepstakes did so in 1909. Americans renamed the Chukchi as Siberian Husky, a more general name but one that has stuck in the States. In Great Britain, the dog is also known as the Arctic Husky.

ESSENTIALS OF THE SIBERIAN HUSKY: Quick and light on his feet, the Siberian Husky is a medium-sized working dog with a moderately compact and fur-covered body. His beautifully balanced and perfectly proportionate structure is a tribute to his power, speed and endurance. Height: 21–23.5 (53–60 cm). Weight: 35–60 pounds (16–27 kg). The gait is effortless and smooth. The back is straight and strong, with level topline from withers to croup. Forelegs are moderately spaced, parallel and straight, with elbows close to the body and turned neither in nor out. The hindlegs likewise, but angulated. Pasterns are slightly slanted. A well-muscled, well-made dog with good bone: the head is of medium size, as is the muzzle in length; the coat is well furred and peltlike, but not so thick as to obscure the dog's clean-cut outline. The

dense soft undercoat is long enough to support the straight smooth-lying guard hairs. Any color is acceptable—black, grays, red and pied are usual. The correct tail is well furred and fox-brush in shape.

Siberian Husky, black and white.

Siberian Huskies, black and white.

Siberian Huskies, (*top left*) black and white, adult and puppy; (*top right*) red and white; and (*bottom*) pied.

Sicilian Branchiero

This little known Italian herdsman exists today as the re-creation of a lost herding dog, the Cane di Macellaio. Its official name is Cane Corso, according to the Italian Kennel Club. Standing about 20–22 inches (51–56 cm) tall, the dog is thick set and mastiff through and through. The head is large and broad across the skull. The dogs do not occur on the Italian mainland but specifically in Sicily. On the island, the breed functioned solely as a butcher's dog, a cattle drover of unyielding abilities. At one time, the breed is believed to have participated in bullbaiting, similar to other butcher's dogs on the Continent. The dog's droving style is unique: the Branchiero does not heel but rather lunges at the head of the herd's leader, thus steering the entire herd in the desired direction. This herding proclivity may indicate a link to the ancient German bullenbeiser.

In the United States, the Branchiero is just beginning to make way. Less than a half dozen puppies were imported in the late 1980s. These dogs will form the stock of any breeding programs in the States. The man responsible for exporting these pups, a Sicilian farmer, passed away shortly after these first exportations. *See also* Cane di Macellaio

Sicilian Hound

See Cirneco dell'Etna

Sickle hocks

The hocks of dogs are usually angulated at approximately 135° with the pastern positioned at a more or less 90° angle. Sickle hocks reflect this desired hock angulation, being sickle-shaped in appearance. Such hock formation is essential to the attainment of great speeds (e.g., Borzoi, Whippet). Straight hocks, on the other foot, would indicate hocks that are angulated more obtusely than the 135° norm.

Sickle tail

A tail carried out and up in a semicircular fashion, not flat against the back.

Side-striped jackal

Canis adustus. See Jackals

Side-winding

See Crabbing

Sight chase

The action of pursuing game according to sight, not scent.

Sicilian Branchiero, brindle.

Sicilian Branchiero, black. Photographs by I. Français.

Sighthounds

Almost without exception, the sighthound group consists of tall, thin, very sleek-looking running hounds. A sight-

hound hunts primarily by sight—pinpointing movement in the distance. The dog's eyes detect movement first: a rabbit sitting quietly in the sand will probably go undetected by the sighthound, but as soon as it adjusts its position or hops, the dog will sight it.

The sighthound prototype developed in the Middle East. The dogs' efficient and well-muscled frame allowed them to course desert prey over relentless terrain. In Arab and other nomadic societies, the dogs must be able to kill a gazelle by the age of two and a boar (or similarly sized beast) by the age of three. A dog is typically retired at the age of seven, due to the extreme exertion of the hunt. The use of sighthounds for the purpose of coursing wolves, gazelles, antelope, deer and hare is a hunting form that dates back to 2000 B.C.

India and Russia have produced a number of sighthound or greyhound types. India has at least four arguably pure purebred dogs. These gazehounds include the Banjara Greyhound, Rampur Dog, Poligar Dog, and the Mahratta Greyhound. These dogs generally have the look of the Greyhound of Britain with slight variations in size and coat textures. The Soviet Union has produced one of the world's most renowned and elegant sighthounds, the Borzoi. Other borzoi types include the Taigan, Tasy, Chortaj, and South Russian Steppe Hound.

Sighthounds were the prized companions of many desert nomads, peoples who despised any dogs other than the sighthound types. Various eastern lands have produced unique sighthound breeds of their own. The sighthounds are among the most numerous of all dog types even though there are

actually few well-known breeds in the Western fancies. This phenomenon is due to the lack of man's intervention and the land expanses between the lands from which the various purebred sighthounds derived. The dogs developed purely to prosper within the ecological niche which Nature intended. The Azawakh of Mali, the Sloughi of Morocco, the Saluki of Iran, the Afghan Hound of Afghanistan and the Pharaoh Hound of Malta are just some examples of distinctive sighthounds each developing in different lands. Britain is credited with the development of the world's most famous race dogs (sighthounds of course): the Greyhound and the Whippet. Ireland and Scotland likewise have fostered sighthound purebreds that they justifiably call their own: the Irish Wolfhound and the Scottish Deerhound, respectively. Italy boasts the Cirneco dell Etna, and Spain, the Ca Eivissencs or Ibizan Hound.

Signal dogs

Signal dogs are canines that are trained to assist the hearing impaired. They are taught to respond to sounds as well as visual and verbal commands.

Signal exercise

This is a section of utility work wherein the handler controls the dog entirely by signals through the complete heeling exercise, i.e., right turn, left turn, about turn, slow, normal, fast, halt, with the final word being recall, with the dog dropping immediately in front of the handler's feet and then being signalled to finish position, heeling at the handler's left side.

Sighthounds illustrated working in conjunction with horsemen in pursuit of hare.

Signals

All signals of obedience are done with the handler using a single command or signal, accompanied by the dog's name. Extra commands and signals are penalized, except in the stay, when command and signal may both be used.

Silent heat

When the bitch comes into season without some of the outward signs, especially a discharge from the vulva. The bitch should mate normally, though the breeder may have difficulty determining the correct day on which to mate. There is no report of increased miscarriages or deformed pups, though mismatings do show a higher incidence or occurrence.

Silky Terrier,
blue/tan.

Silky Terrier

Like his brother the Australian Terrier, the Silky was developed in Australia from British terriers during the 1800s. Crossing the Skye, Australian and Yorkshire Terriers, breeders in New South Wales derived the Silky Terrier, sometimes called the Sydney Silky or the Australian Silky. The breed's coat is worthy of note, and the first recorded blue/tan broken-coated terriers in Australia date to a show in Victoria in 1872. At some point, specimens were transported to England and Dandie Dinmont blood was introduced to improve the Silky's type. Not developed for the purposes of ratting or any work, the Silky was meant to be a companion dog. Some owners today attest that the breed is still capable of managing an anti-vermin campaign if necessary.

The Australian Terrier, closer to the Cairn Terrier in type, was also produced in Australia from British terriers. The histories of these two breeds are difficult to differentiate from each other.

The Silky did not join the ranks of the A.K.C. Toys until 1959, although it was first exhibited in Australia in 1907. The Kennel Club recognized the breed in 1930. England's wealth of terrier and toy breeds perhaps precludes the breed's wide popularity in that country.

ESSENTIALS OF THE SILKY TERRIER: A lightly built, compact dog set moderately low—medium length with refined structure. Parted straight silky hair conveys the desired well-groomed appearance. The head is strong and wedge shaped, the skull is flat and moderately broad between the ears. The neck fits into the sloping shoulders with expected grace. Well laid back shoulders, together with good angulation at the upper arm, set the forelegs nicely to the body. Thighs are well muscled and strong, not appearing heavy. Legs moderately angulated at the stifles and hocks. Feet small and cat-like. The tail is set high and carried erect or semi-erect. Height: 9 inches (23 cm). Weight: 8–10 pounds (3.5–4.5 kg). The Silky Terrier's color is blue/tan. Pronounced diminutiveness is not desired since the general appearance should suggest the required substance of a small functional terrier.

Silky Toy Terrier
See Silky Terrier

Silver eye
See Walleye

Simenia simensis
See Semyen fox

Sindh Hound
Found in the deserts of Sindh and Rajasthan, the Sindh Hounds are said to

resemble the Great Dane. Records indicate that these dogs have bred true for generations and were employed as watchdogs and hunters of wild boar. In height, the dog stands 28–30 inches (71–76 cm), and weighs in excess of 100 pounds (45 kg). It is adaptable and powerful, doing well in rural India.

Sinew
See Tendon

Sinewy
Lean, solid, and visibly strong without excessive muscle, skin, or other tissue. The tendons must be clearly visible beneath the skin. It is a common description of the limbs of short-coated, tight-skinned working and hunting dogs.

Single
A single fall: one bird downed.

Single coat
A coat comprised of one consistent type of hair, without an undercoat (e.g., Italian Greyhound, Maltese).

Single tracking
All footprints fall onto a single travel line. This gait is most usual when a dog begins to travel at faster speeds. Whereas the dog's body is being supported by two legs at a time, to balance the body, the dog angles his legs inwardly. The faster the dog travels, the closer to a single median line will the footprints become.

Sinking
Hunting term that refers to a nearly beaten fox.

Sinusitis
Inflammation of a sinus gland that inhibits breathing.

Sire
The father of a litter.

Sit
In obedience trials, all dogs, but not more than 15 at a time, sit stationary for one minute in the Novice Class with handlers across the ring; three minutes in the Open Class with the handlers out of sight. *See also* Training

Size of dogs
See Measurements, Weight, Height

S.K.C.
States Kennel Club, which *see.*

Skeletal anatomy
The skeletal system of a dog is divided into the axial and the appendicular skeleton. The former consists of the skull, spine, ribs, and pelvis, providing protection for the vital organs. The latter comprises the fore and hind limbs; these essentially cylindrical-type bones are used for locomotion and defense. Each of the bones in the dog's anatomy functions as a storage area of mineral and fats and is

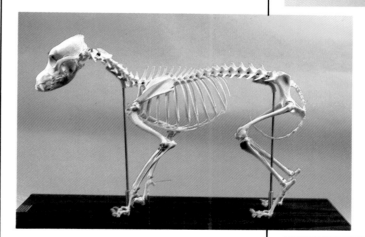

used for leverage. *See also* Forequarters, Hindquarters, Skull

Skewbald
Used to specify the coat color pattern of various unspecific patches or marking of any color other than black upon a white base color. Pied and bicolor are the preferred terms for this coat pattern.

Skijoring
A short race with the driver on skis rather than on a sled. Line is attached around his waist with a slip knot.

Skin
Consisting of two key layers, the dermis (outer layer) and the epidermis (inner layer), the skin is the body's first layer of living defense. From beneath the skin sprout the many hairs out of hair follicles. The skin is also pincushioned by numerous sweat ducts. Though less numerous

Skeletal anatomy of the dog.

than those of humans, sweat ducts are found on the dogs and do serve to cool the heated animal. There are many diseases and conditions that affect the skin: dermatitis, burns, canine pemphigus, allergies, dermatitis, dandruff, eczema, frostbite, abscesses, interdigital pyoderma, itching, lick granulomas, lip-fold pyoderma, which *see*.

Skirter

A hound which, in jealousy, runs wide of the pack.

Skull

All of the many bones of the head, including those of the face and lower jaw and those that surround the brain. The skull and the head are not synony-

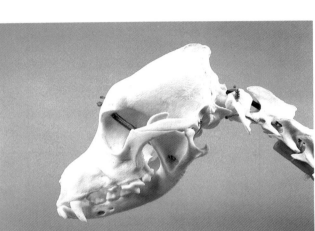

mous, nor does the skull consist only of the bony area that surrounds the brain. In the dog fancy, however, the term skull is sometimes used to refer exclusively to the brain surround, while face is used to include the bony matter thereof. Often the term backskull or topskull is come across. These two terms are synonymous, and both refer to the brain surround, the *cavum cranii*.

Skull types

It is interesting that although the actual size of the canine skull varies from the tiny Chihuahua to the massive Dogue de Bordeaux, with a myriad of shapes and stops in between, the actual "type" of skull can be categorized into three general classes (based on the base-to-width ration), with but a handful more of specialized skull divisions used in the dog fancy. This is astonishing because the canine skull actually varies more in size and shape than that of any other animal species.

The three basic skull classifications are: the brachycephalic, dolichocephalic,

and mesaticephalic skulls. The brachycephalic skull is broad at its base but short in its length. The extant breed with the largest skull is the Dogue de Bordeaux, whose skull is of the brachycephalic type. Other brachycephalic dogs include the Pug and the Bulldog. The dolichocephalic skull is narrow at its base yet long in its length. Examples include many sighthounds, such as the Afghan Hound, Whippet, and Greyhound. Mesaticephalic skulls are balanced in width and length. Many gundogs, including the Brittany and the Vizsla, have mesaticephalic skulls.

Skull types common in the dog world include: arched skull; broad in skull; domed skull; flat skull; oval skull; receding skull; rounded skull; thick in skull; and wedge-shaped skull, which *see*. Other terms used which are synonymous with the already mentioned are: apple, cone-shaped/conical and coarse skull. *See also* Bite types

Skye Terrier

Deriving its name from the "Misty Isle," the Skye Terrier has been recognized for over 400 years. The Skye Islands, islands northwest of Scotland, mark the breed place of inception, although the breed development probably wasn't confined to these islands while not belonging to the whole of Scotland. These terriers enjoyed the favor of the aristocracy during the sixteenth century and didn't associate with the commonfolk and their common dogs. Today's Skye looks somewhat different than its progenitors: nineteenth-century Skyes had less-feathered drop ears, smaller heads and weighed as little as 14 pounds (6.5 kg). This was the most well-known terrier up until the nineteenth century. Today his fans are less in number, though

Skull types: mesaticephalic.

not in enthusiasm. It is said that the duchess would be embarrassed to be seen strolling in the park without her long-coated Skye. At work, he is resilient and ruthless in his expelling of squirmy undesirables. In America, the Skye was a key dog in show circles at the turn of this century. As a companion, he is a one-man dog, undying in his devotion and affection. Usually quite gay with his friends, he is stand-offish with strangers.

ESSENTIALS OF THE SKYE TERRIER: Profusely but elegantly coated, the Skye Terrier possesses a long, flowing outer coat and soft undercoat. It is a sturdy-boned, hard-muscled terrier. Head is long with powerful jaws. The eyes are hazel and medium in size. The body is long and low, with level back. Feet large and pointing forward. The breed's coat, however, is his claim to fame: the moderate-sized head is draped with long, hard hair, veiling the eyes, forehead and ears, when prick. Height: 10 inches. (25.5 cm) Weight: 25 pounds (11.5 kg). Colors: black, blue, dark and light gray, silver platinum, fawn and cream.

Slab-sided
Opposing the typically desired curved ribs that allow for greater chest capacity, slab-sided ribs are "flat," that is they do not allow for maximum chest capacity and thereby inhibit endurance and strength. They are almost universally considered faulty.

Slanting pasterns
The usual requirement in pastern types: the mid-point between upright and broken-down pasterns. Also called sloping pasterns.

Slanting shoulders
See Shoulder types

Skye Terriers, silver platinum and blue.

Skye Terrier. Photographs by I. Français. Courtesy of Barbara Koseff.

Sled dogs

Nordic dogs that are used for draft purposes are known as sled dogs (or sledge dogs). A sled or sledge is a large

vehicle mounted on runners for use on snow, ice, and/or slush. Huskies or Eskimo dogs are the usual sled pullers. All of the nordic draft dog breeds are muscular and double coated. The fitness of these dogs afforded the survival of their Es-

Alaskan Malamute, Siberian Husky, Greenland Dog, Canadian Eskimo Dog, Chinook, and the Northeasterly Hauling Laika. A number of other nordic breeds have occasionally functioned as sled dogs; the Samoyed, Chow Chow, Lapphunds and Wolfspitz among them.

Sled-dog racing

Organized sled-dog racing has been popular in North America for most of the twentieth century. The Alaskan Gold Rush, beginning at the turn of the century, serves as a possible impetus for the sport's development— "there's gold in them there ice caps!" The Nome Kennel Club was organized in 1907 to preserve and assure the performance ability of the husky dogs involved in these excursions. The All-Alaska Sweepstakes is looked at historically as a starting point of the sled-racing sport. The Siberian Husky and the Alaskan Malamute today are among the top contenders in sled-dog racing. Eskimo Dogs and Samoyeds are runners-up; other breeds of the Working Group also make unexpected appearances. As a national sport, sled-dog racing has been gaining much press, principally through the much-talked about sled-Iditarod race, which has been held annually since 1977. This race takes approximately 10–28 days to complete. Or-

kimo owners. No people has ever relied more profoundly on their working dogs. Among the dogs used as sled dogs are the

ganizations presently push for the inclusion of sled-dog racing as an event in the Winter Olympics.

Slicker brush

Wire pin brush with a hook pin that helps break up mats.

Slippage

Not of common canine usage, this term refers to luxation or subluxation of the knee joint.

Slope of pasterns

Angle formed by the longitudinal axis of the pastern and the level ground. About 20° is considered usual although slopes vary from breed to breed, but all breeds must slope to one degree or another.

Slope of pelvis

See Hindquarters

Slope of shoulders

See Forequarters, angulation

Sloping pasterns

See Slanting pasterns

Sloping shoulders

See Shoulder types

Sloughi

The Sloughi or Arabian Greyhound is an ancient greyhound type still to be found in its native areas of Morocco, Tunisia, Algeria and Libya. Just as the Saluki is of undeniably ancient authenticity, so is the Sloughi. Both these breeds have been revered by desert dwellers. The Moslems, who detest all canines except the noble sighthounds, progenerate a special fondness for the Sloughi. Their dogs are treated as members of the tribe and family. As a hunter, the Sloughi proves adept at hare coursing. Arabs believe that by two years of age a Sloughi should be able to kill a wild gazelle and at three years a wild boar.

The breed was first introduced to Europe in 1898, entering the Netherlands only three strong under the discerning eye of artist August Legras. Their impact was so great, however, that the breed has never left the minds nor the homes of European fanciers and has orbited its grace and beauty around the globe. Today the Kennel Club of Great Britain grants championship status to the breed. Native Arabs as well as European enthusiasts work hard at promoting this ancient breed of domesticated canine.

Sloughi, sand. Photo courtesy of Mosica Arabians.

ESSENTIALS OF THE SLOUGHI: The Sloughi is entirely smooth coated on the body, with long fringes on the ears only; the tail is bushy. The coat hair is tough and fine. The breed's general appearance is elegant yet racy, with a frame marked by its muscular leanness. The head is not heavy, but fairly strong with lines not excessively angular; the skull is flat, fairly broad, clearly rounded at rear and curving harmoniously into the sides. The muzzle is wedge-shaped, refined without exaggeration; about equal to skull. The eyes are large and dark. The ears not too large, triangular in shape but with rounded tips. Jaws strong with a perfect scissor bite. Shoulders are well laid and

Sloughi, white with brindle. Photo by I. Français.

clearly visible. Forelegs strong with flat bone and well muscled. Thighs of good length to stifle. Tail fine and well set on. Height: 24–28.5 inches (61–72 cm). Weight: 45–60 pounds (20–27 kg). Colors: all shades of sable or fawn; also possible are various brindles, white, and black with tan points.

Slougui
See Sloughi

Slovak Cuvac
The Slovak Cuvac is Czechoslovakia's big white flock guard. The Liptok or Slovensky Tchouvatch as the Cuvac is variously called has a history that can be documented into the 1600s. The Slovak Cuvac not only looks like the Great Pyrenees, Kuvasz, Greek Sheepdog, and Owczarek Podhalanski, but also performs the same wolf-slaying task. Modern-day technology has treated these European flock guards inconsistently. The Great Pyrenees and Kuvasz remain reasonably popular today, both as workers on the field and as companions in homes.

Sloughi, brindle. Photo courtesy of Mosica Arabians.

Many of the other breeds, however, have not fared so well. The Czech guard became rather scarce as the twentieth century dawned; and without the successful and dedicated efforts of one Dr. Antonin Hruza and the Brno School of Veterinary Medicine, the breed may not have survived. It was this aforementioned team

that revived the breed about fifty years into this century. This is a "no-sleep" canine who is incessantly alert and able to perform well both day and night. In disposition, the Slovak can be stubborn and independent at times but to his immediate human family he is mostly affectionate and more demonstrative than one expects from the average wolf slayer.

ESSENTIALS OF THE SLOVAK CUVAC: Height: up to 28 inches (71 cm). Weight: up to 105 pounds (48 kg). The plush coat is of medium length, with thick, wavy strands. The coat is double with a sufficiently thick undercoat. Its color is ideally white. The head is gracefully chiseled and wedge-shaped, the ears are V-shaped. Moderate stop; rounded head. The legs strongly boned; the chest is rather deep. The tail is well feathered, as are the chest and legs.

Slovakian Hound
See Black Forest Hound

Slovakian Wirehaired Pointer
See Czesky Fousek

Slovensky Kopov
See Black Forest Hound

Slovensky Tchouvatch
See Slovak Cuvac

Small Bernese Hound
See Berner Laufhund

Small Blue Gascony Griffon
Petit Griffon Bleu de Gascogne. *See* Bleu de Gascogne

Small Blue Gascony Hound
Petit Bleu de Gascogne. *See* Bleu de Gascogne

Small French Pointer
See Braque Français de Petite Taille

Small French-English Hound
See Anglo-Français

Slovak Cuvac, white. Photo by I. Français.

Small Münsterländer

Similar and related variety of the Large Münsterländer, the Small Münsterländer is a 20th-century creation from old-time Spanish types of spaniels. The Kleiner Münsterländer was developed in Westphalia, Germany, from small gundogs related to the German Longhaired Pointer and Dutch, French and Spanish gundogs. The breed was "discovered" by Herr Edmund Loens who recognized its above-average abilities and worked toward the establishment of a parent club in 1912. In Germany, he is called the Spion. This is a happy, carefree dog who is equally at home hunting in the woods as he is playing in the back yard. He gets on well with children and has an overall consistently pleasing disposition. His natural retrieving inclinations are strong but can be used effectively in the home as a slipper- or newspaper-fetcher.

Small Münsterländers, liver and white. Photo by I. Français.

ESSENTIALS OF THE SMALL MÜNSTERLÄNDER: Essentially setterlike in appearance, the Small Münsterländer is a tightly skinned, sleekly coated pointing gundog. The skull is noticeably arched; with a defined stop; a strong muzzle; set back ears; and clear, intelligent eyes. The body is rather thinly boned; the chest deep but not wide; the back straight, with a rounded croup; the hindquarters well muscled, with good angulation. In coloration he is invariably brown (liver) and white, with variable amounts of ticking. The coat is of moderate length with considerable feathering on the forelegs, chest and tail. Height: 19–22 inches (48–59 cm). Weight: 33 pounds (15 kg). The tightly lying skin prohibits the existence of dewlap.

Small Portuguese Hound
See Podengo Português

Small Portuguese Rabbit Dog
See Podengo Português

Small Spanish Hound
Name alternatively used for the Sabueso Español Lebrero. *See* Sabueso Español

Small Vendeen Basset
See Petit Basset Griffon Vendeen

Small-eared dog
A rare and distinctive South American wild dog. So unique are its skull, ears, coloration, and movement that the small-eared dog is placed alone in the genus *Atelocynus*, with the species name *microtis*. This is a very short-coated canid that stands 13 to 15 inches (33–38 cm) at the shoulder and weighs around 20 pounds (9 kg). In length the small-eared dog ranges widely from 20 to 40 inches (51–102 cm), with an additional tail length of 10 to 14 inches (25.5–35.5 cm). Catlike in grace, style, and movement, and most peculiar in its head-down, fore-paws-spread, hocks-touching posture, the small-eared dog is a rare sight both in captivity and the wild, resulting in a lack of knowledge concerning its wild behavior and traits.

Smegma
A creamlike yellowish discharge from the sheath on the dog's penis. The discharge is normal.

Smithfield Collie
An English strain of collie used in the development of a number of well-known herding breeds, including the Australian Cattle Dog and Border Collie.

Smålands Hound
See Smålandsstövare

Smålandsstövare

The Smålandsstövare origi-nates in the southern forests of Sweden and is the oldest of the Scandinavian stövare breeds. As is true with many other canines, the Smalandsstövare gets his name from the area in which he originated, Smålands. The Smålands variety of the stövare type has probably been around since the early Middle Ages. Used with great success hunting in the forests of Sweden, the breed was taken seriously, and breeders worked hard to preserve and improve the dogs. They are still em-ployed today as hunters of fox, hare, and other forest game in southern Sweden. The Småland's compact size makes it

more suitable to hunt in the dense woods than in open terrain. This is a deliberate and thorough hound that doesn't rely on speed primarily. In appearance, he is an attractive and even flashy dog who makes a fine show dog.

ESSENTIALS OF THE SMÅLANDSSTÖVARE: This is the shortest yet stockiest of the Swedish hounds. His distinctively stövare body type is built upon well-boned, well-muscled legs. Height, about 17 inches (43 cm); weight, 33–40 pounds (15–18 kg). Color is black with tan mark-ings on muzzle, possibly eyebrows and lower legs. His coat is thick and smooth.

Smooth coat

Coat comprised of short, close-lying hair (e.g., Pointer, Bull Terrier).

Smooth Fox Terrier

One of the two well-known Fox Terri-ers, the Smooth Fox Terrier is believed to have sprouted from smooth-coated black and tan terriers of England, the Bull Ter-rier, the Greyhound, and the Beagle. The Smooth predates the Wire by nearly two decades. Al-though both share the nomencla-ture Fox Terrier, they are hardly the same dog. The Wire is believed to come from the old rough haired, black and tan working terrier of Wales, Durham and Derbyshire. The Smooth Fox Terrier is one of the most widely known and dis-tributed of purebred dogs and his origin is distinctly British. The Fox Terrier was used in conjunction with hounds to drive the fox from its hiding place. The Smooth, la-belled the gentleman of the terrier world, is surely ungentlemanly when facing a badger three times his weight, a feat the Smooth can do again and again with unstinted success.

Practi-cally speaking, the Smooth can be traced back to the mid-nineteenth cen-tury to photographs of "Jock," a prize-

Smooth Fox Terrier, bicolor.

Smålandsstövare, black with tan. Photo postcard issued by the Swedish Kennel Club.

Smooth Fox Terrier, tricolor.

winner whose career began in 1862. Before the breeds were as established, crossings between smooths and wires were common. Today, such crossbreedings are unheard of. The Reverend Jack Russell, although favoring the rough-coated terriers, always kept a few Smooths around. These Smooths are believed to have contributed to the parson's own terrier, the Jack Russell Terrier, which *see.*

less popular than their wiry brothers, are ideal choices.

ESSENTIALS OF THE SMOOTH FOX TERRIER: The coat is straight, flat, smooth, hard, and dense. The importance of good bone and balance cannot be understated. The legs, carried straight forward while travelling, cannot be too long nor too short in order for the Fox Terrier to project the proper appearance. The avoidance of cloddiness and coarseness is sovereign. He must be short backed and level with a moderately narrow skull. The topline of the skull should be almost flat, sloping slightly and gradually decreasing in width towards the eyes, with skull and foreface of equal length. The foreface is chiseled somewhat, and the jaws are punishing. The ears are small and V-shaped with the flaps neatly folded over and forward-drooping. The neck is clean in outline, curving gracefully. Feet compact and round. Height: 15.5 inches (39 cm). Weight: 16–18 pounds (7.5–8.5 kg).

Smooth Fox Terrier, tricolor. Photo by I. Français.

Smooth-muzzled Pyrenean Shepherd Dog
See Bergers des Pyrenees

Smoothhaired Istrian Hound
See Istrian Hound

Smudge nose
See Snow nose

Smutt
Used to refer to the characteristic of a self-colored Bulldog having a black mask.

Show fanciers of the Smooth Fox can be applauded for not exorcising natural ability from this truly talented terrier. Exhibition champions are also known as fine working dogs as well. Home companions or farm dogs, Smooths, though

Smutty
Refers to the occurrence of tan coloration found within the blue coat areas of two Australian breeds: the Australian Terrier and the Australian Silky Terrier. It is undesirable in both breeds.

Snap Dog

The alleged ancestor of the Whippet and certain terriers, the Snap Dog occurred in Great Britain during past centuries.

Snap-on comb

Comblike attachment, available in various sizes, which fits over the clipper head. As the coat is clipped, the hair will be uniformly cut to a predetermined, desired length.

Sneezing

Allergies, dust, fumes, caustic acid, nasal parasites, foxtails, weeds, grass, foreign bodies and tumors comprise the various causes for dogs to sneeze. *Pheumonesis caninum* seems to be the most common of nasal parasites. Vigorous sneezing can cause a dog's nose to bleed if he hits it against a hard surface or wall. Sneezing usually is a normal reaction. Chronic and/or persistent sneezing calls for a visit to the vet.

Snip

The extension of a blaze that extends to the nose.

Snipy

Used mostly in a derogatory sense, it refers to a weak, often narrow, construction to the foreface, mostly the muzzle and jaw, but can refer to the entire foreface in breeds that require a strong, solid construction in this area. Snipiness is the characteristic of a snipy foreface or muzzle. *See also* Pinched muzzle

Snorting

An act in which the dog forcibly brings air in through its nose and expels the air out its mouth. Unless severe or chronically persistent, it is generally little cause for alarm, though investigation of its cause is recommended.

Snow fence

Fencing made of wooden upright slats fastened together with a wire used to mark off areas or to prevent heavy drifting snow from marring the trail.

Snow hook

A hook used to stake a sled team for a temporary purpose.

Snow nose

A black nose that acquires a pink line or marking during the winter months: a normal occurrence in a number of Siberian Huskies and not a fault.

Snowberm

The ridges of snow made along the side of the road by snow plows.

Snowshoe feet

Nature's answer to snowshoes for dogs, these feet are unique to the Arctic sled-pulling breeds. They are oval and compact, equipped with toes well arched and pads well cushioned. Overall the feet are well furred and well webbed to accommodate the dogs' need to work on the ice-ridden landscapes of the Arctic.

Smooth Fox Terrier, bicolor. Photo by I. Français.

Socialization

The process by which a puppy (or dog) learns how to live harmoniously with canine and human family members. The socialization of a dog is a complex proc-

Socialization. The learning and handling process revolves around the dam and the breeder, as these are the first two teachers the puppy will know. Photo by R. Pearcy.

Socialization. Initially, the whelps' exposure to touching and handling should be limited to short periods. Toddler and Old English Sheepdog pups sharing new experiences.

ess because dogs not only live within a higher social structure but also adapt this structure in accordance with the demands of their environment. Turning to the wild, we find the interesting fact that dingoes lead a predominantly solitary existence, while their close relatives the wolves lead a very structured pack existence. It is believed that the different environments in which these animals live could be the single most important factor to understanding their more or less independent natures and different lifestyles. The dog's ability to adapt socially accounts largely for the importance of proper canine socialization: if a puppy is improperly socialized, or not socialized at all, it will adapt its behavior to ways that may well not be welcomed by humans. It will become at least a problem dog, if not a downright dangerous animal. On a positive note, the dog's ability to adapt its social behavior is a primary reason why dogs can be reared and trained to do so many tasks in

so many different settings.

Properly socializing the dog towards both humans and other dogs must be undertaken intelligently and faithfully, and it is of course the dam that begins the socialization process, supervising the whelps' play with one another and correcting overly unruly behavior. In the wild, adult wolves socialize their whelps through constant play and by setting examples daily. Often it is the sire that takes over the play, while the dam rests and supervises. In a conventional domestic dog setting, the sire is likely not available for such an active role in puppy socialization. Additionally, very few breeds are "natural" and undeviant enough to expect the male of the breed to have these strong paternal instincts. Certain breeds among the Nordic spitz dogs may still possess these instincts. Human intervention, handling and playing with the pups, is limited at this early stage to short and simple sessions. Interaction with humans can be limited to the breeder and a couple other individuals with whom the dam is familiar. It is important for the whelps to observe the dam's kind reaction to humans. With continued socialization, the pups will emulate her receptive example in time.

Additionally, the breeder must ensure that the new owner possess the ability

and desire to continue the socializing process. The responsibility rests with the breeder not only because he is the creator and the seller of these lives but also be-

cause human socialization *must* begin during the fourth week of the puppy's life, when the animal becomes more aware of the people around him. The ongoing process continues, with increased intensity, throughout the time that the dog is in the breeder's care. The potential for the dog's future relations with humans (and dogs too) is largely determined by its 12th week, and certainly by its 15th.

At about the fifth week the puppy has developed to the point where more human socialization becomes increasingly important. At this point, and continuing for several more weeks, the puppy will be learning two different social codes: one for the human world, and another for the canine one. It is important that socialization in both contexts be learned by the dog, as behavioral problems can result from either faulty canine or human socialization. For the first few weeks of this period, the pups should be individually picked up and talked to. Each pup should be given some time alone with a human in a short one-on-one interaction. Effectively what the dam has taught the pup should be applicable to its human friends as well.

Between the sixth and and 12th week, most puppies leave for their new homes. By the eighth week, the time when most breeders will let a litter go, puppies require a great deal of human socialization, because at this time their brain develop-

ment has reached the point where the basis of future relationships is being constructed. The transition to the new owners is crucial and any interruption in the pup's socialization can hinder that dog's future social etiquette. Certain breeders prefer to wait till 12 or 15 weeks before allowing the pups to embark on their new lives. Such a long period can be truly unbearable for the dam and for this good reason breeders opt to part with puppies early.

Some other important milestones in the socialization of the puppy include housebreaking, basic training, early crate and kennel restriction, and lead training. Ideally the dam has had ample opportunity to teach the pup the basics of housebreaking and breeders that use crates in their boarding of the new family are laying the groundwork for crate training, making the new owners' jobs that much more simple.

Socialization. Few breeders have the opportunity to allow the sire of the litter to participate in the rearing process. In certain circumstances, the father is able to assume the training–socialization role with considerable adroitness. Danish Broholmer adult and puppy.

Socialization. The human touch. Young whelps quickly accept and trust the humans who handle them regularly. Photo courtesy of Keith Thompson.

SOCIALIZATION

Socialization with each breed is somewhat different. Breeders who crop ears must ensure that puppies' headgear not interfere with play, a vital part of a puppy's development. Photo by I. Français.

Socialization for puppies intended to work with livestock must include exposure to their charges. This Sarplaninac puppy will grow into a fearless protector of its keeper's flock.

To be truly successful in socializing the dog, the breeder and future owner must be fully aware of the innate nature of their breed, and also the breed's family or group. Each breed has its own basic temperament, with individual variations

some degree with the basic character of the breed's group or family. Since most breeders concentrate on a single breed (or at most two breeds), these knowledgeable dog people understand the nuances of his or her breed and experiment with ways of enriching the puppies' environment. For example, packhounds such as Beagles and Basset Hounds, tend to be gregarious and fare well in a multi-dog, large family setting, thriving on the constant company of one another. The spitz breeds, such as the American Eskimo and Keeshond, on the other-hand, more quickly grow out of their dependency on littermates, tending towards greater independence.

While the basic social characteristics of all dogs are the same, an owner, too, should know about the breed, its history and disposition tendency, thereby gearing expectations appropriately.

Certain breeders gear later socialization differently once they know to which homes each pup is intended. In other words, a breeder of Fila Brasileiros, for example, who intends a litter dogs for companions takes specific steps which may differ considerably from the Fila breeder who working for a team intended for heavy-duty guard duty. The history of the Fila reminds us that this large breed was created to be a fierce, not necessarily

thereof occurring in each breed member. This innate character is consistent to

friendly, man-stopper. Thus, the breeder of companion Filas must be sure that his dogs possess a suitable temperament to live happily and peacefully as a pet. Temperament is in part genetic and in part environmental, and it can be tested with some degree of reliability. Regardless of the intention of the animal, all dogs must be consistent, biddable and never be vicious or shy.

Large breeding establishments which produce many different breeds, sometimes called puppy mills, do not have the facility or staff to socialize puppies in an acceptable way. It is not possible to obtain a suitable companion from such an institution. Likewise, breeders who attempt to produce more than two or three litters at one time must be considered suspect as well, since most kennels cannot promise staffs large enough to attend properly to this many dogs.

In all, proper socialization provides the backbone of the human–dog relationship, and while the basis for this relationship is started by the breeder, the owner must consider that all his future interactions will affect and be affected by the social structure that has been constructed in the dog. *See also* Behavior modification, Canine behavior, Housebreaking, Puppies

Society for the Prevention of Cruelty to Animals
See Humane societies

Socks
White markings that extend no further than from the pads to the wrist on the

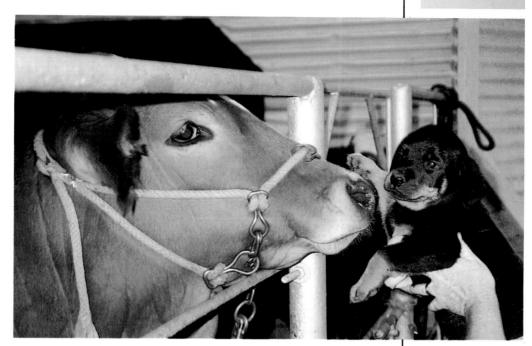

forelegs and/or from the pads to the hocks on the hindlegs on otherwise colored dogs. White markings that extend to the elbow on the forelegs and/or the

thighs on the hindlegs are referred to as "stockings," which *see*.

Socialization. Eliciting a puppy's instincts can assist in nurturing the development of the puppy's personality and confidence. This urchin of a cattle drover (Rottweiler) is meeting the family cow.

Socialization for puppies intended for guard duty must instill an admiration and respect for humans, the same as is necessary for a family dog. Without proper socialization, these Dogue de Bordeaux pups would be unsuitable for any human–dog activity.

Soft Coated Wheaten Terrier

Terriers, long popular in Ireland, have since developed into a number of distinct breeds. The Soft Coated Wheaten Terrier is derived from the general stock of Irish terriers, the Kerry Blue, the Irish and the Glen of Imaal also sprang from Irish stock. The Soft Coated's history, admit-

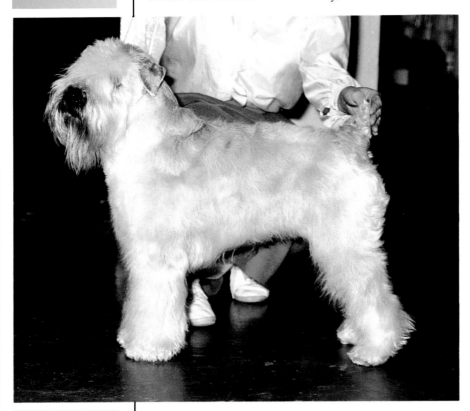

modern disinterest in good grammar.) Nevertheless, its name differentiated it from the other Irish terriers and thus standardized and segregated the Wheaten type. The Wheaten, then, is a latecomer to the world of purebred dogs, even though the dogs have been around for a few centuries. The American Kennel Club did not grant recognition until 1973. As a home companion, he is choice: peace-admiring and devoted.

ESSENTIALS OF THE SOFT COATED WHEATEN TERRIER: An expansive coat, soft, flowing, profuse, never harsh, with a generous amount of loose curls. The body, rectangular in appearance, is compact and relatively short coupled. The head is also rectangular in appearance, with no indication of coarseness. The skull and muzzle are the same length, thus forming a moderately long head. The tail is docked and is carried above. Height: 18–19.5 inches (46–49 cm). Weight: 32–45 pounds (14.5–20.5 kg). A light clear wheaten color is most desirable. Red, white or black guard hairs may be found.

Soft Coated Wheaten Terrier, wheaten. Photo by I. Français.

tedly long, is difficult to discern and has been submerged in tavern suds for many, many rounds (and generations). The Wheaten that was known in Ireland two centuries ago was a peasant dog mostly indigenous to the Kerry and Cork areas. Irish laws penalized the peasants for owning hunting dogs, so terriers were popular with the peasants, who needed the dogs to rid their homes and farms of vermin. The larger Irish terriers have been used as guard dogs, cattle drovers, herders, and hunting dogs. These multifaceted canines were needed to fill the gaps of the dogs which the peasants weren't permitted to own.

The breed known as the Soft Coated Wheaten Terrier was recognized in 1937, when that name was chosen. (The hyphen was dropped in 1989—an unfortunate occurrence quite conversant with

Soft palate

See Palate

Soft-tempered

A sheepdog that shows little assertiveness when pressed by wild or stubborn sheep is called "soft-tempered."

Softening

Losing intensity on point (sometimes accompanied by going down, settling, or squatting). This may occur coincidentally with flagging, but more often as the game moves on or is flushed. Also it may be an indication that a dog is reacting to such reprimand or punishment as was used in breaking. (German-trained dogs are trained to drop on flush as a protection during the multiple shooting that follows the flush in the continental method of bird harvesting.)

Solid color
See Self-color

Somber expression
See Expression

Sonangi
See Alunk

Sound bone
Reference to an adequately strong and thick skeletal structure.

Soundness
Refers to mental and/or physical well being. A dog is said to be physically sound when it can perform well the task(s) for which the breed is intended, i.e., sledge pulling, guard work, etc. For house dogs, or purely pets, soundness can be defined as a dog that is free from disease, has good nutrition, and is well constructed. Mental soundness is a dog's willingness and ability to execute the task(s) for which the breed is intended. Thus, the dog's ability enables it to cope with the mental stress presented to it during the execution of the task(s). For house dogs, mental soundness includes an even temperament, good intelligence, and an overall contented attitude.

South American Foxes
Some of the major South American wild dogs belong to the genus *Dusicyon* and are commonly called the South American foxes. Other wild dogs of South America include the bush dog and the maned wolf, which *see*. There are eight key species of this genus, and together they accumulate a dazzling array of common names, suggestive of our general lack of knowledge (or agreement) about them, the variety of physical specifics that they bear and numerous geographical locations they inhabit. The eight key members of the genus *Dusicyon* are: the culpeo (*D. culpaeus*), the Santa Elena fox (*D. culpaeolus*), the pampas fox (*D. gymnocercus*), the Peruvian fox (*D. inca*), the chilla (*D. griseus*), the Chiloé (*D. fulvipes*), and the Sechura fox (*D. sechurae*).

The culpeo is the head representative of the red foxes of South America and is also the largest member of its genus, with some specimens measuring as much as 60 inches (153 cm) from nose to tip of tail. It is called the red fox because of its distinctive reddish markings on its forehead, jaw, backs of ears, and outer limbs. Known as the Andean wolf in Ecuador, the culpeo is found from the Andes of Colombia to the south of Chile, from Argentina through the Patagonian plateau; it is a temperate-zone inhabitant of various altitudes. Both size and color vary with location, with a noted decrease in size from north to south. Subspecies are reported but little studied, with essential differences being in color and size. The culpeo's color is typically a yellowish and

Soft Coated Wheaten Terrier. Photo by I. Français.

black mix; the tail is distinctively bushy and with a black tip. In habits and diet, the culpeo is similar to other mid-sized wild dogs.

The Santa Elena fox is very similar to the culpeo, so much so that if it were not for the geographic isolation between the two species, the culpeo and the Santa Elena would likely be classified as the same species. The Santa Elena is restricted to a small region of southeast Uruguay. Somewhat smaller than the typical culpeo, the Santa Elena has the same distinguishing color markings and overall appearance.

Whereas the culpeo is the major representative of the red foxes, the pampas fox is the major representative of the gray foxes of South America. The pampas is relatively common in the populated regions of Argentina, Uruguay, and Brazil, while a southern race of the pampas is found in the pampas of southwest Argentina, and a northern race is found in Paraguay and northern Uruguay. Because of its distribution and frequenting of populated areas, the pampas fox is well known: it is a mid-sized wild dog, measuring 31 to 32 inches (79–81.5 cm), with an additional 13-inch (33 cm) tail length; it has a gray coat and a yellowish tail with two black spots, which is characteristic of the species. The pampas fox is known to practice two behavioral peculiarities; it collects and stores objects, such as bits of cloth and leather, which are apparently useless to it; and it lies rigid, apparently faking death, should it encounter a human. Reports of manly men whipping and beating the terror-stricken, possum-playing pampas while it lies rigid suggest that the fox remains immobile until the human threat has passed. Unlike the red foxes of South America, this gray fox is a solitary animal, found in pairs only during the mating season. It lives in dens, which it frequently takes from other animals, and feeds on rodents, especially rats, and birds of all sizes. When food is scarce, the pampas is known to feed on amphibians and reptiles such as frogs and lizards.

The Peruvian fox closely resembles the pampas fox, and its separate species status may have been granted prematurely. Its range is southern Peru and has been found at elevations of 13,000 feet. Its slightly grayer coat color and its skull, which hints of the culpeo (also a dweller of Peru), distinguish it from the typical pampas fox.

From central Chile and western Argentina and Patagonia comes South America's gray fox, the chilla. The chilla is referred to as the southern and western representative of South America's gray foxes. Unlike its close relative the pampas fox, the chilla prefers forested terrain; it has been reported to inhabit elevations exceeding 10,000 feet. There is a notable increase in size of southern specimens, but the chilla is essentially a smallish wild dog, about 30 inches (76 cm) long, of grayish coloration, with large, triangular ears and a pointed muzzle. There is little evidence regarding the chilla's habits in the wild other than that they are similar to the pampas—a rodent eater found around populated areas.

The Chiloé inhabits the Chiloé Island off the coast of Chile and closely resembles the chilla in appearance and habit; some question its designation as a species separate from the chilla. A Chiloé specimen killed by Charles Darwin survives in the museum of the Zoological Society. Darwin and others have noted the trusting nature of these little foxes, and it is believed that this quality contributed to the rapid extinction of the Falkland Island fox, which is closely related to the Chiloé, a few years after the island was first inhabited by man. The Chiloé too has suffered many a hunt but has remained in existence.

The field fox, one of the smallest members of its genus, is native to Brazil and well adapted to the warm climate that it inhabits. Measuring 23 to 24 inches (58.5–61 cm) in body length and weighing about eight pounds (3.5 kg), the field fox has a relatively short muzzle and short molars; it is also known as the short-toothed dog. Found primarily on the open plains of its native land, the field fox feeds on rodents, birds, and insects. It is a timid, shy canid that would rather not receive visits from man.

The Sechura fox has a short muzzle and small teeth that are remarkably similar to those of the field fox, which, however, is found some 2,000 miles distant from the Sechura. Native to the Sechura desert of northwestern Peru, little is actually known about this wild dog, but it has been suggested that the Sechura fox is the transitional form between the field fox and other South American foxes.

South Russian Ovtcharka

The South Russian Ovtcharka is a sheepdog native to the Ukraine, a large, powerful dog designed to protect its flocks from malintending wolves. This Ukrainian guard, however, is no stranger to the English-speaking world. The South Russian Sheepdog (or Ovtcharka) was once a member of the Miscellaneous Class of the American Kennel Club. Although no longer registered by that body, the breed has a noteworthy following in the U.S. In the Soviet Union, the breed is revered for his guard abilities. As the breed was meticulously bred for size, strength and courage, today's Ovtcharka is a competent and competitive worker. His personality, while likable overall, is dominating and possessive, qualities not to be shunned in a flock guardian or watchdog. Not plenteous in the U.S.S.R., the breed is used for military guard purposes, and home-owned specimens may attend an occasional exhibition.

ESSENTIALS OF THE SOUTH RUSSIAN OVTCHARKA: Height: 25–26 inches (63–66 cm) minimum; 30–34 inches (76–86.5 cm) average. Weight: 110–155 pounds (55–74 kg). Color: White with fawn or gray spots on the head. Coat: long, dense, and double. The tail, pump-handle in shape, is long and well feathered, nearly reaching the ground. Ears hang straight; fringe characteristically covers the eyes. The legs are well boned.

South Russian Sheepdog

See South Russian Ovtcharka

South Russian Steppe Hound

The South Russian Steppe Hound graces the Soviet north Caucasus Mountains, the Volga, and the Don River region. These greyhounds are kept by the Kirghiz tribe and thus are commonly referred to as Kirghiz Greyhounds. They are required by the nomads to be solid in color; a uniform white or pale cream is the "standard"—markings of any other color are considered blemishes. The Kirghiz people refer to these noble hounds as *Ahk-Taz-eet*, which means "white Tasy dog." While the nomads do not record pedigrees, great efforts were exerted to keep the strains pure. Although falconry is common in the Steppe area, the Kirghiz do not use their greyhounds for this purpose. The larger boned dogs are reserved for wolf coursing, while the smaller dogs are used on fox, hare, and small deer.

Today, while the Steppe Borzoi is not as pure as its predecessors, this hound is frequently hunted with its close relative, the Chortaj. The Chortaj, also known as the Eastern Greyhound, possesses astounding sight; the South Russian Steppe Hound complements with its super canine speed. Together these two west Russian coursing hounds are an indomitable force. It is generally believed that both these borzois derive from the same stock as the A.K.C. Borzoi. The South Russian Steppe Hound stands 24–28 inches (61–71 cm) in height.

Southern Cur

See Black Mouth Cur

Southern Hound

The Southern Hound was derived from the original St. Hubert Hound, which also begot the modern-day Bloodhound. These much talked-about foxhounds are believed to have contributed to a number of the packhounds of France, including the glorious hounds of the Vendee district. Other reports include the Southern Hound in the composition of the Otter Hound. In appearance, the Southern Hound was a large, heavy dog, with a tricolored pattern coat.

South Russian Ovtcharka, white. Photo by I. Français.

S.P.C.A.
See Humane societies

Spaniel field trials
See Field trials

Spaniels
Known variously since the fourteenth century, the hunting companions known as spaniels are actually pointing setters. All known spaniels derive from setter lines (English, Irish, Gordon, etc.) but later acquired new hunting techniques. Breeds of spaniel developed as these abilities became more and more specialized. *See also* Gundogs, Flushing spaniels, Cocking spaniels, Springing spaniels, American Cocker Spaniel, English Cocker Spaniel, Sussex Spaniel, Field Spaniel, Clumber Spaniel, English Springer Spaniel, etc.

Spanish Greyhound
See Galgo Español

Spanish Mastiff
A guard of cattle and sheep in modern-day Spain, the Spanish Mastiff is a calm and deliberate worker. This native Spaniard has acquired many names, among them: Mastin de Español, Mastin de Extremadura, Mastin de Leon, and Mastin de La Mancha. The Mastin is descended from the dogs that assisted in flock migrations in Europe. Essentially the Spanish Mastiff is the dog that remained in Spain from Phoenician-brought sheepdogs that made their way about the continent. This flock guard, however, looks more mastiffy than most: short hair and a wealth of dewlap. He is overall more tucked up than most mastiffs with lighter boned legs.

Although a gentle dog around farmyard and pasture grazing animals, the Mastin is wary and duly aggressive with other dogs. With people, he is exceptionally even tempered and gracious. Fanciers in the U.S. are doing well to promote the breed as a guard dog and companion.

ESSENTIALS OF THE SPANISH MASTIFF: A large, rather lengthy dog with a massive chest and good length of leg. He has a large but shapely head, and generous dewlap on the neck. Height: 26–29 inches (66–74 cm). Weight: 110–135 pounds

Spanish Mastiff, grizzle. Photo by Ana Mesto.

Spanish Mastiff, fawn. Photo by Carlos Salas.

(50–61 kg). Coat: medium short and very dense. Colors: fawn, brindle, black and white, wolf gray, yellow and white, gray and white, grizzle and red.

Spanish Mastiff, yellow and white. Photo by I. Français.

Spanish Pointer
See Perdiguero de Burgos

Spartiate
The Spartiate of Greece, also known as the Greek Herder, is an ancient breed used by herdsmen and farmers in the native land. It is a medium-sized dog, smaller than its flock-guarding counterpart, the Greek Sheepdog (which *see*). The ears are prick and small; the muzzle short; the head broad with a strongly marked stop. In color the dog is white, sometimes with fawn or orange markings on the ears.

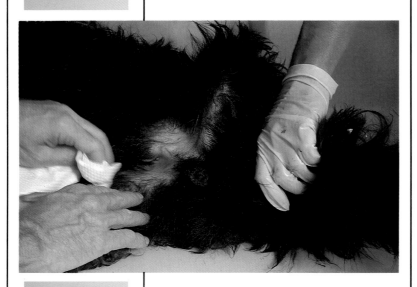

Spaying surgery is simple and inexpensive. Most animal activist groups contend that all pet dogs, not to be bred or shown, should be spayed or neutered. Photo by I. Français.

Spaying
The process by which a portion of the bitch's reproductive system is surgically removed, thereby making her incapable of producing offspring. Should the bitch be spayed? A large number of dog owners are faced with this question; it is one not easily resolved by some. For others, however, the matter is simple: they wish not to breed their bitch, do not want the added responsibilities when she is in season, and know that there is little risk in the spaying operation. Of course, spaying, like all other surgical procedures, does involve some risk, but spaying is a relatively simple, minor procedure that has been performed routinely for many years. One common spaying procedure involves the removal of the ovaries, known as ovarian hysterectomy. It was once believed that the ovaries should not

be removed until after the female matured. Today, spaying before the female reaches her first season is common practice—and a recommended cancer preventative, too. There are various other procedures as well, but these others should be recommended and explained to you by a trained professional.

Many arguments exist for and against the practice of spaying. Persons in favor of spaying cite evidence that spayed bitches are much less inclined to develop breast cancer or other cancers of the reproductive system. Indeed, evidence suggests that bitches who are spayed before their first heat have nearly a zero-percent chance of developing breast cancer. Additionally, any complications that could occur during a bitch's season are of course non-existent in spayed females. Perhaps the strongest argument is based on the fact that there are too many unwanted dogs in existence today. Many unwanted dogs every year die of neglect, others are "humanely disposed of" and many others live on miserably. Spaying can undoubtedly help this situation. Also in favor of spaying are the claims that a bitch will not "miss" her sex drive if she is never mated and that there is little known effect on the physical and mental states of the bitch after the operation (if the operation is performed after the bitch reaches her physical maturity). It is stated that she will lose none of her motherly instincts, etc., which owners fear, but the statement is nearly impossible to prove beyond doubt.

Those in opposition to spaying cite as their major arguments that it is unhealthy, unnatural, and detrimental to a bitch's performance (as a companion, guardian, herder, etc.). The "unnatural" argument is easy to understand. There are many people—some dog fanciers included—who believe in letting nature take its course. They are not without justification, as nature is a relatively effective and efficient process. However, is their stand responsible? Likely it is not. Man has domesticated dog and he must now accept responsibility for its welfare. The claims that it is unhealthy as well as detrimental to performance rest on the similar basis of the dog's chemistry altered as a result of missing secretion-releasing ovaries. Indeed, the chemistry is changed, if for no other reason than the necessary drop in certain hormone levels. Supporters of spaying claim no change in either a dog's health or performance, and many case studies provide evidence of this.

Whatever your stand on spaying, it is a consideration that should be confronted by every dog owner. The decision should rest largely on the individual circumstances and not on individual preference. Both positions have their support; it is recommended that the dog owner discuss the procedure and its effects with a veterinarian and other dog owners who have confronted the decision prior to taking this important step in his dog's welfare. There are many concerned groups that offer assistance and advice, and there are some that can refer or provide free or inexpensive spaying operations. *See also* Breeding

Special for Best of Breed

The highest award that is made within a breed at a dog show. Contrary to the general opinion, it is not a class. It is a special prize for which the specifically entered and otherwise eligible dogs compete. Not being a class, no awards are made other than to the one dog declared Best of Breed.

Specialty dogs

A specialty dog is a dog that is trained to assist a multi-disabled person. Specialty dogs, to an extent, are individually trained to meet the needs of a particular owner. Such dogs are able to handle a blind and deaf person, or a blind person confined to a wheelchair. *See also* Assistance dogs

Specialty show

A show, offering championship points, for a single breed. These may be licensed or member specialty shows. They may be held by a specialty club—a club devoted to the improvement of a single breed. Often, specialty shows are offered for a group or for multi-breeds, e.g., a terrier specialty.

Speckling

Synonymous with ticking, which *see*, this term can refer to the existence of alternative colored tips to otherwise colored hairs. Red speckle, however, refers to the existence of solid red markings on a red roan background of an Australian Cattle Dog. Speckling can also refer to the entire coat color of some Continental hounds and gundogs, e.g., the Braque du Bourbonnais, the Grand Bleu de Gascogne, and the Braques Françaises.

Spectacles

The characteristic light-colored hair surrounding the eyes of the otherwise dark-colored Keeshond.

Speothos venaticus

See Bush dog

Spiked

A racing dog that is injured by claws of a following contestant.

Spinal column

The spinal column is the series of many closely placed vertebrae, only three of which are fused, which together

Specialty show for the Kyi-Leo. Most commonly a single breed is the focus of a specialty show. Photo courtesy of Harriet Linn.

Spinone Italianos, white.

Spinone Italianos, chestnut roan. Photographs by I. Français.

house the spinal cord. Between each vertebra there is a soft cushioning substance that acts as a shock absorber. The construction of the spinal column allows for flexibility and movement. The spinal column extends from the neck region to the base of the tail. The vertebrae of the neck region are called the cervical vertebrae; those of the dorsal chest (thorax) are called the thoracic vertebrae; those of the loin region, the lumbar vertebrae; those at the base of the tail and fused, the sacrum; and those forming the gradually tapering tail, the coccygeal also known as the caudal vertebrae.

Spine

Synonymous with spinal column, which *see*.

Spinone Italiano

An undeniably old breed of Italy that stemmed from native hounds. The exact origin remains a mystery. There are two worthwhile theories about the Spinone's origin. The first makes the breed a descendant of the Segugio Italiano, an ancient hound from the Middle Ages. The second purports that the breed originated in the Alps of Piedmont from the Barbet, Korthals Griffon and other hound types. The breed today is noted for its highly acute scenting ability, super soft mouth, and ability to

endure the elements and terrain. The dog's physical and mental abilities afford quite a variation of hunting proclivities. He is adaptable to any kind of shooting and is particularly suited for heavy cover. The breed's expression is surely a direct line to its temperament. The distinguished, well-salted, great-grandfather look indicates that this is a noble, wise and protective canine companion. He can be either reserved or rowdy and playful. The Spinone fancy in the U.S. is growing steadily and the breed resides in the Miscellaneous Class.

ESSENTIALS OF THE SPINONE ITALIANO: Squarely built and solid, of strong bone and good muscle. The head is long, with the skull flat and lean, and the occiput well developed. The eyes are large, fairly round and open, with eyelids close fitting; the ears are set on level with the corner of the eyes; long, but not more than two inches below the jaw line. Shoulders are strong and well laid back; chest is broad, open, and well let down. The coat is tough, thick and slightly wiry, fitting closely to the body. Eyebrows, moustache and beard comprise the facial furnishings. In color the Spinone is all-white, white with orange, white with chestnut, or either coloration with roan. Height: 24–26 inches (61–66 cm). Weight: 71–82 pounds (32–37 kg). The tail is customarily docked to half its length.

Spion
See Small Münsterländer

Spirochetosis
Diarrhea which cannot be checked through normal anti-diarrhea medication within a few days may indicate spirochetosis; while spirochete are believed by some authorities to be present in and normal to gastrointestinal tracts, unexplainable diarrhea may indicate their presence in great numbers. Large quantities could precipitate diarrhea by upsetting the normal balance of the organ, though it is possible for some dogs which are infected to have no diarrhea at all.

Spitz
Working type nordic dogs that are characterized by their double coats, prick ears, wedge-shaped muzzles, and curled-over-the-back tails. Germany contributes about ten breeds to the group, including the German Spitz, Wolfspitz and Pomeranian. The American Eskimo, Samoyed, Finnish Spitz, and Norbottenspets are examples of these unique types. These are sharp, very alert and independent canines. *See also* Nordic dogs.

Splash
A typically shapeless white marking occurring anywhere on an otherwise colored coat. Splashes are faults in Boston Terriers, for instance.

Splay feet
Feet in which the toes are spread apart. Opposite of tightly knit toes, these feet are usually undesirable and can occur in any foot type. Exceptions exist—in the Irish Water Spaniel, for instance, splay feet are required by the standard.

Spleen
See Circulatory system

Split nose
See Nose types

Split upper lip
Upper lip halves are incompletely joined at the lower borders. *See* Hare lip

Spondylitis
Condition marked by the inflammation and loosening of the vertebra.

Spoon-shaped feet
See Oval feet

Sporting clip
See Clipping the Poodle

Sporting Group
The Sporting Group is essentially an American delineation of the gundog breeds. Included in this group are the spaniels, pointers, setters, retrievers, and European utility breeds. In Britain, these breeds are classified in the Gundog Group. The American Kennel Club Sporting Group includes some of the nation's most popular breeds: the Cocker Spaniel, Labrador Retriever, and Golden Retriever. All of the breeds included are used for feather hunting. *See also* Group Systems, Gundogs

Spinone Italiano, chestnut roan. Photo by I. Français.

Spot

A specific mark on the center skull of the King Charles Spaniel. The mark should be approximately one centimeter in radius, chestnut colored, and surrounded by the white blaze. A similar marking is seen in the Bleu de Gascogne breed. Spot can also be employed as a reference to distinctly colored patches on the coats of other breeds, namely the Dalmatian. *See also* Naming your dog, Speckled

Spot bettor

He who wagers on dog races but waits for what he considers exceptionally favorable prospects and odds.

Spotted nose

See Butterfly nose

Spread

Refers to the extensive width of the chest as seen in the typey Bulldog in good stance.

Spreading feet

See Splay feet

Springing spaniels

Small spaniels used to spring hare from their warrens or grouse from their coverts. Springing is a form of flushing. *See also* Flushing Spaniels, Gundogs, English Springer Spaniel, Welsh Springer Spaniel

Springy action

As a spring, bouncy and buoyant motion. The happy-go-lucky bounce of the Pomeranian is jubilantly springy.

Sprinter

Racing dog with good early speed that weakens at distances of 5–16 miles or greater.

Spot marks the head of the Blenheim English Toy Spaniel. Photo by I. Français.

Square body

A dog is usually said to be square when the distance from withers to the ground equals the distance from the withers to the base of the tail. Some breed standards may use different points of reference, for example, withers to ground equals chest to point of buttocks.

Square muzzle

See Blunt muzzle

Squared-off head

A head that does not appear V-shaped or rounded due to a square muzzle shape.

Squealer

A hound that makes squealing sounds while giving voice.

Squirrel tail

A tail that is carried up and curving forward without resting on the back (e.g., Pekingese).

Stabyhoun

A gundog breed native to the Friesland province of Holland, where he has been known at least since the seventeenth century. The Stabyhoun is most probably the descendant of various setting and couching dogs of Europe that were brought to the Netherlands with the Spanish during their occupation in the mid-sixteenth century. Written documents that refer to the Stabyhoun in its present form date to the early 1800s.

The Stabyhoun is a good hunting dog of fine pointing and soft-mouth retrieving abilities. He is an able water-worker, especially effective on ducks. An enthusiastic and well-rounded gundog who is effective at both retrieving game and pointing. In disposition he is calm, patient, loyal, and obedient. In Holland, the breed is frequently seen larger than the standard indicates—these larger specimens are sometimes used for draft work.

Though the breed has had its trying times in history, it presently rests in the good hands of some native breeders, who are dedicated to the preservation of the breed, its soundness, and its ability. Though rarely seen outside the Continent, the Stabyhoun is a reliable, even-tempered, calm and affectionate canine companion and worker.

ESSENTIALS OF THE STABYHOUN: The skull is broad and slightly rounded; the stop is well defined, and the ears are set high. The back is long; the chest deep; and the hindquarters well muscled. There exists bushy feathering on the base of the tail and the breeches, but the tail tip is covered with smooth hair (together a distinctive feature of the breed). In black, chocolate, or orange—all with white markings—the Stabyhoun is a well-balanced, well-feathered medium-sized dog. He stands 19–21 inches (48–53 cm) and weighs 33–44 pounds (15–20 kg). The coat may or may not be ticked or roaned.

Stacked

A dog set up in show position is said to be "stacked."

Staffordshire Bull Terrier

The Staffordshire Bull Terrier, as so many of the bull and terrier breeds, was developed from crosses of the oldtime ferocious and athletic bull baiters and the game and feisty terriers. The Staff was bred to participate in the "organized sport" of ratting as well as to combat other canines in the dog-fighting rings. The outlawing of both these dubious diversions ushered the Staff out of the pits and into the more respectable arena of the

show ring, where he has enjoyed moderate success. This dog is smaller than the American Staffordshire Terrier, his close relative. At one time these two breeds

Stabyhouns, black with white. Photo by I. Français.

were essentially the same, with only geographic bounds separating them. Through the course of time, however, American and British breeds have strived for different qualities and now the two dogs are two distinct breeds.

Although there is a tendency to joust with fellow canines, the breed is one of

Staffordshire Bull Terrier, black brindle.

Staffordshire Bull Terrier (*right*) and the American Staffordshire Terrier (*left*), brindle. Photo by Michele Pearlmutter.

the most faithful and pleasing of man's canine companions. His devotion, willingness and energy are undying characteristics of the breed. When properly reared, he is an affectionate, outgoing, and intelligent dog sure to provide years of rewarding companionship. *See also* American Staffordshire Terrier, American Pit Bull Terrier.

ESSENTIALS OF THE STAFFORDSHIRE BULL TERRIER: A neat and refined, smooth-coated dog of tremendous musculature and accompanying strength and confidence. The body is close-coupled, with topline level and brisket deep. Neck is muscular and short. Hindquarters well muscled, with hocks well let down and stifles well angulated. The head is short and deep with a broad skull, pronounced cheek muscles and distinct stop. The foreface is short. The medium-sized ears are rose or half-prick—they are never cropped. The body is close coupled, with a level topline and a wide front. The coat is smooth, short and close-lying. Red, brindle, fawn, white, black or blue or any combination of these colors with white comprises the color variations. Height: 14–16 inches (36–41 cm). Weight: 24–38 pounds (11–17.5 kg).

Staghound

The English Staghound represented a large foxhound-type dog used for stag hunting. These dogs originally derived from crosses between the rough-coated Southern Hound and the Bloodhound. Later crosses to the Foxhound of England lightened the build. The Staghound was renowned as the slowest and most persistent of the scenthounds. It is believed that the Normans initially used these dogs to hunt stag deer, following the larger, semi-cumbersome hounds on foot. The large size of the Staghound enabled the dog to move through the heather and open grasses, where the stag deer commonly dwelled. Standing about 30 inches (76 cm) high, these were rugged, fast scenthounds with sensitive, selective noses. In color, the dogs were typically tricolored, with white predominating.

During the early part of the nineteenth century, the last known pack of the larger type Staghounds were sold to a French hunter. These dogs believedly contributed to the bloodwork of many French hounds. The turn of the twentieth century saw a decline in the number of Staghounds; in the mid-1930s there were only eight Staghound packs known in England. Lameness, which was common in the breed, is another reason why the dogs fell into obscurity. Today stag hunting chiefly involves Foxhounds, which may be referred to as staghounds but are not actually the breed once known as the English Staghound.

Stamina

The ability to endure; the quality of a dog that allows it to perform a given task for a prolonged period of time. The Chi-

nook and other husky breeds are known for their stamina in sledge pulling; the gundogs and scenthounds are renowned for their all-day work loads. In dog racing, a dog with great stamina is called a stayer.

Stance

The positioning of a dog on all fours; typically, as in show stance, it is the dog in his "best" possible standing position for judging purposes. *See also* Stacked

Stance, propped
See Propped

Stanchion
Vertical parts of a sled.

Stand-off coat
A type of double coat consisting of long, harsh hairs that stand out from the body and a supporting, soft undercoat (e.g., Shiba Inu, German Wolfspitz).

Standard
See Breed standard

Standard American Eskimo
See American Eskimo

Standard Dachshund
See Dachshund

Staghound. Today's working foxhound breeds of England and France may have derived from the Staghound packs of yesterday, though no direct lineage has been traced. Running pack photographed by I. Français in France.

Standard Schnauzer, pepper and salt, cropped.

Standard Mexican Hairless Dog
See Xoloitzcuintli

Standard Pinscher
See Pinscher

Standard Poodle
See Poodle

Standard Schnauzer

One of three breeds of Schnauzer, the Standard is the middle-sized, the oldest, and the prototype. References in art and literature verify that the Schnauzer was a popular dog in Germany at least as far back as the fifteenth century. Likely, these dogs are as ancient as any modern breed, but accurate sources pointing to the exact beginnings of the dog are lacking. It is known that the renowned German artist, Albrecht Durer, owned one of the breed and that the portrait of the dog occurs several times in the artist's work (circa 1492–1504). Standard Schnauzers are also presented by other artists of centuries ago, including Rembrandt, Lucas Cranach the Elder, and Sir Joshua Reynolds. Supporting the antiquity of the breed, there stands a statue dating to the fourteenth century in Mecklenburg, Germany, of a hunter with his dog, a dog which closely resembles the Standard Schnauzer of today.

The probable crosses to achieve the Schnauzer involve the black German Poodle, the Gray Wolfspitz and roughhaired pinscher types. German breeders have always regarded the Standard as a working dog, versatile and universally effective; in the U.S., the breed is classified as a terrier. His calling in his homeland was principally that of a ratter but it was demanded that he perform as a watchdog and guard dog as well. Today the breed retains its full degree of sagacity and fearlessness. The breed is also a good water dog and can be easily taught to retrieve. As a flock guardian, the Standard Schnauzer has ended many a coyote's life.

The first exhibition of the Schnauzer was at the third German International Show at Hanover, in 1879. At this show the breed was shown as a Wire-Haired Pinscher (*pinscher* translated to English is terrier). The first standard for the breed was adopted in 1890, and the Standard Schnauzer was quick to gain popularity in the show ring, an asset which he retains to this day.

The Standard Schnauzer is an alert and reliable canine, ideally sized and tempered. He is a popular and handy house dog that doesn't require a lot of exercise. A likeable, never pugnacious personality is never indiscernible through his wiry brow.

ESSENTIALS OF THE STANDARD SCHNAUZER: The general appearance of the Standard Schnauzer is that of a robust, heavy-set dog, solidly and squarely constructed of good muscle and plenty of bone. The head is strong, rectangular and elongated, narrowing slightly from the ears to the eyes and again to the tip of the nose; there is a slight stop which is accentuated by the wiry brows. The skull must be moderately broad, flat, and clean; the muzzle strong, and both parallel and equal in length to the topskull; the jaws must be set in a strong, scissors bite. The neck is strong, moderately thick and long, and elegantly arched.

Shoulders are arched and strongly muscled yet flat and well laid back so that the rounded upper ends are in a nearly vertical line above the elbows. The chest is medium wide with well-sprung ribs. The body is compact, short coupled and substantial, allowing for great agility and flexibility. The back is strong, stiff, straight and short, with a well-developed loin section. Forelegs straight, vertical, without any curvature, set moderately far apart; elbows are set close to the body and point directly to the rear. Feet are small and compact, round with thick pads. Tail is set moderately high and carried erect; it is customarily docked to not less than one inch nor more than two inches in length. The coat is tight, hard, wiry and as weatherproof and as thick as possible; it is double. The outercoat is trimmed (by plucking) only to accentuate the body outline. Color: pepper and salt, solid black; though not recognized, all-white specimens are found. Height: 18–20 inches (46–51 cm). Weight: 33 pounds (15 kg).

Staphylococci
Round bacteria that grow in strings.

Star
Typically a small white marking on the forehead.

Starter
Welsh name for the Welsh Springer Spaniel, which *see.*

States Kennel Club
The States Kennel Club is a new American dog association, organized to promote the interest of all purebred dogs and their fanciers on a country-wide level. Proud of its all-American basis: "it is a club of the fancy, by the fancy and for the fancy." Shortly after its 1989 inception, 49 states had registered dogs with the S.K.C. The club recognizes all breeds of the American and Canadian Kennel

Standard Schnauzer, white. Solid white dogs would be faulted in the American show ring. Photo by I. Français.

Clubs, as well as any dog club affiliated with the F.C.I., in addition to the Australian Shepherd, Toy Fox Terrier and American Eskimo of the United Kennel Club. Over three dozen rare, non-A.K.C.-recognized breeds have become involved with this new club.

For purebred fanciers, the development of an "alternative" kennel club is most exciting. In addition to providing similar (but different) events to the A.K.C., S.K.C. also offers performance events including herding competitions, weight-pulling competitions, herding instinct tests, terrier trials, coursing trials, agility races, and other instinct and performance competitions. Events are awarded in a similar fashion to the A.K.C., with the additional award of C.M. (Certificate of Merit). For more information about the S.K.C., write: States Kennel Club, Ltd., P.O. Box 389, Hattiesburg, MS 39403-0389.

Station

The comparative distance from the withers to the point of the elbow versus the distance from the point of the elbow to the ground. A greater distance from the withers to the elbow than from the elbow to the ground makes a dog rela-

Station. The Scottish Deerhound illustrates high in station. Photo by I. Français.

tively low in station, whereas the converse makes the dog relatively high in station. *See also* Height

Staunch

The quality of remaining on point as originally established until the arrival of the gun.

Stayer

Dog with the courage and stamina to race long distances.

Steady

To remain in original pointing position after the birds are flushed and the shot is fired.

Steady to wind and shot

To remain in the original position of the point after the flush or the shot respectively. (Some dogs will break upon flush, others upon hearing the shot or seeing the bird fall.)

Steep

An adjective commonly used to modify angles of body parts, suggesting undesirable obtuse angulation, i.e., steep hocks, steep pasterns, or steep shoulders.

Steep front

Viewed from the side, forequarter angulation appears steeper than desired.

Steep in shoulders

See Shoulder types

Steep pasterns

See Upright pasterns

Steirischer Rauhaarige Hochgebirgsbracke

See Roughhaired Mountain Hound

Stenezkajapastuschja

See Nenets Herding Laika

Stenosis

A narrowing or constriction of a vent or opening, especially of the heart, in which the condition can lead to congestive heart failure.

Stenotic nares

A condition in which the passage of air through the dog's nasal passages is obstructed by some anatomical abnormality. It is noticeable by the dog's forced breathing through its nose, and the degree varies according to the severity of the obstruction. Corrective surgery is often necessary.

Steppe Borzoi

See South Russian Steppe Hound

Sterility

In both the male and the female, sterility signifies the physical inability to create offspring; due to a lack of or defective sperm in the male, and lack of or abnormal eggs in the female. Prostatitis, testicular abnormalities or conditions, and nutritional insufficiency are all likely causes of sterility in the male. Ovarian cysts or other conditions affecting the ovaries, hormonal irregularities, and nutritional deficiency are common causes of sterility in females. Depending on the cause and the severity of the condition, sterility may be treated, either chemically or surgically. *See also* Nutrition, Ovaries, Prostate gland

Stern

As in the stern of a ship, the term "stern" is used to denote the hindmost part of the dog, the tail.

Sternebrae

The breastbone.

Sternum

The breastbone; reference typically includes the fleshy and sinewy matter as well as the sternebrae.

Stephens Cur

See Stephens Stock

Stephens Stock

Hugh Stephens's "little blacks," after a century of breeding pure, were deemed a separate breed in 1970. These dogs are among the five "recognized" strains of mountain curs in the American South. Their vocal versatility and love of the hunt make the Stephens strain preferred by many hunters. Although too small to work alone on mountain lion or bear, these are mighty and courageous hunters. These dogs possess a strong desire to work and therefore are not recommended to non-hunters who might otherwise be attracted to their small size and easycare attributes.

ESSENTIALS OF THE STEPHENS STOCK: A small, compact houndlike mountain cur that standardly comes in black (with white markings permissible); colors other than black occur but disqualify. Height: 16–23 inches (40–59 cm). Weight: 35–55 pounds (16–25 kg). He is lean and short coated. A small head and a narrow muzzle complement his sleek look. The breed has a distinctive rat tail. The body shows every indication of developed musculature—it is sinewy and taut, with no sign of excess.

Stephens Stock, black.

Steward

1) One of the sled-dog officials placed along the trail to avoid trouble at heavy traffic spots, sharp curves, etc. He must stay on the trail until the last team has passed. 2) One who acts as ring assistant to a judge. His duties do not include the judging of dogs.

Stichelhaar, white and brown roan. Photo by I. Français.

Stichelhaar

A rough-coated German gundog that has evolved from stock similar to other German wirehaired dogs, namely the Pudelpointer, the Pointing Griffon, and the German Wirehaired Pointer. It is likely that the Stichelhaar has been crossed at one time or another to any or all of the aforementioned breeds. Each breed, however, has developed into a distinct breed, each with an individualized nature. Consequently, the present-day Stichelhaar is much different than it was in the Germany of old, with more refined type and greater scope of hunting ability. Additionally, the infusion of German Shepherd blood has made for the Stichelhaar's less narrow and long muzzle. Incidentally, with all the emphasis on coat type, the breed has undergone a few name changes, each of which attempted to describe the coat more accurately. In English-speaking places, the breed is sometimes called the Broken-Coated Pointer. Straufhaarig (hard-haired) and Stichelhaarig (prick-haired)

are among the names that still stick out from yesterday. Many Stichelhaars today are registered as Drahthaars (German Wirehairs) and the differences between the two are continually dissolving. With registration numbers totaling under 20 each year, the Stichelhaar is facing the danger of extinction as a distinct breed type.

ESSENTIALS OF THE STICHELHAAR: Deutscher's bearded chin and brow. The Stichelhaar is relatively indistinguishable from the German Wirehaired Pointer. He is medium sized, standing 22–26 inches (56–66 cm) and weighing 44 pounds (20 kg). Body composed with good proportion and balance. The coat measures 1.5 inches (4 cm), although appearing shorter for it necessarily lays flat against the body; coat quality is paramount with the Broken-Coat as is the appropriate feathering on the muzzle, eyebrows, hindlegs and tail, which are to accentuate the overall coat covering. In color the Stichelhaar is white and brown in a roan pattern.

Stifle

Occasionally called the knee, the stifle is the joint of the hindlegs where the tibia is joined with the femur. The angle of the stifle determines the "hindquarter angulation." The common stifle-specific terms are: rugged stifle, straight in stifle, and well-turned stifle. Rugged stifles are clearly defined. Straight in stifle refers to dogs with very obtuse angles formed by the femur and tibia. Well-turned stifles are moderate angles formed by the femur and tibia; these are the most commonly desired. *See also* Hindquarters, angulation

Stilbestrol

A drug that has been used to treat various glandular conditions.

Stilted gait

The up and down, choppy gait of a

straight-hocked dog; the stiff, jerking gait caused by joints that are not flexing.

Stock dog

Term used to refer to a dog or breed of dog which works cattle, sheep, pigs, and/or numerous other farm/ranch animals. These dogs are typically agile, fearless, highly intelligent animals which perform an indispensable service to the livestock farmer. Stock-dog trials, which test the dog's ability to manipulate stock under given conditions, are increasing in popularity throughout the English-speaking world. Some breeds renowned for their stock-working ability include the Australian Cattle Dog, Australian Kelpie, English Shepherd, and Border Collie, which *see*. *See also* Herding dogs

Stockard's syndrome

A congenital condition cause by a triple set of dominant genes. It typically occurs in pups of three months of age but can occur anywhere between two and four months. It is marked by a motor neuron degeneration in the lumbar sections of the spinal cord. It appears more commonly in large breeds and cannot be treated. Signs include progressive paralysis and atrophy of the hindlegs, which are held in extension.

Stockings

White markings covering the feet and extending to cover a considerable portion of the legs. White markings that cover the feet and extend only to cover a maximum to the wrists in the forelegs

and to the hock in the rear legs are called socks, which *see*.

Stomach

The saclike organ found at the lower end of the esophagus and into which swallowed food enters and is partially digested by the acidic juices secreted into the saclike organ. The walls of the stomach are elastic to accommodate the varied amounts of food that enter at any given time. These elastic walls also mix their contents through expanding and contracting, churning motion. See also Digestive system, Vomiting.

Stomach, referring to the region of the dog's abdomen, is an unusual reference in the dog fancy.

Stomatitis

Mouth infection. Bleeding or swollen gums or excessive salivation may indicate this infection. Dirty teeth are usually the cause. Antibiotics and vitamin therapy are indicated; and, of course, scraping the teeth eliminates the original cause. *See also* Gingivitis

Stool eating

See Coprophagy

Stock dog. The Australian Shepherd, for a small herding dog, works terrifically on larger stock such as Hereford cattle. Photo courtesy of Joseph Hartnagle.

Stop

Located between the eyes, the stop is the sloping down of the skull at this area. The angle of the drop as well as the pronouncement of the area varies among breeds. Generally speaking, brachycephalic dogs have a pronounced stop while dolichocephalic dogs have a slight stop. Mesaticephalic dogs tend to have either defined or average stops.

Stop of the Cavalier King Charles Spaniel should be shallow. Photo by I. Français.

Stop to flush

Stopping by command, or preferably of the dog's own initiative, until commanded to go on, when a bird is accidentally or inadvertently flushed.

Stopper pad

A pad located above the wrist. It acts as a protective covering of the accessory bone and can serve a similar function to the pads of the feet when circumstances demand its coming into contact with surfaces.

Stove up

When a sled dog pulls up lame or stiff.

Straddle

A standing position in which the hindlegs form a wide angle, pointing away from the body, while the forelegs are positioned at a 90° angle with the body.

Straight

First place in a dog race; winning position at finish. Straight also refers to a hound running only one kind of game such as a Redbone Coonhound that is "straight on raccoon."

Straight front

The desired normal anatomical front structure: forearms running perpendicular to the ground, paralleling one another. Also called true front.

Straight hocks

See Hock types

Straight in shoulders

See Shoulder types

Stray dogs

Most cities and towns enforce licensing and leash laws to regulate the wandering of dogs, unsupervised, unowned, and unruly. It is, however, a fact that dogs stray and that stray dogs carouse at night in practically every locale that enforces a law against it. Humane societies and "dog catchers" help keep the lost, romantically adventuresome and/or riffraff canines off our streets—and back to their owners or to new, better confining homes. Owners who suspect that their dog has strayed from their property (either the dog is in the back yard or it's not!) should act immediately. Shelters for stray dogs are able to maintain the dogs for only a limited period, due to the high expense of operating such a service center and the sheer number of dogs.

There are many laws that pertain to stray dogs. Persons who adopt a straggly stray for a short period do not legally own the dog without the proper licensing. A veterinarian may euthanize a stray dog without the owner's consent in the case of an emergency. Many vets care for stray dogs without ever being compensated. It is refreshing to know that the veterinary profession is well stocked with sincere animal lovers as well as knowledgeable medical experts.

Streaming

The pack of hounds going across open country at full pace and cry.

Strellufstöver

The Strellufstöver, also known as the Danish Dachsbracke, was developed by Frands Christian Frandsen of Denmark. This breeder selectively crossed three hounds to acquire the desired features. The three contributors include the Westphalian Dachsbracke, the Smålandsstövare, and the Berner Laufhund. By the 1920s, the breed caused quite a ruckus in Denmark, with hunters quickly acclaiming the breed an instant expert on fox, hare and deer. Later the breed contributed to the make-up of the Drever, whose flashy jacket ironically has made him more popular. In Sweden alone, the Drever outnumbers the Strellufstövare 22 to 1.

ESSENTIALS OF THE STRELLUFSTÖVER: A close-coated, low-bodied hound that occurs in any color, the Strellufstöver stands 12–15 inches (30–38 cm) tall; despite the diminutive size, this is a powerful and muscular dog. The chest is deep, and the head is cleanly sculpted. Tail is long; the coat is efficient and all-purpose.

Streptococcus

Spherical, gram-positive bacteria that divide in only one plane and occur generally in chains. Streptococcus are common causative agents in infections of the intestines, bones and brain, as well as numerous other body parts of the dog, including the mucus tissues. When the bacteria attack red blood cells, their attack can lead to anemia.

Strike

To come upon the scent left by an animal in passing.

Strike hounds

Those hounds that possess the best ability in finding traces of a line.

Strip

The surface on which dogs race.

Stripping

Ridding a terrier's coat of dead hair by use of a stripping knife against one's thumb. When a plucking comb is used for the same purpose, it is called plucking. Stripping, like plucking, should not be attempted without professional guidance. *See also* Grooming

Stripping knife

Comes in fine, medium, and coarse

styles. Generally, fine is used on the head, ears, and areas where hair is fine and delicate. Medium and coarse blades are usually used on the body.

Stroke

Irreversible damage or even death may result from bleeding or hemorrhaging in the brain, known as apoplexy or stroke. The extent of damage is in direct relation to both the location of the ruptured vessel and the total area affected. Strokes are rare in dogs, but they do occur. With few to no warning signs, a stroke comes on quickly and unexpectedly. Partial or total unconsciousness may occur. Vomiting, anxiety, loss of balance or coordination and strength, paralysis, and uncontrolled movements are common signs in the partially unconscious victim. Prompt veterinary treatment is imperative.

Strellufstöver, tricolor.

Strongylidosis

Disease caused by strongylid worms that enter the body through the skin and lodge in the wall of the small intestine. Bloody diarrhea, stunted growth, and thinness are general symptoms, as well as shallow breathing. Heavy infestation or neglect leads to death. Isolation of an affected animal and medication will help eliminate the problem, but the premises must also be cleaned thoroughly since the eggs are passed through the feces.

Stubby muzzle

See Short muzzle

Stud book

A record for the breeding particulars of dogs of recognized breeds. Each registry has an official stud book which represents a breed's ancestry since its induction into the registry. Each kennel club maintains a stud book for each breed recognized; some clubs also hold the stud book of dog breeds whom they do not recognize. For instance, the A.K.C. holds the stud books for the Treeing Walker Coonhound and the Peruvian Inca Orchid, breeds which are not yet awarded Miscellaneous Class status. Miscellaneous breeds, and of course other completely unrecognized breeds, are not included in the official Stud Book. The English Setter "Adonis" was the first to enter the American Kennel Club's Stud Book in 1878.

Stud dog

A male used for breeding purposes. The stud dog is typically prepotent, that is, he has the ability to pass on his genetic superiority regardless of the quality of the female. Of course, the female should also be an outstanding specimen, for her faults can appear not only in her litters but also in the litters of her litters. Most all kennels have at least one resident stud for their own use and which is often hired for stud work to outside breeders.

The term "stud fee" refers to the sum exchanged for the services of the stud dog. Usually this involves a monetary sum and a pick of the litter. The stud fee can vary considerably depending on the quality and breeding history of the stud and the relative rarity of the breed.

The stud dog should be carefully considered in relation to the strengths and weaknesses of the bitch and his close conformation to the breed standard. The pedigree of the stud also should be investigated, for it is not unheard of for a dog of great quality to emerge from an otherwise mediocre line. Such a dog may not pass desirable traits with the same reliability as a dog from a solid, excellent line, but such matters are highly subject to variability. Several studs should be reviewed before selection, and only the best possible complement to the bitch should be chosen. *See also* Breeding, Bitch

Stuffy neck

A short, block neck that lacks elegance and is usually over muscled.

Stumpy tail

A tail that is naturally shorter than might be desired in a particular breed. In the Stumpy-tail Cattle Dog, a dog virtually the same as the Australian Cattle Dog except for its tail, a stumpy tail, the breed's hallmark, is certainly desirable. In Schipperke, a similar tail is desirable.

Stumpy-tail Cattle Dog

The Stumpy-tail Cattle Dog of Australia is essentially the tailless version of the Australian

Stumpy tail usually refers to a tail shorter than desired. The Entelbucher has a docked tail.

Cattle Dog. The first specimens recorded were known as Timmins' Biters, and selective breeding fixed the tailless type. In appearance and herding abilities, the dog emulates its tailed cousin. The Stumpy-tail breed is recognized by the F.C.I. even though its numbers are few today.

ESSENTIALS OF THE STUMPY-TAIL CATTLE DOG: An Australian Cattle Dog without a tail. *See* Australian Cattle Dog

Stuttgart disease

See Leptospirosis

Styptics

Styptic pencils or powders prove useful to have on hand when clipping a dog's nails. Applying these to a cut nail, if bleeding should occur, will tend to halt bleeding by contracting the tissues or blood vessels. Alum is one such substance used in pencils and powders. *See also* Nail clipping

Styrian Roughhaired Mountain Hound

The Styrian Roughhaired Mountain Hound is known in its native Austria as the Steirischer Rauhaarige Hochgebirgsbracke; for short, he is sometimes called the Peintinger, after his founder. Herr Peintinger developed the breed from indigenous Austrian hounds as well as German hounds and the Roughhaired Istrian Hound of Yugoslavia. Within 20 years of Peintinger's initial crossings in 1870, the breed was recognized. The Styrian is robustly constructed to withstand the extreme climatic conditions under which he would have to work. Good voice and untiring stamina were required of this little hound that was to be used extensively on the hunt. He is also able to silent trail. Although not widely known outside Austria, the Peintinger has a solid basis at home and a club to insure its

continual sound hunting ability.

ESSENTIALS OF THE STYRIAN ROUGHHAIRED MOUNTAIN HOUND: Relatively long in the body, it is a rough-coated hound—the coat is hard and coarse but not shaggy. The wire coat is inclined towards feathering. Alternatively, the breed can have a short straight jacket that is without shine. Height: 17–21 inches (43–53 cm). Weight: 33–38 pounds (15–17.5 kg). The breed's coloration varies from red to wheaten; a white spot on the chest is permissible. The head is straight with a noticeable stop; the feet are small and the toes are well arched.

Subluxation

Not a true dislocation of a joint, it is a partial or mild separation, a common complication of the shoulder.

Substance

Refers to the bone development. It is most commonly preceded by an adjective such as good, heavy, or insufficient.

Sudan Greyhound

A small coursing dog native to Sudan used on small game.

Styrian Roughhaired Mountain Hound, wheaten. Photo by I. Français.

Sussex Spaniel,
golden liver.
Photo by I.
Français.

Sumatra Battak

Sumatra, a large island of Indonesia just south of the Malay peninsula, has produced in the Sumatra Battak an extraordinary alarm and hunting dog. This active, compact dog was bred as a guard, watchful but shy, never fierce. As a hunter, the dog exhibits a moderately good nose and works almost exclusively in packs. The Battak people select their dogs for hunting based on special physical characteristics, not testing their ability. A fine hunter should have a tail that fits into the middle of the back or that curls three times into itself; hair that twists behind the ears, on the loins and on the feet; a white muzzle and white tail tip. A quality hunting dog has a value equivalent to a male slave or a young girl (on the island). The dogs are said to be particularly fearful of Caucasians and are shy overall. The dog's flesh is also prized by the natives, who consider it a delicacy. Roasted Battak is said to taste much like veal or chicken. The dogs participate in the tribe's lifestyle, bathing with the women and keeping guard over their clothes, and remaining indoors much of the time. Like the larger Telomian of Malaysia (which *see*), this pariah-type dog climbs ladders to enter its master's sleeping quarters. Ladders can be up to 15-feet high.

In appearance, the Sumatra Battak is a strong little dog with a short thick-set neck, firmly attached to the shoulders. Its expression is lively and clever. The back is straight with well-arched ribs. The head resembles that of a German Spitz. The coat is hard, short and thick, with little hair on the chest. In color the dog is red with black markings, rust brown or gray-brown brindle. Clay and soot, yellow/white and solid black also occur. Height: 12–18 inches (30.5–46 cm).

The tail is curly and brushlike. Stumpy tails are common, especially in the northern Malayan states, where docking is used to distinguish the hunters from the watchdogs. Additionally, a piece of the ear is cut off or cropped entirely for this same reason, or simply out of superstition. *See also* Dogs as delicacy

Sunken pasterns

Same as down in pasterns, which *see.*

Sunstroke

See Heatstroke

Suomenajokoira

See Finnish Hound

Suomenpystykorva

See Finnish Spitz

Superciliary ridges

The region of the skull above the eyes.

Superintendent

One who acts in a professional capacity in handling many or all of the arrangements in connection with a show for a dog club.

Sussex Spaniel

The Sussex can be truthfully described as a hard-working dog, although today and historically he has been perceived as a companion dog first. The truth is that he is an extraordinary flusher in dense undergrowth, equally on birds and small fur-bearing animals. This race of spaniels has been peculiar to Sussex County, England, where the first and vital kennel of a Mr. Fuller was located. It is at this kennel that the distinctive rich golden color was developed. The physical characteristics of the Sussex—the heavy skin, long low-set ears, compact massiveness, and prominent flew—would suggest that the low-stationed hounds were important contributing ancestors of the Sussex. Unlike the other spaniels, the Sussex chimes in with a bell voice, giving tongue on the trail; his vocal inflection tells the hunter what kind of game is being pursued. When the terrain is tough and the game is plentiful, the Sussex has proven himself highly successful. His numbers are limited in the U.S. and Canada, however, where the hunting conditions are different.

Perhaps the breed's similarities to the Cocker Spaniels or its meandering between working and toy dog explain the breed's moderate popularity as a show dog. It certainly cannot be attributed to his abilities or personality. He is cheerful and easily trained, a consistently good retriever and an unswervable scenter.

ESSENTIALS OF THE SUSSEX SPANIEL: Light liver tinged with gold, low stationed and long, the Sussex Spaniel is a truly unique spaniel. The coat is abundant and flat with a slight wave. Feathering is generous. Golden liver (rich) is the only acceptable color, and it is a distinguishing feature of the Sussex breed. Height: 13–15.5 inches (33–38 cm). Weight 40–45 pounds (18–20 kg). The body is solid—the back is long and very muscular, both in length and in width; the chest is round, deep and wide, giving good girth. The legs are heavily boned, short, and muscular; the hindlegs are short from the hock to the ground, and wide apart. The tail should be docked from 5–7 inches (13–17 cm), set low, and not carried above the level of the back.

Swan neck
Goose neck. A swan neck is a listed fault in the Dachshund standard.

Sweater
1) Dog that loses weight, through fretting, or sweating while in holdout kennels while waiting its turn to race. Some dogs lose as much as four pounds while in such confinement. Also called "weight loser."

2) Sweater, in smaller-dog circles, refers to specially tailored garments worn by toy dogs, especially smoothhaired or hairless ones.

Swedish Cattledog
See Swedish Vallhund

Swedish Dachsbracke
See Drever

Swedish Elkhound
See Jämthund

Swedish Grey Dog
This elkhound type is essentially the same as the Gray Norwegian Elkhound, belonging to the Peat Dog group, the northern ancestor of *Canis familiaris ladogensis*. It, like a Norwegian dog, is referred to in literature as the Grahund. The breeds evolved in Scandinavia from local dogs, as did the other elkhound types. The dog is medium sized, being smaller than the Jämthund and about the same size as the Norwegian Elkhound.

Sweater sported by a sporty Italian Greyhound. Photo by I. Français.

Swedish Lapp Spitz
See Swedish Lapphund

Swedish Lapphund, black. Photo by I. Français.

Swedish Lapphund

The development of the breed today known as the Swedish Lapphund traces back to the dogs that were kept by the Lapp people. These European natives lived in the area known as Lapland, which includes Sweden, Finland and parts of northern Russia and Norway. The Lapland Dogs or Swedish Lapp Spitz, as they were once known, were brought to England by the Normans. The dogs that were adopted by Swedish dog lovers became known as the Swedish Lapphund, while the dogs that endeared themselves to the Finns became known as the Finnish Lapphund. The F.C.I. recognizes each as a separate breed. They are especially useful as draft dogs and adept at reindeer herding, their most natural activity.

ESSENTIALS OF THE SWEDISH LAPPHUND: A medium-sized, well-coated nordic-type dog with a sturdy square body and squarish head, high set triangular ears and a prominent muzzle. The coat is abundant and harsh, feathers persist throughout, even onto the legs. The tail is fully plumed and rests on the back. Height: 17.5–19.5 inches (44–49 cm). Weight: 44 pounds (20 kg). The undercoat is thick and woolly. In color the breed is usually solid black or liver, although white marks are neither uncommon nor objectionable.

Swedish Vallhund

Called also the Vasgotaspets and Swedish Cattle Dog, the breed is an old and indigenous dog of Sweden, known for its cattle herding ability. The Vallhund is undoubtedly a hardy dog of good strength and all-weather ability.

Cynologists and others have argued for years over the origin of the Vasgotaspets. Certainly old, this small cattle dog, closely resembling the Pembroke Corgi in conformation, may have been transported by Vikings to Britain or spawned from imported Pembies brought to Sweden. Although to Western eyes the Swedish Vallhund is less attractive than the Pembie, he is no less of a utility dog. The *Vallhund*, translating as forest dog, is a canine of many talents: a cattle drover, watchdog, ratter and versatile farmhand. A responsive and even-tempered companion, the Vallhund is both intelligent and affectionate, a comfortable blend of heart and mind. He is a more and more common sight at European exhibitions. Among the clubs that recognize the breed is the Kennel Club of Great Britain.

ESSENTIALS OF THE SWEDISH VALLHUND: A small, sturdily built working dog of long body and watchful, alert, and energetic character. The head is rather long and clean cut, a blunt wedge with an almost flat skull and well-defined stop. The muzzle, when viewed from the side, appears almost square, slightly shorter than the length of the skull. A well-defined mask with lighter hairs around the eyes is highly desirable, and a foxlike expression is paramount. The ears are medium size, pointed, pricked, and of hard leather from base to tip, but smoothhaired and mobile. Shoulder blades are long and well laid. Back is level and well muscled. Chest is long, with good depth and well sprung ribs. The belly is slightly tucked up. The harness marking should be clearly defined. The coat is medium in length and harsh in texture. The top coat is close and tight. Height: 13–16 inches (33–40.5 cm). Weight: 20–32 pounds (9–14.5 kg). In color the Vasgotaspets can be steel gray, grayish brown, grayish yellow, reddish yellow, or reddish brown. A fractional amount of white markings are tolerated.

Sweep
A mild curve to the tail. Same as swirl.

Swine mouth
See Bite

Swinford Bandog
See Bandog

Swing dog
A sled dog that runs directly behind the leader either on the right side of the tow line (right swing dog) or on the left side (left swing dog).

Swirl
A mild curve to the tail.

Swiss Hound
See Schweizer Laufhund

Switching
In hunting, leaving one bird or the area of one fall for another.

Sword tail
If carried upright, a sword tail is synonymous with a flagpole tail. A sword tail, however, is naturally carried down without deviation.

Sydney Silky
See Silky Terrier

Symmetry
A dog with symmetry has balance and harmony between its parts and regions, with no one component (such as the head, shoulders, legs, or hindquarters) dominating or detracting.

Systems
In conformation and obedience competitions, various systems have been de-signed to measure the performance of dogs in the given area, ranking dogs according to a specific point or accomplishment criteria. The Phillips Systems, compiled by Mrs. Irene Phillips (Schlintz), began as an annual feature in

Swedish Vallhund, grayish brown. Photo by I. Français.

Popular Dogs magazine in the mid-1950s. It is designed to measure performances of show dogs in conformation competition in direct correlation with the number of dogs in a given show. This system acknowledges that a win over 1,000 dogs is more significant than a win over 100 dogs, and thereby awards points in accordance with the number of competitors over which the win was scored. In obedience competition, there are two leading systems, the Shuman System and the Delaney System. The former, the Shuman, was developed in 1974 by Nancy Shuman and Lynn Frosh to record the top ten obedience dogs in the U.S. The latter system, the Delaney, came forth the following year (1975) and was first published in *Front and Finish*. All three systems discussed here are based on point accumulations as reported in the *American Kennel Gazette,* the official publication of the A.K.C.

Tahltan Bear Dog and the Nova Scotia Duck Tolling Retriever honored on postage stamps by Canada, the dogs' native country.

T.A.F.

Transfer of ownership applied for with the Kennel Club of Great Britain.

Tachycardia

Abnormal acceleration of the heartbeat. A rapid pulse signaling a disruption in the heart action. Contact a vet at once.

Tahltan Bear Dog

The Tahltan's small size is no indication of its hunting abilities or fearlessness. The Tahltan Indians who bred him were very protective of their dogs and passed the breeding stock down from generation to generation. The Indians used the dogs to hunt black bears and grizzlies, as well as lynx. The Tahltan's hunting style was to distract the victim by circling it

and pelting it with its staccato yelps. Although not standing more than 15 inches (38 cm) at the shoulder, the Tahltan was fierce and brave enough to confront bears many times its size—darting and nipping at the bear and retreating swiftly before the deadly black-pawed retaliation. Its astounding hunting abilities, like its cry, are pervadingly vulpine. The Indians felt it necessary to engage in preparatory hunting rites to rouse the Tahltans for the kill. This ritual involved stabbing the dogs in the hindquarters with a wolf's fibula bone and then canvas-sacking the dogs until bear tracks were sighted. The dogs were toughened through this ritual which incidentally made the chore of porcupine hunting that much more tolerable. The decline in the number of Tahltans is associated with the lack of demand for bearskins, leaving the remaining specimens to rest unemployed on bare, uncovered floors.

In appearance, the Tahltan resembled a cross between a fox and a terrier, with a distinctive, and comical, shaving-brush tail standing at attention and glassy electric eyes dancing wildly in their sockets. The coat is short and dense. The color is black/white or blue-gray/white. Height: 12–15 inches (30.5–38 cm). Maximum weight did not exceed 15 pounds (6.5–7 kg). The tail, the Tahltan's flag of uniqueness, is long, thick, carried erect, and finishes with rather an explosive-cigar effect. The dogs usually had solid black heads with irregular black-and-white patches over the body. The dog's thick coat, tolerance to icy inclemency and hunting proclivities have allowed certain cynologists to include the dog with nordic breeds instead of pariahs. Depending on criteria, either categorization is apropos, although the breed is assuredly of pariah lineage.

The "missing" Mrs. Harriet A. Morgan was the last breeder of Tahltans in Canada before she picked up herself, sacked her Tahltans, and moved to California in 1951. No one knows what became of Mrs. Morgan and her odd kennel of Indian dogs. No new dogs have been registered since that time. The Canadian Kennel Club recognizes this native North American breed and is the only registry to grant status. The Canadian Post Office issued a commemorative stamp featuring the Tahltan Bear Dog in 1988 to mark the centennial of the nation's kennel club.

Taigan

The Taigan was for many years a commonly recognized sighthound in his native Russian homeland. Along the Russo-Chinese border extends a land rugged and steep. Elevations can exceed 7,000 feet (2,100 m). For coursing the fox, marmot, badger, hare, wildcat, wolf, and various hooved game of the area, a strong enduring dog was required. Inhabitants of the area selectively bred a classic sighthound type to yield a hunter effective on this terrain. The Taigan was this hunter. However, as the game and necessity of procuring food by the hunt waned, the glorious Taigan experienced less demands. His numbers declined as a result, as have so many native working dogs. Most dogs today are probably crossbred due to the general scarcity. The sleekness, the grace, the elegance, the beautiful coat, the courage, strength, endurance, and long history of dedicated service are all qualities of the Taigan which make it undeserving of the near extinction it now faces.

ESSENTIALS OF THE TAIGAN: The chest is deep, allowing for excellent lung capacity; his build is lithe, with fine bone, tight muscle, lean neck, and good tuck-up. The head is lean and tapered; the eyes, commonly hazel in color, express determination. The warm coat is thick and double, with heavy feathering on the tail, ears, thighs, shoulders, and front legs. Height: 22–28 inches (56–71 cm).

Tail

The tail is the hindmost portion of the dog's anatomy; it is the portion of the spinal column where the coccygeal or caudal vertebrae gradually taper to a tip. Not all dogs have tails. And not all dogs that have tails have tails of the same length, thickness, or curve. Some American standards state a preference for a docked tail, often stating the specific vertebrae at which the docking should occur. Docking tails has been outlawed in Great Britain. *See also* Tail types, Docking

Taigan, white with black. Photo by V. Pcholkin.

Tail base

The base of the tail is that portion of the tail located just prior to the point where the caudal vertebrae are continued with the lumbar vertebrae by the intercession of the sacrum. The point where the base is joined to the sacrum is commonly known as the set-on of the tail.

Tail carriage

The way in which the caudal vertebrae are presented, or carried. This can vary depending on activity and attitude.

Tail docking

See Docking

Tail feather

See Feather

Tail hounds

Dogs at the rear of the pack.

Tail root

See Tail base

Tail types

Within the world of dogs there exist numerous different tails, distinguished by shape, length, thickness, and degree of

Tail types. The desired tail for the Sloughi must have a strong curve at the end, reach at least to the point of hock; when moving, tail should not be carried higher than level of back. Photo courtesy of Mosica Arabians.

coat coverage. The commonly used tail-type terms are listed alphabetically in this text. They are: bee sting tail; bob tail; brush tail (fox-brush and round fox-brush tail); carrot-shaped tail; cocked-up tail; cork screw tail; crank tail; crook tail; curled tail; docked tail (syn. clipped); flagpole tail; flat tail; gay/gaily carried tail; gnarled tail; hook tail; horizontal tail; kink tail; making the wheel tail; merry tail; otter tail; pipe stopper tail; plume tail; pot-hook tail; rat tail; ring tail; ropy tail; saber tail; scimitar tail; screw tail; sickle tail; squirrel tail; stumpy tail; sword tail; tapering tail; tufted tail; twisted tail; upward hook tail; and whip tail, which *see*.

Tajgan
See Taigan

Talbot Hound
The Talbot Hound is the white variety of the black and tan Southern Hound which contributed to the make up of the Bloodhound. St. Hubert is known to have bred and hunted both Talbots and Southern Hounds.

Tall Transylvanian Hound
See Transylvanian Hound

Tally-ho
The cheer announcing the viewing of a fox. Used in formal hunting.

Tapering head
Head V-shaped and long with a mostly imperceptible stop.

Tapering muzzle
Wedge-shaped muzzle, also called pointed muzzle.

Tapering tail
A short-coated, lengthy tail that tapers to a point (e.g., English Toy Terrier).

Tapeworm
There are many types of tapeworms, the most common being the variety passed along by the flea. It is a white, segmented worm which lives off the wall of the dog's intestine and keeps growing by segments. Some of these are passed and can be seen in the stool or adhering to the hairs on the rear areas of the dog or even in his bedding. It is a difficult worm to get rid of since, even if medication eliminates segments, the head may remain in the intestinal wall to grow again. Symptoms are virtually the same as for other worms: debilitation, loss of weight, occasional diarrhea, and general listlessness. Medication and treatment should be under the supervision of a veterinarian. *See also* Parasites

Tarsal bones
See Hocks, Hindquarters

Tarsus
See Hock

Tartar
Dental calculus that builds up on a dog's teeth. Large accumulations of tartar contribute to bad breath odor, bacterial infection, gum recession and tooth decay. The dog's teeth must not go unattended. Severe cases of infection can lead to tooth loss, heart problems and arthritis. A veterinarian is able to clean your dog's teeth—this should be done on an annual basis. Scaling and cleaning a

dog's teeth is one method of preventing tartar accumulation. Additionally, owners need to provide the dog with a hard chew bone. The nylon type bones have proven the safest and most effective. *See also* Dental care, Periodontitis, Nylon bones, Chewing

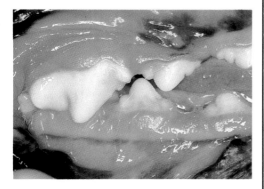

Tasy

Like a strong breeze off the Caspian Sea, the Tasy courses the vast deserts of the windswept area east of this sea, where he is used to great effect on hare, marmot, fox, various hooved game, and even an occasional wolf. Unlike many coursing hounds, who rely purely on their acute eyesight for effectiveness, the Tasy has a nose sensitive enough to track game and begin the chase before the victim is in sight. So necessary were these dogs to the survival of men in years past that they were prized above any other animal as a possession. A report states that a purebred Tasy could once command a price of 47 horses in his native land. The incessant march of modernization, however, has trampled the breed to near extinction. Presently a few dedicated individuals are working hard to preserve this deserving breed. Tasy should not be confused with Tazi, which is a name given to the Afghan Hound.

ESSENTIALS OF THE TASY: The tapered head, the lissome body, the deep chest, good tuck, and runner's legs all suggest coursing hound. Though a tough, enduring fleet hound, the Tasy lacks the refinement desired in most westernized greyhounds. Some notable features are his ring tail and silky yet protective coat, with heavy fringe on the ears, legs and tail. Height: 22–28 inches (56–71 cm). Color: tan, black and tan, or gray.

Tatra Mountain Sheepdog
See Owczarek Podhalanski

Tartar encrusting the teeth causes bad breath, gum disease, and tooth loss.

Tasy, tan. Photo by V. Pcholkin.

Tattooing is the most positive means of identifying a dog. As illustrated by this upstanding member of canine society, the Greyhound, tattoos most often are engraved on a dog's thigh.

Teacup Poodles represent the tiniest Poodle possible, though many breeders have giant reservations about producing super tiny dogs. Photographs by R. Pearcy.

Tattooing

In recent years, tattooing has become a well-accepted form of identifying dogs, purebreds and mixed breeds alike. The purpose of tattooing is the positive identification of your dog in the case of theft or loss; additionally, breeders should subscribe to the notion of tattooing to prove the true identity of a puppy, in this day of such unscrupulous puppy switching. Tattooing the dog's registration number or the owner's social security number on the dog's groin has a 90-percent success rate, and many dog clubs and kennel organizations have programs to help locate tattooed dogs in case of loss or theft. Tattooing is inexpensive and will not detract from a purebred's show career (indeed, it could save it!).

Taut coat

Wrinkleless, tightly stretched skin (e.g., German Shorthaired Pointer).

Tawny Britanny Basset

See Basset Fauve de Bretagne

Tax deductions

No matter how many dogs you own, these beloved family members cannot be written off as dependents. Nor is the master of a one-person, eighteen-dog household legally considered the head of a household and therefore eligible for such tax benefits. Guide dogs for the blind or signal dogs for the deaf are the only exceptions and are generally written off as medical expenses. If indeed other dog owners out there have devised ways to convince the I.R.S. to accept the Poodle as a person, do not hesitate to contact the authors!

Tazi

See Afghan Hound

T.D.

Suffix for Tracking Dog; this signifies that the dog, having acquired at least the C.D. degree under the rules, has been "passed" by two judges officiating at the same time, in an outdoor tracking test under rules set forth by the appropriate governing body.

T.D.X.

Suffix meaning Tracking Dog Excellent, which *see.*

Teacup Poodles

Teacup Poodles or Tiny Toy Poodles, as they are sometimes called, are the smallest type of Poodle. These miniatures are derived from crosses of the smallest Toy Poodles available. They are not quite small enough to fit into a teacup as the name suggests, but could sit cozily in a tea kettle. These dogs, like other tiny breeds, have certain breeding and health considerations that owners and breeders must be aware of. The dogs often tend toward hypoglycemia and may need a spoonful of honey if such an attack occurs. Only experienced breeders should ever toy with these tiniest of tots. At present, these dogs are not recognized by any national registry as a separate breed (i.e. differing from Toy Poodle).

Team dogs

Dogs hitched into the team between the swing dogs and the wheel dogs, which *see*.

Tears

Specifically, tears are drops of the salty substance secreted by the lacrimal gland, which normally serves to lubricate the eyeball. The maintenance of a regular flow of this lubricating substance is essential to the optical health of your dog. Dry eyes, the absence of sufficient lacrimal fluid, is a serious condition that requires prompt veterinary attention. The possible causes are many, treatment varies accordingly. Excessive tearing is also an abnormal condition, but is one of less concern. The cause is often bacterial in nature and cured with antibiotics.

Teckel

German term for dachshund or short-legged dog.

Teeth, cramped

Crowded, irregular alignment. In the short-faced breeds, cramped teeth can be due to molars or premolars; generally the condition is caused by inadequately wide dental arches.

Teething

Puppies at the age of about 10–15 weeks begin to lose their baby teeth (or milk teeth); 12 weeks is about average. The milk teeth will simply fall out; while the puppy's mouth may be sore and bloody, swallowing these temporary teeth should have no effect on him. Within a few days, the permanent teeth begin to come through. A puppy that receives a well-balanced diet (including a mineral supplement) should have no problem in developing strong, straight teeth. If you notice that your puppy's permanent teeth are beginning to surface before the milk teeth have fallen out, it is wise to con-

sult your veterinarian. This high-traffic situation can result in crooked perma-

nent teeth. Milk teeth can be extracted by a vet with little trouble.

Teething is generally uncomfortable for puppies, just as it is for babies. The process may last up to six months, with the problem-potential times early in this period. Puppies differ in the length of time that teething takes as well as in the level of discomfort they experience. Providing the puppy with a hard chew object will satisfy his teething needs and prevent him from damaging furniture (or his teeth) by gnawing on whatever his new choppers decide to experiment on. A Gumabone® is most ideal for teething puppies. *See also* Nylon bones, Chewing

Teething is a trying process for all puppies. Necessarily owners must provide puppies with proper outlets for chewing with their changing teeth. Belgian Sheepdog pup (*above*), photographed by V. Serbin, and English Setter clan (*below*), photographed by R. Reagan.

Telomian

Perhaps the missing link between the Basenji and the Dingo, the Telomian is an ancient breed of dog that originated in Malaysia and was fostered by the aborigines. The aborigines and the Telomian share many aspects of everyday life. In

Telomian, sable with white. Photo by Carole May Easley.

order to sleep with his master, the Telomian climbs a ladder each night to the aborigine's stilt-standing hut. His diet, the same as his master's, consists mostly of tapioca, fish and fruit. The Telomian's great intelligence and lack of fear makes him an ample protector (from snakes and other slimy, injurious types) and an avid catcher of fish. Dr. Orville Elliot is responsible for discovering the Telomian dogs in 1962. These dogs were kept by aborigines in Malaysia. The islanders were cooperative with Dr. Elliot, who obtained a pair and who is responsible for introducing the breed to the Western world. The breed entered the public eye in 1970. Dogs today grow to be a tad larger than the Telomians of yesterday, due to their more substantial diets. The Telomian is similar to the Basenji in many respects, including the growl-like crow and single estrus cycle.

The breed is extremely sociable with humans if properly socialized and accli-mated to people at an early age. These are clever and uncannily smart dogs that are a constant source of diversion and delight for their masters, who insist that they are difficult to confine because of their proclivity for climbing.

ESSENTIALS OF THE TELOMIAN: An efficiently sized pariah-type dog with a sleek and amiable appearance. The Telomian has a medium-sized head topped by slightly rounded ears, always erect. Height: 15–19 inches (38–48 cm). Weight: 18–28 pounds (8–13 kg). The coat is short and smooth and can occur in any shade of sable with white. Speckling may occur in the white areas. The Telomian's face is wrinkled similarly to the Basenji.

Temperament Test

Test performed to evaluate the behavior of a dog when confronted with various threatening, non-threatening, and unusual stresses. The leading organization in the field of temperament testing is the American Temperament Test Society, Inc. (A.T.T.S.). This organization was founded by the late Alfons Ertlet, who believed that the most important quality of any dog was its good temperament. After much field testing of its evaluation concept, the A.T.T.S. held its first official testing in late 1977. Since that first test, the A.T.T.S. has evaluated thousands of dogs and continues to hold evaluations on a regular basis. The test is open to all dogs, purebred and mongrel alike, over one year of age. The dog, handled by the owner or trainer on a six-foot lead, is subjected to a series of standardized stress situations, during which the dog's reaction and recovery time (the two most important considerations in the test) are

evaluated by a registered A.T.T.S. tester. The test also considers the individual dog's age, breed, background, training, and sex. There is no competition in the evaluation: each dog is evaluated on an individual basis and is granted simply a pass or fail for its performance. Purebred dogs which pass the temperament test are awarded a T.T. certificate and are entitled to bear the T.T. suffix in their title. Additionally, all dogs and owners are provided by the A.T.T.S. with a critique of the dog's performance. In this way, dog owners can see their dog's temperament strengths and weaknesses and take any steps or make any adjustments necessary.

Despite the many merits and growing popularity of temperament testing, some dog fanciers are less than satisfied with the state of testing today. Critics point especially to the fact that the tests are standardized, which they claim allows owners to train their dogs specially to pass the test—thus earning the T.T., and thereby becoming more valuable as breeding stock. Critics claim that awards based on such testing prove little about the actual temperament of the dog and strongly encourage the A.T.T.S. to "unstandardize" their testing procedures. Nonetheless, many dog owners and breeders remain committed to the work and benefits which the A.T.T.S. has thus far provided to the dog fancy and congratulate them on their efforts. The ulti-

mate goal of temperament testing is to remove shyness, viciousness, and other undesirable behavioral characteristics from our dogs.

Temperature
The dog's normal body temperature is 101.5° F. Smaller breeds have higher body temperatures, as high as 102° F., and larger breeds have lower ones, as low as 99.5° F. As in humans, body temperature can be a measuring device for infection. *See also* Fever

Temples
The slight depression or hollow on either side of the skull just behind the orbit or eye socket. The trumpet, as the temples are called in canine terminology, are comparable to man's temples.

Temperament Tests involve exposing the dog to a series of unfamiliar and potentially stressful situations to determine how the dog will react. These three illustrations by R. Pearcy capture distinct moments where dogs undergoing testing encounter strange obstacles or new sensations.

Tendon

Sinews or tendons are the relatively inelastic fibrous tissues that form at the end of a muscle in its attachment to the bone. The Achilles tendon is the largest and most powerful tendon in the dog.

Tenerife dogs

The modern-day Bichon Frise is the likely descendant of the dogs of Tenerife which arrived in France in the 1700s. These dogs also gave way to other bichon types, including the Bolognese of Italy and the Havanese of Cuba. *See also* Bichon Frise, Bolognese, Havanese

Terrier Group. Three of the largest members of the Terrier Group: the Kerry Blue Terrier, Soft Coated Wheaten Terrier, and Airedale Terrier. Photo by R. Pearcy.

Tepeizeuintli

See Mexican Hairless

Terrier Brasileiro

See Brazilian Terrier

Terrier front

The long-legged forequarters with parallel-running forearms and a wide chest typical of the bigger terriers or other similarly constructed dogs. Term is sometimes used to describe a fault.

Terrier Group

Most kennel clubs categorize the terrier breeds together in a group appropriately called the Terrier Group. Dogs which are included are those which would have once all been called simply "terriers"; since the specification of breeds came about, a variety of specific types (or breeds, if we must) are treated separately, though all placed together in the show ring for competition. Pinschers, schnauzers, terriers—terriers all! *See also* Group systems

Terrier Noir Russe

See Black Russian Terrier

Terriers

Terriers derive from hounds, as is suggested by the ever popular Dachshund, a hound that functions much in the manner of a terrier. Terriers are to digging as the sighthounds are to running and scenthounds are to tracking. The Latin *terra* means earth, hence these dogs were once referred to as "earth dogges." The terriers' quarry varies: rats, badgers, foxes, otters, snakes, weasels, marmots and mice.

Size and temperament were crucial to the dog's success in its prescribed task. The general small size of the dog allowed the individual terrier to enter a badger or other ground hole. Going to ground required not only a small size dog but also a fearless and tough dog, with no qualms about going head to head with an infuriated rat or badger.

Terriers were the much loved and much needed companions of farmers throughout the ages. As rats have been a source of irritation and destruction since the dawn of humanity, dogs were used to exterminate the grain-eating rats. Terriers were also used in the rat pit in England and Ireland. Terriers would be clocked and the number of rats killed in that period recorded. This parallels animal baiting and dog fighting in tastefulness. Terrier companions today have strong hearts and strong stomachs.

While most of the terriers are rather

diminutive (the Norwich, Skye, Cairn, Dandie Dinmont, and Jack Russell), there are a few very tall exceptions (the Airedale, Soft Coated Wheaten, and Kerry Blue).

In days gone by, times when specialization was a term undefined, terriers were terriers and there weren't breeds divided as such. Hunters and farmers, breeders and fanciers, began to hunt, work, breed and fancy particular qualities in their terriers. The differences between the Cairn, Skye, West Highland White, and Dandie Dinmont evolved as dog people selected for a trait (coat color, ear set, size, etc.).

people are very active in both worlds. Other terriers that infrequently participate in the show world today are strictly

The terrier temperament is exhibited in the show ring, a competition gratefully far removed from England's rat pits of yesterday. Sparring terriers—facing two or three dogs against each other—is still practiced to verify their gameness. Many of the show ring terriers are also working terriers. Lakeland, Welsh and Border

workmen: the Patterdale, German Hunting, Jack Russell and Glen of Imaal. Many of the terriers have been miniaturized so effectively that they reign as true monarchs over the toy group: the Miniature Pinscher, Brussels Griffon, English Toy Terrier, Silky Terrier, and AmerToy (or Toy Fox Terrier).

The Fox Terriers have been hailed among the British terriers as the "gentlemen of the terrier world." In their elegance, good looks and outstanding working ability, both the Smooth and Wire have strong dog world followings.

Terriers. Working Jack Russell bitch being commissioned into a large fox den by terrier man Greg Mousley at a hunt in Derbyshire, England.

Terriers. The gameness and spirit of the Patterdale Terrier can scarcely be denied. Training often involves working a hide on a wheel. Photo by I. Français.

Terriers. Welsh Terriers exploring a woodchuck hole. Photo courtesy of Bardi McLennan.

Testicles

Spermatozoa-producing and -storing gonads of the male. The testes store the male sex hormone testosterone.

Testosterone

A male steroid hormone found in both sexes but in greater levels in the male. The major production factories in the male are the testes.

Tetanus

Lockjaw. An acute infectious disease caused by the specific toxin of a bacillus, *Clostridium tetani*, which usually enters the body through wounds, especially puncture wounds. Signs include involuntary actions and contractions (including spasms) and the characteristic stiffening of some or all of the voluntary muscles, especially those of the jaw, face, and neck. The disease can prove fatal but is typically treatable with antibiotics and antitoxins.

Thai Ridgeback Dog

Contrary to the common belief that the Siamese cat is the only domestic purebred animal to derive from Thailand, the Thai Ridgeback Dog is an ancient purebred which has survived in the rural parts of Thailand for centuries, without ever stirring the interest of West-ern purebred-dog enthusiasts. Originating in the eastern part of the country, the breed is a multi-functional hound-like dog that works for Thai peasants as a home protector, hunting companion, and cart escort.

While the Siamese cat was the national favorite in cities—as urbanites had no use for such a sizeable, fierce canine—the Thai Ridgeback found favor and employment in the rural areas in the eastern part of the country. This geographical factor figures both into the breed's lack of international fame as well as the breed's purity. Until around 1940, such eastern regions as the Trad Province remained virtually without any communication or access to major urban centers, such as Thailand's capital city, Bangkok. (Transportation, mostly by cart, would have taken perhaps months—by car, of which there were hardly any, the trek would require two days.) It is known that keepers of the dogs never crossed the dog with non-Ridgebacks, and therefore the breed has been preserved as a single race for countless generations, if in only relatively small numbers. Such breeding practices are typically associated with the Thai people, renowned for their propensity to maintain a great number of rich traditions and customs.

Not until 1975 had any international attention been given the Thai Dog; it was in this year that the Dog Association of Thailand was established. F.C.I. had been slow to take notice of the breed. Not unlike the Siamese cat, whose fame exceeds the fame of the Thailand nation itself, the Thai Ridgeback is a striking purebred, whose devotion to his master and desire to please parallel the character of that svelte, upstaging feline.

Available literature on the breed speaks of the dog's usefulness as a guardian. This is a fierce, highly protective and devoted dog, whose principal occupation was as a guard dog for farmers and other ruralites. The Thai stayed home while the family worked. Additionally, the dog's speed and intelligence made it a helpful hunting dog, chasing down such prey as rabbit and deer. The breed's guard duty was also extended to "escort," and commonly the Thai was used to follow the family cart on outings.

While the dog is extremely fierce as a home guardian, away from home it is not nearly as "attack-oriented."

The Thai is an easycare, rather unique-looking dog that should soon receive attention from the West. The Rhodesian Ridgeback, a similar hound-like breed from South Africa, can no longer boast the only ridge and whorl in the canine world. Offering more colors than the wheaten Rhodesian, the Thai Ridgeback adds a new, hopefully welcome, dimension to the scope of purebred dogs. It appears that native breeders are anxious to promote the dog in the United States, so all interested parties are duly encouraged to seek contacts!

ESSENTIALS OF THE THAI RIDGEBACK DOG: Well muscled and agile, the Thai Ridgeback is a dog of substance and endurance. The hallmark of the breed, as the name reveals, is the ridge on its back, which must be clearly defined, symmetrical and tapering, beginning behind the shoulder and continuing to a point between the prominence of the hips, and necessarily containing two identical crowns opposite each other. The head is wide; the skull is flat, broad between ears. Eyes are almond shaped. The muzzle is long, deep and powerful. Ears are pointed and carried erect. Viewed head-on, the head appears wedge-like. In color the dog is fawn, black or blue, with white markings on chest and paws permitted; nose must be black; a black mask is greatly desired, as well as a black-marked tongue. Weight: 50–75 pounds (23–34 kg). Height: 22–26 inches (56–66 cm). The coat is dense and very short. The chest is deep with well-sprung ribs. The back is long but strong and firm. The front legs are straight; the hindlegs should be short and sharply defined. The tail, carried with a slight curve, is well set-up—the proper tail is very important to the correct appearance of the dog.

Thallotoxicosis

Thallium sulfate is a cellular-toxic metal used as a pesticide or rodenticide and a ready cause of poisoning in dogs. Thallium can be detected in the urine by a thallium spot test or by spectrographic analysis by the veterinarian. Gastrointestinal disturbances signal the onset with vomiting, diarrhea, anorexia and stomach cramps. Sometimes a cough or difficulty in breathing occurs. Other intestinal disorders may also manifest themselves as well as convulsions. In mild cases the diseases may be simply a skin eruption, depending upon the damage to the kidneys. Enlarged spleens, edema or nephrosis can develop. Antibiotics and medication called dimercaprol are helpful but the mortality rate is over 50 percent. Known also as thallium poisoning.

Thai Ridgeback Dog, fawn. Photo courtesy of Rick Tomita and Thai Dog Club of Thailand.

Thambai
See Chippiparai

Therapy dogs
Therapy dogs are dogs that are used as comforters and companions to the physically and mentally disabled, as well as confined and elderly patients. Some therapy dogs are used to visit prisoners. Programs which promote therapy dogs are dedicated to the idea that dogs help persons relieve their tensions and forget about their problems for a while.

Thick in skull
Synonymous with coarse skull, a dog's skull is said to be thick when it bulges excessively, especially when at the hinge of the jaw due to excessive bone. Seen in American Pit Bull Terriers.

Thigh
The body region between the hip joint and the stifle consisting of the muscle groups that surround the femur. On the dog, three individual thigh regions are commonly referred to: the inner thigh, upper thigh, and lower thigh. The lower thigh is sometimes referred to as the gaskin or the second thigh. *See also* Hindquarters

Thigh bone
Femur. *See* Hindquarters

Thinning shears
The type of thinning shears you use depends on the type of coat you are working on. Styles include those with a double or single edge, 30–46 teeth. *See also* Grooming

Third eyelid
Unlike the upper and lower eyelids, the dog's third eyelid (*Membrana nictitans*) is not consciously controlled by the dog. Its function is essentially for protection, a shield from injury and a cleaner or wiper of sorts. The third eyelid or nictitating membrane is usually pink in pigmentation and more apparent in some breeds than in others and is subject to infection. *See also* Haw-eyedness

Thirst

On hot days and during exercise sessions, your dog will consume more water than usual. Sometimes, however, excessive thirst can be an indicator that something is wrong. Diabetes mellitus (sugar diabetes), more common in fat or middle aged dogs, can be identified by excessive thirst. Diabetes insipidus, a rare form of the disease, is also marked by great thirst. Unquenchable thirst can also be an indicator of rabies. Kidney disorders or uterine infection can also be characterized by excessive thirst. Not to frighten our faithful reader-owner, but safe is better than sorry and a visit to the vet is the best and safest option.

Thorax

See Chest

Throat

Neck's upper portion near the head junction.

Throat latch

Below lower jaw angles, the head/throat junction.

Throatiness

A desirable or undesirable appearance marked by loose folds of skin under the throat and neck underside. In the Basset Hound, this is desirable, while in the Pointer, it is most infelicitous.

Throaty neck

Wet neck. A neck that is not tightly skinned but instead is loose with dewlap and wrinkles prevalent.

Thrombus

A clot in the blood vessel or the heart.

Thrown out

When a hound or horseman loses his position in the chase.

Thumb marks

Marks or spots on the coats of some breeds which are usually black in color (i.e., diamond on the Pug's forehead, mark on English Toy Terrier's chin, pastern marks on Manchester Terrier).

Thyroid gland

This gland is located in the neck and lies on either side of the esophagus. The thyroid is most significant for its secretion of thyroxin, an important chemical body regulator. Thyroxin contains about 60 percent iodine, and an iodine defi-

Thirst quenched at the faucet. Spinone Italiano photographed by I. Français.

ciency is likely to affect the thyroid gland first. Through its secretion of thyroxin the thyroid regulates the metabolism of the animal. An overactive thyroid can cause hyperactivity, while an underactive one can cause lethargy and obesity. The common complaint or justification that the dog has an underactive thyroid is not valid in most cases of obesity. More often it is lack of exercise and stimulation as well as overfeeding that leads to fatness. Dogs in general have well-working thyroid glands. Chronic excitement or lethargy are warning signs, however, and deserve attention. Blood tests, simple and relatively inexpensive, can be clinically performed and a diagnosis given regarding an under- or overactive thyroid gland.

Tibetan Hound

The Tibetan Hound is known for its unusually short coat, the shortest of all Tibetan dogs. The Khampas are a nomadic tribe that keep these swift, lean dogs. They are described as ugly.

Tibetan Mastiff, black.

Tibetan Mastiff

Originating in the central tableland of Asia and occurring in Syria and Arabia, the Tibetan Mastiff is a real mountain dog and a true mastiff. Revered for their fighting and defensive skill, these dogs were prized animals of inhabitants and travelers of the region. Admired for their tremendous size (Marco Polo reported dogs as big as donkeys), Tibetan Mastiffs were presented to Alexander the Great by an Asiatic king to combat lions and elephants. The Romans, during their zenith, also had their hands on the dogs, and they too were no doubt impressed. Tibetan Mastiffs were once commonly employed in the Himalayas and other areas of Central Asia as guard dogs and herders of flocks. Today the breed enjoys Kennel Club recognition and a moderate but faithful following of fanciers. The size of today's Mastiffs is far less than a donkey; such hyperbolic descriptions render these moderate-sized mastiffs a disappointment to some.

ESSENTIALS OF THE TIBETAN MASTIFF: Well-built and heavy dog with a large and massive head and a strong punishing jaw. The ears set high and folded. A straight back, well-developed musculature, deep chest, well-laid shoulders, fairly broad head. European owners indicate that the dog can weigh over 220 pounds (99 kg), although a maximum of 175 pounds (80 kg) or less is more reasonable. Other reliable sources convey that an average of 120 pounds (55 kg) is realistic for a healthy show dog. The coat is thick, double and long. The hair is fine but hard, stand-offish and straight. The tail is well plumed and carried in a curl over the back. In color the dog is rich black, black and tan, brown, various shades of gold or gray. Height: 22–28 inches (56–71 cm).

Tibetan Mastiff, black and tan, puppy. Photo by I. Français.

Tibetan Mastiff (*opposite*), gold. Photo by I. Français.

Tibetan Spaniel

Tibet, like neighboring China, has favored small, pug-faced dogs for centuries. Small dogs were often given as peace

Tibetan Spaniel, fawn with black mask.

Tibetan Spaniels, fawn and particolor. Photographs by I. Français.

offerings from one nation to another. The Tibetan Spaniel, of Tibetan origins, was likely sent to Chinese emperors. These tiny spaniel types probably contributed to the creation of the Pekingese, through crosses to the Pug. Some purport that the Pekingese predates the Tibetan Spaniel and that it was the reverse peace offering that yielded the Tibetan Spaniel, admittedly less distinct than the Peke but more natural.

Regardless of his origin, the Tibetan Spaniel, residing in Tibetan monasteries for centuries, earned his keep as a "Prayer Dog," turning the prayer wheel for intercessing monks. Prayers were written on parchment and put into a revolving box. The little monastery dwellers (the dogs, not the monks) were trained to turn the prayer wheels. The Tibetan Spaniel is the only dog in the world to have this unique claim to fame, a most fascinating use of dog by man—a bookmark of sorts.

The breed was popular outside the monasteries as well and was raised in certain villages throughout Tibet, chiefly as watchdogs and companions. Although the word spaniel promises hunting or gundog implications, the dogs were not used for this purpose. Of course, the Eastern philosophy of dog breeding differed substantially from the West's. Since the crossings of the Tibetan Spaniels were not carefully supervised (as they would have been in Picadilly or Boston), a pure Tibetan Spaniel could only be found inside the monastery, where the dogs, like the monks, had no outside romantic encounters.

Although not as popular as his relation the Pekingese, the Tibetan Spaniel is equally as attractive. Once described as "a Pekingese gone wrong," the Tibetan Spaniel has survived such biased comparisons. The breed surely is the more natural and cleancut of the two. Perhaps leading a rather sheltered existence in

times past explains the Tibetan Spaniel's shyness with strangers, which is vari-

ously interpreted as aloof or reserved. With his own, he is gay and assertive. The first dogs to enter Great Britain came with medical missionaries in the 1920s. The dog did not take hold in England because the Peke and other Oriental toys had saturated the toy-dog market. The breed wasn't recognized in the U.S. until 1983.

ESSENTIALS OF THE TIBETAN SPANIEL: A well-balanced overall impression is complemented by the breed's gay and assertive expression. The body is slightly longer from the point of the shoulder to the root of the tail than at the withers. The tail is set high and richly plumed in a gay curl. The neck is embellished by a mane or "shawl" of longer hair. The hindquarters are well made and strong, hocks well let down and straight. Forelegs slightly bowed but firm at well-placed shoulder, moderately boned. The top coat is silky but lies rather flat. The undercoat is fine and dense. Height: 10 inches (25 cm). Weight: 9–15 pounds (4–7 kg). The standard states no color preference, and all colors and combinations occur and are acceptable.

Tibetan sand fox

A wild dog and a member of the genus *Vulpes*. *See* Foxes.

Tibetan Terrier

Raised as mascots or talismans, the Tibetan Terrier is one of the small native breeds of Tibet. The Lost Valley, a virtually inaccessible area, employed these monastery-raised tykes as St. Christopher medals (of sorts), given to adventuresome travelers as good-luck charms (pets). The breed's alleged ancestors include the North Kunlun Mountain Dog and the poodlelike Inner Mongolian Dog. Many dogs herded sheep in the Tibetan hill country, with the massive Tibetan Mastiff on guard duty. The smaller specimens, too petite for the rugged task of herding, were given to Tibetan lamas to raise. Some Tibetan Terriers were and still are employed as watchdogs or lost article retrievers ("when any possession falls over the khud and lands in a place inaccessible to man or dog").

Equally prized in Tibet as herders and companions, these shag-covered dogs are insightful and industrious. Although they are not true terriers, they can be just as fearless and assertive. Their long coats require some attention—incidentally, a Tibetan summer finds these dogs clipped (like the sheep they herd) and their hair mixed with yak's hair to be woven into

Tibetan Terrier, particolor. Photo by Carter. Courtesy of Anne Keleman.

fine, impervious cloth.

The breed makes a lively, good natured and loyal companion dog: outgoing, alert, intelligent, and game. A fine watchdog, the Tibetan Terrier remains sparing with strangers. This is truly a breed on the move.

ESSENTIALS OF THE TIBETAN TERRIER: Compact and powerful, the body is sturdy, medium sized and generally square in outline. The skull, medium in length, is neither broad nor coarse and narrows slightly from ears to eyes; it is neither completely flat nor domed between the ears. The head is well furnished with long hair, falling forward over the eyes, and the lower jaw carries a small but not exaggerated amount of beard. The eyes are large and round, but neither prominent nor sunken; they are set fairly wide apart. The pendant ears are V-shaped, not too large, and heavily feathered. Jaws are strong, with a perfect and complete scissors bite. Shoulders well laid. Back level over ribs. Chest well ribbed up. Stifles well bent; hocks low set. The tail is of medium length, set fairly high and carried in a gay curl over the back. The coat is double: the top coat is profuse and fine, not silky nor woolly; the undercoat is fine and woolly. The head is furnished with long hair that drapes generously over the eyes. Height: 14–16 inches (35.5–40.5 cm). Weight: 18–30 pounds (8–12 kg). White, golden, cream, gray or smoke, black, particolor and tricolors are all common; any color except liver and chocolate is permissible in the ring.

Tibetan Terrier, particolor. Photo by MikRon Photos.

Tibetan Terrier, tricolor. Photo by Vicky Fox Foto. Courtesy of Anne Keleman.

Tibia

One of the bones of the lower thigh. *See also* Hindquarters

Tick fever

See Rocky Mountain spotted fever

Ticking

Dark marks on a white coat pattern usually typical of hounds or gundogs. Speckles and flecks are used synonymously. Some breeds are ticked more heavily than others. The Bluetick Coonhound and the English Coonhound, for instance, are very heavily ticked, while a number of German Shorthaired Pointers are but slightly ticked.

Ticks

Forever a common parasite of man and dog, ticks have achieved new infamy with their transmission of Lyme disease. Dog and man have long combated the ranks of ticks, including the brown dog tick (*Rhipicephalus sanguineus*), American dog tick (*Dermacentor variabilis*), Rocky Mountain spotted fever tick (*D. andersoni*), Gulf Coast tick (*Amblyomma maculatum*), black-legged tick (*Ixodes scapularis*), and the lone star tick (*Amblyomma americanum*), among others. Truly debili-

tating, ticks not only suck the vital blood of our dogs but they are carriers and transmitters of many diseases, including ehrlichiosis, babesias, Rocky Mountain spotted fever, and Lyme disease, which *see*. The skin wounds of tick bites are highly subject to secondary infections, and tick predation opens the doors to toxemia, screwworm infestation, anemia, and death.

Ticks which infest livestock come from two families, the Argasidae and the Ixodidae. The Argasidae involves some 155 species, most of which infect birds but a few of which have adapted to other lifestyles, affecting both man and his dog. These argasid ticks are soft-bodied and specialize in hiding in tiny niches and crevices. Once infestation occurs, eradication is often difficult. Most of these leathery parasites inhabit tropical or warm temperate climates with long dry spells.

The Ixodidae family houses over 650 species, and these are the true tick parasites of the dog. They are more adaptable than the Argasidae, affecting a wider variety of animals and surviving in a wider range of climates. Most ixodid species (about 600) have three host life cycles, which means that through the course of their development these ticks parasitize three different animals, species or kinds of animal. An example is *Ixodes dammini*, one carrier of Lyme; in its larval stage it primarily affects rodents and birds, on which it matures to its nymphatic stage and moves to such mammals as dog and man. On these higher animals the ticks reach their mature stage, at which time they seek their chosen prey. This is a typical life cycle of the three-host ixodids. Other ixodids, particularly those of the Old World, have developed two-host cycles in which the immature feed on one animal, mature, molt, and the adults feed on another. Like the three-stage ticks, the host may be of the same or different species depending on the species of tick. The remaining ixodids are one-host ixodids, meaning that throughout their life cycle they feed on one host until the female is mated and drops off to oviposit. Among the one-host ixodids are some of the most caustic of all tick species.

All species of tick have their preferred feeding sites on the host animal. Many that prey on the dog, including the common dog tick, prefer the head area. As a concerned owner, one should carefully check the entire dog, from nose to tail, from withers to ground. Look especially in the fold of the ears, limbs, and tail, for these are common tick hideouts. Sprays, powders, collars, and dips are all available to aid the tick-ridden dog and its owner. These should be applied judiciously and with caution; it is not uncommon for a dog to have side-effects to any one of these. Pills, including garlic tablets, are also employed by some owners, and moderate success is reported. Ticks are a serious matter and must be dealt with as such.

When removing an embedded tick, do not touch the tick with your bare hand; doing so may subject you to secretions from the tick that can be disease-causing. Use tweezers or another suitable object that allows you an unslippable grip and riskless contact with the parasite. Clasp the tick between its head and abdomen. It is important that the embedded head of the tick not be left in the host, your dog. A head left buried likely causes infection and toxemia. By twisting the tick and gently pulling, you can easily remove the whole tick. Before destroying the pest, check, with a magnifying glass if necessary, that the entire tick is in your grip. Glowing match sticks, petroleum jelly, iodine, alcohol, and peanut butter have all been

tried as aids in removing an embedded tick, all with varied degrees of success and tastefulness.

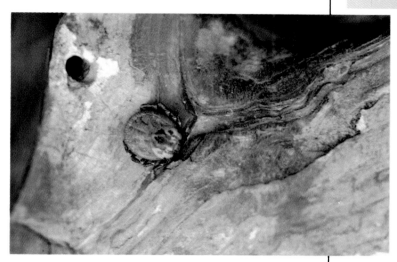

Tie

When the male has successfully penetrated with his penis the vagina of the bitch, the "tie" is said to be made. The terms stem from the fact that after penetration there is a bulbous swelling to the base of the penis that prevents retraction until some time after ejaculation. Although many persons become unduly alarmed, ties can last from 12 mintues to over an hour. *See also* Breeding

Tied-in shoulders
See Shoulder types

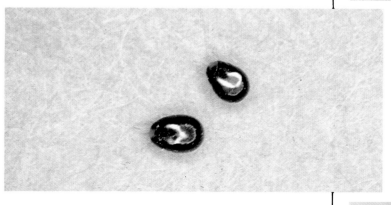

Tiger Dog
See Kai Dog

Tight mouthed
The condition of not having enough voice on the trail.

Ticks vary considerably in size, shape and color pattern. Many different species can be found on dogs and often can be transferred to humans. Photographs by Michael Gilroy and R.T. Zappalorti.

Timber

Multiple meanings in the dog world: 1) Leg bone of the dog. 2) A wooden fence, gait, stile or rail found on the foxhunting course. 3) In dog racing, a timber is a hurdle.

Timer

1) Person in charge of the timing of races. 2) Timing mechanism, usually an electric clock which is automatically started when dogs leave the starting box and stopped by the winner's body breaking a light beam at the finish line.

Timid

1) Shy. 2) A dog that refuses to race in closely bunched packs.

Tiny Toy Poodle

See Teacup Poodles

Toad poisoning

Some species of toad secrete a potent toxin. If while chasing a toad your dog takes it in his mouth, more than likely the toad will release a toxin from its parotid glands that will coat the mucous membranes of the dog's throat. The dog will salivate excessively and suffer prostration and cardiac arrhythmia. Some tropical and highly toxic species cause convulsions that result in death. All members of the genus *Bufo* are poisonous to dogs— *Bufo marinus*, *Bufo americanus* and *Bufo bufo* are among the more common toads in America and Britain. Caught in time, there are certain drugs that can be used to counteract the dire effects. Try washing the dog's mouth with large amounts of water and get him to a veterinarian quickly for proper treatment.

Toe anatomy

See Feet anatomy

Toe types

Constituted of phalanges, series of tiny bones, the dog's toe is usually arched to various degrees, depending upon the breed. Feet types such as hare foot (where the toes are flat) and cat foot (where the toes are well arched) are, of course, closely related to the toe structure. Toes which are said to be well split-up are clearly separated and distinct from one another (e.g., Pug, Chihuahua), as contrasted with the webbed toes of the water breeds or sled pullers. As this reveals, dog's toes often differ in their relationship to one another. Some terms that describe the relationship of toes to one another or their type in general include tightly knit toes, close cupped toes, closely knit toes, compact toes, well-padded toes, spread toes, and well-knuckled-up toes.

Toeing-in

Forefeet not in direct continuation of the pastern line instead rotate towards one another and the center line.

Toenail

Claw. The extension of the third phalanx of each toe. The nail is curved and compressed in a beaklike formation from side to side. In color the toenail is black or brown, or a lighter color altogether. Within the toenail is the quick or blood supply. Dogs that do not usually run on cement or gravel pavements will need to have their toenails clipped more regularly than those that do. Owners must not clip too close to the quick or else the nail will bleed. Application of a styptic powder will usually control this bleeding even though the experience is most unpleasant for the dog and he may grow uncooperative if the nail clipping experience is a continually painful one. Veterinarians will often demonstrate the proper nail clipping procedure to their clients. Dogs whose nails are excessively long make their usual tightly knit toes spread and this eventually interferes

with their ability to walk. Lameness has resulted from such poor keeping.

Tomarctus
See Ancestors of the dog

Tongue worm
An uncommon parasite of dogs. Tongue worms are three-quarters to five inches long and cannot survive for long outside their host. Treatment involves mechanical removal.

Tongue, in scenthunting
See Cry

Tongue, lolling
A tongue that protrudes from the mouth due to its excessive length. If not caused by panting, a lolling tongue is a breed defect. Such a protruding tongue is most typical of the brachycephalic breeds of dog.

Tonsillitis
Inflammation of the tonsils, typically the result of bacterial infection and treatable with antibiotics. The condition is common in dogs, especially in the small breeds and brachycephalic breeds, and chronic cases in any dog are cause for concern. Signs are red, inflamed, and irritated tonsils and throat, difficulty in swallowing, loss of appetite, fever, and excessive salivation.

Topcoat
The outer coat. *See* Coat.

Topknot
Atop the head of some breeds, the tuft of long, woolly, or silky hair (e.g., Shih Tzu, Afghan Hound).

Topline
The dog's outline from just behind the withers to the set-on of its tail.

Topskull
Dome or crown.

Tora Dog
See Kai Dog

Torso
Body.

Tosa Inu
Born on the island country of Japan, the Tosa represents the biggest attempts of Japanese dog-fighting enthusiasts to create the preeminent pit fighter. The Tosa traces his beginnings to the Kochi prefecture where, in the mid-nineteenth century, Bull Terriers, Bulldogs, and Mastiffs were crossbred with the indigenous fighting dogs to produce the Tosa. The rules of Japanese dog fighting demanded that the dogs fight in silence, without ever cowering; the mighty Tosa Inu never disappointed spectators and attacked its opponent head-on, relentlessly, unceasingly, fighting with forever-silent stoicism.

Toenails should be attended to regularly to avoid the dog's discomfort and potential problems. Gordon Setter photographed by I. Français.

Tosa Inu, red. Photo by I. Français.

As a defender of one's home, the Tosa is fearless; his mere appearance deters more would-be intruders than the loudest of alarm systems. To be truly effective as a guard and companion, however, the breed requires considerable work and early training.

Tosa Inu, one of the world's largest and most fearless mastiffs and guard dogs. Photo courtesy of Carl Semencic.

ESSENTIALS OF THE TOSA INU: A stately manner and robust build impose the Tosa's presence. The body musculature is well defined and massive. The chest is broad, deep and very powerful. The skull too is broad, with a moderate amount of wrinkle. The jaws are punishing and powerful. The coat is short, hard and dense. The ideal color is solid red on which white markings are tolerated; brindles, fawns and dull blacks also oc-

cur. Height: 24.5–25.5 inches (62–65 cm). Weight: up to 200 pounds (90 kg).

Tosa Ken
See Tosa Inu

Tosa Token
See Tosa Inu

Tottering action
Faulty motion that is teeteringly uncontrolled and swaying. The Boxer's gait expressly should not be tottering.

Tourniquets
Devices used in emergencies to stop profuse bleeding by completely cutting off the flow of blood to the body part concerned: they often result in the necessary amputation of the body part due to excessive cell necrosis and should only be used in extreme emergencies.

Tout
One who solicits wagers at a dog race, for a commission or gratuity, generally by aid of a pretended exclusive knowledge of prospective winners.

Towline
The center line fastened to the sled to which the dogs are hitched. Same as gangline.

Toxemia
A term used to refer to the condition of poisonous substances accumulating in the bloodstream. Commonly these substances are bacterial in nature and most often are the secondary result of another condition or disease.

Toxoplasmosis
Caused by the protozoan *Toxoplasma gondii*. Although cases have been reported in warm-blooded animals around the world, the disease is essentially rare. Signs of the infection are similar to most diseases and include fever, weakness, anorexia, coughing, diarrhea, and jaundice. Clinical diagnosis is necessary.

Toy American Eskimo
See American Eskimo

Toy Bull Terrier

The Toy Bull Terrier is the smallest variety of Bull Terrier ever to be produced. These dogs were as tiny as three pounds, and rarely bigger than ten. Today's Miniature Bull Terrier ranges from 10–40 pounds (4.5–18.5 kg) and is not troubled by the same breeding difficulties which the Toy variety experienced. The Bull Terriers, like the Bulldog, have distinctive large skulls and promise birthing difficulties for any breeders who attempt to bantamize them to inane extremes. *See also* Miniature Bull Terrier, Bull Terrier

Toy dogs

The definition of a toy dog is no minuscule matter. Essentially a toy dog is an indoor dog that lives to provide its owner with companionship. Toy dogs are small, never *too* big; many are furry, others are shorthaired (one or two are coat-free); they are always friendly (to their owner) and enjoy sitting around (and running around). Toy dogs have been snoozing on pillows, laps, and thrones for thousands of years. The Oriental people, with a keen eye for miniaturization, favored their toy companions. The Pekingese, for example, was adored with cultlike devotion by the Chinese empress. These dogs were fondled and pampered like the emperor's children themselves. Causing

harm to one of the empress's Pekes would be punished by slow torture.

Ofttimes these Oriental toys were called sleeve dogs, since their size made them conducive to sleeping in the emperor's sleeve. Lap dogs and pillow dogs also arise as terms, indicating the various places these companions could fit, sit, and sleep.

While many dogs were intentionally bantamized solely to become companions (and otherwise functionless), certain toys are so ancient that it is difficult to pinpoint their derivation. The Italian Greyhound, Pug and Chihuahua are ancient toys with unclear ancestry. Most every kind of dog has been miniaturized: sighthounds, mastiffs, gundogs, terriers. Hence, the toy group is bountiful with all kinds of canines. The temperament of the Papillon, a miniaturized gundog, is quite different than the temperament of the Miniature Pinscher, a miniaturized terrier.

Toy dogs. The Yorkshire Terrier reigns as one of the tiniest of toy dogs, weighing as little as three pounds (1.5 kg). Photo by I. Français.

Toy dogs enjoy a little spoiling from teatime to teatime. This cavalcade of Cavaliers patiently awaits kind service and crumpets.

Historically, the toy dogs have been associated with the ladies, since the place

Toy dogs stereotypically are cast on laps and pillows and always primping for the next dog show. This lounging Lhasa in braids readies himself for the ring (as an American, however, he'll compete in the Non-Sporting Group!).

Toy Fox Terrier, tricolor. Photo courtesy of Sherry Baker-Krueger.

of the women used to be in the home. Men were surely terrier or hound men. Today men and women alike admit freely and shamelessly to loving toy breeds. As companions and alarm dogs, toys cannot be beat.

The smallest toy dog is (arguably) the Chihuahua. Small Chihuahuas can be as featherlight as one pound! The Yorkshire Terrier and Toy Fox Terriers can weigh in at as little as three and a half pounds. "Pocket" Beagles and "Teacup" Poodles (yes, both fit into the employed adjective

more or less) are among these tiny toy breeds. Tiny Toy Poodles tend toward hypoglycemia as well as certain breeding difficulties unavoidable in these diminutive miniatures.

Certain other dogs fall into the toy category quite inconsequentially. The Lhasa Apso, Bichon Frise and the Australian Terrier are categorized as toys in certain countries and in other countries they are not.

Toy Fox Terrier

The Toy Fox Terrier is an American attempt to produce its own red, white and blue toy terrier. Despite having to settle somewhat for color, Americans happily have been more successful with the AmerToy than the British with the Toy Bulldog or Toy Bull Terrier, both of which were hindered by poor bone quality and weak conformation. The AmerToy, however, is bred down from the already small Smooth Fox Terrier, and therefore is quite free of these unfortunate complications. The originators of the AmerToy were Smooth owners that were fascinated by the "runts" in their litters, which consistently turned out to be scrappier than the other siblings. Crosses to the Chihuahua and the English Toy Terrier completed the mix that created the pint-sized AmerToy. A single armful, the Toy

Fox Terrier is a comical and intelligent companion and surely the ideal toy dog for anyone desiring such a delightful

not coincidentally, are all petite and refined housemates. Many dogs have been created specifically for inclusion in this

Toy Fox Terrier, white/tan. Photo by I. Français.

mate. Puppyhood frivolity remains with him throughout his life; this, mixed with his scrappy nature, makes him a truly smile-evoking pet.

ESSENTIALS OF THE TOY FOX TERRIER: A well-put-together lively squirt, the Toy Fox Terrier is a handsomely balanced dog with a smooth easycare coat. The body is essentially square. The ears are pointed Vs and erect. The head is slightly dome shaped, never apple. The preferred coat is tricolor: white and black with tan trim. However, white/tan and white/black are acceptable as well. Height: 10 inches (25 cm). Weight: 3.5–7 pounds (1.5–3.5 kg).

Toy German Spitz
See German Spitzen, Pomeranian

Toy Group
Most major kennel clubs have a category which they refer to as the Toy Group. This group includes dogs whose role in life is companionship. These dogs,

group, others simply have slipped into the company of their fellow microcanines. See also Group systems, Toy dogs

Toy Manchester Terrier
Today's Toy Manchester Terrier, known in Britain as the English Toy Terrier, is linked to the black and tan terriers of England documented by Caius as early as the sixteenth century. The Manchester district of England was known for its game terriers—dogs that excelled in the sports of rat baiting and rabbit coursing. Early crosses to a Whippet, a similarly talented sportsman, explain the breed's characteristic roach back. The development of the Toy variety occurred rather spontaneously, not intentionally at first. The charm of the underdog—a.k.a. runt—inspired the beginning of the Toy. The Italian Greyhound may have been used to stabilize the desired smaller size, but that breed's influence is not apparent today. Yesterday's devoted breeders are

responsible for the breed's existence today, as bouts with overexaggerated petiteness and ear carriage were so oppressive that many fanciers abandoned the Toy. British legislation banning ear cropping badly doused the spirits of many fanciers—even the later perfection of the Toy's candle-flame ears couldn't rekindle the breed's former popularity. The breed may sometimes be called the Black and Tan Toy Terrier.

Toy Manchester Terrier,black/tan. Photo by I. Français.

ESSENTIALS OF THE TOY MANCHESTER TERRIER: Excepting weight, which must not exceed 12 pounds (5.5 kg), the Toy abides by the exact standard as the Standard Manchester Terrier. In the Toy variety, the ears are of moderate size, flame-shaped, and naturally erect. Cropped ears are a disqualification. *See also* Manchester Terrier

Toy Poodle
   See Poodle

Toy Xoloitzcuintli
   See Mexican Hairless

Tracheobronchitis
   See Kennel cough, Tracheitis

Tracheitis
   Inflammation of the trachea, or windpipe. *See also* Kennel cough

Tracking

An activity designed primarily to test a dog's ability to discriminate scent. There are two possible degrees that can be earned exclusively in tracking, namely the T.D., or Tracking Dog, and the T.D.X., or Tracking Dog Excellent. To attain the T.D. degree, a dog must successfully pass a tracking test under at least two different judges. To attain the T.D.X. degree, the dog must first possess the T.D. degree and then pass a T.D.X. test under at least two different judges, all of course in accordance with A.K.C. rules and regulations. Additionally, there are the degrees of U.D.T. or Utility Dog Tracker, and U.D.T.X., or Utility Dog Tracker Excellent. The U.D.T requires that the dog acquire the C.D., C.D.X. and U.D. degrees under the rules of the A.K.C., as well as pass at least one tracking test under two different judges. The U.D.T.X. requires that the dog acquire the C.D., C.D.X., U.D., U.D.X., and T.D., as well as the T.D.X. degrees. To enter a T.D. test, a dog must first be approved by a tracking judge, who will test the dog on a regulation course. If the dog passes this trial test, he is awarded four certificates. These certificates are then turned in at each tracking test in which the dog is to compete. These certificates expire in one year. If they expire before they are used or before the dog attains its T.D. degree, the dog must be re-approved in the same manner to continue competing.

To enter a T.D.X. test, the dog must possess its T.D. degree. However, because of the design of T.D.X. tests, only six dogs can be run per test. All applicants are entered into a draw, with dogs that have not yet attained their T.D.X. degree given preference. Dogs that are not selected in the draw are held as alternates, in case one or more of the selected dogs drops from the trial.

The competing dog must follow a stranger's scent over an inconspicuous trail of 440 to 550 yards (800 to 1,0000 yards for T.D.X.), which has aged from 30 minutes to two hours (three to four hours for T.D.X.). The track layer is to wear leather-soled shoes and leave a leather object for the dog to find. Dogs work on a lead of 30 to 60 feet in length. There is also a specific number of turns, cross tracks,

degrees earned by American dogs. In 1980, just one year after the addition of the T.D.X. degree, nine dogs, of 151 competing (from five groups), earned the T.D.X. degree. In 1985, 60 dogs, of 366 competing (from six groups), earned this degree. And in 1990, 89 dogs, of 479 competing (from seven groups), earned their T.D.X. degree.

In the U.S., the most common groups competing in tracking tests are the sporting and herding groups, with the working group running a distant third. In terms of breeds, German Shepherd Dogs and Golden Retrievers have each earned more than twice as many tracking titles than any other breed between 1980 and 1990. Labrador Retrievers rank third, with English Springer Spaniels and Rottweilers not far behind in fourth and fifth. *See also* Obedience trials, Instinct tests

obstacles, and other factors that determine the difficulty of the track.

In the U.S., the American Kennel Club sponsors tracking events, which are governed by the Obedience Regulations, although since 1947 tracking has been separate from other Obedience events. As stated in the "Tracking Regulations" pamphlet of the A.K.C.:

"The fundamental feature of a Tracking Test/ T.D.X. is to show unquestionably that the dog has the ability to discriminate scent and possesses the stamina, perseverance and courage to do so under a wide variety of conditions."

With its origins in Germany, tracking remains a relatively popular and growing dog sport around the world. To consider its growing popularity in the U.S., one can look at the number of T.D.X.

Tracking tests excite the natural instincts of a scenthound like the Basset Hound. Photo by V. Serbin.

Tracking. Most breeds perform admirably in tracking tests. The Rottweiler enjoys a long success story as a tracker: this modern-day T.D. follows in the footsteps of the first Rottie T.D., who earned the degree in 1941.

Tracking Dog

A title indicating that a dog has passed the American Kennel Club-licensed or

member tracking test. T.D. is the suffix employed. *See also* U.D.T., Tracking Dog Excellent, T.D.

Tracking Dog Excellent

A title used to indicate that a dog has passed an American Kennel Club-licensed or member Tracking Dog Excellent test. *See also* U.D.T., U.D.T.X.

Trail

Term shouted by mushers to ask another driver for the right of way.

Trailing

The habit some dogs have of following a bracemate with no regard for hunting independently. *See also* Scenthounds

Training

The canine pack instinct makes most dogs very trainable. Training is accomplished with ease when the trainer consistently employs correction and praise. Loyal to the leader, the dog will obey, but it must first learn the language in order to heed the command. Instinctively a dog knows what is meant when another dog growls, crouches, tucks its tail, or rolls on its back; dogs have a language of their own, one that is easily understood by them. The desires and commands of humans, however, have to be translated to the dog. Praise and correction lay down the laws of grammar, leading the dog to a mastery of command language.

An example: to train the dog to sit, you must teach the dog the meaning of the word "sit." The dog is standing in front of you; you say "sit" in a commanding voice while gently pressing the hindquarters of the dog to the ground (this is the correction phase); when the dog is in the sitting position, you praise the animal. The dog associates being forced to sit with his being in the standing position when "sit" is com-

manded; he associates praise with sitting after the command is given. Because the dog desires praise and dislikes correction, he will quickly learn the appropriate response to avoid the one and receive the other. This simplified explanation serves as a general model for shaping the dog's behavior. The process of training a dog to retrieve water fowl or to cease attack upon command are necessarily more complex and require considerably more time and effort. But the basics remain the same: the dog is corrected into performing the appropriate response and praised for its completion. Correction need not be physical manipulation, but can also come in the form of visual learning, as is the case with many retrieving dogs, or other learning processes. In short, the dog is an animal capable of remembering and therefore learning about his environment and the responses appropriate for successful and happy existence in it.

A note on the appropriateness of correction, especially for owners who choose to scold their dog, an action totally unnecessary for all successful dog training: correction must precisely occur with the action that is corrected. A dog who runs away and is scolded upon return is scolded for his return and not for running away, at least as far as the dog is concerned. Such correction is most detrimental to the development of a dog. A dog who is corrected upon return will be just as likely to run away but less likely to return. The same applies to housebreaking. A pup that is corrected for going on the carpet hours after it has done so is corrected for whatever it is doing at the moment of correction and not for messing the carpet. No dog can be successfully trained if correction does not coincide with the behavior to be corrected and,

most importantly, if the dog is not praised coincidentally with his performance of the desired behavior. Always be patient but persistent. *See also* Behavior modification, Housebreaking

Sit, Stand, Come, Heel, and Stay are known as the five basic commands. Most authorities agree that every dog should be taught these essential behaviors. Obedience advocates assure owners that these commands could very well save your dog's life one day.

Sit. This command is a fine one with which to start the dog on his road to obedience. Easy to follow and to retain, the dog can quickly feel good about himself for his mastery, and the master feel pleased with his accomplishment. The necessities are few; all that is needed are a leash, a collar, a few treats (optional), and a place to sit. Begin with a brief walk prior to a meal to relax both you and the dog. Return, let the dog free, call him to you, and praise him when he comes.

Training the dog to sit is the most basic of commands. Professional trainers of show dogs often opt to not teach this command to avoid the dog's sitting in the show ring when it should be standing. Greater Swiss Mountain Dog photographed by I. Français.

Now you and the dog are ready to commence training. Hold the dog's lead tightly in your right hand. Face the dog and have him face you, pulling up gently on the lead if necessary. As eye contact is made, say "sit" in an authoritative voice while pressing gently on the dog's hindquarters. The moment your dog reaches the sitting position, give him warm and earnest praise (supplement with a little tidbit if desired). The dog may look a little confused, but he will appreciate the attention and soon learn what is being asked. Allow the dog to stand again. Repeat the command again while pressing on the hindquarters. Give reward when he assumes the sitting position. Repeat several times, keeping the first lessons short (about five minutes). The dog should master the "sit" command in about three sessions. Reinforcement will be necessary every few days for the first few weeks, after which the dog should never forget the "sit" command. It is important to remember, with this and all training commands, that every dog is an individual and every dog learns at his own rate. Do not expect miracles; be patient, and training will prove rewarding.

Stay. To teach the "stay" command, first command the dog to a sitting position. Place your hand in front of the dog's nose and hold it there. Give the command "stay" in a firm voice and take a step forward. If the dog makes a motion to rise, which he likely will do the first few times, pull sharply on the lead to prevent the dog's rising. Try again. When the dog learns to stay as you step forward, begin to circle around him. Whenever the dog makes motion to rise, pull sharply on the lead. Soon you will be able to walk completely around the dog. Keep lessons

brief. When the dog proves to be learning, increase the radius of the circle you walk around the dog. Eventually you will have to exchange the lead for a long cord or rope, always making certain that the tug you exert will keep the dog in the sitting position. Training the dog to stay takes considerable patience. Whereas the sit command may take only three lessons, the stay command may require eight or ten. Don't be discouraged if it takes more.

Heel. In preparation for the "heel" command, the dog should be walked several times on a lead. Walk the dog on your left side and hold the lead in your right hand so that it forms a J-loop in front of your body. Begin walking. The dog is likely to be excited and pull and romp considerably. When the dog pulls or moves from your left, give a sharp pull on the lead. When his tugging stops, praise him. The dog will soon associate the discomfort of the tug and the warmth of praise with his corresponding behavior and amend it to the appropriate way of walking. Two walks a day for two to three days normally suffice as preparation for heel training. Have the dog stand at your left side. Place your left hand in front of his nose, which should be even

with your left leg. Commence the walk as before, with your dog on your left, the lead in your right hand, and a J-loop formed to the front of you. Now the rules of walking will be more restrictive. The dog must not move too far in front of your leg nor too far behind it. When he does, a sharp tug on the lead will tell him that his walking is not in agreement with your expectations. When he returns close to your side, praise him with a pat, a kind word, and a tidbit if desired. Heel training is normally accomplished in about six to ten sessions.

Down. Teaching the "down" command ideally begins while your dog is still a pup. During puppyhood your dog frequently will lie down, as this position is one of the dog's most natural positions. Invest some time in keeping close watch over your pup. Each time he begins to lie down, repeat in a low convincing tone

the word "down." If, for the first day of training, you coincide a majority of the dog's sitting with your commands and continue with reinforcement and moderate praise, your pup should conquer the "down" command in no time.

Teaching the "down" command to a mature dog likely will require more effort. Although the lying position is still natural to a dog, his being forced into it is not. Some dogs may react with fear, anger, or confusion. Others may accept the process and prove quick learners. Have your dog sit and face you. If he is responsive and congenial, gently take his paws, and slowly pull them towards you; give the "down" command as he approaches the proper position. Repeat several times: moderate reinforcement of this procedure should prove rewarding and successful.

For the dog that responds with anger or aggression, attach a lead (and a muzzle) and have the dog sit facing you at a close distance. There should be a J-loop formed by the lead. With moderate force, relative to the size and strength of your dog, step on the J-loop, forcing the dog down, while repeating the command "down" in a low forceful tone. When the dog is down, moderate praise should be given. If the dog proves responsive, you may attempt to extend his legs to the "down" position—leaving the muzzle on, of course. Daily reinforcement of the training method will soon yield the desired results.

Come. The "come" command is actually the first command and should begin soon after the pup is brought to his new home. Every time the pup's meal is set down, the word "come" should be expelled in a firm tone. The pup will soon associate the word "come" with something that is pleasing, namely his food. Once outdoors, however,

Training the Poodle to come. Photo by R. Pearcy.

Training the Sheltie down. Photo by I. Français.

Training the Great Dane to stay. Photo by R. Pearcy.

the conditions change, and training the "come" command will require a little work. Let the dog reach the end of a long lead, then give the command, gently pulling him towards you at the same time. As soon as he associates the word "c o m e" with the action of moving towards you, pull only when he does not respond on command. As he starts to come, gradually increase the distance until it is considerable. The dog must learn to come to you regardless of the distance between you. Reward is essential after each successful compliance with the come command.

After these five basic commands are well learned, you and your dog can move on to more specialized training or you can settle into a comfortable pet-to-owner relationship, free of the many stresses presented when the dog is untrained.

Training tests

Hunting scenarios used in field trials to examine a dog's skill. The two ba-

Training. Teaching a dog tricks, like standing on his hindlegs, can follow the basic commands. Some talented dogs serenditiously happen upon unique party stunts. Schipperke photographed by I. Français.

Transylvanian Hound, Tall, black and tan. Photo by I. Français.

sic types are marked and blind, each occurring over a variety of terrain, with varied distractions, and with either one or more felled game. In the single marked retrieve, for example, the dog must retrieve a single felled bird, either on land or over water, with the dog able to see the bird fall. In the double blind, two felled birds are involved and the dog cannot see either bird fall. Triple retrieves are also common, often with scenarios involving both water and land in the same retrieve.

Transcaucasian Ovtcharka

The Caucasian region of the old Soviet Union has two known ovtcharkas. The Transcaucasian Ovtcharka is the older type of working dog from the Caucasus Mountains. It is found in Georgia, Azerbaijan, Armenia, Dagestan, Stavropol, Krasnodar, Rostov, Grozny, and Astrakhan; the best specimens today, however, are to be found in the Georgian republic. The Caucasian Ovtcharka, the second ovtcharka recognized by the F.C.I., is also found in this general area. Type on each of these dogs varies considerably. These are ferocious guardians.

Transylvanian Hound

There are two breeds of Transylvanian Hound, divided by size: Tall and Short. While the Short variety is too invitingly flirting with extinction, the Tall can still be found, although it too is quite low in numbers. Efforts to preserve the breed have made use of other hounds, probably laufhunds of Switzerland. These practices have been curbed to savor the tradi-

Transylvanian Hound, Tall, black and tan with white chest blaze, photographed by I. Français.

tional characteristics of the Transylvanian dogs. These very ancient Hungarian foxhounds were developed for hunting in the game-filled woods of the Transylvanian region. The larger variety was used on bigger game, while the smaller hunted mainly hare and fox. The Tall has also been successfully trained as a retriever. The Tall Transylvanian once enjoyed the favor of Hungarian kings and noblemen who worked him on wolf and bear in the mountainous regions. These sleek-coated dogs needed to be sturdy and adaptable to survive the cold and harsh environment of the mountains.

ESSENTIALS OF THE TRANSYLVANIAN HOUND: This sleek, short-coated hound comes in two size varieties: the Tall variety stands 22–26 inches (56–66 cm) and weighs up to 77 pounds (35 kg); the Short variety stands 18–22 inches (46–56 cm). The variation continues in color as well: the Tall is black and tan with a white chest; the Short is red and tan. The Tall is longer than he is tall and appears lean and elegant. Both sizes possess sleek appearances and stunning good looks. The tricolor pattern is particularly brilliant and the head beautifully sculpted.

Traumatic hernia
See Hernias

Traveling with your dog. Afghan Hound motoring in auto with his owner. Photo by R. Pearcy.

Traveling with your dog. Travel by train requires careful planning, or else you may be forced to leave your Chow at the tracks.

Traveling with your dog

The favored Afghan peering out of the portholes of Noah's Ark, the warlike Ibizan sitting securely upon Hannibal's elephant, Leopard Curs atop a covered wagon in colonial America, sennenhunds pulling carts, huskies pulling sledges— "Fala," F.D.R.'s Scottie, riding in the President's convertible, the Queen's Royal Corgis flying first class, rescue-trained German Shepherds lifted by helicopter, the gallant "Laika" on the lunar-bound space launch: traveling with a dog surely has changed over the centuries.

When traveling with a pet, there are many considerations to account for: legality, safety, and efficiency. Additionally, as we have seen, there are many different modes of travel. The most common method of travel of course is the automobile. A sensible approach to car travel will yield the best results. Get the dog accustomed to short trips when he is still young. The safest approach is the well-ventilated crate;

crate prior to the first trip is the most effective way of introducing the dog to crate travel. Giving the dog his favorite toy or bone or another familiar item will also ease the process. The dog should relieve himself prior to traveling and eat a few hours before leaving. During the trip, only water should be offered while in the car. Frequent stops for nature's calls or food are advised. It is not acceptable to leave a dog unsupervised in a car. In some countries and/or states, there are laws which prohibit leaving a dog in a parked car. In hot weather, leaving a dog in a closed car is particularly dangerous (not to mention inhumane). When traveling in hot weather, be sure the car is air conditioned or bring along a couple of cool towels for the dog. Not every dog will enjoy driving. Some dogs become car-sick and will never enjoy traveling. Other dogs thrive on frequent trips to and from the grocery store.

Wise owners make sure that the hotel or motel in which they plan to stay ac-

such a device is useful for both short and long trips. Acclimating the dog to the

cepts dogs. Not all such facilities do. Such regulations can put a damper on a much-waited-for vacation.

In cities, bus travel is extremely common. However, unless your dog is an assistance dog, he most likely will not be allowed to board a bus. Train lines are generally more accommodating than bus lines. Some railways permit dogs to stay in the owner's cabin, while others require that the dog be kept in the baggage compartment. The latter situation promises to cost the owner more for excess baggage. Always check with the railway and train station about regulations concerning traveling with a dog—before leaving. Additionally, one may wish to schedule short exercise periods during the train's rest stops. While ship travel is less popular than it once was, similar accommodations can be acquired. Always look into the specifics before venturing forth into unknown waters, as it were.

Air travel can be a more difficult matter. Airlines most usually allow dogs to fly on their flights. Small dogs can be "carried on" while larger ones need to be kept in the excess baggage compartment. Of course the appropriate crate is required for any dog traveling by air. Another popular option is reserved air freight, in which your pet travels in a compartment

similar to the human passengers. Travel agents are usually well informed and will advise you on such decisions.

If you are planning to leave the country, it is necessary to familiarize yourself with the various regulations regarding quarantines, inoculations, and other importation affairs. In the United States, crossing state lines with a dog may also require looking into. Contact the proper authorities in the state of your destination to alert yourself to any regulations of which you need to be aware. Often a health certificate from a veterinarian is necessary for international travel. Since airlines are notorious for losing baggage, damaging cargo, delaying flights, misloading luggage, etc., many dog owners are hesitant to travel by air with their "live" luggage. Although some airlines have become most effective in accommodating dog owners, other airlines have proven consistently brainless and irresponsible. You are well advised to look into your chosen airline before you subject your dog to a stressful, potentially harmful situation.

Traveling with your dog by air has become increasingly more convenient, particularly when the pilot himself (and your chosen airline) are disposed to canines.

Traveling with your dog to a dog show must be well-thought-out and safe. Keeping the dog in a crate is the most practical mode of transport. Soft Coated Wheaten Terriers photographed by V. Serbin.

Treeing Tennessee Brindle, brindle.

Trawler Spaniel

An old miniature spaniel breed of England that was bantamized from local spaniel types for companion purposes. The dog no longer exists.

Tree bark

The bark a hound employs when it has the quarry treed or bayed. It is usually quite different from the voice on line to one familiar with the hound. Most tree barks are shorter and more insistent. They are more regular than voices on line, which vary with the scenting conditions. *See also* Coonhounds

Treeing Tennessee Brindle

The Treeing Tennessee Brindle is one of America's mountain cur breeds. Its stock, similar to that of the coonhound breeds, includes various treeing coon dogs from all over the U.S. Not exactly the most specific analysis of a breed's origin ever put in print, one must consider that the breed's founding enthusiasts, like most hunters, particularly in the American South, were not overly concerned with naming or labelling the hounds that worked for them. The dogs that went into their initial stock were simply working dogs—the only actual similarity they shared was their coloration: brindle! Hunters employed these small brindle dogs for generations, never giving them a second thought. These men (and women) were keenly aware of the dogs' exceptional open-trailing and locating ability. At one time, the Tennessee Treeing was bunched with the Mountain Cur and the Stephens Stock, but today each has individual breed status. Coon, squirrel and opossum comprise the breed's list of quarry. Treeing Brindle enthusiasts today are among the most responsible of hunting dog owners.

Demonstrative and placid, the Brindles delight owners with their boldness and outward displays of affection. Puppies demonstrate these qualities at an early age. Its intelligence eases its training, but heightens its sensitivity to scolding or neglect.

ESSENTIALS OF THE TREEING TENNESSEE BRINDLE: The solid body of the Treeing Tennessee is muscular and square. The coat, which may vary in shades of brindle, is short and dense and smooth to the touch. Height: 16–24 inches (40–61 cm). Weight: 40–50 pounds (18–22.5 kg). The legs are powerful and well developed, giving the dog speed and coordination.

Treeing Walker Coonhound

The Foxhounds of England and their close Virginia hound relations are responsible for the lineage of the Treeing Walker Coonhound. The Walker Foxhound, a direct descendant of the English Foxhound, is the "middle dog" in the evolutionary chart yielding the Treeing Walker. The breed still possesses a strong resemblance to the English Foxhound. An undying sense of game coupled with untiring speed and manly drive make this coonhound unstoppable.

This efficient and obedient hunter is used on a variety of game: coon, squirrel, opossum, and even deer (the latter an illegal activity in some areas). The coonhound lineage continues to produce new dogs for various purposes. Treeing Walker enthusiasts have also developed a smaller dog to move faster than the Treeing Walker; it is known as the Running Walker Coonhound. These dogs are intelligent and proficient. Training is accomplished with little trouble, as these dogs are able to learn from example.

ESSENTIALS OF THE TREEING WALKER COONHOUND: The Treeing Walker is a medium-sized, efficiently built hound with an elastic and durable frame. The coat, like that of the other coonhounds, is tight, smooth and glossy. The tricolor pattern is preferred, although bicolor dogs are also acceptable. Height: 20–27 inches (51–69 cm). Weight: 50–75 pounds (22.5–34 kg).

Trench mouth

This disease of the mouth is often the result of decreased resistance of the oral mucosa caused by another disease, condition, or state. It is more common in cats than in dogs. Signs begin with a reddening and swelling of the gum area near the base of the teeth; the affected area bleeds easily and causes considerable discomfort to the dog. The infection can then spread, causing increased tissue damage and an odor. If not treated, the infection can easily spread to the lungs, causing pneumonia. Early detection and treatment are important.

Trespassing

Not all jurisdictions protect the trespassers mauled or maimed on a dog's own property. A trespasser, someone without invitation—explicit, implied, or written—may be protected if the dog's owner was aware of the dog's vicious propensity. The postman, U.P.S. delivery man, and milkman have implied invitations on one's property, unless a sign warning to the contrary is posted (i.e., No

Treeing Walker Coonhound, tricolor. Photo by I. Français.

Treeing Walker Coonhound pup at eight weeks of age getting a nose for coon! Courtesy of Danny May.

Floral Deliveries Please or simply, No Trespassing—Man-Eating Canine!). Some courts will allow an owner to raise contributory or comparative negligence defenses; or the alleged trespasser may be permitted to demonstrate that the owner acted unreasonably. Children cannot be considered trespassers since they are not reasonable creatures; therefore, children must be protected from any potentially harmful dogs.

Triangular ears

In one respect or another, the ears are triangular in shape; ofttimes, an equilateral triangle (e.g., Samoyed) or the upper half of the ear is triangularly shaped (e.g., Great Pyrenees).

Triangular eyes

More angulated than oval eyes though similar (e.g., Afghan Hound).

Tricolor Treeing Walker Coonhound tree barking. The saddled tricolor pattern in the hound breeds is most standard and usually desired over other possible markings. Photo courtesy of Danny May.

Trichiasis

Condition caused by abnormally erupting eyelashes occurring in incorrect positions or directions. This condition is related to entropion (which *see*). Potential injury is resultant from continual eyeball to eyelash contact. Believed by some to be an inherited trait.

Trichinosis

A parasitic disease established through the intake of infected, insufficiently cooked meat, typically pork. The parasite is *Trichinella spiralis*, the larvae of which are encysted in the striated muscles of various animals. Infection occurs after consumption, the larvae mature and reproduce, and new larvae travel to the striated muscles of the new host, where they can live for ten years or more. The infection is not too common in domestic dogs, and most cases that occur are mild and go undiagnosed, most clearing solely by the dog's defense system. The disease is "incurable," which means there is no treatment for it other than rest and the alleviation of symptoms—therefore it must be prevented. Prevention involves not feeding poorly cooked meat or allowing your dog to catch, kill, and eat other animals.

Tricolor

Indicating black/tan or chocolate/tan in combinations of white. There are several forms of the color. 1) *Pied tricolor*: White and black spots broken over the entire body, plus tan marks over eyes, on cheeks, under ears, on feet and around vent (e.g., English Toy Spaniel, Prince Charles variety). 2) *Saddled tricolor*: White and tan spots evenly distributed, plus the black saddle (e.g. Foxhound and the Chien Français Tricolore). 3) *Patterned tricolor*: A true black/tan color plus white blaze, chest, feet, tail tip (e.g., Bernese Mountain Dog). *See also* Belton

Tricolor Chien Français

See Chien Français

Trigg Hound

A foxhound type similar to the Treeing Walker Coonhound which also developed in the U.S. It is less commonly used and lesser in number than the other coonhound breeds of America; it is not registered by the United Kennel Club as are many of the other hunting dog types. In height, the dog stands 23–25 inches (58.5–63.5 cm) and can be any color.

Trimming

Grooming a coat by plucking or clipping. *See* Grooming

Triple

Refers to a triple fall: three birds shot down at the same time.

Triple Champion

A dog that has won all three dog sport champion titles: bench show, field trial, and obedience trial.

Trot

A rhythmic two-beat gait in which the feet at diagonally opposite ends of the body strike the ground together; i.e., right hind with left front and left hind with right front. Trot differs from the pace in that the feet are diagonally associated instead of being on the same side of the body.

Trousers

Longish hair at the back of both upper and lower thighs of some breeds. *See* Breeches, Culottes

Trowel-shaped ears

Peculiar, though self-defining, term referring to the desired ear type of the Stabyhoun.

True front

See Straight front

Truffle Dog

A highly specialized kind of dog that is used for the locating of truffles. In France they are of Poodle type and known as Truffleurs. They stand about 17–18 inches (73–46 cm) high. Many dogs (and even pigs!) have been employed to hunt the truffle fungus—in Norway, Sweden and other Scandinavian countries as well as in France. The fungi is a gourmet edible valued by Europeans for generations. The successful dogs of the late truffle hunter Eli Collins were typically offered a piece of bread in exchange for their found fungus. Truffle Dogs were generally believed to have descended from the Spanish Poodles that were utilized by John Stone, a Spaniard who hunted near Stonehenge in the 1600s. Truffle Dogs today have undergone many transformations, and various Poodle strains have been drizzled into the Truffle Dogs to protect them from extinction. Today a stock of working Truffle Dogs exists in Italy, where they are called Lagotas. Coloration is commonly white with slight tan and black markings on the ears, head, flanks and set-on. The dogs, properly trained, ignore all animal game, no matter how enticing, and can scent the truffle fungus from considerable distances. In various countries and regions, many different breeds are used as truffle hunters and some have been incorporated in Truffle Dog stock: Strel-

Trot enthusiastically performed by a Löwchen.

Truffle Dogs called Truffleurs and Lagotas in Europe are dogs of Poodle type used to locate the truffle fungus from the ground. Photographs by I. Français.

lufstöver, Basset Hound, Dachsbracken, Dachshunds, Lapphunds, Buhunds, and spaniels, for starters. The dog's typical curly water dog coat still indicates the Poodle as its most prominent ancestor. It should be understood that these dogs compose a *kind* of dog instead of a *breed* of dog.

Truffle Dog is a medium-sized dog with a curly coat and a water-dog-type conformation. Photo by I. Français.

Tulip ears, in the European sense, (upright with slight curve) on a handsome Frenchie.

Trumpet
See Temples

Tschika
See Chinese Greyhound

T.T.
Suffix indicating that a dog has undergone Temperament Testing. *See* Temperament Testing

Tuareg Sloughi
See Azawakh

Tuberculosis
Canine tuberculosis is far less common today than it was some years ago. Tuberculosis is still contracted by dogs, however, and a higher incidence is reported in dogs that dwell in urban environments. Additionally, short-nosed breeds appear to be at higher risk, and male dogs show a higher incidence of contraction than do females. Dogs can contract the disease from man, and can also transmit the disease to man, especially children. Neoplasms, generally in the form of carcinomas, affect the lung and liver tissue, leading to death. Tests

are available that can diagnose the disease, with radiographs and clinical history proving instrumental for conclusion. Dogs struck with this dreaded disease are best put down and in many localities are required to be so dealt with.

Tuck-up
Appearance of loin created by the sweep of the abdomen upwards into the hindquarters region. In the sighthounds, the tuck-up is more pronounced and acute. In general, the tuck-up is more subtle and less exaggerated.

Tufted tail
A tail whose end is tufted. In the Chinese Crested, a tufted tail is natural; in the Poodle, such a tail is groomed into a pom-pom.

Tugline
Line from harness to the towline; same as backline.

Tulip ears
Ears that stand upright with slightly forward-curving edges, resembling a tulip petal. Sometimes synonymous with bat ears. An alternate interpretation of

the terminology defines tulip ears as rose or semi-erect ears gone erect—a Bulldog with such cartilage erection is frowned upon. *See also* Bat ears

Tumor

An uncontrolled growth of tissue. Tumors can occur anywhere on a dog's body, internal or external. Tumors that do not spread, though they may grow slowly, are termed benign, or nonmalignant. So long as these growths are not large and do not impede any of the functionings of the dog, they are generally of little concern. As should all growths, however, they should be reported to a veterinarian. Tumors that spread and grow rapidly are often malignant. All malignant tumors are termed cancerous. They spread via metastasis and destroy normal cells of the body, quickly leading to death. Malignant tumors, if caught early, can be removed, often with no further complications. Large tumors, however, are very often untreatable, leaving euthanasia as the only real alternative. *See also* Cancer, Lipoma

Turn-up

Upward-bending configuration of the mandible or lower jaw in many brachycephalic breeds (e.g., Boxer).

Tusks

Canine teeth. *See* Dentition

Twist

The Pug's tail.

Twisted tail

A tail peculiar to the Tasy, a sighthound of the Soviet Union, not to be confused with the Afghan Hound, who is sometimes called Tazi. Other "twisted tails" are more correctly termed curled, spiral, double curl, etc.

Two-angled head

When viewed in profile, a head whose planes appear to diverge separately as opposed to the desired parallel planes (i.e., listed as fault in the Shetland Sheepdog standard).

Two-ply coat

Double coat.

Type variation exists within all breeds of dog, although in some it is more evident. The Jack Russell Terrier experiences large dissension in this respect. These two breed representatives show the stockier Bull Terrier type (*left*) and the leggier, leaner Fox Terrier type (*right*).

Type

The term "type" when discussing dogs is not synonymous with breed. Rather it refers to the general appearance of an animal's body or of a specific anatomical part. There are numerous body types: sighthound, collie, mastiff, bichon, etc.; likewise, there are coat types, ear types, eye types, face types, etc. Within a breed, sometimes different types develop, depending on where the dogs work or live. For instance, there are two Sloughi types: a mountain type and a desert type; there are two Jack Russell

progenitors. *See also* Coat types, Eye types, etc.

Typhus
A potentially deadly rickettsial disease that is transmitted mostly by ticks. Typhus is most common in Brazil, Co-

Type variations in coat greatly change the way a breed appears. The Wire and Smooth Fox Terriers share the same physical structure with the important exception of the coat. Photo by M. Pearlmutter.

types: a lighter fox-terrier type and a heavier bull-terrier type. Such divergence in type can be a cause of problems in a breed: Shar-Pei, Anatolian Shepherd, and American Eskimo fanciers contend with such dissension.

Coat types vary considerably within a breed, oftentimes with one type predominating over the other. Many of the sighthound type dogs have different coat types. There are long- and short-coated Salukis and Whippets; there are smooth- and wire-coated Galgos Españoles, Podengos Portugueses, Ibizan Hounds. Scenthounds even more typically have different coat types; most of the French packhounds underwent *griffon* phases, some of which still exist and have become more popular than their smooth

lombia, Kenya and in other tropical or subtropical regions.

Tyrolean Hound
See Tyroler Bracke

Tyroler Bracke
Originating in the western area of Austria, the Tyroler Bracke is the product of line and crossbreeding with various German, Austrian, French, Swedish, and possibly Swiss hounds. Although type probably was secured many years ago, the breed still shares a look common to many of the well-established hounds of the contributing countries. The first of the breed to be exhibited appeared in 1896. As a hunter, the Tyroler is useful on most any terrain and in high altitudes espe-

cially. Its fancy is moderate and does not extend outside Austria.

ESSENTIALS OF THE TYROLER BRACKE: Standing no greater than 19 inches (48 cm) high, usually 18 inches (46 cm) or smaller, and being black and tan (sometimes red) with white markings some-times occurring on the chest. This dog comes in three coat types (rough, hard, and smooth), and each are sometimes registered as individual breeds. Regardless of texture, the coat of the Tyroler is thick and resistant to ex-

tremes in temperature. The rough variety may show slight fringing, otherwise the dog will have a moderately tight appearance overall.

Tyroler Bracke, yellow, smooth.

Tyroler Bracke, black and tan. Photographs by I. Français.

U-shaped ears

Unusual terminology used to describe the drop ears of the Komondor.

U.D.T. was awarded to this proven yellow Labrador Retriever, Champion Broad Reach's English Muffin—the first bitch of her breed to be awarded this suffix. Owner, Martha Lee K. Voshell.

U-CD

Companion Dog degree awarded by the United Kennel Club.

U-CDX

Companion Dog Excellent degree awarded by the United Kennel Club.

U.D.

Utility Dog. This suffix signifies that the dog, having acquired the C.D. and C.D.X. degrees under the rules of the American Kennel Club, has completed three tests in the Utility Class, under at least two judges, and with two or more dogs in competition; has made scores of 170 or better of the possible 200; and has received each time at least 50 percent of the valuation in each individual exercise.

U.D.T.

Suffix indicating that a dog has been recorded as a Utility Dog Tracker. This signifies that the dog has acquired the C.D., C.D.X. and U.D. degrees under the rules of the American Kennel Club, as well as having been marked "passed" in at least one tracking test by two judges.

U.D.T.X.

Suffix indicating that a dog has been recorded as both a Utility Dog and a Tracking Dog Excellent. The U.D.T.X is the highest award a dog may receive in obedience test trials. Winning this degree does not bar the dog from further competition and the owner may carry the dog into as many Open and Utility classes, or as many tracking tests, as desired. *See also* Obedience trials, Tracking

U.K.C.

Abbreviation for United Kennel Club, which *see.*

Ulceromembranous stomatitis

See Trenchmouth

Ulcers

Stomach ulcers are very rare in dogs. If your dog shows signs of an ulcer, i.e., abdominal pain, loss of appetite, or digestive upsets, it is more likely a gastrointestinal infection, which can be treated with antibiotics.

Ulmer Dog

The Ulmer Dog is believed to be a prior form of the German Mastiff or Great Dane, which *see.*

Ulna

See Forequarters

Umbilical hernias

See Hernias

Umbrella

A rather short veil found on a number of long-coated flock guardian breeds (e.g., Komondor, Puli). *See* Veil

Unbalanced head

Head demarcated by a skull and foreface unproportionally balanced. A fault expressly listed in the Rough Collie standard.

Uncoiling

Hunting hound's working and moving from the point of check in a spiral or helical pattern.

Undercoat

The dense soft, short coat concealed by the longer topcoat. *See* Coat

Undercoat rake

Excellent for loosening up the coat and removing dead undercoat. Especially good on breeds like the German Shepherd Dog.

United Kennel Club

The second largest all-breed registry in the United States, the United Kennel Club (U.K.C.) is sometimes referred to as the "other kennel club" (o.k.c.). The organization was founded in 1898 by Chauncey Z. Bennett arguably as a registering body for the Pit Bull fraternity. Today it remains a privately owned enterprise with the nation's only fully computerized registry system, and it records about as many breeds as the American Kennel Club. This remarkably efficient system enables the U.K.C. to provide any

United Kennel Club formed allegedly as a registry for the American (Pit) Bull Terrier fraternity. This clamor of pit bulls was bravely snapped by R. Pearcy—a true tribute to the biddability and patience of smartly reared bulldogs.

Underhung

Undershot. *See* Bite types

Underline

The combined contours of the brisket and the abdominal floor.

Undershot

The front teeth or incisors of the lower jaw project beyond the front teeth of the upper jaw when the mouth is closed. *See* Bite types

Unilateral cryptorchid

An adult male whose testicles on one side are abnormally retained or hidden with the other testicle descended. *See* Cryptorchidism

accepted registrant with a six- or seven-generation pedigree.

The U.K.C. is noteworthy for its liberal, perhaps cavalier, acceptance of breeds. Although the American Kennel Club has usurped the word "American," in actuality the U.K.C. is perhaps more American than the A.K.C. The United Kennel Club registers all five breeds of American Coonhound: the American Black and Tan, Redbone, Bluetick, English, and the Treeing Walker. Of course, the Coonhound breeds, along with the cur types of the South, are America's contribution to the scenthound group. Additionally, the organization has always recognized the American Pit Bull Terrier. A breed in recent times that has caused incredible controversy—legal and ethical chaos—is also a breed that was once unconditionally the national model of the canine companion. The Toy Fox Terrier or AmerToy and the American Eskimo are two uniquely American breeds registered by the U.K.C. that have not acquired fancies outside the States. Other expressly "Yankee Doodle" breeds registered include the English Shepherd and the Australian Shepherd, herding dogs fashioned in the States but named for their contributing forebears. *See also* Purple Ribbon pedigree

Unproductive
A situation in which game cannot be produced after a positive point.

Unsoundness
An undesirable quality indicating that a dog is incapable, mentally or physically, of performing its intended function.

Untraining
The process of undoing a learned behavior. *See* Behavior modification, Training, Obedience trials

Un-united anconeal process
See Non-uniting anconeal process

Upper arm
Arm. *See* Forequarters

Upper jaw
See Jaws

Upper thigh
See Thigh

Upright ears
See Erect ears

Upright pasterns
Steep pasterns: the longitudinal pastern axis is nearly perpendicular. Down in pasterns would be the opposite situation. Dogs with upright pasterns tend to have less stride and stamina. Certain foxhounds require pasterns more upright than are usually desirable.

Upright shoulders
See Shoulder types

Upsweep
See Turn-up

Upward hook tail
A hanging tail that swirls upward at the hook (e.g., Briard).

Uremia
A condition of toxemia caused by failed kidneys, which causes uric acid to enter and pollute the blood. Uremia is a common cause of death in the older dog but rarely occurs in younger animals. Signs include consistently vomiting the entire contents of the stomach, including water; listlessness and discomfort; great thirst or no thirst at all; and a strong urine odor on the breath. Once signs are evidenced in the dog, there is usually little hope.

Urinary incontinence
See Incontinence

Urine
Average urine from the average dog is about 95 percent water. Urea makes up about 2.3 percent; salt about 1 percent; and the remainder is other solids. The color and content of urine can tell many qualities of the dog. For example, high sugar content may suggest diabetes while albumin can suggest kidney disease, especially if great thirst accompanies the albu-

Urine. Scent marking functions as the dog's primary means to identify its territory. Male dogs, more actively than females, mark trees and other objects with their urine. Beagle photographed by Ian Dunbar.

min content. Very dark urine and urine containing blood are signs of acute bacterial infection, especially leptospirosis. Both excessive and infrequent urination can be signs of trouble, likely kidney inflammation or failure. Urine samples should be a regular part of veterinary examinations.

Corrective measures include antibiotics, with corrective surgery often necessary.

Utility
In this class of obedience trials, the breed and sex eligibility is the same as in other classes, except that the dog must have acquired the C.D.X. degree. Ama-

Utility class finds this West Highland White Terrier performing in scent discrimination and retrieve. Photo by R. Reagan.

Urine is also an important means by which dogs mark their territory, leaving their scent. *See also* Canine behavior

Urocyon cinereoargenteus
See Gray fox

Urticaria
See Hives

Uterine infections
The three common infections of the uterus are metritis, endometritis, and pyometra. Metritis is the inflammation of the whole uterus. Endometritis is the inflammation of the lining of the uterus. Pyometra is pus in the uterus. Metritis and endometritis can cause swelling through the whole of the reproductive tract, including the vulva. These two diseases result mostly from injury accrued while giving birth, although they can stem from other causes. Pyometra is not directly related to the birthing process but occurs between mating cycles: bacteria fills the resting uterus, causing the accumulation of pus. The accumulated pus causes swelling, often great, and other organs, especially the kidneys, may become stressed. All three uterine infections require medical treatment.

teur or professional may compete and the dog may be entered in these classes an unlimited number of times. *See also* Obedience trials, Open, Novice

Utility Dog
A dog that has won certain minimum scores in Utility Classes at a specified number of A.K.C.-licensed or member obedience trials. U.D. is the suffix used.

Utility Dog Tracker
A dog that has achieved the required minimum scores in Utility Classes at a specified number of A.K.C.-licensed or member obedience trials as well as having passed the tracking dog test.

Utility Group
This useful kennel club designation for the show ring is one employed principally by the British registry and essentially compares with the American Non-Sporting Group. The group includes a variety of breeds, all of which perform in a working, herding, or sporting function—primarily. Among the breeds which Britain categorizes here are the Poodles, Shar-Pei, Dalmatian, and Bulldog. *See* Group systems

V-shaped ears

Triangular shaped ears that tend to bend forward (not by definition, though). V-shaped ears that are not carried drop are more standardly referred to simply as triangular ears. The Vizsla and Bullmastiff have dropped Vs, while the Alaskan Malamute and German Shepherd have triangular Vs.

V-shaped head

When viewed in profile, a head that is triangular or wedge-shaped, not necessarily of equal dimensions; thus the base of one dog can be appreciably narrow while the length short, and vice-versa, and both dogs possess V-shaped heads.

Vaccinations, as scheduled by your breeder and veterinarian, serve to keep a dog as disease-free as possible. Photo by R. Pearcy.

Vaccinations

The health of our dogs is greatly dependent upon preventive care. Vaccinations are the most important form of such prevention. There are five essential vaccinations that all dogs must receive. The first of these is a canine distemper vaccination which should be given at six to eight weeks. This inoculation will immunize till about three months of age. The second and third vaccinations should be administered at the same time as the second distemper shot; these are the canine hepatitis vaccination and the canine parainfluenza inoculations. Additionally, the canine leptospirosis vaccination is given at this time as well. The last vaccination is the rabies shot, which is necessary at six months of age and followed up annually. A live virus vaccine, however, can be administered every three years instead of this annual booster. Rabies vaccinations are common requirements in most locales, in most states and countries. Such a vaccination usually precludes a dog's receiving its license. While free rabies clinics are less common than planned parenthood clinics, they do exist from time to time. Veterinarians most often administer such vaccinations and are required to issue a report to the appropriate authorities. For exporting purposes, proof of a rabies vaccination is usually requisite.

Vaghari Dog

Used as hunters, the Vaghari Dogs dwell with the nomadic tribe known as the Vaidava Vaghari of Suarastra in India. These dogs are versatile hunters with exquisite noses. Their talents are used on rabbit, wolf, jackal, and boar; they are sometimes used to track wounded game; with little training, the dogs can hunt effectively in packs and can attack and kill a wild panther. They stand 20–24 inches (51–61 cm) at the shoulders. The common colors are tan, brown or black. In shape, they resemble the Greyhound, excepting the tail which turns over the back.

Vagina

The canal found in female animals that leads from the vulva to the uterus and is instrumental in reproduction. Unlike the uterus, the vagina is relatively trouble free. Many of the infections that can occur in the vagina are either lived with by the bitch with no obvious signs or are eradicated quickly by her defense system. Herpes virus can cause great grief, however. Other possible problems include: persistent hymen and clitoris enlargement and vaginitis. Persistent hymen refers to the condition in which the hymen, a web of tissue found in the vagina of some bitches, is too thick to be broken either by the penis of the male or the instrument of the owner and therefore requires surgical correction if mating is to occur. Clitoris enlargement is a disorder that also prevents mating: during excitement, the bitch's clitoris swells so greatly that the male's penis cannot enter. The condition can be dangerous to both the stud and the bitch if it occurs subsequent to the penis's intrusion. Surgical correction may be necessary if the bitch is to be mated. Vaginitis means simply inflammation of the mucus lining of the vagina. It can be of several causes and is often the result of unhygienic conditions. The real danger of vaginitis is its propensity to spread to the uterus, possibly resulting in a serious condition ending in sterility. Vaginitis, in its early stage, is easily treatable under your veterinarian's care.

Vaginitis
Inflammation of the vagina. *See* Vagina

Valee Sheepdog
See Polish Lowland Sheepdog

Vallhund
Swedish for forest dog.

Vanjari
See Banjara Greyhound

Vasgotaspets
See Swedish Vallhund

Veadeiro Catarinense
See Brazilian Greyhound

Veil
The portion of the dog's forelock hanging straight down or partially covering the eyes.

Veins
See Circulatory system

Venereal disease
Any of the many diseases that are

transmitted primarily by sexual activity, primarily sexual intercourse. Dogs typically do not have venereal diseases in the sense that humans do. The one seeming exception is a disease called brucellosis, which *see*.

Vent
Anal opening.

Vent, barreled
Describes an anal sphincter that protrudes when viewed from side.

Ventral
Adjective, of the belly.

Verminous pneumonia
See Pneumonia

Vertebra
See Spinal column

Vertebral column
See Spinal column

Veil enshrining the face of the once-sacred Lhasa Apso. Photo by I. Français.

Veterinarian

At risk of a doggy cliché, your veterinarian is the most important person in your dog's life, next to you. Who is a veterinarian or veterinary surgeon? Essentially any professional or qualified individual who is certified or has earned a degree in veterinary medicine. In the U.S., D.V.M. is the most common title for a vet, although a lexicon of titles exists; in England, no actual doctorate is necessary.

While your veterinarian will have a great many responsibilities (adminstering shots, providing prescriptions, diagnosing illnesses, giving advice and counsel), it is the owner's role to find the *right* vet for his dog. Unless you live in a secluded rural area, you likely have many choices. Don't settle for a vet because he's ten minutes closer. You should ask your fellow dog keepers for recommendations and not commit to one practice immediately. Your vet should show genuine concern for your animal and you, as well as have the knowledge and experience to provide the professional care you need. Being happy with your vet is vital to your dog's health. Work fast but find the one who makes you comfortable and secure. Trusting your vet also means heeding his advice about spaying, surgery and other important decisions that affect your dog's life.

Viciousness

A vicious dog is one that attacks unprovoked and uncontrollably. The dog's primary offensive and defensive weapon is its teeth, which are fused in strong, well-constructed jaws and which can inflict lethal damage. Laws regarding vicious dogs exist in most countries but they often fall under local or regional jurisdiction and therefore can vary from place to place and time to time. Some laws apply specifically to the act of viciousness, while others may apply to the owner's knowingly housing, selling, or giving away a "vicious" dog. Viciousness itself is often defined by the governing body, and the definition can also vary from body to body. A dog can be condemned as vicious if it bites but once for any reason—no exceptions—under certain law. The many attacks by vicious dogs make difficult the keeping of dogs by those who wish to own a dog but are bound by laws that are the result of irresponsible owners making the law necessary for the protection of the people. *See also* Pit bull

Pertinent to the show ring, viciousness, demonstrated by a dog's attempting to bite or biting a judge—or showing hostility, not aggressiveness, towards other dogs, is grounds for that dog's disqualification.

Victorian Pom
See German Spitzen, Pomeranian

Vikhan
This breed from Chitral, India, derives his name from the Sanskrit word for broken or noseless, *Vikh*. The word also means hermit and aptly describes the dog's intense need for independence. These dogs are large and ferocious and capable of protecting flocks from attacking leopards. Like many of the European flock guards, the Vikhan is provided with an iron collar to protect it from sharp-fanged assailants.

Vincent's infection (angina)
See Trenchmouth

Vine-leaf ears
Comparatively small, triangular-shaped ears that narrow gradually toward the tip. British term for desired ear type in Clumber and Welsh Springer Spaniels.

Viral disease
Transmitted through bites or ingestion depending on the specific nature of the virus. Viruses themselves are micro-organisms that form one of the three major groupings of living organisms. Though the signs of viral infections are largely similar to those of bacterial infections, virus and bacteria are quite distinct. A virus cannot reproduce outside a host. Viruses invade host cells, take them over, and command them to produce viral DNA or RNA. Viral diseases can result in mass tissue loss and damage. Rabies, a deadly virus, is transmitted via a bite from an infected animal. Many intestinal viruses can be acquired by simply breathing the same air as an infected animal. Immunity to viral diseases can be acquired either by naturally overcoming a viral infection or through vaccinations. Rabies and parvovirus are two very serious viral infections against

which all dogs should be vaccinated. *See also* Rabies, Parvovirus

Virelade
See Gascon-Saintongeois

Vitamins
Vitamins are not food, but they are necessary for the proper absorption and utilization of food: vitamins act as catalysts in the transformation of food to energy. For the average dog, a balanced diet, with occasional treats and scraps, provides all the necessary vitamins in the required amounts, with little to no need for vitamin supplements. The pregnant bitch, the sick and/or weak animal, and

the dog in training for a sled pull or other physical competition are exceptions, and they may demand vitamin and mineral supplementing. The expectant mother needs plenty of calcium and vitamin D; it is likely that your veterinarian will recommend added milk, cottage cheese, and other products rich in nutrients that the bitch needs for her and her pup's sound health. The sick animal may demand a multi-vitamin, or if suffering from a secondary vitamin deficiency (a result of the initial condition), the dog may require high doses of a few specific vitamins. In the case of a dog in training, multi-vitamin and mineral supplements may be essential for the dog's system to meet the demands placed upon it. In all cases, vitamins should not be given liberally or

Vitamins occur naturally in your dog's food. Additionally, many commercial dog foods are fortified with vitamin and mineral supplements. Chow puppy photographed by I. Français.

without consideration of the dog's condition. A vitamin excess is undesirable and can be dangerous.

Vitamin A Growth, vision, appetite, nerve function, coat condition, digestion are all aided by sufficient levels of vitamin A, which also helps in the prevention of infection.

Vitamins. Many professional breeders recommend supplementing commercial dog foods with home-cooked meats and vegetables to ensure a generous allowance of vitamins in their dogs' meals. Boxer puppies photographed by I. Français.

Vizsla, golden rust, wire, puppy. Coat not accepted in U.S. Photograph by I. Français.

Vitamin B complex A group of B vitamins, including B1 (thiamine), B2 (riboflavin), B6 (pyridoxine), and B12; all of which are required for the health and smooth functioning of most vital organs. The B vitamins also promote appetite, deter anemia, add tone to muscle, and ease bowel movements.

Vitamin C Ascorbic acid, though an important vitamin to the dog, rarely causes complications. Research indicates that dogs are able to manufacture some vitamin C in their system. Dogs respond well to vitamin C supplements should they require them, and it is a rare dog who has scurvy, the condition which occurs from the lack of this vitamin.

Vitamin D Essential for the development and maintenance of strong bones and teeth and the utilization of calcium. A deficiency of D can result in rickets, but an excess can cause hardening of the tissues, tooth deformation, bloody diarrhea, and other undesirables.

Vitamin E For lactation, muscle tone, and healing.

Vitamin K Most importantly, vitamin K is necessary for blood clotting. Other necessary elements include folic and pantothenic acid and choline, all of which are known as trace elements for they are found in minute quantities only within the dog's body.

Vixen

The female fox.

Vizsla

A refined yet all-around hunting dog believed to have originated in Hungary. The Vizsla enjoys world-wide popularity. The exact origin of the breed remains undocumented and authorities remain in antithetical disagreement: some assert that the breed is ancient, while others contend the breed is a twentieth-century development. The Vizsla's accepted native region is the heated plains area in the center of present-day Hungary. The re-

gion is known for its fertile ground and abounding wild game; the terrain demands a most hardy dog, making the Vizsla's refinement the more remarkable. Etchings dating back nearly 1,000 years depict dogs and falcons worked by Magyar huntsmen. It is known that the Magyars (early settlers of the region of Hungary) had dogs and used them for hunting purposes. Additionally, legends remain that point to the "Yellow Turkish Hunting Dog" as component stock used in the creation of the Vizsla. Even some adamant believers in the breed's antiquity concede, however, that the perfecting of this pointer's type and ability is a twentieth-century occurrence, in part due to outcrosses to other European pointers. The Vizsla was ravaged in Europe during the two World Wars and exists today largely because some dogs were taken out of their native land. Presently two coat varieties exist: a wire and a smooth, the wire providing added protection in cold, wet weather and heavily thicketed terrain. While not recognized in the U.S. or U.K. but accepted in Canada, the wirecoated Vizsla, known as the Drótszörü Magyar Vizsla, is often preferred by hunters who know the value of a wire coat when in harsh conditions.

The Vizsla is a multi-functional dog that is particularly useful on upland game and the retrieving of waterfowl. He is an impressively intelligent and gentle-mannered dog. The Vizsla is a natural hunter that is too easy to train. As a home companion, he is clean and his instinctive protective nature makes him a reliable guardian.

ESSENTIALS OF THE VIZSLA: The lean but muscular, Vizsla is a medium-sized dog of power and drive in the field. The head is lean and muscular. The skull is moderately wide between the ears, with a median line down the forehead. Stop is moderate. Muzzle is square and deep. The neck is strong, smooth and muscular. The shoulders well laid back. The back short. The chest moderately broad and deep, reaching to the elbows. Hindquarters well developed, with moderately angulated stifles and hocks. The tail, set just below the croup line, is customarily

docked one third off. Color of the Vizsla is solid golden rust in different shadings. Height: 22–24 inches (56–61 cm). Weight: 49–62 pounds (22–28 kg). The traditional coat is short, smooth, dense, and close-lying, without woolly undercoat; the coat of the wirehaired Vizsla, although not accepted in the U.S. or Britain (but accepted in Canada), is coarse and bristly but not very long. Hair on the muzzle and skull is short and coarse but smooth-lying, except for the beard and the eyebrows, which are prominent and bushy. The gait is far-reaching, light-footed, graceful and smooth.

Vlaamsche Trekhond
   See Belgian Mastiff

Voice
   The bark or cry of a hound.

Vizsla, golden rust. Photo by I. Français.

Volpino Italiano

Spitz dogs are certainly not exclusive to Germany, although it seems that most trace themselves to Germanic origins. Although the connection seems indicative, the moot issue is mottled with speculation. Early sources suggest that the Volpino is but an Italian Pomeranian,

and triangular. The coat is long and abundant on the entire body. Today the most common color is white, although times past enjoyed the Volpino Italiano in solid fawn, black and sable. Some sable dogs still exist but these are rare. Height: 11 inches (28 cm). Weight: under 10 pounds (4.5 kg).

Volpino Italiano, white. Photo by I. Français.

as white is certainly a color option in the German Spitz family. *Volpe* in Italian means fox, which is certainly descriptive of the breed. The Volpino Italiano has enjoyed popularity with Italian ladies for centuries and were decorated with ivory bracelets, symbols of their keepers' affection and affluence. The Volpino may indeed be to Italy what the American Eskimo is to the United States—small white German Spitzen taken home and claimed as natives.

ESSENTIALS OF THE VOLPINO ITALIANO: A profusely coated, solid white spitz-type dog, the Volpino curls a sporty tail, with pointed erect ears and a foxy expression. It is a cobby, small dog with a short, small head. The skull is somewhat stretched from the ears and slightly rounded. The muzzle is short, straight and pointed. It is essential that the Volpino not resemble a toy spaniel. The eyes are large and rounded, dark in color; the ears are small

Vomiting

The abnormal ejection of the contents of the stomach through the mouth. There are two types of vomiting: involuntary and voluntary. Typically involuntary vomiting is infrequent to rare and not usually a sign of trouble. A dog can vomit involuntarily during play, exercise, or other activity in which a sudden movement can cause the stomach to contract, expelling its contents. So long as such an occurrence is rare, there is little cause for concern. If recurrent, the action deserves the attention of a veterinarian. Voluntary vomiting involves active contractions of the abdomen and the cooperation of other body parts for the expellation of the stomach contents. Voluntary vomiting is often recurrent within a given period and is a common sign of an unhealthful condition. Vomiting can signal parasites, reaction to diet, bacterial or viral infection, and other conditions.

Acute vomiting occurs when the dog ingests a toxic substance, particularly poison. Once ingested, the substance irritates the lining of the stomach and/or infiltrates the bloodstream and affects the brain and nervous system, either of which can cause the dog to expel its stomach contents. Therefore, vomiting is a protective reaction that eliminates toxic material from the body. Some poisons, such as alkalis and others, cause severe damage if they are regurgitated, and the dog should be treated otherwise to prevent vomiting and to dilute or counteract the poison. *See also* Poisoning

Whenever a dog suffers acute vomiting, food must be considered as a factor. The dog's digestive system is somewhat sensitive to change. A dog who is subjected to a drastic change in diet will often exhibit vomiting and/or diarrhea for a period. The key to changing a dog's diet is moderate graduation. New dog and puppy owners should find out to which foods or formula the dog is accustomed and continue feeding the same, changing gradually if necessary or desirable. Food poisoning should also be considered, as the bacteria present in decomposing food can easily affect the dog's system and multiply to the point of causing toxemia, large quantities of bacteria in the blood. In addition, many dogs have a physical aversion to a particular food and will vomit whenever it is ingested. The particular substance can be determined by starting with a nutritionally balanced homemade diet of a few basic foodstuffs, i.e., meat, cooked rice or meal, and a boiled vegetable or two, and adding other substances one at a time or replacing one substance and adding a similar one to the diet.

Acute vomiting can also signal disease, particularly intestinal infections, kidney malfunction, and many others. The most common sign of intestinal tract infection is diarrhea. When vomiting accompanies diarrhea, it can be assumed that the upper tract of the small intestine is affected. If vomiting does not accompany, it is assumed that only the lower digestive tract (colon, etc.) is affected. Vomiting as a sign of intestinal infection thereby helps diagnosis and treatment. In older dogs, vomiting is frequently a sign of failing kidneys. Unable to eliminate the toxins of the bloodstream, the kidneys let pass and let accumulate these toxins, causing toxemia, of which vomiting is a sign.

Intestinal parasites can cause vomiting, particularly in heavy infestations. Tapeworms are notorious for causing vomiting. As their numbers increase in

Vomiting. The puppy's digestive system is very delicate. To avoid upset, changes in diet should be undertaken gradually. Belgian Sheepdog pup photographed by V. Serbin.

the digestive tract, so does their release of toxin, which eventually causes vomiting. Some intestinal parasites are visible to the naked eye in the dog's stool, while others require clinical observation. Visiting your veterinarian with a stool sample is a regular part of good health care for your dog.

Acalasia is believed to be an inherited defect that can cause vomiting. Acalasia refers to the existence of a pouchlike development along the esophagus that fills with swallowed food, which after a time forces the dog to "vomit" the accumulated substance. This vomiting is more a spitting up than actual vomiting, but other than the connoisseur may not be able to distinguish the difference.

Vorstehhund

German term for the all-purpose hunting dog. The quest for the vorstehhund involved crossing various schweisshunden (bloodhounds) and pointers. Today the Longhaired Pointer of Germany stands out as an exceptional vorstehhund, as does the Weimaraner.

female reproduction system. A bloody discharge, bright at the beginning and pinkish to colorless towards the end, lasts several days during the bitch's heat period. The tapering off of the discharge marks the readiness of the bitch to mate. A bloody discharge towards the end of a pregnancy signals that whelping is near.

Vorstehhund astutely demonstrated by the Weimaraner, an all-purpose hunting dog able to track and point its game. Wild boar is exceptionally difficult game to work for any dog.

Vulpes spp.

Wild dogs commonly known as vulpine foxes, which include *V. vulpes, V. velox, V. corsac, V. bengalensis, V. cana, V. ferrilata, V. rüppelli, V. pallida, and V. chama. See* Foxes

Vulva

Consists of three parts: the vestibule, clitoris, and labia. It is located below the anus and marks the external end of the

An infection of the vulva, marked by irritation and blood and pus discharge, requires immediate treatment, especially during pregnancy. An infection of the vulva can easily spread to the vagina and then to the uterus and/or ovaries, causing miscarriage and sterility, depending on the conditions and severity of the infection. The vulva should be checked regularly. *See also* Breeding, Brood bitch, Vagina, Reproductive system

Waddling gait

Awkward and pendulumlike tottering from side to side, appearing clumsy. Not to suggest that all ducks are clumsy, this ducklike kinesis is propelled by bow hocks causing the back feet to cross when moving. Usually most undesirable.

Waist

The narrowing portion of the body at the lumbar region, when compared to the chest width.

Walk

Gait pattern in which three legs are in support of the body at all times, each foot lifting from the ground, one at a time, in regular sequence. Sequentially: right front, left rear, left front, right rear, etc., etc. *See also* Gait

Walleye

A condition marked by uneven, incomplete melanin distribution. The iris appears blue with flecks throughout. This condition has acquired a cornucopia of synonyms: china eye; fish eye; glass eye; jeweled eye; marbled eye; blue eye; and silver eye. This condition is most common in merle-colored dogs and can affect one or both eyes.

War dogs

Dogs have always been inextricably associated with man throughout the course of his history. Contemporary historical studies habitually outline the passage of time and define historical periods by their relationship to the wars or revolts that occurred. Periods are defined as pre-Civil War, post-WWII, pre-Bolshevik Revolution, or post-French Revolution. Likewise, dogs have participated in these wars, side by side with man. While all war dogs do not actually combat, they have other equally demanding and crucial wartime functions: carriers of supplies, messengers, sentries, watchdogs, and enemy or mine scenters.

Homer mentions messenger dogs in his writings, verifying that dogs have been involved in battles for many centuries. Three hundred years before Christ, mastifflike dogs with enormous heads, short muzzles and erect prick ear were collared with heavy multi-angled spikes; these lethal collars would injure horses and men as the dogs charged through enemy lines. Attila the Hun was known to have kept packs of dogs around his camp for protective purposes. The mastiff dogs have long been revered for their power and battling propensity. The Romans took ancient British mastiff types back home to perform in the arena. Henry VIII impressed his ally Charles V of Spain by sending a brigade of 800 St. Hubert-type hounds, trained to fight against the French.

In more modern times, dogs have played key roles in both great wars. In World War I, dogs were used to search out the wounded and to carry equipment and accessories. French and Belgian draft dogs performed many such tasks, for instance. The Germans were quite successful in training and developing the potentials of the Airedale Terrier for wartime purposes. Ironically, the Airedale fought gallantly for the Germans against the British, in whose land the dog was chiefly conceived. Among

Walleye commonly occurs in merle-colored dogs. Cardigan Welsh Corgi photographed by I. Français.

War dogs. Rottweilers performing in military service. Even with the advancement of military technology, the need for dogs in the armed forces has not declined.

the other breeds frequently employed as war dogs are the Giant Schnauzer, German Shepherd Dog, Rottweiler and Doberman Pinscher. In World War II, dogs were extensively used by all nations involved. Germany alone trained over 200,000 dogs for military service during the Second World War, and the U.S. trained nearly 150,000. Equally ironic is the fact that while dogs are out in the fields carrying supplies, messages or ammunition, the kennel dogs in the home countries are starving, being neglected or spited, or worse—eaten in times of desperation. The U.S. is the only major military power that does not offer a canine medal for bravery. In times of peace, would-be war dogs work as guard dogs and night watchmen for military bases and the like. *See also* Police dogs, Airedale Terrier, Schutzhund, Guard dog

Warrigal
   See Dingo

Warts
   Hard skin growths, usually caused by a virus. Dogs, like humans get warts periodically, often with increased age. The Azawakh is renowned for its requisite "warts" on its head—warty growths prized by the native nomads.

Wash
   The trail of scent-filled bubbles left by an animal, such as an otter, when swimming under water.

Watchdog
   See Guard dog

Water
   Vital to life, water should be available to the dog at all times. Water should be clean and fresh, changed at least daily, and provided in sturdy, easy-to-clean bowls or containers. Water must be kept away from possible contaminants, such as flies, mosquitoes, and even rain. *See also* Puppies, Nutrition, Urine

Water Dog of Spain

El Perro de Agua de Español, diluted into English, the Water Dog of Spain, is indeed not a water dog in the traditional sense, nor is this newly discovered breed a spin-off or variant of the well-known Cão de Agua, the Portuguese Water Dog. The Perro de Agua has functioned for Spanish shepherds for hundreds of years as a herder and all-around working dog, who has a lusty affinity for the water. Like the Portie, whose origins nonetheless are likely connected, the Water Dog of Spain has webbed feet, making swimming a natural task. However, unlike his Portuguese relation who chased fish and tackle much of the time, this Spaniard had been employed to move sheep from the south of Spain to the north in the summer time, since the southern part of the country was too hot for grazing. In the winter, the dogs would move the sheep back to the south. Working in conjunction with *El Mastin de Español*, the Spanish Mastiff, who guarded the royal *cañadas* or cattle paths, the Perro de Agua lead the way for the shepherds. Today this trip is principally undertaken by train, so the dogs have found different jobs. The breed is a very active and happy dog that is always willing to work. One keeper of these dogs in Spain attests to the fact that his dogs can swim underwater as deep as 10 feet (3 m).

Believably this ancient Spanish dog has played a significant role in the development of the world's spaniels. The

Water Dog of Spain, brown. Photo by I. Français.

French spaniels, in particular, have been tied to this breed, and it is commonly said that Napoleon, during his invasion of Spain, was much enamored of these kinky little workhorses and took examples back home. The Épagneul Pont-Audemer, with its incriminating curly locks and water dexterity, is but one of the spaniels who likely developed from the Water Dog of Spain. Called a variety of names, such as La Mesta and La Medera, the Perro de Agua de Español until recently was considered simply a working dog and companion. Presently pro-

Water Dog of Spain, black.

moters of the purebred Perro have been in contact with the Fédération Cynologique Internationale and a standard has been drawn up. While no English standard is available presently, we know that this dog is substantially smaller than the Perro de Pastor de Catalan (or Catalan Sheepdog), the larger herding dog of Spain, and weighs approximately 20 pounds (9 kg), standing from 16.5–19 inches (42–50 cm). The dogs come in a wide range of colors including fawns, blacks and browns. The coat is curly and thick and may have a tendency to cord. It is a fairly square-bodied breed with a deep chest and moderately large head. The face is fully furnished with hair and the drop ears are carried flat to the head in repose.

Water Dog of Spain, fawn. Photographs by I. Français.

W.C.
Abbreviation for Working Certificate, which *see*.

Weaning
The period during which the pup learns to acquire its foodstuffs from sources other than its mother. Thus, it is an important time in

Water dogs

While many dogs take to the water, "water dogs" most often refers to those gundog breeds which are used primarily for water work. Examples of these dogs are the Barbet, Poodle, Curly-Coated Retriever, and Portuguese Water Dog. Like the retrievers, these dogs are able to retrieve. Retrievers more often retrieve on both land and water. Certain retrievers, of course, have an undissolvable affinity for the water: the Chesapeake Bay Retriever and the Nova Scotia Duck Tolling Retriever. The water dogs are distinguished by their curly coats and are believed to be descendants of the Oriental sheep-herding breeds and certain gundogs. Many of the early water dogs were used as fishermen's on-board helpers. Many European hound breed histories attest to these dogs' swimming to shore as progenerators of the wirehaired scenthound and gundog varieties.

These curly-coated dogs have been sculpted by groomers for centuries. The peculiar clips of the Poodle, Portuguese Water Dog and Barbet were initiated by hunters to maximize the dog's water abilities: agility, protection and speed. Today the clips have been maintained to remain true to tradition. *See* Gundogs, Clipping the Poodle

Weak hocks
See Hock types

the development of the pup in that the young animal is moving towards greater independence. Weaning is marked by the first instance in which the pup eats solid food, beginning with its first meal and ending when exclusively solid food is eaten. The weanling's food must be easily swallowed and highly digestible. A commercial weaning preparation is often recommended, and alternative recipes can be acquired from experienced breeders and veterinarians. In the wild, and sometimes still in our domestic dogs, weaning is initiated by the nursing dam's regurgitation of food for the pups. At times, the father too may regurgitate for the young ones. In domestic dogs, weaning typically runs its complete course during the third through fifth weeks of life and is usually initiated by the nursing dam. On occasion, the breeder must initiate the process, especially in the case of first-time mothers. *See* Puppies, Feeding

Weaselness

Opposite of legginess (which *see*), appearance of a long, lean snakelike body (e.g., fault for Old English Sheepdog).

Weight pulling demonstrated by a hard-working American Pit Bull Terrier.

Weaving

Unsound gait which begins with twisting elbows and ends with criss-crossing and toeing out. Also known as crossing over, plaiting, dishing and knitting, weaving is considered faulty.

Webbed feet

Feet in which the skin and tissue between the toes are well developed to accommodate the dogs' need to work in the water. The Chesapeake and Otter Hound are fine examples of webbed-footed breeds. The snowshoe-footed breeds (huskies, laikas, etc.) also experience a good amount of webbing on their feet.

Wedge-shaped muzzle

See Tapering muzzle

Wedge-shaped head

See V-shaped head

Weediness

Light and insufficient bone.

Weight

Tall tales (and very heavy ones) have exaggerated the size of dogs through the years. Many sources still regard the pony-sized Tibetan Mastiff as the heaviest dog, weighing in at 220 pounds (100 kg). This breed in reality is much smaller. The heaviest breed today is likely the Saint Bernard, which can weigh nearly 250 pounds (113 kg), with the Mastiff a close second at a maximum of about 210 pounds (95 kg). On the opposite end, the smallest breed is likely the Chihuahua, which as an adult can weigh as little as one pound (.5 kg); the lightest adult on record weighed 10 ounces. Other lightweight contenders are the Yorkshire Terrier and Toy Poodle at around three pounds (1.5 kg).

Weight pulling

Organized competitions for weight pulling have become popular in the dog fancy, along with obedience and agility trials. Weight pulling is a common event in agility trials and all breeds participate—from the Tosa Inu to the Chinese Crested. The draft and sled dogs have an added instinctual pull; the mastiffs, the shear muscle to get the job done. The record for heaviest load goes to a Saint Bernard who pulled 6,400 pounds. Pound for pound, the undefeated champion is the American Pit Bull Terrier. Cart pulling is also incorporated into the competition—Rotties, Newfs and Berners are among celebrated cart pullers.

Weil's disease

See Leptospirosis

Weimaraner

An outstanding gundog of German descent, having a distinctive gray coat coloration and light amber, gray, or blue-gray eyes. The breed takes its name in memory of the sporting nobles of the court of Weimar who enthusiastically supported the breed in its early days. The Weimaraner is a study in selective breeding, though without all breed components known with certainty, the products of the inquiry can be discerned only with question. It is believed that the Weimaraner comes from stock similar to that of the German Shorthaired Pointer, with suggested drops of Bloodhound blood added early and perhaps indirectly, through crosses with one or more of the various schweisshund varieties. Various European brackes and the Spanish Pointer are other probable contributors. The dog's silver-gray color is unique in the dog world and no explanation based entirely on fact really exists.

Once used on big game, wolves, wildcats, deer, mountain lion, bear, etc., the Weimaraner had to be a strong, active and courageous dog able to work in packs. With the disappearance of big game in Europe, the breed became somewhat of a rarity by the late 1800s. With continued selective breeding, the Weimaraner became a suitable small game hunter and bird dog and the breed's usefulness and popularity soon grew. The Weimaraner entered the U.S. in 1929, under the skilled eye of American sportsman and breeder, Howard Knight, a member of the Weimaraner Club of Germany. The dog became largely used as a personal hunting companion and a field-trial competitor. In 1943 the AKC granted official recognition to these most able and attractive hunting dogs. The breed today is actively employed in obedience and field trials and is a popular hunting companion. His show numbers are relatively strong and many excel in the ring. There exists a longhaired Weimaraner variety which is not accepted in the U.S. but enjoys recognition in Europe.

In character, he is a loving family dog of unstinting devotion to his household members. He is also, of course, a competent hunter of small game and a skilled tracker of large game. He is adaptable and highly trainable.

ESSENTIALS OF THE WEIMARANER: Most importantly, the dog's conformation must indicate the abil-

ity to work with great speed and endurance in the field. The breed is known for its grace, speed, stamina, alertness, and balance. The light gray coloration of the Weimaraner, however, is the true hallmark of the breed. The eyes, in shades of amber, gray or blue-gray, complement the "gray ghost's" unique appearance. The coat can be shorthaired or longhaired. The smooth coat is short, fine and hard; the long coat is about 1–2 inches (3–6 cm) in length and fringed like a setter's coat. Height: 23–28 inches (58–66 cm). Weight: 70–85 pounds (32–38 kg). The dog is essentially medium sized. The head is moderately long and aristocratic, with moderate stop and slight median line. Occiput rather prominent. The flew should be straight, delicate at the nostrils; skin drawn tightly. The neck to be clean-

Weimaraner, light gray, shorthaired. Photo by J. Ashbey.

Weimaraner, light gray, longhaired. Coat type not accepted in U.S. Photo by I. Français.

Weimaraner. The amber eye coloration of the breed sustains its reputation as the "gray ghost." Photo by I. Français.

cut and moderately long. The ears are long and lobular, slightly folded and set high. The nose is gray. The back should be moderately long, strong, and straight, set with a slight slope from the withers; the chest well developed and deep with the shoulders well-laid back; the forelegs straight and strong; the tail is customarily docked to 6 inches (15 cm). Gait should be smooth, effortless, and coordinated.

Weimaraner Vorstehhund
  See Weimaraner

Well cut-up
  See Tuck-up

Well-angulated
  See Angulation

Well-angulated hocks
  See Hock types

Well-angulated shoulders
  See Shoulder types

Well-coupled
  Short-coupled, strongly coupled. See Coupling

Well-knit
  Body parts firmly enjoined by well-developed musculature. Often synonymous with short or well coupled, which would indicate a strong loin section joining the chest and hindquarters.

Well-knuckled-up
  Cat foot, which see.

Well-laid back shoulders
  See Shoulder types

Well-laid shoulders
  Well-angulated shoulders.

Well-set neck
  The desired placement of the neck into the shoulder region with a nearly indiscernible blend-in.

Well-sunken eyes
  Deep-set eyes.

Welsh Collie
  See Welsh Sheepdog

Welsh Hound
  The Welsh Hound is a large rendition of the English packhounds, looking much like a thick, rough-coated foxhound. In color they were tricolor or tan-pied. The ears are pendant and the tail long. It was valued by Welsh hunters who relied on it for its consistency and pack instincts.

Welsh Setter

A distinct, though now extinct, cross between a black setter and the white curly coated Llanidloes; it once occurred in West Wales.

Welsh Sheepdog

The Welsh Sheepdog, sometimes referred to as the Welsh Collie, is one of the oldest and least known of British herding dogs. Since breed purity was not of utmost importance to the Welsh shepherds, a number of types of these sheepdogs occurred. The native and semi-native dogs are the purest of the types. The mongrelized Welsh Sheepdogs could range in appearance from a Deerhound to a Corgi, speaking for the extent of variation. The old Welsh Grey and the Red Herders are among the most ancient of Welsh Sheepdog types. The former resembled a small, stiff-coated Old English Sheepdog, the latter a deep-red-coated Corgi. Many native dogs, especially those in black and tan, resembled the Scottish Deerhound. Collie blood from the Cumberland area was introduced to the Welsh herders, creating dogs that resemble working Shelties. The existing Welsh Collie looks much like the Border Collies of today, with comparable dexterity and versatility. These herders work on everything from bulls to chickens.

Welsh Springer Spaniel

It is believed that the Welsh Springer has existed as a breed for centuries as a hunting dog found principally in Wales and the west of England. In studying the available sources, we learn that for centuries the most common gundog type is the one closely resembling the Welsh Springer of today. The breed, as far as we know, has always had its exclusive and distinctive red and white coloration. A reference in Dr. Caius's volume of 1570, entitled *Of English Dogges*, is one source of support for these claims: " . . . the Spanniells whose skynnes are white, and if they are marcked with any spottes, they are commonly red. . . "

Welsh Sheepdog, orange and white.

Welsh Sheepdog, merle. Photographs by I. Français.

After centuries of utilitarian existence in Wales, these Springers, once known as "Starters," made their way east to England and north to Scotland, where they

Welsh Springer Spaniel, red and white.

proved useful in both the hunt and in breeding programs. It can also be surmised that crosses were conducted between the Springer and the Welsh Sheepdog and Corgi. It cannot be determined with certainty that the dogs were always used as gundogs, but it is known that they were also employed for shepherding and cattle droving. The versatile abilities and outstanding hunting instincts of the breed made it a prime candidate for world-wide ownership. The breed soon found homes in India, Australia, the U.S., and other countries during the nineteenth and twentieth centuries. The coat of the Welsh Springer, as well as his body conformation, enables him to adapt to and function in a wide variety of climates and terrains. His outer coat is naturally flat and even, with a soft undercoat that prevents the impediment of water, thorns, and burrs.

The Welsh Springer is a keen, hard-working dog known for his never-ending endurance. He has an excel-

Welsh Terrier, black and tan. Photo courtesy B. McLennan.

lent nose and takes naturally to water. He can be used on almost any game.

Before acceptance into the Kennel Club of Great Britain in 1902, the breed was exhibited as "Welsh Cockers." The breed today enjoys world-wide distribution and recognition as the Welsh Springer Spaniel. With kind and careful handling, these dogs can be tireless and efficient hunters. They are high-spirited and good-natured companions that resent harsh treatment, expecting their delightful, polite manners to be reciprocated by their human master.

ESSENTIALS OF THE WELSH SPRINGER SPANIEL: Of very ancient origin, the Welsh Springer is a very distinct spaniel that has been bred and preserved purely for working purposes. The skull is proportionate, of moderate length, and slightly domed. The muzzle is medium in length, straight, and fairly square. Jaw is strong; eyes are hazel or dark, not prominent nor sunken, nor showing haw. Ears are set moderately low and carried close to the cheeks. Built for endurance and activity, the Welsh Springer is symmetrical and compact. The body is not long but strong and muscular with deep brisket. The neck is long and muscular, clean in throat, and set neatly into long and sloping shoulders. The coat is straight and flat, with a silky texture. It is not wiry nor wavy. In color the Welsh dog must be

white with rich red markings. Height: 18–19 inches (46–48 cm). Weight: 35–45 pounds (16–20 kg). The tail is well-set-on low and carried above back level. It is customarily docked.

Welsh Terrier

Although the Welsh Terrier of today appears much like the ancient Old English Terrier (or Broken-Coated Terrier), the breed is so likely strictly indigenous to the principality of Wales that it is

For well over two and a half centuries, the breed was used for the pack hunting of otters and badger. In England, an 1885 Carnarvonshire exhibition marks the breed's first record of separate classification. Even until the turn of the twentieth century, the Welsh was grouped as Old English Terrier at American shows. American recognition came in 1901.

Often the Welsh Terrier has been likened to the Wire Fox Terrier; in appearance the Welshie is quite similar (excepting color of course). Suitable as a companion and workman, the Welshie is of a gay, volatile nature. He is game and fearless, but never vicious or overly pugnacious.

ESSENTIALS OF THE WELSH TERRIER: This is a medium-sized terrier with a square body appearance. The skull is flat and appears wider between the ears than does the Wire Fox Terrier. The jaw is clean-cut and punishing. Ears V-shaped and small. Neck of moderate length and thickness, slightly arched. Shoulders should be long and sloping, well-set-back. The legs straight and muscular. The back short and well ribbed, the loin strong. Thighs muscular, hocks well-let-down. Ample bone. Feet small, round and catlike. Coat is wire-textured and colored black and tan. He is long-legged for a terrier, the topline is level, and he possesses excellent substance. Height: 14–15.5 inches (35.5–38 cm). Weight: 20 pounds (9 kg). The jacket is double coated, close fitting, with furnishings on muzzle, legs and quarters.

Welsh Terrier, black and tan. Photo courtesy of B. McLennan.

probably not the direct descendant of that long-gone English breed. Lengthy Welsh pedigrees and reasonably credible accounts verify this assertion. Its original name, the Carnarvonshire Welsh Terrier, indicates the breed's founding principality. Residents in Carnarvonshire as far back as 1737 were said to pride themselves on the purity of their Welsh Terrier. Informally *y-clept* Hunt Terriers, these dogs worked with packs of Otter Hounds and Foxhounds in North Wales. One John Jones, the squire of Ynysfor, an Otter Hound worker from the mid-1700s, is known to have specialized in the use of Welsh Terriers. This particular line of Welshies can be traced for over 200 years.

West Highland White Terrier

Today's popular West Highland White Terrier was once but a variety of the Cairn Terrier. These white Cairns were known as Poltalloch Terriers, marking the contribution of the Malcolms family who began collecting and breeding these white outcasts. These white Cairns were then crossed with Sealyhams in order to generate a longer bodied white terrier. This cross was ill-conceived, as the longer body was not suitable for game terrier work. Selective breeding helped to restore the breed, which today looks more like a Cairn in body type than a Sealyham. The Poltalloch dogs were very successful for sporting purposes, making brave fox hunters.

Generally speaking, breed nomenclature was thrown around without consideration or immediate consequence. Roseneath Terriers, Roseneath Poltalloch Terriers and Poltalloch Terriers are names that have been all associated with the Westie.

The West Highland White Terrier has proven itself a world-wide all-around companion dog. Adaptable to a variety of lifestyles, this energetic and pleasing terrier needs no fussing and is an ideal apartment dweller. The show Westie, somewhat sculpted, requires a considerable deal of grooming.

ESSENTIALS OF THE WEST HIGHLAND WHITE TERRIER: With a foxy-faced head and a compact body, the West Highland White Terrier is pure white. The coat, the breed's hallmark, is rarely seen to perfection: a double coat, properly blending the two-inch outer coat of straight hard hair with the plenteous, soft undercoat. Silkiness and curliness are insufferable. A flattish side appearance is supported by a level back and deep, well-arched ribs. The skull is slightly domed, tapering from ears to eyes. Head should be thickly coated. Distinct stop, jaws level, nose black. Loins broad and strong, chest deep, ribs well arched, Legs short and muscular, hocks bent, forefeet larger than the hind, round, thickly padded and covered in hard hair. Desired appearance possesses both a high-esteemed and "varminty" quality, unknown in any other terrier.

West Highland White Terrier (*opposite*) photographed by Missy Yuhl. Courtesy of Nancy Spelke.

West Highland White Terrier photographed by J. Ashbey. Courtesy of Robert and Susan Ernst.

West Siberian Laika, piebald tan.

West Siberian Laikas, piebald tan.

West Siberian Laika, red. Photographs by I. Français.

West Siberian Laika

Of the two Siberian Laikas, the West dog is more numerous and more firmly established in type, than the East Siberian Laika, which *see*. The Russian laikas are used over ice-ridden terrain as sledge dogs and hunters of large game (including bear, elk and reindeer). The prized sable or ermine, however, is this sturdy hunter's specialty. The hunters from Khantu and Mansi breed the dogs for their working purposes. In origin, the West Siberian Laika comes from the indigenous stock from which the other laikas also descend. An individual dog does not work for the span of a decade because the work is so demanding. Without the laikas, the hunters surely would not survive.

ESSENTIALS OF THE WEST SIBERIAN LAIKA: The brawny and robust West Siberian Laika is immensely powerful, complete with stamina. The Siberian hunting/sledding laikas are rather long-legged and light, giving them agility and endurance in the deep snow. Height: 21–24 inches (53–61 cm). Weight: 40–50 pounds (18–23 kg). The coat, short and stand-off, is solid or piebald in white, tan, red, or black in color.

Westfälische Dachsbracke

See Westphalian Dachsbracke

Westminster Kennel Club

The Westminster Kennel Club Show is indisputably the most prestigious dog show in the United States. Its 1877 inception deems it the second oldest sporting event in the nation; the Kentucky Derby began in 1875. The first Westminster spectacle attracted over 1,200 dogs from all over the United States and was staged in Gilmore's Garden (also known as the Hippodrome). The show moved to its present hosting "drome" (Madison Square Garden) in 1880. Today's Madison Square Garden show limits its entrants to 2,500 Champions of Record only. Not everyone perceived the glorious success of the first Westminster exhibition through like eyes. Shirley Dare,

true to her name, wrote in *The Spirit of the Times*, a men's periodical, with unprecedented audacity: "Speaking out of the depth of native ignorance, I assert that the extremely high-bred dogs of the bench show were the ugliest of their kind . . . the standard seems to be a select and formulated ugliness . . . It is hard to understand the predilection of the ladies for the tiny, useless pet dogs that formed so large a class. The toy terriers and Greyhounds, thin, shivering, palpitating morsels, were an affliction to anyone used to healthy, natural dogs."

The Westminster Kennel Club itself was formed by a small herd of sportsmen that met in the lounge of the Westminster Hotel. It was the effort of these enthusiasts in training and boarding hunting dogs that eventually reaped the country's most prestigious pure-bred dog exhibition.

A breed that does well at Westminster can be sure to get additional attention in the year to come. It was the two-time winning of H.E. Mellenthin's Champion My Own Brucie, a Cocker Spaniel, that initiated the puppy-mill Cocker craze that ensued in the early 1940s. While winning is surely an honor for the breed (and dog) chosen, at times it can prove problematic. "Brucie," however, does not boast the most consecutive wins. This honor was earned by Winthrop Rutherford's Smooth Fox Terrier, Champion Warren Remedy, who won Best in Show in 1907, 1908, and 1909. Incidentally, the title was usurped in 1910 by a Champion Sabine Rarebit, another Smooth Fox Terrier. The Fox

Terrier's record at Westminster is nothing short of amazing: the Wire Fox Ter-

rier alone has taken the Best in Show title twelve times.

Westphalian Dachsbracke

The Westphalian Dachsbracke developed through knowledgeable breeding of the Dachshund to various foxhound types. German breeders combined the best of two different hunter types: the

strength and proven ground ability of the Dachshund and the speed and quickness of the more leggy dachsbrackes. Though opinion differs on the origin of the breed,

Westphalian Dachsbracke, red with white.

Wetterhoun, black. Photographs by I. Français.

evidence suggests that the breed has existed for centuries in the areas of Westphalia and Sauerland. This latter city gives the breed its alternative name, the Sauerlander Dachsbracke. The Westphalian was used on hare, fox, wild boar and rabbit in his native Germany. Recently he has been employed for schweisshund (blood trailing) work.

image of thrusting power set with a low center of gravity. His height is between 12–14 inches (30–36 cm); he typically weighs between 35–40 pounds (16–18 kg). The coat has a clean, hard, and smooth appearance. Colors include tricolor or red with white.

Wet neck
Opposite of dry neck.

Wetterhoun

A hard-working, water-oriented, versatile gundog native to the Netherlands, the Wetterhoun is also known as the Dutch Spaniel and the Otterhoun, not to be confused with the Otter Hound of Great Britain. The history of the breed traces at least back to the 1600s and likely further. The Frisian people, credited with their own culture and language, are also credited with the creation of the Wetterhoun, which literally translates to "water dog." The breed is believed to descend directly from the old Water Dog of Europe. The Wetterhoun was developed as a skilled hunter of otters—locating and killing them. Later, with the diminished otter population and the all but non-existent need or reason to hunt them, breeders focused on developing the breed's small-land-game-hunting ability. Today the breed is highly effective on both land and water. He is a fine close-working flusher, searching for game, notifying the hunter of its location, and retrieving the fallen game. He is an all-purpose, all-weather dog that is a popular canine companion and farmhand in his native Holland. When properly trained from

ESSENTIALS OF THE WESTPHALIAN DACHSBRACKE: This short, broad-chested hound is set square on four stocky legs. He has good tuck-up, a thick neck, and a chiseled head; these features convey the

puppyhood, he is a highly biddable guard dog with a strong will and a sometimes coarse temperament.

ESSENTIALS OF THE WETTERHOUN: This rugged and soundly built working water dog is an effective gundog, especially adept at flushing game in the manner of a spaniel and retrieving game both on the land and in the water. The dog's appearance should suggest endurance and hardiness. The coat is thick, with tight curls covering the body (except the head and legs, which are smooth); it should provide sufficient protection to allow the dog to perform well even in freezing water conditions. The head is strong and sizable; the body is broad and deep, standing stoutly and square on four legs. In color the Wetterhoun can be liver or black or a combination of either with white—with or without ticking or roaning. Height: 21–23 inches (53–59 cm). Weight: 33–44 pounds (15 kg).

Wheaten
Pale yellow or fawn color often associated with the terrier breeds (e.g., Soft Coated Wheaten Terrier, Norwich and Norfolk Terriers).

Wheel dogs
The two sled dogs directly in front of the sled which determine the direction of the sled.

Wheeling
In quiniela and daily double wagering where a bettor selects a key entry and combines it with all other entries in a race.

Whelp
A very young puppy.

Whelping
See Breeding

Whip tail
A tail that is carried out stiffly straight and tapering or pointed.

Whipper-in
The huntsman's assistant in controlling hounds.

Whippet
The Whippet derives from various coursing, sporting, running dogs. The breed is a rather recent creation, originating in the 1800s, during the lull of bull- and bear-baiting, for the gentry's dog-racing desires. Among the breeds often considered its forerunners are small Greyhounds, Italian Greyhounds, Bedlington Terriers, Manchester Terriers, and old English White Terriers. His original nickname, Snapdog, ricocheted out of his ability to kill rats and rabbits in a "snap," with a "snap," revealing his remarkable instinct. In the areas of

Wetterhoun, black with white.

Whippets, brindle and brindle with white. Photographs by I. Français.

Newcastle and Durham, the Whippet was the favorite whipper-snapper of the miners and colliers. Their enthusiasm for the breed was linked to dog racing, the

Whippet, brindle with white. Photo by R. Pearcy.

Whippet on the move. Photo by V. Serbin.

sport at which the Whippet has whipped all others. For his weight, the Whippet is the fastest domesticated animal, attaining speeds up to 35 miles (56 km) per hour. This ability is primarily directed to the dog tracks, where the Whippet is renowned for his competitive nature and awesome ability to excite those inclined to the sport. He is also a fine coursing hound, especially capable on rabbit and hare. The colliers who kept the Whippet treated him with utmost affection. The Whippet's frailty and delicacy are a tad deceiving. These are not wimpy, spineless, oversized toy dogs. The Whippet is a personable, hardy canine well worthy

of the attention he receives. Though graceful, affectionate, and willing to please, the Whippet may be high-strung. His racing heritage necessitates substantial exercise.

While the Whippet is one of the smoothest canines, recently some commotion has been stirred up by the promotion of a longhaired variety, an admittedly handsome dog with a charm all its own. The authors do not know the derivation of the Longhaired Whippet (which *see*) and therefore refrain from further comment. In Europe, a rough-haired version once gained notice but was never recognized by the Kennel Club in Britain.

ESSENTIALS OF THE WHIPPET: The Whippet is built for the race. His moderate size, balance, and force allow maximum ground coverage with a minimum of superfluous motion. He is a lean yet muscular dog, with excellent cardiovascular capacity, enabled by his deep chest and aerodynamic body design. The head is long and lean, flat on top, tapering to muzzle with slight stop, rather wide between the eyes, jaws powerful and clean cut. The eyes are oval and bright. The ears are rose-shaped, small and fine in texture. The neck is long, muscular, and elegantly arched. The loin gives the impression of strength; ribs well sprung. Thighs broad and strong; stifles well bent. Feet very neat. No feathering on tail. Height: 18–22 inches (46–56 kg). Weight: 28 pounds (13 kg). The coat is short, fine, and close; the color is unimportant, and any color is accepted. The coat of the Longhaired Whippet is long and silky, with feathering; conformation is assumedly like.

Whipworms

Trichuris vulpis, the whipworm, is found in the cecum and upper part of the large intestine of the dog. Three-quarters of the total length of the two-inch worm is hairlike and the last quarter is about double the thickness. They are hard to find unless one strains the feces, and this is best left to a veterinarian. Whipworm eggs are slow to develop, taking three to four months for the larvae to reach maturity. Signs of whipworm infection include slothfulness, apathy, diarrhea, vomiting, and bloody stools. Veterinary treatment is imperative, for a whipworm infestation can lead the dog to death.

Whirl

Hair which grows circularly on a ridge. *See also* Ridge

Whiskers

Longer hairs on muzzle sides and under jaws. In most breeds, particularly smooth-muzzled breeds, trimming the whiskers is optional for the show ring.

White and Black French Hound

See Chien Français

White and Orange French Hound

See Chien Français

White German Shepherd Dog

In America, white German Shepherds have been disqualified from the show ring since 1968 (though have remained registrable). Breed experts, however, admit that many of the exceptional Shepherds of the past were white and that these dogs do not possess genetic defects. Today the white variety has been reared as a separate breed and is a popular choice in rare-breed circles. The White GSD is legitimately handsome and intelligent, ideal for protection and obedience work. *See also* German Shepherd Dog, Color

Whitney reflex

Dr. Leon Whitney first described a reflex action of the male dog that has been used to the advantage of many breeders. The reflex involves the pinching of the male's penis at its base with the right hand, while holding the bitch's vulva with the left hand so as to guide the penis. If the penis is then pinched, a reflex occurs causing the male to thrust forward and gain entry to the vagina. Once a lock is formed, copulation can occur as usual.

Wide front

A front assembly that is wider than usual or desired. In a number of breeds (e.g., Bulldog), however, a wide front is desirable.

Whippet, black with white.

Whiskers being trimmed from a Whippet's muzzle. Photographs by R. Reagan.

Wide thighs
Thighs whose muscular development is optimum and ideal.

Widow's peak
Triangularly shaped markings on the forehead of some breeds, usually bicolored or sable dogs. In the Afghan Hound, referred to as domino. Apex of the triangle always faces forward (e.g., German Shepherd Dog, Collie).

Widow's peak on a winsome windhound, the Afghan Hound. Photo by I. Français.

Wills
Since only a person can be the beneficiary of a will, and a dog is not a person, it cannot inherit an estate, a Swiss bank account or even a life-time supply of its favorite nylon bone. Nevertheless, owners often want their beloved dog cared for after their death. This is typically the concern of elderly dog owners of very young dogs. The most valid and practical approach to providing for your dog after your earthly departure is to choose a close friend or relative to care for the dog. Key to the success of this plan is the new owner's acceptance of the responsibility and his ability. Therefore, leaving money for the dog's continued upkeep to the new owner is an appropriate and responsible gesture on your part. It is also acceptable to leave money to a veterinarian to care for the dog, since an older dog typically has more "doctor's bills" than does a younger one.

Windhound
Alternative term for sighthound, which *see*.

Winners
An award given at dog shows to the best dog (Winners Dog) and best bitch (Winners Bitch) competing in regular classes.

Winners Bitch
The bitch that is declared to be the best in the Winners class, which class consists of the first prize winners from the other five regular official classes.

Winners class
The Winners class for Winners Dog and Winners Bitch represent the best two dogs from the classes. These two dogs then compete for Best of Breed with the champions. *See* Classes at shows

Winners Dog
The dog (male) which is declared to be the best in the Winners class, which class consists of the first prize winners from the other five regular official classes.

Wire coat
A coat of harsh, crisp, wiry texture. Broken coat or bristle coat are similar coats. *See also* Coat

Wire Fox Terrier

The more popular of the world's Fox Terriers, the Wire Fox Terrier is hailed as a dog that often nears perfection in its conformation. The winner of more Westminster competitions than any other breed, the Wire Fox Terrier is 20 years or so younger than its Smooth brother. The two breeds, although sharing the same name (Fox Terrier) are probably not derived from the same stock. The Wire comes from the old roughhaired, black and tan working terrier of Wales, Durham and Derbyshire; the Smooth, however, comes from smooth-coated black and tan terriers of England, the Bull Terrier, the Greyhound, and the Beagle. The Wire Fox's forebears are believed to have roamed Britain as long ago as 55 B.C.

The function of a Fox Terrier is rather self-explanatory, and it was this fox hunting ability that translated into the breed's sole virtue. Conformation was of no concern, as long as the dog could move and gallop. Coat also was of little importance, as indicated by the commonplace crossings of Smooths and Wires, a thought that makes the present-day Fox Terrier breeder shudder. Furthermore, other terriers, rough-coated usually, were crossed in as necessary or available. As long as the dogs were working and working well, there was no need to bother about "establishing a purebred dog."

The Wire Fox is a popular dog, more so in England of course. Not a dog for uncouths, this Fox Terrier is designed for connoisseurs only! His abilities on the field, comparable to his show wins, are undeniable and astounding. In temperament and personality, this dog defines demonstrative and intelligent.

Wire Fox Terrier, tricolor.

Wire Fox Terrier, tricolor. Photo by Eileen.

ESSENTIALS OF THE WIRE FOX TERRIER: The Wire Fox Terrier is the epitome of the desired anatomical terrier type. Its balanced conformation and straight-legged movement give it propulsive power, the

Wire Fox Terrier, tricolor.

quintessence of terrier gait. He must be short-backed and level with a moderately narrow skull. The topline of the skull should be almost flat, sloping slightly and gradually decreasing in width towards the eyes, with skull and foreface of equal length. The foreface is chiseled somewhat; the jaws are punishing. The ears are small and V-shaped, with the flaps neatly folded over and forward drooping. The neck is clean in outline, curving gracefully. Feet compact and round. The proper coat appears broken and feels "crinkly"; the hairs have the tendency to twist and are wiry, "like coconut matting." Height: 15.5 inches (39 cm). Weight: 16–18 pounds (35–39.5 kg). The dog is predominantly white; liver, brindle, red, or slaty blue is objectionable.

Wirehaired Pointing Griffon, chestnut with white. Photo by I. Français.

Wirehaired Continental Pointer
See Wirehaired Pointing Griffon

Wirehaired Istrian Hound
See Istrian Hound

Wirehaired Pointing Griffon
Though undoubtedly a gundog native to the Netherlands, the breed is sometimes attributed to France, and interestingly enough, faintly resembles the German Wirehaired Pointer. In fact, the originator of the breed, Edward K. Korthals, was a Dutchman who later moved to Germany. The Wirehaired Pointing Griffon was born, in Holland, during the 1860s and 1870s, and much of the breed's later development occurred in France. The Pointing Griffon's base stock was various griffons of Barbet origin. The exact crosses that E. K. Korthals performed are not known, but it is believed that he used various British and European setters and/or pointers. German Shorthairs and Small Münsterländers are likely contributory breeds, and many suggest that the Braque Français played a part.

The Korthals of France had to be a truly diversified hunter—"Pointing" in its English name refers to but a small part of the breed's overall ability. The Griffon d'arret á poil dur, as he is known in France, had to point and retrieve partridge and other small game, beat hedge-

row and brush, chase the wily ducks; it also pursued roebuck, fox, and cat and functioned as a vermin-ridder. The breed's intelligence and physical conformation make it a remarkable hunting companion and home guardian. The Korthals history of working alone makes it an independent and decisive canine with the instinct and trained skill to back up its confidence and determination. The breed was the first all-around Continental hunting dog recognized by the A.K.C.

ESSENTIALS OF THE WIREHAIRED POINTING GRIFFON: A strongly limbed, medium-sized dog that is fairly short-backed and rather low on the leg. The head is long, furnished with a harsh coat, forming a mustache and eyebrows. The skull is long and narrow, and the muzzle is square. Eyes are large and open; eye color is yellow to light brown. Neck rather long with no dewlap. Shoulders rather long and sloping. Ribs slightly rounded. The coat is coarse and harsh—the standard compares the coat to "the bristles on a wild boar." Height: 22–24 inches (56–61 cm). Weight: 50–60 pounds (23–27 kg). The tail, generally docked to

one-third its length, is carried straight. Colors are steel gray with chestnut splashes, gray-white with chestnut splashes, chestnut, and dirty white mixed with chestnut, but never black.

Wiry coat
Harsh, crisp and hard hair.

Withers
The highest point of the shoulders, immediately behind the neck.

Withers, low in
See Flat withers

Wolf hybrids
Neither dog in wolf's clothing nor wolf in dog's clothing, wolf hybrids cannot be classified as wolf or dog—these are wild canines, not domesticated nor domesticatable. Despite the howling truth here undressed, wolf hybrids have swept the United States in popularity. Because of legal complications, it is difficult to know the exact number of animals in the country; estimates vary from 80,000–600,000 and all indications are that numbers continue to climb.

Wirehaired Pointing Griffon, chestnut with white. Photo by I. Français.

Wolf hybrids are defined as any dog with a percentage of wolf blood. Photo by I. Français.

Perhaps more in vogue than strolling through the park with a purebred Shar-Pei or Cavalier King Charles is the ownership of a wolf hybrid, perceived by a

Wolf hybrids are extremely sensitive to socialization, as these animals are naturally timid and not responsive to human handling. Photo by R. Pearcy.

Wolf hybrids. The Saarlooswolfhond is a breed developed from a wolf hybrid during the 1930s in the Netherlands. Photo by I. Français.

great many owners as super status symbols. Such owners allegedly concern themselves with the preservation of the wolf, though others regard the "bastardization" of the wolf as a grave abomination, more an insult to the noble beast than a fight to preserve its race. Only the most knowledgeable and dedicated owner is able to keep a hybrid wolf as a pet and watch the animal thrive. Experts relay that, while these animals can be more trustworthy and responsive than domestic dog, the majority of hybrid wolves cannot be trained or housebroken, combining the timidity of the wolf with the lack of aggression control of the domestic dog.

A consummate understanding of wolf instincts as well as of canine behavior is needed in order for the individual to relate to this non-domesticated animal. In spite of myths and fairy tales to the contrary, wolves are not man-eaters but rather are highly social creatures which expend

vast amounts of energy nurturing young, maintaining the pack and hunting in accord to the laws of Nature. Wolves intentionally avoid humans.

A hybrid wolf by definition is any domestic dog with wolf "blood," and such a hybrid is gauged by the percentage of wolf "blood in its veins," which, due to the variance of inheritance, is a dubious calculation. The most common dogs used in these crosses are of Northern derivation: Siberian Huskies, Alaskan Malamutes, and Eskimo Dogs are likely candidates for hybridization. These breeds are favored for their reliably calm temperaments; more aggressive breeds, such as Akitas and Chow Chows, are less effective in these crosses in terms of the temperament of the offspring.

The integrity and good intentions of breeders, in many cases, cannot be shunned, although the overbreeding of hybrid wolves has become a problem to be reckoned with. Due to the high social needs of these animals, constant companionship and supervision are absolute necessities. Hybrids cannot be kept indoors, as they typically eat furniture, scent mark the home with urine, and do not respond to training or discipline. Once abused, these animals will likely never again trust humans; second-owner successes are unheard of, thus these half-breeds are better euthanized than transferred to a second owner. The lack of understanding by owners has led to miserable lives for these animals, who often manifest neurosis and aggression.

Legality of ownership varies from

state to state, and country to country. In the States, the U.S. Wolf Hybrid Association serves as the leading registry of hybrids. Certain states, such as New York, have banned the ownership of hybrid wolves, and most areas apply exotic-animal legislation to the ownership of these animals. *See also* Wolves, Domestication of the dog

Wolf-sable
See Sable

Wolfspitz
See Keeshond, German Spitzen

Wolves

The two species of wolf in the genus *Canis* are the gray wolf and the red wolf. The gray wolf, *Canis lupis*, is a carnivorous animal of notable intelligence and an elaborate social structure. Once of wide distribution, the gray wolf was a prime predator of shepherds' flocks and weary travelers. As evidenced in numerous tales, legends, and other histories, the gray wolf deeply instilled a fear in man that has largely led to his demise. The gray wolf today is very limited in its numbers and territory. Regional names for the gray wolf include: timber wolf, European wolf, northern wolf, and lobo. For many, however, the simple word wolf immediately brings to mind the feared gray wolf. The size of a gray wolf can vary considerably, with small specimens standing about 26 inches (66 cm) and large specimens as high as 38 inches (96.5 cm) at the shoulder. Weight too can vary, with wolves of the southern climes weighing around 60 pounds (27 kg), while those of the north weigh between 100 and 175 pounds (45–79 kg). Wolves are known for their survival instincts. Cubs are often raised communally, with both adults and yearlings eager to contribute regurgitated food, protection, and moments of play and affection. Growing cubs are known to require as much 11 pounds of food daily, and yet they have been known to survive the death of both parents, which speaks well for the communal instinct of the wolf.

The red wolf, *Canis rufus*, is an endangered species native to the U.S. The red wolf's range is now severely limited to a relatively small region of the southern U.S., and the animals survive largely on a diet of rabbit, muskrats, and an occasional water fowl, though they once fed on wild turkey, deer and other large animals. The red wolf hunts in pairs, small family groups, and packs. At one time a government bounty was placed on the species. Then, in the 1970s, the red wolf was granted protection as an endangered species. Approximately 17 specimens (a

Wolves. The gray wolf, *Canis lupis*.

large fraction of the total population) were transported to a breeding colony in the far northwestern U.S.; their captors intentionally treated the wolves in a way that would not cause them to lose their fear of man. In the 1980s, the number of specimens in the breeding colony reached over 100, and six specimens, three male-female pairs, were experimentally re-introduced to the wild in a protected park in the Carolinas. Specialists believe that the red wolf fears man and avoids him at all costs. They assert that the red wolf should not be feared and most certainly should not be hunted, at least until its numbers are stable.

In physical appearance, the red wolf resembles a large, leggy, tawny-colored coyote, standing approximately 24–30 inches (61–76 cm) at the shoulder and weighing 50–80 pounds (22.5–36 kg), and studies confirm that extensive hybridization between the red wolf and the coyote, two believed separate and distinct species, has occurred in the wild. At one time there was a black phase of the red wolf common to Florida, but poisoning, wan-

ton shooting, and diminished refuge has cost all such specimens extinction. It must be mentioned that wolves and dogs

are not commonly crossed, as many owners of bad German Shepherd Dogs or Siberian Huskies would have one believe. Though some dog-to-wolf crosses have been conducted, resulting most notably in the Saarlooswolfhond (which *see*), most efforts have proven less successful or futile. Crossing a dog to a wolf does not produce the ultimate dog; rather, it results in a timid animal given to straying and lacking the desirable qualities of either species. *See also* Wolf hybrids, Maned wolf

Wood utility comb

Excellent for very long coats, like that of the Collie. Easy on the hand, it is excellent for combing deep into a heavy coat and removing undercoat.

Working Certificate

An award earned by dogs who have proven their hunting ability and who are not gun-shy.

Working dogs

Although most of the world's domestic canines function primarily as pets, there are thousands of dogs in the United States, Europe, India, the Soviet Union—most every country of the world, in fact—that serve primarily in a working capacity. The Eastern countries still use a number of borzois, working sighthounds, for hunting and coursing purposes. Many European countries as well as the U.S. employ a vast population of sheepdogs—herders and guard dogs. Sportsmen, particularly on the Continent and in the southern U.S., also hunt with packs of scenthounds, dogs which often function first in working capacities.

While most registries claim that the desired conformation described in their breed standards emphasizes the functional abilities of the working breeds first, there is still more emphasis on superficial detail than necessary. The ideal test for the accuracy and appropriateness of what the breed standard requires for "perfection" would be to compare the standard to the "perfect" working dog. If the perfect working Collie does not have tipped ears or an abundant mane, then these details are superfluous. Granted, not all show dogs feign to be working dogs, and a beautifully groomed Collie is a far more esthetically pleasing sight than a conditioned Border after a day of heeling cattle. Nevertheless, the working breeds should continue to strive for verisimilitude to their type and avoid the details which too commonly exaggerate a feature or quality to absurd extremes.

Working Group

The kennel club designation of dogs that serve man in a given working capacity: police, guard, protection, draft, rescue, herding, etc. The American Kennel Club, unlike the Kennel Club of Great Britain, does not include the herding dogs in this group since its formation of the Herding Group. Dogs that fit into the Working Group are dogs that either still perform in their given capacity or at least originally performed as such. *See also* Group systems

Worms

Worms can enter the body in many ways: ingestion, insect bites, penetration of the skin, and prenatal infection. Some worm species require an intermediate host before they can infect the dog, for example, tapeworm. In general, signs of worm infestation include: lethargy, poor coat, anemia, malnutrition, emaciation, diarrhea, and vomiting. The common worm infestations that affect dogs include: roundworms, hookworms, whipworms, tapeworms, and heartworms, which *see.*

Wrinkle

Loose, folding skin on forehead or foreface. *See* Shar-Pei

Wrist

Carpus. Term borrowed from human anatomy. *See* Forequarters

Wry mouth

The upper and lower jaws are un-

aligned due to the twisting to one side of the lower jaw. In the Bulldog, Pekingese and many other brachycephalic breeds, this fault is reasonably common.

Wurtemburg Pointer

A large, heavy gundog that occurred in the Wurtemburg district of Germany. These slow but steady dogs were raised by a number of huntsmen in this and the surrounding districts.

Working dogs. The conformation of a working dog adheres more to function on the field than to the type necessarily described in written standards; such black-and-white guidelines for type are more useful to show dogs.

Wrinkles in abundance on a Shar-Pei puppy.

Xiphoid process

A portion of the sternum.

Xoloitzcuintli

The "wildlife" of Mexico puzzled most every Spanish explorer who visited there. The inhabitants were unlike any European quadruped, and the earliest accounts of explorers' findings continue to prove remarkable, revealing and pe-

Xoloitzcuintli, puppy. Photo by I. Français.

ripherally absurd. The conquistadors described a number of "doglike" animals which were hairless and mute and climbed trees with dexterity. Writing post-Cortes, Bernardino de Sahagun's multi-volume *Natural History* provides the earliest description of the Xoloitzcuintli: "The little animals that they call down here 'xoloitz-cuintli' have no hair on their bodies, and the natives cover them at night with their blankets. But these little dog-like animals are not born

like this, but the natives use a resin that they call 'oxtli', and that they spread on the animals, and that way they pull all of its hair, leaving the body smooth."

The Modern Dog Encyclopedia, first published in 1949 by the Stackpole Company, confidently demystifies the mystery of the Xolo: "Now it seems certain that the xoloitz-cuintli, the little 'dog-like' animal mentioned by Friar de Sahagun, was a Guinea pig."

Hairless dogs in Mexico, most sources concur, occurred after the conquest of Mexico, despite faulty translations of exploration treatises and the like. Trading between Spain and the Spice Islands brought the ancestors of both the Xolo and the Chihuahua to Mexico; such exchanges began around the year 1580. Dogs arrived on North American shores from Africa and the Orient. Some scientists believe that most hairless dog breeds stem from *Canis africanis*, which spread from Africa to New Guinea, Manila and China, before arriving in North America. Others reject this long-purported assertion as romantic, though swell, swill.

The Xoloitzcuintli, the dog, the larger of Mexico's hairless breeds, comes to the modern-day dog fancy with neither resin residue or rat relatives. The Aztec Indians called the hairless dogs "Biche," which meant naked. These dogs fulfilled rather peculiar tasks for the Indians and were used as bed warmers, communicants to the gods, and general delicacy. These pets were also revered for their palliative powers, capable of curing rheumatism and other physical unpleasantries. The breed's present name is believed to have been acquired from a religious cult (based in Acapulco) which favored this hairless *chiquito*.

The Xoloitzcuintli is the larger of two Xolo types; the smaller and more popular is the Mexican Hairless (which *see*), which was derived from the larger (or Standard) Xolo. The general body type of both these Mexican hairless dogs suggests a relation to the pariah group. Some

thinly textured. The neck is carried high, flexible, with the grace of an antelope. The skin is smooth and soft. Uniform dark colors are preferred—charcoal, slate, dark reddish gray, liver or bronze. Pink and coffee stains occur (areas that lack pigmentation). Height: 13–22.5 inches (33–57 cm).

Xoloitzcuintli, liver.

writers still consider the hairless dogs the missing link between the pariahs and the sighthound breeds. Hairless dogs constitute a specific type: they are mostly terrierlike in appearance, with long legs and prick ears.

Interest in showing Xolos and in the breed as a pet has suffered due to the Chinese Crested's growing popularity. Despite the Xolo's most peculiar appearance, there lies a sporting and affectionate canine underneath for the daring dog fancier.

ESSENTIALS OF THE XOLOITZCUINTLI: The foremost characteristic is the total or nearly total absence of hair. Its calm, graceful way has a harmonious effect. The body is rather long in comparison with the height. The head is somewhat broad and strong; the stop is not very pronounced; the nose is blunt. Both the Xolo and Toy Xolo (Mexican Hairless) are devoid of premolars. The ears are large and expressive—long and

Xoloitzcuintli, coated.

Xoloitzcuintlis, liver and charcoal. Photographs by I. Français.

Xoloitzcuintli, charcoal.

Xoloitzcuintli, dark reddish gray. Photographs by I. Français.

Yellow Black Mouth Cur
See Black Mouth Cur

Yoick
An old hunting cry.

Yorkshire Terrier

Produced by the working men of the West Riding region of Yorkshire, the Yorkie was created in the late nineteenth century as companion to the industrial classes. The first dogs produced, of course, were larger than today's Yorkie.

this extreme petiteness, extraordinary and knowledgeable selective breeding was essential. Certain specimens (full-grown) weighed in at 2.5 pounds (1.13 kg). As the breed was making its initial rounds, it was referred to as the Broken-haired Scotch Terrier, but this name was quickly replaced by the present one. Coincidentally, Yorkie pups look a great deal like Airedale pups—both breeds trace to the Airedale district.

Much of the Yorkie's character comes from its humble beginnings. The fact that

Yorkshire Terrier, blue/tan.

The three breeds used to create the dog likely were the English Black and Tan Terrier, the Skye Terrier, and the Maltese. (The Maltese was once known as the Maltese Terrier—so the Yorkie is really pure terrier.) In order to produce a dog of

this is one of the most attractive dogs is perhaps coincidental, as are the soundness and joy of its temperament. The Kennel Club recognized the breed in 1886, the A.K.C. followed much later in the present century. Today the Yorkie, with his flowing coat (touching or almost touching the floor), is among the world's most prominent toy dogs, known in Canada, Australia, South Africa and throughout most of Europe.

ESSENTIALS OF THE YORKSHIRE TERRIER: A unique blue-tan long coat of perfectly straight glossy hair hanging evenly down each side with a part extending from the nose to the end of the tail. The

blue is steel, and the tan is darker at the roots; puppies are born black.

Yugoslavian Herder
See Sarplaninac

Yugoslavian Mountain Hound
The Yugoslavian Mountain Hound, an indigenous scent hunter of the Planina range in the southwestern region of

Yorkshire Terrier, blue/tan.

head is rather small and flat, not too prominent. The forelegs should be straight; the hindlegs also straight, when viewed from behind, but stifles bend moderately. The body is compact and well proportioned. The back is rather short with a level line. Feet are round with black toenails. The tail is customarily docked to medium length and furnished with plentiful fur. Height: 9 inches (23 cm). Weight: 7 pounds (3.5 kg) and less. The Yorkie color is blue/tan: the

Yugoslavia, is known there as the Jugoslavenski Planinski Gonic . Like the Yugoslavian Tricolor Hound, which derives from like stock, the Mountain Hound is used on fox, hare, deer, and sometimes wild boar. The Yugoslavian scenthound breeds are unique in their lighter builds and keen eyesight. The Phoenician sighthounds and hounds of Gaul are the believed forerunners of this hound as well as the other eight scenthounds indigenous to Yugoslavia. To-

day both the Mountain Hound and the Tricolor are quite rare.

ESSENTIALS OF THE YUGOSLAVIAN MOUNTAIN HOUND: A medium-sized hound, strong and capable of great endurance. The length of the body should exceed the height at the withers by ten percent. The head is long, rather narrow, with a slightly marked furrow running along the forehead. The muzzle is somewhat longer than the skull. The stop is moderately defined. The ears are set above the eyeline, leather moderately thick, of medium length, hanging close to the side of the head. The back is well muscled, somewhat short, with like loins. The chest is long, deep, broad, with moderately sprung ribs. The belly and flanks are short-coupled and rounded. The legs are muscled and of medium length. In color the Mountain Hound is deep red or wheaten, with a black saddle. The cover should reach the head where it forms a black patch on either side of the temple. White blaze on the throat, collar, chest, up to one-third of the body. Height: 17.5–21.5 inches (45–55 cm). The coat is short and dense, with undercoat.

Yugoslavian Tricolor Hound

The Yugoslavian Tricolor Hound represents the Yugoslavian scenthound breed that developed in the southernmost part of that country. The influence of the Phoenician sighthounds is evident in the conformation of the swift-moving scenthounds of Yugoslavia, whose long legs and excellent vision enhance hunting abilities. The Tricolor, known at home as the Jugoslavenski Trobojni Gonič, is believed to share similar origins to the other hounds of his area and, like his fellow Slavs, hunts fox, hare and other small game. Today the Tricolor Hound is very rare and not frequently seen, even in Yugoslavia.

ESSENTIALS OF THE YUGOSLAVIAN TRICOLOR HOUND: A brawny body carried on long straight legs, the Tricolor is a picture of sleek, running elegance. The skull is the broadest part of the head, which becomes progressively narrower towards the eyes and is terminated by a wedge-shaped muzzle. The topline is straight and slightly sloping towards the croup. Withers are defined but not prominent. Chest is long, broad and deep. The legs are rather short. His

Yugoslavian Mountain Hound, red with black saddle.

Yugoslavian Tricolor Hound, tricolor. Photographs by I. Français.

eared fox. The dog figures into the development of a number of other African dogs and does not occur any longer, in all likelihood.

Zulu Dog

The square-muzzled Zulu Dog denotes power and efficiency. Like the Basenji, the tail is carried tightly curled, its color is fawn and it is shorthaired. Although used as a consistent hunting dog, its temperament remains wild and it cannot be fondled even by the Zulu tribesmen. The Zulu people are a pastoral tribe of the Natal province of South Africa, along Indian Ocean shores. The Zulu Dog, along with the Bantu Dog, numbered among this peoples' native working dogs.

Zwergpinscher

See Miniature Pinscher

Zygomatic arch prominently displayed by a Rottweiler.

coat, mostly tan with black areas and white on the front, distinguishes him from the similar Yugoslavian Mountain Hound, who is black/tan. This is essentially a medium-sized hound with a rectangular body. Weight: 44–55 pounds (20–25 kg). Height: 18–22 inches (46–56 cm). The coat is flat, dense and brilliant.

Zanzibar Dog

This East African hunting dog has a distinct wedge-shaped head and a pointed muzzle. The ears are carried horizontally, a most unique feature which it shares with fellow canid, the bat-

Zwergschnauzer

See Miniature Schnauzer

Zwergspitz

See German Spitzen

Zygomatic arch

Bony ridge that forms the lower part of the orbit (or eye socket). The arch is an extension of the malar bone or zygomatic, located at the rear of the skull. The zygomatic arch varies in prominence, shape and contour, from breed to breed. In the Rottweiler, for instance, it is desirably prominent.

Selected Annotated Bibliography

Anderson, Moira K. *Coping With Sorrow on the Loss of Your Pet.* **Los Angeles CA: Peregrine Press, 1987.**
A much needed book on a timely subject, this impassioned offering has been welcomed by all dog lovers. The book delicately deals with the death of one's pet and offers consolation and encouragement to readers to help themselves, family members, as well as other pet owners.

Barrie, Anmarie. *Dogs and the Law.* **Neptune NJ: TFH, 1990.**
A handy little book that scans the laws from federal to local jurisdictions...interesting and helpful. May not be in print forever so readers should look for it soon. Great cartoons too by the talented Andrew Prendimano.

Battaglia, Dr. Carmelo L. *Dog Genetics: How to Breed Better Dogs.* **Neptune NJ: TFH, 1978.**
Fundamental coverage of genetics and breeding dogs. Clearly presented for breeders who are not too keen on genetics. Dr. Carmen deserves high praise for this work and while TFH no longer offers the book, it may be available from other sources.

Benjamin, Carol. *Mother Knows Best: The Natural Way to Train Your Dog.* **New York: Howell Book House, 1985.**
No one does without this book. It has quickly become the "standard of the breed" for puppy rearing. Carol is lucid and perceptive and her keen love of dogs and many years of experience are evident to anyone who opens this book.

Bueler, Lois E. *Wild Dogs of the World.* **New York: Stein and Day, 1973.**
Dog lovers like all other animal lovers will find Bueler's work on the wild dogs a truly fascinating read. This book breaks down the family by genera and describes each member, its range, habits and survivor status. Highly worthwhile and not merely a reference book—you'll read this cover to cover.

Burke, Lew. *Dog Training.* **Neptune NJ: TFH, 1982.**
Lew Burke is an expert at his profession, and this book remains a tribute to his talents. Various aspects of training are covered, from the basic "sit" to some real difficult tasks; exceptional is the section on protection work.

Burris, Christopher. *The Proper Care of Dogs.* **Neptune NJ: TFH, 1991.**
This book has quickly gained high regard from the pet world. Breeds are discussed in a simple manner and the basic needs of each breed are outlined. Very up-to-date and an easy read.

Carlson, Delbert G., D.V.M., and James M. Giffin, M.D. *Dog Owner's Home Veterinary Handbook.* **New York: Howell Book House, 1980.**
A very practical book that clearly presents the signs, symptoms, and basic treatments for hundreds of canine ailments. Particularly useful in its coverage of prevention and husbandry.

Cavill, David. *All about the Spitz Breeds.* **London: Pelham Books Ltd., 1978.**
While somewhat out-of-date and not completely in accord to these authors' findings, this book is a good source on the Nordic breeds of dog.

Clark, Ross D., D.V.M., and Joan R. Stainer, eds. *Medical and Genetic Aspects of Purebred Dogs.* **Edwardsville KS: Veterinary Medicine Publishing Company, 1983.**
Great resource on different breeds and their medical profiles. Each breed is discussed in terms of growth, recognized problems, breeding and whelping, and advanced age. Somewhat technical in places but never too weighty.

Dangerfield, Stanley, and Elsworth Howell, eds. *The International Encyclopedia of Dogs.* **New York: Howell Book House, 1974.**
In its day, this encyclopedia may have been regarded as the cat's meow, although today it is shy in its coverage of many breeds and topics. Printed in the U.S., the book originated in England and was designed by Rainbird Reference Books Ltd. The information set forth is well researched and the book is sensibly organized.

Davis, Henry P., ed. *The Modern Dog Encyclopedia.* **Harrisburg PA: The Stackpole Company, 1958.**
Covers thoroughly many areas of the dog sport and despite its age offers some insightful details on lots of topics. Many authorities were consulted for the compilation of this encyclopedia and the photographs are nostalgic and representative of good typey dogs of the period.

De Prisco, Andrew, and James B. Johnson. *The Mini-Atlas of Dog Breeds.* **Neptune NJ: TFH, 1990.**
The first collaboration by the authors and one which has led to many good things. We've been told that this book is thorough, entertaining and a great dog-watchers' guide, but you be the judge!

Dunbar, Dr. Ian. *Dog Behavior: Why Dogs Do What They Do.* **Neptune NJ: TFH, 1979.**
Dunbar has long been an expert doggie shrink and covers many deep topics in laymen's language. The book will prove helpful to trainers and pet folk alike for its insight into behavior modification and general canine instincts.

Fraser, Clarence M., Asa Mays, et al., eds. *The Merck Veterinary Manual.* **6th ed. Rahway NJ: Merck and Co., 1986.**
The standard reference work for the veterinary professional. Very technical but will clarify certain otherwise difficult maladies. Virtually every canine disease and disorder is described, treatments are included. Excellent information on dog nutrition and the different body systems.

Gannon, Dee. *The Rare Breed Handbook.* **2nd ed. Hawthorne NJ: Golden Boy Press, 1991.**
A rare book on rare breeds! This looseleaf book compiles all of the current standards for the non-AKC breeds that are currently being promoted in the dog world. In addition, the author offers a brief history and photo of each breed. Dee is a noted rare-breed aficionado and a major contributor to rare-breed activity on the East coast.

Glover, Harry, ed. *A Standard Guide to Pure-bred Dogs.* **New York: McGraw Hill, 1977.**
A compilation of histories and illustrated breed standards. Short entries on the many FCI breeds divided by their groups offer some lesser known facts about these European dogs. The book was originally published by Trewin Copplestone Publishing Ltd. in England.

Hubbard, Clifford L.B. *Working Dogs of the World.* **London: Sidgwick and Jackson Ltd., 1947.**
A staple in every dog lover's library, Hubbard's fascinating account of the working dog breeds proves timeless. This is a real collector's item book with in-depth information on some breeds that has never been imitated.

Hutchinson, Walter, ed. *Hutchinson's Popular and Illustrated Dog Encyclopaedia.* **3 vols. London: Hutchinson and Co., no date.**
Most every dog book enthusiast has at least seen these three volumes, although few persons are fortunate enough to acquire them. Published in the 1930s, the volumes are difficult to come by but offer priceless information and photographs of England's beloved breeds as well as Continental dogs. From its onset, its British master architects knew they were crafting a lasting monument to the dog: "An invaluable work of international importance on breeds of dogs of every country, with full veterinary advice in cases of accidents or ailments, etc., on their care and home treatment, contributed by the most eminent authorities."

Johnson, Norman H., D.V.M. *The Complete Puppy and Dog Book.* **New York: Atheneum, 1977.**
A classic in dog care originally printed in 1965. Handy for general coverage of health care and puppy development for different-sized dogs.

Mandeville, John J., and Ab Sidewater, eds. *The Complete Dog Book.* **18th ed. New York: Howell Book House, 1992.**
This is the American Kennel Club official publication of its breed standards. The book offers brief but romantic histories of each breed in the U.S. as well as general maintenance chapters.

Nicholas, Anna Katherine. *Successful Dog Show Exhibiting.* **Neptune NJ: TFH, 1981.**
Anna Katherine has been in the dog show ring since the 1920s, and there is hardly a soul in the fancy who doesn't respect this woman's experience, writings, and knowledge. Who better to introduce the novice to the exhibition world? The authors recommend this book and any of Anna's specialized breed books which are beautifully illustrated and informative. Published principally by TFH, Anna has written around 75 books and has been published more than any other dog writer in history.

Rutherford, Clarice, and David H. Neil, M.R.C.V.S. *How to Raise A Puppy You Can Live With.* **Loveland CO: Alpine, 1981.**
A good book on puppy care that has become immensely popular. While its title is a tad off-color, the book has much to recommend it and has true yuppy over-achiever appeal.

Schneider-Leyer, Dr. Erich. *Dogs of the World.* **Trans. Dr. E. Fitch Daglish. London: Popular Dogs, 1964.**
This ambitious survey of the world's dog breeds, originally published in 1960 in Germany by Albert Müller Verlag, is still an enchanting source of information on many breeds. The author provides good scope on the breeds discussed and breaks them down by specific function. Photographs are an interesting study in breed development.

Schwartz, Charlotte. *The Howell Book of Puppy Raising.* **New York: Howell Book House, 1978.**
Written by an outstanding breeder and all-around knowledgeable dog person, this book offers a detailed account of puppy development, including physical, psychological, and sociological needs. Charlotte's approach to puppy raising is accessible and her writing style inviting. The puppy development charts are the finest we've seen.

Semencic, Dr. Carl. *Pit Bulls and Tenacious Guard Dogs.* **Neptune NJ: TFH, 1991.**
Dr. Carl Semencic is a well-known, much respected rare-breed man and deserves credit for bringing recognition to such breeds as the Canary Dog, American Bulldog, Dogo Argentino and other great imported mastiffs. This book (don't be confused by the title) is a marvelous first-hand account of over 20 guardian breeds which the doctor feels are most suitable for protection work. His writing is candid and impassioned, and, like most of the dogs in the book, Carl holds no punches. The photography is terrific and really brings these home-worthy monsters to life!

——. *The World of Fighting Dogs.* **Neptune NJ: TFH, 1981.**
Dr. Carl's first book concentrates on the fighting breeds of dog and offers a rare source of information on this taboo subject. Both sides of the issue are well represented in the book, and, while controversy has surrounded the publication of this book, it has prevailed for its candor and historical relevance. The author's firsthand experience with pit bulls and other fighting dogs gives him an advantage in advising potential suitable owners.

Spira, Harold R. *Canine Terminology.* **New York: Harper and Row, 1982.**
An excellent reference source for decifering the language of breed standards, Spira's book has been widely acclaimed. The line drawings by Mary and Peggy Davidson make the book remarkable and are clearly effective. American readers may be disappointed by the heavy leaning towards Australian terminology, but all in all will find it worthwhile to peruse.

T.F.H. All-Breed (160) Dog Grooming Book. **Neptune NJ: TFH, 1987.**
Detailed and illustrated, this volume offers expert grooming techniques on the most common of breeds. Not necessarily for the average reader, the book must be applauded for its great utility to beginning and professional groomers, and may be helpful to potential owners to gauge the necessary grooming needs of their intended breed (e.g., Cockers vs. Poodles vs. Bichons).

Whitney, Leon F., D.V.M., and George D. Whitney, D.V.M. *The Complete Book of Dog Care.* **Garden City NY: Doubleday and Co., 1985.**

The classic work by Leon Whitney, originally published in 1950, has been revised by his son George for this more recent release. Coverage of care-related topics is exhaustive and practical, although be aware that some information is already somewhat dated. Charts and tables, as well as its super index, add to the user-friendly nature of the book.

Wilcox, Bonnie, D.V.M., and Chris Walkowicz. *The Atlas of Dog Breeds of the World.* **Neptune NJ: TFH, 1989.**

The widely acclaimed labor of love of two great dog ladies and authors, *The Atlas* is the first recent book of its kind to reacquaint the dog fancy with the hundreds of breeds in the world and surely paved the way for this *Canine Lexicon.* As remarkable for its 1000+ color photographs as for its well-researched, impeccably written accounts of rare and common breeds, this book will remain a monument to the dog and its authors. Despite its daunting heft and size, this book is inviting and unimposing—for its ten-plus pounds, it's in fact easier to pick up than it is to put down!

AUTHORS' NOTE: This bibliography represents selected volumes which were referred to during the process of compiling this lexicon. In addition to these books, countless magazines and journals were consulted. While no breed-specific books have been included, the authors acknowledge that many such books were used in our research, in addition to personal conversations and interviews with the authors of those books and books-in-progress. Especially noteworthy and supportive were Maryann Akers-Hanson, Moira Allen, Lloyd Alton, Barbara J. Andrews, Olga Baker, Nona Kilgore Bauer, Alice Bixler-Clark, John Blackwell, Joan McDonald Brearley, Dr. I. Lehr Brisbin, Jr., George Caddy, Chris Carter, Dick Dickerson, Dr. Samuel Draper, Kitty Drury, Christine Eicher, Dr. Dieter Fleig, Marcia Foy, Isabelle Francais, Jackie Fraser, Dee Gannon, Bill Gorodner, Mr. and Mrs. Samuel Hardy, Mike Harlow, Joseph Hartnagle, Ann Hearn, Andre Humblet, Connie Jankowski, Diane Jessup, Anne Keleman, Dean Keppler, Muriel Lee, Frederick Mayo, Charlotte McGowan, Bardi McLennan, Sonja Neu, Anna Katherine Nicholas, Don Robinder, Charlotte Schwartz, Bill Scolnik, Dr. Carl Semencic, Dr. John Slack, Richard Stratton, James Taylor, Richard Tomita, Kimberly Tudor, Guy Vandenbossche, Chris Walkowicz, Jerry Walls, Dr. Bonnie Wilcox, Yvonne Wilson, and Dr. Berney Ziessow.